The
SOURCE
A Guidebook of American Genealogy

Revised Edition

*Edited by Loretto Dennis Szucs
and Sandra Hargreaves Luebking*

Ancestry.

Szucs, Loretto Dennis
 The source : a guidebook of American genealogy / edited by Loretto
Dennis Szucs and Sandra Hargreaves Luebking. — Rev. ed.
  p. cm.
 Includes bibliographical references and index.
 ISBN 0-916489-67-1
 1. United States—Genealogy—Archival resources. I. Luebking, Sandra
Hargreaves. II. Title.
CS49.S9 1996
929'.1'07273—dc20   96-41402

© 1997

Ancestry Incorporated

P.O. Box 476

Salt Lake City, Utah 84110-0476

First printing 1996

10 9 8 7 6 5 4 3 2 1

Printed in the United States of America

CONTENTS

Ethnic Origins

Time and Place

Appendixes

FOREWORD

America, the Great Melting Pot—a theme many of us have heard repeatedly. However, this concept of many people from every corner of the world coming to the American continent, settling together in communities, and mixing in the great cauldrons of urban and suburban areas to become simply "Americans" is at least a little misleading. I have always much preferred this analogy: *America, the Great Tapestry.*

The great tapestries of both today and yesteryear are woven with variegated threads from a nearly infinite palette of colors. Each thread's unique qualities contribute to the beauty and strength of the entire piece. The complete tapestry is only as rich to the eye, as pleasing to the touch, and as wonderful in its creation as the individual threads are rich, pleasing, and wonderful; this is how I prefer to think of the settling and peopling of America. The idea of such a tapestry accurately reflects our history and heritage—the history and heritage of the many peoples who have woven a great American tapestry.

Increasing numbers of individuals from every walk of life, from every corner of the continent, and of every ethnic persuasion are pursuing their family histories, thirsting to discover their unique threads in the tapestry. A 1995 survey performed by Maritz Marketing Research and published in *American Demographics* indicated that roughly 19 million Americans are "involved a great deal in tracing their lineage." With such large numbers of individuals engaged in the field of genealogy, it is increasingly important for consequential encyclopedic works relating to tracing and documenting family heritage to be offered to these researchers. *The Source* is such a work.

In compiling *The Source,* Ancestry's editorial team has taken great pains to engage knowledgeable experts in the many subject areas covered in the work. They spent much time working with these experts to craft sections and chapters that are informative, accurate, comprehensive, and readable for the widest range of individuals engaging in family history research. The many source citations further enhance a most useful text.

This compilation is an essential research aid for beginning, intermediate, and advanced researchers. The first-time user will be quickly guided to important sources as he or she is exposed to discussions and demonstrations of sound research methodology. Intermediate and advanced researchers will appreciate this tome for its thoroughness and true reference utility. In its nearly unique readability it presents itself to the reader as a volume that may be read from cover to cover, but it can just as comfortably be engaged by reading pertinent sections or chapters. It is truly a work for all in the genealogical field.

Whether you are just beginning your quest to discover the richness of your "threads" in the great American tapestry, continuing to trace the many threads of your ancestors throughout your research, or assisting others in uncovering their parts in the great history and heritage of the United States, *The Source* will assuredly be your steady research companion.

Curt B. Witcher
Manager, Historical Genealogy Department
Allen County Public Library
Councilor, National Genealogical Society
President, Federation of Genealogical Societies

PREFACE

Loretto Dennis Szucs and Sandra Hargreaves Luebking

Since the first edition of *The Source* was published in 1984, it has become a standard reference in the field of genealogy and family history. Indeed, it received the coveted "Best Reference" award from the American Library Association in 1984. Ancestry's maiden publication can now be found on the shelves of homes and research facilities across the United States. To say that it was a formidable challenge for the present editors to attempt to match what our predecessors achieved would be a great understatement.

While a number of credible genealogical guides were available before 1984, *The Source* was the first to provide the wide scope and the depth of description of so many potentially rich sources for family historians. Editors Arlene Eakle and Johni Cerny broke new ground with a work that assembled the knowledge of twelve experts in the field. Each chapter of the volume was crafted to describe information that can be gleaned from the records or secondary sources, where to locate the materials, and the inherent problems or limitations of researching specific materials. A virtual encyclopedia of sources, *The Source* was aimed at genealogists with varying levels of experience and expertise, but it soon became a favorite reference for historians, archivists, and librarians as well.

Since *The Source*'s debut, some record collections have shifted, some record access policies have changed, some have become available to the public for the first time, and many more have been newly discovered. Consequently, almost every chapter of this new edition reflects significant growth in the number of records that have become available, and in the great number of indexes and finding aids that have been created or published in print or electronic format since *The Source* was originally published.

This new edition of *The Source* is intended to identify and describe the rich body of original research materials that is available, and to facilitate the use of these materials so that family history can be preserved and enjoyed. It explores information sources that are available for researchers of every level of experience, including beginners, who are addressed in chapter 1, The Foundations of Family History Research. This chapter acquaints the novice with home sources, such as family photographs and documents, and introduces the basic skills and concepts to be mastered initially.

Every chapter in this edition of *The Source* has been updated and fine-tuned. Because of the dramatic changes that have taken place in the field of genealogical research, some chapters that appeared in the original *Source* have been completely revised. This volume also offers two chapters that emphasize contemporary usage. The all-new Twentieth-Century Research chapter (chapter 18) has been added for the ever-growing segment of our reading audience whose research is focused on this period. Chapter 2, Databases, Indexes, and Other Finding Aids, addresses the influence of computer-linked finding aids while exploring the rich and ever-growing collection of source material available in print and electronic format.

We hope that this revised and enhanced edition of *The Source* will prove as useful as the previous one, and we invite readers to become our collaborators by writing to offer suggestions for improving and expanding the future editions of *The Source*.

ACKNOWLEDGMENTS

Any compilation such as *The Source* depends upon the scholarship and experience of many individuals. Because no one individual can be an expert in every aspect of the multifaceted field of genealogical research, we relied upon the knowledge of twenty experts who contributed specialized and current information. This volume is built upon the knowledge of the contributing authors; we are indebted to all of them.

We gratefully acknowledge the tremendous accomplishment of Arlene Eakle and Johni Cerny in compiling the original version of *The Source,* which was published in 1984. Their groundbreaking work, together with the exceptional vision and resources dedicated by Ancestry's founder, John Sittner, combined to make the first edition of *The Source* a standard in the field.

For this revised edition of *The Source,* we are indebted to Robert Anderson, who took time away from his own important projects to read and comment on every chapter of this volume, for his guidance in bringing all of the pieces together.

Every chapter was independently peer reviewed. We have relied greatly upon the many colleagues who offered critiques and suggestions, and we wish to thank them all collectively. Certain individuals who helped to evaluate the material in this volume deserve special gratitude. They include Desmond Walls Allen, Judith Allen, Thomas Allen, Debra Anderson, Gale Williams Bamman, Noel Barton, Susan Hawkes Cooke, David Dilts, Joan Fletcher, Linda Woodward Geiger, Jeanne Gentry, Eric Grundset, Ruth Land Hatten, Margaret M. Hoffman, Birdie Monk Holsclaw, Donald Jackanicz, Miranda Levin, Karen Livsey, Laura Ann Kathryn Luebking, Wayne Moore, Ted Naanes, Elizabeth Nichols, Charles F. Rehkopf, Judith P. Reid, Marsha Rising, Jayare Roberts, Juliana Marie Smith, Lynette Strangstad, Rabbi Malcolm Stern, Chuck Sherrill, David S. Van Daff, and Paula Stuart Warren.

In addition to contributing their own parts for this book, these individuals took time to review and comment on other chapters: Robert Anderson, Johni Cerny, James Hansen, Gordon Remington, David Thackery, and Curt Witcher. This volume would not have been possible without them.

Matt Grove, senior editor for Ancestry, contributed greatly by integrating the ideas and writing styles of the various writers in this single volume. We are also grateful for the very constructive criticism and suggestions offered during the earlier stages of this volume's production by Anne Lemmon during her tenure as managing editor of Ancestry.

INTRODUCTION

Robert Charles Anderson

The purpose of *The Source* is to indicate to you what sorts of records are available to family historians and how to find them. In the course of reviewing this material, you, the researcher, will find much information that will assist you in the careful documentation of these records, as well as some guideposts toward the first steps in analyzing the documents.

It is a commonplace to state that the records created by various government and non-government agencies and by individuals—and which we use in our genealogical research—were not created with the genealogist in mind but for some more immediate reason. The genealogical researcher's role is to see past the original purpose for which a record was created and to discern those meanings that will aid in constructing pedigrees. To begin that process we need to understand some widely used but frequently confused and misunderstood categories into which documents can be placed.

A common distinction is that between primary and secondary sources. Many definitions have been given for these two terms. We will say that a primary record is one that was created in near chronological proximity to an event by someone who had reasonably close knowledge of the event. A secondary record, then, is one that was created at some remove from the event in question; it represents editorial conclusions based on primary records. The distinction between the two categories is not always obvious. A marriage certificate, a census entry, or a deed would qualify as a primary source, while a family history created some generations after the events recorded in the deed or census entry and resulting from a combination and interpretation of many such documents would be a secondary source.

The Source attempts to introduce the reader to the main varieties of primary sources which the researcher will find useful. The presence of such sources as newspapers in this book may cause some to question their inclusion, for there is a widespread belief that newspapers are secondary sources at best. But a single newspaper issue may contain material of all levels of usability. One news story might be an excellent eyewitness account of a fire, more accurate and closer to the event than any other account (even court testimony), while another article may represent the writer's own opinion about an event he himself did not witness. The lesson is that categorical distinctions such as primary versus secondary should not be applied too rigidly; each record should be taken on its own merits.

ARRANGEMENT OF *THE SOURCE*

There is a set of perspectives from which we may examine the sources which genealogists use, based on the type of problem being solved or the particular stage of research that has been reached. Three perspectives of this sort have determined the way in which *The Source* is organized.

The first of these perspectives—the commonest and most traditional—is the distinction of records by the type of agency that generated them and the purpose for which they were originally created. This perspective, of course, involves the usual approach of studying census, church, vital, or court records, the basis of most genealogical textbooks. This way of looking at the records should be applicable to all genealogical problems, regardless of time or place.

The second perspective requires us to be especially aware of the unique history of one segment of the population, for whom some of the usual varieties of records have not been created or for whom one or another of the ordinary record types becomes unusually important. This perspective would most commonly apply to various ethnic or minority groups, whether indigenous or immigrant.

Finally, for any locality and for any population, the particular combination of records that will most easily and most frequently lead to a solution of a genealogical problem changes over time. In most instances those changes are taken for granted and accommodated as research proceeds. But over the last one hundred years, with the increased mobility and urbanization of the population, new approaches to genealogical problems have become necessary, and a special emphasis on urban and twentieth-century research is appropriate.

This introduction is devoted to a brief summary of each of the chapters in *The Source*'s three main sections, which correspond to the three perspectives just discussed: Record Types, Ethnic Groups, and what might be called the Genealogy of Time and Place. Remember that these three ways of looking at the records are complementary and not exclusive. City directories, for instance, are an important record type, and they receive treatment in a chapter in the first section. But these same records are very important in the study of some ethnic groups and in research in modern cities, so references to directories appear in many chapters.

RECORD TYPES

In chapter 1, The Foundations of Family History Research, Sandra Luebking and Loretto Szucs open the discussion of record types where the genealogical quest should always begin: with those persons and events closest to us. They discuss the process of recovering the living memories of those relatives who still survive and then go on to cover the sorts of documents likely to be found in the home, such as family Bibles, birth and marriage certificates, and certain family heirlooms.

Although home sources, whether oral or written, may "feel" different from public and more official records simply because they are so familiar to us, Luebking and Szucs point out that they must be regarded and analyzed as rigorously as all the other records we encounter. They discuss the need to critically evaluate family traditions and oral history so that we can separate the myth from the solid historical basis upon which the tradition was built. They also describe how to go about dating an object or a document found in the home. Although the methods for dating home sources may differ from the process of dating a manuscript record found in a courthouse or library, the creation of a sound chronological framework for our research is a consideration to be kept in mind at all stages of our work.

Having introduced the researcher to this first record type, Luebking and Szucs pause to examine a number of aspects of the research process that are important regardless of what types of records we are examining. They begin with an explanation of the network of resources with which the genealogist must become familiar—the societies and libraries and knowledgeable individuals who will help provide access to new information. This explanation is linked to a discussion of the broader areas of historical and geographic knowledge, which support genealogical research.

The authors follow this up with a very important section on note-taking and documentation. The act of copying a record always includes the possibility of introducing errors or of degrading the information content of the record in some way. Even an excellent photocopy will lose some of the contrast created by differing inks in a manuscript record. Thus, every effort that can be made to minimize this information loss will be repaid at a later stage of research. The more accurate your note-taking, the less the likelihood that you will need to go back and examine a source again. But if you do need to return to a source, an accurate record of the location and identification of that source is vital. This requirement is true not only for your own research but for the person who comes after you and who wishes to follow up on a point of disagreement or of additional research.

Continuing the discussion of general methodology, in Databases, Indexes, and Other Finding Aids, Kory Meyerink sets forth various methods by which all varieties of records may be found, and also methods for searching these records. He introduces the researcher to the massive databases, library catalogs, indexes, and other points of entry to the world of information that must be used at the beginning of any research project.

As Meyerink notes, many of these research tools are now available in electronic form, whether on CD-ROM or as part of larger online computer services. The time has arrived when the genealogist has to master these technologies in order to research effectively.

Returning to the discussion of specific record types, Johni Cerny and Arlene Eakle devote two chapters to the important category of vital records. The first of these chapters discusses birth records, death records, and cemetery research. Cerny gives a brief history of the registration of births and deaths in the colonies and the states, and then she describes the content of typical records. Eakle describes the types of cemeteries and the related records, and then she discusses the recommended procedures for researching cemeteries, including, most importantly, the process of researching in the cemeteries themselves.

In providing examples of death records, Cerny makes an important distinction between "a photocopy of the certificate filed at the time of death" and "a transcript of the basic information on a preprinted form." Many vital records registries will send the researcher a transcript of the record rather than a photocopy; frequently, a transcript includes less information than the original certificate—and may even introduce new errors. This lesson about copies and transcripts may be applied to all record groups, for we should always be alert to the lineage of the record itself and to how close the copy we hold in our hands is to the earliest version of the record.

In the chapter on marriage and divorce, Cerny lists the great variety of jurisdictions that recorded and maintained marriage records, and she explains the many different sorts of records of marriages which exist, including bonds, licenses, intentions, and certificates. Eakle covers divorce records, presenting the many different ways in which divorces might be granted, whether by legislatures or courts, and she provides information on the location of divorce records.

The section on marriage records gives Cerny an opportunity to explore a source variant that can arise in regard to a wide range of record sources. She examines the situation in Hamilton County (Cincinnati), Ohio, where the early marriage records were destroyed. Many interested parties worked together to reconstruct the records, going to churches, families, and newspapers to rebuild what had been lost. Such reconstructed records will, of course, have problems that the earlier, more contemporaneous versions of the same data would not have, but they should not be shunned on that account.

One of the record categories that is of broadest application, and that every genealogist uses early in the research process, is the census—especially the federal census. Loretto Szucs covers these records in great detail, beginning with a section on the history of census taking and moving on to a longer discussion of the strengths and limitations of census records. This is followed by a description of each of the federal censuses taken from 1790 to 1920, and the chapter concludes with a listing of indexes and finding aids.

An excellent feature of Szucs' census chapter is the census-by-census description, which makes it clear that, even in this relatively homogeneous record category, each census has to be taken on its own merits. Szucs presents the questions that were asked on each census, and then she describes peculiarities of that census which could affect the information it might contain or the way in which we might interpret it. When this information on a given census is combined with the more general discussion of strengths and limitations of census records, the researcher has a powerful tool for interpreting the census entries that might affect a particular genealogical problem.

In his chapter on church records, Richard Dougherty describes the genesis of the different religious denominations that exist in the United States and how their evolution has affected the nature and the quality of the records which they have created. He describes how to go about finding church records—sometimes a very difficult task—and he discusses some printed church records. Finally, he gives addresses and other useful information for several dozen denominations, including, for those that exist, the locations of the denominations' central archives.

Especially helpful in the chapter is a section on "Suggestions for Research." Dougherty presents a number of ideas on interpreting church records and on the tactics of obtaining those records. This last point is extremely important with records of this sort, which may be privately held or whose custodian may not understand what it is the genealogist wants. The suggestions in this section can be used for a wide variety of records that are not held in large, professionally-managed repositories but are unique documents held by small, local organizations or that are even in private hands.

Arlene Eakle surveys the vast topic of court records, providing information on court procedures and on the organization and variety of courts. Of greatest importance to genealogists, Eakle discusses here the records of probate courts throughout the country; but the chapter also includes descriptions of many lesser courts which may be of interest, such as admiralty courts and the records of mining districts.

This chapter includes many examples of documents preserved by various courts, which not only help us understand the workings of a particular court but also alert us to the unusual and unexpected information that may be included in such records. For example, a bill of costs in a lengthy lawsuit, seemingly a dull and irrelevant piece of paper, includes entries which give a narrow range for the date of death of a person connected to the suit—a date which might not otherwise be available.

Perhaps no category of records is more important to the genealogist than those relating to land. Chapter 8, revised by Sandra Luebking, examines these from various perspectives. First discussed are the older states, where most or all of the land was granted by the colony or state and not by any higher authority. As might be expected, the systems of land granting and land tenure in these jurisdictions varied widely, and each must be studied separately. The chapter also presents information on the much larger number of states that were established after the formation of the federal government, in which most or all of the land was originally granted by that government and not by the states. Finally, it includes a section on each of the fifty states and the District of Columbia, pointing out what is unique to their governments and including some bibliographic items.

The maps included in this chapter add to its usefulness. The discussion indicates how these graphic documents assist in locating the lands of our ancestors. It goes beyond that, however, to demonstrate also how the platting of individual pieces of land can be vital in solving difficult genealogical problems.

Johni Cerny next provides a systematic survey of military records. She first covers the surviving service records, beginning with seventeenth-century colonial wars and continuing through the twentieth century. She moves on to records of veterans' benefits, again proceeding chronologically, and including bounty land grants, pensions, and other records. The chapter concludes with an extensive bibliography, arranged by war and going through the Civil War.

When we think of directories, what comes to mind most immediately is city directories. Gordon Remington describes for us seven types of directories, starting with the obvious category but including also such types as professional and religious directories. He discusses the content and likely location of each variety of directory and then presents a brief methodological example based on each category.

As might be expected, the greater part of Remington's chapter is devoted to city directories, including this latter methodological section, where we are treated to a detailed examination of how one type of record relates to another. We discover how city directories can lead us to census records, to death and probate records, to church records, and even to naturalization and land records. This interconnection between different sources is one of the most important lessons that any genealogist must learn, because very few genealogical problems can be solved using only one record.

Many researchers classify newspapers as "secondary" sources—ones created after the fact—and they evaluate the evidence supplied by newspapers accordingly. More than any other source, however, newspapers are not so easily categorized. Of two items on the same newspaper page, one can be the best evidence available anywhere on a given point, and another can be of no evidentiary value at all. Only comparison with other sources allows the determination of the value of a piece of evidence from a newspaper.

James L. Hansen surveys newspapers from all aspects, first discussing the various types of information to be found in them and how to evaluate this evidence. In describing obituaries, for example, he points out that this information was sometimes provided directly by close relatives of the deceased, and in other instances was filtered through a professional obituary writer. Hansen then describes the techniques necessary to find newspapers appropriate to the researcher's problem, and how to carry out the search once the newspaper has been found. He concludes with an extensive bibliography of inventories of newspapers, indexes and abstracts of their contents, and other related items.

ETHNIC ORIGINS

To begin this section, Kory Meyerink and Loretto Szucs tackle the subject of immigration. They begin with the necessary step of looking for all records created by the immigrant and the immigrant's known family in the United States as a basis for beginning research in the country of origin. The authors follow this discussion with the historical background of immigration and an explanation of the immigration process itself.

This explanation leads naturally to an examination of the records most directly involved in immigration. Most important among these are the passenger lists and naturalization records. Beginning researchers usually want to move directly to these records, but the thrust of this chapter is that much work should be done before these record categories are approached. In this way, the correct record will be found more easily and will have more meaning in the context of what is already known.

Two approaches are taken to the study of the records of Native Americans. First, Curt Witcher surveys the sources that everyone researching such ancestry must use. These sources include a wide range of government documents, ethnohistorical studies, and publications pertaining to one or more of the tribes.

George Nixon then provides a case study, probing in detail the records available for research on Native Americans in Oklahoma. He begins with coverage of records relating to all tribes in Oklahoma and proceeds through the records agency by agency, including material both in Washington and in Oklahoma.

In his chapter on African American genealogy, David Thackery greatly assists the researcher by providing the historical background in which the relevant records were created. Concentrating on the time immediately before and after Emancipation, the author discusses census records, deeds, probates, and plantation records, among others. He emphasizes especially the documents created by the Freedmen's Bureau and related agencies.

Thackery makes an important point about African American research in the period before Emancipation when he notes that, for those years, records for free blacks will be found intermixed with the records for the general population. At the same time, much of the useful documentation for slaves will be found among the records of the white owners and is not limited to plantation records. In other words, if engaged in genealogical research on this ethnic group before 1865, you should not limit yourself to records generated by or for the African American population; examine the full range of material for the appropriate time and place.

In his presentation of research for those with Hispanic ancestry, George Ryskamp opens with a sequence of steps that should be taken by each researcher. Then ensues a lengthy conspectus of the records available both in this hemisphere and in Spain, whether in print or in manuscript, including material in several archives in Spain.

Ryskamp emphasizes the importance of what he calls "locality analysis." This process involves more than finding an ancestral village on a map or in a gazetteer. It requires the researcher to learn as much as possible about the place from which an ancestor came—not merely for general historical context but to assist in locating and interpreting records that might be peculiar to a locality.

Gary Mokotoff begins his treatment of Jewish-American ancestry by surveying the history of Jewish migration, first outlining the movements of Jews throughout the world during the full course of their history, and then describing six phases of Jewish immigration to the United States in more detail. The author makes an important point here, observing that each of these periods "has its own sources of information for doing genealogical research." This insight has broad application for all genealogical research, for the sources which may be appropriate for the eighteenth century in a certain locality will not necessarily be useful (or even available) for research of the nineteenth century.

Mokotoff then examines at length the sources available for the study of Jews during the Holocaust, after which he surveys access to records of Jews in Central and Eastern Europe, paying special attention to developments after the fall of the Iron Curtain and the dissolution of the Soviet Union. This chapter concludes with a bibliography of reference works relevant to research into Jewish ancestry and a list of pertinent record repositories.

TIME AND PLACE

A few decades ago, when the first guides to genealogical research were being compiled, most of us could talk with relatives who had been born in the nineteenth century. Armed with their unique knowledge, we were able to go immediately to records of that century as we began to study a line of ancestry. But as we rapidly approach the twenty-first century, a generation or two of ancestors who were born in this century are already deceased and not available to share their knowledge.

For these reasons, twentieth-century research is emerging as a separate research category, and Kathleen Hinckley's chapter introduces us to this subject. To do this she points out those types of records which have become more useful in finding people in this century of increased population and high mobility. City and telephone directories, for example, become very important. Hinckley also tells us how to research Social Security records, a source which will rapidly become one of the most important for twentieth-century research.

The author also discusses matters of privacy and other restrictions. With most records of the nineteenth century and earlier there are no privacy restrictions, and we expect to be able to see any document we might be interested in. This is not the case with more recent research, and the genealogist must always be alert to this problem, know the ways to gain access to records, and be prepared to use another approach when any given class of records is closed to us.

Another feature of the twentieth century is increased urbanization. In this century, the percentage of the American population living in urban settings has overtaken the percentage of the rural population. Loretto Szucs covers the subject of research in cities, both in the twentieth century and in earlier times. She first provides general guidance, describing the sorts of finding aids that will lead to records and the institutions that hold them. She then covers in detail each of the varieties of records that are especially important for urban research, which include (from a different perspective) not only many of the sources of value for twentieth-century research, but also sources of particular importance in cities, such as business records and the files of municipal courts.

Szucs includes a lengthy section on maps, which are useful to the genealogist in any setting but even more so to the genealogist researching urban subjects. Maps include such different cartographic categories as the Sanborn fire insurance maps, bird's-eye views, and ward maps. Szucs shows how these maps can be used in conjunction with other record types to help narrow the field of search in the census—for example, where reading an entire city directory for one name would be impractical.

SUMMARY

In this introduction I have attempted to show that, in many cases, the specific suggestions offered in a chapter on one record type or ethnic group are equally applicable in other areas. This ability to transport concepts of methodology between chapters creates a synthesis of sorts in how we approach research. But there is a caution here. When we are collecting records and documents in the early stages of our work, the temptation is great to begin the synthesis immediately, adding these records directly to our family group sheets or compiled genealogical sketches. This urge should be resisted, for your first impressions may not be correct. Later reflection and analysis, or other records, may change your early conclusions dramatically.

For this reason the raw data, in the form of specific records collected with the aid of what you have learned from *The Source*, should be maintained separately from your synthesized family groups. Do not enter census entries or baptismal records directly onto a family group sheet! Keep these records separate and distinct; you can always rearrange your reconstructed families at a later date, but it is much harder to do this if your only copy of the raw data is mixed in with unrelated material on some other family.

The location and correct identification of records is the underpinning of all we do in genealogical research, and if we are careful at this early stage, the rest of our genealogical work will benefit. *The Source* is designed to accomplish just that.

THE FOUNDATIONS OF FAMILY HISTORY RESEARCH

CHAPTER CONTENTS

THE FOUNDATIONS OF FAMILY HISTORY RESEARCH

Sandra Hargreaves Luebking and Loretto Dennis Szucs

The goal of every family historian is to discover and preserve the family's history through a permanent and accurate record. This chapter is about beginnings: beginning a research journey, beginning to acquire knowledge about the past, and beginning to record that knowledge for the future. Your efforts will enable future generations to know your ancestors—and you.

This chapter is intended to start you "on the path" of family history research. Thus, only the essential first steps are discussed: (1) to consider your personal knowledge of the family; (2) to interview all persons who have information about the family; (3) to identify and catalogue items often found in the home; (4) to evaluate family traditions and seek clues from these interviews; and (5) to maintain a written record of all you discover and to link each discovery to its proper source.

The importance of participating in the genealogical community through organizations or programs of education is emphasized in this chapter, as is the importance of geography (especially the use of maps) and history to your research. Finally, a discussion of the ethical and legal considerations is included to clarify the current status of public record access and copyright laws.

It is expected that, before you continue in your research, you examine one of the how-to guides available. Many titles are available through local libraries. Read more than one, and read them with a discriminating eye. The best guides are those that stress good record-keeping techniques, linkage of information to sources, and an orderly, systematic approach to family history research.

THE FIRST STEPS

In family history research, we begin with the present. The first steps in research include consideration of what is known about the family by observation or from the traditions and stories passed down through the generations. Conversations and interviews with family members, friends, former neighbors, and perhaps people familiar with the history of the local area supplement our own memories. Home sources, such as a military medal, photographs, the family Bible, a grandparent's baptismal certificate, or the patent to your great-great-grandparents' homestead, enhance these recollections and interviews.

Any of these items could hold clues about your family his-

tory. Is the medal from the Civil War service of an ancestor? Does a newspaper clipping describe the accidental death of a great-uncle's first wife? Did your maternal line immigrate in 1878, as tradition states, and your paternal line in 1778, as Grandmother was fond of saying?

The clue might be a date inscribed on a wedding ring which leads you to an entry in the session minutes of a Presbyterian church. A memory that the family once lived in upstate New York might later be verified by finding a land deed at a courthouse. First steps involve discovering these clues, organizing them into a coherent pattern, and then following them on what might be the most remarkable and compelling journey of your life: the reconstruction and preservation of your own family's history.

As first steps become a journey, you will extend your searches to libraries and archives, courthouses, and other public record offices. As your curiosity grows, so will the collection of paper you accumulate. Unless you begin with good record-keeping practices, you may be overwhelmed by the amount of information you acquire.

Just as important as taking those first research steps is maintaining a clear record of them. Memories and observations are vulnerable to the ravages of time, and they should be preserved as soon as possible. Begin by writing down what you remember and what you learn. This written record will do more than document and preserve your findings. Completing record-keeping forms, maintaining a log of research activities, citing all sources of information, and periodically summarizing your findings will structure your investigation, enabling you to use your research time more wisely and productively.

There are many forms and organizational systems from which to choose. Some record-keeping systems require handwritten entry notes on preprinted forms. Other systems comprise software designed for use with personal computers. Whether using a computer or entering information by hand, it is critical to link every entry to its origin. This connects your findings to the specific document or other source that provided the information. Examples of this linkage on a manual set of forms and a computer-generated chart are shown later in this chapter.

Two other record-keeping skills assume great importance in genealogical research. The first is that of taking notes clearly and concisely. The second skill is drafting regular summaries of your findings. One basic summary style is to present the information as a timeline of important events. A timeline can help focus on immediate research needs while providing a stepping-stone to the long-term goal of publication. A timeline is readily updated and can include specific statements about people, places, and treasured moments.

Another style of summary is the narrative form. A narrative can range from informal paragraphs about a single ancestor to a multi-generational family history suitable for publication. Novices and experienced researchers alike can benefit from creating short narratives at every stage of their work. Techniques for note-taking and methods of summarizing findings are discussed later in this chapter.

MEMORIES

Your recollections, and those of others, are unique and vital to your family's story. As these memories undergo the rigors of examination, selection, evaluation, and recording, they become the foundation upon which additional research will be built.

Knowing the date and place of your grandparent's marriage from family conversations could save weeks of frustration and expense in locating the official record of that event. One family's belief that "Great-Grandpa was a twin" was a key element in subsequent record searches in England. Although untrue, this conviction ultimately helped locate the birth record of a sibling; it had been filed less than a year before that of the great-grandfather. Both fact and fiction have their place in your study, and both can provide important clues for future searches.

Oral interviewing is the primary technique by which the fact and fiction of memories can be collected from family members or family friends and acquaintances. Information obtained in this manner can be extremely useful as long as one acknowledges that "human memory is a fragile historical source; it is subject to lapses, errors, fabrications and distortions."[1]

Good interviews do not just happen. You must prepare well for interviewing others. There are several helpful guides to conducting interviews; one of the most respected, although dated, in the oral history field is Cullom Davis, Kathryn Bake, and Kay MacLean, *From Tape to Type* (Chicago: American Library Association, 1977). This guide offers techniques for planning, conducting, and transcribing the interview. One of the most important cautions for new family historians who do not have interviewing experience is that "An interview is not a dialogue. The purpose of oral history interviews is to learn the *narrator's* story."[2]

Other essential considerations include making advance arrangements and letting the narrator know what topics you want to discuss. Compile a list of questions, but let the narrator carry the discussion as long as it does not go too far astray. Watch for signs of tiredness and do not overstay your welcome. It is far better to have a narrator count the hours until you return than the minutes until you leave. If you take notes during the interview, examine them as soon as possible after the meeting. Elaborate on entries that are unclear. Consider topics that were not covered or questions that remain unanswered.

The use of a tape recorder (with the permission of the person being interviewed) is most successful if you have practiced with the recording equipment in advance. Be sure to bring spare tapes and batteries to the session. It is important to transcribe the resulting tapes immediately. An interview might be reconstructed from your notes and recollections if they are fresh in your mind despite equipment failures or unintelligible conversation.

Video cameras and tape recorders can produce powerful supplements to your written record. The use of such equipment and interviewing techniques can be acquired from guides, such as Duane and Pat Sturm, *Video Family History* (Salt Lake City: Ancestry, 1989), or Living Family Albums, *Grandparents' Video Interview Kit: The Producer's Handbook, The Camera Person's Guide, The Interviewer's Guidebook,* and *Script Packet* (Westlake, Ohio: Living Family Albums, 1989). These last four booklets provide step-by-step instructions for creating hour-long oral or video histories. Again, common sense prevails: make the narrator aware of the use of such equipment well in advance, practice with the equipment so that its use will not distract the speaker, and review the results as soon as is practical.

Video cameras can move interviews away from the realm of "two chairs and a table." Interview sessions can be more informative if speakers can perform routine tasks as they talk. Your grandmother may agree to bake bread as she has done for years, without a recipe. A great-uncle might demonstrate how he painstakingly sands the rungs on the seventh baby cradle he has made. Your mother, an avid gardener, could divide and re-plant bulbs as she recounts tales of ancestors. Use the camera to tour the family home, filming the rooms and the outside environs. Visit the schools attended and parks frequented. Capture the past—even the recent past—as part of your family history worthy of preservation.

Of course, a personal visit may not be practical. You may not know where all your relatives are, especially if your family has been separated by divorce or adoption. Try to gather relevant names and addresses from those with whom you are in contact. Chapter 18, Tracking Twentieth-Century Ancestors, provides suggestions for locating others. Initiate contact with a letter and include a self-addressed, stamped envelope.[3] Be sure to attend to the oldest folks first; don't risk losing their knowledge.

Interviews also provide opportunities to locate, identify, catalog, and preserve what family historians term "home sources." Home sources (see the section later in this chapter) include heirlooms, such as furniture, small collectibles, and photographs; manuscript materials, such as diaries, letters, and family bibles; and copies of public records, such as certificates of birth, marriage, and death, land patents, and wills. Your interview could capture details about a piece of furniture as the current owner describes its importance to your family. Or remarks about the people in an early family portrait can be retained along with a copy of the portrait.

Recalling memories, interviewing others, and examining home sources will immerse you in the past and will pay dividends as your search progresses. You will come to appreciate the necessity of preserving these memories and personal attributes of people who could move out of your life at any moment. Public records and archival collections, in all likelihood, will outlast the relatives and acquaintances who have knowledge of the family to share. That is why people, not objects or records, provide our first source of information.

TRADITIONS

Tradition is "the handing down of statements, beliefs, legends, customs, etc., from generation to generation, especially by word of mouth or by practice, i.e., a story that has come down to us by tradition."[4] Some cultures, such as African American and Native American, hold tradition in high regard as a way of preserving a past for which few written records survive. Anthropologists have found that when tradition is the medium by which culture and family history are transmitted, the completeness and accuracy of the spoken word are likely to be carefully maintained by the storyteller.

Discovering information about the parents of an Austrian woman who had married a Native American of the Lakota Sioux tribe depended upon oral interviews with those who recalled the woman through tribal tradition. The details proved surprisingly accurate and led to the discovery of death dates and burial information about the woman's parents. The mother and father had followed their daughter to the Dakota reservation but soon departed. Oral tradition placed their destination as Chicago, and in this city was found the father's estate papers, which indicated that contact had been lost with one daughter—a daughter who resided on an Indian reservation.

Unfortunately, not all traditions contain as much truth as the one described above. It is not uncommon for less-factual stories to follow a pattern, perhaps of separation, lost wealth, or thwarted opportunity. One common theme is that of the "separated brothers." While there can be truth in such an account, it occurs so often as to be suspect. Usually, in this account, three brothers immigrated and separated soon after their arrival in the United States. One disappeared into the "West" and is lost to the others, although it is suspected that he became famous and, no doubt, wealthy.

Be skeptical about tales of unclaimed wealth. Southern variations may cite treasure buried to conceal it from Union soldiers during the Civil War. The East Coast version may include a castle and inheritance in Nottinghamshire, Devon, or Surrey, denied the American immigrant. In the Midwest, lost wealth supposedly results from the Great Chicago Fire of 1871, the family having hired a wagon to transport them and their goods from the scene and the wagonmaster speeding away with their possessions before the family could board.

Most traditions, however, contain a core of truth, an element that is surprisingly accurate and useful in research. The difficulty in proving these truths might be because the storyteller has assigned the activities to the wrong generation. More than one researcher has found "blended" generations a challenge to sort: was it Jacob's father who fought in the American Revolution or his grandfather? As your research skills grow, you may want to consult articles such as Helen F. M. Leary, "Finding Truth in a Family Tradition: Sumner Antecedents of Demsey S. Goodman," *National Genealogical Society Quarterly* 81 (3) (September 1993), as examples of methodology used to detect myth and evaluate evidence.

Record all the stories, even those that seem doubtful. Attempt to substantiate each through verification by other people (it is wise to have another person repeat the story rather than for you to offer leading questions) or through public documents. Include the traditions in your written record, but carefully identify them as such and note the sources of the information. These citations will be useful as you analyze information with an eye to proving or disproving parts of it.

HOME SOURCES

Home sources come in many shapes, sizes, and textures. A home source can be a wedding band etched with a date of marriage; a quilt with the name of the quilter and the date of completion stitched on it; the account book of a nineteenth-century female entrepreneur who supported a young family as a dressmaker for the wealthy; a drop-leaf desk with a secret compartment containing an unrecorded deed; or century-old letters chronicling the Civil War from the perspective of a young soldier from Mississippi.

Funeral prayer cards, resumes, even articles of clothing can be home sources. The criterion is not an object's monetary worth or research potential. Instead, value may be purely intrinsic. An object might symbolize a previous owner you've come to know through narratives and research; or an artifact might bring another place or time to life. Among one researcher's most prized possessions is a rough, flat rock—a piece of the stone door frame that still marks the valley home of an eighteenth-century Yorkshire Dale's ancestor. The stone provides an almost tangible link to the men and women who populated those rugged, remote regions of northern England.

Home sources offer three significant opportunities to a family historian. First, the very fact of their survival can tell much about the caretaker—the person or persons who found them to be worthy of saving. Second, they can be genuine sources of evidence: the will preserved for generations that names all of a great-grandfather's children (even the illegitimate ones) or the record of an infant's baptism. Third, a home source can be a key that unlocks the approach to an official record, such as a vital record, a cemetery record, or a court case, to name a few possibilities.

Two faded newspaper clippings offered important clues in one research project. The clippings, pasted in a scrapbook, were reports of deaths. One was determined to be the obituary of a merchant who died while visiting family members in the European village of his birth. The translated information provided countless avenues of research. The name of the deceased, his residence, occupation, and date of death led to local historical writings, business and employment sources, a death certificate, and cemetery plot plans. The name and denomination of the minister who conducted the memorial service also proved useful. The listing of other family members, siblings, his widow, and children was especially helpful.

The other clipping contained significantly less detail but its value soon became apparent. This shorter notice included the sentence "Cincinnati papers, please copy." Cincinnati proved to be the home of many family members of the deceased, a woman without close relatives at her place of death, where the original notice was published.

Discussed below are some of the sources most likely to be found among your possessions.

Photographs

Perhaps the most durable of home sources are pictorial items that depict people as they were: photographs that capture the essence of a lifetime in a second, outlasting the people portrayed. Sometimes family history research results from the need to identify the people in a particularly captivating photograph or to learn what secrets their lives held.

Such was the case with one researcher who discovered, amidst several boxes of photographs, an intriguing portrait of a mother and her five children (figure 1-1). This print was the key to a series of important discoveries about the finder's family. The photograph held the name and city of the studio in which it was taken. This knowledge led to a death certificate for the woman; one entry provided the city of her birth. This information led the researcher to a search site in a different state, providing a breakthrough to the family's past.

Your research goal for home sources is to organize and catalogue these links to the past and, if you are reasonably skilled or very fortunate, to identify them in time and place. While few clues may be offered, knowledge of dating techniques for a particular object may provide a breakthrough. For example, although a photograph may not contain the name and location of the studio, tracking the changes in photographic processes could help in identification and dating.

Figure 1-1. Julia Smith Stone with her children, ca. 1890, Port Huron, Michigan. Courtesy of Sandra Luebking.

The photographic process dates from 1839, when physicist Louis Daguerre invented the daguerreotype process. It utilized a silver-plated copper plate and was used in America almost exclusively until the late 1850s. A pocket-size case, sometimes ornately decorated and with a hinged cover, protected the plate.

The ambrotype (a photograph on glass) achieved popularity from about 1855 into the 1860s. Also mounted in a case, the glass that held the negative was backed with dark paint, cloth, or paper. Often confused with the ambrotype is the tintype, or ferrotype, invented in 1856. In it, a plate of sheet iron holds the image. The tintype was more durable and less expensive than the ambrotype. Tintypes could be placed in cases or even be covered with glass, but more often they were unmounted. Tintypes continued being made into the early 1900s, mostly in rural areas.

Carte-de-visite photographs were often displayed in albums on parlor tables after 1860. These paper photographs measured approximately 2 ½ by 4 ¼ inches and were produced in great quantity through about 1890. From about 1870 until 1910, the larger cabinet-size photograph won favor among portrait sitters, and the images of well-known people, such as movie stars, became popular collector's items (figure 1-2).

Modern gelatin dry plates, first manufactured in the United States in 1878, were slow in winning acceptance, but in 1888 George Eastman's Kodak began to move photography into the amateur realm. After 1900, card-mounted prints were superseded by durable paper photographs produced by home cameras.

Postcards

Although not as personal as family photographs, picture postcards are an intriguing enhancement to a family history. Picture postcards can depict places where your family once lived, including the European village from which the family emigrated, the ships ancestors might have sailed upon, or events conceivably witnessed by past generations. The messages written on postcards can add to your knowledge about the family while providing important insights into the lives of your ancestors.

Postcards were introduced into the United States from Austria in the 1870s. Designed to convey brief messages, these cards were used for special occasions or as souvenirs. Before World War I, holiday greeting postcards were a popular choice for Christmas, Halloween, and Valentine's Day messages.

Topical postcards encompass advertisements or announcements of special events, such as the cards introduced by the 1893 World's Columbian Exposition. Topical cards were also used to depict disasters (such as fires), to provide entertainment, and to promote political figures. View cards are realistic portraits of actual places, people, or objects, tourist attractions and landscapes being the most favored subjects (figure 1-3).

Family Bibles

The written record endures in many forms. Letters and personal accounts of events or eras are highly valued for the information they contain—but it is the family Bible that most often becomes the object of diligent searching.

Should you be fortunate enough to possess a family Bible, the following techniques might help you to evaluate its usefulness as a source of information. First, note the date of its publication. Match the publication date against the span of events written upon the page for family history. If the handwritten entries predate the publication, it is clear indication that they were recorded not as they occurred but at a later date. Next, examine the handwriting used for each entry. Is it all in the same script, indicating that they were written by the same person? Are the entries in the same ink, suggesting that all were made at one sitting? Is there an inscription?

Check each page of a Bible or inherited book for notations or enclosures. Some owners recorded the dates of events, such as memorial services, weddings, and christenings, in the margin adjacent to the Bible text used for the occasion. Others used favorite books to hold prayer cards, obituaries from newspapers, significant scraps of church bulletins, and handwritten notes. Such a note enclosed in one book contained, in German script, the full name and birth date of each child born to the finder's great-grandparents.

Diaries and Journals

Diaries and journals are valued highly by family historians. It is easy enough to verify the accuracy of news and events: weather, surroundings, world and local happenings the diarist might have chosen to record. The accuracy and completeness of such entries can in part indicate the care with which other, more family-oriented, news was recorded.

Official Documents Held by Family Members

Did family members save copies of documents created by public rather than private entities? Birth, marriage, and death certificates; naturalization papers; military discharges; and legal papers from court actions are among the official records families may chose to retain. Valuable in themselves, such documents become priceless when the original documents have been lost through fire or neglect or are otherwise unavailable to you.

What do the records tell you? Are the names recognizable? Is there evidence of where the original record might be, or perhaps the name of the county or church that created the record? Such tips can be springboards to finding other information. A will might be only one of dozens of documents pertaining to an estate that are on file at a county courthouse.

Of course, it is possible that your home copy of a document may never have been in a courthouse. People sometimes found it inconvenient or too expensive to officially record certain events. An early deed or mortgage, an original will, or the marriage certificate of a penniless couple might be the only record of a particular event. Such semi-official records should be stored in a safe place that will slow or prevent their deterioration. (See "Restoration, Preservation, and Disposal," below.)

Privately held documents should be evaluated without bias and with some understanding of their history. Be especially careful to avoid reaching unfounded conclusions about their value. For example, take care with land patents (documents that transferred property from the federal government to private citizens). Patents dated before 2 March 1833 were signed by the president of the United States; after that date, designated officials signed on the president's behalf.

DELLA FOX, IN "THE LITTLE TROOPER."
Copyright 1894, by Napoleon Sarony.
87 UNION SQR., N. Y.

Figure 1-2. Performer Della Fox in an 1894 publicity shot by Napoleon Sarony of New York. Courtesy of Sandra Luebking.

Samplers

> When I this little Record see
>
> I think how haPPy it would be
>
> If Pa and Ma should live to say
>
> Our children walk in wisdoms way.
>
> And when the Parting stroke is come
>
> And they and we are called home.
>
> May we all meet in heaven above
>
> And sing redeeming grace and love.

When nine-year-old Mary A. Richards (1814 to 1873) of Jaffrey, New Hampshire, applied crinkled silk floss to linen, she began a family record sampler that has survived more than a century. Her wish, above, is a pleasant suggestion of the era. But it is the family record embroidered above this little poem that provides the data so avidly sought by family historians:

Figure 1-3. A postcard dated 1911 announcing the birth of a child (see the writing on the back side). Courtesy of Sandra Luebking.

Family Record

Mr. Luther A. Richards born sept. 26 1785/Miss Mary Page born/June 8 1794/Luther Richards & Mary Page married July 5 1813/Mary Adeline born Jan 1 181[4]/Roderick Streat born June 22 18[15]Abijah born APril 10 Died APril 18/1817/ Luther Abijah born APril 12 1818/Sarah Ann born June 15/1820/Amanda born August 7 1822/ Harriet born Oct 1 1824/Huldah Hopkins born April 13 ?/M.[5]

For more than two hundred years, the making of samplers was part of a young American woman's education. Introduced in the seventeenth century by settlers from England and northern Europe, samplers soon acquired distinctively American characteristics. Mary Jaene Edmonds, an authority on samplers, has determined that samplers were created in the classroom according to the instructions of women teachers. Edmonds has traced numerous samplers back to the influence of private schoolmistresses, whose teachings can be seen in the selection of patterns and the methods of execution.[6]

Other Artifacts

Not all home sources contain as much obvious family information as does the sampler described above, yet even the most unlikely of trinkets can be revealing by providing identifiers that direct or define a search.

One researcher discovered a police badge among her family's home possessions. There was little on it to connect the original owner to a particular police department or time period, yet it opened doors otherwise closed. This object provided an indicator, in this case an occupation, that distinguished the ancestor from the many other urban dwellers of the same name. Knowledge of the police connection enabled the researcher to track its owner through several years of city directories, providing a given name for the family member, an approximate year of death, and the year of arrival in the city. With these facts, the researcher was able to venture into records of immigration, death, and probate, a difficult task in an urban area.

Jewelry is often a valued family heirloom. If a piece has monetary value, it may be fairly easy to date. Two books that offer discussions of valuable jewelry are Joseph Sataloff and Alison Richards, *The Pleasure of Jewelry and Gemstones* (London: Octopus Books, 1975), which focuses on English jewelry and has useful information on mourning jewelry, including pieces containing locks of hair of the departed; and Margaret Flower, *Victorian Jewellery* (South Brunswick, N.J.: A.S. Barnes & Co., 1967), which is helpful in dating late nineteenth-century jewelry and may identify a place or manufacturer of origin.

DATING HOME SOURCES

Placing photographs in specific time periods and locales may help to identify the persons featured. Consult books such as Karen Frisch-Ripley, *Unlocking the Secrets in Old Photographs* (Salt Lake City: Ancestry, 1992). Photographic processes, discussed earlier, are critical to classifying a photograph within a decade or so of its origin. Once the general period of origin has been established, other indicators offer more precise dating. A book of photographic portraits edited by Alison Mager, *Children of the Past* (New York: Dover Publications, 1978) provides the opportunity to compare studio backdrops and props, such as period playthings and furniture, with those in an unidentified photo.

An examination of clothing styles over decades might also help to demystify a photograph in your possession. Joan Severa, *Dressed for the Photographer: Ordinary Americans and Fashion, 1840–1900* (Ohio: Kent State University Press, 1995), shows Americans, rich and poor, black and white, rural and urban, and how they chose to dress for the photographer.

Other clues to dating a photograph are the style of moustaches, sideburns, and beards on men and hairstyle for both genders; setting or environment (if a studio portrait, the objects used in the setting); even the pose can be revealing of the era in which the subject lived (figure 1-4).

A photograph depicting one of the first African American-owned banks in Memphis, Tennessee, provides insights into a workplace of its period. Note the telephone at the teller's window and the electrical fixture hanging from the ceiling. These items are not only interesting; they may provide inclusive dates for the photograph (figure 1-5).

Postcards can be dated through their inscriptions, stamps, or postmarks. Those marked "Private Mailing Card" are likely to have been printed between 1898 and 1902 or, if printed in Europe, between 1899 and 1918. Cards on which correspondence was prohibited on the address side and overlaid onto the photograph or illustration predate 1907. Penny postcards were manufactured after 1898, when postal regulations established the penny postcard rate, while cards requiring two cents of postage date from 1873 to 1898.

The dating of antiques, such as furniture or other collectibles, is more complicated. Few family historians are experts in this art, and most will benefit from the professional help available from museums and historical societies. Take the object or a photograph of it to a curio shop or antique show where there are knowledgeable and reliable dealers. Seek more than one opinion, but be willing to pay for such consultations.

Once you have acquired some information about an object's origin or the date of its creation, prepare a written record of it. Create a "home sources album"—sometimes called an "heirloom book"—by taking photographs of each precious item and arranging them in an archival photo album. Leave space to record all that is known about the object, including professional opinions you have received regarding value, origin, and age. Instructions for preparing such an album will be found in "Leaving a Legacy: How to Preserve Your Research, Photos and Heirlooms" in *Ancestry,* the quarterly of the Palm Beach County (Florida) Genealogy Society, 28 (2) (April 1993). Here, too, is the perfect place to identify the person to whom the object is to go upon your demise.

INVENTORYING AND CATALOGING HOME SOURCES

The home sources album is good for insurance purposes as well as for preserving background information. It provides a photographic record for the identification of possessions and can help to manage an otherwise overwhelming collection of artifacts or written materials. The amount of organizing and the system you employ will depend on how many home sources you have. Small collections can be grouped by type: artifacts, wearables, or photographs. If you have a Bible, two diaries, several letters, and a journal, the category might be "communication or written." Larger collections of a single category can be subdivided chronologically.

Regardless of the type or amount of material you possess or the system you adopt, organizing possessions makes good sense and enables you to effectively use the information without excessive handling of the objects. Substituting photographs of home sources (especially those most often referred to for research purposes) allows you to place the originals in a safe location.

After the collection is divided into categories, the inventory begins. Design a simple inventory form that has headings for inventory date, person or persons conducting the inventory, category of home source, and its ultimate destination. List each item, provide a description, note its condition, context (where

Figure 1-4. Mabel Banks Fletcher, born 1 August 1899, age three. Courtesy of Joan Fletcher.

Figure 1-5. The Scott Wilkerson Bank—one of the first African-American-owned banks in Memphis, Tennessee—ca. 1905. Courtesy of Joan Fletcher.

it was found or is usually kept), any genealogically relevant information it contains, and whatever is known or surmised about its origin.

Computer database programs provide an excellent way to organize such information. A carefully designed database will allow you to print a list of holdings in a variety of ways: by type of object, by date or origin, by name of original possessor, or by present or future caretaker, for example. The database can be enhanced by adding similar information on all family holdings—even those that some family members may refuse to share or exchange. Family members who cannot bear to part with objects may permit photographs or written summaries to be made. They are more likely to do so if, in exchange, they receive similar information from other holders of home sources.

RESTORATION, PRESERVATION, AND DISPOSAL OF HOME SOURCES

The condition of some items may require an attempt at restoration. If you are not familiar with the techniques necessary to restore or preserve antiques or manuscript material, two options are available. First, you can study a manual on restoration and determine if you are capable of restoring the artifact to

your satisfaction. A useful publication is Barbara Sagraves, *A Preservation Guide: Saving the Past and the Present for the Future* (Salt Lake City: Ancestry, 1995).

If time or skill limitations prohibit a do-it-yourself project, a second option is to call upon professionals. Obtain the names of qualified persons by contacting area museums or historical societies. Talk to neighbors or antique dealers who have had good experiences with persons who restore or prepare items for preservation.

Important and irreplaceable photographs or picture postcards can be duplicated, often inexpensively. Artifacts, jewelry, clothing, and samplers can be photographed. Correspondence, Bible pages, diaries, and journals not durable enough to be photocopied can be transcribed (in script or type). Every care should be taken to ensure that the original is duplicated or described carefully in a permanent record.

One of the best methods of preservation is sharing. Provide other family members with items from your collection that may be of emotional value but are not critical to your genealogical record. Any item that can be reproduced in some fashion should also be shared. Not only does your benevolence lessen the risk of a major catastrophe destroying all family treasures, your kindness may encourage others to share with you.

Finally, when these most precious of objects need care beyond what you can provide, consider disposal. With whom will you entrust your collection of memorabilia and home sources? An unmarried son? A museum or archive? A local historical society? Whatever you decide, contact the recipient in advance to be sure the person or organization is willing to accept the collection and to determine in what form or condition it would be most welcome. Plan wisely. Leaving a collection of fragile glassware to a niece who plans to live in small apartments as she pursues an acting career or to a library that specializes in printed matter may not be the best disposal decisions.

"HOME" SOURCES OUTSIDE THE HOME

Not every family is fortunate enough to possess a collection of home sources. For those who have scarcely a photograph or a piece of heirloom jewelry, the initial steps will include a search for artifacts or manuscripts that may have been moved to other places.

A distant relative, a former neighbor, or a one-time business associate of the family may possess photographs or correspondence exchanged a generation or more ago. Or these persons may have knowledge of more distant holders of such artifacts. A researcher who practices tact, patience, and persistence could discover a treasure trove of memorabilia in another's possession. If so, do not expect instant access to what may be valued materials. Instead, establish yourself as a caring, considerate seeker of information and one who is willing to share what you have acquired.

Flea markets, antique dealers, and county fairs in the region from which a family came are all potential places to find materials that, even if not specifically linked to your family, can reveal much about the era and location in which they lived. The notebook of Reverend John Webster Bailey illustrates the possibilities. Rev. Bailey painstakingly recorded entries on more than nine hundred names of members of churches in Indiana, New York, and Vermont from May 1882 through September 1890. Mary Balderston, a family historian from West Chicago, Illinois, purchased this book at a local flea market in 1976. The entries identify those who were baptized, married, or buried by Rev. Bailey during his ministry in Presbyterian, Reformed, and Congregational churches. Entries for the Cambridge City Presbyterian Church were published in "Presbyterian Church, Cambridge City, Indiana. Rev. J. W. Bailey, Pastor," *Hoosier Genealogist* 22 (1) (March 1982); they proved helpful to researchers of that era and locale.

Do not overlook the possibility of finding what you seek in an archive or museum. When visiting the hometown or city where family members once lived, take time to view photographs or collectibles exhibited by area museums or historical societies. These agencies may hold important collections of manuscript materials that might include Civil War correspondence, business records of companies that employed relatives, or the private papers of former neighbors who were prominent in the community.

There are a number of good finding aids to locate collections of family materials. *The National Union Catalog of Manuscript Collections*, described in chapter 2, Databases, Indexes, and Other Finding Aids, is one aid. In particular, the two-volume *Index to Personal Names in the National Union Catalog of Manuscript Collections 1959-1984* is helpful.

Andrea Hinding, *Women's History Sources: A Guide to Archives and Manuscripts Collections in the United States* (New York: R.R. Bowker, 1979), indexes collections by the geographical location and the name of the female most prominently featured in the collection. *American Diaries: An Annotated Bibliography of Published American Diaries and Journals* (Detroit: Gale Research Co., 1983) is another source for locating manuscript materials no longer in private possession.

The Library of Virginia, formerly known as the Virginia State Library and Archives, holds more than 4,000 family Bible records and registers that reflect Virginia connections. The library has been diligent in adding to this collection, which is housed at Eleventh Street at Capitol Square, Richmond, VA 23219-3491.

Some collections of Bible records from other areas have been indexed and published. Memory Aldridge Lester, in *Old Southern Bible Records, Transcriptions of Births, Deaths and Marriages from Family Bibles, Chiefly of the 18th and 19th Centuries* (Baltimore: Clearfield Co., 1990), transcribed genealogically significant data from the family Bibles of 581 Southern families.

Libraries have been the recipients of published and manuscript family histories. These include the Family History Library of The Church of Jesus Christ of Latter-day Saints (LDS church) in Salt Lake City, Utah, the Library of Congress in Washington, D.C., and the Newberry Library in Chicago. See chapter 2 for information about accessing these collections. Watch for news of less-well-known collections in genealogical periodicals.

Private, local museums can offer serendipity of a similar nature. A German immigrant named Curt Teich spent the 1890s photographing the United States. He printed his pictures as postcards at his business establishment in Chicago. The Teich Company became the largest postcard printer of its kind in the world, producing cards for more than seventy-five years. The business archives of more than 320,000 postcards and the original production files are now housed in a small museum in Lakewood Forest Preserve near Wauconda, Illinois. Perhaps a card, when fully catalogued by geographic area, would reveal something about the neighborhood in which your family lived.

Your personal knowledge and memories, the interviews you conduct, and the home sources you locate are the first steps in family history research. Findings from such seemingly humble origins will thrust you into the larger arena of public records and, perhaps, more detailed facts, but you will return to these beginning steps often—each time with a new awareness of the information previously collected.

THE GENEALOGICAL NETWORK

Networking—making contact with other people who share similar interests—can save you much time and energy in accomplishing your research goals. Have a research question? Try networking. At a crossroads and not sure in which direction to turn? Try networking. Need someone to talk to about your successes? Again, try networking.

Networking can take place in the form of classroom participation, attendance at conferences, or society membership.

Genealogists are generally positive and energetic, and most are ready to share their findings or research experience with anyone they can help. This camaraderie and interest in exchange results in a vast system of societies, projects, and communication. The sooner you become part of this network, the sooner you will be drawn into a very special group. Knowledge of the genealogical community will place you in the midst of much activity, increase your productivity, and alert you to the importance of research standards and etiquette.

SOCIETIES

There are hundreds of genealogical societies at the grass-roots level, many formed by amateur researchers who sense a need for meetings and instruction. Because much family history research utilizes records found at the county level, many local societies represent counties. Organizations also form around shared interests. Ethnic or religious origins account for many such groups, such as the Polish Genealogical Society of America and P.O.I.N.T.—Pursuing Our Italian Names Together. Societies also form around common locales of origin for members' ancestors; hence, the Palatines to America and Germans from Russia societies. Some of these local groups, including the two just mentioned, are chapters of national groups.

For almost every state there is a state genealogical society, a state council, or both. To locate other societies, use Elizabeth Bentley, *The Genealogist's Address Book* (Baltimore: Genealogical Publishing Co., 1994). In addition to work of their own, these state-level groups sometimes help coordinate the efforts of local societies within the state. Their publications, newsletters and quarterlies, supplement those produced by the local societies. Some state organizations, such as the Ohio Genealogical Society, offer chapter membership in the organization. Other state organizations operate on a less-formal basis.

At the national level, a number of organizations seek to serve individual genealogists or societies. The Federation of Genealogical Societies (FGS) is an umbrella organization for local, state, and other organizations, such as genealogical societies, libraries, archives, and institutes. The National Genealogical Society (NGS) is comprised of individual researchers. The oldest society is the New England Historic Genealogical Society, which celebrated its sesquicentennial in 1995. Appendix E is a list of some major state and national societies and their addresses.

Most societies undertake valuable indexing and preservation activities and produce newsletters, journals, and other publications that benefit the genealogical community. Societies also provide educational opportunities for members and non-members in their areas. These can range from sponsoring adult education courses to hosting nationally known lecturers in one- or two-day seminars.

Some organizations sponsor week-long institutes—intensive, multi-track programs oriented toward a variety of interests and skill levels. The institutions that have operated for three or more years include the Institute of Genealogy & Historical Research (held in June in Birmingham, Alabama), the Genealogical Institute of Mid-America (July in Springfield, Illinois), the National Institute of Genealogical Research (July in Washington, D.C.), and the Institute of Genealogical Studies (July in the Dallas, Texas, area). In 1996, institutes began in Salt Lake City, Utah, and in Rosslyn, Virginia. In 1996 also a summer camp was conducted in Philadelphia, and the Disney Institute added genealogy to its program selections for guests at Walt Disney World resorts in Orlando. For details on these and other institutes, see the current Winter issue of *Forum*, the magazine of the Federation of Genealogical Societies.

For those who prefer not to travel, an award-winning home study course, American Genealogy: A Basic Course, is offered by the National Genealogical Society, Education Department, 4527 17th Street North, Arlington, VA 22207-2399.

National conferences are held annually in different parts of the United States. Members of the National Genealogical Society met in Nashville, Tennessee in 1996 and San Diego, California, in 1995. The Federation of Genealogical Societies' 1995 conference was in Seattle, Washington, and 1996's was in Rochester, New York. Write to the National Genealogical Society, Conferences, 4527 17th Street North, Arlington, VA 22207-2399, and to the Federation of Genealogical Societies, Conferences, P.O. Box 830220, Richardson, TX 75083-0220, for details of future events. The publications of these two organizations, the *NGS Newsletter* and the FGS *Forum*, provide in-depth information (including multi-page programs) about their respective conferences in appropriate issues. The *Forum* maintains an international calendar of major events with contact information.

PROFESSIONAL GROUPS

In the United States, there are several groups that serve the interests of professional genealogists and their clients. The Association of Professional Genealogists (3421 M Street N.W., Suite 236, Washington, DC 20007) is a membership organization that does not administer tests, award credentials, or otherwise endorse individual researchers. The association does offer arbitration in the event a dispute arises between any association member and the genealogical public. A publication that lists members' names, addresses, and areas of expertise is the *APG Directory of Professional Genealogists*. This can be ordered from the APG office; it is revised every two years.

The Board for Certification of Genealogists (P.O. Box 14291, Washington, DC 20044) screens applicants through a testing process and offers several classes of certification. It will also provide a roster of certified genealogists for a small fee.

A long-standing program to examine and certify researchers in specialized geographic areas has been conducted by the Family History Library. A roster of researchers who have met the requirements is available (include a self-addressed, stamped envelope) from Accredited Genealogists, Family History Library, 35 North West Temple, Salt Lake City, UT 84150.

For information on other professional groups, see chapter 2.

REPOSITORIES

There are many libraries, archives, and societies which have excellent and well-known collections of genealogical research materials. The names and addresses of some of these are given within the chapters and appendixes of this book.

LDS FAMILY HISTORY LIBRARY

The LDS Family History Library in Salt Lake City, Utah, has been acquiring and preserving genealogical data since its founding in 1894. The library, owned by the LDS church, has collected vital information on hundreds of millions of deceased individuals. The Family History Library has books and microform copies of records from all over the world that are available at the library in Salt Lake City and through LDS family history centers, which are located throughout the United States and in many foreign countries. Many of the records described in this volume have been microfilmed. Appendix D provides further information about the Family History Library. Also see Johni Cerny and Wendy Elliott, *The Library: A Guide to the LDS Family History Library* (Salt Lake City: Ancestry, 1988).

THE GEOGRAPHIC DIMENSION

Genealogical research requires knowledge of the times and places inhabited by our families. A good example of the importance of this knowledge was cited in the introductory pages of the original edition of *The Source*:

> . . . one census might have John Smith born in Mississippi in 1813, while another might say Alabama. In this case, you would need to know that Alabama was created from Mississippi Territory in 1817. A death certificate might list a nonexistent Yellow Bush, Mississippi, but a check of Mississippi place-names might produce Yalobusha County. The problem of shifting political boundaries should be obvious: a householder can appear in various counties or New England towns without ever having moved. The solution in such cases is to find a guide to those changing political boundaries; those containing maps are especially helpful.

MAPS, ATLASES, AND LOCALITY COLLECTIONS

You might use maps to locate an ancestral home or to find a reference to a town that no longer exists. In "Gazetteers: Identifying Research Localities," *Ancestry* 12 (4) (July/August 1994), David Thackery notes that "Genealogy is, among other things, an exercise in geography. Successful research often hinges on identifying the locality in which one's ancestors lived. Once we know the locality, we are in a position to consult the records and histories for the area in an effort to piece together the lives of our forebears."

Pinpointing modern place-names can begin with Frank R. Abate, ed., *Omni Gazetteer of the United States of America,* 11 vols. (Detroit: Omnigraphics, 1991). The work is subtitled *Providing Name, Location, and Identification for Nearly 1,500,000 Populated Places and Geographic Features in the Fifty States, the District of Columbia, Puerto Rico, and U.S. Territories.* Modern towns can also be sought in *Bullinger's Postal and Shipper's Guide to the United States and Canada* (Westwood, N.J.: Bullinger's, 1982) or *American Places Dictionary: A Guide to 45,000 Populated Places, Natural Features, and Other Places in the U.S.,* 4 vols. (Detroit: Omnigraphics, 1994). The latter details all of the "populated places" in the United States and is arranged by county within state chapters. Every place that is incorporated or has a functioning government—nearly 40,000 cities, towns, townships, and boroughs—is contained in the four regional volumes for the Northeast, South, Midwest, and West. Volume 4 also contains a national index and entries of interest covering Native American reservations, military bases, and major geographical features.

Maps, atlases, and gazetteers are necessary tools for any genealogist. For a broad introduction to types of maps, see Joel Makower, ed., *The Map Catalog: Every Kind of Map and Chart on Earth and Even Some Above It,* 2nd ed. (New York: Vintage Books, 1992). Genealogists doing much U.S. research should at least own an inexpensive atlas such as the Rand McNally's annual *Road Atlas*. Locate on maps each place-name in a research problem and relate the place to nearby rivers, mountains, valleys, large towns and cities, ports, and adjoining political jurisdictions.

In one family research project, the ancestor had reportedly moved back and forth between three towns—one in Missouri, one in Kansas, and one in Nebraska. While some researchers would simply pick a state and begin the chase, a smarter genealogist would start with maps and discover that the three towns lay in adjoining counties where the states came together. In fact, the three towns were within ten miles of each other. Suddenly the problem shifted from a vague project spanning three states and became a neighborhood puzzle that happened to straddle three state lines. No long-distance migrations had occurred.

Maps can be either topographical or historical in nature, though either type can show cultural features such as the town and creek names that are so important to genealogical research. Sheet maps can be more difficult to use than books and manuscripts. They are hard to photocopy because they are large; libraries find them inconvenient to store and retrieve; and their titles often fail to accurately convey their contents. You may quail when faced with a score of maps, each listed in a catalog as "Map of Connecticut"; poring over two hundred pages of bibliography listing pre-1900 Connecticut maps may not narrow your choices much unless the editor supplies descriptive notes on map contents. The map user must accept such frustrations as normal. Major map collections are listed by state and thereunder by city in David A. Cobb, ed., *Guide to U.S. Map Resources* (Chicago: American Library Association, 1990). Cobb provides a subject index to specialized content, such as collections with many land ownership maps and railroad maps.

Atlases are bound collections of maps. Atlases may also include charts and illustrations, tables, and detailed explanations of the maps featured. The types of atlases vary. They include thematic atlases (those which pertain to a specific event, such as the Civil War) as well as location atlases. A useful reference to the latter is Norman J. W. Thrower, "The County Atlases of the United States," *Surveying and Mapping* 21 (1961): 365-73. This article identifies parts of the United States for which county atlases are available.

The small scale of a road atlas necessarily omits hamlets and most rivers. The Rand McNally *Commercial Atlas,* found in nearly all U.S. public libraries, supplies a somewhat greater scale. For much larger scales there are the United States Geological Survey (USGS) maps, which show just about every named cluster of houses. Likewise, many states and even counties have published place-name guides. Several national gazetteers that were published in the nineteenth century list many small towns that have since vanished or been renamed. Figure 1-6 is an 1876 map of Allen County, Indiana, from such a gazetteer. To discover the place-name guides and gazetteers that do include smaller communities, use the catalogs of research libraries, including the microfiche/computer catalog of the Family History Library. The catalog is also available at LDS family history centers across the United States. Also see Richard B. Sealock, *Bibliography of Place-Names Literature: United States and Canada* (Chicago: American Library Association, 1982).

The USGS publishes several series of maps in different scales designed to fit together to cover the entire United States. Statewide indexes to topographic maps may be ordered from Topographic Maps, U.S. Geological Survey Map Distribution, P.O. Box 25286, Building 810, Denver Federal Center, Denver, CO 80225. Such maps are described and elaborately illustrated in Morris M. Thompson, *Maps for America: Cartographic Products of the U.S. Geological Survey and Others* (Washington, D.C.: Government Printing Office, 1987).

Map scales are expressed as proportions, such as 1:24,000, 1:500,000, etc., meaning that the map reproduces a real feature at 1/24,000th or 1/500,000th of its actual size. There are 1:1,000,000 and 1:500,000 single sheets of the states in black and white that show towns, rivers, swamps, railroads, and county lines. The more esoteric maps, especially those in abandoned scales, are listed in Riley Moore Moffat, *Map Index to Topographic Quadrangles of the United States, 1882-1940* (Santa Cruz, Calif.: Western Association of Map Libraries, 1986). The USGS also has many specialty maps for metropolitan areas, national parks, battlefields, and historical sites.

The 1:250,000 topographical series in color shows the above-mentioned features and elevations as well, thus revealing mountain and valley systems. Topographical maps of the Appalachian Mountains, for example, can show you how roads, and therefore people, tended to go in the directions of least resistance. The 1:250,000 series covers sizeable regions in a good topographical scale. Fourteen sheets cover Virginia in this scale, but these maps include portions of the neighboring states, also covering most of Maryland and half of Delaware.

Hikers often buy the 1:24,000 maps for their large-scale topographical features. Genealogists drawing land-grant tracts find this to be the best scale. Approximately eight hundred sheets cover Virginia in 1:24,000.

The USGS maps are authoritative and inexpensive. The USGS has published two booklets for each state that summarize the topographic maps available: *Index to Topographic and Other Map Coverage* and *Catalog of Topographic and Other Published Maps*. These booklets are (as of this writing) free upon request. Write to Map Distribution, U.S. Geological Survey, Box 25286, Federal Center, Denver, CO 80225. You can buy maps in person at the USGS's field offices—called Earth Science Information Centers—currently located in Alaska (Anchorage), California (Los Angeles, Menlo Park, and San Francisco), Colorado (Denver), Mississippi (Stennis Space Center), Missouri (Rolla), South Dakota (Sioux Falls), Utah (Salt Lake City), Virginia (Reston), Washington (Spokane), and Washington, D.C.

The USGS has a National Cartographic Information Center, 507 National Center, Reston, VA 22092; (800) USA-MAPS. This center can assist you with more exotic items, such as aerial photographs or color separations of topographical maps, which can be used for reproducing maps in a book you may plan to publish. (Such technical matters are of no concern to most genealogists, but a few may benefit.)

Microfilm copies of out-of-print USGS topographic map series can be purchased. These are black-and-white microfilms of the 1:24,000 series (and occasionally other scales), with each state's maps in alphabetical order by the names of the sheets. (The USGS topographic collection was microfilmed state by state, then two additional, more recent, issues were microfilmed, so check the title listings in three places for a particular state.) For a genealogist who expects to do very extensive research in a particular state, or who perhaps specializes in professional work in one state, these reels are much less expensive and far easier to store than a full set of 1:24,000 topographical sheets of the state. Such microfilms are available at some libraries, of course, including the Family History Library, which has microfilms for every state.

Historical maps are not so uniform or easily described as topographical maps, nor can they be so conveniently purchased. "Historical" refers both to modern maps that present historical information, such as colonial roads, migration routes, former county boundaries, and land-grant bounds; and to old maps valuable for their outdated information, such as nineteenth-century county and land ownership maps and property tax maps. The surest way to see the best maps for an area is to visit a major research library specializing in that area.

Anyone who enjoys keeping current on geography and cartography publications can do so by reading the quarterly *Bulletin* of the Special Libraries Association, Geography and Map Division.

An estimated 2 million maps in the National Archives are briefly described in the *Guide to Genealogical Research in the National Archives* (Washington, D.C.: National Archives Trust Fund, 1982). If you want a copy of a particular old map, inquire of the Cartographic and Architectural Branch (NNSC), National Archives at College Park, 8601 Adelphi Road, College Park, MD 20740-6001. Also, the Library of Congress has a vast map collection in its Geography and Map Division, from which you can obtain reproductions.

MIGRATION AND SETTLEMENT PATTERNS

The wise researcher keeps migration routes in mind. A good historical overview, such as Ray Allen Billington and Martin Ridge, *Westward Expansion,* 5th ed. (New York: Macmillan, 1982) will provide general background that can lead to more-specific investigation. Historical atlases present history in cartographic form. (See "Migration and Settlement Patterns" in the chapter bibliography.)

COUNTY BOUNDARIES AND BOUNDARY CHANGES

Conducting genealogical research in the United States requires an understanding of county and New England town boundaries. Both usually changed several times before stabilizing. Unfortunately, no complete list of all present and defunct United States counties has been published. The three standard listings of counties in the United States are George B. Everton, Sr., *The Handy Book for Genealogists* (Logan, Utah: The Everton Publishers, 1988); Ronald V. Jackson, *Encyclopedia of Local History and Genealogy: U.S. Counties* (Bountiful, Utah: Accelerated Indexing Systems, 1977); and Joseph Nathan Kane, *The American Counties: Origins of Names, Dates of Creation and Organization Data, and Published Sources,* 4th ed. (Metuchen, N.J.: Scarecrow Press, 1983). Everton and Jackson omit many defunct counties; Kane lists only surviving modern counties.

Figure 1-6. 1876 map of Allen County, Indiana.

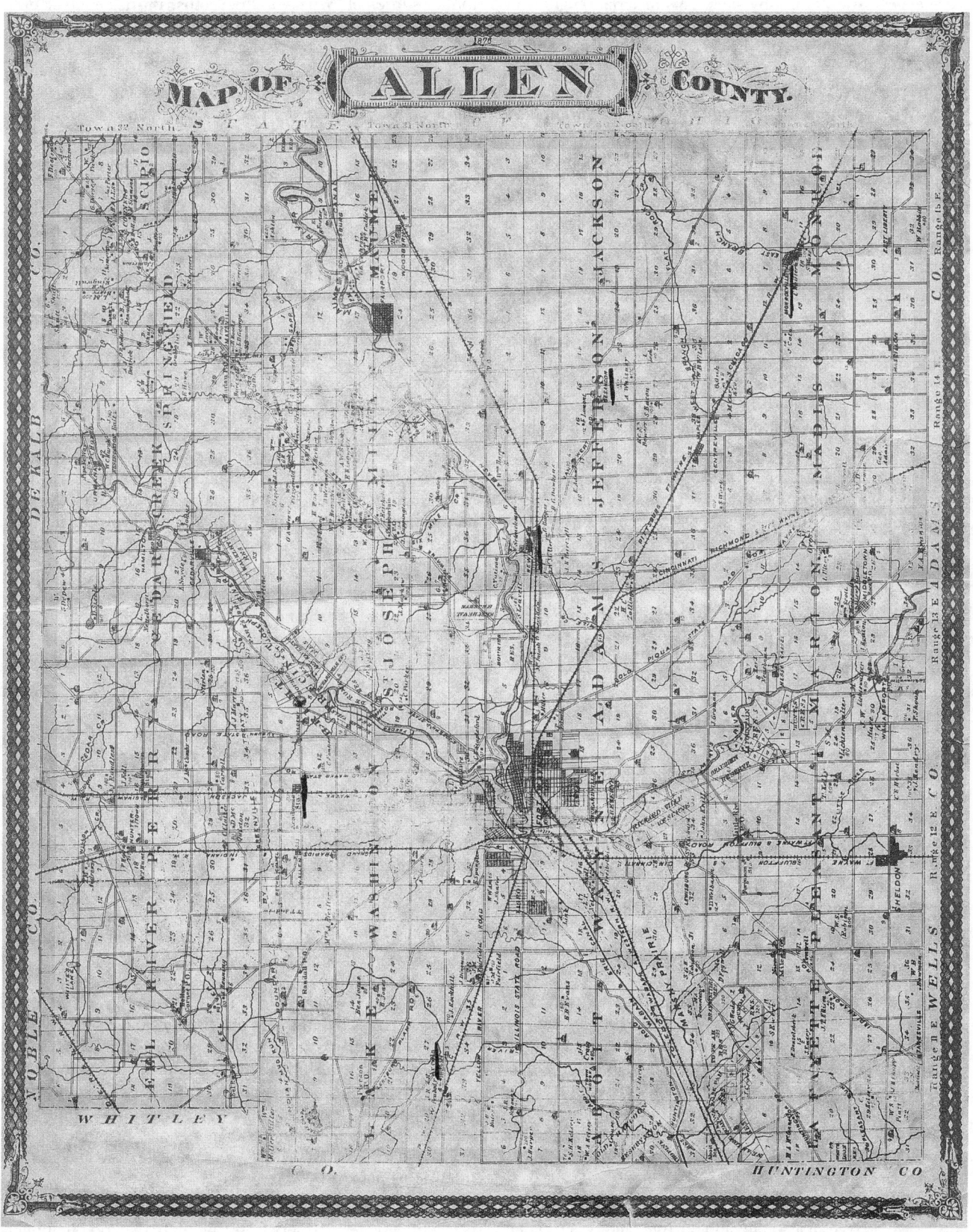

The amount of material published regarding county boundary changes varies widely by state. This material ranges from outstanding books that map the boundaries, such as for California, Indiana, and New Jersey; to listings of laws on boundary changes (without maps), as for Virginia and North Carolina; to practically nothing. Many titles appear in the bibliography by William Thorndale and William Dollarhide, *Map Guide to the U.S. Federal Censuses, 1790-1920* (Baltimore: Genealogical Publishing Co., 1987). The *Map Guide* also shows county boundary changes for all states and territories, but only at ten-year intervals. For state and territorial lines only, see Franklin K.Van Zandt, *Boundaries of the United States and the Several States* (Geological Survey Professional Paper 609. Washington, D.C.: Government Printing Office, 1976).

Chicago's Newberry Library, with funding from the National Endowment for the Humanities, has initiated a project to draw all county boundary changes since 1788. It has completed more than fourteen states in five volumes: John H. Long, ed., *Historical Atlas and Chronology of County Boundaries, 1788-1980* (Boston: G.K. Hall, 1984). These volumes are a vital resource for the genealogist doing extensive research in those states.

A parallel project of The Newberry Library is the creation of a multi-volume series titled *Atlas of Historical County Boundaries*. Publication commenced in 1992, with plans to produce one volume per state (except for very small states, such as Delaware, which will be combined with adjacent states). Each volume will include chronologies; separate, detailed maps for each county's different configurations; county areas; tables of censuses; state outline maps for the censuses; and a bibliography. A list of current volumes is available from The Newberry Library, 60 West Walton, Chicago, IL 60610.

THE HISTORICAL DIMENSION

As a genealogist, you need to know about the historical eras of your ancestors. Problem solving often becomes easier when you know the historical context in which a situation existed. For instance, some Southern families in the years between the American Revolution and the Civil War tended to wander from one area of newly opened Native American lands to the next. To understand which Native American lands were opened for settlement, you could start with the technical listing by Charles C. Royce, *Indian Cessions in the United States* (1900. Reprint. New York: Arno Press, 1971. From this source you could go on to explore local histories.

A great many examples can be marshaled to prove the importance of understanding history. As a hypothetical example, suppose an ancestor was a Methodist circuit rider, an occupation about which you might be vague. Could circuit riders be married? How long were they assigned to one circuit? What and how large was a circuit? Where and in what sorts of Methodist records would you look for records about a rider? What is the difference between a circuit rider, a regular Methodist preacher, and a lay exhorter?

Assume the immigrant ancestor whose British origins are not known arrived in a colony around 1690 and was soon appointed as the crown's legal officer for a county. What sort of legal education would such a person likely have? Could he have been a lawyer in the colonies without having gone to the London Inns of Court? Was there any other school in England

that trained lawyers? Would a degree from Cambridge or Oxford be sufficient? What was the Scottish or Irish equivalent of these English schools? Would study in them permit the practice of law in the colonies? Could one be a lawyer in 1700 just by apprenticing with a practicing lawyer? Would such an apprentice-trained lawyer likely be chosen as King's Counsel? Is this legal background even a plausible avenue to search for the man's British birthplace?

Suppose a family tradition says ancestress Mary Jones was born a Catholic but was adopted as an eight-year-old by Quakers after the French and Indian War. It helps to know that adoption did not exist under colonial law and that the earliest adoption law in the United States seems to have been the 1851 Massachusetts law. Perhaps this "adoption" was really a guardianship. If her parents were Catholic, were there laws suppressing the Catholic Church about 1763, and would there ever have been a Catholic Church register naming Mary? Was it illegal to practice Catholicism in New York in 1763 but legal in Pennsylvania?

Such examples could continue endlessly. Obviously, a genealogist needs such information. It is easy, however, to put off background reading because the appropriate book or article can be hard to find. Which books explain anti-Catholic laws in the Mid-Atlantic colonies? A good local library is an obvious boon, though the interlibrary loan of history books is practical. Helpfully, many college libraries offer borrowing privileges for nonstudents for a quarterly or yearly fee.

Finding the history book or article you need is a hit-and-miss affair that is called developing a bibliography. Even the most expert historian or genealogist suffers from the frustrations of trying to learn what has been published. Take such frustrations in stride. Certain finding aids will help.

The bibliographic *Harvard Guide to American History,* edited by Frank Freidel, 2 vols. (Cambridge, Mass.: Belknap Press of Harvard University Press, 1974), is a good place to begin. It leads the user directly to specific history titles by topics. Do not overlook using the *Family History Library Catalog* of the LDS Family History Library as a subject index. (See chapter 2.) This catalog is also available at the many LDS family history centers located across the United States.

American associations compile yearly bibliographies. The two major services are *America: History and Life* and *Writings on American History*, also online at university library computer-search centers. If Annadel N. Wile, et al., *C.R.I.S.: The Combined Retrospective Index Set to Journals in History, 1838-1974,* 11 vols. (Washington, D.C.: Carrollton Press, 1977), is available, check it for articles on obscure subjects. Many state bibliographies also exist either in book form or as yearly bibliographies in state historical journals. If you are concentrating on a particular area and have access to the back issues of historical journals devoted to that area, first seek a cumulative index to the periodical and, if there is none, examine the title pages of each issue to see what was published. Also check the titles in the book review sections.

This scattershot approach is the way things are done. There is usually no one-stop service for building the good bibliography you want. And without that in-depth knowledge of the world of your ancestors, you stand a much smaller chance of solving lineage problems.

ORGANIZING DATA AND PUTTING IT INTO PERSPECTIVE

Whether family information is gathered from home, local, or federal government sources, a good record-keeping system is essential for easy retrieval, for preservation, and for analysis. Notes may be kept on standard notepaper, specially designed genealogical forms, or on your computer. The important thing is that the information you find be preserved in an efficient and consistent manner that is easily understandable to you and to others. What will a box or notebook full of jumbled research notes and documents mean to the person who may come across it months or years from now? Good record-keeping practices allow you to keep track of where you are at every stage of research: What have I found in my research, and what has yet to be accomplished? A well-organized record-keeping system is like a road map that allows you visualize and analyze all the parts as well as the whole of the project, and to set clear goals.

Every family historian should adopt a comfortable note-keeping system. No one system is exclusively correct. You may want to study the various methods explained in the "how-to" genealogy guides. These guides are available from booksellers and libraries everywhere. Experts differ widely on how to keep notes, so don't be afraid to experiment and modify systems so that they will meet your specific needs. Beverly DeLong Whitaker, *Beyond Pedigrees: Organizing and Enhancing Your Work* (Salt Lake City: Ancestry, 1993) describes and illustrates more than twenty-five form options for preserving research information. Whitaker also suggests various methods of organizing family information, whether you are using three-ring binders or a computer.

SURVEYING AVAILABLE SOURCES

Relatively few people are able to link themselves to families whose genealogies have been researched, well documented, and published. While recent technology has made genealogy more accessible and attractive to a much larger segment of the population, most of us will have to do our own research. It is always wise, however, to investigate the possibility that someone may have published a genealogy or otherwise made available information on your family. But even if you are fortunate enough to find collected information on your family or about an individual in your family, the compiler's work and the sources used to compile the work should be checked for accuracy. A good starting point is to survey the published and unpublished records pertaining to the subject or family of interest. (See chapter 2.)

RANKING INFORMATION SOURCES

This volume is replete with potential sources for exploring your family history. Some records will be easily accessed and have a reputation for yielding the kind of biographical information that is essential for building reliable accounts of individuals and families. Before focusing on any specific kinds of records to be searched, read Robert C. Anderson's introduction and scan the subject outlines that begin each chapter in this volume. Rank the available records according to priority in the search process. Records that are accessible and most likely to solve problems should be consulted first. From the beginning, decide exactly what you want to learn and which records are most likely to produce the desired results.

CORRESPONDENCE

Eventually, every family historian finds the need to write letters in order to obtain or share genealogical information. Because of the importance of correspondence, almost every genealogical guide published devotes significant space to the subject. Almost all experienced researchers agree on some basic rules:

- Keep your letter short. Lengthy letters usually overwhelm the recipient. The chances of accomplishing the goal of a letter are greatly diminished if the reader must wade through unnecessary words.

- Keep letters clear and to the point. Unnecessary details confuse the issue. Make the question stand out from the body of the letter so that the reader can quickly find it and refer back to it without rereading the entire letter.

- Maintain a cordial tone in all of your correspondence.

- Do not request too much information at once. Whether asking for information from a family member or from a county clerk or a federal agency, limit your request. One question per letter is best; more than three questions will almost certainly stall the process or eliminate entirely your chances of getting an answer. Depending on the results of your first inquiry, you can probably write again with additional questions.

- Keep letters clean and neat. Type them whenever possible. Most people do not have the time to decipher unfamiliar handwriting, and most will not have the inclination to cooperate with a letter writer who has not taken the time to be neat.

- Make a duplicate copy of every letter, note, or form that you send and keep it on file so that you can refer back to it when necessary.

- Do not expect anything for nothing. Try to offer an exchange of information for family members, or some monetary compensation that may be appropriate for the information you are requesting.

- Never send cash in the mail.

- Never send money in any form until you know the current fees or policies of researchers or research institutions.

- When writing to individuals or private institutions, it is not only a courtesy but sometimes absolutely necessary to enclose a stamped, self-addressed envelope (SASE) for a reply.

- When sending letters to federal or other tax-supported government agencies, a stamped, self-addressed envelope is not required and will usually be returned to the sender.

- When writing to a person or office in a foreign country, it is advisable to use International Reply Coupons, which are available from most post offices.

RESEARCH AND CORRESPONDENCE LOGS

Some researchers purchase various printed forms from genealogical societies or genealogical vendors; others generate their own by computer. Two popular forms for keeping track of copied information are the research log and the correspondence log. The research log, also called a calendar, is a running list of sources checked; annotations can indicate whether a particular

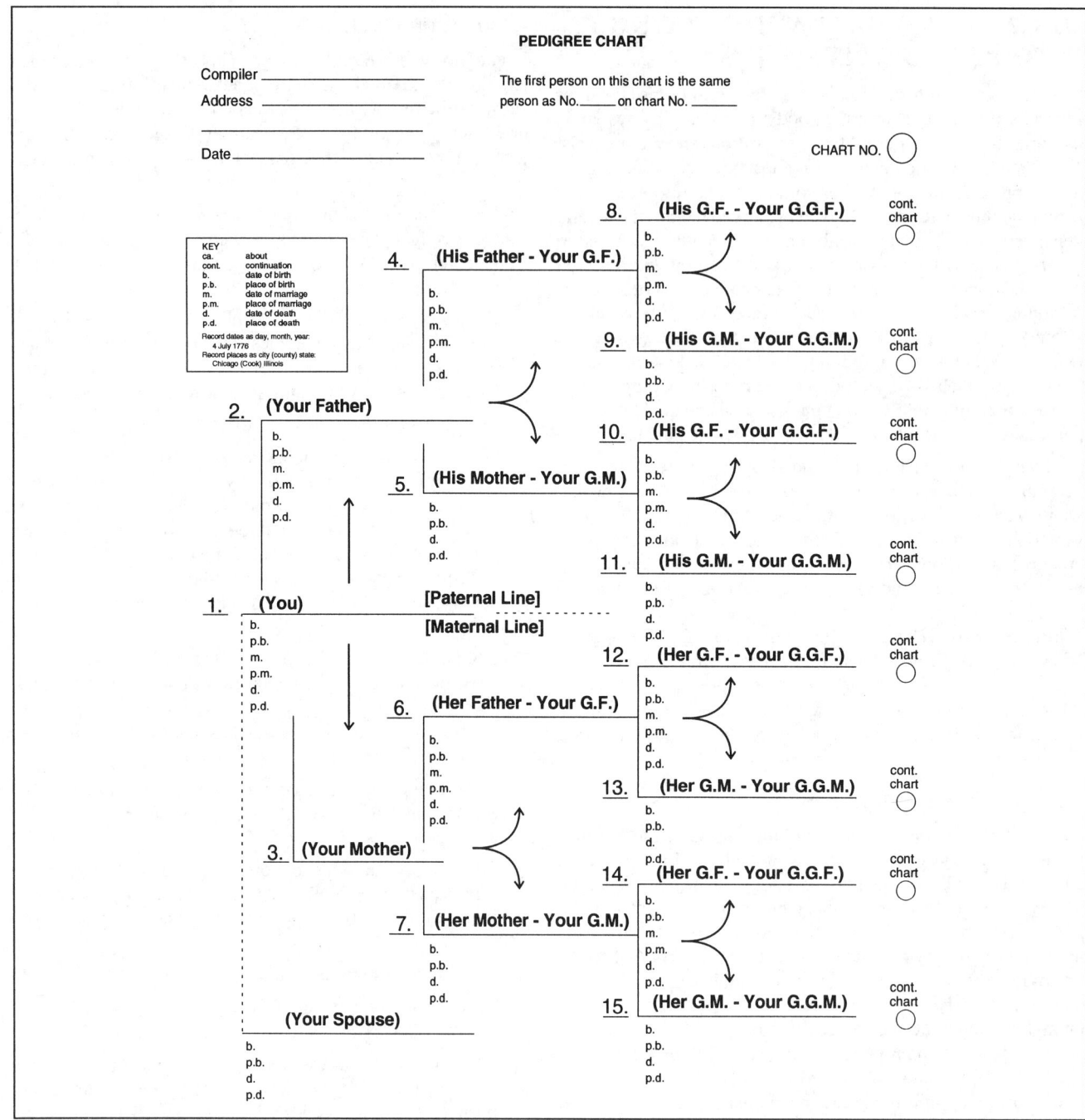

PEDIGREE CHART

Compiler _____

Address _____

_____

Date _____

The first person on this chart is the same
person as No.____ on chart No. ____

CHART NO. ◯

KEY
ca.   about
cont.   continuation
b.   date of birth
p.b.   place of birth
m.   date of marriage
p.m.   place of marriage
d.   date of death
p.d.   place of death
Record dates as day, month, year:
    4 July 1776
Record places as city (county) state:
    Chicago (Cook) Illinois

8. (His G.F. - Your G.G.F.)   cont. chart ◯
    b.
    p.b.
    m.
    p.m.
    d.
    p.d.

4. (His Father - Your G.F.)
    b.
    p.b.
    m.
    p.m.
    d.
    p.d.

9. (His G.M. - Your G.G.M.)   cont. chart ◯
    b.
    p.b.
    d.
    p.d.

2. (Your Father)
    b.
    p.b.
    m.
    p.m.
    d.
    p.d.

10. (His G.F. - Your G.G.F.)   cont. chart ◯
    b.
    p.b.
    m.
    p.m.
    d.
    p.d.

5. (His Mother - Your G.M.)
    b.
    p.b.
    d.
    p.d.

11. (His G.M. - Your G.G.M.)   cont. chart ◯
    b.
    p.b.
    d.
    p.d.

1. (You)   [Paternal Line]
    b.   [Maternal Line]
    p.b.
    m.
    p.m.
    d.
    p.d.

12. (Her G.F. - Your G.G.F.)   cont. chart ◯
    b.
    p.b.
    m.
    p.m.
    d.
    p.d.

6. (Her Father - Your G.F.)
    b.
    p.b.
    m.
    p.m.
    d.
    p.d.

13. (Her G.M. - Your G.G.M.)   cont. chart ◯
    b.
    p.b.
    d.
    p.d.

3. (Your Mother)

14. (Her G.F. - Your G.G.F.)   cont. chart ◯
    b.
    p.b.
    m.
    p.m.
    d.
    p.d.

7. (Her Mother - Your G.M.)
    b.
    p.b.
    d.
    p.d.

15. (Her G.M. - Your G.G.M.)   cont. chart ◯
    b.
    p.b.
    d.
    p.d.

(Your Spouse)
    b.
    p.b.
    d.
    p.d.

Figure 1-7. The arrangement of a pedigree chart. Courtesy of National Genealogical Society, 4527 Seventeenth St. N., Arlington, VA 22207-2399.

source revealed anything. The log shows all sources checked and acts as a table of contents to the research notes. The correspondence log lists all the letters you send and receive, perhaps with a number key written on the letters so they can be stored and easily retrieved. The correspondence log tells you if you did or did not reply to your aunt or if it has really been six months since you sent to New York City for a birth certificate. Some family historians prefer to keep track of all research activity, including correspondence, in a single research log.

PEDIGREE CHARTS

Most genealogical experts agree that the first step one should take in a genealogical research project is to sketch out what-

ever knowledge is available on a given family. As noted earlier in this chapter, research and documentation should begin with oneself and proceed backward in time, one generation at a time. Pedigree charts (figure 1-7) provide an overview of the family and enable you to track research progress. All information recorded on the sheet (names, dates, and places) should be accompanied by a notation showing how that information was obtained. If names, dates, or places indicated on a pedigree chart are a product of speculation (unproven or undocumented), that fact should be indicated in some way on the chart.

FAMILY GROUP SHEETS

A portrait of the Raymond F. Dyer family (figure 1-8) contained notations on the back indicating the family's location in Brooklyn, New York, and the names of the family members. To organize what is known about a couple and their children, researchers usually use family group sheets (figure 1-9), which include spaces for names, parents, dates and places of events, children, spouses, sources, and other information to help identify members of a particular family. But the family group sheet note-keeping system goes a step further: it uses family group sheets to keep the actual notes. One family group sheet is used for each source entry. Thus, information about a man and his family described in a revolutionary war pension file would be copied onto family group sheets. The sources of the information must be included also for a complete and accurate record. Each additional source of information (census, deed, will, newspaper obituary, or other record) gets its own family group sheet, with only that file's information recorded. The same approach is used for every family shown on the pedigree chart.

This system makes it easier to compile summary family group sheets with everything known about the couple. After extensive research, all of the family group sheets for censuses, probates, deeds, Bibles, newspapers, printed biographies, and anything else used are combined and sorted into groups—by head of household, for example. Bringing together all of the sheets for one name makes it easy to see if they seem to represent one person or more than one. This system also requires in-depth evaluation of each record as it is searched. The process of placing information into a set format is an analytical one. Clues for follow-up and discrepancies in dates, spellings, or places of origin, obvious during the extraction process, might be forgotten or overlooked later.

TIMELINES AND NARRATIVES

It is important to draft regular summaries of your findings. Two of the forms such summaries can take are the timeline and the narrative.

The timeline is a chronologically arranged listing of events in the life of a particular person or a span of time in the existence of a family. The timeline should reflect the research principle that we work from the present to the past. Thus, a timeline on a particular person should begin with his or her death, as shown in figure 1-10. It may prove helpful to introduce historical events into the timeline—particularly those of regional significance, which may dictate the availability of records (a tornado that destroyed a courthouse, for example).

A narrative can be as simple as an informal collection of paragraphs about an ancestor, or as elaborate as a multi-generational family history suitable for publication. For most researchers, the more simple paragraph narrative is the precursor to publication. You need not be an award-winning author to present your findings in this manner. Simply compose an accurate and concise summary of your research steps and a condensed version of your findings. Consider such a narrative to be a research status report that can help you to spot inconsistencies in your evaluations as it highlights potential pursuit opportunities.

Lawrence Gouldrup, *Writing the Family Narrative* (Salt Lake City: Ancestry, 1992), and the accompanying *Workbook* (Salt Lake City: Ancestry, 1993) provide guidelines on in-depth narrative writing. Other works are listed below in the bibliography which follows this chapter. Keep in mind that, however you choose to summarize your findings, the organizational forms and the summaries produced should insure that others can reconstruct your research activities. This is achieved by identifying, either through footnote citations or full citations immediately following the entry, the sources of the information and indicating when and from where it was acquired. Richard S. Lackey, *Cite Your Sources: A Manual for Documenting Family Histories and Genealogical Records* (Jackson: University Press of Mississippi, 1986), gives examples.

RESEARCH ACTIVITY LOGS

The research activity log (figure 1-11), used in conjunction with the timeline, is an efficient way to keep track of the origins of information provided on the family group sheet and in a chronological account. A well-kept research activity log will serve as a quick reference for sources of information, allowing you to see at a glance what work remains to be done The source numbers serve as a cross-reference to the sources used in entering information on the family group sheet and the timeline.

DOCUMENTATION

Unfortunately, many family historians have made it a practice

Figure 1-8. The Raymond F. Dyer family of Brooklyn, New York, 1907.

to publish or otherwise disseminate research results with incomplete or even without citations of the sources from which their information was derived. As Patricia Law Hatcher states in a chapter titled "How Do You Know?" in *Producing a Quality Family History* (Salt Lake City: Ancestry, 1996) ". . . for every statement of fact—a date, a place, a name, or a relationship—you must provide a citation. A citation states where you found that piece of information."

The specific footnote style is up to the author. *The Source* uses the widely accepted *Chicago Manual of Style*, 14th ed. (Chicago: University of Chicago Press, 1993), supplemented on genealogical points by Lackey, *Cite Your Sources: A Manual for Documenting Family Histories and Genealogical Records* (cited above). The important point is to indicate sources in an economical yet comprehensive format so that other researchers can judge the quality of the proof and know where to find the cited sources. If the source is "Personal interview, 12 Feb. 1978, with Mable Ann (Alton) Jones, Upper Fairfax, Pierce Co., Wash.," say so. If the information is from a will not seen but given in a published abstract of probates, indicate so: "Halifax Co., N.C., wills 3:377, Edward Montford, 3 Nov. 1801, proved Aug. ct. 1802, as cited in Margaret M. Hofmann, *Genealogical Abstracts of Wills 1758 through 1824, Halifax County, North Carolina* (Weldon, N.C.: Roanoke News Co., 1970), p. 121." Unless you are meeting the requirements of a publisher, it is far more important to be consistent, complete, and efficient than it is to use any given style.

Numbering Systems

Family pedigrees require a numbering format that allows the user to easily follow lines down through descendants or back toward the original ancestors. It is best to adopt a system that has been well-established, refined as needed over the years, and is easily understood. "Three basic numbering systems are already in use by experienced genealogists worldwide," according to attorney and certified genealogist Donn Devine. In "How to Number People in Pedigrees and Genealogies," *Ancestry Newsletter* 4 (1) (January-February 1986), Divine describes and illustrates these widely accepted methods: "(a) the pedigree system; (b) the compiled genealogy system; and (c) the expansible genealogy system, based on the use for which each is most appropriate." Joan Ferris Curran, *Numbering Your Genealogy: Sound and Simple Systems* (Arlington, Va.: National Genealogical Society, 1992), elaborates on the "two user friendly formats for compilers of descending genealogies"—the National Genealogical Society Quarterly System (NGSQ, also known as the Modified Register System and sometimes The Record System) and the Register System originated in 1870 by the New England Historic Genealogical Society.

Analyzing Data

Analyzing data and assigning people to the correct families requires a combination of common sense, a knowledge of history, and a marshaling of sources. How-to books will give some suggestions, though, beyond obvious matters, such as a plausible chronology, it is very difficult to explain analytical techniques in a brief discussion. One book devoted to the subject is Noel C. Stevenson, *Genealogical Evidence: A Guide to the Standard of Proof Relating to Pedigrees, Ancestry, Heirship and Family History* (Laguna Hills, Calif.: Aegean Park Press, 1979). This book overemphasizes *legal* standards of proof but is well worth reading nonetheless.

Experienced genealogists are distinguished by an ability to analyze record sources. Anyone can extract names from ap-

Family Group Record

Prepared By MARGARET MARY PYBURN — Relationship to Preparer GRANDDAUGHTER

Address 4124 TROWBRIDGE STREET EL PASO, TEXAS — Date 16 JAN 1972 — Ancestral Chart # 1 — Family Unit # 3

Husband RAYMOND FRANCIS DYER — Occupation(s) CARPENTER — Religion ROMAN CATHOLIC

	Date — Day, Month, Year	City	County	State or Country	
Born	31 MAY 1869	BROOKLYN	KINGS	NEW YORK	
Christened	12 JUNE 1869	BROOKLYN	KINGS	NEW YORK	Name of Church ST. JAMES
Married	27 NOV 1895	BROOKLYN	KINGS	NEW YORK	Name of Church SACRED HEART
Died	17 FEB 1952	BROOKLYN	KINGS	NEW YORK	Cause of Death HEART DISEASE
Buried	20 FEB 1952	Cem/Place HOLY CROSS CEMETERY	KINGS	NEW YORK	Date Will Written/Proved NONE

Father EDWIN BROUGH DYER — Other Wives NONE

Mother MARGARET DONER (DOONER)

Wife maiden name MARGARET ELLEN HOWLEY — Occupation(s) HOUSEWIFE — Religion ROMAN CATHOLIC

	Date	City	County	State or Country	
Born	14 FEB 1875	BROOKLYN	KINGS	NY	
Christened	UNKNOWN	BROOKLYN			Name of Church
Died	9 MARCH 1911	BROOKLYN	KINGS	NY	Cause of Death TYPHOID
Buried	12 MARCH 1911	Cem/Place HOLY CROSS CEMETERY	KINGS	NY	Date Will Written/Proved NONE

Father THOMAS HOWLEY — Other Husbands NONE

Mother JANE GOSSON (GOSSEN)

X	Sex M/F	Children Given Names	Birth Day Month Year	Birthplace City	County	St./Cty.	Date of first marriage/Place; Name of spouse	Date of Death/Cause; City, County, State/Country	Computer I.D. #
X	F	1 MADELON VERONICA	16 JUN 1897	BROOKLYN	KINGS	NY	8 OCT 1923; PAUL FRANCIS PYBURN	13 SEP 1958 · CANCER; EL PASO, EL PASO, TEXAS	–
	M	2 EDWIN BROUGH	18 AUG 1899	BROOKLYN	KINGS	NY	NANETTE TAYLOR	1 DEC 1926 · BROOKLYN; EFFECTS OF WWI MUSTARD GAS	
	F	3 MURIEL AGNES	3 JAN 1902	BROOKLYN	KINGS	NY	27 NOV 1929; JOSEPH RAYMOND DENNIS	26 NOV 1960 · CANCER; BROOKLYN, KINGS, NY	
	F	4 ETHEL MARIE	16 OCT 1903	BROOKLYN	KINGS	NY	15 JAN 1928; EDWIN C. ROSS	29 JAN 1992; LARKSPUR, DOUGLAS, CO	
	F	5 MARJORIE ELLEN	27 SEP 1906	BROOKLYN	KINGS	NY	NEVER MARRIED	30 OCT 1945 · PNEUMONIA; BROOKLYN, KINGS, NY	
		6							
		7							

Figure 1-9. Family group sheet for the Raymond F. Dyer family.

propriate records; but if you can't identify relationships and find meaning in these extractions, the records are essentially useless. All genealogical conclusions must be based on accurately recorded, carefully documented, and exhaustively analyzed records. No possible clue should be ignored, no stone left unturned. Because of the ample record sources that are available—the chapters that follow will impress even experts—there is no reason to assemble a pedigree without convincing proof.

A second important point is that you seek explicit proof for asserting that any two records apply to the same person. Far too many erroneous pedigrees have used slapdash "name's-the-same" assumptions. Say, for example, that a birth record for a John Smith dated twenty-five years prior to the marriage of another John Smith in Allegheny County, Pennsylvania, was found. Because the groom is known to have been approximately twenty-five years old when he married, can he be correctly assumed to be the John Smith of the birth record? No. He may well be, but without analysis of other records and the family situation, you cannot responsibly make such a conclusion.

A comprehensive discussion of the analytical process and evaluation of evidence can be found in Johni Cerny and Arlene H. Eakle, *Ancestry's Guide to Research* (Salt Lake City: Ancestry, 1984). See also the old but still sound Derek Harland, *Genealogical Research Standards* (Salt Lake City: Bookcraft, 1970), chapters 2-4, and the lively and eccentric Eugene Aubrey

Stratton, *Applied Genealogy* (Salt Lake City: Ancestry, 1988). A helpful essay is Robert C. Anderson and Neil D. Thompson, "Evaluating Evidence: The Test of a Good Genealogist" (a paper presented at the Third Annual Conference in the States, National Genealogical Society, Fort Worth, Texas, 16 April 1983).

FRAUDULENT PEDIGREES

Supplying phony noble ancestries for the newly rich has been a profitable business for centuries. Just as there have been forgeries in the arts and letters, so there have been forgeries in genealogy. An entire issue of the *Genealogical Journal* (19 [1 and 2] [1991]) was devoted to case studies in fraud. The editor, Gordon L. Remington, addressed the topic at a national conference and proposed the following guidelines to detect genealogical fraud ("Charlemagne or Charlatan: Case Studies in Genealogical Fraud," 1994 Federation of Genealogical Societies/Virginia Genealogical Society Conference):

1. Suspicious, inadequate, or no citations.

2. The ancestry provided is "too good to be true."

3. The reasoning doesn't make sense.

COMPUTERS AND GENEALOGY

Computers have dramatically accelerated interest and growth

Timeline	Raymond Frances DYER
1869, May 31	born 117-119 Tillery St., Brooklyn, NY[1]
1879, June	confirmed at St. James Cathedral, Jay St., Long Island, NY[1]
1883, June	graduated from Christian Boys School, St. James academy[1]
1883	employed at Artist Engravers (Wood) Office, 90 Nassau St., NY[1]
1890, May 31	self-employed at 47 State St.[1]
1895, Nov. 27	married[1] Raymond F. and Margaret A. "Hawley" [Howley] married at Church of the Sacred Heart[3]
1897, June 16 June 27	daughter Madelon born at 480 Halsey St.[1] "Madeleine" born 12 June 1869, baptised 27 June 1869[2]
1899, Aug 19	son Edwin born at 15 Brooklyn Ave.[1]
1902, Jan. 03	daughter Muriel born at St. Andrews Place[1]
1903, Oct. 16	daughter Ethel born at 1234 Bedford Ave.[1]
1906, Sep. 27	daughter Marjorie born at 51 Madison St.[1]
1902, Dec. 01	employed by Board of Education at C.H. School[1]
1905, June 01	employed by Board of Education at P.S. 8[1]
1923, Oct. 08	daughter Madelon Veronica married Paul Francis Pyburn[4]
1936, Sep 01	retired[1]
1952, Feb. 17	died in Brooklyn, Kings County, New York[5]

Figure 1-10. A timeline for the Dyer family. It was created from five different sources. The superscript numbers refer to sources of information identified on the research activity log (see figure 1-11).

Date of Search	Results and Source Citation	Source No.
24 June 1971	Autobiographical sketch written in 1945 by Raymond DYER, in possession of L.D. Szucs	1
30 Aug. 1971	"Madeleine," child of Raymond and Margaret Howley, born 16 June 1897, baptized 27 June 1897. Baptism register 1895-1900, page 298, Holy Rosary Church, Brooklyn, N.Y.	2
12 Oct. 1971	Raymond F. Dyer and Margaret A. Hawley [Howley], married 27 Nov. 1895. Marriage Register 1895-1900, page 29, Church of the Sacred Heart, Brooklyn, N.Y.	3
02 May 1972	Marriage of Madelon Veronica to Paul Francis Pyburn, Jr., 08 Oct. 1931, Brooklyn, N.Y. Wedding invitation in possession of L.D. Szucs.	4
24 July 1972	Raymond F. dyer died 17 Feb. 1952, Brooklyn, Kings Co., N.Y. Death certificate no. 62045, recorded 24 Feb. 1952, Kings County Courthouse, N.Y.	5

Figure 1-11. The research activity log shows when a search was conducted and the results of the search.

in the field of family history. New technology has changed the way we conduct research and organize the results of our research, and in the way we publish information and share it on a global scale. Whether using personal computers or the online networks at libraries, family historians are locating and accessing research materials with a few keystrokes. Thousands of reference works and other items that were previously hidden or unaccessible are now identified and put within our reach. Technology and a great surge of interest in the field have expedited the publication of enormous databases of census records, vital records, military records, cemetery records, and the like.

Word processing has saved researchers countless hours that would have been wasted in transcribing original records and organizing materials. Electronic scanning allows text, illustrations, and photographs to be reproduced in almost any format. Desktop publishing has opened new avenues for disseminating family information through personal letters, newsletters, and books.

A wide variety of computer software that facilitates and enhances genealogical research is available. For those who can't even fathom doing things "the old-fashioned way," such software offers endless possibilities.

Raymond S. Wright, *The Genealogist's Handbook: Modern Methods for Researching Family History* (Chicago: The American Library Association, 1995), includes a chapter devoted to "Organizing Your Records with a Computer." As Wright points out, not only can a personal computer make organizing and maintaining family records a relatively simple activity, but with a genealogy program you can "organize your forebears and descendants into families and link them from one generation to the next by showing from whom you and your direct ancestors descended." Additionally, Wright notes:

"Your computer can also connect with networks or other computers through modems—devices that connect computers to telephone lines over which they transmit information."

Because new genealogical software programs regularly come on the market, and those already in use are constantly being upgraded, it would be inappropriate to endorse any particular computer products here. A good way to stay informed of what is happening in this quickly changing arena is to subscribe to a specialty publication such as *Genealogical Computing,* published quarterly by Ancestry Incorporated (P.O. Box 476, Salt Lake City, UT 84110). Another option is to participate in one of the many computer interest groups associated with genealogical societies.

TRADITIONAL RECORD-KEEPING FORMS VERSUS COMPUTER-GENERATED ORGANIZATION

While the paper forms that have been used to organize genealogy projects for decades remain popular, an ever-growing number of family historians are relying on computers to keep records in order and to share the results of their research. Many individuals have no interest in working with computers, however. The tried and true method of manually recording and documenting research findings will always be favored by some. Again, it is the quality of the research being recorded and documented that is most important, not the medium that is used. Standard organizational forms are available from many genealogical societies and from some genealogical libraries, specialty shops, and through mail-order catalogs. Ancestry Incorporated, for example, offers a full array of forms for genealogical record keeping.

There are many advantages to using a computer to organize your research. Most computer-generated genealogical forms follow the same general format of the traditional pedigree charts and family group sheets that have been in use for decades. Instead of the time-consuming work of recording information about an individual manually on multiple sheets of paper, however, genealogical programs make it possible for you to enter names, dates, places, and relationships for an individual into the computer only once, whereupon the program will automatically recognize the individual and link him or her to the appropriate family and generation.

ETIQUETTE

Helen F. M. Leary and Maurice R. Stirewalt have expressed their concern with the demands on the time, funds, and patience of directors of depositories in which genealogical research is conducted. They point out that

> . . . the responsibility for an individual researcher's work rests with that individual researcher, not with the staff of the repository in which the records are kept. The responsibility for keeping those repositories open and their records available also rests with the individual researcher; foolish questions, arrogant behavior, and unreasonable demands by one researcher place additional obstacles in the path of the researcher who follows.[7]

Research etiquette makes good sense. The basic premise is common courtesy—treating others respectfully and complying with the rules and expectations of the repository in which you find yourself. Compliance may mean a consideration of the clothing you wear (bare feet, even in tropical climates such as summertime Florida, is simply not acceptable) or the type of writing instrument you use (in many institutions a pencil, not a pen, is the required tool).

Standards of conduct dictate that conversations among researchers in a library or other research facility be limited to necessary exchanges, as the constant talking of people working together can be distracting to others. It is also to your advantage not to waste the time of the librarian or archivist who is attempting to answer a question by telling him or her more than is necessary. Family history enthusiasts who preface each question with a detailed description of their family or research not only irritate the person who is attempting to help, they absorb more than their share of valuable time, thus angering those who may be waiting for assistance.

For suggestions on correct etiquette in public or private record repositories and libraries, consult Ann Ross Baltheizen, *Searching on Location: Planning a Research Trip* (Salt Lake City: Ancestry, 1992). This book is a guide to planning and carrying out a successful research trip and offers basic suggestions for being a courteous and thus successful researcher.

ETHICS

Although genealogical research might seem to be a solitary exercise, this is simply not true. Family historians, professional and amateur, are often viewed by the general public and even occasionally by the institutions that serve them as a collective entity. However, this community of researchers is sometimes judged by the actions of a single individual. To maintain easy access to institutions, to preserve record availability, and to

ensure an excellent reputation, every researcher must behave in an exemplary manner when collecting family history material or presenting it.

Many genealogical societies publish codes of ethics which they require or encourage their members to sign. Most conform to the following guidelines:

General Code of Ethics

To protect the integrity of public records and published materials:

1. I will be courteous and respectful to all record custodians, librarians, archivists, and others who serve the public.

2. I will handle carefully all books or records entrusted to me and return them to the designated space.

3. I will not tear, erase, mark, or remove any document, book, or film, nor will I mutilate, deface, destroy, or otherwise change any part of such document, book, or film.

4. I will present my genealogical findings with honesty and integrity, using permission when necessary and attributing work that is not my own to the proper entity.

LEGAL CONSIDERATIONS

While it is not feasible, nor is it the intent of this work to address all of the legal questions that one might encounter in conducting genealogical research, a few points are worth considering. At some stage in your research you may need to know what rights you have or do not have to see certain records described in this volume. Who is and what records are protected by the Privacy Act? How might copyright laws restrict use of letters, diaries, and excerpts or other published works that might be used in family histories? The Freedom of Information Act, the Privacy Act, and copyright laws all affect our research in some way. A brief discussion of those laws follows, along with sources for learning more about them.

FREEDOM OF INFORMATION ACT

The Freedom of Information Act (FOIA) generally provides that any person has a right, enforceable in court, of access to federal agency records, except to the extent that such records (or parts of them) are protected from disclosure by one of nine exemptions or one of three special law enforcement record exclusions. The FOIA does not affect local or state records. Most states have their own laws covering these local records.

Most family history researchers will never have to resort to the FOIA. The vast majority of federal records used by family historians are easily accessed. Researchers with additional questions should study the *Freedom of Information Act Guide and Privacy Act Overview* (U.S. Department of Justice, September 1994 Edition) from which the following information on the Freedom of Information and Privacy acts was extracted:

Enacted in 1966, the FOIA established for the first time an effective statutory right of access to government information. The basic purpose of the FOIA is to ensure an informed citizenry, vital to the functioning of a democratic society and necessary to check corruption and to hold the governors accountable to the governed.

Under the FOIA, virtually every record possessed by a federal agency must be made available to the public in one form or another, unless it is specifically exempted from disclosure or specially excluded from the act's coverage in the first place. The nine exemptions of the FOIA (below) ordinarily provide the only bases for nondisclosure and generally are discretionary, not mandatory, in nature. Dissatisfied record requesters are given a relatively speedy remedy in the United States district courts, where judges determine the propriety of agency withholdings *de novo* and agencies bear the burden of sustaining their nondisclosure actions.

"Agency records" are documents which are (1) either created or obtained by an agency, and (2) under agency control at the time of the FOIA request. Each federal agency is required to publish in the Federal Register the procedural regulations governing access to its records under the FOIA. These regulations must inform the public of where and how to address requests; of what types of records are maintained by the agency; of its schedule of fees for search, review, and duplication; of its fee waiver criteria; and of its administrative appeal procedures.

FOIA requests can be made for any reason whatsoever, with no showing of relevancy required; because the purpose for which records are sought "has no bearing" upon the merits of the request, FOIA requesters do not have to explain or justify their requests. The FOIA specifies only two requirements for access requests: that they "reasonably describe" the records sought and that they be made in accordance with agencies' published procedural regulations.

Once an agency is in receipt of a proper FOIA request, it is required to inform the requester of its decision to grant or deny access to the requested records within ten working days. Agencies are not necessarily required to release records within ten days, but access to reasonable records should be granted promptly thereafter.

Exemption 1 of the FOIA prohibits disclosure of national security information.

Exemption 2 exempts from mandatory disclosure records related solely to the internal personnel rules and practices of an agency.

Exemption 3 incorporates the disclosure prohibitions that are contained in various other federal statutes.

Exemption 4 protects "trade secrets and commercial or financial information obtained from a person that is privileged or confidential."

Exemption 5 protects "inter-agency or intra-agency memorandums or letters which would not be available by law to a party . . . in litigation with the agency."

Exemption 6 permits the government to withhold all information about individuals in "personnel and medical files and similar files" where disclosure of such information would constitute a clearly unwarranted invasion of privacy. This exemption cannot be invoked to withhold from a requester information pertaining only to himself.

Exemption 7, as amended, prohibits disclosure of records or information compiled for law enforcement purposes.

Exemption 8 covers matters that are contained in or related to examination, operating, or condition reports prepared by, on behalf of, or for the use of an agency responsible for the regulation or supervision of financial institutions.

Exemption 9 covers geological and geophysical information and data, including maps, concerning wells.

PRIVACY ACT

You must understand privacy rights to determine who has access to records. Broadly stated, the purpose of the Privacy Act is to balance the government's need to maintain information about individuals with the rights of the individuals to be protected against unwarranted invasions of their privacy stemming from federal agencies' collection, maintenance, use, and disclosure of personal information about them. The historical context of the act is important to an understanding of its remedial purposes. In 1974, Congress was concerned with curbing the illegal surveillance and investigation of individuals by federal agencies that had been exposed during the Watergate scandal; it was also concerned with potential abuses presented by the government's increasing use of computers to store and retrieve personal data by means of a universal identifier, such as an individual's Social Security number. The act focuses on four basic policy objectives:

1. To restrict disclosure of personally identifiable records maintained by agencies.

2. To grant individuals increased rights of access to agency records maintained on themselves.

3. To grant individuals the right to seek amendment of agency records maintained on themselves upon a showing that the records are not accurate, relevant, timely, or complete.

4. To establish a code of "fair information practices," which requires agencies to comply with statutory norms for collection, maintenance, and dissemination of records.

COPYRIGHT LAW

A knowledge of current laws pertaining to copying or duplicating records or pages from reference books will prevent copyright violations. Copyright is a protection provided by the laws of the United States (title 17, U.S. Code) to the authors of "original Works of authorship," including literary, dramatic, musical, artistic, and certain other intellectual works. This protection is available to both published and unpublished works. Section 106 of the Copyright Act generally gives the owner of copyright the exclusive right to do and to authorize others to do the following:

- To reproduce the copyrighted work in copies or phonorecords

- To prepare derivative works based upon the copyrighted work

- To distribute copies of phonorecords of the copyrighted work to the public by sale or other transfer of ownership, or by rental, lease, or lending

- To perform the copyrighted work publicly, in the case of literary, musical, dramatic, and choreographic works, pantomimes, and motion pictures and other audiovisual works

- To display the copyrighted work publicly, in the case of literary, musical, dramatic, and choreographic works, pantomimes, and pictorial, graphic, or sculptural works, including the individual images of a motion picture or other audiovisual work

It is illegal for anyone to violate any of the rights provided by the act to the owner of copyright. These rights, however, are not unlimited in scope. Sections 107 through 119 of the Copyright Act establish limitations on these rights. In some cases, these limitations are specified exemptions from copyright liability. One major limitation is the doctrine of "fair use," which is given a statutory basis in section 107 of the act. In other instances, the limitation takes the form of a "compulsory license" under which certain limited uses of copyrighted works are permitted upon payment of specified royalties and compliance with statutory conditions. For further information about the limitations of any of these rights, consult the Copyright Act or write to the Copyright Office.

Who Can Claim Copyright
Copyright protection exists from the time the work is created in fixed form; that is, it is an incident of the process of authorship. The copyright in the work of authorship immediately becomes the property of the author who created it. Only the author or those deriving their rights through the author can rightfully claim copyright.

Copyright protection is available for all unpublished works, regardless of the nationality or domicile of the author.

What Is and Is Not Protected by Copyright
Copyright protects "original works of authorship" that are fixed in a tangible form of expression. The fixation need not be directly perceptible, so long as it may be communicated with the aid of a machine or device. Copyrightable works include the following categories:

1. Literary works

2. Musical works, including any accompanying words

3. Dramatic works, including any accompanying music

4. Pantomimes and choreographic works

5. Pictorial, graphic, and sculptural works

6. Motion pictures and other audiovisual works

7. Sound recording

8. Architectural works

These categories should be viewed quite broadly. For example, computer programs and most "compilations" are registrable as "literary works"; maps and architectural plans are registrable as "pictorial, graphic, and sculptural works."

Several categories of material are generally not eligible for statutory copyright protection. These include, among others:

- Works that have not been fixed in a tangible form of expression

- Titles, names, short phrases, and slogans; familiar symbols or designs; mere variations of typographic ornamentation, lettering, or coloring; mere listings of ingredients or contents

- Works consisting entirely of information that is common property and containing no original authorship. For example: standard calendars, height and weight charts, tape measures and rulers, and lists or tables taken from public documents or other common sources

- Works by the U.S. government are not eligible for copyright protection

Duration of Copyright Protection
- A work that is created (fixed in tangible form for the first time) on or after 1 January 1978 is automatically protected from the moment of its creation and is ordinarily given a term enduring for the author's life, plus an additional fifty years after the author's death

- For works made for hire, and for anonymous and pseudonymous works (unless the author's identity is revealed in copyright records), the duration of copyright will be seventy-five years from publication or one hundred years from creation, whichever is shorter

- Works that were created but not published or registered for copyright before 1 January 1978 have been automatically brought under the statute and are now given federal copyright protection. The duration of copyright in these works will generally be computed in the same way as for works created on or after 1 January 1978; the life-plus-fifty or seventy-five/one-hundred-year terms will apply to them as well

- Under the law in effect before 1978, copyright was secured either on the date a work was published or on the date of registration if the work was registered in unpublished form. In either case, the copyright endured for a first term of twenty-eight years from the date it was secured. During the last (twenty-eighth) year of the first term, the copyright was eligible for renewal. The current copyright law has extended the renewal term from twenty-eight to forty-seven years for copyrights that were subsisting on 1 January 1978, making these works eligible for a total term of protection of seventy-five years

For more detailed information on the copyright term, write to the Copyright Office and request Circulars 15, 15a, and 15t.

For information on how to search the Copyright Office records concerning the copyright status of a work, request Circular 22.

The above information was culled from *Circular 1: Copyright Basics* (U.S. Government Printing Office, 1994). For a list of other material published by the Copyright Office, request *Circular 2: Publications on Copyright* (Copyright Office, LM-455, Library of Congress, Washington, DC 20559-6000. To speak to a copyright information specialist, call (202) 707-3000 between 8:30 a.m. and 5:00 p.m. Eastern Time, Monday to Friday.

NOTES

1. *History With a Tape Recorder: An Oral History Handbook* (Springfield, Ill.: Oral History Office, Sangamon State University, n.d.), 2.

2. *History on Tape: A Guide for Oral History in Indiana* (Indiana Historical Bureau, 1979), 11.

3. Research courtesy requires that a self-addressed, stamped envelope (commonly referred to as an SASE) accompany genealogical requests in which no payment is enclosed or expected.

4. *The Random House Dictionary of the English Language* (New York: Random House, 1966).

5. *Samplers and Samplermakers: An American Schoolgirl Art 1700-1850* (New York: Rizzoli International Publications, 1991).

6. Ibid.

7. Helen F.M. Leary and Maurice R. Stirewalt, eds., *North Carolina Research* (Raleigh, N.C.: North Carolina Genealogical Society, 1980), 56.

BIBLIOGRAPHY

Abate, Frank R., ed. *Omni Gazetteer of the United States of America: Providing Name, Location, and Identification for Nearly 1,500,000 Populated Places and Geographic Features in the Fifty States, the District of Columbia, Puerto Rico, and U.S. Territories.* 11 vols. Detroit: Omnigraphics, 1991.

American Diaries: An Annotated Bibliography of Published American Diaries and Journals. Detroit: Gale Research Co., 1983.

American Places Dictionary: A Guide to 45,000 Populated Places, Natural Features, and Other Places in the U.S. 4 vols. Detroit: Omnigraphics, 1994.

Anderson, Robert C., and Neil D. Thompson. "Evaluating Evidence: The Test of a Good Genealogist." Paper presented at the Third Annual Conference in the States, National Genealogical Society, Fort Worth, Texas, 16 April 1983.

Baltheizen, Ann Ross. *Searching on Location: Planning a Research Trip.* Salt Lake City: Ancestry, 1992.

Bannister, Shala Mills. *Family Treasures: Videotaping Your Family History, A Guide for Preserving Your Family's Living History as an Heirloom for Future Generations.* Baltimore: Clearfield Co., 1994.

Bentley, Elizabeth Petty. *The Genealogist's Address Book.* Baltimore: Genealogical Publishing Co., 1994.

Billington, Ray Allen, and Martin Ridge. *Westward Expansion.* 5th ed. New York: Macmillan, 1982.

Brackman, Barbara. *Clues in Calico: Identifying and Dating Quilts.* McLean, Va.: EPM Publications, 1989.

Bullinger's Postal and Shipper's Guide to the United States and Canada. Westwood, N.J.: Bullinger's, 1982.

Cerny, Johni, and Arlene H. Eakle. *Ancestry's Guide to Research.* Salt Lake City: Ancestry, 1984.

_____, and Wendy Elliott. *The Library: A Guide to the LDS Family History Library.* Salt Lake City: Ancestry, 1988.

Clifford, Karen. *Genealogy and Computers for the Complete Beginner.* Baltimore: Genealogical Publishing Co., 1992.

_____. *Genealogy and Computers for the Determined Researcher.* Baltimore: Genealogical Publishing Co., 1993.

Cobb, David. A., ed. *Guide to U.S. Map Resources.* Chicago: American Library Association, 1990.

Curran, Joan Ferris. *Numbering Your Genealogy: Sound and Simple Systems.* Arlington, Va.: National Genealogical Society, 1992.

Davis, Cullom, Kathryn Back, and Kay MacLean. *Oral History: From Tape to Type.* Chicago: American Library Association, 1977.

Devine, Donn. "How to Number People in Pedigrees and Genealogies." *Ancestry Newsletter* 4 (1) (January-February 1986).

Dollarhide, William. *Managing A Genealogical Project.* Rev. ed. Baltimore: Genealogical Publishing Co., 1991.

Edmunds, Mary Jaene. *Samplers and Samplermakers: An American Schoolgirl Art 1700-1850.* New York: Rizzoli International Publications, 1991.

Eichholz, Alice, ed. *Ancestry's Redbook: American State, County and Town Sources.* Rev. ed. Salt Lake City: Ancestry, 1992.

Elbert, E. Duane, and Rachel Kamm Elbert. *History from the Heart: Quilt Paths Across Illinois.* Nashville: Rutledge Hill Press, 1993.

Everton, George B., Sr. *The Handy Book for Genealogists.* Logan, Utah: The Everton Publishers, 1988.

Flower, Margaret. *Victorian Jewellery.* South Brunswick, N.J.: A.S. Barnes & Co., 1967.

Folklife Program, Office of American and Folklife Studies, Smithsonian Institution. *Family Folklore Interviewing Guide and Questionnaire.* Washington, D.C.: Government Printing Office, 1976.

Frisch-Ripley, Karen. *Unlocking the Secrets in Old Photographs.* Salt Lake City: Ancestry, 1992.

Gouldrup, Lawrence. *Writing the Family Narrative.* Salt Lake City: Ancestry, 1992.

_____. *Writing the Family Narrative: Workbook.* Salt Lake City: Ancestry, 1993.

Guide to Genealogical Research in the National Archives. Washington, D.C.: National Archives Trust Fund, 1982.

Harland, Derek. *Genealogical Research Standards.* Salt Lake City: Bookcraft, 1970.

Harvard Guide to American History. Edited by Frank Freidel. 2 vols. Cambridge, Mass.: Belknap Press of Harvard University Press, 1974.

Hatcher, Patricia Law. *Producing a Quality Family History.* Salt Lake City: Ancestry, 1996.

Hinding, Andrea. *Women's History Sources: A Guide to Archives and Manuscripts Collections in the United States.* New York: R.R. Bowker, 1979.

Hogan, Roseann R. "Oral Histories." *Ancestry* 13 (4) (July-August 1995), 13 (5) (November-December 1995).

Jackson, Ronald V., et al. *Encyclopedia of Local History and Genealogy: U.S. Counties.* Bountiful, Utah: Accelerated Indexing Systems, 1977.

Kane, Joseph Nathan. *The American Counties: Origins of Names, Dates of Creation and Organization Data, and Published Sources.* 4th ed. Metuchen, N.J.: Scarecrow Press, 1983.

Lackey, Richard S. *Cite Your Sources: A Manual for Documenting Family Histories and Genealogical Records.* Jackson, Miss.: University Press of Mississippi, 1986.

_____, and Donald R. Barnes. *Write it Right: A Manual for Writing Family Histories and Genealogies.* 2nd ed. Ocala, Fla.: 1988.

Leary, Helen F.M. "Finding Truth in a Family Tradition: Sumner Antecedents of Demsey S. Goodman." *National Genealogical Society Quarterly* 81 (3) (September 1993).

"Leaving a Legacy: How to Preserve Your Research, Photos and Heirlooms." *Ancestry* (quarterly of the Palm Beach County [Florida], Genealogy Society) 28 (2) (April 1993).

Lester, Memory Aldridge. *Old Southern Bible Records: Transcriptions of Births, Deaths and Marriages from Family Bibles, Chiefly of the 18th and 19th Centuries.* Baltimore: Clearfield Co., 1990.

Living Family Albums. *Grandparents' Video Interview Kit: The Producer's Handbook, The Camera Person's Guide, The Interviewer's Guidebook,* and *Script Packet.* Four booklets. Westlake, Ohio: Living Family Albums, 1989.

Mager, Alison, ed. *Children of the Past.* New York: Dover Publications, 1978.

Maida, Pamela, ed. *Freedom of Information Act Guide and Privacy Act Overview.* September 1994 Edition. Washington, D.C.: Office of Information and Privacy, U.S. Department of Justice, 1994.

Neubauer, Joan R. *From Memories to Manuscript: The Five-Step Method of Writing Your Life Story.* Salt Lake City: Ancestry, 1994.

"Presbyterian Church, Cambridge City, Indiana. Rev. J. W. Bailey, Pastor." *Hoosier Genealogist* 22 (1) (March 1982).

Przecha, Donna, and Joan Lowrey. *A Guide to Genealogy Software.* Baltimore: Genealogical Publishing Co., 1994.

Royce, Charles C. *Indian Cessions in the United States.* 1900. Reprint. New York: Arno Press, 1971.

Rubincam, Milton. *Pitfalls in Genealogical Research.* Salt Lake City: Ancestry, 1987.

Sagraves, Barbara. *A Preservation Guide: Saving the Past and the Present for the Future.* Salt Lake City: Ancestry, 1995.

Sataloff, Joseph, and Alison Richards. *The Pleasure of Jewelry and Gemstones.* London: Octopus Books, 1975.

Sealock, Richard B., et al. *Bibliography of Place-Names Literature: United States and Canada.* Chicago: American Library Association, 1982.

Severa, Joan. *Dressed for the Photographer: Ordinary Americans and Fashion, 1840–1900.* Ohio: Kent State University Press, 1995.

Shull, Wilma Sadler. *Photographing Your Heritage.* Salt Lake City: Ancestry, 1989.

Stevenson, Noel C. *Genealogical Evidence: A Guide to the Standard of Proof Relating to Pedigrees, Ancestry, Heirship and Family History.* Laguna Hills, Calif.: Aegean Park Press, 1979.

Stratton, Eugene Aubrey. *Applied Genealogy.* Salt Lake City: Ancestry, 1988.

Sturm, Duane, and Pat Sturm. *Video Family History.* Salt Lake City: Ancestry, 1989.

Swisher, Linda Herrick. "Oral History: Tell Me 'Bout the Good Old Days." *Ancestry* 12:4 (July/August 1995).

Thackery, David. "Gazetteers: Identifying Research Localities." *Ancestry* 12 (4) (July/August 1994).

_____. "Oral History and Genealogy." FGS *Forum* 5 (3) (Fall 1993).

Weinstein, Robert A., and Larry Booth. *Collection, Use, and Care of Historical Photographs.* Nashville: American Association for State and Local History, 1989.

Whitaker, Beverly DeLong. *Beyond Pedigrees: Organizing and Enhancing Your Work.* Salt Lake City: Ancestry, 1993.

Wile, Annadel N., et al. *C.R.I.S.: The Combined Retrospective Index Set to Journals in History, 1838-1974.* 11 vols. Washington, D.C.: Carrollton Press, 1977.

Willoughby, Martin. *History of Postcards.* Book Sales, 1992.

Wright, Raymond S., III. *The Genealogists Handbook: Modern Methods for Researching Family History.* Chicago: The American Library Association, 1995.

MAPS, ATLASES, AND PLACE NAME LITERATURE

American Geographical Society. *Index to Maps in Books and Periodicals.* 10 vols. Boston: G.K. Hall, 1968. 1st and 2nd supplements. 2 vols. 1971, 1976.

Bancroft Library. *The Bancroft Library, University of California, Berkeley: Index to Printed Maps.* Boston: G.K. Hall, 1964.

Carrington, David K., and Richard W. Stephenson. *Map Collections in the United States and Canada: A Directory.* 4th ed. New York: Special Libraries Association, 1985.

William L. Clements Library. *Research Catalog of Maps of America to 1860 in the William L. Clements Library.* 4 vols. Boston: G.K. Hall, 1973.

Department of the Interior. *Catalog of the United States Geological Survey Library.* 25 vols. Boston: G.K. Hall, 1964. 1st and 2nd supplements. 15 vols. 1972, 1974.

Hargett, Janet L. *List of Selected Maps of States and Territories.* Washington, D.C.: National Archives, 1971.

LeGear, Clara Egli. *United State Atlases: A List of National, State, County, City, and Regional Atlases in the Library of Congress.* 2 vols. Washington, D.C.: Library of Congress, 1953.

Library of Congress. *The Bibliography of Cartography.* 5 vols. Boston: G.K. Hall, 1973. 1st supplement. 2 vols. 1979.

Long, John H., ed. *Historical Atlas and Chronology of County Boundaries, 1788-1980.* 5 vols. Boston: G.K. Hall, 1984. Vol. 1: Delaware, Maryland, New Jersey, Pennsylvania; vol. 2: Illinois, Indiana, Ohio; vol. 3: Michigan, Wisconsin; vol. 4: Iowa, Missouri; and vol. 5: Minnesota, North Dakota, South Dakota.

Makower, Joel, ed. *The Map Catalog: Every Kind of Map and*

Chart on Earth and Even Some Above It. 2nd ed. New York: Vintage Books, 1992.

Moffat, Riley Moore. *Map Index to Topographic Quadrangles of the United States, 1882-1940.* Santa Cruz, Calif.: Western Association of Map Libraries, 1986.

Newberry Library. *Checklist of Printed Maps of the Middle West to 1900.* Edited by Robert W. Karrow. 13 vols. Boston: G.K. Hall, 1981.

New York Public Library, Research Libraries. *Dictionary Catalog of the Map Division.* 10 vols. Boston: G.K. Hall, 1971.

Thompson, Morris M. *Maps for America: Cartographic Products of the U.S. Geological Survey and Others.* Washington, D.C.: Government Printing Office, 1987.

Thorndale, William, and William Dollarhide. *Map Guide to the U.S. Federal Censuses, 1790-1920.* Baltimore: Genealogical Publishing Co., 1987.

Thrower, Norman J.W. "The County Atlases of the United States." *Surveying and Mapping* 21 (1961): 365-73.

Van Zandt, Franklin K. *Boundaries of the United States and the Several States.* Geological Survey Professional Paper 609. Washington, D.C.: Government Printing Office, 1976.

MIGRATION AND SETTLEMENT PATTERNS

Billington, Ray Allen, and Martin Ridge. *Westward Expansion.* 5th ed. New York: Macmillan, 1982.

Cappon, Lester J., et al. *Atlas of Early American History: The Revolutionary Era, 1760-1790.* Princeton, N.J.: Princeton University Press, 1976.

Jackson, Kenneth T. *Atlas of American History.* 2nd. rev. ed. New York: Scribner's, 1984. Includes fifty-one more maps than the 1942 edition by James Truslow Adams.

Kirkham, E. Kay. *A Genealogical and Historical Atlas of the United States of America.* N.p., 1976.

National Geographic Society. *Historical Atlas of the United States.* Washington, D.C.: National Geographic Society, 1988.

Paullin, Charles O., and John K. Wright. *Atlas of the Historical Geography of the United States.* Washington, D.C.: Carnegie Institution of Washington and the American Geographical Society of New York, 1932. Reprint. Westport, Conn.: Greenwood Press, 1975.

DATABASES, INDEXES, AND OTHER FINDING AIDS
CHAPTER CONTENTS

2

DATABASES, INDEXES, AND OTHER FINDING AIDS

Kory L. Meyerink

Agenealogist reconstructing a family history or pedigree faces mountains of records that may contain some reference to the family or ancestor of interest. This chapter focuses on the major finding aids that enable genealogical researchers to obtain data faster and more efficiently. Finding aids include *databases,* which are compiled collections of genealogical information; *indexes,* which identify where in a record or set of records information about an individual, organization, or geographic location can be found; *catalogs*, which help determine where records are; *bibliographies* that identify records; *directories* of organizations and other researchers; and *dictionaries,* which can explain the meaning of a record.

Databases and indexes, especially in the last decade, have become essential tools in genealogical research. In fact, with the present information explosion and the increased availability of earlier records, databases and indexes are the best tools with which genealogists can search large collections of records successfully.

DATABASES

A database is any collection of information that is organized for rapid search and easy retrieval. Usually the term refers to computerized (electronic) records, but it can also refer to manual (non-electronic) records. More and more databases are now being published on microfilm and microfiche (manual records) or on CD-ROM (compact discs—an electronic form). Databases are of great interest to genealogists because they are easily usable sources of information that reflect the previous research of others.

Many databases are referred to as indexes, even though they may include much more information than the traditional indexes genealogists use. How do databases differ from indexes? A database is more than an index *if it includes significant information about its subjects.* Typically, an index includes only enough information to identify a subject and a reference to another source where the researcher can get further information on the subject. While databases usually refer to source information, they may also include some, if not all, of the known information about their subjects. The distinction may seem minor, but it is important to understand from a research perspective. A database may contain sufficient information for a researcher's needs, while an index usually only points to the information—the researcher must still retrieve it from some other source. Access to that source may not be easy and entails another step in the research process. Therefore, databases are usually preferred by researchers.

Some manual databases have existed for several decades, existing even before the term "database" became popular. The more recent development of automated (computerized) databases allows access from more than one location. Access options include CD-ROM, floppy diskettes, and modem connection to a mainframe or personal computer. Manual databases are often unique and accessible at only one location—usually at the institutions where they were created—although some have been published, usually on microfilm.

Because databases are compiled from other records, they contain secondary information—facts, such as names and the dates of events, that were recorded after the events took place. Thus, the information found in a database must be used with caution. The data provided should be verified from the original records because, when databases are created, errors are often introduced during the data entry process. Some of the major databases available for genealogical research are discussed below.

FAMILYSEARCH®

FamilySearch is a remarkable collection of genealogical databases. It is an "umbrella" computer program developed by the Family History Department of The Church of Jesus Christ of Latter-day Saints (LDS church). FamilySearch includes a number of databases, indexes, and catalogs that are useful to genealogists, and more are being added every year. As of 1996, the following databases, indexes, and catalogs were part of FamilySearch:

- Ancestral File™
- International Genealogical Index™
- Social Security Death Index
- Military Index (Korea and Vietnam war dead)
- TempleReady
- Personal Ancestral File®
- *Family History Library Catalog*™ (discussed later under "Catalogs")

FamilySearch runs on personal computers using CD-ROM technology. Each part of FamilySearch is stored on one or more CD-ROMs that are updated on a regular basis as information is added. FamilySearch and its accompanying programs are available from the Family History Library or through any of the many LDS family history centers located across North America, and in many libraries that have genealogical collections. As FamilySearch grows, it will become more and more important for every genealogist to be familiar with it. Each of the tools presently in FamilySearch is discussed below. For more information on FamilySearch and its current files, see Elizabeth Nichols, *Genealogy in the Computer Age: Understanding FamilySearch*, rev. ed. (Salt Lake City: Family History Educators, 1994).

Ancestral File™

Ancestral File is a lineage-linked database that contains significant genealogical information on more than 15 million persons. First released in 1989, Ancestral File offers genealogists a way to share their findings about their ancestors with others. The initial data in the file came from nearly 200,000 family group records submitted by LDS church members. Most of these records have been microfilmed; the submission code is listed with the submitter's name, helping the user determine the sources of the information. Millions of subsequent entries have been contributed by thousands of genealogists from throughout the world, both members of the LDS church and nonmembers.

The key feature of Ancestral File is its ability to link individuals to their relatives. A researcher can enter the name of a person and, if that person is in the database, learn the names of any ancestors and/or descendants who are also in the database; thus, Ancestral File is "lineage linked." Although still in its infancy, it could become the most important compiled source a genealogist can use when beginning research on a family.

Ancestral File was designed for the novice computer user. When a name is entered, the program retrieves the alphabetical portion of the database index for that surname. The index gives the name, year of birth, state or country, and a parent or spouse's name. Usually, this information is enough for the researcher to determine if any of the index entries pertain to the person being researched. The researcher can then choose to view more-detailed individual information, a pedigree, family groups, or a descendent list for the subject. The information can be printed or downloaded to floppy diskette for use on a personal computer.

Because the file began with the four-generation ancestry of many LDS families, it does have limitations for some researchers. However, as more researchers contribute their ancestry, the file will gain in usefulness. Because of rights of privacy requirements, details about living people are not displayed in Ancestral File.

International Genealogical Index (IGI)

The International Genealogical Index (IGI) is an international personal-name database (though it is called an index) of birth, christening, and marriage information about persons now deceased. As of 1995, this database contained more than 200 million entries. Updated versions are issued regularly to include the 7 to 10 million names added to the database each year. The IGI exists in microfiche and CD-ROM form.

Although millions of U.S. names are added each year, the following numbers indicate the breadth and depth of this significant database as of 1995. The U.S. section has nearly 49 million entries; the greatest number are for Massachusetts and Ohio—more than 4 million and 3 million names, respectively. For New York and Pennsylvania there are more than 2 million names each. Other states for which there are more than 1 million names include Connecticut, Virginia, Tennessee, Missouri, North Carolina, Kentucky, Maine, and New Jersey. There are more than 1.5 million for Canada, including 800,000 for Quebec.

The entries in the IGI have come from two main sources: names supplied by researchers from family records and the results of their own research, and names extracted by trained volunteers from selected sources, such as church registers, birth and marriage records, and probate and census documents from many areas of the world. Each entry includes the name of the person, names of parents or spouse, sex, date and place of a genealogical event (usually birth or marriage), LDS ordinance dates, and a reference number for the input source. The names are arranged alphabetically by common spellings. The input source, called a batch number, is coded to indicate the type of record used and whether it was submitted by a researcher or as part of the extraction project. The batch number refers to the original input source, where additional data may be recorded for each person.

Although the same data has been used to create the microfiche and CD-ROM versions, there are important differences in the search approaches used with the two versions. The microfiche version is arranged by state. Within each state, the birth and marriage entries are listed alphabetically by standardized surname. For example, Pierce, Peirce, and Pearce are all interfiled. Within a surname, the entries are listed by first name(s) and then by date. Figure 2-1 is an annotated example. This arrangement makes it easy to browse all the entries for a state and to see all the information without having to look at other screens. Also, the microfiche version is available for purchase by private individuals and libraries, making it easy to access.

The CD-ROM version of the IGI first requires the user to specify the region of the world to be searched—such as North America, Germany, or the British Isles. The IGI can then be searched by the individual's name (for births or marriages), by the parents' names (births only), or by a married spouse's name (marriages only). The computer responds with a list of persons matching the search request. The list includes the name, type of event recorded, year, state or county, and spouse or parents' names. The batch number (input source) and the Family History Library microfilm or book number for the record are also available. A single entry or up to two hundred entries can be printed or downloaded to a diskette for use on a personal computer.

Complete instructions for using the IGI are available wherever copies of it are found (section U on the microfiche version). The instructions include details about sources of information, uses and limitations, format, LDS ordinance dates, and how to interpret the IGI. A second document on the microfiche version explains the Batch Number Index—the master list of sources that have been extracted for inclusion in the IGI. For additional information on the CD-ROM version of the IGI, see Elizabeth L. Nichols, "The International Genealogical Index,

Figure 2-1. A portion of the International Genealogical Index (IGI).

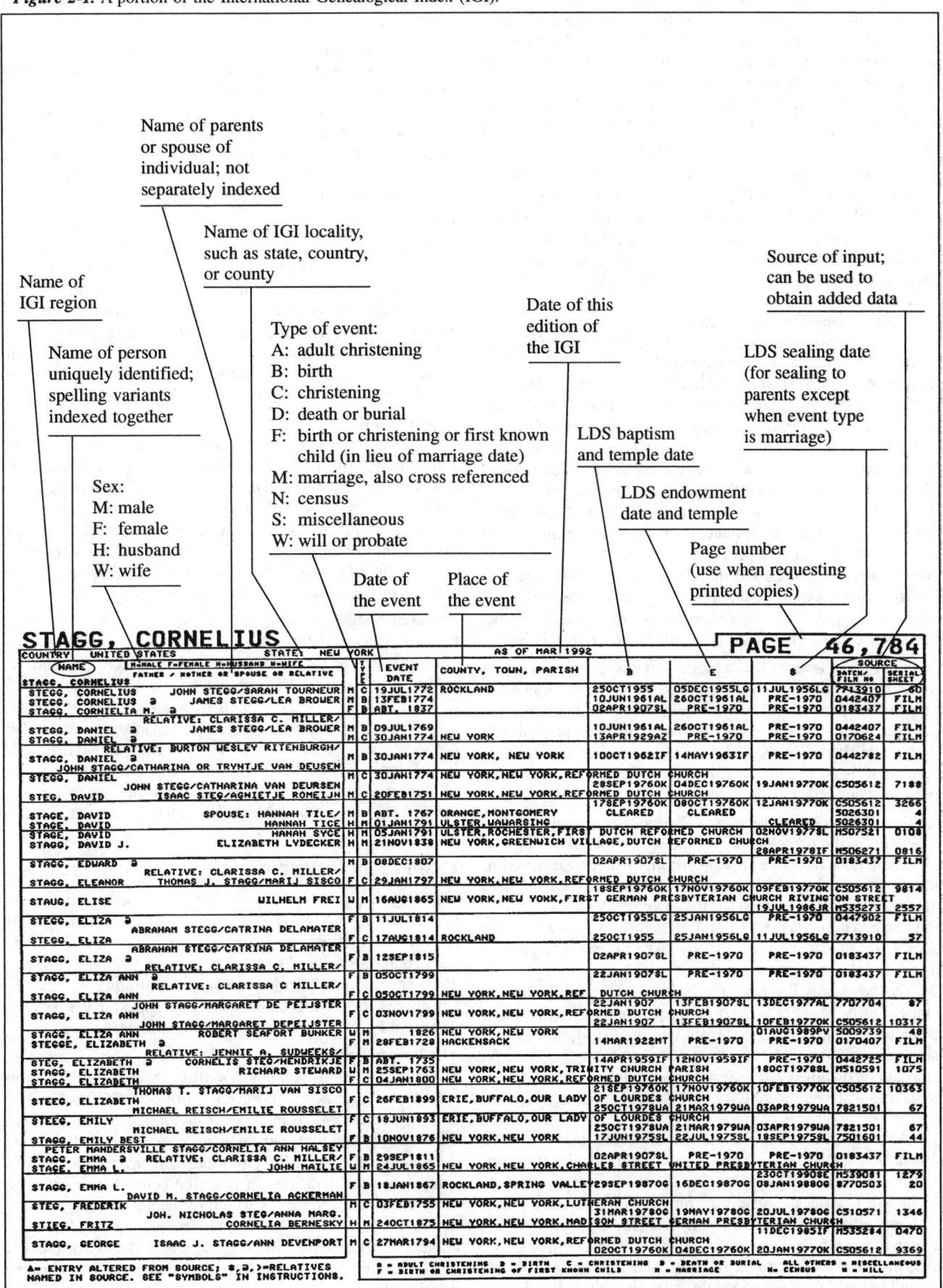

1993 Edition," FGS (Federation of Genealogical Societies) *Forum* 5 (4)–6 (3) (1993–94). This five-part series includes a step-by-step guide on using the IGI as well as details on how to trace an entry back to the original source. The seven-disk 1994 addendum, which updates the 1993 edition of the IGI, is discussed in Elizabeth L. Nichols, "International Genealogical Index (IGI) Updated by Addendum," FGS *Forum* 7 (3)–7 (4) (1995).

Two articles that discussed the current (1992) microfiche edition of the IGI appeared in the *Genealogical Journal*: Elizabeth Nichols, "The International Genealogical Index 1992 Microfiche Edition," *Genealogical Journal* 20 (1) (1992) and David Dilts, "1992 International Genealogical Index: Another Perspective," *Genealogical Journal* 20 (2) (1992).

U.S. Social Security Death Index

The federal government is one of the largest creators of records in the United States. Several government agencies have information about persons who have lived in the United States. One of the most important collections of information is kept by the Social Security Administration. Charged with providing Social Security benefits to all eligible citizens, the agency has had to keep track of millions of Americans. While their records of living persons are protected by rights of privacy, records of deceased persons are available. The Social Security Administration has developed a computer database with minimal information about most of the persons in its files, and the records of deceased individuals have been released as the Social Security Death Index. Several commercial firms make these records available for public searches. The Family History Library has added this database to its FamilySearch collection on CD-ROM.

The Social Security Death Index includes information about more than 50 million people who lived in the United States and had a social security number. Virtually all of the persons in the database died after 1961. The database is updated periodically by its publishers. The 1994 FamilySearch version included information up to 1993. There are also a very few records for persons who died from 1937 to 1961.

The FamilySearch version of the index is arranged alphabetically by the name of the person. It includes the complete birth date (day, month, and year), the month and year of death, the state where the Social Security number was issued, the state and zip code for the person's last known residence, and where the death benefit was sent (if all of this information was in the file). Also indicated are what towns have the zip codes given. The person's residence at the time of death may not appear in the file, especially if the person died before receiving any Social Security benefits or died at a place other than the legal place of residence. An added feature of the FamilySearch version provides, for each state, the address where a death certificate can be obtained. The information can be printed or downloaded to a diskette in ASCII or GEDCOM formats.

Although the Social Security Death Index contains some 50 million names, not all post-1962 deaths are listed. Many persons were not eligible for Social Security death benefits, including federal and state government workers (who had a different retirement program), many self-employed persons (including farmers), and spouses who did not earn incomes. Other persons are not in the index because their deaths were not reported to the Social Security Administration, they died before

the records were computerized, or incorrect information was in the files.

While the FamilySearch version does not permit searches by Social Security number, commercial versions do. The FamilySearch version is updated every few years, while private vendors update it as frequently as four times per year. As with every database, it is not perfect; yet it is the largest of the databases and indexes available for deceased U.S. residents. For more details about the Social Security Death Index, see chapter 18, Twentieth-Century Research.

Military Index

Another database available on FamilySearch is the Military Index. It is a list of known U.S. military dead from the Korean and Vietnam conflicts. The index provides an individual's birth date and home residence, date, rank, and service number for the tour of duty, date and location of death, religious affiliation, marital status, and race. The Military Index does not include all service personnel nor prisoners of war (unless determined to have died); only those who died are included.

TempleReady

The LDS church's interest in genealogy has led it to create TempleReady for its members. This new program is not available for purchase; rather, it is part of FamilySearch and enables LDS church members and other interested persons to prepare the names they have researched to be submitted to LDS temples. Subsequently, these names will appear in the IGI. Most researchers do not need to use TempleReady but should be aware of its purpose because it is a part of FamilySearch.

Personal Ancestral File (PAF)

Personal Ancestral File is a genealogy software package for use on home computers. PAF (in FamilySearch) does not include data to be searched; rather, it allows users of FamilySearch to input, store, and retrieve their own genealogical data. Like commercially produced software, PAF is available for individual purchase and supports the GEDCOM standard. (GEDCOM [Genealogical Data Communications] is a file format that allows transfer of data between dissimilar software programs.) Also see "Genealogical Computer Software" later in this chapter.

FAMILY GROUP RECORDS COLLECTION

The Family Group Records Collection is a lineage-linked database that is not a part of FamilySearch. It is a microfilm collection of family group sheets submitted by members of the LDS church from 1924 to 1978. The almost 10 million family group sheets represent approximately 40 million people, living and deceased. Many of these names also appear in the IGI or in Ancestral File. The collection is divided into sections.

The Patron Section

The patron section includes 2 million sheets submitted from 1962 to 1978 for people born *since* around 1850 (the last four or five generations). It includes many duplicate family sheets submitted by different genealogists who descended from the same families. Comparing all of the different versions will reveal names and addresses of potential cousins who share the same ancestors; references to family Bibles, letters, and diaries in the possession of living family members and personal accounts written by family members now deceased; clues to family naming patterns, spelling variants of surnames, migrational routes and places of residence for family members; and exact dates of birth and death known only by the families. Variations of family traditions can also be discerned in these sheets. Most of the sheets in the patron section pertain to the immediate ancestry of U.S. LDS families. Another section, referred to as the Old Patron Section, contains sheets submitted from 1924 to 1962. The original sheets of the Old Patron Section are no longer available, but they were microfilmed separately in 1952 and 1965. The 1965 microfilming represents the most complete copy of these early sheets. Sheets submitted from 1962 to 1968 have been microfilmed annually. The original sheets are presently available in the FamilySearch Center in the Joseph Smith Memorial Building in Salt Lake City.

The Main Section
The main section includes approximately 8 million sheets, most of them for deceased persons born before 1870 (beyond the third generation). These sheets were submitted between 1942 and 1969. While documentation was called for on the sheets, the documentation cited is often limited. Usually "family records" was indicated if the information was based on personal records or knowledge. Sheets based on research usually rely on printed family and local histories and parish registers. Some of these family group sheets are the products of professional research by the former Research Department of the Family History Library. Such sheets usually include three initials with the name of the submitter. Patron (client) files of the Research Department may include more research information and are available on more than 4,000 microfilms in the Family History Library's collection under the title Research Department Patron Files.

Asterisks (*) mark cross references to show if other group sheets exist (or once existed) for a person as a member of another family. For example, an asterisk on a parent's name might indicate that a sheet showing him or her as a child is or was available. This feature makes the Family Group Records Collection a manual, lineage-linked database.

Though these family group sheets were submitted by members of the LDS church, they document families from which any researcher may have descended. The names and addresses of those who submitted the sheets are also recorded on them, but, as they predate 1969, submitters may have moved or died since preparing the sheets. Submitters who are still living can usually be reached by sending an unsealed, stamped letter to the LDS Membership Department, 50 East North Temple, Salt Lake City, UT 84150. The Membership Department will forward the letter to the person's last known address.

The group sheets in both sections are filed in strict alphabetical order by the name of the husband of each family and chronologically by date where there are two or more sheets showing husbands with the same names. There is some duplication between the two sections, but it is limited. The original group sheets (available at the Family Search Center in Salt Lake City) are incomplete because some have been unofficially removed or worn out from constant use and photocopying. A more complete version is available on microfilm at the Family History Library and its family history centers. Call numbers are listed in the Family History Library Catalog in the author/title section under the title Family Group Records Collection.

The Family Groups Record Collection is an alphabetized, compiled source, making it a manual database—not an index. The information in it is only as accurate as the care used in compiling the records. The Family History Library has not verified the research, and some family group sheets are known to have errors, especially those for colonial American lines going into England and Europe. Sources are usually given at the bottom of group sheets; however, a careful analysis of the data will show that not all entries came from the sources listed.

PRIVATE RESEARCH DATABASES
As genealogy has become a more popular pursuit, and as computers have become more inexpensive and widely available, many individuals and companies have developed private databases. Several major private databases are described below. No such listing can be complete because, at present, there is no clearinghouse for such projects. However, the National Genealogical Society and the Family History Library are cooperating to encourage the growth of a "Genealogical Projects Registry." Such a registry would be a boon to researchers wanting to determine if someone has already found a particular ancestor. You can learn more about such databases, both national and regional in scope, from research handbooks for specific localities or topics and from genealogical periodical articles and advertisements.

Automated Archives
Automated Archives, now owned by the Banner Blue Division of Brøderbund Software, P.O. Box 6124, Novato, CA 94948-6125, pioneered the commercial use of CD-ROM as a storage medium for genealogical information. This company has produced numerous disks containing several databases and indexes for sale to individuals and institutions. As of 1996, available databases included marriage records from several southern and midwestern states, the Social Security Death Benefit Records, several CD-ROMs containing linked family pedigrees, indexes to most federal censuses through 1860, and many other sources.

Lineages
Lineages, a professional research company, also maintains a significant lineage-linked database consisting of client pedigrees. Many of the more than 1.65 million names in the database have been researched by Lineage's staff. Lineages also has a database that identifies the places of origin of more than 320,000 German-speaking immigrants. The company will share its information and add information from other researchers to its files for a fee. For information, write to Lineages, P.O. Box 417, Salt Lake City, Utah 84110-0417.

Mormon Pioneer Genealogy Library
The Mormon Pioneer Genealogy Library is a manual database that includes thousands of pedigrees and family group records showing the American ancestry of hundreds of early LDS (Mormon) families. Many Mormon pioneers were of New England ancestry, making this a valuable database for many families. Sources are given for each family. Although compiled chiefly from the Family Group Records Collection (see above) of the Family History Library, much additional research has gone into these families to resolve discrepancies and conflicts and to better link them. For more information, write to the Mormon Pioneer Genealogy Library, P.O. Box 11488, Salt Lake City, UT 84147.

Torrey's New England Marriages to 1700
Torrey's New England Marriages to 1700 is a manual database that was created by Clarence A. Torrey, an accomplished genealogist. He spent much of his lifetime searching every genealogy of New England families published prior to the 1950s for

evidence of marriages that took place before 1700. The result is this list of 74,000 New England adults of the seventeenth century. It probably identifies more than ninety-five percent of the marriages for that period. Although appearing as a set of marriage records (or evidences), this database serves to alert the researcher that a published genealogy exists for an ancestor. It includes almost every couple from more than 2,000 published New England genealogies. Torrey's *New England Marriages Prior to 1700* (Baltimore: Genealogical Publishing Co., 1985) serves as an index to his files; however, the source of the information is not given in it. Rather, the researcher must search Torrey's handwritten notes, which are arranged on seven rolls of microfilm alphabetically by the groom's name. The original notes are at the Library of the New England Historic Genealogical Society; microfilm copies of Torrey's files are available from that society or the LDS Family History Library. The notes include cryptic, abbreviated references to published genealogies. Torrey made no attempt to evaluate the information in the genealogies; hence, the index, and his notes, may contain conflicting information. The researcher must determine which, if any, of the sources are correct. Two supplements to Torrey's index were created by Melinde Lutz Sanborn and published by the Genealogical Publishing Company of Baltimore in 1991 and 1995.

FAMILY OR SURNAME ORGANIZATIONS

In addition to the services described above, there are hundreds of organizations devoted to research of particular families or surnames, and many have compiled databases containing the genealogies of their members, or at least their genealogy relative to the family or surname of interest. Such organizations exist to share data and are very willing to respond to queries, even from researchers who do not belong to them. Usually there is no charge, except for copies and postage. Refer also to Elizabeth Bentley's *Directory of Family Associations,* cited below under "Directories."

LOCAL SOCIETIES

Many county historical and genealogical societies maintain files of their members' interests. Such files usually include families from the locality served by the society. The information in them reflects the findings of society members as they have researched families of their areas. Since the societies' focus is on serving their members, they are usually quite helpful in connecting inquiries to members with the same family or surname. Refer to Bentley's *Directory of Family Associations,* cited below under "Directories," for the addresses of local societies.

ETHNIC SOCIETIES

Societies devoted to researching particular ethnic groups can provide information from data submitted by their members. Two databases that pertain to specific ethnic groups are P.O.I.N.T. (Pursuing Our Italian Names Together), managed by Thomas Militello, P.O. Box 2977, Palos Verdes, CA 90274; and the Jewish Genealogical People Finder, operated by Gary Mokotoff, *Avotaynu,* P.O. Box 900, Teaneck, NJ 07666.

RESEARCH EXCHANGES

Research exchanges are much like query files (see below under "Indexes"), except that they comprise files (databases) of genealogical information. Typically, they rely on subscribers to submit family group records to build the database. Then, for a fee, they provide copies of family group records for requested surnames. Some of the older and larger exchanges include Everton's "Family File," based in Logan, Utah; Yates' "Family Group Sheet Exchange" (Ozark, Missouri, and Stevensville, Montana); Nationwide Surname Index (Bend, Oregon); Ray's Surname Index File (McCook, Nebraska); Researcher's Surname Index (Lockport, New York); and TapRoots Research and Publications (Amarillo, Texas). Research exchanges can usually be found among the advertisers in major genealogical magazines. Many are also listed in Bentley's *The Genealogist's Address Book,* cited below under "Directories."

GENEALOGICAL COMPUTER SOFTWARE

Important tools for family historians are the increasing numbers of personal computer software programs designed to help manage genealogical data. Individuals can use these programs to create their own databases and share them with family members and other researchers. The database may comprise the ancestry of one person (such as the researcher), the members of a genealogical organization (with or without their ancestry), or the genealogical information in a set of records, among many other uses. While some genealogists use word processing and database management programs for these purposes, most use one of several programs designed specifically for genealogical data. Most genealogical programs now use the GEDCOM (Genealogical Data Communications) standard, which allows transfer of information between different programs. GEDCOM files can be uploaded to Ancestral File or downloaded from Ancestral File or other FamilySearch files. For more information, see Paul A. Andereck and Richard A. Pence, *Computer Genealogy: A Guide to Research Through High Technology*, rev. ed. (Salt Lake City: Ancestry, 1991).

Linked Database Managers

The most common genealogical programs are those that enable researchers to record and track the relationships between people. A person's name and associated information can be entered and linked with parents, children, and other relatives already in the file. These programs can arrange the data to produce a variety of reports, such as pedigree charts and family group records. A growing number of commercial programs are available for DOS, Windows, and most other computer operating systems. Personal Ancestral File (PAF) has received the most attention because it was one of the first linked database managers to be developed, is inexpensive, and is distributed by the LDS church. However, most of the other programs, while more expensive, have many more features. A number of shareware programs—software available on computer networks to anyone for a minimal registration fee—are available as well, including Brother's Keeper. Reviews of these programs and announcements of new software appear regularly in periodicals devoted to computing, such as Ancestry's *Genealogical Computing* and the *Computer Interest Group Digest*, now part of the *Newsletter* of the National Genealogical Society. A directory of programs available by 1993 is George Archer, *Archer's Directory of Genealogical Software* (Bowie, Md.: Heritage Books, 1993). However, this guide was published before the explosion of Windows-based software in 1994 and 1995. A directory of genealogical software is published annually in the July-August-September issue of Ancestry's *Genealogical Computing* quarterly.

Research Databases

Some programs have been designed to help researchers track all individuals found while researching many different records. Depending on the capabilities of these programs, many different reports that help researchers analyze their findings can be generated. Such a program is Comsoft's Sesame. A simple file system is Research Data Filer, part of PAF.

INDEXES

While databases include actual genealogical data that researchers want, indexes generally give very little genealogical information; rather, indexes are primarily finding aids—they refer the user to other sources of information about a subject. Most family historians seek references to their ancestors in indexes as well as in databases. Indexes are crucial to successful research because they free the researcher to search many more sources then would be possible if it was necessary to read each record completely without knowing if a name was in it. While many indexes are topical—that is, they indicate where particular topics are treated—the following discussion focuses on nominal (name) indexes.

Some genealogical indexes have broad application; others have very limited uses. Generally, indexes cover two different categories of records: compiled sources (which usually contain secondary information, such as family or local histories, genealogies written by others, journal articles, and family group sheets); and original sources (which generally provide primary information, such as military rolls, immigration lists, census records, etc.).

Indexes that list individuals may include the given names of each subject (personal name indexes) or the last name only, with page references for each occurrence of that name (surname indexes). They can be comprehensive (every name in the source indexed) or selective (only the major occurrences of the name indexed). In selective indexes, the name of the head of the family may be the only name indexed, although the whole family is described by name in the record entry itself. There may be locality, topical, or major-entry indexes as well.

Indexes compiled by government clerks for wills, deeds, and court cases are personal-name indexes; they refer only to the principals in each transaction. Witnesses, jurors, clerks, and others mentioned in the documents are rarely indexed. In government records particularly—though not exclusively—indexes may not be strictly alphabetical. For example, all of the *A* entries may be grouped together but may not be alphabetized—Abbott may come after Arnold. In some indexes, names are arranged by the first letter of the given name, the first three letters of the surname, or the first and third letters of either name; some are alphabetized by the given name irrespective of the first letter of the surname. Others, like the Soundex indexes, are arranged so that names *pronounced* alike are indexed together.

The original indexes found in most compiled histories generally include topical or surname entries only. Comprehensive, every-name indexes are sometimes compiled later for genealogical use. These supplements may be bound into the original record, written, typed, or printed in a separate volume, or added to the pages of a reprint edition. As you search a record, whether it is compiled or original, check carefully for multiple indexes. You may find them at the end, in the middle, or, conveniently, at the front of the record. Indexes may be indicated in the table of contents as well.

No index is perfectly accurate or complete. Whether prepared manually or by computer, indexes contain errors of omission, incompleteness, and typography. The key to using any index is to understand who created it and why. Successful researchers spend as much time getting to know the index as in using the index itself. The preface or introduction to the index, "how-to" books and articles, other researchers, and experimenting with the index itself can reveal much about its usefulness.

An index is only as accurate as the source itself. If a family history has errors, those errors will be indexed. Misspelled words, garbled names, and incorrect page references will be indexed as well. It is not the indexer's place to correct errors—even when they are obvious—although some add prefaces or footnotes to warn users. If a record is in a foreign language or has been damaged, names may be indecipherable or illegible. Even a skilled indexer, dealing with unfamiliar names, may misinterpret spellings, placing a name in an entirely different part of the index than it belongs. Cross references for spelling variants and for multiple entries may be omitted due to space, time, or financial considerations.

Indexers select entries according to their own criteria. The best ones describe their selection processes for the reader's benefit. For example, Schneider and Snyder may be indexed together or separately in a surname index. If the index is topical, who chose the topics? Are public officials indexed together, individually by name, or by separate government agencies? Entries in a family history index may be divided into descendants, spouses who married into the family, ancestors of the central couple, and places where the family lived—each in a separate index. Check them all.

Women may have been omitted from an index. If you're looking for Mary Loomis and the index lists only John, Joseph, Michael, and Stephen Loomis, check those entries; the indexer may have included only Mary's brothers and father. Children and grandparents may have been treated similarly.

Any name can be spelled some other way. The Cole family of New York sometimes appears as Kool due to Dutch influence or Kohl due to German influence, yet many families with this name stem from the New England Coles. In strictly alphabetical indexes, such spelling variants must be checked to get all of the data. Be especially watchful for variations with a vowel as the initial letter. Even simple names, such as Ott, can appear as Ot, Otte, Utt, or Autt. Thompson is often spelled without the letter *p,* giving it a different Soundex code in the census and other government indexes.

Both given names and family names may have been translated from other forms. Jacob is the Latin and German form of James. The Slavic Vojtech becomes Adelbert or Albert in English. Polly and Mary are interchangeable, as are Sarah and Sally. The Huguenot Le Counte becomes the Dutch de Graff; and de la Maiste' becomes Delamater. Some Germans translated their surnames into English: Zimmerman becomes Carpenter and Schwartz becomes Black. Be wary when you are dealing with the first and second American generations.

When searching indexes, look for less-common names first. For example, for a Mary Loomis-John Smith marriage, check Loomis first because it is less common. If searching a Loomis family history, however, reverse the process: check for John Smith married to Mary Loomis. This method is faster and usually more effective.

An excellent article on the use of printed indexes is Donald Lines Jacobus, "Tricks in Using Indexed Genealogical Books," *The American Genealogist*, 30 (April 1954): 85. In it, Jacobus covers some of these rules in greater detail. Keep in mind that indexes are tools—not sources.

The following discussion of specific indexes includes only the largest, most commonly available, and most useful of the dozens available.

GENEALOGY AND BIOGRAPHY INDEXES

Before conducting extensive research, find out if a genealogy (or family history) for the surname of interest has already been published. Such a find can be of great value, allowing you to build on previous research instead of redoing the same work. Tens of thousands of such works have been published. Many trace the descendants of one person through several generations; others trace the ancestors of a couple. Various combinations also exist but, generally, such books are based on one surname. To determine if someone has compiled a history or genealogy on your family, you must use indexes, catalogs, and bibliographies.

American Genealogical-Biographical Index (AGBI) (Rider's Index)

The largest and most comprehensive index to family histories is Fremont Rider, ed., *The American Genealogical-Biographical Index (AGBI)*, Series 2 (Middletown, Conn.: Godfry Memorial Library, 1952–present. Vol. 181 published 1995). This work is also known as Rider's Index. An ongoing project, it will contain references to more than 12 million individuals in articles, books, and brief biographies when complete. An average of four to six volumes are published each year. Volume 181 ends with the surname Tups.

The *AGBI* is an extensive personal-name index that excludes only persons mentioned incidentally or those unrelated to the subjects being indexed, such as witnesses and authors. The primary emphasis is on family genealogies to 1950, but other valuable genealogical collections are included, such as the *Boston Transcript* (a genealogical column with a wide circulation), the complete United States 1790 census, and published revolutionary war records from most of the colonies.

Each entry contains the subject's complete name, year and state of birth (if known), abbreviated biographical data, and the book and page citation. Every volume contains an explanation of the index. Full bibliographical citations for the sources indexed are in volumes 1, 10, 34, and 54; a supplement is in volume 70. More than 850 sources are being indexed. A similar work in forty-eight volumes appeared as series 1 and can be used for the remainder of the alphabet because it indexes most of the same family histories. Series 1, however, does not include many of the additional sources that are in series 2. Both series are available at major genealogical libraries as well as public and university libraries with large genealogy collections.

Biography and Genealogy Master Index (BGMI)

Approximately 8 million Americans have been the subjects of biographical sketches in collective biography volumes. While many of these sketches are in local histories, more than 3 million appear in books with a nationwide scope, such as *Who's Who in America* and *Men and Women of Science*. In fact, approximately 2,000 such volumes exist and have been indexed by Mirana C. Herbert and Barbara McNeil in the *Biography and Genealogy Master Index* (Detroit: Gale Research Co., 1980–). It is an ongoing indexing project; a five-volume index first appeared in 1980. Supplemental volumes have been issued every year, with cumulations occurring every fifth year (1985, 1990, and 1995). Each cumulative set and supplementary volume contain one alphabetical sequence. The index gives the name of the subject of the biographical sketch, years of birth and death (if known), and an abbreviation for the source of the sketch. It is an invaluable tool for locating more than 8 million references to notable people. It concentrates heavily on the twentieth and late nineteenth centuries and includes many living people, making it valuable for locating distant cousins. However, significant numbers of early Americans are also included. The *BGMI* is also available in some libraries on microfiche, as an online database, and on CD-ROM.

Old Surname Index

From its early years, the Family History Library, like many genealogical libraries, indexed articles, genealogies, and family histories in periodicals as well as books. By around 1964, however, it was no longer feasible to analyze the articles and chapters in the new books the library was receiving, and this indexing project was ended. The original index cards, now available only on microfilm, were arranged alphabetically by surname. Approximately 100,000 cards were created; most of these entries apply to early American and English families. Each card includes the surname, and sometimes given name, the source and page number where the article was found, and an old library call number. Use the library catalog where you research to determine if the indicated source is available. All of them are available at the Family History Library, and most should be available through the library's family history centers.

Greenlaw Index

An index similar to the Old Surname Index is William Prescott Greenlaw, comp., *The Greenlaw Index of the New England Historic Genealogical Society,* 2 vols. (Boston: G.K. Hall, 1979). Greenlaw was the librarian of the New England Historic Genealogical Society from 1894 to 1929. The citations refer only to works carrying a family through three or more generations in books published from 1900 to 1940. The more than 35,000 entries are arranged alphabetically by surname and given names on three-by-five-inch cards reproduced in two large volumes. The citations also include the ancestor, residence, time period, and source. This index is similar in size and scope to the Munsell and Newberry indexes (see below). Oriented toward New England, as is Munsell's Index, Greenlaw's nicely complements the Midwest orientation of the Newberry Index (see below) and the general coverage of the Old Surname Index.

LOCAL HISTORY INDEXES

Many printed genealogies and biographies are buried in the thousands of local histories that have been published throughout the United States in the last century and a half. Once found, they can produce added insight on a particular ancestor—a father's name or place of origin, for example—or add several generations to a lineage. The proper use of available indexes can greatly assist in finding these sources. Those that are generally nationwide in scope are the following.

Index to American Genealogies (Munsell's Index)

One of the first attempts to index every printed genealogical work was by Joel Munsell's Sons, an Albany publishing house of the late nineteenth century. The greatest value of the *Index to American Genealogies* lies in the inclusion of genealogical material from town, county, and local histories. First printed in 1862, five cumulative editions had been produced by 1900; a later supplement covered 1900 to 1908. Munsell's Index was reprinted by Gale Research Company of Detroit in 1966 and is currently available in a 1979 reprint edition from Genealogical Publishing Company of Baltimore. Although somewhat dated, it is still very useful. Many local histories, which typically include lengthy genealogies, were published before 1908.

This work indexes surnames; brief titles and page numbers indicate where a family history may be found. The approximately 55,000 references are not comprehensive but do include the major occurrences of family information in the books cited. Many of the brief citations can be located in a companion volume, *The American Genealogist*, 5th ed. (Albany, N.Y.: Joel Munsell's Sons, 1900. Reprint. Detroit: Gale Research Co., 1975), which is a bibliography of family histories published in America to 1900. This volume should be available in every genealogical library collection. A helpful description of this index and how to use it is in Roger Scanland, "The Munsell Genealogical Indexes," *Genealogical Journal* 2 (September 1973): 103–8.

Genealogical Index of the Newberry Library (The Newberry Index)

The Newberry Library in Chicago is one of the largest genealogical libraries in the United States. Between 1896 and 1918, its staff compiled a detailed surname index to genealogical periodicals, local history books, and genealogies. The *Genealogical Index of the Newberry Library*, 4 vols. (Boston: G.K. Hall, 1960), contains 512,000 entries arranged alphabetically by surname. Although not an every-name index, it is fairly comprehensive. The references include brief mentions of the surname as well as biographies and family genealogies. Very brief citations are included for the books indexed—usually a short title, author, and year of publication. They are arranged by region or state. The index was discontinued in 1918, so no books published after that date are included. (Note that catalog numbers published in the index are no longer valid.)

Library of Congress Index to Local History Biographies

Another card file for biographical material in local histories was made by the Library of Congress and published on forty reels of microfilm: *The Library of Congress Index to Biographies in State and Local Histories* (Baltimore: Magna Carta Book Co., 1979). This index includes approximately 170,000 names of persons whose biographical sketches appear in 340 local histories. Most are state histories but, for some states, significant county, regional, and city histories were indexed. The names are arranged alphabetically, but the index is not comprehensive; of the 340 histories indexed, twenty-six states are represented only once. The remaining twenty-four states have the following distribution:

Alabama:	8	Louisiana:	21
Alaska:	3	Maryland:	2
Arkansas:	10	Mississippi:	13
Arizona:	6	Nevada:	11
California:	34	North Carolina:	10
Connecticut:	3	North Dakota:	3
Delaware:	3	New York:	2
District of		Oklahoma:	3
Columbia:	3	Ohio:	2
Georgia:	36	South Carolina:	13
Hawaii:	3	Tennessee:	32
Idaho:	3	Texas:	27
Kentucky:	50		

Comparatively extensive coverage for the South makes this tool especially helpful. An excellent review of this index is J. Carlyle Parker, "Book Reviews," *Genealogical Journal* 9 (March 1980): 39. When the Magna Carta Book Company ceased operation in the mid-1980s, the rights to this index were given to the Family History Library. Copies can be obtained from the library.

American Biographical Index

Another important index to biographical information in local histories is the *American Biographical Index* (*ABI*) (New York City: K.G. Saur, 1993), an index of approximately 300,000 biographies from more than 600 volumes for local and national leaders in the United States and Canada. The six-volume index identifies every subject, including dates of birth and death and occupation. The 368 sources used for this collection were published between 1702 and 1956, but fully ninety-two percent of the titles were published before 1920; fifty-five percent of them were published before 1900. Relatively few were published in the early years of this range. In fact, half of the indexed titles were published between 1880 and 1909. Virtually all of the subjects were born in the nineteenth century.

The selection of sources is quite broad, geographically and by scope. The set complements the *BGMI* very well because many state and regional sources were used, thus identifying thousands of obscure persons of only local importance. Approximately two-thirds of the sources are not indexed in the *BGMI*. Even fewer are indexed in the *Library of Congress Index to Local History Biographies*. It appears that less than ten percent of the individuals included have more than one entry. Therefore, approximately 275,000 distinct individuals are cited in the index. The geographic coverage is also very broad. Virtually every state is represented by at least one title, several by two or more.

Statewide Indexes

A relatively recent development is the creation of statewide indexes to local histories. Many every-name indexes have been published for individual local histories; now works are appearing that include many histories in one alphabetical index. These are personal-name indexes to those for whom a sketch or important information is available. However, they are not every-name indexes to all the books included. When using these indexes, check every sketch in an area of interest (county, city) for all people having the surname of interest. In this way the ancestor may be found, even if not the subject of a sketch. Statewide biographical sketch indexes are available (usually published as books, but sometimes existing only as card files) for Alabama, Alaska, Arkansas, California, Colorado, Connecticut, Florida, Idaho, Illinois, Indiana, Iowa, Kentucky, Maryland, Michigan, Minnesota, Mississippi, Montana, Nevada, New Hampshire, New Jersey, New York, North Dakota, Ohio, Oregon, Pennsylvania, Rhode Island, South Carolina, South Dakota, Texas, Utah, Virginia, Washington, Wisconsin, and Wyoming. An annotated bibliography that includes most of these is in J. Carlyle Parker, *Going to Salt Lake City to Do Family History Research,* 2nd ed. (Turlock, Calif.: Marietta, 1993).

PERIODICAL INDEXES

For almost 150 years, genealogists and genealogical societies have been printing periodicals (serials, journals, or magazines) that include a large variety of original sources, abstracts, transcripts, how-to articles, and compiled family histories. Periodicals spawn periodical indexes, which, even though not every-name indexes, are very helpful. Some of the indexes mentioned above include some genealogical periodicals, but the following focus exclusively on periodicals.

Index to Genealogical Periodicals (Jacobus' Index)

One of the foremost modern genealogists, Donald Lines Jacobus, saw the need to access the information hidden in periodicals. He published three volumes (1932 to 1953) as a partial index to major genealogical periodicals. Reprints, some of them three volumes in one (Baltimore: Genealogical Publishing Co., 1978), are available in all genealogical libraries and collections. A 1983 edition, *Donald Lines Jacobus' Index to Genealogical Periodicals,* Carl Boyer III, ed. (Newhall, Calif.: Boyer Publications, 1983) combines the seven separate indexes of the three original volumes into two: name and place. The index includes approximately 20,000 references to people, places, and records appearing in periodicals from 1870 to 1952 by surname, given name, and locality. However, Jacobus did not index periodicals that had their own comprehensive indexes, and he only indexed articles by their main subjects; therefore, his work is not an every-name index (e.g., the family record of the Wilsons of Newport is indexed as: Wilson; Family Record, Newport). No individuals are specified. Jacobus' introductions in each volume are invaluable for understanding the scope of the index.

Genealogical Periodical Annual Index (GPAI)

Since 1962 (except for a gap from 1970 to 1973), the *GPAI* has been a boon to genealogists. Several editors have accepted the task of producing it over the years. Currently, Leslie K. Towle and Laird C. Towle produce the *Genealogical Periodical Annual Index* (Bowie, Md.: Heritage Books, 1974–present). This index is in virtually every genealogy library collection. It is not cumulative from year to year, so each year must be searched separately. It is not an every-name index and includes a personal name only when the individual is the subject of an article. Book reviews and other articles, such as those concerning research methodology, are also indexed. Approximately 300, or roughly one-half of the genealogical periodicals currently available—specifically, those periodicals that are provided to the indexers at no charge—are indexed. While most major periodicals are included, many small, local periodicals are not. As with many major indexes, compiling the *GPAI* is a lengthy process; the index to 1992 periodicals was published in 1994.

PERiodical Source Index (PERSI)

PERSI is an indexing project of the Historical Genealogy Department of the Allen County Public Library in Fort Wayne, Indiana. This library has long been known as having one of the best genealogical collections in the United States. The first volume appeared in 1987; it covered periodicals published in the calendar year 1986. Subsequent annual volumes have been published. The library has also published a sixteen-volume retrospective *PERSI* covering periodicals published from 1847 through 1985. The last of its four sections was published in 1995.

Like the *GPAI, PERSI* is not an every-name index. Rather, it is a subject index; only the subjects of the articles are included. Because families and individuals are often the subjects of articles, many of the citations are for given and family names. *PERSI* also indexes articles dealing with sources in localities, which are the staple of local periodical publishing. Each annual volume of PERSI includes more than 45,000 entries.

Information in *PERSI* is presented in a column format in five separate alphabetical parts: U.S. Places, Family Records, Canada Places, Foreign Places, and Research Methodology. Each of these parts is arranged alphabetically by the place (two-letter postal abbreviation for states), surname, or type of record (methodology section), followed (in separate columns) by the title of the article, journal abbreviation, volume number, issue number, month, and year. The three geographic parts list articles pertaining to the same locality by record type, then by title.

PERSI indexes many more periodicals than does the *GPAI.* The entire project will index more than 4,100 titles, including defunct, merged, and renamed periodicals. The index also includes many foreign periodicals from Canada, Germany, England, and other countries. Both historical periodicals and genealogical periodicals are included. A four-letter abbreviation identifies the journals. However, no addresses are given, nor are cross references to other (older) titles. The PERSI book volumes are available at most major genealogical libraries. There are plans for a CD-ROM version to be issued in 1996. PERSI is also available on microfiche at U.S. and Canadian LDS family history centers.

The Allen County Public Library has also published a comprehensive *Bibliography of Genealogical and Local History Periodicals With Union List of Major U.S. Collections* (Fort Wayne, Ind.: Allen County Public Library Foundation, 1990). This list serves to more fully identify the titles indexed in PERSI and also identifies which of several significant libraries throughout the United States have copies of the periodical. It also includes citations for hundreds of family and surname periodicals *not* included in the index.

Individual Periodical Indexes.

The publishers of many long-lived genealogical periodicals have created comprehensive, cumulative indexes for their own magazines. While most publish annual indexes, those with cumulative indexes are more helpful to the genealogist. A partial list of such periodicals and the volumes covered in each cumulative index follows. Most of them are every-name indexes.

The American Genealogist, vols. 1–60 (subject index).

Daughters of the American Revolution Magazine, vols. 1–84, then every five years to vol. 104 ("Genealogy Index").

Detroit Society for Genealogical Research Magazine, vols. 1–10, then every five years to vol. 30.

Genealogical Journal, vols. 1–16 (subject index).

Mayflower Descendant, vols. 1–34 ("Index of Persons").

National Genealogical Society Quarterly, vols. 1–50 (topical indexes).

New England Historical and Genealogical Register Index of Persons, vols. 1–50, 51–148. NEHGS plans to publish a CD-ROM edition of the full run of the *Register* (through 1994), with consolidated index, in 1996.

New Jersey Genealogical Magazine, vols. 1–30, 31–40, 41–50.

New York Genealogical and Biographical Record, vols. 1–113, (subject only).

Notes and Queries Relating to Pennsylvania, 7 vols. 1st–4th series. See Eva D. Schory, *Every Name Index to Egle's Notes and Queries* (Decatur, Ill.: Decatur Genealogical Society, 1981.)

South Carolina Historical and Genealogical Magazine, vols. 1–40, 41–71.

Virginia Genealogist, vols. 1–20.

Statewide Indexes to Genealogical Periodicals
The following indexes provide subject coverage for many periodicals within the state indicated.

The *Connecticut Periodical Index* and a collection of more than 200 periodicals are at The Pequot Library, 720 Pequot Ave., Southport, CT 06490.

Bell, Carol Willsey. *Ohio Genealogical Periodical Index: A County Guide*. 4th ed. Youngstown, Ohio: C. W. Bell, 1983.

Buckway, G. Eileen. *Index to Texas Periodicals*. Salt Lake City: Family History Library, 1987.

Finnell, Arthur Louis. *Minnesota Genealogical Periodical Index*. Marshall, Minn.: Finnell Richter and Assoc., 1980.

Grover, Robert L. *Missouri Genealogical Periodical Index: A County Guide, 1960–1982*. Independence: Missouri Territory Pioneers, 1983.

Quigley, Maud. *Index to Family Names in Genealogical Periodicals*. Grand Rapids, Mich.: Western Michigan Genealogical Society, 1981.

_____. *Index to Michigan Research Found in Genealogical Periodicals*. Grand Rapids, Mich.: Western Michigan Genealogical Society, 1979.

Swem, Earl Gregg. *Virginia Historical Index*. 2 vols. in 4, 1934–36. Reprint. Gloucester, Mass.: Peter Smith, 1965.

Trapp, Glenda K., and Michael L. Cook. *Kentucky Genealogical Index*. Evansville, Ind.: Cook Publications, 1985.

University of Arizona Library. *The Arizona Index: A Subject Index to Periodicals About the State*. 2 microfilms. Boston: G.K. Hall, 1978.

Subject Index to Genealogical Periodicals (Sperry)
The *GPAI* and *PERSI* indexes are strong on geographic and personal names while maintaining a lesser focus on research and methodology articles. Articles on research procedures, descriptions of genealogical collections, sources, histories of localities, and other topical material of interest are dealt with in Kip Sperry, *Index to Genealogical Periodical Literature 1960–1977* (Detroit: Gale Research Co., 1979). While Sperry's index does not include compiled genealogies or printed source records, it is helpful for genealogists who need information about a source or area.

QUERY FILES
A useful but often overlooked form of index is the query file. A query is a kind of "want ad" that is published in genealogical periodicals. Individual researchers write brief descriptions of the family they are seeking in the hopes of locating others who know more about the family. The query is a popular approach in genealogy for learning if others are researching a particular family. Almost every society or periodical maintains or prints a query file for its members or subscribers. In addition, some periodicals exist specifically to publish queries. In a very real sense, queries are indexes to ongoing research. The query seldom contains significant genealogical material, but it does, like other indexes, refer to a source for more information. If a researcher is not a member of the society or does not subscribe to the periodical, there is usually a small fee to place a query. The files or publications, however, are usually available for research at no cost. Over time, the addresses associated with queries often become out of date as researchers move. However, the society that maintains the file may have the researcher's present address.

Family Registry
Microfiche indexes for more than 300,000 forms registered by individual researchers and family organizations are available for search and inquiry at the Family History Library and its family history centers. These forms were submitted to the Family History Library (then the Genealogical Library) beginning in 1983. The purpose was to allow individual researchers and family organizations to register the family lines they were researching. In this way, research efforts could be shared and coordinated rather than duplicated. With the advent of Ancestral File and its option to "register a research interest," the importance of Family Registry has waned. The library no longer encourages new registrations, and, as of 1996, plans were to make Family Registry a static or closed file. Eventually, the information in it should be added to Ancestral File. Family Registry is still a good source, however, to learn if others have been researching a particular person.

Computerized "Roots" Cellar
The "Roots" Cellar is a computerized query service of The Everton Publishers in Logan, Utah, offered through Everton's periodical, *Everton's Genealogical Helper*. Most genealogical periodicals have query sections in which subscribers can advertise for information on a surname or a research "dead end"; this one is by far the largest. By 1994, some 48,000 participants had submitted more than 500,000 names for computer input. Updates are printed in each issue of *Everton's Genealogical Helper*, and the entire database can be searched for a surname or an individual for a fee. Details are in each issue of the *Genealogical Helper*. Microfiche copies of the Roots Cellar can be found at many family history centers, and the file is available on CD-ROM from the Banner Blue Division of Brøderbund Software (see above under "Databases—Private Research Databases—Automated Archives").

Genealogical Research Directory
An annual query book published since 1981, each issue of the *Genealogical Research Directory* contains approximately

100,000 new entries from all over the world. Edited by Keith A. Johnson and Malcolm R. Sainty, this source is available at most major genealogical libraries, although most of the purchasers are individual researchers. Any researcher may pay a small fee to list the individuals being sought. (Purchase of the book is not required for a listing.) Its worldwide scope makes it especially useful for finding researchers in other countries who are interested in the same family. Back issues usually remain in print for from three to five years. The U.S. distributor is Jan Jennings, 3324 Crail Way, Glendale, CA 91206. Similar books exist specifically for England, Germany, and for some other countries.

Query Magazines

While some magazines focusing solely on queries have been published since the 1960s, they have become increasingly popular in the last few years. The following magazines specialize in queries:

Family Puzzlers. 1964–. Mary Bondurant Warren, Heritage Papers, 170 Windsor Ct., Athens, GA 30606.

Genealogical Queries Magazine. 1989–. Robert J. Wilson, 169 Melody Lane, Tonawanda, NY 14150.

Genealogical Query Index. 1983–. P.O. Box 15153, Dallas, TX 75201.

Lost and Found: National Genealogical Query Newsletter. 1984–. Ethel M. Weber, P.O. Box 207, Wathena, KS 66090.

The National Queries Forum. 1990–. Michael Cooley, P.O. Box 593, Santa Cruz, CA 95061-0593.

Southern Queries. 1990–. Steve Smith, P.O. Box 726, Durham, NC 27702-0726.

INDEXES TO ORIGINAL RECORDS

Census Indexes

As of early 1996, statewide census indexes existed for all federal censuses taken through 1860 and for all but thirteen states for the 1870 census. No part of the 1870 census has been indexed for Connecticut, Maine, Maryland, or Vermont. For the other eight states that are still incomplete, large portions have been indexed; these include the larger states from Illinois to Massachusetts. Book indexes for later censuses (1880, 1910) for many western states are available.

Observe caution when using census indexes. For example, blacks may have been omitted from some indexes. Additionally, the indexers may not have been well trained in early American handwriting; most census indexes have been made from microfilm copies, and the writing may have been faded or difficult to read. Most indexes for the 1850 and later censuses contain only the heads of households and persons in the households with different surnames. Often, two or more indexes exist for the same census; if possible, use them all. However, do not depend on the index alone. If an ancestor was known to have lived in a county when a census was taken but does not appear in the index, search the entire township or county. In larger cities for the post-1850 period, city directories may be helpful as a type of index; see chapter 19, Tracking Urban Ancestors, and chapter 11, Research in Directories. See chapter 5, Research in Census Records, for a thorough discussion of census records.

Significant nationwide census indexes are now available. The 1790 census is included in the *American Genealogical-Biographical Index (Rider)*. Also, *Century of Population Growth 1790–1900* (1909. Reprint. Baltimore: Genealogical Publishing Co., 1967) includes (pp. 227–70) a table of names from the 1790 census, grouped by similar spellings, showing in which states each name appears; it thus serves as a quasi-index for 1790. In 1984, the Family History Library obtained on microfiche the then-available census indexes from Accelerated Indexing Systems (AIS) for the library's family history centers. These microfiche indexes are also available at some research libraries. This includes all U.S. federal census indexes for 1850 and earlier, but few for later years. The AIS index is divided into nine searches. Searches 1 through 4 cover the entire United States for, respectively, 1607 to 1819, 1820 to 1829, 1830 to 1839, and 1840 to 1849 (a few state and colonial lists are also indexed). Search 5 includes thirteen southern states for 1850 and some for 1860. Search 6 covers eleven northeastern states for 1850, and search 7 includes the remaining midwestern and western states for 1850 and some later dates. Search 7a combines searches 5, 6 and 7 into one alphabet, while search 8 includes only some mortality schedules for 1850 to 1885. The Family History Library has no plans to update this index. However, Banner Blue Software, a division of Brøderbund Software (see above under "Databases—Private Research Databases—Automated Archives"), has produced these and other more current census indexes on CD-ROM.

Military Indexes

Almost every United States genealogist has one or more ancestors who served in the military. Many lineage societies have been formed around service in a particular war, thus creating great interest in military records. A few select military indexes are mentioned below; others are discussed in chapter 9, Research in Military Records.

Revolutionary War. Most colonial states have published books listing state residents who served in the revolutionary war. There are, however, three nationwide indexes of note: The *Index of Revolutionary War Pension Applications in the National Archives*, National Genealogical Society Special Publication No. 40 (Washington, D.C.: NGS, 1976) is an alphabetical index of all those who applied for a pension or who received bounty land based on revolutionary war service (some *see* references are included). The index thus includes only those soldiers and sailors who lived until pension laws went into effect and widows who could prove their husbands' revolutionary war service—approximately 80,000 names. The index is available in most genealogical libraries. The original pension files are in the National Archives. The Family History Library and many other repositories have microfilm copies.

In 1991 and 1992, Virgil White published *Genealogical Abstracts of Revolutionary War Pension Files* in four volumes (Waynesboro, Tenn.: National Historic Publishing Co.), providing indexed abstracts for each of these files.

The DAR *Patriot Index Centennial Edition* (Washington, D.C.: National Society DAR, 1994), is a list of more than 125,000 people who aided the cause of the American Revolution with one descendant or more who joined the Daughters of the American Revolution (DAR) by 1990. In most cases, lineage papers are available showing some documentation for the patriot and family. An updated, combined index is being prepared by the society. The DAR lineage books have been published through National Number 164,000 (Vol. 164). The *Index of Rolls of Honor in the Lineage Books* (Washington, D.C.: DAR, 1939–present) may also help identify a patriot ancestor. See chapter 20, Tracking Through Heredity and Lineage Organizations, for more information on lineage societies.

Civil War. Statewide indexes exist for those who served from specific states in the Civil War (both Union and Confederate), but the major indexes are in the National Archives or genealogical libraries that have purchased microfilm copies. The three-by-five-inch card index to Civil War pension applications is the largest single index for this war: *General Index to Pension Files 1861–1934* (Washington, D.C.: National Archives), microfilm T288, 544 rolls, is available at many major genealogical libraries. It covers only those who served the Union cause or former Confederate soldiers who changed sides.

Compiled service records have also been indexed for every known soldier—not only those who applied for pensions. However, they are arranged by state. No consolidated, nationwide index of service in the Civil War exists. However, a project is under way to create such a nationwide index. Called the Civil War Soldier's System, it will contain the names taken from 5.2 million General Index cards. Contact the Federation of Genealogical Societies (FGS), P.O. Box 83022, Richardson, TX 75083-0220, for details.

Many books have been compiled on those who served in other U.S. wars, as described in chapter 9, Research in Military Records, and chapter 18, Tracking Twentieth-Century Ancestors. Also see the discussion of lineage societies in chapter 20.

IMMIGRATION INDEXES

The topic of immigration to the United States is also discussed in chapter 13, Immigration: Finding Immigrant Origins. Immigration records are generally available in two forms: printed lists taken from manuscripts or compilations and unpublished manuscript lists. A mammoth, ongoing work seeking to index all printed immigration records is P. William Filby, ed., *Passenger and Immigration Lists Index* (Detroit, Mich.: Gale Research Co., 1980–). This work contains more than 2,200,000 personal names filed alphabetically and includes age (if given), destination, and source citations for approximately 2,000 printed immigration lists. Supplements add approximately 150,000 names every year. The annual supplements are cumulated every five years. Approximately 2,600 printed sources are identified in P. William Filby, ed., *Passenger and Immigration Lists Bibliography 1538–1900* (Detroit: Gale Research Co., 1988). Eventually, all of these and many newly printed lists will be indexed. Two excellent articles by P. William Filby in the *Genealogical Journal* explain this project: "Published Passenger Lists" (8 Dec. 1979): 177 and "Published Passenger Lists" (Fall 1983): 112. Several other projects and indexes are mentioned in the latter article.

More than 20 million people who came to the United States in the nineteenth century are not included on printed immigration lists. Many arrival lists compiled by ports of entry survived and have been microfilmed by the National Archives.

Indexes exist for arrivals at the following ports for the years indicated:

Baltimore: 1820–74, 1852–97, 1853–66

Boston: 1848–91

Mobile, Alabama: 1820–62

New Bedford, Massachusetts: 1823–74

New Orleans: 1820–50 and 1853–99

New York City: 1820–46 and 1897–1902

Philadelphia: 1800–1906, 1820–74

These indexes are available at the National Archives and its regional branches and at the Family History Library, as well as larger genealogical libraries. Also see *Genealogical Research in the National Archives* (Washington, D. C.: National Archives and Records Service, 1982) and Loretto Dennis Szucs and Sandra Hargreaves Luebking, *The Archives: A Guide to the National Archives Field Branches* (Salt Lake City: Ancestry, 1988).

OTHER NAME INDEXES

Several other indexes and lists of indexes that can be a boon to the genealogist exist. A sampling is included below.

Anita Cheek Milner, *Newspaper Indexes*, 3 vols. (Metuchen, N.J.: Scarecrow Press, 1977–82), indicates where newspapers indexes are located and their scope. It is arranged by state and subdivided by city or county. See also Milner's "Newspaper Indexes," *Genealogical Journal* 8 (Dec. 1979): 185, and chapter 12, Research in Newspapers.

Ronald V. Jackson, Jr., *Early American Series* (Salt Lake City: Accelerated Indexing Systems, 1981–84) is a set of personal-name indexes in book form, much like his census indexes. These indexes are statewide and typically cover the colonial and early periods. Tax lists, state censuses, and passenger lists are included in the indexes. Many of these books are available at large genealogy libraries.

Betty M. Jarboe, *Obituaries: A Guide to Sources,* 2nd ed. (Boston: G.K. Hall, 1989), identifies 3,547 published collections and indexes to death notices and cemetery listings throughout the United States and some foreign countries. An appendix identifies obituary card files in eighteen states.

The growing popularity of genealogy and the increasing number of genealogical publications mean that more and more indexes are being created and published each year. Additional indexes are mentioned throughout this book. The purpose of all of these indexes generally remains the same: to help researchers find individuals faster and to locate important information more easily.

LIBRARY CATALOGS

A number of genealogical libraries have published catalogs of their holdings in some form. Such catalogs can serve as indexes to published genealogies if the genealogies are cataloged by family surname. Catalogs should be the first sources consulted when research on a new family is begun or when new information about an earlier generation has been found. If catalogs were not thoroughly searched during earlier research, they can also help solve "dead-end" problems. Remember that libraries continue to acquire books after their catalogs are published, so published catalogs are out of date as soon as they are printed. Often, libraries issue supplements to previous publications to inform readers of their new holdings.

One product of the numerous efforts made over the last two decades to automate libraries has been the "online" availability of library catalogs. Many major academic libraries and an increasing number of key research libraries have made their catalogs available to the public through various "dial-up" services, allowing almost anyone with a personal computer and modem to access them. They include libraries of great interest to genealogists, such as the Allen County Public Library in Fort Wayne, Indiana, and the New York (City) Public Library. Other libraries, including the Family History Library and many state libraries, have published their catalogs on CD-ROM so that individuals and institutions can purchase them, avoiding telecommunication fees. Consult your favorite research libraries about such services.

The growth of the Internet and the so-called information superhighway will make increasing numbers of such catalogs available to more and more researchers. Many libraries, however, have not yet automated their entire collections, so in some cases only portions of a catalog may be accessible through such media. Also, of course, catalogs contain only descriptions of the actual books or sources. Access to most actual documents via personal computer is still years away.

FAMILY HISTORY LIBRARY CATALOG

The Family History Library has the largest single collection of genealogical records in the world. Consequently, the *Family History Library Catalog* is the largest bibliography and finding aid for genealogical research. The catalog entries include detailed, analytical descriptions for each source, book, and manuscript in the collection. The main purpose of the catalog is to describe the records fully enough that practical choices for research can be made.

The catalog is available on microfiche and CD-ROM. Each version includes the same catalog entries, but they have slightly different features. The microfiche version has four sections that list records by author or title, surname, subject, and locality. The CD-ROM version includes the two most popular sections of the catalog: the surname and locality sections. It also allows searches by microfilm, microfiche, or computer number. Copies are available at each of the library's more than 2,000 family history centers. Both versions of the catalog are generally updated annually.

As of 1996, the Family History Library collection included more than 115,000 separate family histories cataloged according to one or more surnames. Up to 1,000 new titles are added each month. Approximately twenty percent are surname newsletters, manuscript collations, and biographies; the remainder are genealogies or family histories. Furthermore, eighty percent of the titles in the surname section of the catalog pertain to U.S. or Canadian families. Thus, this catalog lists more than 66,000 family histories for North American families, making it the most important and comprehensive bibliography of genealogies available. Each family history is listed under an average of five to seven names, yielding upwards of 400,000 references.

The *Family History Library Catalog* is available at family history centers and for purchase by individuals (microfiche only) and institutions (microfiche or CD-ROM version). Each microfiche section can be purchased separately. Researchers can purchase the locality section by state or country and the surname section in smaller segments of the alphabet.

DICTIONARY CATALOG OF THE LOCAL HISTORY AND GENEALOGY DIVISION, NEW YORK PUBLIC LIBRARY

The New York Public Library (Fifth Avenue and Forty-second Street, New York, NY 10018) houses an excellent collection of genealogical research material. The eighteen-volume catalog for its genealogical collection, *Dictionary Catalog of the Local History and Genealogy Division* (Boston: G.K. Hall, 1974), consists of duplications of the typed and handwritten, alphabetically arranged card catalog. Copies of this catalog are available at most major libraries in the United States. It includes approximately 300,000 references to the 100,000 volumes that were in the collection before 1972. Although most of the books are local histories, approximately 26,000 titles, and perhaps 75,000 references, are genealogies and family histories. The catalog indexes only the major surnames in each book, but it remains very useful. Like most published catalogs, this one has not been added to since publication. However, new acquisitions are identified in the annual *Bibliographic Guide to North American History*, published by G. K. Hall of Boston.

GENEALOGIES IN THE LIBRARY OF CONGRESS

The Library of Congress has one of the largest collections of genealogies and family histories in the United States. A 1919 bibliography has been superseded by Marion J. Kaminkow, *Genealogies in the Library of Congress: A Bibliography*, 2 vols. (Baltimore: Magna Carta Books, 1972; supps. 1976, 1987). This catalog can be found in most genealogical and research libraries. It lists the 20,054 genealogies in the library's collection as of 1972. Be sure to check the addenda in each volume, where approximately 700 of the titles are listed. The Library of Congress has added about 12,000 cross-references for surnames mentioned prominently in books about other families.

Arranged alphabetically by surname, the entries contain complete bibliographic citations. *See* and *see also* entries lead the user to genealogies that would usually be overlooked. The books indexed are, of course, available in the Library of Congress, but many can also be found at other major genealogical libraries.

Three supplements have been published to update this catalog. They cover books from 1972 through 1976; between 1977 and 1986; and from 1986 to 1 July 1991. Combined, the supplements list approximately 22,000 titles of recent genealogies.

A COMPLEMENT TO GENEALOGIES IN THE LIBRARY OF CONGRESS

Contrary to popular opinion, the Library of Congress does not have a copy of every book ever printed in the United States. Especially lacking are genealogies and family histories. Such books are often printed in small quantities and distributed through personal networks. Realizing this, the editor of *Genealogies in the Library of Congress* set out to locate genealogies *not* in the Library of Congress. The result was *A Complement to Genealogies in the Library of Congress* (Baltimore: Magna Carta Books, 1981). It is a bibliography of 20,000 genealogies found in one or more of twenty-four major libraries outside of the Library of Congress collection. The format is the same as that of the earlier volume (without cross references). It also indicates in which library the book can be found.

This book includes the more obscure titles and gives their locations. However, it is not comprehensive; several libraries surveyed only portions of their collections. Also, some libraries with major genealogical collections did not participate. The same titles may be in many other libraries as well, so be sure to check the catalog of any local research library.

NATIONAL SOCIETY DAUGHTERS OF THE AMERICAN REVOLUTION, LIBRARY CATALOG

This catalog is another important tool for locating compiled genealogies. While the Daughters of the American Revolution (DAR) Library includes most major published genealogies, its collection is unique for its holdings of genealogies that were published in very small numbers—sometimes fewer than a dozen copies. Many of its typescript genealogies can be found in no other research library. They are listed in National Society Daughters of the American Revolution, *Library Catalog, Volume One: Family Histories and Genealogies* (Washington, D.C.: DAR, 1982). This catalog, along with a small supplement published in 1984, lists 15,031 titles of family histories and genealogies. It is arranged alphabetically by the names of the primary families treated. The entries include complete bibliographic citations as well as DAR Library call numbers. In addition to an author index, the catalog has a surname index with approximately 26,000 entries that indicate in which books a surname is prominently mentioned, even if the name is not included in the title of the book. Volume 3 of the catalog, published in 1992, includes references to 4,123 family histories acquired by the library within the previous decade.

OTHER PUBLISHED LIBRARY CATALOGS

The catalogs discussed above probably identify more than ninety-five percent of the published genealogies and family histories of North American families. All, or most, of these catalogs are available in every major genealogical library. There are, however, several other library catalogs that researchers should be aware of. These should be consulted if you have access to the library described or if more thorough research is needed.

Several library catalogs have been published by the G.K. Hall Company of Boston (in addition to the New York Public Library Catalog described above.) They include those of the Peabody Library (Baltimore), Boston Athenaeum, Los Angeles Public Library, American Antiquarian Society (Worcester, Massachusetts), and others. These can be found in most university and some public libraries.

Many significant regional libraries have published catalogs of their genealogical holdings. An example is Mary L. Strong, comp., *Library Shelf List of the Genealogical Forum of Portland* (Portland, Oreg.: Genealogical Forum of Portland, 1983). More than 6,000 histories, genealogies, and source books are listed in it.

LIBRARY CATALOG NETWORKS

Online Computer Library Center

Many major public, private, and university libraries continue to explore the many aspects of automation and take advantage of the opportunities the computer age provides. These libraries are connected to one of several computer networks that allow them to locate and catalog books faster by sharing information with other repositories that use the network. One of the major networks is the Online Computer Library Center (OCLC). This network is an online card catalog for more than 5,000 public, private, and some academic libraries that subscribe to the service. New books are then cataloged only once—by the library that enters the book in the OCLC first. Other libraries flag the book as being in their collections and download the description for their catalogs. At libraries that have FirstSearch, patrons can conduct searches themselves. Librarians also can search the OCLC for specific requests. For example, if you know a specific title or an author's name, you can retrieve the full citation and locate the copy nearest to you, which you can then borrow through interlibrary loan.

Research Libraries Network

Several hundred major academic and research libraries belong to the Research Libraries Network (RLIN). While it operates cooperatively, much like OCLC, RLIN offers different search capabilities. In addition to author, title, and subject searches, key words and phrases can be found using sophisticated search techniques. Most major university libraries subscribe to RLIN and will help patrons make searches, although there may be fees. A similar network, Western Library Network (WLN), operates in many libraries in the Pacific Northwest.

Within the last few years, several states have begun publishing union catalogs on CD-ROM. These catalogs list every book in each cooperating library in the state, thus providing a larger set of research materials and identifying which libraries have copies. The WLN catalog is available on CD-ROM, as are catalogs for Iowa, Kansas, Louisiana, Maine, Mississippi, Missouri, Pennsylvania, Virginia, Wisconsin, and others. Contact the respective state library organizations to learn more about these catalogs.

MANUSCRIPT CATALOGS

Thousands of libraries across America have manuscript collections that include genealogies, family histories, and the research notes of professional and amateur genealogists on the many families they have researched. Any unpublished document—journals, diaries, letters, business records, and church registers, among others—is a manuscript. A genealogy, pedigree chart, or a family history neatly typed or written in almost illegible, abbreviated notes is a manuscript as well. And a printed volume that has handwritten annotations can be a manuscript. In a genealogy or family history, these notes may be corrections to previously printed errors or new information, such as previously missing maiden surnames. In addition to the various library catalog networks, which can also help in locating manuscripts, two important tools are also available.

National Union Catalog of Manuscript Collections

Since 1959, the Library of Congress has solicited detailed descriptions of manuscript collections in public, private, and academic libraries. These indexed and cross-referenced descriptions are published in the *National Union Catalog of Manuscript Collections* (Washington, D.C.: Library of Congress, 1962–present). Published annually since 1962, this catalog, often referred to as the *NUCMC*, provides brief descriptions of approximately 65,325 different collections at 1,369 different repositories (through the 1991 catalog). While most of these collections are not genealogical, many are biographical, and approximately 10,000 of them include genealogical information. A two-volume cumulative *Index to Personal Names in the National Union Catalog of Manuscript Collections, 1959–1984* (Alexandria, Va.: Chadwyck-Healey, 1988), is an alphabetical arrangement of all the "personal and family names appearing in the descriptions of manuscript collections cataloged from 1959 to 1984." Many of the 200,000 names in the index are entries for family information, which is typically genealogical. It is an excellent place to start a search for research notes that someone else may have compiled on a specific family.

Check also for the specific locality where your ancestors lived, the churches and schools they attended, other families they were associated with, and so on. These entries sometimes disclose invaluable sources—the location of a family Bible, diaries, letters, etc.

These volumes are especially valuable for records taken to places not associated with your family by relatives or family friends who moved away. For example, the personal papers of Zachariah Johnston, a resident of Rockbridge County, Virginia, were found in Durham, North Carolina. Searches in Rockbridge County disclosed the location of some of his papers in the Virginia Historical Society in Richmond, but failed to disclose that a much larger collection had been deposited in Duke University at Durham, North Carolina, where one of the family members later settled. This collection was cataloged in the *NUCMC*.

National Inventory of Documentary Sources (NIDS)

Many manuscript collections are too large to be fully described in the brief paragraph that appears in *NUCMC*. Most repositories create inventories or finding aids for their large manuscript collections, so researchers can often determine if a manuscript collection has information of value by consulting such finding aids. Unfortunately, most such finding aids have very limited distribution—often only within the library or archive that houses the collection. Recognizing the value of these tools, Chadwyck-Healey, Inc. (1101 King St., Alexandria, VA 22314), has begun publishing the finding aids for many research libraries on microfiche. The microfiche is accompanied by an index to the key subjects and persons mentioned in the finding aid. The *National Inventory of Documentary Sources (NIDS)* allows the researcher to get one step closer to the manuscript collection and to learn whether its contents will be of value. While most of these collections have little information of genealogical value, many that do include genealogical information are also described. *NIDS* is available at large research libraries, including government repository libraries. Beginning in 1993, the index to the various inventories was also published on CD-ROM.

For more information on locating manuscript collections using these sources, as well as online networks, see Mary McCampbell Bell, et al., "Finding Manuscript Collections: NUCMC, NIDS, and RLIN," *National Genealogical Society Quarterly* 77 (3): 208–218 (September 1989).

BIBLIOGRAPHIES

A bibliography is a list of books, articles or records. Bibliographies are important tools for researchers because they identify sources of information. Usually published as a book or as part of a book, bibliographies usually have a specific topical focus. They may be arranged by subtopic or strictly alphabetically.

Many are annotated, including brief descriptions of the books cited. Bibliographies are usually created by scholarly researchers seeking to identify important works pertaining to a specific topic or field. Booksellers' catalogs are also kinds of bibliographies, although they are usually not as comprehensive as other sources. Some major bibliographies are described below.

GENEALOGICAL AND LOCAL HISTORY BOOKS IN PRINT

The major source in this field is Netti Schreiner-Yantis, *Genealogical and Local History Books in Print*, (Springfield, Va.: Genealogical Books in Print, 1976–). Four editions have been printed (there is little overlap between them). The present (fourth) edition was first published in two volumes in 1985 and later reprinted in three volumes. Two supplements have been printed as volumes 4 (1990) and 5 (1992) of the fourth edition. Plans are under way for a new, fifth edition.

More than one thousand vendors list genealogical books for sale in this bibliography. One of its larger sections is the "Family Histories for Sale" section. Approximately 5,500 genealogies and family histories are included in the third and fourth editions (1981 and 1985). The index to family histories provides approximately 26,750 references to these titles—an average of almost five surnames for each book. The 1990 supplement to the fourth edition included an additional 815 titles, while the 1992 supplement included an additional 1,432 titles. Brief descriptions are given for each family history, as is the location of the vendor. One great value is that many of these are new books not included in other indexes or catalogs. The volumes are not cumulative, so all four of them and the supplement should be checked. Most genealogical libraries have this bibliography. In 1996, the Genealogical Publishing Company, 1001 N. Calvert St., Baltimore, MD 21202, acquired *Genealogical and Local History Books in Print*. The company plans to publish the fifth edition in several volumes, beginning with a family history volume.

AMERICAN AND BRITISH GENEALOGY AND HERALDRY

An excellent listing of most books published through mid-1985 that deal with genealogy in the English-speaking world is P. William Filby, comp., *American and British Genealogy and Heraldry: A Selected List of Books,* 3rd ed. (Boston: New England Historic Genealogical Society, 1983), and its *Supplement* (1987). This bibliography and its supplement list more than 12,800 titles of published genealogical sources. The primary emphasis is on United States sources; however, this bibliography usually excludes county and local histories, family histories, and immigration sources.

LIBRARY SERVICE FOR GENEALOGISTS

Many librarians have recognized the need to serve genealogists, but they often find it challenging to do so. A helpful guide by J. Carlyle Parker, *Library Service for Genealogists,* Gale Genealogy and Local History Series, 2nd ed. (Detroit: Gale Research Co., 1981), lists many indexes and other tools that a libraries would find useful. Although dated, it is an excellent bibliography of sources that researchers should be familiar with. A second edition is being prepared for publication by Marietta Publishing of Turlock, California.

UMI CATALOGS

University Microfilms International (UMI), 300 North Zeeb Road, Ann Arbor, MI 48106, supplies microfilm and photocopies of hundreds of out-of-print family histories. UMI's "Genealogy" catalog lists some 1,300 books currently on microfilm. If you know the title of a book you want and where a copy is located, UMI will obtain permission to copy it (including copyright clearance, if needed) and supply a microfilm or photocopy.

GENEALOGY AND LOCAL HISTORY SERIES

Since 1979 the Genealogy and Local and History Series, now produced by UMI, has been providing a growing collection of genealogical materials on microfiche. Published genealogies are a major part of UMI's Genealogy and Local History collection. Several hundred titles are collected, copied on microfiche, and cataloged as sets or "parts" of the collection. These parts are then sold (as separate units) to libraries and archives. Each part is described by a guide that includes complete catalog information with subject, title, and surname indexes. By 1995, thirty separate parts had been produced; they included a total of almost 6,000 genealogies. Many are rare titles, usually published before 1920 and in limited numbers. A number of research libraries subscribe to this collection. In 1990, UMI published *UMI Guide to Family and Local Histories*, a cumulative catalog of the first ten parts. Volume 2 of the catalog, covering items in the second ten parts, was published in 1993. The individual titles in the two catalogs are now available on microfiche for purchase by institutions and individuals. These volumes identify 4,367 genealogies and 6,185 local histories.

PERIODICAL LISTINGS

Two periodical sources are available. The Allen County Public Library's *Bibliography of Genealogical and Local History Periodicals* was mentioned previously (see "Periodical Indexes—Periodical Source Index [PERSI]," above). Also useful is Dina C. Carson, *Directory of Genealogical and Historical Publications in the US and Canada* (Niwot, Colo.: Iron Gate Publishing, 1992). This directory identifies approximately 5,500 family, historical, ethnic, and genealogical journals, newsletters, and magazines by title. An index of publishers helps locate periodicals published by organizations.

PUBLISHERS AND BOOKSELLERS CATALOGS

Other sources for family histories are the catalogs of various publishers that sell new, old, (used or rare), and reprinted books, especially family histories. These are surname catalogs (or they have surname sections), and they are arranged similarly to library catalog indexes.

The following publishers' catalogs may also be helpful:

American Genealogies. Higginson Book Co., 14-R Derby Square, Salem, MA 01970. Many family histories and genealogies, once out of print, have been reprinted and are available in paperback or hardcover. This is one of the largest collections of in-print family histories.

Genealogy and Local History Catalog. Tuttle Antiquarian Books, Inc., P.O. Box 541, Rutland, VT 05701

Genealogy, Heraldry, Local History Catalogs. Genealogical Publishing Co., 1001 North Calvert Street, Baltimore, MD 21202.

Genealogical and Historical Books. Picton Press, P.O. Box 1111, Camden, ME 04843.

ONLINE SEARCH SERVICES

Many libraries have integrated computer technology, CD-ROM databases, and online searching into their reference services. Library personnel can obtain information from hundreds of databases, including *America, History and Life, Historical Abstracts, Comprehensive Dissertation Abstracts, Encyclopedia of Associations, National Newspaper Abstracts, Standard and Poor's News Service, Social Science Citation Index, ERIC (Educational Resources Information Center)*, and many others.

Usually these databases are accessed through vendors, such as DIALOG, EPIC, and BRS (Bibliographic Retrieval System). Such systems are popular at academic and many public libraries. Many people find it useful to access such services from their homes; all that is needed is a personal computer with a modem. Many vendors do not charge minimum fees; rather, they charge for time spent using the individual databases.

Such databases require little time to search. They can provide bibliographies of books and articles of interest, including locations of specific reference materials that can be borrowed through interlibrary loan. Users are charged by the minute for computer time and by the entry for the bibliographies generated. As an example, one search required twenty-two minutes to search 9,000 periodicals covering a ten-year period, yielding thirty-two entries of specific interest at a cost of $28.45. It would have taken at least four months to physically search those periodicals, even with the best of indexes.

Many of these databases are now being distributed on CD-ROM and are available at local research libraries. In such cases, there is often no charge for the researcher to use them because the library pays no online connection charges. Sources of interest to the genealogist now on CD-ROM (and still available online) include *Biography Index, America, History and Life, Biography and Genealogy Master Index, Congressional Masterfile*, and others.

Many experienced genealogists conduct research in academic libraries. Although large and organized for academic studies, these facilities have the funds to purchase some of the most important research tools available—many of them discussed throughout this book. Sign up as a Friend of the Library or an Associate (a fee is required) to gain borrowing privileges and a library card, then explore the computer services department and investigate what it has to offer.

DIRECTORIES

Directories are important tools for genealogists because they help locate people and organizations that can assist in research. For more information on directories as research tools, see chapter 11, Research in Directories. *Everton's Genealogical Helper* includes different directories of interest to genealogists in five of the six issues published each year:

January–February: locality periodicals

March–April: family organizations and surname periodicals

May–June: genealogical libraries

July–August: genealogical societies

September–October: professional genealogical researchers

These directories are not comprehensive. The magazine is available in most genealogical libraries.

DIRECTORIES OF ORGANIZATIONS, SOCIETIES, AND INSTITUTIONS

American Library Directory, edited by Jacques Cattell Press. New York: R.R. Bowker Co., 1908–. This annual (since 1978) directory lists thousands of academic, public, private, and special libraries in the United States and Canada.

Bentley, Elizabeth Petty. *County Courthouse Book.* 2nd ed. Baltimore: Genealogical Publishing Co., 1995. This directory provides addresses, telephone numbers, and county organization dates for more than 3,300 county offices. A list of the records available, search fees, and other information is included for the courthouses that responded to the compiler's survey.

_____. *Directory of Family Associations.* Baltimore: Genealogical Publishing Co., 1995. This directory, issued every two years, is an A to Z directory that provides addresses, telephone numbers, contact persons, and publications (if any) for more than 5,000 family and surname organizations.

_____. *Genealogist's Address Book.* Baltimore: Genealogical Publishing Co., 1994. This directory, updated every two years, provides addresses and telephone numbers for thousands of national, state, and local organization of interest to genealogists. It includes libraries; historical, lineage, and genealogical societies; ethnic and religious organizations; publishers; booksellers; professional organizations; and periodicals. Additional information, such as hours of operation, contact persons, publications, and services is included for those organizations that responded to the compiler's survey.

The *Genealogist's Address Book* is a useful, single-volume tool that identifies many of the organizations and institutions genealogists seek. However, for more comprehensive listings, refer to the following "subject-specific" directories.

SUBJECT-SPECIFIC DIRECTORIES

Carson, Dina C. *Directory of Genealogical and Historical Societies in the US and Canada* (cited earlier). This directory includes family, historical, ethnic, and genealogical societies in the same listing, arranged by state and thereunder by town. An index provides access by the name of the society.

Directory of Historical Organizations in the United States and Canada. Edited by Mary Bray Wheeler. 14th ed. Nashville: American Association for State and Local History, 1990. A comprehensive list of approximately 13,000 organizations interested in history, including virtually all local and special interest history groups.

Encyclopedia of Associations. Detroit: Gale Research Co., 1987–. This annual directory includes current addresses, functions, and membership requirements of fraternal, ethnic, veteran, hereditary, patriotic, and other associations.

Filby, P. William. *Directory of American Libraries With Genealogy or Local History Collections.* Wilmington, Del.: Scholarly Resources, 1988. Briefly describes the genealogical collections and services of more than 1,500 public and university libraries, state archives, historical societies, and other libraries.

Meyer, Mary K. *Directory of Genealogical Societies in the USA and Canada.* 10th ed. Maryland: the compiler, 1994. This biennial publication identifies almost all genealogical societies and describes their services and publications. It also includes a list of independent genealogical periodicals (periodicals that are not affiliated with a society).

National Historical Publications and Records Commission. *Directory of Archives and Manuscript Repositories in the United States.* 2nd ed. Phoenix: Oryx Press, 1988. This volume identifies hundreds of manuscript collections in a variety of repositories. It includes many references to collections for ethnic and immigrant groups.

Zakalik, Joanne A., ed. *Directory of Special Libraries and Information Centers.* 17th ed. Detroit: Gale Research Co., 1994. An annual, comprehensive list of more than 21,000 libraries that have special collections and purposes.

TELEPHONE DIRECTORIES

Local telephone books have always been useful to genealogists—especially for locating living relatives. Recently, access to telephone books or residential address listings has become easier. Bell and Howell publishes *Phonefiche,* an annual microfiche collection of almost all telephone books published by the various Bell System companies. However, to use this source, you must know the town in which the person lives.

With the advent of CD-ROM technology, large databases, such as telephone lists, can be collected in a single collection. Two former Bell System companies, U.S. West and NYNEX (New York and New England), have published CD-ROM databases that each contain 10 to 15 million telephone numbers from their respective areas of operation. *PhoneDisc* (Digital Directory Assistance, 5161 River Road, Building 6, Bethesda, MD 20816) is a three-CD-ROM collection (two containing names, one containing business addresses and telephone numbers) that includes approximately 70 million households covering the entire country. Many of the 100 million telephone numbers in this directory are represented by two, three, or even four entries (e.g., husband, wife, and adult children), making it easier to find individuals than in a regular telephone directory. Another telephone directory on CD-ROM (usually including only one entry for each telephone number) is *ProPhone* (Pro CD, Inc., 222 Rosewood Dr., Danvers, MA 01923). Both of these directories provide names, addresses, and telephone numbers.

Such databases do not come exclusively from telephone company records. They are collected from various sources, including mailing lists and utility company records. Consequently, some addresses may be out of date. Recent court decisions declaring that telephone company lists are not proprietary will likely encourage the publication of more telephone directories by commercial companies.

DIRECTORIES OF PROFESSIONALS AND OTHER RESEARCHERS

Occasionally, researchers want to contact other genealogists known to be working on the same family lines or in the same area. Or, a genealogist might want to engage a professional to conduct research on a lineage, topic, or locale. Generally, their names become known from previous publications by them or through the recommendations of others. To find addresses and other information, several directories and indexes of genealogists are available.

Who's Who in Genealogy and Heraldry, 2nd ed., edited by P. William Filby and Mary K. Meyer (Savage, Md.: Who's Who in Genealogy and Heraldry, 1990), gives much information about 1,100 genealogists chosen for their contributions to the field. Many of them are professional genealogists.

The Association of Professional Genealogists publishes a *Directory of Professional Genealogists* listing its several hundred members and, for those who contributed, providing detailed background information. The four indexes are by geographic specialties, research specialties, related services, and member residence. It is available in most genealogy libraries and from the Association of Professional Genealogists, 3421 M Street N.W., Suite 236, Washington, DC 20007.

The Board for Certification of Genealogists publishes an annual list of genealogists and record searchers it has certified for competency in specific areas. It is arranged alphabetically by state and includes areas of specialization. It is available for a small fee from the Board for Certification of Genealogists, Box 14291, Washington, DC 20044.

The Family History Library maintains a list of accredited genealogists who have been tested for ability in specific regions and countries. Updated quarterly and listed by area of accreditation, this list is available free of charge from the Family History Library, 35 North West Temple, Salt Lake City, UT 84150.

The Genealogical Speakers Guild offers a directory of presenters, their topics, and fees. Listings are confined to those who are members of the guild. Order from the Genealogical Speakers Guild, 3421 M Street N.W., Suite 329, Washington, DC 20007.

For information on genealogists who may now be deceased there are fewer indexes. The best is Frederick A. Virkus, ed., *The Handbook of American Genealogy*, vols. 1–4 (Chicago: Institute of American Genealogy, 1932–43). This source includes a list of 2,341 amateur and professional genealogists, with some background information. Volume 4 (1943) is the most complete, but it omits some names from earlier volumes. It also includes a list of almost 11,000 genealogies in progress with the names of the researchers who were working on them, and a state and county breakdown of genealogists.

DICTIONARIES

Another important tool for genealogists is the dictionary. Many genealogical records were created in time periods, places, or societies that researchers are not familiar with. Dictionaries are excellent tools to help understand such records. For many, a standard desk or library dictionary is sufficient. Major, unabridged dictionaries available at every library are also useful. Especially note the following specialized dictionaries that are useful for understanding older records:

Black, Henry Campbell. *Black's Law Dictionary*. 4th ed. St. Paul, Minn.: West Publishing Co., 1968. This dictionary defines the terms and phrases of American and English juris-

prudence, ancient and modern, and is useful for understanding terms in court records and other legal records.

Evans, Barbara Jean. *The New A to Zax: A Comprehensive Genealogical Dictionary for Genealogists and Historians*. 2nd ed. Champaign, Ill.: B. J. Evans, 1990. This is an excellent list of terms often encountered by genealogists and their definitions. It also includes a list of nicknames and their usual given names.

Harris, Glen, and Maurine Harris. *Ancestry's Concise Genealogical Dictionary*. Salt Lake City: Ancestry, 1989.

Lederer, Richard. *Colonial American English: A Glossary*. Essex, Conn.: Verbatim Book, 1985. This dictionary explains words found in early American documents that are now archaic, obscure, obsolete, or have different meanings.

Oxford English Dictionary. Oxford, England: Clarendon Press, 1931–1986. This is the "master" dictionary of the English language. Its seventeen volumes identify virtually every word ever found in written English. The definitions are arranged chronologically to indicate what a word meant at different times. Definitions also include examples of word usage. Its size and expense limit it to larger libraries, although a CD-ROM version was released in 1990. A two-volume edition, *The New Shorter Oxford English Dictionary*, edited by Lesley Brown, became available in 1993 (Oxford University Press) and includes annotations of changing meanings.

ON THE HORIZON

It is difficult and perhaps unwise to peer into the "crystal ball" to see what tools the future genealogist might have access to. Many good intentions will not be fulfilled, while others will take much longer than anticipated to materialize. However, a glimpse of things to come is encouraging and perhaps will inspire similar plans. Further, such a glimpse can remind us to keep watching for and learning about new tools and indexes.

FAMILYSEARCH

With FamilySearch (see "Databases—FamilySearch" above) still in its infancy, many great sources can be expected to be available from it in the future. Some automated sources that are being considered for FamilySearch include:

- 1880 U.S. Census. An 1880 U.S. census database on CD-ROM would be the culmination of an ongoing extraction project that has been under way for several years. The database would include all of the significant genealogical data from the census for all persons. The first edition may not include all of the names on the census.

- Immigration lists. Many immigration lists and indexes have been computerized in preparation for printing. Several of these are planned as resource files.

- Scottish Old Parochial Registers. All of the old church records of Scotland have been extracted. They are now available on microfiche and may later appear on CD-ROM, arranged much like the International Genealogical Index.

- Other church and civil records. Millions of names have been extracted from parish and civil records. A separate file for such names, before they are ready for the International Genealogical Index, will be a boon to researchers.

- 1881 British census. Thousands of British genealogists are currently extracting this vital census. When completed, it will also be published on CD-ROM.

- Civil War Soldiers System. A cooperative indexing project with the Federation of Genealogy Societies, the National Archives, the National Park Service, and the Family History Library will eventually produce this database of Union and Confederate soldiers with cross-references.

OTHER TOOLS AND INDEXES

While many major automated tools and indexes may become part of FamilySearch, other important aids will not. It is difficult to determine what will actually be done or what will prove worthwhile after completion, but some projects under way include:

- Genealogical Projects Registry. Major organizations are encouraging the establishment of a clearinghouse of project ideas. Genealogical societies will greatly benefit by encouraging completion of projects and reducing duplicate or similar projects.

- Commercial CD-ROM sources. As technology becomes less expensive and as digital scanning becomes more accurate, more books, such as family and local histories, will be available on CD-ROM. The search capabilities of such databases will make research much easier.

- More indexes. Indexing is becoming easier and more profitable, and new indexes will continue to be published.

CONCLUSION

Databases, indexes, and other finding aids are perhaps the most important sources genealogists use. They provide access to information that may previously have been difficult, if not impossible, to search. Computer technology makes indexing simultaneously more feasible and more necessary.

How can genealogists learn about new tools and indexes? Involvement with colleagues in professional societies and local genealogy societies is important. So are regular surveys of major genealogical periodicals and those in your area of interest. Some periodicals, such as *Genealogical Computing* and the *Computer Interest Group Digest* (NGS), referred to earlier, provide regular updates on new databases and software. Other periodicals offer book reviews that can reveal new sources. Some periodicals recommended for this purpose are *Everton's Genealogical Helper,* the *Genealogical Journal,* the *National Genealogical Society Quarterly, the New England Historical and Genealogical Register,* and the FGS *Forum.*

BIBLIOGRAPHY

American Biographical Index (ABI). New York City: K.G. Saur, 1993.

The American Genealogist. 5th ed. Albany, N.Y.: Joel Munsell's Sons, 1900. Reprint. Detroit: Gale Research Co., 1975.

American Library Directory. Edited by Jacques Cattell Press. New York: R.R. Bowker Co., 1908–.

Andereck, Paul A., and Richard A. Pence. *Computer Genealogy: A Guide to Research Through High Technology.* Rev. ed. Salt Lake City: Ancestry, 1991.

Archer, George. *Archer's Directory of Genealogical Software.* Bowie, Md.: Heritage Books, 1993.

Bell, Carol Willsey. *Ohio Genealogical Periodical Index: A County Guide.* 4th ed. Youngstown, Ohio: C. W. Bell, 1983.

Bell, Mary McCampbell, et al. "Finding Manuscript Collections: NUCMC, NIDS, and RLIN." *National Genealogical Society Quarterly* 77 (3): 208–218 (September 1989).

Bentley, Elizabeth Petty. 2nd ed. *County Courthouse Book.* Baltimore: Genealogical Publishing Co., 1995.

_____. *Directory of Family Associations.* Baltimore: Genealogical Publishing Co., 1995.

_____. *Genealogists's Address Book.* Baltimore: Genealogical Publishing Co., 1994.

Bibliographic Guide to North American History. Boston: G.K. Hall.

Bibliography of Genealogical and Local History Periodicals With Union List of Major U.S. Collections. Fort Wayne, Ind.: Allen County Public Library Foundation, 1990.

Buckway, G. Eileen. *Index to Texas Periodicals.* Salt Lake City: Family History Library, 1987.

Carson, Dina C. *Directory of Genealogical and Historical Publications in the US and Canada.* Niwot, Colo.: Iron Gate Publishing, 1992.

Century of Population Growth 1790–1900. 1909. Reprint. Baltimore: Genealogical Publishing Co., 1967.

A Complement to Genealogies in the Library of Congress. Baltimore: Magna Carta Books, 1981.

Crowe, Elizabeth Powell. *Genealogy Online: Researching Your Roots.* Blue Ridge Summit, Penn.: Windcrest/McGraw-Hill, 1994.

Dictionary Catalog of the Local History and Genealogy Division. Boston: G.K. Hall, 1974.

Dilts, David. "1992 International Genealogical Index: Another Perspective." *Genealogical Journal* 20 (2) (1992).

Directory of Family Associations. Baltimore: Genealogical Publishing Co., 1995.

Encyclopedia of Associations. Detroit: Gale Research Co., 1987–.

Evans, Barbara Jean. *The New A to Zax: A Comprehensive Genealogical Dictionary for Genealogists and Historians.* 2nd ed. Champaign, Ill.: B. J. Evans, 1990.

Filby, P. William, comp. *American and British Genealogy and Heraldry: A Selected List of Books.* 3rd ed. Boston: New England Historic Genealogical Society, 1983. Supplement, 1987.

_____. *Directory of American Libraries With Genealogy or Local History Collections.* Wilmington, Del.: Scholarly Resources, 1988.

_____, ed. *Passenger and Immigration Lists Bibliography 1538–1900* Detroit: Gale Research Co., 1988.

_____. "Published Passenger lists." *Genealogical Journal* (8 December 1979): 177.

_____. "Published Passenger Lists." *Genealogical Journal* (Fall 1983): 112.

Filby, P. William, ed. *Passenger and Immigration Lists Index.* Detroit, Mich.: Gale Research Co., 1980–.

Finnell, Arthur Louis. *Minnesota Genealogical Periodical Index.* Marshall, Minn.: Finnell Richter and Assoc., 1980.

Genealogical Abstracts of Revolutionary War Pension Files. 4 vols. Waynesboro, Tenn.: National Historic Publishing Co., 1991–92.

Genealogical Guide Master Index of Genealogy in the Daughters of the American Revolution Magazine Volumes 1–84 (1892–1950) with Supplement Volumes 85–89 (1950–55) Combined Edition. Compiled by Elizabeth Benton Chapter, NSDAR, Kansas City, Mo., 1951. Reprint. Baltimore: Genealogical Publishing Co., 1994.

The *Genealogical Index of the Newberry Library.* 4 vols. Boston: G.K. Hall, 1960.

Genealogical Research in the National Archives. Washington, D.C.: National Archives and Records Service, 1982.

Genealogist's Address Book. Baltimore: Genealogical Publishing Co., 1994.

Greenlaw, William Prescott, comp. *The Greenlaw Index of the New England Historic Genealogical Society,* 2 vols. Boston: G.K. Hall, 1979.

Grover, Robert L. *Missouri Genealogical Periodical Index: A County Guide, 1960–1982.* Independence: Missouri Territory Pioneers, 1983.

Herbert, Mirana C., and Barbara McNeil. *Biography and Genealogy Master Index.* Detroit: Gale Research Co., 1980–.

Index of Revolutionary War Pension Applications in the National Archives. National Genealogical Society Special Publication No. 40. Washington, D.C.: NGS, 1976.

Index of Rolls of Honor in the Lineage Books. Washington, D.C.: DAR, 1939–present.

Index to Personal Names in the National Union Catalog of Manuscript Collections, 1959–1984. Alexandria, Va.: Chadwyck-Healey, 1988.

Jackson, Ronald V, Jr. *Early American Series.* Salt Lake City: Accelerated Indexing Systems, 1981–84.

Jacobus, David Lines. "Tricks in Using Indexed Genealogical Books." *The American Genealogist* 30 (April 1954): 85

_____. *Index to Genealogical Periodicals.* Edited by Carl Boyer III. Newhall, Calif.: Boyer Publications, 1983.

Jarboe, Betty M. *Obituaries: A Guide to Sources.* 2nd ed. Boston: G.K. Hall, 1989.

Kaminkow, Marion J. *Genealogies in the Library of Congress: A Bibliography,* 2 vols. Baltimore: Magna Carta Books, 1972; supps. 1976–87.

Lederer, Richard. *Colonial American English: A Glossary.* Essex, Conn.: Verbatim Book, 1985.

Library Catalog, Volume One: Family Histories and Genealogies. Washington, D.C.: DAR, 1982.

Meyer, Mary K. *Directory of Genealogical Societies in the USA and Canada.* 10th ed. Maryland: the compiler, 1994.

Directory of Archives and Manuscript Repositories in the United States. 2nd ed. Phoenix: Oryx Press, 1988.

The Library of Congress Index to Biographies in State and Local Histories Baltimore: Magna Carta Book Co., 1979.

Milner, Anita Cheek. *Newspaper Indexes.* 3 vols. Metuchen, N.J.: Scarecrow Press, 1977–82.

_____. "Newspaper Indexes." *Genealogical Journal* 8 (Dec. 1979): 185.

National Union Catalog of Manuscript Collections, Washington, D.C.: Library of Congress, 1962–present.

The New Shorter Oxford English Dictionary. Edited by Lesley Brown. 2 vols. Oxford, England: Oxford University Press, 1993.

Nichols, Elizabeth L. "The International Genealogical Index 1992 Microfiche Edition." *Genealogical Journal* 20 (1) (1992).

_____. "International Genealogical Index (IGI) Updated by Addendum." FGS *Forum* 7 (3)–7 (4) (1995).

_____. "The International Genealogical Index, 1993 Edition." FGS *Forum* 5 (4)–6 (3) (1993–94).

_____. *Genealogy in the Computer Age: Understanding Family Search.* Rev. ed., Salt Lake City: Family History Educators, 1994.

Oxford English Dictionary. Oxford, England: Clarendon Press, 1931–86.

Parker, J. Carlyle. "Book Reviews." *Genealogical Journal* 9 (March 1980): 39

_____. *Going to Salt Lake City to Do Family History Research.* 2nd ed. Turlock, Calif.: Marietta, 1993.

_____. *Library Service for Genealogists.* Gale Genealogy and Local History Series. 2nd ed. Detroit: Gale Research Co., 1981.

Patriot Index Centennial Edition. Washington, D.C.: National Society DAR, 1994.

Quigley, Maud. *Index to Family Names in Genealogical Periodicals.* Grand Rapids, Mich.: Western Michigan Genealogical Society, 1981.

_____. *Index to Michigan Research Found in Genealogical Periodicals.* Grand Rapids, Mich.: Western Michigan Genealogical Society, 1979.

Rider, Fremont, ed. *The American Genealogical-Biographical Index (AGBI).* Series 2. Middletown, Conn.: Godfry Memorial Library, 1952–present.

Sanborn, Melinde Lutz. *Supplement to Torrey's New England Marriages Prior to 1700.* Baltimore: Genealogical Publishing Co., 1991.

_____. *Second Supplement to Torrey's New England Marriages Prior to 1700*. Baltimore: Genealogical Publishing Co., 1995.

Scanland, Roger. "The Munsell Genealogical Indexes." *Genealogical Journal* 2 (September 1973): 103–08.

Schreiner-Yantis, Netti. *Genealogical and Local History Books in Print*. Springfield, Va.: Genealogical Books in Print, 1976–.

Sinclair, Donald Arleigh. *A New Jersey Biographical Index: Covering Some 100,000 Biographies and Associated Portraits in 237 New Jersey Cyclopedias, Histories, Yearbooks, Periodicals, and Other Collective Biographical Sources Published to About 1980*. Baltimore: Genealogical Publishing Co., 1992.

Sperry, Kip. *Index to Genealogical Periodical Literature 1960–1977*. Detroit: Gale Research Co., 1979.

Strong, Mary L., comp. *Library Shelf List of the Genealogical Forum of Portland*. Portland, Oreg.: Genealogical Forum of Portland, 1983.

Swem, Earl Gregg. *Virginia Historical Index*. 2 vols. in 4. 1934–36. Reprint. Gloucester, Mass.: Peter Smith, 1965.

Szucs, Loretto Dennis, and Sandra Hargreaves Luebking. *The Archives: A Guide to the National Archives Field Branches*. Salt Lake City: Ancestry, 1988.

Torrey's *New England Marriages Prior to 1700*. Baltimore: Genealogical Publishing Co., 1985.

Towle, Leslie K., and Laird C. Towle. *Genealogical Periodical Annual Index*. Bowie, Md.: Heritage Books, 1974–present.

Trapp, Glenda K., and Michael L. Cook. *Kentucky Genealogical Index*. Evansville, Ind.: Cook Publications, 1985.

University of Arizona Library. *The Arizona Index: A Subject Index to Periodicals About the State*. 2 microfilms. Boston: G.K. Hall, 1978.

Virkus, Frederick A. ed., *The Handbook of American Genealogy*. Vols. 1–4. Chicago: Institute of American Genealogy, 1932–43.

White, Virgil. *Genealogical Abstracts of Revolutionary War Pension Files*. 4 vols. Waynesboro, Tenn.: National Historic Publishing Co., 1991–92.

Who's Who in Genealogy and Heraldry. Edited by P. William Filby and Mary K. Meyer. 2nd ed. Savage, Md.: Who's Who in Genealogy and Heraldry, 1990.

Zakalik, Joanne A., ed. *Directory of Special Libraries and Information Centers*. 17th ed. Detroit: Gale Research Co., 1994.

RESEARCH IN BIRTH, DEATH, AND CEMETERY RECORDS

Chapter Contents

3

RESEARCH IN BIRTH, DEATH, AND CEMETERY RECORDS

Johni Cerny

Vital records, as their name suggests, are connected with central life events: birth, marriage, and death. Maintained by civil authorities, they are prime sources of genealogical information; but, unfortunately, official vital records are available only for relatively recent periods. Marriage records are discussed in detail in chapter 4, Research in Marriage and Divorce Records, while birth and death records will be considered here. These records, despite their recent creation in the United States, are critically important in genealogical research, often supplying details on family members well back into the nineteenth century.

BIRTHS AND DEATHS IN PUBLIC RECORDS

Many British and European countries began keeping birth and death records nationally in the nineteenth century. Before then, churches maintained registers of christenings and burials, and colonial settlers in America brought British laws and customs with them. Thus, churches were initially the sole keepers of vital records; ministers in many colonies were required by law to report christenings and burials to civil authorities. In some areas, consequently, these events are recorded in both civil and church records. Eventually, some colonies, primarily those in New England, passed laws requiring local town or county clerks to maintain records of births and deaths. Massachusetts had the most comprehensive laws pertaining to birth and death registration, and many of its early records have been published. Figure 3-1 is an example of published vital records from Rehoboth, Massachusetts.

During the nineteenth century, England and other European countries instituted national registration systems, primarily to compile medical statistics as information on epidemic diseases. The United States did not implement the practice until much later. The majority of the states did not require registration until the first quarter of the twentieth century, and then the responsibility for registering births and deaths was left to the individual states rather than the federal government, accounting for different starting dates and differences in the data called for. The earliest cities to require civil registration were New Orleans (1790), Boston (1848), Philadelphia (1860), Pittsburgh (1870), and Baltimore (1875). Fourteen states also initiated registration before 1880:

Delaware:	1860	New Jersey:	1878
Florida:	1865	New York:	1880
Hawaii:	1850	Rhode Island:	1853
Iowa:	1880	Vermont:	1770
Massachusetts:	1841	Virginia:	1853
Michigan:	1867	Wisconsin:	1876
New Hampshire:	1840	Washington, D.C.:	1871

The U.S. Department of Health and Human Services periodically compiles *Where to Write for Vital Records—Births,*

Declarations of Intentions to Marry

MUNRO Joseph of Swanzey and Anne Goff of Rehoboth, Jan. 9, 1741-2.
    Elizabeth and Henry West, both of Rehoboth, Aug. 1, 1747.
    Sarah and Ichabod Bowen, Jr., both of Rehoboth, June 11, 1757.
    Nathaniel of Rehoboth and Ellis Hazard of South Kingetown, R. I., Dec. 13, 1774.
    Samuel and Molly Blake, both of Rehoboth, July 8, 1780.
    John of Rehoboth and Mary Osborn of Long Island, Aug. 8, 1780.
    Waitstill and Asa Daggett, both of Rehoboth, Dec. 27, 1780.
    John, Jr., of Rehoboth and Parthania Cornell of Swanzey, June 20, 1782.
    Merebah of Swanzey and Joshua Round of Rehoboth, Aug. 24, 1813.

Births

3 90	MUNRO Benjamin, of Benjamin and Mary,	July 18, 1775
8 90	Joseph,	July 21, 1777
3 90	Benjamin,	Aug. 24, 1779
3 90	Allice Allen, of Benjamin and Rahamnah,	Dec. 30, 1803
3 90	Jacob,	March 22, 1805
3 90	Phebe Luther,	Dec. 6, 1806
3 90	Thomas Jefferson,	Jan. 29, 1809
3 90	Margaret Richards,	May 17, 1811
3 168	Hugh, of Hector and Miriam,	Dec. 29, 1765

Deaths

3 364	MUNRO Betty, of Nathan,	Dec. 26, 1758
4 221	Major Nathan, 76 years,	March 6, 1806
8 3	Roanah, widow, 79y 10m 5d,	Jan. 16, 1847
8 12	Charles N., of John N. and Louisanna, 9m 15d,	July 17, 1854
8 16	Ruth, wife of Benjamin, 75 years,	Dec. 22, 1857
3 360	Samuel, of John,	March 23, 1758
11 5	Benjamin, of B. and Mary, 83y 0m 22d,	Sept. 15, 1862

Figure 3-1. Vital records published in James H. Arnold, *Vital Records of Rehoboth, Massachusetts, 1642–1895,* 2 vols. paged continuously (Providence, R.I.: Narragansett Historical Publishing Co., 1897), 479, 688, 854.

Deaths, Marriages, and Divorces, DHHS Publication No. (PHS) 93-1142. (The 1993 edition is reproduced in this volume as appendix F.) It lists, for each state, the dates on which the records began, the types of records kept, the cost of certified copies, and the address of the records custodian in each state. The fees listed in it are subject to frequent increase. Future editions can be obtained from the Government Printing Office, Washington, DC 20402-9328.

Even in areas with early registration laws, enforcement was haphazard, particularly in rural and frontier areas. West Virginia is a good example of the incompleteness of early vital records. The initial law requiring registration was passed by the Virginia legislature to become effective in 1853, when West Virginia was still part of Virginia. The exact extent of citizen compliance is difficult to estimate, but professional genealogists know that many births and deaths were not registered. Property owners were more likely to register the birth of a slave than the birth of their own children because registering a slave was a protection of personal property rights. Sometimes a couple registered one or more children but not all. Undoubtedly the difficulty of traveling long distances over rough terrain contributed to the lack of compliance. Table 3-1 lists some available statewide birth and death indexes and records.

Even when early vital records are incomplete, you should examine them. Of course, you are not limited to vital records alone for birth and death information. A natural beginning for research is a survey of available family records. Family Bibles, family record books, journals, diaries, and letters often note births and deaths of family members. (For a discussion of some sources of birth information found in an average family, see chapter 1, The Foundations of Family History Research.)

During the period when civil authorities did not require vital records, births and deaths were regularly recorded in the family Bible among literate, religious families. These entries often supply the only complete birth and death dates for individuals who were born or died before the twentieth century, although other forms of family records sometimes contain mention of births and deaths as they occurred. Various groups of the Daughters of the American Revolution (DAR) have compiled many volumes of family Bible records, frequently including evaluations of the accuracy and authenticity of the records. The DAR collections are available at the DAR Library in Washington, D.C., and in libraries of state and local DAR groups throughout the United States (see appendix E). The Genealogical Society of Utah has microfilmed the DAR main collection and many state publications; they are available through the family history centers of the Family History Library of The Church of Jesus Christ of Latter-day Saints (LDS church). The library of Brigham Young University in Provo, Utah, is indexing every name in the DAR Bible records and diaries for the South. Eventually, this index will be available online through computer terminals in major libraries.

Other government and legal documents also contain birth and death information: New England town records, coroners' reports, probate records, land records, mortality schedules, and military records, among others. These sources, including family records, are discussed in other chapters, so mention of them in this chapter will be limited.

A coroner's report is issued when an inquest is held to investigate unusual or unknown circumstances related to a death. When the inquest is complete, the report includes the causes of death, the autopsy findings, where held, testimony about the circumstances existing at the time of the death, and the findings of the coroner's jury. Coroner's reports are public records

Table 3-1. Some Statewide Birth and Death Indexes and Records in the Family History Library's Vital Records Collection as of Late 1995

State	Birth Indexes	Birth Records	Death Indexes	Death Records	Comments
Alabama	1917–1919		1917–19		
California			1905–1988		
Delaware	1861–1913		1855–88	1855–1910	
Florida			1877–1969		
Hawaii	1896–1909 1909–44 1859–1939[1]	1859–1903[1] 1896–1903 1909–16 1916–49 1904–05[1]	1896–1909 1909–49	1896–1903 1909–16	
Idaho			1911–32	1911–37	
Illinois			1916–38[2]	1871–1933[5] 1916–42[2]	
Chicago		1871–1922 1871–1915 1896–1933	1871–1933	1878–1915 1916–22	Chicago stillbirths, 1916–42 (missing years)
Cook County	1871–1915[3]	1878–94[4] 1916–22 1916–18[1]		1878–1909 1914 1906–22	Also Cook County coroner's death records, 1879–1904
Iowa	1880–1934				
Kentucky	1911–54		1911–86		
Maine[6]			1892–1922		
Massachusetts	1893–1970[1] 1841–1900	1841–1895	1841–1971	1841–99	

State	Birth Indexes	Birth Records	Death Indexes	Death Records	Comments
New Jersey		1848–1900		1848–1900	
New York City		1881–1965	1900–65		Coroner's inquisition, 1823–98
Manhattan		1847–73	1888–94 1895–97[7]		Manhattan bodies in transit, 1859–94
North Carolina			1901–67	1906–94	
Ohio			1908–32	1941–64 (veterans)	
Oregon			1903–70		
Rhode Island	1853–1900		1853–1900 1901–43		
South Dakota	1880–1990		1880–1990		
Tennessee	1908–12	1908–12[8]	1914–42 1908–12[8]	1914–42	
Texas	1900–45[1]		1900–45		
Vermont[9]	1871–1908		1871–1908		
Washington	1907–54 1936–53[1]	1907–36	1907–79	1907–52	
West Virginia[10]					
Wisconsin	1852–1907[11]		1862–1907 1959–84	1862–1907 1959–84	

1. Corrected and/or delayed birth registrations.
2. Excluding Chicago.
3. Corrections with indexes.
4. Two sets: (1) Chicago births and (2) other county births.
5. Deaths in the city of Chicago.
6. Index to vital records, 1892–1907; 1908–22; index to vital records of eighty towns prior to 1892.
7. Includes Brooklyn.
8. Enumerator records.
9. General index to vitals, early to 1870; general index to vitals, 1871–1908.
10. Birth, marriage, and death records by county, 1853–1860.
11. Births in this index are found in county records.

Entries provided by Lineages, Inc., 1994, and Kathleen Hinckley, CGRS, 1996, from the *Family History Library Catalog.*

---

available for use by researchers, and they may be requested from the state, county, or city coroner's office. Not all deaths of unknown or suspicious nature result in a coroner's inquest; but when there is evidence that an ancestor died in an unusual manner or was murdered, coroners' records should be examined. There are medical examiners (as coroners are more frequently called today) at city, county, and state levels, and their records may be found at all three levels. (See chapter 10, Business, Employment, and Institutional Records.)

Probate records can also contain birth and death information. In them, the exact date of death may be listed for the individual whose estate is in probate; the names and dates of birth of his or her minor heirs may also be found in the record. These records are usually found in the probate court or the court having probate jurisdiction in a town or county. They are also public records and are available to the genealogist upon request to the probate clerk. (See chapter 7, Research in Court Records.)

Court minutes seem to be a "catchall" for miscellaneous items recorded to give them public credibility. For example, John Wills, clerk of the Council for West Jersey, an administrative court, entered a complete list of his brothers and sisters followed by his own children at the end of his minute book, vol. 3 (18 April 1712 to 6 February 1721/22), just before the index (figure 3-2). Thus, the clerk made his family vital records a matter of public record.

Occasionally, land and property records contain birth and death information. Sometimes the death date of a person leaving property to heirs appears in a deed executed after his or her death. Birth information is sometimes included in applications for public lands or homesteads filed with the federal government. (See chapter 8, Research in Land and Tax Records.)

Mortality schedules were included as part of the decennial (every ten years) census enumerations between 1850 and 1900. These schedules give the name, age, sex, color, occupation, birthplace, month and year of death, cause of death, number of days ill, the attending physician, and other details for persons who died within the year prior to the taking of the census. The 1890 and 1900 mortality schedules were destroyed. To locate those still in existence, see chapter 5, Research in Census Records. The Genealogical Society of Utah has microfilmed a large number of mortality schedules. They are available at the Family History Library and through its family history centers.

Military pension files also contain valuable birth and death records. The date and place of birth of the veteran, the dates of birth of his children, and the date and place of birth of the veteran's widow (if she received a pension) are included in the

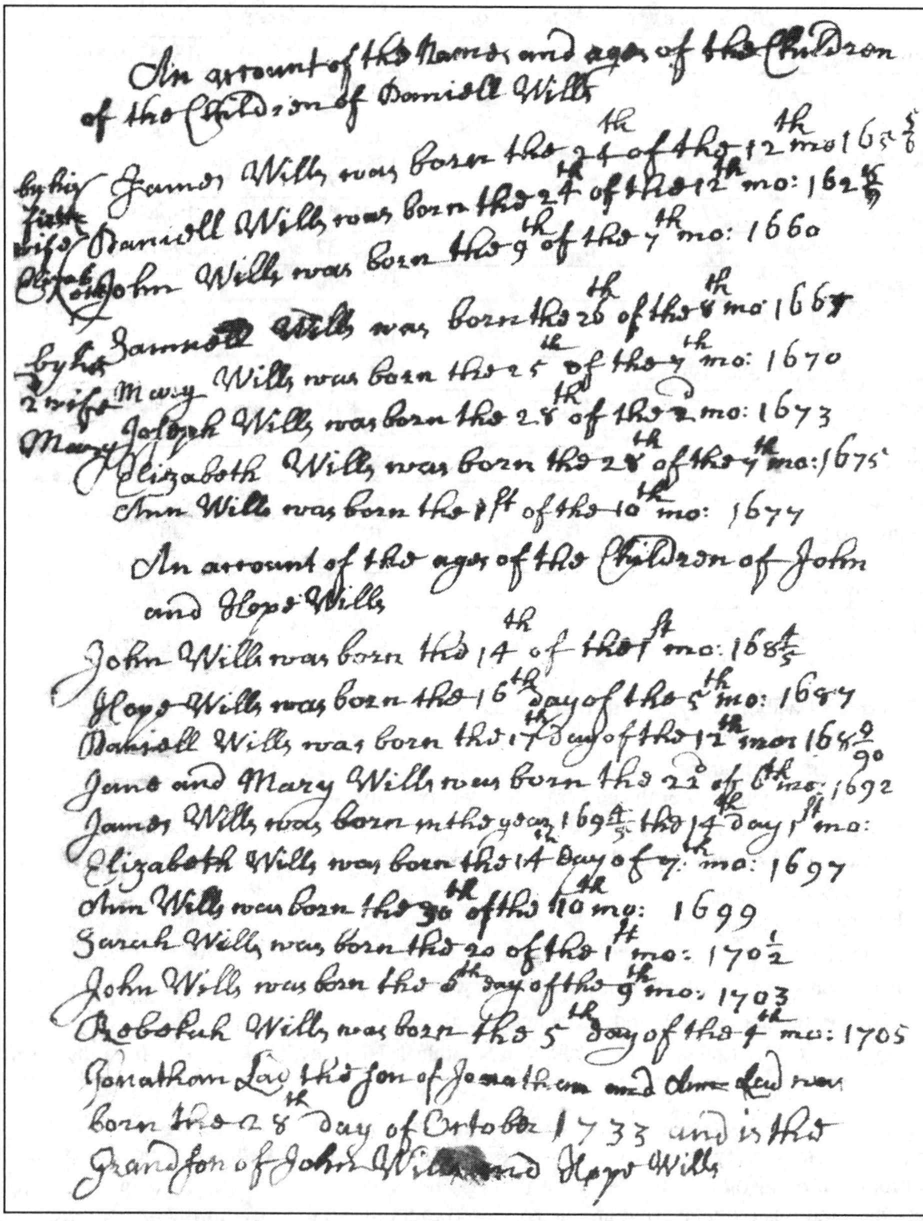
An account of the Names and ages of the Children
of the Children of Daniell Wills
by his James Wills was born the 24th of the 12th mo 165 5/6
first Daniell Wills was born the 24th of the 12th mo: 165 8/9
wife Daniell Wills was born the 9th of the 7th mo: 1660
Elizabeth John Wills was born the 26th of the 8th mo: 1664
by his Samuell Wills was born the 25th of the 7th mo: 1670
2 wife Mary Wills was born the 28th of the 2 mo: 1673
Mary Joseph Wills was born the 28th of the 7th mo: 1675
Elizabeth Wills was born the 1st of the 10th mo: 1677
Ann Wills was born the 1st of the 10th mo: 1677
An account of the ages of the Children of John
and Hope Wills
John Wills was born the 14th of the 1st mo: 168 4/5
Hope Wills was born the 16th day of the 5th mo: 1687
Daniell Wills was born the 17th day of the 12th mo: 1689/90
Jane and Mary Wills was born the 22 of 6th mo: 1692
James Wills was born in the year 169 4/5 the 14th day 1st mo:
Elizabeth Wills was born the 14 day of 7th mo: 1697
Ann Wills was born the 30th of the 10 mo: 1699
Sarah Wills was born the 20 of the 1st mo: 1701/2
John Wills was born the 8th day of the 9th mo: 1703
Rebekah Wills was born the 5th day of the 4th mo: 1705
Jonathan Lad the son of Jonathan and Ann Lad was
born the 28th day of October 1733 and is the
Grandson of John Wills and Hope Wills

Figure 3-2. Listing of John Wills' siblings and children in Minutes of the Council of West Jersey, vol. 3, 18 April 1712–16, February 1721–22 following p. 138; Rutgers University Library, New Brunswick, NJ 08903; Family History Library (hereafter FHL) microfilm 888,812.

file in some cases. (See chapter 9, Research in Military Records.)

Birth and death records are also found in church records, such as parish registers, which list christenings, burials, births, and deaths. Some churches took special church census enumerations that are of use to the researcher. Some ministers and evangelists kept vital records for their members in personal journals and diaries, and some churches have established historical societies or departments to collect and maintain official church membership records. The headquarters of the affiliate churches ordinarily maintain the records, but some may be found in local church offices. Inquire at a local church about the existence and location of the records of interest. (See chapter 6, Research in Church Records.) Personal records of ministers and other church officials can be found by consulting the *National Union Catalog of Manuscript Collections (NUCMC)*. (See chapter 2, Databases, Indexes, and Other Finding Aids, for more information on indexes.)

As the twenty-first century approaches, insurance and business records will play an increasingly important role in establishing genealogical facts. An excellent example of such records is Connie Bell and Vernell Walker, comps., *Union Pacific Railroad Life Insurance Claims Data* (Salt Lake City: microfilmed by the Genealogical Society of Utah, 1990). These alphabetically arranged records contain vital records and other documents supporting insurance claims. The compilers attempted to abstract all information of genealogical importance. Some of the details include name of the deceased, Social Security number, sex, race, occupation, date and place of birth, address, parents' names, date of marriage, date and cause of death, place of burial, and spouse's name. This collection is available on microfilm through the Family History Library.

Other insurance companies and businesses have compiled similar records, but researchers are just beginning to locate and abstract them. Check repository catalogs periodically and inquire at national and local genealogical societies about "works in progress" to determine if a source of interest is in the making.

Military records are discussed at length in chapter 9, but one military record source deserves special mention as a source of vital information: *Records, 1861–1936, of the Central Branch (Dayton, Ohio) of the National Home for Disabled Volunteer Soldiers.* The original records, located at Wright State University Library, were microfilmed by that repository and are available through the Family History Library. The records include the name of the disabled soldier, name of his regiment, home state, dates of admission and discharge or death, record of conduct and discipline while living at the home, administrative records and minutes of the managers, meetings, and death records (1875 to 1936).

Fewer vital records exist for the period prior to 1900, so researchers must search more obscure records on the chance of finding the details needed to identify people and document relationships. An example that is an excellent source for pre-1900 vital information is *The Gentleman's Magazine,* a periodical published in Great Britain that contained information about people from the United States, Jamaica, Antigua, Barbados, and the West Indies. David Dobson compiled *American Vital Records From the Gentleman's Magazine, 1731–1868* (Baltimore: Genealogical Publishing Co., 1987). The periodical published columns listing births, marriages, and deaths of British citizens at home and abroad.

Private sources, such as newspapers, morticians' records, hospital and doctors' records, business and employment records, and local published histories, also contain birth and death information. Some of these records are also discussed in detail in other chapters.

CONTENTS OF BIRTH RECORDS

Early birth records gave little information beyond the name of the child, date and place of birth, and parents' names. Some localities listed only the name of the father—particularly in early New England town and church records, as the following example from the town records of Simsbury, Connecticut, shows.

SIMSBURY RECORDS.   119

James the firft Son of James Tullar was Born the firft Day of January A : D : 1737/8

Eli Tullar Son of James Tullar was Born the: 14th Day of february A : D 1740/41:

[226] Jerufha the Daughter of Return Holcomb was Born aprill the : 3 : anno : Dom : 1734 :

Stephen the Sone of Return Holcomb was born September the : 23 : A : D : 1736 :

Timothy Cafe the Son of Richard Cafe was born the 2nd Day of February A : D 1759.

Lucy the Daughter of Gillet Adams was born feb : 14th A : D : 1731/2 :

Anne Granger the Daughter of George Granger was born July the : 19th : 1732 :

Rhoda the Daughter of George Grainger was born Aprill : 26th A : D : 1735 :

Simsbury Connecticut Birth, Marriage and Deaths (Hartford: Albert C. Bates, 1898), 119.

Early birth records are distressingly sparse, with a heavy concentration found in New England only. In the colonial period, church records that can serve as birth records were kept in Pennsylvania, New York, New Jersey, and Virginia, with Virginia trailing far behind the others. Quaker records for all of the states mentioned above are far superior to most others, providing the exact dates of birth and death for members of that faith. They have been well preserved; many are included in William Wade Hinshaw, *Encyclopedia of American Quaker Genealogy,* 7 vols. (1969. Reprint. Baltimore: Genealogical Publishing Co., 1991–94), available in most genealogical libraries in the United States. Willard Heiss has expanded coverage for Indiana with seven additional volumes of Quaker entries. These books are also widely available.

By the mid-nineteenth century, birth records in the United States began to include more detailed information. Figure 3-3 is from the birth register of Kanawha County, West Virginia. All Virginia and West Virginia counties used this format beginning in 1853. Some entries in these registers list the mother's maiden name instead of her married name—obviously helpful information in identifying the maternal ancestry of a child.

Early birth records can be obtained from town or county clerks in the area in which an ancestor was born. These records, too early to fall under the jurisdiction of recent privacy laws, are public records. However, when writing for a birth or death record, state your relationship to the ancestor of interest in case the clerk requires it. Your inquiry should indicate the specific record desired; give the ancestor's full name and as much identifying information as possible (especially if the ancestor has a common surname). Providing the exact date of birth, if known, or an estimated five-year birth period is especially helpful. The average fee for birth or death records at the county level is seven dollars; send that amount with your request. If additional funds are required, the clerk will either request the balance in advance or send the material and ask you to forward the balance. Most jurisdictions will search their records for a five-year period, but few will search further unless specifically requested to do so.

The Genealogical Society of Utah has microfilmed birth records of thousands of towns and counties throughout the United States, concentrating heavily upon the states east of the Mississippi River. These microfilms are available at the Family History Library and upon request through its family history centers). The printed vital records of New England towns are also available at the Family History Library; those that have been microfilmed can be borrowed through the family history centers). The printed vital records of New England towns are also available at the Family History Library; those that have been microfilmed can be borrowed through the family history centers. Many state and local historical society libraries also have copies, and many of the larger metropolitan city libraries with genealogical collections, such as the New York Public Library and the Los Angeles Public Library, also have copies of these printed records. The Holbrook Research Institute, 57 Locust St., Oxford, MA 01540, has microfiche copies for those Massachusetts towns that were never printed; a price list is available on request.

Even though births were not widely recorded during the early years of America's existence, those records that do exist

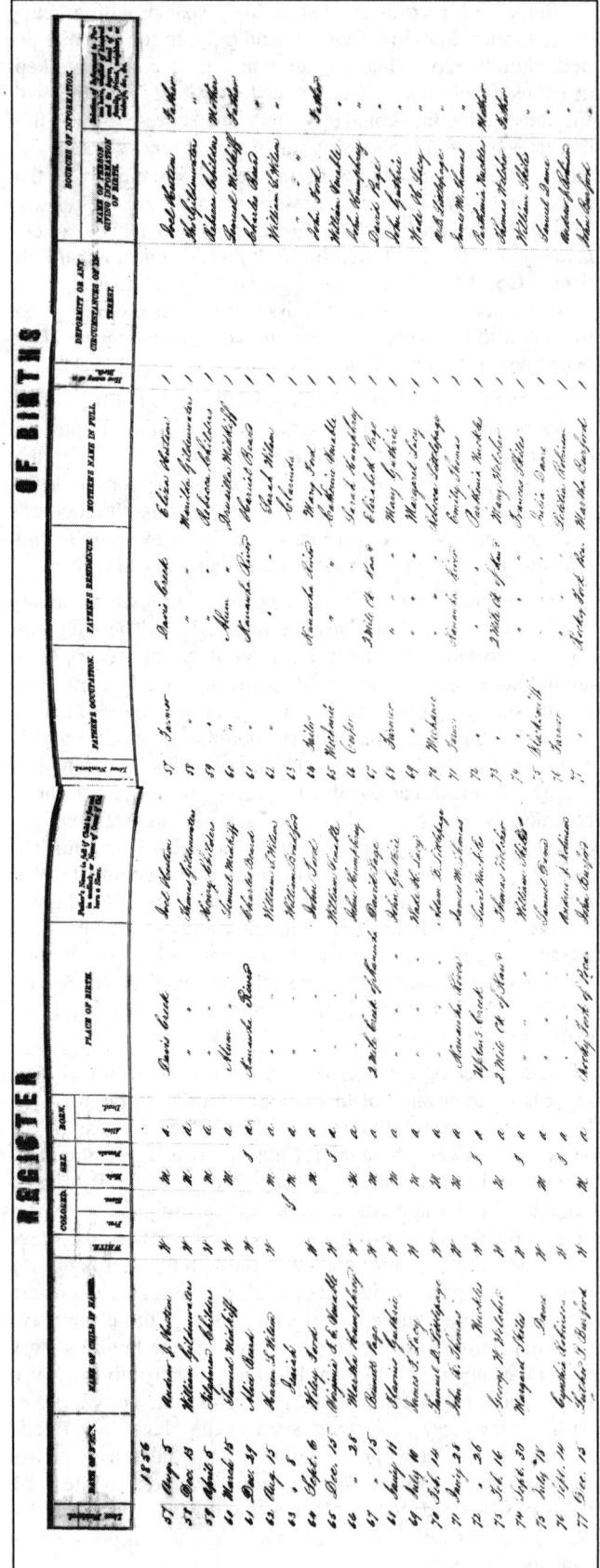

Figure 3-3. Register of births, Kanawha County, West Virginia, 1856; FHL 521,891.

may provide the only source of exact birth data for your ancestors. They should always be searched.

Modern (post-1910) birth records are maintained by the states. They are extremely valuable, but many researchers, learning birth information from home sources, fail to obtain birth certificates. This reluctance is most unfortunate and can result in an inaccurate or incomplete family genealogy. Modern birth records contain much more information than earlier records. Although birth certificates vary from state to state, most of them share much information in common.

Figure 3-4 is a birth certificate that is fairly representative of those compiled in most states. It contains the following information about the child and its parents:

Child	**Mother**
Name	Name
Birthplace	Race
Date of birth	Birthplace
Sex	Age
Hospital	Occupation
Time of birth	Residence
	Term of residence in the community
Father	
Name	Term of pregnancy
Race	Marital status
Birthplace	Number of other living children
Age	Number of other deceased children
Occupation	Number of children born dead

Most modern birth records are protected by the privacy laws passed by the federal government during recent years. However, some states have allowed microfilming of births after masking entries for illegitimate and stillborn births.

Despite such gaps, these records are obviously useful. Most states require a request form to be completed before they will issue a copy or abstract of a birth certificate. Such a form will often request more information than you have, but you should fill it out as completely as possible, estimating dates and places as accurately as you can. Some states will search more than a five-year period, while others limit the search to a single, approximate year of birth. If the record cannot be found in the year listed, a few states refund the fee; most do not. Each request should state your relationship to the individual and the purpose for which you will use the data. Family history and genealogical research purposes are acceptable reasons in most states. For state addresses, see appendix F.

A rarely used form of birth record is the delayed birth certificate. When Social Security benefits were instituted in 1937, individuals claiming benefits had to document their births even if their states of residence had not required birth registration at the time of their births. The 1880 and 1900 federal census enumerations were partially or fully indexed to help provide this documentation. Another method was to file evidence as part of an application for a delayed birth certificate. Figures 3-5 and 3-6 show a petition and delayed birth certificate from Lake County, Florida. They are representative of the types of records maintained by other states.

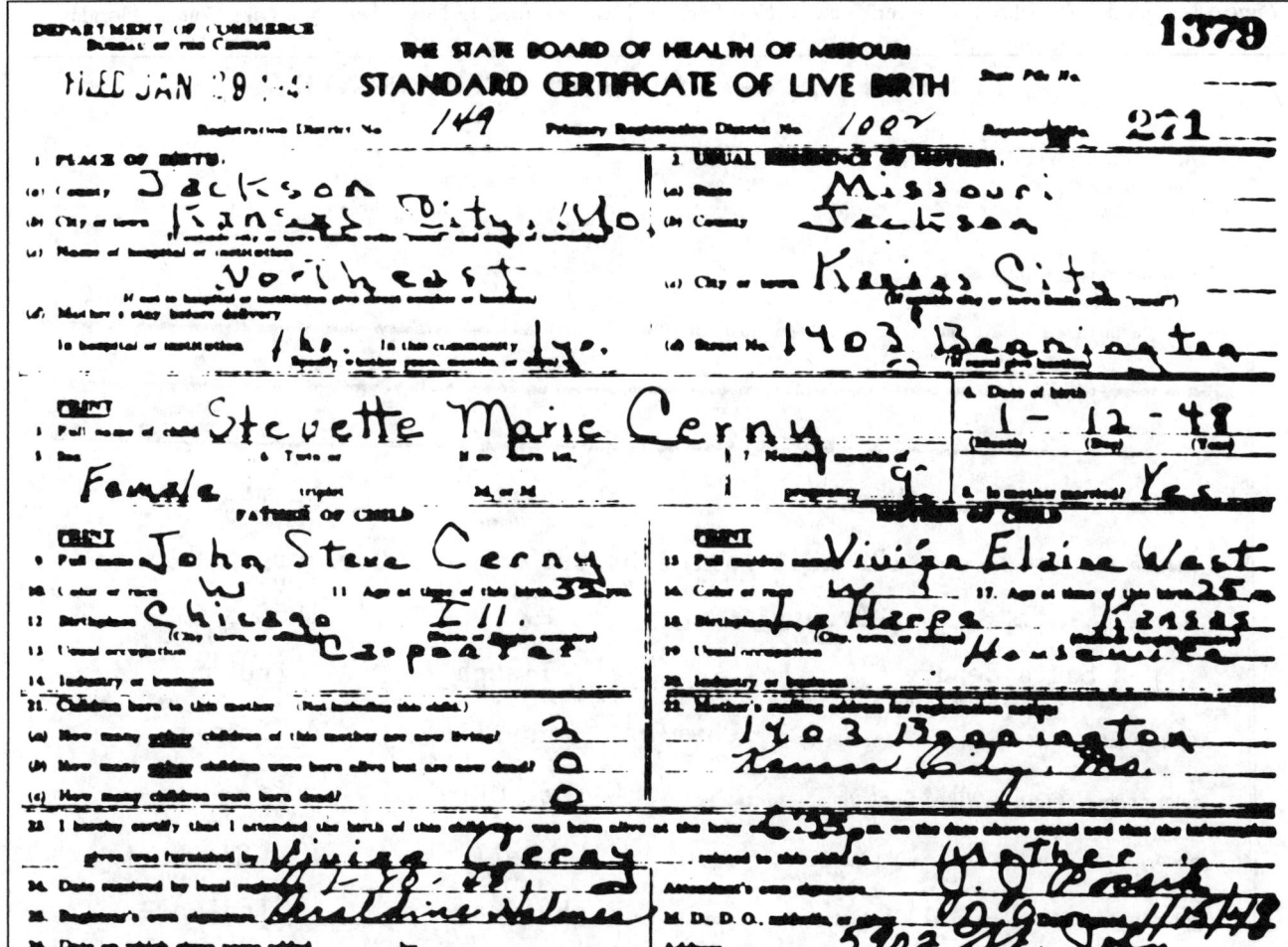

Figure 3-4. Birth certificate of Stevette Marie Cerny, 12 January 1948, Kansas City, Jackson County, Missouri.

The individual applying had to submit a petition to the county court stating his or her name, address, date and place of birth; father's name, race, and place of birth; and evidence to support the facts presented. The evidence could be in the form of a baptismal certificate, Bible record, school record, affidavit from the attending physician or midwife, application for an insurance policy, birth certificate of a child, copy of an application for a Social Security account number, or an affidavit from a person having definite knowledge of the facts.

Delayed birth certificates list vital information abstracted from the supporting evidence. Most states have delayed birth records, some of which are indexed and easily usable. Some delayed birth records have been filed for individuals born as early as 1840. These records are usually filed in the county where the individual applied—not in the county of birth. Though relatively uncommon, these records provide information about individuals and their parents for periods when vital records were not widely kept. The records and testimony used as supporting evidence for the document can lead you to other information sources and also show which relatives were living at the time the certificate was applied for.

Families in transition when children were born present a research problem. Often, a family moving when a child was born waited just long enough for the mother to recover and then moved to an adjoining town or state, where the infant's

birth was recorded. In such cases, if you move back in time from the known to the unknown, you will know where the birth was recorded when you may know nothing of where the birth occurred—so check the obvious; find out if the birth was recorded after the fact. The resulting document will give you the actual place of birth, and you can then make searches there also.

CONTENTS OF DEATH RECORDS

Early death records in the United States provide little more than the name of the deceased, the date of death, and the place of death. Burial records contain basically the same information. Occasionally the record will list the name of the deceased's spouse. These early records appear in town, county, and church records, most extensively in New England, where they were kept as late as 1900.

Death records of the nineteenth century are more detailed in many jurisdictions. They often include the name of the deceased, date, place, and cause of death, age at the time of death, place of birth, parents' names, occupation, name of spouse, name of the person giving the information, and the informant's relationship to the deceased. Race is listed in some records. Some southern states also note if the deceased was a slave. For example, in figure 3-7, the published death records of Pulaski indicate "slave."

Figure 3-5. Petition for delayed birth certificate of Neal Eberhart Newman, filed 15 November 1943, Lake County, Florida.

PETITION FOR DELAYED BIRTH CERTIFICATE

In the County Judge's Court,
State of Florida,
County of   Lake

County Judge's
File Number   101

Petitioner respectfully says that:

No birth certificate has heretofore been filed for him (or her) ~~and as evidence thereof, petitioner has attached hereto an official statement to that effect from the official custodian of the birth records of the State of _____ being the State of his (or her) birth.~~

Petitioner's full name is   Neal   (First)   Eberhart   (Middle)   Newman   (Last)

His (or her) residence is   102 West Dozier, Street   (Street Address)   Leesburg   (City)   , Florida

He (or she) was born on   February   (Month)   20   (Day)   1886   (Year)

at   South Bend   (City or Town)   St. Joseph   (County)   Indiana   (State)

That petitioner's father's name was (or is)   Charles   (First)   William   (Middle)   Newman   (Last)

color or race of father   White   birthplace of father   Clyde, Ohio

maiden name of mother   Sylvia   (First)   Bell   (Middle)   Eberhart   (Last)

color or race of mother   white,   birthplace of mother   Mishawaka,   Indiana

and petitioner prays that an order be entered by this court, certifying such facts.

(Signature)   *Neal Eberhart Newman*

If not signed by petitioner,
state relationship to petitioner _____

Subscribed and sworn to before me this   15th   day of   November   , 19   43

(Signed)   *Marie Lane*

_____
(Official Title)

(Seal)

As corroboration of the petitioner's sworn statement of the facts of birth, there may be presented:

Baptismal Certificate
Family Bible.
School Record.
Application for Insurance Policy.
Affidavit from the Attending Physician or Midwife.
Application for Marriage License.
Birth Certificate of Petitioner's Child.
Copy of Application for Social Security Account Number.
Affidavit from Person Having Definite Knowledge of the Facts.

Figure 3-6. Delayed birth certificate of Neal Eberhart Newman, filed 16 November 1943, Tavares, Lake County, Florida.

DELAYED BIRTH CERTIFICATE

In the County Judge's Court,
State of Florida

State File No.

County of __Lake__

County Judge's
File Number __101__

THIS IS TO CERTIFY THAT: It has been made to appear to me that

| Neal | Eberhart | Newman | was born on |
| (First Name) | (Middle Name) | (Last Name) | |

February (Month)   20 (Day)   1886 (Year)

at   South Bend (City or Town)   St. Joseph (County)   Indiana (State)

to   Charles William Newman (Full Name of Father)   White (Color or Race)

who was born at   Clyde, Ohio (Father's Birthplace)   and

Sylvia Bell Eberhart (Full maiden name of Mother)   White (Color or Race)

who was born at   Mishawaka, Indiana (Mother's Birthplace)

Evidence that no birth certificate has heretofore been filed for this person was presented in the form of an affidavit ~~official statement~~ to that effect ~~from the official custodian of the birth records of the State of~~

ABSTRACT OF SUPPORTING EVIDENCE

Affidavit of Mother and older sister show the date and place of birth and parentage as above.

Birth Certificate of applicant's child shows date and place of birth as above.

Application for Fidelity Mutual Life Insurance policy #531253 issued October 8, 1935, shows date and place of birth as above.

Given under my hand and seal, at   Tavares, Lake County   , Florida.

this   16   day of   November   , 1943.

(Seal)

(Signature) _____

County Judge of   Lake   County.

Margin Reserved for Binding

Write on Typewriter using 1.
Stamped Signature of Judge Not Acceptable.

Margin Reserved

Figure 3-7. From Clarita H. Morgan, *Births and Deaths 1853-1871 on Record in Pulaski County Court House, Pulaski, Virginia* (n.p, n.d.), 7.

Page 1

DATE	NAME	SEX	FATHER OR SLAVE OWNER	PLACE	DISEASE OR CAUSE	AGE	BIRTH	OCCUPATION	CONSORT OF OR UNMARRIED	PERSON GIVING INF. OF DEATH
1853										
Mar	NOT NAMED (S)	F	Malvina Hinkle	Pulaski	Cold	2	Mont.			Phebe Hinkle, aunt
Jun	NOT NAMED (S)	F	James Hoge	"	Unknown	3	Pulaski			J. Hoge, master
7-11	SARAH J. HARROLD	F	M. & S. Harrold	"	Scarlet Fever	3-10	"			M. Harrold, father
9-17	CHARLOTTE E. MOE	F	J. & C. Troillager	"	Unknown	23	"		J.B. Hoge	J.B. Hoge, husband
12-25	MARY (S)	F	William Hoge	"	Pneumonia	20	"			Wm. Hoge, master
Oct	LUCINDA HILL	F	A. & S. Odel	"	Consumption	35	"		Harvey Hill	H. Hill, husband
Aug	JOHN H. HILL	M	H. & L. Hill	"	Diarria	11	"			H. Hill, father
Feb	PETER (S)	F	James B. Hoge	"	Old Age	70	"			J.B. Hoge, master
12-22	JAMES B. HOWARD	M	J.D. & A. Howard	"	Dropsy of Heart	13-01-18	"			J.D. Howard, father
4-15	JAMES M. HOLMES	M		"		1-02	"			H. Miller, neighbor
Mar	HARRISON (S)	M	Joseph Graham	"		4	"			J. Graham, master
Feb	HARRIET (S)	F	Harvey Shepherd	"	Scarlet Fever		"			H. Shepherd, master
Oct	NOT NAMED (S)	F	Elizabeth Kent	"	Not Known	18	"			E. Kent, mistress
8-8	MARY F. LITTLE	F	S. & A. Little	"	Scarlet Fever	3-01-25	"			S. Little, father
8-11	WALTER C. LITTLE	M	"	"	"	6-15	"			"
Oct	NOT NAMED (S)	F	F.A. Morgan	"	Unknown	6	"			Mrs. Morgan, mistress
Oct	NOT NAMED (S)	M	"	"	"	3	"			"
4-5	SARAH L. MARTIN	F	W. & M. Martin	"		3	"			M. Martin, mother
2-22	WILLIAM MARTIN	M	W. & M. Martin	"	Old Age	84	"			Mrs. Shepherd, daughter
12-31	DOLLY ODEL	F	R. & S. Day	"	Unknown	35-06	"		Abram Odel	A. Odel, mistress
8-11	RICHARD (S)	M	James M. Pierce	"	Smothered	5	"			Mrs. Pierce, mistress
Jan	BALLARD QUESENBERRY	M	Crockett E. Quesenberry	"	Fever	8	"			C. Quesenberry, father
Feb	MARTINA QUESENBERRY	F	"	"	"	6	"			"
12-7	JOHN SUTTON	M	Unknown	"	Cholic	64	"	Farmer	Eliz. Sutton	E. Sutton, wife
Mar	ALEX (S)	M	H. Shepherd	"	Old Age	10	"			H. Shepherd, master
6-24	THOMAS THORTON	M		"	Scarlet Fever	54-06	"		Rob. Thorton	B. Thorton, wife
	REBECCA THORTON	F		"	Unknown	70	"			daugh.-in-?
Aug	ELIZABETH VICKERS	F	W. & S. Vickers	"	Unknown	1-06	"			H. Vickers, father
6-20	JOHN W. WALLACE	M	C. & H. Wallace	"	Worms	20-11	"			C. Wallace, father
10-1	FRANCIS (S)	M	Edwin Watson	"	Unknown	5	"			E. Watson, master
Sep	PARTINA (S)	F	John Wygal	"	Cold	2	"			J. Wygal, master
Dec	GEORGE W. (S)	M	"	"	"	1-06	"			"
2-5	NOT NAMED (S)	F	J. & M.S. Wygal	"	Infant Cholery	5	"			father
1852										
8-15	URBAN C. ALLISON	M	Wm. & N.A. Allison	"	Typhoid Fever	1-00	"			W. Allison, father
2-11	NOT NAMED	M	J. & M.A. Akers	"	Jaundice	21	"			F. Akers, "
Mar	HETTY ANDERSON	F	J. & E. Carper	"	Infl. Stomach	51-03	Mont.	Housekeeper	Wm. Anderson	W. Anderson, husband
Nov	CHARLES (S)	M	Francis Allison	"	Choaked	35				F. Allison, master
Sep	EASTER (S)	F		"	Cold	40	"			
Jul	WILLIAM (S)	M	Thurman Bullard	"	Palsey	1-01	"			T. Bullard, master
Apr	CAROLINE (S)	F	Chester Bullard	"	Whooping Cough	15	"			C. Bullard, "
Jun	SARAH (S)	F		"	Unknown	2	"			
					Whooping Cough					
6-31	NOT NAMED	M	J. & S. Black	"	Unknown	1-15	"			J. Black, father
2-28	REBECCA CARPER	F	L. & B. Carper	"	Cramp	7	"			L. Carper, "
3-10	JOSEPH W. COCKE	M	J. & M. Cocke	"	Infl. Brain	2-06-21	Mont.			T. Cocke, "
May	GEORGE W. (S)	M	Sebastian W. Cecil	"	Hives	1	"			S. Cecil, master
Feb	ANDREW ROBBINS	M	Melvina Robbins	"	Infl. Brain	3	Pulaski			
1-20	ALICE DRAPER	F	J. & J. Draper	"	Pneumonia	76	Wythe			S. Draper, niece

Modern (post-1910) death records, though comparatively recent, are steadily increasing in value. People are living longer, and death records often provide information about birth as well as death.

Modern death certificates have not been standardized throughout the United states; but, like birth certificates, most of them contain the same types of information. Figure 3-8, a death certificate from Oklahoma, is representative of most contemporary death certificates. It includes the deceased's name, sex, race, date of death, age at the time of death, place of death, date of birth, place of birth, marital status, name of spouse, Social Security number, occupation, residence, father's name, mother's name, cause of death, and place of burial. Records from other states generally provide the birthplace of the deceased's parents. The Social Security number is not always included, but, when it is, it can be invaluable because other records (subject to right-of-privacy laws) may be accessible if you have the Social Security number.

As any experienced researcher knows, death records are only as accurate as the knowledge of the person who provided the information. Many informants are unaware of the name of parents or are unsure about dates and places of birth. Always try to find additional information about parents and dates and places of birth whenever possible.

In response to a request, some states will supply a photocopy of the certificate filed at the time of death, while some make a transcript of the basic information on a preprinted form, certifying it as a true copy. A photocopy is much preferable. Not only does it eliminate the danger of errors in transcription; it will also include more data. The clues of cemetery, undertaker, informant, residence at time of death, and other details that take you from the death certificate to other records are found only on the original.

Below is an example. When genealogist Harry L. Carle first requested the death certificate of his grandfather, Harry Chester Lee, he requested a certification of death abstracted from the death register (figure 3-9).

Harry received this certification with a request for payment. He sent a check and a request for the original certificate, explaining what information he was looking for. Note that it did not need to be certified ("sealed"). The court clerk's reply provided the name of the physician, L.E. Hedgecock, and the undertaker, Ray A. Fox. The clerk also suggested writing the Department of Vital Statistics in Des Moines and provided the address.

When Harry pursued his request to the Des Moines office, he received a photocopy of the original certificate filed with the state (figure 3-10). It was obviously worth the extra correspondence to get this certificate. From it, Harry discovered that Harry Lee had lived in Hampton only six years before his death; that his wife, Sylvia Smith Lee, the informant, was fifty-six years old; that Harry had been born in Chicago; and that he had been a stage worker. It also gave his parents, names and places of birth, the date and place of burial, the attending physicians' names, and the fact that Harry Lee had suffered from heart disease for about five years before it proved fatal.

Death records are valuable corroborating evidence for family traditions handed down generation after generation without verification. They also help distinguish between two or more people with the same name. For example, one prominent Texas family gave me its personal files and family sources to produce a family history. Their records included a maternal ancestor named Nettie Green, who was married to Robert Michael. Public records produced a Nettie Green who was also married to a Robert Michael. Thinking they were the same Nettie Green, I extended that family line back two hundred years to the immigrant ancestor. The paternal ancestors were less accommodating; in the process of identifying them, I requested the death certificate of Nettie's husband. It clearly stated that he had married Nettie Bunting. Furthermore, Albert Robert Michael had always used his middle name. His descendants did not even know that he had a different given name. The marriage records supported the death record; Nettie Bunting was indeed the ancestor, and we bade farewell to two hundred years of the Green family.

Death records, both early and modern, can help you identify others related to the decedent. The information provided in the records is usually given to the authorities by a close relative. If the relative is a married daughter, the record will state her married name. Aunts, uncles, in-laws, cousins, and other relatives are listed as informants on death records. Each new name is a clue to the identity of other ancestors that should be pursued.

The death record informant may not have been the person who provided vital statistics to the funeral director or to the cemetery sexton. The death certificate names both the funeral home and the place of burial, so check both the mortician's records and the sexton's records to confirm the information on the death record and to look for additional information not included in the death certificate. Once you know the exact date of death, you can more easily look for an obituary notice in a local newspaper. Obituaries usually at least summarize the deceased's life, sometimes including other towns of residence. They may also list all of the living heirs, as well as the names of parents, brothers, and sisters. Tracking backward with these clues, you can look for other members of the family and additional historical information.

In short, you should routinely request birth and death records for ancestors who were born or who died during the period for which records are available in a particular locale. They are rich in genealogical information and may serve to clarify discrepancies in family records.

PROBLEMS WITH VITAL RECORDS

The use of vital records is not without its difficulties. The problem of informants being unaware of (or not knowing) dates and places of birth when providing death information has already been mentioned. Many record collections are incomplete, necessitating additional searches in other records to fill the gaps.

Legibility is also a problem in many handwritten records. It is sometimes worthwhile to ask for help from someone skilled in reading various types of handwriting when a certificate or register entry is not easily decipherable.

A third problem is that early records may contain a variety of surname spellings—none of them spellings currently used by branches of the family. Early record clerks, like early census enumerators, often spelled people's names as they heard them pronounced. When looking for birth or death records from earlier periods, consider all possible spellings—especially pho-

Figure 3-8. Certificate of death of Charles Henry West, Oklahoma, 22 May 1978, file number 011047.

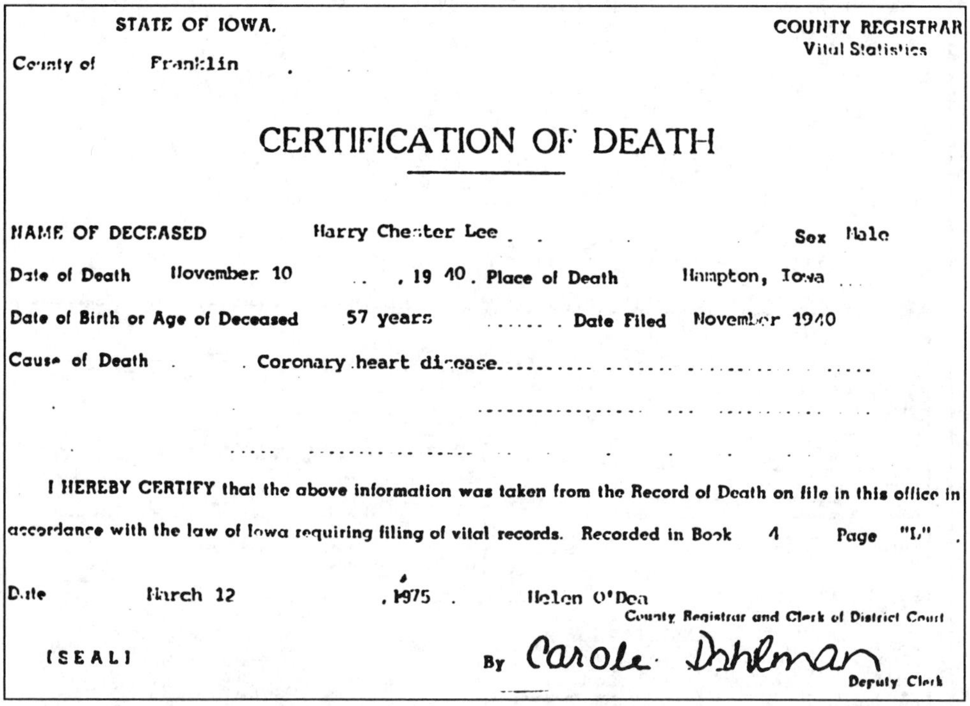

STATE OF IOWA.

County of   Franklin   .

COUNTY REGISTRAR
Vital Statistics

CERTIFICATION OF DEATH

NAME OF DECEASED   Harry Chester Lee   .   Sex Male

Date of Death   November 10   . , 19 40 . Place of Death   Hampton, Iowa

Date of Birth or Age of Deceased   57 years   .... Date Filed   November 1940

Cause of Death   .   Coronary heart disease.......... ....

I HEREBY CERTIFY that the above information was taken from the Record of Death on file in this office in accordance with the law of Iowa requiring filing of vital records. Recorded in Book   4   Page "L" .

Date   March 12   , 1975 .   Helen O'Dea

County Registrar and Clerk of District Court

[SEAL]   By *Carole Dahlman*

Deputy Clerk

Figure 3-9. Certificate of death of Harry Chester Lee, 10 November 1940, Franklin, Iowa; in possession of Harry L. Carle, 8035 168th S.W., Edmonds, WA 98020. This and subsequent documents are used with permission.

netic spellings—before concluding that no record exists for an ancestor. This is especially important for urban areas, where more than one person having the same name is the rule rather than the exception.

A related problem is that records were often indexed many years after they were compiled. The person doing the indexing had to interpret the handwriting in the record just as the researcher must, and his or her skills may not have been well developed. The obvious errors in indexes are a *T* read as an *F,* a *P* as an *R,* and an *L* as an *S.* Take these possibilities into consideration, too, as you try to determine all the possible spellings of a surname.

Some researchers stop searching if they cannot find an ancestor's name in an index. But some indexes have an error rate in excess of twenty-five percent, meaning that more than twenty-five percent of the individuals in the indexed records were not included in the index. If you know the approximate date of a birth or death, settle down to a page-by-page search before concluding that your ancestor is not in the records.

Legally restricted access represents an important limitation of modern vital records. Different states regulate in different ways who can have access to vital records and under what circumstances. Some new laws attempt to reduce the assumption of a false identity for fraudulent purposes (for example, assuming the identity of a deceased person to obtain credit cards to be used for defrauding merchants). Other laws protect the privacy of people still living. Regardless of the reasons behind such laws, you should research the access-restriction laws that exist in the states where you will be conducting research. (See the discussion of right-of-privacy laws in chapter 1, The Foundations of Family History Research.)

FINDING AIDS

There are numerous aids for locating vital records. Appendix F, Where to Write for Vital Records, is a good place to begin.

Most towns and counties have indexes to birth and death records. Even if they are not complete, they can often facilitate research. Many local historical and genealogical societies have published birth and death records in their periodicals, newsletters, and journals; they should be examined whenever available. Family members may be able to send photocopies of birth and death records in their possession. It is worth a letter or telephone call to inquire.

Always check for duplicate copies at county, city, town, and state levels. Many counties kept vital records before the states did. After state registration began, counties and cities continued to maintain registers of vital events. If one set of records is lost or incomplete, you can check the other.

The Family History Library has a significant collection of microfilmed birth and death records and indexes. Table 3-1 is a state-by-state list of those available as of 1996. This collection is expanded regularly, so consult the *Family History Library Catalog* (see chapter 2) for the most current entries.

SUMMARY

Vital Records, despite their relatively recent origin, are becoming increasingly useful to the genealogist and will become more valuable as generations pass. They have limitations, but they can be used effectively to support or disprove existing evidence, to clarify the direction of future research, and to contribute to a more complete genealogy.

CEMETERY RECORDS

Cemetery records and headstone inscriptions are also sources of birth and death information. The custom of burying the dead in areas set aside for that purpose goes back thousands of years, but the genealogist's interest focuses mainly on historic periods in Jewish and Christian communities. The records of this type most commonly found are church burial registers, sextons, records, cemetery deed and plot registers, burial permit

Figure 3-10. Certificate of death of Harry Chester Lee, 15 April 1975, state of Iowa. Certified copy owned by Harry L. Carle.

I HEREBY CERTIFY THAT THIS IS A TRUE AND CORRECT COPY MADE OF THE ORIGINAL CERTIFICATE ON FILE IN THIS OFFICE IN ACCORDANCE WITH THE LAW OF IOWA REQUIRING FILING OF VITAL RECORDS. THIS RECORD IS NOT VALID IF THIS PHOTOCOPY HAS BEEN ALTERED OR IF IT DOES NOT BEAR THE RAISED SEAL OF THE DEPARTMENT OF HEALTH.

Norman L. Pawlewski
NORMAN L. PAWLEWSKI
STATE REGISTRAR

Carson E. Whitlow
CARSON E. WHITLOW, CHIEF
DIVISION OF RECORDS & STATISTICS DATE APR 15 75

DEPARTMENT OF COMMERCE
Bureau of the Census

IOWA STATE DEPARTMENT OF HEALTH
Division of Vital Statistics
Certificate of Death

State Office No. 35 -4- 139

1. PLACE OF DEATH: (a) County Franklin Township Washington
(b) City or Town Hampton (If outside city or town write RURAL NEAR and give town)
(c) Hospital or Institution: Name and Street Address
(d) Length of stay in Hospital or Inst. (yrs., or mos., or days)
In this community (yrs., or mos., or days) 6 years

2. USUAL RESIDENCE (HOME) OF DECEASED: For newborn infant give residence of mother
(a) State Iowa (b) County Franklin
(c) City or town Hampton (If outside city or town limits write RURAL NEAR and give town)
(d) Street No. (If rural give LOCATION)
(e) If foreign born, how long in U. S. A.? years
3. (b) IF VETERAN, NAME WAR

3. (a) FULL NAME Harry Chester Lee
3. (c) Social Security Account Number 475-03-3422

4. Sex Male
5. Color or Race White
6. (a) Single, married, widowed or divorced Married
6. (b) Name of husband or wife Sylvia Smith
6. (c) If alive, give age 56 years
7. Birth date of deceased (mo., day, yr.) June. 21. 1883
8. Age Years 57 Months 4 Days 19 If less than 1 day hrs. min.
9. Birthplace Chicago, Ill (Town, county, and state or foreign country)
10. Usual Occupation Stage Worker
11. Industry or business
Father: 12. Name Benjamin Lee
13. Birthplace Peoria, Ill (City, town or county) (State or foreign country)
Mother: 14. Name B Hinkle
15. Birthplace Glee ford, Ill (City, town or county) (State or foreign country)
16. (a) Informant's own signature Mrs Sylvia C Lee
(b) Address Hampton, Iowa
17. (a) Burial (b) Date thereof Nov. 13. 40
Burial, cremation, or removal (specify) (Month) (Day) (Year)
(c) Place of burial or cremation Hampton Cemetery
Location Hampton, Iowa
Funeral Director: 18. (a) Signature [signature]
(b) Address Hampton, Ia (c) License No. 2026
Local Registrar: 19. Signature [signature] District 359
Date received Nov. 13 1940 Filed No. 43
Cx. DEC 14 40

MEDICAL CERTIFICATION
20. DATE OF DEATH Nov. 10 1940 (Month, WRITE OUT) (Day) 19 (time)
21. I CERTIFY that death occurred on the date above stated; that I attended deceased from 11/10 1940 to 11/10 1940, and that I last saw h im alive on 11/10 1940
Immediate cause of death Coronary Heart Disease DURATION 5 yrs?
Due to Hypertension &
Due to arteriosclerosis.
Other conditions (Include pregnancy within 3 months of death)
OPERATION: Date of
MAJOR FINDINGS: Of operation / Of autopsy
PHYSICIAN: Please underline the cause to which the death should be ascribed
22. If death was due to external causes, fill in the following:
(a) (b) Date of (Accident, suicide or homicide)
(c) Where did injury occur? (City or town) (County) (State)
(d) Injured at home, farm, industry, public place (where?)
(e) Injured at work? (Yes or no)
(f) Means of injury
(g) Nature of injury
23. (a) Signature L. E. Hedgecock M.D. (M. D. or other)
(b) Address Hampton, Iowa
(c) Date signed 11/13/40
(OVER)

records, grave opening orders, and monument (gravestone) inscriptions.

Such records usually supplement standard sources of genealogical information, but sometimes they represent the only information that can be found pertaining to the birth and death of an ancestor. Using these records effectively requires specific knowledge of their content, availability, and location. The following section, based on Arlene Eakle, *How to Search a Cemetery* (Salt Lake City: The Genealogical Institute, 1974), appeared in the first edition of *The Source.* It has since undergone extensive revision by Jeanne Gentry, president of the Oregon Historic Cemeteries Association, and Lynette Strangstad, a consultant on burial ground preservation and author of *A Graveyard Preservation Primer* (Nashville: American Association for State and Local History, 1988). Laura Ann Luebking assisted in revising the bibliography.

Cemetery Research

Searching in cemeteries compensates for the effort it requires if only for the information cemeteries provide about children under the age of twenty-one. In the twentieth century, where the death rate for children is fewer than 8 per 1,000 live births, we often fail to realize that the local cemetery may contain the only evidence of some young nineteenth-century lives.

The cemetery is also, sadly enough, sometimes the only real evidence of some women's lives. A woman, hidden in her father's household during her growing years and recorded in pre-1850 censuses as "female 5-10 years of age," may be located under her own name for the first time on her headstone.

For example, James Bell, born in 1773, was married three times and lost two wives in childbirth (figure 3-11). His first wife, twenty-five-year-old Sarah, died four hours after giving birth to twins, both of whom survived. His second wife, also named Sarah, died at age seventeen, thirty-five days after giving birth to a namesake daughter who also died thirty-one days later. The third wife, Margaret, died at age sixty-eight. Their son James is buried between his parents in the cemetery of the old Stone Church in Fort Defiance, Virginia. The family Bible and the cemetery plot are the only records of the existence of these women.

Even though colonial gravestones are often long since gone or illegible, the surviving gravestones in a cemetery are important sources of information for immigrants. Sometimes the only recording of the original surname is on a gravestone, overlooked by a genealogist who was unaware that the family name had been Americanized and thus missed the original spelling in the alphabetical list. Had the grave plot itself been checked, the person's juxtaposition to known family members would have drawn attention to the difference in the name. The period of time when the largest number of immigrants arrived—1820 to 1920—coincides with gravestones which have survived.

TYPES OF CEMETERIES

The Church Burial Yard
Most churches, until around World War II, were constructed on lots large enough to provide their members with burial grounds. Even churches in large cities had adjacent burial yards. Some of these still exist; however, as cities grew, church membership increased, and real estate values rose, the need for larger burial facilities developed and burial grounds were established in the suburbs while the old plots were used as building sites. Sometimes the graves were moved; sometimes they were not.

Public Cemeteries
Most local civil jurisdictions in the United States have some sort of public burial ground. Some are maintained by the counties; however, most of them are village, town, township, or city burial sites. Some national and state jurisdictions maintain burial facilities for veterans and their families.

Family Burial Plots
Still common in rural areas of the United States are family burial grounds. With the enforcement of health codes that require burial permits, the use of licensed morticians, and regulations governing health hazards, such private plots are disappearing. In the nineteenth century or earlier, most rural families had family burial sites; usually the site was on the farm first settled by the family in the area. These cemeteries are the most difficult to locate, but obviously they are most valuable for establishing family identity. Today properties on which those cemeteries are located are often in the hands of unrelated persons. Fences are left in disrepair and gravestones are often overturned, broken, buried, carried away, or otherwise lost. Some, however, are still well preserved and cared for by descendants or local historical societies.

Commercial Memorial Parks
Since World War II, with the development of large, highly transient city populations, a new sort of burial institution has come into being: the commercially owned and operated nonsectarian facility.

TYPES OF RECORDS

Written Sources
Entries in burial registers are chronological as the funerals occurred. If the registrar noted which plot the person was buried in, you can sometimes deduce relationships, a valuable clue because gravestones may have been destroyed or never placed on the grave, women's maiden names are often not recorded, and children may not have been mentioned in previous records.

Church Burial Registers. Churches that have affiliated burial grounds usually maintain records of interments in their burial

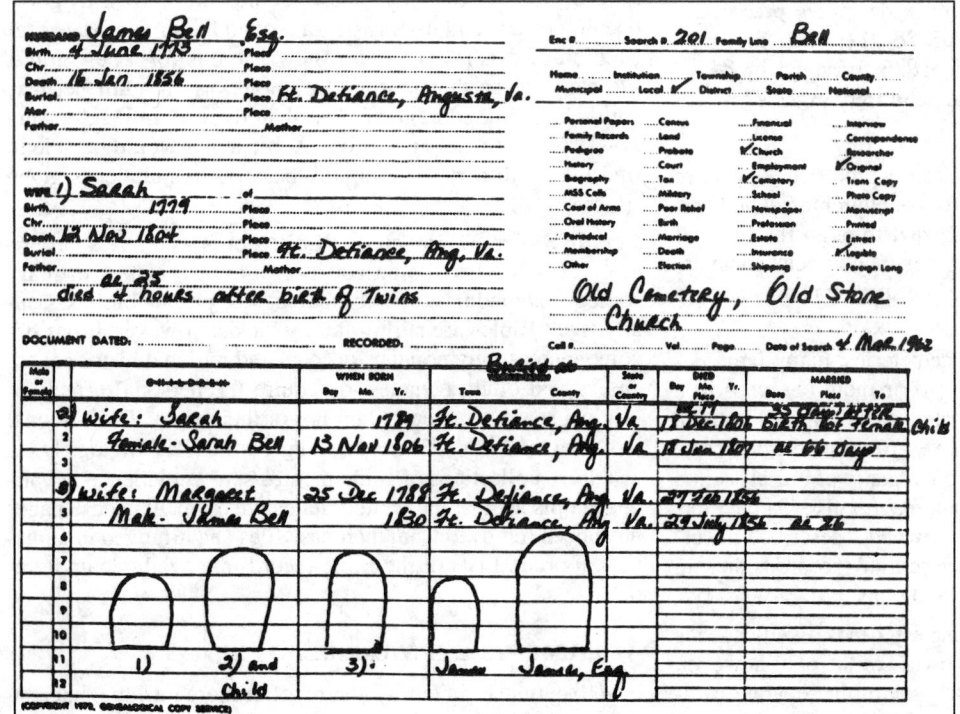

Figure 3-11. Family group sheet of James Bell, Esq., 4 March 1962; in possession of Arlene H. Eakle.

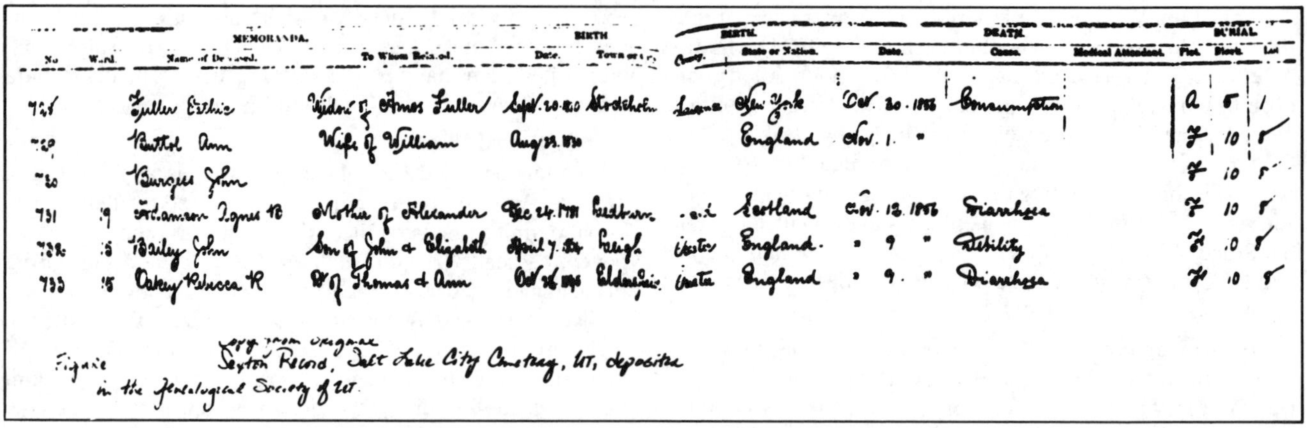

No	Ward	Name of Deceased	To Whom Related	Birth Date	Town or City	County	State or Nation	Death Date	Cause	Medical Attendant	Plat	Block	Lot
728		Fuller Esther	Widow of Amos Fuller	Sept. 20 1800	Stockholm	Lawrence	New York	Oct. 30. 1856	Consumption		A	5	1
729		Bartol Ann	Wife of William	Aug 23 1830			England	Nov. 1. "			F	10	8
730		Burgess John									F	10	8
731	19	Adamson Agnes R	Mother of Alexander	Dec 24 1781	[illegible]		Scotland	Nov. 13. 1856	Diarrhoea		F	10	8
732	15	Bailey John	Son of John & Elizabeth	April 7 18[illegible]	Raleigh	Chester	England	" 9 "	Debility		F	10	8
733	15	Oakey Rebecca R	D of Thomas & Ann	Oct 26 1846	[illegible]	Chester	England	" 9 "	Diarrhoea		F	10	8

Figure copy from original Sexton Record, Salt Lake City Cemetery, UT, deposited in the Genealogical Society of Ut.

Figure 3-12. Sexton's record, Salt Lake City Cemetery, Utah, 1856; in Genealogical Society of Utah, Salt Lake City.

registers. These records sometimes include the names of other family members, as the following register from Killinger's Church shows.[1]

> (62) 1826. Jan. 7, Buried Isaac *Lotch*, son of Johannes & Elisabeth Lotch. b. May 20, 1822; bapt. May 10, 1823, by Rev. Hemping. d. Jan. 6, 1826, cause: Gichtern. age: 3 yrs. 8 most less 4 days.
>
> Jan. 10, Buried Daniel *Deiwler*, in the David's cong. son of Albrecht & Catharina Deiwler. b. Febr. 16, 1771, in Upper Paxton twp. Dauphin county. bapt. by Rev. Mr. Enderlein. married in 1795 to Anna Maria Fissler. They had 11 children, 5 sons & 6 daughters. d. Jan. 9, 1826, Cause: Hitziges Fieber. age 54 yrs. 10 most 24 days.
>
> Jan. 11, buried in Hoffman's congr. Margaretha *Hoffman*, da. of Johannes & Catharina Herman. b. Nov. 7, 1753 in Heidelberg twp. Berks county. bapt. & confirmed in Lutheran religion. married Apr. 22, 1772, Johann Nicolaus Hoffman. They had 12 children, 6 sons & 6 daughters. 2 daughters preceded her as also her husband, d. Apr. 28, '14; cause of death: Pilger's Fieber. d. Jan 9, 1826, survived by 84 grandchildren & 21 great-grandchildren. Age: 72 yrs, 2 most 2 days.

Finding such registers today presents a problem. Some have been placed in central church archives or church-affiliated university libraries;[2] some have descended through the heirs of ministers or clerks along with other personal effects; some are stored in the original meetinghouses. In short, you may have to hunt for them. (See chapter 6.)

Sexton's Records. All municipal cemeteries, many large denominational facilities shared by two or more churches in a community, all commercially operated memorial parks, and a few large family burial grounds have offices or official caretakers where you can expect to find a registry of burials called the sexton's book (figure 3-12). Such records also list the plots available—occupied, owned, or not owned—described in sufficient detail for sale and resale. The sexton's record is thus an accurate record of cemetery deeds and plats.

Cemetery Deeds. The original cemetery deeds, like the deeds to any real estate, are given to the owner of the plat; however, recorded copies are retained by the sexton in separate cemetery deed books. Sales, transfers, and bequests of title to this property are duly recorded also.

Plat Records. In areas before local governments were functioning effectively, graves were dug where convenient with no concept of plots; often, the burial wasn't recorded. With the platting of cemeteries, selling plots, and registering deeds, attempts were made to record earlier burials. In many instances, the names and burial dates could be obtained, but the actual location of the grave was lost. Figure 3-13 is a plat record that was reconstructed after burials in the last four decades of the nineteenth century; for that reason, it is incomplete.

Burial Permit Records. Since around 1920, state health departments have regulated burials. Today, very few jurisdictions permit burials except by licensed morticians, who either obtain or determine that someone else has obtained a certified burial permit from the city or county authority. These records constitute another valuable source of burial information (figure 3-14).

Grave Opening Orders. Most cemeteries preserve records of all grave openings, whether for burial, postmortem exhumation, or transfer of body. These records are known as grave opening orders and usually begin around the time of state registration of deaths. The order shown here is for a new grave. We can deduce that Matilda Bennion was an adult because children are buried in graves less than five feet in length. Amy Fowler was probably a relative. A researcher would be able to find the death certificate rapidly because its number is given (figure 3-15).

Family Bibles. While family Bible records are more appropriately classified as home sources, they are also a primary source— sometimes the only source—for private burials. Usually, such Bibles are still in family hands; however, it has become increasingly popular for local and regional historical societies and other agencies to acquire the personal effects of original settlers and early families of their areas. The National Archives and the Library of Congress in Washington, D.C., also have collections of Bible records sent as evidence in various claims against the United States government. These pages have been removed from their case files and arranged in alphabetical order. Lists of the Bible records are available upon request.

Monuments and Memorials

Few experiences in family history offer more intrigue, interest, and even recreation than searching for monuments and their inscriptions. Even when written records are available and seemingly complete, these sources should always be used.

Prominent, influential, and affluent families often present special gifts—stained glass windows, altar pieces, sacramental services, confessionals, ornaments, statues—in the name and memory of their deceased relatives. Plaques or inscriptions give names, dates, and relationships of those involved with such gifts.

Sometimes the family may make contributions in lieu of flowers toward a special trust fund, organization, or project in the memory of a deceased loved one. Records are often maintained of all who contribute, the amount of the contribution, and the date made. Indications of this type of memorial will be found in newspaper accounts, court records, home sources, and the records of the person or institution responsible for the fund or project.

The burial of a loved one in a tomb or raised vault rather than a grave is customary among some ethnic groups and is the practice of some families. These tombs are normally in a special part of the cemetery or in mausoleums created expressly for this purpose. The inscriptions found on the tombs themselves are similar to regular monument inscriptions. The decoration of the tomb is an important part of the memorial. Burial registers may be stored in a special cupboard inside the tomb.

The ashes of the cremated are usually placed in urns and preserved in vaults at the crematory itself, at the cemetery where the other family members are interred, or in the home of a family member. Inscriptions may be etched on a plaque or other label.

Monuments with inscriptions are extremely varied, ranging from wooden crosses rotted into illegibility to long marble slabs with paragraphs of biography inscribed upon them. Dates of birth and death, places of birth and death (especially when far removed from the place of burial), names of parents, names of spouses, occupation, brothers and sisters, and special circumstances of life can be found. Below are some typical inscriptions.

From a cemetery in Manchester, Vermont:

> In Memory of Rufus Munson, who Died Sept. 13th, 1797 in the 35th year of his Age & left a Widow & four children of the first two letters of thare names is thus:
>
> C.M: G.M: B.M: P.M:

From Old Burying Ground, Newport, Rhode Island:

> Wait daughtr of   Also William
> William and   their son
> Desire Tripp   died March
> died April 24   7th 1784 Aged
> 1780 aged 10   22 mo
> mo 10 days
>
>   Also his Wife's Arm
>   Amputated Feby 20th 1786

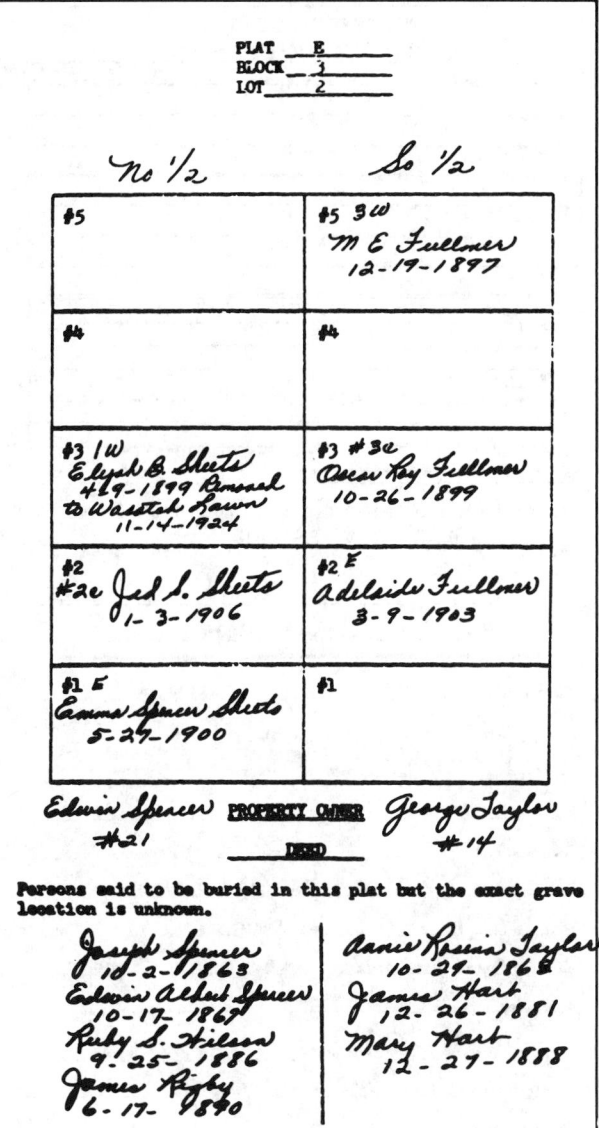

Figure 3-13. A reconstruction from existing records of Plat E, Block 3, Lot 2, sexton's office, Salt Lake City Cemetery.

From a cemetery in Norton, Massachusetts:

> In Memory of
> Mr Joseph Hill
> Who Died
> Dec 6, 1826
> Aged 66 years
> My sledge & Hammer ly reclined
> My Bellows too have lost their wind.
> My fire's extinct My forge decayed
> And [in] the dust my vice is laid;
> My iron's spent my coals are gone
> My nail are drove My work is done.

From a cemetery in Mottville, Michigan:

> Ransom Beardsley
> Died Jan 24 1850
> Aged 56 yr. 7 mot 21 days

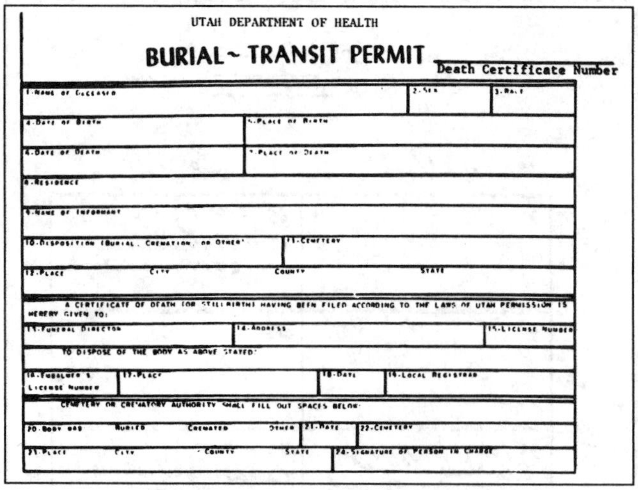

UTAH DEPARTMENT OF HEALTH

BURIAL ~ TRANSIT PERMIT

Death Certificate Number

1-Name of Deceased | 2-Sex | 3-Race
4-Date of Birth | 5-Place of Birth
6-Date of Death | 7-Place of Death
8-Residence
9-Name of Informant
10-Disposition (Burial, Cremation, or Other) | 11-Cemetery
12-Place City County State

A CERTIFICATE OF DEATH (OR STILLBIRTH) HAVING BEEN FILED ACCORDING TO THE LAWS OF UTAH PERMISSION IS HEREBY GIVEN TO:

13-Funeral Director | 14-Address | 15-License Number

TO DISPOSE OF THE BODY AS ABOVE STATED:

16-Embalmer's License Number | 17-Place | 18-Date | 19-Local Registrar

CEMETERY OR CREMATORY AUTHORITY SHALL FILL OUT SPACES BELOW:

20-Body was Buried Cremated Other | 21-Date | 22-Cemetery
23-Place City County State | 24-Signature of Person in Charge

Figure 3-14. Burial-transit permit, Utah State Department of Health, Division of Vital Statistics.

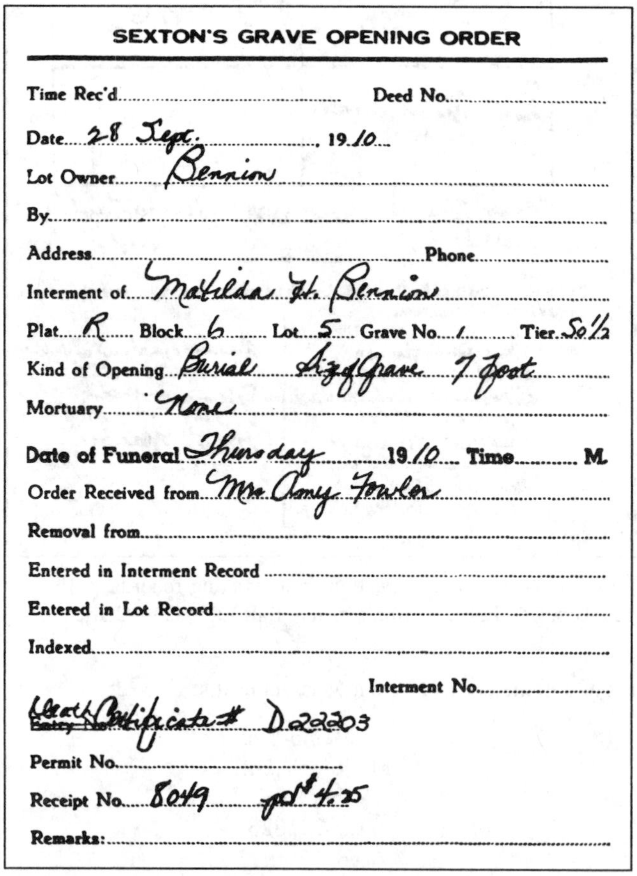

SEXTON'S GRAVE OPENING ORDER

Time Rec'd. .... Deed No. ....

Date 28 Sept. 19 10

Lot Owner Bennion

By ....

Address .... Phone ....

Interment of Matilda H. Bennion

Plat R Block 6 Lot 5 Grave No. 1 Tier So½

Kind of Opening Burial Size of Grave 7 foot

Mortuary None

Date of Funeral Thursday 19 10 Time .... M.

Order Received from Mrs. Amy Fowler

Removal from ....

Entered in Interment Record ....

Entered in Lot Record ....

Indexed ....

Interment No. ....

Entry No. Death Certificate # D22203

Permit No. ....

Receipt No. 8049 pd $4.25

Remarks: ....

Figure 3-15. Sexton's grave opening order for Matilda H. Bennion, 28 September 1910, Salt Lake City Cemetery, Utah.

A Vol. in the War of 1812
No Pension!

Genealogists should also be aware of indirect evidence that can be found in monument decorations. Decorations can express occupations, age, sex, interests, cause of death, religious affiliation, membership in ethnic and fraternal organizations, and philosophies of life (figure 3-16). Such details are rarely recorded by transcribers, but sketches photographs, and rubbings can preserve these symbolic messages.

The date when the stone was placed on the grave is very important. Obviously, one placed two days after the funeral is usually more reliable than one placed fifty years later, although there are exceptions. Gravestones, like cars, have distinctive styles and materials depending upon the year they were made that can provide clues about the time of placement. Figure 3-17 provides some typical examples.

By carefully studying the vintage of the gravestone, the researcher can more accurately determine the validity of its inscription. Modern gravestones with ancient dates indicate replacement of an earlier gravestone or considerable time lapse between death and grave marker.

Most older and some new graves sink, leaving a slightly depressed area outlining the dimensions of the grave. If no age or birth date is given, you can determine which graves are those of children and which are of adults by measuring which are more than five feet in length.

Research Preparation

When you search a cemetery, you should arrive with as many clues as you can: surname variants, people who married into your family, maiden names of women on your pedigree, and dates of settlement and migration into and out of the area. Be sure to check land records and county or town histories to learn precisely when and where the first family member settled in the area, when and from where subsequent members of the family arrived in the area, precise property descriptions for graveyards located on family land or nearby farms, land reserved for burial grounds or conveyed to church or township authorities, bequests in wills to maintain a graveyard, location of families in relationship to churches in the area, church affiliations of family members, and the location of families in relationship to cities and villages in the county.

Check death certificates for the names of all cemeteries in which family members are buried. Usually, family members are buried in clusters. Even where surnames are familiar, consider the probability that persons buried nearby are related to you. Acquire death certificates for all children of the pedigree ancestor you are seeking.

Check printed compilations of cemetery inscriptions. Earning the gratitude of all researchers, county and state genealogical societies, in cooperation with Boy Scout troops, the U.S. Department of Energy, the U.S. Army Corps of Engineers, university and college units, and other interested parties have restored, copied, indexed, and otherwise preserved the information from gravestones. The results are printed in scattered volumes of local proceedings, newsletters, and journals. The printed compilations usually have inexpensively available every-name indexes. The inscriptions are copied by people who know local surnames and who may know where persons are buried for whom there are no gravestones. The volume will also have a location map showing where cemeteries are in relation to modern roads.

Cemetery Associations

Consult card indexes to inscriptions of cemetery associations (where they exist) for locations of cemeteries and plots. These can save you hours of searching time and provide evidence of family members unknown to you buried nearby. Some active in the United States today are:

Association for Gravestone Studies
30 Elm St.
Worcester, MA 01609

Membership includes a newsletter, conferences, and access to photographic and field notes archives housed at the Worcester Historical Museum in Worcester, Massachusetts. The association can provide names and addresses of other statewide groups. Enclose a stamped, self-addressed envelope.

Kentucky Cemetery Project
Kentucky Historical Society
300 W. Broadway
Frankfort, KY 40601

Maine Old Cemetery Association
2 Sylvan Rd.
Farmingdale, ME 04344

Maryland Coalition to Protect Maryland Burial Sites
P.O. Box 153
Ellicott City, MD 21042

Missouri Burial Grounds
118 Fairview
Warrensburg, MO 64093

National Catholic Cemetery Conference
710 N. River Road
Des Plaines, IL 60016-1296

New Hampshire Old Cemetery Association
7 Maple Court
Tilton, NH 03276

Oregon Historic Cemeteries Association
P.O. Box 802
Boring, OR 97009-0802

Vermont Old Cemetery Association
P.O. Box 132
Townsend, VT 05353

Wisconsin Old Cemetery Association
P.O. Box 141
4370 Windsor
Windsor, WI 53598

Figure 3-16. Miner's tombstone (left); physician's tombstone (right). Photographs taken in 1975, Mt. Olivet Cemetery, Salt Lake City, Utah.

Figure 3-17. Collage of grave marker styles, 1800 to the present. Photographs taken in 1975, City Cemetery, Salt Lake City, Utah.

Before 1800: Slender, square sandstone or slate slabs with or without elaborate carvings.

1830–1910: Moderately sculptured stones of white marble and soft gray granite; subject to lichen and weathering.

1880–present: Polished granite or marble, machine-cut, often lying flat on the ground.

1860–80: Square, towering marble stones, often elaborately shaped or with ornate sculpture.

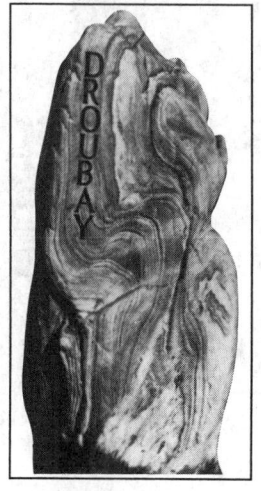

Some associations publish newsletters and hints on how to copy gravestone data or how to preserve cemeteries, including funding resources and work assignments. Some publish maps showing locations of cemeteries.

Cemetery Research Projects

Check cemetery research projects in the area of your ancestry. Some are one-person operations and some are large-scale projects carried out under the supervision of a project director. An international project being implemented by the American Jewish Genealogical Society will index and document all Jewish cemeteries. Using volunteers to index each cemetery, the American Jewish Genealogical Society intends to create a master index of all names in Jewish cemeteries throughout the world.

Consult the National Projects Registry, being compiled by the Family History Library in conjunction with the National Genealogical Society's Genealogical Projects Registry.

Finding Cemeteries

Procure a detailed county or city map with churches and cemeteries marked on it. County road maps are usually available through county or state highway departments, assessors' offices, or registrars of deeds. In rural areas, it is also helpful to have a U.S. Geological Survey quadrangle map for the area you are researching, for some inactive cemeteries may not be indicated on the current county map. Mark the cemeteries nearest the land holdings or residences of family members directly on your map.

If this process seems elaborate, consider that a county may cover more than six hundred square miles. You could spend hours driving and asking local residents who may know less than you do about the area without ever locating the cemetery where your ancestors are buried.

When searching for family burial plots, you are dependent upon your own keen observation and the help of local residents once you are within half a mile of the cemetery's location. Since the 1930s, increasingly large acreages left unattended have succumbed to weeds, brambles, and trees. Some of this land is in the federal land bank. Some has been left by owners who now work in industry. It is not uncommon to find a property owner who is unaware of a burial plot in his or her woods. The best help may come from older residents who have lived in the area for years or young boys who enjoy rabbit and grouse hunting.

RELOCATED CEMETERIES

In areas where land use has changed from agricultural to urban or industrial, few local people actually know where cemeteries have been relocated, but local historical societies have done much to preserve records of them.

When a dam is built, with subsequent flooding of local areas, or a freeway planned or an energy reservation set aside, surveys of local cemeteries are made to determine if any will be disturbed and, if so, where the bodies will be reinterred. These reinterment projects produce generally accurate records of all graves and inscriptions. Efforts are made to identify the occupants of unmarked graves using family records, the memories of local residents, and public documents.

These interments are usually recorded on file cards that are arranged alphabetically within geographic areas. They are open to the public through mail or telephone requests, and the information is usually available without charge or for a minimal copying fee. A good example is the Tennessee Valley Authority, with its thousands of maps, cemetery inscriptions, and other valuable materials all along the Tennessee River. Some maps and cemetery inscriptions are available through the TVA Mapping Services, (HB 2A) 1101 Market Street, Chattanooga, TN 37402-2801.

Military facilities sometimes relocate graves as well. Fort McPherson National Cemetery in Maxwell, Nebraska, opened in 1873 to consolidate twenty-two cemeteries in Colorado, Wyoming, South Dakota, Idaho, and Nebraska. By 1947, the project had been completed. The cemetery is carefully plotted and indexed with control markers throughout the grounds; even so, there are 584 "unknown" graves. Copies of these records are in the National Archives and at Fort McPherson in Maxwell, Nebraska.

Churches that were moved during the years of their existence usually have more than one burial ground. For example, the old cemetery of the Augusta Stone Church in Fort Defiance, Augusta County, Virginia, is walled and stands behind a screen of trees. The grave of Rachel (Crawford) Berry, who was born on 18 April 1812 and died on 23 May 1832, wife of Thornton Berry, lies alone on the side of the hill. One hundred yards away in the Crawford family plot lies her ten-year-old son, James. Across the main highway and over a block lies a new portion adjoining the new Augusta Stone Church. There lies Thornton Berry, who died on 11 December 1882 at age seventy-two, and his second wife, Nancy, who died in April (year illegible) at age eighty-one, and other members of his family. Had the old portion, which is not visible from the road, been neglected, Thornton's first wife and son would have been overlooked.

It was fairly common for congregations to split during controversies and for the dissenting unit to build separate facilities—meetinghouse and cemetery—a few miles away. An example is found in Virginia. New Providence congregation broke with Old Providence over the procedure of singing hymns in meetings in the early nineteenth century. As a result, there are two churches and two cemeteries located only two miles apart. Sometimes the two congregations reunite at a later time and build a third meetinghouse, closing down the previous two. Furthermore, because it is common for members of the same family to have belonged to different churches, you should plan to search all cemeteries in the immediate vicinity of the family home, regardless of religious affiliations.

The procedure to follow in locating graves differs somewhat depending upon the size of the cemetery. The sexton's records, when they exist, should be searched first regardless of the size or type of gravestone. By looking at the names, you can locate females with surnames of interest who are buried under married names in the plots of other relatives who have surnames unknown to you.

Family cemeteries are usually very small and without sexton's records. You should, therefore, read every gravestone to determine which graves are those of ancestral families. For very large public, church, and private cemeteries, consult the various kinds of sexton's records to determine when family members were buried and the exact locations of each one. Then check the master plat or map showing the individual cemetery plats and their smaller subdivisions (sections, blocks, tiers, etc.) to determine the locations of graves for the period of time in which you are interested. Some cemeteries provide smaller map reproductions on which you can mark the grave sites in which you are particularly interested.

SEARCHING IN CEMETERIES

It is best to explore cemeteries with one or more companions rather than conducting a search alone. Drive through or walk around the cemetery before examining individual gravestones. Absorb some of the atmosphere of the setting. Consider the location, the upkeep and condition, size, presence of above-ground burials, fenced-off or enclosed sections, plantings, artwork and statuary, presence of the graves of prominent citizens, positioning of gravestones and their relationship to others, and color and material of the stones. These elements provide evidence of ethnic graveyards, the economic base of the community, historical events, lifestyle and outlook of local residents, and other details.

Next, focus on individual gravestones, looking for naming patterns in the plots. A large name stone in the center with smaller stones around it bearing only given names may indicate Swedish origins. If the smaller gravestones have relationships or initials only, it may indicate German origins.

Note the dates of death. Many gravestones with proximate death dates can indicate an epidemic, a weather disaster, a mine accident, or the close of a generation. For example, in the Darling, Minnesota, Swedish cemetery, burials took place starting about 1870. They were the children of the immigrant generation who arrived in Minnesota just before the turn of the century with their parents or were born shortly after their arrival in America.

A Swedish cemetery will have gravestones in gray, sand, pink, and other warm, soft colors. The setting will be uncluttered, with open spaces around the plots and scanty data on the stones. Polish graves have large, heavy black or red gravestones in rows, with precise dates and frequently the original spelling of the surname. Early New England and Virginia origins show up in ornate carvings of death's heads, weeping willows, and all-seeing eyes on gravestones large enough to include the essential facts and a scriptural verse. These gravestones are liberally interspersed with flat, biographical gravestones giving full details of family relationships. Quaker gravestones were exactly twelve inches high until well into: the nineteenth century. Quaker stones with incomplete or missing inscriptions may have been "oversize" monuments that Quaker leaders ordered trimmed to customary size.

Many cemeteries have special sections set aside for specific kinds of burials. The sexton's records for the paupers' section will be found among poor relief or workhouse records; blacks, Asians, and Native Americans may be buried in "colored" sections; religious sections may contain Catholics, Jews, or Muslims. Those who died without the sacraments of a church may be found in an unconsecrated section of a religious cemetery. In Masonic sections, burials are in crypts or wall vaults. Watch for other sections as well.

The best time of year to conduct cemetery searches is in the early spring, after winter has killed the weeds and before spring briars and grasses begin growing or snakes come out of hibernation. Snow and winter rain will have removed some of the moss from the faces of the gravestones.

Many cemeteries, especially abandoned ones, harbor snakes, chiggers, poison ivy, thorns, and other natural hazards. Wear protective clothing, including gloves and sturdy shoes. Be alert for animals, uneven ground, and other hazards. A can of Mace or another eye-stinging mist may deter dogs. Again: knowledgeable cemetery searchers advise never going to a cemetery alone.

Reading and Photographing Gravestones

Whether an "expedition" to read cemetery stones is a personal or group effort, secure permission from the proper authorities before beginning. Explain the nature of your work and be specific about how you intend to approach the reading or photography. Become familiar with the proper methods of care for these valuable and irreplaceable artifacts.

The popular stones for markers in years gone by were often soft. Often, old inscriptions are so weathered they can hardly be deciphered. Furthermore, there may be an accumulation of moss or lichen on the gravestones. It is improper to use harsh abrasives or wire brushes to remove such growth because these measures further damage the inscriptions and are of questionable value even to the immediate user. Chalking is not a good practice; it can actually stain porous stone. If a gravestone must be cleaned, preservationists recommend gently brushing away loose material with a natural bristle brush, then wetting the gravestone with clean water. Carefully remove organic growth with a natural bristle brush, using a smaller brush to clean incised areas. Thoroughly rinse the stone with clean water and pat the surface dry with a soft towel.[3]

While photographing produces an exact copy of the gravestone itself, it may not give you a legible reproduction. Use a polaroid camera or, if you use a regular camera, copy the inscription in your notes in case the photograph does not turn out.

For details on how to make a documentary photograph (as opposed to an artistically pleasing photograph), see Daniel and Jessie Lie Farber, *Making Photographic Records of Gravestones,* a leaflet published by The Association for Gravestone Studies, 30 Elm St., Worcester, MA 01609. The Farbers advise that documentary photographs be made only in brilliant sunlight. The light should fall across the face of the gravestone at an angle of approximately thirty degrees. If necessary, a mirror can be positioned to reflect sunlight across the stone. Never attempt to straighten a leaning or fallen gravestone. Doing so could result in permanent damage to the marker. Instead, tilt the camera to correspond with the lean of the stone. A thirty-five millimeter camera is recommended. For black-and-white photographs, tri-X film shot at a shutter speed of 1/250th of a second produces good results. Using a tripod and light meter can further enhance results.

After developing, handle the photographs carefully. Obtain clear, archive-quality sleeves to protect them from fingerprints. Include labels with the photographs, but do not mark directly on the photograph itself.

Special Problems Encountered When Recording Gravestone Data

Making Gravestone Rubbings. The following caution, from *Preservation of Historic Burial Grounds,* Information Series

No. 76, 1993 (Washington, D.C.: National Trust for Historic Preservation, 1993), is worth repeating. "Gravestone rubbing should be strongly curtailed or eliminated due to potential damage to markers. Irreparable and significant damage has been done by people who thought themselves to be both careful and knowledgeable. In addition to the damage caused by pigment residue, most visitor are not able to accurately distinguish between sound gravestones and unstable ones. Because of the potential damage, rubbing is best avoided altogether."

Fallen Markers. Markers frequently fall and are buried under an accumulation of undergrowth and topsoil. When working in poorly kept cemeteries, carry a probe long enough to gently check the ground eight to ten inches deep. Carefully check fence lines and hedgerows. Fallen markers that could not be easily replaced may have been carried to the side and propped against a fence or left on the ground. Though they cannot be readily identified with the appropriate plot, the inscriptions are still valuable. Notify the proper authorities of the locations of fallen markers; do not attempt to replace or repair them yourself.

Duplicate Gravestones. When a new gravestone is prepared for a grave, there is always the possibility that the stone cutter will leave the original stone in place; you may thus find two gravestones for the same person. In very old cemeteries, you may also discover some apparent duplicates that are really a headstone and a footstone. A gravestone for the same person may appear in a family cemetery or plot with a second gravestone in the cemetery where the person is actually buried.

Recording Cemetery Data

The more times you copy an inscription, the greater the chance of error. Therefore, take an ample supply of family group worksheets or research notepaper with you and transcribe the data directly on the worksheet or notepaper.

Most researchers copy only the direct genealogical data: dates and places of birth and death, parents, husband, and wife. Such a practice, however, can cause you to overlook the clues indicated in the selection of epitaphs: church affiliation, survivors, occupations, military service, cause of death, physical description, citizenship, and migrational patterns.

Another reason for recording all that you find is the fragility of the site. Once you leave the site, the information may no longer be available to you. Many cemeteries are destroyed through vandalism, development, or other circumstances, and what you record on your visit may soon thereafter prove to be the only information available. Consider the potential needs of those working in related fields—landscape historians, archaeologists, folklorists, and preservationists, as well as future family historians who could benefit from your data. Always reread your notes for accuracy and completeness before leaving the cemetery, comparing them to the gravestones.

One manner of insuring a complete recording of data is to plot the site. Because people are usually buried in family units, drawing a diagram of each plot enables you to analyze graves in their relationships to others: size, location, gravestones, etc. On the backs of your worksheets, sketch the gravestones as they appear in the plot; number each one, then list the inscription and description of the stone by the same number on the worksheets. Where family units are definite, record them on the same worksheet as a family; but where there is any question, list each one on a separate sheet and refer by number back to the plot you have drawn for the relationship of each individual grave to the entire plot. Figure 3-18 is an example taken from the Lexington Presbyterian Church Cemetery in Lexington, Virginia. The numbers refer to the inscription notes, which made it possible to analyze some family relationships.

Unit 1

1. Margaret McDowell, wife of Robert McDowell, died 14 Feb. 1830, age 70.

2. Robert McDowell, born 10 Mar. 1767, died 2 Aug. 1838. Both stones were identical (despite the difference in the sketch).

Unit 2

3. Zachariah Johnston, died 7 Jan. 1800, age 57.

4. Ann Johnston, died 25 Aug. 1818, age 77.

Unit 3

5. Sally W. Johnston, wife of Alexander Johnston, born 29 Jan, 1776, died 30 Apr. 1818, age 43.

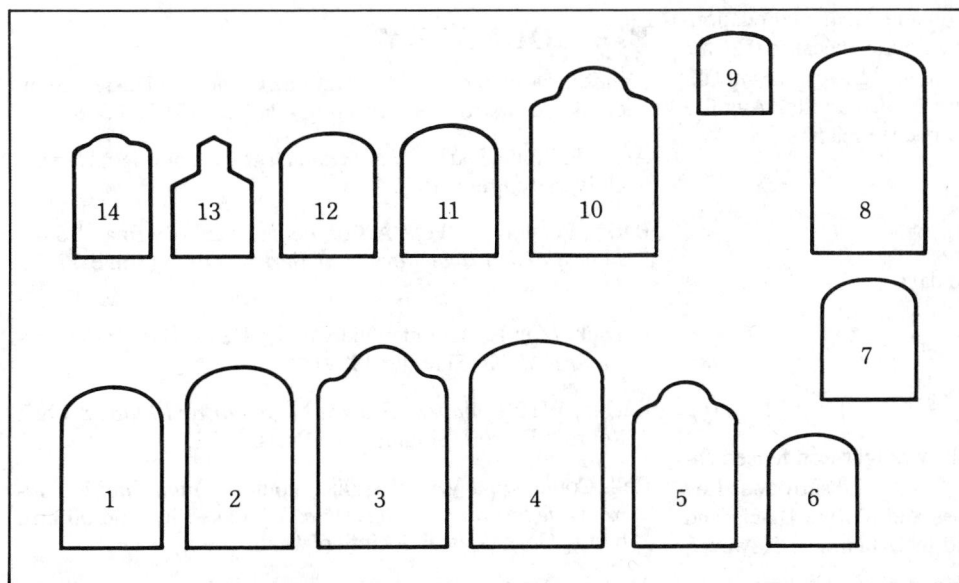

Figure 3-18. Researcher's hand-drawn plot of gravestones showing comparative sizes, shapes, and proximity. All of the markers are of sandstone with legible inscriptions. They were copied from Lexington Presbyterian Church Cemetery, Virginia.

6. Zechariah G. Johnston, born 18 June 1807, died 28 June 1815, age 6. This inscription was rather hard to read.

7. A.J., no date, child's grave with no other inscription, probably part of the Johnston family and a grandchild of Zachariah and Ann.

Unit 4

8. Ann, daughter of Susan and Thomas Johnston, born 10 Apr. 1803, died 7 oct. 1834.

9. William G. Johnston, son of Susan and Thomas Johnston, born 27 Jan. 1819.

10. Susan, daughter of Susan and Thomas Johnston, died 10 April 1832, age 22.

11. Susan Johnston, wife of Thomas Johnston, died 19 Nov. 1857, age 81.

12. Thomas Johnston, born 10 Jan. 1773, died 27 Dec. 1847.

Individual Burials

13. Elizabeth McDowell, "Our Loving Aunt," born 28 Sept. 1796, died 29 May 1861.

14. Rebecca (Our Sister), wife of William C. Lewis, died 2 April 1857, age 57.

In this plat, family groupings are clear in most cases, and certain hypotheses can be made and tested with evidence from other sources.

Although compiled records cannot fully replace a personal search, historical, genealogical, and patriotic societies have performed a valuable and commendable service in preparing compilations of gravestone inscriptions, especially in view of the annual toll taken on grave markers through neglect, highway construction, suburban development, and reclamation projects. Beware, however, the compiled source that obscures family relationships because the entries are artificially arranged in an alphabetical sequence. The value of such works is dramatically increased when the inscriptions are listed as found in the graveyard, cross-referenced to their specific locations on a map of the cemetery, and indexed by surname on separate pages.

Another weakness of these compilations comes from including only the names, dates of birth and death, and relationships. Indirect evidence and clues are omitted because they are too voluminous. In a printed compilation of gravestones in Tinkling Spring Presbyterian Cemetery in Fisherville, Augusta County, Virginia, the alphabetical sequence reads:[4]

Cynthia Johnson
Born 19 Dec 1799
Died 15 Aug 1887
Aged 87 years 7 months and 26 days
Wife of Thomas Johnson
Thomas Johnson
died 19 Dec 1865
Age 75 years, 4 months and 25 days

In the cemetery itself, in a lovely, wrought-iron fenced enclosure, the graves of Cynthia and Thomas lie surrounded by Cynthia's family: her parents, James and Martha Black; and several of her brothers, sisters, and their families. However, nothing in the printed volume connects Cynthia with the Black family.

PRESERVATION OF CEMETERIES

All researchers need to be concerned about and supportive of the ongoing efforts of cemetery preservation organizations and genealogical and historical societies seeking to bring conservation procedures to the attention of cemetery officials. Individuals and groups interested in familiarizing themselves with this process (which certainly should be done before any cemetery projects are undertaken) would benefit from a study of Lynette Strangstad, *A Graveyard Preservation Primer* (cited earlier). This work was published in cooperation with the Association for Gravestone Studies (30 Elm Street, Worcester, MA 01609) and is a landmark in the field. Write for a current list of the association's publications.

In the original edition of *The Source,* Arlene Eakle closed this section with words that are still apt. "I confess to a weakness for the emotional impact of searching a graveyard, but the wealth of direct and circumstantial evidence a cemetery can provide would still justify a search on the least sentimental of grounds. Although the extra time, expense, and inconvenience of on-site searches may deter a genealogist, examining these sources with the same care and thoroughness you would bring to library research pays off."

NOTES

1. St. David's Reformed Church (also known as Killinger Church), Death Register, Dauphin County, Pennsylvania. Microfilm copy of typescript at the Family History Library, GSU-020,348, item 7.

2. Consult August Suelflow, *Preliminary Guide to Church Records Depositories* (Madison: Society of American Archivists, 1969).

3. These procedures are from *Gravestone Rubbing Instructions,* a pamphlet distributed in 1994 by the Oregon Historic Cemeteries Association, P.O. Box 802, Boring, OR 97009-0802.

4. Howard M. Wilson, *Tinkling Spring: Headwater of Freedom* (Fisherville, Va.: for the congregation, 1954), Appendix E.

BIBLIOGRAPHY

Annese, Domenico. "Construction: Cemetery Design Standards." *Landscape Architecture* (January 1983): 85–87.

Aries, Philippe. *Images of Man and Death.* Cambridge: Harvard University Press, 1985.

Barba, Perston A. "Folk Art on Pennsylvania German Tombstones." *Historical Review of Berks County* (June 1955): 43–47.

Barrick, Mac E. "Cumberland County Death Lore." *Pennsylvania Folklife* (Summer 1979): 37–46.

Beable, W.H. *Epitaphs: Graveyard Humor and Eulogy.* 1925. Reprint. Detroit: Singing Tree Press, 1971.

Bell, Connie, and Vernell Walker, comps. *Union Pacific Railroad Life Insurance Claims Data.* Salt Lake City: microfilmed by the Genealogical Society of Utah, 1990.

Benes, Peter. "Abel Webster, Pioneer, Patriot, and Stonecutter." *Historical New Hampshire* 28 (1973): 221–40.

Bondurant, Lynn, Jr. "Science: A Grave Situation." *The Instructor* (April 1977): 110–14.

Breisocher, E. H., and Sandra Lorentzen. *Last Resting Places, Being a Compendium of Fact Pertaining to the Mortal Remains of the Famous and Infamous.* Princeton, N.J.: Darwin Press, 1992.

Brown, John Gary. *Soul in the Stone: Cemetery Art From America's Heartland.* Lawrence, Kans.: University Press of Kansas, 1994.

Bunnen, Lucinda, and Virginia Smith. *Soaring in Heaven: Gravestones and Cemetery Art of the American Sunbelt States.* New York: Aperture, 1991.

Burek, Deborah, ed. *Cemeteries of the United States.* Detroit: Gale Research Co., 1994.

Burns, Stanley B. *Sleeping Beauty: A History of Memorial Photography.* Pasadena, Calif.: Twelve Trees Press, 1990.

Carmack, Sharon DeBartolo. "Carved in Stone: Composition and Durability of Stone Gravemarkers." *NGS Newsletter* 17 (May–June 1991): 69–70.

_____. "Digging in Cemeteries." *Reunions* 1 (Spring 1991): 22–24.

_____. "There's More Here Than Meets the Eye: A Closer Look at Cemetery Research and Transcribing Projects." FGS *Forum* 7 (3) (Fall 1995).

Dethlefson, E.S., and K. Jensen. "Social Commentary from the Cemetery." *Natural History* 86 (1977): 32–39.

Dobson, David, comp. *American Vital Records From the Gentleman's Magazine, 1731–1868.* Baltimore: Genealogical Publishing Co., 1987.

Dreyfuss, Henry. *Symbol Source Book: An Authoritative Guide to International Graphic Symbols.* New York: McGraw-Hill, 1972.

Duval, Francis. *Early American Gravestone Art.* New York: Dover Publishing, 1979.

Eakle, Arlene. *How to Search a Cemetery.* Salt Lake City: The Genealogical Institute, 1974.

Eiedesel, Gordon M. "The Geography of Saunders County Rural Cemeteries from 1859." *Nebraska History* 61 (1980): 215–18.

Ellis, Nancy, and Parker Hayden. *Here Lies America.* New York: Hawthorn Books, 1978.

Farber, Daniel, and Jessie Farber. *Making Photographic Records of Gravestones.* Leaflet available from Association for Gravestone Studies, 30 Elm Street, Worcester, MA 01609.

Frenza, Paula J. "Communities of the Dead: Tombstones as a Reflection of Social Organization." *Markers VI: The Journal of the Association of Gravestone Studies* (1989): 137–57.

Gillespie, Angus K. "Gravestones and Ostentation: A Study of Five Delaware County Cemeteries." *Pennsylvania Folklife* (Winter 1969– 70): 34–43.

Habenstein, Robert W., and William M. Lamers. *Funeral Customs the World Over.* Milwaukee: Bulfin Printers, 1960.

Hinshaw, William Wade. *Encyclopedia of American Quaker Genealogy,* 7 vols. 1969. Reprint. Baltimore: Genealogical Publishing Co., 1991–94.

Howett, Catherine. "Living Landscapes for the Dead." *Landscape* 21 (1977): 9–17.

Jack, Phil R. "A Western Pennsylvania Graveyard, 1787–1967." *Pennsylvania Folklife* (Spring 1968): 41–48.

Jackson, Kenneth T., and Camilo Jose Vergara. *Silent Cities: The Evolution of the American Cemetery.* New York: Princeton Architectural Press, 1989.

Jeane, D. Gregory. "The Upland South Cemetery: An American Type." *Popular Culture* 11 (1978): 895–903.

_____. "Southern Gravestones: Sacred Artifacts in the Upland South Folk Graveyard." *Markers IV: The Journal of the Association of Gravestone Studies* (1987): 55–84.

Kay, J.H. "Sixty Million Graves: The Virginia Cemetery Extravaganza." *Nation* (19 February 1977): 209–12.

McDonald, Frank E. "Pennsylvania German Tombstone Art of Lebanon County, Pennsylvania," *Pennsylvania Folklife* (Autumn 1975).

Meyer, Richard E., ed. *Cemeteries and Gravemarkers: Voices of American Culture.* Ann Arbor: UMI Research Press, 1989.

Montell, William Lynwood. *Ghosts Along the Cumberland: Deathlore in the Kentucky Foothills.* Nashville: American Association for State and Local History, 1971.

National Trust for Historic Preservation. *Preservation of Historic Burial Grounds.* Information Series No. 76, 1993. Available from Preservation Forum, NTHP, 1785 Massachusetts Ave. N.W., Washington, DC 20036.

Nishiura, Elizabeth. *American Battle Monuments: A Guide to Battlefields and Cemeteries of the United States Armed Forces.* Detroit: Omnigraphics, 1989.

Roberts, Allen D. "Where Are the All-Seeing Eyes?" *Sunstone* (May–June 1978): 22–37.

Roberts, Warren E. "Tools on Tombstones: Some Indian Examples." *Pioneer America* (June 1978): 106–11.

Shushan, E.R. *Grave Matters.* New York: Ballantine Books, 1990.

Slater, James A., and Ernest Caulfield. "The Colonial Gravestone Carvings of Obadiah Wheeler." *American Antiquarian Society Proceedings* 84 (1974): 73–104.

Sloane, David C. *The Last Great Necessity: Cemeteries in American History.* Baltimore: Johns Hopkins University Press, 1991.

Strangstad, Lynette. *A Graveyard Preservation Primer.* Nashville: American Association for State and Local History, 1988.

"Two Cemeteries Are Last Remains of Black Colony of Pleasant Ridge." *Wisconsin Then and Now* (November 1974): 2–3.

Vallentine, John F. "Locating the Correct Cemetery." *Genea-logical Journal* 4 (1975): 107–09.

Vlach, John. "Graveyards and Afro-American Art." In *Long Journey Home: Folklife in the South*. Chapel Hill, N.C.: Southern Exposure, 1977).

Wallis, Charles L. *American Epitaphs: Grave and Humorous*. New York: Dover Publications, 1975.

Weil, Tom. *Cemetery Book*. New York: Hippocrene Books, 1991.

Weitzman, David. *Underfoot: An Everyday Guide to Exploring the American Past*. New York: Charles Scribners & Sons, 1976.

Winkler, Louis. "Pennsylvania German Astronomy and Astrology IV: Tombstones." *Pennsylvania Folklife* (Winter 1973): 42–45.

Yeich, Edwin B. "Die Leich: The Old-Fashioned Country Funeral." *Historical Review of Berks County* (July 1954): 110–11.

RESEARCH IN MARRIAGE AND DIVORCE RECORDS

CHAPTER CONTENTS

4

RESEARCH IN MARRIAGE AND DIVORCE RECORDS

Johni Cerny and Sandra H. Luebking

The registering of marriages and granting of divorces in the United States are quasi-religious, quasi-legal social functions that have been influenced by religious beliefs, custom, and English law since the earliest colonial settlements. The effective genealogist needs a complete understanding of the jurisdictions responsible for maintaining these records, the types of records kept by each jurisdiction, periods in which various types of records were maintained, the circumstances peculiar to each colony and state that created the necessity for registering marriages and divorces, and the factors that produced changes in these registrations.

A complication is the fact that the United States, unlike England and some European countries, does not have a national registration program. Instead, marriage registration is the responsibility of the individual states. Furthermore, marriage registration was never uniformly implemented among the states. Prior to state registration requirements, towns in New England and counties in the remainder of the nation were the primary jurisdictions charged with maintaining marriage records. Thus, records can ordinarily be found dating from when a town or county was created. Some states, however, such as Pennsylvania and South Carolina, have not required subordinate jurisdictions to keep marriage records until more recent times.

JURISDICTIONS

Marriage records in the United States have been, and in some cases still are, kept by churches, ministers, justices of the peace, state boards of health, colonial governors, military personnel, and local (county and town) governments.

STATE BOARDS OF HEALTH/BUREAUS OF VITAL STATISTICS

The most important record-keeping agencies for marriages and divorces in the united States today are the state boards of health or bureaus of vital statistics (or their equivalents). Even though these agencies are primarily state bodies, large cities usually have their own registries. However, few states had them until after 1850. Vermont (1770) and Washington, D.C. (1811), were the first to form them; Colorado (1968) was the last. Even when the requirement existed, the laws were seldom enforced; consequently, many genealogists are reluctant to spend the time necessary to search for marriage records on file with these agen-

cies for early periods. However, residents of heavily populated cities are not often mentioned in local histories or biographical publications. Quite often they can be found only in major record sources. Thus, it is imperative to search for whatever records may exist. Appendix F is a state-by-state list with the dates each began keeping vital records and the address of the responsible agency (reprinted from the U.S. Department of Health, Education, and Welfare Public Health Services booklet *Where to Write for Vital Records—Births, Deaths, Marriages, and Divorces,* DHHS Publication [PHS] 93-1142). Addresses and certificate fees change often; future editions of the booklet can be obtained for a fee from the U.S. Government Printing Office, Washington, DC 20402-9328.

COLONIAL GOVERNORS

Many of the earliest marriage records were kept by the offices of colonial governors. While not numerous, many of these records are still in existence, usually in state archives. Some are now in print.

MILITARY PERSONNEL

Colonial, state, and federal military officers and ships' officers (military and civilian) often performed marriages and recorded them in ships' logs, daybooks, and private journals. Those records can be found among military records maintained by the federal government and in historical societies, libraries, and museums.

TOWN AND COUNTY GOVERNMENTS

Town clerks in New England and county clerks elsewhere have been responsible for registering most marriages in the United States. Marriage records were kept in New England beginning in the 1600s and in the South beginning in the 1700s. Clerks issued documents granting permission for a couple to marry, and then they received notification that the ceremony had taken place from the ministers and justices of the peace in the towns or counties. The remainder of this chapter will discuss in detail the records on file in these town and county jurisdictions.

There is no uniformity among U.S. marriage records. Researchers should thus become familiar with the laws and customs of each area and time period to be researched. Some jurisdictions required more than one form of document, and the information required on different documents often varied. For example, Kentucky marriage registers usually include the names of the bride and groom, the date and place of the marriage, and the officiating authority. The marriage license, issued as a separate record for the same couple, could also include residence, age, place of birth, names of parents, and occupation.

CHURCHES

Churches were among the earliest keepers of marriage records. By 1640, Virginia and Massachusetts had passed laws requiring ministers to present records of the marriages they performed to civil officials in the county or parish. Records of marriages in areas that did not require periodic reporting remained with the minister or the church.

Many churches, especially in the frontier areas, did not keep extensive records, and many records have been lost or destroyed. New England churches, Quaker Monthly Meetings, and the German churches kept and have preserved the most complete records. (See chapter 6, Research in Church Records.)

JUSTICES OF THE PEACE

Most states have authorized the election or appointment of justices of the peace who can perform marriages. Like ministers, justices have also been required to submit records of the marriages they performed to civil authorities. Justices also maintained their own registers, often in the personal account books in which they recorded the fees paid. These sometimes contain marriage and other genealogical information not forwarded to the civil authorities and they should not be overlooked by the researcher, even when civil records are available. Justices' registers can be found in the care of county clerks, local historical societies, libraries, and descendants of the justices themselves. Several are on microfilm at the Family History Library of The Church of Jesus Christ of Latter-day Saints (LDS church), and some have been published by local genealogical societies.

TYPES OF MARRIAGE RECORDS

CONSENT AFFIDAVITS

The minimum legal age for marriage varies from one place to another. While some jurisdictions have required consent regardless of age most demanded consent affidavits from a parent or legal guardian only for those under the minimum age—usually twenty-one for males, eighteen for females. Sometimes a parent or guardian appeared with the underage person and gave verbal permission. The record will show that the parent was present and was known to the clerk but may not record the name. A detailed, printed consent form was part of the marriage license in a few localities.

The father of the underage person usually gave consent, especially in the South. When a mother has given consent, the father was likely deceased. When both parents were deceased, the legal guardian granted permission to marry. If the guardian is related to the person getting married, their relationship may be stated.

Figure 4-1 is an application for a marriage license by David Hoard for Chester B. Hoard and Martha S. Huffman in Medina County, Ohio. In it, David Hoard states that he is Chester B. Hoard's guardian and gives his consent to the marriage.

Consent documents are found in town and county jurisdictions throughout the United States, but they are more numerous in the South and former frontier regions, where early marriages were encouraged.

DECLARATIONS OF INTENT

Declarations of intent to marry have been required in one form or another in all colonies and states from colonial times. The practice may have been abandoned in a particular place for a period of time, only to be reinstated later. There are many types of declarations of intent, both written and oral.

BANNS

The publishing of banns was a church custom during the colonial period. Banns were usually read in church on three consecutive Sundays (sometimes during public meetings); in some areas, they were posted in public places as well. Their purpose was to give local residents the opportunity to state their objections to a marriage. Below is a sample of what might be included in a published banns:

> I publishe the Banns of Marriage between Robert Preston of New Haven and Priscilla Fuller of Milford. If any known cause or just impediment why these two persons should not be joined together in Holy Matrimony, ye are to declare it. This is the 1st time asking.
>
> Daniel Stout, Reverend.

INTENTIONS

These records were similar to banns but were filed with the town or county clerk. Not generally read aloud, they were posted in public places for a prescribed period of time to give others the opportunity to voice objections to the union.

Many intentions filed in New England have been published. Below are some marriage intentions from the town records of Beverly, Massachusetts.

Marriage Intentions

Jofiah Hall of Exeter in the Prouince of new Hampfheir and Mary Woodbery of Beverly their Intention of—Publifhed March 30th Day 1712

William Grouer and Elizabeth Hull Boath of Beverly their Intention of Marriage publifhed may ye 18th 1712

John Stone Junr of Beverly and Ruth Waldran of Wenham their Intention of Marriage Publifhed May 18th Day 1712

Roger Hafkins and Elizabeth Shaw Boath of Beverly their Intention of Marriage Publifhed auguft 10th 1712

Phillip Piles & Return Ellinwood Boath of Beuerly their Intention of Marriage Publifhed on August 24th 1712

Benjamin Webfter & Ruth Gray Boath of Beuerly there Intention of Marriage publifhed on Nouember 8th 1712

Ifaac Hull Junr & Ann Wood Both of Beuerly their Intention of marriage publifhed on Nouembr 22d 1712

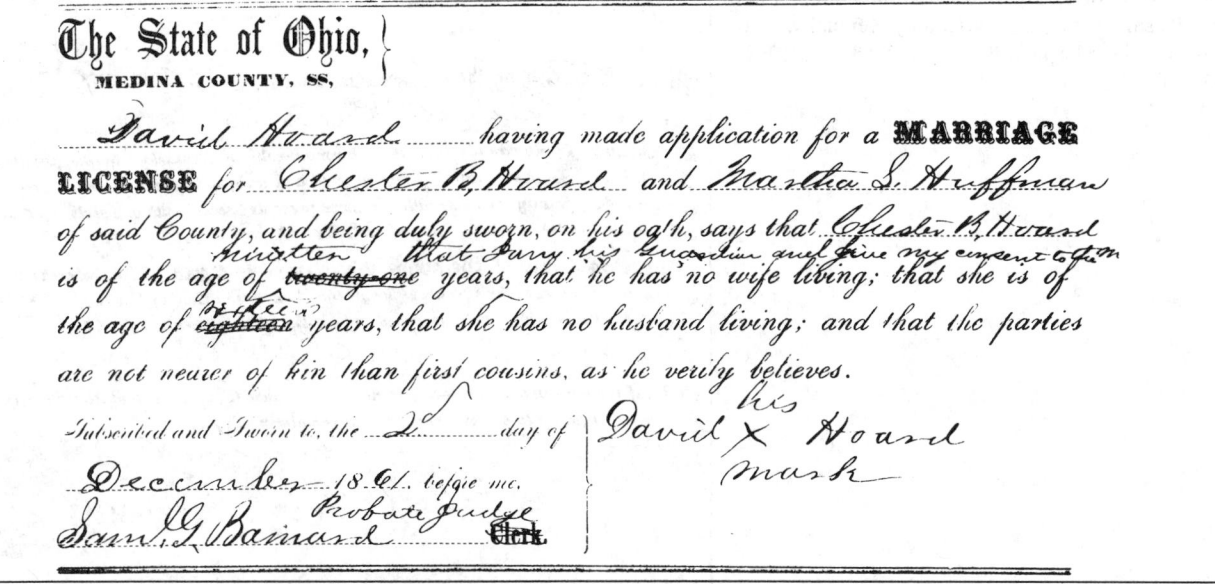

Figure 4-1. David Hoard's application for a marriage license for Chester B. Hoard and Martha S. Huffman, Medina County, Ohio, 2 December 1861, book 1, p. 29; Family History Library (hereafter FHL) microfilm 55,536, pt. 3.

Ebenezer Cleues. & Sarah Stone Boath of Beurley their Intention of Marriage Publifhed Nouember 21ˢᵗ 1712

Samuel Harris and Sarah Biles boath of Beuerly their Intention of Marriag publifhed Decemb: 5ᵗʰ 1712

Jonathan Ober and Rebeckah—— their Intention of Marriage publifhed December 28ᵗʰ day 1712

James Afhby and Abigel Reed Both: of Beuerly their Intention of marriage publifhed December 28ᵗʰ day 1712

Samuel Woodbery of Beuerly and hannah Dodge of Salem their Intention of marriage publifhed Auguft 22ᵈ 1713

Augustus A. Galloup, comp., *Early Records of the Town of Beverly, Essex County, Mass.* (Boston: Eben Putnam, 1907), 43.

BONDS

Marriage bonds were not required by all colonies or states but have been common in the South. Bonds were posted prior to the issuing of the required marriage license in some states and were the sole documents required in others. Bonds were posted by the groom alone or with a second person, usually the father or the brother of the bride, to defray the costs of litigation in the event the marriage was nullified.

Bonds were posted in the jurisdiction where the marriage was to take place, often in the bride's home county. These bonds, the only marriage records maintained in some jurisdictions, were usually annotated with the marriage date after the ceremony. It was rare for a marriage not to take place within a few days of the posting of the bond, even though many bonds do not bear the annotation. Although the missing information could mean that the marriage did not take place, more often it reflects poor record keeping or failure of the justice or minister to report the

marriage to local officials. Figure 4-2 is an example of a bond typically found in the South.

CONTRACTS

Marriage contracts are relatively uncommon. They were usually drawn up when one or more of the parties was wealthy or an heir to wealth and wished to protect the inheritance rights of heirs.

Marriage contracts have also been used in second marriages. Property left to a widow by her first husband could be protected with a marriage contract. Such documents guarantee the distribution of property to the children of the first husband. Without such a contract, the property inherited at the death of the first husband became the property of the second husband at the time of marriage. He could dispose of that property as he desired, without provision for his stepchildren. Marriage contracts are recorded among marriage records, filed in the court records, or with the deeds.

Marriage contracts were widely used in Louisiana during the colonial period. Under civil law, the French and Spanish used formal marriage contracts to protect their property, regardless of their social position or wealth. These documents are of unequaled value in genealogical research because they list extended family relationships and often the place of origin of the French immigrant ancestor. The contract between Charles de Lavergne and Marie Joseph Carriere, below, illustrates the superb detail of the documents.

June 16, 1739

CHARLES de LAVERGNE, Lieutenant on half-pay, of this Province of Louisiana, son of Mr. PIERRE de LAVERGNE, Counsellor at Chatelet of Parish, and of Dame ELIZABETH BILLET his father and mother, a native of parish, Parish of St. Eustache

with

Demoiselle MARIE JOSEPH CARRIERE, minor

Figure 4-2. Marriage bond for Robert French and Priscilla Duvall, Edmundson County, Kentucky, 8 November 1843, Marriage Bonds 1843–58, p. 11; FHL 367,211.

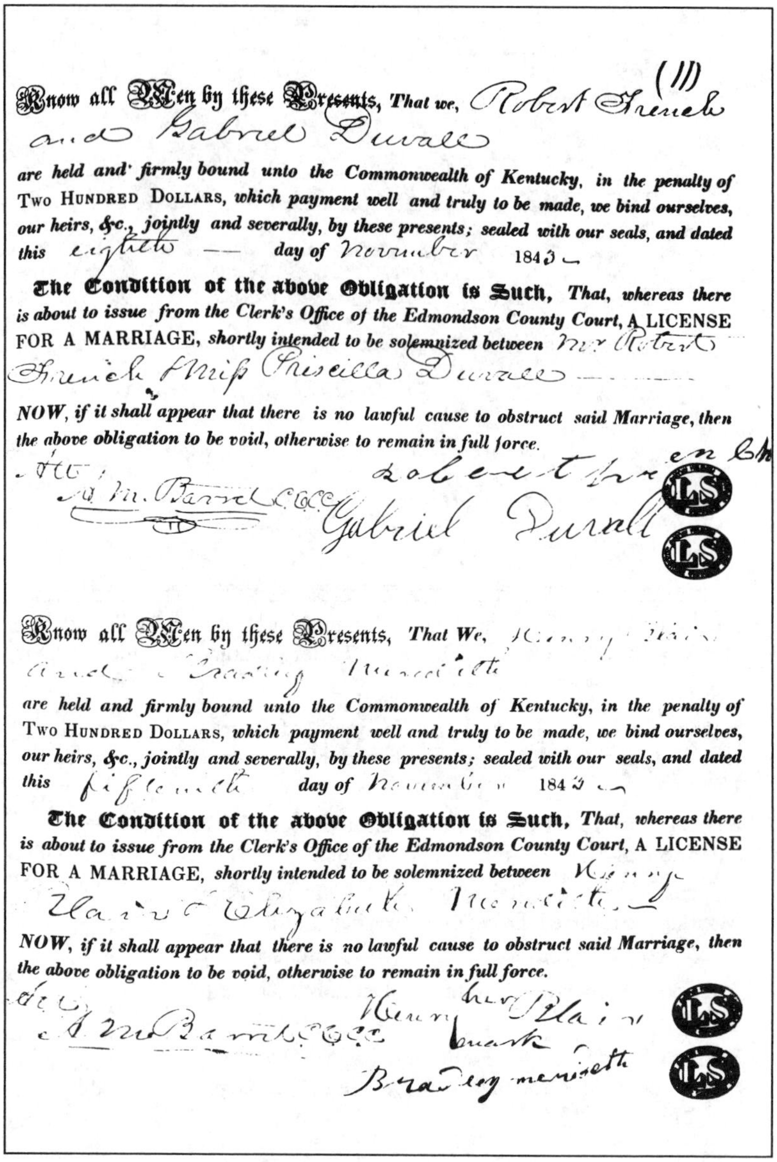

(11)

Know all Men by these Presents, *That we,* Robert French and Gabriel Duvall

are held and firmly bound unto the Commonwealth of Kentucky, in the penalty of Two Hundred Dollars, *which payment well and truly to be made, we bind ourselves, our heirs, &c., jointly and severally, by these presents; sealed with our seals, and dated this* eighth — *day of* November 1843 —

The Condition of the above Obligation is Such, *That, whereas there is about to issue from the Clerk's Office of the Edmondson County Court,* A LICENSE FOR A MARRIAGE, *shortly intended to be solemnized between* Mr Robert French & Miss Priscilla Duvall —

NOW, *if it shall appear that there is no lawful cause to obstruct said Marriage, then the above obligation to be void, otherwise to remain in full force.*

Att. A. M. Barrel C.C.C. Robert French L.S.

Gabriel Duvall L.S.

Know all Men by these Presents, *That We,* Henry Blair and Bradley Meredith

are held and firmly bound unto the Commonwealth of Kentucky, in the penalty of Two Hundred Dollars, *which payment well and truly to be made, we bind ourselves, our heirs, &c., jointly and severally, by these presents; sealed with our seals, and dated this* fifteenth *day of* November 1843 —

The Condition of the above Obligation is Such, *That, whereas there is about to issue from the Clerk's Office of the Edmondson County Court,* A LICENSE FOR A MARRIAGE, *shortly intended to be solemnized between* Henry Blair & Elizabeth Meredith

NOW, *if it shall appear that there is no lawful cause to obstruct said Marriage, then the above obligation to be void, otherwise to remain in full force.*

Att. A. M. Barrel C.C.C. Henry his mark Blair L.S.

Bradley Meredith L.S.

daughter of the deceased Sieur ANDRE CARRIERE and of Dame MARGUERITTE HARLUT her father and mother, a native of Mobile, Bishopric of Quebec. The named Dame MARGUERITTE HARLUT now wife of Sieur LOUIS TIXERRANT being present.

Consenting for the minor being Sieur JOSEPH CARRIERE her uncle and tutor.

Consenting on the part of the named Sieur de LAVERGNE, Mr. de BIENVILLE, Chevalier of the Royal and Military order of St. Louis, Governor of this Province, of Louisiana, Mr. de SALMON, Commissioner of the Marines of this Province and Madame his wife, Mr. DIRON DARTAGUETTE, Chevalier of the Royal and Military Order of St. Louis, Commandant at Mobile, Mr. BELLUGA Captain of the King's vessel, Mr. DeVILLER FRANSSURE, Lieutenant of the King's vessel, presently of this Colony, his friends and friends of his deceased parents.

And for the named Demoiselle MARIE JOSEPH CARRIERE, Sieur and Dame TIXERRANT her step-father and her mother, Sieur JOSEPH CARRIERE her uncle and tutor, Sieur JACQUES CARRIERE also her uncle, Dame FRANCOISE JALOT widow CARRIERE, Aunt of Demoiselle MARIE MARGUERITTE CARRIERE, her sister, Sieur LOUIS TIXERRANT her brother, Mr. and Madame de LIVAUDAIS her cousin, Mr. the Chevalier de LOWBOY, of the Royal and Military Order of St. Louis, Captain of the Infantry of the Marines, Mr. D'AUTHERIVE, Chevalier of the Royal and Military Order of St. Louis, Mr. de BELISLE, Mr. BOBE DESCLOSEAUX, comptroller of the Marines, Mr. DUBREUIL VILLARS, contractor for the King's fortifications in this colony.

This marriage to be solemnized in the Holy Roman Apostolic Catholic Church.

This document collated and entered in the minutes of the Royal Notary, at New Orleans on the 17 of June of 1768. /s/ Garic, Notary.[1]

Marriage Licenses

Marriage licenses are the most common marriage records in the United States. They are issued by the appropriate authority prior to the marriage ceremony, and they have come to replace the posting of banns and intentions. Marriage licenses, which grant permission for a marriage to be performed, are returned to civil authorities after the ceremony.

Applications for marriage licenses have been required in some jurisdictions in addition to or in place of bonds. Applications are often filled out by both the bride and groom and typically contain a large amount of genealogical information. They may list the full names of the bride and groom, their residences, races, ages, dates and places of birth, previous marriages, occupations, and their parents, names, places of birth (state or country), and occupations. Recent laws require health certificates attesting to the absence of diseases that could be passed on to children.

For most locations, marriage license applications can be found for periods beginning after the Civil War. Indiana, Wisconsin, and Utah counties maintained them earlier. The application form does not include the marriage date.

Marriage licenses exist in varying forms. Figure 4-3, a certified copy of a marriage license issued in the Illinois county where the marriage took place, is much like licenses from most towns or counties. A standard form generally asks for the names of the bride and groom, their residence at the time of application, the date the marriage was performed, the date the license was issued, the place of the marriage, and the name of the person performing the marriage ceremony.

A license from Spencer County, Kentucky (figure 4-4), illustrates the style of license used during earlier periods in the South. Note that the return after the ceremony is annotated at the bottom of the license in the minister's handwriting.

Certified copies of marriage records are certified to be correct, but there is a possibility of error in any typescript. It is best to request photocopies when you write a town or county clerk.

Marriage Certificates

Marriage certificates are given to the couple after the ceremony is completed and are thus usually found among family records. There are exceptions, however. Figure 4-5 is from a volume of marriage certificates on file in Medina County, Ohio. These certificates, however, are similar to marriage licenses issued in other places. The bride and groom usually receive a marriage certificate for their family records containing similar historical information, signatures of witnesses, etc.

Marriage Registers and Returns

Colonial and state governments have required that marriages performed within their jurisdictions be reported to civil authorities. The town or county clerk then compiles marriage registers, though these registers are rarely complete. Those who officiated at marriages in rural areas were often reluctant to travel the distances required to comply with the law. Sometimes, also, ministers' records were lost or destroyed before the marriages were properly reported. Itinerant preachers, who crossed jurisdictional boundaries, rarely registered marriages at all. Couples

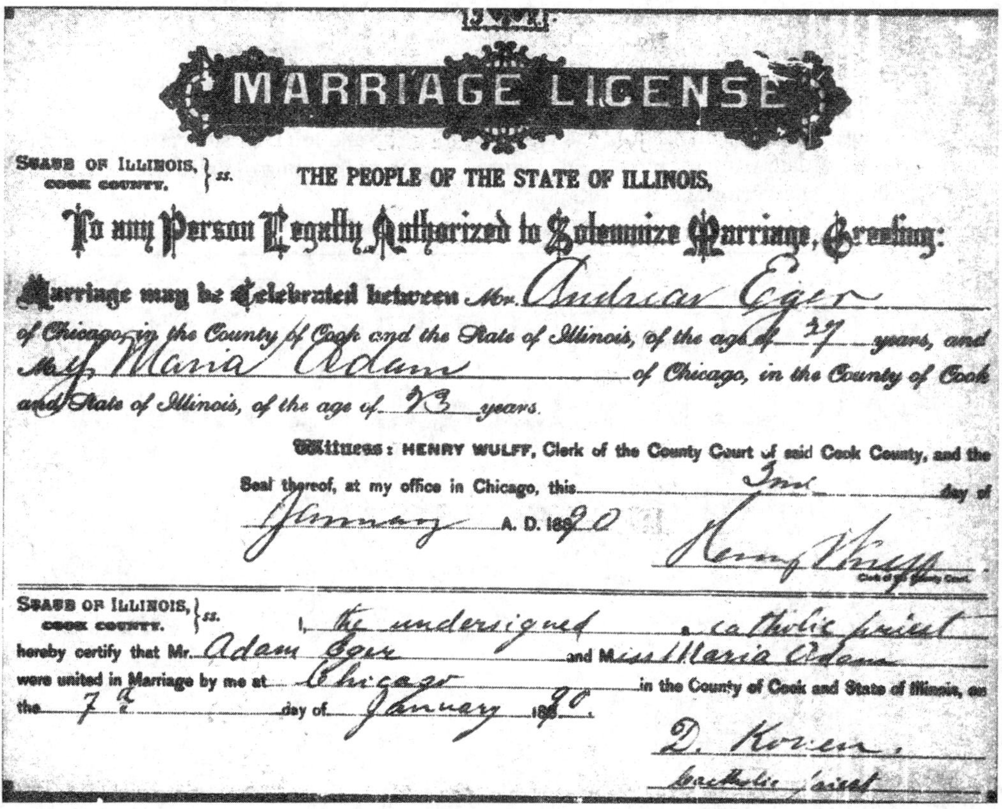

MARRIAGE LICENSE

State of Illinois, Cook County, } ss. THE PEOPLE OF THE STATE OF ILLINOIS,

To any Person Legally Authorized to Solemnize Marriage, Greeting:

Marriage may be Celebrated between Mr. Andreas Eger of Chicago in the County of Cook and the State of Illinois, of the age of 27 years, and Miss Maria Adam of Chicago, in the County of Cook and State of Illinois, of the age of 23 years.

Witness: HENRY WULFF, Clerk of the County Court of said Cook County, and the Seal thereof, at my office in Chicago, this 3rd day of January A. D. 1890

Henry Wulff
Clerk of the County Court.

State of Illinois, Cook County. } ss. I, the undersigned, a catholic priest hereby certify that Mr. Adam Eger and Miss Maria Adam were united in Marriage by me at Chicago in the County of Cook and State of Illinois, on the 7th day of January 1890.

D. Koren,
Catholic priest

Figure 4-3. A certified copy of a marriage license issued in the Illinois county where the marriage took place. It is much like licenses from most towns or counties.

Spencer County Court.

These are to license and permit you to join together, in the holy state of Matrimony, John S Summers and Mary C Reynolds, according to the rites and ceremonies of your Church; and for so doing this shall be your sufficient warrant: the said John S Summers. having executed bond with security, in my office, conditioned as the law directs, and the said parties being of lawful age

Given under my hand, this 25th day of December 1863

To any Minister of the Gospel, legally authorized to solemnize the rites of Matrimony. } Jos. B. Cox C.C.

Dated 16th day of Febuary 1864 I did sollemnize the rites of Matromony between the above named John S. Summers and Mary C. Reynolds at the house of James Reynolds in Spencer County in presents of William Summett and Mark Summers on the 16th day of Febuary 1864

William Pugh Minister of Methodist E.S. church south

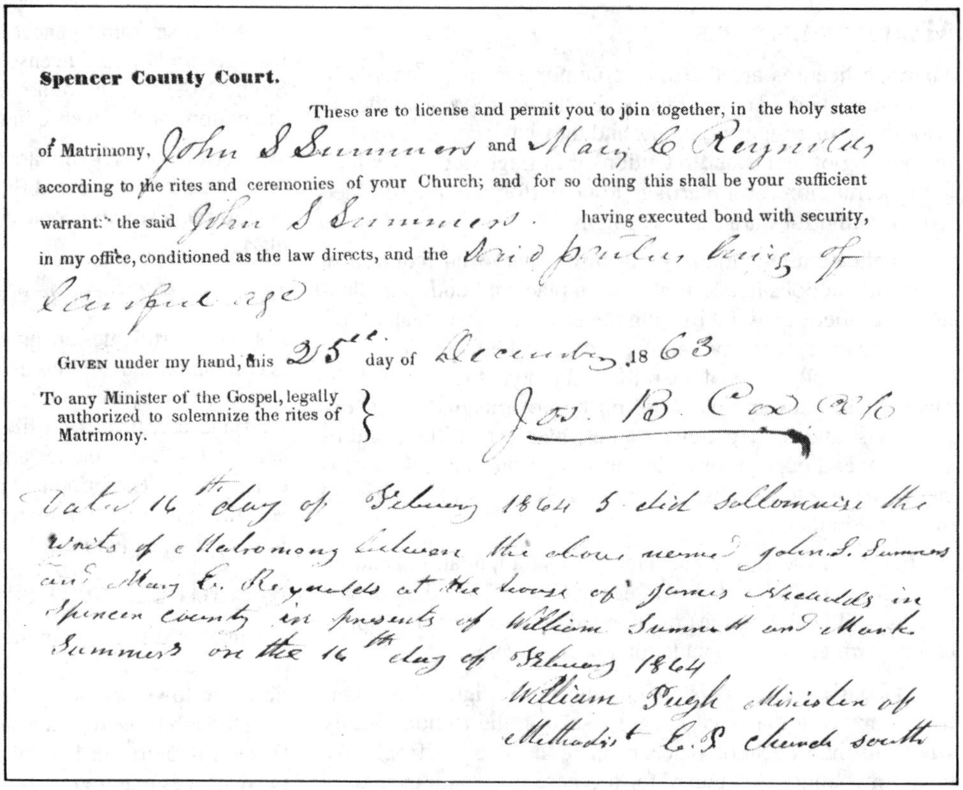

Figure 4-4. Marriage license of John S. Summers and Mary C. Reynolds, Spencer County, Kentucky, 25 December 1863, Marriage Book B, p. 22; FHL 482,642, certificate 412.

sometimes obtained a license, filed a bond, or made applications in one jurisdiction and then married in another, but ministers filed returns only in their own counties. Still, marriage returns are the only documents that provide evidence that the marriage actually took place.

Marriage registers differ from one jurisdiction to another. Some required only the names of the couple and the date of the marriage. Registers are normally arranged in chronological order by year, though there can be overlap in registers that were infrequently updated. The Spencer County, Kentucky marriage register shown in figure 4-6 provides the date of marriage, names of the parties, name of the person who performed the marriage, the place of marriage, the names of witnesses, and the certificate number.

Some registers exist in the absence of licenses. This is true for registers in Virginia and West Virginia after 1853, which provide the marriage date, minister, names of the parties, their ages, places of birth, residences, parents, and occupations. Many of these registers have been transcribed.

Most marriage registers are compiled from written returns submitted by ministers and justices. The lists are copied into the register by a clerk and are thus subject to transcription errors. Figure 4-7 is from the returns register of Daviess County, Kentucky.

14

5 cts U. S. REVENUE STAMP. Cancelled.

MARRIAGE CERTIFICATE.

THE STATE OF OHIO, MEDINA COUNTY, SS.

I hereby Certify, That on the ninth day of January A. D. 1865, I joined together in Marriage, Mr. Charles H Bennett and Miss Elizabeth Painter

Philander Green Minister.

Filed, February 15th 1865 .... Justice of the Peace.

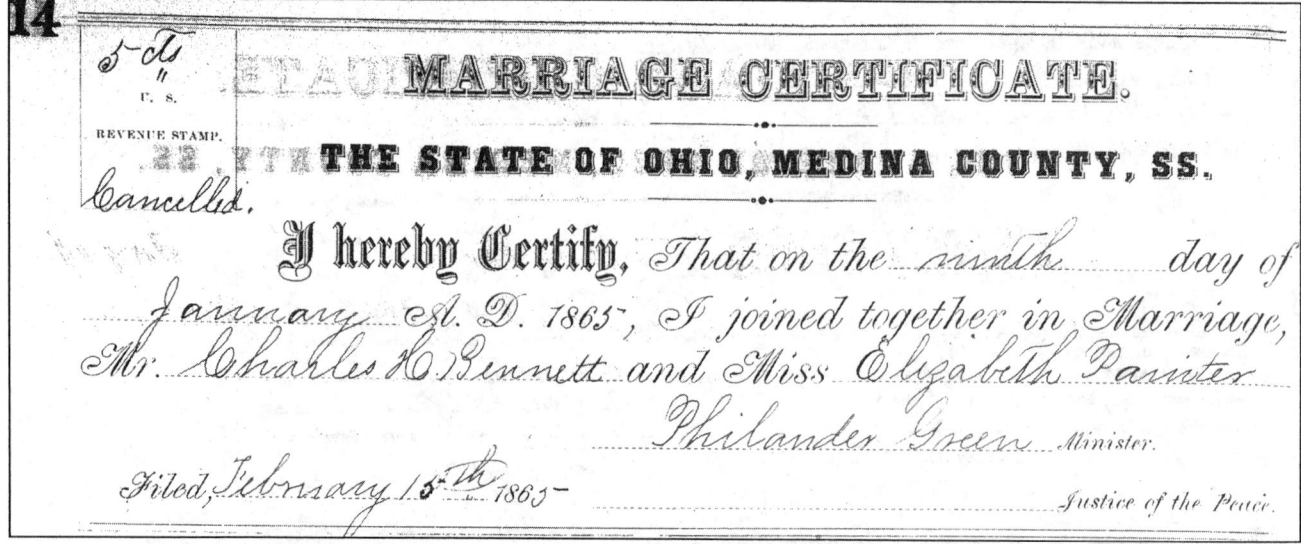

Figure 4-5. Marriage certificate of Charles H. Bennett and Elizabeth Painter, Medina County, Ohio, 15 February 1865, Book 2, p. 14; FHL 55,537, pt. 3.

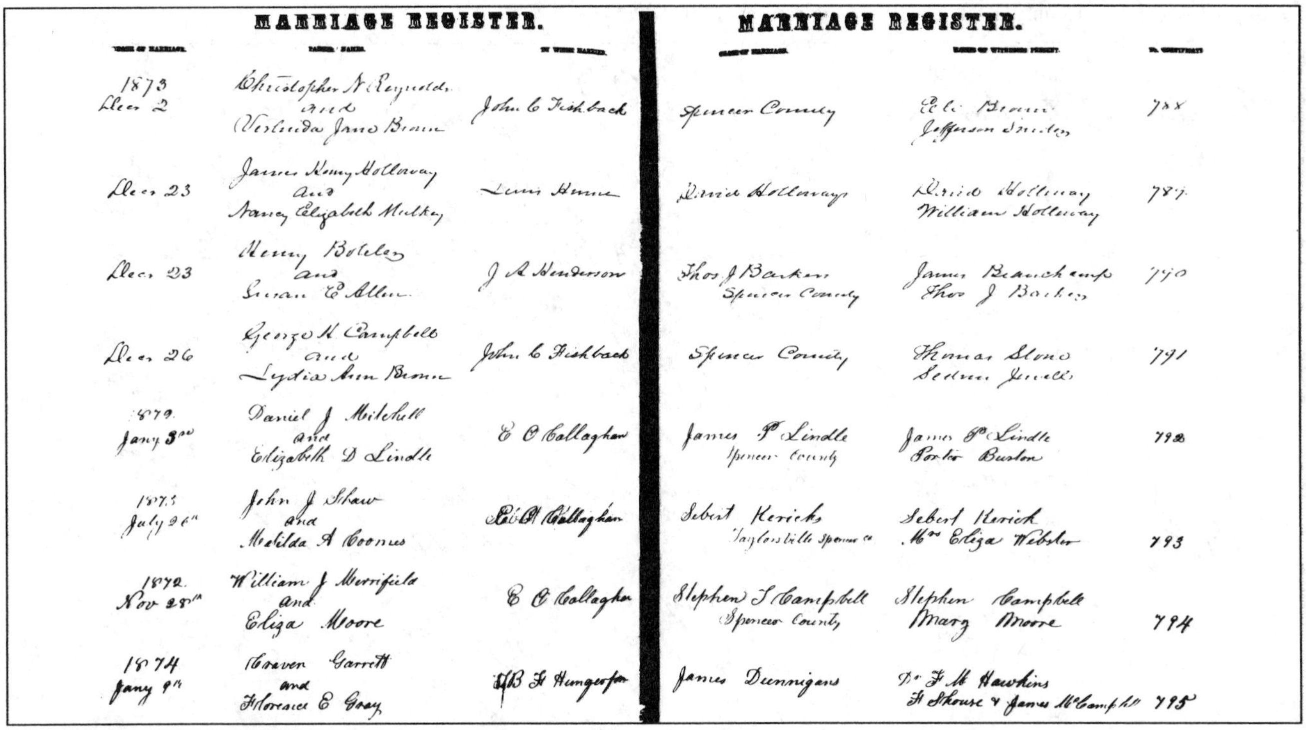

Figure 4-6. From the Spencer County, Kentucky, marriage register, 10 April to 31 July 1862; FHL 482,494.

Not all marriage returns were entered into a register. Some were simply noted on the license or bond; others were written on scraps of paper filed loosely in the clerk's office, either in alphabetical order or by the first letter of the groom's surname. Most loose returns have been microfilmed for easier use.

LOCATING MARRIAGE RECORDS

Marriage records were issued and maintained by town and county jurisdictions before state registration was established. Marriage records are usually indexed by the surname of the groom, but a few jurisdictions have compiled cross-indexes. Some states are collecting these early marriage records from the local jurisdictions—but because no comprehensive list of these repositories exists, you must write to the town or county first.

Addresses, including zip codes, for every county and town clerk are in the current edition of *Ancestry's Red Book: American State, County and Town Sources,* rev. ed. (Salt Lake City: Ancestry, 1992). At least one state has undertaken a project to index the early marriage records: The Illinois Statewide Marriage Index is an ongoing joint project of the Illinois State Archives and the Illinois State Genealogical Society that seeks to index pre-1900 marriages for all Illinois counties. Write to the Illinois State Archives, Springfield, IL 62756, for details.

GENEALOGICAL SOCIETY OF UTAH

The Genealogical Society of Utah, operated by the LDS church, has created the Family History Library. The world's largest genealogical library, it houses millions of sources, including microfilmed records from most states east of the Mississippi River and some western states. Microfilming continues in many counties. The collection is available in its entirety in Salt Lake City, but copies of the microfilms can be obtained through LDS

family history centers located throughout the United States (see appendix D for locations). This collection includes thousands of original marriage registers and collections of bonds, consents, licenses, and applications. The library also has, in book or manuscript form, marriage entries that have been transcribed by the Daughters of the American Revolution (DAR) or Work Projects Administration (WPA). Where originals and transcripts both exist, it is wise to check both. The transcripts often have cross-indexes to brides, annotations from ministers' journals and account books, newspaper announcements, and even the personal knowledge of the compiler. Table 4-1 contains a list of marriage indexes and marriage records available through the Genealogical Society of Utah as of mid-1994.

WRITING FOR MARRIAGE RECORDS

Researchers who cannot use the Family History Library's collection can write to town or county record custodians. For a fee, clerks will search the local records and send a copies of the information requested. This process can be lengthy, and clerks are not always thorough in their searches. (I made three separate requests for a single marriage license to the same county. The clerk wrote back each time saying that there was no record on file. Upon visiting that county myself a few years later, I found the document in less than five minutes.) Make repeated requests or hire an agent to obtain a record when the marriage location is certain.

Because of recently passed privacy laws, state boards of vital records and bureaus of vital statistics may require you to file a form stating your relationship to the bride and groom and the purpose of the request, but they will usually provide records for family history purposes.

Marriage records can be obtained from numerous sources. Some counties registered marriages in court records and deed

Figure 4-7. Daviess County, Kentucky, marriage returns; FHL 582,231.

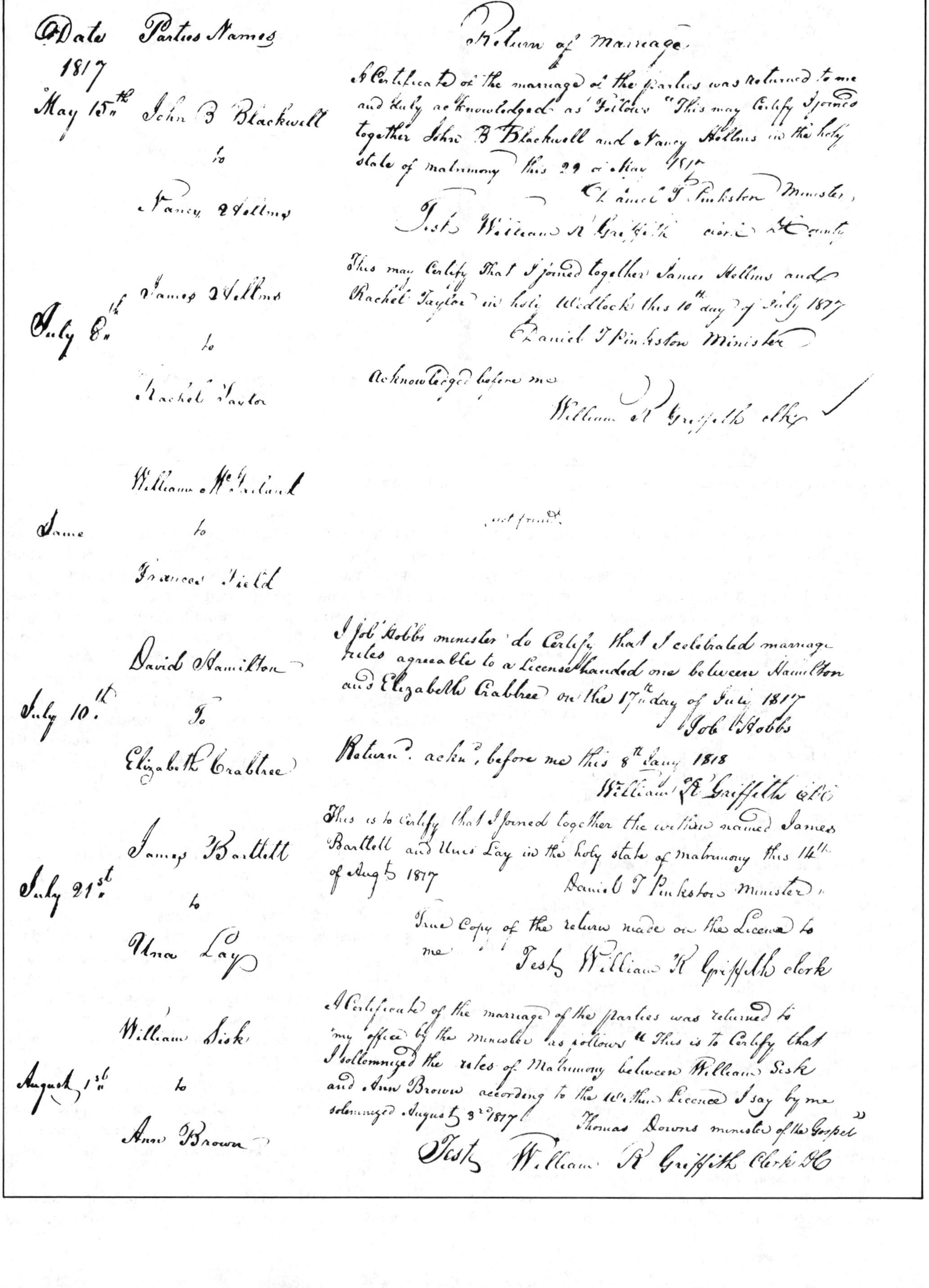

Date Parties Names

Return of marriage

1817

May 15th John B Blackwell to Nancy Hollins

A Certificate of the marriage of the parties was returned to me and duly acknowledged as follows "This may Certify I joined together John B Blackwell and Nancy Hollins in the holy state of matrimony this 29 of May 1817
Daniel T Pinkston Minister
Test William R Griffith clerk D County

July 8th James Hollins to Rachel Taylor

This may Certify That I joined together James Hollins and Rachel Taylor in holy Wedlock this 10th day of July 1817
Daniel T Pinkston Minister
acknowledged before me
William R Griffith clk

Same William McFarland to Frances Field

not found

July 10th David Hamilton To Elizabeth Crabtree

I Job Hobbs minester do Certify that I celebrated marriage rites agreeable to a License handed one between Hamilton and Elizabeth Crabtree on the 17th day of July 1817
I Job Hobbs
Return. ackn. before me this 8th Jany 1818
William R Griffith clk

July 21st James Bartlett to Una Lay

This is to Certify that I joined together the within named James Bartlett and Unes Lay in the holy state of matrimony this 14th of Augt 1817
Daniel T Pinkston minister
True Copy of the return made on the Licence to me
Test William R Griffith clerk

August 1st William Sisk to Ann Brown

A Certificate of the marriage of the parties was returned to my office by the minester as follows "This is to Certify that I sollemnized the rites of Matrimony between William Sisk and Ann Brown according to the within Licence I say by me solemnized August 3rd 1817
Thomas Downs minester of the Gospel"
Test William R Griffith Clerk DC

**Table 4-1. Statewide Marriage Indexes and Records From the
Family History Library's Vital Records Collection as of Mid-1996**

State	Marriage Index	Marriage Records	Comments
Alabama	1936–59	1936–92	Indexed by year
California	1960–85	By county	
Colorado	1900–39, 1975–92	By county	No index 1940–74
Connecticut	1638–1850s	By town	Barbour collection
Delaware	1680–1850	1855–61, 1889–94	
Florida	1927–69	By county	Indexed by year
Hawaii	1826–1910, 1909–49	1884–96, 1909–15	
Illinois	1760–1900	By county	Chicago, 1871–1916
Kentucky	1972–90	1874–78, 1906–14	
Maine	Pre-1892, 1892–1907, 1908–22	By town	Bride index, 1895–1953
Massachusetts	1841–1900	By town	Indexed by five-year sets
Nevada	1968–91		
New Hampshire	1640–1900	By town	
New Jersey	1670–1900, 1848–78	1670–1800, 1711–1878, 1848–1900	
New York City	1866–1937		Pre-1888 Manhattan only
North Carolina	1741–1868	By county	Index to bonds
Rhode Island	Pre-1853, 1853–1900	By town	
Vermont	1760–1908	By town	
Wisconsin	1852–1907, 1973–84	By county	

books. Common law marriages, if referred to at all, would be found in court records, which are rarely indexed (unlike deed books) and require substantial research time. However, they should not be overlooked.

FAMILY RECORDS

Family records, such as family Bibles, journals, diaries, and personal histories, often include marriage documents or references to marriages. Certificates, contracts, and divorce records can also be found in personal collections. Some family records have been donated to local historical societies, libraries, universities, or state archives. Manuscripts of unpublished family histories contain valuable genealogical information and are also found in these kinds of libraries, all of which usually have guides to their manuscript collections.

PRINTED RECORDS

The number of printed volumes of marriage records grows daily as genealogy enthusiasts continue to make contributions to the field. These volumes are available through libraries, historical and genealogical societies, booksellers, publishers, and private distributors. They vary in usefulness. Some collections improve upon a poor original record by adding details about a couple and their families. However, the quality of such a volume always depends on the skill of the transcriber in reading illegible handwriting and damaged records. Because a transcribed copy rarely includes all the information contained in the original record, you should also look at the original entry whenever possible.

Below is an example of the alphabetized and printed marriage records kept by two brothers who were justices of the peace in Washington County, Pennsylvania: Squires Isaac and Joseph F. Mayes. They married more than 3,000 couples, most of whom eloped to the Mayes' border town from West Virginia and Ohio because Pennsylvania did not require a marriage license.

DEGARMO, MARTHA
to John Stiger
both of Triadelphia,
Ohio Co., WV
14 January 1871
DEGARMO, MARTHA E.
to Eli Johnston
both of Ohio Co., WV
17 June 1882

—

DELANEY, JONATHAN
of Wheeling, Ohio Co., WV
to Rosabella Faulkner
of Belton, Marshall Co., WV
5 November 1865
DELANY, William C.
to Mary Virginia Crow
both of Wheeling, Ohio Co., (W)VA
24 August 1862[2]

Genealogical periodicals published by state and county genealogical societies also include marriage records. You can find large collections of these periodicals in many local libraries, or you can receive your own copies of such publications by joining the societies.

Newspapers have printed marriage announcements and engagements for decades. These articles often contain such information as the names of the parents of the bride and groom, place of residence after the marriage, and names of those in attendance at the wedding.

SPECIAL PROBLEMS ENCOUNTERED WHEN USING MARRIAGE RECORDS

An estimated thirty percent of the marriage records in this country are incomplete. Many marriage returns were never submitted to civil authorities, and countless others have been lost. Hamilton County, Ohio, which recorded marriages for Cincinnati, is an interesting example. Many records were lost in a courthouse fire. Years later the WPA copied those that survived, combining applications, licenses, and returns and then indexing them. Local genealogists reconstructed some from ministers' daybooks, original certificates, and newspaper accounts. The DAR also collected marriage records from family and local sources. Because each of these collections came from different sources, the researcher must check them all; even so, some marriages will not have been recorded. Careful checking of all versions becomes important upon considering that Cincinnati, like many American cities, was a "Gretna Green" (a no-questions-asked marriage locale in Scotland) for couples from up and down the Ohio River and from a wide circle of counties in Indiana and Kentucky, as well as Ohio. Therefore, if there is no record in the nearby county where a couple may have lived, chances are good that the entry may be found among the Cincinnati marriage records, even though they are incomplete.

Marriage records are often inaccurate. Brides and grooms have sometimes provided deliberately falsified information. To reduce their workloads, clerks often entered the date of the marriage at the time the license was issued instead of waiting for the return. Thus, marriage information should be compared with other facts known about an individual. Additional research may be necessary to resolve discrepancies.

Spelling variants are also a problem in marriage records. Many clerks did not ask couples how their names were spelled but wrote them based on their pronunciation instead. All possible spellings of a surname should be checked before assuming that a couple is not in a given record.

Many marriage records are virtually illegible due to faded entries, damaged ledger books, poor handwriting, and poorly microfilmed originals. Published marriage records can assist in clarifying unreadable entries. If poor microfilming is the problem, write to the county or town and request a photocopy or certified copy of the original. Sometimes more than one type of marriage record can be obtained.

If a marriage record is not on file for an ancestor, other records can reveal an approximate date of marriage. The 1900 Federal Census lists the number of years a couple had been married; the marriage date can be calculated from that entry. Civil War pension application files contain marriage information. If a veteran's widow filed for a pension, she had to produce proof of the marriage by obtaining an affidavit from the appropriate minister or civil authorities, supplying a copy of the marriage certificate, or sending sworn statements from persons who could testify to the marriage date and place.

DIVORCE

Today, one in every three marriages ends in divorce. Divorce was also common in early America as the colonies reacted against the severely restrictive divorce tradition inherited from England.[3] Divorce in England at the time of the founding of America was expensive, time-consuming, against Anglican law, and frowned upon socially. The only cause recognized was adultery. Three types of divorce existed in England in the early modern period: (1) a trial before an ecclesiastical court for a divorce from "bed and board" (legal separation), the legal right to live apart as though single but not the right to marry again (an oath or bond promising the parties would not remarry was filed); (2) a suit for damages in a civil court against the spouse's lover; and (3) a petition presented to the House of Lords for a hearing which ended with the grant of an absolute divorce—the dissolution of a legally valid marriage leaving both parties free to remarry.

Before 1715, the House of Lords granted only five divorces in the entire British Empire. From 1715 to 1775, sixty were granted; from 1776 to 1800, seventy-four; and from 1800 to 1850, ninety. Only four of these divorces were granted to women, who had to prove extreme cruelty as well as adultery.[4]

A less expensive but equally elaborate way to dissolve a marriage was to obtain an annulment from the Church of England, which declared the marriage void from the beginning because undue force or fraud had been used or the parties were too closely related by blood, were underage, or one or both of the parties had been under contract to someone else. Children born to an annulled union were declared illegitimate and could not inherit from their parents unless the church made special exception. Still, many annulments were sought.

American colonists were not anxious to establish ecclesiastical courts in the New World. Divorce law in the United States is almost entirely derived from statute. A study of the system the colonists knew at the time they left England, which thus formed the basis of divorce law in all the colonies, is Lawrence Stone, *Road to Divorce: England, 1530–1987; Uncertain Unions: Marriage in England, 1660–1753;* and *Broken Lives: Separation and Divorce in England, 1660–1857,* 3 vols. (Oxford Press, 1990–93).

In New England, where marriage was considered a civil contract, courts granted civil divorces from early times. In the middle colonies—New York, New Jersey, and Pennsylvania—divorces were handled either by the governor and his council or by petition to the Assembly. Adultery or prolonged desertion were the only grounds recognized. In the South, where the Church of England had greater influence, few civil divorce laws were in effect until after the American Revolution. A married couple could separate by mutual consent, apply for legal recognition of their separation, and petition for alimony. The parties were usually not free to marry again. In all of the original colonies and several of the states, divorce by legislative petition was allowed. As petitions became numerous, however, overburdened legislatures gave this judicial function to the regular courts.

Profound differences still exist from one state to another. Each state determines which court will handle divorce cases—superior court, equity court, probate court, or family or domestic court. The procedure basically allows the judge to decide what is just and equitable in each case within the limits set by the law. Because of this lack of uniformity, a researcher must study the development of divorce in each relevant jurisdiction. (See the suggested readings on divorce in the chapter bibliography.)

DIVORCE RECORDS

Divorce is a court action recorded in court records: dockets that list plaintiff and defendant and the specific term or day of the court; minute books, which record court judgments and case descriptions (often in terse legal language); and case files, which provide affidavits, lists of children with their ages, property inventories, and other data. The date and place of marriage, ages or dates of birth of the couple, places of birth, and the grounds for the divorce are usually included. In addition, the record may list the names of other family members, since the children may be in the custody of grandparents, uncles, or close family friends.

Divorce records may be recorded in volumes with the regular court cases, in separate volumes reserved for divorce cases, or in a series of separate volumes for each kind of record. The examples that follow introduce the kinds of records that exist.

County Minutes
Charles County, Maryland

Minutes for 1658–59.

Elizabeth Robins Pit   (

Robert Robins Deft   (

Elizabeth Robins petitioneth the court that she may have the privilege to choose an Aturnie to pleade her cause which was granted her and she not finding nor naming any Aturnie the court proceeded and Robert Robins housband to the said Elizabeth Robins taxeth her with adulterie and divers dispositions being read concerning the said buisnes which doe not declare any such thing as she is taxed with by her said husband it is thearfor ordered by the Court that the sayd Robert husband to the said Elisabeth his wife that he take the sayd Eliza: his wife againe, & provid for her & her children and further it is ordered that in case the sayd Robert Robins shal make apears by testimonie that shee hath formerlie confessed that the child now in her Arms was not begotten by her sayd housband but by some other that then tree shal not bee charged either to mayntaine her or her Sayd Child.

At a Countie Court held at Humpherie Atwikses the 4th day of June 1658.

The 18th of June 1659 Robert Robins and his wife Elisabeth Robins did come to the office of the Recorder of Charleses Counties and before Josias Fendall Governour and Mr John Hatch and the Clarke of the sayd office did macke this their Particular declaratione which was taken in writing by mee George Thompson Clarke of Charleses Countie which the sayd Robert Robins Caused to bee Recorded:

"I Robert Robins doe hereby disclayme my wife Elizabeth Robins for ever to acknowledge her as my wife and I doe hear oblige myself and everie one from mee never to molest or trouble her any further."

"I Elisabeth Robins doe hereby disclayme my husband Robert Robins for ever to acknowledge him as my husband and I doe hear oblige my selfe and everie one from mee never to Molest or trouble him any further for mayntainance or any other necessaries.

This to bee their owne declaration is affirmed by mee, George Thompson.[5]

This interesting example shows how first the husband tried to gain his freedom by accusing his wife of adultery—the only grounds recognized as valid for divorce or separation in Maryland at the time. When that failed he evidently persuaded his wife to believe that the best course was to mutually consent to the separation.

Legislative Act
Connecticut Legislative Resolves and Private Acts, 1837

Upon the petition of Polly M. Mead of Danbury, Fairfield County, and State of Connecticut, praying a bill of divorce from her husband, Martin Mead of said Danbury, which petition was duly served and returned:

Resolved by the Assembly, that the said Polly M. Mead be, and she is hereby divorced from the said Martin Mead, and is and forever hereafter shall be absolved from all obligations to the said Martin Mead by virtue of said marriage contract, and is hereby declared to all intents and purposes, sole, single, and unmarried.

This entry points to the original petition, which may contain case papers and testimony submitted by the parties involved. See Henry S. Cohn, "Connecticut's Divorce Mechanism, 1636–1969," *American Journal of Legal History* 14 (1970): 35–54. Multi-volume sets of selected abstracts for most of the original colonies have been printed in archive series at government expense and can be found in most large research libraries throughout the United States (see chapter 7, Research in Court Records, for a list of these). Abstracts should be used as indexes to the originals.

Civil Divorce
Weber County, Utah, Civil Divorce Case File, 1866

Christina Anderson   (

In the Probate Court County of Weber   (

SS for said County   (

Special Term July 1866   (

Hon. A. F. Farr, Judge   (

Christina Anderson vs. In Divorce Peter Anderson

Now comes the aforesaid Christina Anderson, on this 4th day of July A.D. 1866, and petitions the aforesaid court for a Bill of Divorce against her husband the said Peter Anderson for abuse and maltreatment. Your petitioner for the past two years has lived a very unhappy life with her said husband on account of this conduct towards her, he being quarrelsome in his disposition, and he has in numerous instances shamefully beat her. Your petitioner therefore on these grounds would ask a decree of court dissolving the marriage relations between us.

her

Christina X Anderson

mark

Sworn to and subscribed
this 4th day of July 1866
Walter Thompson
Clerk of Court

Inventory of Belongings

70 acres of land	cooking utensils
1 house & lot (unfenced)	bedding &c
2 cows	30 yards of cloth
2 calves	10 tons hay
2 yearlings	50 bushels (approx.)
22 sheep	grain raised this year
2 pigs	1 wagon
1 yoke oxen	1 plow
25 bushels wheat due for one cow sold	potatoes in the garden

Territory of Utah

In the Probate Court for said
County

County of Weber

SS Special Term July 4th 1866

Hon. Aaron F. Farr, Judge

Christina Anderson vs. In Divorce - Peter Anderson

The aforesaid cause came up for hearing before the aforesaid court on the day and year above written, upon the petition of the plaintiff. The court having heard the case became satisfied that the parties could not live in happiness as husband and wife and that the petitioner had just grounds for petitioning for a Bill of Divorce against her said husband, Peter Anderson. It was therefore ordered and decreed that the bonds of matrimony theretofore existing between the said Christina Anderson and Peter Anderson be and the same are hereby dissolved.

It was also ordered that the petitioner have the house and lot that the said parties now occupy, 1/2 of the sheep, 1/4 of the grain and vegetables, in the measure raised on the farm the present season, 1/2 of the bedding and household utensils and any other articles that they may have gathered since their marriage, her wearing apparel and any furniture or other articles she may have brought with her when married.

In testimony whereof I hereunto set my hand and affix the seal of said court the day and year first above written.

Walter Thompson, Clerk[6]

Early Utah quickly gained the reputation of being a divorce "mecca," with its broad grounds for divorce, inexpensive court procedures, and lack of residence requirements. Thus, Christina Anderson could obtain a divorce for abuse and maltreatment, grounds that were not allowed in eastern courts. When out-of-state people began arriving to take advantage of this situ-

ation, Utah stiffened its residency requirements and lengthened the waiting period.

A second example from a case file shows a pretrial notification:

Cuyahoga County, Ohio, Publication of Divorce, 1933

Lola Loe v. (Publication of Divorce Lawrence Loe)

Lawrence Loe, whose place of residence is unknown, will take notice that on March 22 the undersigned, Lola Loe, filed her petition against him in the Court of Common Pleas of Cuyahoga County, Ohio, praying for a divorce and relief, on the grounds of gross neglect of duty. Said cause will be for hearing on and after the 26th day of April, 1933.

Lola Loe by Martin H. Blood, Esq., her attorney.[7]

If the location of the defendant had been known, he could have been served with papers by a court official. Instead, the notice was published in the newspapers. During the colonial period, notices were posted on the town bulletin board at the courthouse, church, or city hall. News notices often ran as long as forty weeks. As communications improved, the time was gradually decreased to three to four weeks.

Some states require a certificate of divorce, with a copy filed at the state bureau of vital statistics. New Hampshire has issued certificates since 1880; other states did not begin this practice until well into the 1930s. Court records are public records, but those issued in the past fifty years are often protected by privacy legislation, and the permission of the divorced party may be required to get the data. Some states do not have certificates on file but can verify dates and refer queries to the court that has the record.

LOCATING DIVORCE RECORDS

Divorce records can be found in such diverse places as a well-lighted archive search room, a basement storage vault, or a warehouse. For addresses of the depositories of twentieth-century divorce records in each state, see appendix F.

Nineteenth-century divorces and some earlier divorces will most often be found in county or circuit courts or their counterparts. Divorces filed in the years immediately following statehood may be in the proceedings of the state's legislative body. Legislative divorces continued to be granted in some areas long after the same powers were granted to the regular courts, so researchers should check the records of assembly and council as well as the court records. Printed volumes can serve as name indexes to the original files.

Divorces filed before statehood may be found in territorial or colonial legislative records. In addition to legislative or court files, there are other sources where early divorces are recorded. Colonial assemblies were required to submit copies of every law passed to the British government for ratification or veto. Private acts for divorce were included. Sometimes acts of divorce were disallowed by the crown. Because colonial laws were valid and legal until they were disallowed, couples who may even have remarried were sometimes ordered back together after a royal review period that sometimes lasted three to six years. By 1773, the increase in divorces caused alarm in England, and governors were ordered not to approve any further divorce bills. Hence, there were fewer divorces until after the American Revolution.

Acts submitted to the crown are recorded in the Colonial Office volumes, available in print in large research libraries. Each volume is individually indexed for all documents abstracted or calendared. Originals are in the Public Record Office, Ruskin Ave., Kew, Richmond, Surrey, TW94DU, UK.

Local newspapers publish legal notices and also lists of divorces granted. Early issues carried notices placed by husbands to warn local tradesmen that they would no longer be responsible for debts incurred by their ex-wives. On occasion, wives also placed notices of freedom. (See chapter 12, Research in Newspapers, for instructions on how to find old newspapers.)

The disposition of property in any divorce case is determined by state statute or by equitable decision of the court. Alimony is the allowance a woman is entitled to receive from her husband during separation and after divorce. The amount is usually set by the court based on the financial circumstances of the husband and the needs of the wife. In rare instances, a husband may be granted alimony from his wife. Alimony can be paid in monthly or annual installments or as a single lump sum, and the obligation usually ends when the spouse remarries. In some jurisdictions, a wife guilty of adultery is denied alimony; in others she receives payment regardless of such circumstances.

In South Carolina, which did not recognize divorce, or states that severely limited the grounds for divorce, courts accepted petitions for alimony to provide for the needs of family members who wished to live apart. In areas in which there were many Shakers, for example, courts addressed the needs of spouses abandoned when the other spouse joined the celibate group. A woman was given a share of the husband's property and custody of the children. No divorce was granted, and the parties were still legally married, although living apart.

In most jurisdictions, until recently, if the wife was not guilty of adultery, she was entitled to her full dower and one-third of her husband's property at his death, even though a divorce had taken place. Some jurisdictions subtracted from the dower the amount already received in alimony. A husband could claim, by right of curtesy, one-third of the wife's property.

Courts outline provisions for children of dissolved marriages at the time the divorce is granted. The law generally stipulates that the father must help pay for the upbringing of the children. The amount is determined by the court, based upon the earning ability of the father and the number of children. In cases of non-payment, the court can order arrears to be made and enforce its decrees, even to the point of garnishing wages if necessary.

The custody of children is usually awarded based upon individual circumstances, although some jurisdictions today permit children above a certain age (eight to fourteen) to choose which parent they wish to live with. Visiting rights may be granted or denied to the other spouse at the discretion of the court.

DIVORCE MECCAS

Certain states (or colonies) gained reputations for easy divorce. Stringent laws in one area led to migration into areas where divorces were easier to obtain. Pennsylvania and New England attracted New Yorkers. Ashtabula County in Ohio, which was readily accessible from New York, Pennsylvania, and Ontario, Canada, granted many divorces to non-Ohio residents. Chicago granted four hundred divorces in 1868 alone. Utah Territory had no residency requirements until 1878, and even today Utah requires only three months' residency. Indiana had no residency requirements until 1859, and the residency requirements in other states vary widely: twenty-nine states require one year; Delaware, New Jersey, Rhode Island, Tennessee, and Arkansas require two years; Connecticut and Massachusetts require three years; North Carolina and Virginia require six months; Utah three months; Arkansas, Florida, Idaho, Wyoming, and Nevada seem to compete to lower their requirements to attract the divorce trade. Louisiana, New York, Wisconsin, and South Carolina have no specific residency requirement, but the grounds are more stringent in those states.[8]

After the Civil War, the frontier was often the most practical resolution to a bad marriage. In earlier periods this had been true of immigration to the New World as well. A ride into the sunset by one or both parties was easier and less expensive than petitioning for a legislative divorce. Numerous examples of runaway spouses can be found among the advertisements in early newspapers, a bonus for genealogists.

NOTES

1. Marriage Contract of Charles de La Verge and Marie Joseph Carriere in Alice Daly Forsyth and Ghislaine Pleasanton, comps., *Louisiana Marriage Contracts* (New Orleans: Polyanthos Press, 1980), 85.

2. Helen L. Harris, CG, Elizabeth J. Wall, and Betty Treat Petrich, comps., *Marriage Records of Squires Isaac and Joseph F. Mayes* (Pittsburgh: 1978), 59.

3. This section is adapted, with permission, from *Sources of Birth, Marriage, and Death Prior to 1900* (Salt Lake City: The Genealogical Institute, 1974), 39–50.

4. Nelson M. Blake, *The Road to Reno: A History of Divorce in the United States* (New York: Macmillan, 1972), 32.

5. Liber A, p. 4, *Maryland Archives,* (Baltimore: Maryland Historical Society, 1934), vol. 53.

6. Petition for Divorce and Decree of Divorce, Christina Anderson vs. Peter Anderson, "Ancient Civil Divorce Files," 2 Feb. 1859–21 Feb. 1887, 2nd District Court, Utah, Civil Trials Record, H-2, 01-181, Utah State Archives.

7. Copy of original notice filed 22 March 1933, Cuyahoga County court clerk, Cleveland, Ohio.

8. See appendix F, Where to Write for Vital Records.

BIBLIOGRAPHY

MARRIAGE

Basch, Norma. "Women's Rights and the Wrongs of Marriage in Mid-Nineteenth Century America." *History Workshop Journal* 22 (3) (Autumn 1986): 18–40.

_____. "Invisible Women: The Legal Fiction of Marital Unity in Nineteenth Century America." *Feminist Studies* 5 (2) (Summer 1979): 346–66.

Cook, Frank G. "Marriage Celebration in the Colonies." *Atlanta Monthly* 61 (1888).

Cook, Mrs. Henry Lowell. "Maids for Wives." *Virginia Magazine of History and Biography* 51 (1943): 71–86.

Goodsell, Willystine. *A History of Marriage and the Family.* Rev. ed. New York: Macmillan, 1934.

Howard, George E. *History of Matrimonial Institutions.* 3 vols. Chicago: University of Chicago Press, 1904.

North, S.N.D., comp. *Marriage Laws in the United States, 1887–1906.* Reprint. Conway, Ark.: Arkansas Research, 1994.

Semonche, John E. "Common Law Marriage in North Carolina: A Study in Legal History." *American Journal of Legal History* 9 (1965): 320–49.

DIVORCE

Bamman, Gale. W., and Debbie W. Spero. *Tennessee Divorces, 1797–1858.* Thorndike, Mass.: Van Volumes Unlimited, 1990.

Basch, Norma. "The Emerging Legal History of Women in the United States: Property, Divorce, and the Constitution." *Signs* 12 (1) (Autumn 1986): 97–117.

Bell, Carol W. *Ohio Divorces: The Early Years, 1794–1947.* Youngstown, Ohio: the author, 1994.

Blake, Nelson M. *The Road to Reno: A History of Divorce in the United States.* New York: Macmillan, 1972.

Blattner, Theresa. *Divorces, Separations, and Annulments in Missouri, 1769 to 1850.* Bowie, Md.: Heritage Books, 1992.

Cohen, Sheldon S. "The Broken Bond: Divorce in Providence County, 1749–1809." *Rhode Island History* 44 (1985): 67–79.

Cohn, Henry S. "Connecticut's Divorce Mechanism, 1636–1969." *American Journal of Legal History* 14 (1970): 35–54.

Cott, Nancy F. "Divorce and the Changing Status of Women in Eighteenth-Century Massachusetts." *William and Mary Quarterly,* 3rd Series, 33 (1976): 586–614.

———. "Eighteenth-Century Family and Social Life as Revealed in Massachusetts Divorce Records." *Journal of Social History* 10 (1976): 20–43.

"Divorce in Colonial New York." *New York Historical Society Quarterly* 3 (October 1955): 422.

"Early Statutory and Common Law Divorce in North Carolina." *North Carolina Law Review* 604 (1973).

"Harding vs. Harding, a 1753 Virginia Divorce." *Kentucky Ancestors* 14 (1978–79): 15–16.

Hartman, Margaret S. "Annulments and Divorces in Kentucky." *Kentucky Genealogist* 20 (1978): 60–64.

Index to Divorce Cases of the Thirteenth Judicial Circuit Court of Alabama, 1816–1918. Mobile: University of South Alabama Archives, 1995.

Ireland, Gordon, and Jesus de Galindez. *Divorce in the Americas.* New York: Dennis and Co., 1947.

Johnson, Guion G. *An Evaluation of North Carolina Divorce Law in Antebellum North Carolina: A Social History.* Chapel Hill: University of Carolina Press, 1937.

Knapp, Paul R. "Divorce in Washington." *Washington Historical Quarterly* 5 (1914): 121–28.

McCracken, George E. "New Jersey Legislative Divorces, 1778–1844." *American Genealogist* 34 (1958): 107–12.

Newhard, Malinda E.E. *Divorces and Name Changes Granted by the Indiana General Assembly Prior to 1852.* Harlan, Ind.: the author, 1981.

Riley, Glenda. *Divorce: An American Tradition.* New York: Oxford University Press, 1991.

Salmon, Marylynn. "Divorce and Separation." In *Women and the Law of Property in Early America.* Chapel Hill, N.C.: University of Carolina Press, 1986.

Stanley, Lois, et al. *Divorces and Separations in Missouri, 1808–1853.* Greenville, S.C.: Southern Historical Press, 1990.

Stone, Lawrence. *Road to Divorce: England, 1530–1987; Uncertain Unions: Marriage in England, 1660–1753;* and *Broken Lives: Separation and Divorce in England, 1660–1857.* 3 vols. Oxford Press, 1990–93.

"To Parts of the World Unknown: The Circumstances of Divorce in Connecticut, 1750–1797." *The Canadian Review of American Studies* 9 (1980) 275–93.

Van Ness, James S. "On Untieing the Knot: The Maryland Legislature and Divorce Petitions." *Maryland Historical Magazine* 67 (1972): 171–75.

Venier, Chester G. *American Family Laws.* Vol. 2. Stanford, Calif.: Stanford University Press, 1931.

RESEARCH IN CENSUS RECORDS
CHAPTER CONTENTS

5

RESEARCH IN CENSUS RECORDS

Loretto Dennis Szucs

Whatis the name, age, sex, color, occupation, and birthplace of each person residing in this house? Which of these individuals attended school or was married within the year? Who among them is deaf and dumb, blind, insane, "idiotic," a pauper, or a convict? Is there anyone in the household over twenty years of age who cannot read and write? What is the name of the slave owner? How many slaves belong to the owner? What is the tribe of this Indian? What were the places of birth of the person's parents? In what year did this person immigrate to the United States and, if naturalized, what was the year of naturalization?

For answers to these and other questions, researchers look to census records. While not all of these inquiries were made in every census year, each of the decennial (occurring every ten years) enumerations of the inhabitants of the United States has its own potential for solving mysteries of the past. Few, if any, records shed as much light on individuals, families, or communities as do population census schedules. From the first federal census of 1790 to the 1920 census (the most recent census available to the public), the records present a vast resource that is rich in personal information and very accessible.

This chapter will provide a brief history of the U.S. federal population censuses from 1790 to 1920, followed by a section describing strengths and limitations of census records. Suggestions in the "General Strengths and Limitations of Census Records" section, below, will be useful not only for searching federal schedules but also for searching special and state censuses described later in the chapter. The contents and special features of each federal decennial census are described in chronological order, followed by a section on related census indexes. Where and how to use census records is discussed in the last part of this chapter.

HISTORICAL BACKGROUND

The actual records of civilization's first population counts have apparently not survived, but it is known that in early Babylonia, Egypt, and China the inhabitants were counted on a regular basis. There are ancient written accounts of the Greeks and Romans having taken censuses, but those tallies, too, seem to have been lost over the centuries. On the North American continent, the Spaniards led the way in census-taking, counting heads in what was then Mexico in 1577.

Since 1790, the U.S. government has taken a nationwide population count every ten years. Though never intended for genealogical purposes, the federal censuses are among the most frequently sought records for those looking for links with the past. Unique in scope and often surprisingly detailed, the census population schedules created from 1790 to 1920 are among the most used of federally-created records. Over the course of two centuries, the United States has changed significantly, and so has the census. From the six basic questions asked in the 1790 census, the scope and categories of information have changed and expanded dramatically.

Article I, Section 2, of the U.S. Constitution required that an enumeration of the people be made within three years after the first meeting of the Congress. In March 1790, after President Washington signed the first census act, Secretary of State Thomas Jefferson sent a copy of the law to each of the seventeen U.S. marshals and instructed them to appoint as many assistants as they needed to take the census.

From 1790 to 1880, census districts were aligned with existing civil divisions. The district marshals were authorized to subdivide each district into reasonable geographical segments to facilitate supervision of the enumeration. Enumeration districts were limited in size to 10,000 individuals by the Census Act of 1850, but final tallies show that the number was usually less than 6,000. In 1880, the Census Office appointed supervisors to further subdivide the districts. In that year, the average population of each of the 28,000 enumeration districts was less than 2,000.[1]

Early censuses were essentially basic counts of inhabitants, but as the nation grew, so did the need for statistics that would reflect the characteristics of the people. The logical means for obtaining a clearer picture of the American populace was to solicit more information about individuals. In 1850, the focus of the census was radically broadened. Going far beyond the vague questions previously asked heads of households, the 1850 census enumerators were instructed to ask the age, sex, color, occupation, birthplace, and other questions regarding every individual in every household. Succeeding enumerations solicited more information; by 1920, census enumerators asked twenty-nine questions of every head of household and almost as many questions of everyone else in the residence. As W.S. Rossiter, chief clerk of the Bureau of the Census around the first part of the twentieth century, stated, "The modern census is thus the result of evolution."[2]

THE CENSUS BUREAU

Although the Constitution, ratified in 1787, called for a census every ten years, there was no special government agency to conduct and tabulate the results of this massive survey. Until 1840, federal marshals managed the process as best they could. In 1850, the first Census Office was opened in Washington, D.C. However, it was disbanded after the 1850 census and only reestablished in time to take the census and tally the results in 1860, 1870, 1880, 1890, and 1900.

Not until 1902 was the Bureau of the Census established as a permanent bureau in the Department of the Interior. In 1903 the bureau was transferred to the Department of Commerce. The Bureau of the Census is responsible for providing statistics about the population and economy of the nation and collecting, tabulating, and publishing a wide variety of statistical data for government and private users.[3]

GENERAL STRENGTHS AND LIMITATIONS OF CENSUS RECORDS

Few, if any, records reveal as many details about individuals and families as do the U.S. federal censuses. The population schedules are successive "snapshots" of Americans that depict where and how they were living at particular periods in the past. Census records since 1850 suggest dates and places of birth, relationships, family origins, changes in residence, schooling, occupations, economic and citizenship status, and more.

Once home sources (see chapter 1, The Foundations of Family History Research) have been exhausted, the census is often the best starting point for genealogical research. The availability of statewide indexes for almost every census year makes them logical tools to locate individuals whose precise residence is unknown. While some inaccuracies are to be expected in census records, they still provide some of the most fascinating and useful pieces of personal history to be found in any source. If nothing else, census records are important sources for placing individuals in specific places at specific times. Additionally, information found in the census will often point to other sources critical to complete research, such as court, land, military, immigration, naturalization, and vital records.

The importance of census records does not diminish over time in any given research project. It is always wise to return to these records as discoveries are made in other sources because, as new evidence about individuals is found, some data that seemed unrelated or unimportant in a first look at the census may take on new importance.

When family, vital, or religious records are missing, census records may be the only means of documenting the events of a person's life. Vital registration did not begin until around 1920 in many areas of the United States, and fires, floods, and other disasters have destroyed some official government records. When other documentation is missing, census records are frequently used by individuals who must prove their age or citizenship status (or that of their parents) for Social Security benefits, insurance, passports, and other important reasons.

PROBLEMS CREATED AT THE TIME THE CENSUS WAS TAKEN

When evaluating any source, it is always wise to consider how, when, and under what conditions the record was made. By examining how enumerations were conducted, it becomes easy to understand why some individuals cannot be found in the census schedules or in the indexes to them.

From the first enumeration in 1790 to the most recent in 1990, the government has experienced difficulties in gathering the precise information it desired for a number of reasons. At least one of the problems experienced in extracting information from individuals for the first census continues to vex officials today: There were and still are many people who simply do not trust the government's motives. Many citizens have worried that their answers to census questions might be used against them, particularly regarding issues related to taxation, military service, and immigration. Some have simply refused to answer enumerators' questions; others have lied.

BOUNDARIES

In the days before regular mail service, government representatives conducted door-to-door canvasses of their appointed districts. Supervisors subdivided districts using existing local boundaries. The town, township, military district, ward, and precinct most often constituted one or more enumeration districts.[4] Boundaries of towns and other minor civil divisions, and in some cases of counties, were ill defined, so enumerators were frequently uncertain whether a family resided in their or an adjoining district. For this reason, it is not unusual to find individuals and families listed twice in the census and others missed entirely. Robert C. Anderson, et al., provide excellent examples and an analysis of this rather common problem in "Duplicate Census Enumerations," *The American Genealogist* 62 (2) (April 1987): 97–105; 62 (3) (July 1987): 173–81; 62 (4) (October 1987): 241–44.

Over the years, state, county, township, and city ward boundaries have changed. Any census search can be thrown off by these changes and inconsistencies. For a thorough discussion of boundaries and detailed maps, see William Thorndale and William Dollarhide, *Map Guide to the U.S. Federal Censuses, 1790–1920* (Baltimore: Genealogical Publishing Co., 1987). The introduction to this work includes a discussion of duplication in census records.

HISTORICAL PERSPECTIVE

For a better sense of how census takers carried out their duties in a given year, it is useful to imagine the landscape and the modes of travel available in the specific time period. In the earliest census years, travel was obviously more difficult and, sometimes, very dangerous—conditions that did not improve for decades in the more rural states and territories of the "Wild West."

To complicate the situation further, a large portion of the young nation's population lived in small villages and isolated farms that were dispersed over a large area. It was not uncommon for a census enumerator to make a long trip to a remote farm, only to find no one at home. In these instances, he was left to make a decision—whether to try again on another day, or question farm or household help, neighbors, or even young children. The latter appears to have been an option taken by many. In some situations, enumerators probably found it easier to guess themselves.

Obtaining answers directly from the head of household or an adult in the house was no guarantee of accuracy. For a number of reasons, ages are always suspect in census records. Many people tend to be secretive about their age; women may have been particularly sensitive about revealing the truth. One woman tracked in the census taken in New York from 1850 to 1880 claimed to have aged only twelve years in the thirty-year period. According to the 1850 and 1860 censuses of Springfield, Illinois, Mary, wife of Abraham Lincoln, aged only seven years in the ten-year period (figure 5-1). She, or someone reporting for her, claimed that she was twenty-eight in 1850 and only thirty-five in 1860. Dozens of cases have been similarly noted; undoubtedly, some honestly could not remember how old they were. If a person's age was not exactly known, it was frequently rounded off to the closest decade, making ages reported as thirty, forty, fifty, and so on somewhat suspect. Therefore, unless an age reported in the census can be corroborated with another source, it should not be considered totally reliable.

When questions were answered by someone other than the subject of the inquiry, the likelihood of error increased. A husband or wife might not always know the birthplaces of a spouse's parents. A child being quizzed might easily be unsure of the birthplaces of his or her parents. Census schedules do not tell us *who* may have answered the enumerator's questions.

An important point to remember is that enumerators simply wrote down the responses given to them. They were not authorized to request any kind of proof, such as birth, marriage or property ownership records. However, every individual contacted by a government representative was required by law to answer truthfully. Anyone refusing to answer or willfully providing false information was guilty of a misdemeanor and subject to a fine. As early as 1790, offenders were fined twenty dollars, to be split between the marshals' assistants and the government. But relatively few individuals were hauled into court for refusing to answer or for not answering truthfully. It would have been an impossible task for the government to follow through and to investigate everyone's answers.

It was not until 1830 that the census office supplied printed questionnaires or "schedules." The enumerators of the 1790, 1800, 1810, and 1820 censuses returned the results of their canvassing on whatever paper they had. Each also had to post copies of their censuses in two public places in their assigned areas. Presumably, people who could read would see discrepancies or omissions and call them to the attention of officials. Unfortunately few, if any, of these duplicates have survived.

Another factor that comes into play in the accuracy of every census record is the competency of the enumerator who recorded the information. Individuals were not necessarily well educated or qualified for the job, and anyone who has studied census records knows that good penmanship was not a requirement. Census takers were political appointees who were frequently chosen because they were of the correct political affiliation in a particular time and place, or just knew the right people.

Wages were definitely not an incentive for would-be census takers. In 1790, even the highest pay rate, one dollar for fifty persons, barely covered an enumerator's expenses. In 1920, payment was on a per-capita or per-diem basis—sometimes a combination of the two. An enumerator was paid between one and four cents per person, depending on the urban or rural setting of the district to be counted.

The United States has always been home to a large number of immigrants, and those who did not speak English well presented still another problem for the census taker. Often, enumerators could hardly understand the information given to them by people with foreign accents. Names were frequently misunderstood and misspelled by enumerators to the extent that they may not even begin with the correct letters, making them hard to find in census schedules and almost impossible to find in indexes. The German name Pfeiffer could easily be heard and committed to paper as Fifer, for example. An Irish census taker in Cleveland recorded the Polish name Menkalski as McKalsky in the 1920 census. Places of birth may have been equally difficult to translate into English.

Whether recording information from a foreign-born or American-born individual, some enumerators took the quickest way to get the job done. Some used initials rather than given names, some used nicknames, and some omitted places of birth, value of real estate, occupations, and other details. In boarding houses, hotels, and clusters of workers' cottages, enumerators could easily overlook entire families.

While enumerators were given basic instructions as early as 1820, it was not until 1850 that the Census Office printed uniform instructions for the enumerators, explaining their responsibilities, procedures, the specifics of completing the schedules, and the intent of each question asked. In 1850, the Census Office also provided enumerators with a large portfolio to accommodate the oversize forms (which measured twelve by eighteen inches), pens, a portable ink stand, ink, and blotting paper. Enumerators were instructed not to fold the pages and not to allow anyone to "meddle with [their] papers." Pages were numbered consecutively as they were completed. Each page was dated on the day it was begun, even if it was not completed until another day. Every page was to include the enumerator's signature, the name of the civil division, county, and state and, after 1870, the local post office.

According to the 1850 census instructions, the enumerator, on completing the entry for each family, farm or shop, was to read the information back to the person interrogated so that errors could be corrected immediately. But if an informant was unclear or incorrect in giving information in the first place, this procedure did little to correct errors. A significant portion of the American population could not read nor write in the last century, so, if an enumerator misspelled the family surname, it could easily have stayed that way, whether or not it was repeated by the enumerator.

As the enumeration of each subdistrict was completed, the enumerator was to make two copies that were to be carefully compared to the original for accuracy. Hand copying, of course, brings the very strong possibility of mistakes that are often unknown to the creator of the copy. Experience with the various copies of the census shows that most copies were not error free. It was cumbersome and tedious to copy names and endless columns of personal information. It is unlikely that enumerators envisioned the copies ever being read again once the statistical tabulations were completed, so it is easy to believe that many became careless as the job wore on.

As the process was completed, the enumerator was to sign

Figure 5-1. 1850 (p. 120) (top) and 1860 (p. 140) (bottom) federal census entries for the household of Abraham Lincoln, Springfield, Sangamon County, Illinois.

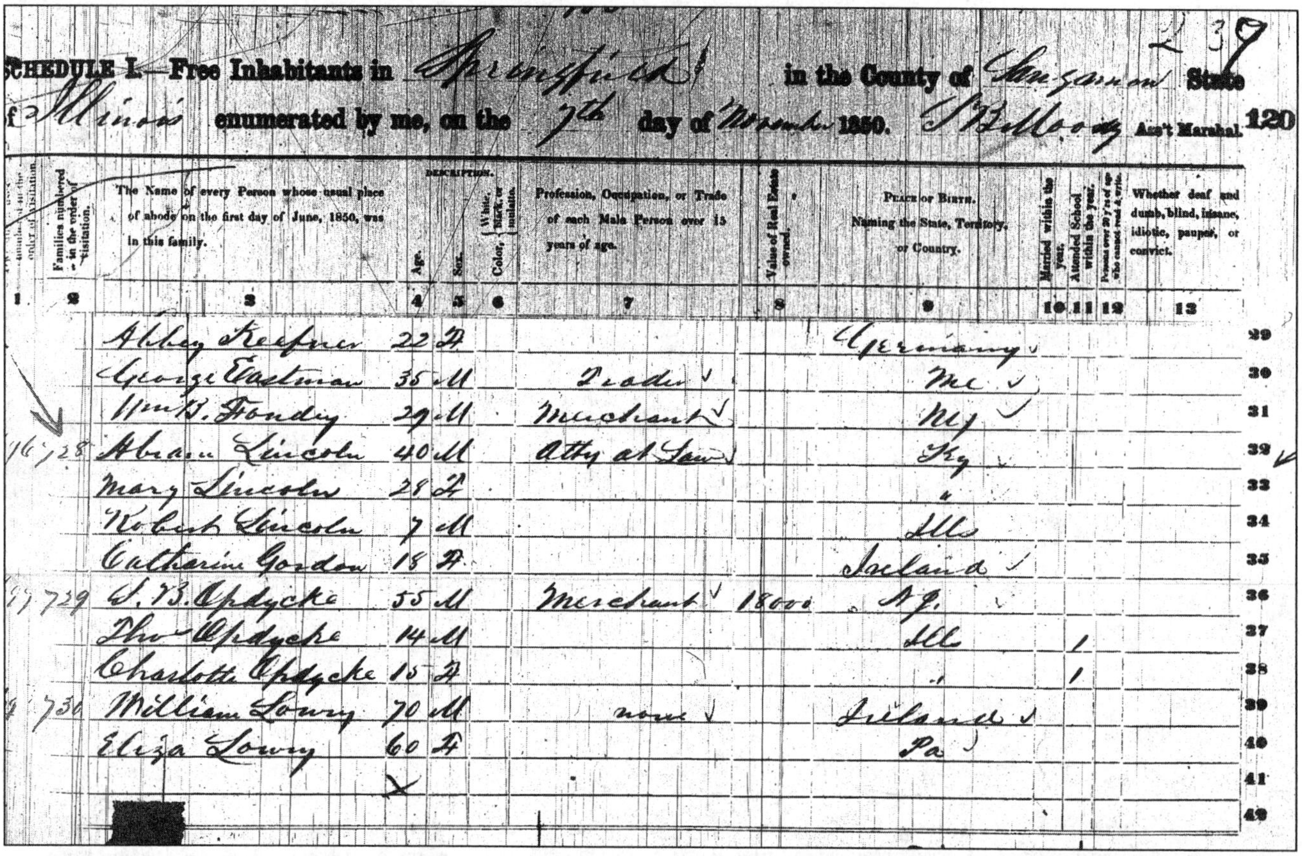

SCHEDULE I.—Free Inhabitants in Springfield in the County of Sangamon State of Illinois enumerated by me, on the 7th day of November 1850. T. Billoo Ass't Marshal. 120

	Dwelling-houses numbered in the order of visitation	Families numbered in the order of visitation	The Name of every Person whose usual place of abode on the first day of June, 1850, was in this family.	Age	Sex	Color	Profession, Occupation, or Trade of each Male Person over 15 years of age.	Value of Real Estate owned.	Place of Birth. Naming the State, Territory, or Country.	Married within the year.	Attended School within the year.	Persons over 20 y'rs of age who cannot read & write.	Whether deaf and dumb, blind, insane, idiotic, pauper, or convict.
	1	2	3	4	5	6	7	8	9	10	11	12	13
29			Abby Keefner	22	F				Germany				
30			George Eastman	35	M		Trader		Me				
31			Wm B. Fondey	29	M		Merchant		NY				
32		728	Abram Lincoln	40	M		Atty at Law		Ky				
33			Mary Lincoln	28	F				"				
34			Robert Lincoln	7	M				Ills				
35			Catharine Gordon	18	F				Ireland				
36		729	S. B. Opdycke	55	M		Merchant	18000	NJ				
37			Thos Opdycke	14	M				Ill		1		
38			Charlotte Opdycke	15	F				"		1		
39		730	William Lowry	70	M		none		Ireland				
40			Eliza Lowry	60	F				Pa				
41													
42													

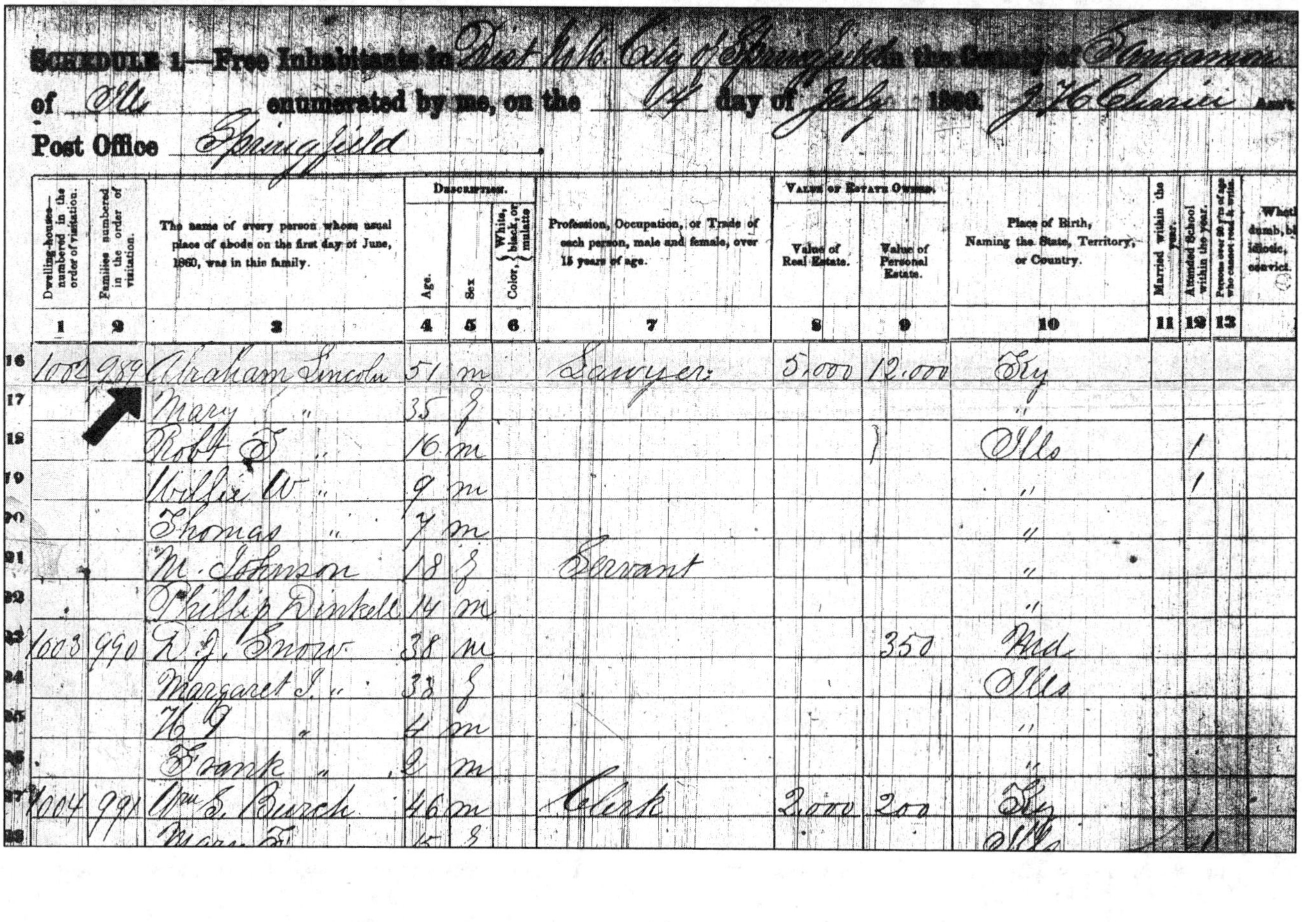

SCHEDULE 1.—Free Inhabitants in Dist No 6 City of Springfield in the County of Sangamon of Ill enumerated by me, on the 04 day of July 1860. J. H. Claine Ass't
Post Office Springfield

	Dwelling-houses numbered in the order of visitation.	Families numbered in the order of visitation.	The name of every person whose usual place of abode on the first day of June, 1860, was in this family.	Age.	Sex.	Color, { White, black, or mulatto.	Profession, Occupation, or Trade of each person, male and female, over 15 years of age.	Value of Real Estate.	Value of Personal Estate.	Place of Birth, Naming the State, Territory, or Country.	Married within the year.	Attended School within the year.	Persons over 20 y'rs of age who cannot read & write.	Whether deaf and dumb, blind, insane, idiotic, pauper, or convict.
	1	2	3	4	5	6	7	8	9	10	11	12	13	
16	1002	989	Abraham Lincoln	51	m		Lawyer	5,000	12,000	Ky				
17			Mary "	35	f					"				
18			Robt T. "	16	m					Ills		1		
19			Willie W "	9	m					"		1		
20			Thomas "	7	m					"				
21			M. Johnson	18	f		Servant			"				
22			Phillip Dinkell	14	m					"				
23	1003	990	D. J. Snow	38	m				350	Md				
24			Margaret J. "	33	f					Ills				
25			H. J. "	4	m					"				
26			Frank "	2	m					"				
27	1004	991	Wm S. Burch	46	m		Clerk	2,000	200	Ky				
28			Mary F.	15	f					Ills		1		

each page of the census and, at the end of each set of copies, to certify that the census had been taken and copied according to instructions. One set was to be filed with the clerk of the county court, and the other two were to be forwarded to the supervisor. As the supervisor received the completed schedules, it was his or her duty to see that every part of the district had been visited and that the copies were in good order. One set was then sent to the state or territory, and the other was forwarded to the U.S. Census Office for statistical analysis. Unfortunately, it is almost impossible to distinguish the original census taken by the enumerator—the one likely to be most accurate—from the copies, which were prone to additional inaccuracies due to mistakes in the copying process. While it is usually not possible to know if the original census or a copy was sent, it is relatively easy to recognize the census that was sent to the Census Office. "Researchers can distinguish the latter set from the other two because the Census Office made tabulations directly on the schedules; consequently, the central office copy bears pencil, crayon, and red ink markings on virtually every page."[5]

In 1880, the procedure of making three sets of returns was abandoned. Enumerators forwarded the originals to the Census Office and did not make any copies. In an attempt to correct errors, however, the Census Act of 1880 called for "public exhibition of the population returns," and for this purpose it authorized enumerators to make a list of names with age, sex, and color of all persons enumerated in the district, to be filed with the clerk of the county court. If any of these lists have survived, they will be found at the county level.

In most enumerations, census takers were instructed to number each dwelling consecutively in the order of visit, though it was not always clear how the instructions may have changed or been interpreted from year to year. It should be emphasized that there was no connection between the household numbers (usually the number listed in the first column to the left of the census page) and the locality or address.

Census instructions defined a dwelling as any structure in which a person was living, including a room above a store, warehouse, or a factory or a wigwam on the outskirts of a settlement. Institutions, such as hospitals, orphanages, poorhouses, garrisons, asylums, and jails, were counted as single-dwelling houses. It was not until the 1880 census that the character and name of the institution were required to be written in the margin. The 1880 census was also the first to include street addresses in cities.

In most years, census instructions stated that all persons temporarily absent on a journey or visit were to be counted with the rest of their family in their usual abode. However, children away at school and living near the school or college were to be enumerated with that family or institution. According to the instructions, "seafaring men" were to be reported at their homes on land, no matter how long their absence, if they were believed to be still alive. Sailors residing in boardinghouses were not to be counted there but rather at their permanent residences, if they had any. Expressmen, canalmen, railroad employees, and others engaged in transportation were to be enumerated with their families if they returned to their homes at regular intervals.

Census instructions were quite specific as to how enumerators were to map out and proceed through their assigned areas so that no one would be missed. The 1920 instructions, for example, stated:

> 68. Method of canvassing a city block - If your district is in a city or town having a system of house numbers canvass one block or square at a time. Do not go back and forth across the street. Begin each block at one corner, keep to the right, turn the corner, and go in and out of any court, alley, or passageway that may be included in it until the point of starting is reached. Be sure you have gone around and through the entire block before you leave it.

> 69. The arrows in the following diagram indicate the manner in which a block containing an interior court or place is to be canvassed:

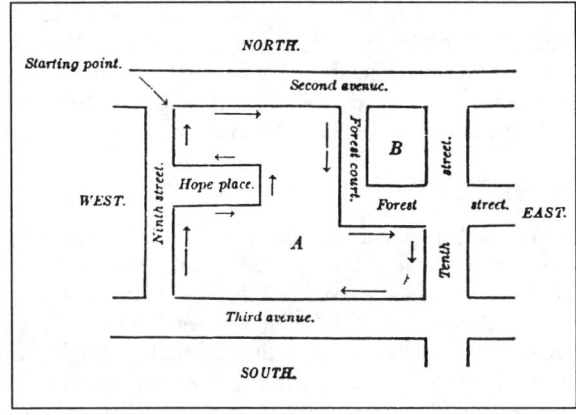

Department of Commerce, Bureau of the Census, *Fourteenth Census of the United States. January 1, 1920: Instructions to Enumerators* (Washington, D.C.: Government Printing Office, 1919).

MISSING CENSUSES

According to most authorities, the 1790 census schedules for Delaware, Georgia, Kentucky, New Jersey, Tennessee, and Virginia were burned during the War of 1812. Some records, such as the 1790 records for Virginia, have been reconstructed from state enumerations and tax lists. In later enumerations, city blocks, neighborhoods, townships and sections of townships, and even entire counties are known to be missing from the census schedules, simply because no census was taken in the particular area in a given year or because they were lost before they reached Washington, D.C.

Probably the most noted loss of the federal enumerations is that of the 1890 census. Most of the 1890 schedules were destroyed in a fire in the Commerce Department in 1921.

FALSE CENSUS ENTRIES

Another confusing situation can arise in census research when names show up in a district where they do not belong—sometimes more than once! According to Arlene Eakle, Ph.D., "padding the totes," or adjusting the census for political reasons, was not uncommon. "Frontier areas, anxious for statehood, often added bogus names. In 1857, seven counties in Minnesota had wild population totals, complete with fake names on the schedules. Jurisdictions facing increased taxes might also understate their populations to keep overall per capita taxes lower. The 1880 Utah census juggled households to disguise polygamy at a time when federal officials were seeking evidence for the prosecution of those convicted of unlawful cohabitation."[6]

MISSING PERSONS

Bogus entries may have been a frustration in some times and places, but a far greater problem in every census year has been that of undercounting. Whether families or individuals were not counted because they lived in remote areas or because they would not tolerate an enumerator's personal questions, millions have been missed since official government census-taking began. The Census Bureau, still searching for a remedy, has acknowledged "that the 1990 census which put the U.S. population at 248.7 million, missed an estimated 5 million people—ranging from 1.7 percent of whites to 5.2 percent of Hispanics" (*Chicago Tribune*, Tuesday, 17 March 1992, sec. 2, page 4). While no stone should remain unturned in the search for an individual in the census, the unfortunate truth is that a significant portion of the population has been missed entirely.

LEGIBILITY

Probably no other factor causes more frustration for a researcher than finding the general area in which an individual or family should be found in the census and then not being able to read the page or pages of interest. Often, worn and torn pages, faded or smeared ink, and the disintegrating paper of the original census are to blame. Most frequently, however, poor microfilming techniques caused unfocused and blurred sections, overexposed and underexposed pages, and words to be obscured because of tightly bound volumes or mending tape.

Microfilming of federal census records took place in the 1940s, when the technology was in its infancy and techniques had not yet been perfected. Because of the poor quality of the original microfilming, some of the 1850, 1860, and 1870 schedules were microfilmed a second time. The versions can be distinguished because the earlier microfilming included two pages to a frame, the newer having only one census page per frame. Unfortunately, the original census schedules for 1900, 1910, and 1920 have been destroyed by acts of Congress, so records that are not legible cannot be re-microfilmed.

The quality of microfilms may vary from one copy to another. Generally, the original microfilm will be better than later generations of the same. Census microfilms have been duplicated a number of times in order to make the records available to as many researchers as possible. In some cases, the National Archives in Washington, D.C., may have the best copy.

HANDWRITING

Poor penmanship, archaic handwriting styles, and symbols are other leading causes of researchers' inability to find or read specific names or information in census records. Many letters can be misinterpreted unless a study is made of the enumerator's handwriting style. For example, uppercase letters *L* and *S* are frequently difficult to distinguish. In one district of the 1850 census, the word "lawyer" looks more like "sawyer." Likewise, a birthplace of Missouri might look more like "Mifouri" or "Mipouri" to someone unfamiliar with the long *s* character that took the place of a double *s* in some manuscripts.

Despite the many imperfections of the census, it should again be emphasized that census records are one of the first sources used in almost every genealogical project. They are invaluable for placing an individual in a particular time and place and for connecting the individual to other sources. The foregoing descriptions make it fairly easy to see why census records are not perfect or entirely reliable. But, as noted author Val Greenwood suggests, "no research on an American genealogical problem after the beginning of census is complete until all pertinent census schedules have been searched."[7]

SUGGESTIONS FOR MICROFILM SEARCHES

Courtesy of Arlene Eakle

Because most censuses must be searched on microfilm, below are some suggestion to save time.

1. Become familiar with the surnames in your area so that you can recognize them with only half of their letters distinct. Study a county history, a tax list, or a landowner's atlas.

2. Create a "pony" from the actual entries in the census. How does the writer make *a, h, s, p, j,* and other letters which could be misinterpreted? Draft an alphabet with uppercase and lowercase letters for comparison. An easy way is to slip a piece of plain paper onto the viewing surface and trace the letters from the page.

3. Use a reader in a darkened room, with a strong light to project the image. Slip a colored piece of paper—pink, yellow, and green are effective—onto the viewing surface.

4. Copy the microfilmed page, enlarging or reducing the image to make it clearer and sharper. Many microfilm copiers have interchangeable lenses.

5. Review the whole schedule so that you don't miss important entries that appear out of place. Record all columns for each entry, even if the information seems unimportant, and *record all members of the household* whether they are familiar or not. In multiple-family dwellings, record all family units living in the building. These families are often related, especially in immigrant settlement areas.

6. Copy the data exactly as it appears in the record. If the given name is abbreviated, copy the abbreviated form. Do not expand it. If the entry is crossed through or changed, copy the entry, the cross-through line, and the changes. Note carefully the last entry on each page. Family units may be split between two pages without a repeat of the surname.

7. Use finding tools and indexes to get into the census quickly, then search the census carefully to get all the data it contains (see the chapter bibliography). If all the data is available, it is possible to block out the pedigree for several generations from this source alone. Then, proof can be sought in other records to insure that names in the pedigree really belong there. If you are researching a common name like Brown or Foster, the censuses can help eliminate those that do not fit, making searches in other sources less time consuming.

INTERPRETING CENSUS INFORMATION

Professional researchers recommend that photocopies be made of census pages whenever possible. The advantages of photocopies over transcriptions are several: the possibility of mistakes being made in the transcription process are eliminated; a photocopy will include neighbors and provide an overview of the population makeup of the area; and a photocopy makes it easy to go back and reevaluate information as new discoveries are made in the research process.

While information in the census may be quite accurate, at times the order in which data has been entered can be misleading. For example, a head of household recorded in 1820, 1830, or 1840 may not be the oldest person in the house. With only age ranges to distinguish, it is impossible to know who may be a grandparent, a younger brother, or a man with both parents still living at home. Individuals listed in early censuses in any age grouping could be servants, visitors, or boarders not related to the family. Even in 1880 and later, the relationships noted apply to heads of household only. Children listed as sons and daughters of the head of household may be unrelated to the wife.

CENSUS RECORDS AND THE ROLE OF THE NATIONAL ARCHIVES

The National Archives has custody of the federally-created census records, including the published 1790 census schedules, negative photostatic copies of the 1800, 1810, 1820, and 1830 census schedules, originals of the 1840, 1850, 1860, and 1870 census schedules, the surviving fragments of the 1890 schedules, and microfilm copies of the 1900, 1910, and 1920 schedules. Due to their fragile condition, some of the original schedules have been retired and are not available to researchers. The original 1880 census schedules went back to the states, and they are no longer in the custody of the National Archives. National Archives and Records Administration, *Guide to Genealogical Research in the National Archives,* rev. ed. (Washington, D.C.: National Archives Trust Fund Board, 1985), provides detailed information on federally-created census records from 1790 to 1910. According to the *Guide,* "Because copies of the census records are now available at the archives field branches, NARA no longer searches schedules in response to mail requests. The National Archives will furnish photocopies of census pages only when the researcher can cite the state, county, enumeration district for 1880, 1900 and 1910, volume number, and exact page on which a family is enumerated."

MICROFILM COPIES

The National Archives has reproduced all of the available federal population census schedules on microfilm. Copies of available 1790 to 1920 censuses for all states and territories can be used in the Microfilm Research Room in the National Archives in Washington, D.C., regional branches of the National Archives, at the Family History Library of The Church of Jesus Christ of Latter-day Saints in Salt Lake City, and at many other private and public libraries. The added options of borrowing census schedules from microfilm lending companies and purchasing microfilm copies from the National Archives make the census one of the most readily available record sources.

LIMITATIONS OF MICROFILM COPIES

As noted earlier, microfilming of the census schedules, indexes, and other heavily-used records in the National Archives took place in the 1940s, when the technology was in its infancy. The microfilms of most of the censuses for most years are quite

legible. However, there are thousands of census pages from various states and years that cannot be read because of poor focusing or because of too much or too little lighting. Pages of original census schedules were inadvertently skipped when microfilming took place—some pages may have stuck together when turned, and some may have been missing when the microfilming began. For example, nine pages were missed during the microfilming of the 1820 Virginia schedule. They were subsequently identified and indexed by Gerald M. Petty in "Virginia 1820 Federal Census: Names Not on the Microfilm Copy," *Virginia Genealogist* 18 (1974): 136–39. In another case, more than 1,000 Illinoisans with names beginning with the letter O were somehow missed when the rest of the 1880 Soundex index was microfilmed. The missing section for the letter O was later transcribed from the original cards by Nancy Gubb Frederick, *1880 Illinois Census Index, Soundex Codes O-200 to O240* (Evanston, Ill.: the compiler, 1981).

Unfortunately, the 1900, 1910, and 1920 census originals were destroyed in 1946 (with the approval of the Archivist of the United States and Congress), so it will be impossible to remicrofilm any illegible pages or pages missed in the original microfilming of schedules for those census years.

RESTRICTIONS ON ACCESS TO POST-1920 CENSUS RECORDS

To protect the privacy of living individuals, access to population schedules is restricted for seventy-two years after the census is taken, so they are not available to researchers during that time. The Personal Service Branch, Bureau of the Census, P.O. Box 1545, Jeffersonville, IN 47131, will provide, for a fee, official transcripts of census records from 1930 to 1990. Access is restricted to whomever the information is about, their authorized representatives, or, in the case of deceased persons, their heirs or administrators. Use Form BC-600 to request information.

FEDERAL POPULATION CENSUS RESEARCH PROCEDURES

1. HOW TO FIND CENSUS RECORDS

All available federal census schedules, from 1790 to 1920, have been microfilmed and are available at the National Archives in Washington, D.C.; at the National Archives' regional archives in twelve states; at the LDS Family History Library and LDS family history centers throughout North America; at many large libraries; and through microfilm lending companies. Some state and local agencies may have census schedules only for the state or area served.

2. STARTING INFORMATION

It is usually best to begin a census search in the most recently available census records (1920) and to work from what is already known about a family. With any luck, birthplaces and other clues found in these more recent records will point to locations of earlier residency.

3. ARRANGEMENT OF CENSUS RECORDS

The census schedules are arranged by census year and thereunder alphabetically by name of state; then, with a few exceptions, alphabetically by name of county. To begin research, a researcher must know in which state the subject of interest lived during the census year, and may need to know the county and an exact address if the name is common.

In early census years or in sparsely populated areas, one roll of microfilm may contain all the schedules for one county or several small counties. However, in heavily populated areas, there may be many rolls for a single county. The arrangement of surnames on a page of the schedule is usually in the order in which the enumerator visited the households. To search for a particular name in the schedules may necessitate scanning every page of a district, however, the increasingly numerous indexes to federal censuses and finding aids have dramatically reduced such tedious work.

4. INDEXES

Federal census indexes have been compiled and published for every state up to and including 1850; many states have been indexed up to and including 1870, and a few have been completed for 1880. Indexes may be in book, microfilm, computer diskette, or CD-ROM form. There are microfilmed indexes or partial indexes for the 1880, 1900, 1910, and 1920 censuses. Archives and libraries that have copies of census microfilm generally have indexes to complement their collections.

5. CATALOGS

Four catalogs produced by the National Archives Trust Fund Board are especially helpful in conducting research in federal census records. Each catalog may be purchased for a small fee from the National Archives Trust Fund, NEPS Dept. 735, P.O. Box 100793, Atlanta, GA 30384. They are:

National Archives Trust Fund Board. *The 1790–1890 Federal Population Censuses: Catalog of National Archives Microfilm.* Washington, D.C.: National Archives Trust Fund Board, 1993. This catalog is arranged chronologically, thereunder by state or territory, and then by county. Given for each microfilm publication is the series number and the total number of microfilm rolls in the enumeration. The catalog further identifies each microfilm roll by number and contents.

_____. *1900 Federal Population Census: A Catalog of Microfilm Copies of the Schedules.* Washington, D.C.: 1978. This catalog lists the 1,854 rolls of microfilm on which the 1900 population census schedules appear. The census schedules are arranged by state or territory and then by county. Numbers for the 7,846 rolls of 1900 Soundex indexes appear in the second half of the book.

_____. *The 1910 Federal Population Census: A Catalog of Microfilm Copies of the Schedules.* Washington, D.C.: 1982. This catalog lists the 1,784 rolls of microfilm on which the 1910 population census schedules appear. The census schedules are arranged by state or territory and then by county. Numbers for the 4,642 rolls of 1910 Soundex/Miracode indexes appear in the second half of the catalog.

_____. *The 1920 Federal Population Census: Catalog of National Archives Microfilm.* Washington, D.C.: 1991. This catalog lists the 8,585 rolls of 1920 Soundex indexes in the front portion of the book. The catalog lists 2,076 rolls of 1920 census schedules arranged by state or territory and then by county.

1790 CENSUS

The 1790 census was begun on 2 August 1790. The marshals were expected to finish the census within nine months of the Census Day—by 1 May 1791. Although most of the returns were in long before the deadline, Congress had to extend the count until 1 March 1792. By that time some people probably were counted who had not been born or present in 1790.

QUESTIONS ASKED IN THE 1790 CENSUS

Name of family head; number of free white males of sixteen years and older; number of free white males under sixteen; number of free white females; number of slaves; number of other persons; and sometimes town or district of residence.

The 1790 census instructed the marshals to identify, by age brackets, free white males sixteen years of age or older and those under sixteen. It was designed to determine the country's industrial and military capabilities. Additionally, the first census was to count the number of free white females; all other free persons regardless of race or gender; and slaves. A twenty-dollar fine, to be split between the marshals' assistants and the government, would be levied against anyone who refused to answer the enumerator's questions.

OTHER SIGNIFICANT FACTS ABOUT THE 1790 CENSUS

The Constitution called for a census of all "Persons . . . excluding Indians not taxed" for the purpose of apportioning seats in the House of Representatives and assessing direct federal taxes. The "Indians not taxed" were those not living in the settled areas. In later years, Native Americans everywhere were considered part of the total population, but not all were included in the apportionment figures until 1940.

The government did not provide printed forms or even paper until 1830. It was up to each assistant to copy his census return on whatever paper he could find and post it in two public places in his assigned area. Those who saw and could read them were supposed to check for discrepancies or omissions. The highest pay rate, two cents per person, barely covered expenses, especially where settlers were scattered and living in places that were difficult to find or access.

The jurisdictions of the thirteen original states stretched over an area of seventeen present-day states. Census schedules survive for only two-thirds of those states. The surviving schedules were indexed by state and published by the Bureau of the Census in the early 1900s. Bureau of the Census, *Heads of Families at the First Census of the United States Taken in the Year 1790,* 12 vols. (Washington, D.C.: Government Printing Office, 1908), can be found in most research libraries; it has been reprinted by various publishers over the years.

Both the original and printed 1790 census schedules are available on microfilm for Connecticut, Maine (then part of Massachusetts), Maryland, Massachusetts, New Hampshire, New York, North Carolina, Pennsylvania, Rhode Island, South Carolina, and Vermont (figure 5-2). The schedules for Delaware, Georgia, Kentucky, New Jersey, Tennessee, and Virginia were burned during the War of 1812 (there are substitutes for most of these). Published and microfilmed 1790 schedules for Virginia were reconstructed from state enumerations and tax lists.

Figure 5-2. From *1790 Federal Census, Albany County, New York* (Baltimore: Genealogical Publishing Co., 1971), 13. All extant 1790 census schedules have been published and reprinted more than once. Copies are readily available in most public and research libraries.

HEADS OF FAMILIES—NEW YORK. 13

ALBANY COUNTY—Continued.

NAME OF HEAD OF FAMILY.	Free white males of 16 years and upward, including heads of families.	Free white males under 16 years.	Free white females, including heads of families.	All other free persons.	Slaves.
ALBANY CITY, FIRST WARD—continued.					
Yates, Peter W	2		8		2
Staats, Henry	3	1	5		2
Radlie, Philip	1		2		2
Hilton, William	1	1	1		
ALBANY CITY, SECOND WARD.					
Cuyler, Jacob	2	3	1		4
Groesbeck, John	2	5	4		1
De Garmo, Bastian	4	1	4		
Rogardus, Jacob	1				
Cavenaugh, William	2	1	3		
Groesbeck, David	2		1		2
Woodruff, Hanlock	2	1	4		2
Hanson, John	2				1
Blucker, Catherine		2	5		3
Beekman, John J	1	1	4		6
Fellows, William	2		1		
Batist, ——*	2			1	
Hagerdy, William	1	2	1		1
Lansing, Jacob	1		1		2
Bradt, Aaron	2	3	1		
Nehemiah, John	1	3	3		
Bradt, John A	1	3	1		
Dunkavy, James	1	1	3		
Barrington, Nicholas	1		3		
Pruyne, Margaret			2		
Muclaroy, Richard	1	1	1		
Devenbagh, Frederick	1	1	3		
Brower, John	1	4	3		
McKenney, John	1	1	5		
Groesbeck, Cornelius	1	1	2		
Van Vrankin, Moses R	1	1	3		1
Willitt, Edward, Junr	2		2		(*)
Kennear, James	1	1	2		(*)
Ruby, Conradt	2	1	5		(*)
Park, Henry	1		2		(*)
Davis, Peter	1	1	3		(*)
Sturges, Isaac	1	1	3		(*)
Milligan, James	1		2		(*)
Giles, William	1		1		(*)
Winne, Jacob	1	4	1		(*)
Finch, Isaac	1	1	2		(*)
Van Ness, John	2	2			(*)
Fadon, John	1	4	2		(*)
Hawk, Christopher	1	2	5		(*)
Bulson, John	1		5		(*)
Shaw, Ezra	1	2	4		(*)
Roberts, John	1	1	1		(*)
Amos, Thomas				2	(*)
Stoop, Catherine		1	4		(*)
Visscher, Sarah	1	1	2		(*)
Van Dusen, Aaron	1	1	4		(*)
Fonda, Isaac D	1		2		(*)
Visscher, Tuenis G	1		3		(*)
Johnston, John	1		1		(*)
Driskile, Jeremiah	1	3	1		(*)
Blecker, Nicholas	1	2	1		(*)
Edgar, Gregg	1		3		(*)
Patrick, James	1		1		(*)
Vanloan, Jacob	1	3	3		(*)
Bleecker, John J	4	2	3	(*)	(*)
Bleeker, Jacob	1			(*)	(*)
Bleeker, Jacob, Junr	1	2	1		4
Cameron, William	1	2	2		
Andrew, John	2	1	1		
Blecker, John R	1		2		3
Lansing, Gerandus	1		1		5
Bleeker, John N	1	3	6		1
Bleeker, Catelintia	1		4		2
Brower, Cornelius	1	1	4		2
Lyn, Aaron	1	1	3		
Barrington, Lewis	2	2	4		
Magee, John	1		3		
Boyd, John	1	4	2		
Hanson, Albert	1	2	2		
Staats, Barent G	1	1	1		2
Van Zant, John W	1	1	2		
McDurmot, Michael	2	1	2		
Rider, Barent	1	1	3		
Carson, John	1	4	3		
Fuller, James	1	5	2		
Meggs, Seth	1	1	2		
Pruyn, John F	1		2		6
Merchant, George	3	2	5	1	
Viss her, Matthew	3		2		2
Ten Eyck, Hendrick	1	1	6		3
Jackeum, Jack	1	1		7	
Metcalf, Simon	2	2	4		1
Fonda, Nicholas	1		2		4
Brown William	1	2	4		

NAME OF HEAD OF FAMILY.	Free white males of 16 years and upward, including heads of families.	Free white males under 16 years.	Free white females, including heads of families.	All other free persons.	Slaves.
ALBANY CITY, SECOND WARD—continued.					
McFarson, Hugh	1	1	1		
Barber, John	3		2		
Watson, Matthew	2	2	2		1
Easterly, Thomas	2	3	4		
Norwood, Mary	1		4		
Fonda, Jacobus	1	1	3		
Bogert, Barent	1	1	5		
Mersales, Gysbert	1		4		2
Cuyler, Philip	1		1		
Hooker, Samuel	3	3	3		
Hanson, John J	1	3	4		
Switz, Cornelius	2	1	3		
Van Schaaick, Cornelius	1	1	1		
Mersailes, John	1		3		
Pruyn, Casparus	3	1	2	1	3
Tiffany, Silvester	3	2	2		1
Whipple, Benjamin	4		5		
Cuyler, Abraham	2		5		5
Ten Eyck, Harmanus	1	2	4		2
Vn Rensselaer, Jeremiah	1		2		3
Vn Schurlyne, Cornelius	2		3		12
Bogert, Abraham	1		1		1
Douglass, Thomas	1	3	4		
Ryan, Patrick	2		2		
McGurgy, Edward	1		2		
Dale, William	1	2	2		
Cammeron, John	1	1	1		
Campbell, John	1	1	2		
Haynes, Thomas	1		1		(*)
McDonald, Donald	1		1		(*)
Bruce, Robert	1		1		(*)
Archer, George	1	1	2		(*)
Andrews, Joseph	1	1	2		(*)
Hannah, Samuel	1		3		(*)
Smith, James	2	1	1		(*)
McGourk, James	1		2		(*)
McGourk, Robert	1	1	2		(*)
Welch, Joseph	1		1		(*)
Ackerson, James	1		3		(*)
Mersielus, John G	2		5		1
Watson, Alexander	1		1		(*)
Crom, John			1	3	
Burgess, John	1		3		(*)
Mulhance, Peter	1		4		(*)
Ellison, Abraham	1		4		(*)
Lawson, Henry	1	1	1		(*)
Stevenson, Mary			2		(*)
Legrange, Jacobus	1		3		(*)
Cheseham, George	1		3		(*)
McCloud, Donald	1	1	4		(*)
Forsight, Alexander	1	3	2		(*)
Barkley, James	1	1	2		(*)
McMurray, Thomas	1	1	3		(*)
Hendrick, Jacob	1		1		(*)
Ostrander, John	3	1	2	(*)	(*)
Myer, Carol	1		2		
Waggoner, Andrew	1	1	2		
Wilmot, John	1	1	5		
McManac, William	1	1	3		
Keating, Garret	2	1	1		
Snyder, Daniel	1		2		
Heath, John	1	3	1		
Staals, Henry	2		1		
Carson, Alexander	1		2		
Bromley, Samuel	1		2		
Horse, George	1		1		
Hay, Alexander	1		3		
McMickle, John	3	2	4		
Christie, John	1		1		
Whitney, William	1	2	2		
McKown, William	2	4	2		1
Bradt, Daniel	1	2	3		
Truax, John J	1	3	5		
Kagle, Cornelius	1	1	3		
James, John		1		3	
Winne, Killian D	2	1	2		
ALBANY CITY, THIRD WARD.					
Lansing, Abraham A	1	1	4		6
Blair, James	1	1	5		
Sharp, Conradt	1	3	3		
Van Iveren, Rynier	1		2		
Van Duser, Peter	1	2	2		
Young, Peter	1	1	3		
Truax, Isaac	1	1	1		2
Van Arnam, Isaac	1		3		2
Lansing, John, Junr	1	1	4		4
Lansing, Sanders	1		1		2
Walsh, Dudley	1	1			
Ten Broeck, Dirick	1	1	3		6

NAME OF HEAD OF FAMILY.	Free white males of 16 years and upward, including heads of families.	Free white males under 16 years.	Free white females, including heads of families.	All other free persons.	Slaves.
ALBANY CITY, THIRD WARD—continued.					
Stringer, Samuel	2	1	2		2
Lush, Stephen	1	3	3		2
Wendell, *—— H	1	1	3		2
Douw, Volkert A	1		3		4
Lansing, John Jacob	1	1	1		3
Evertson, Bernardus	2	5	4		
lansing, Garrit	1		1		1
lush, Richard	1	1	4		
Graham, John	2		2		
Defrust, Isaac	2	3	3		4
Veeder, Abraham	2	2	1		
Vn Vechten, Teunis T	2	3	3		2
Dexter, Samuel	2		1		
Douw, Peter W	2		1		3
Beekman, Elizabeth	1		2		5
Glen, Cornelius	1		1		6
Caldwell, James	5	3	6		1
Maley, John	2		3		5
Willett, Elbert	2		8		1
Sim, Peter	2	2	2		(*)
Orr, Isabel	1		2		(*)
Waters, David	1				(*)
Hale, Daniel	4	1	3		2
Bloodgood, James	6		2		5
Bower, Barent	1		1		(*)
Roseboom, Eve			3		3
Fonda, David	1	3	5		2
Groesbeck, Garrit	1		2		(*)
Cuyler, John	2				(*)
Kirk, John	1	1	3		(*)
Boyd, John	3	2	1		2
Hunn, Thomas	2		2		
Gansevoort, Harman	1	1	1		7
Gansevoort, Leonard, Junr	1	1	6		(*)
Bleeker, Barent	1		1		(*)
McMillen, John	1	1	1		(*)
Evertson, Henry	2	1	2		(*)
Yates, Abraham, Junr	2	5	5		(*)
Westerlo, Ellardus	1	1	3		(*)
Gansevoort, Peter	3	1	4		(*)
Ten Broek, John	3	2	4	(*)	(*)
Truax, Henry	1	1	2	(*)	(*)
Glen, Henry	3	1	3		7
Schuyler, Abraham	2		3		9
Cuyler, Jacob, Junr	2	1	1		2
Wallace, Benjamin	3		2		
Vesscher, Nanning H	1		4		
Bisbrown, Thomas	1		1		1
Lansing, Jeremiah	1	2	2		2
Beauman, Charles	1		2		
Visscher, Teunis	1		2		6
Vandebergh, William	2		2		
Van Husen, Cathelina			3		3
Chesney, James	1		4		
Wendell, Barbara			3		5
Bradford, Thomas	1		1		
McGibbon, Peter	1	1	6		
Tolbert, William	1	3	3		
Richards, Ezra	1	1	2		
Vander Zee, Walter	1	5	2		
Killburn, York				3	
Ram, John	1		4		
McHargh, John	1		2		1
Van Iveren, Rynier	2		3		5
Ten Broeck, Abraham	1		3		12
Vander Heyden, Jacob	1	2	4		3
Hunn, William	2	2	5		1
Williamson, Timothy	1		1		
Dunbar, William	1	3	3		
Visscher, Garrit T	4		1		1
Icebrass, Hannah		1	2		
McReady, William	1	3	7		
Miller, Philip, Junr	1	1	4		1
Van Vronkin, Garrit	1		1		
Gates, John	1	2	3		
Vanderburg, Garrit	1		1		1
Graverato, Henry	2		2		1
Slingerland, Jacob	1		2		
Graham, Theodorus Van Wyck	2	1	3		4
Roff, John	1	1	1		
Bradt, Henry	1		1		
Douw, Catherine		1	3		2
Leonard, Enock	1	1	2		2
Wynkoop, Jacobus	2		3		2
Sharp, Peter	2	2	2		
de frust, Philip	1	1	2		
de frust, Philip, Junr	1		3		
Verplank, William	2		1		2
Winne, Jellis	1	2	3		1
Lansing, Philip	1	2	8		5

Illegible.

RESEARCH TIPS FOR THE 1790 CENSUS

Because of the availability of the printed 1790 census schedules, researchers tend to overlook the importance of consulting the original schedules, which are readily available on microfilm. As in most cases, the researcher who relies on printed transcripts may miss important information and clues found only in the original version.

The 1790 census records are useful for identifying the locality to be searched for other types of records for a named individual. The 1790 census will, in most cases, help distinguish the target family from others of the same name; identify immediate neighbors who may be related; identify slaveholders; and spot spelling variations of surnames. Free men "of color" are listed as heads of household by name. Slaves appear in age groupings by name of owner. By combining those age groupings with probate inventories and tax list data, it is sometimes possible to determine names of other family members and the birth order of those individuals.

For a state-by-state listing of census schedules, see *The 1790–1890 Federal Population Censuses: Catalog of National Archives Microfilm* (Washington, D.C.: National Archives Trust Fund Board, 1993). For boundary changes and identification of missing census schedules, see William Thorndale and William Dollarhide, *Map Guide to the U.S. Federal Censuses, 1790–1920* (Baltimore: Genealogical Publishing Co., 1987).

1800 CENSUS

The 1800 census was begun on 4 August 1800. The count was to be completed within nine months.

QUESTIONS ASKED IN THE 1800 CENSUS

Name of family head; number of free white males and females in age categories: 0 to 10, 10 to 16, 16 to 20, 16 to 26, 26 to 45, 45 and older; number of other free persons except Indians not taxed; number of slaves; and town or district and county of residence.

OTHER SIGNIFICANT FACTS ABOUT THE 1800 CENSUS

Most 1800 census entries are arranged in the order of visitation, but some have been rearranged to appear in alphabetical order by initial letter of the surname.

RESEARCH TIPS FOR THE 1800 CENSUS

The 1800 census records are useful in identifying the locality to be searched for other types of records for a named individual. The 1800 census will, in most cases, help distinguish the target family from others of the same name; help to determine family size; locate possible relatives with the same name; identify immediate neighbors who may be related; identify slaveholders; and spot spelling variations of surnames. Free men "of color" are listed as heads of household by name. Slaves appear in age groupings by name of owner. By combining those age groupings with probate inventories and tax list data, it is sometimes possible to determine names of other family members and the birth order of those individuals.

For a state-by-state listing of census schedules, see *The 1790–1890 Federal Population Censuses: Catalog of National Archives Microfilm (Washington, D.C.: National Archives Trust Fund Board, 1993)* (cited earlier). For boundary changes and

identification of missing census schedules, see William Thorndale and William Dollarhide, *Map Guide to the U.S. Federal Censuses, 1790–1920* (cited earlier).

1810 CENSUS

The 1810 census was begun on 6 August 1810. The count was due within nine months, but the due date was extended by law to ten months.

QUESTIONS ASKED IN THE 1810 CENSUS

Name of family head; number of free white males and females in age categories: 0 to 10, 10 to 16, 16 to 20, 20 to 26, 26 to 45, 45 and older; number of other free persons except Indians not taxed; number of slaves; and town or district and county of residence.

RESEARCH TIPS FOR THE 1810 CENSUS

The 1810 census records are useful in identifying the locality to be searched for other types of records for a named individual. The 1810 census will, in most cases, help distinguish the target family from others of the same name; help to determine family size; locate possible relatives with the same name; identify immediate neighbors who may be related; identify slaveholders; and spot spelling variations of surnames. Free men "of color" are named as heads of household. Slaves appear in age groupings by name of owner. By combining those age groupings with probate inventories and tax list data, it is sometimes possible to determine names of other family members and the birth order of those individuals. Manufacturing schedules are scattered among the 1810 population schedules.

For a state-by-state listing of census schedules, see *The 1790–1890 Federal Population Censuses: Catalog of National Archives Microfilm* (Washington, D.C.: National Archives Trust Fund Board, 1993). For boundary changes and identification of missing census schedules, see William Thorndale and William Dollarhide, *Map Guide to the U.S. Federal Censuses, 1790–1920* (Baltimore: Genealogical Publishing Co., 1987).

1820 CENSUS

The 1820 census was begun on 7 August 1820. The count was due within six months but was extended by law to allow completion within thirteen months.

QUESTIONS ASKED IN THE 1820 CENSUS

Name of family head; number of free white males and females in age categories 0 to 10, 10 to 16, 16 to 20, 20 to 26, 26 to 45, 45 and older; number of other free persons except Indians not taxed; number of slaves; and town or district and county of residence. Additionally, the 1820 census for the first time asked the number of free white males 16 to 18; number of persons not naturalized; number engaged in agriculture, commercial, or manufacture; number of "colored" persons (sometimes in age categories); and number of other persons except Indians.

RESEARCH TIPS FOR THE 1820 CENSUS

The 1820 census records are useful in identifying the locality to be searched for other types of records for a named individual. The 1820 census will, in most cases, help distinguish the target family from others of the same name; help to determine family size; locate possible relatives with the same name; identify immediate neighbors who may be related; identify slaveholders; and spot spelling variations of surnames. Free men "of color" are listed as heads of household by name. Slaves appear in age groupings by name of owner. By combining those age groupings with probate inventories and tax list date, it is sometimes possible to determine names of other family members and the birth order of those individuals.

The added questions in the 1820 census break down ages so that it is possible to gauge the age of young men more accurately. However, the redundancy of asking the number of free white males "Between 16 and 18," and "Of 16 and under 26," "Of 26 and under 45," "Of 45 and upwards," is frequently cause for confusion in attempts to calculate the total number of persons in a given household. The column regarding naturalization status may be some indication of length of residency in the United States and the possibility of finding naturalization papers in a local court.

The questions asked regarding number and nature of those involved in agriculture, commercial, or manufacturing enterprises allow researchers to make some distinctions about the occupation of the head and any others in the household who were employed. Some, though admittedly not much, identifying information is available where schedules go beyond stating the number of "colored" persons and provide an age breakdown as well. The 1820 manufacturing schedules are on twenty-nine separate rolls of microfilm.

For a state-by-state listing of census schedules, see *The 1790–1890 Federal Population Censuses: Catalog of National Archives Microfilm* (Washington, D.C.: National Archives Trust Fund Board, 1993). For boundary changes and identification of missing census schedules, see William Thorndale and William Dollarhide, *Map Guide to the U.S. Federal Censuses, 1790–1920* (Baltimore: Genealogical Publishing Co., 1987).

1830 CENSUS

The 1830 census was begun on 1 June 1830. The enumeration was to be completed within six months but was extended to allow completion within twelve months.

QUESTIONS ASKED IN THE 1830 CENSUS

Name of head of household; number of free white males and females in age categories 0 to 5, 5 to 10, 10 to 15, 15 to 20, 20 to 30, 30 to 40, 40 to 50, 50 to 60, 60 to 70, 70 to 80, 80 to 90, 90 to 100, over 100; number of slaves and free "colored" persons in age categories; categories for deaf, dumb, and blind persons and aliens; town or district; and county of residence.

OTHER SIGNIFICANT FACTS ABOUT THE 1830 CENSUS

The 1830 census was the first for which the government provided uniform, printed forms to enumerators for the purpose of recording answers to census questions.

RESEARCH TIPS FOR THE 1830 CENSUS

The 1830 census records are useful in identifying the locality to be searched for other types of records for a named individual. The 1830 census will, in most cases, help distinguish the target

family from others of the same name; help to determine family size; locate possible relatives with the same name; identify immediate neighbors who may be related; identify slaveholders; and spot spelling variations of surnames. Free men "of color" are listed as heads of household by name. Slaves appear in age groupings by name of owner. By combining those age groupings with probate inventories and tax list data, it is sometimes possible to determine names of other family members and the birth order of those individuals.

The 1830 census went a step further in breaking down ages, thus allowing more precise knowledge of the household configuration. With the age categories expanded to include those one hundred years and older, it is possible to have a better idea of life spans during that time period. The addition of information regarding those who were deaf, dumb, and blind is an indication that there may be related guardianship or institutional records. The presence of aliens in a household suggests the possibility that those individuals may eventually have been naturalized in a nearby court.

For a state-by-state listing of census schedules, see *The 1790–1890 Federal Population Censuses: Catalog of National Archives Microfilm* (Washington, D.C.: National Archives Trust Fund Board, 1993). For boundary changes and identification of missing census schedules, see William Thorndale and William Dollarhide, *Map Guide to the U.S. Federal Censuses, 1790–1920* (Baltimore: Genealogical Publishing Co., 1987).

1840 CENSUS

The 1840 census was begun on 1 June 1840. The enumeration was to be completed within nine months but was extended to eighteen months.

QUESTIONS ASKED IN THE 1840 CENSUS

Name of head of household; number of free white males and females in age categories 0 to 5, 5 to 10, 10 to 15, 15 to 20, 20 to 30, 30 to 40, 40 to 50, 50 to 60, 60 to 70, 70 to 80, 80 to 90, 90 to 100, over 100; number of slaves and free "colored" persons in age categories; categories for deaf, dumb, and blind persons and aliens; town or district; and county of residence.

Additionally, the 1840 census, asked for the first time, the ages of revolutionary war pensioners and the number of individuals engaged in mining, agriculture, commerce, manufacturing and trade, navigation of the ocean, navigation of canals, lakes and rivers, learned professions and engineers; number in school, number in family over age twenty-one who could not read and write, and the number of insane.

RESEARCH TIPS FOR THE 1840 CENSUS

The same research strategies used in the previous census apply to the 1840. A significant bonus comes from the question regarding revolutionary war pensioners. A search of revolutionary war sources (see chapter 9, Research in Military Records) may provide a wealth of genealogical information. A refinement of the occupation categories makes it possible to pursue other occupational sources and easier to distinguish individuals of the same name in the ever-growing population. Reading and writing skills and some indication of the educational level attained add an interesting and more personal dimension to a family history. An indication of the "insane" within a household might point to guardianship or institutional records.

For a state-by-state listing of census schedules, see *The 1790–1890 Federal Population Censuses: Catalog of National Archives Microfilm* (Washington, D.C.: National Archives Trust Fund Board, 1993). For boundary changes and identification of missing census schedules, see William Thorndale and William Dollarhide, *Map Guide to the U.S. Federal Censuses, 1790–1920* (Baltimore: Genealogical Publishing Co., 1987).

1850 CENSUS

The 1850 census was begun on 1 June 1850. The enumeration was to be completed within five months.

QUESTIONS ASKED IN THE 1850 CENSUS

Name; age; sex; color; territory or country of birth; whether the person attended school or was married within the year; whether the person could read or write if over age twenty; whether the person was deaf-mute, blind, insane, or "idiotic"; and whether or not a fugitive from the state. The census also asked the occupation of males over age fifteen.

Separate slave schedules for 1850 asked the name of each slave-owner, the number of slaves owned, and the number of slaves manumitted (released from slavery). While the schedules, unfortunately, do not name individual slaves, they asked the age, color, sex, and whether or not slaves were deaf-mute, blind, insane, or idiotic; and whether or not a fugitive from the state.

OTHER SIGNIFICANT FACTS ABOUT THE 1850 CENSUS

The 1850 census is frequently referred to as the first modern census because of dramatically improved techniques employed for it and repeated in later years. Printed instructions to the enumerators account for a greater degree of accuracy compared with earlier censuses. The instructions explained the responsibilities of enumerators, census procedures, the manner of completing the schedules, and the intent behind census questions. "In the 1850 census and thereafter, enumerators were required by law to make their count by personal inquiry at every dwelling and with every family, and not otherwise."[8] As enumerations of districts were completed, the enumerator was instructed to make two additional copies: one to be filed with the clerk of the county court, one to be sent to the secretary of the state or territory, and one of the three to be sent to the Census Office for tabulation.

The census was to show the names of persons who died after 1 June of the census year and to omit children born after that date. It should be noted that many of the census takers did not get around to their assigned districts until late in 1850; some were as late as October and November.

The enumeration was to list every person in the United States except Indians living on government reservations or living on unsettled tracts of land. Indians not in tribal relations, whether of mixed blood or not, who were not living among the white population or on the outskirts of towns, were counted as part of the taxable population. The count was designed to determine the apportioning of representatives among the states.

RESEARCH TIPS FOR THE 1850 CENSUS

The 1850 Schedules included the free population and slave population and mortality, agriculture, and industry data. The inclusion of so much personal data for the first time in the 1850 census is an obvious boon to genealogists and social historians. For the first time it is possible to identify families and other groups by name. The inclusion of birthplaces for every individual allow for the plotting of migrational routes.

Ages provided in the 1850 census allow researchers to establish dates for searching vital records. While few states officially recorded vital records that early, religious and other records may be pursued with estimated dates of birth gleaned from the census.

The identification of previous residences points to still other record sources to be searched in named localities. The indication of real estate ownership would suggest that land and tax records should be searched. The 1850 census may provide starting information for searching marriage records, probates, and a number of other genealogically important records. Probable family relationships may also be determined through 1850 census records, though it is easy to come to the wrong conclusions. The 1850 census provides valuable insights into occupations and property value. It may also make it possible to spot remarriages and step-relationships and to determine approximate life spans.

For a state-by-state listing of census schedules, see *The 1790–1890 Federal Population Censuses: Catalog of National Archives Microfilm (Washington, D.C.: National Archives Trust Fund Board, 1993).* For boundary changes and identification of missing census schedules, see William Thorndale and William Dollarhide. *Map Guide to the U.S. Federal Censuses, 1790–1920.*

1860 CENSUS

The 1860 census was begun on 1 June 1860. The enumeration was to be completed within five months.

QUESTIONS ASKED IN THE 1860 CENSUS

For all free persons, the census asked: name; age; sex; color; occupation of persons over age fifteen; value of real estate; value of personal estate; name of state, territory, or country of birth; whether the person was married during the year; and whether the person was deaf-mute, blind, insane, an "idiot," a pauper, or a convict.

The information in the slave schedules is the same as those for 1850.

OTHER SIGNIFICANT FACTS ABOUT THE 1860 CENSUS

The 1860 census was the first to ask those being queried to reveal the value of their personal estates. As enumerations of districts were completed, enumerators were instructed to make two copies: one to be filed with the clerk of the county court, one to be sent to the secretary of the state or territory, and the third to be sent to the Census Office for tabulation.

The birthplaces of individuals were to be specific as to the state or territory in the United States and the country of birth if foreign born. For example, designations of England, Scotland, Ireland, and Wales and the German states of Prussia, Baden, Bavaria, Württemberg, and Hesse-Darmstadt were preferred to Great Britain and Germany.

RESEARCH TIPS FOR THE 1860 CENSUS

Research strategies remain the same as those suggested for the 1850 census because information included in the 1850 and 1860 schedules is essentially the same, except for the addition of a question concerning personal estates. While the added column may be a general indicator of a person's assets, it is doubtful that individuals were likely to disclose true figures for fear of being taxed accordingly.

For a state-by-state listing of census schedules, see *The 1790–1890 Federal Population Censuses: Catalog of National Archives Microfilm* (Washington, D.C.: National Archives Trust Fund Board, 1993). For boundary changes and identification of missing census schedules, see William Thorndale and William Dollarhide, *Map Guide to the U.S. Federal Censuses, 1790–1920* (Baltimore: Genealogical Publishing Co., 1987).

1870 CENSUS

The 1870 census was begun on 1 June 1870. The enumeration was to be completed within five months.

QUESTIONS ASKED IN THE 1870 CENSUS

The 1870 census form called for dwelling houses to be numbered in the order of visitation; families numbered in order of visitation; and the name of every person whose place of abode on the first day of June 1870 was with the family. The census further asked the age of each individual at the last birthday. If a child was under one year of age, months of age were to be stated in fractions, such as 1/12. Additionally, the census asked the sex, color, profession, and occupation or trade of every male and female. There were also columns for disclosure of value of real estate and personal property. The 1870 census asked for the place of birth, specifically in which state or territory of the United States, or in which country if foreign born (including the province if born in Germany). The schedule provided space to indicate whether or not the father and the mother of the individual was foreign born, and if an individual was born or married within the year, the month in which the event occurred was to be entered. The census also asked for those who had attended school within the year; those who could not read; those who could not write; and the deaf and dumb, blind, insane and the "idiotic" to be identified. Finally, the schedules had space to identify any male citizen of the United States of age twenty-one and older, and any male citizen of the United States age twenty-one and older whose right to vote was denied or abridged on grounds other than rebellion or other crime. (Also see "Non-Population Schedules and Special Federal Censuses," below.)

OTHER SIGNIFICANT FACTS ABOUT THE 1870 CENSUS

The 1870 census may identify survivors of the Civil War, thus suggesting that military records may be found. Conversely, if an individual does not appear in the 1870 census as expected, it may be a clue that the person was a casualty of the war. In the absence of so many other records from the South for this era, information from the 1870 census can be especially important. A caveat, however, is found in *Map Guide to the U.S. Federal Censuses 1790–1920,* in which it is stated that "The 1870 census in the Southern States omits a great many persons."

RESEARCH TIPS FOR THE 1870 CENSUS

The 1870 census is the first census in which parents of foreign birth are indicated—a real boon in identifying immigrant ancestors. Immigrants who were naturalized and eligible to vote are identified, suggesting follow-up in court and naturalization sources. Indications of a person's color that were intended to be more precise—white (W), black (B), Chinese (C), Indian (I), mulatto (M)—may be helpful in determining individuals' origins. (Also see "Non-Population Schedules and Special Federal Censuses," below.)

For a state-by-state listing of census schedules, see *The 1790–1890 Federal Population Censuses: Catalog of National Archives Microfilm* (Washington, D.C.: National Archives Trust Fund Board, 1993). For boundary changes and identification of missing census schedules, see William Thorndale and William Dollarhide, *Map Guide to the U.S. Federal Censuses, 1790–1920* (Baltimore: Genealogical Publishing Co., 1987).

1880 CENSUS

The 1880 census was begun on 1 June 1880. The enumeration was to be completed within thirty days, or two weeks for communities with populations of 10,000 or more.

QUESTIONS ASKED IN THE 1880 CENSUS

For each person in every household, the census asked name; whether white, black, mulatto, Indian, or Chinese; sex; age; month of birth if born within the year; relationship to the head of the household; whether single, married, widowed, or divorced; whether married within the year; occupation and months unemployed; name of state, territory, or country of birth; parents' birthplaces; school attendance within the year; whether unable to read if age ten or older; and whether sick or temporarily disabled on the day of enumeration and the reason therefor. Those who were blind, deaf-mute, "idiotic," insane, or permanently disabled were also indicated as such.

OTHER SIGNIFICANT FACTS ABOUT THE 1880 CENSUS

In addition to identifying the state, county, and other subdivisions, the 1880 census was the first to provide the name of the street and house number for urban households. The 1880 census was also the first to identify relationship to the head of household; illness or disability at the time the census was taken; marital status; number of months unemployed during the year; and the state or country of birth of every individual's father and mother. Individuals who were born or died after 1 June 1880 were not to be included in the 1880 census, even though the enumerator may not have questioned them until well after that date. Indians not taxed are not in regular population schedules. Some may appear in special Indian schedules. (Also see "Non-Population Schedules and Special Federal Censuses," below.)

RESEARCH TIPS FOR THE 1880 CENSUS

The 1880 census makes it possible to identify the state or country of birth for parents—especially important for tracing movements of immigrant ancestors. The census may be used to supplement birth or marriage records for the census year or even to partially replace them where vital records are not recorded elsewhere. The census may also be useful in discovering previously unknown surnames of married daughters, mothers-in-law, cousins, and other relatives living with the family. This is the first census to state relationship to the head of household, but the wife may not be the mother of the children. The

1880 census may also provide clues to genetic symptoms and diseases in earlier generations of a family.

For a state-by-state listing of census schedules, see *The 1790–1890 Federal Population Censuses: Catalog of National Archives Microfilm* (Washington, D.C.: National Archives Trust Fund Board, 1993). For boundary changes and identification of missing census schedules, see William Thorndale and William Dollarhide, *Map Guide to the U.S. Federal Censuses, 1790–1920* (Baltimore: Genealogical Publishing Co., 1987). Also available are 1885 territorial censuses for Colorado, Florida, Nebraska, Dakota Territory, and New Mexico.

1890 CENSUS

The 1890 census was begun on 1 June 1890. The enumeration was to be completed within thirty days, or two weeks for communities with populations of more than 10,000.

QUESTIONS ASKED IN THE 1890 CENSUS

The surviving 1890 schedules provide the address, number of families in the house, number of persons in the house, and number of persons in the family. Individuals are listed by name; whether a soldier, sailor, or marine during the Civil War; and whether Union or Confederate or whether the widow of a veteran; relationship to head of family; whether white, black, mulatto, quadroon, octoroon, Chinese, Japanese, or Indian; sex; age; marital status; whether married during the year; if a mother, number of children and number living; place of birth of the individual and his or her father and mother; if foreign born, how many years in the United States;, whether naturalized or in the process of naturalization; profession, trade, or occupation; months unemployed during census year; ability to read and write; ability to speak English; if not, language or dialect spoken; whether suffering from acute or chronic disease (if so, name of disease and length of time afflicted); whether defective in mind, sight, hearing, or speech; or whether crippled, maimed, or deformed (with name of defect); whether a prisoner, convict, homeless child, or pauper; whether the home is rented or owned by the head or a member of the family (if so, whether mortgaged); if the head of family was a farmer, if he or a family member rented or owned the farm; and, if mortgaged, the post office address of the owner.

OTHER SIGNIFICANT FACTS ABOUT THE 1890 CENSUS

Most of the original 1890 population schedules were destroyed or badly damaged by a fire in the Commerce Department in 1921. Records enumerating only 6,160 individuals—less than one percent of the schedules—survived. Unfortunately, no complete schedules for a state, county, or community survived, but only the following fragments:

1. Alabama: Perry County (Perryville Beat No. 11 and Severe Beat No. 8).

2. District of Columbia: Q. Thirteenth, Fourteenth, R.Q. Corcoran, fifteenth, S.R. and Riggs streets, Johnson Avenue, and S Street.

3. Georgia: Muscogee County (Columbus).

4. Illinois: McDonough County, Mound Township.

5. Minnesota: Wright County, Rockford.

6. New Jersey: Hudson County, Jersey City

7. New York: Westchester County, Eastchester, Suffolk County, Brookhaven Township.

8. North Carolina: Gaston County, South Point Township and River Bend Township; Cleveland County, Township No. 2.

9. Ohio: Hamilton County (Cincinnati) and Clinton County, Wayne Township.

10. South Dakota: Union County, Jefferson Township.

11. Texas: Ellis County, J.P. no. 6, Mountain Peak, and Ovila Precinct; Hood County, Precinct no. 5; Rusk County, Precinct no. 6 and J.P. no. 7; Trinity County, Trinity Town, and Precinct no. 2; Kaufman County, Kaufman.

See the following indexes to these schedules:

Index to the Eleventh Census of the United States. National Archives microfilm M496.

Nelson, Ken. *1890 Census Index Register.* Salt Lake City: Genealogical Society of Utah, 1984.

Swenson, Helen Smothers. *Index to 1890 Census of the United States.* Round Rock, Tex.: the author, 1981.

RESEARCH TIPS FOR THE 1890 CENSUS

Because it is well known that the 1890 census records were destroyed by fire, few researchers think to check the index to the remaining schedules. (See "Federal Population Census Indexes and Finding Aids," below.)

Special 1890 schedules enumerating Union veterans and widows of Union veterans of the Civil War are sometimes useful as a substitute for the missing 1890 population schedules. (Also see "Non-Population Schedules and Special Federal Censuses," below.)

For a state-by-state listing of census schedules, see *The 1790–1890 Federal Population Censuses: Catalog of National Archives Microfilm* (Washington, D.C.: National Archives Trust Fund Board, 1993). For boundary changes and identification of missing census schedules, see William Thorndale and William Dollarhide, *Map Guide to the U.S. Federal Censuses, 1790–1920* (Baltimore: Genealogical Publishing Co., 1987).

1900 CENSUS

The 1900 census was begun on 1 June 1900. The enumeration was to be completed within thirty days, or two weeks for communities with populations of more than 10,000.

QUESTIONS ASKED IN THE 1900 CENSUS

The 1900 population schedules provide the name of each person in the household; address; relationship to the head of the household; color or race; sex; month and year of birth; age at last birthday; marital status; the number of years married; the total number of children born of the mother; the number of those children living; places of birth of each individual and the parents of each individual; if the individual was foreign born, the year of immigration and the number of years in the United States; the citizenship status of foreign-born individuals over age twenty-one; occupation; whether the person could read, write, and speak English; whether the home was owned or rented; whether the home was on a farm; and whether the home was mortgaged.

OTHER SIGNIFICANT FACTS ABOUT THE 1900 CENSUS

The 1900 census is the only available census that provides columns for including the exact month and year of birth of every person enumerated. Previous censuses, and even the 1910 and 1920 censuses, include only the ages. The 1900 census is also the only census to include space to record the number of years couples were married, the number of children born to the mother, and how many were still living. This census was also the first to indicate how long an immigrant had been in the country and whether naturalized; whether a home or farm was owned or rented and whether the owned property was free of mortgage; and whether the person was a Civil War veteran or the widow of one.

RESEARCH TIPS FOR THE 1900 CENSUS

Because the Soundex index to the 1900 census is regarded as one of the most inclusive and accurate of the federally-created indexes, it is recommended as a good starting point for beginning researchers. Most beginning researchers have or are able to find some knowledge of family names and residences that will serve as a starting point for searching the 1900 Soundex index. (See "Federal Population Census Indexes and Finding Aids," below.) The 1900 census is an excellent tool for determining dates and places to search for marriage records, birth records of children, deaths of children, and the marriages of children not listed. It is also a means of verifying family traditions, identifying unknown family members, and linking what is known to other sources, such as earlier censuses, naturalization records (especially declarations of intent to become citizens), school attendance rolls, property holdings, and employment and occupational records. These records can help to verify Civil War service, trace and document ethnic origins, and identify overseas and shipboard military service.

Note that some Indian schedules are kept at the end of the schedules for the state instead of the county.

For additional information on the 1900 census, see *National Archives, 1900 Federal Population Census: A Catalog of Microfilm Copies of the Schedules* (Washington, D.C.: 1978). For boundary changes and identification of missing census schedules, see William Thorndale and William Dollarhide, *Map Guide to the U.S. Federal Censuses, 1790–1920* (Baltimore: Genealogical Publishing Co., 1987).

1910 CENSUS

The 1910 census was begun on 15 April 1910. The enumeration was to be completed within thirty days, or two weeks for communities with populations of more than 5,000.

QUESTIONS ASKED IN THE 1910 CENSUS

The 1910 census schedules record each person's name and relationship to the head of household; sex; color or race; age at last birthday; marital status; length of present marriage; if a mother, number of children and number of living children; birthplace and parents' birthplaces; if foreign born, year of immigration and citizenship status; language spoken; occupation; type of industry employed in; whether employer, employee, or self-employed; number of weeks unemployed in 1909 if applicable; ability to read and write; if attended daytime school since 1 September 1909; if home was rented or owned; if owned, whether free or mortgaged; if home was a house or a farm; if a veteran of the Union or Confederate army or navy; if blind in

both eyes, and if deaf and dumb. The Indian schedule also recorded the tribe and/or band.

RESEARCH TIPS FOR THE 1910 CENSUS

The quality of the microfilming of the 1910 census seems especially poor when compared to other census schedules. Overexposure in microfilming schedules for Mississippi, for example, rendered hundreds of pages illegible. Additionally, the omission rate in the 1910 Miracode/Soundex appears to be greater than in most other indexes. In many cases, individuals not indexed are indeed present in the census schedules, so it is especially advisable for researchers to continue a search in the actual schedules even though a name fails to show up in an index.

The 1910 census, while not providing as much precise information as the 1900 census (such as exact birth month, years married, and number of children born to the mother), is still a good tool for determining approximate dates and places to search for marriage records, birth and death records of children, and the marriages of children not listed. The 1910 census sometimes makes it possible to verify family traditions, identify unknown family members, and link what is known to other sources, such as earlier censuses, naturalization records (especially declarations of intent to become citizens), school attendance rolls, property holdings, and employment and occupational records. These records will also verify Civil War service, trace and document ethnic origins, and locate military and naval personnel in hospitals, ships, and stations and those stationed in the Philippines.

For additional information on the 1910 census, see National Archives, *The 1910 Federal Population Census: A Catalog of Microfilm Copies of the Schedules* (Washington, D.C.: 1982). For boundary changes and identification of missing census schedules, see William Thorndale and William Dollarhide, *Map Guide to the U.S. Federal Censuses, 1790–1920* (Baltimore: Genealogical Publishing Co., 1987).

1920 CENSUS

The 1920 census was begun on 1 January 1920. The enumeration was to be completed within thirty days, or two weeks for communities with populations of more than 2,500.

QUESTIONS ASKED IN THE 1920 CENSUS

Name of street, avenue road, etc.; house number or farm; number of dwelling in order of visitation; number of family in order of visitation; name of each person whose place of abode was with the family; relationship of person enumerated to the head of the family; whether home owned or rented; if owned, whether free or mortgaged; sex; color or race; age at last birthday; whether single, married, widowed, or divorced; year of immigration to United States; whether naturalized or alien; if naturalized, year of naturalization; whether attended school any time since 1 September 1919; whether able to read; whether able to write; person's place of birth; mother tongue; father's place of birth; father's mother tongue; mother's place of birth; mother's mother tongue; whether able to speak English; trade, profession, or particular kind of work done; industry, business, or establishment in which at work; whether employer, salary or wage worker, or working on own account; number of farm schedule.

OTHER SIGNIFICANT FACTS ABOUT THE 1920 CENSUS

The date of the enumeration appears on the heading of each page of the census schedule. All responses were to reflect the individual's status as of 1 January 1920, even if the status had changed between 1 January and the day of enumeration. Children born between 1 January and the day of enumeration were not to be listed, while individuals alive on 1 January but deceased when the enumerator arrived were to be counted.

Unlike the 1910 census, the 1920 census did not have questions regarding unemployment, Union or Confederate military service, number of children, or duration of marriage. It did, however, include four new question columns: one asked the year of naturalization and three inquired about mother tongue. The 1920 census also asked the year of arrival and status of every foreign-born person and inquired about the year of naturalization for those individuals who had become U.S. citizens. In 1920 the census included, for the first time, Guam, American Samoa, and the Panama Canal Zone.

Also unlike the 1910 census, the 1920 census has a microfilmed index for each state and territory.

Due to boundary modifications in Europe resulting from World War I, some individuals were uncertain about how to identify their national origin. Enumerators were instructed to spell out the name of the city, state, province, or region of respondents who declared that they or their parents had been born in Germany, Austria-Hungary, Russia, or Turkey. Interpretation of the birthplace varied from one enumerator to another. Some failed to identify specific birthplaces within those named countries, and others provided an exact birthplace in countries not designated in the instructions. See Department of Commerce, Bureau of the Census, *Fourteenth Census of the United States, January 1, 1920: Instructions to Enumerators* (Washington, D.C.: Government Printing Office, 1919).

There are no separate Indian population schedules in the 1920 census. Inhabitants of reservations were enumerated in the general population schedules.

Enumerators were instructed not to report servicemen in the family enumerations but to treat them as residents of their duty posts. The 1920 census includes schedules and a Soundex index for overseas military and naval forces.

Soundex cards for institutions are found at the end of each state's Soundex index. It is important to note that many institutions, even if enumerated at their street addresses, are found at the end of the enumeration section.

The original 1920 census schedules were destroyed by authorization of the Eighty-third Congress, so it is not possible to consult originals when microfilm copies prove unreadable.

RESEARCH TIPS FOR THE 1920 CENSUS

Since nearly everyone has some knowledge or access to knowledge of family names, relationships and the family's state of residence in 1920, most genealogical instructors recommend the 1920 census as the best starting point for research in federal records. Working from known information about the most recent generations, an efficient researcher works backwards in time to discover family relationships and to determine where additional records may be found.

The 1920 census is a good tool for determining approximate dates and places to search for marriage records, birth and death records of children, and the marriages of children not listed. The 1920 census sometimes makes it possible to verify family traditions, identify unknown family members, and link what is known to other sources, such as earlier censuses, school attendance rolls, property holdings, and employment and occupational records. In several instances, women, rather than men, have been listed as head of household in the 1920 Soundex index (figure 5-3); therefore, a search focused on a male name may be unsuccessful.

The 1920 census asked the foreign-born for the year of their arrival in the United States, making it easier to pinpoint the date of passenger arrival records. It also asked the naturalization status of every foreign-born person and inquired about the year of naturalization for those individuals who had become U.S. citizens, thus facilitating searches in naturalization records.

Due to the more specific questions asked of immigrants from Germany, Austria-Hungary, Russia, and Turkey regarding their birthplaces and those of their parents, many researchers will be able to discover the exact towns or regions from which their families emigrated. The fact that the 1920 census asked for the mother tongue of each respondent and that of each parent will further help to define the origins of many families.

For additional information regarding the 1920 census, see the following sources:

Green, Kellee. "The Fourteenth Numbering of the People: The 1920 Census." *Prologue* (Summer 1991): 131–45.

National Archives. *The 1920 Federal Population Census: Catalog of National Archives Microfilm.* Washington, D.C.: National Archives Trust Fund Board, 1991.

Shepard, JoAnne (Bureau of the Census). *Age Search Information.* Washington, D.C.: Government Printing Office, 1990.

For boundary changes and identification of missing census schedules, see William Thorndale and William Dollarhide, *Map Guide to the U.S. Federal Census, 1790–1920* (Baltimore: Genealogical Publishing Co., 1987).

FEDERAL POPULATION CENSUS INDEXES AND FINDING AIDS

The census is a clear reflection of population growth in the United States. The millions of names and figures added to the census totals in the last half of the eighteenth century have made indexing, particularly of the most populous states, a formidable and expensive task. Indexes have been widely available for census schedules for the states and territories up to and including the 1850 enumeration. Recent developments in technology have facilitated indexing and publication, however, and now a significant and ever-growing number of 1860, 1870, and 1880 statewide census schedules have been indexed.

Unlike the 1880 Soundex, which is only a partial index, the newer 1880 works are every-name compilations. An ambitious project is currently under way to complete the 1880 index series for the remaining states. It will probably not be long before all of the gaps are filled and all states up to 1900 will be indexed and available in either book or CD-ROM (compact disk) format. Fortunately for researchers, libraries with good genealogy collections usually make it a priority to acquire these

Figure 5-3. 1920 federal census schedule (below) and Soundex index card (right) showing Caroline Levins as head of household, in spite of the fact that her husband, Joseph, is also listed in the schedule.

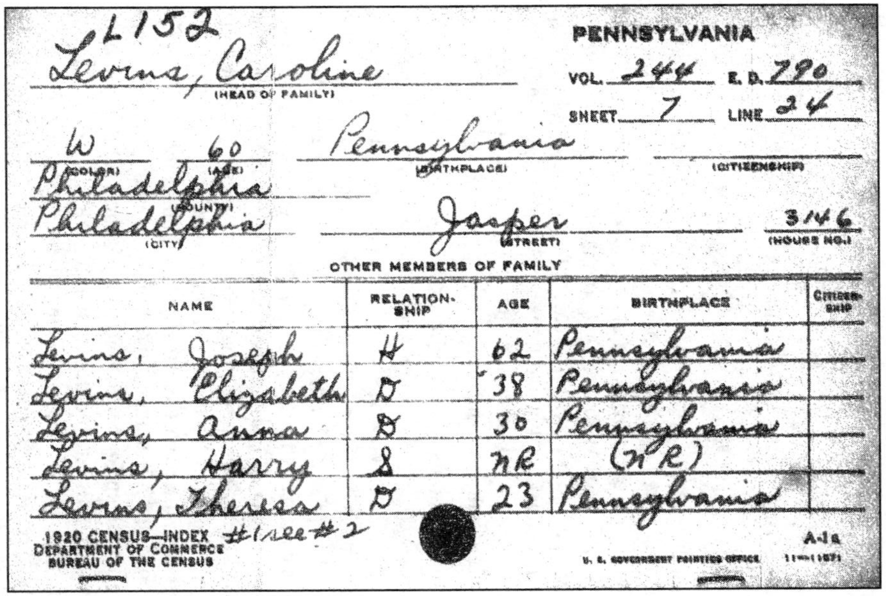
L152

PENNSYLVANIA

Levins, Caroline (HEAD OF FAMILY) VOL. 244 E.D. 790

SHEET 7 LINE 24

W (COLOR) 60 (AGE) Pennsylvania (BIRTHPLACE) (CITIZENSHIP)

Philadelphia (COUNTY)

Philadelphia (CITY) Jasper (STREET) 3146 (HOUSE NO.)

OTHER MEMBERS OF FAMILY

NAME	RELATION-SHIP	AGE	BIRTHPLACE	CITIZEN-SHIP
Levins, Joseph	H	62	Pennsylvania	
Levins, Elizabeth	D	38	Pennsylvania	
Levins, Anna	D	30	Pennsylvania	
Levins, Harry	S	NR	(NR)	
Levins, Theresa	D	23	Pennsylvania	

1920 CENSUS—INDEX #1 see #2
DEPARTMENT OF COMMERCE
BUREAU OF THE CENSUS

A-1a

U. S. GOVERNMENT PRINTING OFFICE

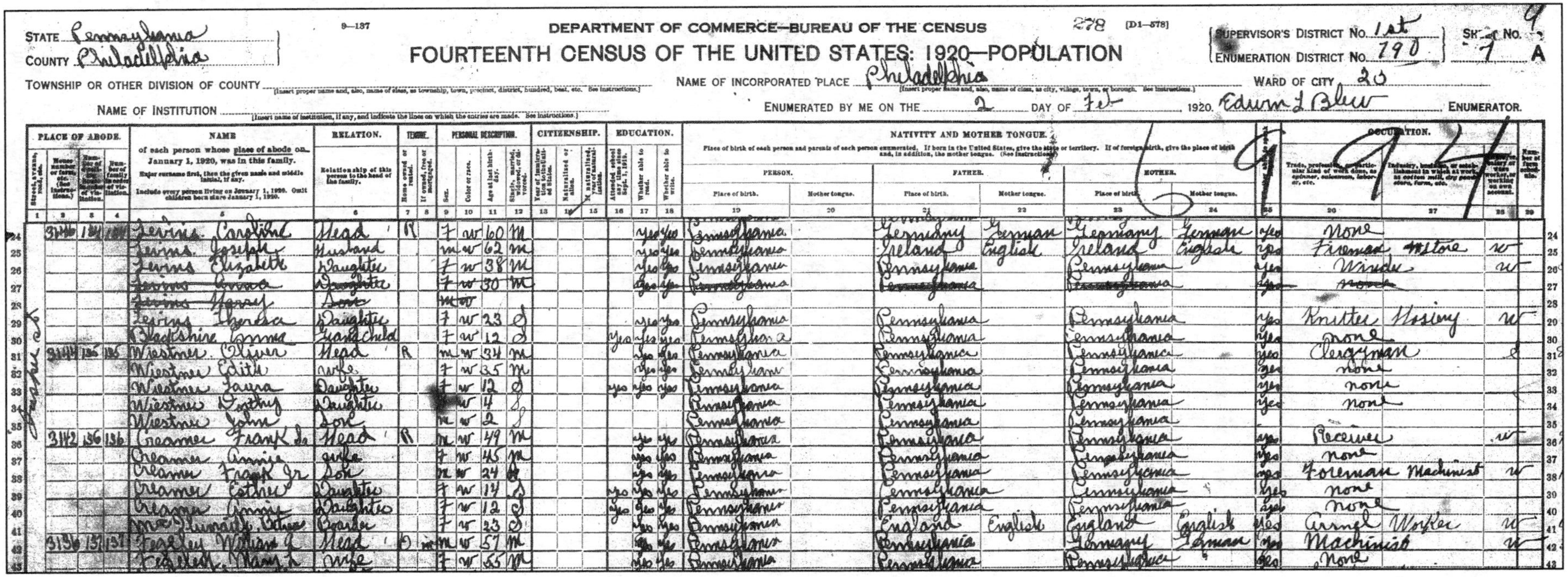
DEPARTMENT OF COMMERCE—BUREAU OF THE CENSUS

FOURTEENTH CENSUS OF THE UNITED STATES: 1920—POPULATION

STATE Pennsylvania COUNTY Philadelphia

SUPERVISOR'S DISTRICT NO. 1st ENUMERATION DISTRICT NO. 790 SHEET NO. 7 A

TOWNSHIP OR OTHER DIVISION OF COUNTY ______ NAME OF INCORPORATED PLACE Philadelphia WARD OF CITY 20

NAME OF INSTITUTION ______ ENUMERATED BY ME ON THE 2 DAY OF Feb 1920. Edwin L Blew ENUMERATOR.

Line	Name	Relation	Sex	Color	Age	Marital	Place of birth	Occupation
24	Levins Caroline	Head	F	W	60	M	Pennsylvania	none
25	Levins Joseph	Husband	M	W	62	M	Pennsylvania	Fireman
26	Levins Elizabeth	Daughter	F	W	38	M	Pennsylvania	Winder
27	Levins Anna	Daughter	F	W	30	M	Pennsylvania	none
28	Levins Harry	Son						
29	Levins Theresa	Daughter	F	W	23	S	Pennsylvania	Knitter Hosiery
30	Blackshire Emma	Grandchild	F	W	12	S	Pennsylvania	none
31	Wiestner Oliver	Head	M	W	34	M	Pennsylvania	Clergyman
32	Wiestner Edith	Wife	F	W	35	M	Pennsylvania	none
33	Wiestner Laura	Daughter	F	W	12	S	Pennsylvania	none
34	Wiestner Dorothy	Daughter	F	W	4	S	Pennsylvania	none
35	Wiestner John	Son	M	W	2	S	Pennsylvania	
36	Creamer Frank Jr	Head	M	W	49	M	Pennsylvania	Receiver
37	Creamer Annie	Wife	F	W	45	M	Pennsylvania	none
38	Creamer Frank Jr	Son	M	W	24	S	Pennsylvania	Foreman Machinist
39	Creamer Esther	Daughter	F	W	17	S	Pennsylvania	none
40	Creamer Annie	Daughter	F	W	12	S	Pennsylvania	none
41	McDonald Esther	Boarder	F	W	23	S	Pennsylvania	Carpet Worker
42	Fesley William J	Head	M	W	57	M	Pennsylvania	Machinist
43	Fesley Mary L	Wife	F	W	55	M	Pennsylvania	none

popular and important state indexes as soon as they become available.

While federal census records are an important component in almost every American genealogy, the lack of indexes to millions of names on census microfilms has delayed, if not completely stymied, many a project. The U.S. government, commercial publishers, and even volunteers have responded to the need for finding aids by producing, in various formats, indexes to the federal censuses for almost every state, up to and including the 1860 census.

CENSUS INDEX LIMITATIONS

A common mistake made by beginners is to consult an index, find a name, extract the index information—and go no further. Many seem unaware that census indexes are simply finding aids. While there is a certain element of excitement in discovering an ancestor's name in an index, there is greater satisfaction in store for those who view the fuller picture provided in the actual census schedules.

A well-prepared index includes a preface explaining the index parameters (for example, whether it is an every-name index or if only heads of household are included) and identifying specific problems encountered in the process of compiling the index. The wise researcher will read every preface carefully.

In most published census indexes, only the heads of households are listed. If an ancestor was a child when the census was taken, and if the name of his or her father, mother, or other head of the household in which he or she lived is not known, a long and tedious search may be in store. It may be necessary to look at different census schedules for every entry for a given surname in an index before her household is found.

Regardless of the care taken by the creator of an index to make it accurate, no index is perfect. Omissions, misinterpreted names, and misspellings creep into virtually all census indexes. Some indexes are not useful for tracing individuals because information was culled from microfilm that was nearly impossible to read, and sometimes the microfilmed version itself lacks certain information. Examples of the latter are the published federal census indexes from 1790 to 1840. Like the censuses themselves, the indexes are of limited use in finding individuals because only heads of household are listed. Likewise, most post-1840 census indexes include only heads of household and "strays."

Frequently, names are actually included in an index but cannot be found because they are misspelled to the extent that they are unrecognizable. Some surnames have been incorrectly alphabetized when indexers could not decipher even the first letter of a surname. In some handwriting styles, the letter *L* resembles an *S*; thus, the handwritten surname Lee might become See in an index. Handwriting styles have caused indexing problems when certain similar-appearing letters have been confused, including *T* and *F; J, G,* and *Y; I* and *J; K* and *R; O* and *Q; P* and *R; U* and *W.*

PAGE NUMBERING PROBLEMS

Pages of census schedules were originally numbered by the census taker; when the schedules were later arranged and bound, they were often renumbered with a hand stamp. It is common for some volumes to have two or more series of page numbers.

A stamped number, when it is present, is usually the page reference used in printed census indexes.

HISTORY AND QUALITY OF CENSUS INDEXES

Computer technology has revolutionized the process of indexing census schedules. Computer-produced census indexes are becoming increasingly available in book, microfiche, floppy disk, and CD-ROM forms. Despite the advanced technology, however, no index is error-free. Misinterpretations of handwritten census manuscripts and transcription mistakes continue to thwart research, particularly when the first letter of a name is entered into an index incorrectly.

While a number of individuals and genealogical societies have used computers to create census indexes, most such indexes have been created by commercial firms. The oldest of these firms is Accelerated Indexing Systems. Accelerated Indexing has produced indexes for every extant state and territory census through 1860 and some for later years, as well as a number of special censuses and census substitutes. During the 1980s, Index Publishing produced thirty-one census indexes in paper and microfiche editions. Precision Indexing, a subsidiary of the American Genealogical Lending Library (AGLL), has more recently entered the census indexing business and has taken a step further than its competitors. While most census index publishers include in their indexes only the names of heads of household or individuals living alone (strays), their county of residence, minor civil division, and census page number, Precision Indexing includes age, sex, race, birthplace, and census microfilm reel and number for each of the entries in its indexes.

Automated Archives, the dominant producer of census indexes on CD-ROM, was acquired by Banner Blue software in 1994. The Master Name Index—an index of names on all CD-ROMs published by Automated Archives/Banner Blue Software, Inc., is distributed with deluxe editions of Banner Blue's popular and widely marketed Family Tree Maker software. The advantage of the Master Name Index is in its ability to find all CD-referenced names in a single index; the disadvantage is that it does not provide complete information for locating individuals in original indexes or the sources from which the indexes were compiled. While the Master Name Index is a useful tool, it is only an index to many other indexes, including a large number of census indexes.

1790–1840

The federal government led the way in publishing census indexes when, in the early 1900s, it published indexed volumes of the extant 1790 census schedules for each state. The individual state volumes have since been privately reprinted and are widely available in libraries with genealogy collections.

1850–1870

Most statewide indexes for censuses after 1850 include only heads of household and the names of persons in households whose names were different than that of the household head. Obviously, then, a large percentage of the actual population of a state is excluded from such an index. This is especially a problem with common names, and when a child's or woman's name is known but that of the head of household is not.

The schedules for some states and areas have been indexed more than once by different organizations and commercial publishers. But though the year and the locality indexed may be the same, formats and contents can differ dramatically. Names may have been interpreted differently; some publications may include names missed by others; and some may include much more than county, township, and page and microfilm numbers after the names of heads of households. It is wise to check every index when more than one is available for a given time and place. For example, compare the two indexes below for the surname Hall in the 1850 federal census for Tennessee.

```
HALL,  RANDOLPH              SUMN 29A 16TH DIS
HALL,  RANDOLPH              RUTH 251 MC CRACK
HALL,  REBECCA               OVER 042 ATH DIST
HALL,  REBECCA               ANDE 074 14TH SUB
HALL,  REBECCA               COFF 033 ATH CIVI
HALL,  REESE R.              KNOX 205 19TH SUB
HALL,  REUBEN                MEDE 212 20TH CIV
HALL,  REUBIN                CANN 391 CRAFTS 5
HALL,  RHODA                 DAVI 303 2ND SUB
HALL,  RHODA                 MORG 292 13TH SUB
```

HALL, Randolph 50, Mary 45, Va Va, Sa-10-502
HALL, Randolph 54, Mary 44, Judy A. 27, John R. 13,
    Abner E. 12, May M. 10, Levander J. 8, Mormon R.
    6, Lambert C. 3, Jarmon C. 1, Va Va, Ru-63-505
HALL, Rebecca 55, William 21, T T, Ov-823-120
HALL, Rebecca 45, John 21, Rachel 19, Richard 15, James
    10, Rebecca 7, T T, A-52-7
HALL, Reese B. 24, Sarah 20, William Mc. 3, Charles
    TALIFARRO 12, T NC, K-1596-410
HALL, Rhoda 40, T, Mg-232-583
HALL, Rhoda 70, Albert PAYNE 38, Susan 25, James
    GRANT 38, Jane 28, Mary 2, LeRoy ARMSTRONG
    27, Mary 17, Henry SCHNIDER 24, Ann 20, Romulus
    2. Va T. D-532-607

Federal Census Indexing Systems: Accelerated Indexing Systems, Salt Lake City, 1975, and Byron Sistler & Associates, Evanston, Illinois, 1975.

Many indexes, up to and including the 1920 census, cover individual counties only. They can prove especially useful when a name or names cannot be found in a statewide compilation. Because local indexes are frequently compiled by genealogical societies and indexers who tend to be familiar with local name spellings and geographical distinctions, their reliability is sometimes greater than the larger indexes.

Statewide censuses are sometimes interfiled with other sources in single personal name indexes available in state archives. The addresses of state archives and state historical societies are given in appendixes B and C.

1880

Until recent years, the fastest method for finding names in the 1880 census for most states was to use the Soundex, a partial index that includes only households with children ten years old and under in residence. Compiled by the Work Projects Administration (WPA), the Soundex index was designed to identify those who would be eligible for Social Security. (An explanation of the Soundex coding system follows this section.)

Important to remember when using the 1880 Soundex is that, while a large portion of the population is not indexed because many families had no children ten years old or under, all individuals and families were supposed to have been included in the original census schedules. Some of the original Soundex index cards survive and have been distributed among various state and local agencies; others have apparently been destroyed.

Some of the 1880 cards were lost or misfiled before or when they were microfilmed. Nancy Gubb Frederick, for example, noting the omission of some 1,000 cards in the "O" section in the microfilming of the Illinois Soundex, compiled and published the missing section in *1880 Census Index, Soundex Codes O-200 to O240* (Evanston, Ill.: the compiler, 1981).

Use the Soundex to determine surname distribution throughout the state. This can be an important clue if you don't know which county to search for a family. You can identify family naming patterns (because each person in the family is listed on the Soundex card with relationships stated), find orphaned children living with persons of other surnames, and identify grandparents living under the same roof. They are listed in the census schedule, even though they may not be indexed separately (figure 5-4).

1890

A card file to the names on the surviving 1890 schedules is available on two rolls of microfilm titled *Index to the Eleventh Census of the United States,* 1890 (National Archives microfilm M496). The index is also available in printed form.

Ken Nelson, comp., *1890 Census Index Register* (Salt Lake City: Genealogical Society of Utah, 1984), is an index to the 6,160 names in the surviving fragments of this census. Available on microfilm (1,421,673, item 11), it is also to be found in the reference area of the Family History Library (Family History Library book Ref 973 X2n 1890). Also see Helen Smothers Swenson, *Index to 1890 Census of the United States* (cited earlier), and "Veterans Schedules, 1840–1890," below.

1900

The Soundex index to the 1900 census is regarded as one of the most inclusive and accurate of the federally-created indexes. It serves as an efficient key to locating households and individuals in the most genealogically informative census ever taken. Unlike the 1880 census, the 1900 census identifies all heads of household and every adult whose name is different from that of the head of household (figure 5-5).

1910

The most notable problem with the 1910 census is the lack of indexes for most states. Miracode/Soundex indexes exist for only twenty-one states: Alabama, Arkansas, California, Florida, Georgia, Illinois, Kansas, Kentucky, Louisiana, Michigan, Mississippi, Missouri, North Carolina, Ohio, Oklahoma, Pennsylvania, South Carolina, Tennessee, Texas, Virginia, and West Virginia. Since Soundex/Miracode indexes are not available for the remaining states, researchers must rely on city directories, county landowners' atlases, enumeration districts, or specially created finding tools (such as the special index to streets and enumeration districts for certain cities), or conduct tedious, page-by-page searches of the census schedules. (For a detailed description, see "Federal Population Census Indexes and Finding Aids," below.)

Soundex and Miracode (a slightly modified version of Soundex) indexes were created by the Bureau of the Census for the twenty-one states that lacked a centralized vital statistics bureau at the time the indexes were created. The Miracode system uses the same phonetic code and abbreviations as the Soundex system, but Miracode cards list the visitation numbers assigned by the enumerators, while Soundex cards show the page and line numbers on the appropriate census schedules. With the exception of Louisiana, which uses both, the

Figure 5-4. 1880 federal census schedule for St. Patrick's Orphan Asylum, Rochester, New York, p. 39.

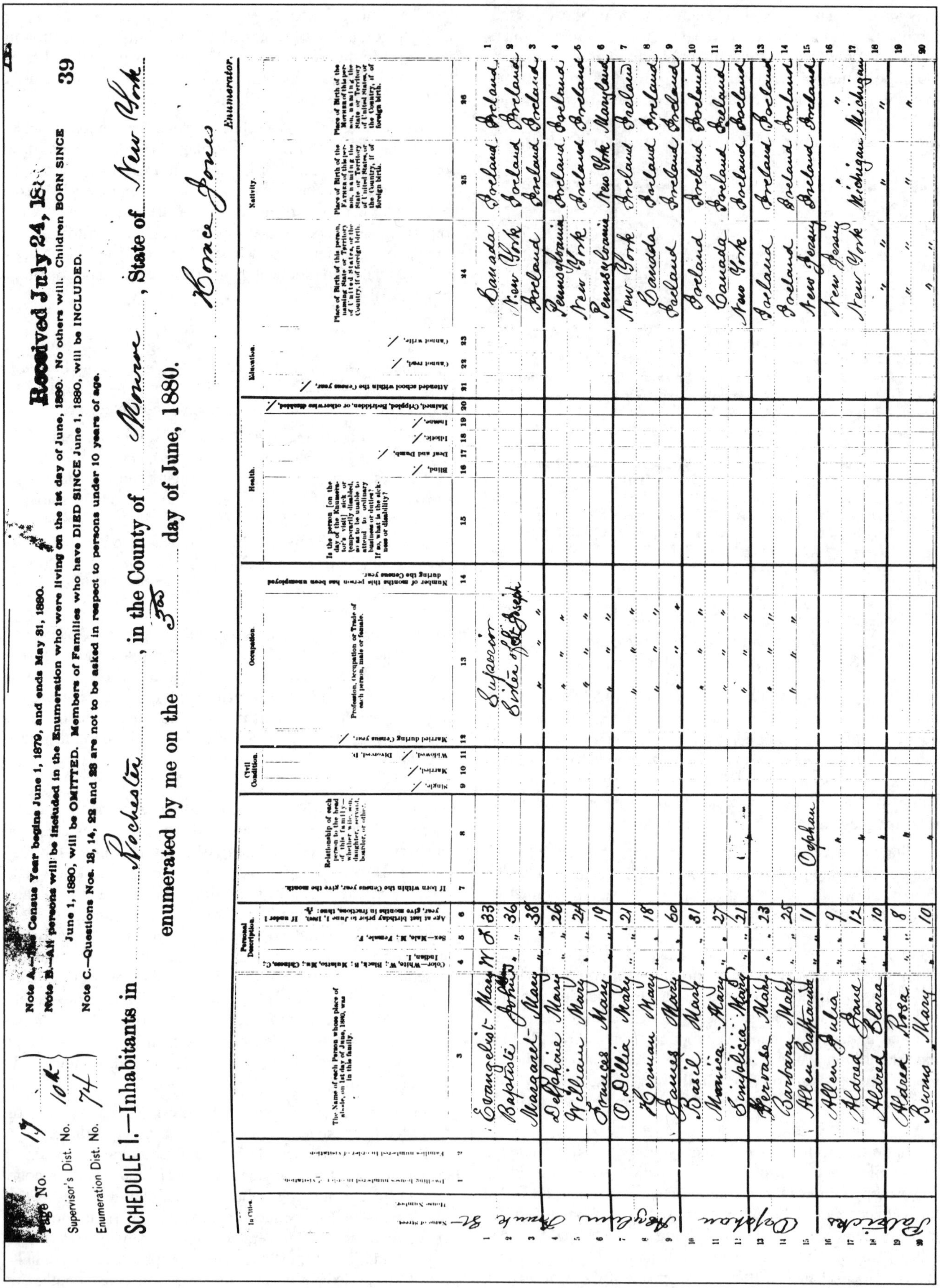

following states have been indexed using either the Soundex or Miracode systems: Alabama, Arkansas, California, Florida, Georgia, Illinois, Kansas, Kentucky, Louisiana, Michigan, Mississippi, Missouri, North Carolina, Ohio, Oklahoma, Pennsylvania, South Carolina, Tennessee, Texas, Virginia, and West Virginia. Both indexing systems give the surname, first name, state and county of residence, city (if applicable), race, age, and place of birth as well as the volume number and enumeration district number of the census schedule from which the information was obtained. Some large cities are indexed separately in the 1910 census. Be sure to see separate Soundex listings in the National Archives microfilm catalog for some metropolitan areas in Alabama, Georgia, Louisiana, Pennsylvania, and Tennessee.

The 1910 Census City Street Finding Aid

The Federation of Genealogical Societies (FGS) promoted and coordinated the funding to microfilm an important finding aid for the 1910 census. A city street finding aid, it was created by the Bureau of the Census to facilitate its work of searching the original schedules for age and other personal data in response to inquiries from individuals and government agencies. This index to city streets and census enumeration districts for thirty-nine cities in the 1910 federal population census is widely available on fifty sheets of microfiche. The index enables users of the population schedules to translate specific street addresses into the appropriate enumeration district number and corresponding volume number of the microfilmed schedules. The city schedules were selected for indexing by the Bureau of the Census based on the frequency of requests for information. The indexes were originally in bound volumes, but they were disbound for microfilming. With the exception of several of the larger cities, the index for each city occupied a single volume. The original arrangement of the indexes has been preserved, with the exception that the boroughs of Manhattan and the Bronx, Richmond (Staten Island), and Brooklyn have been placed under the heading "New York City." There is no index for the borough of Queens.

Entries in the index give for each city a list of city streets and house numbers and show the appropriate enumeration district. The records are arranged alphabetically by name of city and thereunder by street. Named streets, arranged alphabetically, are listed first, followed by numerical streets. Immediately preceding the index portion of each volume is a table listing the enumeration districts covered in the volume, with a cross-reference to the corresponding volume of the original population schedules.

The thirty-nine cities included in the 1910 index are:

Akron, Ohio	Newark, New Jersey
Atlanta, Georgia	New York City (excluding
Baltimore, Maryland	Queens)
Canton, Ohio	Oklahoma City, Oklahoma
Charlotte, North	Omaha, Nebraska
Carolina	Patterson, New Jersey
Chicago, Illinois	Peoria, Illinois
Cleveland, Ohio	Philadelphia, Pennsylvania
Dayton, Ohio	Phoenix, Arizona
Denver, Colorado	Reading, Pennsylvania

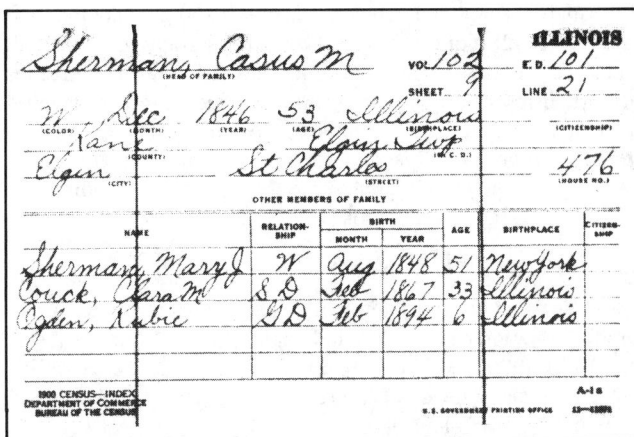

Figure 5-5. Illinois Soundex household card for Casus M. Sherman in *1900 Federal Population Census: A Catalog of Microfilm Copies of the Schedules* (Washington, D.C.: Government Printing Office, 1978), appendix.

Detroit, Michigan	Richmond, Virginia
District of Columbia	San Antonio, Texas
Elizabeth, New Jersey	San Diego, California
Erie, Pennsylvania	San Francisco, California
Fort Wayne, Indiana	Seattle, Washington
Gary, Indiana	South Bend, Indiana
Grand Rapids, Michigan	Tampa, Florida
Indianapolis, Indiana	Tulsa, Oklahoma
Kansas City, Kansas	Wichita, Kansas
Long Beach, California	Youngstown, Ohio
Los Angeles and Los Angeles County	

The 1910 street index can dramatically reduce the problems and time expenditure involved in searching large cities for which there are thousands of pages of census entries.

1920

The 2,074 rolls of microfilm for the 1920 census are Soundex indexed on 8,590 rolls of microfilm. The Soundex includes all of the states as well as the then territories of Alaska and Hawaii. The Canal Zone, Puerto Rico, Guam, American Samoa, the Virgin Islands, and military, naval, and various institutions are also indexed.

While the percentage of mistakes and omissions in census indexes is disappointingly high, it is generally agreed that even an imperfect index can be invaluable time-saver and is certainly better than no index at all. Improved technology and better editing are making most new compilations more inclusive and more accurate.

BEYOND THE INDEX

Experienced researchers know that there is much more to a census search than merely checking an index—whether that index is a book, a microfilmed version of the Soundex, or a computerized database. Unfortunately, too many beginners give up the search if the name sought does not appear in the index; if it does appear, they often seem content with the minimal information found in the index. Those who do not take the time to get the full picture provided by careful study of the actual census schedules usually miss important information and clues to further research. The study should include not only the subject of the search but the general area in which that person lived. To focus on only one name or one family in a given census is to see only a partial picture—somewhat like reading one chapter of a fascinating book.

THE SOUNDEX INDEX SYSTEM

An index and filing system called the Soundex is the key to finding the names of individuals among the millions listed in the 1880, 1900, 1910, and 1920 federal censuses. The Soundex indexes include heads of households and persons of different surnames in each household.

The Soundex indexes are coded surname (last name) indexes based on the progression of consonants rather than the spelling of the surname. This coding system was developed and implemented by the WPA in the 1930s for the Social Security Administration in response to that agency's need to identify individuals who would be eligible to apply for old-age benefits. Because early birth records are unavailable in a number of states, the 1880 census manuscripts became the most dependable means of verifying dates of birth for people who would qualify—those born in the 1870s. Widespread misspelling caused so many problems in matching names, however, that the Soundex system was adopted. Because locating eligible Social Security beneficiaries was the sole reason for creating the 1880 Soundex, only households with children ten years of age or under were included in that index. All households were included in the Soundex indexes for the 1900, 1910, and 1920 censuses.

HOW THE SOUNDEX WORKS

Soundex index entries are arranged on cards, first in Soundex code order and then alphabetically by first name of the head of household. For each person in the house, the Soundex card should show name, race, month and year of birth, age, citizenship status, place of residence by state and county, civil division, and, where appropriate for urban dwellers, the city name, house number, and street name. The cards also list the volume number, enumeration district number, and page and line numbers of the original schedules from which the information was taken.

Coding a Surname

To search for a name it is necessary to first determine its Soundex code. Every Soundex code consists of a letter and three numbers; for example, S655. The letter is always the first letter of the surname. The numbers are assigned according to the Soundex coding guide below.

Code key letters and equivalents:

1	B, P, F, V
2	C, S, K, G, J, Q, X, Z
3	D, T
4	L
5	M, N
6	R

The letters *A, E, I, O, U, W, Y,* and *H* are disregarded. Consonants in each surname which sound alike have the same code.

Use of Zero in Coding Surnames

A surname that yields no code numbers, such as Lee, is L000; one yielding only one code number, such as Kuhne, takes two zeros and is coded as K500; and one yielding two code numbers takes just one zero; thus, Ebell is coded as E140. No more than three digits are ever used, so Ebelson would be coded as E142, not E1425.

Names With Prefixes

Because the Soundex does not treat prefixes consistently, surnames beginning with, for example, Van, Vander, Von, De, Di, or Le may be listed with or without the prefix, making it necessary to search for both possibilities. Search for the surname vanDevanter, for example, with and without the "van-" prefix. Mc- and Mac- are not considered prefixes.

Names With Adjacent Letters Having the Same Equivalent Number

When two key letters or equivalents appear together or one key letter immediately follows or precedes an equivalent, the two are coded as one letter with a single number. (Surnames may have different letters that are adjacent and have the same number equivalent.) Pfeiffer, for example, is coded P160. Because the *P* and the *F* are both coded as 1, only one (*P*) is used. The letters *e* and *i* separate the coded Pf from the second and third appearance of the letter *f*, so one of these is coded. The double *f*'s again require that only one be considered in the code. The letter *r* is represented by 6, and in the absence of additional consonants, the code is rounded off with a zero. Other examples of double-letter names are Lennon (L550), Kelly (K400), Buerck (B620), Lloyd (L300), Schaefer (S160), Szucs (S200), and Orricks (O620). Occasionally the indexers themselves made mistakes in coding names, so it may be useful to look for a name in another code.

Different Names Within a Single Code

With this indexing formula, many different surnames may be included within the same Soundex code. For example, the similar-sounding surnames Scherman, Schurman, Sherman, Shireman, and Shurman are indexed together as S655 and will appear in the same group with other surnames, such as Sauerman or Sermon. Names that do not sound alike may also be included within a single code: Sinclair, Singler, Snegolski, Snuckel, Sanislo, San Miguel, Sungaila, and Szmegalski are all coded as S524.

Alphabetical Arrangement of First or Given Names Within the Code

As described above, multiple surnames appear within most Soundex codes. Within each Soundex code, the individual and family cards are arranged alphabetically by given name. Marked divider cards separate most Soundex codes.

Mixed Codes

Divider cards show most code numbers, but not all. For instance, one divider may be numbered 350 and the next one 400. Between the two divided cards there may be names coded 353, 350, 360, 365, and 355, but instead of being in numerical order they are interfiled alphabetically by given name.

Soundex Reference Guide

For those who are unsure of their Soundex skills, most genealogical libraries have a copy of Bradley W. Steuart, *The Soundex*

Reference Guide: Soundex Codes to Over 125,000 Surnames (Bountiful, Utah: Precision Indexing, 1990).

Soundex Abbreviations

In addition to the letter/numerical codes, Soundex also uses a number of abbreviations, most of which relate to residents' relationships to the head of the household (see table 5-1). NR (not recorded) is a frequently found abbreviation.

Native Americans, Asians, and Nuns

Names of nuns, Native Americans, and Asians pose special problems. Phonetically spelled Asian and Native American names were either coded as one continuous name or by what seemed to be a surname. For example, the Native American name Shinka-Wa-Sa may have been coded as Shinka (S520) or Sa (S000). Nuns were coded as if "Sister" were the surname, and they appear in each state's Soundex under the code S236, but not necessarily in alphabetical order.

SOUNDEX RESEARCH TIPS

The Soundex indexes can be especially useful in identifying family units, because all members of the household are listed on the Soundex cards under the name of the head of the household. Often, census searches begin with only a surname and the name of the state in which a person or family lived in a given census year. In such cases, the Soundex can be a means of determining surname distribution throughout the state. A search can often be narrowed to a smaller geographic area within a state. Once the county of origin is determined through census work, whole new paths of research open up. The Soundex can also be used to locate orphaned children living with persons of other surnames and to identify families with grandparents living under the same roof. They are sometimes listed on the Soundex cards, even though they may not be indexed separately.

1900, 1910, AND 1920 CENSUS ENUMERATION DISTRICT DESCRIPTIONS

Because of errors in transcribed names and because of variant spellings of names, a researcher may not be able to locate an entry in the Soundex system for a given head of family or individual living in a specific area. And though a name does not appear in the Soundex, the possibility exists that the individual being sought was indeed enumerated but was somehow missed or incorrectly coded in the indexing process. Those wishing to bypass the 1900, 1910, or 1920 Soundexes and to consult the actual schedules for a given town, a minor civil division or geographic area, or a ward of a large city need to know the enumeration district numbers assigned to the particular place.

Arranged alphabetically by state and thereunder by county, the Census Enumeration District Descriptions identify the specific enumeration district numbers assigned within states, counties, and cities. Note that the district boundaries are described in the microfilm series as they were when the censuses were taken and may have changed significantly since then.

Further information on Census Enumeration District Descriptions for the 1900, 1920, and 1920 censuses is provided in the introduction pages of the following National Archives catalogs:

1900 Federal Population Census. National Archives Trust Fund Board, 1978.

The 1910 Federal Population Census. National Archives Trust Fund Board, 1982.

The 1920 Federal Population Census. National Archives Trust Fund Board, 1991.

CENSUS LOCATOR MAPS AND TOOLS FOR CITIES

Even though an ever-growing number of indexes are available to facilitate research in cities and towns, few, if any, indexes are complete. A significant number of city dwellers, though present in the actual census schedules, were missed or misplaced in the indexing process. To remedy the situation, historians, researchers, and librarians have compiled finding aids for a number of metropolitan areas. Historian Keith Schlesinger devised a system to locate individuals overlooked by Soundex and other indexing processes. Schlesinger gleaned addresses from city directories, which he found both accurate and accessible, then plotted them on maps of census enumeration districts, which normally followed the boundaries of voting pre-

---

Table 5-1. Soundex Abbreviations: Relationships to Head of Household

A	Aunt	GF	Grandfather	Nu	Nurse	SM	Stepmother
AdD	Adopted daughter	GGF	Great-grandfather	O	Officer	SML	Stepmother-in-law
AdS	Adopted son	GGM	Great-grandmother	P	Patient	SS	Stepson
At	Attendant	GGGF	Great-great-	Pa	Partner (share	SSi	Stepsister
B	Brother		grandfather		common abode)	SSiL	Stepsister-in-law
BL	Brother-in-law	GGGM	Great-great-	Pr	Prisoner	SSL	Stepson-in-law
Bo	Boarder		grandmother	Pri	Principal	Su	Superintendent
C	Cousin	GM	Grandmother	Pu	Pupil	U	Uncle
D	Daughter	GNi	Grandniece	R	Roomer	W	Wife
DL	Daughter-in-law	GS	Grandson	S	Son	Wa	Warden
F	Father	GU	Great-uncle	SB	Stepbrother		
FB	Foster brother	Hh	Hired hand	SBL	Stepbrother-in-law	**Citizenship Status**	
FF	Foster father	I	Inmate	Se	Servant	A	Alien
FL	Father-in-law	L	Lodger	SF	Stepfather	NA	Naturalized
FM	Foster mother	M	Mother	SFL	Stepfather-in-law	PA	First papers filed
FSi	Foster sister	ML	Mother-in-law	Si	Sister		
GA	Great aunt	N	Nephew	SiL	Sister-in-law	NR	Not recorded
GD	Granddaughter	Ni	Niece	SL	Son-in-law		

cincts in most cities. By narrowing the search for a non-indexed individual to one or two enumeration districts, this scheme permits the researcher to escape the confinement of the Soundex. The technique is described in Keith Schlesinger and Peggy Tuck Sinko, "Urban Finding Aid for Manuscript Census Searches," *National Genealogical Society Quarterly* 69 (3) (September 1981): 171–80.

The staff of the Newberry Library in Chicago has created enumeration district maps for Chicago for the 1880, 1900, and 1910 censuses. Similar maps are available for other cities, and at least one, Mary Lou Craver Mariner and Patricia Roughan Bellows, *A Research Aid for the Massachusetts 1910 Federal Census* (Sudbury, Mass: Computerized Assistance, 1988), has been published.

The Family History Library has some unpublished finding aids for some cities that are filed in notebooks with other materials in the census area of the library. The library has also compiled or revised some census finding aids for cities. *Guide to the Use of the United States Census Office 10th Census 1880 New York City* was originally compiled by Barbara Hillman in 1963 for use at the New York Public Library. This unpublished finding aid was revised in 1985 by Raymond G. Matthews. The newer, forty-one-page guide reproduces 1880 Manhattan street maps and assembly and election districts, and converts ward numbers to corresponding Family History Library census microfilm call numbers. The 1880 finding aid has been published on microfiche (Family History Library microfiche no. 6047913).

The U.S. 1910 Federal Census: Unindexed States, A Guide to Finding Census Enumeration Districts for Unindexed Cities, Towns, and Villages is a Family History Library finding aid compiled by G. Eileen Buckway, Marva Blalock, Elizabeth Caruso, Raymond G. Matthews, and Ken Nelson. It is an alphabetical directory, arranged by state, that lists the names of cities and towns not indexed by Soundex or Miracode. It provides the name of the county, enumeration district number, and Family History Library microfilm number for the corresponding 1910 census. For large cities, it gives additional aids, such as call numbers for city directories, street address indexes, enumeration district maps, and others. It is in the reference area at the Family History Library (Family History Library book Ref 973 X2bu 1910; microfiche no. 6101340)

Street Indexes to the 1910 Census: Boston, Massachusetts; Des Moines, Iowa; Minneapolis, Minnesota; Queens, New York; Salt Lake City, Utah (Malmberg, Malmberg, Blalock, Atwood, and Payne, 1990) is yet another Family History Library finding aid. It is a time-saving directory that lists street addresses for the named densely populated areas that were not indexed in 1910. This uncataloged finding aid may be located in reference binder 49b on the second floor of the library or on microfiche (no. 6104151).

For those having problems locating addresses for the New York Metropolitan area in the state's 1915 census, The Family History Library has made available two important finding aids: *New York City 1915 State Census Street Address Index* vol. 1, *Manhattan,* is an alphabetical listing of all Manhattan addresses, giving the assembly district, election district, block, and Family History Library microfilm numbers. It was compiled by Elaine Justesen and Ann Hughes and edited by Raymond G. Matthews in 1992 (Family History Library book 974.71 X22m

v.1.; microfiche no. 6101203). Vol. 2, *Brooklyn,* an equally valuable finding aid, was compiled by Lois Owen and Theodore R. Nelson and edited by Raymond G. Matthews in 1993 (Family History Library book 974.71 X22m, v.2; microfiche no. 6101620).

NON-POPULATION SCHEDULES AND SPECIAL FEDERAL CENSUSES

In addition to the population schedules, the federal government requested special information for administrative decisions. These special schedules can be quite useful for genealogy.

1885 CENSUS

An act of 3 March 1879 provided that any state could take an interdecennial census with partial reimbursement by the federal government. Colorado, Florida, Nebraska, and the territories of Dakota and New Mexico returned schedules to the secretary of the interior. The schedules are numbered 1, 2, 3, and 5.

- Schedule No. 1, inhabitants, lists the number of dwellings and families. It also identifies each inhabitant by name, color, sex, age, relationship to head of family, marital status, occupation, place of birth, place of birth of parents, literacy, and kind of sickness or disability, if any.

- Schedule No. 2, agriculture, gives the name of the farm owner and his tenure, acreage, farm value, expenses, estimated value of farm products, number and kind of livestock, and amount and kind of produce.

- Schedule No. 3, products of industry, lists the name of the owning corporation or individual, name of business or products, amount of capital invested, number of employees, wages and hours, number of months in operation during the year, value of materials used, value of products, and amount and type of power used.

- Schedule No. 5, mortality, lists the name, age, sex, color, marital status, place of birth, place of birth of parents, and occupation, and gives the cause of death for every person who died within the year ending 31 May 1885.

The schedules are interfiled and arranged alphabetically by state and then by county. Schedules for a number of counties are missing. The National Archives has microfilmed the Colorado (M158, eight rolls) and Nebraska (M352, fifty-six rolls) schedules. The originals are in the National Archives.

RESEARCH TIPS FOR THE 1885 CENSUS

The 1885 census is useful for locating data about individuals who were living on rapidly growing frontiers: Arizona, Colorado, New Mexico, Nebraska, Florida, and North and South Dakota; for locating and documenting newly arrived immigrants from Europe; and for documenting small businessmen and farmers—many of them immigrants—who were just getting started in their businesses. The manufacturers schedule for 1885 is the latest one available for research.

MORTALITY SCHEDULES, 1850–1885

The 1850, 1860, 1870, 1880, and 1885 censuses included inquiries about persons who had died in the twelve months immediately preceding the enumeration. Mortality schedules list deaths from 1 June through 31 May of 1849–50, 1859–60, 1869–70, 1879–80, and 1884–85. They provide nationwide, state-by-state death registers that predate the recording of vital statistics in most states. While deaths are under-reported, the mortality schedules remain an invaluable source of information (figure 5-6).

Mortality schedules asked for the deceased's name, sex, age, color (white, black, mulatto), whether widowed, place of birth (state, territory, or country), month in which the death occurred, profession/occupation/trade, disease or cause of death, and number of days ill. In 1870, parents' birthplaces was added. In 1880, the place where a disease was contracted and how long the deceased person was a citizen or resident of the area were included (fractions mean months when less than one year).

Before the National Archives was established in 1934, the federal government offered the manuscripts of the mortality schedules to the respective states. Those schedules not accepted by the states were given to the National Library of the Daughters of the American Revolution. Copies, indexes, and printed schedules are also available in many libraries (summarized in table 5-2).

The *United States Census Mortality Schedule Register* is an inventory listing microfilm and book numbers for the mortality schedules and indexes at the Family History Library. An appendix lists where the records are found for twelve states whose schedules are not at the library. Originally compiled by Stephen M. Charter and Floyd E. Hebdon in 1990, the thirty-seven-page guide was revised by Raymond G. Matthews in 1992. The second edition includes twelve pages of introduction to this important material. While the reference is not available in book form outside the second-floor reference area of the Family History Library, the library has reproduced it on microfiche that can be borrowed through LDS family history centers and a few other libraries (microfiche no. 6101876).

Frequently overlooked by family historians, mortality schedules comprise a particularly interesting group of records. Until recently, few were indexed. Lowell M. Volkel indexed the Illinois mortality schedules for 1850 in *Illinois Mortality Schedule 1850,* 3 vols. (Indianapolis: Heritage House, 1972); for 1860 in *Illinois Mortality Schedule 1860,* 5 vols. (Indianapolis: Heritage House, 1979); and those that survive for 1870 (the 1870 mortality schedules for more than half of the counties in Illinois are missing) in *Illinois Mortality Schedule 1870,* 2 vols. (Indianapolis: Heritage House, 1985). A more recent compilation is James W. Warren, *Minnesota 1900 Census Mortality Schedules* (St. Paul, Minn.: Warren Research & Marketing, 1991–92). As computers make indexing projects more manageable, we can expect more of these obscure yet genealogically valuable materials to be indexed. All statewide mortality schedules are indexed from 1850 to 1880 and for 1885 (South Dakota only) on microfiche by Accelerated Indexing Systems, and there is a CD-ROM index by Automated Archives, Inc.

RESEARCH TIPS FOR MORTALITY SCHEDULES

Mortality schedules are useful for tracing and documenting genetic symptoms and diseases and verifying and documenting African American, Chinese, and Native American ancestry, although African Americans are often included, especially if they were slaves. By using these schedules to document death dates and family members, it is possible to follow up with focused searches in obituaries, mortuary records, cemeteries, and probate records. They can also provide clues to migration points and supplement information in population schedules.

VETERANS SCHEDULES, 1840–1890

Revolutionary War pensioners were recorded on the reverse (verso) of each page of the 1840 population schedules. It is

Name	Age	Sex	Birthplace	Month of Death	Trade	Disease	Days Ill
Benton County, Sauk Rapids District							
AYR [AYER], Frederick	13	M	Minnesota	August		Affect lungs	[not given]
CRAWFORD, Leonard	1	M	Maine	February		Chronic	"
Ramsey County							
GERVAIS, Pierre	8	M	Minnesota	May		Unknown	42
DONNAR, Magdelin	60	F	Canada	April		Fever	15
BOUVAIS, Antoine	80	M	"	January	Farmer	Pulmonary	30
BIBOT, Zoe	25	F	"	April		Cholera	2
BAPTISTE, John	2	M	"	December		Pulmonary	30
PONCIN, Sophie	7	F	Minnesota	July		Cholera	3
RAMSEY, Alex, Jr.	4	M	Pennsylvania	"		Fever	14
FORBES, W. A.	6/12	M	Minnesota	March		Brain inflammation	21
GLASS, Phoebe	8	F	Wisconsin	February		Burned	2
BARBER, Mary Jane	3	F	Iowa	August		Conjestion	3
Albert	2	M	"	"		"	3
LUMLEY, John	23	M	Ohio	July	Stonemason	Cholera	1
GREEN, James	40	M	Pennsylvania	"	Trader	"	1
GLADDEN, Elijah	35	M	Ohio	"	None	"	5
ROBERT, Francis	25	M	Missouri	December	Trader	Consumption	90
GOODHUE, James, Jr.	2	M	Wisconsin	"		Teething	20

Figure 5-6. From Patricia C. Harpole and Mary Nagle, eds., *1850 Mortality Schedule, Minnesota Territorial Census* (St. Paul: Minnesota Historical Society, 1972), 100.

Table 5-2. Mortality Schedule Depositories

An asterisk (*) indicates publication. An underline (_)indicates that it has been indexed. For addresses, see appendix A, National Archives Regional Archives; appendix B, State Archives; appendix C, Historical Societies and; appendix D, Family History Library and Its Centers.

	1850	1860¹	1870	State Census Taken With Federal Funds 1880	1885	FHL¹	DAR²	NARA³ Micro-publications	State Archives	State Historical Society	Comments
Alabama	•	•	•	•					•		
Arkansas			•*	•*		•	•	T655			
Arizona	•*	_•*_	_•*_	_•*_	•				•		Printed and indexed; State Department of Archives
California	•	•	_•_	•			•				DAR has 1870 only
Colorado			•*	•*	•	•	•	T655			
Connecticut	•	•	•	•		•			•		
Delaware	•	•	•	•					•		
District of Columbia	_•_	_•_	_•_	_•*_			•	T655			
Florida	•	•	•	•	•			•	•		NARA has 1885 only
Georgia	•*	•	•	•			•	T655			
Idaho			•*	•*	•					•	
Illinois	•*	•*	•	•				T1156	•		
Indiana	•*	_•_	_•_	_•_			•		•		DAR has Jefferson County only
Iowa	•	•	•	•				T1156		•	
Kansas		_•*_	_•*_	_•*_	•		•	T1130			
Kentucky	•*	_•_	_•_	_•_		•	•	T1130			
Louisiana	•*	_•_	_•_	_•_		•	•	T655			
Maine	•	•	•	•	•						Originals in Office of Vital Statistics
Maryland	_•_	•	•	•					•		
Massachusetts	_•_	•	•	•			•	T1204			DAR has 1850 only
Michigan	•*	•*	•*	•*			•	T1163	•		
Minnesota	•	•	•			•	•	•		•	NARA has 1870 only
Mississippi	•*	•	•	•					•		
Missouri	_•_	_•_	•	•			•			•	DAR has 1850–60 only
Montana		•	•				•	GR6	•		
Nebraska		•*	•*	•*	•		•	T1128	•		NARA has 1885 only
Nevada		•	•				•		•		DAR has 1870 only
New Hampshire	•	•	•	•	•				•		
New Jersey	•	•	•	•			•	GR21	•		
New Mexico	•	•	•	•	•				•		NARA has 1885 only
New York	•	•	•	•			•		•		DAR has 1850 and city of Buffalo only
North Carolina	•	•	•	•	•			GR1	•		
North Dakota		•	•	•*	•	•				•	FHL has 1880 only
Ohio	•*	•		•	•	•		T1159	•		
Oregon	•*	•*	•*	•*					•		
Pennsylvania	•	•	•*	•		•	•	T956	•		DAR has Mifflin County only
Rhode Island	•	_•_	_•_	_•_		•					
South Dakota only		•	•	•	•*	•					FHL has 1880 only; NARA has 1885
Tennessee	•	•		•		•	•	T655			FHL has 1850–60 only
Texas	•*	•*	•	•		•		T1134	•		FHL has 1850–60 only
Utah	•	•	•	•		•		T1134			State copy, LDS Historical Department, Salt Lake City; FHL has 1870 only; originals at Texas State University

| | 1850 | 1860[1] | 1870 | State Census Taken With Federal Funds | | FHL[1] | DAR[2] | NARA[3] Micro-publications | State Archives | State Historical Society | Comments |
				1880	1885						
Vermont	•*	•*	•	•				GR7	•		NARA has 1870 only
Virginia	•	•	•	•			•	T1132			State library has 1850, 1870–80; Duke University has 1860; FHL has 1870
Washington		•	•	•			•	T1154			
West Virginia	•*	•*	•*	•*	•				•		
Wisconsin	•	•	•	•			•			•	Milwaukee Public Library has 1860–70; DAR has 1850–70 only
Wyoming			•	•			•				Originals in State Law Library, Cheyenne, Wyoming

1. FHL: LDS Family History Library, Salt Lake City, Utah.
2. DAR: Daughters of American Revolution, Washington, D.C.
3. NARA: National Archives and Records Administration, Washington, D.C.

easy to miss these names, especially in parts of the United States where few or no slaves were recorded. (Slaves were also recorded on the verso of the schedules.) Also, many elderly veterans or their widows were living in the households of married daughters or grandchildren who had different surnames or who lived in places not yet associated with the family. By government order, the names of these pensioners were also published in a volume called *A Census of Pensioners for Revolutionary or Military Services* (1841, various years. Reprint. Baltimore: Genealogical Publishing Co., 1996). The names of some men who had received state or Congressional pensions were inadvertently included with the revolutionary war veterans. The Genealogical Society of Utah indexed the volume in *A General Index to a Census of Pensioners . . . 1840* (Baltimore: Genealogical Publishing Co., 1965). These volumes are available in most research libraries. Figure 5-7 is the pensioner's list for Maine.

The National Archives has the surviving schedules of a special 1890 census of Union veterans and widows of veterans. They are on microfilm M123 (118 rolls). The schedules are those for Washington, D.C., approximately half of Kentucky, and Louisiana, Maine, Maryland, Massachusetts, Michigan, Minnesota, Mississippi, Missouri, Montana, Nebraska, Nevada, New Hampshire, New Jersey, New Mexico, New York, North Carolina, North Dakota, Ohio, Oklahoma, Oregon, Pennsylvania, Rhode Island, South Carolina, South Dakota, Tennessee, Texas, Utah, Vermont, Virginia, Washington, West Virginia, Wisconsin, Wyoming, Indian territories, and U.S. ships and navy yards. Schedules for other states were destroyed in the 1921 fire that destroyed the population schedules. The schedules are arranged by state or territory, thereunder by county, and thereunder by minor subdivisions.

Each entry shows the name of a Union veteran of the Civil War; name of his widow, if appropriate; veteran's rank, company, regiment, or vessel; dates of enlistment and discharge and length or service in years, months, and days; post office address; nature of any disability; and remarks (figure 5-8). In some areas, Confederate veterans were mistakenly listed as well.

Unlike the other census records described in this chapter, these schedules are part of the Records of the Veterans Administration (Record Group 15). They are discussed in Evangeline

Thurber, "The 1890 Census Records of the Veterans of the Union Army," *National Genealogical Society Quarterly* 34 (March 1946): 7–9. Printed indexes are available for some of the 1890 census.

RESEARCH TIPS FOR SPECIAL VETERANS SCHEDULES

Veterans schedules can be used to verify military service and to identify the specific military unit in which a person served. A search of the state where an individual lived in 1890 may yield enough identifying information to follow up in service and pension records at the National Archives; it can often trace Civil War veterans to their places of origin. The 1890 veterans schedules have been indexed for every state for which schedules are extant (except Pennsylvania).

SLAVE SCHEDULES, 1850–1860

Slaves were enumerated separately during the 1850 and 1860 censuses, though, unfortunately, most schedules do not provide personal names. In most cases, individuals were not named but were simply numbered and can be distinguished only by age, sex, and color; the names of owners are recorded. Figure 5-9 is a slave schedule for Kentucky. Few of the slave schedules have been indexed. (Also see chapter 15, Tracking African American Family History.)

AGRICULTURE SCHEDULES, 1840–1910

Agriculture schedules are little known and rarely used by genealogists. They are scattered among a variety of archives in which they were deposited by the National Archives and Records Service. Most are not indexed, and only a few had been microfilmed until recently, when the National Archives asked that copies be returned for historical research. The schedules for 1890 were destroyed by fire, and those for 1900 and 1910 were destroyed by Congressional order. See table 5-3 for the locations of existing schedules.

RESEARCH TIPS FOR AGRICULTURE SCHEDULES

Agriculture censuses can be used to fill gaps when land and tax records are missing or incomplete; to distinguish between people with the same names; to document land holdings of

Figure 5-7. Revolutionary war veterans and military pensioners of Maine, 1840, in *A Census of Pensioners for Revolutionary or Military Services* (1841. Reprint. Baltimore: Genealogical Publishing Co., 1954), 1.

CENSUS

OF

PENSIONERS FOR REVOLUTIONARY AND MILITARY SERVICES,

AS

RETURNED UNDER THE ACT FOR TAKING THE SIXTH CENSUS,

IN 1840.

STATE OF MAINE.

Names of pensioners for revolutionary or military services.	Ages.	Names of heads of families with whom pensioners resided June 1, 1840.	Names of pensioners for revolutionary or military services.	Ages.	Names of heads of families with whom pensioners resided June 1, 1840.
YORK COUNTY.			**YORK COUNTY—Continued.**		
WATERBOROUGH.			**SHAPLEIGH.**		
Noah Ricker	78	Noah Ricker.	Keziah Warren	81	John Pitts.
Jonathan Knight	77	Simeon C. Knight.	Jonathan Horn	85	Simon Ross.
Moses Deshon	76	Moses Deshon.	Jonathan Ross	91	Gideon Ross.
Abigail Hutchens	87	Abigail Hutchens.			
Elizabeth Smith	85	Abner Thing.	**SACO.**		
Thomas Carpenter	76	Thomas Carpenter.	Stephen Googins	86	Alexander Googins.
Sarah McKenney	74	Rufus McKenney.	John Grace	79	Moses Grace.
John Hamilton	75	John Hamilton.	Abraham Tyler	77	Abraham Tyler.
Caleb Lassell	79	Ivory Parcher.			
Moses Rhodes	74	Moses Rhodes.	**PARSONSFIELD.**		
			Noah Wedgwood	81	Allen Henry.
SOUTH BERWICK.			Levi Chadbourn	82	Levi Chadbourn.
Mary Chambertin	90	Josiah W. Seaver.	James Brown	83	Edmund Chase.
Lydia Jay	92	Ivory Jay.	Jacob Eastman	77	Jacob Eastman.
Henry Beedle	80	Henry Beedle.	Josiah Davis	90	Enoch Hale.
Timothy Berdens	76	John Brooks.	Wentworth Lord	84	Wentworth Lord.
Peliliah Stevens	83	John Welch.	William Campnell	80	Nathan Moulton, jr.
Barsham Allen	76	Barsham Allen.	George Newbegin	76	George Newbegin.
Charles Sargent	86	Charles Sargent.	Thomas Pendexter	58	Thomas Pendexter.
Lydia Marr	72	Reuben Bennett.	John Stone	82	John Stone.
John Hearl	85	John Hearl.	Thomas Towle	98	Thomas Towle.
Peace Peirce	69	Samuel Peirce.	Nathan Wiggin	80	Nathan Wiggin.
Hannah Peirce	81	Hannah Peirce.	Jonathan Wingate	82	Lot Wedgwood.
Betsey Nasan	81	Betsey Nasan.			
Seammon Chadbourn	85	Seammon Chadbourn.	**NORTH BERWICK.**		
Benjamin Nealey	58	Benjamin Nealey.	Ichabod Wentworth	52	Ichabod Wentworth.
			Absalom Stacpole	88	Absalom Stacpole.
WELLS.			Jacob Allen	82	Jacob Allen.
Aaron Warren	83	Walter Warren.	Simeon Applebee	88	Benjamin Applebee.
Samuel M. Jefferd	77	Samuel Jefferd.	Jonathan Hamilton	85	Abraham Henderson.
Mary Gawen	73	James Goodwin.			
Joseph Hilton	85	Joseph Hilton.	**NEWFIELD.**		
Miriam Littlefield	85	Joseph Littlefield, 3d.	Simeon Tibbets	88	Silvester Tibbets.
Daniel Stuart	87	Joseph Stuart.	Ebenezer Colby	81	Ebenezer Colby.
William Eaton	85	William Eaton.	Paul Roberts	78	Nathaniel Roberts.
Abigail Hobbs	72	James Hobbs.			
David Hatch	79	David Hatch.	**LYMAN.**		
Joseph Williams	90	Moses Williams.	Nathan Raymond	86	Francis Eldreg.
Benjamin Penny	79	Benjamin Penny.	Thomas Murphey	85	Joseph Murphey.
Joseph Wheelwright	88	Joseph Wheelwright.	Joshua Gilpatrick	82	Benjamin Goodwin.
			Silas Grant	86	Peter Grant.
SANFORD.			Jeremiah Roberts	86	Jeremiah Roberts.
John Hurton	77	John Hurton.	Rebecca Ricker	83	George W. Ricker.
Hepribeth Jacobs	85	Theodore Jacobs.	Simeon Chadbourn	91	Simeon Chadbourn.
Betsey Leavitt	72	Daniel L. Littlefield.	Elizabeth Lord	78	Elizabeth Lord.
Eunice Goodwin	72	John Lard.	John Burbank	88	Reuben Goodwin.
John Quint	79	John Quint.	Uriah Hanscomb	59	Felard Davis.
Samuel Shaw	83	Samuel M. Shaw.	William Clark	88	William Clark.
Samuel Shackford	79	Christopher Shackford.	Amaziah Goodwin	77	James Goodwin.
Robert Tripp	76	Robert Tripp.	Isaac Coffin	84	Issaac Coffin.
William Worster	86	Samuel Worster.			

Figure 5-8. 1890 federal census (veterans schedule), Allegeny County, Maryland.

[7-741.]

Page No. _1_

Supervisor's District No. _3_

Enumeration District No. _17_

Eleventh Census of the United States.

SPECIAL SCHEDULE.

SURVIVING SOLDIERS, SAILORS, AND MARINES, AND WIDOWS, ETC.

Persons who served in the Army, Navy, and Marine Corps of the United States during the war of the rebellion (who are survivors), and widows of such persons, in _Lonaconing_, County of _Allegany_, State of _Maryland_, enumerated in June, 1890.   _Hugh Muir_, Enumerator.

From Schedule No. 1. House No.	Family No.	NAMES OF SURVIVING SOLDIERS, SAILORS, AND MARINES, AND WIDOWS.	Rank.	Company.	Name of Regiment or Vessel.	Date of Enlistment.	Date of Discharge.	Length of Service. Yrs.	Mos.	Days.	
1	2	3	4	5	6	7	8	9			
7	7	James Atkinson	Corpl	I	10 R P a	v 15 Mo 1861	15 June 1864	3	1	+	1
16	16	John M. Gardner	Private Private Comp	a a	2 Md P H B	August 20 1861	Septem. 28 1864	3	1	8	2
168		Joseph Stewart	Private	cony I	R 10 Pen Vol	July 21 1861	October 31 1862	1	3	10	3
138		Michael Kenney	Private	a 2 Md 2	2 Md 2 H B	august 20 1861	septem + 28 1864				4
143		Andrew Scugler	Private	D 2	2 M P H B	September 29 1861	Septem 29 1864	3	+	+	5
198		Isaac Cochrane	Private	K	14 Indian Inf	10 June 1861	10 Septem 1864	3	2	+	6
64		John Shearer	Corp.	B	3 west virgine cavalry	12 September 1861	24 Septem 1864	3	+	12	7
224		William Whitfield	Private	D	2 Md P H B	September 29 1861	Discharge Septem 29 1864	3	+	+	8
85		John Stewart	Sergent	a	2 Md P H B	august 20 1861	Discharge Septem 28 1864	3	1	8	9
43		Casper Slade	Private	a	2 Md P H B	august 20 1861	Septem 28 1864	3	1	8	10
15		Adam McMillan	private	a	2 Md P H B	august 20 1861	september 28 1864	3	1	8	11
30		James Jonston	Private	a	2 Md P H B	august 20 1861	1865	3			12

	POST-OFFICE ADDRESS. 10	DISABILITY INCURRED. 11	REMARKS. 12	
1	Lonaconing Md			1
2	Lonaconing Md			2
3	Lonaconing Md	Gun Shott in Cheek		3
4	Lonaconing Md			4
5	Lonaconing Md			5
6	Lonaconing Md	Chronic Diarrhea		6
7	Lonaconing Md			7
8	Lonacoic Md			8
9	Lonaconing Md			9
10	Lonaconing Md			10
11	Lonaconing Md	Chronic Diarrhea		11
12	Lonaconing Md	in Andersonville P q	got no date of discharge	12

(19644—200,000.)   240

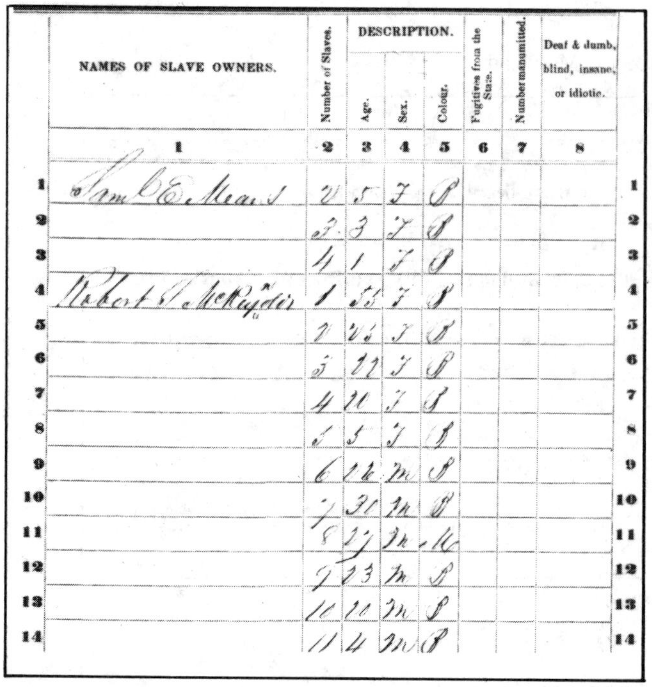

	NAMES OF SLAVE OWNERS.	Number of Slaves.	DESCRIPTION. Age.	Sex.	Colour.	Fugitives from the State.	Number manumitted.	Deaf & dumb, blind, insane, or idiotic.	
	1	2	3	4	5	6	7	8	
1	Saml E. Means	2	5	F	B				1
2		3	3	F	B				2
3		4	1	F	B				3
4	Robert S. McReyder	1	55	F	B				4
5		2	25	F	B				5
6		3	22	F	B				6
7		4	10	F	B				7
8		5	5	F	B				8
9		6	16	M	B				9
10		7	30	M	B				10
11		8	27	M	M				11
12		9	23	M	B				12
13		10	20	M	B				13
14		11	4	M	B				14

Figure 5-9. 1850 federal census (slave schedule), Fayette County, Kentucky.

ancestors with suitable follow-up in deeds, mortgages, tax rolls, and probate inventories; to verify and document black sharecroppers and white overseers who may not appear in other records; to identify free black men and their property holdings; and to trace their movements and economic growth.

MANUFACTURERS SCHEDULES

The first census of manufacturers was taken in 1810. The returns were incomplete, and most of the schedules have been lost except for the few bound with the population schedules. Surviving 1810 manufacturers schedules are listed in appendix IX of Katherine H. Davidson and Charlotte M. Ashby, comps., *Preliminary Inventory of the Records of the Bureau of the Census,* Preliminary Inventory 161 (Washington, D.C.: National Archives and Records Service, 1964).

The second census of manufacturers, taken in 1820, tabulated the owner's name, the location of the establishment, the number of employees, kind and quantity of machinery, capital invested, articles manufactured, annual production, and general remarks on the business and demand for its products. The schedules have been arranged alphabetically by county within each state to make research easier. The originals, deposited in the National Archives (Record Group 29), have been microfilmed with an index on each roll (M279, twenty-seven rolls). The Southeast, New England, Central Plains, and Mid-Atlantic regional archives of the National Archives have copies of the series. These indexes have been compiled and printed as *Indexes to Manufacturers' Census of 1820: An Edited Printing of the Original Indexes and Information* (Reprint. Knightstown, Ind.: Bookmark, n.d.).

No manufacturers schedule was compiled for the 1830 census. The 1840 schedules included only statistical information. Except for a few aggregate tables, nothing remains of these tallies.

From 1850 to 1870, the manufacturers schedule was called the "industry schedule." The purpose was to collect information about manufacturing, mining, fisheries, and mercantile, commercial, and trading businesses with an annual gross product of $500 or more. For each census year ending on 1 June, the enumerators recorded the name of the company or the owner; kind of business; amount of capital invested; and quantity and value of materials, labor, machinery, and products. Some of the regional archives of the National Archives have microfilm copies of the schedules for the specific states served by the region.

In 1880, the census reverted to the title "manufacturer's schedule." Special agents recorded industrial information for certain large industries and in cities of more than 8,000 inhabitants. These schedules are not now extant. However, the regular enumerators did continue to collect information on general industry schedules for twelve industries, and these schedules survive for some states. The manufacturer's schedules for later years were destroyed by Congressional order. See table 5-3 for the locations of extant schedules.

SOCIAL STATISTICS, 1850–1880

Social statistics schedules compiled from 1850 to 1880 contain three items of specific interest for the genealogist: (1) The schedules list cemetery facilities within city boundaries, including maps with cemeteries marked; names, addresses, and general description of all cemeteries; procedures for internment; cemeteries no longer functioning; and the reasons for their closing. (2) The schedules also list trade societies, lodges, clubs, and other groups with addresses, major branches, names of executive officers, and statistics showing members, meetings, and financial worth. The 1880 schedules were printed by the Government Printing Office, and most government document sections of public and university libraries have them. (3) The schedules list churches with a brief history, a statement of doctrine and policy, and a statistical summary of membership by county. The schedules for 1850 through 1900 are not listed in Davidson and Ashby, *Preliminary Inventory of the Records of the Bureau of the Census.* Those for 1906, 1916, and 1926 are printed; the originals were destroyed by order of Congress. Church records are especially helpful for researching immigrants, and the census of social statistics is a finding tool to locate the records of a specific group. See table 5-3 for the locations of extant schedules.

Special schedules are valuable because they document the lives of small businessmen and merchants who may not appear in land records. If population schedules give manufacturing occupations connected with industry, search the manufacturing schedules for more clues. It is also possible to trace the involvement of an individual in a fraternal club, trade society, or other social group.

STATE AND LOCAL CENSUSES

Population counts taken by state and local governments, though generally harder to find than the federal decennial censuses, can be very useful in family history research. In some cases state and local census details will supplement information found in the federal counts; in others they may provide the only census information to be found for a given family or individual.

Table 5-3. Summary of Special Census Schedules, 1850–80

For addresses, see appendix A, National Archives Regional Archives; appendix B, State Archives; appendix C, Historical Societies; and appendix D, Family History Library and Its Centers.

State	Schedule	1850	1860	1870	1880	Location/Comments
District of Columbia	Agriculture	•	•	•	•	Duke University, Durham, N.C.
	Social statistics	•	•	•	•	
	Industry		•	•	•	
	Manufacturers				•	
Georgia	Agriculture	•	•	•	•	Duke University
	Social statistics	•	•	•	•	
	Manufacturers	•	•	•		
Illinois	Agriculture	•	•	•	•	State Historical Library
	Industry	•	•	•		
	Social statistics	•	•	•	•	
	Manufacturers				•	
Kentucky	Agriculture	•	•	•	•	Duke University
	Industry	•	•	•		
	Social statistics	•	•	•		
	Manufacturers				•	
Louisiana	Agriculture	•	•	•	•	Duke University; copy in state Department of Legislature Reference, Baton Rouge, La.
	Social statistics	•	•	•		
	Manufacturers				•	
Maryland	Agriculture	•	•			Hall of Records; social statistics schedule for Baltimore City/County only surivess
	Industry	•	•			
	Social statistics	•				
Massachusetts	Agriculture		•	•		State archives
	Industry		•	•		
	Social statistics		•			
Minnesota	Agriculture		•	•	•	Minnesota Historical Society
	Industry				•	
	Social statistics		•	•		
	Manufacturers		•	•	•	
Mississippi	Agriculture	•	•	•	•	Department of Archives
	Industry	•	•	•		
	Social statistics	•	•	•		
	Manufacturers				•	
Montana	Agriculture			•	•	1870, State Historical Society; 1880 agricultural schedule at Duke University; other schedules at State Historical Society
	Industry			•		
	Social statistics			•		
	Manufacturers				•	
Nebraska	Agriculture		•	•	•	National Archives and Records Administration
	Industry		•	•	•	
	Social statistics		•	•		
	Manufacturers				•	
Nevada	Agriculture				•	Duke University
North Carolina	Agriculture	•	•	•	•	Department of Archives
	Industry	•	•	•	•	
	Social statistics	•	•	•		
	Manufacturers				•	
Pennsylvania	Agriculture	•	•	•	•	National Archives and Records Administration
	Industry	•	•	•	•	
	Social statistics	•	•	•		
	Manufacturers	•	•	•		
Tennessee	Agriculture	•	•	•	•	Duke University
	Industry	•	•	•		
	Social statistics	•	•	•		
	Manufacturers				•	
Texas	Agriculture	•	•	•	•	State library
	Industry	•	•	•	•	
	Social statistics	•	•	•		
	Manufacturers				•	
Utah	Agriculture	•	•	•	•	Genealogical Society of Utah has a microfilm of the three schedules; originals in LDS Historical Department
	Industry	•	•	•		
	Manufacturers				•	
	Mining			•		
Vermont	Agriculture	•	•	•		Public Records Commission
	Industry	•	•	•		

State	Schedule	1850	1860	1870	1880	Location/Comments
Virginia	Slave		•			Duke University, Durham, N.C.
	Agriculture		•			
	Industry		•			
	Social statistics		•			
Wisconsin	Agriculture	•	•	•	•	State Historical Society of Wisconsin
	Industry	•	•		•	
	Social statistics	•	•	•		
	Manufacturers				•	
Wyoming	Agriculture				•	Duke University

For those states not included in this table, check with the state archive or library first. (When these schedules were disposed of by the National Archives, state archives were given first rights to them.) Then check with the state historical society or state university with historical collections. Addresses are in the appendixes.

STATE CENSUSES

State censuses were often taken in years between the federal censuses. In some places, local censuses were designed to collect specific data, such as the financial strengths and needs of communities; tallies of school-age children and potential school populations to predict needs for teachers and facilities; censuses of military strength, cavalry horse resources, and grain storage; enumeration for revenue assessment and urban planning; and lists to monitor African Americans moving into northern cities.

As noted by Ann S. Lainhart in her comprehensive study *State Census Records* (Baltimore: Genealogical Publishing Co., 1992), tallies taken at the state level take on special importance for researchers attempting to fill in gaps left by missing censuses. For example, state and territorial censuses taken in Colorado, Florida, Iowa, Kansas, Nebraska, New Jersey, New Mexico, New York, North Dakota, and Wisconsin in years between 1885 and 1895 can partially compensate for the missing 1890 federal census schedules.

Additionally, some remarkably detailed state censuses are available for recent years. The Florida State Archives, for example, has 1935 and 1945 state enumerations. Like most other state schedules, the Florida state manuscripts are not indexed; they are arranged alphabetically by county and then geographically by election precincts. As with research in most state censuses, users must obtain election precinct numbers to expedite a search.

Probably no other state enumeration surpasses the 1925 Iowa state census in terms of genealogical value. In that year, Iowa asked for the names of all its residents and their relationship to the head of that household; place of abode (including house number and street in cities and towns); sex; color or race; age at last birthday; place of birth; marital status; if foreign born, year naturalized; number of years in the United States; number of years in Iowa; level of education; names of parents (including mother's maiden name); places of birth, age if living, and place of marriage of parents; nine specific questions relating to military service; nine questions regarding occupation; church affiliation; and six questions related to real estate, including the amount for which each listed property owner's house was insured.

A useful indication of what the Family History Library has on state and other censuses is "U.S. State and Special Census Register: A Listing of Family History Library Microfilm Numbers." It is an inventory, arranged by state and census year, describing the contents of each census and providing microfilm numbers for most known existing state censuses. The unpublished listing, compiled by G. Eileen Buckway and Fred Adams, was revised in 1992 and is available in the reference area of the Family History Library (Family History Library book Ref 973 X2be 1992; CCF 594855).

Below is a summary of state census schedules for the years 1623 to 1950 that includes the date, comments on them, and their current locations. (The notation "Ltd." following the census year indicates that only a partial census of the state was completed or is available. A census date is only included if at least the name of the head of the household is listed. Territory censuses are also included where applicable. Special thanks to Ann S. Lainhart for her assistance in preparing this summary.) The vast wealth of data available in these local enumerations can take several forms as the discussion will show.

Alabama
1818 Ltd., 1820 Ltd., 1821 Ltd., 1823, 1850, 1855, 1866, 1907 Ltd.

Alaska
1878 Ltd., 1879 Ltd., 1881 Ltd., 1885 Ltd., 1890–95 Ltd., 1904 Ltd., 1905 Ltd., 1906–07 Ltd., 1914 Ltd., 1917 Ltd.

Arizona
1866 Ltd., 1867 Ltd., 1869 Ltd., 1872 Ltd., 1874 Ltd., 1876 Ltd., 1880 Ltd., 1882 Ltd.

Arkansas
1823 Ltd., 1829 Ltd., 1865 Ltd., 1911 Ltd.

California
1788 Ltd., 1790 Ltd., 1796 Ltd., 1797–98 Ltd., 1816 Ltd., 1836 Ltd., 1844 Ltd., 1852

Colorado
1861, 1866 Ltd., 1885

Connecticut
No record of an applicable state census has been found.

Delaware
1782 Ltd.

District of Columbia
1803, 1867, 1878

Florida
1825, 1855 Ltd., 1866 Ltd., 1867 Ltd., 1868 Ltd., 1875 Ltd., 1885, 1895, 1935 Ltd., 1945 Ltd.

Georgia
1798 Ltd., 1800 Ltd., 1810 Ltd., 1827 Ltd., 1834 Ltd., 1838 Ltd., 1845 Ltd., 1852 Ltd., 1853 Ltd., 1859, 1865 Ltd., 1879 Ltd.

Hawaii
1878 Ltd., 1890, 1896 Ltd.

Idaho
No record of an applicable state census has been found.

Illinois
1810 Ltd., 1818 Ltd., 1820 Ltd., 1825 Ltd., 1830 Ltd., 1835 Ltd., 1840 Ltd., 1845 Ltd., 1855 Ltd., 1865 Ltd.

Indiana
1807 Ltd., 1853 Ltd., 1857 Ltd., 1871 Ltd., 1877 Ltd., 1883 Ltd., 1889 Ltd., 1901 Ltd., 1913 Ltd., 1919 Ltd., 1931 Ltd.

Iowa
1836 Ltd., 1838 Ltd., 1844 Ltd., 1846 Ltd., 1847 Ltd., 1849 Ltd., 1851 Ltd., 1852 Ltd., 1854 Ltd., 1856, 1885, 1895,1905, 1915, 1925

Kansas
1855 Ltd., 1865, 1875, 1885, 1895, 1905. 1915, 1925

Kentucky
No record of an applicable state census is available.

Louisiana
1853 Ltd., 1858 Ltd.

Maine
1837 Ltd.

Maryland
1776 Ltd., 1778 Ltd.

Massachusetts
1855, 1865

Michigan
1837 Ltd., 1845 Ltd., 1854, 1864, 1874, 1884, 1888 Ltd., 1894, 1904

Minnesota
1849 Ltd., 1853 Ltd., 1855 Ltd., 1857 Ltd., 1865 Ltd., 1875, 1885, 1895, 1905

Mississippi
1801 Ltd., 1805 Ltd., 1808 Ltd., 1810 Ltd., 1816 Ltd., 1818 Ltd., 1820 Ltd., 1822 Ltd., 1823 Ltd., 1824 Ltd., 1825 Ltd., 1830 Ltd., 1833 Ltd., 1837 Ltd., 1840 Ltd., 1841 Ltd., 1845 Ltd., 1850 Ltd., 1853 Ltd., 1860 Ltd., 1866 Ltd.

Missouri
1797 Ltd., 1803 Ltd., 1817 Ltd., 1819 Ltd., 1840 Ltd., 1844 Ltd., 1852 Ltd., 1856 Ltd., 1860 Ltd., 1864 Ltd., 1876 Ltd., 1880 Ltd.

Montana
No record of an applicable state census is available.

Nebraska
1854 Ltd., 1855 Ltd., 1856 Ltd., 1865 Ltd., 1869 Ltd., 1885

Nevada
1862–3 Ltd., 1875

New Hampshire
No record of an applicable state census has been found.

New Jersey
1855 Ltd., 1865 Ltd., 1875 Ltd., 1885, 1895, 1905, 1915

New Mexico
1790 Ltd., 1823 Ltd., 1845 Ltd., 1885 Ltd.

New York
1790 Ltd., 1825 Ltd., 1835, 1845, 1855, 1865, 1875, 1892, 1905, 1915, 1925

North Carolina
1786 Ltd.

North Dakota
1885 Ltd., 1915, 1925

Ohio
No actual state censuses were taken, but there are lists of eligible voters called quadrennial enumerations.

Oklahoma
1890 Ltd., 1907 Ltd.

Oregon
1842 Ltd., 1843 Ltd., 1845 Ltd., 1849 Ltd., 1850 Ltd., 1853 Ltd., 1854 Ltd., 1855 Ltd., 1856 Ltd., 1857 Ltd., 1858 Ltd., 1859 Ltd., 1865 Ltd., 1870 Ltd., 1875, 1885 Ltd., 1895, 1905

Pennsylvania
No record of an applicable state census has been found.

Rhode Island
1774 Ltd., 1777 Ltd., 1782 Ltd., 1865, 1875, 1885, 1905, 1915, 1925, 1935

South Carolina
1825 Ltd., 1839 Ltd., 1869 Ltd., 1875 Ltd.

South Dakota
1885 Ltd., 1895 Ltd., 1905, 1915, 1925, 1935, 1945

Tennessee
1891 Ltd.

Texas
1829–1836

Utah
1852 Index to Bishops Report, 1856 Territorial Census

Vermont
No record of an applicable state census has been found.

Virginia
1782 Ltd., 1783 Ltd., 1784 Ltd., 1785 Ltd., 1786 Ltd.

Washington
1856 Ltd., 1857 Ltd., 1858 Ltd., 1860 Ltd., 1871 Ltd., 1874 Ltd., 1877 Ltd., 1878 Ltd., 1879 Ltd., 1880 Ltd., 1881 Ltd., 1883 Ltd., 1885 Ltd., 1887 Ltd., 1889 Ltd., 1891 Ltd., 1892 Ltd., 1898 Ltd.

West Virginia
No record of an applicable state census has been found.

Wisconsin
1836, 1838 Ltd., 1842, 1846 Ltd., 1847 Ltd., 1855 Ltd., 1865 Ltd., 1875, 1885, 1895, 1905

Wyoming
1875 Ltd., 1878 Ltd.

LOCAL CENSUSES

Local population schedules usually resemble those of corresponding federal enumerations, but those taken in New York and Boston during the colonial period included details later incorporated in federal censuses. Beginning as early as 1703, some cities required that a census be taken of their population. Although these city/town censuses are not as numerous as the federal population schedules, some may be worth the time it takes to find them.

CENSUS SUBSTITUTES

In the absence of official census records, genealogists and historians have shown ingenuity in filling the resulting gaps. An interesting 1776 census was compiled from oaths of allegiance ordered by the colonial government of Maryland. Several of the lists are arranged in family units, with ages given for each person (figure 5-10). The pattern was later used for U.S. federal schedules. In 1778, a second census tallied those who opposed the American Revolution. Included on this second list are Quakers, Mennonites, and others who refused to take oaths, as well as some remaining Tories. Tax lists often make acceptable substitutes for missing censuses.

SCHOOL CENSUSES

Traditionally, school censuses have been taken to insure that local facilities and teachers are adequate and to plan for future appropriations. These schedules count the children of school age. Some lists are in family units with parents' names included. Some list children with ages only (figure 5-11).

CONSTABLE'S OR SHERIFF'S CENSUS

The constable or sheriff's census (also called a police census) actually had little to do with law enforcement; but the local constable, often under the eye of the sheriff, was the official most often used to assemble data required for administrative decisions. For example, in 1769–1770, the governor of Connecticut required an enumeration of "how many parsons partayn to ech family, and how many boshels of wheat, and of Indian corne, ech famyly hath."

Another sheriff's census was taken to the Committee of Safety and Relief, 16 April 1814, to account for settlers on the Niagara Frontier (western New York) who were "victimized during the War of 1812." Money was raised in Albany by voluntary donation to provide aid for these settlers.

Pennsylvania's tax assessors took septennial (every seven years) censuses from 1763 to 1807, listing taxable inhabitants by township. Occasionally, the list covered males age sixteen to forty-five only, thus making a militia census. Tax assessors were exempt along with teachers, physicians, provincial and state government leaders, militia captains, and others. Their names were not included on the same lists. Exempt status was set by law.

CHURCH/CIVIL CENSUSES

In areas where a church was established and supported by the civil government, enumerating the population was often the responsibility of church officials. The most common examples come from New England, but others can be found among church-wardens' records in Virginia and South Carolina.

As a more modern example, The Church of Jesus Christ of Latter-day Saints enumerated its members in Pottawatomie, Iowa, as part of the Iowa state census ordered in 1847 for all residents. These church schedules contain the standard information asked for in the Iowa tally but also include wagons, guns, number of family members ill, aged, or infirm, and oxen/

cattle/horses. These data suggest a dual function for the census to comply with the Iowa law and to prepare for transporting a large body of people westward, a project even then under way (figure 5-12). Emigrating companies were enumerated in tens and hundreds before they embarked the organization under which they traveled to Utah.

Other censuses were taken in Utah in 1852 and 1856. These tallies are valuable because many people did not survive the trek across the Great Plains and the Rockies; comparing the two censuses helps clarify mortality figures. Many of the companies that Brigham Young sent to colonize the Mormon Corridor before 1872 (Rocky Mountain valleys stretching from Mexico to Canada and from Las Vegas to San Bernardino, California) made summaries of individuals, professions, states of health, wagons, cattle, and weapons. Many of these schedules are among the collections of the LDS Church Historical Department, 50 North West Temple, Salt Lake City, UT 84150. More widely known are the twentieth-century census cards (1914 to 1960), which enumerate all LDS families in organized wards. They are available for research on microfilm at the Genealogical Society of Utah (figure 5-13).

SETTLERS CENSUS

Still another example is the Holland Land Company Census of 1806 (figure 5-14). The Holland Land Company had great difficulty getting payments from settlers on their lands in central and western New York. Its census assessed the resources of these settlers and, hence, their ability to pay. The 1806 data is especially valuable, as many of these people moved on before the 1810 federal census. For some, it is the only record of their stop in New York City.

IMPORTANCE OF LOCAL CENSUSES

Local censuses can be useful in discovering the names of children who are listed in pre-1850 census schedules by age groupings only. Similarly, these censuses may be used to determine the number living in a household and compared with birth and death records. They may also verify specific residences of individuals who moved too rapidly to be recorded in other sources; and they may identify neighbors and other community members whose records can provide additional clues for tracing families and individuals back in time. Comparing local census schedules with tax records and other property sources is often one of the best ways to distinguish individuals of the same or similar names.

AFRICAN AMERICAN CENSUS SCHEDULES

From about 1830 on, northern cities increasingly felt the need to monitor African Americans who were moving from the South seeking freedom and work. In 1863, in the midst of the Civil War, Ohio called for the number and names of African Americans who had immigrated to Ohio from other states since 1 March 1861, their current township of residence, and their state of origin. Thirteen counties in southeastern Ohio submitted schedules. Hamilton County refused because the numbers were too great and its staff too limited.

Household censuses of Philadelphia's African American population were taken in 1838 and 1856 by the Pennsylvania Abolition Society and in 1847 by the Society of Friends. In addition to the variables listed in the federal census, the records

1776 CENSUS OF SUSQUEHANNAH HUNDRED, HARFORD COUNTY, MD.
Taken by Charles Gilbert

Small, Robert	30	Horton, William	33	Macantraus, Hugh	24		
Elizabeth	21	Elisabeth	32	Feeby	31		
John	9mos.	William	14	Mary	3mos.		
Beacor, George	15	Mary	12				
Hare, Patience	11	James	10	Hall, Josias	24		
		Sarah	8	Mecarty, Owing	22		
Small, John	27	Elisabeth	5	3 negroes			
		Ruth	1				
Wilson, Andrew	46	2 negroes		Choislin, Thomas	41		
Lidiea	36			Young, Thomas	40		
James	10	Cummins, Paul	35	Chisholm, Thomas	11		
Cathron	8	Hannah	27	Chisholm, John	7		
Benjamin	4	Samuel	9				
Andrew	2	James	3	Hampton, John	85		
Hallett, John	25			Ann	84		
Prigg, Mary	25	Barns, Joseph	45				
Brown, George	14			Mitchel, John	31		
		Horner, James	29	Mary	34		
Hare, Sarah (Widow)	39	Mary	28	Gaberil	19		
Mary	17	Elisabeth	7	Elisabeth	6		
Sarah	6	Thomas	6	Rachel	4		
Daniel	3	Casandrew	4	Fredrick	1		
		Mary Gilbert	1	Purkins, Ritchard	16		
Rigdon, Charles	27	Baker, Jenny Mary	11	Taylor, Ritchard	12		
Molton, Mathew	15	2 negroes					
Sulliven, Nathaniel	13			Cortny, Thomas	32		
		Clarke, Elizabeth	18	Sarah	27		
Donovan William	23			Jonas	10		
Rachel	19	Culver, Benjamin	24	John	8		
Anos	6mos.	1 negro		Hollas	6		
		Culver, Ann	62	Semelia	5		
Durbin, Avariller	25	1 negro		Sarah	3		
Delila	2	Suillovon, John	27	Thomas	2mos.		
		Margret	18	Brown, James	13		
Judd, Daniel	40	Coolley, John	21	1 negro			
Hanah	39	Rigdon, Sarah	62				
William	17	Sarah	23	Knight, Jonathan	56		
Daniel	11	Pritchart, Mary	12	Ellender	46		
Joshua	9			Holliday, Mary	12		
Rachel	8	Bedelhall, John	27				
Ann	6	5 negroes		West, Thomas	45		
Elisabeth	3			Ann	39		
James	3mos.	Michael, Belsher	48	Elisabeth	17		
		Ann	28	James	14		
Thomson, Edward	45	John	14	Thomas	12		
Jamine	30	James	13	Samuel	6		
Martha	10	Bennet	8	Sarah	6		
Mallon	6	Jacob	6	Mary	3		
Mary	3	Susannah	4	Isaac	1		
William	1	Daniel	2				
Sullavin, James	17	William	8mos.	Wright, Charles	30		
		Horten, John	23	Blackford, Thomas	66		
Johns, Richard	43	4 negroes					

108

Figure 5-10. 1776 census of Susquehannah Hundred, Barford County, Maryland, from *1776 Census of Maryland* (published by B. Stirling Carothers, 14423 Eddington Dr., Chesterfield, MO 63017).

of 11,600 households contain information describing membership in church, beneficial, and temperance societies; income, education level, and school attendance; house, ground, and water rent; how freedom was acquired; and the amount of property brought to Pennsylvania. These superb records constitute the most detailed information we have describing any population group in the mid-nineteenth century; they are being computer-processed as part of an urban-immigrant study of African Americans in Philadelphia conducted by Temple University.

The National Archives has issued a separate list of "Free Black Heads of Families in the First Census of the U.S. 1790" as Special List 34. This compilation by Debra L. Newman is available free upon request from the National Archives. An expanded version for New York is Alice Eichholz and James M. Rose, comps., *Free Black Heads of Households in the New York State Federal Census 1790–1830,* Gale Genealogy and Local History Series, vol. 14 (Detroit: Gale Research Co., 1981).

RECONSTRUCTED 1790 CENSUS SCHEDULES

Census schedules are extant for only two-thirds of the thirteen states originally covered in the 1790 census. Concerned genealogists have reconstructed substitute schedules for the missing states using tax lists and following the pattern set by the Bureau of the Census in *Bureau of the Census Records of State Enumerations, 1782–1785* (1908. Reprint. Baltimore: Genealogical Publishing Co., 1970). These substitutes for 1790 schedules include:

Figure 5-11. First Monday of August, 1821, school census, Glastonbury, Connecticut, p. 2. The originals are in the Connecticut State Library, Hartford.

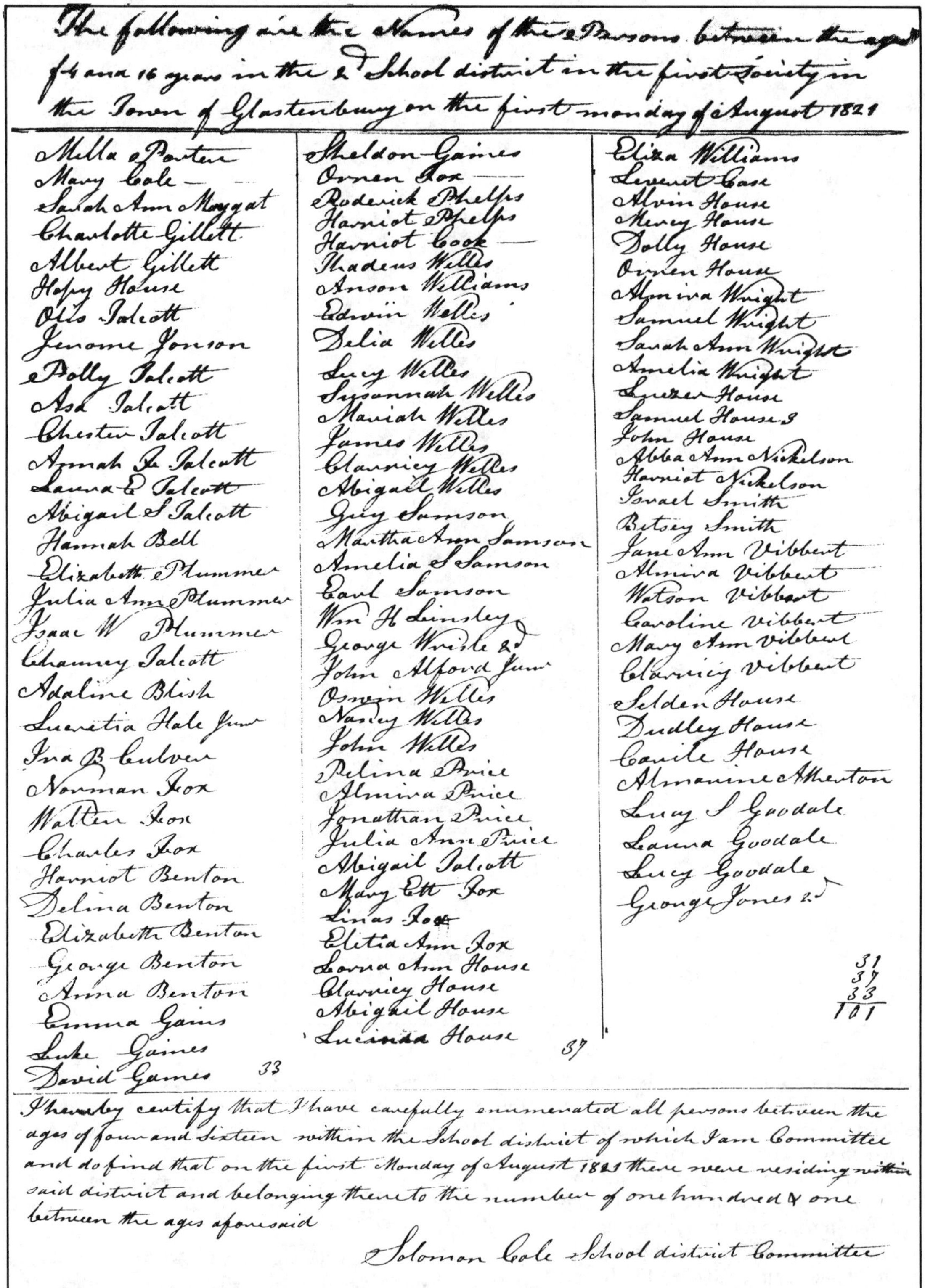

The following are the Names of the Persons between the ages of 4 and 16 years in the 2d School district in the first Society in the Town of Glastenbury on the first monday of August 1821

Milla Porter	Sheldon Gaines	Eliza Williams
Mary Cole	Orren Fox	Levrett Case
Sarah Ann Moggat	Roderick Phelps	Alvin House
Charlotte Gillett	Harriot Phelps	Mercy House
Albert Gillett	Harriot Cook	Dolly House
Hopy House	Thadeus Welles	Orren House
Otis Talcott	Anson Williams	Almira Wright
Jerome Jonson	Edwin Welles	Samuel Wright
Polly Talcott	Delia Welles	Sarah Ann Wright
Asa Talcott	Lucy Welles	Amelia Wright
Chester Talcott	Susannah Welles	Luther House
Azmah F. Talcott	Mariah Welles	Samuel House 3
Laura E Talcott	James Welles	John House
Abigail S Talcott	Clarrisy Welles	Abba Ann Nickelson
Hannah Bell	Abigail Welles	Harriot Nickelson
Elizabeth Plummer	Guy Samson	Israel Smith
Julia Ann Plummer	Martha Ann Samson	Betsey Smith
Isaac W Plummer	Amelia S Samson	Jane Ann Vibbert
Chauncey Talcott	Earl Samson	Almira Vibbert
Adaline Blish	Wm H Linsley	Watson Vibbert
Lucretia Hale Jun	George Wriste 2d	Caroline Vibbert
Ira B Culver	John Alford Jun	Mary Ann Vibbert
Norman Fox	Oswin Welles	Clarrisy Vibbert
Walter Fox	Nancy Welles	Selden House
Charles Fox	John Welles	Dudley House
Harriot Benton	Pelina Price	Carile House
Delina Benton	Almira Price	Almarine Atherton
Elizabeth Benton	Jonathan Price	Lucy S Goodale
George Benton	Julia Ann Price	Laura Goodale
Anna Benton	Abigail Talcott	Lucy Goodale
Emma Gains	Mary Ett Fox	George Jones 2d
Luke Gaines	Linas Fox	
David Gaines	Eletia Ann Fox	
	Lorra Ann House	
	Clarrisy House	
	Abigail House	
	Lucinda House	
33	37	31 37 33 101

I hereby certify that I have carefully enumerated all persons between the ages of four and Sixteen within the School district of which I am Committee and do find that on the first Monday of August 1821 there were residing within said district and belonging thereto the number of one hundred & one between the ages aforesaid

Solomon Cole School district Committee

On this 30th day of August 1821 personally appeared the above named Committee and made oath to the truth of the above return by him Subscribed

Saml Welles Justice Peace

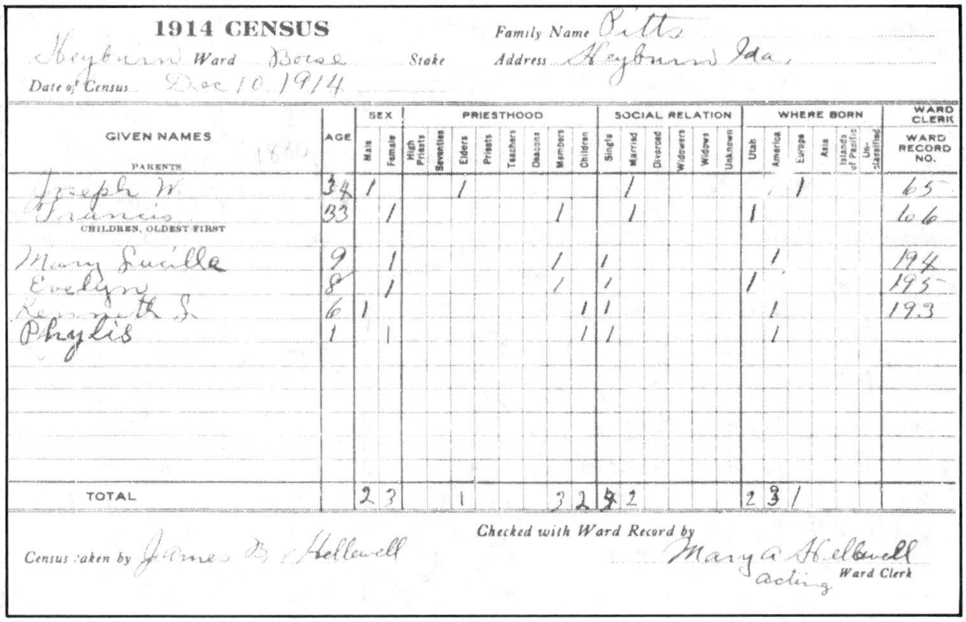

1914 CENSUS

Heyburn Ward Boise Stake Family Name Pitts Address Heyburn Ida.

Date of Census Dec 10. 1914

GIVEN NAMES	AGE	Male	Female	High Priests	Seventies	Elders	Priests	Teachers	Deacons	Members	Children	Single	Married	Divorced	Widowers	Widows	Unknown	Utah	America	Europe	Asia	Islands of Pacific	Unclassified	WARD RECORD NO.
PARENTS																								
Joseph W.	34	1				1							1							1				65
Francis	33		1							1			1					1						66
CHILDREN, OLDEST FIRST																								
Mary Lucille	9		1							1		1							1					194
Evelyn	8		1							1		1						1						195
Kenneth S.	6	1									1	1							1					193
Phylis	1		1								1	1							1					
TOTAL		2	3			1				3	2	4	2					2	3	1				

Census taken by James B. Helliwell

Checked with Ward Record by Mary A. Helliwell acting Ward Clerk

Figure 5-12. Entry for the Joseph L. Pitts family from the 1914 census of LDS church members; FHL 245155.

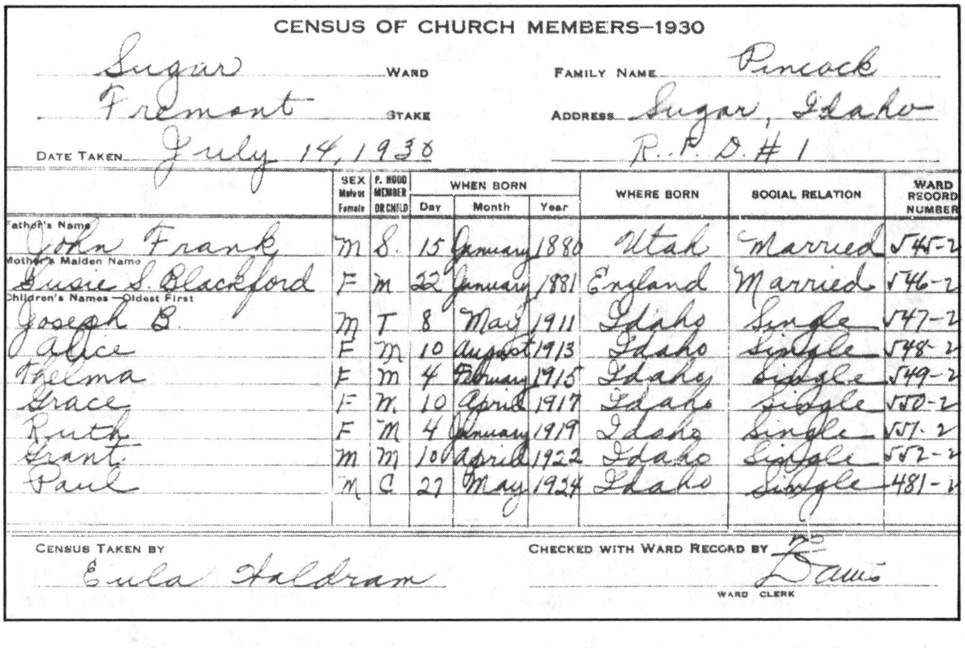

CENSUS OF CHURCH MEMBERS—1930

Sugar WARD FAMILY NAME Pincock

Fremont STAKE ADDRESS Sugar, Idaho

DATE TAKEN July 14, 1930 R. F. D. #1

	SEX Male or Female	P. HOOD MEMBER OR CHILD	WHEN BORN Day	Month	Year	WHERE BORN	SOCIAL RELATION	WARD RECORD NUMBER
Father's Name John Frank	M	S.	15	January	1880	Utah	Married	545-2
Mother's Maiden Name Susie S. Blackford	F	M	22	January	1881	England	Married	546-2
Children's Names—Oldest First Joseph B.	M	T	8	May	1911	Idaho	Single	547-2
Alice	F	M	10	August	1913	Idaho	Single	548-2
Thelma	F	M	4	February	1915	Idaho	Single	549-2
Grace	F	M	10	April	1917	Idaho	Single	550-2
Ruth	F	M	4	January	1919	Idaho	Single	551-2
Grant	M	M	10	April	1922	Idaho	Single	552-2
Paul	M	C	27	May	1924	Idaho	Single	481-2

CENSUS TAKEN BY Eula Haldram

CHECKED WITH WARD RECORD BY Davis WARD CLERK

Figure 5-13. Entry for the John Frank Pincock family from the 1930 census of LDS church members; FHL 245155.

Delaware

Leon deValinger, Jr. *Reconstructed Census for Delaware.* Washington, D.C.: National Genealogical Society, 1954.

Georgia

Georgia Department of Archives and History. *Some Early Tax Digests of Georgia.* Atlanta: Department of Archives, 1926. Also available are several volumes of printed land lotteries, 1805 to 1820, available in most research libraries, and a pamphlet which describes the state's head-right (land bounty for attracting new settlers) and lottery system, including eligibility qualifications. This pamphlet is available upon request from the Georgia Department of Archives and History, 330 Capitol Avenue S.W., Atlanta, GA 30334. Lotteries include precise description of qualifications for land ownership for each person drawing land in specific counties created as a result of the land awards. Figure 5-15 shows which years applied to which counties for lotteries.

Kentucky

Heinemann, Charles B. *"First Census" of Kentucky, 1790.* 1940. Reprint. Baltimore: Genealogical Publishing Co., 1971.

New Jersey

Norton, James S. *New Jersey in 1793.* Distributed by The Everton Publishers, Box 368, Logan UT 84321. Based on military census lists and ratables.

Stryker-Rodda, Kenn. *Revolutionary Census of New Jersey: An Index, Based on Ratables of the Inhabitants During the Period of the American Revolution.* New Orleans: Polyanthos, 1972.

The Library of the Daughters of the American Revolution,

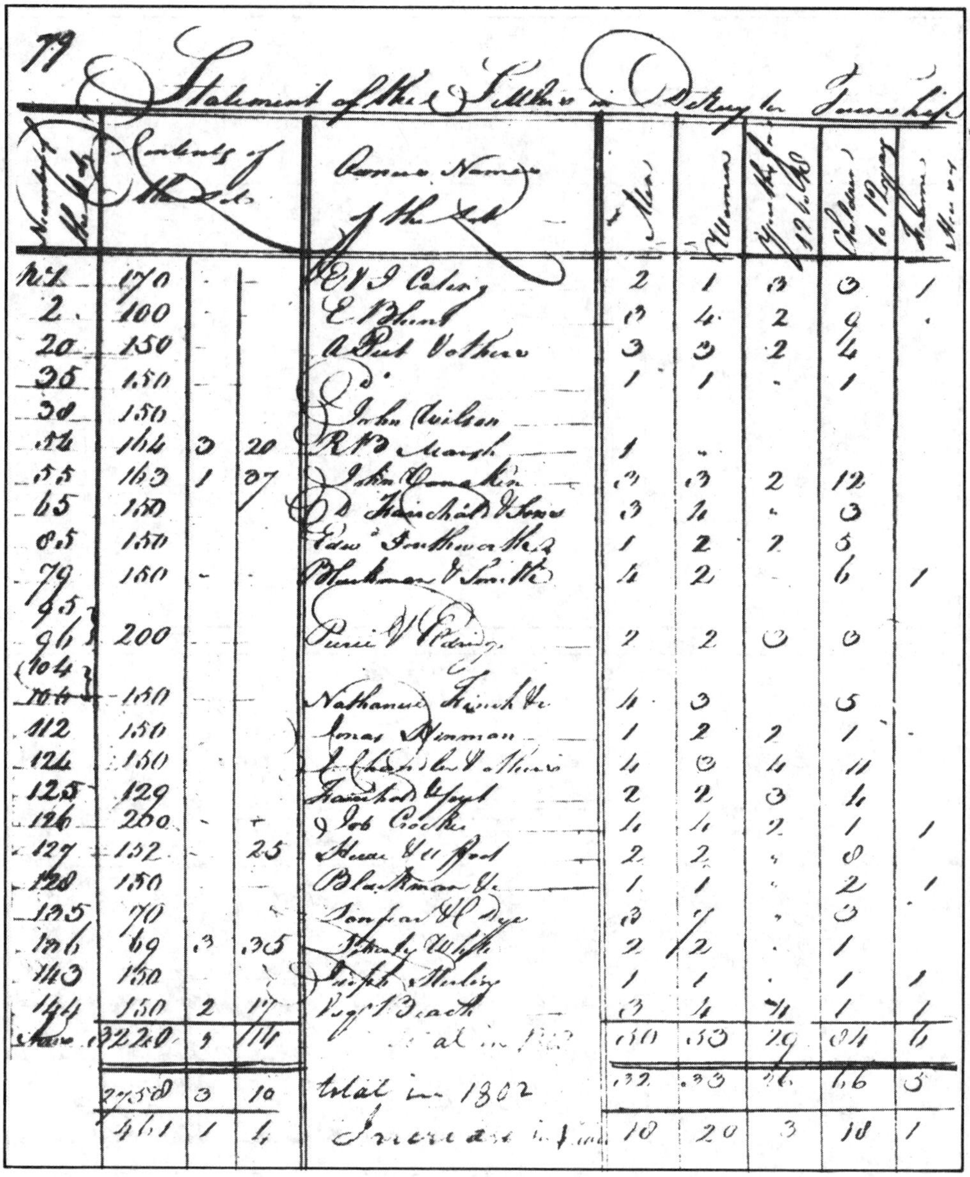

Figure 5-14. Statement of settlers, Holland Land Company census, 1806. The original papers are in the possession of Central New York Park and Recreation Commission; microfilm copies are in Cornell University, Department of Manuscripts and Archives, Ithaca, NY 14853. The facing page (not shown) includes information about livestock and equipment.

Washington, D.C., has twenty-four microfilm rolls of New Jersey tax lists for 1783 which can also substitute for 1790 data.

TENNESSEE

Creekmore, Pollyanna. *Early East Tennessee Tax-Payers.* Easley, S.C.: Southern Historical Press, 1980. Originally printed in East Tennessee Historical Society Publications beginning in 1951.

Sistler, Byron, and Barbara Sistler. *Index to Early East Tennessee Tax Lists.* Nashville: Byron Sistler & Associates, 1977.

VIRGINIA

Bureau of the Census Records of State Enumerations, 1782–1785. 1908. Reprint. Baltimore: Genealogical Publishing Company, 1970.

Fothergill, Augusta B., and John M Naugle. *Virginia Tax Payer 1782–1787. Other Than Those Published in the United States Census Bureau.* 1940. Reprint. Baltimore: Genealogical Publishing Co., 1971.

Schreiner-Yantis, Nettie, and Viriginia Love. *The 1787 Census of Virginia.* Baltimore: Genealogical Publishing Co., 1987.

Because substitutes for the 1790 census have been so useful, numerous reconstructions of other missing schedules are also under way. Tax lists, oaths of allegiance, land entities, militia lists, petitions, road records, and other sources, though never as complete as censuses, can go far toward filling the gaps left by lost or destroyed census schedules. Table 5-4 is a checklist of census substitutes.

In order to use substitutes effectively, it is important to know what specific categories of people are included in each source and which ones were left out. Most potential census substitutes are described in detail in other chapters of this book, and some can be found printed with indexes. Still other sources have been stored, and sometimes forgotten, in various state archives, courthouses, and historical agencies.

CENSUSES OF NATIVE AMERICANS

In some years, separate censuses of Native Americans were taken by the federal government and the Bureau of Indian Affairs. While some early Native American populations were tabulated by missionary priests and colonial authorities, specific examples of such tallies have not been located.

The 1860 and 1870 federal censuses noted only Native Americans living in non-Native American households. Native Americans who were not taxed (living on reservations) and members of nomad tribes in unsettled territories were not counted. It is safe to say that those enumerations of Native Americans made before 1880 are incomplete and, frequently, inaccurate. Additionally, in many instances, Native American origins are not indicated.

1880 NATIVE AMERICAN CENSUS

In 1880, a special enumeration was taken of Native Americans living near military reservations in the Dakota and Washington territories and the state of California. The census included the name of the tribe, the reservation, the agency, and the nearest post office; the number living in the household with a description of the dwelling; the Native American name with English translation for each family member; relationship to head of household; martial and tribal status; and occupation, health,

education, land ownership, and source of sustenance. Some enumerators also added customs and lifestyle data.

The "1880 Census of Indians, Not-Taxed" is in four volumes in National Archives Record Group 29. Volumes 1 and 2 cover Fort Simcoe, Washington, and Tulalip, Washington Territory. Volume 3 covers Fort Yates, Dakota Territory, and volume 4 covers California.

1885–1940 NATIVE AMERICAN CENSUSES

The 1885 to 1940 Indian census rolls are on National Archives microfilm M-595 (692 rolls). Census enumerations were taken regularly, though not annually, by Indian agents on each reservation from 1885 to 1942. Throughout these rolls are scattered letters written by agents describing why returns were not taken with instructions to enumerators on how to take the census. Vital records are noted in the age column or appended in separate lists.

In 1978, E. Kay Kirkham, Field Operations, Genealogical Society of Utah, updated and corrected the National Archives listing of Native American bands and tribes in these 692 microfilm rolls. He compiled an index for all tribes and bands, with Indian agency, National Archives reel number, and Ge-

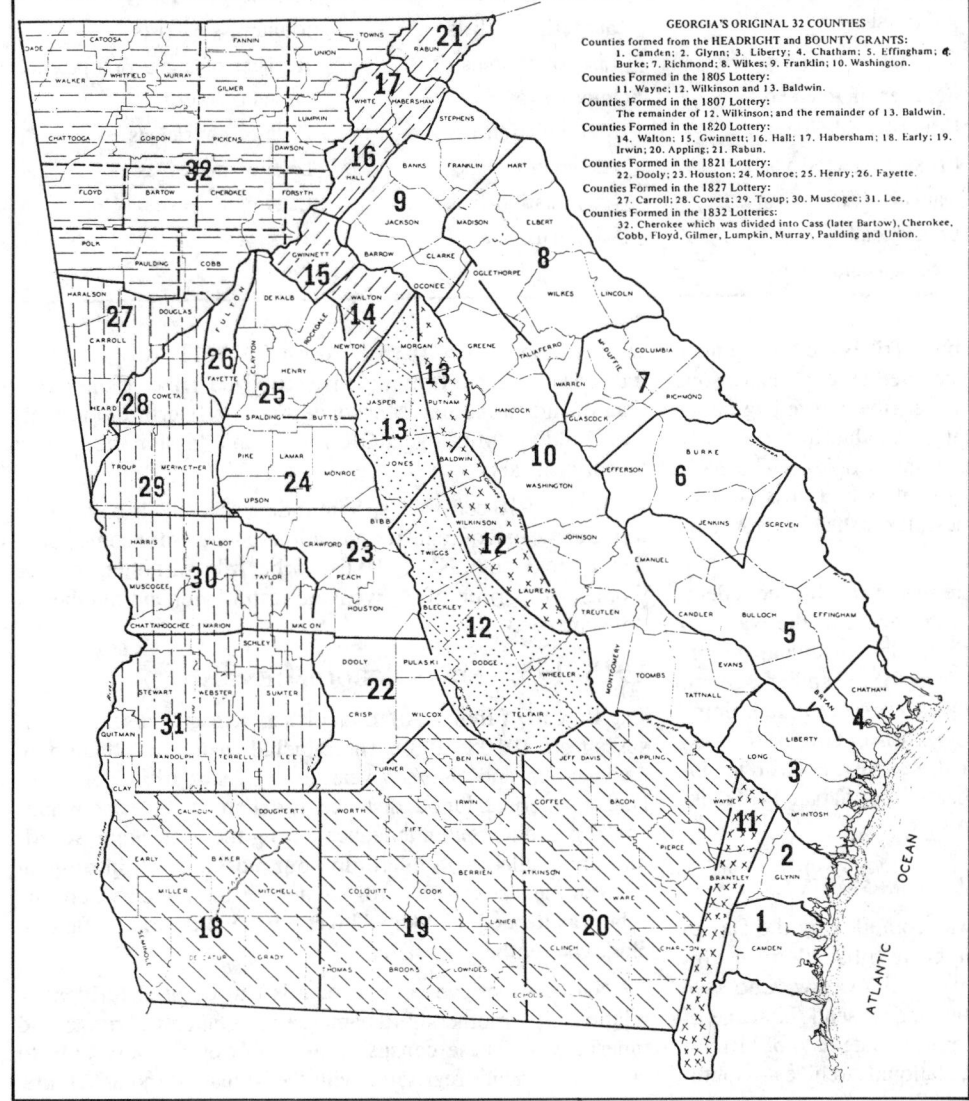

Figure 5-15. From the Rev. Silas Emmett Lucas, Jr., *The Creation of Georgia Counties, 1777–1932;* a separately published map, copyright 1982. Used with permission.

Table 5-4. A Checklist of Census Substitutes

Tax Rolls
__Poll tax
__Personal property
__Real estate
__1863 income tax
__1798 property tax
__Assessors' lists
__Faculty lists
__Rate lists

Land Records
__Entries plats
__Plat maps
__Lotteries
__Processioning lists
__Perambulations
__Ground rents
__Quitrents
__Debt books
__Permits to settle
__Land grant lists
__Suspended land grants
__Headright claims
__Lists of indentured servants
__Immigrant land allowances
__Inquisitions
__Devises' lists
__Heir lists

Court Records
__Oaths of allegiance
__Registers of papists
(Roman Catholics)
__Lists of attorneys
__Lists of constables
__Lists of jurors
__Jury pay lists
__Jury attendance lists
__Commissions of officiials
__Appointments of Justices
of the peace
__Lists of gamekeepers

Road Records
__Petitions
__Plats
__Appointments of road officials

Voters' Records
__Voters' register
__Voters' lists
__Poll books
__Register of intended voters
__Register of freemen
__Lists of freeholders
__Lists of rejected voters
__Oaths of office
__Loyalty oaths
__Freemen admissions

Militia Records
__Militia lists
__Muster rolls
__Muster-in rolls
__Muster-out rolls
__Payrolls
__Lists of males over age 16
__Troop returns
__Enlistments
__Enrollments
__Lists of recruits
__Substitutes
__Lists of rejected men
__Wagoners' rolls
__Casualty lists

Church Records
__Pew rents
__Membership lists
__Rate rolls
__Collection lists
__Subscription lists
__Lists of paupers

School Lists
__Matriculation lists
__Attendance lists
__Examination lists
__Tuition lists

__Subscription lists
__Pupil lists
__Teacher lists

Legislative Records
__Petitions
__Memorials

Ships' Records
__Crew lists
__Register of seamen
__Seamens' oaths
__Seamens' certificates
__Officers' lists
__Sick rosters
__Death registers
__Casualty lists

Miscellaneous Records
__Register of prisoners
__Register of slaves
__Register of free negroes
__Prisoners of war
__Manumission lists
__Register of unmarried persons
__Orphans' register
__Lists of physicians
__Lists of midwives
__Lists of strangers

---

nealogical Society of Utah call number. Tribes are found under several agencies during the period covered by the census, so it is important to study the history of the tribe before beginning research. Copies of this register are available in the Family History Library's American Reference area. Copies can be made on request for use in family history centers to access the lists more easily. There is no master name index to the Native Americans themselves.

Three copies of the census were made: one for the federal government in Washington (now transferred to the National Archives); a second for the Superintendent at Indian Affairs (Bureau of Indian Affairs); and a third for the Indian agency. Many Bureau of Indian Affairs copies were destroyed. Some local copies are still in agencies' possession or have been transferred to National Archives regional archives. For further information on Native American research, see chapter 14, Tracking Native American Family History.

1898–1906 INDIAN CENSUS CARDS INDEX

The Indian Census Cards Index was compiled by the Dawes Commission to verify individual rights to tribal allotments for the Five Civilized Tribes (Cherokee, Chickasaw, Choctaw, Creek, and Seminole). To search this index, send the name of the tribe, name of the individual, approximate date of birth or death, and location to the Director, National Archives—South-

west Region, Box 6216, Fort Worth, TX 76115. Copies of the index are available from the Five Civilized Tribes Center, Bureau of Indian Affairs, Muskogee Agency, Fourth Floor, Federal Building, Muskogee, OK 74401, and through the Family History Library.

In the 1910 census, a special Indian schedule is sometimes found at the end of regular population schedules for some counties. For example, NV 1910 lists tribe, tribe of father, tribe of mother, proportion of Native American blood, and number of times married.

1910–1939 INDIAN SCHOOL CENSUS

The Bureau of Indian Affairs took separate Indian school censuses from 1910 to 1939. These include names of all children between six and eighteen years of age, sex, tribe, degree of Native American blood, distance from home to the school, parent or guardian, and attendance during the year. Some schedules are available on microfilm, but most are still in original form in the Federal Records Center for the region where the tribe was located. Unlike white census records, these often include the mother's surname.

Native American census records can be used to identify relationships, mothers' full names, aliases, ancestral rights, and inheritances. These census records, however, apply only to Native Americans registered with the Bureau of Indian Affairs.

Many Native American families never enrolled with the government. These persons are recorded in the regular census schedules, usually without evidence of their Native American ties.

Other miscellaneous records document Native American populations. Supplementary rolls list births, deaths, and sometimes marriages. Deduction rolls give deaths or removals from the jurisdiction. Additional rolls include arrivals and births. Allotment rolls list those entitled to payment and the payments received. For a more detailed description of these and other Native American sources, see chapter 14.

NOTES

1. Carmen R. Delle Donne. *Federal Census Schedules, 1850–80: Primary Sources for Historical Research.* Reference Information Paper 67 (1973). Filled with interesting details on why and how the census was taken, 1850 to 1880.

2. U.S. Department of Commerce. Bureau of the Census. *A Century of Population Growth from the First Census of the United States to the Twelfth, 1790–1900.* Washington, D.C.: Government Printing Office, 1909. Reprint. Baltimore: Genealogical Publishing Co., 1967. Includes much information about the 1790 census and a list of common surnames and their distribution in the states.

3. Szucs, Loretto Dennis, and Sandra Hargreaves Luebking. *The Archives: A Guide to the National Archives Field Branches.* Salt Lake City: Ancestry, 1988.

4. Delle Donne, 1973.

5. Ibid.

6. Arlene H. Eakle. "Census Records" in *The Source: A Guidebook of American Genealogy.* Salt Lake City: Ancestry, 1984.

7. Val D. Greenwood. *The Researcher's Guide to American Genealogy.* 2nd ed. Baltimore: Genealogical Publishing Co., 1990.

8. Delle Donne, 1973.

BIBLIOGRAPHY

Anderson, Robert C., et al. "Duplicate Census Enumerations." *The American Genealogist* 62 (2) (April 1987): 97–105; 62 (3) (July 1987): 173–81; 62 (4) (October 1987): 241–44.

Barrows, Robert G. "The Ninth Federal Census of Indianapolis: A Case Study in Civic Chauvinism," *Indiana Magazine of History* 73 (1) (March 1977): 1–16.

Bureau of the Census. *Heads of Families at the First Census of the United States Taken in the Year 1790.* 12 vols. Washington, D.C.: Government Printing Office, 1908.

Bureau of the Census Records of State Enumerations, 1782–1785. 1908. Reprint. Baltimore: Genealogical Publishing Co., 1970.

Carpenter, Niles. *Immigrants and Their Children 1920: A Study Based on Census Statistics Relative to the Foreign Born and the Native White of Foreign or Mixed Parentage.* Census Monographs VII. Washington, D.C.: Department of Commerce, Bureau of the Census, 1927.

Census Enumeration District Descriptions, 1830–1890 and 1910–1950. National Archives Microfilm Publication T-1224, 146 rolls.

Census Enumeration District Descriptions, 1900. National Archives Microfilm Publication T-1210, 10 rolls.

A Census of Pensioners for Revolutionary or Military Services. 1841, various years. Reprint. Baltimore: Genealogical Publishing Co., 1996.

Conzen, Michael P. "Spatial Data from Nineteenth Century Manuscript Censuses: A Technique for Rural Settlement and Land Use Analysis." *The Professional Geographer* 21 (5): 337–43 (September 1969). A primer on mapping the enumerator's route.

Creekmore, Pollyanna. *Early East Tennessee Tax-Payers.* Easley, S.C.: Southern Historical Press, 1980.

Davenport, David P. "Duration of Residence in the 1855 Census of New York State," *Historical Methods* 18 (1) (Winter 1985): 5–12.

Davidson, Katherine H., and Charlotte M. Ashby, comps. *Preliminary Inventory of the Records of the Bureau of the Census.* Preliminary Inventory No. 161. Washington, D.C.: National Archives and Records Service, 1964.

Department of Commerce, Bureau of the Census. *Fourteenth Census of the United States, January 1, 1920: Instructions to Enumerators.* Washington, D.C.: Government Printing Office, 1919.

deValinger, Leon, Jr. *Reconstructed Census for Delaware.* Washington, D.C.: National Genealogical Society, 1954.

Dubester, Henry J. *State Censuses: An Annotated Bibliography of Censuses of Population Taken After the Year 1790 by States and Territories of the United States.* Washington, D.C.: Bureau of the Census, 1948. Reprint. Knightstown, Ind.: The Bookmark, 1975.

Eichholz, Alice. *Ancestry's Red Book: American State, County and Town Sources.* Rev. ed. Salt Lake City: Ancestry, 1992. Chapters appear alphabetically by state. Within each state chapter is a description of available federal, state, special, and local censuses and their respective finding aids.

_____, and James M. Rose, comps. *Free Black Heads of Households in the New York State Federal Census 1790–1830.* Gale Genealogy and Local History Series, vol. 14. Detroit: Gale Research Co., 1981.

The 1790–1890 Federal Population Censuses: Catalog of National Archives Microfilm. Washington, D.C.: National Archives Trust Fund Board, 1993.

Fishbein, Meyer H. *The Censuses of Manufacturers, 1810–1890.* Reference Information Paper 50 (1973).

Fothergill, Augusta B., and John M. Naugle. *Virginia Tax Payers 1782–1787. Other Than Those Published in the United States Census Bureau.* 1940. Reprint. Baltimore: Genealogical Publishing Co., 1971.

Franklin, W. Neil, comp. *Federal Population and Mortality Census Schedules, 1790–1890 in the National Archives and the States: Outline of a Lecture on Their Availability, Content and Use.* Special List no. 24. Washington, D.C.: National Archives and Records Service, General Services Administration, 1971. The greater part of this work describes the federal censuses and their availability in 1971. However, a discussion of mortality schedules is still valid. The compiler's bibliography cites some relatively obscure but important finding aids.

Frederick, Nancy Gubb. *1880 Illinois Census Index, Soundex Codes O-200 to O240*. Evanston, Ill.: the compiler, 1981.

A General Index to a Census of Pensioners . . . 1840. Baltimore: Genealogical Publishing Co., 1965.

Georgia Department of Archives and History. *Some Early Tax Digests of Georgia*. Atlanta: Department of Archives, 1926.

Giltner, Charlotte L. "Interpreting the 1790 Census." *Detroit Society for Genealogical Research Magazine* 51 (3) (Spring 1988): 110, 112.

Green, Kellee. "The Fourteenth Numbering of the People: The 1920 Federal Census." *Prologue: Quarterly of the National Archives* 23 (2) (Summer 1991): 131–45.

Greenwood, Val D. *The Researcher's Guide to American Genealogy*. 2nd ed. Baltimore: Genealogical Publishing Co., 1990. Particularly pp. 181–253.

Guide to Genealogical Research in the National Archives. Washington, D.C.: National Archives, 1983. Particularly pp. 9–38.

Heinemann, Charles B. *"First Census" of Kentucky, 1790*. 1940. Reprint. Baltimore: Genealogical Publishing Co., 1971.

Hollingsworth, Harry. "History and Availability of United States Census Schedules, 1850–1880," *Genealogical Journal* 7 (3) (September 1978): 143–50.

Indexes to Manufacturers' Census of 1820: An Edited Printing of the Original Indexes and Information. Reprint. Knightstown, Ind.: Bookmark, n.d.

Justesen, Elaine, and Ann Hughes, comps. *New York City 1915 State Census Street Address Index*. Vol. 1, *Manhattan*. Edited by Raymond G. Matthews. Salt Lake City: Family History Library, 1992.

Lainhart, Ann S. *State Census Records*. Baltimore: Genealogical Publishing Co., 1992.

McLeod, Dean L. "Record Source Failure; Some Implications for Analysis." *Genealogical Journal* 7 (2) (June 1978): 98–105.

Mariner, Mary Lou Craver, and Patricia Roughan Bellows. *A Research Aid for the Massachusetts 1910 Federal Census*. Sudbury, Mass.: Computerized Assistance, 1988. An index by towns and counties of enumeration districts, wards, and precincts and where to locate them on the microfilm. Enables a researcher to find town by roll, volume, and page number. Includes a large foldout street map of 1910 Boston with the wards indicated, plus county maps for the entire commonwealth.

National Archives and Records Administration. *Federal Population and Mortality Schedules, 1790–1910, in the National Archives and the States*. Washington, D.C.: National Archives, 1986. Two microfiche.

_____. *Guide to Genealogical Research in the National Archives*. Rev. ed. Washington, D.C.: National Archives Trust Fund Board, 1985.

National Archives and Records Service. *Cartographic Records of the Bureau of the Census*. Preliminary Inventory No. 103. Washington, D.C.: 1958. Includes a concise administrative history of federal census-taking. Following the inventory is a list showing the availability in the National Archives of maps of enumeration districts for each of the censuses, 1880 to 1940. The list is arranged by state, thereunder by county, and thereunder by locality.

_____. *Geographic Index to Census Microfilm (Major Subdivisions)*. This is the title of National Archives and Records Service Form NAR T56, bound, processed sets of completed copies of which comprise this finding aid. The forms are arranged alphabetically by state and thereunder alphabetically by county and major city. The forms show, for each subdivision, where applicable, the numbers assigned the rolls of microfilm that reproduce the schedules for that subdivision for each of the decennial censuses, 1800 to 1880. Sets of this finding aid are available for use in the Microfilm Reading Room of the National Archives.

_____. *Population Schedules, 1800–1870: Volume Index to Counties and Major Cities*. National Archives and Records Service Lists, No. 8. Washington, D.C.: 1969. Each bound volume of schedules in the National Archives bears an identifying number which is shown in this publication. Its arrangement is alphabetical by name of state and thereunder by name of county.

_____. *Records of the Bureau of the Census*. Preliminary Inventory No. 161. Washington, D.C.: 1964. Includes an administrative history of census-taking, an outline of preservation problems, and a description of the population schedules (1790 to 1950).

National Archives Trust Fund Board. *Federal Population Censuses, 1790–1890: A Catalog of Microfilm Copies of the Schedules*. Washington, D.C.: National Archives Trust Fund Board, 1979. This catalog is arranged chronologically, thereunder by state or territory, and then by county. Given for each microfilm publication is the series number and the total number of microfilm rolls in the enumeration. The catalog further identifies each microfilm roll by number and contents.

_____. *1900 Federal Population Census: A Catalog of Microfilm Copies of the Schedules*. Washington, D.C.: 1978. This catalog lists the 1,854 rolls of microfilm on which the 1900 population census schedules appear. The census schedules are arranged by state or territory and then by county. Numbers for the 7,846 rolls of 1900 Soundex appear in the second half of the book.

_____. *The 1910 Federal Population Census: A Catalog of Microfilm Copies of the Schedules*. Washington, D.C.: 1982. This catalog lists the 1,784 rolls of microfilm on which the 1910 population census schedules appear. The census schedules are arranged by state or territory and then by county. Numbers for the 4,642 rolls of 1910 Soundex/Miracode appear in the second half of the catalog.

_____. *The 1920 Federal Population Census: Catalog of National Archives Microfilm*. Washington, D.C.: *1991*. This catalog lists the 8,585 rolls of 1920 Soundex in the front portion of the book. The catalog lists 2,076 rolls of 1920 census schedules arranged by state or territory and then by county.

Nelson, Ken. *1890 Census Index Register.* Salt Lake City: Genealogical Society of Utah, 1984.

Norton, James S. *New Jersey in 1793.* Distributed by The Everton Publishers, Box 368, Logan UT 84321.

Owen, Lois, and Theodore R. Nelson, comps. *New York City 1915 State Census Street Address Index.* Vol. 2, *Brooklyn.* Edited by Raymond G. Matthews. Salt Lake City: Family History Library, 1993.

Parker, J. Carlyle. *City, County, Town and Township Index to the 1850 Census Schedules.* Detroit: Gale Research Co., 1979. Designed to identify cities, counties, towns, and townships in every state as they were in 1850, this alphabetically arranged list matches localities with appropriate census microfilm numbers. Its usefulness is not limited to the 1850 census because it can be used as a gazetteer to locate places that no longer exist and places that have been lost due to boundary changes.

Petty, Gerald M. *Virginia 1820 Federal Census: Names Not on the Microfilm Copy.* Virginia Genealogist 18 (1974): 136–39.

Schedules of the Colorado State Census of 1885. National Archives Microfilm Publication M-158 (eight rolls).

Schedules of the Florida State Census of 1885. National Archives Microfilm Publication M-845 (thirteen rolls).

Schedules of the Nebraska State Census of 1885. National Archives Microfilm Publication M-352 (fifty-six rolls).

Schedules of the New Mexico Territory Census of 1885. National Archives Microfilm Publication M-846 (six rolls).

The schedules of the 1885 Dakota Territory census are divided, the appropriate portions being held by the state historical societies of North and South Dakota. In addition to the federally supported 1885 state censuses, other states took censuses without federal support (see the sources listed above).

Schlesinger, Keith R. "An 'Urban Finding Aid' for the Federal Census," *Prologue* 13 (4): 251–62 (Winter 1981).

_____, and Peggy Tuck Sinko. "Urban Finding Aid for Manuscript Census Searches." *National Genealogical Society Quarterly* 69 (3) (September 1981): 171–80.

Shepard, JoAnne (Bureau of the Census). *Age Search Information.* Washington, D.C.: Government Printing Office, 1990.

Sistler, Byron, and Barbara Sistler. *Index to Early East Tennessee Tax Lists.* Nashville: Byron Sistler & Associates, 1977.

Stephenson, Charles. "The Methodology of Historical Census Record Linkage: A User's Guide to the Soundex," *Journal of Family History* 5 (1) (Spring 1980): 112–15. Reprinted in *Prologue* 12 (2) (Fall 1980): 151–53.

Steuart, Bradley W. *The Soundex Reference Guide: Soundex Codes to Over 125,000 Surnames.* Bountiful, Utah: Precision Indexing, 1990.

Straney, Shirley Garton. "1800 Census, Cumberland County;

A Contribution," *The Genealogical Magazine of New Jersey* 60 (1) (January 1985): 27–34.

Street Indexes to the 39 Largest Cities in the 1910 Census. National Archives Microfiche Publication M-1283.

Stryker-Rodda, Kenn. *Revolutionary Census of New Jersey: An Index, Based on Ratables of the Inhabitants During the Period of the American Revolution.* New Orleans: Polyanthos, 1972.

Swenson, Helen Smothers. *Index to 1890 Census of the United States.* Round Rock, Tex.: the author, 1981.

Thorndale, William. "Census Indexes and Spelling Variants." *APG [Association of Professional Genealogists] Newsletter* 4 (5) (May 1982): 6–9. Reprinted in *The Source: A Guidebook of American Genealogy,* edited by Arlene Eakle and Johni Cerny. Salt Lake City: Ancestry, 1984, pp. 17–20.

_____, and William Dollarhide. *Map Guide to the U.S. Federal Censuses, 1790–1920.* Baltimore: Genealogical Publishing Co., 1987.

Thurber, Evangeline. "The 1890 Census Records of the Veterans of the Union Army." *National Genealogical Society Quarterly* 34 (March 1946): 7–9.

U.S. Bureau of the Census. *200 Years of U.S. Census Taking: Population and Housing Questions, 1790–1990.* Washington, D.C.: Government Printing Office, 1989. Earlier editions had different titles: *Population and Housing Inquiries in U.S. Decennial Censuses, 1790–1970* (1973) and *Twenty Censuses: Population and Housing Questions, 1790–1980* (1979).

U.S. Census Office. Eighth Census, 1860. *Eighth Census, United States—1860. Act of Congress of Twenty-third May, 1850. Instructions to U.S. Marshals. Instructions to Assistants.* Washington, D.C.: G. W. Bowman, 1860. Enumerator's instructions for the 1860 census (omitted from Wright and *200 Years of U.S. Census Taking*).

U. S. Congress. Senate. *The History and Growth of the United States Census.* Prepared for the Senate Committee on the Census by Carroll D. Wright. S. Doc. 194,56 Cong., I sess., Serial 385b. Reprint. 1967. In the appendixes are reproduced the schedules of inquiry of each of the decennial censuses from 1790 to 1890 and the instructions for the taking of each of the decennial censuses from 1820 to 1890.

U.S. Library of Congress. Census Library Project. *State Censuses: An Annotated Bibliography of Censuses of Population Taken After the Year 1790 by States and Territories of the United States.* Prepared by Henry J. Dubester. Washington, D.C.: Government Printing Office, 1948.

_____. *Index to the Eleventh Census of the United States, 1890.* National Archives Microfilm Publication M-496 (two rolls).

_____. *Special Schedules of the Eleventh Census (1890) Enumerating Union Veterans and Widows of Union Veterans of the Civil War.* National Archives Microfilm Publication M-123 (118 rolls). The schedules for the states alphabetically from Alabama through Kansas and part of Kentucky were destroyed before the veterans schedules were acquired by the National Archives in 1943. Only the schedules for the states in the latter part of the alphabet are thus available for use. In recent years, state-by-state indexes for the veterans schedules have become available. They must, of course, be used with the same caution as any census indexes.

U.S. National Archives. *Federal Population Censuses, 1790–1890.* Washington, D.C.: National Archives, various dates.

_____. *1900 Federal Population Census.* Washington, D.C.: National Archives, 1978.

_____. *1910 Federal Population Census.* Washington, D.C.: National Archives, 1982.

_____. *1920 Federal Population Census.* Washington, D.C.: National Archives, 1991.

Vallentine, John F. "Effective Use of Census Indexes in Locating People." *Genealogical Journal* 4 (2) (June 1975): 51–58.

_____. "State and Territories Census Records in the United States." *Genealogical Journal* 2 (4) (December 1973): 133–39.

Volkel, Lowell M. *Illinois Mortality Schedule 1850.* 3 vols. Indianapolis: Heritage House, 1972.

_____. *Illinois Mortality Schedule 1860.* 5 vols. Indianapolis: Heritage House, 1979.

_____. *Illinois Mortality Schedule 1870.* 2 vols. Indianapolis: Heritage House, 1985.

Warren, James W. *Minnesota 1900 Census Mortality Schedules.* St. Paul, Minn.: Warren Research & Marketing, 1991–92.

Warren, Mary Bondurant. "Census Enumerations: How Were They Taken? Do Local Copies Exist?," *Family Puzzlers* no. 475 (November 1976): 1–16.

Wright, Carroll D. *The History and Growth of the United States Census.* Washington, D.C.: Government Printing Office, 1900. Reprint. New York: Johnson Reprint, 1966. A basic source for background and details of the census-taking process, 1790 to 1890. There is nothing as detailed for later censuses.

RESEARCH IN CHURCH RECORDS
CHAPTER CONTENTS

6

RESEARCH IN CHURCH RECORDS

Richard W. Dougherty

Church records rank among the most promising of genealogical records available. Indeed, for periods before the advent of civil registration of vital statistics (a very late development in many American states), church records rank as the best available sources for information on specific vital events: birth, marriage, and death.

They are also among the most under-used major records in American genealogy. Part of the reason lies in the number of denominations—there are hundreds of them. Identifying and locating the records of these various churches makes even professional genealogists hesitate. Yet the task is not impossible. Microfilming, photocopying, and indexing techniques make church records more accessible now than ever before.

Church records vary a great deal in content and emphasis according to the basic theology and social role of each denomination. However, a useful distinction is the difference between "state" churches and so-called "free" churches. State, or "established," churches in Europe considered every Christian in the state or kingdom to be a member. Free, or "gathered," churches emphatically rejected this inclusive view of belonging from birth. Rather, only those who had been "born again" in Christ could be considered true members of his church. The sign of this rebirth in Christ was another baptism (adult baptism) that took precedence over the person's baptism as an infant. For this practice they were called Anabaptists—from the Latin for "rebaptizers." The descendants of the Anabaptists include Mennonites, Hutterites, many smaller groups associated with the Pennsylvania Germans, and their British cousins, the Baptists, who form the dominant religion in much of America today.

Because Anabaptists saw the most important event in a person's life as his or her rebirth in Christ, not his or her physical birth, their records reflect the difference. Baptist records contain much valuable historical information about the activities of adult members, but they do not always deliver accurate birth information. In contrast, Lutherans meticulously recorded infant births and subsequent parish baptisms.

Of course, theology is not the only factor that has determined the types of records kept. In Scandinavia and many German states, the Lutheran church was the established church. Thus, the pastor was a quasi-public official who was the official recorder of births, deaths, and marriages. Similarly, in England, a 1538 Act of Parliament required all ministers of the Church of England to record baptisms, marriages, and burials in their parishes. In 1597, another parliamentary act reinforced the original law, requiring that duplicates of parish records be sent annually to the bishop of the pertinent diocese, initiating the valuable "bishops' transcripts."

In Scotland, the Netherlands, Switzerland, and certain German states where Calvinism became the established faith, pastors were also official record keepers. Not all German Protestants were Lutherans. In many German states, most notably in Prussia, the state church combined Lutheran and Calvinist elements, resulting in long-range consequences when German immigrants organized churches in the New World.

In areas of Europe where Roman Catholicism was the established faith, parish priests were the official recorders of baptisms, marriages, and burials. They were accountable to more than local parliaments, however. In 1563, the church's Council of Trent issued a decree requiring proof of baptism before marriage. Subsequent decrees reinforced this edict, notably that of Pope Paul V in 1614, which made parish registers obligatory.

Church record-keeping transcended national and religious boundaries. It was a manifestation of a stage of European civilization that emphasized rationality and bureaucracy. Human memory and oral tradition no longer sufficed. The written record prevailed.

This background is relevant to discussion of American church records because habits, attitudes, and ecclesiastical edicts crossed oceans with the emigrants. The various immigrant churches, including those that developed in Plymouth Colony in the 1620s, reflected European philosophy and practices. In fact, most of the American colonies promptly established state churches. In New England, the Congregational Church generally held preferred status. In the southern colonies (Virginia, Georgia, and South Carolina), the Church of England (Protestant Episcopal) became the established church, as it was in Maryland for a time, even though that colony was originally founded as a haven for Roman Catholics. As long as the Dutch controlled New Netherland (now New York), the Dutch Reformed Church served as the established church.

Some of these established churches functioned on a state level until well after the American Revolution, but the variety of immigrant groups and religious preferences ultimately defeated all attempts to impose religious uniformity. The Founding Fathers recognized this fact, totally separating church and state nationally when they drew up the Constitution. The wisdom of this decision was verified by the Great Awakening of the eighteenth and early nineteenth centuries, which shook established churches to the core and guaranteed that American religious life would be fundamentally different from that of the Old World.

The United States possesses a tremendous, sometimes bewildering, variety of religious groups that have widely differing record-keeping practices. Nevertheless, certain basic types of records found at the parish, or local, level can be identified.

TYPES OF CHURCH RECORDS

BAPTISM AND CHRISTENING RECORDS

Baptism or christening records almost always list at least the name of the person baptized, the date and place of birth, and the date and place of the baptism. For infant baptisms, the pastor usually recorded the parents' names and often their place of residence, particularly if the pastor was serving a circuit rather than a single parish. Quite often, the register lists the date of birth or at least the age of the person being baptized. In addition, many baptismal records list the names of sponsors or godparents, who are often close relatives of the parents.

Figure 6-1 is a transcription of the christening register of Albemarle (Protestant Episcopal) Parish, Surry and Sussex Counties, Virginia, from around 1739–1741. These entries predate the change from the Julian to the Gregorian calendar in September 1752. Before then, the year began on 25 March. Dates between 1 January and 25 March listed both the current and succeeding year—for example, 5 January 1746/47. Under the present calendar this date would be 5 January 1747. The transcriber retained the original double-dating system to avoid confusion.

The rector of Albemarle parish, the Reverend William Willie, was an unusually diligent record keeper; on page 384 of the same christening register is a page of unusual entries. Below are three:

> Suky, f.; o. Col Allen; i. —b. Nov.3, 1774; c. May 14, 1775.
>
> Cuba, f.; o. Mrs. Lightfoot; i.–; b. March 31, 1775; c. May 14, 1775.
>
> Ede, f.; o. Capt. Thompson; i. –; b. Dec. 1774; c. May 14, 1775.

These infants are the children of slaves. The adults listed are not their parents but their owners. Thus, church records can sometimes aid in the extremely difficult task of tracing blacks before the Civil War. A second example, figure 6-2, is from the records of the First English Reformed Church of Baltimore, Maryland, around 1867–1868.

This register does not contain as much genealogical information as the Albemarle register, which preceded it by 120 years. It lists no sponsors except the parents themselves. (This situation—later church records providing less information than earlier ones—is by no means unique.) Five baptisms include only the mother as a parent, which does not necessarily mean that she was widowed or that the child was illegitimate but more probably that the mother was the only parent who belonged to that church.

MARRIAGE RECORDS

The second major type of church records are marriage records. Almost all American denominations have recorded marriages, although there are some interesting exceptions. For instance, the early Puritans viewed marriage as a civil contract. Hence, marriages were performed by a civil magistrate and were not recorded in the church registers. This was not a typical situation, however. In most areas, church marriage records predate civil marriage records by many decades and sometimes even centuries. For instance, South Carolina did not record marriages (except for marriage contracts) at the county or state level until 1911. In such situations, church marriage records acquire greater importance.

Church marriage records vary widely in content. Some provide nothing more than the names of the bride and groom and the date. Figure 6-3 is a published transcription of records of the First (Congregational) Church in Huntington, Long Island. This record yields an additional dividend to the genealogist: the pastor recorded the previous residences of the couple.

The other extreme is demonstrated by a Roman Catholic marriage register from a parish in south-central Texas (figure 6-4). It records the date of the marriage; the names, ages, residences, birthplaces, and religion of the bride and groom; the occupation of the groom; the place where the ceremony was held; the names and birthplaces of the parents of the nuptial pair; and the name of the officiating priest. As with most Catholic records, these are in Latin, a custom often cited as an obstacle to their use by genealogists. If so, it is a minor obstacle. When the records are in columnar form, as is the case here, you can decipher the Latin headings using common sense and a Latin word list. Admittedly, this example is unusual, especially in listing the parents' birthplaces. But Catholic, Lutheran, and German Reformed marriage records frequently list the birthplace of the bride and groom.

DEATH RECORDS

Church marriage records are often useful in locating an immigrant ancestor's birthplace, but, in my professional experience, church death registers have been the single most valuable source for tracing an immigrant's place of birth. Figure 6-5 is an alphabetized translation of the death records of Saint John's Lutheran Church, Ruma, Illinois. Originally, churches recorded burials rather than deaths, and some churches still do. However, most American church records also list the date of death, and often they record a great deal more information.

In one instance, I researched a county history that listed a German immigrant's birthplace as Gubeardstadt, Prussia. I found no such village in any gazetteer. Fortunately, the county history also stated where the family attended church. A letter to the church (then German Evangelical, now United Church of Christ) produced a photocopy of the pertinent page of the death register, which noted that the individual had been born in Gross Bierstadt in the province of Saxony, Prussia. I then easily located the village using a standard atlas.

Figure 6-1. From Gertrude Richards, trans. and ed., *Register of the Albemarle Parish Surrey and Sussex* [counties, Virginia], *1739–78.* Indexed by Florence M. Leonard (Richmond: National Society Colonial Dames of America in the Commonwealth of Virginia, 1958), 9.

ALBEMARLE PARISH REGISTER   9

Arthur s. of John Burnham and w. Mary; b. June 14; c. Oct 21, 1740; gdpts. William Willie, Arthur Smith, Jean Bennet.

Anne d. of Benja Adams and w. Agnes; b. Sept 29; c. Dec 4, 1740; gdpts.---.

Agnes and Jane, 2 of 3 d. of John Stigal and w. Winnifred; b. Feb 3; c. Feb 4, 1740/1; gdpts.---

Anne d. of Robert Newman and w. Catharine; b. Jan 11; c. March 15, 1740/41; gdpts. Francis Walker, Mary Bobbit, Amy Bobbit.

Amy d. of Charles Hay and w. Sarah; b. Nov 9; c. 1737; gdpts.---.

Amy d. of Charles Mabry and w. Rebecca; b. Dec 9, 1740; c. March 29, 1741; gdpts. Simon Gale, Amy Freeman, Mary Gillum.

()ne d. of Nathl Hawthorn and w. Susanna; b. April 7, c. June 17, 1739; gdpts. Peter Hawthorn, Frances Hawthorn, Eliza Weaver.

Anne d. of Joseph Clarke and w. Margaret; b. July 11, 1740; c. May 4, 1741; gdpts. William Willie, Eliza Willie, Mary Berry.

()y d. of John Weaver and w. Eliza; b. April 15; c. June 28, 1741; gdpts. John Vincent, Mary Shelton, Bridget Tatum.

()y d. of Thomas Musslewite and w. Sarah; b. Sept 4, 1740; c. June 28, 1741; gdpts. John Stigal, Eliza Tatum, Eleanor Smith.

()my d. of Philip Bailey and w. Mary; b. June 19; c. July 19, 1741; gdpts. Alexr Dickens, Lydda Dickens, Mary Shelton.

Arthur s. of Charles Delahay and w. Eliza; b. July 13; c. Sept 13, 1741; gdpts. Henry Freeman, jr, Francis Hutchins, Sarah Ellis.

Amy d. of Abraham Evans and w. Eliza; b. June 19; c. Sept 13, 1741; gdpts. Joshua Rolland, Hannah Bell, Eliza Rolland.

Abigail d. of Thomas Davis and w. Jean; b. Dec 1, 1740; c. Oct 4, 1741; gdpts. Richard King, Mary (), Mary Emmery.

Anne d. of Stephen Pepper and w. Jean; b. Sept 16; c. Nov 12, 1741; gdpts. Richard Pepper, Simon Murphy, Sarah Alsobrook, Susanna Ellis.

Anne d. of Wm Freeman and w. Eliza; b. Dec 28, 1741; c. Jan 24, 1741/2; gdpts. Wm Moss, Susanna Freeman, Anne Sandefour.

() d. of Robert Sandefour and w. Anne; b. Dec 11, 1741; c. Jan 24, 1741/2; Wm Freeman, Susanna Freeman, Eliza Denton.

Confirmation Records

While most genealogists are aware of the value of baptismal, marriage, and death records, they sometimes overlook other types of church records that also contain valuable genealogical and historical information; confirmation records are a case in point. Most how-to books dismiss them as mere name lists, which, admittedly, is often the case. However, those of the Scandinavian Lutheran denominations contain voluminous information, as figure 6-6 shows, as do present-day Episcopal churches.

Obviously, a reading knowledge of Norwegian is a more specialized skill than reading Latin, but this basic record is intelligible even without language expertise. I do not have a good command of Norwegian, but, with an inexpensive Norwegian-English dictionary, I deciphered the confirmation entries. The first column contains the date of the confirmation; the second column, the name of the confirmed; the third, the age; and the fourth, the names of the parents. The fifth column offers a somewhat greater challenge but, as is often the case, commensurate rewards—it states the place of baptism. Most of those confirmed were baptized in "this congregation" (*menigheden her*),

Baptisms.

№	Names.	Parents.	Birth	When Baptized.
1	Sidney Harry.	Benj. G. & Susan M. Kent.	July 14- 1867.	December 5- 1867.
2	Daniel Henry.	Daniel G. & Albenia E. Biser.	March 9- 1867.	December 26- 1867.
3	Howard Lee.	William & Sarah Randall.	March 25- 1867.	January 5- 1868.
4	Henrietta Jerome.	Benj. & Christiana Reynolds.	March 23- 1865.	January 5- 1868.
5	Emma Virginia.	Benj. F. & Jane E. Sweeting.	January 20- 1868.	March 12- 1868.

Figure 6-2. Entries from the baptismal register of the Baltimore First English Reformed Church, 1867–74, vol. 1, p. 1; Family History Library (hereafter FHL) microfilm 940,423.

MARRIAGES.

A record of Marriages Consummated by Me E. P. Ab Anno 1723 Ad Annum &c.

Place of Marriage	Year	Mo.	Day	Names of Parties Married	Places of their abode before Marriage.
Huntington,	1723	Octobr.	31	Epenetus Platt and Sarah Scuddar	Huntington
		Decemr.	18	Jonathan Foster and Elisabeth Chichester	Huntington
	1724	June	1	Daniel Keleg and Unice Jarvis	Norwalk In Connecticot Huntington
			30	Stephen Miller and Sarah Warin	Bedford On ye main Oysterbay
		Decemr.	21	Richard Drage and Mary Coone	Oysterbay.
			22	Samuel Plumbe and Anna Roe	Huntington
	1724/5	Feby.	10	Jonathan Smith and Temperance Whitman	Stamford in Connectcot Huntington.

Figure 6-3. From Moses L. Scudder, comp., *Records of the First Church in Huntington, Long Island, 1723–79* (Huntington, N.Y.: the compiler, 1899), 61.

but Edvart Olson and Karin P. Hausland were baptized in Hjelmedard, Norway. Again, the crucial piece of information needed to find the family's place of origin in Europe is provided. The sixth column refers to the degree of "Christian knowledge" possessed by the confirmed. Most received a "good," three received a "very good," and three received "less good." The last column refers to the membership status of the parents of those confirmed. All were members of the congregation except for Albert and Anne Olson ("nonmembers") and Ole Olson ("outsider").

Scandinavian-American Lutheran confirmation records typically contain exceptionally valuable genealogical information. German-American Lutheran and Reformed confirmation records often contain the date of baptism and sometimes the place. Episcopal churches include records of baptism in the confirmation records and file a report with the bishop. In my experience, Catholic confirmation records seldom contain the place of baptism. Most American Protestant denominations, if they perform confirmations at all, merely list the names of those confirmed and the date of the event, marking the young person's entry into full membership in the congregation. Some also give the ages of those confirmed, yielding more precise estimates of birth data and identities.

MEMBERSHIP RECORDS

Confirmation records lead to another category of church sources: membership records. One type of membership record is communicant lists. While not as valuable to the genealogist as the records already discussed, they can be of great help in reconstructing a family history. The sudden disappearance of a couple from the communicant lists may signify their departure from the community. The disappearance of one but not the other may indicate death, an important clue if the death records no longer exist.

Usually, the regular membership list is of greater genealogical value. In some cases, however, it too may be only a name list. But by the late nineteenth century, many Protestant churches kept fairly good membership records. Figure 6-7 is a page from a membership record of one family in a Methodist Church in Indiana between 1895 and 1927. The particular value of this record is in the information it contains about the movement of members in and out of the congregation. Some of these "removals" or "dismissals" occurred well after 1920, the date of the latest federal census available to the public. The implications for the genealogist seeking heirs rather than ancestors are obvious. Church records should not be dismissed as irrelevant for periods after civil registration began in a given state or community.

OTHER TYPES OF CHURCH RECORDS

In addition to the types of records discussed above, local parishes or congregations created many other genealogically valuable types of church records: minutes of the church council or vestry, disciplinary records, pew rentals, and family registers, among others. If the ancestor was active in church affairs, such records can be invaluable for reconstructing the family's history.

Figure 6-4. Entries from the Saint Rose of Lima Catholic Church, Schulenberg, Texas, marriage register, vol. 2, p. 2; FHL 025,499.

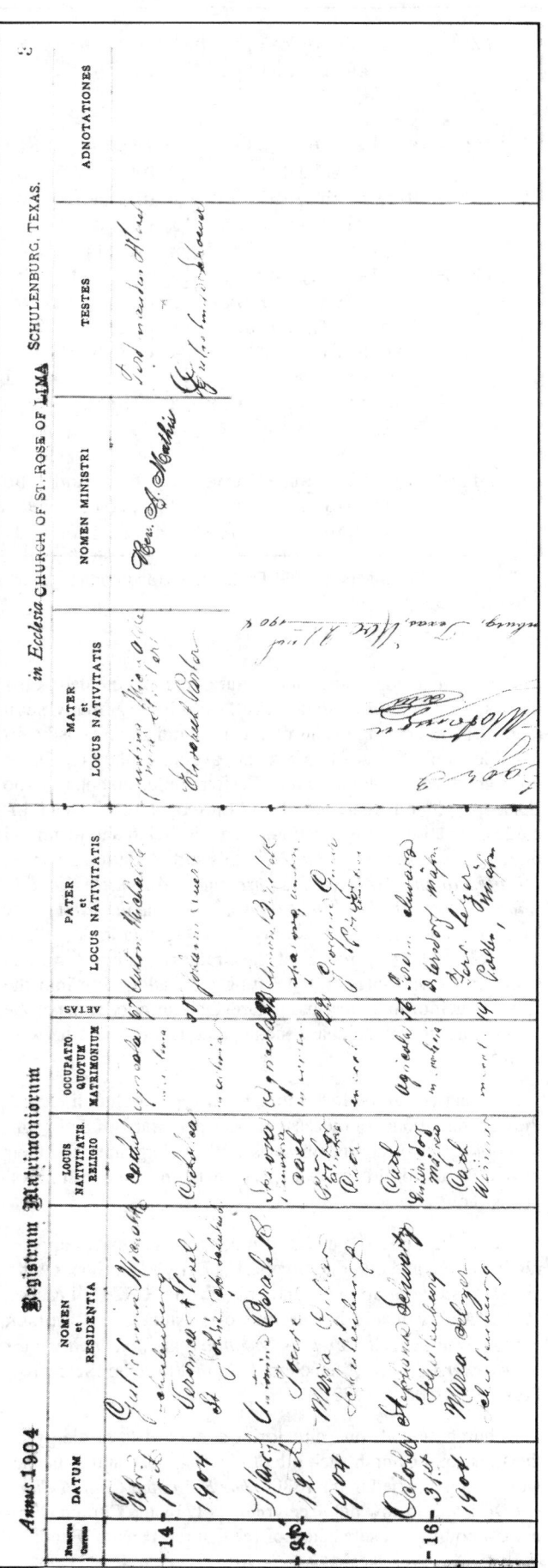

```
#245--Lina Schenkel,a child, born at Mascoutah, Ills., living bei Evansville,
       died 12 März 1879, i. 14 März, aged 13 years, 3 months, 3 days, pages
       190-191


#281--Christian Schlimme, widower, born Hannover, living near Ruma, Ills., died
       17 Dec 1883, i. 19 Dec 1883, aged 60 years, 11 months, 17 days, pp. 194-195
#364--Heinrich Schlimme, husband, born in Borstel, kingdom of Hannover, Germany,
       living at Ruma, Ills., died 10 Jan 1900, i. 12 Jan 1900, aged 47 years,
       11 months, 26 days--Matthew 24, 44--pages 204-205
#213--Maria Dorothea Schlimme, wife, born in Borstel in Kingdom of Hannover,
       living at Horse Creek, died 19 May 1877, i. 20 May, aged 47 years, 3
       months, 24 days, pages 186-187
#308--Maria Elisabeth Louise Schlimme, a child, born near Ruma, Ills., living
       near Ruma, Ills., died 26 Oct 1888, i. 27 Oct, aged 12 days, pp. 196-197
#73 --Rosette Maria Carolina Schlimme, a child, living at Horse Creek, died at
       11 Sep 1869, i. 12 Sep, aged 7 years, 10 months, 25 days, pages 168-169


#156--Joseph Schmellemeier, husband, born Siegmaringen im Kingdom Würtemberg,
       living at Evansville, died 19 März 1874, i. 20 März 1874, aged 49 years,
       1 month, 4 days, pages 178-179
```

Figure 6-5. From Mrs. Harold Drake, trans. and comp., *Church Records of St. John's Lutheran Church, Ruma, Illinois* (Watseka, Ill.: the compiler, 1975), 16.

Many genealogists overlook church records created at the diocesan or denominational level. Admittedly, many such records lie moldering in church archives and are not easily accessible. But when such records are available, they can be of very great genealogical value. For example, bishops of the Episcopal Church keep records of "Episcopal Acts," which include ordinations, confirmations, and admission and dismissal of clergy. An excellent example of this sort of church record is *Minutes of the Methodist Conferences Annually Held in America; From 1773 to 1813 Inclusive Volume the First* (New York: 1813. Reprint. Swainsboro, Ga.: Magnolia Press, 1983). This volume lists the names of the circuit riders in the various districts of the church, often listing their admission into the church, their ordinations, and tenure. Obituaries of some of the pastors provide invaluable genealogical data that is otherwise unavailable.

Obituaries can be found in another type of church record: the denominational or diocesan newspaper. Many of these contain obituaries of lay members as well as clergymen and their wives. Space forbids an extensive treatment of church newspapers here.

A useful guide to published indexes of obituaries appearing in church and other newspapers is Betty M. Jarboe, *Obituaries: A Guide to Sources*, 2nd ed. (Boston: G.K Hall & Co., 1989). Also valuable in this regard is Anita Cheek Milner, comp., *Newspaper Indexes: A Location and Subject Guide for Researchers,* 3 vols. (Metuchen, N.J., and London: Scarecrow Press, 1977, 1979, 1982).

Church annuals and directories contain lists of clergy. In the Episcopal Church such directories, annuals, and almanacs were first published in the 1830s. *The Episcopal Church Clerical Directory* is now published biennially by the Church Hymnal Corporation, a subsidiary of the Church Pension Fund.

CHURCH RECORDS PROJECTS

Several projects that make access to church records easier and more effective are listed below. Some are readily available in most research libraries; some, however, access special collections, requiring you to visit the repository or send an agent to search for you.

PENNSYLVANIA AND MARYLAND GERMAN RECORDS

Dr. Frederick S. Weiser, a Lutheran pastor of Pennsylvania German ancestry, has translated, transcribed, and edited many of the Lutheran church registers of colonial Pennsylvania. He has also re-translated many records originally translated by William J. Hinke. Typewritten copies are on deposit in the A.R. Wentz Library in Gettysburg, Pennsylvania, and at the Family History Library of The Church of Jesus Christ of Latter-day Saints (LDS church) in Salt Lake City. Microfilm copies of most are also available through LDS family history centers located throughout the United States. Pastor Weiser has also compiled a valuable series of *Guides to Central Pennsylvania Lutheran Church Records;* there is one for each county. These are also available at the two libraries mentioned; you can order copies from Pastor Weiser, 55 Kohler School Rd., New Oxford, PA 17350-9415.

In 1986, Pastor Weiser extended his translating activities to Maryland, inaugurating a new series: *Maryland German Church Records,* published by the Noodle-Doosey Press, Manchester, MD 21102. Thus far, seven separate volumes have appeared; they are divided approximately equally between German Reformed and Lutheran congregations.

LOUISIANA CATHOLIC RECORDS

Reverend Father Donald J. Hebert has translated and transcribed parish records for several Louisiana Parishes. These registers are available in some forty printed volumes to date: *Southwest*

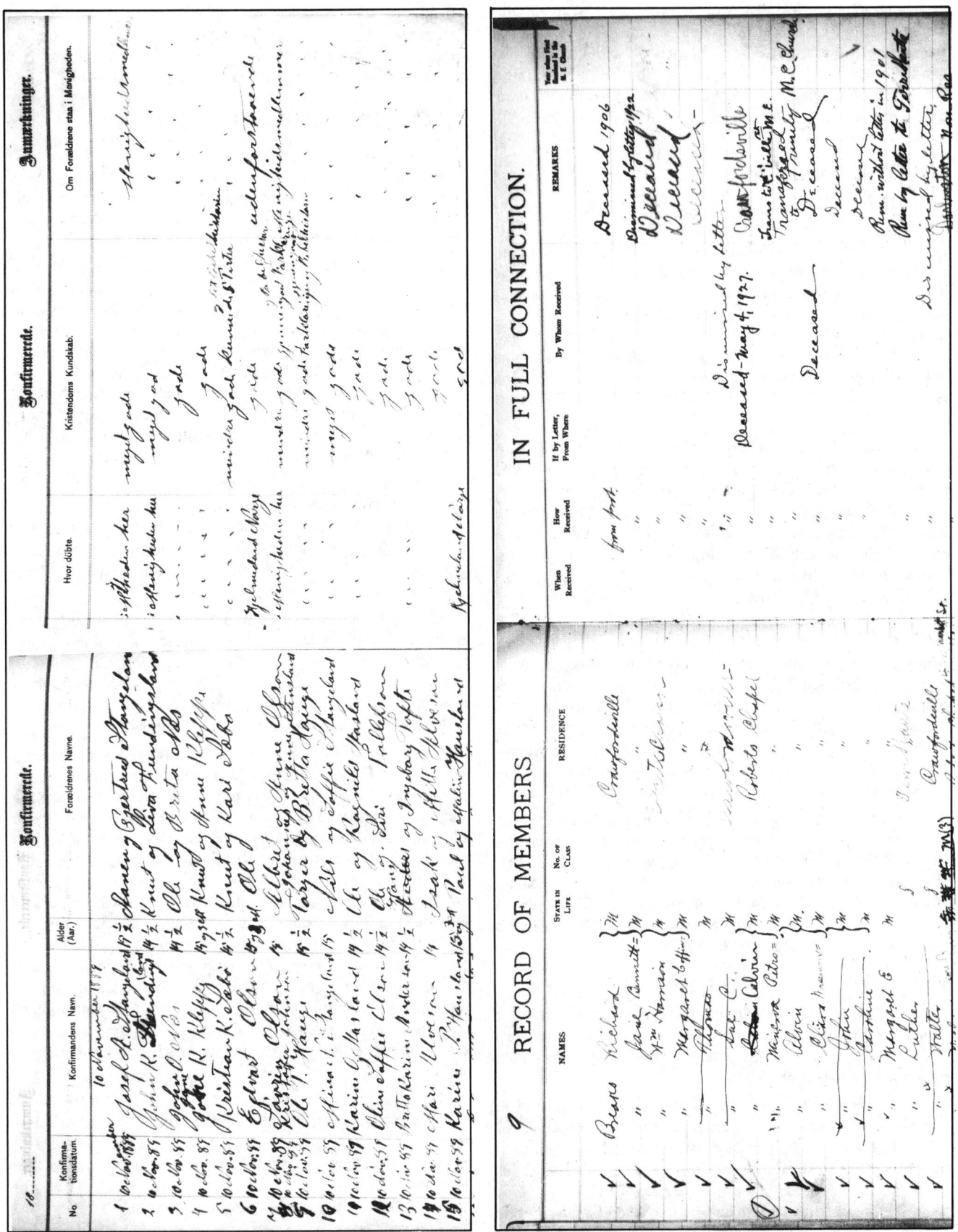

Figure 6-6. Entries from the Stavanger Norwegian Evangelical Lutheran Church, Fayette County, Iowa, confirmation register, 1884–1910, p. 68; FHL 1,034,242.

Figure 6-7. Entries from the Roberts Chapel Methodist Episcopal Church, Crawfordsville Circuit, Crawfordsville, Indiana, record of members, p. 9; FHL 877,714, item 3.

Louisiana Records, to 1897, twenty-eight volumes, and *Southern Louisiana Records,* to 1895, nine volumes. These volumes are available in many research libraries. To acquire your own copies, order them from Hebert Publications, Box 31, Eunice, LA 70535. Reverend Father Hebert has also compiled *A Guide to Church Records in Louisiana* (Eunice, La.: the author, 1975). It covers all denominations.

New York State Church Records Collections

The Study Center for Early Religious Life in Western New York, headquartered at Ithaca College, has microfilmed or photocopied three hundred collections of church records for that area. The center is no longer in existence, and the records have been deposited in the Regional Collection, Cornell University Library, for general use. Because Cornell's is a research library, the staff available to answer queries is limited. Expect some delay in receiving a response. A list of records in the collection is available on request with a self-addressed, stamped envelope.

A second collection of New York state church records worthy of special mention has been transcribed, compiled, and published by Arthur C.M. Kelly. He has focused primarily on Dutch Reformed churches of the Hudson River Valley, but he has published transcriptions of other churches' records as well—for example, Lutheran. For a complete list of his publications, contact Arthur C.M. Kelly, Kinship Press, 60 Cedar Heights Rd., Rhinebeck, NY 12572.

The Shane Collection—Kentucky and Ohio

Many genealogists are familiar with the collection of the Reverend John Dabney Shane's papers in the Draper Manuscript collection at the State Historical Society of Wisconsin in Madison. However, half of Shane's papers are housed in the archive of the Presbyterian Historical Society in Philadelphia. Microfilm copies of the Draper collection and the Shane papers in Philadelphia are available from the Family History Library.

Until recently, the wealth of genealogical information contained in that portion of Shane's papers housed in the Presbyterian archive has remained largely unrecognized and inaccessible. A recently published book should help to remedy the situation: William K. Hall, *The Shane Manuscript Collection: A Genealogical Guide to the Kentucky and Ohio Papers* (Galveston, Tex.: Frontier Press, 1990).

Other Published Church Records

The collections listed above might be described as the tip of an iceberg. A vast number of American church records have been transcribed and more appear every month; it would be quite impossible to list them all here.

Many transcriptions of church records have appeared in genealogical periodicals—for example, the *New England Genealogical Register.* Fortunately, indexes have been published that make this information accessible to the genealogist. Arguably the most important of these is the *Periodical Source Index (PERSI),* prepared and published by the Allen County Public Library Genealogy Department in Fort Wayne, Indiana. Another extremely important index to genealogical periodicals is Donald Lines Jacobus, *Index to Genealogical Periodicals* (1952. Reprint. Baltimore: Genealogical Publishing Co., 1978).

An important complement to that index is the *Genealogical Periodical Annual Index (GPAI),* 1962 to the present. For a thorough discussion of *PERSI* and other periodical indexes, see chapter 2, Databases, Indexes, and Other Finding Aids.

LOCATING CHURCH RECORDS

Two real difficulties with American church records are, first, locating them and, second, obtaining access to them. Various denominations have differing policies on public access to their records. See the denomination-specific listing at the end of this chapter for information on availability.

Determining the church your ancestor attended is the first task in locating church records. In some families this poses no great problem due to a continuing religious tradition. Even in cases of changing affiliations, the family's Bibles and other papers—baptismal certificates, wedding announcements, etc.—should be searched for clues. County marriage records, if they exist, often give the name of the clergyman who officiated. If a county history exists, it will usually list the various churches and their clergymen, thus enabling you to identify the clergyman's denomination.

In large cities, the task becomes a bit more complicated, for the county history may not list every clergyman for every church. Fortunately, city directories usually list the clergymen and their churches. Larger libraries often possess microfilm copies of city directories dating back to the first half of the nineteenth century.

Of course, the ancestral pair may have been married by the local justice of the peace, which complicates the problem. However, their siblings may have preferred a religious ceremony; and since a wedding customarily takes place in the bride's church, the marriages of the groom's sisters are worth seeking to determine which church his family attended.

The same basic procedure can be followed with the civil death records. The death certificate may list the name of the clergyman who conducted the funeral. If not, it may state the name of the undertaker. If it does, a check of a current city or telephone directory may yield the present address of the funeral establishment. A letter to the firm could produce the name of the clergyman, as well as other extremely valuable genealogical information. Some mortuaries also cater to persons of specific religious affiliations, so ask their morticians directly for this information. If the ancestor was hospitalized before his or her death, hospital records may contain information about religious affiliation and additional genealogical data. Another approach for determining religious affiliation is the obituary column of the local newspaper. Obituaries vary greatly in quality, but they usually list the time and place of the funeral and burial.

But what if the ancestor died before civil registration of vital statistics began or before newspapers carried obituaries? As the late Derek Harland stated, "In no other aspect or phase of genealogy is a knowledge of the history or geography of the area in which research is to be carried out more essential than in the study of the church records of the United States."[1]

Using other types of available records—census returns, land records, and county plat maps—you can pinpoint where the ancestor actually lived, then determine what churches existed in the area. Sometimes the task is simpler if the area was settled by a single national or ethnic group with a historically dominant religion, such as Polish (Catholic), Norwegian (Lutheran), or Scottish (Presbyterian). However, many European immigrants, even those who came from countries dominated by a state religion, chose other religions after they arrived in the United States. For instance, the state church of Sweden was Lutheran, but many Swedes became Baptists or Methodists in America. Many Germans who immigrated to Pennsylvania in the eighteenth century were not Lutherans but religious dissenters—Amish, Mennonites, or Baptists. The LDS church conducted an extremely successful missionary program in Sweden and Denmark in the mid-nineteenth century.

To further complicate the situation, various German states adopted Calvinism, or a blend of Lutheranism and Calvinism, as the state church—among them the Rhenish Palatinate and Prussia. Some immigrant pastors from these areas organized German Reformed or German Evangelical churches in the New World. Today these churches form part of the United Church of Christ. German pastors of Methodist persuasion successfully organized many congregations that are today part of the United Methodist Church.

Generally speaking, immigrants, if they went to church at all, attended churches where their native language was spoken. People needed a community where they could function as equals. Family members of some denominations may have crossed denominational lines to serve as sponsors or witnesses in religious events for friends and relatives. Therefore, try to find all the churches of your ancestor's language group in the area.

In the South, even though it never experienced a major influx of non-English-speaking immigrants in the nineteenth century, church records are crucial for genealogical success and, at the same time, problematic. They are crucial because no other records exist and problematic because they do not always contain needed information. The South was the last area of the United States to establish statewide civil registration, viewing vital records as the business of churches.

In colonial times, the Protestant Episcopal Church was the established church in many southern colonies. In frontier communities, such as Augusta County, Virginia, there were more Presbyterians (Scots-Irish) than Protestant Episcopalians or Anglicans (English), so the established parishes were presided over by Presbyterians and held Presbyterian services. The Augusta Church physically housed the Revolutionary Committee of Safety and even the Virginia Provincial Assembly for a period of time during the break with England. It is always wise to check the established church records even if your ancestors were known to belong to another faith.

With the advent of the Great Awakening in the eighteenth century, the emotional and spiritual declaration of independence so crucial to the formation of the American character, record-keeping received less priority. The date of a person's rebirth in Jesus was often considered more important than his or her physical birth. The continuing westward migration of settlers made exact record-keeping difficult as well.

A useful guide through the maze of denominational history in the United States is Frank Mead and Samuel S. Hill, *Handbook of American Denominations*, 8th ed. (Nashville: Abingdon Press, 1985). For current information, consult the *Yearbook of American and Canadian Churches,* published annually by Abingdon Press under the editorial direction of the National Council of Churches. (This extremely useful volume is described more fully in the list at the end of this chapter.) Another source of information about local church records is the *Family History Library Catalog*. The Family History Library has made considerable efforts to obtain American church records at all levels. As a result, you can often find microfilms or printed transcriptions of local church records of given townships or counties in its holdings. (See chapter 2.)

The International Genealogical Index (IGI), established by the Genealogical Society of Utah and available at the Family History Library and its family history centers, contains entries from many American church records—for example, Dutch Reformed records for New York and New Jersey, Lutheran and German Reformed records for Pennsylvania, and Congregational records for the New England states. There are also Presbyterian, Quaker, and Roman Catholic sources in the IGI. See chapter 2 for instructions on using the IGI.

In some states, the state historical society has become the official archives for certain denominations. For example, the State Historical Society of Wisconsin is the official archive for the United Church of Christ in that state. Often, however, the records you need are still in the possession of the local church. If the church is still in existence and the name has not changed, the telephone directory may solve the problem. If an individual church has merged with another one of the same denomination, the yearbook of the denomination should have the name, address, and current pastor of the merged church. If the denomination has merged or split, Mead and Hill's *Handbook of American Denominations* can be extremely useful. If the church is defunct, contact another church of the same denomination in the area and inquire about the locations of the records. If the denomination requires that the records of defunct churches be sent to a central archive, the local minister may know the address and whom to contact. Another source of information could be the state organization of the denomination.

If you locate the church but the older records are missing, discuss the problem with the current minister. He may know which archive they are stored in. If not, he may know descendants of former pastors who have kept records, or he may be able to refer you to older members of the congregation who are well versed in local church history.

Next, contact the local historical or genealogical society. If that does not prove productive, write or visit the denominational archive. Older records of a particular church may have been deposited there years before. The state office of the denomination can sometimes help in your quest.

For a complete list of private and state historical libraries, see *The Directory of Archives and Manuscript Repositories* (Phoenix: Oryx Press, 1988). Do not overlook each state's Historical Records Survey of the Work Projects Administration (WPA), undertaken in the later years of the Great Depression (1930s). Among its projects is a compilation of church records at the state and local level—incomplete, but still the most comprehensive attempt of its kind ever made. The results were summarized in the *Check List of Historical Records Survey Publications* (WPA, 1943. Reprint. Baltimore: Genealogical Publishing Co., 1969). It is essentially a bibliography of research project reports. The individual states, in turn, published detailed lists of the church records available at the local level. Figure 6-8, from the *Inventory of the Church Archives of New York City*, illustrates the approach generally taken by the survey.

A more recent guide to the WPA Historical Records Survey that covers unpublished material is Loretta L. Hefner, *The WPA Historical Records Survey: A Guide to the Unpublished Inventories, Indexes, and Transcripts* (Chicago: Society of American Archivists, 1980). Another, much older guide to unpublished material in church archives is William H. Allison, *Inventory of Unpublished Material for American Religious History in Protestant Church Archives and Their Repositories* (Washington, D.C.: Carnegie Institute, 1910). Some of these archives are still functioning, making the inventory still relevant. A current source of new acquisitions and microfilming projects of church records is the "New Notes" section of *The American Archivist*, the quarterly journal of the Society of American Archivists.

If the records are known to have been destroyed—in a fire, perhaps—the personal records of former pastors sometimes prove effective substitutes. Many clergymen kept their own private record of baptisms, marriages, and funerals at which they officiated. In fact, in areas where no permanent churches existed, the private records of the circuit-riding pastors may be the only records ever made. The first place to look for these is the denominational archive; however, some of these pastoral records have found their way into private or state archives. An extremely useful guide to these private pastoral records and other church records is the *National Union Catalog of Manuscript Collections (NUCMC)* (see chapter 2). The index entry and full entry in figure 6-9 illustrate the type of information provided.

If, after all of your efforts, you are unable to learn the denomination of your ancestor, the local historical or genealogical society can often be of great assistance. If you do not know whether a local society exists, consult the current edition of the *Directory of Historical Societies and Agencies in the U.S. and Canada* (updated every five years) or *Meyer's Directory of Genealogical Societies in the USA and Canada*. Because the leadership of such groups can change from year to year, it may require additional effort to identify the current president and his or her mailing address—but it is usually worth the effort. I have received very good cooperation from various county historical societies, the staffs of which will often perform research for modest fees.

Another resource is the local public library. In some communities, the public library is the repository of genealogical material, including old church records. Larger public libraries may have a genealogical reference specialist who can assist you. You can usually locate public libraries through directory assistance, but the *American Library Directory* will also list the local library.

Many communities possess neither a local historical society nor a public library. If a town has a weekly newspaper, the editor can sometimes be a good source of local historical information or can refer you to someone who is. The county or town clerk's office may not have sufficient staff to conduct genealogical searches and may refer all requests to a local researcher. Often, these individuals know a great deal about local history, including church history.

A vexing situation involving church records can occur when they fall into private hands. Sometimes a clerk of the parish kept the records for so many years that he came to regard them as his personal possessions. More typically, a minister has died and his private records, or those of a defunct church he served, remain in the possession of his family, never finding their way to a public or private archives. I pursued one such set of minister's records for two years. A descendant of the minister recalled having seen her great-grandfather's old records in the house when she was a child. However, they had been lent to someone in the 1930s to verify a marriage and had never been returned. Perhaps the best way to solve problems of this sort is to visit the area and contact as many relatives and former parishioners of the pastor as possible. If time and money do not permit this approach, you might hire a local researcher who is well acquainted with the area. This problem does not lend itself to easy solutions.

Still another important source of defunct church records is college libraries, particularly denominational colleges. For instance, Swarthmore College in Swarthmore, Pennsylvania, possesses an extremely important collection of Quaker records. The same holds true for many other church colleges. In fact, some serve as official or quasi-official repositories for their denominations. *The Yearbook of American and Canadian Churches* contains a list of all church-related colleges, with the denominational affiliation noted.

Also, certain private libraries not affiliated with any religious denomination contain a vast amount of genealogical data, including church records. The Library of the National Society, Daughters of the American Revolution, in Washington, D.C., is undoubtedly the best known of these (see appendix C).

SUGGESTIONS FOR RESEARCH

Effective use of church records requires following some basic rules of genealogical research and knowing the particular hazards associated with church records. Be sure to search other available records from the locality. If the church death registers are missing, try the county probate records. Note the names of witnesses at weddings and baptisms and look for your direct ancestors as witnesses; very important family relationships can be discovered in this manner. If the congregation is of a particular ethnic group, note the birthplaces of other members as listed in the marriage or death records. Even if your ancestor's place of origin is not given, he or she may have come from the same town or area.

In frontier communities, people often attended whatever church or circuit-riding services existed, regardless of affiliation. Thus, a Methodist family may have attended a Baptist church at one time.

Knowing the particular doctrines and discipline of a denomination helps in using the record. If a church did not practice infant baptism, you need to know this or you could make serious errors in calculating birth dates.

Some churches have devised standard forms to reply to requests for information from their records. Some of these date from the 1930s, when the primary object was to verify a person's age. Often, therefore, they do not contain all the information found in the original record. Hence, you should request *all the information* in the pertinent entry. If you are interested in finding an ancestor's place of birth in Europe, indicate so.

Figure 6-8. From Historical Records Survey, Work Projects Administration, *Inventory of the Church Archives of New York City: Reformed Church in America* (New York: Historical Records Survey, 1939), 14.

- 14 -

NEW YORK CITY CHURCH ARCHIVES

Reformed Church in America   Entry A

Reformed Dutch Church, Constitution of the Reformed Dutch church in the United States of America, New York, William Durell, 1793. 354 pp. Edward Tanjore Corwin, D.D., A Digest of Constitutional and Synodical Legislation of the Reformed Church in America, New York, Board of Publications, 1906, pp. 307-12. Charles E. Corwin, Manual of the Reformed Church New York, Board of Publications, 5th ed., 1922, pp. 91-95. Willard Dayton Brown, A History of the Reformed Church in America, New York, Board of Publications, 1928, 140 pp. William Henry Steele Demarest, Notes on the Constitution of the Reformed Church in America, Princeton, N.J. Princeton University Press, 1929. Loc. NN.

MINUTES: General Synod, vol.-1, 1771-1812 (includes minutes of Original and Particular Synods, 1794-99. Minutes of the Coetus, 1738-54. Proceedings of the Conferenti; 1755-67). Vol.-2A, 1813-20, vol.-2B, 1821-26, vol.-3, 1827-31, vol.-4, 1832-36, vol.-5, 1837-41, vol.-6, 1841-45, vol.-7, 1846-49, vol.-8, 1850-55, vol.-9, 1855-60, vol.-10, 1861-65, vol.-11, 1866-69, vol.-12, 1870-73, vol.-13, 1874-77, vol.-14, 1878-81, vol.-15, 1881-85, vol.-16, 1886-89, vol.-17, 1890-93, vol.-18, 1894-97, vol.-19, 1898-1901, vol.-20, 1902-04, vol.-21, 1905-07, vol.-22, 1908-10, vol.-23, 1911-13, vol.-24, 1914-16, vol.-25, 1917-19, vol.-26, 1920-22, vol.-27, 1923-25, vol.-28, 1926-28, vol.-29, 1929-31, vol.-30, 1932-34, vol.-31, 1935-36.
Particular Synod of Albany (Separate yearly booklets kept in cardboard file boxes). Box-1, 1877-1905, box-2, 1906-24, (1909 missing), box-3, 1925-37.
Particular Synod of Chicago (Separate yearly booklets kept in cardboard file boxes), box-1, 1885-86,1887-91,1892-93,1895-1915 (inclusive), box-2, 1916-37.
Particular Synod of Iowa (Separate yearly booklets kept in cardboard file box). Box-1, 1920-37.
Particular Synod of New Brunswick (In 5 bound vols.), vol.-1, 1869-79, vol.-2, 1880-89, vol.-3, 1900-09, vol.-4, 1910-19, vol.-5, 1920-29. (Separate yearly booklets kept in cardboard file box). Box-1, 1930-36.
Particular Synod of New York (Separate yearly booklets kept in cardboard file boxes). Box-1, 1850-74, box-2, 1875-99, box-3, 1900-15 (1914 missing), box-4, 1916-29, box-5, 1930-37.
FINANCIAL: Ledgers, 11 vols., 1876-95,1896-1908,1908-19,1919-23, 1924-29,1929-35,1935--; petty ledgers, 1885-89,1889-95,1896-1900,1901-19. General, Cash books, 12 vols., 1869-96,1896-1901,1901-06,1906-11,1911-14, 1914-19,1919-24,1924-37,1937--. Real Estate - Widow's Fund - Disabled Fund, Cash books, 1882-89,1889-95,1895-1922. Journals, 2 vols., 1934-37,1937--. Day Books, 4 vols., 1876-84,1884-93,1893-1904,1904-14. Cancelled Check Stubs, about 50 vols.
Magazine of the Reformed Dutch Church (monthly booklets bound in 4 vols.). Edited by William Craig Brownlee, D.D. Rutgers Press. Printed by Terhune and Letson, New Brunswick, Vol.-1, 1826-27, vol.-2, 1827-28, vol.-3, 1828-29, vol.-4, 1829-30. Vols.-3 and 4. printed by William A. Mercein, 1 Burling Slip, N.Y.
The Mission Field (monthly booklets bound in 23 vols.), 1888-89, 1890-91,1892,1893,1894-96,1896-98,1898-1900,1900-02,1902-04,1904-06,1906-08, 1908-09,1910-11,1911-12,1912-13,1913-14,1914-15,1915-16,1916-17,1917-18,1918-19,1919-20,1921-22.
Christian Intelligencer paper issued weekly - bound in yearly vols. (107 vols.). Issues complete from 1830-1937, with exception of year 1873 which is missing. Printed and published by William A. Mercein, 240 Pearl Street, N.Y.C.

Be aware of some of the inherent limitations of church records. Even in churches which practiced infant baptism, a significant amount of time might elapse between the date of a child's birth and baptism. Be wary when it appears that entries have been made some time after the rite occurred. Errors often creep in when this happens.

Particularly problematical are typewritten or printed transcriptions of church records, especially if they have been translated from another language. In spite of the best efforts of the translator or transcriber, mistakes occur. Quite often, transcriptions do not include all of the data in the original entry. The names of baptismal sponsors or occupations may be omitted, for example. Sometimes alphabetized information may conceal important clues, such as children baptized in the same family or a brother and sister marrying the same day. Therefore, make every effort to locate the original record or, at least, a microfilm copy. Do not let a foreign language deter you. With common sense and a dual-language dictionary you may be able to decipher it. If not, find someone who can. The results may be worth the extra effort.

If the original record is still in the custody of the church, obtaining permission to see it may pose a problem. In several years of genealogical research, I have encountered this situa-

tion only once. A Lutheran pastor in Wisconsin felt that his congregational records were too fragile for public use and insisted that he check the records himself, while I watched. His concern was legitimate, as the records clearly needed rebinding. Depending upon the situation, you may suggest that the records could be microfilmed for safekeeping. One genealogist of my acquaintance brought some nineteenth-century church records from Ohio to Salt Lake City to be microfilmed by the Genealogical Society of Utah, the originals then being returned to the owner. Several states also have microfilming programs.

Traditionally, Catholic records have been kept at the parish level, so the vast majority of sacramental records (baptism, marriage, communion, confirmation, burial, and other original records) will be found in the church in which the event took place. However, older records and those of closed parishes have often been moved (usually by order of the diocese) to diocesan archives, or occasionally to historical societies or university archives. Locating records of older churches can be challenging. When a family is known to have lived in a particular county or in a specific neighborhood in a city, yet the parish is unknown or has been closed, local diocesan sources can at least provide information on where those records can be found. Virginia Humling, *U.S. Catholic Sources: A Diocesan Research Guide* (Salt Lake City: Ancestry, 1995) provides information on the more than one hundred archdioceses and dioceses in the United States, together with a description of the area encompassed by the archdiocese or dioceses, and addresses, telephone numbers, historical information, fees (if applicable), addresses, and other information on how to obtain newspapers for each archdiocese or diocese.

The press of pastoral duties has forced many priests to delegate the responsibility for answering genealogical inquiries to the parish secretary or a parish volunteer. An increasing number of Catholic diocesan archives—that of Newark, for example—have permitted the Genealogical Society of Utah to microfilm their older records. Hence, a check of the *Family History Library Catalog* for the locality in question is highly recommended.

When you request data from local church records, do not expect the pastor or the parish secretary to do your genealogical research for you. If your initial inquiry proves unsuccessful, visit the church yourself or hire a local genealogist. Sometimes a church officer can suggest a member of the congregation who is proficient in genealogical research. Include a check as well as a self-addressed, stamped envelope with your initial request. Five to ten dollars is a reasonable minimum; send a larger amount if your request covers more than an entry or two. Some churches will return your check. Most churches are very cooperative, certainly in answering the first inquiry.

BAPTISTS (Continued)

Kentucky.   70-2056, 72-1858, 72-1851

Massachusetts.   72-15

Mississippi.   72-1569

New York.   71-1439

New York City.   71-13, 71-1439, 71-1440, 72-158

MS 72-1569
Mississippi Baptist church records, 1819-1957. (MS 66-888)
———— Addition, 1837-1968.   6 reels of microfilm (negative)
    In Mississippi State University Library (State College, Miss.)
    Microfilm of originals which have been returned to owners.
    Minute books, lists of church members, histories, constitutions, and other records. Churches represented include Bethel, Wilkinson Co. (1853-93); Liberty, Lauderdale Co. (1845-87); Mt. Pleasant, Chickasaw Co. (1868-1950);
Pleasant Ridge, Union Co. (1842-1945); Siloam, Clay Co. (1850-1968); and Toxish, Pontotoc Co. (1837-1967).
    Unpublished guide in the library.
    Information on literary rights available in the library.
    Acquired from various sources.
    Additions to this collection are anticipated.

Figure 6-9. From Library of Congress, *National Union Catalog of Manuscript Collections* (Washington, D.C.: J.W. Edwards, 1972), vol. 11, index (top), and p. 224 (bottom).

DENOMINATION ARCHIVES, REPOSITORIES, AND RECORD-KEEPING PRACTICES

Space forbids an exhaustive treatment of all denominations. For a complete list that includes the names and addresses of current officers, see the current edition of the *Yearbook of American and Canadian Churches* (New York and Nashville: Abingdon Press).

ADVENTIST

Inquire at:

Andrews University Library
Berrien Springs, MI 49104

Dr. Linden J. Carter Library
Berkshire Christian College
Lenox, MA 01240

Seventh-Day Adventists General Conference Archives
6840 Eastern Ave. N.W.
Washington, DC 20012

BAPTIST

Encyclopedia of Southern Baptists. 3 vols. Nashville: Broadman, 1958.

Helmbold, F. Wilbur. "Baptist Records for Genealogy and History." *National Genealogical Quarterly* 61 (September 1973): 168–78. Contains valuable background and a list of record locations by state.

_____. "Family History in the Bible Belt: Southern U.S. Church Records." *World Conference on Records: Preserving Our Heritage,* 12–15 August 1980, vol. 3, series 336. Salt Lake City: Church of Jesus Christ of Latter-day Saints, 1981. FHL microfiche no. 6070692. Emphasizes Baptist records.

McLaughlin, William G. *New England Dissent, 1630–1833: The Baptists and Separation of Church and State.* 2 vols. Cambridge: Harvard University Press, 1971. Essential reading for genealogists with ancestors who migrated from New England to New York, Pennsylvania, and Ohio. Studies individual congregations and records.

Menkus, Belden. "The Baptist Sunday School Board and Its Records." *American Archivist* 24 (1961): 441–44.

Piepkorn, Arthur Carl. "The Primitive Baptists of North America." *Baptist History and Heritage* 7 (January 1972): 33–51.

Starr, Edward Caryl. *A Baptist Bibliography, Being a Register of Printed Material By and About Baptists.* 25 vols. Rochester, N.Y.: American Baptist Historical Society, 1947–76. In progress.

Try to determine the kind of Baptist church your ancestor might have joined, narrowing your search to a state and county. Few records have been published, so begin in the locality rather than the library. Use the suggestions made by Wilbur F. Helmbold in the two articles cited above.

Today, many Baptist archives acquire material for Baptist churches besides their own. Because your ancestor was not a Southern Baptist does not mean the records are not now held by a Southern Baptist archive.

Major Baptist Collections

American Baptist Historical Society (including the Samuel Colgate Baptist Historical Collection)
1106 S. Goodman St.
Rochester, NY 14620-2532

This is the major repository for the American Baptist Convention (formerly known as the Northern Baptist Convention).

Andover Newton Theological School
(including the Backus Historical Society)
169 Herrick Rd.
Newton Centre, MA 02159

Baptist Historical Collection
Z. Smith Reynolds Library
Wake Forest University
Winston-Salem, NC 27109

Contains valuable vertical files for every North Carolina Baptist Church, both extant and extinct, and for Baptist ministers. Detailed indexes are available.

Bethel Theological Seminary Library
3949 Bethel Dr.
St. Paul, MN 55112

Swedish Baptist Records

For microfilmed copies of Swedish Baptist records, contact the Swenson Swedish Immigrant Research Center, Box 175, Augustana College, Rock Island, IL 61201.

Historical Commission of the Southern Baptist Convention
127 Ninth Ave. N.
Nashville, NC 37234

One of the largest collections of original congregation minutes, correspondence, annual reports, and missionary records.

Special Collection
Samford University Library
800 Lakeshore Dr.
Birmingham, AL 35229

The Baptist collection is recognized as the world's most complete on Alabama Baptists. It includes histories of Baptist organizations, agencies, and institutions; histories of Baptist associations in Alabama; Alabama Baptist church histories; printed minutes of the Baptist state convention and the Southern Baptist Convention; a biographical compendium and individual biographies of Alabama Baptists; and many manuscript materials pertaining to Baptists.

Seventh Day Baptist Library
Seventh Day Baptist Building
Plainfield, NJ 07060

Has German Baptist collections.

Seventh Day Baptist Historical Society Library
3120 Kennedy Rd.
P.O. Box 1678
Janesville, WI 53547

Library
Southern Baptist Theological Seminary
Louisville, KY 40206

Particularly important for Kentucky Baptist records.

Library
Southwestern Baptist Theological Seminary
Fort Worth, TX 76122

Serves as the Texas Baptist repository

Primitive Baptist Archives
Elon College
Elon, NC 27244

BRETHREN IN CHRIST CHURCH

Archives of the Brethren in Christ Church
Messiah College
Grantham, PA 17027

CHURCH OF CHRIST, SCIENTIST

The First Church of Christ, Scientist
Archives and Library of the Mother Church
Boston, MA 02115

CHURCH OF GOD

For all bodies under this name, see the current *Yearbook of American and Canadian Churches.*

THE CHURCH OF JESUS CHRIST OF LATTER-DAY SAINTS

Church of Jesus Christ of Latter-day Saints, Family History Department, *Series LDS* No. 1, LDS Records. Salt Lake City: Church of Jesus Christ of Latter-day Saints, 1992.

Jaussi, Laureen Richardson, and Gloria D. Chaston. *Genealogical Records of Utah.* Salt Lake City: Deseret Book, 1974.

_____. *Register of Genealogical Society Call Numbers.* 2 vols. Provo, Utah: Genealogy Tree, 1982. Includes record-by-record detail for holdings of LDS records.

Records of local Mormon congregations (wards) through the 1960s are available at the Family History Library. Membership records for the 1970s and later are confidential and are kept at church headquarters in Salt Lake City. Four types of records that are of general interest to genealogists are:

1. The International Genealogical Index (IGI) includes names submitted for processing in LDS temples. Many of the names submitted are from historic records. The name index is arranged alphabetically within a designated geographic region. The IGI, available at the Family History Library and its family history centers, includes names extracted from many published parish registers, especially in the eastern states. Hence, a search of the IGI could prove valuable for anyone pursuing research in eastern church records.

2. The *Family Group Record Archives* is a microfilmed collection of 8 million family group records. Copies are available through all family history centers. They are in alphabetical order by the husband's surname followed by his given name(s). This collection is particularly useful for families from England and New England.

3. Ancestral File is an increasingly valuable collection of information submitted to the Family History Library on computer diskette by genealogists of all faiths. Hence, there are many names in the file that do not appear in the IGI. See chapter 2 for more information on these collections and how to use them.

4. The *Family History Library Catalog* lists the holdings of the Family History Library and is available at the Family History Library and its family history centers.

Major LDS collections are in:

Family History Library
35 North West Temple
Salt Lake City, UT 84150

LDS Church Archives
Historical Department
50 East North Temple
Salt Lake City, UT 84150

Brigham Young University
Center for Church History
Provo, UT 84602

Contains personal journals, letters, and congregational records.

CHURCH OF THE BRETHREN

German-American Pietist-Anabaptist background.

Bethany Theological Seminary
Butterfield and Meyers Rds.
Oak Brook, IL 60521

Brethren Historical Library and Archives
1451 Dundee Ave.
Elgin, IL 60120

Juniata College Library
18th and Moore
Huntingdon, PA 16652

CHURCHES OF CHRIST

Harding Graduate School of Religion Library
1000 Cherry Rd.
Memphis, TN 38117

CONGREGATIONAL

Greenwood, Val. *The Researcher's Guide to American Genealogy.* 2nd ed. Baltimore: Genealogical Publishing Co., 1990, pp. 360–62. Contains examples of Congregational records.

Walker, Willeston. *The History of the Congregational Churches in the United States.* New York: ACHS, 1894.

So many New England records have been published or microfilmed that it might be most productive to begin by checking the various periodical indexes—for example, the *Periodical Source Index (PERSI).*

As a result of mergers, schisms, and other historical developments, at least three denominations contain Congregational Churches or former Congregational Churches: Congregational Christian Churches (National Association), Unitarian Universalist Association, and United Church of Christ. Archives of these churches may include old Congregational Church records. The major collection of Congregational records, primarily from New England, is in:

Congregational Library
14 Beacon St.
Boston, MA 02108

Includes large collections of newspapers and local magazines.

DISCIPLES OF CHRIST

Garrison, W.E., and A.T. DeGroot. *The Disciples of Christ, a History*. St. Louis: Bethany Press, 1948.

Major collections are:

Christian Theological Seminary
1000 W. 42nd St.
Indianapolis, IN 46208

Culver-Stockton College Library
Canton, MO 63435

The Disciples of Christ Historical Society
Library Archives
1101 Nineteenth Ave. S.
Nashville, TN 37212

Lexington Theological Seminary
631 S. Limestone
Lexington, KY 40508

Brite Divinity School Library
Texas Christian University
P.O. Box 32904
Fort Worth, TX 76219

EPISCOPAL—see PROTESTANT EPISCOPAL

EVANGELICAL CONGREGATIONAL CHURCH

Historical Society of the Evangelical Congregational
Church
121 S. College St.
Meyerstown, PA 17077

EVANGELICAL COVENANT CHURCH OF AMERICA

Evangelical Covenant Church of America
Archives and Historical Society
5125 N. Spaulding Ave.
Chicago, IL 60625

The congregational records of this denomination, originally Swedish-American, have been microfilmed. Contact the Swenson Swedish Immigration Research Center, Box 175, Augustana College, Rock Island, IL 61201.

EVANGELICAL FREE CHURCH OF AMERICA

Evangelical Free Church of America
1515 E. 66th St.
Minneapolis, MN 55423

Also Swedish-American in origin, the congregational records of this denomination have been microfilmed. Contact the Swenson Center (listed in the preceding paragraph).

EVANGELICAL UNITED BRETHREN CHURCH—see METHODIST

GREEK ORTHODOX

Archives of the Greek Orthodox
Archdiocese of North America
10 E. 79th St.
New York, NY 10021

For other Eastern Orthodox church archives, see the *Yearbook of American and Canadian Churches*.

HUGUENOT

(French Protestants of the Reformed Church)

Allen, Cameron. "Records of the Huguenots in the United States, Canada, and the West Indies with Some Mention of Dutch and German Sources," a paper delivered at the World Conference on Records and Genealogical Seminar, 5–8 August 1969, Area F-10, Salt Lake City, sponsored by The Church of Jesus Christ of Latter-day Saints. FHL Fiche no. 6039362. Much of this material also appears in "Huguenot Migrations" in the American Society of Genealogists, *Genealogical Research: Methods and Sources, 256–90, vol. 2* (Washington, D.C.: American Society of Genealogists, 1971).

Baird, Charles W. *History of the Huguenot Emigration to America*. 2 vols. Reprint. Baltimore: Genealogical Publishing Co., 1991.

A great deal has been published about Huguenots, including original source material. Beginning with library research may be most productive. The major collection is in:

Huguenot Historical Society
Box 339
New Paultz, NY 12561

JEWISH

For a more complete treatment of Jewish records, see chapter 17, Tracking Jewish-American Family History.

Kurzweil, Arthur. *From Generation to Generation: How to Trace Your Jewish Genealogy and Personal History*. New York: Schocken Books, 1982.

Rottenberg, Dan. *Finding Our Fathers: A Guidebook to Jewish Genealogy*. 1977. Reprint. Baltimore: Genealogical Publishing Company, 1986. Especially note chapter 6, Jewish Sources in America.

Stern, Malcolm H. "Church Records of the United States: Jewish Synagogue Records," a paper delivered at the World Conference on Records and Genealogical Seminar, 5–8 August 1969, Salt Lake City, sponsored by The Church of Jesus Christ of Latter-day Saints, Area I, 6 and 7a.

Avotaynu: The International Review of Jewish Genealogy. 1985–. P.O. Box 900, Teaneck, NJ 07666.

Major collections are in local Jewish historical societies and:

American Jewish Archives
3101 Clifton Ave.
Cincinnati, OH 45220

American Jewish Historical Society
10 Thornton Dr.
Waltham, MA 02154

YIVO Institute for Jewish Research
555 W. 57th St.
New York, NY 10019

LUTHERAN

Bodensieck, Julius, ed. *The Encyclopedia of the Lutheran Church.* 3 vols. Minneapolis: Augsburg Publishing House, 1965.

Greenwood, Val. *The Researcher's Guide to American Genealogy*, 2nd ed. Baltimore: Genealogical Publishing Co., 1990, pp. 373–77. Examples from Lutheran records.

Luecker, Erwin L., ed. *Lutheran Cyclopedia.* St. Louis: Concordia, 1975.

Nelson, E. Clifford, ed. *The Lutherans in North America.* Philadelphia: Fortress Press, 1980.

Suelflow, August R. "The Lutheran Family in North America," *World Conference on Records: Preserving our Heritage*, 12–15 August 1980. Salt Lake City: Church of Jesus Christ of Latter-day Saints, 1980, vol. 4, series 368. FHL Fiche no. 6085718.

_____. "Records of the Lutheran Church in America," a paper delivered at the World Conference on records, 5–8 August 1969, Salt Lake City, sponsored by the Church of Jesus Christ of Latter-day Saints, Area I, 6 and 7b. FHL microfiche no. 6039393. Different emphasis from the above, good bibliography.

Wittman, Elisabeth. "The Evangelical Lutheran Church in America Churchwide Archives." *Illinois Libraries* 74 (5): 467–69 (November 1992).

Lutheran church records rank among the best available and are invaluable for tracing German or Scandinavian ancestors, even though the numerous synods may seem baffling. However, as a result of a merger in 1988, the majority of American Lutherans now belong to a unified body called the Evangelical Lutheran Church in America (ELCA). The second-largest Lutheran denomination is the Missouri Synod.

The creation of the ELCA also began an archival system featuring regional repositories. For information concerning ELCA regional archives, contact:

Archives
The Evangelical Lutheran Church in America
8765 W. Higgins Rd.
Chicago, IL 60631-4198
(312) 380-2818

This archive now houses the microfilmed records of thousands of congregations of the former American Lutheran Church (ALC), a synod composed largely of Norwegian-American, Danish-American, and midwestern German-American churches. The former Lutheran Church in America (LCA), composed of Swedish-American, Finnish-American, Danish-American, and German-American churches of the eastern and midwestern United States, has some congregational microfilm via a program to microfilm Swedish-American congregation records (see the Swenson Center information below). Microfilming of the former Norwegian-American Lutheran congregational records up to 1917 is better than ninety-percent complete. The microfilming of the Swedish-American Lutheran congregations for records up to 1930 is almost complete. Microfilms are not available on loan, but they may be used at the Chicago archive, which will respond to short, specific genea-

logical questions. For a fee of $20, two hours (maximum) of genealogical research is available. The regional archives listed below have the original copies of disbanded Lutheran congregations.

ELCA Region 1 Archives (Alaska, Idaho, Montana, Oregon, Washington)

Mortvedt Library
Pacific Lutheran University
Tacoma, WA 98447
(206) 535-7586

ELCA Region 2 Archives (Arizona, California, Colorado, Hawaii, New Mexico, Nevada, Utah, Wyoming)

Pacific Lutheran Theological Seminary
2770 Marin Ave.
Berkeley, CA 94708-1597
(510) 524-5264

ELCA Region 3 Archives (Montana, North Dakota, South Dakota)

2481 Como Ave. W.
St. Paul, MN 55108-1445
(612) 641-3205

ELCA Region 4 Archives (Arkansas, Kansas, Louisiana, Missouri, Nebraska, Oklahoma, Texas)

For Arkansas and Oklahoma:

Arkansas-Oklahoma Synod
4803 S. Lewis Ave.
Tulsa, OK 74105-5199
(918) 747-8617

For Kansas and Missouri:

Bethany College
Wallerstedt Learning Center
421 N. First St.
Lindsborg, Kansas 67456-1897
(913) 227-3311, Ext. 299

For Texas and Louisiana:

The Rev. Arnold Moede
205 Coventry
Seguin, TX 78155
(210) 379-6450

For Nebraska:

Ms. Vivian Peterson
1325 N. Platte Ave.
Fremont, NE 68025
(402) 721-9119

ELCA Region 5 Archives (Illinois, Iowa, Wisconsin, upper Michigan)

333 Wartburg Place
Dubuque, IA 52003-7797
(319) 589-0320

ELCA Region 6 Archives (Indiana, Kentucky, lower Michigan, Ohio)

Trinity Lutheran Seminary
2199 E. Main St.
Columbus, OH 43209
(614) 235-4136, Ext. 71

ELCA Region 7 Archives (New York [except Metropolitan New York City], New Jersey, eastern Pennsylvania, New England, and the non-geographic Slovak-Zion Synod)

Lutheran Archives Center
7301 Germantown Ave.
Philadelphia, PA 19119
(215) 248-4616

For Metropolitan New York Synod:

Lutheran Church Archives
Hormann Library
Wagner College
Staten Island, NY 10301
(718) 390-3100

ELCA Region 8 Archives (Delaware, Maryland, central and western Pennsylvania, northern Virginia, West Virginia, Washington, D.C.)

For western Pennsylvania, West Virginia, and western Maryland:

Archives
Thiel College
Greenville, PA 16125

For central Pennsylvania, Delaware, eastern Maryland, and Washington, D.C.:

A.R. Wentz Library
Lutheran Theological Seminary
Gettysburg, PA 17325
(717) 334-6286

ELCA Region 9 Archives (Alabama, Florida, Georgia, Mississippi, North Carolina, South Carolina, Tennessee, Virginia, and the Caribbean Synod)

For North Carolina:

ELCA North Carolina Synod
1988 Lutheran Synod Drive
Salisbury, NC 28144
(704) 633-4861

For South Carolina:

ELCA South Carolina Synod
P.O. Box 43
Columbia, SC 29202-0043

For Alabama, Florida, Georgia, Mississippi, Tennessee, and the Caribbean Synod:

ELCA Region 9 Archives
Lutheran Theological Seminary
4201 N. Main St.
Columbia, SC 29203

(803) 786-5150

For Virginia:

ELCA Virginia Synod
P.O. Drawer 70
Salem, VA 24153
(703) 389-1000

For further information, contact the central ELCA archives in Chicago.

Swedish-American Churches

The congregational records of the Augustana Evangelical Lutheran Synod (Swedish-American Lutheran) were microfilmed in the 1970s with a grant from the Wallenberg Foundation of Sweden. Since then, microfilming of other Swedish-American congregation records has been completed: Evangelical Covenant, Baptist, Methodist, and the Evangelical Free Church.

Positive copies of these microfilms are in the custody of:

The Swenson Swedish Immigration Research Center
Box 175
Augustana College
Rock Island, IL 61201
(309) 794-7221

The microfilmed records are available for public use at the Swenson Center. The staff of the center will perform limited searches. Enclose a check for $10 for the initial request.

Finnish-American Churches

Finnish American Historical Archives
Suomi College
Hancock, MI 49930

Lutheran Church—Missouri Synod

This church is much more theologically conservative than those that merged to form the Evangelical Lutheran Church in America. Largely midwestern-German in background, it also contains some Slovak and Finnish Lutheran congregations. It supports the Concordia Historical Institute, which publishes a quarterly journal and acts as a clearinghouse for information on Lutheran and other German-American church records.

Concordia Historical Institute
Department of Archives and History
The Lutheran Church—Missouri Synod
801 De Mun Ave.
St. Louis, MO 63105
(314) 721-5934

Wisconsin Evangelical Lutheran Synod

Commonly known as the Wisconsin Synod, it maintains an archive at this address:

Wisconsin Lutheran Seminary
1831 N. Seminary Drive, 65W
Mequon, WI 53092
(414) 272-7200

This denomination is ultra-conservative in its doctrinal position. German-American in background, its congregations are concentrated in the upper Midwest with a scattering elsewhere.

For information about the smaller Lutheran synods, consult August Suelflow's paper, "Records of the Lutheran Church in America," cited previously.

MENNONITE

The Mennonite Encyclopedia: A Comprehensive Reference Work on the Anabaptist-Mennonite Movement. 4 vols. Hillsboro, Kan.: Mennonite Brethren Publishing House, 1955–59.

Major collections are in:

The Archives of the Mennonite Church
1700 S. Main
Goshen, IN 46526

Center for Mennonite Brethren Studies
4824 E. Butler
Fresno, CA 93727

Mennonite Historical Library
Bluffton College
Bluffton, OH 45817

Mennonite Library and Archives
Bethel College
North Newton, KS 67117

Simons Historical Library and Archives
Eastern Mennonite College
Harrisonburg, VA 22801

Lancaster Mennonite Historical Society
2215 Millstream Rd.
Lancaster, PA 17602

METHODIST

General Commission on Archives and History of the United Methodist Church. *The Directory.* Madison, N.J.: United Methodist Church, 1981. Contains a current listing of the Commissions on Archives and History for each Annual Conference in the United States. These commissions are beginning to preserve local records.

Harmon, Nolan B., ed. *The Encyclopedia of World Methodism.* 2 vols. Nashville: United Methodist Publishing House, 1974. Prepared and edited under the supervision of the World Methodist Council and the Commission on Archives and History. Locations of some archives of some of the smaller Methodist churches are listed under the heading "Archives." Since publication there may have been some changes.

Little, Brooks R. *Methodist Union Catalog of History, Biography, Disciplines, and Hymnals.* Lake Junaluska, N.C.: Association of Methodist Historical Societies, 1967.

Ness, John, Jr. "Church Records of the United States: Methodist Records," a paper delivered at the World Conference on Records and Genealogical Seminar, 5–8 August 1969, Salt Lake City, sponsored by The Church of Jesus Christ of Latter-day Saints, Area I, 4 and 5b. FHL Fiche no. 6039392.

Williams, Robert H. "Methodist Church Trials in Illinois, 1824–1960," *Methodist History* 1 (1962): 14–32.

Major collections are in:

United Methodist Archives Center

General Commission on Archives and History of the United Methodist Church
P.O. Box 127
Drew University
Madison, NJ 07940

This archive is making a concerted effort to collect microfilm copies of the many newspapers published by the various state conferences of the Methodist church. It also houses microfilm copies of foreign-language newspapers published by churches such as the Evangelical United Brethren, which later merged with the Methodist church. For a fee of $10, the archive will search the newspaper holdings for an obituary if provided with a place and time of death and precise denominational affiliation. This archive does not maintain records of defunct congregations. These are housed in the pertinent state repository. However, the general archive will inform correspondents of the location of the state repository most likely to have the records in question.

Center for Evangelical United Brethren Studies United Theological Seminary
1810 Harvard Blvd.
Dayton, OH 45406

Indiana United Methodist Archives
Roy O. West Library
DePauw University
Greencastle, IN 46153

William R. Perkins Library
Manuscript Department
Duke University
Durham, NC 27706

Pitts Theology Library
Emory University
Atlanta, GA 30322

Interdenominational Theological Center Library
671 Beckwith St. S.W.
Atlanta, GA 30314
Has an African American Methodist Collection.

Garrett Evangelical Theological Seminary Library
2121 Sheridan
Evanston, IL 60201

The Historical Center of the Free Methodist Church
Winona Lake, IN 46590

Bridwell Center for Methodist Studies
Perkins School of Theology
Southern Methodist University
Dallas, TX 75222

New England Methodist Historical Society Library
Boston University
School of Theology
745 Commonwealth Ave.
Boston, MA 02215

Pacific School of Religion
Charles Holbrook Library
1798 Scenic Ave.
Berkeley, CA 94709

For Swedish-American Methodist congregational records, contact:

The Swenson Swedish Immigration Research Center
Box 175
Augustana College
Rock Island, IL 61201

MORAVIAN

Hamilton, Rt. Rev. Kenneth G. "The Resources of the Moravian Church Archives." *Pennsylvania History* 27 (1960): 263–72.

Wallace, Paul A. W. "The Moravian Records." *Indiana Magazine of History* 48 (1952): 141–60.

The Archives of the Moravian Church
1228 Main St.
Bethlehem, PA 18018

Moravian Archives
Southern Provinces of the Moravian Church
Drawer M
Salem Station
Winston-Salem, NC 27108

Moravian Historical Society
Nazareth, PA 18064

PENTECOSTAL

Oral Roberts University Library
7777 S. Lewis
Tulsa, OK 74105

Dir., Wayne Warner
Assemblies of God Archives
1445 Boonville Ave.
Springfield, MO 65802

Dir., Joseph Bryd
Pentecostal Research Center
Church of God (Cleveland, Tenn.)
P.O. Box 3448
Cleveland, TN 37320

PRESBYTERIAN

Miller, William B. "Church Records of the United States: Presbyterian," a paper delivered at the World Conference on Records and Genealogical Seminar, 5–8 August 1969, Salt Lake City, sponsored by The Church of Jesus Christ of Latter-day Saints, Area I, 4 and 5c. FHL microfiche no. 6039392.

Union Catalog of Presbyterian Manuscripts, Presbyterian Library Association, 1964. Lists Presbyterian and Reformed records.

Local church records are generally scattered because, until recently, no uniform provision was made to preserve local records.

Major collections are in:

Historical Foundation of the Presbyterian and Reformed Churches
Assembly Drive
Box 847
Montreat, NC 28757

Strongest on Presbyterian Church records in the South. See Thomas H. Spence, Jr. *The Historical Foundation and Its Treasures.* Montreat, N.C.: Historical Foundation, 1960.

McCormick Theological Seminary
McGaw Library
800 W. Belden Ave.
Chicago, IL 60614

Presbyterian Historical Association & Department of History
Presbyterian Church in the U.S.A.
425 Lombard St.
Philadelphia, PA 19147

This large collection includes the Presbyterian Biographical Index, a card index to periodicals, newspapers, and books for both clergy and laypersons.

Princeton Theological Seminary
Speer Library
Mercer St. and Library Place
P.O. Box 111
Princeton, NJ 08540

PROTESTANT EPISCOPAL

Bellamy, V. Nelle. "Church Records of the United States: Protestant Episcopal," a paper delivered at the World Conference on Records and Genealogical Seminar, 5–8 August 1969, Salt Lake City, sponsored by The Church of Jesus Christ of Latter-day Saints, Area I, 6 and 7d. FHL microfiche no. 6039393. A good explanation; no bibliography.

Greenwood, Val. *The Researcher's Guide to American Genealogy.* Baltimore. Genealogical Publishing Co., 1990, pp. 363–73. Good examples of Protestant Episcopal records.

McQueen, Edith E. "The Commissary in Colonial Maryland." *Maryland Historical Magazine* 25 (1930): 190 ff. The church exercised probate authority in early Maryland.

Oliver, David B. "The Society for the Propagation of the Gospel in the Province of North Carolina." *Proceedings, North Carolina Historical Society.* Beaufort: North Carolina Historical Society.

Painter, Bordon W. *The Anglican Vestry in Colonial America.* New Haven, Conn.: Yale University Press, 1965. The vestry exercised local government functions as well as church administrations. Vestry minutes for most of the Episcopal parishes in Virginia have been printed by the Virginia Historical Society and can be found in many research libraries. These are also available on microfilm through the LDS family history centers.

The Episcopal Church maintains its national archive in Austin, Texas.

Mark Duffy, Archivist
Episcopal Church Archives
P.O. Box 2247
Austin, TX 78768

The archive holds microfilm copies of colonial records of the Church of England in what is now the United States and records of the Protestant Episcopal Church since the American Revolution. There are few parochial or diocesan records other than official reports, but the staff can direct researchers to the location of such.

Do not overlook the collection at Lambeth Palace Library in London, which includes correspondence, reports, subsidies to settlers, and other materials for colonial congregations and the records of the Society for the Propagation of the Gospel in Foreign Parts, which sponsored several European protestant congregations in America and sent more than three hundred missionaries.

Begin searching for genealogical records in the local parish first. If the local rector does not have the requested record, the diocesan registrar or historiographer may be able to indicate where such records may be found. The *Episcopal Church Annual* has current names and addresses of local parishes and clergy, as well as the address of the diocesan office.

Some records may have been deposited in secular libraries and archives. An inquiry to the diocesan office will direct the researcher.

QUAKERS (SOCIETY OF FRIENDS)

Quaker records rank among the very best available. They form a striking exception to the generalization that "dissenting" church records do not match the quality of "established" church records.

Comfort, William W. "Quaker Marriage Certificates." *Friends Historical Bulletin* 40 (1951): 67–80.

Elliot, Erro T. *Quakers in the American Frontier: History of the Westward Migrations, Settlements, and Developments of Friends on the American Continent.* Richmond, Ind.: Friends United Press, 1969.

Greenwood, Val. *The Researcher's Guide to American Genealogy.* 2nd ed. Baltimore: Genealogical Publishing Co., 1990, pp. 377–85.

Heiss, Willard. "American Quaker Records and Family History," *World Conference on Records: Preserving our Heritage,* 12–15 August 1980. Salt Lake City: Church of Jesus Christ of Latter-day Saints, ser. 358. Besides reviewing the Quaker records, he provides a list of records in print, a bibliography about Quakers, and suggestions for locating the records. FHL microfiche no. 6085709.

_____. "Church records of the United States: Quaker Records in America: Records with an Extra Dimension," a paper delivered August 1969, Salt Lake City, sponsored by The Church of Jesus Christ of Latter-day Saints, Area I, 6, and 7c. FHL microfiche no. 6039393. Contains points not discussed in the previously cited paper.

_____. *Guide to Research in Quaker Records in the Midwest.* Indianapolis: Indiana Quaker Records, 1962.

_____. *A List of All Friends Meetings That Have Ever Existed in Indiana, 1807–1955.* Indianapolis: John Woolman Press, 1961.

_____. *Quakers in the South Carolina Back Country: Wateree and Bush River.* Indianapolis: Quaker Records, 1969.

Hinshaw, William Wade, ed. *Encyclopedia of American Quaker Genealogy.* 6 vols. 1936. Reprint. Baltimore: Genealogical Publishing Co., 1969.

Jacobsen, Phebe R. *Quaker Records in Maryland.* Annapolis, Md.: Hall of Records, 1966.

Jones, Rufus M. *The Quakers in the American Colonies.* 1911. Reprint. New York: Russell and Russell, 1962. Describes original congregations in each area.

Williams, Ethel W. "Quaker Records" in *Know Your Ancestors.* Rutland, Vt.: Charles E. Tuttle Co., 1960, pp. 119–37. Contains less detail on the records themselves than on printed records and locations; strong for Indiana Quakers.

Continued for Indiana by Willard Heiss. *Abstracts of Records of the Society of Friends in Indiana.* Vol. 7, *Encyclopedia of American Quaker Genealogy.* 7 vols. Indianapolis: Indiana Historical Society, 1965–77.

Major collections are in:

Friends Historical Library (Hicksite Records)
Swarthmore College
500 College Ave.
Swarthmore, PA 19081

Magill Historical Library
Haverford College
Haverford, PA 19041

Quaker Collection
Guilford College Library
Guilford, NC 27410

Archives of the New England Yearly Meeting of Friends
Rhode Island Historical Society
121 Hope St.
Providence, RI 02906

REFORMED

General

Holland Society of New York
Manuscript Collection
122 E. 58th
New York, NY 10022

Archives of the Reformed Church in America.
New Brunswick Theological Seminary
21 Seminary Place
New Brunswick, NJ 08901

Dutch

Christian Reformed
Colonial Origins Collection
Calvin College and Seminary
Grand Rapids, MI 49046

German—see United Church of Christ
For other Reformed churches, see the *Yearbook of American and Canadian Churches,* cited earlier.

ROMAN CATHOLIC

Curran, Francis X., S.J. *Catholics in Colonial Law.* Chicago: Loyola University Press, 1965. Discusses legal restrictions, which are also useful sources for identifying Catholics, by colony.

Ellis, John Tracy. *Catholics in Colonial America.* Baltimore: Helicon Press, 1963.

Hennesey, James, S.J. "Square Peg in a Round Hole: On Being Roman Catholic in America." *Records of the American Catholic Historical Society of Philadelphia* (1973): 167–95.

Humling, Virginia. *U.S. Catholic Sources: A Diocesan Research Guide.* Salt Lake City: Ancestry, 1995. A state-by-state description of Catholic diocesan sources.

McAvoy, Thomas T. "Catholic Archives and Manuscript Collections." *American Archivist* 27 (1964): 409–14.

O'Toole, James M. "Catholic Records: A Genealogical and Historical Resource." *The Register* (October 1989): 251–63.

_____. "The Roman Catholic Family in North America: Family History as Viewed Through Catholic Church Records." *World Conference on Records: Preserving Our Heritage,* 12–15 August 1980. Salt Lake City, sponsored by The Church of Jesus Christ of Latter-day Saints, Area I, 4, and 5c. FHL microfiche no. 6070677. Includes excellent examples.

Vollman, Edward R., S.J. *The Catholic Church in America: An Historical Bibliography.* New York: Scarecrow Press, 1972.

Start your search in the locality where the ancestral family lived. Inquire at the parish level first and then the diocese. *The Official Catholic Directory,* published annually by P.J. Kenedy & Sons, Box 265, Skokie, IL 60077, provides current addresses for both. *The Official Catholic Directory* is available at most Catholic parishes, schools, universities, and other large libraries.

Some old Catholic records have been deposited in local and state historical societies and other secular libraries. See *Studies in American Church History,* 35 vols. (Catholic University Press) for specific accounts and records in various states.

SALVATION ARMY

Archives and Research Center
615 Slaters Ln.
Alexandria, VA 22313

SCHWENKFELDER

Schwenkfelder Library
Seminary Ave.
Pennsburg, PA 18073

SHAKERS

Western Reserve Historical Society
History Library
10825 E. Blvd.
Cleveland, OH 44106

UNITARIAN AND UNIVERSALIST

Archives of the Unitarian-Universalist Association
25 Beacon St.
Boston, MA 02108

Harvard University Divinity School
Andover-Harvard Theological Library
Manuscript Department
45 Francis Ave.
Cambridge, MA 02138

Meadville Theological School of
Lombard College
Library
5701 S. Woodlawn Ave.
Chicago, IL 60637

UNITED CHURCH OF CHRIST

This church resulted from a merger of the Evangelical and Reformed Church (largely German in background) and the General Council of the Congregational Churches.

Clark, Elmer T. *The Small Sects in America.* New York: Abingdon Press, 1965. Discusses records as well as groups.

Hinke, William J. "German Reformed Church Records in Pennsylvania." *National Genealogical Society Quarterly* 37 (1949): 33–38. An excellent discussion of records.

Rosenberger, Francis C. "German Church Records of the Shenandoah Valley as a Genealogical Source." *Virginia Magazine of History and Biography* 66 (1958): 195–200.

Congregational

Congregational Library
14 Beacon St.
Boston, MA 02108

Divinity Library and University Library
Yale University
New Haven, CT 06520

Hartford Theological Seminary Library
Hartford, CT 06105

Harvard Divinity School Library
Cambridge, MA 02140

Evangelical and Reformed

Eden Archives
475 E. Lockwood Ave.
Webster Grove, MO 63119

Holds materials from the largely Midwestern Evangelical Synod of North America, a German-American body that merged with the Reformed Church in the United States in 1934 to form the Evangelical and Reformed Church and later became part of the United Church of Christ.

Evangelical and Reformed Historical Society
555 W. James St.
Lancaster, PA 17603

Contains a very important collection of early Pennsylvania German Reformed church records.

An extremely useful guide for locating current United Church of Christ (UCC) congregations is *Yearbook United Church of Christ,* published annually by the UCC, 297 Park Ave. S., New York, NY 10010. Usually, a local UCC congregation will have a copy.

NOTES

1. Derek Harland, *Genealogical Research Standards* (Salt Lake City: Bookcraft, 1963).

ACKNOWLEDGMENT

The author wishes to acknowledge the use of an unpublished manuscript by Luana Gilstrap. It was of great assistance in preparing this chapter.

BIBLIOGRAPHY

Allison, William H. *Inventory of Unpublished Material for American Religious History in Protestant Church Archives and Their Repositories.* Washington, D.C.: Carnegie Institute, 1910.

Check List of Historical Records Survey Publications. WPA, 1943. Reprint. Baltimore: Genealogical Publishing Co., 1969.

The Directory of Archives and Manuscript Repositories. Phoenix: Oryx Press, 1988.

Ganstadt, Edwin Scott. *Historical Atlas of Religions in America.* New York: Harper & Row, 1962. An important research tool.

Hall, William K. *The Shane Manuscript Collection: A Genealogical Guide to the Kentucky and Ohio Papers.* Galveston, Tex.: Frontier Press, 1990.

Harland, Derek. *Genealogical Research Standards.* Salt Lake City: Bookcraft, 1963.

Hebert, Rev. Donald J. *A Guide to Church Records in Louisiana.* Eunice, La.: the author, 1975).

Hefner, Loretta L. *The WPA Historical Records Survey: A Guide to the Unpublished Inventories, Indexes, and Transcripts.* Chicago: Society of American Archivists, 1980.

Jacobus, Donald Lines. *Index to Genealogical Periodicals.* 1952. Reprint. Baltimore: Genealogical Publishing Co., 1978.

Jarboe, Betty M. *Obituaries: A Guide to Sources.* 2nd ed. Boston: G.K Hall & Co., 1989.

Kirkham, E. Kay. *A Survey of American Church Records.* 4th ed. Logan, Utah: The Everton Publishers, 1978.

Mead, Frank, and Samuel S. Hill. *Handbook of American Denominations*, 8th ed. Nashville: Abingdon Press, 1985.

Melton, J. Gordon. *National Directory of Churches, Synagogues, and Other Houses of Worship.* Edited by John Kroll. Detroit: Gale Research, 1994. Attempts to list the name, address, and telephone number of every active house of worship in the United States. Each volume covers a distinct geographic area.

Milner, Anita Cheek, comp. *Newspaper Indexes: A Location and Subject Guide for Researchers.* 3 vols. Metuchen, N.J., and London: Scarecrow Press, 1977, 1979, 1982.

Minutes of the Methodist Conferences Annually Held in America; From 1773 to 1813 Inclusive Volume The First. New York: 1813. Reprint. Swainsboro, Ga.: Magnolia Press, 1983.

Pettee, Julia. *List of Churches: Official Forms of the Names for Denominational Bodies With Brief Descriptive and Historical Notes.* Chicago: American Library Association, 1948. Includes names before the many mergers of the ecumenical movement.

Rodda, Dorothy. *Directory of Church Libraries.* Philadelphia: Drexel Press, 1967.

Ruoss, George M. *World Directory of Theological Libraries.* Metuchen, N.J.: Scarecrow Press, 1968.

Suelflow, August R. *A Preliminary Guide to Church Records Repositories.* St. Louis: Church Archives Committee, Society of American Archivists, 1969.

Sweet, William Warren. *Religion on the American Frontier, 1783–1840: A Collection of Source Materials.* New York: Cooper Square Publishers, 1940, 1964. Covers Baptists, Methodists, Congregationalists, Presbyterians; gives history and reproduces minister journals, letters, and diaries, missionary records, and conference minutes.

RESEARCH IN COURT RECORDS
CHAPTER CONTENTS

7

RESEARCH IN COURT RECORDS

Arlene H. Eakle

Even today, few people escape mention in court records at some time during their lives as witnesses, litigants, jurors, appointees to office, or as petition signatories. However, Americans of a few generations ago also expected to attend local court proceedings when they were in session. It was a civic duty—and they could be fined if they did not attend.

IMPORTANCE OF COURTS IN AMERICAN SOCIETY

America's predominantly English heritage established a tradition of equitable and just court processes in which the people have a right to participate actively.[1] A majority of American colonists were English, and they were accustomed to seeking redress in the courts. With relative freedom from royal supervision in the New World and court enforcement of religious as well as civil laws, American courts tried many matters that were not subject to court action in other parts of the British empire and that are now considered too minor to warrant criminal action. In many places, until the time of the Civil War, people were criminally prosecuted for such crimes as gossiping, witchcraft, scolding a husband, being publicly disrespectful to a minister, and refusing to attend church services. Indeed, some of these "blue laws," as they were called, are still on the books today, although they are not enforced.

The benefits for the genealogist are considerable. It is not unusual for a single case to have involved between seventy-five and one hundred people, all of them being named in the course of court action.[2]

Local courts were units of government as well as judicial bodies. They issued licenses to lawyers, physicians, merchants, peddlers, ordinaries (public inns), midwives, ferry operators, and clergy; regulated apprenticeships; established weights and measures; provided for inspection of goods and services; ordered the destruction of harmful pests and beasts; paid bounties for heads, tails, and skins; oversaw education for orphans and the poor; built housing for the maimed and poor, sometimes in conjunction with a local church; built roads and bridges and oversaw their maintenance; called local militia units to muster; assessed taxes and collected them.[3]

Most of these administrative functions are now filled by county commissions, city councils, and other administrative agencies established for that purpose, each with its own records.

Courts also served a social function in bringing a region's people together regularly. Court week (every three months) was a festive occasion. On Monday mornings, courthouses buzzed with activity as people argued about the cases on the docket and gossiped. Deeds were registered, wills probated, taxes paid, county records audited, elections held, courtships begun, and marriages contracted. Sessions were often juggled to avoid planting and harvest time so that most people could attend.

On Saturday afternoons, janitors swept out the courtrooms. The judges shook hands all around and prepared to start hearings in adjoining localities the following Monday. In between, courts measured, almost precisely, the moral, physical, spiritual, and economic condition of the people within their jurisdictions. A scolding wife, a quarrelsome neighbor, a Sabbath card-player, the owner of cattle wandering beyond their bounds, a dangerous liberal who freed his slaves and gave them land, an alien (non-English before 1776 or non-American after) applying for citizenship so he could buy a farm, a blind man applying for tax-exempt status—all of these and many, many more "ordinary" citizens appeared in court.

When court records have been destroyed—as when courthouses have burned—lost records have been reconstructed as far as possible so that legal business can continue. In short, it is safe to say that even the most modest individuals before World War I in America will have appeared in court records at least once during their lifetimes.

If court records are so valuable for genealogical information, why do genealogists hesitate to use them? The answer is simple: They are or appear to be more complicated than census records. Indexes for court records are incomplete, the records themselves seem difficult to decipher, and there are many of them.

This chapter will acquaint you with legal terms, teach you how to read court material, tell you where to find the records, and describe what you can expect to find in civil, criminal, equity, and probate court records.

LEGAL TERMS

Laws—the rules of conduct by which society is governed—consist of case law (decisions of the courts based on local custom and common usage, or "common law") and statute law (legislative enactment). The basic law of most states is the common law, inherited from England and based on custom and usage. It is what "seems fair" in a community but is articulated in judicial interpretations, opinions, minutes, and orders. Legislative assemblies enact laws for situations not covered by common law or where serious disagreement exists about what is fair. In certain instances, a statute is designed specifically to change or nullify local custom. For example, where local blue laws required businesses to close on Sundays so employees could attend church, "fairness" was a hardship for Seventh-Day Adventists and Jews because their Sabbaths fall on Saturday. Local authorities, by drafting laws making Sunday closing optional, have changed the custom.

Judicial jurisdiction is the fundamental authority of a court to hear a controversy between parties, to consider the merits of each side, and to render a decision which is binding upon the parties involved.

Original jurisdiction is the authority to commence a case—to hear it for the first time. Civil cases under forty shillings in value were tried first before a justice of the peace in colonial times, and today before small claims courts. *Appellate jurisdiction* is the authority to review, upon request, questions of law which arise in the trial of a case. Not all cases can be appealed. The jurisdiction of appeals courts determines the cases acceptable for review. *Exclusive jurisdiction* is the sole authority to try a case. Only a federal court can try a case involving citizens of two different states. *Concurrent jurisdiction* means that more than one court may try the same case. Litigants choose which court to use. *General jurisdiction* is the authority to try almost any case brought before the court except for a few limitations set by law. *Special jurisdiction* is the authority to handle specific matters—probate, divorce, military, etc. Often these courts also have exclusive jurisdiction to try their cases. *Limited jurisdiction* is the authority of a court to try cases specified by law only or involving less than certain sums of money. Justice of the peace courts are limited courts.

The parties in a legal conflict include the plaintiff, who seeks a remedy under the law and starts legal action against the defendant, who must answer the charge. Either party may be represented by legal counsel or power of attorney.

All cases brought before courts of law are called legal actions. There are three main types:

1. Civil actions (person versus person) arise over injuries done by one individual to the physical being, the property—real or personal—or the reputation of another. Suit is brought to enforce private rights or to seek compensation for injuries. The parties are often encouraged to settle matters out of court. The most common civil actions are torts—property damage, trespass, libel, assault, negligence, and so on.

2. Criminal actions (state or people versus person) involve the protection of society. These cases can never be settled out of court, although modern plea-bargaining can reduce or eliminate punishment. Criminal offenses include felonies (murder, robbery, burglary, rape) and misdemeanors (petty theft, vagrancy, drunkenness, prostitution, breaking the Sabbath).

The basic difference between civil/equity and criminal actions is apparent with the question, "Does the offense threaten a well-ordered society?" When a man backs his automobile into his neighbor's car, the neighbor can sue for damages. This is a civil case. However, drunk driving threatens everyone on the same road and thus can be prosecuted as a criminal offense.

3. In equity actions, the case is determined by "reasonable justice" and "common good" because legal remedies are inadequate or because enforcing the full letter of the law would be unjust. For example, a man borrows money to buy land. He agrees to repay the money with interest by a specific date or forfeit the land. If he is unable to pay, he could be held to the letter of the law and lose all he has invested. The money owed, however, may be less than the value of the land. The court can order the land sold, pay the money owed, and give the man what remains. This is a fairer solution.

Equity actions usually involve property rights and serve as an extension of civil actions. The remedy of the court can be an order of specific performance—to deliver goods promised, to restore animals to their proper owners, to replace equipment damaged, or to rewrite a document or report. It could be a mandatory injunction to prevent a certain action. It could also be a bill of account for monies spent in a guardianship. Probate, divorce, and adoption are equity actions.

In the early stages of American legal development, civil and equity actions were combined, while a strong distinction was maintained for criminal actions. Few jurisdictions have three separate courts that each handles a specific action. Most have one judicial body which handles them all, although it may clearly indicate which hat is worn: "The Court of Rhea County sitting in equity" or "The Criminal Court of Rhea County."

The U.S. judicial system is a dual one with national (federal) courts, whose personnel are appointed by the federal government to adjudicate (try) cases under the U.S. Constitution or federal statutory law; and a system of state courts, whose personnel are elected or appointed to try cases under state constitutions, statutory laws, and local custom. Both systems have two types of courts:

1. Trial courts, where cases originate. The jury or, in its absence, the judge, decides what happened and whether, within a given rule of law, the facts constitute guilt or innocence of the accused. Trial courts make up the majority of our system.

2. Appellate courts, to which losing parties can appeal for further consideration of a case. These courts may, but usually do not, call witnesses or have juries. The court accepts the evidence of the previous trial presented in the form of a brief or trial resume, and then reviews points of the law where an error has been made in the earlier trial. Some appellate courts also have original jurisdiction.

Figures 7-1, 7-2, and 7-3 show the relationships between trial and appeals courts. They also introduce the variety of courts that can be found in researching family lines.

Genealogists will encounter many new terms and legal phrases in court records—too many to list here. Standard references are *Black's Law Dictionary,* available in every good public library, county law library, and university or college library. Most college bookstores carry the current edition. Another is William C. Burton, *Legal Thesaurus* (New York: Macmillan, 1981). This special thesaurus is designed for quick recall of nuances and double meanings of words with legal applications.

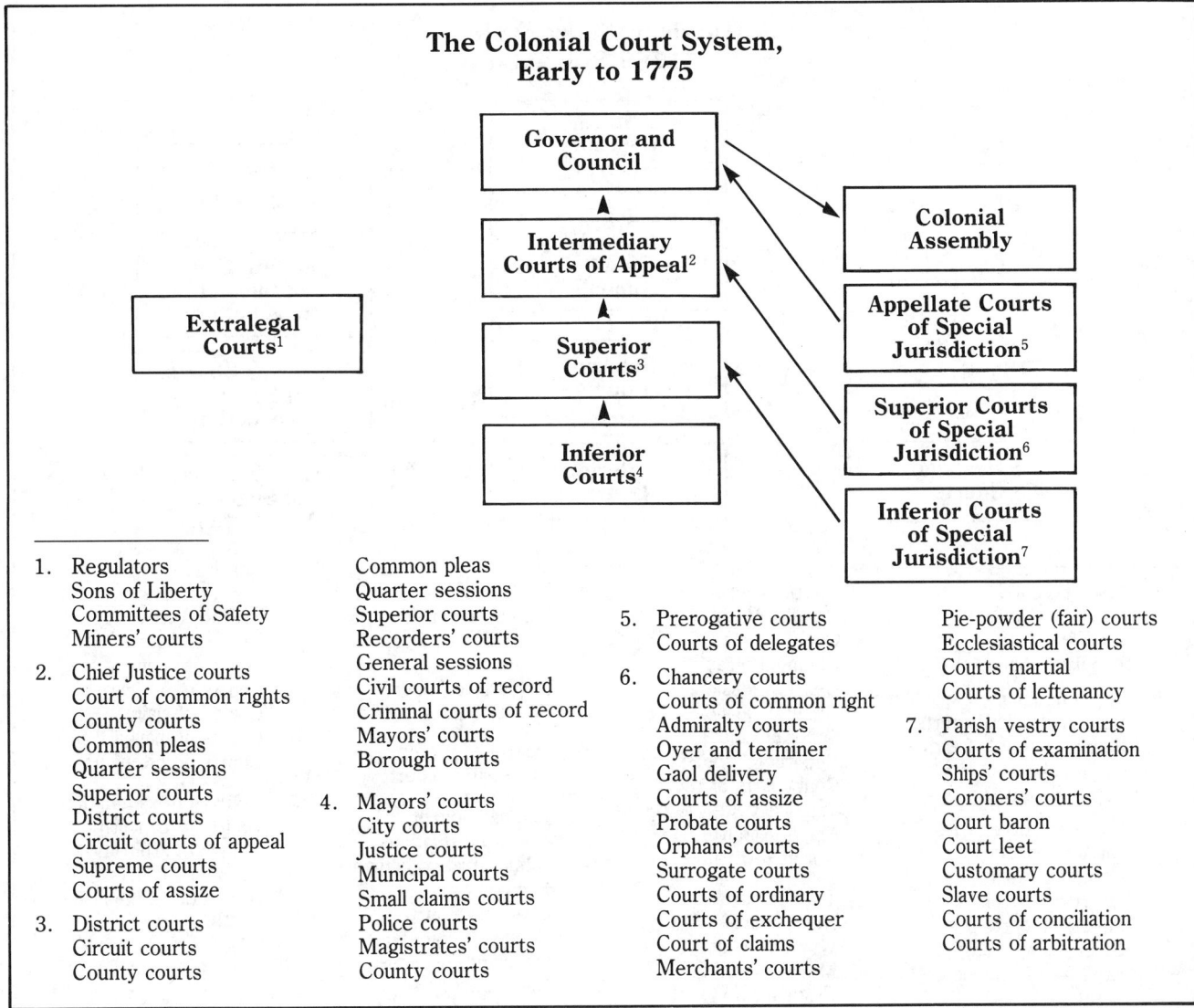

**The Colonial Court System,
Early to 1775**

Governor and
Council

Intermediary
Courts of Appeal[2]

Extralegal
Courts[1]

Superior
Courts[3]

Inferior
Courts[4]

Colonial
Assembly

Appellate Courts
of Special
Jurisdiction[5]

Superior Courts
of Special
Jurisdiction[6]

Inferior Courts
of Special
Jurisdiction[7]

1. Regulators
   Sons of Liberty
   Committees of Safety
   Miners' courts

2. Chief Justice courts
   Court of common rights
   County courts
   Common pleas
   Quarter sessions
   Superior courts
   District courts
   Circuit courts of appeal
   Supreme courts
   Courts of assize

3. District courts
   Circuit courts
   County courts

   Common pleas
   Quarter sessions
   Superior courts
   Recorders' courts
   General sessions
   Civil courts of record
   Criminal courts of record
   Mayors' courts
   Borough courts

4. Mayors' courts
   City courts
   Justice courts
   Municipal courts
   Small claims courts
   Police courts
   Magistrates' courts
   County courts

5. Prerogative courts
   Courts of delegates

6. Chancery courts
   Courts of common right
   Admiralty courts
   Oyer and terminer
   Gaol delivery
   Courts of assize
   Probate courts
   Orphans' courts
   Surrogate courts
   Courts of ordinary
   Courts of exchequer
   Court of claims
   Merchants' courts

   Pie-powder (fair) courts
   Ecclesiastical courts
   Courts martial
   Courts of leftenancy

7. Parish vestry courts
   Courts of examination
   Ships' courts
   Coroners' courts
   Court baron
   Court leet
   Customary courts
   Slave courts
   Courts of conciliation
   Courts of arbitration

Figure 7-1. The colonial court system, early to 1775.

It includes some 5,000 legal terms, definitions of foreign phrases, and a valuable every-word index.

COURT PROCEDURES

Court procedures differ slightly from state to state, and more than three centuries have seen the evolution of American court procedures, yet many procedures date from the Middle Ages. On 1 June 1872, federal courts changed their procedural rules to conform to those of the states within which they were located. An overview of civil, criminal, and equity actions will define basic words and illuminate what is happening in court minutes and on the dockets.[4]

STARTING THE ACTION (PLEADINGS) IN CIVIL CASES

Every civil case starts suit with the issuing of a writ of summons, a command which notifies the defendant to appear before the court to answer charge. The clerk, upon request of the plaintiff or an attorney, issues the writ under the court's authority.

The court directs the sheriff or constable to serve the writ of summons on the defendant. In most jurisdictions, the defendant must receive it personally; but in a few, the sheriff can leave it with an adult member of the family or with someone in charge at the place of business. In most cases, an action cannot proceed until the writ has actually been served. The notable exception is in divorce actions. The writ may be published in newspapers when the defendant is outside of the court's jurisdiction or when his or her whereabouts is unknown. The usual procedure is for the sheriff to produce the original writ, tell the defendant its contents, and provide him or her with a copy. The sheriff will then make out a return, usually on the back of the original writ, stating where, when, and upon whom he has served it, sign it, and return it to the clerk of the court on or before the return day specified in the writ. The writ and the return are filed in the case file or packet as part of the permanent record of the case.

The next step is the filing of the plaintiff's claim. This pleading may be called a statement of claim, a complaint, or a petition. The purpose of the declaration or petition is to explain clearly the plaintiff's reason for taking action so that the defendant knows the nature of the claim and so that there is "a cause

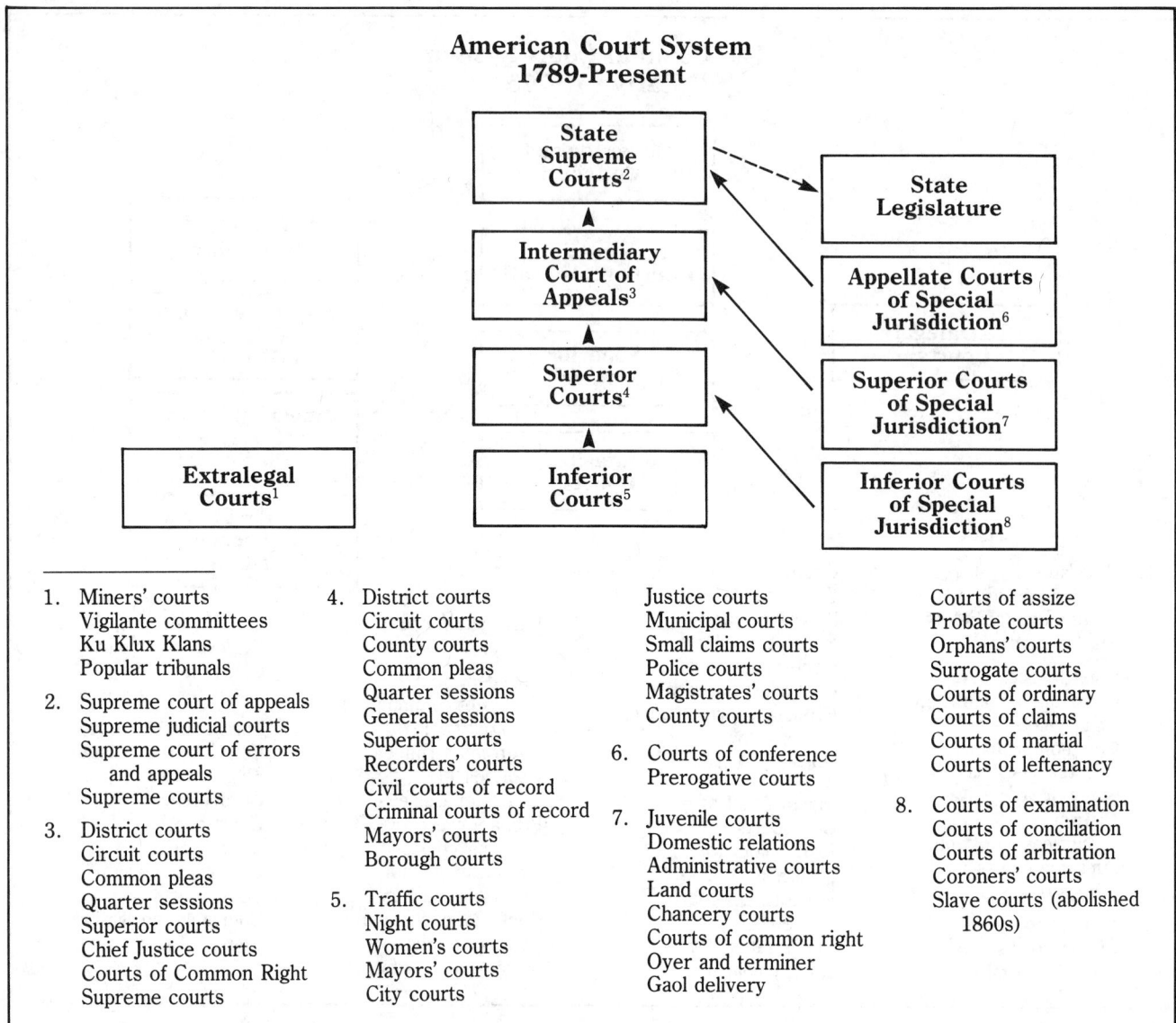

**American Court System
1789-Present**

State
Supreme
Courts[2]

State
Legislature

Intermediary
Court of
Appeals[3]

Appellate Courts
of Special
Jurisdiction[6]

Superior
Courts[4]

Superior Courts
of Special
Jurisdiction[7]

Extralegal
Courts[1]

Inferior
Courts[5]

Inferior Courts
of Special
Jurisdiction[8]

1. Miners' courts
    Vigilante committees
    Ku Klux Klans
    Popular tribunals

2. Supreme court of appeals
    Supreme judicial courts
    Supreme court of errors
       and appeals
    Supreme courts

3. District courts
    Circuit courts
    Common pleas
    Quarter sessions
    Superior courts
    Chief Justice courts
    Courts of Common Right
    Supreme courts

4. District courts
    Circuit courts
    County courts
    Common pleas
    Quarter sessions
    General sessions
    Superior courts
    Recorders' courts
    Civil courts of record
    Criminal courts of record
    Mayors' courts
    Borough courts

5. Traffic courts
    Night courts
    Women's courts
    Mayors' courts
    City courts

Justice courts
Municipal courts
Small claims courts
Police courts
Magistrates' courts
County courts

6. Courts of conference
    Prerogative courts

7. Juvenile courts
    Domestic relations
    Administrative courts
    Land courts
    Chancery courts
    Courts of common right
    Oyer and terminer
    Gaol delivery

Courts of assize
Probate courts
Orphans' courts
Surrogate courts
Courts of ordinary
Courts of claims
Courts of martial
Courts of leftenancy

8. Courts of examination
    Courts of conciliation
    Courts of arbitration
    Coroners' courts
    Slave courts (abolished
       1860s)

Figure 7-2. The American court system, 1789 to the present.

of action sufficient in law" to justify a judgment in favor of the plaintiff. The declaration and notice are filed with the court clerk, and a copy is served on the defendant or his attorney. In some jurisdictions, only the attorneys exchange pleadings, not filing them with the clerk of the court until they have been completed or until a judgment may be entered.

The defendant then counters with an answer or affidavit of defense admitting or denying the various claims contained in the plaintiff's declaration. It may also present new information bearing on the defense. It is filed with the court clerk, and a copy is served upon the plaintiff or his attorney. If the defendant fails to file an answer within the time allowed by law, the plaintiff is entitled upon motion of the court to enter judgment by default for "failure to file and answer." The clerk enters the judgment in the court records, and the court provides for the enforcement of the judgment.

When the declaration and answer have been filed, and if the case has not been judged before, then it is "at issue"— ready for trial before a judge and jury. (In many courts, the parties can waive a jury trial and elect to have their case tried before the judge alone.) The case is then scheduled on the court's docket.

Most jurisdictions encourage litigating parties to settle their case out of court to save time and money. When it happens, the clerk usually notes it in the court records. Some jurisdictions require that civil cases under a certain amount be brought before a court of arbitration or conciliation before a trial. At this point, there are certain motions which can be entered to delay (stay) judgment. These motions pertain to points of law (legal technicalities). A record of them and their disposition is also part of the case file.

STARTING THE ACTION (PLEADINGS) IN CRIMINAL CASES

When a crime has been committed, the offender must be brought, by some legal process, before a tribunal to hear the complaint and take appropriate action. Before the days of organized law enforcement, in any locality, the citizens of a com-

Figure 7-3. The federal court system, 1789 to 1952.

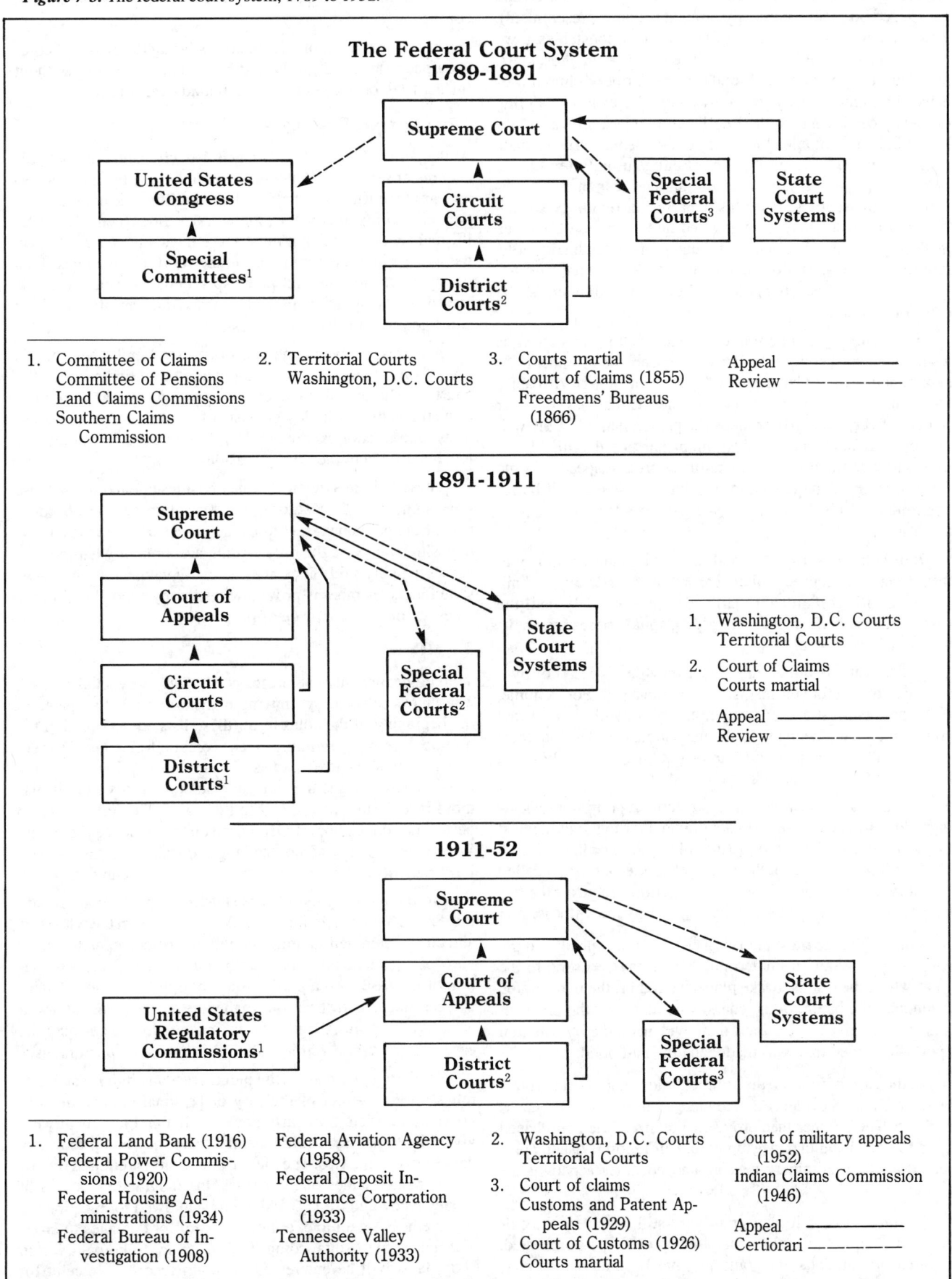

**The Federal Court System
1789-1891**

1. Committee of Claims
   Committee of Pensions
   Land Claims Commissions
   Southern Claims
   Commission

2. Territorial Courts
   Washington, D.C. Courts

3. Courts martial
   Court of Claims (1855)
   Freedmens' Bureaus
   (1866)

Appeal ————————
Review — — — — — —

1891-1911

1. Washington, D.C. Courts
   Territorial Courts

2. Court of Claims
   Courts martial

Appeal ————————
Review — — — — — —

1911-52

1. Federal Land Bank (1916)
   Federal Power Commissions (1920)
   Federal Housing Administrations (1934)
   Federal Bureau of Investigation (1908)
   Federal Aviation Agency
   (1958)
   Federal Deposit Insurance Corporation
   (1933)
   Tennessee Valley
   Authority (1933)

2. Washington, D.C. Courts
   Territorial Courts

3. Court of claims
   Customs and Patent Appeals (1929)
   Court of Customs (1926)
   Courts martial
   Court of military appeals
   (1952)
   Indian Claims Commission
   (1946)

Appeal ————————
Certiorari — — — — — —

munity were responsible to see that offenses were reported and the alleged offenders physically brought to court (presentment). Presentment could be made by private persons, constables, town watchmen, selectmen of the town, elected town presenters, grand jurors, government officials, paid informers, church wardens, tithingmen, or by the court itself. For example, during the seventeenth century, the English tithing system was established in some colonies for short periods of time. Every male over age twelve was enrolled in a tithing (usually ten households), and one was appointed tithingman, responsible to inspect the households under his supervision regularly so that "sin and disorder may be prevented and suppressed," to see that everyone attended church on Sunday and kept the day holy, retired at curfew, and did not play cards or engage in other illegal gaming. The tithingman had to report offenders to the court or be fined.

Today, the injured person, or the state acting for society as a whole, enters a complaint. The court orders the offender to be summoned, usually by means of a warrant or writ of capias issued to an authorized officer (the sheriff, marshal, or other police officer). The officer takes the person named in the writ into custody and usually holds him or her in jail. This officer must produce the accused before the court at a specified time for a hearing. If the detention is legal, the person will be recommitted to jail. If not, he or she will be released on bail to await trial.

Bail is the posting of a bond in a set amount of money to insure that the accused will appear in court. In default of bail, the accused is committed to jail and kept in custody until the case is disposed of by trial or appeal. Capital crimes may have no provisions for bail.

If the crime is minor, the matter may be disposed of by a summary trial before the magistrate without a jury. For example, if the police arrest a vagrant upon the street without a formal complaint having been made, the magistrate decides both facts and law. The amount of the fine or the type of punishment a magistrate may impose is limited by statute.

In most cases, however, the next step is a preliminary hearing held before a magistrate to determine if the evidence against the accused is sufficient to justify holding him or her for trial. Guilt or innocence is not the issue. Witnesses are often called to testify, and the court, in some jurisdictions, requires the testimony to be written, attested, and signed by the witnesses.

The magistrate must prepare a copy of the hearing and the case, usually within a limited number of days, to send to the court where the trial is to take place. It contains the name of the defendant, the nature of the charge, the names of the prosecutors and witnesses (sometimes their evidence), the information upon which the arrest was made, and the bail bond.

In the case of murder, the coroner holds an inquest before a jury, which hears evidence and renders a verdict about the cause of death. The coroner then provides a return to the court based upon this semi-judicial investigation. This report is usually presented at the preliminary hearing and becomes a part of the court record.

In some jurisdictions, a grand jury still considers the evidence and renders an indictment based upon the facts presented. In other jurisdictions, the grand jury has been abolished altogether and the indictment is issued by the court, based upon the preliminary hearing or the returns of the magistrate and coroner.

In the next step, the defendant is brought before the court (arraigned) to plead guilty and be sentenced at once without further trial, or not guilty and be bound over for the trial.

COLLECTING TESTIMONY

At the point when the trial is scheduled, civil and criminal procedures are similar. Witnesses are summoned by subpoena to appear at the trial on behalf of the plaintiff or the defendant. If they must bring documents, the writ describes them. The sheriff, marshal, or constable must serve the subpoena directly on the witness and submit a return to the court. If the witness fails to appear at the time and place specified, a bench warrant is issued on the spot for his or her arrest, and an officer of the court goes out to find the witness.

A representative of the court interviews and takes depositions from witnesses who live outside the jurisdiction of the court or who are ill, maimed, or unable to appear in person. Sometimes the testimony consists of answers to written questions (interrogatories) prepared by the court and forwarded to a local court where the witness resides.

These written statements must be attested, and the witness must sign them. Depositions, and any interrogatories, become part of the permanent record of the court. In early cases, these depositions may be the only written accounts of what the witnesses actually said. They are especially valuable if an out-of-state family member is providing testimony needed to probate an estate or divide a piece of property.

THE TRIAL

Trial procedures may be prescribed by law or by local custom. The jury is selected by drawing names from a list prepared at the beginning of the court term (these lists are recorded in the minutes) or by summoning "twelve good and lawful men, housekeepers" as their names appeared in rotation on the tax rolls. Each party has the right to challenge jurors and dismiss those it feels are "prejudicial to the case." The jury is then to perform its duties impartially, based on the evidence presented. Where jury trial is waived, the judge considers the case. A non-jury trial will usually be shorter, with fewer documents.

Presenting the case includes statements by the plaintiff and the defendant (or their attorneys), testimony from the witnesses and cross-examination, introduction of written depositions, review of documents or other exhibits before the court, summation of the case with a parting speech to the judge and/or jury by each side, and instructions to the jury on the points of law at issue. At this point, the jury or the judge retires to consider the case and arrive at a verdict. The verdict must be unanimous.

Rendering judgment is the judge's responsibility. The judge relies on the verdict of the jury or personal deliberations to arrive at a decision. In early days, verdict and judgment were given the same day. More recently, there may be up to ninety days between the two. The clerk of the court is required by law to record the names of the parties, the judgment, amounts of money recovered (if any) and the time allowed for meeting the judgment. For example, a money award for damages to crops and fences by a stampeding herd of cattle, to be paid within sixty days, will be entered in the court record. A receipt for payment is often filed with the court, and the clerk may paste it at the top or bottom of the page where the judgment is recorded in the case file or packet.

Before 1865, a jail sentence was unusual. Local jails served only to hold the accused for trial. Criminal courts were often called "gaol delivery" because they emptied the jails of prisoners. Instead of "doing time," the convicted person might be whipped, pilloried, submerged in cold water, forced to labor on a public project, or sentenced to pay fines and damages. Capital crimes brought death or banishment.

Imprisonment for debt was common in most jurisdictions during the colonial period and even later. In 1949, two World War II veterans were imprisoned in Vermont for ninety-one days because they could not pay their debts. The state legislature ordered an investigation, which found that 4,091 Vermont residents had been imprisoned for debt and only 2,085 discharged from 1827 to 1829. The Prison Discipline Society of Boston reported that New England jails housed five times as many debtors as criminals during the 1930s.

Consult these studies for specific regions:

Becker, Robert A. "Salus populi supreme lex: Public Peace and South Carolina Debtor Relief Laws, 1763–1788." *South Carolina Historical Magazine* 80 (1979): 65–75.

Connant, H.J. "Imprisonment for Debt in Vermont: A History." *Vermont History* 19 (1951): 67–80.

Few, Robert A. "Imprisonment for Debt in Massachusetts." *Mississippi Valley Historical Review* 48 (1961–62): 252–69.

"Imprisonment for Debt in Colonial Virginia." *Virginia Magazine of History and Biography* 35 (1927): 1–6.

Mittlebeller, Emmet V. "The Decline of Imprisonment for Debt in Kentucky." *Filson Club Quarterly* 49 (1975): 169–89.

Ryan, Edward L. "Imprisonment for Debt: Its Origin and Repeal." *Virginia Magazine of History and Biography* 42 (1934): 53–58.

Thompson, Tommy R. "Debtors, Creditors, and the General Assembly in Colonial Maryland." *Maryland Historical Magazine* 72 (1977): 59–77.

———. "Personal Indebtedness and the American Revolution in Maryland." *Maryland Historical Magazine* 73 (1978): 13–29.

Today, punishment includes fine, imprisonment, or both. "Cruel and unusual punishment" violates the Fourteenth Amendment to the U.S. Constitution.

Enforcing the Judgement (Execution)

Once a judgment is rendered, the court commands the sheriff, marshal, or constable to carry it out. Some courts ordered imprisonment or labor until the judgment had been met.

In the case of debt, imprisonment was often useless because the person in custody had no way to earn the money. "Judgment-proof" debtors—those certified by the court as unable to pay—could laugh at creditors.

If the judgment debtor owned property, the court issued an order for the sheriff to seize and sell it (attachment) to satisfy the creditor's claims. In some jurisdictions, the property must be taken into custody before judgment is given as security that

the creditor can recover if the debtor fails to make payment. A companion action is distraint—property is taken into custody to impel the debtor to come to court. When the person appears in court, the property is returned. Personal property is actually brought to the courthouse, and the officer in charge makes an inventory. In some jurisdictions the creditor must post a bond for the value of the property attached to indemnify the officer against unlawful seizure.

Seizure of real property consists of recording a writ against the title, called a judgment lien, and giving notice to the person in possession that the land has become court property and cannot be disposed of or sold by the owner. Homesteads (dwelling house and a small piece of garden property), pensions, bankrupt property, property in hands of guardians or trustees, cemeteries, tools of trade, and insurance are free from attachment.

If the debtor fails to make payment, the sheriff condemns the property and posts it for sale by publicly advertising on placards, in newspapers, by town crier, or by Sunday notice in church. Then the property is auctioned to the highest bidder and the proceeds go to the creditor for redress, costs, and damages.

Each step generates court records. Brief summaries appear in minutes, orders, and judgments; documents, testimony, and exhibits (plus copies of orders), writs, judgments, and notices will be found in the case packets.

New Trials and Appeals

A litigant, usually the loser but sometimes the winner if he or she received less than petitioned for, can appeal the case within a specified period of time. Each state determines by law which court may hear which appeals. Federal judiciary acts do the same on the federal level. Some states have only one appeals court; some allow only specific cases to be appealed; and some place a limit on the amount of damages an appeals court can handle.

When the appellate court issues a writ allowing the case to be heard, the litigants prepare briefs containing the facts of the case, errors committed, and reasons why appeal is sought. After printing became common, briefs were printed in multiple copies for the judges, attorneys, litigants, case files, and news media.

New trials or appeals are granted if the judge erred on the admissibility of evidence, the verdict was contrary to the evidence, the verdict was contrary to the law, the judge erred in the charge to the jury, and/or new evidence becomes available.

When errors occur, the case is tried only on the legal technicalities involved, not on the evidence offered in the trial. The judges consider the matter individually, then collectively, and render their opinions—usually in writing—at a later date.

If the court grants a new trial, the case is sent back to the trial court and the whole case is retried in accordance with rules laid down by the appeals court.

The two cases that follow are verbatim typescripts of original case papers retrieved from garbage containers in 1962 in Fulton County, Kentucky, where case files were being dumped after they had been microfilmed. As court after court grapples with budget cuts, forced economies, and limited storage space, many files are being culled. Unfortunately, many are not microfilmed; nor are funds available to do so.

Genealogists can and should urge that these records be transferred to local historical and genealogical societies. Pottowattamie County, Iowa, transferred court files to the county historical society in 1976 before building a new courthouse. Lancaster County, Pennsylvania, transferred its documents to the Lancaster County Historical Society several years ago, when the county clerk, who was also president of the society, knew the records were in jeopardy and petitioned for custody.

In the sample civil case that follows, only portions of the case papers are included. Order books, minutes, judgments, and the appeal transcript prepared for the circuit court provide more data. However, these eight documents from the case file will familiarize you with typical legal language and procedures.

In this case, Hubbard, a physician, entered a suit against James Brown for medical services rendered but not paid for. Brown was not a resident of Kentucky and owned a horse. The constable served the summons and attached the horse. Brown posted a bond and took the horse back. Depositions were ordered in Caddo Parish, Louisiana, possible place of residence of James Brown. Brown lost judgment in the county court, appealed to the Fulton Circuit Court, posted bond to cover the action, and entered a counter-suit against Hubbard.

SAMPLE CIVIL CASE

[On back of document:]

55

J. N. Brown

vs.

C. Hubbard

To Sept.

Executed by obtaining a copy of the within summons to Deft June 24th 1854.

[signed] R. C. Pratten S.F.C.

Charles Hubbard vs James Brown

Fulton County Quarterly Court

Kentucky, 1853-54

PLAINTIFF'S DECLARATION

To the Honorable Lewis Scearce Presiding Judge of Fulton County in Chauncry sitting -

Your complainant states that he has an account against James Brown for $14.50 for medical services rendered by pltft to deft as Physician which is now due, unpaid and in no way satisfied.

Compt further states that said Brown is a non resident of this State and is about to remove all his effects out of this state, and your pltff can have no way of making his debt except out of the property now in this State, which is a horse now in Fulton County and within the Jurisdiction of this Court.

Pltff files his account herewith marked (A) and calls on deft to answer if the same is not just and correct and he asks for process and answer against deft, and for an order directing the Constable to sieze and take into his possession a horse belonging to said Brown and him safely keep till further orders herein unless deft will give Bond with good security conditioned to pay off and satisfy any decree rendered him-

Pltff prays for a decree for the amount of his debt and for all proper relief in the premises-

Atty

WRIT OF SUMMONS

The Commonwealth of Kentucky to any Constable of Fulton County—

You are commanded to summon Jas Brown to answer a bill in Chancry, filed against him in my office by Charles

Hubbard, on the 4th Monday in Oct next, and you are directed to seize and take into your possession a horse belonging to said Brown now in this county, and him safely keep till further order herein unless deft should give Bond with good security conditioned to pay and satisfy any order or decree made in this cause-Given under my hand as Presidy Judge of Fulton County this 24th day of September 1853-

[signed] Lewis Scearce P.J. F.C.C.

ATTACHMENT BOND

Know all men by these presents that we Charles Hubbard and A. D. Kingman are held and firmly bound to James Brown in that just and full sum of Twenty Nine Dollars to which payment well and truly to be made we bind ourselves our heirs to so jointly and severally and firmly by these presents, sealed and dated this 24th of Sept 1853.

The condition of the above obligation is such that whereas the above bound Charles Hubbard is about to sue out an attachment against the said James Brown. Now should the said Charles Hubbard well and truly pay to the said James Brown all such damages and costs so he may sustain by reason of the improper suing out of said attachment then this obligation to be void else to remain in full force and virtue.

Sealed and delivered before me

[signed] Charles Hubbard (seal)

[signed] A. D. Kingman (seal)

[signed] Lewis Scearce P.J. F.C.C.

DEFENDANT'S JUDGEMENT BOND

C. Hubbard—Plaintiff   (

   against   (Bond

James Brown—Defendant (

We undertake and are bound to the plaintiff C Hubbard in the sum of Twenty-Eight Dollars that the defendant James Brown shall perform the Judgement of this court in this action or that the undersigned Joseph A. Fawlkes will have the grey horse attached in this action or his value Seventy five Dollars forth coming and subject to the order of the court for the satisfaction of such Judgement.

NOTICE OF DEPOSITION

Charles Hubbard Lis [lawsuit]

Take notice that on the 22nd day of March 1854 at the house

of Mrs. Helen Garret in the Parish of Caddo in the State of Louisiana I shall proceed to take the deposition of Miss Mary L. Elgin to be read as evidence in a cause now pending in the Fulton County Quarterly Court wherein you are Plaintiff & James Brown is defendant if said deposition cannot be taken on the 23rd of March, then on the 24th if not on the 24th then on the 28th if not on the 28th then on the 1st of April 1854 and if not completed on that day then from day to day until completed.

[signed] James Brown

for Atty Roulhac

State of Kentucky(Personally appeared before the under-
Fulton County (signed Presiding Judge of the Fulton County Court - Frank Rouchas who makes oath that he did on the 24th day of March 1854 deliver to C. Hubbard in Hickman, Ky a true copy of the within notice Given un der my hand March 4th 1854

[signed] Lewis Scearce P.J. F.C.C.

DEPOSITION OF WITNESSES

This deposition of David Caddis taken on the 24th day of April 1854 at the office of A. D. Kingman in the town of Hickman Ky to be read as evidence in an action pending in the Fulton Quarterly Court wherein Charles Hubbard is plaintiff and James Brown is defendant- Question by Pltffs Atty. Please state if you know the horse which James Brown had here last fall, and the one attached by Easly in this case.

Ans. Brown said he had bought this mare up in Tennessee and wanted to trade her to a man to get one that match another one he had in a waggon. In a day or two after that he was in my house he could not trade. He said unless he could get a good boot - this was the same horse that was attached by Easly in the case of Hubbard vs Brown - it was of grey color a large fine looking animal.

By Deft. Are you certain [strikeouts omitted] that he claimed the horse as his own property

Ans. He claimed it and said he wished to trade it off or purchase another to match.

By Same. You say it was a mare he spoke to you about so on are you certain it was the same animal which was attached by Easley.

Ans. I cannot say certainly that it was the same animal which was attached by Easly as the attachment was levied at Mr Fowlkes stable when I was not present.

By Same. Did he not also claim a wagon and horse which were in his possession at the same time?

Ans. He did.

[signed] David Caddis

Also the deposition of James Wilson taken at the same time, place and for the same purposes -

Question by Pltffs Atty. Please state if you did not hear James Brown say that pltff had rendered medical services to deft in the year 1832 and was or not pltff a practicing physician at the time -

Ans. I did hear him say the plaintiff had rendered him medical services & plaintiff was a physician at the time I carried the Plaintiffs bill to Mr. Brown and when I hand the Dr's Bill to Mr. Brown he Replyed the bill was high but he would settle it and have nothing more to do with Dr. Hubbard.

[signed] James P. Wilson

Also the deposition of Joseph Fowlkes taken by consent at the same time & place to be read as evidence in behalf of the defendant in an action wherein Charles Hubbard is plaintiff & James Brown defendant -

Question by Defendant. Did you or not during the fall of 1853 keep in your stable a large gray horse which was brought there by the defendant Brown & did you not understand from him that the horse was the property of Miss Mary Elgin & was not the property of the same charged to her?

Ans. Mr Brown the defendant arrived at my stable in fall of 1853 reporting himself directly from the eastern part of Texas in the western part of Louisianna. He was riding a large grey geldin which I judged to be about twelve years old. He put him up at my stable and told me he was the property of Miss Mary Elgin. The horse stayed in my stable the greater part of the time Brown stayed here he always spoke of him as Miss Elgins horse told me who she bought him from and how much she gave for him. My stable bill for feeding said horse was made out ajoint Miss Elgin at Mr Brown request. This was the same horse levied on by Mr Easly and placed in my charge by him.

By Pltffs Atty. Are you or not the security of deft Brown for the forthcoming of the property attached to this case?

Ans. I am

[signed] Joseph A. Fowlkes

APPEAL BOND

Know all men by these presents that we James Brown and Jos A. Fowlkes are held and firmly bound to Charles Hubbard in the penal sum of Twenty nine dollars the payment whereof well and truly to be made we bind ourselves our heirs Executors and administrators jointly severally and firmly by these presents sealed with our seals and dated this 16th day of May 1854. The correction of the above obligation is such that whereas the above bound Brown has obtained an appeal to the Fulton Circuit Court from the judgement of the Fulton County Masterly Court rendered at the April term therof 1854 wherein the said Brown is Deft and the said Charles Hubbard is Pltff now if the said Brown since duly prosecute the said appeal and with effect or shall well and truly satisfy and pay the said Hubbard the amount of his said judgement with interest and costs and all costs and damages which may be awarded so sustained by him the said Brown in case the said judgement is affirmed in while or in part or the said appeal dismissed or discontinued then this obligation shall be void else to remain in full force and virtue.

(seal)

[signed] Jos A. Fowlkes (seal)

WRIT OF SUMMONS

THE COMMONWEALTH OF KENTUCKY

To the Sheriff of Fulton County

You are commanded to summon Charles Hubbard to answer on the first day of the next Sept. term of the Fulton Circuit Court, a petition filed against him in said Court by James Brown and warn him that upon his failing to answer, the petition will be taken for confession, or he will be proceeded against for contempt; and you will make due return of this summons on the first day of the next Sept. term of said Court.

Witness, G.S. Morris Clerk of said Court, this 21st day of June 1854.

[signed] G S Morris

[Note: The testimony in this case is invaluable in tracing the movements of James Brown in Tennessee, Texas, Louisiana, and Kentucky. The testimony given in his behalf constitutes a sort of census of persons who knew him and his movements.]

SAMPLE CRIMINAL CASE

The Commonwealth vs. Woodull & c: James

Wiley

George

Hickman County, Kentucky, 1832   Robert

William

GRAND JURY INDICTMENT

The Commonwealth of Kentucky, Hickman County and Circuit Set: At a circuit court, holdon for the County and circuit aforesaid, at the Court house of said County, on the second day of April in the year one thousand eight hundred and thirty two before Rezin [Reason] Davage, one of the Circuit Judges, appointed and Commissioned, within said Commonwealth and asigned, and allotted, as the Judge of said Court. The grand jurors of the County and Circuit aforesaid then and there duly emppannelled, sworn and charged, to enquire for said Commonwealth and the body of the County aforesaid in the Court aforesaid in the Commonwealth aforesaid present that Robt Woodall, late of said County, yeoman, William Woodall late of said county, yeoman, James Woodall late of said County, yeoman, Wiley Woodall late of said county, yeoman, and George Woodall late of said county yeoman, not having the fear of God before their eyes but being moved and reduced by the ins[tig]ation of the Devil on the third day of December in year one thousand eight hundred and thirty one, in the county of Hickman and Circuit aforesaid, did with force and arms, feloniously, willfully, and of their [malice] aforethought, make an asault, in and upon one Wilson White, and that the Robert Woodall, with a certain piece of oak timber of the value of six cents which he the said Robert Woodall in both his hands, then and there had and held, the said Wilson White in and upon the left side of the head of him the said Wilson White, then and there feloniously, willfully, and of his malice aforethought, did strike, giving unto him, the said Wilson White, then and there with the said piece of oak timber, by the stroke aforesaid, in manner aforesaid, in and upon the side of the head of said Wilson White, one mortal wound of the length, of three inches and of the depth of two inches, of which said mortal wound, he the said Wilson White, on and from the said third day of December in the year one thousand eight hundred and thirty one at the County of Hickman and Circuit aforesaid, until the fourth day of December of the same year at three of the clock in the morning of the said fourth day of December at the County of Hickman and Circuit aforesaid, did languish, and languishing did live, on which said fourth day of December at the hour aforesaid of the said year one thousand and eight hundred and thirty one at the County of Hickman and Circuit aforesaid, he the said Wilson White of the mortal wound aforesaid died. And that said

William Woodall, James Woodall, Wiley Woodall and George Woodall at the time of committing the felony and murder aforesaid, in manner aforesaid, feloniously, willfully, and of their malice aforethought, were present aiding, abbetting, consorting, supporting and maintaining, the said Robert Woodall in the felony and murder aforesaid in manner and form aforesaid, to do, commit, and perpetrate, and so the jurors aforesaid upon their oath aforesaid, do say, that the said Robert Woodall, William Woodall, James Woodall, Wiley Woodall, and George Woodall, him the said Wilson White, in manner and form aforesaid, feloniously, willfully and of the malice aforethought, did kill and murder, against the statute in that case made and provided, and against the peace and dignity of the Commonwealth of Kentucky.

[signature of attorney not legible]

[On back of document:]

We the Jury find the prisoner George Woodall not guilty.

John Campbel

We the Jury find Wiley Woodall not guilty Oct the 2nd 1832.

Wm. Taylor

Commonwealth

v.   (Indictment

(for

(Murder

Robert Woodall

William Woodall

James Woodall

Wiley Woodall

and George Woodall

A true bill

George Reese

Foreman

Patterson

[Note: This report followed the completed trial six months later.]

WARRANT (WRIT OF CAPIAS)

THE COMMONWEALTH OF KENTUCKY

To the Sheriff of Hickman County, Greeting:

We command you to take James Woodall, George Woodall,

Robert Woodall, Wiley Woodall, and William Woodall if they be found within your bailiwick, and them safely keep, so that you have their bodies before the Judge of Honor[able] Hickman Circuit Court, at the Court House in Clinton, on the first day of the next July term, to answer The Commonwealth of and Indictment found against them by the Grand Jury for murder and have then there this writ.

Witness, Richard Taylor, Jr. Clerk of our said Court, at the courthouse aforesaid, this 18th day of May 1832, and in the 4th year of the Commonwealth.

[signed] Richard Taylor J. C. H.C.C.

JURY SUMMONS

James Woodall

The Commonwealth of Kentucky to the Sheriff of Hickman County Greetings: You are hereby commanded to summon and cause to come before the Judge of our Hickman Circuit Court at the Courthouse in the Town of Clinton on the 1st day of the next July Term twelve good and lawful men, housekeepers of your county to pass between the Commonwealth after and James Woodall and his trial for murder who are of no wise a kin to said Woodall and this they shall in no wise omit under the penalty of L100 and have then there this writ witness Richard Taylor Jr Clerk of our said Court at the Courthouse aforesaid this 7th day of June 1832 and in 41st year of the Commonwealth.

[signed] Richard Taylor Jr. C.H.C.C.

[On back of document (jurors' names)]

1. Gabriel David	7. John Johnson
2. Michal Watson	8. Peter Sibert
3. John E. Anderson	9. Asa Vitcherson
4. Porter Brown	10. G. B. Bailey
5. Abraham Watson	11. John Henry
6. Price Edvington	12. Ferral Vincent

Commonwealth

     vs.   (Venirie

Woodall   (facias

To July Term 1832

[Note: This jury summons for James Woodall is repeated for William, Wiley, and George, each with a separate list of jurors.]

SUMMONS FOR WITNESSES (SUBPOENA)

COMMONWEALTH OF KENTUCKY

to the Sheriff of Hickman County, Greetings:

We command you to summon Thomas Griffey, Thomas Wellingham, Robert Tanner, Archibald Appleton, Wright Simpkins, Grey Stone, Benjamin Stacy, Nancy Stacy, John Odeguard, Elijah Bradley, Samuel Sawyer to appear before the Judge of our Circuit Court, at the courthouse of Hickman County, on the 1st day of the October term, to testify and the truth to say, on behalf of the Deft [James Woodall] in a certain matter of controversy in our said court depending and undetermined, wherein The Commonwealth is Plaintiff and [James] Woodall is Defendant; and this they shall in nowise omit, under the penalty of L100. Witness Richard Taylor Jr. Clerk of our said Court at the court house aforesaid, this 21st day of July 1832, and in the 41st year of the Commonwealth.

[signed] Richard Taylor Jr CHCC

[On back of document:]

Executed on all but Tanner and Sawyer.

S. Gibson DS for

Saml Gibson SHC

Wiley Woodall

    vs.

Commonwealth

To October 1832

[Note: Separate subpoenas were issued for different witnesses ordered to appear on behalf of William, Wiley, and George on 21 July and 5 September. It is known from the endorsement on the back of the indictment above that George and Wiley were judged not guilty. The fate of James, Robert, and William is not stated in the surviving papers. A search in Hickman County newspapers could reveal what happened to them. The court docket lists Commonwealth of Kentucky vs. Woodhull. The case includes seventy-five different residents of Hickman County as witnesses, defendants, clerks, and court officers.]

EQUITY CASES

Common equity cases are probate disputes, estate divisions, divorce proceedings, adoptions, dissolution of partnerships, and other cases involving property rights.

THE BILL (DECLARATION OR PETITION)

The action begins by filing a bill stating the plaintiff's case and praying the chancellor (judge) for relief. The bill must state every fact entitling the plaintiff to relief. After printing became more common, many courts required these bills to be printed and presented in court as bound volumes.

FILING AND SERVICE

The bill is filed with the clerk of the court, and a copy is served on the defendant as prescribed by statute or rules of the court. A proof of service (return) must appear on the back of the record. At this point, the bill may be tested to determine if it is sufficient to entitle the plaintiff to a remedy at equity. This is called a demurrer (meaning to delay or stay).

ANSWER

The answer, setting up every circumstance the defendant will use, must be filed within the time stated. If there are several defendants, each may file an answer, although one will suffice.

If the defendant fails to file or admits all the allegations, judgment by default or decree *pro confesse* (judgment because of confession) will be given. The case ends here.

HEARINGS AND PROOF

Equity trials are generally conducted without a jury. The chancellor has the power to decide both questions of fact as a jury and questions of law as a judge. The rules of evidence applicable to suits at law also apply, but the proceedings are more direct. Frequently, in cases without serious dispute over the facts, no oral testimony is introduced. The matter is argued to a conclusion upon the allegations set forth in the bill and answer. If proof is necessary, it is usually brief. There are four common methods of presenting proof:

1. Depositions. Obtained by written questions or through oral examination by counsel, summarized and written. Such depositions are valuable where family members have moved from their birthplaces to unknown places, for their residences are recorded.

2. Reference to special examiners (masters). This is a convenient method where the facts are complicated or where several hearings are necessary. The chancellor commissions a member of the bar to determine the facts of the case and make a report, including testimony and findings on the facts. The chancellor uses the report as a basis for the decree but is not bound to accept the findings of the master.

3. Jury trial. Generally, equity litigants have no right to a jury trial, though the court may submit questions of fact to a jury if it chooses. The chancellor is not bound by the jury's verdict. In some states, however, the right to a jury trial in chancery cases is given by statute and can only be set aside for reasons which would justify a judge in setting aside a verdict in any law action, as, for instance, where the verdict was contrary to the evidence.

4. Hearings before the court itself take place when the trial judge permits litigants or their legal representatives to present oral or written arguments.

DECREES

A decree is the judgment or sentence determining the rights of the parties to the suit. A decree is final when it decides the whole case, reserving no further questions for the future judgment of the court. A decree dismissing a bill or ordering specific performances of a contract would be final. It is interlocutory when it reserves any question for future judicial consideration—for instance, ordering the delivery of property to a receiver or granting a temporary injunction.

A decree in equity is generally easier to enforce than a judgment in law. When the chancellor orders a person to execute a deed, perform a contract, account for trust funds, cancel a mortgage, or any of the various things it may order, the person must comply or be subject to fine or imprisonment. Disobedience to the order is contempt of court. All the machinery of the government, including the army, may be used to enforce a decree of equity.

SAMPLE EQUITY CASE

L. N. Calvert and Wife

vs

Marcus Milners Heirs

Fulton County Circuit Court, Kentucky

and

Kentucky Court of Appeals, 1856-1866

GUARDIAN'S ANSWER

Fulton Circuit Court

L. N. Calvert & wife - pltffs   (

    against   (Answer

Marcus Milners Heirs--Defts   (

The answer of A. D. Kingman as Guardian & John B. Milner, the infant heirs [meaning under twenty-one] of Marcus Milner dec'd for answer to pltffs Petition says - that he admits all the alligations of said petition that are in favor of said infants and desires all that are or may be considered prejudicial to their interest, and calls for full proof, and asks for full protection of their rights as infants under the laws of the land & that they be dismissed with their costs ye

Sept 11 1856   [signed] A. D. Kingman

                             Guardian adlitim

[Note: A minor cannot bring suit in a court of law; therefore, a guardian *ad litem* (in suit) is appointed to serve as litigant in the case. When the case has been terminated, the guardian is released.]

NOTICE OF DEPOSITION

[Note: This notice is usually printed among the legal notices in local newspapers.]

W.R. Bradley Atty for N. S. Calvert & Wife

Take notice that I shall proceed on the 19th day of Nov 1856 at the residence of Wm Milner in Fulton County Ky to take the deposition of John Milner and others to be read in Evidence on the trial of a suit pending in the Fulton Equity & Criminal Court wherein said Calvert & wife are pltffs and I and others are defendants - and if the taking is not completed on that day, it will be continued from day to day till done.

               [signed] Wm Milner

[On back of document:]

    Wm Milner

To   (

    (Notice

    (

    W. R. Bradley

Executed on W. R. Bradley by delivering to him a true copy of within notice 12 Nov 1856.

P. B. Adams Shf

by F L Morse dept.

TRANSCRIPT OF CASE (BRIEF)

The State of Kentucky　　(

The Court of Appeals　　(December 19th 1858

W. Milner et al. Appellant　(

　　　against　　　(　The Fulton Circuit Court

L. Calvert et al. Appeller　(

The Court being sufficiently advised delivered the following opinion herein-

Marcus Millner died in Fulton County in this state leaving an estate in land, slaves etc which was disposed of by his last will between his widow and children.

All of the children except Louisa were of a former marriage and Louisa died soon after the testator, in infancy and without issue -leaving her mother and half brothers and sisters her sole heirs.

This is a contest between the mother of Louisa and the surviving children of the testator as to the mothers rights under the will, and as heir of her deceased child.

Two questions are made: First - what interest she has under the will, and second - In what proportions the mother and half brothers and sisters take the slaves and personalty belonging to the estate of the deceased infant.

The 1st and 9th clauses of the will alone relates to the subject matter in dispute, and must determine the extent of the widows interest as devisees.

They are as follows:

1. I give to my wife Martha the south home quarter - my negro boy Levi and my woman Terry and children to use as she thinks best during her life time, and then to go to my children; and should there be a surplus above her support, the proceeds to be equally divided among my children.

Ninethly, should there be a surplus arising from the farm or tan yard above the support of my family, I desire my Executors to use it to the best advantage for the benefit of my children.

It is concluded that the home quarter and "the farm" are the same; and this controversy is in regard to the "surplus" mentioned in the first clause. Whether the testator intended it as the surplus remaining at the death of the tenant for life, or as the annual surplus to be held by his Executors and used by them for the benefit of his children as it occured as indicated by the nineth clause.

Disregarding the latter clause of the will, no doubt could exist to the meaning of the former. Its language would clearly authorize the view which the court below seems to have taken, and entitled the widow to the surplus whilst she lived giving to the children only what remained at her death. This construction is however in our opinion, not at all allowable in view of the ninth clause of the will, in which the testator clearly indicates a different purpose with regard to such surplus.

Both claims direct that the surplus shall go to the children.

The first is silent as to the character of surplus - whether annual or that remaining at the death of the widow - and also as to the time of enjoyment by the children; but considering the discretion left the widow and the estate conferred upon her, its language would indicate that the testator intended the surplus left at her death. The latter however forbids such an interpretation of the previous clause, because it irrequivocally indicates a very different intention - both as to the character of surplus, and the time of its enjoyment by the children. It shows that he did not mean the surplus remaining at the death of the widow only, but the surplus as it accrued during her life - and also that his children were to have the benefit in their discretion might think most advantageous to them, or, as he says, "to use it to the best advantage".

Our opinion upon this branch of the case, therefore, is, that the widow was only entitled to so much of the rents, and profits of "the farm " or "home quarter" as would support herself and family -that is - the family with her at the death of the testator - including herself - the children of the testator living with her and her servants; and that the Court below erred in adjudging to her and her husband beyond that proposition.

The ruling of the Court is to the proportions in which the mother and half brothers and sisters take as heirs of the deceased infant was obviously correct.

By the Revised Statutes Chapt 30 Sec II, it is provided that "where any person shall die intestate as to his personal estate or any part thereof, the surplus, after payments of funeral expenses, charges of administration, and debts shall pass and be distributed among the same persons and in the same proportions to whom and which real estate directed to descend - except as follows:

"First - the personal estate of an infant shall be distributed as if he had died after full age etc"

Sec 1 of the same Chapter, directs that real estate shall descend, first to children and their descendants, if none, then to the father, if none, then to the mother, brothers and sisters and their descendants etc.

Sec 2 provides that "Collaterals of the half blood shall inherit only half so much as those of the whole blood, or as ascending kindred, when they take with either."

In this case the collaterals are altogether of the last blood - there are none of the whole blood with whom they can take - and the question is, whether they take as brothers and sisters equally with the mother as provided in Sec 1 infra. Restriction imposed by the second section only applies to collaterals of the half blood, when there are collaterals of the whole blood to take with them, and not to a case like the present.

It is difficult to perceive how this position can be maintained in view of the section referred to. It provides not only for cases when there are collaterals of the half and whole blood, but also for such as we are considering.

It limits the shares of collaterals of the half blood to one half in either case - the language, when properly construed, means nothing more nor less than that they shall inherit only half as much as collaterals when they take with them, and the same proportion when they take with ascending kindred.

In this respect, the provision is similar to the 15 Sec of the Act of 1796 -

1. Stat Law. 564 - which declares that "if all be of the half blood, they shall have whole portions only giving the ascendants (if there be any) double portions."

The mother in this case is of the ascending kindred. She is entitled under the 1st Section to take a share equal to a brother or sister of the whole blood - and the chancellor very properly gave her a share double that of either of the collaterals of the half blood.

The judgment is however reversed upon the other ground already indicated, and the cause remanded for further proceedings in conformity with this opinion.

A copy

Att. R. R. Revill C. C. A.

[On back of document:]

Milner et al

(

(Co. Opinions

(

Calvert et al

Filed May 31, 1860

John R. McGhee

Clk

Recovered

Fulton

[Note: The case has been appealed by William Milner as executor of the estate of Marcus Milner. A complete resumé of the case as it was presented to the Fulton Circuit Court was prepared by the county clerk. It contained a brief outline of the facts of the case, the points of law and controversy upon which the appeal is based, and the opinion of the lower court.]

BILL OF COSTS

S. N. Calvert & Wife Plaintiffs   (Fulton Equity Circuit Court

(

(Bill of Costs

(

Milner et al Defendants   (To Decs term 1861 & inclusion

/56 Feb 28	To Fil Ct[11] dec[10] Aty[10] Sums[25] 6 Cefs[60]		
	Ret[10] oath[25]	1.40	
" Sep "	Osdn fil ans[25] fil10 oath[15] Out Out		
	sy wit my of Byland[25]	.75	
" " "	Osdn fr him to be Milners party[25]		
	Order afy Kin Gad L fr	.25	
" " "	Infts[25] One fil In Milner Anst	.25	
	fil[10] oath[15] Out	.75	
" " "	fit Ans of G ad L[25] fil[10] Osd trus		
	fn case	.35	
" " "	to E Cr Ct[25] Cent[25]	.50	4.00
" " "	Oud apty McGelu Comr[25] Doct[10] Ciut[25]	.60	
/57 Jan "	Dock[10] Cuit[25]	.35	
" Dec "	One fil Cunr Rept[25] fil[10]		
	Ord allowance[25]	.60	

" " "	One fil Di ci[25] fil[10] at Di ci /56	.35	
" " "	Owe fr Di ciu to be Recrdur	25	
	Recrdng same[75]	1.00	
" " "	To Kin Appe Bond[50] Sup[25] to Cep[10]	.85	3.75
	Morris Costs	7.75	
pd by Deft "	In R Mcgelu Exr fr Deposition of		
	In Milner	3.50	
pd by Plts "	In R McGelu Exr from Deposition		
	of In R Calvert	3.00	
	McGelu cut (ae paid him)		6.50
"	Serving notice to take in Milner		
	Dep - PB Adams G Co	.25	.25
"	To Sheriff for serving 6 copies of		
	Sum 250 Early P C -	3.00	3.00
"	On McGelu allowance as Comr	10.00	10.00
/60 May "	One fil Ct of Appl of[25] one Ruistery		
	Cou[25] dock[10] fil[10]	.70	
"	Recording172 Curt[25]	2.00	2.70
/60 Dec "	Dock[10] One siz death of Inv B Milner[25]		
	One cuit[25]	.60	
"	Cuit[25]	.25	
/61 May "	Dock May/61[10] Cuit[25]	.35	
" Dec "	One cut _____ fr fife to issue on		
	Judge[25] Dock[10]	.35	
"	One submiss of law[25] Out Surt Death		
	of I B Milner[25]	.50	
"	One Qust Milin fr fifu fr 114[34]/100		
	Dollars to issue[25]	.25	
"	Onthr for said Fifu[25] fifu[50]		
	Amt Cost[25]	1.00	4.10
	Total Costs to Decr/[61] in claim=		34.30
	state tax		.50
			34.80
	Att fee	5.00	
			5.00
			39.80

[Note: Note particularly the first entry for 60 December, which establishes a family death date. The use of abbreviations is a problem for genealogists unfamiliar with legal terms. *Black's Law Dictionary* will help. Several references to specific court volumes in the document can shorten your searches considerably. For example, Dock 10, Doct. 10, refer to Dockets, Vol. 10.]

AMENDMENT TO PETITION

Fulton Circuit Court

L. N. & Martha Calvert Plffs   (

Agst   (Amd Petition

Wm H. Milner & others Defts   (

The Plffs amend their original petition in this they state that Wm Mervin is now the Admr of Decedent Marcus Milner, and that Mary F. Milner has intermarried with I. C. Byland, and that Martha Ann Milner has intermarried with Alexander Burnett.

Wherefore he prays that they be made Defts hereto for proper relief.

L. N. & Martha Calvert

[Note: This valuable document amends the original petition to add two new defendants, the husbands of two of the daughters of Marcus Milner. This writing is in a different penmanship and ink than the rest of the document, and the plaintiffs are cited differently. Thus, although this amendment was filed 20 March 1863, it was probably submitted prior to the appeal, thus placing the marriages not between 1858 and 1863 but rather between 1856 and 1858, when the case was still before the circuit court.]

COMMISSIONER'S APPOINTMENT

State of Kentucky

Fulton Cir Court Sct

March Term March 18th 1864

S. N. Calvert & Wife   (Plaintiff

vs   (

John Milner Exs & Others (Defendants

It is ordered that John R. McGehee be and he is hereby appointed Commissioner to take proof of Rents and Profits in the above entitled cause and Report to the next term of this court.

Copy Attest

W. A. Brevard Clk

[On back of document:]

L N Calvert & Wife

vs

John Milner Exect &

others

Not served

Wm Keenin DpC

JUDGMENT PRELIMINARY

Fulton Equity Court

Calvert & Wife   (

vs   (Judgment preliminary

Milner & Wife   (

It is ordered that John R McGehee be and he is hereby appointed this courts commissioner - He is instructed to take proof & ascertain the value of the yearly rents and profits of the Tan Yard once owned by Marcus Milner as also the value of the rents & profits of the farm upon the South home quarter where Milner resided at his death, commencing and descriminating in his report from the date of Marcus Milners death up to the date of the removal from the said farm by Calvert and wife. And from that date to the commencement of this suit, and from that date to the next term of this court. He is further instructed

to take & ascertain reasonable amount to be allowed to Mrs Calvert for her support taking into view her situation and condition in life and the number of the inmates of her family white & black their age sex and capacity to assist in their own support up to the time of her removal from the farm. But in estimation the assistance she derived from the labor of the slaves she had in her possession - Levy & Terry are not to be estimated as she has the right to their labor in her own right. And also from that time to the next term of this court so far as may be requisite for the support of Mrs Milner & such of the negroes as she may have taken with her from the farm when she removed. Also to take proof and ascertain the age sex and value of the two negroes - Levy - Terry & Child of Terry bequeathed to Mrs. Calvert in the will of her late husband Marcus Milner. The said Commissioner is also instructed to ascertain and report the value of all the personal estate of Marcus Milner decd after payment of debts - the number age sex and value of all the slaves belonging to the estate of said Milner excluding those specifically devised by him - also the yearly hire of said slaves - and whether it is practical so to divide the slaves in kind as to give to the said Mrs Calvert from interest in their equal to a double share out of one sixth of said slaves or whether in his opinion it would most descend to the interest of all concerned that the heirs should pay to the plaintiff Martha if she elects to take the same an amount equal to her portion of the aggregate value of said slaves or whether a sale of any of the slaves would be necessary to a fair decision and if practicable to make division & allott to Mrs Calvert her interest in said slaves and reprt to court & making this division he is instructed to take into the estimate of slaves divided[,] the slaves willed to the plff Mrs Calvert, excluding Mrs Calverts life interest.

[On back of document:]

Calvert & Wife   Filed Dec 8th 1860

Int   O C Gardner Clk

Judgt   LH McDaniels DC

Milner

Recorded

[Note: This document is a type of minute entry recording what has occurred to this point in the case and may signify that no entry has been made in the regular minute book. Reference to other slaves owned by Mrs. Calvert, not part of the estate, is important. If she inherited them from her father, this reference will supply corroborating evidence of relationship.]

COMMISSIONER'S REPORT

Fulton Circuit Court

Calvert & Wife   (

vs   (Commissioners Report

M. Milner & heirs (

Your Commissioners, would beg leave to report as follows - in said case - that he finds the yearly rents & profits of the Tan Yard in Controvercy to be from 1854 to 1866 at $25. per year and the rents of the farm upon south home quarter where sd Milner resided at his death, from 1854 to 1860 to be worth $100. per year and from 1860 to 1866 to be $75. per year. And he would report that it would take to support Mrs. Calvert & the family that resides with her at the death of M. Milner from 1854 to 1866 the sum of $500. per year & in this the labor of the slaves Levi, Terry & her children is not estimated as taken into consideration - That Mrs. Calvert removed from the farm in Nov 1854 and has not returned to it since.

The age of the slaves & their value at date of the order in this case of Levi was 27 years of age his value was $1000. the age of Terry was 40 and her value was $700. Betty was worth $450. Sally worth $700.

The value of the personal effects as come to the hands of Wm Heron as Adms, was in Cash & notes $880. & he has paid out in costs & fee bills the sum of $65. leaving $815. in his hands for distribution.

The number, value, age and sex of all slaves is found in my report of date Dec 17 1857, now on file in this case. And that's what I regarded them worth at that time, but the slaves Levi, Terry, Sally & Betty, Buck, Fayett were specifically devised by M. Milner in his will and the sd slaves all having left and of no service from about the first of Jany 1862. I cannot now report the value of the same unless they were with their masters where they should be, but I can say that their annual hire from 1854 to end of 1861 to be $825. per year and in this I exclude Levi, Terry, Sally & Betty, Buck, & Fayette.

It is not possible to divide sd slaves as they are all now regarded free and worthless to anyone except themselves and not much to them.

Your Commissioners would report that the number of the white family residing with Pltffs Mrs Calvert at the death of M. Milner was seven (vis) Wm1, Jne2, B. Martha3 Fannie4 Mrs Milner, Thos5 & Lue6 Milner all these numbered were children of M. Milner decd.

I further find that the rents of the south home greater & Tan Yard from the profits adduced before me on both sides would not support the widow of M. Milner and the family residing with her at the death of her husband at any time from his death up to the present time. But I find from the evidence offered and introduced before me by the present husband of Mrs. Calvert viz L.N. Calvert that reasonable rents for the South home quarter & Tan Yard would only be $100 per anum. and would not support the widow and her family residing with her at death of M. Milner but that it would take to support the widow and her family residing with her at that time, or at death of M. Milner from 1852 to 1854 the sum of $1000 per year, and from 1854 to 1866 the sum of $600. per year.

All of which is respectfully reported to the Court for Approval.

Sept 10th 1866

Jne R. McGehee (Com)

Commissioners

fee $25.

[Note: This file does not contain the 1857 report.]

JUDGMENT

Fulton Circuit Court

L.N. & Martha Calvert ⎛

agst ⎛ Judgment

Wm Milner & Others ⎛

It appearing from the proscution & filed in the cause that the Defts William Milner, Mary F & I C Byland, Alexander & Martha Burnett & Thomas F Milner, have had the use & Occupation of the Farm and Tan yard willed by Marcus Milner to plff - Martha Milner & new Calvert, since November 1854 & that the same has been worth for rentsuit and that the whole of said rent was not more that sufficient for the support of the said Martha Milner the sum of $100, it is the report adjudged by this Court, that the plaintiffs L N & Martha Calvert, do receive adjudgment against the Defts I. C. Byland, Alexander Burnett and Thomas F Milner for the sum of Sixteen Hundred and fifty dollars with interest on the same from this date at the reate of six per cent per annum, & their costs herein expended for which execution may issue said judgment being for the rent per year at $100, & interest on each years rent as the fill acc.

And the said Mary F Byland & Martha Burnett being firm coverts, no personal judgments can be given against them, but they are ordered to pay to plffs the amount of said judgment interest & cash on or before the first day of the next term of this Court & a payment of said sum of $1650. with interest from this date & costs by them shall be a satisfaction of this judgment, & further orders and proceedings are herein continued -

It is further adjudged that the interest of Mrs. Martha Calvert in the assets in the honor of the Admr of Marcus Milner, Wm Mervin being $815. as reported by Commrs is as heir of her daughter Louisa Twenty six dollars & 60/100 which he is adjudged to pay to her & her husband L N Calvert, but this adjudication is not to effect Mrs. Calverts claim against the former Admrs of M Milner, for assets of said estate pursued with to their honor -

Filed & recorded in open court

Sept 22/66

W A Bevard Clk

COURT RECORDS

Most courts in America are courts of record—that is, they are required by law to keep a record of their proceedings. Inferior courts, not required by law to keep a record, usually do so for their own convenience. They need to know what they did and when. Before the days of shorthand and court transcript machines, the clerk received complete written depositions, testimony of witnesses, summons, writs, and often attorneys' arguments so he had a complete record of the essential parts of the case. From these and his own notes, the clerk prepared minutes, orders, and judgments.

While practices vary from one court to another and between state and federal courts, the kinds of records summarized in table 7-1 can be found. In addition to the records in table 7-1, the court process produces sheriff and constable files, coroners' inquests, jury and jail records, and attorney lists.

Some states file all cases together in one set of volumes, with one set of case files running chronologically by date and number. Other states use a different set for divorces, equity proceedings, and so on. Probate records are almost always separate.

Although the case file is an invaluable collection of testimony and exhibits that may include photographs, marriage certificates, wills, receipts for the division of property in an estate, writs, and subpoenas, it is created only for matters before the court which involve litigants. The administrative activities of the court, such as the binding out of apprentices, the exemption of the elderly from taxes or military service, appointments of road inspectors or militia officers, and memorials for soldiers killed in war are recorded only in the minutes and orders of the court.

INDEXES

Indexes to court records are usually incomplete. Some list only the surnames of the litigants (Potts v. Abernathy, 12 81-3, 289), some approach docket-style entries (William Potts, 12, 81, 82,

83, 289), and some index plaintiffs only (William Potts v. Robert Abernathy. Case in Common Pleas: Warrant, 12; deposition, 81–83; report, 289). Since 1900, some courts have prepared typewritten indexes by plaintiff and defendant, with separate subject indexes for the use of bench and bar. Rarely do these official indexes list jurors, witnesses, attorneys, justices, and other parties mentioned. Administrative court actions are not indexed either. The murder trial, for example, indexed only the Woodall brothers, although seventy-five individuals were named in the case file.

During the 1930s, the Work Projects Administration (WPA) organized several court indexing projects using out-of-work schoolteachers, secretaries, and executives. Projects in West

Table 7-1. Types of Court Records

Record	Type	Bound Volume	Filed Papers	Loose Papers	Case File
Indexes (alphabetical):	Plaintiff	•			
	Defendant	•			
	Reverse	•			
	Every name	•			
Dockets: calendar or waiting list of pending cases, in the order they will be considered by the court	Civil	•			
	Criminal	•			
	Equity	•			
	Chancery	•			
	Estate	•			
	Orphans'	•			
	Guardian	•			
	Probate	•			
	Name change	•			
	Claims	•			
	Insolvents'	•			
	Bankruptcy	•			
	Divorce	•			
	Adoption	•			
	Lunacy	•			
	Reference	•			
	Execution	•			
	Appearance	•			
	Appeals	•			
	New actions	•			
Minutes: descriptive entries of all actions taking place in the court process	Journals	•			
	Register of actions	•			
	Appeal briefs		•		•
Orders: official record of all orders of the judge(s)	Journals	•			
	Writs		•		•
	Summons		•		•
	Warrants		•		•
	Subpoenae		•		•
	Actions	•			
	Indictments				•
	Presentments				•
	Executions	•			•
	Stays (demurrers)	•			•
	Injunctions				•
	Foreclosures				•
	Attachments				•
	Distraints		•		•
	Jury lists				•
Judgements: final decisions, punishments, and awards made by the court	Satisfied	•			
	Short	•			
	Equity	•			
	Decrees	•			
	Fines	•			
	Liens	•			
	Verdicts	•			
	Opinions	•			
	Decisions	•			
	Reports		•		
	Appeals		•		
	Bills of costs		•		

Record	Type	Bound Volume	Filed Papers	Loose Papers	Case File
Case files or packets: all original papers placed in the hands of the court during a court case	Civil				•
	Criminal				•
	Equity				•
	Estate				•
	Orphans'				•
	Probate				•
	Chancery				•
	Divorce				•
	Adoption				•
	Claims				•
	Insolvents'				•
	Lunacy				•
	Bankruptcy				•
	Appeals				•
				Bonds	•
				Depositions	•
				Testimony	•
				Declarations	•
				Inventories	•
				Documents	•
				Exhibits	•
				Receipts	•
				Petitions	•
				Affidavits	•
				Pleas	•
				Pleadings	•
				Allegations	•
				Complaints	•
				Inquisitions	•
				Examinations	•
				Promissory notes	•
				Letters	•
				Appraisals	•
				Arbitration reports	•

Virginia, Tennessee, Ohio, and other parts of the country have made searching for court records almost painless. The WPA index of the 1823-to-1829 minute dockets of Rhea County, Tennessee, includes a Col. George Gillespie who is not mentioned in the original index. The original index lists a George Gillespie, but the WPA index includes sixty-seven entries for him.

DOCKETS

When a judiciary agrees to hear a case, it is placed on the court docket until trial. Abbreviated entries are made on the dockets for all changes in the status or pending action of the case for each term of court until the case is closed, carried over, or settled out of court, or until judgment is rendered. Thus, any time a case is pending, its current status may be determined by examining the docket. Most cases were on docket for at least three or four terms of court.

Most courts maintain several different dockets: criminal, civil, equity (chancery), miscellaneous (condemnations, lunacy commitments, disqualification of voters, adoptions, divorces, tax foreclosures, insolvency, estates, etc.), stets (cases removed from the regular docket because they have been inactive for several years), and claims (claims of creditors against estates and property). A court that maintains separate dockets will usually separate its other records into distinct volumes. Some courts maintain only one court docket for all types of cases. Sometimes duplicate dockets are prepared for judges, attorneys, or court clerks. Many dockets are indexed by plaintiff, by defendant, or by both; naturally, such indexes vary a great deal in form. Dockets may also be called "minute dockets," combining two records into one.

The value of dockets is in their use as an index. They are not alphabetically arranged, but reading them is faster than having to read every page. For example, if searching for the surname Potts, 1813 to 1845, begin with the dockets for the first term of court in 1813. Searching the dockets through twenty-two terms of court to 1 September 1818 reveals "William Potts v. Robert Abernathy Crd o" (carried over). This notation indicates that a case involving William Potts was placed on the docket but that no judgment had been made. Searching the quarterly dockets reveals that the case appeared on the docket and was carried over in December 1818, March 1819, June 1819, September 1819, December 1819, and March 1820.

From these entries can be found information in both the minutes and the orders for each term of court through March 1820, when the case was closed. At this point, most court clerks place all of the miscellaneous papers pertaining to the case into one file labeled with the term of court in which judgment was rendered, the title of the case, and the case number. This case file is now the point of interest, supplementing the minutes and orders. If the court kept judgment records, they too will be arranged chronologically. Thus, entrance to the minutes, the orders, the judgments, and the case files is gained by using the dockets.

COURT MINUTES

All actions of the court are briefly recorded by the clerk in the minutes. Though rarely indexed, minutes are valuable. Where dockets and indexes are missing, minutes will identify terms of court where an ancestor's cases appear. The minutes may not always be complete enough to include the names of all witnesses and jurors; however, it is far easier to search through unindexed minutes than it is to examine the individual papers filed in each case file for each term of court.

The following extracts are typical of the contents of court minute books:

Chester County Court, Pennsylvania, 1865(6)/

Att a Court held att	(John Symcocke Presidt
Chester	
for ye County of Chester	(John Blunstone (
the 1st 3d day in the	(Robert Wade (
1st Weeke of ye 8th	(George Maris (Justices
moneth being ye	(Nicholas Newland(
6th day of ye	(Robert Pile (
moneth 1685	(Thomas Usher (

Jeremy Collett Shreife

Robert Eyre Clerke

After Proclimation made The Constables were Called over ffor to bring In thyr Returns & they Returnd All was well and there were new ones Chosen for to serve for this next yeare: John Pennick Constable ffor the Township off Beathell Richard Barnard Constable for Aishtown: William Vestall of Burmingham: John Boyeter off Middelltowne: John worrola off Edgemont: Joseph Edge: of Springfield: Daniell Broome of marpoole: of Darby William fflower off Chichester: moris Lewellin of Haverford Allixander Edwards of Radnor Robert Scothern In the Room of Josiah ferne

Josiah Taylor and Mary Williamson was Called to Answer the presentment of the Grand Juery ffor being to ffamilier with each other: they appeare and will Travis it

David Loyd their Majestys Attorny: In that Case

The Petty Juery was Called and attested: Thomas Varnon John Worroclaw: Joseph Baker: Robert Barber: Randall mallin: Robert Varnon William Mallin: James SwaFoord: John Beales: Thomas Green: Thomas Minshall: Robert Carter:

John Barbery being taken up as a runaway was ordered to give in Security not to depart untill Certificate should be brought from his master that he is a free man and untill wuch time to have lyberty to worke for himselfe

William Johnson made over a deed dated this Instant for fifty Acres of Land lying on the north side of Chester Creek to Peter Thomas and his heirs for ever he the said Peter Thomas Allowing a Convenient high way through the said land from the house of the said Wm Johnson leading to Chester roade

Jeremy Collett made returne of an Execution granted ye last Court against Henry Renolds for Crowners fees and Constaples Charges &c dated ye 4th 7th moneth 1685 which he levied on an Oxe Appriased at L4 10s

Henry Renolds came into Court and made full Satisfaction for the said Oxe Whereupon the Court Ordered him his Oxe againe

Thomas Usher Presented Henry Renolds for keeping an Ordinary Contrary to Law.

Ordered that William Hues be vewer of Pipe Staves for this County

Robertt Browne came into Courtt & acknowledged himselfe Gilty of Lying with a yonge Woman and haveing ye Carnall knowledge of her Contrary to ye Law in that case made and provided, and Cast himselfe upon ye mercy of ye bench to doe what ye pleased with him; And the Courtt Considering the unlawfull act of unclainess seeing the woman is not be found and ye sd Browne Humbly submiting himselfe & promising for ye future to be carefull & doe soe noe more The Court have been pleased to show him mercey and doe fine him forty shillings to be paid into The sheriff before ye next Court and to be discharged paying his fees. And Thomas Browne Brother to ye sd Robertt, doth Recognize himself in ye sum of Ten pounds for ye payment of ye aforesd fine and Charges &c

The Courtt Adjorned for one hour and mett againe. . . .

ORDERS

Orders of the court are recorded by law in most jurisdictions for future reference. Executions are an important kind of order, often rating a separate volume for recording. They are directed to the sheriff, marshal, or constable to enforce, usually include a brief resume of the court case, and describe the judgment to be carried out. The example below is typical.

Springfield Magistrate's Court, 1640

To John Searles of Springfield: These are in his Majesties name to require you presently uppon the receite hereof That you attach the body of John Woodcoke uppon an execution granted to Mr. George Moxon by the jury against the said John Woodcoke for an action of slander: and that you kepe his body in prison or irons untill he shall take some course to satisfie the said execution of L6 13s 4d granted by the Jury January 2d 1639. That you use what means you can to put him out to service and labor till he make satisfaction to the said George Moxon for the said L6 13s 4d and also to satisfie yourselfe for such charges as you shall be at for the keeping of his person: And when Mr. Moxon and your selfe are satisfied, Then you are to discharge his person out of prison; faile not at your perill.

Springfield this 5 October 1640

Per William Pynchon

Execution October 1, 1640

John Woodcoke not appreainge to give satisfaction to Mr. Moxon according to the liberty tendered to him: Therefore I ordaine the execution as above.[7]

Many items of court business, especially before 1800, have nothing to do with litigation, for courts were administrative bodies as well as courts of law. The following extracts from court minutes and orders will show you the potential value of these records.

Walter V. Ball, in an article titled "Family Records From County Court Order Books," *National Genealogical Society Quarterly* 58 (1970): 3, notes:

> Sometimes it is impossible to trace a family line without checking the county court order books, especially in the absence of any land records. Many of these records are not indexed and must be checked page by page which is a time-consuming task. Most, if not all, of these records have been microfilmed and sent to the state capitals. Unfortunately many of them have been destroyed by fire or otherwise but for anyone having access to them they are a valuable source of information.
>
> My father was born in Tazewell county, Virginia, and as a youth I often hear him say his mother's people, the Cecils, came from Maryland. Several years ago I became interested in genealogy and through research I found so much history that I published a book on the Cecil family. This would not have been possible without reference to the county court order books, and it may be interesting to describe some of the missing links I found in them.
>
> In checking in the Hall of Records, Annapolis, Maryland, I found some reference to William Cecil in the probate records but nothing in the land records. I found that he was in Queen Anne's Parish in Prince George's County and I spent many days checking the court records of that county. The first entry was found in the record of the September, 1696 court, where he was sued for debt of 459 pounds of tobacco. The next entry was so unusual that it is quoted below.
>
> "March, 1697/8 Court: to the Commissioners of Prince Georges County these are humbly to Satisfie you that William Sessell, by the request of my wife as she lay on her death bed I have disposed of my children to Marreen Duval, and his heirs, till they are of age. John Sesell, aged seven years the 24th of December last past, Phillip Sesell, aged five years the 28th day of this instant and Susan Sessell, aged two years of January last /S/WILLIAM SESSELL."
>
> This is the first time I have ever seen a record of children being given away, as they were usually bound out where there were no relatives to take care of them. In 1707 William Cecil appeared as a witness in a trial of Her Majesty vs Doctor Richard Pile. The Queen Ann's Parish Register shows he gave 50 pounds of tobacco to the church in 1709 and his son, John, was married there in 1718. The births of two of Phillip Cecil's daughters were recorded there in 1712 and 1716. In the November 1732 court, he made a petition for tax relief stating that he was 67 years of age and had "spent most of his time in this Province." The Testamentary Proceedings show that Samuel Cecil, of Frederick County, was made administrator for the estate of William Cecil in July, 1749, and John Cecil was the bondsman. John was his son and Samuel was his grandson. In December, 1723, Phillip Cecil, the other son of William, bought 100 acres of land in Prince Georges County but in 1732-33 Phillip died and his wife, Elizabeth, was made Admnx of his estate, which was very small. In March, 1733, Elizabeth filed an inventory of the estate and in 1735 she rendered an account which was a rare find as it mentioned the heirs as "Phillip, John, William, Joshua, Elizabeth, and Mary, children of ye deceased."
>
> Joshua Cecil and his brother, William, moved to Frederick County, Maryland, about 1753 as there is a record of a land patent to William that year. This land later fell into Montgomery County and the county court order books show Joshua Cecil was sued by Conrad Bladensburg for debt in 1775. Joshua Cecil was a soldier in the Revolutionary War and when he was an old man in 1805 he moved to Harrison County, Ohio. He died in 1814 and left a will naming his children including Joshua, Jr., Joshua Cecil, Jr., was married to Mary Reedon in Piscataway Parish, Prince George's County in 1787. Joshua Cecil was the name of my father's grandfather so I next went to Richmond, Va., to check the records of Tazewell County. Here again there were no land records so I had to fall back on the order books of the county court and here I found the following:
>
> Order Book No. 1: Nov. 5, 1800. "The Commonwealth vs. Joshua Cecil cont'd. Sept 17, 1805. Joshua Cecil and Jane, his wife each prove two days attendance as witnesses."
>
> Order Book No. 3: Feb. 27, 1821. "John Wynn is appointed administrator of the estate of Joshua Cecil, deceased." Jan. 28, 1823. "On the motion of John Wynn it is ordered that the overseers of the poor bind George Cecil and Joshua Cecil as the law directs."
>
> By 1850 I could pick up the 3rd Joshua Cecil, and his family, from the census records but I had established proof of four ancestors in one line from the court order books. In the September 1967 issue of the NGS Quarterly an item I had written was published in which I cited another case where an ancestor was bound out in 1805 in Campbell County, Virginia. Copies of these records have been accepted by the Society of Colonial Wars, the Sons of the Revolution, and The Secretary of the War of 1812 as proof of descent. So I suggest that anyone having trouble tracing a family line try to search the county court order books or court judgment records as they are sometimes called.[8]

Memorials

The court may also order a memorial resolution as an expression of the community's respect for the deceased. Here is an 1849 example:

> The death of Chapman Johnson occurred at the residence of John B. Baldwin in Richmond on the 12th of June 1849. The Court expressed respect and admiration for him. A motion to obtain a memorial to such a truly great and good man was made. He had many social and mental virtues and legal abilities, an

ardent and unselfish patriotism, and monumental purity as a statesman.

Ordered that the court present to the presses of Staunton and Richmond for publication and a special copy to the family: 14 June 1849.

Having learned that Chapman Johnson, who was for many years a citizen of their town and acknowledged head of the legal profession, not only here but in the Commonwealth of Virginia, and who departed this life in the city of Richmond on the 12th of June it is due alike to their feelings and the public sentiment of the community that the Augusta County Bar Association gives publically their deep sense of loss, their affectionate regard for his memory, and their sympathy to his estimable family. Mr. Johnson became a resident of the town of Staunton more than 40 years ago. His profound learning as a lawyer and his distinguished eloquence as an orator endeared all to him. More than 20 years ago he removed himself to Richmond, but his removal did not sever the ties which bound him to Augusta County. A portion of each year was spent by him within our borders. In 1829, though of Richmond, he represented Augusta County at the convention to revise the State Convention. Our loss, with yours, is great.

It was further decided that the court would wear the badge of mourning for 30 days.[9]

This entry would be invaluable to a researcher who was unable to locate Chapman's whereabouts or unable to determine when or where he died.

Naturalizations

Often, the only references to early naturalizations are the court orders granting citizenship. An 1851 example from the Augusta County, Virginia, Court Order Book announces:

It is ordered by this court that Samuel Johnston formerly of Ireland who declared his intention to become a citizen of this state some 2 years ago having resided in the United States at least 4 years and in Virginia at least 1 year, be granted United States Citizenship.[10]

Furthermore, swearing-in formalities for a witness or a jury member often require a statement of citizenship status such as, "I, William Patrict, of Trenton, New Jersey, late of Dublin, Ireland, age 42, do declare. . . ." This valuable information will usually only be found in the court minutes.

Appointment of Guardians

The following entry, from the Order Book of the Augusta County Court, Virginia, 1750, is the only indication of the fact that James Berry was the guardian and not the father of these orphans:

Ordered that James Berry be appointed Guardian of John Berry, James Berry, and William Berry orphans of James Berry, dec'd.

This item distinguishes between the three James Berrys.

Re-Recording of Deeds

Order books are usually the places where deeds are re-recorded if the originals are not available. When the Rockingham County, Virginia, deed books were destroyed by fire, the county clerk reconstructed them from court orders and fragments that did not burn. This list of items appears in the February term in the order book:

Deed Bryant to Moyus [Mavis] the wife of Thomas having acknowledged the same & their privy [private] examination taken as the law directs is OR [ordered recorded]

A Deed Harrison to Read ackledged & OR

A.D[eed]. of Lease Hudlow to Jackson proved by Witnefs thereto & OR

A Deed Kyle to Stright proved by the Witnefs thereto & OR

A *Deed Fuzle to George Clemente ackledg wives acklgd taken and OR....*

A notation by the clerk establishes that these "entries are taken from the list of Deeds returned for record . . . and record thereof being wholly lost and neither the Original Deed nor certified copy being found for record."[11]

JUDGMENTS

In some jurisdictions, when judgment is given by the court and the case is closed, the court clerk is required to make an extensive minute entry with abridgement of the case and its resolution in a special book of judgments. These volumes are popular legal sources for lawyers and members of the bench because of their brevity. Before the days of printed court opinions, these judgments formed the precedents for future legal decisions. Below are some examples taken from the Eastowne (Westchester), New York, Mayor's Court for 1657.

Eastowne May ye 1: 1657. where as it doth appeare in court that Roger miles Jarmia Akenes and hendrick corneloson waare the caus of kiling wine to the number of seven yet being a actidentall thing therefore the sentance of the coreut is yt they shall pay thirty shilings to anne quinbe proposinably and cost of coreut which is eighttene shilings and to be performed in ten days

Eastowne may ye 1: 1657. whereas it appears in curuet that Larans Turner is in deted to hendrick Corneloson five pounds Sterling thirteen shilings yet becaus ten of the catel were not keept at winter therfore the sentense of the couert is that Larans Turner shall pay to hendrick Corneluson five pounds Sterling acording to the complaint and [?] cost of coreut which is seven shiling

mary Corneluson plantiv against gorg wright in an action of slander

Eastowne may ye 1: 1657. it being proved in coreut that gorg wright hath ruyestly [illegible word] betwen mary Cornelu son and good wife * * * that was formerly ended therfore the sentens of the cureut is that gorg wright is fined and shall pay to mary Corneluson three gilders and cost of court which is fourtene shilings to be performed in ten days

June ye 12 1657. Richard Ponten plantive in the case of mary corneluson is plantive in atction of batrey against ales martin

whereas Ales martine hath proseeded to the threattening of blodsheed with mary Corneluson and hat allso slandred her in a hey maner and hat charged the couert with in justice and hath charged one of the magstrates with speaking on truth therfor the sentanc of the couert is that Ales martine shall be punished by whipping her naked body as a magstrate or tow shall see caus to omit it and to pay all cost of couert

September ye 1: 1657. Thomas martine plantive against Josiah Gilbord in a aktion of slander

wher as it cannot be proved that Josiah Gilbord hath slanderd Thomas martin therfor for the sentanc of The cureut is that Thomas martin is to pay all cost of cureut which amounts to six shilings and three pense to be pad in 10 days.[12]

CASE FILES

These are among the most valuable of all court records because they contain original copies of evidence, writs, testimony, subpoenas, publications, etc., and thus are usually the most complete. In these files will be found details which are never recorded in the minutes, orders, or judgments. In some jurisdictions, court clerks group all closed case files into one large bundle for each term of court and label it with that term. However, other court clerks assign case numbers to their files and access them through plaintiff-defendant cross-indexes.

Case files may contain one document or hundreds of them. Even before shorthand, most significant testimony was taken down in writing and, if not signed by witnesses, at least attested by the court.

WITNESSES LISTS

Most courts reimbursed witnesses, an arrangement that encouraged participation from those who had to travel long distances or leave employment to appear. Witness books and lists show the names of witnesses and the amounts they received in payment. Some lists even include the addresses and ages of the witnesses named (figure 7-4). These lists may not have been complete. Nevertheless, they provide another means of identifying ancestral families in the cases where they exist.

JURY RECORDS

There are commonly three types of juries: the grand jury, the petit jury, and the coroner's jury.

The grand jury, or indictment jury, consists of one to twenty-three members and holds a preliminary hearing court to consider the evidence against a person accused of a crime and to determine if the evidence justifies holding the defendant for trial. They can also present those suspected guilty of law violations for punishment based upon their own personal knowledge.[13]

The petit jury, or trial jury, consists of six to twelve persons and acts as an impartial body to hear the evidence of the case and to reach a just decision based upon that evidence.

The coroner's jury, or jury of inquiry, consists of three to twenty-four members and is charged with hearing evidence about deaths under questionable circumstances.

Most courts maintain separate records of jury duty. For each court term, a specific number of names is drawn from a list of all those eligible to serve, prepared from the tax records or voters' lists on file in the county. Figure 7-5 shows the jurors' names, addresses, occupations, and sometimes ages. Jurors excused or exempt are indicated with the reason for the dismissal. Each person selected is summoned to appear by the court. Coroners' juries are also called by drawing and summons, but they serve only for specific cases.

In most jurisdictions, a jury call is mandatory unless the person has an acceptable excuse for refusing. Originally, the only records kept were the summons and minute entries made by the court clerk. Before long, however, many jurisdictions began to reimburse jurors for travel costs and loss of employment income while on duty and to keep careful records of jury service as a basis for payment. When the court meets in session each day, a roll call of jurors determines who is present.

Many courts require grand juries to keep careful records of their investigations in separate volumes. These records contain the roll call and description of the case under consideration, including testimony of witnesses, reports, and findings of the jury. The actual trial record of a case after indictment contains a summary of the findings of the grand jury, but its own minutes are usually more complete.

In a jury book, you will find each case listed with the names of jurors who served on the case, the court term, the case number, and the number of the juror. Some courts prefer to record petit, grand, and coroner juries separately, while others use the same volume for all three types.

The attendance record gives the names and addresses of the jurors, the days served, the days defaulted, date excused from service, and the kind of jury—petit, grand, or coroner's—on which each juror served. From this attendance record, payment is made for the number of days served.

Not all jurisdictions use or preserve discharge certificates. Each certification shows the name and address of the juror, the date of discharge from jury duty, and sometimes the reason for discharge—death, disability, end of term, etc.

The genealogical value of jury records lies in such information as names, occupations, and addresses. Jury records can also prove that the person named is still alive at that date, that he or she is a citizen of the jurisdiction, that he or she owns property— real estate or its equivalent—in the jurisdiction, and that he or she is of legal age. If a juror dies or moves from the jurisdiction during service, normally the record will note it.

ATTORNEY RECORDS

The attorneys who appear in court on behalf of the plaintiff or defendant are not always lawyers. In fact, several colonies in early years actually banned the practice of law by attorneys-at-law— professional lawyers educated in techniques and procedures of law. Instead, this role was taken by attorneys-in-fact, proxies for the plaintiff or defendant who pleaded the case for someone else before the court.[14] In most colonies, they were literate and experienced individuals, though not technically trained.

As universities were founded and travel and communication with England improved, the number of attorneys-at-law

Spring Term 1842

Case	Witnesses' Names	No Days	No Miles	Amt	Whole Amt of Bill	Remarks
James B Trimble	John P. Harriman	3			1.59	Del[d]
vs	John Thompson	3	60	.25	4.24	"
Turner Wilson & Co	same	4	70	.25	5.17	"
John Brown	John Supple	3		1.50	3.09	Del[d]
vs	Gowen Hayes	4		.31	2.43	"
P.M. Hall						
Nelson & Gillihand	James Dodson	9		.25	5.02	At Fall Term
abt	same	2		.12	1.18	1841 Del[d]
C.B. Thompson						At this Term Del[d]
George Nevill	Henry Robinson	4			5.12	Del[d]
vs	George Nibert	5		.62	3.27	Del[d]
Noyes & Donnelly	Joseph C Harvey	6			3.18	"
	Thomas Scott	5			2.65	"
Donnelly & Noys	Ben F. Scott	6		.12	3.30	Del[d]
abt						
George Nevill						

Figure 7-4. Transcript from Brooke County, West Virginia, witness book, Spring term 1842. The original is in Brooke County Courthouse, Wellsburg, West Virginia.

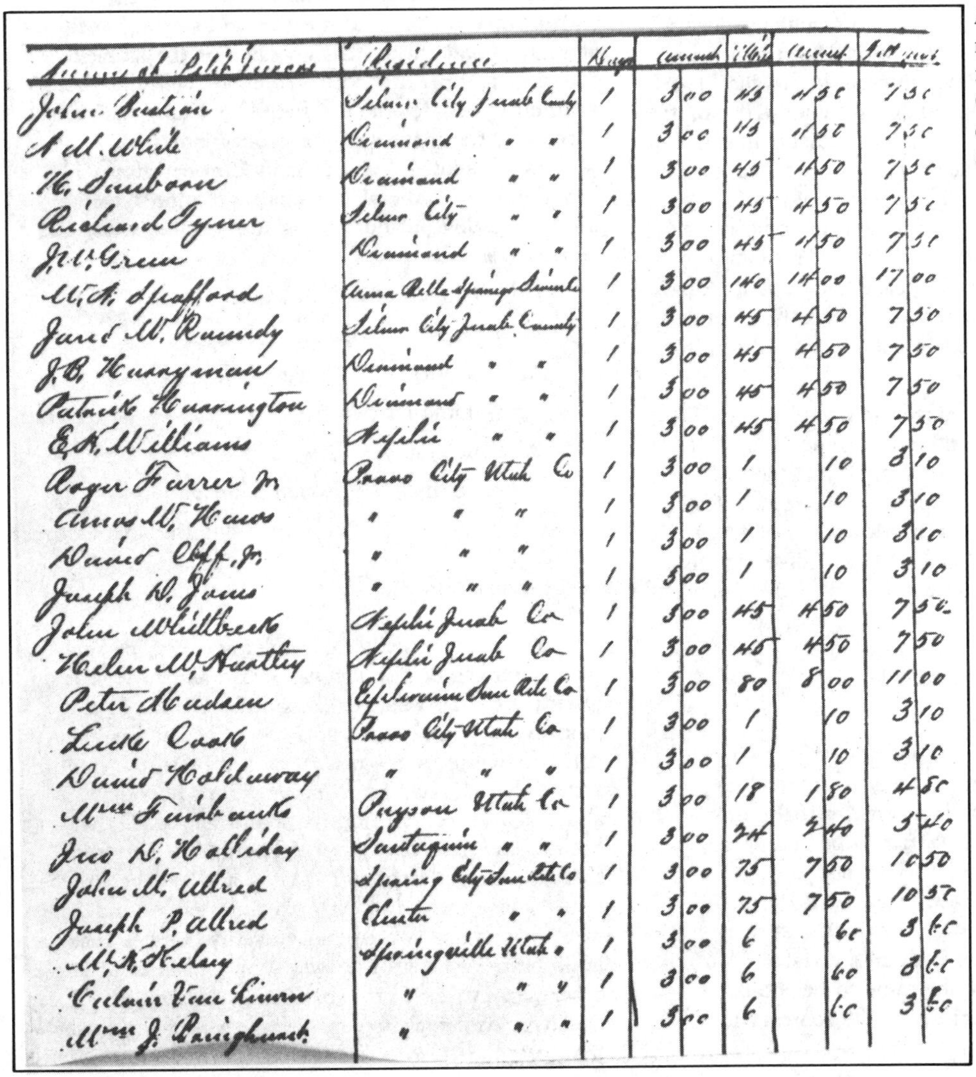

Names of Petit Jurors	Residence	Days	Amount	Miles	Amount	Total
John Bastian	Salem City Juab County	1	3 00	45	4 50	7 50
A. M. White	Diamond " "	1	3 00	45	4 50	7 50
H. Sunborn	Diamond " "	1	3 00	45	4 50	7 50
Richard Tyner	Salem City " "	1	3 00	45	4 50	7 50
J. W. Green	Diamond " "	1	3 00	45	4 50	7 50
W. H. Spafford	Anna Belle Springs Sevier	1	3 00	140	14 00	17 00
James M. Rumsey	Salem City Juab County	1	3 00	45	4 50	7 50
J. B. Harryman	Diamond " "	1	3 00	45	4 50	7 50
Patrick Harrington	Diamond " "	1	3 00	45	4 50	7 50
E. K. Williams	Nephi " "	1	3 00	45	4 50	7 50
Roger Farrer Jr	Provo City Utah Co	1	3 00	1	10	3 10
Amos W. Haws	" " "	1	3 00	1	10	3 10
David Cluff Jr	" " "	1	3 00	1	10	3 10
Joseph W. James	" " "	1	3 00	1	10	3 10
John Whitbeck	Nephi Juab Co	1	3 00	45	4 50	7 50
Helon M. Huntley	Nephi Juab Co	1	3 00	45	4 50	7 50
Peter Madsen	Ephraim San Pete Co	1	3 00	80	8 00	11 00
Leslie Cook	Provo City Utah Co	1	3 00	1	10	3 10
David Holladay	" " "	1	3 00	1	10	3 10
Wm Fairbanks	Payson Utah Co	1	3 00	18	1 80	4 80
Jno W. Holliday	Santaquin " "	1	3 00	24	2 40	5 40
John M. Allred	Spring City San Pete Co	1	3 00	75	7 50	10 50
Joseph P. Allred	Chester " "	1	3 00	75	7 50	10 50
M. H. Kelsey	Springville Utah "	1	3 00	6	60	3 60
Calvin Van Leuven	" " "	1	3 00	6	60	3 60
Wm J. Bringhurst	" " "	1	3 00	6	60	3 60

Figure 7-5. Payroll for petit jurors, April term 1879, probate minutes, Utah County, Utah, 21 October 1879. From the State Archives, State Capitol Building, Salt Lake City, Utah.

increased while attorneys-in-fact decreased in proportion. By the time of the American Revolution, the colonies had trained lawyers and learned judges, but lay attorneys still acted for many decades.

There are two main types of records concerning attorneys. The first is letters of attorney, or permission for an attorney-in-fact to appear before the court on behalf of a plaintiff or defendant. Such a letter is very similar to the letters testamentary or administrative in a probate case and contains the name of attorney, the party granting proxy, the case involved, and the date when permission is granted.

The second is rolls of attorneys. Most courts maintain separate volumes of attorneys and members of the local bar who are licensed and approved to appear before that particular court. Each roll contains the name of the attorney, the sponsor, and the date of the admission to the bar. Some rolls also contain dates of death, disbarment, removal from the jurisdiction, etc. Some jurisdictions require law students to register as prospective bar members. These registrations contain the name and address of the student, the lawyer under whom the intern will serve, school, sponsors, and the report of the board of law examiners concerning qualifications. Sometimes the date and place of birth, age, and even parents' names are included.

Coroners' Records

The coroner's foremost responsibility is to conduct inquests when a death occurs within his or her jurisdiction which involves the possibility of foul play, violence, or suicide. The inquest determines if a criminal act has been committed and, if so, the potential guilty party. No inquest is necessary in deaths from natural causes, illness, and accident with no indication of negligence. In some jurisdictions, the inquest is ordered by the court, in some by justices of the peace, and in some by the county attorney. In fact, in jurisdictions where an official coroner is not appointed, the justice of the peace or the county (district) attorney serves in this capacity. More recently, coroners have been replaced by medical examiners—especially in urban areas.

Below are the documents produced in one coroner's inquest in 1844: the warrant, which convenes the inquest and calls jurors; the inquisition, which determines the facts of the case; and the deposition, which records the witnesses' testimony. The case is titled "The State v. the dead body of a Negro woman Violet, the property of John Dinkins, Edgefield District, South Carolina." The warrant was issued by the coroner in the name of South Carolina.

To the Sheriff or any lawful constable
of Edgefield District

Greating:

These are to require to immediately upon receipt and sight hereof, to summon and warn, verbally or otherwise, 4 men of the said district to be and appear before me the Coroner of said District at John Dinkins as within the said District between the hours of 8 and 9 o'clock on tomorrow am. there and then to inquire upon the view of a body of a certain person there lying dead how she came to her death. Fail not herein as you will answer to the contrary at

your peril. Given under my hand and seal at Edgefield Courthouse

24 Mar AD 1844

by me Dan Holland, Coroner

The coroner's inquisition produced a document summarizing the facts of the case as the jury determined them:

An inquisition indented and taken at John Dinkins in Edgefield District on 25 Mar AD 1844 before me Daniel Holland, Coroner for the said district upon view of the body of a negro woman (slave) named Violet the property of said John Dinkins then and there being dead by the oaths of J.R. Tillman, John Doby, M.L. Gantry, James Dinkins, William Lundy, James Johnson, William Walker, Reuben Cooper, William I. Walker, John Cooper, William Doby, and Joseph Morris being a lawful jury of inquest who being charged and sworn to inquire for the State of South Carolina where and by what means said negro woman Violet came to her death upon their oaths do say, that the said Violet did on yesterday morning about 9 o'clock near the said John Dinkins spring in said District violently, willfully, and feloniously destroy her own life, by hanging herself by the neck with a rope to the limb of a tree and so the jurors aforesaid upon their oaths do say that the aforsaid Violet in manner and form aforesaid then and there voluntarily and feloniously herself did kill, against the peace and the dignity of the county aforesaid. In witness whereof, I Dan Holland Coroner aforesaid and the jurors aforesaid to this inquisition have interchangeably put our hands and seals this day and year aforesaid.

J. R. Tillman	Wm Walker
John Doby	Reuben Cooper
M. L. Gantry	William I. Walker
James Dinkins	Jno Cooper
William Lundy	Wm Doby
James Johnson	Joseph Morris

Danl Holland Coroner

Two depositions follow:

John Dinkins the owner of Violet and first person that found the dead body was sworn and says: that on yesterday the 24 Mar 1844 about 11 o'clock in the morning he found the dead body of Violet near his spring hanging by the neck with a rope to the limb of a tree, that she had been missing from his house about 2 or 3 hours before he found her dead, that himself and several of his neighbors took her from the tree (where hung) last evening and laid her in the house where she now lies, with the rope around her neck, just as she is now and he verily believes that she hung herself without the agency or assistance of any other person that from what he has learned, the hussy had it in contemplation to destroy herself for sometime past Sworn to this 25 Mar Ad 1844

John Dinkins

Before me

Dan Holland Coroner

Simeon Dinkins was sworn and says: that about 3 o'clock yesterday (having previously heard that Violet had hung herself) he came to the spring of John Dinkins and there he saw the dead body of Violet hanging by the neck with a rope to the limb of a tree, that it appeared from all circumstances that she hung herself, that he saw her body taken from the tree and brought to the house just as it is now, with the rope around her neck that he has owned Violet and she was a negro of a very unhappy and ungovernable disposition that he has no doubt (from all circumstances) that she had had it in contemplation for sometime past to destroy herself and he has no doubt but that she hung herself without the agency or assistance of any other person Sworn to this 25 Mar AD 1844

	his
before me	Simeon X Dinkins
Dan Holland Coroner	mark

The coroner is also responsible to carry out the regular duties of the sheriff should he become personally involved in a particular case. However, as the records produced are almost always filed with the sheriff's records, no problem arises from this occurrence.

SHERIFF (MARSHAL, CONSTABLE, CHIEF OF POLICE) RECORDS

In every action filed in the courts of record, a sheriff is called upon to perform some service. The sheriff serves the official writs, summons, and subpoenas and must execute all final judgments of the court. The sheriff is responsible for the preservation of the peace; enforcement of laws; arresting felons and committing them to jail; and executing the mandates, orders, and directions of the court. The sheriff has the power to command every person above fifteen years of age to respond for the protection of the jurisdiction and preservation of the peace in times of emergency or be subject to fine or imprisonment. In so acting, the sheriff represents the sovereignty of the state, and no one in a county is superior to the sheriff.

The counterpart of the sheriff in a large municipality is the chief of police; in the federal court system, the marshal. The constable serves in a like manner within the area served by a magistrate or justice of the peace: he serves as the sheriff in any matter within the jurisdiction of the local magistrate. The constable has the same powers and responsibilities within a more limited sphere of authority.

The records preserved by the sheriff can be conveniently divided into those produced as executive officer of the court and those produced as an instrument of law enforcement.

Records Produced as Court Executive
The sheriff is responsible to serve all writs issued by the court. Original writs are unserved writs. They may be current ones about to be served or old ones for persons whose whereabouts are unknown or whose fees for service have not been paid.

Some jurisdictions require that the sheriff preserve a copy of all writs which he served. Some sheriffs maintain a running list of the writs they have received for service. This list contains the type of writ, the date issued, the names and addresses of the parties, the court term, case number, and the date filed.

In some jurisdictions, record of all writs is kept in the same volume. In others, various kinds of writs are recorded in separate volumes—*capias* (arrest warrants), summons, warrants, executions, sales of condemned property, etc.

Most sheriffs also preserve a docket recording all writs served and any resultant sales of property. This docket will give the names of the parties, court, term and case number, title of the action, date filed, attorney named, costs and fees, disposition (judgment and execution) of the case, and the sheriff's signature.

Some sheriffs keep a special volume recording all deeds transferred by sheriff's sale. These show the description of the property, the date and amount of sale, the name and address of the grantee, and the date of the deed.

A lien book is similar, recording all liens on property within their jurisdiction which have resulted from court order. They will show the date of the lien, the parties involved, date of sale notice, location, and description of property.

Because the sheriff is frequently responsible to select as well as summon the jurors for each court term, he will often have a copy of the court's jury records.

Records Produced in Law Enforcement
Many sheriffs maintain a fingerprint and "mug" file; however, they are of such recent origin that it is rare for the genealogical researcher to encounter them.

In most jurisdictions, the sheriff is responsible for the care and supervision of the local jail and its occupants. Unknown to most researchers, jail records are available as early as 1695 and perhaps earlier. Because the majority of incarcerations in the past were for debt, not crime, many Americans appeared at least once in these records before debt no longer was a cause of imprisonment.[15]

Before the American Revolution, jails were used to detain offenders awaiting trial, debtors, and witnesses. Violators of laws sometimes had to wait as long as a year before being brought to trial, and debtors were held until their property could be condemned and sold to pay the debts. Debtors with no property were released.

Some jurisdictions—Georgia, for example—"farmed out" convicts and debtors for labor and board[16] beginning during the last quarter of the eighteenth century or the first quarter of the nineteenth century. Jail records include journals kept by sheriffs, jail wardens, or deputies. They are similar to daybooks and show the name and sex of every prisoner, the type of sentence and its length, dates of commitment and discharge, and reason for discharge: death, pardon, termination of sentence, etc. (For a more complete treatment of jail records, see chapter 10, Business, Employment, and Institutional Records.)

The register of prisoners contains a physical description of the prisoner (hair, eyes, weight, height—later records contain fingerprints and photograph), name and address, age, occupation, date and place of birth, habits and distinguishing characteristics, crime committed, sentence, education, previous prison record, dates of commitment and discharge, name of committing official, etc. This record can also be called the admission record, commitment register, prisoner's docket, or discharge book; it is required by law in most jurisdictions. Some even include the destinations of discharged offenders.

Some jurisdictions have required medical records since the early days of their jails. This register contains the name, physical description, age, sex, mental condition, and a brief medical history of each prisoner requiring medical attention. As part of this history, names and ages of parents, brothers and sisters, spouses, and children are often included.

The prisoners' daily record shows the daily roll of prisoners, their names, the date, the number of meals served, the total cost per day for each prisoner, etc. Because the United States had no penitentiaries for several decades for those convicted in federal courts under federal laws, separate records were kept on these prisoners in regular jails so that claims for costs could be submitted to the federal government.

Since 1814, jail keepers have been required to keep separate records of all prisoners of war either awaiting trial or imprisoned after conviction—again, for reimbursement by the government. The contents of these registers are similar to the regular registers, but they also contain information concerning capture and military unit.

Most jurisdictions require that the jail keeper prepare an inventory of prisoners' property taken into custody during their term of imprisonment. The prisoner's name and signature is usually found in these records, along with the list of property.

Some jails preserve a record of all prisoners who are transferred to another jail showing the name, date of commitment, date and place of transfer, reason for transfer, etc.

In one family research project, one Bridget Nixon proved decidedly elusive. A family tradition held that her alcoholism alienated her family. Her children were housed with relatives, and the husband finally divorced her, then remarried and reunited the children. Finding documents to support the tradition, however, was difficult until a search of jail records revealed her activities in St. Paul, Minnesota, from 1856 to 1860.

Aug 1856 p. 77	Criminal Court City of St. Paul vs Bridget Nixon Disorderly conduct, no return of process
20 Nov 1856 p. 84	Cited Bridget Nixon for drunkenness arrested by officer White W.R. Miller, City Marshall
Nov 1856 p. 90	Police Court of St. Paul United States vs Bridget Nixon Threats of violence Defendant committed in default of recognizance to keep the peace Orlando Simons, City Justice. . . .
May 26 1857	Report of the Chief of Police W.R. Miller submits claims for boarding of prisoners Mrs. Bridget Nixon, intoxication arrested by Officer Powers 25 May

11 June 1957 [sic]	Mrs. Nixon arrested for intoxication by Officer Wollers, 26 May
21 July 1857	Bridget Nixon arrested for assault and battery by Officer Morton, 16 July. . . .
7 Dec. 1858 p. 156	Arrests— Mrs. Nixon, intoxication by Officer Morton, 1 Dec. . . .
17 June 1859 p. 39	Report, Chief of Police, W. Crosby Mrs. B. Nixon, disorderly conduct arrested by Officer Miller
20 May 1859	City of St. Paul vs Bridget Nixon Disorderly conduct Defendant fined $10.00 and committed in default of payment
27 June 1859	Identical entry [duplicate or repeat of offense not clear][17]
p. 46	

HOW TO SEARCH COURT RECORDS

BEFORE 1800

Search a jurisdiction's records page by page unless an every-name index is available. Begin on the first page for the period of time an ancestor lived in the area and work through each page. Where printed volumes or abstracts are available, use them as indexes to the pages where the ancestor is recorded. Where there are no printed copies, search page by page, entry by entry, and extract entries with pertinent data.

To make positive and direct connections between each pedigree generation, especially if you have one of the 2,000 most common names in America, you will have to be very thorough. Professional genealogists searching records for clients have to take some calculated risks because the costs of page-by-page searching are high in both time and money. Even so, such methodology is often necessary before 1800, for identifying information is otherwise too sketchy to make the right connections.

AFTER 1800

Colin James recommended a search procedure that has proved consistently successful in his "United States Court Records, Part II: Genealogical Data to be Found in Court Records," a paper presented to the Utah Genealogical Association in Salt Lake City, Utah, in 1972.

First, ask for the index to court cases—civil, criminal, or equity—whichever you wish to begin with (figure 7-6). Since around 1840, most courts have both a plaintiff and a defendant (or reverse) index. This index will give the case number or the box in which the case file or packet (also called a case jacket) is stored.

Next, ask the clerk for the case jacket or file by case or box number. You will receive a small packet of documents folded or rolled into a bundle and secured with a string or a rubber band. This file has the loose documents and copies of the important papers of the case.

Then examine the docket book entries, using the dates for the beginning of the case and the date it was closed by judgment, which you will find on the outside of the case file. Entries are either made numerically by case number or chrono-

Index to Cases -- Plaintiff

PLAINTIFF	DEFENDANT	ACTION	Box No.
Davis Jeremah Ex parte	to sell Real Estate	Petition	1
Duncan Joseph	Samuel Duval, etal	Foreclosure	2
Dowler Jeremiah R.	Geo. B. Thompson	Petition	5
Davis James a	Heirs of Philip Schaeffer	Partition	6
Dummer H. E. adm.	John J. Moseley	Foreclosure	6
Dutch John	Alfred Dutch	Foreclosure	6
Davidson R. B.	John T. Goodpasture etal	Petition	1
Detrick Jacob H.	Orpian M. Ross	Foreclosure	1
Decker John etal Gdn.	of Charles Floderer	sell Est te	5
Dutch John R.	Joseph T. Dunbar etal	Foreclosure	9
Dummer Henry E.	John B. Thompson	Enforce Vendor Lien	10
Dutch, Esra J, Gdn. of	Wm. Dutch, etal,	Petition to sell Real Estate	10

Figure 7-6. Index to equity cases, Cass County, Illinois; photocopy of original in Cass County Courthouse, Sigourney, Illinois.

logically by date of case. A quick glance will tell you which applies. Examine all the entries for the case to see if there are other references you need to check. For example, the docket book may note: "Exhibits 1-14 in storage vault" or "Companion case, No. 4321."

From the case packet, decide whether you will begin with the orders, judgments, or other documents. Wherever you find a reference to another document which does not appear in your file, seek it out. Watch carefully for evidence that the case was appealed to a higher court or that the parties settled by arbitration.

Most search strategies suggest that you begin with the index and docket entries and then search the bound volumes for each court case. This procedure works if you don't know the case number or if there is no index to cases. It also takes longer because bound volumes provide fewer details.

Many court records have been microfilmed by the Genealogical Society of Utah, including some case files. Especially noteworthy are the collections for York County, Maine, the eastern counties of Tennessee, much of Georgia, the Northern Neck of Virginia, and the adjoining counties of West Virginia. Some states and counties have microfilmed their early records to provide better access for users without handling fragile volumes. They are kept in state archives and county offices.

The vast majority of court records are still in local courthouse vaults and storage areas. To search these, request a photocopy of the indexes or dockets for the period of time and the surnames you are searching. This is a short, easy request, for which you can expect to pay between five and fifteen dollars depending upon the county. When you get your index copies, order the files you wish, giving specific case numbers. It is

wise to ask for a cost estimate before the files are copied, although some courts will bill you; then you can send the right amount when you order the files. Some courts will supply estimates over the telephone.

If you have an extensive list of cases to check, hire a local genealogist to search them for you and provide extracts or photocopies of both the recorded copies in bound volumes and the case files, omitting duplicate documents. Do not ask court personnel to make extensive searches for you. They have neither the time nor the interest to do a careful job, and a missed entry can be misleading.

PRINTED COURT RECORDS

Court records are being printed in extract form and as verbatim transcriptions so rapidly it is difficult to keep current. While it is usually best to rely upon original documents for research accuracy, the condition of original court records varies considerably: some are still firmly bound and easy to read, some are faded and crumbling, some are torn or have missing pages, some have been restored through lamination, and many have been destroyed or lost. As a result of these circumstances, printed transcripts can prove invaluable to the researcher who knows their limitations and uses them wisely.

Most printed volumes with verbatim transcripts are also indexed, including the names of all witnesses, jurors, court personnel, attorneys, and litigants. In addition, they usually give the volume and page number of the original record and sometimes the case number. Thus, the printed volumes can serve as an effective and accurate index to the originals.

Often, the unfamiliar handwriting of a court clerk, the prevalence of legal terms, Latin and French words, unknown abbreviations, and fading ink can make original court records difficult to read. A well-trained, experienced editor can often make a better transcript then an untrained researcher. Such a copy can be used as a guide to understand the words in each document and can thus save hours of poring over hard-to-read documents.

Many transcripts of early records were made during the 1800s. Since that time, the originals have been destroyed or lost. Although they vary widely in quality, these transcripts may represent the only existing copies of many records.

Extracts and abstracts are abbreviated versions of original documents; no attempt is made to copy them entirely. Below is an example. The numbers in parentheses refer to the original page numbers.

March 16, 1779

(400) Garrat Wheeler exempted from levy.

(400) Commission for examination of Jane, wife of Robert Buchanan. Deed to Philip Sciler.

(402) Elizabeth, wife of James Thorpe, soldier in the Continental Army, with small childre, allowed L25.

(402) Joseph Crouch recommended as Captain, Alexr. Maxwell as Lieutenant, and Patrick Hamilton as Ensign.

(403) John Lewis, Wm. Lowther and Andrew Davidson qualified justices.

(404) William Robertson, Captain, and Nicholas Sybert, as First Lieutenant - qualified.

(406) Commission for priv. examination of Mille, wife of Charles Cummins, as to deed to Robert Cummins.

(406) Joseph Crouch as Captain, Jacob Warwick and Alexr. Maxwell as First Lieutenants - qualified.

(407) Elizabeth Wilson, soldier's wife, with small children, allowed L20.

(407) Admn. of estate of William Wallace granted widow Jane.

(408) Court appoints John Graham guardian of Joseph Graham, orphan of David Graham.[18]

Verbatim transcripts record every word with original punctuation and spelling. The editor will indicate in brackets any additions made by him or her. The following are examples:

Records of the Court of Sessions of Westchester County (New York): (Westchester Historical Society Publications, Vol. 1)

At a Court of Sessions held at Westchester for Ye County of Westchester by their Maj[es]ties Authority p[r]esent John Pell Justice & Quorum presed[en]t of the Court: John Palmer Justice of ye peace & Quorum & Daniel Strang & William Barnes Esqrs Justices of ye peace Decem[ber] ye 1st: 1691 - absent Joseph Theale Esqr Justice of ye Peace [1692 crossed out: 1691 inserted]

The Court opened

The Grand Jury Called & Appeared (Viz.)

Robert Hustead	John fforgeson
John fferis Senjor	Robt Hustead Junjor
John Mullenax	John Hadden Senjor
Joseph Hunt	Edwd Hadden
John Hunt	John Winter
John Quinby Junjor	Tho. Bedient
John Baly	Samll Palmer
	William Chadderton

The Court Adjurnes till Thursday morning
Constables Called

Westchester	
Eastchester	x
Rochell	Same
Momoroneck	x
Rye	x
& per younkers	x
Bedford	x all absent but westchester Rochell Same

[Page 2]

Mary Bayly Enters a Compl[ain]t against her husband Nathan baly by Mr. Antill her Atturney by petition

[next is crossed out] the Court hears the Complt and orders that Nathan Baly shall be sent for by a special warr[an]tt & that he appear on ye 17th Instant to Answer ye above said Complt directed to ye Sherrif or his Deputy And if he doth not appeare at the time appointed at westchester Court the matter is deferred for further Examination unto Justice pell & Justice Theale.[19]

Annotated transcripts are verbatim transcriptions with records from other courts, case files, and/or court opinions to reconstruct the whole case. (Rarely, however, are all papers in the case file used.)

EVALUATING PRINTED RECORDS

As with any copied record, errors are frequently made. Below is a checklist to help you determine the accuracy and completeness of the printed copy.

1. Compare a few pages of the transcribed copy selected at random with the original document, where it exists, to spot errors or omissions.

2. What is the editor's reputation? Is the editor known for correct work or does he or she sacrifice accuracy to save time or money? Does the editor have the proper training, education, and experience to insure a good job?

3. Based on your experience or that of a genealogist specializing in court records, do the number of cases covered appear sufficient for the approximate number of people living in the jurisdiction?

4. Is it listed in an annotated bibliography? Here is the notation

for one work from a bibliography of published New England court records:

> 21. *Records of the Suffolk County Court, 1672–1680.* Edited by Samuel Elliot Morison with an Introduction by Zachariah Chafee, Jr. In publications of the Colonial Society of Massachusetts, *Collections,* vols. 29–30. Boston: Published by the Society, 1933. These volumes represent a high-water mark in the editing of American colonial legal records. The editor has supplemented the records with copious extracts from the relevant file papers, and Professor Chafee has contributed a valuable essay. There is a most ample general index of names and subjects, and a separate table of reference to the General Laws and Liberties. Absolutely definitive for the court and period covered.[20]

What do reviewers say? Reliable publications are the *Journal of American Legal History, The American Genealogist, The Genealogical Journal,* and other specialized historical and genealogical journals.

In the preface or introduction, the editor will explain his or her editorial policies, changes made in the original, and describe the original itself. For example:

> In reproducing these old records the manuscript has been faithfully followed, even when this means repeating obvious slips made by the old scribes, such as omissions of words, repetitions of words, or the use of words clearly wrong. The only liberty taken with the original text has been . . . to supply in brackets the missing word or words, where the old paper . . . has left enough letters of the defective word to justify this.[21]

FINDING PRINTED COURT RECORDS

Many volumes of printed court records are available, but there is no complete bibliography of titles or locations. Below are some suggestions about places to look.

1. Published state archives. Most of the original colonies/states authorized publication of original court records in series called archives. Such compiled volumes as *Pennsylvania Archives* and *Maryland Archives* are examples. Complete sets are available in most research libraries.

2. Local histories, particularly those published around the turn of the nineteenth century, frequently contain extracts or transcribed court records. Some are accurately reproduced with careful indexes; some have many errors. Be sure to check for appendixes, special sections of documents, and quotations in the middle of town and family sections.

3. Extracts, indexes, and complete transcripts of court records can be found in journals, occasional publications, annual volumes, and special series.

4. William Jeffrey, Jr., "Early New England Court Records: A Bibliography of Published Materials," *American Journal of Legal History* 1 (1957): 119–47, reprinted from the *Boston Public Library Bulletin,* contains a listing of the records published, the dates covered, name of court; title, author, and bibliographic data of printed volume; description and index; brief analysis of editing done and omissions.

5. Evarts B. Green and Richard B. Morris, *A Guide to the Principal Sources for Early American History (1600–1800) in the City of New York,* 2nd ed. (New York: Columbia University Press, 1953), contains a separate section of printed sources, including court records, found in various record depositories in New York City. They are arranged by subject and thereunder by state and locality.

6. Bradley Chapin, *Criminal Justice in Colonial America, 1606–1660* (Athens: The University of Georgia Press, 1983), is a valuable description of courts and their jurisdictions, and specific crimes for which punishment was meted out before 1660 in America. The author includes a list of selected cases and a full bibliography of early sources. Since there are no printed reports, few indexes, and missing volumes for this period, the list is especially valuable. The genealogist who is searching for an American ancestor in this early period will benefit from a careful study of this book.

7. Volumes of court records have been published through the American Legal Records Series of the American Historical Association:

Ames, Susie, ed. *County Court Records of Accomack-Northampton, Virginia, 1632–40.* Washington, D.C.: American Historical Association, 1954.

Bond, C.T., and Richard B. Morris, eds. *Proceedings of the Maryland Court of Appeals.* Washington, D.C.: American Historical Association, 1933.

Crowl, Philip A., and Joseph H. Smith, eds. *Records of the Court of Prince Georges' County.* Annapolis, Md.: American Historical Association with Maryland Hall of Records, 1964.

Ferrell, J.T., ed. *The Superior Court Diary of William Samuel Johnson, 1773–93.* Washington, D.C.: American Historical Association, 1942.

Gregoria, Anne K., ed. *Records of the Court of Chancery of South Carolina, 1671–1679.* Washington, D.C.: American Historical Association, 1950.

Morris, Richard B., ed. *Select Cases of the Mayor's Court of New York City.* Washington, D.C.: American Historical Association, 1935.

Reed, H. Clay, and G.J. Miller, eds. *The Burlington Court Book.* Washington, D.C.: American Historical Association, 1944.

Smith, Joseph H., ed. *Colonial Justice in Western Massachusetts (1639–1702): The Pynchon Court Record.* Cambridge: Harvard University Press, 1961.

Towle, Dorothy S., ed. *Records of the Court of Vice Admiralty of Rhode Island.* Washington, D.C.: American Historical Association, 1939.

Since the initial series was completed, other volumes have been published by university or trade press publishers which come within the same scope. For example, the University Press of Virginia published, in 1973, Susie M. Ames, ed., *County Court Records of Accomack-Northampton, Virginia 1640–1645.*

PROBATE

Probate cases are distinctive enough to be discussed separately from civil, criminal, and equity proceedings. The records they generate are among the most valuable genealogical materials we have in America. They are also among the most complicated, filled with pitfalls for the unwary.

The probate process transfers the legal responsibility for payment of taxes, care and custody of dependent family members, liquidation of debts, and transfer of property title to heirs from the deceased to an executor/executrix (where there is a will), to an administrator/administratix (if the person dies intestate—without a will), or to a guardian/conservator if there are heirs under the age of twenty-one years or in cases where a person has become incompetent through disease or disability.

TESTATE ESTATES

When a person makes a last will and testament, he or she leaves a *testate* estate. Originally, a *will* devised (gave) real estate (or land) and property attached to it—buildings, mills, timber, water rights, etc. A *testament* bequeathed personally (personal property) made up of movables (lump sums of money, books, jewelry, furniture, clothing, horses, cattle, pigs, sheep, grain, tools, slaves, services of indentured servants) and receivables (book debts, mortgages, bills of exchange, and loans). American laws generally leave a person free to distribute his or her estate at will as long as it does not leave the heirs dependent for their upkeep on the state.

Wills are of three different kinds: (1) Attested wills are prepared in writing, signed by responsible witnesses who certify to the court that the will was written at the instance of the deceased of his of his or her own free will and choice and that he or she was of sound mind at the time. (2) Holographic wills are handwritten entirely by the person making the will, signed, dated, and not witnessed. If any other person writes on the will, it is invalid. In addition, the will must be found among the individual's important papers. It cannot be filed with an attorney or other third party unless all valuable papers are so filed. In some jurisdictions, this kind of will is not valid. (3) Nuncupative wills are oral, deathbed wills dictated to witnesses who convert them to writing at the earliest possible moment and present them to the court within a specified period of time after the person dies. In some jurisdictions, this kind of will is also invalid.

INTESTATE ESTATES

When a person dies without making a will, his or her property becomes an intestate estate. It is divided according to settlement shares determined by law. In most states, if the deceased is a married man, the widow receives one-third for her lifetime (known as her dower rights) and the rest is divided equally among the children. If a child is dead, his share is divided among his own legal heirs. An illegitimate child is entitled to inherit from his or her mother. Unless the father has acknowledged his parenthood in writing, duly witnessed and accepted by the court, or unless he later marries the mother, a child cannot inherit from the father. Some states allow the father to petition for a legislative act to legitimize his children so they can inherit, and some allow naturalization of deceased persons by special act so their heirs can inherit.

If a person dies without issue, his or her estate passes to the spouse. If there is no spouse, the estate passes to his or her parents and brothers and sisters. In some states, descent of property goes no further than this. In some, lines of descent become quite complicated, with provision even for nephews, second cousins, and others.

In community property jurisdictions (Louisiana, California, Washington, Idaho, etc.), the property that a husband and wife own at the time of marriage and the property that each individually inherits afterward remain separate property; the property which they acquire together during their married life becomes community property in which each has an undivided one-half interest. Upon the death of one, the common estate automatically reverts to the surviving spouse in fee simple— that is, with the right to sell, mortgage, exchange, bequeath, or gift by written document.

In non-community property states, a woman has a dower right or life-estate in one-third of her husband's property. This right must be legally recognized in all transactions, including transfers of land. A man has the right of curtesy—a life-estate in any property his wife owned when they married or in any she inherits in her own right during the marriage—providing they have at least one living child who can inherit from them. Otherwise, he has a right to one-third of her property only.[22] Marriage settlements contracted at the time of marriage can change these provisions. Under recent legislation, however, a woman has the right to renounce her dower claim to her husband's estate. She must acknowledge that full disclosure of the total worth of the estate was made and that she understands what she is renouncing. This protects the estate against undue litigation. A man cannot legally disinherit his wife and leave her destitute, on the public's mercy. In most jurisdictions, welfare help is denied, even in cases of divorce, if the husband is in a position to pay for the wife's upkeep.

GUARDIANSHIP

A guardian is a responsible individual of legal age appointed or acknowledged by the court to manage the property ownership of those incompetent by reason of youth or mental or physical handicap to handle their own affairs. A guardian may also be called a conservator, a curator, a tutor, or a receiver.

An orphan is a minor whose father is dead or whose deceased mother left separately owned property to her child but excluded the father. In both cases, a guardian is appointed to assume the legal responsibilities of property ownership. In other words, the "orphan" may have a living parent in either case. Such a child may also be called a ward or infant. It is also common for a mother or father to be appointed guardian of his or her own children without implying adoption, formal or otherwise.

The appointment of a guardian for a minor may be a separate court process from probate, handled by a different court. Depending on the jurisdiction, the appointment of a guardian for an adult who is incompetent to handle his or her own affairs may require two additional court processes: the first to declare him or her incompetent and the second to appoint someone to act in his or her behalf.

PROBATE PROCEEDINGS

Since the procedures followed in both testate and intestate cases are almost identical, both can be considered together. Most states require that probate begin the first term of court following the death of a property owner, between thirty and ninety days after death.

1. Usually, the principal heir petitions the court for authority to begin the probate process. Until recent years these petitions were made verbally and recorded only in the probate minute books. However, some jurisdictions require written petitions bearing the names of all heirs, their residences, and their ages; these are filed with the original estate papers. Such petitions are especially valuable because they may be the only documents that list all the heirs. Figure 7-7 is an example of a petition to commence probate.

In a testate estate, the executor petitions for letters testamentary or authority to probate the will. In an intestate case, the surviving spouse or oldest son normally petitions for letters of administration or authority to administer the estate according to the laws of the jurisdiction.

It is the responsibility of the executor or the administrator to look out for the best interest of the estate, the needs of the heirs, and the claims of the creditors.

2. Proving the will is a step that applies only to testate cases. The document is presented to the court. The witnesses to the will appear and attest that they saw the individual sign the will, that he or she was in sound mental condition and that he or she expressed his or her own free will. The court, after hearing this sworn testimony, will order that the will be recorded. Wills judged invalid are not proved and, hence, are not recorded in the will book but can often be found among the loose or miscellaneous papers of the courthouse or town hall. They will not appear in the index to probate records, and they are rarely microfilmed. You have to ask for these records to be searched at the courthouse.

Some jurisdictions require that all heirs of the estate be notified and present at the reading and recording of the will. Anyone who would argue against the admission of the will to probate may make claim then or generally forfeit any future right to contest the will.

3. The executor designated in the decedent's will must be formally approved by the court. In intestate cases, the court appoints the administrator. Each state prescribes the order in which persons are entitled to be appointed, but, in general, this order is maintained: spouse, one of the children, parents, grandparents, brothers or sisters, uncles, aunts, nephews, nieces, great-uncles, great-aunts, first cousins, creditors, anyone legally competent, public administrators, etc.

4. An administrator must post a bond equal to the worth of the assets of the estate to insure his or her faithful performance of duty and to protect the heirs in cases of misconduct. In most states, an executor is not required to file a large bond if the decedent's will exempts him or her from that trust.

Bondsmen were usually relatives or family friends until recently, when bonding companies replaced personal sureties. If the wife is executrix, the bondsmen will usually be her relatives. If a brother or son is executor, they will be chosen from the family of the deceased. Bondsmen can also be heirs to the estate.

5. In most testate and all intestate estates, three disinterested people (often relatives who are not potential heirs) are appointed by the court to inventory and appraise all the property of the estate. They are usually ordered to submit the inventory at the

---

Petition for Probate of Will and Letters Testamentary In the County Court of Johnson County, Nebraska In re Estate of George Hindenach Deceased.

PETITION

Your petitioner, Hannah Hindenach who is of legal age, shows: That George Hindenach late a resident of Spring Creek Precinct, in Johnson County Nebraska, died at his residence, in Johnson County Nebraska, on or about the 9 day of September A.D. 1895 leaving a last will and testament, executed in due form of law, as your petitioner believes which is now on file in this Court: that the subscribing witnesses to said instrument are T. Appelget of Tecumseh, Nebraska, and T. E. Fairall of Tecumseh, Nebraska; that said Will nominated Hannah Hindenach as executrix thereof, and that Hannah Hindenach is willing to accept the trust as Executrix that said decedent died seized of real estate in said Johnson County of the estimated value of $5000.00; that the said decedent was possessed of personal property in the said State of Nebrasska of the estimated value of $600.00.

Your petitioner further shows that the devisees, legatees, heirs at law in the absence of a will, and other persons interested in said matter are as follows:

Name	Age	Residence	Relationship to Deceased
Hannah Hindenach	45	P.O. Tecumseh	Widow
George Hindenach Jr.	25	" "	Son
Lillie Hindenach	22	" "	Daughter
Bessie Hindenach	17	" "	"
Ella Hindenach	15	" "	"
Anna Hindenach	13	" "	"
Josie Hindenach	11	" "	"
Charles Hindenach	8	" "	Son
Mary Hindenach	6	" "	Daughter
Stella Hindenach	4	" "	"

Your petitioner therefore prays that a day may be fixed for hearing the proof of the execution of said instrument; that all the persons listed herein may be notified by Publication three weeks prior to said hearing, to show cause if any there be, why said instrument shall not be recorded as the last will and testament of said decedent.

Figure 7-7. Petition to commence probate by Hannah Hindenach, 9 September 1895, Johnson County Court; typescript of a holograph in Johnson County Courthouse, Tecumseh, Nebraska.

---

next term of court or within ninety days. This inventory protected the executor or administrator from excessive claims against the estate and protected heirs against fraud or pilfering of their inheritance. The court also used it to set probate fees, as in modern practice. As a result, the values given to each item were close to current market value, although there seems to have been a tendency to keep them low. Thus, the fees levied against the estate were lower and the sale of items at auction was ensured.

6. As soon as the inventory is made, publication of the pending probate is published. In early times, notices were tacked on the doors of courthouses, town halls, churches, etc. Later, the court required public posting at the town hall and publication three

successive weeks in the major county, town, or district newspaper before probate to give interested parties opportunity to be present to voice disagreement or to present claims against the estate. The law required preservation of those publication notices. Some jurisdictions keep copies of the newspapers in which notices appeared at the county courthouse or town hall, while others clip the notices and preserve them with the case packet. It is thus possible to find missing issues of newspapers at the probate authority.

7. Another step taken before probate begins is assigning an allowance for the dependents from a portion of the estate (usually the amount is determined annually) until the estate is settled and distributed. It may take the form of cash, income-producing property (such as a herd of cattle), or money from the court-authorized sale of certain property. Usually the property so designated is exempt from creditors' claims. At this time, also, the widow's dower right will often be set off to provide for her support.

8. In estates involving minors or incompetent individuals, a guardian is appointed to receive and assume stewardship over their respective shares. Figure 7-8 is a petition of minor children for their mother to be appointed guardian. As with administrators and executors, guardians must post a bond equal to the worth of the orphan's estate. Figure 7-9 is an example of the required bond.

9. To raise funds for the support of the widow and children or to convert perishables to cash, it is frequently necessary to conduct periodic sales of property under the surveillance of the court. First, the administrator/executor or guardian petitions the court for authority to sell, stipulating the items, why the income is needed, and how much is expected to be realized. If the court authorizes the sale, a public auctioneer is appointed

and a careful account is kept of what was sold, how much each item brought, and to whom the item went.

10. In some jurisdictions, executors/administrators or guardians must account annually to the court for income received and expenses paid out of the estate, and for what purposes. In others, executors may only be required to account upon request from heirs or creditors. Because these records show heirs who die and women who marry before final settlement, they are extremely valuable for the genealogist.

11. Prior to the final settlement and distribution of the estate among the heirs, additional publication notices are issued to give claimants one last chance to voice their desires.

12. The executor/administrator must make a final accounting of receipts and disbursements of the estate before the remaining property can be divided and the responsibility ended. Figure 7-10 shows a final accounting.

13. When all parties concerned come to an agreement or when all heirs are twenty-one years of age, the property is divided and distributed to those heirs entitled to receive it; the case is closed; and the executor/administrator is released. In many probate jurisdictions, lengthy division documents will be found listing all heirs and their addresses, husbands of female heirs, and second marriages of widows. In some states, these settlement documents are found in the office of the land recorder— Division of Real Estate.

14. As each heir receives his or her portion of the estate, he or she signs a receipt or release to the executor/administrator. These receipts give the name of the heir, the amount and description of property received, the name of the executor/administrator, the names of guardians of minor children, and the name of the deceased. These releases are filed among the original estate papers.

Figure 7-8. Nomination of guardian petition of Julia A. Adams, 29 March 1881, Salt Lake County, Utah Territory.

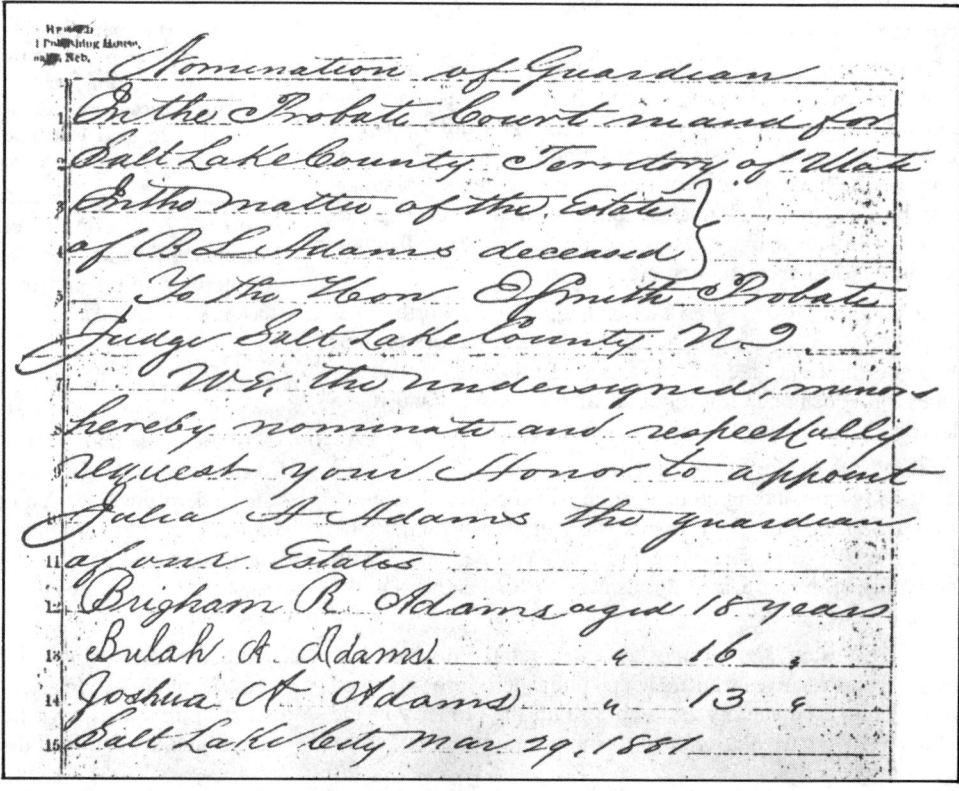

GUARDIAN'S BOND.

Know all Men by these Presents, That Polly Cripe as principal, and Davis Butler & Francis M. Jeffers as Sureties, all of the County of Iowa in the State of Iowa, are held and firmly bound unto said County for the use of Sarah Jane Blackater in the penal sum of Six Hundred Dollars, for the payment of which well and truly to be made, we do jointly and severally bind ourselves, and our lawful representatives. Witness our hands and seals, this third day of June 1865

The condition of the above obligation is such, that if the above named Polly Cripe who has been appointed Guardian of the said Sarah J Blackater shall faithfully discharge the office and trust of such Guardian according to law, and shall render a fair and just account of such Guardianship from time to time, whenever thereunto required by law and render and pay to said minor all moneys, goods and chattles, title papers and effects, which may come to the hands or possession of such Guardian belonging to such minor when such minor shall be entitled thereto, or to any subsequent Guardian, should such Court so direct, then this obligation to be void, or otherwise to remain in full force and virtue.

Polly her X mark Cripe [SEAL.]

[SEAL.]

Davis his X mark Butler [SEAL.]

Francis M Jeffers [SEAL.]

ATTEST, H A Willits County Judge.

The above bond was approved and filed by me, this 3rd day of June 1865

A. H. Willits

Co. Judge of Iowa County, Iowa

Figure 7-9. Guardian's bond of Polly Cripe for Sarah Jane Blackater, 3 June 1865, Iowa County, Iowa. Originals are in the Iowa County Courthouse, Marengo, Iowa.

Recevd Marengo January 2d 1869 of Polly Cripe Guardian of Sarah Jane Blackater minor heir of Henry Blacketar deceased three hundred thirty Eight dollars & twenty six cents in full of all demands against said Guardian for pension Back pay & Baunty together, with all other claims against said Guardian

Sarah ~~Jane Moore~~ formerly

Attest Sarah Jane Blackiter

Isaac Goodin } John his X mark Moore

Figure 7-10. Final account of Polly Cripe, guardian of Sarah Jane Blackater, 3 June 1865. Original is in Iowa County Courthouse, Marengo, Iowa.

Probate records can provide an intimate glimpse into the lifestyle of an ancestor and specific facts about the family. From wills you can discover how often the men on your pedigree entrusted their assets to a wife, whether all sons inherited equally, how the daughters fared in comparison, whether a man distributed his property to his children before his death, and who was instructed to care for the widow and younger children or for incapacitated or handicapped family members. Servants were sometimes released by will and slaves freed.

What provision was made for the widow? Was firewood delivered to her door? Were living quarters and a cash allowance for needed purchases provided? Did the allowance end on remarriage? What was to happen to her portion of the estate if she remarried?

What are the demographics of your family? Who lived in the household? What was the ratio of adults to children, males to females? Did the men live to see their grandchildren? Did the women outlive the men? How many children reached adulthood before their parents died? What were the sizes of your family units? What standard of living did your family have? Did they read and write? Did a bequest include paintings, a family Bible, fine furniture, a carriage, or musical instruments?

Also revealed in a will is biographical information: title, occupation, religious affiliation, age, place of residence, place of property ownership, associates of the family, and relationship to prominent families in the area.

Did your ancestor bequeath assets to charities, such as schools, hospitals, and churches? Did he make a contribution for the upkeep of roads and bridges? Did she support a political party?

How did your ancestor speak? Indications of local dialect and pronunciation can be found in spelling variants, especially when a will is a holograph. It can also reveal personality, character, and level of formal education.

The probate inventory gives other insights into your family's life and how your family compared to others in the community.[23] If items are listed room by room and the rooms labeled, you know who slept where. A man was often judged by the kind of bed he slept in, so inventories usually listed bed and bedding in considerable detail: bed curtains imply a canopied bed to keep out cold drafts. Featherbeds, sheets, coverlets, blankets, and spreads may also be listed separately.

Table linens may be listed (damask, diaper, flaxen, canvas); cooking utensils and dishes (pewter, wood, china, porcelain, silverplate, brass); lighting (candles, lamps, wicks, lantern glass, and lighter fluids). In poor households, a clock might represent almost a quarter of the estate's total value. Pots and pans may be valued by weight, since that is the way they were bought and sold. Unfamiliar items, such as kimblins, piggins, and eshons (cheese vats and presses), may appear.

The processes of cooking, brewing, baking, dairying, and washing are described in the kinds of utility tubs and bowls used. The presence of smoothing tables or boards and flat irons indicate that clothes were ironed before wearing, and bedding may also have been "smoothed." Sanitary facilities inside the house could consist of chamber pots and close stools, often both. The larder hints at diet—butter, cheese, ham, bacon, hanging beef, salt pork, potatoes. Particular trades or occupations emerge from tools, mercantile inventory, record books, contents of barns, granaries, and crops in the field.

A comparison of inventories from one generation of the family to another will show improvements in living conditions—from fireplace cooking to stoves, from enclosed bedsteads to heated bedrooms, from wooden platters to china. Glass in windows, unless bequeathed as heirlooms to a family member, could be sold separately from a house, so panes may be listed in the inventory as well.

Sometimes an item will be missing from an inventory because the owner gave it away before his or her death, because it was sold to cover debts prior to death, or because it is specified in the will and falls in the executor's charge. Some inventories will end with "things unseen or forgotten," a category with an arbitrary dollar value assigned.

An inventory is also useful for distinguishing between persons of the same name by matching inventory contents, such as horses, cattle, and pigs, with tax rolls and agricultural census entries. You can also prove the relationship between a man and his children with property, real or personal, listed in inventories and wills from one generation to the next.

AMERICAN PROBATE LAW

Despite their usefulness, probate records are filled with traps for the unwary genealogist. The first pitfall is contemporary law. Probate is a function of state authority, with only one federal prohibition: primogeniture, or passing a landed estate automatically to the eldest son, is forbidden; by 1811, all former colonies had revoked it by statute. Because probate is a state function, probate procedures vary from state to state and have changed over time.

It is useful to know what laws were in effect in a state at the time an ancestor lived there. The printed laws for several American colonies have been published in eighteen volumes by Michael Glazier, Inc., 1210 King St., Wilmington, DE 19801. Copies can be found at most law libraries. *Sessions Laws of American States and Territories Prior to 1900* is available on microfiche from Redgrave Information Resources Corp., 53 Wilton Road, Westport, CT 06880. For laws not cited in full, references to the revisions in each state law code are given, providing a reference to follow the changes backward in time. The years for which printed laws are available are summarized in table 7-2.

Tracing the history of a law is not difficult. Most law libraries are open for public use. A call before you go can verify public access, hours of operation, availability of copy machines, and fees (if any).

In addition to the pitfalls presented by ignorance of legal language and past laws, another problem may arise if a researcher concentrates only on the case files or probate packet. You should not overlook other records leading to probate which appear among the records of other courts. For example, the Court of Common Pleas in Pennsylvania was responsible for hearing evidence of incompetency and determining the status of such individuals.

Appearance Docket, Vol. A, p. 536, Perry County, Pennsylvania, contains the petition of John River, brother-in-law of Peter Arnold of Buffalo Township, to issue a writ of incompetency since Peter Arnold was a habitual drunkard. His heirs are

Table 7-2. Printed Laws of the United States (Pre–1900)

State	Colony	Territory	Years Available	Special Laws
Alabama		1818	1819–99	
Arizona		1864–99		
Arkansas		1818–35	1836–99	
California			1849–99	
Colorado		1861–76	1876–99	Jefferson Territory, 1859–61
Connecticut	1639–73		1776–1899	Special acts, 1837–99
Dakota		1862–89		
Delaware	1704–41		1776–1899	
Florida		1822–45	1845–99	
Georgia	Dates not given		1787–1899	
Idaho		1863–88	1890–99	
Illinois		1809–17	1818–99	
Indiana		1801–51	1816–99	
Iowa		1838–45	1846–98	
Kansas		1855–61	1861–99	
Kentucky			1792–1898	
Louisiana			1812–99	District (under jurisdiction of Indiana Territory), 1804; Territory of Orleans, 1804–11
Maine			1820–99	Resolves, 1820–39; private and special acts, 1820–49
Maryland	Dates not given		1777–1898	
Massachusetts	Dates not given		1777–1899	Resolves, 1776–1838
Michigan		1821–35	1835–99	
Minnesota		1849–57	1857–99	
Mississippi		1799–1816	1817–98	
Missouri		1813–18	1820–99	
Montana		1864–89	1889–99	
Nebraska		1855–67	1866–99	
Nevada		1861–64	1864–99	
New Hampshire	1680–1726		1783–1899	
New Jersey	1703–22		1776–1899	
New Mexico		1846–99		
New York	Dates not given		1777–1899	
North Carolina	1669–1751		1777–1899	
North Dakota			1889–99	
Northwest		1788–1801		
Ohio			1803–98	
Oklahoma		1890–99		
Oregon		1890–99		
Pennsylvania	Dates not given		1776–1899	
Rhode Island	1647–1719		1776–1899	
South Carolina	1692–1734		1776–1899	
South Dakota			1890–99	
Tennessee			1796–1899	Territory of the U.S.A. South of the River Ohio, 1792–95

State	Colony	Territory	Years Available	Special Laws
Texas			1846–99	
Utah		1851–94	1896–99	
Vermont			1778–1898	
Virginia			1776–1899	
Washington		1854–87	1889–99	
West Virginia			1861–99	
Wisconsin		1836–48	1848–99	
Wyoming		1869–90	1890–99	

listed as George, Peter, William, and daughter Barbara, wife of George Varns. The court confirmed the petition on 16 March 1824. By 10 Nov. 1827, Peter had reformed and petitioned the court to have his rights restored. The court granted his request and released the guardian.[24]

Table 7-3 is a checklist of documents produced by probate courts.[25]

Important supporting legal documents can also be found in these non-probate categories of records:[26]

- Bastardy papers
- Child custody papers
- Aliases
- Unfiled documents
- Manumissions
- Certificates of freedom
- Legitimation of children
- Name changes
- Loose papers
- Inquisitions of lunacy
- Petitions for freedom
- Apprenticeships

- Dower releases
- Marriage settlements
- Foreclosures
- Liens
- Land sold for back taxes
- Congressional petitions
- Annulments
- Orphans court records
- Claims
- Marriage contracts
- Lis Pendens
- Deeds
- Tax liens
- Legislative papers
- Divorces
- Adoptions
- Appeals
- Attachments of property

Also available at law libraries are the state law codes. To locate a law effective when you ancestor was alive, check the current law code (dower rights, for instance, or age when a minor could make a will). Get the reference to the next earliest code when the law was changed or modified and work backward in time until you find the law as it was.

Table 7-3. A Checklist of Documents Produced by Probate Courts

Court Records
__Estate docket
__Guardianship docket
__Claims docket
__Minutes
__Orders
__Decrees
__Judgments
__Executions
__Appeals
__Indexes

Petitions
__Letters testamentary
__Administration
__Guardianship
__Appointment or change of guardian
__Redress for misuse or waste of property
__List of heirs
__Renunciation

Wills
__Written
__Nuncupative

__Holographic
__Codicils

Bonds
__Administrator
__Executor
__Guardian
__Appraiser
__Trustee

Inventories
__Real estate
__Personal property
__Guardians
__Conservators
__Partnership
__Minors' estates
__Appraisals
__Appraisers warrants
__Reports

Publications
__Advertisements
__Announcements
__Notice to heirs
__Notice of sales
__Notice to creditors

Accounts
__Administrator
__Executor
__Guardian
__Trustee
__Conservator

Divisions
__Commission reports
__Settlements
__Decrees of distribution
__Dower rights
__Courtesy rights
__Awards
__Private disbursement
__Ledgers
__Guardians' final report
__Probate decrees
__Certificates of devise
__Assignments of real estate
__Order of distribution
__Decree of heirship

Releases
__Executor
__Administrator

__Trustee
__Guardian
__Heirs
__Conservator

Claims
__Petitions
__Registers
__Accounts
__Appeals

Miscellaneous
__Unrecorded wills
__Widows' allowances
__Orders to find heirs
__Sales documents
__Marriage settlements
__Waivers
__Changes of name
__Legitimization
__Memoranda
__Appeals
__Judgments
__Estate taxes

Although this process seems tedious, it is sometimes necessary and nearly always illuminating. The law determines the specifics in much of the probate process. Court officials do not explain what they are doing or their reasons for acting in a certain way in the records. They expect you to know that already.

The law also determined the ages at which your ancestors could transact legal business. Table 7-4 summarizes the most common ages (and exceptions) in the United States.

When courthouse fires have occurred, these other court documents may have survived if they were filed in other buildings or kept among the personal papers of justices or court officials.

Some of these records are used legally in lieu of probate processes. For example, Jacob Hoofman (Hoffman), Sr., died intestate in Fairfield County, Ohio, leaving sixteen children. The probate clerk, when a search was requested, found no will, but a careful search brought an extremely detailed deed to light.

Jacob had distributed his lands to his children before his death but had died before the deed he executed for his son Simon could be recorded. The property went into his estate. Jacob had recorded the transaction in his own account book and the court accepted the transaction, requiring only that a quitclaim deed be signed by all sixteen children and their spouses. The document is invaluable, but it was found in the deeds, not the probate records.

Many probate records have been published by societies and individuals. As is true with any extract, some transcripts are complete and others are incomplete or have been misread.

For example, the *South Carolina Genealogical Register,* June 1967, pp. 216–17, which extracts Will Books A–D, 1787–1810, shows this will among Newberry District Wills on p. 123:

Mathew SIMS, Sr.

Wife - Jeminah

Sons - Charles, Matthew, Nathan and Reuben

Daus. - Hannah Henderson, Drucilla Backley (deceased), Mary Sanders and Ann Henderson

Executors - Reuben Simms and Bernard Glenn

Witnesses - John Stequart, George Wilson and Fanny Stewart

Will dated - 14 April 1795

proved - 18 May 1795

In contrast, George Leland Summers, *Historical and Genealogical Newberry* (the author, 1950), p. 463, shows the same will as being on a different page and provides much more detailed information:

Matthew Sims, Sr., decd. Will 4-14-1795; proved 5-18-1795. Wife: Jemima (to have all lands remaining

Table 7-4. Ages of Legal Action*

Legal Action	Legal Age	Exceptions/Comments
Inherit	From birth	An unborn child can also inherit
Be enumerated in census	From birth	Usually heads of household only until 1850
Attend school	5	Some schools accepted 3-year-olds
Witness documents	14 (male); 12 (female)	The age of discretion under the common law was 14 (males) and 12 (females). Some exceptions are listed below
Testify in court	14 (male); 12 (female)	
Choose guardian	14 (male); 12 (female)	Must be 21 in New York. No choice until age of discretion; then, if guardian appointed by court is unacceptable, can select another subject to court approval
Serve as apprentice	14 (male); 12 (female)	Standard term was to 21 (male), 18 (female), or time of marriage. If apprenticed before age of discretion, bound only to ages 14/12. Must have written deed which allowed for apprentice's content, except for orphans on the public charge
Show land to processioners	14 (male); 12 (female)	Males only; southern states. (Procession means to walk around the boundary lines of local property owners.)
Be punished for crime	14 (male); 12 (female)	Some general exceptions before 1860. Complicated changes in the 20th century
Sign contracts	14 (male); 12 (female)	May be required to confirm contract after arriving at majority
Act as executor	14 (male); 12 (female)	Usually administrator with will annexed so the court had some controls. Age 17 in Massachusetts, Rhode Island, Missouri; age 18 in Mississippi. Bondsman who could act as co-executor required in Vermont
Bequeath personal property by will	14 (male); 12 (female)	Age 18 in Connecticut, Massachusetts, Virginia; age 18 (male) and 16 (female) in New York; age 21 in Vermont. Property may be held in custody of court pending review

Legal Action	Legal Age	Exceptions/Comments
Marry	14 (male); 12 (female)	Parental consent required in most states until age 21 (male) and 18 (female). Married child not subject to control of parents, could remarry on death of spouse without consent if underage. Age 18 (male) and 14 (female) in Mississippi, Ohio, Indiana; age 18 (male) and 15 (female) in Minnesota; age 17 (male) and 14 (female) in Illinois; age 16 (male) and 14 (female) in Iowa. Marriage is valid without parental consent, but officiator could be fined. Annulment or ivorce only way to void the marriage
Be taxed	16	Males only were counted; females appear as "heirs of . . ."
Muster into militia	16	Males only
Procession land	16	Procession means to walk around the boundary lines of local property owners
Take possession of land holdings	16	"In possession of" on tax rolls signifies that the person named is at least 16
Practice trade	18	Some cities licensed tradesmen to practice their profession/occupation at age 18
Release of guardian	21 (male); 18 (female)	
Own land	21	Some states allowed females these rights at age 18
Devise land by will	21	
Be taxed	21	Full poll responsibility unless exempt
Plead or sue in court	21	
Be naturalized	21	After meeting residence requirements
Fill public office	21	Age 25 or older required for some offices
Serve on jury	21	Grand jury, petit jury, coroner's jury
Vote	21	Linked to 21 as age of land ownership, a prerequisite to voting in colonies

*Based in part on Judge Tapping Reeve, *The Law of Baron and Femme, of Parent and Child, Guardian and Ward, Master and Servant, and of the Powers of the Courts of Chancery; With an Essay on the Terms Heir, Heirs, Heirs of the Body,* 3rd ed. (1862. Reprint. New York: Source Book Press, 1970). This is an important legal treatise on family law describing the common law in America and exceptions created by statute law or specific traditions inherited from Spanish or French law codes. The author assumes legal knowledge on the part of the reader, so use *Black's Law Dictionary.* The original text predates the abolition of slavery and includes a discussion of law relating to slaves and their rights. It also predates much of the legal reform of the late nineteenth century, which substantially changed the laws in several states. For the modern period, consult Chester G. Vernier, *American Family Laws: Comparative Study of the Forty-Eight American States, Alaska, District of Columbia, and Hawaii to 1 Jan. 1931,* 5 vols. (Stanford, Calif.: Stanford University Press, 1931), a state-by-state study of marriage, parent-child relationships and responsibilities, divorce, and probate in all aspects. These volumes have extensive indexes, making it easy to check specifics. Both works can be found in most law libraries.

in her hands during her life or widowhood, under care of the Exrs.). Sons: Charles; Matthew (to his wife, Mary); James (dead) - to his heirs; Nathan (dead) - to his heirs; Reuben; David. After death of my wife, 200 acres whereon I live, on Tyger and Broad Rivers, to be sold and money equally divided among my four daughters, or their children. The daughters; Hannah Henderson, Drucilla Backley, Mary Sanders, and Ann Henderson. If Matthew's wife, Mary, should take her third part or right of dower of a certain tract of land in Hanover County, Va., which land I did purchase from my son, Matthew, and did give to my son, Nathan, I direct my Exrs. to stop and detain out of my son's, Matthew parts, as much as will fully satisfy my son's, Nathan, estate; to pay to Admrs. of estate of said Nathan, dec. In case my widow does not claim dower, my Exrs. are not to detain any part of my son's, Matthew, decd., share. Gr-children: William Sims and Sarah Shelton (the children of my son, Charles Sims). Exrs: Reuben Sims (son), Bernard

Glenn (kinsman). Witnesses: John Stewart, George Wilson, Fanny Stewart.

Even more striking than the differences in content are the errors: the first lists four sons and four daughters, one deceased; the second lists six sons, two deceased, and four daughters, all living. The second also lists two grandchildren unmentioned in the first. Use the printed version as an index to the originals—but check the originals.

Two important printed projects are Carol Willsey Bell, *Ohio Wills and Estates to 1850: An Index,* available from the author at 4801 Mockingbird Court South, Columbia, OH 43229; and Brent Holcomb, *Abstracts of South Carolina Wills* for several counties, available through Southern Historical Press, Box 738, Easley, SC 29740. These two projects are models for needed work in other areas.

Another problem is that New England demographic research comparing wills and probate inventories with tax rolls and other inhabitants' lists shows that less than fifty percent of the male population was included among inventories and less than forty percent left wills. In some areas, the percentage was below twenty-five percent. Less than ten percent of the women had either wills or inventories. While some people had little or no property to inventory, a substantial number seem to have deliberately made provision for their estates to pass to their heirs without probate.[27]

Probate records are of uneven value when it comes to establishing specific death dates. Some probate records include the date of death. Some indexes include the date of death, while the probate record does not. Where the death date is not given, the date of the acknowledgment of witnesses is usually the first record made in the probate process, followed by admission of the will to probate. In some jurisdictions, however, the witnesses acknowledged their signatures and certified the mental soundness of the testator at the time the will was drafted—not after the person's death. To avoid these problems, the safest date to use is the date the will was recorded—between thirty and ninety days after the death of the testator.

Relationships between legatees and testator were seldom defined. As a consequence, brothers and nephews are mistaken for sons, sisters-in-law and daughters-in-law appear as unmarried daughters, and daughters with unknown married names may be unidentifiable. The legatees sometimes are mentioned by first names only.[28] "In-law" was often a synonym for "step" and adopted kin. Because of these ambiguities, it is wise to corroborate all relationships with other sources.

Probate records can provide valuable leads to those relationships. Here are some clues:[29]

1. In states that allowed the eldest son a double portion of his father's estate, an estate with seven shares had six heirs, not seven.

2. Daughters unmarried at the time a will was drafted may have been married by the time it was probated. The will and subsequent documents will contain different names. Watch given names carefully and always check all males listed in the final settlement, especially if they are not listed in the will as potential sons-in-law.

3. Statements such as "my daughters Mary and Martha shall have five shillings each with what I have already given them" and "my daughter Grace shall have £30 to make her equal with her sisters" imply that some daughters were married and had already received their portions.

4. Special terminology may reveal relationships: "a femme sole" is an unmarried woman; "coverture" refers to a married woman.

5. Where two executors are named in a will, one is usually the relative of the testator and the other a relative of the spouse. Both sides of the family were represented to safeguard the interests of all parties and to keep peace.

6. Bondsmen are usually relatives who are willing to stand the risks and who have some leverage over the persons they guarantee. If the wife is executrix, the bondsmen will usually be her relatives. Where her maiden surname is unknown, look carefully at the names of the bondsmen.

7. Guardians are usually relatives who have no potential interest in the estate. With some careful calculations, you can decide who these would be and perhaps identify missing surnames.

8. When the court has to determine who inherits, unless extenuating circumstances dictate otherwise, the estate is usually awarded to heirs of the whole blood (related by blood to both sides of the family) rather than an heir of the half blood (related to one side only). In this way, the property is more likely to stay in the family.

9. Second marriages of widows are most frequently documented among probate and guardianship records, as their new husbands assume responsibilities of the estate. This makes probate records especially valuable.

Sometimes, family members are omitted from a will because they are otherwise provided for. A man can settle a jointure on his wife at the beginning of the marriage in lieu of dower rights or subsequent claims against the estate. During colonial times, when the law of primogeniture was in effect, the eldest son was frequently not mentioned in the will, for the real property descended automatically to him if the estate was entailed. Most American men also owned other lands in fee simple which could be described and left to younger sons.

As daughters married, they were customarily given their portions in cash, land, household furnishings, food, horses, slaves, etc. Sons were given their property when they reached majority or planned to marry. A family account book recorded the property conveyed to each child. If, when the father's estate was later settled, a child contested the settlement, this account showed what each marriage portion was. Thus, children who had received their shares were frequently omitted from the will.

SPECIAL COURT PROCEEDINGS

A number of special court proceedings are invaluable to the genealogist. Some, such as name changes, are straightforward sources with easy-to-use indexes. Others, like the records of extra-legal courts, must be searched for without an index. Yet such special processes can provide the key which opens a locked pedigree:

- Naturalizations
- Oaths of allegiance
- Adoptions
- Appeals and court reports
- Admiralty proceedings
- Claims
- Courts-martial
- Extra-legal courts
- Special courts: Indians, African Americans, and foreign powers

Naturalization and administering of oaths of allegiance are court functions discussed in detail in chapter 13. Divorces, closely related to name changes and often indexed together, are discussed in chapter 4.

NAME CHANGES

Every state provides for legal name changes. The circumstances, however, vary from state to state, and so do the courts having jurisdiction to authorize name changes. Below is a list of finding aids for the states where they exist.

California

"Record of Name Changes, 1866–1883." Typescript, in California State Archives; GS 978-907, item 2.

Georgia

Rowland, Arthur R. "Names Changed Legally in Georgia, 1800–1856." *National Genealogical Society Quarterly* 55 (1967): 177– 210.

Indiana

Newhard, Malinda E., comp. *Names Changes Granted by Indiana General Assembly to 1852.* Available from Malinda Newhard, Box 86, Harlan, IN 46743.

Maryland

Meyer, Mary K., comp. *Divorces and Names Changed in Maryland by Act of the Legislature, 1634–1854.* Pasadena, Md.: the author, 1970; updated in "Names Changed in Maryland, 1855–1867: A Supplement to Divorces and Names Changed. . . ." *Maryland Historical Magazine* 68 (1973): 335–39.

Massachusetts

Matakov, Albert. *List of Persons Whose Names Have Been Changed in Massachusetts, 1780–1892.* 2nd ed. 1893. Reprint. Baltimore: Genealogical Publishing Co., 1972.

North Carolina

McBride, Ransom, comp. "Legal Name Changes by Act of North Carolina Assembly, 1790–1799." *North Carolina Genealogical Society Journal* 1 (1975): 68–74; expanded "1800–1804," ibid. 2 (1976): 18–23; "1805–1808," ibid.: 162–67.

An early source which includes the American colonies to 1782 is W.P.W. Phillimore and Edward A. Fry, comps., *An Index to Changes of Name Under Authority of Act of Parliament 1760–1901* (1905. Reprint. Baltimore: Genealogical Publishing Co., 1968). The original introduction includes an essay on the "Law and Practice of Change of Name" by Phillimore, one of the foremost genealogists of his day.

Legislative control of name changes continued until roughly 1850 to 1865 in America. Some state legislatures still have power to legalize names, although it is rare for them to do so. Regular courts with divorce jurisdiction usually have the power to legalize name changes today. Some have separately indexed volumes in which these are recorded, and some list them in the regular court orders or judgments.

Name changes are especially important where divorce or adoption has occurred. For this reason it is a good idea to search the indexes name by name for all pedigree surnames and for those names that married into your lines. List any entries that appear promising, then check the case files referred to for essential information.

ADOPTION RECORDS

Adoption records usually result from court processes, although there are three methods through which adoption can take place: (1) agreement without judicial proceedings, (2) agreement filed in a court of law and accompanied by court order, and (3) petition filed in a court of law and accompanied by a court order. The first method is not considered legally binding in most states today.

Under Roman civil law, which forms the basis of the legal systems in Louisiana and Texas, adoption was an integral part of family law and was often used to increase prestige and family wealth. Native Americans also practice adoption to varying extents. English common law, upon which the legal systems of most of the states are based, had no provision for adoption until 1926. Even though adoption statutes in America precede

this date by nearly a century in some states, the majority did not provide for legal adoption until the latter half of the nineteenth century. Hence, legal adoption of a child by two people who are not the biological parents is a fairly recent action. Table 7-5 indicates when the first statutes granting adoption were passed in the original thirteen states and selected others and the court that was given jurisdiction by the state codes.

Adoptions, even those later recognized by court action, often begin within the family. For this reason, family traditions are important. Learn what family members know, including favorite nieces and grandsons who have been confidants of family members most likely to know the facts.

Next, check the facts in actual documents. The documents and traditions in the case of Harry Chester Lee, below, are examples. According to a granddaughter:

> Great-Grandma Bandina Hinkle Lee, as you know, was Grandpa's [Harry Chester Lee's] adopted mother. However . . . his . . . real mother was Aunt Mary [Bell Hinkle] Garwood, Bandena's [sic] sister. I know she died [1927] after I was born & indications show Grandpa knew it. It must have been very hard for the poor woman, because she was living in Chicago by that time & she couldn't acknowledge her granddaughter & her first great grandchild. Anyhow the narrative is very interesting.

This Harry Chester Lee was born 21 June 1883, in a Chicago foundling home under the name of Chester Perry. Bandina Hinkle Lee picked him up from the foundling home at the age of three days, and he lived with her and her husband, Benjamin P. Lee, until they adopted him, at age thirteen. Bandina was Mary Bell's half-sister from Peoria County, Illinois.

A 1974 letter requesting the adoption papers brought the information from the presiding judge of Cook County Circuit Court that "all adoption files in Cook County are impounded."

Attempts to find a documented connection between Harry Chester Lee (Chester Perry) and Mary Bell failed. Cook County birth records yielded no data for Chester Perry. An inquiry to Cook Count Court regarding maternity was not answered, and there were no other records on file in Cook County. It is interesting, however, that Harry cared for Mary Bell Garwood in her later years. He was present at her death and provided the information on her death certificate. He also selected and paid for her burial place and funeral marker. Family members concluded that she was Harry's mother.

THE ADOPTION PROCESS

The petition sets out information concerning the child (or sometimes adult requiring custodial care) to be adopted, the biological parents, and the adopting parents. State statutes vary in the amount and type of data required, but generally they contain the name, residence, age or date of birth of the child; a description of any property the child might possess; the agency or person having present custody of the child; sometimes the sex, race, religion, place of birth, brothers and sisters (if any), and names and residences of the parents or guardian; the adoptive parents' names, residences, ages, religious affiliations, marital status, place and date of marriage, and fitness to adopt. In many states, if the child is illegitimate, the father is not recorded.

Table 7-5. Statutes Granting Adoption Jurisdiction

State	Date	Court
Connecticut	1864	Probate
Delaware	1890	Orphans'
Georgia	1855	Superior
Hawaii	1903	Circuit
Kentucky	1860	Circuit, equity, criminal
Maine	1867	Probate
Maryland	1892	Circuit
Massachusetts	1851	Probate
New Hampshire	1862	Probate
New Jersey	1877	Orphans'
New York	1873	Surrogate
North Carolina	1872	Superior
Ohio	1859	Probate
Pennsylvania	1855	Common pleas
Rhode Island	1872	Probate, municipal
South Carolina	1882	Common pleas
Tennessee	1852	County, circuit
Texas	ca. 1848	
Vermont	1853	Probate
Virginia	1891	Chancery
West Virginia	1882	Circuit

Massachusetts, Illinois, New York, and Pennsylvania require that no indication of illegitimacy be given.

All parties who have an interest in the proceedings are notified of the date and time of the proceedings. Copies of these notifications are found in the case file. In Vermont, publication of adoption proceedings and proposed name changes had to appear for three successive weeks in the local newspapers before the hearing was held. Then the clerk of the probate court was required to submit annual returns of all such proceedings and name changes to the secretary of state.[30] In this case, duplicate records are available in newspapers and in state archives.

Consent of the biological parents and their sworn and written statements relinquishing their rights to the child must be part of the case file. If the child is in the care of a guardian or institution, it provides consent. Children over a certain age—varying from eight to fourteen—are also required to give formal consent to the adoption.

Only five states—Alaska, Mississippi, Oklahoma, Oregon, and South Carolina—do not require a formal investigation of the adopting parents and the child. In other states, the proposed home, financial status, health, mental condition, occupation, and social standing in the community of the adopting parents are investigated along with the physical and mental condition and heritage of the child. Reports of these investigations become a part of the case file.

The hearing may be closed or open according to the judgment of the court. Evidence, testimony, and the above documents presented at the hearing provide the basis for a judgment and court decree. The decree may be interlocutory (requiring a waiting period of six months to one year before the adoption is final) or final (no waiting period). Usually, as part of the decree, the child's name is changed to that of the adopting parents and the birth certificate is also changed accordingly.

If any party involved disagrees with the adoption, the case file will contain petitions for pending appeals to reconsider, annul, or revoke the decree. The grounds and procedures for such appeals vary considerably from one state to another.

The records produced in adoption proceedings prior to 1930 are still open in most states prior to 1930. Since that time, however, in an attempt to protect both children and adoptive parents, some states have passed laws restricting the records. Wisconsin, Arkansas, California, Alabama, Minnesota, North Dakota, and Delaware limit access to adoption records only to the parties involved (with court permission). In Pennsylvania, New Jersey, Louisiana, and Texas, the decree is open to the public, but the case files can be examined only with court permission. Most other states leave the choice of access up to the court.[31]

Records of adoptions which predate these laws are usually found among the regular records of the courts having adoption or family law jurisdiction. There is little trouble in searching the early ones if you follow this simple procedure: Ask to see the court docket or indexes covering the period of time of the search. Check carefully all surnames relating to your pedigree, for a relative may have adopted the child. Note the number and name of the case and ask the clerk for the case files you wish by number and name only, not by subject. If you want copies and cannot make them yourself, request them by page or document date, not by name of document.

In some courthouses, there is little problem because the records are in files accessible to the public, and coin-operated copy machines are nearby. For sealed records, you will have to follow the rules of access set down by the court or the legislature. In most cases, the individual concerned must request the records in person.

Rights of Inheritance

The primary purpose behind early adoption laws was to provide a legal heir for the adoptive parent. Hence, in most states adopted children inherit just as though they were "heirs of the body." In some jurisdictions, rights of inheritance are severely restricted. Property which is designated for "heirs of the body" by the testator cannot be inherited by adopted children in Maine, New Jersey, Ohio, Oklahoma, Rhode Island, Vermont, Utah, and West Virginia. Parents cannot inherit from adoptive children in Georgia, Oklahoma, and Tennessee.[32]

Citizenship

Alien children adopted by American parents do not automatically become citizens of the United States; however, the residence requirement is lowered to two years. The proceedings for children are less complicated than for adults.

APPEALS COURTS

Appeals courts review cases begun initially in other courts upon request of one or more litigants in the case. Some appeals courts also transfer cases from lower courts for review upon crucial points of law. This power is called *certiorari*. Few appeals courts are concerned with questions of fact. That is, no witnesses testify, and no jury determines the facts of the case. The court accepts the evidence of the previous trial and reviews questions of law—points on which alleged errors have been committed by the lower court. An exception is the Maryland Provincial Council, which will hold a full retrial. Usually, however, appeals made on new evidence are sent back to the lower court for retrial.

During the colonial period, most appeals courts also had original jurisdiction in cases involving land title, admiralty, probate, equity, divorce, criminal cases involving life or limb (capital cases), and all civil suits over £20 (increased eventually to £100).

Usually these appeals courts consisted of the royal governor and his council in judicial session, following the model of the Privy Council of the King. Naturally, they were reluctant to surrender such judicial powers. These courts were called by various titles: Court of Assistants (Connecticut), Court of Magistrates (New Haven), Supreme Court (New Hampshire), General Court (Virginia), Court of Appeals (New Jersey and Georgia), and Provincial Court (Maryland).

In some of the colonies, the legislative assembly also handled appeals: Connecticut, Maryland, and Virginia assemblies heard divorce and land title cases until 1683, then these were transferred to the governor and council. Rhode Island, New York, and Delaware assemblies heard equity cases. In contrast, Pennsylvania, Rhode Island, and Massachusetts established supreme courts very early with jurisdiction equivalent to that of the English Court of King's Bench.

After the American Revolution, most state constitutions established supreme courts as the highest appellate courts in most states, although, in theory, appeal can be made to the United States Supreme Court.

Appeals courts also issue these standard administrative enforcement writs: *mandamus,* ordering government officials to perform their duties; *certiorari,* ordering the review of a case from a lower trial court; *habeas corpus,* ordering the presentation of the accused before a magistrate for trial; and *quo warrantis,* ordering an officeholder to prove by what authority an office is held.

The courts of ultimate appeal during the colonial period were the King in Privy Council and/or Parliament. Such appeals were expensive and time consuming, involving amounts over £100 to £500 in value and taking almost two years to reach a verdict. As a result, only 265 cases were appealed. Some legislative assemblies restricted appeals to the king, and the Palatines (the Carolinas and Maryland) required the proprietor's permission to appeal.[33]

During the American Revolution, appeals were limited to admiralty and military cases heard by the Continental Congress. The unsettled conditions and costs involved resulted in few appeals until the new government began to function. Then claims and cases were appealed to Congress as well as the supreme Court.

Some state supreme courts did not assume conventional shape until after the revolution. For example, Kentucky, at one point in the early eighteenth century, had two courts of appeal to handle an enormous number of land title disputes, and the Texas Supreme Court in the Reconstruction period was so erratic that its rulings are never cited as serious precedents.[34]

Special courts of appeal were created from time to time to meet specific needs. In Virginia, the General Court (governor and council) heard criminal appeals well into the nineteenth century, before they were transferred to the Virginia Supreme Court. In Tennessee, it was impossible to survey land prior to settlement, resulting in overlapping and duplicate claims. The Tennessee Supreme Court of Errors and Appeals tried these land cases until 1834. In North Carolina, the circuit court judges met regularly in a Court of Conference to discuss important cases and points of law. Gradually, it became a regular supreme court. New Jersey's Prerogative Court and Maryland's Court of Delegates handled probate of wills and administration of estates.

Intermediate appeals courts relieved the workload of the state supreme courts, and they are courts of last resort for most cases. County and superior courts, such as Common Pleas and Quarter Sessions for appeals from justice, and municipal courts are examples.

Records of appeals courts are similar to those discussed above under civil, criminal, and equity cases, with two important exceptions: trial briefs and court opinions.

TRIAL BRIEFS

Since appeals courts did not usually hear trials, summaries of evidence and testimony—trial briefs—transmitted the facts of the case. These summaries have survived in most courts, and they are extremely valuable where the original case files no longer exist. Each judge in the court had a copy, with copies for the case file and trial attorneys. The earliest are in manuscript, but surprisingly soon they were printed. Supreme Court briefs were printed and bound from 1832 on.

COURT OPINIONS

Court opinions are decisions of the judges in each case along with reasoning and references to precedents. The first opinions were given orally and noted briefly in the court minutes or orders. Written opinions were required of all Supreme Court judges by a congressional act of 1834, and they became popular in other appeals courts, for they could be printed, circulated, and cited in similar cases, thus saving a great deal of research and correspondence.

Many appeals court records have been summarized, indexed by plaintiff (some defendant cross-indexes are available), and printed. (See figure 7-11 for courts with printed reports.) More than 6,000 volumes representing some 500,000 different cases were in print in legal libraries across the United States by 1896. Many more have appeared since then.

The multi-volume *American Digest System,* published by West Publishing Co., 50 West Kellogg Boulevard, St. Paul, MN 55102, is a partial index to printed reports of all fifty states from 1658 to the present, and its many volumes are available in most law libraries. The Century Edition or Digest covers cases from 1658 to 1896. The Decennial Edition or Digest covers cases from 1897 to 1906, the Second Decennial Digest covers 1907 to 1916, and so forth to 1966, when the General Digest, fourth edition, begins.

An important feature of the Decennial Digest (vols. 21–25) is the Table of Cases, an alphabetical listing of printed cases from 1658 to 1906, with subsequent tables for each ten-year increment in later volumes. For each case it gives the correct title, parallel citations to the National Reporter System and the State Reports (citations to State Reports are not included in the American Digest Table of Cases since 1966), the history of the case (i.e., whether it has been affirmed, reversed, or modified

on appeal or rehearing), and the topics and key numbers under which the various points of law in the case have been classified.

The Table of Cases has several limitations: (1) Cases are listed by plaintiff only. Defendants are cross-referenced in later digests and may be indexed in state and specialized reports. (2) Reports for county courts are often omitted. If your ancestor was A.P. Beard of Pennsylvania, you would not find his case listed, for it was tried before the county court. Yet the printed reports for Pennsylvania included his case. (3) Cases are described in abbreviated terms, so you must use the glossary carefully to find the case you want. (4) Cases from 1897 to the present require checking several ten-year volumes. In spite of its limitations, every genealogist should be familiar with this reference tool. Including 500,000 cases, it is too valuable to be overlooked.

In addition to the Decennial Digest, you can check the printed reports for the states in which your ancestors lived. Each state has a series of printed reports, and some special courts have reports devoted to their cases. For example, *United States Reports* includes cases tried before the Supreme Court of the United States (see table 7-6). The first ninety volumes were originally designated by the name of the court reporter and are cited as, for example, "1 Dallas 295"; 1 is the volume number, Dallas is the name of the court reporter, and 295 is the page number. Articles in legal periodicals and law reviews are cited in the same volumes with an established abbreviation for the publication in the place of the reporter's name. Volume 91 was the first to carry the title *United States Reports,* but reprints of

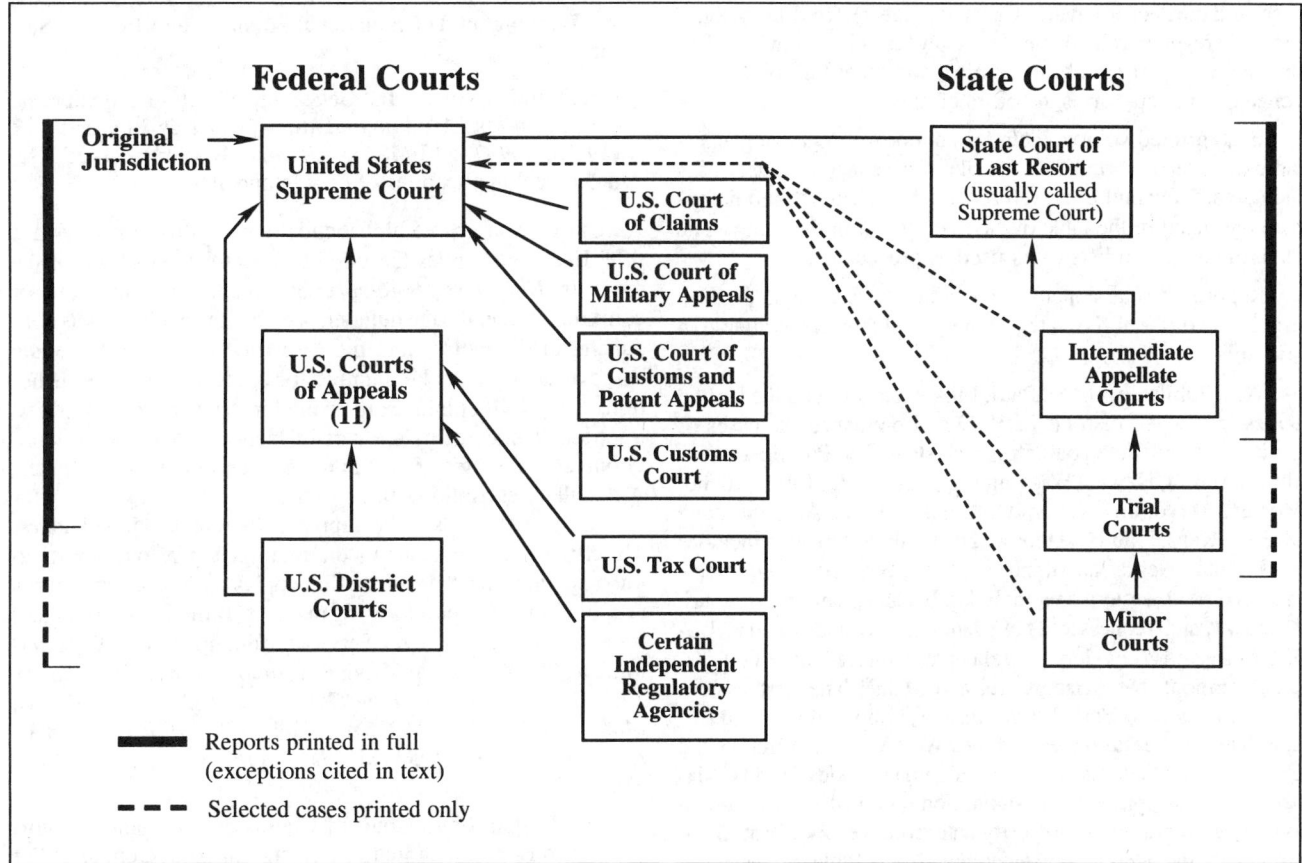

Figure 7-11. Courts for which printed reports are available.

Table 7-6. Summary of U.S. Reports

Number of Volumes	Name of Court Reporter	Years Covered	Report Volume
1–4	Dallas	1790–1800	U.S. Reports 1–4
1–9	Cranch	1801–15	U.S. Reports 5–13
1–12	Wheaton	1816–27	U.S. Reports 14–25
1–16	Peters	1828–45	U.S. Reports 26–41
1–24	Howard	1843–60	U.S. Reports 42–65
1–2	Black	1861–62	U.S. Reports 66–67
1–23	Wallace	1863–74	U.S. Reports 68–90

the first ninety volumes are labeled *U.S. Reports,* with a consecutive volume number, along with the original designation of the reporter's name for ease of identification.

1 Dallas, though the first volume of *U.S. Reports,* contains no decisions of the U.S. Supreme Court. Instead, it covers Pennsylvania reports: the Supreme Court of Pennsylvania, 1754 to 1789; Court of Common Pleas, Philadelphia County, 1785 to 1789; Court of Oyer and Terminer, 1785 to 1788; and Court of Errors and Appeals, 1786 to 1788. The Supreme Court decisions begin in 2 Dallas, which also includes the United States court of Appeals, 1781 to 1787. 4 Dallas includes the decisions of the United States Circuit Court for Pennsylvania, 1799 to 1806, and the Court of Errors and Appeals of Delaware, September Term, 1788.

Each case reported includes names of the plaintiff and the defendant, the court term and case number, the court involved, a summary of the facts of the case, a statement and clarification of the legal issues, a summary of the law pertaining to the case, and the decision reached by the judge(s). Obviously, these reports are prepared for the legal profession, but when they deal with property, probate, divorce, and other family matters, genealogical data forms the basis of the report.

Each printed volume includes an index of legal subjects, a table of cases reported, and a table of cases cited. Later cases include a defendant cross-reference table. Plaintiff and defendant are listed in the table of cases only, not in the index. The table of cases also lists cases used as precedents.

Reports of state appellate and trial courts are also printed, usually by order of the state judiciary, and they are available in law libraries.

West Publishing, of St. Paul, Minnesota, divided the United States into seven districts in 1879 and published the cases of the highest appellate courts for each state. The Pacific area includes Alaska, Hawaii, Washington, Oregon, California, Idaho, Montana, Wyoming, Colorado, Utah, Nevada, Arizona, New Mexico, Kansas, and Oklahoma. The northwestern area includes the Dakotas, Nebraska, Minnesota, Iowa, Wisconsin, and Michigan. The southwestern area includes Texas, Arkansas, Missouri, Kentucky, and Tennessee. The Atlantic area includes Pennsylvania, Maryland, New Jersey, Delaware, Connecticut, Rhode Island, Vermont, New Hampshire, and Maine. The northeastern area includes New York, Massachusetts, Ohio, Indiana, and Illinois. The southeastern area includes West Virginia, Virginia, the Carolinas, and Georgia. The southern area includes Florida, Alabama, Mississippi, and Louisiana. Some published cases begin as early as 1658, but the majority date from the Civil War. These reports are included in the *Decennial Digest* Table of Cases.

As nearly as can be determined, all Supreme Court cases with written opinions from 1790 to 1815 have been printed. From 1816 to 1883, some 351 cases were unreported, with 310 written opinions not included. These cases are listed and described by J.C. Bancroft Davis, the court reporter, in the Appendix to 131 *United States Reports* (1889), lxiv–ccxxxi. Cases with no written opinions are not included.

Table 7-7 is a summary of other published reports from federal courts. Below are three useful sources for using Supreme Court records.

Browning, James R., and Bess Glenn. "The Supreme Court Collections at the National Archives." *American Journal of Legal History* 4 (1960): 241–56. Includes a checklist of records, their description, years covered, and the number of feet per film.

Johnson, Marion M., et al. *Index to the Manuscript and Revised Printed Opinions of the Supreme Court of the United States in the National Archives, 1808–1873.* Special Lists, 21. Washington, D.C.: National Archives and Records Service, 1965.

Cocke, William Ronald, Jr. "Genealogical Notes from Supreme Court Reports." *William and Mary Quarterly* 2nd series, 12 (1932): 167–72; 13 (1933): 49–54; 14 (1934): 24–35. Genealogical applications of data in appellate courts.

Opinions are listed alphabetically by justice, then by case title. Each entry gives the title of the case; the citation of the report in *United States Reports* by volume number, name of court reporter, and page number; whether the decision was concurring or dissenting; and the case file number for appellate cases or the term docket number for cases of original jurisdiction. Almost all opinions are printed in *United States Reports.* Supporting documents are part of National Archives Record Group 267, Records of the Supreme Court of the United States. A detailed description can be found in NARS Preliminary Inventory 139, Records of the Supreme Court of the United States. This finding aid also shows the relationship of the reports to the other court records. Microfilm copies of these court records are available for purchase from the National Archives and Records Service, General Services Administration, Washington, DC 20408. They are from *Revolutionary War Prize Cases, 1776–87* (M213); *Appellate Case Files, 1792–1831* (M214); *Minutes, 1790–1950* (M215); *Dockets, 1797–1950* (M216); *Attorney Rolls, 1790–1951* (M217); and *Index to Appellate Case Files* (M408).

The United States Court of Claims did not handle claims for pensions, although many were submitted to Congress. For further readings on the Court of Claims, see the chapter bibliography.

ADMIRALTY COURTS

Before 1697, no special courts of admiralty existed. Maritime matters were handled by existing common law courts sitting with juries. The English government asked these courts to enforce the Trade and Navigation Acts, but jury members, who had themselves been guilty of violating those same laws, were reluctant to convict their fellow citizens. These breaches included failure to enter, clear, and register vessels, neglecting to carry the proper certificate, trading in ships not English-built, navigating without the proper number of seamen, smuggling, and illicit trade. The Boston Tea Party was a revolt against the harshness of these acts.[35]

In 1697, American Courts of Vice-Admiralty were established by the English government in the chief seaports or districts (groups of colonies). They were completely separate from the courts of the colonies in which the seaports were located. The governor served as vice-admiral of the colony but usually appointed someone to be the judge of the court. Prosecutors attempted to bypass sympathetic juries by bringing their cases before the vice-admiralty, where jury trial was prohibited and prosecutors could hope for convictions. Colonial judges, however, were also hesitant about convicting Americans of violating the admiralty laws, particularly smuggling and illegal trade.

In 1763, a vice-admiralty court for all of America was established in Halifax, Nova Scotia, with British officials and judges. It heard its first cases in 1764, but protests from the colonies forced its removal to Boston, with branch courts at Philadelphia and Charleston. This court gradually fell into disuse, although it was not formally abolished.

With the outbreak of the American Revolution and the collapse of the British courts, the Continental Congress suggested that each state provide a court of admiralty or return admiralty jurisdiction to the regular courts. Jury trial was a prominent feature in the courts. The U.S. Constitution later vested admiralty jurisdiction in the federal district courts. See table 7-8 for a state-by-state summary.

ADMIRALTY JURISDICTION

Originally, admiralty courts limited their coverage to the mouths of rivers and the seacoasts of America. Gradually, their jurisdiction was expanded to cover a wide variety of cases. This breadth of action yields some valuable data for genealogists.

Jurisdiction of matters included seamen's wages—the most common cause the courts treated—bottomry (mortgaging a ship as security for payment of a loan), charter parties (contracts between merchants and mariners for merchandise to be carried), partnership (where two or more agree to share and share alike in some venture and one or more refuses to keep his part of the bargain), salvage (retrieving goods from wrecked vessels), claims for injuries to property or persons, contracts for building and furnishing ships, claims for money loaned or advanced, collisions, brutality, neglect of duty, insufficient food, and impressment (being

Table 7-7. Published Reports From Federal Courts

U.S. Appeals Court/Cases	Dates	Titles and Contents of Reports
Supreme Court	1790 to present	*U.S. Reports.* First 90 volumes identified by court reporter; reprint of vols. 1–90 labeled *U.S. Reports* with reporter's name; vols. 91 on titled *U.S. Reports*
U.S. Court of Appeals	1781 to present	*U.S. Reports* 1781–87 printed in 2 Dallas (vol. 2, *U.S. Reports*)
U.S. District Courts	1789 to present	*The Federal Reporter,* selected cases only.
U.S. Court of Claims	1855–63	*Reports of the Court of Claims Submitted to the House of Representatives*
	1863 to present	*Cases Decided in the Court of Claims in the U.S.* Vol. 30 indexes vols. 1–29; vol. 54 indexes vols. 30–54; vol. 62 indexes vols. 55–61
U.S. Court of Military Appeals		*Decisions of the Court of Appeal*
U.S. Court of Customs and Patent Appeals	1930 to present	*Reports of the Court of Customs and Patent Appeals of the U.S.* Each volume has a plaintiff-defendant index
U.S. Court of Customs Appeals	1909–29	Reports published by the Treasury Department under various titles. Indexes in each volume
Prize Cases Appealed to Continental Congress	1776–80	Includes Committee on Appeals cases referred to Court of Appeals. 109 Cases listed 131 *U.S. Reports* 1889), xix–xlix. Each listing gives the title of the case, a brief description, court from which the appeal was made, dates of appeal and consideration, whether referred to committee or court
Prize Cases of Revolutionary War, Committee on Appeals	1776–80	38 cases
Prize Cases of Revolutionary War, Court of Appeals	1776–80	56 cases from all states except New York, which had no prize court

Source: Lawrence F. Schmechebier, *Government Publications and Their Use,* 3rd. rev. ed. (Washington, D.C.: Brookings Institution, 1961), 266–78.

Table 7-8. State Admiralty Courts, 1776–89

State	Title of Court	Date Formed	Appeals to Congress Allowed	Jury Trial*
Connecticut	County Maritime Courts (Long Island Sound counties)	1776	No	
Delaware	Court of Admiralty	Before 1778	No	
Georgia	Court of Admiralty	1777	No	
Massachusetts Boston	District Admiralty Courts (3)	1775 1776	No No	After 1778
Maryland	Court of Admiralty	1763; renewed 1776	Yes	1776
North Carolina	Court of Admiralty	1777	No	1777
New Hampshire	Court of Admiralty	1776	Yes	
New Jersey	Court of Admiralty	1776 (abolished 1799)	No	
New York	No court established. British-occupied after 1776.			
Pennsylvania	Court of Admiralty for Port of Pennsylvania	1778 (abolished 1780)	After 1780	Before 1780
Rhode Island	Maritime Court Court of Admiralty	1776 1780	Before 1780	
South Carolina	Court of Admiralty	1776	After 1777	1776
Virginia	Court of Commissioners in Admiralty	1775	After 1779, cases between two persons of the state excluded	1776
	Court of Admiralty	1776		

*Almost all states permitted trial by jury for prize cases.

Based upon 131 *U.S. Reports,* Appendix, xx–xxii. Jurisdiction of state admiralty courts transferred to U.S. District Courts in 1789, under the Federal Judiciary Act, 1st Congress, Sess. I, Ch. 20 (Statute 1, 24 September 1789).

kidnapped and forced to serve against one's will). These courts also had jurisdiction over prizes—enemy vessels and their cargo seized during wartime. Such cases were common in New York and South Carolina. Violations of pine masts were also handled by the admiralty courts—the king reserved all white pines of more than twenty-four inches in diameter and three feet in height for ships' masts for the Royal Navy. Anyone caught cutting them was tried before an admiralty court.

Admiralty courts had civil and criminal jurisdiction over merchants who dealt with mariners, owners of ships, and all persons having any relation to maritime transactions: those who built ships; those who equipped, manned and supplied them; those who landed, loaded, and unloaded them; those who freighted them; those employed in their service; those who damaged, injured, or violated their duty to or on public streams, fresh water, ports, rivers, and creeks with the ebbing and flowing of the tides as far as the high-water mark on shores or banks. If your ancestors lived along the shoreline, most of their legal business would have been transacted in admiralty courts, not the local county courts.

Admiralty records have been preserved on both sides of the Atlantic. English records are in the Public Record Office among the records of the Lords of Trade, Board of Trade, and High Courts of Admiralty. Many of them have been calendared or abstracted and printed by order of Parliament. Some English records fell into the hands of American courts during the American Revolution. For example, the records of the Vice-Admiralty Court of New York are at the National Archives—Northeast Region in .[36] American records are found among the files of the court that exercised jurisdiction. Records for the state

admiralty courts are in the state archives; some extracts have been published.

In addition to the regular court records, such as dockets, minutes, and case files, admiralty courts include such evidence as ships' records and records kept by seamen: ship registers, enrollments, licenses, crew lists, manifests, passenger lists, seamen's contracts, clearance papers, logbooks, private letters, and other correspondence carried by ships and seized as part of its cargoes.

For additional reading on admiralty courts, see the chapter bibliography.

CLAIMS COURTS

The right—first guaranteed by the English government and incorporated into federal and state constitutions—to petition the government for redress of grievances provides an excellent source of genealogical data because our ancestors used it so freely.

Common grievances were compensation for supplies and provisions supplied in war; for unfair dealings of the government and its personnel; for unpaid wages, pensions, or other compensation promised; for lack of protection against local enemies and foreign powers; and for jurisdiction and boundary changes.

Although this discussion is limited to claims against the U.S. government and its courts, equivalent actions and records can be found in state court files and among the records of counties, towns, and cities.

Table 7-9 is a summary of the types of claims made from 1774 through World War II with the agency responsible to deal

Table 7-9. Claims Made Against the U.S. Government

Table of Claim	Date	Name Index	NARA Record Group	Comments/Description
Claims Barred By Statute of Limitations, Adjusted and Allowed	1810	See comments		Printed in *American State Papers* (036-216), available in most government documents sections of public and university libraries. Some claims indexed in Phillip W. McMullin, *Grassroots of America* (Provo, Utah: Gendata, 1972). Volume indexes are unreliable
Claims of Persons, Circumstances Barred by Limitations	1792	Yes		1,500 revolutionary war soldiers pensioned under an act of 27 March 1792. See Mary G. Ainsworth, "Recently Discovered Records Relating to Revolutionary War Veterans Who Applied for Pensions Under the Act of 1792," *National Genealogical Society Quarterly* 46 (1958): 8-13, 73-78
Private Claims Submitted to Congress	1774-89	Yes	360	*Papers of the Continental (and Confederation) Congress*, 204 rolls (microfilm no. 247); *Journals of the Continental Congress* (includes Confederation), 34 vols., printed by the Library of Congress, 1904-37. Every-name indexes: *Index: Journals of the Continental Congress, 1774-1789* (NARA, 1976); *Index: Papers of the Continental Congress, 1774-1789*, 5 vols. (NARA, 1978). Microfilm and indexes are available in National Archives regional archives and other research libraries
	1789 to present		233(House) 46 (Senate)	Published as *Congressional Documents*. Arranged alphabetically to form an easily accessible index, 1789-1891 (House), 1815-1909 (Senate)

Congress	Date	Congressional Document Containing List*
Senate		
14th-16th	1815-81	46th Cong., 3rd Sess., S. Misc. Doc. 14, serials 1945-46
47th-51st	1881-91	53rd Cong., 2nd Sess., S. Misc. Doc. 266, serial 3175
52nd-55th	1891-99	56th Cong., 1st Sess., S. Doc. 449, serial 3881
56th-57th	1899-1903	57th Cong., 2nd Sess., S. Doc. 221, serial 4433
58th	1903-05	59th Cong., 1st Sess., S. Doc. 3, serial 4917
59th-60th	1905-09	60th Cong., 2nd Sess., S. Doc. 646, serial 6165
House of Representatives		
1st-31st	1789-1851	32nd Cong., 1st Sess., H. Misc. Doc. (unnumbered), serials 653-655
32nd-41st	1851-71	42nd Cong., 3rd Sess., H. Misc. Doc. 109, serial 1574
42nd-46th	1871-81	47th Cong., 1st Sess., H. Misc. Doc. 53, serial 2036
47th-51st	1881-91	53rd Cong., 2nd Sess., H. Misc. Doc. 213, serial 3268

*These claims have been reprinted in three volumes by Genealogical Publishing Co., Baltimore, Maryland. Senate documents more than 50 years old are open for research. House documents may be used only by permission of the clerk of the House. Contact your congressman for authorization. For details see Arlene H. Eakle, *American*

Table of Claim	Date	Name Index	NARA Record Group	Comments/Description
				Congressional Records (Salt Lake City: The Genealogical Institute, 1974); Preliminary Inventory 113: Records of the U.S. House of Representatives, 2 vols.; Preliminary Inventory 46: Records of the United States Senate; and Special List 32: Hearing in the Records of the U.S. Senate and Joint Committees of Congress; Special List 35: Printed Hearings of the House of Representatives Found Among Its Committee Records, 1824-1958. For pension claims, see also Leroy P. Graf, et al., "The Pension Office to Congressman Andrew Johnson: A List, 1843-1853," *East Tennessee Historical Society Publications* 38 (1966): 97-108 for a list of pension claims Johnson introduced; originals are in possession of the U.S. Pension Office
Quartermaster Claims	1839-60	Volume indexes	92	Four manuscript vols., claims relating to services, supplies, or transportation furnished to or requisitioned for the army. Supporting documents may have been destroyed. Includes Mexican War claims, 1847-58, and civilian claims (mostly Mexican War teamsters), 1848-60
Fourth of July Claims	1861-70	Volume indexes	92	Sixty-eight vols. (manuscripts with supporting case files); include rejected claims. Volumes arranged by auditors' numbers, related papers filed by register numbers. 29 vols. (manuscripts with supporting case files); arranged by year. Rejected claims arranged by box numbers. Incomplete 2-vol. register to rejected claims. Must prove loyal citizen of loyal state. Valuable, covers country. 36 vols. (manuscripts with supporting correspondence and case files)
	1871-90	Partial indexes only		
Civil War Claims	1861-94	Some volume indexes	92	Transportation, personal services for persons later deceased, horses and mules, extra duty, bounty arrears, property damage, rents, and other matters. Indexes, where they exist, are incomplete. See *Genealogical Research in the National Archives* (NARA, 1982), p. 230; and Preliminary Inventory 135, Records Relating to Civil War Claims, U.S. and Great Britain
Transportation Claims	1871-87	Some volume indexes	92	131 registers, including ocean and lake vessels, railroad accounts connected with military operations, ferries
Confederate Horse Claims	1901-14	No	92	Claims for paroled Confederate soldiers whose arms and horses were seized by Union soldiers in violation of the terms of surrender. Files arranged by members from general correspondence of the quartermaster general, 1890-1914
Alabama Claims	1872	Yes		List of documents and correspondence in the cases of U.S. and Great Britain indexing the claims for losses to Confederate ships Alabama, Shenandoah, Florida, Tallahassee. Description of cases in Revised List of Claims . . . Known as the Alabama Claims
Southern Claims Commission	1871-80	Yes	217	Approved claims
			233	Disallowed claims filed with records of House of Representatives. Gary B. Mills, comp., *Civil War Claims in the South: An Index of Civil War Damage Claims Commission, 1871-1880* (Laguna Hills, Caif.: Aegean Park Press, 1980). 22,298 claims were submitted by Southerners who swore they were loyal to the Union; 7,092 were allowed. Includes interrogatories (detailed questionnaires) filled out by all applicants. See Frank W. Klingberg, *The Southern Claims Commission* (Berkeley: University of California Press, 1955), and Sarah Larson, "Records of the Southern Claims Commission," *Prologue* (1980): 207-18
Claims of Citizens of Kansas	1858-61	Volume indexes		35th Cong., 2nd Sess., H. Misc. Doc. 43, serial 1017 (1858-59); 36th Cong., 2nd Sess., H. Reports

Table of Claim	Date	Name Index	NARA Record Group	Comments/ Description
				104, serial 1106. Indexes are incomplete. Claims awarded for property damage by marauding raiders, e.g., Quantrell
Hearings, Committee on War Claims claims	1910-14	Volume indexes		63rd Cong., 2nd Sess., H. Reports 124. Many available on microfiche
Claims Commissions, United States and Mexico	1839-1938	Yes	76	Include cases of seizure of property, quartering of troops, illegal arrest and maltreatment of prisoners, boundary claims, prize cases submitted by local residents. Several thousand claims were accepted. See Preliminary Inventory 136: Records of United States and Mexican Claims Commission
War Relocation Authority (Japanese Americans)	1941-46	Master index of evacuees (microfilm of cards)	210	9,000 Japanese-Americans moved out of military zones in California, Oregon, Washington, Arizona, Arkansas, and Hawaii voluntarily. More than 100,000 were forced to evacuate by the War Relocation Authority. See Preliminary Inventory 77: Records of the War Relocation Authority
World War II Exclusion Files	1941-48		153	Relocation of German and Italian aliens, U.S. citizens of German and Italian heritage in military zones. Alphabetically arranged by surname

with them, the record group number, and a brief description of the contents and/or location.

Most claims against the U.S. government before 1855 were presented to Congress and referred to committees on claims of the Senate and the House of Representatives. The inability of these committees to examine in detail all the claims submitted, together with the difficulty of getting Congress to appropriate the necessary funds to pay favorable claims, amounted to a denial of justice to many citizens. In addition, the number of claims became too great. A separate Court of Claims, established in 1855, did not solve the problem because it had no authority to render judgment. Its job was to investigate claims and forward all evidence, testimony of witnesses, law briefs of solicitors and claimants, and opinions and recommendations of the court to the Committee of Claims, House of Representatives, for final consideration of those cases recommended favorably. Those reported unfavorably were placed upon the calendar for Congressional consideration. This amounted to having each case tried twice and solved nothing. In 1863, the court was given power to render final judgment in all cases with the right of appeal to the Supreme Court for cases involving more than $3,000. From 1855 to the end of 1881, it heard more than 13,000 cases. By an amendment passed in 1868 to the Act of 1863, the clerk of the court was required to submit an annual return to Congress containing a list of all judgments rendered by the court, the amount of redress granted, the parties involved and a brief synopsis of the nature of the claim. See William S. Richardson, "History, Jurisdiction and Practice of the Court of Claims of the United States," *Southern Law Review,* New Series, 7 (1882): 790. Such reports would be valuable, but I have been unable to locate any reference to them among the records of Congress.

The procedures and practices of the Court of Claims are very similar to those followed in regular courts of law except that all testimony and evidence is in writing. Twenty-five printed copies of all briefs must be filed (if the case is under $3,000, the briefs are printed at public expense) with the clerk of the court at least one day prior to the hearing of the case. No court costs are required except those of the claimant's personal attor-

ney. Cases must be presented by legal counsel. There is no jury. Before 1868, all claimants had to prove that they had been loyal citizens of the Union during the Civil War. Since that time, the amnesty oath pardoning Confederates has voided this provision. Table 7-10 is a summary of the court's growing jurisdiction.

The records of the Court of Claims are similar to the records found in any court—dockets, minutes, judgments, and case files. The National Archives has published listings of the case files and related records with descriptions of what they contain, how they are filed, and indexes which can be used in Preliminary Inventories 47 and 58. Therefore, it is not necessary to go into detail concerning these records here. Table 7-11, prepared for the convenience of the researcher from these inventories, indicates the kind of records produced, the dates covered, and the locations of the original records themselves. Congressional records—both original and printed—contain pertinent information concerning the Court of Claims and its cases through the annual reports submitted by the court. The procedures outlined above for use with claims presented to Congress can be followed to use Court of Claims information.

Even though the court and parts of its jurisdiction were not established until the latter half of the nineteenth century, documents and evidence sometimes date from the revolutionary war period. In addition, many claims are submitted by and awarded to heirs of the original claimants.

For example, the French Spoliation cases include ledgers, account books, insurance policy registers, notarial records, letter books, day books, executors' accounts of liquidation of estates, ships' registers and logs, lists of crew members who served aboard vessels, etc. (See Appendix 1 in Preliminary Inventory 58.) Case files also include certificates of appointments of administrators, executors, legal representatives, powers of attorney, and proof of death. The Court of Claims, in an effort to substantiate the claims submitted, ordered evidence collected from customs and marine records in French ports and archives. Authenticated copies of these French materials, together with English translations, were sent to the State Department, and certified copies were introduced as evidence in the claims cases.

Table 7-10. United States Court of Claims

Jurisdiction	Date Established	Date Abolished	Indexes Located
Investigate, report findings to Congress. General jurisdiction, violations of contracts entered into by government agencies, violations of Indian treaties, patent infringements, unlawful imprisonment, overassessment of overpayments of taxes, payment of army, navy, civilian personnel, and unlawful seizure of property.	1855	1863	Court of Claims
Try claims, render final judgement.	1863		Court of Claims
Admiralty claims.		1930*	Court of Claims
Equity claims	1870		Court of Claims
Appeals to Supreme Court, plaintiff over $3,000, defendant all cases.	1866**	1925***	Supreme Court records in the National Archives
District of Columbia—jurisdiction cases.	1880	1915†	Court of Claims
Cases originally handled by Congressional committees. The majority were claims for seizure of stores, supplies, and damages resulting from the occupation of Union troops during the Civil War.	1883, 1887		Court of Claims
Claims under interdepartmental agencies. Also includes naval bounty claims arising from the Spanish-American War.	1883, 1887		Court of Claims
Claims arising from depredations by French warships and privateers on American commerce, 1793–1801 (French spoliations). Court to investigate and report to Congress. The U.S. abandoned all claims for reparations against France in 1801, but the claimants continued to press for payment. 5,574 claims were filed with the court; all claims were settled with heirs.	1885	1908	Court of Claims Section, Dept. of Justice, National Archives Record Group 205. Lists of claimants; 16th Cong., 2nd Sess., Sen. Doc. 118, serial 45; 19th Cong., 2nd sess., H. Doc. 68, serial 157; 22nd Cong., 2nd Sess., H. Doc. 147, serial 235; 38th Cong., 1st Sess., Sen. Reports 41, serial 1178; 48th Cong., 1st Sess., Sen. Exec. Doc. 205, serial 2168; 49th Cong., 1st Sess., Sen. Exec. Doc. 102, serial 2340; 50th Cong., 1st Sess., H. Exec. Doc. 309, serial 2561. See Donald L. Jacobus, "Genealogy, the Law, and French Spoliation Claims," *American Genealogist* 46 (1970): 81–84
Concurrent jurisdiction given to federal district courts under $1,000; to circuit courts $1,000–$10,000.	1887		Pertinent district or circuit courts
Claims for property taken or destroyed by Indians under treaty with the U.S. government, 1814–91 (Indian Depredations). Cases usually involve isolated miners, ranchers, towns, stage coaches, wagon trains, and railroad lines.	1891†† 1915	1920 1920	Same as French cases above. List of claims 49th Cong., 1st Sess., H. Exec. Doc 125, serial 2399
Indian claims. In 1946, Indians were given the right to present claims against the U.S. government like other U.S. citizens.	1946		Court of Claims, 400 cases to 1960

* Since 1930, only foreigners can sue for admiralty claims in this court. Citizens must petition federal admiralty courts.

** The law of 1863 gave right of appeal to the Supreme Court, but the court refused to hear appeals that were reviewable by the Department of the Treasury. Treasury jurisdiction was abolished in 1866.

*** Since 1925, the Supreme Court has had the right to choose the cases it hears.

† A large number of cases arising from long-standing Civil War claims were canceled. The number of cases handled after 1915 was small.

†† From 1796 to 1891, cases heard by Department of the Interior and its predecessors, report made to Congress. Few awards were made before 1891.

Table 7-11. Court of Claims Record Locations

Original Records	*Dates Covered*	*Located*
Original indexes, dockets, minutes, judgments books, register of attorneys	1855 to present	Court of Claims
Case files: general jurisdiction Archives	1855–1939	Court of Claims, Record Group 123, National
	1939–46	Federal Records Center, Suitland, Maryland
	1946 to present	Court of Claims
Other	1855–1943	Court of Claims, Record Group 123, National Archives
	1943 to present	Court of Claims
Attorney general records	1855–1945	Court of Claims Section, Department of Justice, Record Group 205, National Archives
	1945 to present	Attorney General Office, Department of Justice
Reports to congress	1855–63	Committee on Claims, records of House of Representatives, Record Group 233, National Archives
Printed Records		
Reports to Congress	1855–63	Congressional Documents and Reports, government documents libraries
Court reports	1863	Cases Decided in the Court of Claims of the United States, vols. 1 to present available in most large law libraries. Each volume indexed separately, general indexes vol. 30 (vols. 1–29); vol. 54 (31–54); vol. 62 (55–62)

Even though these records are copies of copies and thus subject to error, most originals have since been destroyed or lost. Maritime records kept by United States Customs officials at ports of entry—registrations, registers, oaths, proofs of ownership, licenses, enrollments—were also included.

Among the case files of the Congressional-jurisdiction records are muster rolls, certificates of death and burial, oaths of allegiance, inventories of property, statements and records of military service, records of courts-martial, and tax lists. The naval bounty claims contain lists of seamen who served on vessels during the Spanish-American War.

The United States Court of Claims did not handle claims for pensions, although many were submitted to Congress.

For further readings on the Court of Claims, see the chapter bibliography.

COURT-MARTIAL RECORDS

The purpose of military courts is to insure orderly operations and exact obedience. The United States has traditionally maintained a small standing army during times of peace, depending upon local militia or civilian conscripts to supplement these soldiers in times of war.

Local militias and state-authorized troops made up the bulk of American armed forces from colonial times until the Civil War. During the Revolutionary war, the soldiers who formed the Continental Army were drawn from these local units. As a result, records exist both at the federal level for the continental troops and at the colonial/state level.

Before 1689, all military offenses were tried before regular law courts. With the passage of the English Mutiny Act in 1689, courts-martial heard military violations at the county/town and colonial levels.

Every able-bodied man from the ages of sixteen to sixty (except those specifically exempted by law), fully armed at his own expense, was required to serve in the county or town militia. These militia units were required to hold at least four private (local) musters and one or two general (county) musters per year at which they were to drill and to become proficient in the use of arms. At all musters, the captains of the companies were to keep an attendance record on each man and a record of the offenses and delinquencies of attendance and equipment of all men of the respective companies and report the same to the court-martial. The court-martial convened once a year in each county after the general muster of the county. In this militia court sat a majority or all of the captains of the county. They reviewed the ages and capabilities of all those on the muster lists, dropped those too old or disabled, inquired into the absences and delinquencies reported, and imposed fines. Militia watches were outlined, assigned, and reported on also. In some jurisdictions, the militia captain was also responsible for tax assessment, and tax districts coincided with militia districts.

The professional, standing army of the United States dates from 1789. In times of war, it is supplemented by National Guard and reserve units, state militias, and conscripted civilians. There are three types of military jurisdiction: military law, or the Code of Military Justice; martial law, or temporary rules enforced by soldiers governing both military and civilian populations; and military governments, or administrative functions exercised by military personnel and organizations over civil populations.

The Code of Military Justice outlined by Thomas Jefferson and John Adams in 1776 to govern Washington's volunteers has evolved into the Uniform Code of Military Justice, which was adopted on 31 May 1951 to make all branches of the armed forces subject to the same courts, trial procedures, and appellate review.

The National Guard is subject to this system when nationalized, in training, and under police actions. Reserve units are subject to military law while on active duty and during annual

Table 7-12. Types of United States Courts-Martial

Court	Membership	Offenses	Punishment
Court of inquiry	Appointed upon request of the accused	Any non-capital or capital offense	Determined by the nature of the offense. If there is sufficient evidence for court martial, records are admissible as evidence in later trial
Summary court-martial*	One commissioned officer	Any non-capital or capital offense	Confinement at hard labor for 1 month, restriction for 2 months, or forfeiture of 1/2 of 1 month's pay
Special court-martial	Three or more commissioned officers	Specific cases of a non-capital nature	Discharge, confinement at hard labor for 6 months, forfeiture of 2/3 of 6 month's pay, reduced rank. Officers punishable only 60 days by confinement and forfeiture
General court-martial	Five or more commissioned officers and 1 law officer**	Any offense, especially subject to capital cases and those punishable by death	Any punishment not forbidden by the Military Code

 * Cadets and officers cannot be tried in a summary court-martial.
 ** The law officer instructs the court on points of proper law.

training camps. All members of the U.S. armed forces are subject to the code at all times. This code is enforced in military courts-martial. Although provided for by the Constitution, these tribunals derive their authority from the executive branch rather than the judicial and thus are completely separate from the regular system. Cases are not reviewable by civil courts nor can appeal be made to civil courts. Table 7-12 summarizes the types of courts-martial

Courts-martial exercise exclusive jurisdiction over all persons subject to military law for violation of the military code. Military offenses under the code include insubordination, failure to obey orders, being absent without leave, and disrespect for officers; courts-martial exercise concurrent jurisdiction with civilian law courts over offenses such as murder, theft, rape, and burglary. Under this system, violators may be tried, convicted, and punished twice for the same crime.[37]

Court-martial files deposited in the National Archives, Judge Advocate General's Office, contain records of the general courts-martial, courts of inquiry, and military commissions for the period 1809 to 1938. Included are documents describing the personnel and organization of the courts, changes and specifications, pleas and arraignments of the defendants, papers and exhibits submitted to the court for consideration, proceedings, findings, and sentences, reports of reviewing authorities, and statements of actions by the secretary of war and the president. Table 7-13 is a summary of these records.

In 1776, when Congress established authority for military courts, no sentence of a general court-martial could be carried out until confirmed by Congress. This proved to be impractical and was soon modified to apply only to high-ranking officers or death sentences. A little later, the president of the United States had to confirm all convictions of the death penalty in military trials. Noncommissioned soldiers could appeal only to the authority which appointed the military court. Under the National Defense Act of 4 June 1920, a Board of Review was established for review of all general court-martial cases before punishment could be carried out. In 1952, Congress provided

for a Court of Military Appeals through which civilian judges could review all military convictions and appeals from lower tribunals. In its first year, it heard 108 suits on appeal and in fifty percent of the cases reversed the decision rendered by the Board of Review.[38]

Martial Law and Military Governments

Martial law consists of rules temporarily applied to civilians under the direction of military officers. Authority for martial law must originate from Congressional grant or presidential power and is enforced by military tribunals. If local units of government are unable to cope with war, insurrection, invasion, or other disruptive forces, Congress or the president can order a military government to replace these local units and supply administrative controls. Examples include federal occupation of Southern territory during the Civil War (martial law) and the Reconstruction government exercised in Southern states following the end of the Civil War, when the South was physically and financially unable to direct its own affairs (military government). The jurisdiction of military forts in Indian territory of the American West is another important example.[39]

EXTRALEGAL COURTS

In the colonial "back country," as on the frontiers of Texas, Wyoming, and Arizona, outlaw elements of society, both organized and disorganized, lived by plundering established settlements. Law and order were ineffective or nonexistent. Vigilante movements were a citizens' response.

Between 1765 and 1769, for instance, lawlessness reached its height in the Carolinas. Armed outlaw bands and individuals congregated in outlaw communities throughout the "back country." A Ranger-Regulator unit, organized with the approval of the South Carolina governor and Assembly to deal with these outlaw bands, drew up a "plan of regulation" and began acting. People without a fixed residence were apprehended, tried before Regulator courts, and punished—whipped, deported, put to work, or, occasionally, executed. Immoral persons were whipped, and negligent fathers and mothers were returned to their family responsibilities. To prevent interference from colonial officials and judicial personnel who neither understood nor cared about frontier problems, the only processes from Charleston allowed were actions for recovery of debts. The Regulators became the government in this area, deciding all disputes at militia courts on the muster field. On 25 March 1769, the Regulator movement ended peaceably when circuit courts were created to provide local justice. Estimates of the number of men who actually participated range from 3,000 to 5,000. Richard Maxwell Brown, in *The South Carolina Regulators* (Cambridge: Harvard University Press, 1963), has made a detailed study of 118 participants. Records of Regulator actions are sparse, consisting of correspondence, diaries, and militia court-martial minutes. The governor pardoned on 31 October 1771 the seventy-six men officially identified as part of the movement.[40]

In North Carolina, a similar Regulator movement was much more violent. The colonial government flatly refused to consider the grievances of the back country Regulators and called out the state militia. In a short battle with some 2,000 Regulators at the Alamance River on 16 May 1771, eighteen men were killed. Fifteen of the movement's leaders were tried for treason, and six were hanged. The governor proclaimed amnesty for those who would take an oath of allegiance, and some 6,000 did.[41]

Ethan Allen and his Green Mountain Boys in Vermont and Bacon's Rebellion in Virginia are two more examples of such movements.

The difference between extralegal and illegal is narrow. A legislative act prohibiting group action (mob rule) renders a specific action illegal. The banding of a group of citizens together for mutual protection usually involves appointment of leader(s) and a secretary, keeping a written record of proceedings, and making group decisions (rules) binding upon all regardless of approval. This kind of action is extralegal—outside the law.

Extralegal courts do produce records—a wide variety of "official" or approved documents as well as reports of investigations, newspaper accounts, and correspondence between participants, witnesses, and government officials. For a provocative and fact-filled description of archives relating to extralegal bodies, see Richard Maxwell Brown, "The Archives of Violence," *American Archivist* 41 (1978): 431–44.

To provide legislative, executive, and judicial functions when regular government institutions had ceased to function effectively during the revolutionary war, the colonials used the same system adopted by the Puritans a century earlier when they overthrew and executed Charles I in England.

By 1774, two separate governments functioned in most of the colonies: assemblies and governors under British control, and those created by the revolutionary colonial leadership. These two governments met in immediately successive sessions, frequently with the same membership. When Parliament abolished the regular assemblies, the revolutionary governments assumed complete control. Each colony sent representatives to the Continental Congress; each appointed a provincial assembly, a provincial council, and various district, county, and town governing committees. By the time the war started, each of the colonies had created a functioning system of local and provincial self-government. They operated under a combination of martial and civil law until state constitutions could be ratified and regular government reestablished.

Some meetings of freeholders (freemen) had been organized as early as 1766. In Westmoreland County, Virginia, 114 freemen joined for common defense and safety, forming the basis for subsequent citizen action as the revolution approached and selecting patriot representation for their extralegal provincial congress in the 1770s.[42]

Committees of Correspondence (observation) corresponded with members in the colony and with committees in other colonies. They provided political information, creating and consolidating pre-Revolutionary sentiment with frequent meetings.

Table 7-13. Records of United States Courts-Martial

Records	Dates	Record Group Number	Comments
Records of general courts-martial and courts of inquiry, U.S. Navy	1799–1867	125, microfilmed in 198 reels, no. M237	Originals cover 1799–1943. Partially name-indexed. Must know approximate date; for some records must know offense as well. Records include name, rank, ship or station, alleged offense, place and date of trial, sentence. May include medical fitness for duty, prison reports, requests to change discharge from dishonorable to honorable. Dossiers include transcript of testimony.
Proceedings of general courts-martial, Marine Corps	1798–1866	27	Arranged chronologically, must know date of court-martial.
Court-martial records, Office of Judge Advocate General (U.S. Army)	1805–1939	153	Case files for general courts-martial, courts of inquiry, military commissions. Arranged by case number. Name index, 1891–1917. The National Archives is compiling a name index for pre-1891 files. Some files include dates of birth, places of residence, dependents, as well as transcripts of trial. Separate series of files exist for 1805–15 (incomplete) and for 1861–65. Registers showing name, rank, unit, place, and date of court provide a partial index to all series. Files dated before 1812 are incomplete.

By 1774, every colony but Pennsylvania and North Carolina had Committees of Correspondence.

Committees of Safety were the executive powers that carried out the orders of the Continental Congress and enforced the Articles of Association which all colonies had signed. County-level committees frequently usurped the powers of the regular county courts, some even requiring that every suit brought before a regular court of law had to be authorized by the committee. They also appointed military officials and judicial personnel for certain courts; appointed patrols to control African Americans; exchanged prisoners; fined militia members for refusal to serve; relocated, paroled, or jailed Loyalists (Tories); punished counterfeiters; administered loyalty and test oaths; supervised elections to provincial congresses and the Continental Congress; ordered lists of taxable property and census rolls; censored publications and speech, frequently jailing offenders; passed moratoria on collection of debts or confiscations to be paid to creditors; corresponded and cooperated with other committees; offered bounties and premiums for manufacture of needed items—cotton, wool, lime, steel, etc.—regulated travel; controlled horse racing, billiard playing, and dances; seized vessels and prizes; made lists of inhabitants to submit to Provincial Councils; and inventoried estates of suspected Loyalists.

The local militias were under their direct control. They tried all cases of disobedience and reported to the provincial congresses. Once state constitutions were ratified, the extralegal units were replaced by regular governments.

The original minutes, correspondence, and loose papers of these committees are located, almost without exception, in state archives. Unfortunately, they are almost never used in genealogical research, although they are often the earliest indications of revolutionary war activity. Their minutes also provide judicial records for the years 1774 to 1782, between the discontinuance of crown courts and the establishment of state courts. Figure 7-12 is an example of judicial proceedings.

Some Committee of Safety records have been published:

Connecticut
Public Records of the State of Connecticut: Journals of the Council of Safety. Hartford, Conn.: Case, Lockwood, and Brainerd Co., 1894–1942. Vols. 1–4 include Committees of Safety, 1776 to 1784.

Maryland
"Committees of Observation." *Maryland Historical Magazine* 3 (1908): 387.

"Committee of Observation for Elizabethtown District." *Maryland Historical Magazine* 13 (1918): 28–53, 227–48.

"Journal of the Committee of Observation of the Middle District of Frederick County, Maryland." *Maryland Historical Magazine* 10 (1915): 301–31; 11 (1916): 50–66, 157–75, 237–60, 304–21; 12 (1917): 10–21.

Hoyt, William D., Jr. "Civilian Defense in Baltimore, 1814–15: Minutes of the Committee of Vigilance and Safety." *Maryland Historical Magazine* 39 (1944): 199–224; 293–309; continued in vol. 40.

"Journal and Correspondence of the Maryland Council of Safety, 1775–1793." *Archives of Maryland* 11 (1892); 12 (1893); 16 (1897); 21 (1901); 43 (1924); 45 (1927); 47 (1930); 48 (1931); 71 (1970); 72 (1972).

"Proceedings of the Eastern Shore Branch of the Council of Safety of Maryland." *Maryland Historical Magazine* 5 (1910): 153–66.

Vivian, Jean H. "Thomas Stone and the Reorganization of the Maryland Council of Safety, 1776." *Maryland Historical Magazine* 69 (1974): 271–78.

Massachusetts
Brown, Richard D. *Revolutionary Politics in Massachusetts: The Boston Committee of Correspondence and the Town, 1772–1774.* Cambridge: Harvard University Press, 1965.

Fisch, Theodore. "The Revolutionary Committee System in Massachusetts, Virginia, and New York, 1772–1775." Master's thesis, University of Illinois, 1945. Comparative study; describes records used and their locations.

North Carolina
Waddell, Alfred M. "Proceedings of the Safety Committee of the Town of Wilmington, With Occasional Minutes of Joint Meetings of a Committee of New Hanover County and the Committees of the District of Wilmington, 1774–1776." In *A History of New Hanover and the Lower Cape Fear.* Wilmington, Del.: 1909, pp. 85–165.

Whitaker, Bessie Lewis. *The Provincial Council and Committee of Safety in North Carolina.* Chapel Hill: University of North Carolina Press, 1908. Includes a list of meetings in sixteen counties and descriptions of records.

Pennsylvania
Minutes of the Pennsylvania Provincial Council. 10 vols. Philadelphia: J. Stevens, 1851–52. Includes "Council of Safety Minutes."

"Minutes of the Committee of Safety." *Pennsylvania Archives,* 1st series, 4–6; 2nd series, 1,3,15; 3rd series, 10; 4th series, 3.

South Carolina
"Miscellaneous Papers of the General Committee, Secret Committee, and Provincial Congress, 1775." *South Carolina Historical Magazine* 8 (1907); 9 (1908).

"Papers of the First Council of Safety of the Revolutionary Party in South Carolina, June–November, 1775." *South Carolina Historical Magazine* 1 (1900); 2 (1901); 5 (1904); 6 (1905); 7 (1906).

"Papers of the Second Council of Safety of the Revolutionary Party in South Carolina, November, 1775–March, 1776." *South Carolina Historical Magazine* 3 (1902); 4 (1903).

"Revolutionary Association in Public Defense of South Carolina, 1775." *National Genealogical Society Quarterly* 18 (1930): 1–2.

Virginia
Bowman, Larry. "The Virginia County Committees of Safety, 1774–1776." *Virginia Magazine of History and Biography* 79 (1971): 321–27.

Coleman, Charles W. "The County Committees of 1774–75 in Virginia." *William and Mary Quarterly,* 1st series, 5 (1896–97): 9–106, 245–55.

Harwell, Richard B. *The Committees of Safety of Westmoreland and Fincastle: Proceedings of the County Committees, 1774–1776.* Richmond: Virginia State Library, 1956.

Leake, James M. *The Virginia Committee System and the American Revolution.* Baltimore: Johns Hopkins University Press, 1917.

McIlwaine, H.R. "Proceedings of the Committee of Safety: Caroline and Southampton Counties, 1774–76." *Bulletin of the Virginia State Library* 17 (1920).

_____. "Proceedings of the Committee of Safety for Cumberland and Isle of Wight Counties, Virginia, 1775–76." In *Fifteenth Annual Report, Virginia State Library Board.* Richmond: Virginia State Library (1919).

Miller, E.I. "The Virginia Committee of Correspondence, 1759–70." *William and Mary Quarterly,* 1st series, 22 (1913–14): 1–19, 99–113.

"Proceedings of the Virginia Committee of Correspondence, 1759–1767." *Virginia Magazine of History and Biography* 10 (1902–03); 11 (1903–04); 12 (1904–05).

Westerberg, Frank B. "Vehicles of Discontent: The Committees of Correspondence in the Southern Colonies, 1773–1776." Ph.D. dissertation, University of North Carolina, 1967.

The Sons of Liberty, artisans and professional men organized in urban areas, were another extralegal revolutionary group. Samuel Adams and his Boston Tea Party "Indians" were Sons of Liberty.[43]

Other important extralegal groups were the "Associators" who drafted the first instruments of government in new communities. These extralegal articles of association, signed by all males over age twenty-one, enabled settlers to handle basic legal needs. Examples are the Mayflower Compact of the early Pilgrims, the Watauga Association of Tennessee, and the Kentucky Resolves.[44]

MINING DISTRICTS AND THEIR RECORDS

In areas richly endowed with mineral resources—Pennsylvania, West Virginia, Alabama, Georgia, and the entire western United States—are many jurisdictions called mining districts. Like the New England towns, they kept order until county local governments functioned smoothly. In 1866 there were 500 districts in California, 200 in Nevada, 100 in Arizona, 100 in Idaho, 100 in Oregon, 50 in Montana, 50 in New Mexico, and 50 in Colorado. Twelve California counties were called mining counties for their principal industry.[45]

Here, as on a county level, are found the recording of deeds, transfers of title, claims, abstracts, surveys, mortgages, probates, and other court processes. For example, the Mining Records of Buckskin Joe District, Park County, Colorado, record the election of officers, mining claims, and transfers of title:

July 12, 1860

Meeting in house of J.T. Berger.

Discussion to who was to be regular recorder some claiming the office for D.J. Grist others for J.B. Stansell.

Grist and Stansell retired.

Charles Hitchcock moved meeting vote on recorder and Stansell was elected by a vote of 26 to 18.

Moved by Stansell that meeting be held regularly the

Mar. 11, 1777

The Committee met acording to adjournment, Mr. Thomas Jordan in the Chair.

Upon complaints being made by a certain Allis Read, of Wyoming Township, that he the said Read, had a horse strayed or stolen from him some time ago, and was found in the custody of a certain John Drake, when said Read replevied [sic] the horse and got him and kept him in his possession for about six months, and then the widow of said Drake came and took him forcibly out of said Read's stable, he not being at home himself, and now keeps the horse and absolutely refuses to give him up again to the said Read.

Resolved, That Messrs. James McClure, Peter Milleck and John Clingman, with the assistance of the Committee of Wyoming Township, be a joint committee to meet at the house of James McClure in said township, on Saturday the 22nd day of this instant, March, to hear the complaint and defence of both parties concerning the said Horse, and that the Chairman of this Committee issue summons for the evidences of the complainer to attend at said meeting, which summons are to be served by the complainer himself, as also a summons for the said Widow Drake to attend with the horse and her evidences or reasons, if any she have, why the complainer should not have his horse upon proper proofs being made of his being his property, and the aforesaid persons are hereby authorised to judge and determine betwixt both parties, and upon proper proofs being made, give their final judgment in the matter.

A certain Captain Jacob Links, of Buffalo Township, appealed to this Committee in consequence of a resolve of the Committee of said township, a copy of which is as follows, viz:

Resolved, That Jacob Links does return several sums of money which a nuymber of the inhabitants of this township did deliver to him for the use of purchasing salt, he, said Links, acknowledging he could have had salt, but it being troublesome times he was afraid he should suffer loss if he would purchase the salt, and a certain evidence did declare that he said he was going on his own business to Philadelphia, and he, said Links, did not bring salt.

Dec. 21, 1776. By the Committee of Buffalo Township.

WILL IRWIN, Chairman.

In consequence of said appeal, Mr. Links was called in before this Committee and asked if he had evidence to produce. He said he had, but that he had them not then ready. *Resolved,* That Mr Links's appeal be referred till the next meeting of Committee, and that his evidence be summoned to attend.

Figure 7-12. Minutes of the Northumberland County, Pennsylvania, Committee of Safety, 11 March 1777. From *Pennsylvania Archives,* 2nd series, vol. 14, pp. 375–77.

first Saturday in each month at 4 of the clock P.M. at the house of J.T. Berger . . .

Buckskin Joe Diggins May 23d 1860 . . .

Know all men that I Buck Skin Joe Claim 100 feet of min^g ground for min^g purposes it being situated in Buck Skin Diggins Bounded on the Lower End by D. Griest and on upper end by Moore and Company.

Buck Skin Joe.

May 22, 1860

Know all men by these presents that I, Frank

Obena of Buckskin Diggins, J.T. (Jefferson Territory) for and in consideration of the sum of $50 to me in hand paid, the receipt of which is hereby acknowledged and receipted. Do sell Transfer and assign unto A. Fall my right title and interest in and to certain mining claims situated in Buckskin Diggins between Mr. Belden and Buckskin Joes claim, said claim being 50 feet up to the creek and 300 feet across. In testimony of which I have hereunto set my hand and seal this 28th day of April A.C. 1860.

F. Obena

W.G. Swimez (Witness

B.S. Peabody (Witness[46]

Almost every mining district kept written records of some sort from the beginning, as claims had to be registered, although many did not survive fire, migration, or a thin vein. In other areas, major mining camps became county seats, and their records were the first public records.

Mining district records, though rare, are valuable precisely because of that rarity. Almost invariably they are the only written evidence available for their period. In California, where the population in 1848 was 14,000 and, by the end of 1849, more than 100,000, no government records could hope to be comprehensive.

Miners' Courts

In the absence of legally appointed law enforcement personnel, citizens of mining communities had to provide their own systems of justice. Although the criminal cases confronting these "popular tribunals" have caught the public imagination, the miners' courts or *alcades*[47] dealt much more frequently with civil problems. They fixed the size of claims (which varied greatly from one camp to another), determined the boundaries of districts, and made simple rules governing the working and abandoning of claims and trespassing on the claims of others.

These courts were active only when occasion arose. In smaller camps, guilt and punishment were often determined by the whole assembly of miners; in the larger mining communities, this responsibility was delegated to a jury, and sometimes legal counsel was available for the litigating parties. Justice was usually summary.

Compared with the "lynch-law" of cattle ranges, vigilante committees in mining towns represented a more formal administration of justice, more closely paralleling indictment and trial in statutory courts. Justice in Montana and other territorial mining camps was based in part on the examples set in the preceding decade in California, from which many of the Montana miners had come. For further study, see the chapter bibliography.

VIGILANTE SOCIETIES

Around 1830–1840, some whites in northern cities became alarmed about the flow of African Americans fleeing slavery. Other whites openly encouraged the blacks to come, operating the underground networks and providing new identities, work, and schooling once they arrived. Both types of groups kept records; the Vigilance Committee of Philadelphia is one example.[48]

New Jersey's numerous vigilante groups have been docu-mented in Anthony S. Nicolosi, "The Rise and Fall of the New Jersey Vigilant Societies," *New Jersey History* 68 (1968): 29–53, a comprehensive study by location, county, name, place of meeting, date established, earliest meeting, latest meeting, and date dissolved. He also includes mutual protection associations for merchants, and his notes include locations of records.[49]

Many frontier vigilance committees disbanded as soon as a specific emergency ended. Others had a long tenure.[50] An example of a formal vigilance society is one organized in 1851 in San Francisco with a constitution, bylaws, and newspaper publication. The organization grew from 200 initial signatories, keeping painstaking records, until it was superseded by state-organized court systems in August 1859. It continued to meet as an organization until late in 1859. Between 6,000 and 8,000 men were formal members.[51]

Ku Klux Klan

At the close of the Civil War, the South faced not only the momentous task of reconstruction but also the punitive acts of Congress and a frequently corrupt "carpetbag" administration. Federal armies were quartered on Southern soil, and martial law was exercised in the five newly established military districts. All those loyal to the Confederacy in some areas were stripped of their civil rights, while blacks were permitted to vote, hold public office, and bear arms.

Ex-Confederate soldiers, ignored by the government and judiciary, organized the first Ku Klux Klan in Pulaski, Giles County, Tennessee, on 24 December 1865.[52] Initially a social organization, within a month it had taken a political slant, initiating several hundred members. From Tennessee it spread to every southern state. In May 1867, at a conference in Nashville, Tennessee, of individual Klans, the Invisible Empire of the South was established under the leadership of General Nathan B. Forrest, a trusted and experienced Confederate officer. Each member took an oath in which he swore to "defend the Constitution and laws of the United States in their original purity[,] care for widows, females, and their households [,] aid brothers in distress[,] abstain totally from intoxicating liquors[,] oppose the radical [Reconstruction] party [, and] never divulge membership or activities."

In September 1878, five years after a federal investigation of terrorist activities, the Klan formally disbanded. Forrest estimated 550,000 men had participated during its existence.[53]

In 1915, Georgia granted a charter to a new group of Ku Klux Klansmen who had organized themselves into a patriotic society of white, Protestant, native-born Americans. Shortly after World War I, legal Klans appeared throughout the South and in many other states of the Union. By 1926, there were more than 15 million members. Several of these Klans are still in existence today.

Since Klan activities are secret, few written records have survived. However, the 1871–1872 Congressional investigations generated testimony that included firsthand biographical accounts and oral descriptions of neighbors, relatives, business associates, and deaths, violent and otherwise. They contain many family history details. These transcripts are extremely valuable for tracing African American (indexed as "colored") ancestry.

Poore, *A Descriptive Catalog of the Government Publications of the United States, 1744–1881,* compiled by order of

Congress, 1885, identifies the volumes containing Ku Klux Klan investigations. Each volume is indexed. Lesser parties and witnesses are not included. A review of the index for Alabama in the *House Reports, Testimony, Alabama,* vol. 6, shows several entries for William Henderson, a witness whose stepson, Mark, is not indexed, though he was also a witness. Figure 7-13 is the Henderson index entry, while figure 7-14 shows the kinds of information included in these reports.

Other extralegal jurisdictions include claims clubs and land and cattle companies (both described in some detail in chapter 8, Research in Land and Tax Records).

SPECIAL COURTS

The American court system has included separate courts for such specific population groups as Native Americans, who were treated as a foreign power; slaves, who had few civil rights (in some areas, "free persons of color" were legally treated as slaves); Confederates, whose governments abolished federal power in local courts; and citizens of foreign powers, who exercised jurisdiction over American soil at varying times. Only the Native American courts still function.[54]

Indian Courts

Records of Native American-white cases, settled according to treaty provisions, are scattered among state records for New York, North Carolina, and many of the western states. Sometimes they are clearly identified in archival finding aids, but usually they are filed with treaty papers or among court or commission case files, so the genealogist must read archive inventories carefully. See the chapter bibliography.

Native Americans not living on reservations and not enrolled on tribal rolls have assumed American citizenship. Their records will be found in the local courts. Because Native Americans could expect juries to rule in favor of whites, they avoided court processes as much as possible. Jail records and cases brought before justices of the peace may be more common but are also more difficult to locate.

Black Courts

Slaves were usually tried in a separate set of courts presided over by one or two justices of the peace with assistance from local land holders. Free persons "of color," although not slaves, were rarely treated as were whites and sometimes were required to appear before slave courts.

Manumission—setting a slave free—was a court process. A certificate of freedom was issued to each member of the family manumitted and also recorded by the court. Look for a formal marriage ceremony following manumission, since freedom brought with it other rights as well.

Some jurisdictions distinguished between freedmen and free African Americans who had never been slaves or whose freedom had been won very early in their ancestry. Both are usually identified by color in the records and thus are distinguishable from whites of the same name.

The Inferior Court minutes for Jones County, Georgia, contain the petition of a free black for recognition of his freedom. He had been seized as property of a debtor, sold at a sheriff's sale in 1811 and, finally, eight years later, had come to court seeking his freedom again. The same court granted a petition for a guardian for three free black minors to protect their property.[55]

North Carolina records show cases where a man would free his slaves by will at the time of his death. Some even provided them with land or other property. Because emancipation was against the law in North Carolina, the county records rarely disclose such details. Usually, the land was left by will in the hands of an executor who was instructed privately about the wishes of the testator. Among the appeals cases, however, will be details from relatives who felt slighted or neighbors who resented living next to African Americans.

In South Carolina, the Magistrates and Freeholders Court handled all matters under the laws for "the better ordering of slaves" under authority originally granted in 1690 and revised in 1740, 1743, and 1783. This court could inflict any punishment allowed by law. Death sentences were carried out immediately. Before 1783, the proceedings were written and sent to the clerk of the crown in Charleston. Later they were recorded in the district courts. This duplication is important because fires in some South Carolina courthouses destroyed their early records, as occurred in Abbeville County.

Slave courts and proceedings have not been studied in any depth, but the chapter bibliography contains several references.

OTHER COURTS

Other powers have exercised jurisdiction on American soil at varying times. Examples are the Confederate courts, 1861 to 1865; the Spanish systems in Florida, the Mississippi River delta area, Texas, and the American Southwest; the French control of the Mississippi River Valley and its tributaries; the Mexican claims and jurisdiction in the Southwest; and the Dutch occupation of New Netherlands. See the chapter bibliography for an introduction to these systems and their records.

NOTES

1. The word "people" is misleading. At first, it meant all white men, then all men regardless of color eligible to vote, and finally, in 1918, all adults eligible to vote. It did not then, and does not now, mean all persons.

2. Bradley Chapin, *Criminal Justice in Colonial America, 1606–1660* (Athens, Ga.: University of Georgia Press, 1983), 99–142.

3. See Bruce C. Daniels, *Town and County: Essays on the Structure of Local Government in the American Colonies* (Middletown, Conn.: Wesleyan University Press, 1978).

4. Based on Clarence N. Callender, *American Courts: Their Organization and Procedures* (New York: McGraw-Hill Book Co., 1927).

5. See H.J. Connant, "Imprisonment for Debt in Vermont: A History," *Vermont History* 19 (1951): 67–80.

6. Chester County Court, Penn., 1685, *Records of the Court at Upland in Pennsylvania, 1681–92,* vol. 8 (Philadelphia: Pennsylvania Historical Society, 1860).

7. Joseph H. Smith, ed., *Colonial Justice in Western Massachusetts, 1639–1702: The Pynchon Court Record* (Cambridge, Mass.: Harvard University Press, 1961), introduction.

8. In *National Genealogical Society Quarterly* 58 (1970): 171–72; reprinted with permission.

9. Memorial Upon the Death of Chapman Johnson, Order Book, Spring Term 1849, Augusta Co., Va. Transcribed from original in Augusta County Courthouse, Staunton, Virginia.

Figure 7-13. Index, *House Reports,* 42nd Cong., 2nd sess. From 4 Dec., vol. 2, pt. 8, no. 22. *Testimony, Alabama,* vol. 6, p. 28.

Henderson, William, attempt to drown 540, 557, 558, 577–581, 583, 584, 636–638
character of 636
HENDERSON, WILLIAM, (colored,) testimony of.......................... 576–590
lives in Huntsville; lived last August at Mr. Calvin Goodloe's, Colbert County; is married.. **576**
details of outrage upon him by disguised men, and their attempt to drown him...577–581, 583, 584
character of the disguises worn 579
recognizes three of the party... 579, 580
previous difficulty with some of them.................................. 581, 582
the parties arrested, tried before the United States commissioner, and acquitted...582, 583, 584
alibis proven.. 588
accounts between witness and Mr. Malone.............................. 589, 590

Figure 7-14. *House Reports, Testimony, Alabama,* 42nd Cong., 2nd sess., vol. 6, pp. 628, 631.

The following is the record of the evidence in the trial of Holscapple, Lindsay, and Malone, before United States Commissioner Day, at Huntsville, Alabama, September 1, 1871, referred to in the testimony of Lionel W. Day, page 590.

UNITED STATES
vs.
HOLSEAPPLE, LINDSAY, MALONE. } Trial September 1, 1871.

WM. HENDERSON:

Question. What is your name?
Answer. William Henderson.
Question. Where do you live?
Answer. With C. Goodloe.
Question. In what county?
Answer. Colbert County.
Question. How long have you been living there?
Answer. Moved there two weeks after Christmas.
Question. Men came to your house disguised; how many?
Answer. On Tuesday night, the 15th day of August, I had been talking to Mr. Goodloe until 11 o'clock at night, and then went to bed. Four men came to my room and woke me up and told me to strike a light. I shook Mack, my boy; woke him up instead of getting up myself. He got up and made a light, and they then told me to get up and put on my clothes; that they wanted me to go and show them where Cater Thompson was. I told them I did not know where he was and did not know him when I saw him. At that time I had a gun in the south corner of the house. One man was standing between me and the gun. I aimed to get at it and he shoved me back. Two of the men had pistols and two of them shot-guns, which they presented at me and told me to go out of the door; and as I turned around to go out of the door. I saw Mr. Duco Lindsay, who put his hand on my shoulder; did not hurt me. I knew him by a veil on his hat being turned back over his hat from over his face. The veil came down over the face and the shoulders behind. Am well acquainted with him and knew it was him.

MARK HENDERSON: Uncle Henderson is my father; he is my mother's husband. I live with him. Some men came one night; been three weeks to-day, five men came. I was asleep when they came; they told Uncle Henderson to make up a light; Uncle Henderson woke me up, and I made up a light. Three of them came into the house and two stood in the door. Knew Holseapple; saw his face; had on a straw hat; am well acquainted with him; he did nothing. I started out of the door, and he told me to go back. They took William Henderson out of the house. I staid in Lewis's house the balance of the night; the houses adjoined. I saw William Henderson 8 o'clock the next day; went after Dr. Cross. William Henderson came after me; do not know what he wanted; I got back home before he saw me. I don't know where William Henderson was the day before the night they took him out.

Cross-examined:

Never told anybody what I would swear before I came here. Uncle Jim Carter asked me a while ago, but I did not tell him. Henderson told me this morning to tell nothing, only what I had seen and heard. Three men came in; Holseapple stood at the door; I saw his face; had a small piece of a veil over his face; I looked through the veil and saw his face; am certain only three men came in; did not look in the faces of the rest. Mr. Holseapple had on a straw hat; wore a little straw hat about there; he spoke to me, and I knew his voice; could see his features through the veil. No one in Lewis's house but himself and wife; I staid all night. Don't know where Henderson was the day before. I wasn't there.

his
MARK × HENDERSON.
mark.

10. Order of Naturalization for Samuel Johnston, July Term, 1851, Order Book, Augusta Co., Va. Transcript from original in Augusta County Courthouse, Staunton, Va.

11. Re-recorded Deeds, Feb. Term 1800, Court Orders, vols. 0– 0000, 1778–1810, Rockingham County, Va. Originals in Rockingham County Courthouse, Winchester, Va. Microfilm copy, Family History Library microfilm 033,452.

12. Minutes of the Mayor's Court, Borough Town of Westchester, New York. Printed in "Minutes of Court of Sessions, 1657–78," *Westchester County Historical Publications* 2 (1926): 1–39.

13. An excellent description of how a grand jury functions is Richard D. Younger, "The Grand Jury on the Frontier," *Wisconsin Magazine of History* (Autumn 1956): 3–8 ff. Not consecutive.

14. See Anton H. Chroust, *The Rise of the Legal Profession in America,* 2 vols. (Norman Okla.: University of Oklahoma Press, 1965).

15. A very interesting, well-documented study of the use of jails and punishment in New York State is Philip Klein, *Prison Methods in New York State* (New York: Columbia University Press, 1920). It traces the development and history of most of the penal institutions in the state. See also Douglas Greenberg, "The Effectiveness of Law Enforcement in Eighteenth Century New York," *American Journal of Legal History* 20 (1976): 173–207.

16. See Derrell Roberts, "Joseph E. Brown and the Convict Lease System," *Georgia Historical Quarterly* 44 (1960): 399–410.

17. Police Court Minutes, St. Paul, Minn. Printed as appendix in Annual Report of City Council, St. Paul, Minn., 1856–60. Copies available in rare book vault, St. Paul Public Library, St. Paul, Minnesota.

18. Lyman Chalkley, *Chronicles of the Scotch-Irish Settlement in Virginia, Extracted From the Original Court Records of Augusta County, 1745–1800,* 3 vols. (1962. Reprint. Baltimore: Genealogical Publishing Co., 1965).

19. "Records of the Court of Sessions of Westchester County (New York)," *Westchester Historical Society Publications* 1 (1924): 33, 44 ff.

20. William Jeffrey, Jr., "Early New England Court Records: A Bibliography of Published Materials," *American Journal of Legal History* 1 (1957): 119–47.

21. "Introduction" in *Archives of Maryland: Proceedings of the Court of Chancery of Maryland, 1669–1679,* vol. 51 (Baltimore: Maryland Historical Society, 1934).

22. For a more complete discussion, see "Dower Rights in the United States," *Harvard Law Review* 61 (1948): 42 ff., and George L. Hoskins, "Curtesy in the United States," *University of Pennsylvania Law Review* 100 (1951): 196–223.

23. "Inventories as a Source of Local History: Houses, Farmers, Industries, and Professions," *Amateur Historian* 4 (1958–59): 157–61, 186–95, 227–31, 320–24; and B.C. Jones, "Inventories of Goods and Chattels," *Amateur Historian* 2 (1955–56): 76–79.

24. As cited in Harry A. Focht, "Hidden Genealogical Data in Court Records," *The Perry Historians* 8 (1923): 2–3. The record also documents Peter Arnold's second marriage.

25. From Vincent L. Jones, et al., *Family History for Fun and Profit* (Salt Lake City: The Genealogical Institute, 1972). Used with permission.

26. See Juliette Tomlinson, "Local History in Legal Records," *Old Time New England* 58: 1–7, for other examples.

27. Kenneth Lockridge, "A Communication," *William and Mary Quarterly,* 3rd ser., 25 (1968): 516–17; and Daniel Scott Smith, "Underregistration and Bias in Probate Records: An Analysis of Data From Eighteenth Century Hingham, Massachusetts," *William and Mary Quarterly,* 3rd ser., 32 (1975): 100–110.

28. Gilbert S. Walker, "Old Land Deeds," *Pennsylvania Magazine of History and Biography* 41 (1917): 365–67.

29. Donald L. Jacobus, "Probate Law and Custom," *American Genealogist* 9 (1932): 4–9.

30. *General Statutes of Vermont (1863)* (Reprint. Wilmington, Del.: Michael Glazier, 1987), 416–17.

31. See Walter Lee Sheppard's interesting article "Confidential and Sealed Records: Their Effect on Genealogical Research," *American Genealogist* 50 (1974): 203–9.

32. Jean J. McVeetney, "Comparative Study of Laws of Adoption of Minors," *Women Lawyers Journal* 47 (1961): 13–21.

33. See A.M. Schlesinger, "Colonial Appeals to the Privy Council," *Political Science Quarterly* 28 (1913): 279–97; and Joseph Henry Smith, *Appeals to the Privy Council From the American Plantations* (New York: Columbia University Press, 1950). For Palatine jurisdiction, see Baillard Lapsley, *The County Palatine of Durham* (Cambridge, Mass.: Harvard University Press, 1900). There was little difference in the powers granted the Palatinate in England and America; the problems arose in enforcing them so far away from the support of the royal government.

34. Edward H. Hilliard, "When Kentucky Had Two Courts of Appeal," *Filson Club Historical Quarterly* 34 (1960): 228–36; and George Shelley, "The Semicolon Court in Texas," *Southwestern Historical Review* 48 (1944–45): 449–68.

35. See O.M. Dickerson, *The Navigation Acts and the American Revolution* (Philadelphia: Lippincott, 1951).

36. Some of these records have been edited by Judge Charles M. Hough, *Reports of the Cases in the Vice-Admiralty of the Province of New York* (New Haven: Yale University Press, 1925), but these represent only about forty percent of the total number. See Loretto Dennis Szucs and Sandra Hargreaves Luebking, *The Archives: A Guide to the National Archives Field Branches* (Salt Lake City: Ancestry, 1988).

37. See Hubert D. Hoover, "Army Courts-Martial," *Legal Essays in Honor of O.K. McMurray* (Berkeley: University of California Press, 1935), 165–86.

38. See Daniel Walker and C. George Niebank, "The Court of Military Appeals: Its History, Organization and Operation," *Vanderbilt Law Review* 6 (1952–52): 228–40.

39. John R. Kirkland, "Military Occupation in the South Atlantic States During Reconstruction, 1865–1876," Ph.D. dissertation, University of North Carolina, 1967; "The Reconstruction Courts of Texas, 1867–1873," *Southwestern Historical Quarterly* 62 (1958): 141; and James E. Sefton, *The U.S. Army*

and Reconstruction, 1865–1877 (Baton Rouge: Louisiana State University Press, 1967).

40. Regulator Pardon of 31 October 1771 in *Miscellaneous Records, South Carolina Department of Archives and History,* vol. PP, (Charleston, n.d.): 45–47. Published by government order.

41. See John S. Bassett, "The Regulators of North Carolina, 1765–1771," *American Historical Association, Annual Report, 1894* (Washington, D.C.: AHA, 1895), 143–212; Arthur P. Hudson, "Songs of the North Carolina Regulators," *William and Mary Quarterly,* 3rd ser., 4 (1947): 470–85; Elmer Douglas Johnson, "The War of the Regulators: Its Place in History," master's thesis, University of North Carolina, 1942; William S. Powell, ed., *The Regulators of North Carolina: A Documentary History, 1759–79* (Raleigh: State Department of Archives and History, 1971); and James P. Whittenburg, "Planters, Merchants, and Lawyers: Social Change and the Origins of the North Carolina Regulation," *William and Mary Quarterly,* 3rd ser., 34 (1977): 215–38, 693–95.

42. "Westmoreland Resolutions," *Virginia Historical Register* 2 (1849): 15–18. Originals in Virginia Historical Society, Richmond, Va.

43. "The Baltimore Artificers Company," *Maryland Historical Magazine* 2 (1907): 367–68; Richard Walsh, *Charleston's Sons of Liberty: A Study of the Artisans, 1763–1789* (Columbia: University of South Carolina Press, 1959); "Charleston's Sons of Liberty: A Study of the Mechanics, 1760–1785" (Ph.D. dissertation, University of South Carolina, 1958); and Henry B. Dawson, *The Sons of Liberty in New York* (1959. Reprint. New York: Arno Press, 1969). Read footnotes carefully for locations of records.

44. See "Associations and Associators in the American Revolution," *Maryland Historical Magazine* 6 (1911): 241–54; and "Records of the Cumberland Association," *American History Magazine* 7 (1902): 114–35, 254–66.

45. *Reports on U.S. Mineral Resources* (Washington, D.C.: Government Printers, 1866), 236.

46. As cited in Roy A. Davidson, "Some Early Manuscript Records of Park County, 1859–1863," *Colorado Magazine* 18 (1941): 168–79.

47. An *alcade* was a Mexican court after which many miners' courts were patterned and named. See Charles H. Shinn, *Land Laws of Mining Districts* (Baltimore: Johns Hopkins University Studies in History and Political Science, 2nd ser., 1884).

48. Joseph A. Borone, "The Vigilant Committee of Philadelphia," *Pennsylvania Magazine of History and Biography* 92 (1968): 320–51.

49. Anthony S. Nicolosi, "The Rise and Fall of the New Jersey Vigilant Societies," *New Jersey History* 68 (1968): 29–53. See also "The Vigilance Committee: Richmond During the War of 1812," *Virginia Magazine of History and Biography* 7 (1900): 225–41, 406–18.

50. J.W. Caughey, "Their Magesties the Mob: Vigilantes Past and Present," *Pacific Historical Review* 26 (1957): 217–34.

51. Richard Maxwell Brown, "San Francisco Vigilantes of 1856," in John Alexander Carroll, ed., *Reflections of Western Historians* (Tucson: University of Arizona Press, 1969); and Porter Garnett, "Papers of the San Francisco Committee of Vigilance, 1851," *Academy of Pacific Coast History* 1 (1910); 2 (1911); 4 (1913), edited by Mary Floyd Williams. See also Williams's *History of the San Francisco Committee of Vigilance of 1851* (1921. Reprint. New York: De Capo Press, 1970). The original papers are deposited in the Huntington Library, San Marino, Calif. For a careful analysis of 2,500 applications for membership, see Richard Maxwell Brown, *Strain of Violence: Historical Studies of American Violence and Vigilantism* (New York: Oxford University Press, 1975).

52. See Allen W. Trelease, *White Terror: The Ku Klux Klan Conspiracy and Southern Reconstruction* (New York: Harper & Row, 1971). Based in part on personal testimony of ex-Klansmen is Margaret S. Bearnson, "The Ku Klux Klan," M.A. thesis, University of Utah, 1931, containing a copy of the prescript (constitution and bylaws) and a cipher code used in the Klan in Pulaski, Tennessee, for all messages. See also William D. Bell, "The Congressional Investigations of the Ku Klux Klan, 1871–1972," Ph.D. dissertation, Louisiana State University, 1967.

53. The reports of this investigation, which contain reports of trials, testimony of witnesses, names of Klansmen, and descriptions of their activities, can be found in *Reports of Committees of the House of Representatives and of the Senate,* 2nd sess., 42nd Cong., 1871–72, *Affairs in the Late Insurrectionary States: The Ku Klux Klan Conspiracy.*

54. Jack Kleiner, "United States Law on American Indians," *Case and Comment* (July–August 1971): 3–7, summarizes the legal rights of Native Americans on reservations; the impact of the Civil Rights Act of 1968, which included the Indian Bill of Rights; tribal judicial systems; and the impact of recent legislation.

55. See Inferior Court Minutes, 13 April 1819, Jones County, Georgia, pp. 61–63, and January Term, 1817, p. 97, for examples. Originals in Jones County Courthouse, Georgia.

BIBLIOGRAPHY

This bibliography begins with guides, bibliographies, and sources of general interest on law in the colonies and early states, then continues with specific subject bibliographies. Some attempt has been made to avoid duplicating sources cited in the notes unless they apply to more than one subject area.

Alaska State Archives. *Record Group Inventory: District and Territorial Court System.* Juneau: Alaska State Archives, Department of Administration, 1987.

Ames, Susie M., ed. *County Court Records of Accomack-Northampton, Virginia 1640–1645.* University Press of Virginia, 1973.

Bailey, Robert E., et al., eds. *A Summary Guide to Local Government Records in the Illinois Regional Archives.* Springfield: Illinois State Archives, Office of the Secretary of State, 1992.

Barker, Bette Marie, et al., eds. *Guide to Family History Sources in the New Jersey State Archives.* Revised edition. Trenton, N.J.: Division of Archives & Records Management, New Jersey Department of State, 1992.

Barr, Charles Butler. *Records of the Choctaw-Chickasaw Citizenship Court Relative to Records of Enrollment of the Five*

Civilized Tribes, 1898–1907. Independence, Mo.: C.B. Barr, 1990.

Beckstead, Douglas S. *The Judicial System in Utah: Organic Act to the Twentieth Century.* Salt Lake City: Utah State Archives, 1988.

Bell, Carol Willsey. *Ohio Guide to Genealogical Sources.* Baltimore: Genealogical Publishing Co., 1988.

Bentley, Elizabeth P. *County Courthouse Book.* Baltimore: Genealogical Publishing Co., 1992.

Black, Henry C. *Black's Law Dictionary,* 6th ed. St. Paul: West Publishing, 1991.

BRB Publications Research and Editorial Staff. *The Sourcebook of Federal Courts, U.S. District and Bankruptcy: The Definitive Guide to Searching for Case Information at the Local Level Within the Federal Court System.* Tempe, Ariz.: BRB Publications, 1993.

Brown, Richard Maxwell. "The Archives of Violence." *American Archivist* 41 (1978): 431–44.

Burton, William C. *Legal Thesaurus.* New York: Macmillan, 1981.

Corriston, Mark A. "Discovering Frontier History Through Territorial Court Records." *Prologue: Quarterly of the National Archives* 21 (3): 222–29 (Fall 1989).

Devine, Donn. "The Widow's Dower Interest." *Ancestry* 12 (5): 20–22 (September–October 1994).

_____. "Probate Records: An Underutilized Source." *Ancestry* 12 (3) (May–June 1994): 14–15.

Dolan, John P., and Lisa Lacher. *Guide to Public Records of Iowa Counties.* Des Moines, Iowa: Connie Wimer, 1986.

Eichholz, Alice, ed. *Ancestry's Red Book: American State, County and Town Sources.* Rev. ed. Salt Lake City: Ancestry, 1992.

Evans, Barbara Jean. *The New A To Zax: A Comprehensive Genealogical Dictionary for Genealogists and Historians.* 2nd ed. N.p., 1990.

Greenwood, Val D. *The Researcher's Guide to American Genealogy.* 2nd ed. Baltimore: Genealogical Publishing Co., 1990.

Guzik, Estelle M., ed. *Genealogical Resources in the New York Metropolitan Area.* New York: Jewish Genealogical Society, 1989.

Hendrix, GeLee Corley. "Backtracking Through Burned Counties: Bonds of Louisiana, Mississippi, Georgia, and the Carolinas." *National Genealogical Society Quarterly* 78 (2) (June 1990): 98–114.

Hogan, Roseann Reinemuth. *Kentucky Ancestry: A Guide to Genealogical and Historical Research.* Salt Lake City: Ancestry, 1992.

Minnesota Historical Society Library and Archives Division. *Genealogical Resources of the Minnesota Historical Society.* St. Paul: Minnesota Historical Society Press, 1989.

Morris, Richard B., ed. *Select Cases of the Mayor's Court of*

New York City, 1674–1784. Washington, D.C.: The American Historical Association, 1935. Reprint. Millwood, N.Y.: Kraus Reprint Co., 1975.

Morris, Robert C. "From Piracy to Censorship: The Admiralty Experience." *Prologue: Quarterly of the National Archives* 21 (3) (Fall 1989): 186–95.

Naanes, Ted, and Loretto D. Szucs. "Dead Men Do Tell Tales: Coroner's Records." *Ancestry* 12 (2): 6–11 (March–April 1994).

Neagles, James C. *Military Records: A Guide to Genealogical and Historical Research.* Salt Lake City: Ancestry, 1990.

New York State Archives. *List of Pre-1874 Court Records in the State Archives.* Albany: Office of Cultural Education, New York State Education Dept., 1984.

Nicolosi, Anthony S. "The Rise and Fall of the New Jersey Vigilant Societies." *New Jersey History* 68 (1968): 29–53.

Owens, James K. "Documenting Regional Business History: The Bankruptcy Acts of 1800 and 1841." *Prologue: Quarterly of the National Archives* 21 (3) (Fall 1989): 178–85.

Phillimore, W.P.W., and Edward A. Fry, comps. *An Index to Changes of Name Under Authority of Act of Parliament 1760–1901.* 1905. Reprint. Baltimore: Genealogical Publishing Co., 1968.

Plowman, Robert J. "An Untapped Source: Civil War Prize Case Files 1861–65." *Prologue: Quarterly of the National Archives* 21 (3) (Fall 1989).

Ray, Susanne Smith, et al., comps. *A Preliminary Guide to the Pre-1904 County Records in the Archives Branch.* Richmond: Virginia State Library and Archives, 1987.

Ride, Millard Millburn, ed. *This Was the Life: Excerpts from the Judgment Records of Frederick County, Maryland 1748–1765.* 1979. Reprint. Baltimore: Genealogical Publishing Co., 1984.

Ruple, Jack Damon. *Genealogist's Guide to Arkansas Courthouse Research.* Arkansas, 1989.

Rust, Barbara. "The Right to Vote: The Enforcement Acts and Southern Courts." *Prologue: Quarterly of the National Archives* 21 (3) (Fall 1989): 231–38.

Ryskamp, George R. "Fundamental Common-Law Concepts for the Genealogist: Marriage, Divorce, and Coverture." NGS *Quarterly* 23 (3): 165–79 (September 1995).

Salmon, Marylynn. *Women and the Law of Property in Early America.* Chapel Hill: University of North Carolina Press, 1986.

Scott, Kenneth, ed. *New York Historical Manuscripts: Minutes of the Mayor's Court of New York, 1674–1675.* Baltimore: Genealogical Publishing Co., 1983.

Szucs, Loretto Dennis. "To Whom I Am Indebted: Bankruptcy Records." *Ancestry* 12 (5) (September–October 1994): 26–27.

_____. "Court Records: Far Beyond Probate." *Ancestry* 14 (4) (July–August 1996): 5–8.

Szucs, Loretto Dennis, and Sandra Hargreaves Luebking. *The*

Archives: A Guide to the National Archives Field Branches. Salt Lake City: Ancestry, 1988.

Ulasek, Henry T., and Marion Johnson. *Records of the United States District Court for the Southern District of New York.* Preliminary Inventory 116. Washington, D.C.: National Archives and Records Service, 1959.

Washington Division of Archives and Records Management. *Frontier Justice: Abstracts and Indexes to the Records of the Territorial District Courts, 1853–1889.* Olympia, Wash.: secretary of state, 1987.

Watkins, Beverly. "To Surrender All His Estate: The 1867 Bankruptcy Act." *Prologue: Quarterly of the National Archives* 21 (3) (Fall 1989): 207–14.

Wilson, Don W. "Federal Court Records in the Regional Archives System." *Prologue: Quarterly of the National Archives* 21 (3) (Fall 1989): 176–77.

Wolfe, William A., and Janet B. Wolfe. *Names and Abstracts from the Acts of the Legislative Council of the Territory of Florida, 1822–1845.* Tallahassee: Florida State Genealogical Society, 1991.

Guides

Important guides to National Archives records include numerous references to court documents. These guides are available in most research libraries—sometimes in government document sections.

Guide to Genealogical Research in the National Archives. 1982. 304 pp.

Guide to the National Archives of the United States. 1974. 884 pp.

Guide to Federal Archives Relating to the Civil War. 1962. 721 pp.

Guide to Archives of the Government of the Confederate States of America. 1968. 536 pp.

Handbook of Federal World War Agencies and Their Records, 1917–1921. 1943. 666 pp.

Federal Records of World War II. Vol. 1: *Civilian Agencies.* 1950. 1,075 pp. Vol. 2: *Military Agencies.* 1951. 1,061 pp.

List of Record Groups in the National Archives and the Federal Records Centers. 1981. 70 pp.

National Archives Microfilm Publications. 1974. 137 pp. Updated with titles 1974–82.

Szucs, Loretto Dennis, and Sandra Hargreaves Luebking. *The Archives: A Guide to the National Archives Field Branches.* Salt Lake City: Ancestry, 1988.

In addition to these guides, the National Archives has issued preliminary inventories describing in detail the holdings of specific record groups. These inventories are so detailed that you can often order documents directly from them. Special lists provide finding aids for selected record series. The microfilm publications of the National Archives and Records Service have accompanying pamphlets which list the specific contents of microfilm rolls and give the historical background to help you use the records more effectively. These publications are free upon request. Institutions and local genealogical societies can be placed on the regular mailing list to receive inventories and lists as they are produced. A catalog is available on request from the National Archives and Records Service, General Services Administration, Washington, DC 20408.

Bibliographies

Blume, William, and Elizabeth Gaspar Brown. *Digests and Lists Pertaining to the Development of Law and Legal Institutions in the Territories of the United States: 1787–1954.* 6 vols. Ann Arbor: University Microfilm, 1965–79.

Flaherty, David H. "A select Guide to Manuscripts Court Records of Colonial New England." *American Journal of Legal History* 9 (1967): 107–26.

Gersack, Dorothy Hill. "Colonial, State, and Federal Court Records: A Survey." *American Archivist* 36 (1973): 33–42.

Greene, Jack P. "The Publication of the Official Records of the Southern Colonies." *William and Mary Quarterly,* 3rd ser., 14 (1957): 268–80.

Hasse, Adelaide R. *Materials for a Bibliography of the Public Archives of the Thirteen Original States Covering Colonial Period and State Period to 1789.* 1908. Reprint. New York: Argonaut Press, 1966.

Jeffrey, William, Jr. "Early New England Court Records: A Bibliography of Published Material." *Boston Public Library Quarterly* 1954, as reprinted in *American Journal of Legal History* 1 (1957): 119–47.

Kammen, Michael G. "Colonial Court Records and the Study of Early American History: A Bibliographical Review." *American Historical Review* 70 (1965): 732–39.

Keitt, Lawrence. *An Annotated Bibliography of Bibliographies of Statutory Materials of the United States.* Cambridge: Harvard University Press, 1934.

Low, Erick Baker. *A Bibliography on the History of the Organization and Jurisdiction of State Courts.* Williamsburg: National Center for State Courts, 1980.

McReynolds, Michael. *List of Pre-1840 Federal District Court Records Located in Federal Record Centers.* Washington, D.C.: Government Printing Office, 1972. Special List, 31.

National Association of State Libraries. *A Checklist of Legislative Journals of the States of the U.S.A.* New York: Oxford Press, 1938.

———. *Preliminary Checklists of Sessions Laws, to 1933.* New York: Oxford Press, 1934.

Nunis, Doyce B., Jr. "Historical Studies in United States Legal History, 1950–59: A Bibliography of Articles Published in Scholarly Non-Law Journals." *American Journal of Legal History* 7 (1963): 1–27.

Prager, Herta, and William W. Price. "A Bibliography on the History of the Courts of the Thirteen Original States, Maine, Ohio, and Vermont." *American Journal of Legal History* 1 (1957): 336–62; 2 (1958): 35–52, 148–54.

Sell, Gary L. *Legal Materials on Microform: A Bibliography.* 3rd ed. Provo, Utah: Brigham Young University, 1976.

Tompkins, Dorothy Campbell. *Court Organization and Administration: A Bibliography.* Berkeley: University of California Press, 1973.

USING LEGAL RECORDS

Ball, Walter V. "Family Records from County Court Order Books." *National Genealogical Society Quarterly* 58 (1970): 3.

Bramwell, B.S. "Frequency of Cousin Marriages." *Genealogists' Magazine* 8 (1939): 305–16.

Connor, Seymour V. "Legal Materials as Sources of History." *American Archivist* 23 (1960): 157–65.

Dorman, John Frederick. "Colonial Laws of Primogeniture." World Conference on Records, 1969 (Salt Lake City, Utah: Genealogical Society of Utah, 1969).

Dumbauld, Edward. "Legal Records in English and American Courts." *American Archivist* 36 (1973): 15–32.

Farnham, Charles W. "Lower Court Cases: A Genealogist's Tool." *National Genealogical Society Quarterly* 49 (1961): 200.

Gilliam, C.E. "Mr. in Virginia Records Before 1776." *William and Mary Quarterly,* 3rd ser., 19 (1939).

Greenwood, Val D. "Court Records in the United States." *Genealogical Journal* 6 (1977): 159–68.

_____. *The Researcher's Guide to American Genealogy.* Baltimore: Genealogical Publishing Co., 1973.

Haskins, George L. "Court Records and History." *William and Mary Quarterly,* 3rd ser., 5 (1948): 547–52.

_____. "Curtesy in the United States." *University of Pennsylvania Law Review* 100 (1951): 196–223.

Jacobus, Donald Lines. "Probate Law and Custom." *American Genealogist* 9 (1932): 4–9.

Johnson, Guion G. "Courtship and Marriage Customs in Antebellum North Carolina." *North Carolina Historical Review* 8 (1931): 384–402.

Johnston, G.D. "Legal Terms and Phrases." *Amateur Historian* 3 (1956–57): 249–52.

Jordan, Philip D. "In Search of Local Legal Records." *American Archivist* 33 (1970): 79–82.

Keim, C. Ray. "Primogeniture and Entail in Colonial Virginia. *William and Mary Quarterly,* 3rd ser., 25 (1968): 545–86.

King, George H.S. "Maiden Names Used After Marriage." *American Genealogist* 47 (1971): 44.

Klein, Fannie J. *Federal and State Court Systems: A Guide.* Cambridge: Ballinger Publishers, 1977.

MacLeod, D. "Natural Child." *Genealogists' Magazine* 5 (1930): 250. In America, "natural birth" means the legitimate "heirs of the body," as opposed to stepchildren or adopted children.

Maduell, Charles R. "Genealogy from Law Books." *New Orleans Genesis* 9 (1972): 42–43. Includes specific examples from state court reports.

Merritt, H.A., Jr. "Preservation of Court Records." *Wisconsin Bar Bulletin* 33 (1960): 43.

Morris, Richard B. "Early American Court Records: A Publication Program." In *Anglo American Legal Series.* New York: New York University School of Law, 1941.

_____. "Primogeniture and Entailed Estates in America." *Columbia Law Review* 27: 47.

_____. *Studies in the History of American Law With Special Reference to the Seventeenth and Eighteenth Centuries.* New York: Columbia University Press, 1930, 82–125.

"Mrs. for Unmarried Women." *Genealogists' Magazine* 10 (1950): 493, 538, 579–80.

Myrick, Shelby, Jr. "Legal Terminology in Genealogical Research in the U.S.A." Salt Lake City: World Conference on Records, 1969. Area 1–10. Includes a useful glossary with terms often omitted from modern dictionaries.

Padgett, Patricia Ann. "Legal Status of Women in Colonial Virginia, 1700–1785." Master's thesis, College of William and Mary, 1967.

Pound, Roscoe. *Organization of Court.* Boston: Little, Brown, 1940.

Russell, George Ely. "Court Depositions and Affidavits as Evidence of Age in Maryland, 1637–1657." *Maryland Magazine of Genealogy* 2 (1979): 68–75.

Rutman, Darrett B., and Anita H. Rutman. "Now-wives and Sons-in-law: Parental Death in a Seventeenth Century Virginia County." In *Chesapeake in the Seventeenth Century.* Chapel Hill: University of North Carolina Press, 1979, 153–82.

Semonche, John E. "Common-Law Marriage in North Carolina: A Study in Legal History." *American Journal of Legal History* 9 (1965): 320–49.

Stevenson, Noel. "Genealogical Research in the Law Library." *American Genealogist* 18 (1941): 100–03. Genealogical applications of printed court reports.

Surrency, Edwin C. "The Courts in the American Colonies." *American Journal of Legal History* 11 (1969): 253–76, 347–76.

"Terms of Relationship in Colonial Times." *American Genealogist* 55 (1979): 52–54.

Southwick, Neal S. "The Coordinate Use of Wills and Deeds." *Journal of Genealogy* 2 (1973): 154–56.

Walker, Gilbert S. "Old Land Deeds." *Pennsylvania Magazine of History and Biography* 41 (1917): 365–67.

Weinberg, Allen. "Court Records: Orphans Among Archives." *American Archivist* 23 (1960): 167–74.

Weiner, Carol Z. "Is a Spinster an Unmarried Woman?" *American Journal of Legal History* 21 (1977): 27–31.

Wyatt-Brown, Bertram. *Southern Honor: Ethics and Behavior in the Old South.* New York: Oxford University Press, 1982.

ADMIRALTY COURT RECORDS

Andrews, Charles M. *The Colonial Period of American History: England's Commercial and Colonial Policy.* Vol. 4. New Haven: Yale University Press, 1938. An excellent historical treatment of the courts of admiralty in the colonies.

Towle, Dorothy S. *Records of the Vice-Admiralty Court of Rhode Island: 1716–1752.* Washington, D.C.: American Historical Association Committee on Legal History, 1939. Contains incomplete extracts of cases and a history of admiralty jurisdiction in Rhode Island.

Ubbelhide, Carl. *The Vice-Admiralty Courts and the American Revolution.* Chapel Hill: University of North Carolina Press, 1960. A good description of the courts before 1763 and their influence on the American Revolution.

Whitney, Edson L. *Government of the Colony of South Carolina.* Baltimore: Johns Hopkins Press, 1895. Chapter 2 describes South Carolina's pre-revolutionary admiralty courts.

ADOPTION RECORDS

Much information has become available in the past ten years for adoptees seeking access to information. Resources, support groups, and texts are listed here. The many studies on current adoption laws seldom cover the historical changes which affect tracing family lines. The impact of current law on pre-1930 adoption has been primarily to make access to early records more difficult. See chapter 1 for a discussion of freedom of information laws that may be used to get access.

"Adoption in South Carolina." *South Carolina Law Quarterly* 9 (1957): 210.

Askin, Jayne. *Search: A Handbook for Adoptees and Birthparents.* New York: Harper & Row Publishers, 1982.

Barran, Annette, et al. "The Dilemma of Our Adoptees: Secret Adoption Records." *Psychology Today* (December 1975): 38.

Broenan, J.F. "The Law of Adoption (New York)." *Columbia Law Review* 22 (1922): 332.

Cavanaugh, Karen B. "Adoption and Genealogy." *Indiana Genealogical Informer* 2 (July 1981): 88–89; 3 (August 1981): 1–2.

Cutter, Simon. "Parent and Child, The Law of Adoption in Massachusetts." *Boston University Law Review* 15 (1935): 171.

Howard, Mary. "I take After Somebody; I Have Real Relatives; I Possess a Real Name." *Psychology Today* (December 1975): 33–37.

Huard, Leo Albert. "The Law of Adoption: Ancient and Modern." *Vanderbilt Law Review* 9 (1955–56): 743.

Kupersmith, Nancy. "The Fight to Open Up Adoption Records." *Reader's Digest* (June 1978).

Leary, Morton L. *The Law of Adoption Simplified.* New York: Oceana Publications, 1948.

McLeod, R.M. "Adoption in Virginia." *Virginia Law Review* 38 (1952): 627.

Murphy, Harry J. *Where's What: Sources of Information for Federal Investigators.* New York: Warner Books, 1976. Important reference on how to access current records.

Merlin, William. "The Tennessee Law of Adoption." *Vanderbilt Law Review* 3 (1950): 627.

Neier, Aryeh. *Dossier: The Secret Files They Keep on You.* New York: Stein and Day, 1965. Provides insights into consulting records protected by privacy laws.

Rillera, Mary Jo. *The Adoption Searchbook: Techniques for Tracing People.* Huntington Beach, Calif.: Triadoption Publications, 1981. Available from the publisher, Box 5218, Huntington Beach, CA 92646, or from The Everton Publishers, Box 368, Logan, UT 84321.

Robie, Diane C. *Searching in Florida: A Reference Guide to Public and Private Records.* ISC Publications, P.O. Box 10857, Costa Mesa, CA 92627.

Sanders, Patricia. *Searching in California: A Reference Guide to Public and Private Records.* Costa Mesa, Calif.: Independent Search consultants, 1982. Available through ISC Publications, P.O. Box 10857, Costa Mesa, CA 92627, or from The Everton Publishers, P.O. Box 368, Logan, UT 84321.

Silberman, Curt C. "Adoption in New Jersey: An Analysis of Its Legal Effects and Consequences." *Rutgers University Law Review* 1 (1947): 250.

Strahorn, John S., Jr. "Adoption in Maryland." *Maryland Law Review* 7 (1943): 275.

Zainaldin, Jamil. "The Emergence of a Modern American Family Law, Child Custody, Adoption and the Courts, 1796–1851." *Northwestern University Law Review* 73 (1979).

_____. "The Legal Origins of Modern Adoption." Ph.D. dissertation, University of Chicago, 1976.

COURTS OF CLAIM RECORDS

Field, Kate. "Notable and Curious Cases in the Court of Claims." *Green Bag* 7 (1895): 12.

National Archives. *Genealogical Research in the National Archives.* Washington, D.C.: General Services Administration, 1982.

_____. "Records of the Court of Claims Section of the Department of Justice." Preliminary Inventory 47 (1953).

_____. "Records of the United States Court of Claims." Preliminary Inventory 58 (1954).

INDIAN COURT RECORDS

Brown. "The Choctaw-Chickasaw Court Citizens." *Chronicles of Oklahoma* 16 (1938): 425.

Davis. "Court of Reform in the Navajo Nation." *Journal of American Judicature Society* 43 (1959): 52. Describes the establishment of the tribal court.

Fullerton. "Courts in the Quapaw Country." *Indian Territory Bar Association Proceedings* 4 (1903): 63.

Givens. "The Creek Courts." *Indian Territory Bar Association Proceedings* 4 (1903): 43. Describes the establishment of Creek courts in 1850 following resettlement.

Hastings. "The Cherokee Courts." *Indian Territory Bar Association Proceedings* 4 (1903): 39.

Hill, Edward E. *Guide to Records in the National Archives of the United States Relating to American Indians*. Washington, D.C.: NARS, 1981. This guide is well indexed and gives specifics on the courts maintained by Indian agencies. The records themselves are not described in detail.

Kawashima, Yasu. "Legal Origins of the Indian Reservation in Colonial Massachusetts." *American Journal of Legal History* 13 (1969): 42–56.

Knight. "Fifty Years of Choctaw Law, 1834–1884." *Chronicles of Oklahoma* 31 (1953): 76.

"Notes and Documents: The Brush Court of Indian Territory." *Chronicles of Oklahoma* 46 (1968): 201.

Reid, John. *A Law of Blood: The Primitive Law of the Cherokee Nation*. New York: New York University Press, 1970.

Sharp. "The Chickasaw Court." *Indian Territory Bar Association Proceedings* 4 (1903): 54. Describes the creation of Chickasaw courts in 1867.

Thompson. "Courts of the Cherokee Nation." *Chronicles of Oklahoma* 2 (1924): 63.

MINING DISTRICT RECORDS

Directory of Nevada Mines. Rev. ed. Reno: Mining Press, 1940.

Greever, William S. *The Bonanza West: The Story of the Western Rushes, 1848–1900*. Norman: University of Oklahoma Press, 1963.

Griffen, Helen S. *California Mining Town Newspapers, 1850–80*. Glendale, Calif.: J.E. Reynolds, 1954.

Griswold, Don L., and Jean H. Griswold. *The Carbonate Camp Called Leadville*. Denver: the authors, 1951.

Hult, Ruby. *Lost Mines and Treasures of the Pacific Northwest*. 3rd ed. Portland: Binfords and Mort, 1968. Includes descriptions by "old-timers" of mines open for only a short time.

Marshal, Thomas Maitland. "Miners Laws of Colorado." *American Historical Review* 25 (1919–20): 426.

Mumrey, Nolee. *Early Mining Laws of Buckskin Joe*. Boulder, Colo.: the author, 1961.

_____. *History and Proceedings of Buckskin Joe*. Boulder, Colo.: the author, 1961.

Records of R.C. Barry, Justice of the Peace, Sonoma, California, 1850–51. Printed in *Miners and Business Directory*. Columbia, Calif.: Heckendorf and Wilson, 1856.

Shinn, Charles H. *Institutional Beginnings of a Western State*. Johns Hopkins University Studies in History and Political Science, 2nd ser. Vol. 7. Baltimore: 1880. Discusses the lead mines of Iowa.

_____. *Mining Camps: A Study in American Frontier Government*. 1884. Reprint. New York: Harper Torchbooks, 1965.

_____. *Land Laws of Mining Districts*. Johns Hopkins University Studies in History and Political Science, 2nd ser., vol 12. Baltimore: 1884.

Smith, Duane A. *Rocky Mountain Mining Camps*. Indianapolis: Indiana University Press, 1975.

OTHER COURT RECORDS

Aiken, John. "New Netherlands Arbitration in the 17th Century." *Arbitration Journal* 29 (1974): 145.

Brown. "Legal Systems in Conflict: Orleans Territory, 1804–1812." *American Journal of Legal History* 1 (1975): 35.

Dart. "Influence of the Ancient Laws of Spain on the Jurisprudence of Louisiana." *InterAmerican Law Review* 1 (1959): 303.

Dupuy. "The Earliest Courts of the Illinois Country." *Illinois Law Review* 1 (1906): 81.

Fielder, George. *The Illinois Law Courts in Three Centuries 1673–1973: A Documentary History*. Chicago: Physician's Record Company, 1973.

Ford, Jeanette W. "Federal Law Comes to Indian Territory." *Chronicles of Oklahoma* 58 (1980–81): 432–39.

Gilbert. "Mexican Alcades of San Francisco, 1835–1846." *Journal of the West* 2 (1963): 245.

Grivas, Theodore. *Military Government in California, 1846–1850, With a Chapter on Their Prior Use in Louisiana, Florida and New Mexico*. Glendale, Calif.: Arthur H. Clarke Co., 1963.

Hershkowitz, Leo. "The Troublesome Turk: An Illustration of Judicial Process in New Amsterdam." *New York History* 46: 299.

Lang, Margaret. *Early Justice in Sonora*. N.p.: Mother Lode Press, 1963.

McKnight. "The Spanish Legacy to Texas Law." *American Journal of Legal History* 3 (1959): 222, 229.

Robinson, William M., Jr. *Justice in Grey: A History of the Judicial System of the Confederate States of America*. Cambridge: Harvard University Press, 1941.

Shinn, Charles H. *Mining Camps: A Study in American Frontier Government*. 1884. Reprint. New York: Harper Torchbooks, 1965. Includes an excellent description of the Spanish/Mexican legal system.

Twitchell. "Spanish Colonization and the Founding of the Cuidades and Villas in the Time of Don Juan Onate." *New Mexico Bar Association Minutes* (1919): 27.

Wiener, Frederick B. *Civilians Under Military Justice: British Practice Since 1689, Especially in North America*. Chicago: University of Chicago Press, 1967.

SLAVE COURT RECORDS

Crawford, Paul. "A Footnote on Courts for Trial for Negroes in Pennsylvania." *Journal of Black Studies* 5 (December 1974): 167–74.

Klebaner, Benjamin J. "American Manumission Laws and the Responsibility for Supporting Slaves." *Virginia Magazine of History and Biography* 63 (1955): 443–53.

McCain. "Magistrates' Courts in Early North Carolina." *North Carolina Historical Review* 48 (1971): 23.

McPherson, Robert G. "Georgia Slave Trials, 1837–1849." *American Journal of Legal History* 4 (1960): 257–84; 364–77. Includes cases.

Senesè, Donald J. "The Free Negro and the South Carolina Courts, 1790–1860." *South Carolina Historical Magazine* 68 (1967): 140–53, 265.

Sisk. "Crime and Justice in the Alabama Black Belt, 1875–1917." *Mid-America* 40 (1958): 106.

Steel, Edward M., Jr. "Black Monongalians: A Judicial View of Slavery and the Negro in Monongalia County, 1776–1865." *West Virginia* 34 (1972–73): 331–59.

RESEARCH IN LAND AND TAX RECORDS
Chapter Contents

8

RESEARCH IN LAND AND TAX RECORDS

revised by Sandra Hargreaves Luebking

Land records provide two types of important evidence for the genealogist. First, they often state kinship ties, especially when a group of heirs jointly sells some inherited land. Second, they place individuals in a specific time and place, allowing the researcher to sort people and families into neighborhoods and closely related groups. By locating people with reference to creeks and other natural features, the deeds, land grants, and land tax lists help distinguish one John Anderson, son of Mark, from another John Anderson in the same county. Prior to the Civil War, most free adult males owned land; so if the land records of an area have survived but do not mention your ancestor, you should reevaluate the assumption that he or she lived in the area.

Most beginning genealogists underestimate the importance of using land records to pin persons to specific locales. Donald Lines Jacobus, considered the founder of scientific New England genealogy, wrote of Connecticut: "The most important town records, genealogically, are the land records."[1] In the South, which has far fewer vital records than New England, the land records are even more crucial to genealogical success.

This chapter on land is divided into two major parts. The first describes deeds, survey systems, military bounty land, and taxes and offers some information on real property law. The second half is a synopsis of each state's land grant records, along with historical notes and bibliographic references. Observe especially the distinction between "state-land states" (where the state or colony made the land grants) and "public-domain states" (where the federal government made the grants). The first part of the chapter explains these two systems; the state-by-state synopsis indicates which system was used in each state.

Many of the land records mentioned in this chapter have been microfilmed. The Genealogical Society of Utah (parent organization of the Family History Library of The Church of Jesus Christ of Latter-day Saints in Salt Lake City) includes state land grants and county and some city deeds among its routinely microfilmed records. Consult its catalog at the branches listed in appendix D.

The society formerly microfilmed deed books only up to 1850, later up to the Civil War, and still later—in some cases but not all—the subsequent volumes. Sometimes cumulative deed indexes exist but were not microfilmed. Thus, despite the society's vast number of land records on microfilm, you should not regard its catalog as a complete inventory of what survives.

Other microfilmed records belong to libraries and archives that have made their manuscript collections of private land company papers and other records available. The millions of federal land patents have also been microfilmed and are available through the Bureau of Land Management, as described in the state-by-state synopsis of public-domain states later in this chapter.

DEEDS

Deeds form the bulk and backbone of American land records. They are fairly uniform in format and content, can normally be located in routinely predictable jurisdictions—usually the county—and generally present few difficulties for the average researcher. Being one of the most important components of the workaday civil law (as opposed to criminal law), deeds contain a fair measure of legal terms. Val Greenwood, with the advantage of a law degree, has discussed some basic legal concepts about land in his *Researcher's Guide to American Genealogy* (Baltimore: Genealogical Publishing Co., 1990), pp. 345–57. *Black's Law Dictionary* also provides definitions. An authoritative encyclopedia such as the *Encyclopedia Britannica* in an older edition will contain a good review of "real property and conveyancing." Also check indexes in encyclopedias under "deeds." This section contains an overview of deeds and other records found in deed books. Some remarks on more technical aspects are given below in the section on the "Use of Land Records."

The term "deed" can be used broadly to mean a legal document of transfer, bargain, or contract, or narrowly for a warranty deed by which the seller warrants (guarantees) the title to the land being sold. Deed books contain many types of title conveyances and contracts: deeds in fee simple granting absolute ownership, mortgages transferring property rights as security for a debt, dower releases waiving a wife's rights, quitclaim deeds releasing whatever title or right is held whether valid or not, deeds of gift transferring land without a reciprocal consideration except perhaps "love and affection," powers of attorney appointing legal agents, marriage property settlements between spouses either before or after the marriage, bills of sale transferring property that is usually not land, and various forms of contracts, such as leases, partnerships, indenture papers, and other performance bonds. These last four were not ordinarily recorded, though probate bonds were common in probate volumes. Deed books from before the Civil War and especially in colonial years were more miscellaneous in their contents, even including animal brands, occasional wills, slave manumissions, apprentice papers, petitions, depositions, tax lists, and whatever else the clerk decided to preserve on a convenient page.

European settlers and their governments brought to the colonies the principle that before land could be privately owned the government had to pass title into private hands. Thus, for any tract of land there should be a first-title deed, which is normally called a grant or patent. Usually the authorities sought from the local Indian tribes a cession of Indian title, though this concept of owning land was foreign to the Indian view of communal occupancy. Once the Indian title was terminated to the satisfaction of the whites, the government could grant title for a tract to an individual, corporation, or, in the case of federal grants, even to a state. All subsequent transfers of a tract are by deed or analogous conveyance, or by inheritance.

In the United States, responsibility for guaranteeing legal title rests with the buyer and seller, who nowadays usually employ professional title searchers and lawyers to trace the chain of title back to the first-title grant if possible, attempting to verify a valid, unencumbered title transfer at each step. The government limits itself to the role of a referee—supplying the rules, recording the results, and adjudicating disputes brought to court. To simplify such title searches, title abstract and insurance companies have arisen to make professional searches and sell insurance against defective titles. Such companies have compiled indexes to title transfers in their local areas. If a genealogist can afford the high expense, such a title company could compile an ancestor's local land records. Also, there are cases where the local deed office has been destroyed recently but abstracts survive in the private title company records.

An important fact follows from the American system of deed registrations: The records are usually sought by the names of the buyer or seller rather than the tract name or number. This means that a break in the chain of recorded owners can complicate a genealogist's understanding of why, in the absence of a deed, John Smith now owns land that Mary Smith owned ten years ago. The land could have passed from mother to son by will with proof only in the probate records, or it could have passed by intestate probate and not be recorded at all. It could also be that the two persons are unrelated and that Mary sold the land to Paul Williams, who then sold it to John Smith, neither of the deeds being recorded, perhaps to save the cost of the clerk's fees. Or perhaps the deed from Mary Smith to John Smith was by sheriff's sale and indexed under the sheriff's name as seller. Such a sheriff's sale for delinquent taxes raises the point that tax foreclosures affecting the land would be in court records, while a bankruptcy suit might be processed in another county entirely.

A registry system called Torrens attempts to resolve some of these problems. Named for Robert Richard Torrens, the South Australian legislator who developed it in the late 1850s, Torrens ideally records in one place under the title of the tract all former owners and all rights, interests, and liens to which the property is subject. Having established the registry as mandatory and complete, the government can then issue guaranteed certificates of title to a new owner. While available in about twenty states, Torrens has not operated in the United States as intended for several reasons, including constitutional questions of right of appeal to the courts, the great expense of the registration, inadequate insurance funds to insure title guarantees, the statutory exclusion of certain encumbrances from the Torrens records, and—it is said—sabotage by private title companies and lawyers fearing loss of business.

For the genealogist, the advantage of a Torrens chain of title may be offset where the deed indexes are by tract rather than buyer and seller, a situation said to operate in parts of Iowa. Usually there are two sets of indexes, one by tract and one by buyer and seller. If there are no buyer and seller indexes, the genealogist would need to search each tract record to insure comprehensive coverage of an ancestor's land transactions in the county. However, Torrens has never flourished in the United States, so the chances are small that the researcher will encounter this particular problem.

The variety of records in deed books requires the user to develop certain searching and abstracting skills. Because few researchers have the time to read, page by page, the forty, fifty, or one hundred volumes of deeds in an average county or independent city, the user usually turns to the index. Seller indexes are also called direct and grantor indexes; buyer indexes are indirect and grantee indexes. Some counties have alphabetical indexes only for sellers, which requires reading all index entries from A to Z to check the buyers (for example, the buyers would be listed next to the sellers, but only the sellers are alphabetized). Before relying on a deed index, it is wise to make an informal sampling of the contents of the deed volumes to see if they contain records significantly different from deeds and if these different sorts of records are indexed along with the deeds. There actually exist deed volumes containing wills omitted from the deed index and not found in the probate indexes either.

While cumulative deed indexes are usually in alphabetical order ("alpha" order), running indexes cannot be because more names are continually being added. Some running indexes merely group surnames under their first letter (initial order), so all *A* surnames are together (unalphabetized), all *B* surnames together, etc., with special pages for *Mc* and *O'*. Occasionally, a clerk ignored the patronymic prefix and indexed MacDonald, for example, with *D* surnames and O'Carroll under *C*. More elaborate running indexes were sold commercially by companies vying for sales by inventing unique, eye-catching systems. Such complicated indexing systems must be mastered when encountered, though usually there are instructions in the front of the volume. Some allocate separate pages for vowels (surnames *Ba, Be, Bi* . . .), some for consonants (the l-m-n-r-t system brings Chalkley, Cullison, and Czeskleba to the same page, because each has an *l* as the first internal "key" letter). Some running indexes use an initial surname order subdivided by initial letters of the given name (so Gregory Buck, Gary Ball, and Gertrude Brown are all on the same page). Several other approaches are illustrated in Morris L. Radoff, et al., *The County Courthouses and Records of Maryland. Part Two: The Records* (Annapolis: Hall of Records Commission, 1963), pp. 20–36.

Other problems with indexes are sins of omission—creating only a grantor index, mistakenly omitting a name, or ignoring non-deed items. This last problem is fairly common, especially in alphabetized master-deed indexes compiling all the deed volumes of the last one hundred or two hundred years. Whether the indexer will consider the barrel brand of Thomas Forehall, cooper, worth indexing is doubtful, especially because it was recorded 150 years ago and can serve no contemporary purpose. The researcher must always choose between trusting the index or checking the book or needed years page by page. Deeds with more than one buyer or seller may be indexed under the first's name only, another reason to take the time to read page by page if the problem warrants it. There is also the occasional deed that provides information on a surname different from either the seller or buyer. On 7 May 1763, William and Betty Eskridge of Northumberland County, Virginia, sold land to Thomas Williams and, in passing, the deed gave a beautiful account of the Neale family, former owners of the land.[2]

Having found an actual entry in the deed volume, either by using the index or by page-by-page scanning, you should have a fairly standard format for abstracting entries. It is wise to train yourself to *first* write down the source (or, if you have photocopied the entry, to immediately write the source on the photocopy). The source includes the archive or library where you found the record, as well as the record type, volume, and page. Below are three examples.

> Maryland Hall of Records—Charles Co., Md., deeds 10:231 (microfilm)
>
> King Co., Wa., courthouse, county auditor's office, deeds 27:13
>
> Draper Papers (State Historical Society of Wisconsin, Madison), 6BB35 (microfilm 889,101, Family History Library, Salt Lake City)

Printed notekeeping forms help some people remember to copy such sources. Be sure also to include your name and the date when you found the record.

As for abstracting a deed, the style is up to the researcher. Find a format you like and try to standardize it within adaptable limits. Records tend to follow standard formats, which makes abstracting easier. Below is an example of an abstracted deed.

> Barnwell Dist, SC, deeds vol. H, 1814-15, p. 318, 27 Oct 1813: Samuel Sprawls, Barnwell Dist, to John Ashley, residence not given, $20, 46 acres on branch of Tinkers Creek, adj Mary Collins and said John Ashley
>
> signed: Samuel Sprawls
>
> wit: Edmond Brown, J.C. Starpkins (also Starkin)
>
> recorded 21 Nov 1814

Some users forget that the deed book is a copy of an original paper and that, therefore, the deed book signatures are usually in the clerk's handwriting—they are not holographs. Some jurisdictions, however, did require a signature on the copy they retained, so watch for them. Likewise, the seal—in wax and later in paper—beside the seller's signature was real on the original; but, in the deed book, the clerk drew a stylized circle surrounding the word "seal." The use of personal wax seals has long been out of fashion; but in the colonies, men were

expected to have or borrow some sort of sealing device, which usually supplemented the illiterate's mark. Even English peasants as early as the thirteenth century were required by law to seal their signatures; in fact, there was a time when the seal was the official attestation and the person's mark was auxiliary. By the late seventeenth century, the seal was merely a traditional ornament.[3] Consequently, heraldic devices on colonial seals probably do not prove a signer had a coat or arms. In fact, George Washington had a seal with a device different from the family coat of arms, a fairly typical situation.

Seals and signatures are, however, minor problems compared to late recording. Since running indexes show names in chronological order, a 1735 deed recorded in 1802 is so out of place that the researcher may not carry the search far enough to spot it. Actual examples include a deed dated 31 March 1800 and recorded 21 March 1896 in Montgomery County, Georgia, with another in the same place dated 30 December 1791 and recorded 110 years later on 30 July 1901.[4] In the same general category are deeds re-recorded after a courthouse or town hall burned. Also be alert to indexes that show only the recording date, because behind the 1827 date could be an 1818 deed. If the ancestor died in 1823, the researcher might mistakenly conclude from the index that an 1827 deed could not be the ancestor's.

STATE-LAND STATES

Deeds normally locate the land tract by some legal description with a survey. The thirty states where the federal government granted land use the federal township and range system and include a special subcategory called private land claims. First, however, will be described the remaining twenty states, called state-land states, which granted their own lands and have various surveying systems.

The twenty state-land states are the thirteen original states from New Hampshire to Georgia and Maine, Vermont, West Virginia, Kentucky, Tennessee, Texas, and Hawaii. For the last two, consult the "Summary of State Land Records" at the end of this chapter. The remaining eighteen can be divided between the six New England states, which used the New England town system, the transitional state of New York, and the remaining states from Pennsylvania and New Jersey southward, which used the southern system of metes and bounds.

SOUTHERN LAND GRANTS

The "tomahawk" grant is part of American folklore. The buckskin-clad squatter cut blazes on a perimeter of trees that surrounded his newly picked tract of wilderness, and then off he went to a land office to get a deed. He entered his claim (the petition) and got official authorization (a warrant) to have the tract surveyed to produce a legal description (the plat) so that the government could grant title to that piece of land (the first-title deed, usually called a grant or patent).

In the absence of a surveyed grid of meridians, baselines, townships, and ranges by which the land can be legally described, the description must use local features, usually called "metes and bounds," which requires the "measuring" and "naming" of boundary features. The distances in patents and deeds were usually in poles, rods, or perches (all synonyms) of sixteen and a half feet.

Here is part of a simple description: "Starting at the ash

tree in the split rock, then 139 poles to where the spring branch enters Crooked Creek, then up said creek its meanders to a three-notch oak, then. . . ." A surveyed compass course reads: "Starting at the ash tree in the split rock, then North 41 degrees East 139 poles to where the spring branch enters Crooked Creek, then up said creek its meanders South 14 poles, South 3 degrees West 25 poles, South 9 degrees East 13 poles to a three-notch oak. . . ."

Strictly speaking, because they used compass bearings, nearly all southern tracts were not in metes and bounds. A more correct term is the "indiscriminate" survey, meaning that the survey was not part of any larger survey grid. This chapter, however, will employ the common composite term of "indiscriminate metes and bounds." Since the natural or man-made features of the description tended to disappear over the years, the property owner, in the company of local officials, neighbors, and sometimes a surveyor, might retrace the property bounds and mark again from memory or from a new survey those points that were disappearing or lost. This walking and remarking of the bounds was called "processioning."[5]

Unlike in New England, lands in the southern system were usually allotted directly to individuals. In New York, a transition zone, large grants were often made to wealthy individuals who subdivided and sold the grants in small parcels. In Pennsylvania, New Jersey, and the colonies to the south, the allotted lands were usually farm-size tracts that went directly to individuals. There were some very large grants in the southern colonies, especially Virginia. Two of the largest were 92,000 acres to Benjamin Borden and 118,000 acres to William Beverley, both in 1739 in the upper Shenandoah Valley, both part of the total 539,000 acres granted by 1740 to eight individuals or partnerships.[6] (Incidentally, Beverley's papers, including account books for his valley tract, are in the New York Public Library, which illustrates how far the genealogist might have to look for pertinent records).

Land offices handled the paperwork of petitioning and obtaining the individual grants. It is extraordinary that in the colonies from Pennsylvania to Georgia and their offspring of West Virginia, Kentucky, and Tennessee, no land offices were destroyed in a major fire. In the Civil War, the state capitals of Virginia and South Carolina were burned, yet the land office records survived. Nearly every one of the early states south of Pennsylvania still has a land office either as a distinct section of the state archive or as a division of an active state office.

The authority granting colonial lands was not always the government. There were three variations: (1) The English monarch controlled the government and granted the land through the governor. Examples are New York after 1689, South Carolina after 1729, and Georgia after 1754. (2) The monarch controlled the government but gave a private citizen or citizens (proprietors) the right to grant the land; examples are the Northern Neck Proprietary of Lord Fairfax in Virginia and the Granville District of Earl Granville in North Carolina. Or (3) the English monarch allowed a private citizen or citizens to control the government and grant the land, as in Pennsylvania under the Penns and in Georgia under the trustees, 1733 to 1754. Where the proprietors were distinct from government, there will be land office records distinct from government records, as in New Jersey, Virginia, and North Carolina, though these

records may later have been added to the government archives, as in Virginia and North Carolina but not New Jersey. (See the state-by-state summary at the end of this chapter.)

There were several ways to acquire first title to lands, but usually they followed the four steps of petition, warrant, survey/plat, and grant/patent. (*Patent* and *grant* sometimes have different meanings; for example, the colony made patents but the state gave grants. In this chapter, however, they are used interchangeably to mean the first-title deed.)

The *petition* is a request to take up land. The petitioner may have gone before the appropriate officials—the colony's council or the land office clerk—and presented a satisfactory reason for getting land, such as paying the purchase price, being promised land for military service, bringing an immigrant into the colony and thus becoming eligible for the headright land bounty (especially used in the South), or being able to produce a government order for a specified amount of land.

The *warrant* certifies the right to a specific acreage and authorizes an official surveyor to survey it, assuming no prior and conflicting claims.

The *plat*, sometimes called a *survey*, is the surveyor's drawing of the legal description so that the land is identifiable—his certification that everything is in order so far as the warrant, approved acreage, and legal description are concerned.

The *patent/grant* is the government's or proprietor's passing of title to the patentee/grantee. This is the first-title deed and the true beginning of private ownership of the land.

The government or proprietor usually entered a copy of the patent in a bound volume as a permanent, official record. The plats were sometimes recorded in volumes, and the surveyor's loose copy was sometimes also kept. The North Carolina Land Office, for example, has many loose surveys. Some land offices kept permanent warrant records; some did not. The petition was rarely recorded because the warrant was the formal statement of an authorized petition, though petitioner information is occasionally found in council minutes—especially for colonial headrights.

Bringing oneself or another person to the colonies entitled the importer to a "headright" of land at specific historical periods. Virginia granted fifty acres per importation, but sailors abused it by claiming fifty acres every time they sailed to Virginia, then sold their claims. In the case of indentured servants, the fifty acres went to the person who paid the servant's passage. These headrights could be bought and sold, so the person claiming two hundred acres for importing four persons was not necessarily the person who actually paid the passage costs. Thus, if Mark Randle claimed 450 acres for transporting nine persons, including Mary Randle, it is possible Mark merely bought headrights to nine persons and never saw or knew Mary. It is also possible that Mary paid her own passage and sold her headright rather than claim the land. Furthermore, the nine persons need not have come on the same ship nor arrived in the same year.

New England did not have this system of headrights as a rule, though granting free land to town settlers was a form of reward for immigration. The Southern proprietors rarely gave headrights—the Calverts did for a time—because they sold land for a profit. The crown tried at times to make the colonies grant lands to indentured servants at the end of their service, but this was uncommon. Despite these caveats, the headright lists are valuable as the major or only immigration record for most colonial immigrants from the British Isles to the South.

The patent and related documents rarely give kinship information, so their great value is in locating the grantee in a specific time and place. On 11 August 1774, the following grant was made by the royal colony of South Carolina:

> George the Third by the Grace of God, of Great Britain, France and Ireland, King, Defender of the Faith, and so forth. To all to whom these presents shall come, Greeting Know ye, that we of our special grace, certain knowledge and mere motion, have given and granted, and by these presents, for us, our heirs and successors, do give and grant unto Ezekiel Backler his heirs and assigns, a plantation or tract of land containing four hundred & fifty acres on Four Hole Swamp St. Mathews Parish Berkley County bounding northeast on Samuel Young & Ezekiel Backler Senr's land and all other sides on vacant land. . . .[7]

This grant names the owners of two adjoining tracts: Samuel Young and Ezekiel Backler, Sr. Is this Ezekiel, Sr., the same person as the grantee? Or is the grantee a younger Ezekiel living next to his father or uncle? Are there other Backlers in the area? What are the names of other neighbors? Could any be in-laws? Did these neighbors come from the same former home as the grantee? A beginning toward answering these questions would be to draw the surveyed tracts in the area. Drawing a plat map is laborious and time-consuming, but such a map can identify neighbors with considerable precision. Researchers may want to consider platting software (a list appears at the end of this chapter).

The surveys of the 1600s were quite crude. Early Virginia surveys often merely gave a distance along a river and indicated that the rectangle into the woods was a certain number of acres. Descriptive bounds giving only "up the meanders of the creek" must be approximated based on the remaining precise bounds, sometimes with the help of neighboring tracts. Copy errors by clerks—N 56 degrees E 76 poles instead of the correct N 56 degrees W 176 poles—can make it impossible to close the tract's perimeters, but the contiguous tracts may supply the corrections. Figure 8-1 explains how to draw plat maps.

Some early colonial descriptions have strange directions, such as SE 1/2 E or ES 1/2 S or even WNW 1/4 N. These refer to the thirty-two-point compass card, which is described in Sarah S. Hughes, *Surveyors and Statesmen: Land Measuring in Colonial Virginia* (Richmond: Virginia Surveyors Foundation and The Virginia Association of Surveyors, 1979), a book worth reading by anyone interested in Southern indiscriminate surveys. In the thirty-two-point card, the directions beginning at north toward east are:

north	N	N
north by east	N by E	N 11° 15' E
north northeast	NNE	N 22° 30' E
northeast by north	NE by N	N 33° 45' E
northeast	NE	N 45° E
northeast by east	NE by E	N 56° 15' E
east northeast	ENE	N 67° 30' E
east by north	E by N	N 78° 45' E
east	E	E

Fortunately, these compass card directions were rarely used. Dividing ninety degrees into eight parts gives eight 11-degree, 15-minute sections, which, given the imprecision of a modern small protractor and surveyors' very rough angles in the 1600s, means the angles can be treated as N = 0 degrees, N by E = 11 degrees, NNE = 22 degrees, N = 34 degrees . . . , E by N = 11 degrees, E = 0 degrees. Sometimes the angle is NE by N½ N, meaning halfway between NE by N and NNE.

When researching deeds and surveys, you must decide whether to copy the detailed bounds. Much depends on whether the records will be easily available for future checking. Photocopies can help but are expensive when they start accumulating. A wise approach may be to not copy the precise bounds (unless time is no problem or platting is planned) but instead to abstract the usual information, noting carefully all neighbors. Thus, copies can later be ordered of those descriptions that seem to adjoin. If the bounds are to be copied, a simple notekeeping system is:

John Lemon, Northern Neck patent K171, 1 Jly 1760, Frederick Co., Va., survey by Thomas Rutherford, Jr., Begin locust and black oak,

w/ Lemon	S 10 W 38	locust
w/ Francis Lilburn	N 80 W 40	white oak
	S 20 W 190	black oak
	N 70 W 200	locust on hill
	N 20 E 240	2 black oaks
	S 70 E 235	to beginning

311 acres[8]

Sometimes a course says "with Francis Lilburn's line" and gives the bearings and distance; sometimes it gives a bearing and direction and then tells what feature is met. Centering the bearing and distance information on the page leaves space right and left for such descriptions. These natural features and adjoining landowners are important because they help match contiguous tracts. The difficulty of drawing tract maps is well worth the trouble for difficult lineage problems.[9]

NEW ENGLAND TOWNS

While the Southern and New England land systems shared most of the same terminology, they differed fundamentally in that New England grants usually went to a group of men called town proprietors. Upon receipt of a block of land, these town proprietors surveyed parts of their large tract, apportioned out village home sites and field strips for themselves and others, and oversaw the subsequent disbursements of "divisions" of land until all the grant had passed into private ownership except for the town commons and local government lots. Thus, whereas the Southern grants to individuals created a rural landscape of scattered farms with very few towns, the New England grants created a society of villages.

The origin of the New England town extends back to the first settlers of Plymouth and Massachusetts Bay, where the Pilgrims and Puritans strove to establish a congregation-community uniting church and civil government into God's commonwealth. As new lands were needed to feed the growing population, groups of prospective settlers would petition a colony's government for land to establish a new town, praying

Figure 8-1. How to draw a plat map in indiscriminate metes and bounds.

Drawing Plat Maps

To plat a tract using metes and bounds bearings, you need only an ordinary protractor, pencil, scissors, and lined paper to provide constant east-west lines to orient the protractor.

The degrees begin at the first direction—cardinal point: north, south, east, west—and move toward the second given direction. Thus N 53° E is 53° east of north. If, as is occasionally done, the bounds read E 53° N, this is 53° north of east. N 53° E and E 53° N are not the same; N 53° E and E 37° N are.

For distance, which is measured in 16½—foot lengths called poles/rods/perches (synonymous terms), a homemade scale can be made of 320 parts to the mile (320 poles × 16½ feet = 5280 feet). To make such a scale, cut a narrow strip of paper perhaps a quarter-inch wide to the length you want one mile to equal. Double, redouble, and redouble again.

Folding three times creates a strip divided into eight parts each 40 poles long. Then visually divide each 40 poles into four parts, thus creating a scale of ten poles to each mark. The U.S. Geological Survey's 1:24,000 topographic maps are a very good scale for drawing plats because small tracts such as thirty and forty acres come out at a good working size, not so tiny that they easily get lost. To fix exactly on the topographic map where a tract lay, it is usually necessary to bring together enough adjoining tracts to create sufficient known points on a creek so the whole series can be adjusted to match the bends of the creeks and rivers.

To order topographic maps, request the appropriate state index to maps from Branch of Distribution, USGS, 1200 South Eads Street, Arlington, VA 22202.

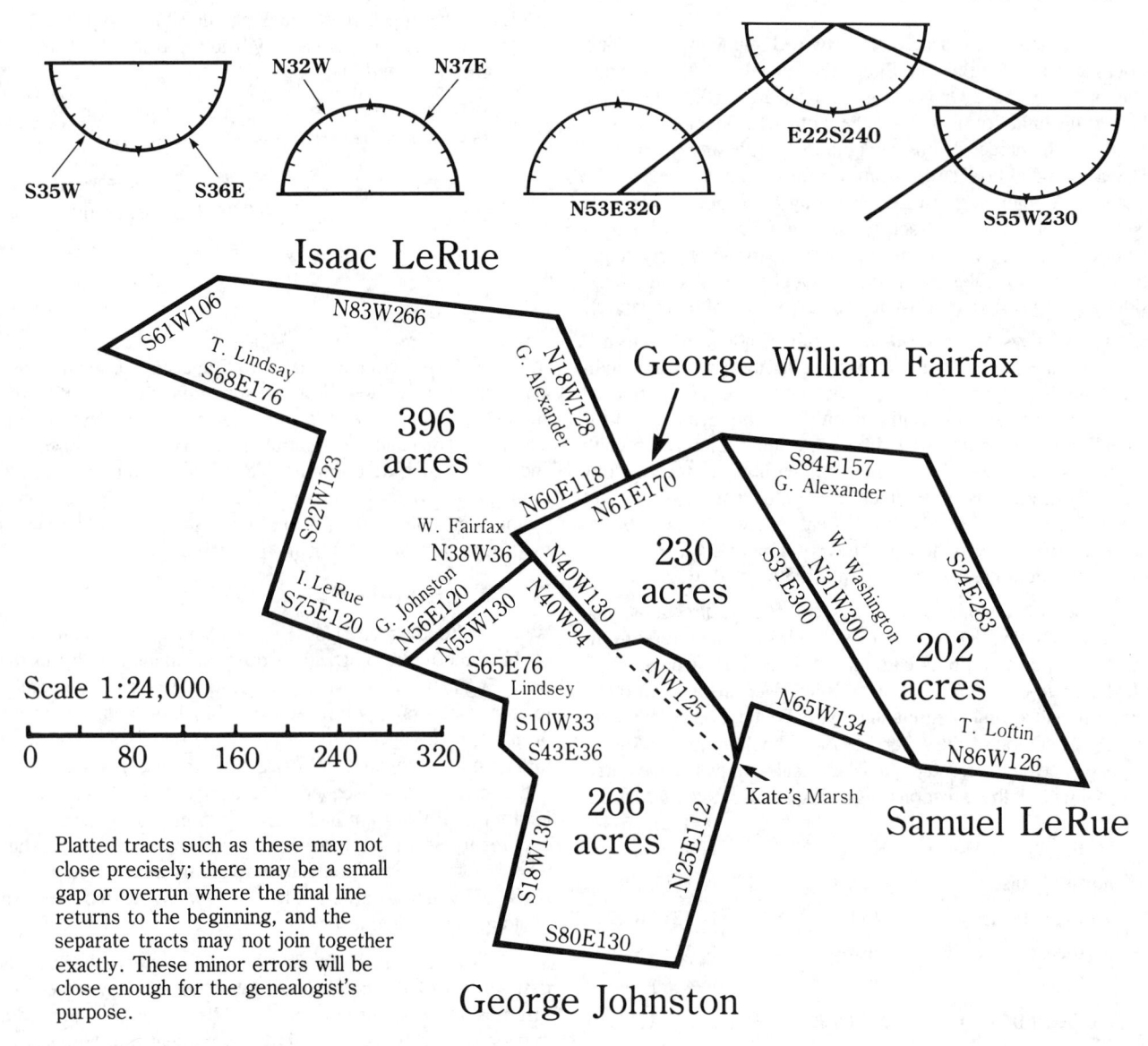

Platted tracts such as these may not close precisely; there may be a small gap or overrun where the final line returns to the beginning, and the separate tracts may not join together exactly. These minor errors will be close enough for the genealogist's purpose.

to be constituted the official proprietors to distribute the land within the town. The town was a geographical unit extending beyond the village to some agreed boundaries with the neighboring towns. The early towns were irregularly shaped; the later ones tended to run six miles by six miles in size. Thus, the town bounds had to be established so that a formal grant could be issued to the proprietors. The religious fervor of Puritanism later declined, but the town form of the congregation-community survived and was carried throughout most of New England and even into eastern New York and northeastern New Jersey. There was, however, a pressing tendency for people to move out of the village to be nearer their fields, which led to the buying and exchanging of land parcels to consolidate property into farms.

The classic analysis of the origins of the New England town is Sumner Chilton Powell, *Puritan Village: The Formation of a New England Town* (Middletown, Conn.: Wesleyan University Press, 1963), a book with valuable English local sources on the origins of English immigrants. The literature is accessible through David Grayson Allen, *In English Ways: The Movement of Societies and the Transferral of English Local Law and Custom to Massachusetts Bay in the Seventeenth Century* (Chapel Hill: University of North Carolina Press, 1981). For colonial land history in New England, see Marshall Harris, *Origin of the Land Tenure System in the United States* (Ames: Iowa State College Press, 1953); and Roy Hidemichi Akagi, *The Town Proprietors of the New England Colonies: A Study of Their Development, Organization, Activities and Controversies, 1620–1770* (Philadelphia: Press of the University of Pennsylvania, 1924).

The New England town system has several implications for genealogists, starting with the need to determine what records are on the county level and which are on the town level. Early Massachusetts Bay towns recorded their own deeds until counties were created in 1643. Early towns on eastern Long Island also recorded their own deeds until the Duke of York's New York proprietary required registration in Suffolk County. Connecticut, Rhode Island, and Vermont recorded and still record deeds on the town level. Aside from deeds, the researcher should also check for early proprietor minutes on the town level. More generally, New England research requires that towns be treated as mini-counties. Thus, while counties are not as important as in the South, there are three levels of jurisdiction in New England—state, county, and town.

Some of the technical aspects of the New England land system have been well summarized by genealogist David Stoddard:

A. *Commoners and Non-Commoners* . . . The term[s] "commoner" and "proprietor" are synonymous. "Proprietor" simply replaces "commoner" as the proper legal term.

Commoners were originally those to whom the General Court [the legislature] had made a grant of land in common for settlement, very often without giving them entire control. They formed a quasi-corporation. The right of a commoner might be conveyed in a land transaction or inherited and one who thus became entitled to a right was not necessarily entitled to vote in the town meetings when township privileges had been

conferred upon the inhabitants. On the other hand, because a man was entitled to a vote in the town did not entitle him to a voice in the control of the common lands. . . . The land community and the political community were distinct and separate bodies.

The town could enter into transactions with the proprietors; and they in turn could make grants to the town. In plantations where the inhabitants were all commoners, the two bodies acted as one and there would be no "proprietors' records" kept. For instance, Groton, Mass., was settled in 1655, yet there are no proprietors' records until 1713.

As the population of the towns increased, it became necessary to protect the commoners' rights. Hampton, now in New Hampshire, is a good example: (1) 1641—Persons who were not freemen present at town meetings; (2) 1662—Voted "that no man be considered an inhabitant, or act in town affairs but he that hath one share at least of commonage, according to the first division"; (3) 1700—Voted that no one should vote unless a freeholder and none to vote to dispose of lands, unless he is a commoner. In towns such as these, the serious researcher will generally find separate proprietors' records either in a separate book or as the initial part of the first town book. . . .

Two ways existed for the satisfying of claims by non-commoners: (1) Increase the number of commoners; (2) Grant lands to newcomers without accompanying the rights to commonage, either to an individual by name or to all of a given class; such as Barnstable granting 4 acres to every widow.

B. *Division of Common Lands* . . . The valuation of a man's estate, made from the tax-list, was the principal basis of division (Haverhill, Ipswich, Dedham, Hartford, many Connecticut River towns, settlements along Long Island Sound).

C. *Restrictions Upon Alienation* . . . Great care was taken to preserve the original character of the community and to control its membership. A Connecticut law of 1659 declared no inhabitants shall make sale of house and lands until put forth to the town for approval; an item in Guilford, Connecticut, Town Book refers to no one being able to sell OR purchase unless by consent of the community; Watertown, Massachusetts, in 1638 had a provision "against selling town lots to forrainers."

D. *Common Field* . . . The proportions of land cultivated in common varied greatly throughout New England; largely based on necessity. Connecticut and Massachusetts laws gave authority to townsmen or selectmen, or, when there were none, to the major part of the freemen.

Common fields were found in most towns. They were formed: (1) Due to lack of means to fence separately; (2) Due to difficulty of fencing (land along the Connecticut River); (3) Due to convenience. Fences were maintained by each owner according to his share of land enclosed.

E. *Home Lots, Acre Rights, Pitches* . . . Home/house

lots differed in size in different New England towns, and quite often in the same town; (1) Barnstable, 6 to 12 acres; (2) Haverhill, 5 to 22 acres; (3) Groton, 10 to 20 acres. They were often proportioned as to the "quality and estate" of the possessor. . . .

Acre rights or lots indicate the share owned by any one person in the common lands. It is entirely different from home/house lots. Value varied greatly. In Billerica a 10 acre lot or right in common land was equivalent to 113 acres of upland or 12 acres of meadow. In Groton there were 60 acre rights; 20 acre rights, etc. with 755 rights in all. A 60 acre right would have entitled the owner one complete partition to 3242 acres of common land.

Pitches are rights drawn in a division which entitled the drawer to lay out a lot of land in the commons wherever he might choose.[10]

The New Hampshire town of Bow (see figures 8-2 and 8-3) illustrates how town divisions of land were made.[11] In 1725, some residents of Haverhill, Massachusetts, petitioned the Massachusetts General Court (the legislature) for a town grant in the Merrimack River Valley at what is now Concord, New Hampshire. The legislature approved a town of about seven by eight miles, and the first proprietors arrived in the winter of 1726 at this new town called Pennycook. The valley was also claimed by New Hampshire, whose coastal ruling establishment in 1727 received from its legislature an overlapping grant of eighty-one square miles called Bow. Among the proprietors (each promised five hundred-acre shares) were the governor, lieutenant governor, president, and four members of the council, both the colonial secretary and the treasurer, and various members of the legislature. This was, in short, a land speculation in the guise of a town grant, far different from Pennycook and its Massachusetts farmers.

In 1728, the Massachusetts General Court granted a town called Suncook, next to Pennycook, to the heirs and survivors of an Indian expedition two years previous in which thirteen soldiers had died. Suncook, predecessor of modern Bow, was surveyed in 1729, confirmed by the Massachusetts General Court, and made its first division of land in 1730. Field lots averaging fifteen to twenty acres were laid along both sides of the Merrimack River. All houses were built on the east side. The rival New Hampshire proprietors also declared a land division on the east side of the river, the first lots being forty acres. Thus rival town proprietors granted lands.

In 1740, George II established the Massachusetts-New Hampshire line as it is today, placing Pennycook and Suncook inside New Hampshire and directing that existing property titles be honored. This ruling made the Bow proprietors the sole legal proprietors, but the ex-proprietors of Suncook had the advantage of possession. The resulting legal battles were long and expensive, going all the way to England more than once. The present modern town gained a grant of town government from New Hampshire in 1767. When the Bow proprietors ceased functioning in 1786, the town of Bow was finally free of absentee land speculators.

PUBLIC-DOMAIN STATES

The U.S. government has sold or given away more than 1 billion acres of land (not including Alaska). In the process it granted more than 5 million patents kept in 8,978 bound volumes in the Springfield, Virginia, office of the Bureau of Land Management (BLM). An even greater mass of records in the National Archives represents the paperwork granting those patents. Searching for the record of a particular land grant from the federal government requires contacting both the BLM and the National Archives. To know what to request means understanding something of how the federal government processed the paperwork.

FEDERAL LAND GRANTS

From 1776, when Congress promised land to German auxiliaries (sometimes incorrectly known as "Hessians"), and for a quarter of a century afterward, it experimented, mostly in Ohio, to find a workable public land policy. By 1803, when Ohio became a state, the major characteristics of the federal land system had been set:

1. The federal government, not the state, would dispose of the western lands which the original states had ceded, Georgia in 1802 being the last to surrender its western claims.

2. Before any grants were made, the Indian title had to be removed and the land surveyed in rectangular townships of six-mile squares. Some partial townships would exist due to the curvature of the earth.

3. The disposal of the vacant land would be handled through land offices located near settlers.

4. War service (at least prior to the Civil War) usually brought the veterans a right to free land.

5. Legally registered entry claims and military bounty land could usually be sold before a patent was obtained (homesteads could not).

6. Valid land titles obtained from previous French, Spanish, and British governments would be honored.

By 1880, Congress had passed more than 3,500 laws dealing with public lands. In summary, the federal government granted lands in seven broad categories:

Disposed Public Domain	Approximate Acreage
1. Sales and miscellaneous	300,000,000
2. Homesteads	285,000,000
3. Grants to states	225,000,000
4. Military bounty	73,000,000
5. Private land claims	22,000,000
6. Railroad grants	91,000,000
7. Timber culture, etc.	35,000,000
Total disposed	1,031,000,000
Remaining federal lands	411,000,000
State-owned lands	462,000,000
Total U.S. acreage	1,904,000,000[12]

Thus, the disposed public domain was more than 1 billion acres. It included all states west of the Mississippi except Texas and Hawaii, all states north of the Ohio River west of Pennsyl-

Figure 8-2. Pennycook and Suncook in relation to Bow, New Hampshire. Adapted from David A. Bundy, *100 Acres More or Less: The History of the Land and People of Bow, New Hampshire* (Canaan, N.H.: Bow Town History Committee and Phoenix Publishing, 1975), 28, 32, 44.

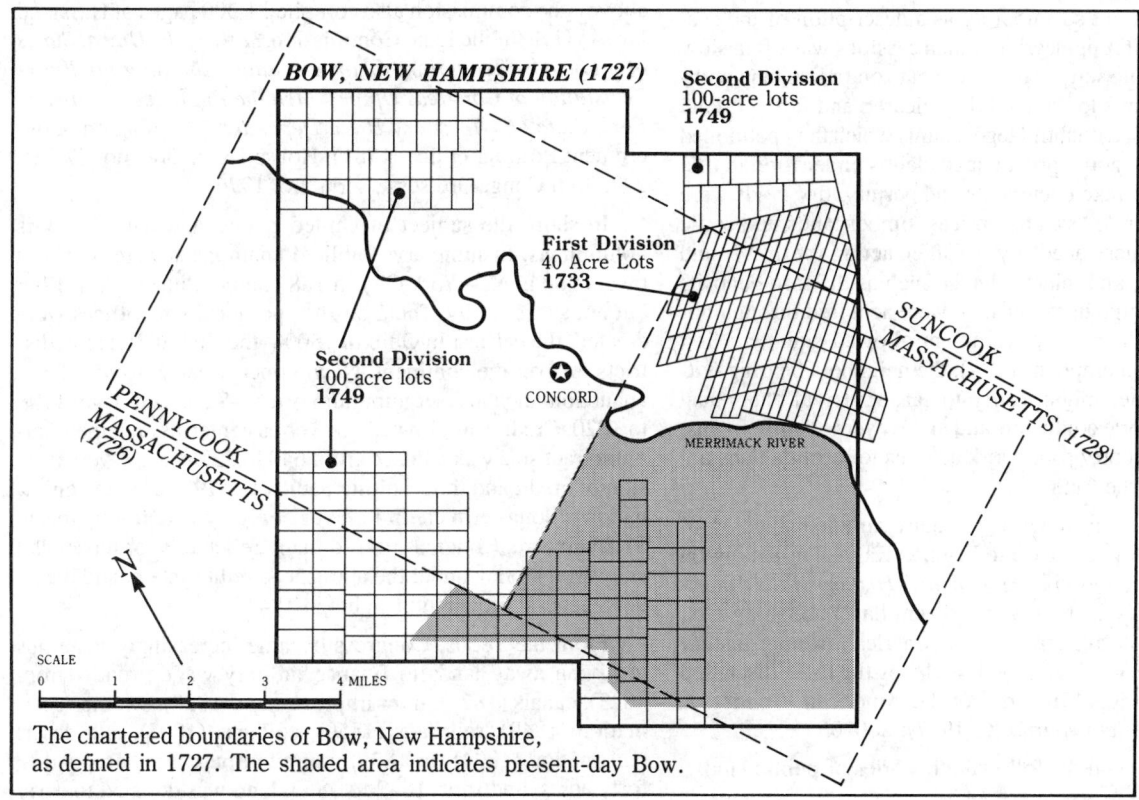

Figure 8-3. Modern Bow, New Hampshire, showing its surveyed lots. Adapted from Bundy, *100 Acres More or Less,* p. 106.

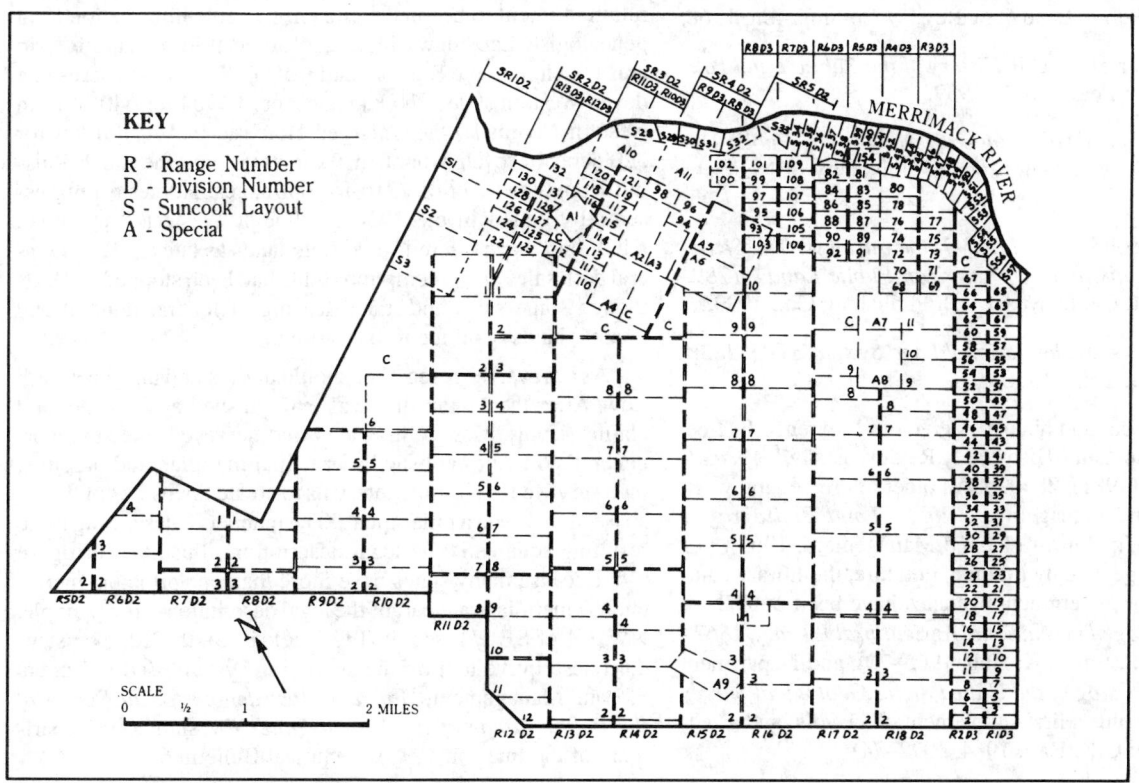

vania, and the four Gulf states of Louisiana, Mississippi, Alabama, and Florida.

Much of the public domain was transferred to private or state title, though not so smoothly as a description of the system might suggest. Engineering Indian cessions was often slow and deceitful; white settlers lived for years on Indian land without any legal claims to the land they cleared and farmed; land speculators amassed doubtful legal claims which they petitioned Congress to make good; private land claims under foreign title were proven with fake documents and perjury; dry lands were purchased at cut-rate "swamp" prices; timber lands and cattle ranges were "homesteaded" by frontmen acting for timber and cattle companies; and mineral lands, such as the iron deposits of the Mesabi Range in Minnesota, were acquired through bogus entrymen. When the government allowed squatters first claim on lands (preemption rights), the neighbors bearing witness for each other might testify to earlier arrival dates than were true. In short, confusion and fraud were common. Just because the land-entry paperwork adheres to formula does not mean it presents the truth.

Clearly, good genealogy may require an understanding of frontier history. A good place to begin is Ray Allen Billington and Martin Ridge, *Western Expansion, A History of the American Frontier*, 5th ed. (New York: Macmillan Publishing Co., 1982). It is a masterful summary of American frontier history with an extensive bibliography. It includes the titles discussed in John F. Vallentine, "Histories of the American Frontier: A Series," *Genealogical Journal* 6 (1977): 200–05.

I also recommend the following histories of public lands:

Donaldson, Thomas. *The Public Domain: Its History With Statistics.* New York: Johnson Reprint Corp., 1970 reprint of 1884 GPO original. House Misc. Doc. 45 pt. 4, 47th Cong., 2nd Sess.

Gates, Paul W. *History of Public Land Law Development.* Washington, D.C.: Public Land Law Review Commission, 1968.

Hibbard, Benjamin Horace. *A History of the Public Land Policies.* New York: Peter Smith, 1939.

Robbins, Roy Marvin. *Our Landed Heritage: The Public Domain, 1776–1970.* 2nd ed. Lincoln: University of Nebraska Press, 1976.

Rohrbough, Malcolm J. *The Land Office Business: The Settlement and Administration of American Public Lands, 1789–1837.* Belmont, Calif.: Wadsworth Publishing Co., 1990.

Treat, Payson Jackson. *The National Land System, 1785–1820.* New York: E.B. Treat, 1910.

Recent work on land history is given in Lawrence B. Lee, "American Public Land History: A Review Essay," *Agricultural History* 55 (1981): 284–99. An older, more general work is Bureau of Land Management, *Public Land Bibliography* (Washington, D.C.: Bureau of Land Management, 1962). For those wishing to get deeply into the literature, the library catalogs of two major government agencies have been published: *Dictionary Catalog of the National Agricultural Library, 1862–1965*, 73 vols. (Boston: G.K. Hall, 1965–70); and Department of the Interior, *Catalog of the United States Geological Survey Library*, 24 vols. plus a first supplement of 11 vols. and a second of 4 (Boston: G.K. Hall, 1964, 1972–74).

In 1879, Congress created the U.S. Public Land Commission to take stock of past and future land policies. In addition to its general report and Donaldson's 1,500-page history (cited above), the commission also compiled 1,300 pages of U.S. land laws in U.S. Public Land Commission, *Laws of the United States of a Local or Temporary Character and Exhibiting the Entire Legislation of Congress Upon Which the Public Land Titles in Each State and Territory Have Depended* (Washington: Government Printing Office, 1881), House Exec. Doc. no. 47, pts. 2–3, 46th Cong., 3rd sess., serial no. 1976.

In short, the subject of United States land law history is voluminous. In summary: Public domain lands were first sold by auction in New York City in 1787 and in Pittsburgh in 1796 but not successfully. Then, on-the-spot local land offices were created, the earliest in Ohio in 1800—the first of 362 land districts to span the continent. Newly opened lands were offered at auction, then at a set minimum price—$2 an acre from 1796 to 1820. Credit was allowed on ever-easier terms, and the minimum tract size was reduced from 640 to 320 acres. Overextension of credit and the resulting panic of 1819 caused the elimination of long-term credit in favor of eighty-acre minimums at $1.25 an acre. Congress passed many relief acts for those who still owed money under the abolished credit system, and it also gave general preemption rights in 1841.

From the 1820s, Congress became increasingly generous in giving away lands to finance military wagon roads (from 1823), canals (1827), river improvement (1828), swamp reclamation (1849), railroads (1850), colleges (1862), and desert reclamation (1894). In 1832, minimum purchases dropped to forty acres, and from 1842 to 1853, land was donated to early settlers in Florida, Oregon/Washington, and New Mexico/Arizona. The famous 1862 Homestead Act gave a settler 160 acres (80 within railroad grant areas) for living on the land for 5 years and improving it. The donation and homestead acts required the claimant to show U.S. citizenship or an already-filed declaration of intent to become a citizen, valuable information for a genealogist. Later laws increased homestead acreage in arid areas, including the Desert Land Act of 1877 for 640 acres in a dozen Western states; the Kincaid Act of 1904 for 640 acres in western Nebraska; the Enlarged Homestead Act of 1909 for 320 acres in seven Mountain West states; and the Stock-Raising Homestead Act of 1916 for 640 acres. Homesteading essentially ended in the 1930s, although Western "sagebrush rebellions" have offered some state lands as late as 1983. General cash sales and preemption rights had been stopped in 1891, though some sales and much leasing of federal mineral and grazing lands continue to the present.

As always, the researcher should understand the paperwork flow. After the Indian title was extinguished and private land claims, if any, were adjudicated and surveyed, the surveyor-general's office established a principal meridian and baseline, then surveyed at six-mile intervals to create townships of thirty-six sections, each a mile square. The manner of describing these resulting squares is the legal description, illustrated in figure 8-4. Because many states have more than one principal meridian, the meridians are part of the legal description—for example, NW 1/4 of SE 1/4, sec. 9, T13S, R11E, Sixth P.M. The standard descriptive text on the surveying system used is Bureau of Land Management, *Manual of Instructions for the Survey of the Public Lands of the United States* (Washington: Department of the Interior, 1973), Technical Bulletin 6.

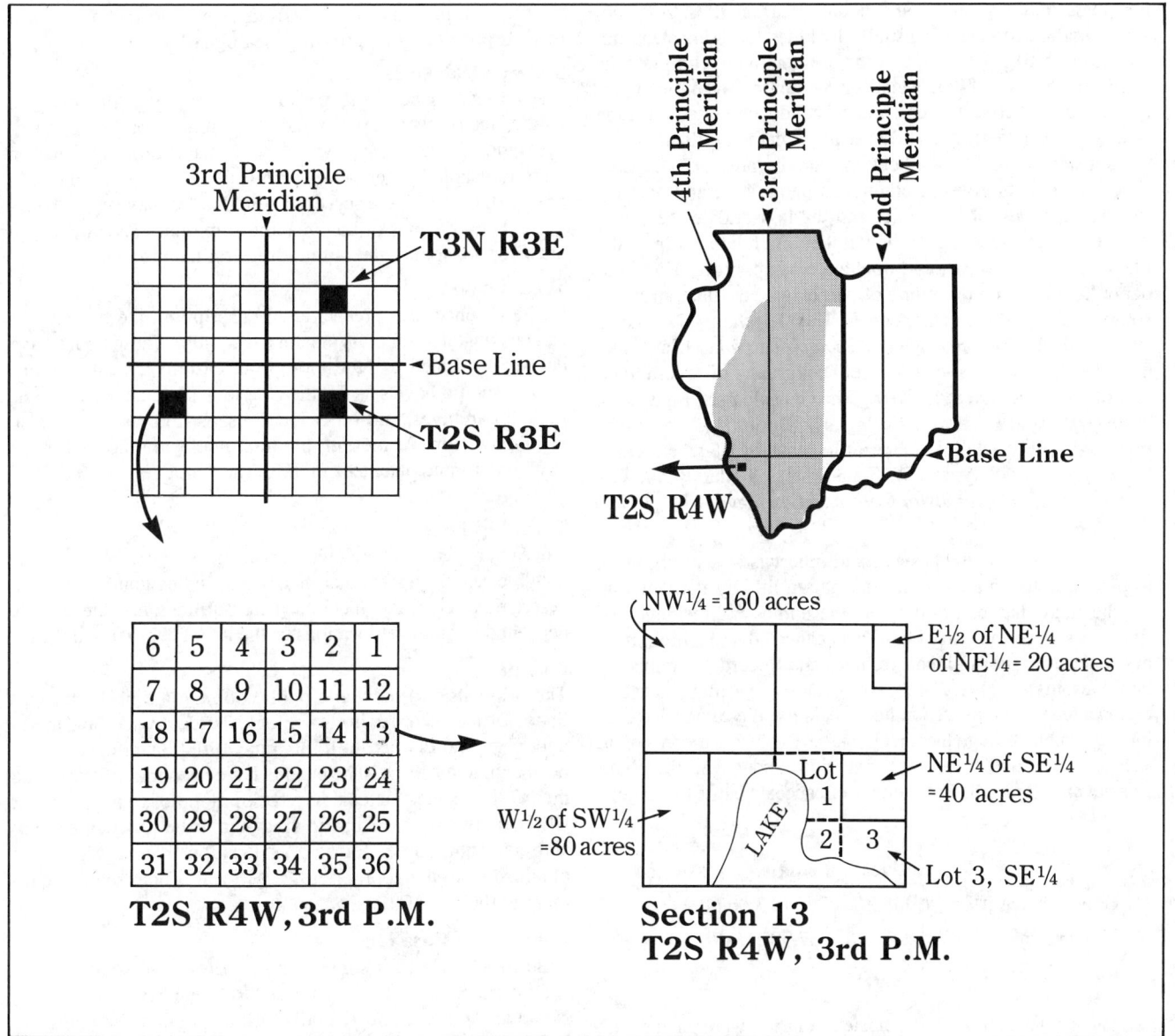

Figure 8-4. Legal descriptions in the federal township and range system.

Once the land was surveyed and could be legally described, a local land office was opened, the auction was held, and land was available at the minimum price to claimants/entrymen who paid a credit installment (before 1820) or a down payment on a cash purchase. Homesteads required a very small fee. Each land office was run jointly by two officials: a registrar, who recorded entries and kept track of which tracts were claimed or still open, and a receiver, who handled the money. These officials kept daily journals and account ledgers and sent periodic summaries to the national headquarters—first the Treasury Department and, from 1812, the newly created General Land Office (GLO). The local land office kept a separate file for each entry and two indexes by area: (1) the tract book, which was a written description of each entry on sheets arranged by township and range (figure 8-5), and (2) a township plat (figure 8-6), which was a map of entries for each township showing patented tracts.

Once the entryman had fulfilled the requirements of pur-

chase or homesteading, the local officials sent the case file (the entryman's paperwork and the final certificate of entitlement to a patent) to GLO headquarters in Washington, which confirmed that all paperwork was in order and issued a patent (first-title deed) transferring the land from the government to the private individual (or to the states, railroads, canal companies, etc.). The GLO headquarters recorded chronologically a copy of the patent in a bound volume by state and district and stored the land-entry case file. After 30 June 1908, patents were recorded chronologically in one continuous, national series regardless of state. This series is indexed for all patentees. The new owner may then have had the patent recorded in the county deed book, or the state may have had an agreement with the GLO that the appropriate county and state authorities would be automatically informed of all patents, because the new lands were often exempt from property taxes for a set term, such as five years.

Homestead case files are richer in genealogical information than the cash, credit, and bounty-warrant files. A homestead final certificate file usually includes the homestead application, certificate of publication of intention to complete the claim, final proof of homesteading (testimony from the claimant and his or her witnesses), and a final document authorizing issuance of a patent. A certified copy of the naturalization papers, if needed for the application, may be present. The final proof documents give the claimant's name, age, and post office address, describe the tract and the house, date the establishment of residence, give the number and relationship of the members of the family, and note citizenship, crops, acres under cultivation, and testimony of witnesses. For illustrations of some of these documents, see E. Kay Kirkham, *The Land Records of America and Their Genealogical Value* (Salt Lake City: Deseret Book, 1964). A brief background of federal land records is in Richard S. Lackey, "The Genealogists' First Look at Federal Land Records," *Prologue* 9 (Spring 1977): 43–45; reprinted with additional material in 1981 by Natchez Trace Genealogical Society; and W. Frank Meek, "Federal Land Office Records," *University of Colorado Law Review* 43 (1971–72): 177–97.

Not all claims—homestead and otherwise—were brought to patent. If the entryman did not obtain title by the deadline for the final charges or complete the homestead residency of five years, then the entry claim was canceled and stored, now available from the National Archives and Records Administration, Washington, D.C. 20408. However, some went to state and regional federal archives. For the genealogist, these canceled case files, traceable through the tract books, are valuable records of an ancestor's life and sometimes give clues about why the claim was never completed. The number of canceled entries is large:

	Entries	Patents	Percent Canceled
Homestead Act	1,968,264	783,053	60.2
Timber Act	290,300	67,382	76.8
Desert Land Act	87,247	23,984	72.5

More than 1,185,000 homestead entries were never patented but should have files containing some of the same information as patented case files, plus a date and reason for the cancellation.

Bureau of Land Management

In 1946, the GLO and the Grazing Service were consolidated into the Bureau of Land Management (BLM), which today holds many GLO records or is the agency title under which the National Archives and its regional branches store GLO records—Record Group 49. The BLM (as of 1996) is divided into eastern and western states. Its working records—the tract books, plats, and patents—for all the eastern states are at the Eastern States Office, 7450 Boston Blvd., Springfield, VA 22153. The eastern states comprise all public-domain states east of the Mississippi River and all states on the river's west bank (Louisiana to Minnesota). Most western states have their own offices; however, Washington's is with the Portland, Oregon, office, and the Great Plains states are under adjoining states farther west. The local land offices and GLO headquarters made duplicate tract and plat books, so the researcher often has a choice of several repositories for microfilm or original records (see the summary at the end of this chapter).

Each step of the process from survey to patent has left records potentially helpful to genealogists:

Survey Field Notes
The surveyor general's records for a state may be in the state's land office (most common), the state archive, or the appropriate regional federal archive. Surveys have little information directly usable by genealogists; but for ancestors on the land prior to the survey, the surveyor's field notes may supply background descriptions of the area and sometimes specific, crude drawings of homes and outbuildings on the property.

Tract Books
In the absence of a precise legal description, the tract books can be consulted for entrymen in a township. These books have been microfilmed, and the appropriate eastern or western states offices should have sets for their regions. Some state archives, regional archives, and other local research libraries may also have microfilm. At present, the tract books are the best index to claimants and patentees in those states not yet computerized (see figure 8-5).

Township Plats
After many years of being written on and over, the plats may be illegible, and the tract books are a better finding tool for the legal description. The plats have been microfilmed and are usually deposited in the same locations as the tract books (figure 8-6).

Patents
The originals for the whole public domain are in the Eastern States Office, recorded in chronological order by state and thereunder by land district up to 30 June 1908. The indexes have been explained above. The patents have been microfilmed, and the Western states' patents have been mounted, one patent per IBM card (aperture card), allowing them to be sorted into township and range order for ease of location. Patents should be obtained from the appropriate BLM local office (see the summary at the end of the chapter).

Land-Entry Case Files
Case files (except for some canceled files never sent to GLO headquarters) are held at the Textual Reference Branch (NNRI), National Archives and Records Administration, Washington, DC 20408. These files contain such things as the entryman's declaration of intent, supporting documents, witness testimonies, bounty-land warrants (if used in lieu of cash), and final naturalization papers. No copy of the patent is in the file except under unusual circumstances, such as inability to deliver the patent to the patentee. The files are arranged by acts, state, and land district and thereunder numerically. The tract book or patent should supply the necessary information, but the Textual Reference Branch does not have either, so the information must accompany the request for the case file. The case files are briefly described in Harry P. Yoshpe and Philip P. Brower, *Preliminary Inventory of the Land-Entry Papers of the General Land Office*. Preliminary Inventory 22 (Washington, D.C.: National Archives, 1949. Reprint. San Jose, Calif.: Rose Family Association, 1996).

Finding Patents

GLO Automated Records System
Federal patents or deeds dated from the late 1780s to 1 July 1908 are indexed for the states of Alabama, Arkansas, Florida, Louisiana, Michigan, Minnesota, Mississippi, Missouri, Ohio, and Wisconsin in a computerized master index to patentee

Figure 8-5. Typical page from a General Land Office tract book. Courtesy of the Bureau of Land Management.

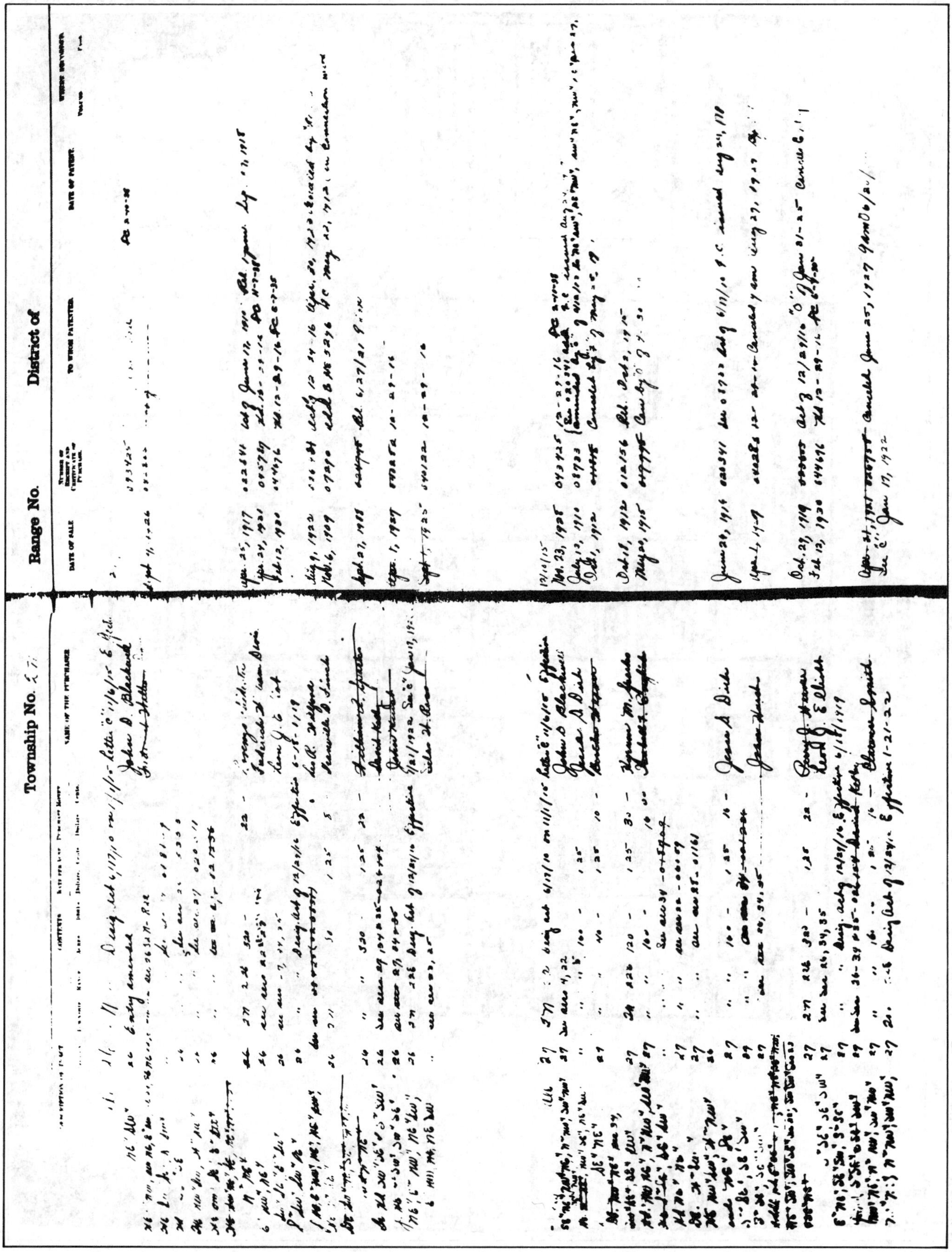

Figure 8-6. Typical page from a General Land Office township plat map. Courtesy of the Bureau of Land Management.

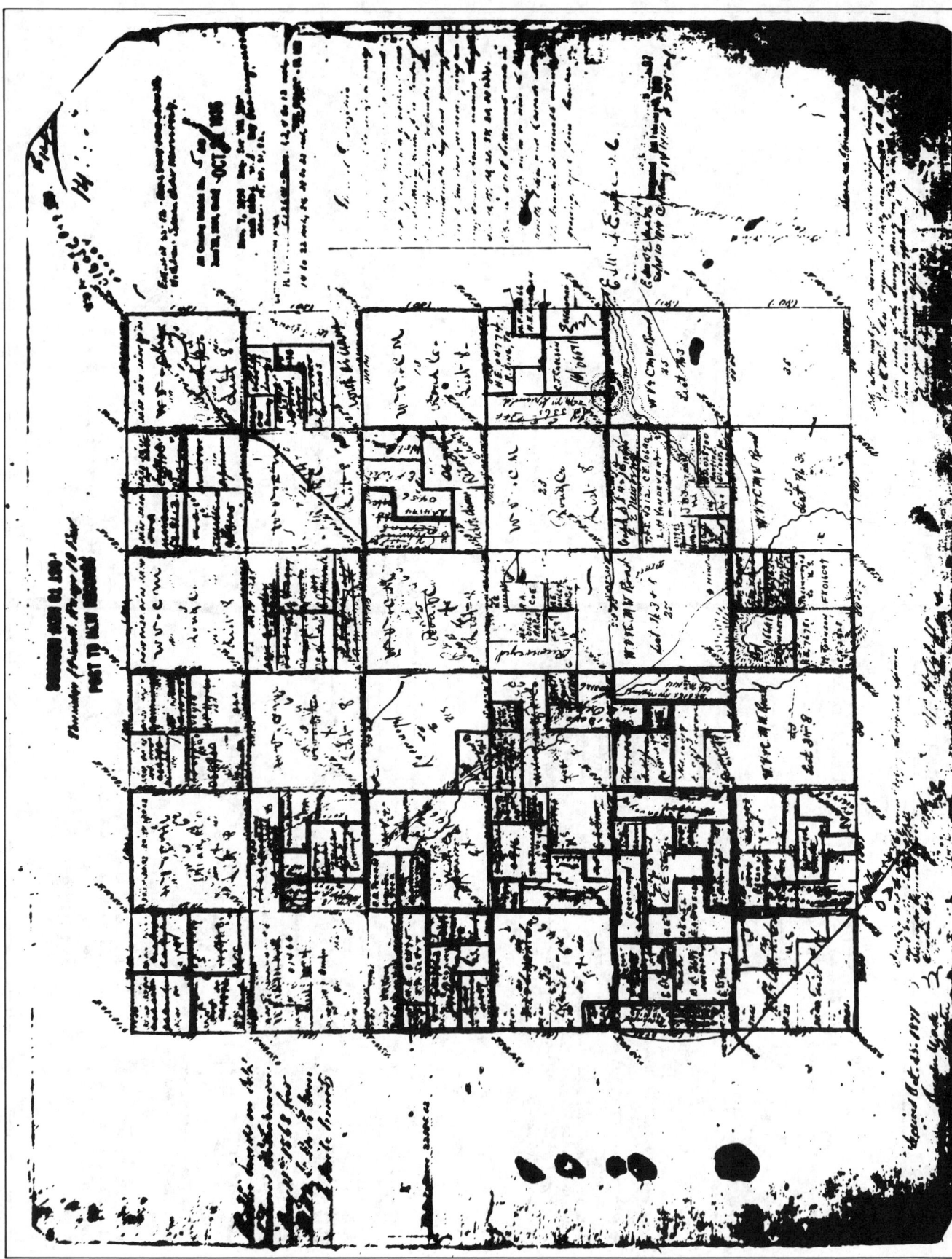

names. More than 1 million homestead and cash patents or deeds issued by the United States can be accessed by computer terminals at the BLM's office in northern Virginia. The BLM proposes to automate the remainder of the eastern public-domain states—Illinois, Indiana, and Iowa—and the remaining patents (those dated after 1908) by the year 2000.

Information in these records is also accessible by remote, dial-in access (modems). To use a modem, an account must be established with the BLM Eastern States Office. This can be done by mail or telephone. When an account is established, the user receives an access code and password, a communications diskette, and a user guide. More information on the GLO Automated Records System is available from 7450 Boston Blvd., Springfield, VA 22153, or by calling (703) 440-1600.

There is a non-computerized index to patents dated before 1 July 1908 for Alaska, Arizona, Nevada, and Utah. This index does not include private land claims. It is available through the BLM at the address above.

Obtaining a Legal Description

For those states that have not been indexed as described above, the legal description is the key to finding a patent and case file except for post-30 June 1908 records. The BLM state offices will perform research by the quarter hour (prepaid), but genealogists may find this does not work well for "fishing expeditions." The cost is too high, and genealogists usually want the names of the kin and in-laws living in the ancestor's neighborhood and cannot usually afford to send all the possible names. Therefore, try to search the tract books yourself at a convenient repository or use a private agent, first confirming where the tract books are in original and/or microfilm form. Microfilm copies of the tract books are increasingly available at nearby research libraries.

Two other ways to obtain the legal description may be even easier: (1) a reference in the county deeds either recording the original patent or making reference to the tract in a deed, and (2) the legal description calculated from a historical atlas. These historical atlases are often called plat books because they featured land ownership plat maps. Some good discussions concerning these atlases are Richard W. Stephenson, *Land Ownership Maps* (Washington: Library of Congress, 1967); Library of Congress, *List of Geographical Atlases in the Library of Congress,* 8 vols. (Washington, D.C.: Library of Congress, 1909–74); Michael J. Fox, "The Map Collection," in James P. Danky, ed., *Genealogical Research: An Introduction to the Resources of the State Historical Society of Wisconsin* (Madison: State Historical Society of Wisconsin, 1979). Historical atlases—and subscription county histories, for that matter—were a midwestern phenomenon, which makes especially valuable the Newberry Library, *Checklist of Printed Maps of the Middle West to 1900,* 11 vols. (Boston: G.K. Hall, 1980), which lists all known pre-1900 plat maps and plat books for the states of Indiana, Illinois, Iowa, Kansas, Michigan, Missouri, Nebraska, North Dakota, Ohio, South Dakota, and Wisconsin.

For the early years, the patent references may be in Clifford Neal Smith, *Federal Land Series,* 4 vols. to date (Chicago: American Library Association, 1972–). Among the records listed in it are the outgoing correspondence of the GLO and its predecessor office, which include the cover letters to transmitted patents as found on National Archives microfilm M25. Volumes 1 and 3 bring this correspondence down to August 1814.

INDIAN RESERVATIONS AND PREEMPTION RIGHTS

From 1830 to 1934, the government dissolved many Indian reservations by first allotting each Indian a tract of land, then selling the remainder. The records of such allotments are voluminous, and many have been microfilmed as Bureau of Indian Affairs agency records. For instance, the records of the Winnebago Agency, Nebraska, are in the National Archives—Central Plains Region in Kansas City, Missouri, and include land sales, 1902 to 1910; Santee acknowledgments of allotments, 1885; lists of Ponca and Santee tribe members never receiving allotments, 1936–1941, etc.

The problem of settlers claiming land before surveyors arrived was a very pressing one which Congress attempted to solve by preemption rights. That this was not a complete solution is shown by the existence of claims clubs, which were private associations sworn to enforce their members' claims when local land was offered for sale or homesteading. Often armed and intimidating, members would attend land office auctions as a group to convince non-members not to enter lands the members claimed. Such clubs were often quite formal in organization and kept records, some of which have survived. Claims clubs may be more interesting for historians than for genealogists, but they are definitely worth searching where they exist. Claims clubs were especially numerous and active in Iowa and Minnesota and the adjoining states to the west.

Such extralegal policing of land claims existed wherever the federal government's land title system came later than the settlers. The mining camp law of the California Gold Rush is an obvious instance of trying to avoid the violence of claim-jumping. In Utah, settlers arrived twenty-two years before the land office and were openly worried about their legal position. Brigham Young once threatened, "If they jump my claim here, I shall be very apt to give them a preemption right that will last them to the last resurrection."[13]

State land offices of the public domain states will not be described here. These states received title to large acreage from the federal government and in turn sold or leased it to individuals. These records are in state land offices and archives. If you suspect that your ancestor had land dealings with a state, you can write either the state archive or the state secretary of state's office and ask where the records are. In many states, they are still held by the equivalent of a state land commissioner or by a state land board (as in Colorado).

Private Land Claims

There was a special type of federal land grant called the private land claim, wherein the American government recognized as valid certain land grants made by the earlier French, Spanish, and British governments in areas acquired by the United States after the American Revolution. These areas were the Old Northwest north of the Ohio River, the Gulf states from Florida to Louisiana, the tier of states on the west bank of the Mississippi, and the Spanish Southwest from New Mexico to California but not including Texas.

Sometimes the foreign legal titles were quite old and meticulously documented; often they were vague claims without clear bounds. Near villages it was common to find communal fields divided into long, individually owned arable strips surrounded by a communally maintained fence. Also characteristic, though not universal, were the "long lots"—narrow, adjoining tracts, each a few hundred feet wide, along a road or

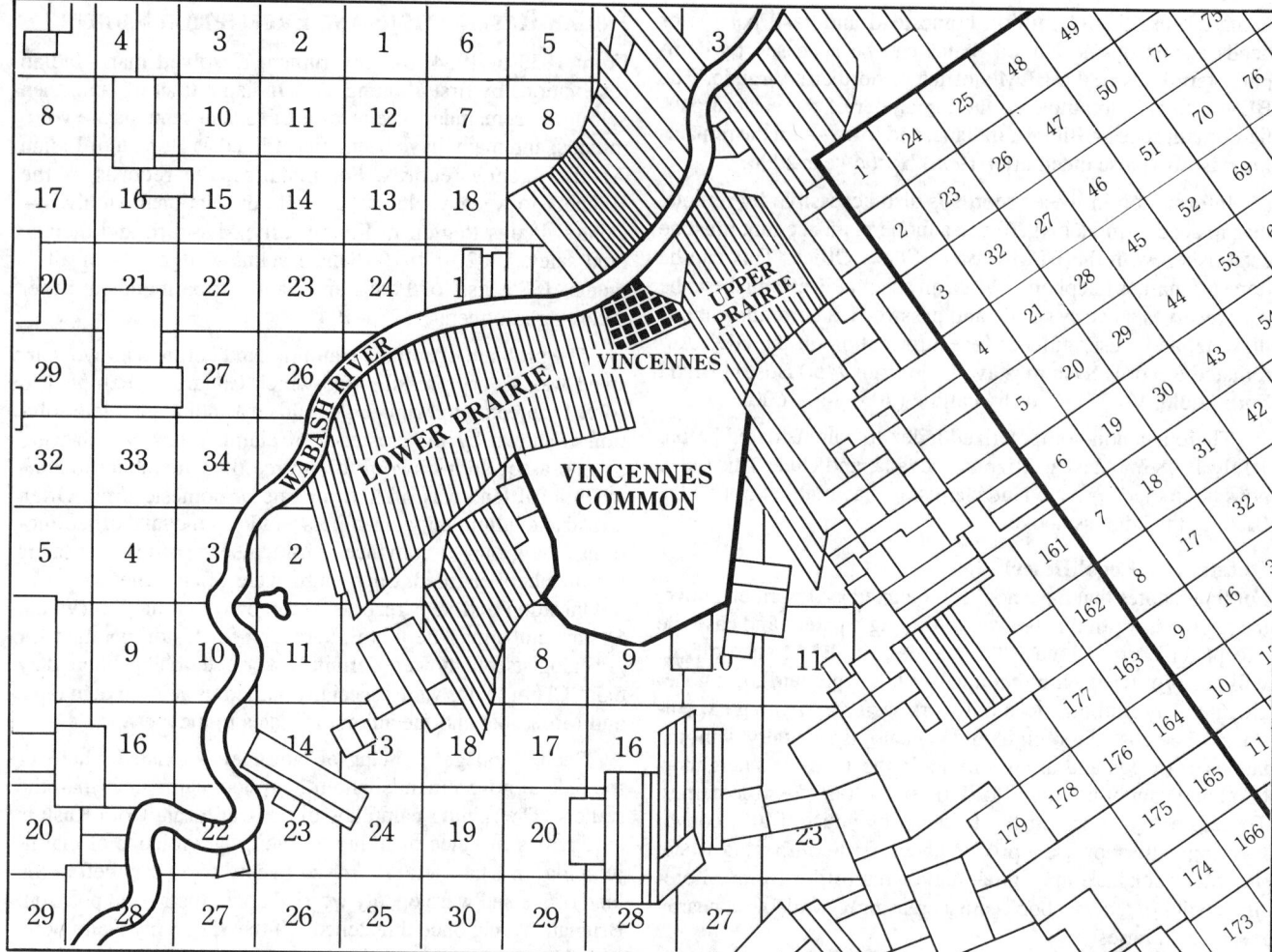

Figure 8-7. Private land claims surveyed within the federal township and range system in Vincennes, Indiana. Adapted from Leonard Lux, *The Vincennes Donation Lands* (Indianapolis: Indiana Historical Society, 1949), map in pocket.

river and each running far back into the woods or prairie—sometimes a mile or more. The French and Spanish authorities also made larger grants, such as the square leagues common in Texas and the rancheros in California. Barring the usual losses, the Spanish and French administrations usually kept adequate records, and land titles were recorded and preserved. The Texas General Land Office today has a series of sixty-nine volumes of Spanish and Mexican records. (See chapter 16 for a discussion of Hispanic records.) The Spanish land system is discussed in detail for Texas, New Mexico (with Colorado), Arizona, and California in Henry Putney Beers, *Spanish & Mexican Records of the American Southwest: A Bibliographical Guide to Archive and Manuscript Sources* (Tucson: University of Arizona Press and the Tucson Corral of the Westerners, 1979), 44–60, 141–56, 247–68, 328–39.

When the U.S. government assumed control of areas containing Spanish and French grants, it had to create private land claims commissions to separate the authentic and legal titles from the fraudulent and dubious. (It is said that nine hundred Kaskaskia, Illinois, claims were perjured.[14]) By international law, the new government was obliged to recognize the valid property titles of the previous regime.

The private land claims ruled valid by the claims commissions of the U.S. state and federal courts are first-title deeds

surveyed outside the regular federal system of townships and ranges. For example, on figure 8-7, a survey of Vincennes, Indiana, the federal survey lines stop at the irregular lots and tracts of the private land claims of the old French outpost called Vincennes Common. Even today, the legal titles run back to the confirmed first-title patents of the Vincennes private claims validated by the governor of the Northwest Territory, as directed by a Congressional resolution of 1788. The legal description of this land is not in terms of sections, townships, and ranges, but in terms of the lot numbers the governor assigned to the validated and surveyed private land claims at Vincennes. The general system of private land claims, however, did not always run smoothly. Some perfectly good pre-American titles were not presented to claims commissions, engendering litigation much later.

"Private land claims" can also refer to the claims directly presented to Congress for private relief. These papers could be in different archives, depending on the administrative route taken. Claims to 1837 are recorded in U.S. Congress, *The American State Papers, Class VIII, Public Lands* and *The American State Papers, Class IX, Claims* (Washington, D.C.: Gales and Seaton, 1832–61. Reprint. Greenville, S.C.: Southern Historical Press), and are indexed in Phillip W. McMullin, *Grassroots of America* (Reprint. Greenville, S.C.: Southern Historical Press,

1994). The National Archives has congressional records, case files, and plat maps of private claims. According to the *Guide to Genealogical Research in the National Archives:*

> Originals of the committee reports to Congress on private land claims are among Records of the U.S. Senate, Record Group 46, and Records of the U.S. House of Representatives, Record Group 233. They are filed by Congress, thereunder by name of committee, and thereunder chronologically.

Committee reports on individual land claims considered from 1826 to 1876 by the two congressional committees on private land claims are collected and published in *Reports of the Committees on Private Land Claims of the Senate and House of Representatives,* 2 vols. (45th Cong., 3d sess. Misc. Doc. 81, serial 1836). Each volume is indexed by name of claimant or subject, but many names are omitted. There is also an "Index to Reports of Committee on Private Land Claims, House of Representatives" on pages 5–20 of *House Index to Committee Reports* by T.H. McKee (Y1.3:C73/2). The Congressional Serial Set provides digested summaries and alphabetical lists of private claims presented to the U.S. Congress from the 1st to 51st Congress (1789–1891).[15]

Table 25 in the *Guide* shows which congressional documents list private claims brought before Congress. Major university libraries and other large research libraries are usually repositories for such government publications, and many of the early publications have been microfilmed.

Private land claims are also found in various court records, because disapproved claims could be taken to court. In fact, Congress, in abolishing particular claims commissions, routinely authorized the holders of unsettled claims to prosecute their cases through the courts.

For further reading, see Paul W. Gates, *History of Public Land Law Development* (Washington, D.C.: Public Land Law Review Commission, 1968), 87–119; his "Private Land Claims in the South," *Journal of Southern History* 22 (1956): 183–204; Louis Pelzer, "The Private Land Claims of the Old Northwest Territory," *Iowa Journal of History and Politics* 12 (1914): 363–93; T.P. Martin, "The Confirmation of French and Spanish Land Titles in the Louisiana Purchase" (M.A. thesis, University of California, Berkeley, 1914); Lemont K. Richardson, "Private Land Claims in Missouri," *Missouri Historical Review* 50 (1955–56): 132–44, 271–86, 387–99; Clark S. Knowlton, ed., "Spanish and Mexican Land Grants in the Southwest: A Symposium," *Social Science Journal* 13 (October 1976): 1–63.

MILITARY BOUNTY LAND

The granting of military bounty land in the United States to encourage enlistments or reward previous service began in colonial times, but its legislative heyday was from 1788 to 1855, though claims were still being received by the federal government in the 1960s. Genealogists find bounty-land records especially attractive because they serve the dual role of locating persons in time and place and of proving military service. Applications sometimes contain a wealth of information, especially when heirs claimed lands.

Colonial legislatures gave land for military service, such as for the Narragansett campaign of King Philip's War, 1675 to 1676, but these were mostly private acts passed to reward meritorious service to the colony. In 1701, Virginia passed an act promising two hundred acres free of quitrents for twenty years to those who would make armed settlements on the Indian frontier. The Crown's proclamation of 1763 ordered the colonies to give bounty land for service in the French and Indian War to "reduced" (indigent) officers and to British Army privates mustered out in the colonies who intended to remain there. This did not include militia units. In 1776, Congress promised so-called "Hessian deserters" fifty acres but had few takers. Also in 1776, Congress promised bounty land to soldiers of the Continental line, with privates and noncommissioned officers to get one hundred acres, captains three hundred acres, and other ranks various amounts. States that likewise promised or afterwards gave bounty lands were Connecticut, Massachusetts (with Maine), New York, Pennsylvania, Maryland, Virginia, the Carolinas, and Georgia. Lloyd D. Bockstruck, *Revolutionary War Bounty Land Grants Awarded by State Governments* (Baltimore: Genealogical Publishing Co., 1996), is a master index to approximately 35,000 persons named in the grants from these nine states. The states that did not give revolutionary war bounty lands were New Hampshire, Rhode island, Connecticut, New Jersey, and Delaware.

North Carolina was the most generous, giving 640 acres (a square mile) to a private in the Continental line. Maryland gave the smallest amount, fifty acres to a private, but the state had very little western land to give. Figure 8-8 and table 8-1 show the locations of the military reserves and the acreage for each rank for each state and the federal government. Massachusetts grants were in Maine but were in no specific reserve. Privates who got a one hundred-acre warrant from the federal government were not eligible for a Massachusetts state grant. Soldiers of the Continental line from other states could take both the federal and their state land bounties. (See the state summaries at the end of this chapter for brief references to bounty-land records. For Massachusetts, see Maine.) Paul Gates, *History of Public Land Law Development,* discusses aspects of various state grants. Gates states, without elaborating, that Connecticut gave bounty land; but this seems to refer to the Fire Lands in Ohio granted to individuals burned out in the revolution rather than to grants to soldiers.[16] Virginia is discussed below because its bounty-land records are widely scattered; some are in the National Archives.

Congress was slow to redeem its promise of land for its soldiers. In 1788, it directed that bounty-land warrants be issued to those applying. But the U.S. Military District in Ohio, the only federal lands where federal revolutionary warrants could be used until 1830, did not open until 1796—a full fifteen years after victory at Yorktown. A planned second federal reserve at the southern end of Illinois was not created; instead, the district in Ohio was enlarged. The Ohio Company and John Cleves Symmes in 1787 and 1788 had purchased millions of Ohio acres on credit from Congress and were permitted to pay one-seventh of the price in federal bounty-land warrants. Therefore, land offices of the two speculations accepted some federal warrants, the earliest locales where they could be used. Congress also created three military reserves for veterans of the War of 1812, but there were no federal reserves after these three in Illinois, Arkansas, and Missouri. Warrants usable in the Virginia and U.S. military districts in Ohio were made redeemable by scrip acts in 1830 and 1832, respectively, in any

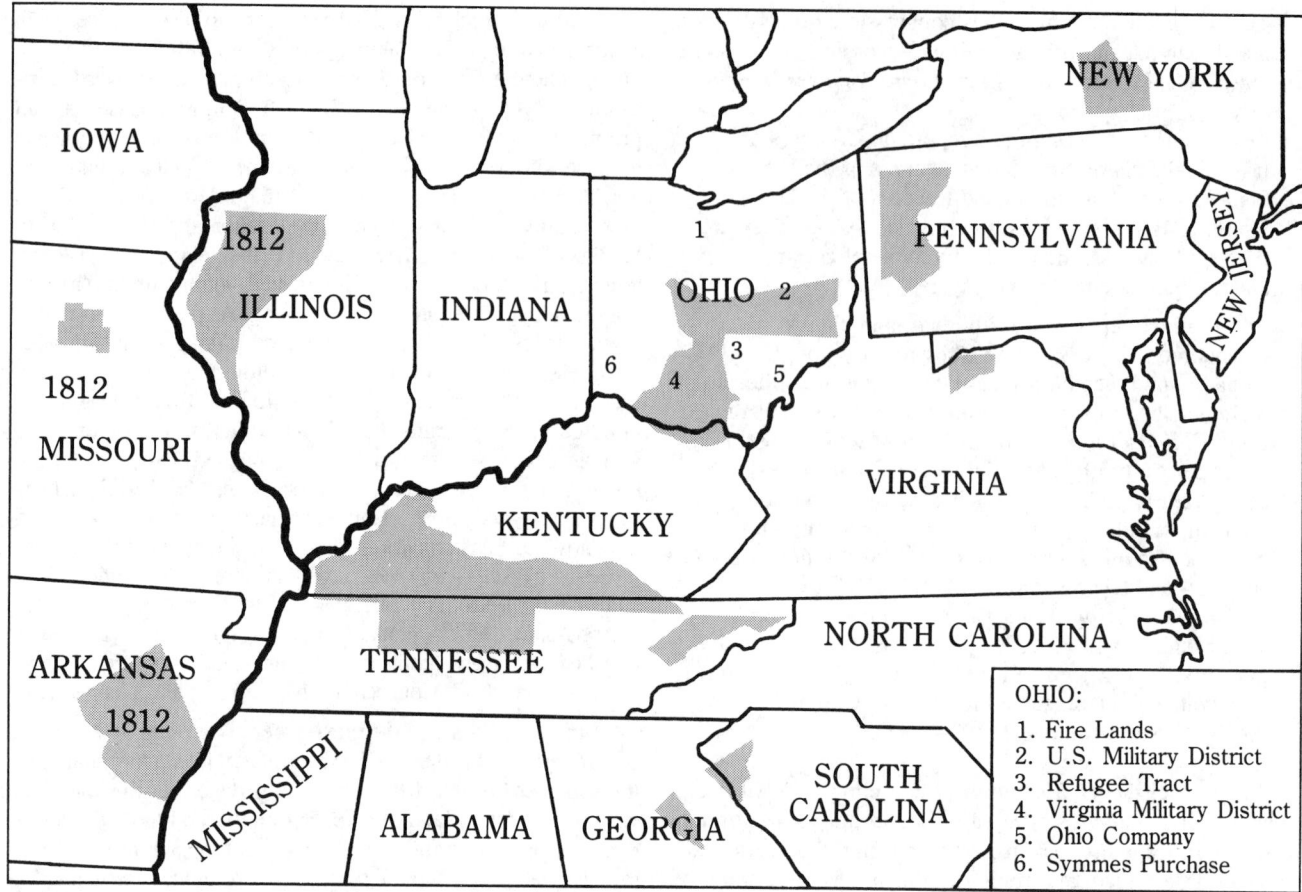

Figure 8-8. Federal and state military land reserves for veterans of the revolutionary war and the War of 1812.

GLO land offices in Ohio, Indiana, and Illinois. In 1842, all federal bounty-land warrants were made good for purchases at any GLO land office.

The 1788 act stipulated that warrants were assignable, meaning the soldier could sell his warrant and not wait to take the land. This created an instant market in bounty warrants and allowed land speculators to accumulate large quantities of warrants and land. Paul Gates shows that less than one soldier (or his heirs) in ten got land by using his warrant under any federal bounty-land act. Because few soldiers actually used their warrants to patent land, patents and land-entry case files are much less valuable than the warrants and the warrant applications for locating a soldier's military service. Most soldiers sold their rights, using the back of the warrant to assign it to the buyer, who might in turn assign the warrant to another buyer. Sometimes the assignment left the buyer's name blank, to be filled in by the last purchaser. The warrant certificates issued to Mexican War veterans were folios, with the insides and back unprinted so they could be used for assignments.

The warrant market was big business, especially when warrants were no longer restricted to military reserve lands. Major brokerage firms dealt extensively in warrants, buying in the eastern states and selling to western land brokers and settlers. Financial newspapers in the boom years of the 1850s frequently carried price quotations. The government set a price ceiling from 1820 by charging a flat $1.25 per acre for most of its lands. The average market price peaked at about $1.20 an acre in 1854–55 for 160-acre warrants, just before the market

was flooded by the act of 1855.[17] More warrants were used in Iowa than in any other state, and it is estimated that half of Iowa was purchased with bounty-land warrants.

The federal government gave no bounty land for service after 1855, but Union veterans of the Civil War received special homestead rights: in 1870, the right to claim 160 acres within railroad grant areas (other homesteaders got only 80), and in 1872, the right to deduct the length of their war service from the five-year residency needed to prove a homestead.

To get a federal bounty-land warrant it was necessary, under any act from 1788 to 1855, for the soldier or heirs to apply. The warrant applications are in Record Group 15 in the Military Service Records section of the National Archives. The surrendered warrants (those used to obtain land) are in land-entry case files of the patentees in Record Group 49 in the National Records Center, Suitland, Maryland. The case file categories are briefly described in Harry P. Yoshpe and Philip P. Brower, *Preliminary Inventory of the Land-Entry Papers of the General Land Office* (cited earlier), pp. 7–9, known as Inventory No. 22. The patents, obtained by using land warrants, were like any other GLO patents. The official copies are in the Eastern States Office of the BLM in Springfield, Virginia. In seeking the various records related to a federal bounty-land warrant, the researcher should try to learn the warrant number, the acreage claimed, and the act used—for example, warrant no. 8256, forty acres, act of 1852. This information could be unnecessary because the National Archives may handle the searching, but having it in full or in part allows for more precise re-

Table 8-1. Federal and State Bounty-Land Acreage, Revolutionary War

Rank	U.S.	Georgia	Maryland	Massachusetts	New York	North Carolina	Pennsylvania	South Carolina	Virginia
Major General	1,100	—	50	100	5,500	—	25,000+	2,000	100	15,000
Brigadier General	850	1,955	50	100	4,250	—	12,000	1,500	100	10,000
Colonel	500	1,150	50	100	2,500	2,000	7,200	1,000	100	6,667
Lieutenant Colonel	450	1,035	50	100	2,250	2,000	5,760	800	100	6,000
Major	400	920	50	100	2,000	2,000	4,800	600	100	5,333
Captain	300	575–690	50	100	1,500	1,500	3,840	500	100	4,000
Lieutenant	200	460	50	100	1,000	1,000	2,560	400	100	2,666
Ensign	150	460	50	100	1,000	1,000	2,560	300	100	2,666
Noncommissioned Officers	100	345	50	100	500	500	1,000	250	100	200–400
Private	100	230–287½	50	100	500	500	640	200	100	100–300

quests, thereby increasing the chances of success. The best source is the bounty-land application files.

The following summary of the various warrant acts is from Inventory No. 22, to which explanatory remarks are added. The number of warrants issued gives the researcher an idea of how many soldiers or their heirs applied under each act. Reference citations are to the respective acts of Congress. (Citation 2 *Stat.* 236 means volume 2 of *U.S. Statutes at Large*, p. 236. M804 means National Archives microfilm publication M804.)

1. Revolutionary War Warrants in the U.S. Military District in Ohio

9 July 1788	Continental Congress *Journals* 34: 307	#1–14220
16 March 1803	2 *Stat.* 236	1–272
15 April 1806	2 *Stat.* 378	273–2500

Initially, these assignable warrants were redeemable only for land in the U.S. Military District in Ohio. Privates and non-commissioned officers of the Continental line from any state received 100 acres, ensigns 150, lieutenants 200, captains 300, majors 400, lieutenant colonels 450, colonels 500, brigadier generals 850, and major colonels 1,100. The initial minimum grants in the district were for quarter townships of the five-mile dimensions—i.e., five miles to a side or 16,000 acres, thereby requiring warrantees to band together through an agent to reach 4,000 acres or sell out to get some value from their warrants. By 1800, lots as small as one hundred acres were available. In 1832, entries in the district were ended, and those still holding warrants were allowed to trade them for scrip negotiable at GLO land offices in Ohio, Indiana, and Illinois. From 1842, such scrip was accepted at any GLO land office.

Many warrant application files for the 1788 act have been destroyed. Where the warrantee's name is known, a substitute card was made with the note "no papers." These cards and the surviving application files are interfiled with the surviving revolutionary war pension files, all microfilmed on M804, *Revolutionary War Pension and Bounty-Land Warrant Application Files,* in 2,670 rolls. This series is indexed for pensions and warrantees in National Genea-

logical Society, *Index of Revolutionary War Pension Applications in the National Archives* (Washington, D.C.: National Genealogical Society, 1976).

To aid soldiers who had not met the deadline of the 1788 act, Congress passed a time extension in 1803 that was amended in 1806. The warrants of these acts are numbered in one sequence. Nearly all surrendered warrants, from numbers 1–6912 of the 1788 act, were destroyed. Surviving surrendered warrants of the 1788, 1803, and 1806 acts are filed in land-entry case files and are on M829, *U.S. Revolutionary War Bounty Land Warrants Used in the U.S. Military District of Ohio and Related Papers (Acts of 1788, 1803, 1806),* in sixteen rolls. Since patents were rarely placed in the case files, the U.S. Military District land-entry case files usually contain only the surrendered warrant. The files were microfilmed sequentially, and missing warrants were either lost, misplaced, or never surrendered for land. The few surrendered for scrip under the 1832 and later acts are in that series, but they are cross-referenced on M829. On roll 1 of M829 are two ledgers indexed in Smith's *Federal Land Series*, vol. 2, once used to record the issuance of warrants. Roll 1 of M829 also has indexes to the ledgers done and/or microfilmed by the National Archives. The pamphlet accompanying M829 describes these records and is available upon request from the National Archives.

2. War of 1812 Warrants in U.S. Military Districts in Illinois, Arkansas, and Missouri

24 Dec. 1811	2 *Stat.* 669	
11 Jan. 1812	2 *Stat.* 672	#1–28085 for 160 acres
6 May 1812	2 *Stat.* 729	
27 July 1842	5 *Stat.* 497	
10 Dec. 1814	3 *Stat.* 147	1–1101 for 320 acres

The acts of 1811 and 1812 promised 160 acres to privates and non-commissioned officers who enlisted in regiments raised by Congress and who served for five years, unless discharged sooner or killed. The 1814 act doubled the acreage for those who enlisted after 10 December 1814. Officers were given no bounty lands until the acts of 1850 to 1855. The warrants were not legally assignable except by inheritance, and the GLO retained the warrant certificates, issuing the veteran a certificate of notification. These warrants were redeemable only in military reserves in Illinois, Arkansas, and Missouri until the act of 1842 made them redeemable at any GLO land office. The warrants became legally assignable in 1852.

These War of 1812 warrants, preserved mostly in bound volumes, are on M848, *War of 1812 Military Bounty Land Warrants 1815–1858,* in fourteen rolls. Patentees in the Arkansas and Missouri reserves are indexed on roll 1, as are Illinois patentees with surnames beginning with C and D. The Illinois State Archives' computer index, referenced under Illinois, following, which records almost all original public domain sales, should include the military reserve. Because War of 1812 warrants were not legally assignable until 1852, the patent indexes should serve as indexes to prior warrantees, though Gates shows that the land speculators got large parts of the reserves, presumably by having the patents processed in the names of the warrantees. This means many veterans patented land they probably never saw. The pamphlet accompanying M848 describes these records and is available upon request from the National Archives. Aside from these microfilmed warrants, there should also be unmicrofilmed warrant application files and land-entry case files in Record Groups 15 and 49, respectively.

3. Applications for Bounty-Land Scrip

30 May 1830	4 *Stat.* 422	#1–1994
13 July 1832	4 *Stat.* 578	
2 March 1833	4 *Stat.* 665	1–225
3 March 1835	4 *Stat.* 770	1–970
31 Aug. 1852	10 *Stat.* 143	1–1689

The land available for patenting in the Virginia and U.S. military districts ran out long before all the outstanding warrants were redeemed, so Congress issued scrip for the remaining warrants. At first good only in GLO land offices in Ohio, Indiana, and Illinois, the scrip, printed in acreage denominations, was good at any GLO land office from 1842.

4. Mexican War Bounty-Land Warrants

11 Feb. 1847 9 *Stat.* 125 —— #1–7585 for 40 acres
1–80689 for 160 acres

Congress, in the Mexican War, authorized ten regiments and offered privates and non-commissioned officers (but not officers) 160 acres for serving one year or more and 40 acres for serving less than a year. Alternately, the veteran could apply for $100 or $25 in scrip at six percent interest, acceptable for any payment due to the U.S. government. (This dollar scrip was different from the acreage scrip mentioned in entry 3 above.) There were no military districts created for Mexican War bounty land, the warrants being redeemable at any GLO land office. They were assignable. As usual, few warrantees or their heirs actually patented land using their warrants. The surrendered warrants are in the land-entry case files of the patentees. The best finding aid to Mexican War warrantees is their warrant application files.

5. The Acts of 1850–1855

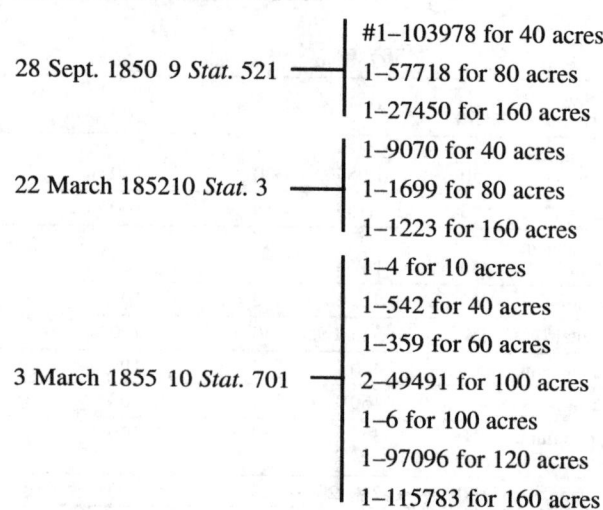

28 Sept. 1850 9 *Stat.* 521 —— #1–103978 for 40 acres
1–57718 for 80 acres
1–27450 for 160 acres

22 March 1852 10 *Stat.* 3 —— 1–9070 for 40 acres
1–1699 for 80 acres
1–1223 for 160 acres

3 March 1855 10 *Stat.* 701 —— 1–4 for 10 acres
1–542 for 40 acres
1–359 for 60 acres
2–49491 for 100 acres
1–6 for 100 acres
1–97096 for 120 acres
1–115783 for 160 acres

The acts of 1850 to 1855 were not to encourage enlistments but to reward former service. The act of 1850 extended bounty land to officers and enlisted men who had not previously received land and who had served in any war since 1790, including the Indian wars. Nine month's service brought 160 acres, four months' service 80 acres, and one month's service 40 acres. Since there was initial confusion over whether the act made warrants assignable, the GLO commissioner later ruled that it did not. The act of 1852 explicitly made them assignable and extended the 1850 act to militiamen who served after 1812.

The 1855 act extended bounty-land privileges even further by making 160 acres the minimum entitlement and reducing service to fourteen days or even less. Those who traveled 1,200 miles in service were eligible even if they served less time. A veteran or his heirs who had previously received fewer than 160 acres could apply for the balance. Eligibility was extended to chaplains, wagon masters, militia rangers, and volunteers of certain campaigns such as Kings Mountain, the Nickojack Campaign in Tennessee, and the Cook County volunteers in the Black Hawk War. An act of 14 May 1856 extended the 1855 benefits to naval veterans and any revolutionary war service.

Using these figures as given by Inventory No. 22 and omitting scrip because it redeemed already issued warrants, the warrant totals issued by these categories of acts are:

Revolutionary war	16,720
War of 1812	29,186
Mexican War	88,274
Acts of 1850 to 1855	464,419
Total	598,599

Considering that 77.6 percent of these bounty-land warrants are in the miscellaneous categories of the 1850 to 1855 acts and that each warrant should have an application file with the veteran's documentation of service of kin documenting their relationship to him, how do genealogists locate what they need?

National Archives Trust Fund (NATF) Form 80 should be used to request pre–World War I pension and military service records and pre-1856 bounty-land warrant application files. The cost will be listed on the form. If the requester has: (1) such definite information as service in a specific war or unit, (2) a soldier of uncommon name, or (3) extensive background information on the person sought, there should be few unanticipated problems. But many requests are "fishing expeditions" with little background identification on men with ordinary names, or the genealogist attempts to compile branches of a large family by plowing page-by-page through collections. It is difficult to see how these problems can be solved comprehensively by mail with much confidence. In such cases, a personal search or the services of an agent already in Washington, D.C., should be considered.

A special problem is fraudulent warrant applications, especially where heirs claimed a soldier's rights. Mrs. Ellen Reed and her two children received bounty-land warrant no. 61,656 in 1849 for the Mexican War service of Richard Reed, private, Company D, First U.S. Artillery Regiment. Two months later, Richard's mother applied as his next of kin and showed that, on his supposed marriage day in Mississippi, he was fishing on the Kennebec in Maine. Ellen's warrant was canceled and a new one issued to the mother.[18] This problem of potential fraud is large enough to be a major contaminant. Gates notes 59,190 warrants for which caveats against delivery had been filed by 1856, thus suspecting further action on patenting.[19] Why waste research time worrying about such obscure points? Double and triple proofs and forays into collateral lines may seem like expensive overkill, but experienced researchers know that solutions often come from unpredictable quarters.

For example, bounty-land eligibility for service in the War of 1812 was first limited to able-bodied enlisted men age eighteen to forty-five. Mrs. Abigail O'Flyng's husband and three sons had served. Two sons had been killed, yet none of the four was eligible for bounty land. Her husband had been over forty-five, one son was under eighteen, and the two dead sons had been promoted to officers just before they died. The Abigail O'Flyng Act of 1816 ended the age restrictions and allowed enlisted men promoted to officers to receive land. Also, by private act of Congress, her husband received 480 acres, the youngest son 160 acres, and the heirs of the dead sons their half pay for five years.[20]

Such a case tests a genealogist's expertise. Does he or she understand the scope and intent of the record group searched? Nearly all government records—federal, state, and local—are created as a result of statutes that should be read. Would a check of bounty-land applications filed have "proved" that none of the four O'Flyng men served in the war? Have unlikely records, such as private acts of Congress, been searched? Has the researcher screened other records many years later in which some legal actions resurface?

This last question is not rhetorical. Col. Robert Porterfield was killed in the revolution. His son Robert received from Congress a warrant for "about 6,000 acres." But the land was in Kentucky and from superior conflicting claims was lost. In 1860, Congress authorized scrip for Robert's heirs, to whom 153 warrants for forty acres each were issued. In 1900, twenty-one of these warrants were still outstanding and unlocated for land given on revolutionary war service.[21]

For background on bounty lands, see National Archives, *Guide to Genealogical Research in the National Archives* (Washington, D.C.: National Archives and Records Service,

1982), 133–39; Rudolf Freund, "Military Bounty Land and the Origins of the Public Domain," *Agricultural History* 20 (1946): 8–18; Paul Gates, "Military Bounty Land Policies," in *History of the Public Land Law Development* (Washington, D.C.: Public Land Law Review Commission, 1968), 249–84; C. Lichtenberg, "Beginnings of the United States Military Land Bounty Policy, 1637–1812" (M.A. thesis, University of Wisconsin, 1945); Paul V. Lutz, "Land Grants for Service in the Revolution," *New York Historical Society Quarterly* 48 (1964): 221–35; Jean H. Vivian, "Military Land Bounties During the Revolutionary and Confederation Periods," *Maryland Historical Magazine* 61 (1966): 231–56; A.M. Lingegren, "The History of the Land Bonus of the War of 1812" (M.A. thesis, University of Wisconsin, 1922); James W. Oberly, "Military Bounty Land Warrants of the Mexican War," *Prologue* 14 (1982): 25–34; and Oberly, *Sixty Million Acres: American Veterans and the Public Lands Before the Civil War* (Kent, Ohio: Kent State University Press, 1990).

VIRGINIA MILITARY DISTRICT

An extraordinary flood of revolutionary war bounty-land warrants poured from Richmond, partly because Virginia had the largest state population and partly because it granted warrants not only to its Continental line but to its state line as well. The distinction rests on who paid the soldiers—Congress or Virginia.

The first military reserve was created south of Green River in Kentucky and subsequently expanded west of the Tennessee. There were no bounty lands within present-day Virginia or West Virginia. In 1784, Virginia ceded its claim to the area north of the Ohio River, reserving the 4 million acres between the Scioto and Little Miami rivers for redemption of its bounty-land warrants. This Virginia Military District in Ohio was federal land for which first-title land grants were reserved solely for the Virginia warrants of veterans of the continental line. A series of ever more liberal acts broadened where warrants could be used and by whom until, in 1852, Congress agreed that all Virginia revolutionary war warrants could be exchanged for scrip accepted at any GLO land office. Large numbers of these assignable warrants were sold; an estimated one-quarter of the Virginia Military District was acquired by twenty-five men.[22]

The paperwork flow was: (1) warrant application to Richmond, (2) warrant issued to warrantee; (3) selection of desired land in Kentucky or Ohio reserves and survey by official surveyor; (4) paperwork for Kentucky lands to the Virginia Land Office or, from 1792, the Kentucky Land Office, or the federal capital for Ohio lands; and (5) patent for Kentucky land sent to patentee or federal patent sent to Richmond for relay to Ohio patentee.[23]

Thus, there should be four major repositories today for Virginia bounty-land records. There are, however, actually six. The land offices of Virginia, Kentucky, and Ohio are described in the state summaries at the end of this chapter. The microfilmed federal patents are in the BLM Eastern States Office in Springfield, Virginia. The surrendered warrants are in Record Group 49 at the Textural Reference Branch in Washington, D.C. The sixth major collection is the Illinois Historical Survey Collection in the University of Illinois Library, Urbana-Champaign, which has the papers of Richard Clough Anderson, surveyor of the Virginia Military District in Ohio. Clifford Neal Smith has brought this collection to the attention of a wide audience by his indexes in the *Federal Land Series*, especially vol. 4, which is devoted to the district. He estimated that "about 64 percent of Virginia's obligations to its veterans were satisfied by the land grants in the Virginia Military District of Ohio."[24]

Also see Clifford Neal Smith, "Virginia Land Grants in Kentucky and Ohio, 1784–1799," *National Genealogical Society Quarterly* 61 (1973): 16–27; John Salmon, "Revolutionary War Records in the Archives & Records Division of the Virginia State Library," *Genealogy* no. 70 (July 1982): 2–10; Gaius Marcus Brumbaugh, *Revolutionary War Records . . . Virginia Army and Navy Forces With Bounty Land Warrants for Virginia Military Scrip; From Federal and State Archives* (Washington, D.C.: 1936); Willard Rouse Jillson, *Old Kentucky Entries and Deeds: A Complete Index to All of the Earliest Land Entries, Military Warrants, Deeds and Wills of the Commonwealth of Kentucky*, Filson Club Publication No. 34 (Reprint. Baltimore: Genealogical Publishing Co., 1971).

LOYALIST LANDS

The confiscation of Loyalist lands in the revolution—what might be called "negative bounty land"—is a subject that deserves both extended research and a bibliographical source essay. Below is a brief discussion.

The British government made a commendable effort to compensate Loyalist losses, and Loyalists had to list their lost property to claim that compensation. One of the best sources is Alexander Fraser, ed., *United Empire Loyalists Inquiry into the Losses of Services in Consequence of Their Loyalty. Evidence in the Canadian Claims*, 2 vols. (Toronto: The King's Printer, 1905), Second Report of the Bureau of Archives for the Province of Ontario. From this excellent source book comes the example of John Fowler. The claim (p. 293) of Fowler, formerly of Stockbridge, Massachusetts, indicates he was a native of Guilford, Connecticut, lived in Stockbridge, fled to New York during the war and hired a farm on Long Island, was carried a prisoner to Stamford, Connecticut, and ultimately settled in Kingston, Ontario. "Produces deed dated 19th July, 1770, whereby Mark Hopkins in considn. of £30 lawful Conveys to Claimt. forty acres in Stockbridge. Says he purchased 35 acres adjoining, from his Br., in 1770 for about £25," and so on. "Produces a letter from his Father in Law saying that his Personal Property had been sold to the amount of £100 Lawful." Aside from separating the various John Fowlers, this record helps fill a page in the Fowler family genealogy.

Such claims name only a small percentage of Loyalists. Two New Jersey studies revealed that of 275 known Loyalists of Bergen County, only twenty-nine claims could be found, while for the approximately 1,200 estates confiscated in New Jersey, there exist only 239 Loyalist claims.[25]

The official files of Loyalist claims are in the Public Record Office in London, partly summarized in Peter Wilson Coldham, *American Loyalist Claims: Abstracted from the Public Record Office, Audit Series 13, Bundles 1–35 & 37* (Washington, D.C.: National Genealogical Society, 1980). The manuscript sources are identified in Gregory Palmer, ed., *A Bibliography of Loyalist Source Material in the United States, Canada, and Great Britain* (Westport and London: Meckler Publishing and the American Antiquarian Society, 1982), a helpful book but one intended for experts. Another bibliography which is useful but which may be hard to find is Robert S. Allen, *Loyalist Literature: An Annotated Bibliographic Guide to the Writings on the Loyalists of the American Revolution* (Toronto and Charlottetown: Dundurn Press, 1982). There is no comprehensive bibliography to literature on the confiscation of Loyalist estates. (Also see chapter 9, Research in Military Records.)

One land record of potential help in identifying children is the land given in Canada and Nova Scotia to Loyalists under royal instructions of 1783, which promised one hundred acres to heads of Loyalist families and fifty acres each to their children and to single men.

TAXES

Things taxed have included carriages and watches, windows and whiskey, land and slaves. Taxes on documents and tea helped start a war. Arkansas Territory's sudden tax on bounty lands in the 1820s was enacted and due before the news had time to reach out-of-state owners, permitting the quick seizure and sale of "delinquent" lands. As this variety suggests, name lists of such taxes must be used with a cautious understanding of who should be on the list and who should not.

Colonial and antebellum counties and towns usually taxed free adult males a set, uniform amount called the poll (head, capitation) tax, which became due when a young man reached age twenty-one (sixteen or eighteen in some areas) and ceased to be due when a man reached some age, such as fifty or sixty. Searching a series of such annual tax lists can locate sons coming of age. Sometimes the law made a father liable for a head tax for sons sixteen to twenty so that sons first moved through the yearly tax lists as unnamed tallies under their father's name. The great failing of the system is that it seldom works for women, who were usually not subject to such a poll tax but who might own and be taxed for land. North Carolina illustrates the variability of the poll tax ages. In colonial years, it set the white male poll at ages sixteen and upward, changed it to twenty-one and upward from the revolution, exempted men over fifty from 1801, made it twenty-one to forty-four beginning in 1835, and from 1868 laid the poll tax on males between twenty-one and fifty.[26] The wary researcher must be aware of these shifting limits.

However, for all their limitations, poll tax lists can be combined with property tax lists as a substitute census. To identify clearly who owed what, clerks sometimes added useful descriptors. For example, the 1799 list for Warren County, Kentucky, has John Taylor Slick, John Taylor Cooksland, John Taylor gambler, John Taylor one eye, and John Taylor hatter.[27] The first two mean "on Salt Lick Creek" and "on land owned by Cook." A long series of such county tax lists can be crucial to identifying men with common names and showing when men entered and left the county, though lists often omit a man for a year or two when he is obviously still living on the same land. This means researchers should read at least eight years before and after a man first appears and disappears.

Names are often listed in initial order, meaning all surnames beginning with *A* are grouped together—but not alphabetically. Apparently, clerks received tax lists from various justices of the peace, constables, or militia captains and copied from each list first all the *A* surnames, then all the *B* surnames, etc. While some of the neighborhood proximities are lost, initial name order lists are easy to search for one surname. Researchers should always check the end of the county list, where the clerk would often add the names of the late, delinquent, and insolvent.

Other typical omissions are children, slaves and indentured servants (except as unnamed but taxed property), landless men over the poll tax age, paupers, ministers, justices of the peace, militia officers, tax assessors, and men granted exemption for whatever reason. An Indiana statute of 1826 exempted "all persons who had served in the land or naval service of the United States, during the Revolutionary War, from the payment of a poll tax, and a tax upon personal property" if the veteran gave an affidavit to a justice of the peace.[28] There are also, inevitably, those who were overlooked.

Original lists as received by the clerk survive for 1771 Bute County, North Carolina, and have been compared to the final county-wide copy.[29] On the left are nine adjoining entries of a local list compared with the poll entries on the right of the final county list (in initial order of the original):

Local List	County List With Polls	
Joshua Taylor	not listed	
John Linch Jr.	John Lynch Jr.	1
John Faulcon, Henry Brown	John Falcon	2
John Baxter, John Weedon, Sharp Balthrop (& 1 sl.)	John Baxter	4
Rossen Allen, Drury Allen	Rossen Allan	2
Geo. Elliott Sr., Wm Stevenson (& 7 sl.)	George Elliott	9
James Elliott, Thos. Rosser	James Elliott	2
Richd. Towns	Richard Town	1
David Towns, sons David & John	David Towns	3

Obviously, the final county list has significantly fewer names. It is surprising that so many of the hidden surnames differ from that of the head of the household.

Several reconstituted state "censuses" have been compiled from county tax lists, such as the substitute for 1790 Kentucky and 1840 Texas "censuses." They can be great time-savers in localizing a man's state residence, but calling these reconstitutions "censuses" runs counter to the need of researchers to understand the nature of their sources. The 1790 federal census attempted to record everyone under some head of household. The 1790 Kentucky tax lists did not. Thus, the 1790 reconstituted Kentucky census cannot completely replace the lost 1790 Kentucky census schedules.

One great advantage of the county tax lists is that many states also received and stored copies. Thus, when the records of Buckingham County, Virginia, were destroyed by fire, its main surviving records became the yearly tax lists in Richmond.

The quitrent was a land tax typical of colonies from New York south; New Englanders took pride in being free of this remnant of feudal dues. In English manorial society the land obligations due the manor, such as plowing and haying the lord's land, were commuted to an annual money payment. Upon payment, the obligations were "quit" for the year. Land patents in New York and colonies to the south stipulated a yearly quitrent

that went either to the crown, as in Virginia south of the Rappahannock River, or to the proprietor, as in Virginia in the Northern Neck. The revolution generally saw the abolishing of quitrents.

Broken runs of annual quitrent books survive, along with the related rent rolls, though no colony has complete yearly series. Locating surviving quitrents is not simple, especially because many were the private property of proprietors and thus were lost during and after the revolution. Significant numbers of landowners successfully avoided the lists, and there was great resistance to paying quitrents in general, especially for lands held for speculation and not farmed. Producing even approximately complete lists was often administratively impossible. One massive effort was made in Virginia in 1704; it provides a good but incomplete survey of surnames south of the Rappahannock River, the area north of the river being in the Northern Neck and its quitrents due not to Virginia but to the proprietary. The standard, though dated, general study is Beverley W. Bond, Jr., *The Quit-Rent System in the American Colonies* (New Haven: Yale University Press, 1919).

There have been three federal direct tax series that produced name lists, all to raise money for armies. In 1798, the French war scare led to a direct tax on real property and slaves (1 *Stat.* 580 and 597), which produced extensive name lists, though how complete and far down the economic scale is not clear. One local historian praises the comprehensiveness of this tax on dwelling houses: "In common with other towns, the Federal Direct Tax on Rehoboth [Massachusetts] lists the names of the owners and tenants of every dwelling house in the town, data which are found in no other record. . . . This 1798 dwelling house list, together with the census for 1800 . . . enables us to reconstruct a far more complete record for Rehoboth at the end of the eighteenth century than is possible in any other period of that century."[30]

Unfortunately, the 1798 direct tax has survived only in fragments. (A janitor of the Boston Customs House used sections of the Massachusetts/Maine lists to fire his stoves.[31]) Most surviving lists have been microfilmed, though not in a single series. The known manuscripts, many very incomplete, follow. (The addresses of state historical societies are in appendix C):

Maine, New Hampshire, Massachusetts: New England Historic Genealogical Society

Vermont: none found

Rhode Island: Rhode Island Historical Society

Connecticut: Connecticut Historical Society

New York (vicinity of Clinton and Franklin counties): Vermont Historical Society

New Jersey: none found

Pennsylvania: National Archives (717 volumes filmed as M372)

Delaware: Historical Society of Delaware

Maryland and District of Columbia: Maryland Historical Society; Maryland State Archives (formerly Hall of Records)

Virginia/West Virginia: none found

Kentucky: none found

Tennessee: Tennessee State Library

North Carolina: none found

South Carolina: none found

Georgia (part of Burke County): Georgia State Archives

To raise money for the War of 1812, the federal government again resorted to a direct tax from 1814 to 1816. Even fewer lists survive. The Connecticut Historical Society holds lists for 1814 to 1816 "for many towns," and Hancock County, Maine, survives for 1815. The 1813 law directed that $3 million be collected and apportioned among the states by population. The state governments were allowed to pay the federal treasury the amount levied on their citizens (less fifteen percent for saving the cost of collection) and in 1814 seven states did so, with four states doing the same in 1815 and 1816.[32] Perhaps this explains why few lists are extant—few were made.

The greatest number of federal direct tax lists, called assessment lists, are those from the Civil War to as late as 1917, when the government levied income taxes, property taxes, and license fees. These taxes were directed more to wealth rather than the broader earlier taxes and therefore capture a smaller proportion of the adult male population; however, they do provide specific information on propertied individuals. The records are in Record Group 58, Records of the Internal Revenue Service. The National Archives has microfilmed the assessment lists for most states, focusing primarily on lists of 1862 to 1866. These microfilms are listed in Loretto D. Szucs and Sandra H. Luebking, *The Archives: A Guide to the National Archives Field Branches* (Salt Lake City: Ancestry, 1988), 215–20, which also identifies those manuscript assessment lists found only in the regions of the National Archives.

As the Confederate states were conquered, the direct taxes were extended to them. Since many Southerners were unable to pay, the government sold much Southern land for taxes. In using the National Archives microfilms of Civil War direct taxes, note that each state has a different microfilm publication number—M754 for Alabama, M756 for California, M764 for Illinois, etc.—and therefore a separate pamphlet explaining each state's lists. These pamphlets are available from the National Archives upon request. (New York and New Jersey were microfilmed together as M603.)

USE OF LAND RECORDS

With some exceptions, American land law still reflects its English origins. The important exceptions are the French civil law in Louisiana, Spanish law in the Southwest, and Polynesian communal-use concepts in Hawaii. English property law, which means both land conveyance and inheritance law, was extremely complex and plagued by a nearly crushing mass of technicalities. This was especially true in the seventeenth and eighteenth centuries, when the United States was founded. The colonies lacked the judges, lawyers, law schools, and elaborate court system to implement English property law in all its complexity, but most of the basic concepts crossed the Atlantic and exist in the land records genealogists use.

One major distinction is between *real* and *personal* property, which arose in Norman England to distinguish between property the courts could restore to a dispossessed owner and property for which the courts would grant compensation for losses. The distinction is conveniently—if only roughly—be-

tween land (and its "fixtures") and movables. Because leases were deemed personal property and because deed registries record mostly real property, leases were normally not recorded. Hence, for reasons of early English law, tracing Americans who rented rather than bought farms can be very frustrating because their leases probably do not appear in the land records.

Another English concept is between *freehold* and *copyhold,* the first being for lands held in England by free men and the latter by *villeins* (i.e., peasants bound legally to the manor). The villein succeeded to the lands of his father upon payment of customary dues (fines), whereupon the record of such holdings was copied into the manor court roll—hence the name copyhold. In the American colonies, such copyhold was never successfully established because feudal and manorial structures did not exist in the colonies. The few instances where provincial proprietors tried to establish them, such as in Maryland and the Carolinas, were short-lived experiments in the face of all the unoccupied land surrounding these artificial manors. Thus, the American genealogist encounters freehold law that developed in contrast to a concept—copyhold—not normally found in American records. The one important remnant of feudalism that did gain a partial foothold in the colonies from New York to Georgia was the quitrent, which was explained in the section on taxes.

A third aspect of property law in England was the doctrine of estates, which assumed that all land in England was owned only by the crown and thus any subject held merely an "estate" in that land. Such holdings (tenures) could be with right to will or deed the land to another (fee simple), with right to a life interest that ended at the tenant's death (life estate), or with right for the land to pass inalienably to one's direct descendants so long as any existed (fee tail). The last—"to X and the heirs of his body"—might be land entailed without a sex restriction or it might be entailed only to male heirs (tail male) or, rarely, only to female heirs (tail female).

Out of these various historical concepts from the feudal-manorial world as they survived in English common law came legal records that genealogists encounter and need to understand. Not only did copyhold fail to flourish in the colonies, the idea that the crown "really" owned all the land also failed. Therefore, American law was centuries ahead of English law in developing the legal sense of fee simple as an absolute (allodial) ownership. "Absolute" in this sense is restricted by eminent domain, taxation, zoning, and the public interest. Public interest, as an example, might restrict a private citizen from damming a fishing stream that ran through his land.

Two remnants of English law encountered in colonial records, mostly south of New England, are *livery of seizin* and the *lease and release.* Livery of seizin was a very old method of transferring land tenure by actually handing pieces of the property to the new owner. It means to take delivery of possession. Here is how lawyer William Blackstone described it:

> Livery in *deed* is thus performed. The feoffor [seller], lessor, or his attorney, together with the feofee [buyer], lessee, or his attorney . . . come to the land, or to the house; and there, in the presence of witnesses, declare the contents of the feoffment or lease, on which livery is to be made. And then the feoffor, if it be of hand, doth deliver to the feofee, all other persons being out of

the ground, a clod or turf, or a twig or bough there growing, with words to this effect. 'I deliver these to you in the name of seizin of all the lands and tenements contained in this deed.'[33]

Whether Americans performed all these steps is conjectural. Certainly such deeds were occasionally used in the colonial period in both New England and the South. In 1714, in Westmoreland County, Virginia, Arthur Harris "made Livery and Seizin of the Lands and Appurtinances within mentioned by delivering Turff and Twigg and the Ring of the Door of the Chief Mansion House on the Lands."[34] These odd phrases were formula; nothing individual should be read into them.

Though livery of seizin was uncommon, the system of lease and release—two parts—flourished in Southern colonies in the 1700s. The intent of this document in seventeenth-century England was to avoid the legal fee of having deeds recorded publicly. Under Henry VIII, the Statutes of Uses dictated that the person having the use of any land had the obligations of that land as well, such as taxes, feudal dues, etc. If land was leased, then by the Statute of Uses the only interest remaining to the lessor was the reversion of the land at the end of the lease's term. If that reversion was then released to the lessee, the land was sold without a bargain and sale, thus circumventing the law requiring public registration and fee. Here again, the form is formula and not a lease at all. The genealogist should read both documents because the lease often omits the wife's name because her husband could lease property without her consent. Also, the two serve as duplicate copies for such easily miscopied information as intricate metes and bounds descriptions and difficult-to-read proper names.

English property law (land law and inheritance) prior to the Victorian reforms was extraordinarily complex, dependent on technicalities, and steeped in a vocabulary now long obsolete. The manner in which land was inherited contains many subtle clues which nearly all researchers will pass by in ignorance. It is unfortunate that legal history studies in America are both rare and usually inadequate and that genealogists have few convenient compilations of American property law that are aimed toward the non-lawyer. Three important exceptions are Carole Shammas, Marylynn Salmon, and Michel Dahlin, *Inheritance in America From Colonial Times to the Present* (New Brunswick: Rutgers University Press, 1987); Marylynn Salmon, *Women and the Law of Property in Early America* (Chapel Hill: University of North Carolina Press, 1986); and "An American Law of Property" and "The Land: And Other Property" in Lawrence M. Friedman, *A History of American Law,* rev. ed. (New York: Simon and Schuster, 1985).

Property was divided into the real (mostly land) and the personal (usually movables). In seventeenth- and eighteenth-century England, in intestate cases where no legal will existed, the personal property, but not land, was probated through the ecclesiastical courts with equal distribution to all children, while land was given under the common law to the heir-at-law. These differing courts for personal and real property account for why, at least in the colonial South, land is rarely mentioned in estate inventories: in England, such inventories were generally made by the ecclesiastical probate courts only, which did not usually probate land.

Primogeniture developed elaborate rules for identifying the

heir-at-law in the absence of children. If there were children, the heir-at-law was the eldest son (or, if dead, his heir-at-law). In the absence of a son, the daughters jointly inherited as heirs-at-law. After 1540, the testator (maker of the will) could bequeath land, but lands not mentioned in the will were treated as intestate and went to the heir-at-law. The major exception was entailed lands, meaning lands bequeathed by an ancestor to a person and that person's lineal descendants. The legal entailing phrase was "to X and the heirs of his [of her] body lawfully begotten." (The phrase "to his heirs and assigns forever" is not an entail.) Such land entailed to X could not be bequeathed by will so long as it remained entailed, because entailed lands went to the heir-at-law. Widows had a right to a life interest in one-third of their husband's lands, to be surrendered if they remarried. An excellent case study is Margaret Hickerson Emery, "The Adeustone-Rogers Families of Virginia: Tracing a Colonial Lineage through Entailment and Naming Patterns," *National Genealogical Society Quarterly* 77 (2) (June 1989): 89–106.

The genealogist interested in colonial lineages should note how the land was inherited and how the personal property was disposed, if the inheritance existed in a time and colony governed by primogeniture and entail. If something strange seems to be happening, try to determine the local inheritance laws governing that time and place. Entailed lands and dower rights were protected from the debts owed by the estate, which may also give clues.

A summary of "Inheritance Laws Circa 1720 in the American Colonies" appears as Table 1.1 in Shammas, et al., *Inheritance in America From Colonial Times to the Present*, pp. 32–33. But there is no simple summary for each colony showing which laws were in effect for which years for real/personal property or for other years for testate/intestate probates. John Frederick Dorman, "Colonial Law of Primogeniture," I–12, World Conference of Records (Salt Lake City: Genealogical Society of Utah, 1969) is helpful. Richard B. Morris, "Colonial Law Governing the Distribution and Alienation of Land," in *Studies in the History of American Law With Special Reference to the Seventeenth and Eighteenth Centuries* (New York: Columbia University Press, 1930), pp. 69–125, asserts that colonial practice was varied, uncertain, and debatable even to the colonial judges.

Two English laws worth knowing are the 1670 Statute of Distribution (22 & 23 Charles II c. 10 as amended 1 James II c. 17) and the 1677 Statute of Frauds (29 Charles II c. 3). (An English statute is cited by chapter number of the acts passed by the Parliament sitting in a regnal year of the sovereign. Thus, the 1677 act is chapter 3, 29th regnal year of Charles II.) The 1670 statute dictated that personal property (not real property) was distributed like this:

1. To children where no widow survived: whole property was divided equally among the children; a lone child received all.

2. To children and widow: two-thirds to the children or their heirs and one-third to the widow.

3. To widow where no children survived: one-half to widow and one-half to the father of the deceased if alive or, failing him, to mother or the brothers and sisters.

4. When no widow and children survived, property went to

father if alive or, failing him, to mother or the brothers and sisters.

The Statute of Frauds provided that personal property could no longer be disposed by oral testament and that executors/administrators must distribute such property as stipulated by will. Personal property not disposed by will was treated as intestate.

Although there are many local exceptions, English law was in force in the colonies to some degree where more specific colonial statutes did not exist, but the colonies could and did enact differing laws if "not repugnant" to English law and custom. The New England colonies, Pennsylvania, and Delaware granted equal divisions of land and movables in intestates with a double share to the eldest son. (The eldest daughter, in the absence of brothers, had no like double portion.) If the land could not be conveniently divided, it could go to the inheriting son provided he justly compensated the other heirs. Rhode Island seems to have used primogeniture until 1770 (except from 1718 to 1728). Maryland abolished primogeniture in 1715, substituting equal division. The remaining colonies, all royal, retained primogeniture until the American Revolution: New York, New Jersey, Virginia, the Carolinas, and Georgia. Georgia, in its earliest years, experimented with entailing lands by patent to male heirs, but it was an unpopular system.

If the heir-at-law automatically inherited entailed and intestate lands, then the eldest son need not be mentioned in his father's will. For example, in 1713, a John Taylor of Julian Creek, Norfolk County, Virginia, made a deed stating that the will of his brother Richard (Richard was alive) did not leave seventy-five acres to Richard's eldest son and in fact did not name this eldest son at all. Since the land had come to Richard from their father, John feared that if the land were not specifically transferred to the eldest son, he himself or his heirs would inherit this tract because John was the eldest son and primogeniture was the law in Virginia. Therefore, John, in his deed, gave seventy-five acres belonging to Richard to Richard's eldest son, Richard, Jr. Richard, Sr.'s, will survives and indeed does not mention the seventy-five acres or his eldest son.[35]

No English law required a testator, in disinheriting a child, to name him or her or to leave such a disinherited child the proverbial one shilling. As an unfortunate result, many wills ignore some children, leaving the genealogist in doubt as to whether the omission means the person was disinherited, dead, or not a child of the testator. Other records must be used to establish such points.

However, good genealogy is a conjunction of many types of records that together reinforce a pedigree and simultaneously test it. Land records are an essential strand in that web of proof but are only one part. For example, the problem was to identify which of several Isaac Lindseys in Maury County, Tennessee, married in 1808 and died in Navarro County, Texas, in 1852.[36] An 1810 will by John Lindsey named a son, Isaac, who was a good chronological fit for the Texan, but this John had no deeds in Maury. Because Maury was opened to white settlement by an 1805 Indian cession and because the Lindsey family was certainly there by 1807, this absence of deeds or patents from the state of Tennessee was puzzling until local history provided an explanation.

In 1783, North Carolina had allowed the purchase of Tennessee lands still held by Indians. The Maury County area had been claimed in 5,000-acre tracts by wealthy North Carolinians, but only in 1805 and 1806 could whites actually settle there. The Lindseys had arrived to legally "new" lands that had actually been long owned.

The deeds, court minutes, tax lists, marriages, and other usual records sorted out four groups of Lindseys—a justice of the peace who lived in the eastern part of the county, a latecoming family who settled in the southwestern corner, two brothers who owned land but never settled in the county, and the group to whom the Texan apparently belonged.

In the absence of deeds, the Texan's family was localized by three steps: (1) the 1809 court minutes contained an oath about a lease from Long heirs to John Lindsey; (2) various road overseer appointments placed the targeted Lindseys on Little Bigby Creek in the center of the county; and (3) the 5,000-acre tract of the Long family, purchased in 1783, was plotted, locating it on Duck River, which runs through the center of Maury County, and overlying Little Bigby Creek. Thus, the Long acres included Little Bigby Creek. Clearly, John Lindsey had leased his Little Bigby land from the Longs, not purchased it.

The rest of the proof included tracing the family back through Georgia into South Carolina. John had a brother who died, leaving three small sons who had come to Maury with their uncle John. One of these sons was named Isaac, while a second son had a son of his own named Isaac, neither being the Isaac who had married in 1808 and gone to Texas. Thus, the Texan was the one named in the 1810 will. By reading many volumes page by page, by plotting land grants, by following clues through several states, and through the fortunate survival of records, it was possible to see these Lindseys in Maury in the years 1805 to 1830, to sort out the different families, and to single out individuals. Land records underlie the whole proof, though alone they could never have untangled the lineage.

MAPPING SOFTWARE

Compiled by Birdie Monk Holsclaw

It is strongly recommended that the researcher gain a basic understanding of manual mapping techniques before attempting to use mapping software. Also, new software is always being developed, so watch for announcements and reviews in genealogical journals and newsletters.

Black Oak Mapper 6.0 (IBM/compatible). Black Oak Systems, 7472 Mt. Sherman Rd., Longmont, CO 80503-8678. Compiles single "metes and bounds" tracts for printers or to popular graphic file formats. Replaces and updates a previous freeware version.

DeedMapper 2.0 (IBM/compatible). Direct Line Software, 71 Neshobe Rd., Newton, MA 02168. Compiles and prints "metes and bounds" maps. Topographic map overlays are available at additional charge.

Deed Plotter + for WIndows 1.0 (IBM/compatible). Greenbrier Graphics, Inc., P.O. Box 1000, Spring Dale, WV 25986. IBM/compatible. Compiles single or multiple tracts on screen or printer; allows rotation. Handles "metes and bounds" as well as "rectangular" surveys. Curves and labels allowed in Deed Plotter + Series II. For Windows only.

Farmer's Plotter (Macintosh). Older Kids & Co., 8547 E.

Arapahoe Rd. No. J144, Greenwood Village, CO 80112. Generates "metes and bounds" and "rectangular" survey maps.

LANDcalc 1.13 (Macintosh). COMPUneering, 113 McCabe Crescent, Thornhill, Ontario L4J 2S6 CANADA. Comprehensive map drawing program for surveyors; very technical. Compiles single or multiple tracts on screen or printer; many labeling options. More features available in LANDesign.

L-Plot 5.2 (IBM/compatible). Lan/Scan, Inc., P.O. Box 6863, Abilene, TX 79608-6863. Can compile single or multiple tracts on screen or printer; allows rotation and labeling. Handles both "metes and bounds" and "rectangular" surveys.

SUMMARY OF LAND RECORDS BY STATE

The following persons contributed to the revision of this summary: Desmond Walls Allen (Arkansas), Robert Charles Anderson (Massachusetts), Gale Williams Bamman (Tennessee), Eric Grundset (Virginia), Ruth Land Hatten (Mississippi), Margaret M. Hofmann (North Carolina), Birdie Monk Holsclaw (Colorado), Donald Jackanicz (Illinois), Karen E. Livsey (New York), Sandra H. Luebking (Illinois), Wayne Moore (Tennessee), Marsha Hoffman Rising (Missouri), Paula Stuart Warren (Minnesota). These revisions make current the 1984 version by William Thorndale.

The following summary locates the first-title grants for each state, although it is painfully brief. Because all states except Connecticut, Rhode Island, and Vermont have recorded deeds and mortgages in the county and independent city, the deeds are assumed to be there unless otherwise stated. In short, the deeds should be easy to find, assuming they have not been destroyed. By contrast, the location of the land grants is complicated, varying widely from state to state.

The addresses of state land offices (where relevant) and the appropriate BLM office are given. For addresses of state archives and state historical societies, see appendixes B and C. The BLM's Eastern States Office is at 7450 Boston Blvd., Springfield, VA 22153. The regional archives of the National Archives are listed in appendix A. Questions involving private land titles are usually referred first to *American State Papers, Public Lands 1789–1837 and Claims*, 9 vols. (1832–61. Reprint. Greenville, S.C.: Southern Historical Press, 1994), as indexed in Philip W. McMullin, *Grassroots in America* (Reprint. Southern Historical Press, 1994). Inventory No. 22 refers to Harry P. Yoshpe and Philip P. Bower, *Preliminary Inventory of the Land-Entry Papers of the General Land Office*. The titles cited are obviously only a small part of what is available. I have doubtless overlooked still other titles.

Finally, remember that generalizations have exceptions and that records are sometimes transferred. Joseph Martin Glynn, Jr., summarizes:

> Suppose I say, 'The 1880 Soundex cards are at the National Archives in Washington, D.C., and on microfilm.' This statement was true in 1945 but false by 1975. After some New England states cards were destroyed the remainder were sent to the Waltham Branch [of the National Archives]. If I say that[,] it's true in 1975 but false by 1979 because the cards were given to NEHGS [New England Historic Genealogical

Society] where they now [1982] are. Suppose I say the Waltham Branch has no ship passenger records. It's true in 1973 but later surplus copies of the films were given to them. What a repository doesn't have [it] can acquire and what [it has] can be lost, stolen, destroyed, transferred, abstracted, microfilmed, and indexed, etc.[37]

This summary attempts to provide record locations as of 1996. Always send a mailed inquiry or telephone to verify locations before beginning research.

ALABAMA

Public-domain state with two principal meridians (established 1805 and 1807) and fifteen GLO land districts. The first opened at St. Stephens in 1806, and the last closed at Montgomery in 1927. The GLO local records were sent to the National Archives in Washington, D.C. Obtain patents from the BLM Eastern States Office, which also has copies of the tract books and township plats. The National Archives has the land-entry case files as described in Inventory No. 22, and a card index to Alabama federal patentees to 30 June 1908 (excluding private land claims). Alabama federal patents are indexed in the GLO Automated Records System. State and some county copies of ledgers, tract books, and plats are in the state archives and the Lands and Trademark Division, 528 State Office Building, Montgomery, AL 36130. See "Old Land Records of Madison County, Alabama," *Family Puzzlers* no. 622 (20 September 1979): 2–3. Marilyn Davis Barefield is abstracting GLO district records, using mostly state duplicates rather than GLO originals. In addition to *Old Cahaba Land Office Records & Military Warrants, 1817–1853* (Greenville, S.C.: Southern University Press, 1986), she has published, in eight volumes, the land office records and military warrants for Demopolis; Huntsville; Mardisville, Lebanon, and Centre; Montgomery; Sparta and Elba; Tuskaloosa; and St. Stephens. Many private land claims were processed through the St. Stephens office, and this volume contains entries from the *American State Papers*. Pre-1813 records for Alabama south of thirty-one degrees should be in Tallahassee in the West Florida archive. Also see James F. Doster, "Land Titles and Public Land Sales in Early Alabama," *Alabama Review* 16 (1963): 108–24; and David Lightner, "Private Land Claims in Alabama," ibid. 20 (1967): 187–204.

ALASKA

Public-domain state with five principal meridians (three established from 1905 to 1911 and two in 1956). Alaska was under the jurisdiction of the Russian-American Company until 1867; the company's papers (1802–1867) are microfilmed on M11, seventy-seven rolls. Trade, not settlement, was the company's goal, and the NARS pamphlet accompanying the microfilm collection does not mention any land title collection. An act of 1884 first authorizing a civilian governor expressly excluded general U.S. land law from Alaska except for mines and mining claims. The earliest of three GLO land districts opened at Sitka in 1885. Inventory No. 22 lists exactly fifty-six cash entries and 133 homestead patents for all of Alaska. The National Archives in Washington, D.C., has the land-entry case files as described in Inventory No. 22, and a card index to Alaska patentees to 30 June 1908 (excluding private land claims). Obtain patents from the BLM Alaska State Office, No. 13, 222 W. 7th

Ave., Anchorage, AK 99513-5076. The office also has copies of the tract books and township plats. Researchers with access to the Alaska Region of the National Archives should inquire there concerning Alaska tract books, township plats, and the records of the GLO local Alaska land districts. Seek deeds in the judicial districts (Alaska's equivalent to counties).

ARIZONA

Public-domain state with two principal meridians (established 1865 and 1869). The earliest of Arizona's three GLO land districts opened in Prescott in 1870. Obtain patents from the BLM Arizona State Office, P.O. Box 16563, 3707 N. 7th St., Phoenix, AZ 85011, which also has copies of the tract books and township plats. The National Archives in Washington, D.C., has the land-entry case files as described in Inventory No. 22, the GLO headquarters tract books and township plats, and a card index to Arizona patentees to 30 June 1908 (excluding private land claims). *The Archives: A Guide to the National Archives Field Branches* (Salt Lake City: Ancestry, 1988), p. 230, reports some GLO local office records in the National Archives—Rocky Mountain Region in Denver, but most are in the Pacific Southwest Region at Laguna Niguel, California. For private land claims, write to the BLM New Mexico State Office, P.O. Box 27115, 1474 Rodeo Rd., Santa Fe, NM 87502-0015.

ARKANSAS

Public-domain state with one principal meridian (established 1815). There were eight GLO land districts, beginning and ending with Little Rock, 1821 to 1933. The GLO local office records are in the Arkansas State Land Office, Room 109, State Capitol, Little Rock, AR 72201. Obtain patents from the BLM Eastern States Office, which also has copies of the tract books and township plats. The National Archives in Washington, D.C., has the land-entry case files as described in Inventory No. 22. Arkansas had one of the War of 1812's three military reserves. The warrants and an index are available on NARS microfilm M848, *War of 1812 Military Bounty Warrants, 1815–1858,* fourteen rolls. A ca.-1860 listing of patentees in the reserve is Katheren Christensen, *Arkansas Military Bounty Grants (War of 1812)* (Hot Springs, Ark.: Arkansas Ancestors, 1971). Desmond W. Allen has published *Arkansas Land Patents Through 1908* (Conway, Ark.: Arkansas Research, 1990), a fifty-seven-volume series with information taken from the BLM database described above. Arkansas federal patents are indexed in the GLO Automated Records System. Arkansas land patents are available for purchase on CD-ROM from the GLO. For private land claims, see the *American State Papers, Public Lands* as indexed in McMullin, *Grassroots of America*.

CALIFORNIA

Public-domain state with three principal meridians (established 1851 to 1853). The first of ten GLO land districts opened at Los Angeles and Benicia in 1853. The records of these offices are at the National Archives—Pacific Sierra Region at San Bruno, except for the Los Angeles local district records, which are at the Pacific Southwest Region in Laguna Niguel. Obtain patents from the BLM California State Office, Room E-2841, 2800 Cottage Way, Sacramento, CA 95825-1889, which also has copies of the tract books and township plats. The National Archives has the land-entry case files as described in Inven-

tory No. 22, and the GLO headquarters has originals of the tract books and township plats. For private land claims, see the state archives (indexed) and the Bancroft Library at the University of California, Berkeley. A Board of Land Commissioners met from 1852 to 1856 to adjudicate Spanish and Mexican grants. Its files and other private claims papers, mostly collected at the surveyor-general's office in San Francisco, were destroyed in the earthquake and fire of 1906, but some parts or duplicates survive. See J.N. Bowman, "Index to the Spanish-Mexican Private Land Grant Records and Cases of California" (microfilmed typescript at Bancroft Library, Berkeley, 1958). The Mexican Archives (1833–1845) of the surveyor-general's office are on microfilm (fourteen rolls) at the state archive. The National Archives has microfilmed federal California court records regarding private land claims (NARS microfilms T910, T1207, T1214, T1215, and T1216).

Because the government could not control the hordes of 1849 miners, it pretended they did not exist, and there are no GLO records of 1849 gold rush claims. See Joseph Ellison, "The Mineral Land Question in California, 1848–1866," *Southwestern Historical Quarterly* 30 (1926): 34–55; William Wilcox Robinson, *Land in California, the Story of Mission Lands, Ranchos, Squatters, Mining Claims, Railroad Grants, Land Scrip [and] Homesteads* (Berkeley: University of California Press, 1948); Rose H. Avina, *Spanish and Mexican Land Grants in California* (New York: Arno Press, 1976); and Paul W. Gates, "Public Land Disposal in California," *Agricultural History* 49 (1975): 158–78.

COLORADO

Public-domain state with three principal meridians (established 1855 and 1880). The earliest of thirteen GLO land districts opened at Golden City in 1863. The National Archives—Rocky Mountain Region in Denver holds GLO local office records for the more than seventy land districts formerly covering Colorado, New Mexico, Montana, the Dakotas, and Utah. Obtain patents from the BLM Colorado State Office, 2850 Youngfield St., Lakewood, CO 80215-7076, which also has copies of the tract books and township plats. The National Archives in Washington, D.C., has the land-entry case files as described in Inventory No. 22, and the GLO headquarters originals of the tract books and township plats. See LeRoy R. Hafen, "Mexican Land Grants in Colorado," *Colorado Magazine* 4 (1927): 82–93; George L. Anderson, "The Canon City or Arkansas Valley Claim Club, 1860–1862," ibid. 16 (1939): 201–10; "The Middle Park Claim Club, 1861," ibid. 10 (1933): 189–93; and a series of articles collectively titled "Spanish Land Grants in New Mexico and Colorado," *Journal of the West* 19 (July 1980): 1–99. Also see Joseph O. Van Hook, "Mexican Land Grants in the Arkansas Valley," *Southwestern Historical Quarterly* 40 (1936–37): 58–75.

CONNECTICUT

State-land state surveyed in variations of the New England town. First settled 1634 to 1635 in the Connecticut River Valley, its river towns formed a united government in 1639 without a charter from England. The New Haven colony was founded in 1638 and absorbed into Connecticut under the royal charter of 1662, which authorized a corporate colony (one that chooses its own governor). Connecticut was thus always free to grant its own lands, which it did through the General Court (legislature), usually to town proprietors but sometimes to individuals by grant or sale. The records are at the state archive in the Connecticut State Library; the colonial land records are being microfilmed. The Connecticut State Library also has such pertinent papers as the Robert C. Winthrop Collection, 1631 to 1794, and the William F.J. Boardman Collection, 1661 to 1835, both of which include land papers. Conveyances are recorded in the towns, not the counties. Proprietor records are rich in land records. See Nelson P. Mead, "Land System of the Connecticut Towns," *Political Science Quarterly* 21 (1906): 59–76; and Dorothy Deming, *The Settlement of the Connecticut Towns* (New Haven: Tercentenary Commission, 1953).

DELAWARE

State-land state surveyed in indiscriminate metes and bounds. Delaware is unique among the thirteen colonies in not having some colonial jurisdiction within its bounds that granted first titles to its lands. See Edward F. Heite, ed., *Delaware's Fugitive Records: An Inventory of the Official Land Grant Records Relating to the Present State of Delaware* (Dover: Delaware Division of Historical and Cultural Affairs, 1980), Hall of Records Inventory No. 2. The successive absorption of New Sweden into the Dutch colony of New Netherlands and then into the English proprietary of James, Duke of York, means the early Delaware grants were made in New York. In 1682, the Duke of York conveyed his claims in present-day Delaware to William Penn, whose Pennsylvania proprietary granted Delaware's lands until the Revolution. In 1770, the Delaware legislature ordered the New York grants transcribed, since published as *Original Titles in Delaware Commonly Known as the Duke of York Records 1646–1679* (Wilmington: Delaware General Assembly, 1903), abstracted in the *Maryland and Delaware Genealogist*, vols. 5–15, 18 (1964–74, 1977). See also B. Fernow, *Documents Relating to the History of the Dutch and Swedish Settlements on the Delaware River* (Albany: Argus, 1877). Warrants and surveys from the Penn proprietary, 1682 to 1776, are in the Delaware Hall of Records in Dover, as are tax records of the levy courts. The proprietary quitrents are at the Historical Society of Pennsylvania in Philadelphia. Forty-five Maryland grants are listed in Percy G. Skirven, "Durham County: Lord Baltimore's Attempt at Settlement of His Lands on the Delaware Bay, 1670–1685," *Maryland Historical Magazine* 25 (1930): 157–67. Also see A.R. Dunlop, "Dutch and Swedish Land Records Relating to Delaware . . . ," *Delaware History* 6 (1954–55): 25–51.

DISTRICT OF COLUMBIA

Federal district of the United States, originally a ten-mile square taken from Maryland and Virginia by an act of 1790. The federal government arrived in 1800. Two counties divided by the Potomac River were created in 1801: Washington County, to use Maryland law, and Alexandria County (renamed Arlington in 1920), to use Virginia law. Within these counties were the chartered cities of Georgetown, Washington, and Alexandria. The land records (1792–1886) of the district's Recorder of Deeds have been microfilmed in 694 rolls. For various land-related records of the district, see the *Guide to Genealogical Research in the National Archives*, p. 242. In 1846, Alexandria County was retroceded to Virginia. During its years within the District of Columbia, it recorded its own deeds, as did the city of Alexandria. See John Frederick Dorman, "A Guide to the Counties of Virginia: Alexandria County (Arlington County)," *Virginia Genealogist* 3 (1959): 126–27.

FLORIDA

Public-domain state with one principal meridian (established 1824). Of the five GLO land districts, the earliest opened at Tallahassee in 1825; the last closed at Gainesville in 1933. Obtain patents from the BLM Eastern States Office, which also has copies of the tract books and township plats. Florida's federal patents are indexed in the GLO Automated Records System. A CD-ROM of Florida land patents is available from the GLO. The National Archives in Washington, D.C., has the land-entry case files and a card index to Florida patentees to 30 June 1908 (excluding private land claims). The National Archives also has Florida donation entry files (ca. 1842) under the Florida Armed Occupation Act of 1842, which granted 160 acres to settlers able to bear arms. In 1821, Spain surrendered to the United States present-day Florida, including British/Spanish East Florida and, west of the Apalachicola River, the portion of British/Spanish West Florida that remained after the United States had seized western West Florida in 1810. Parts of the surviving British/Spanish provincial archives formerly at Saint Augustine and Pensacola are now in the Florida state archive in Tallahassee.

Several Congressional land commissions and many courts grappled with private land claims. The East Florida private land claims (1824–1828) are on microfilm (seventeen rolls), as are East Florida Spanish land grant archives (1764–1844) (eight rolls). The Historical Records Survey published five volumes on *Spanish Land Grants in Florida* (Tallahassee, 1940–41). The county tax rolls of 1839 to 1891 in the Florida Tax Commission have been microfilmed. See also George C. Whatley and Sylvia Cook, "The East Florida Land Commission: A Study in Frustration," *Florida Historical Quarterly* 50 (1971): 39–52; Charles L. Mowat, "The Land Policy in British East Florida," *Agricultural History* 14 (1940): 75–77; and S.W. Martin, "The Public Domain in Territorial Florida," *Journal of Southern History* 10 (1944): 174–87.

GEORGIA

State-land state surveyed partly in indiscriminate metes and bounds and partly in lottery lots. The Georgia Surveyor-General Department in the Georgia State Archives and Records Building, Atlanta, holds the grants, surveys, and related papers for Georgia from the colony's founding. Its major records and indexes are microfilmed. The department is one of the most active in the United States in indexing land records and publishing guides, including an admirable work by Marion R. Hemperley, *Georgia Surveyor General Department: A History and Inventory of Georgia's Land Office* (Atlanta: State Printing Office, 1982). A sampling of other titles issued by the department include Marion R. Hemperley and Pat Bryant, *English Crown Grants, 1755–1775*, 9 vols. (1972–74); Pat Bryant, *Entry of Claims for Georgia Landholders, 1733–1775* (1975); Alex M. Hitz, *Authentic List of All Land Lottery Grants Made to Veterans of the Revolutionary War By the State of Georgia (1820, 1827, 1832)* (1955), and his *Georgia Bounty Land Grants,* reprinted from the *Georgia Historical Quarterly* 38 (1954): 337–48. For a price list, write to the Georgia Surveyor-General Department, Archives and Records Building, Atlanta, GA 30334.

The three major means of granting land in Georgia were headrights (usually two hundred acres for heads of households plus fifty acres for each family member and slave), revolutionary war bounty warrants (for citizens purportedly loyal to the revolutionary government), and lotteries. The headrights are listed in *Index to the Headright and Bounty Grants of Georgia, 1756–1909* (1970. Reprint. Greenville, S.C.: Southern Historical Press, 1992). The revolutionary war bounty warrant files are very incomplete. The lotteries began with an act of 1803 and disposed of public lands in ceded Indian territories in 1805, 1807, 1820, 1821, 1827, and 1832. Eligibility required Georgia residency with extra draws for special categories, such as revolutionary war service. See Robert Scott Davis, Jr., *Research in Georgia* (1981. Reprint. Greenville, S.C.: Southern Historical Press, 1991), for a summary of qualifications for each lottery. The statewide lists for all lotteries have been published but give only winning draws—except for the 1805 list, which shows all persons eligible under the enabling act of 1803. Its year's residency requirement from May 1802 makes it a good substitute for the missing 1800 Georgia federal census. There are some county eligibility lists in manuscript for later lotteries, and these might identify additional revolutionary war veterans. See also Robert S. Davis, Jr., and Silas Emmett Lucas, Jr., *The Georgia Land Lottery Papers, 1805–1914: Genealogical Data From the Loose Papers Filed in the Georgia Surveyor General Office Concerning the Lots Won in the State Land Lotteries and the People Who Won Them* (1979. Reprint. Greenville, S.C.: Southern Historical Press, 1987). Prior to 1777, Georgia conveyances were recorded only in Savannah and survive mostly in the state archives. See *A Preliminary Guide to Eighteenth-Century Records Held by the Georgia Department of Archives and History* (Atlanta: Georgia Department of Archives and History, 1976). The R.J. Taylor, Jr., Foundation of Atlanta has published indexes to several of these colonial records and promises more. The State Tax Commission lists for 1787 to 1899 have been microfilmed. For essential background on headright grants, subsequent laws, Indian treaties, land reserves, boundaries, maps, county surveys, surveyors' field notes, frauds, and land transfers in Georgia see Farris W. Cadle, *Georgia Land Surveying: History and Law* (Athens: University of Georgia Press, 1991).

Hawaii

State-land state unique in the Union for the Polynesian origins of its land titles. Hawaiian lands have never been part of the federal public domain. Prior to European settlement, the idea of absolute fee-simple land title did not exist. Instead, there was a hierarchy of right of use descending from the king through chiefs and subchiefs to commoners. The royal family or high chiefs gave Europeans and Americans similar rights of use which the foreigners interpreted as absolute ownership. In 1848, a Royal Land Commission sought to resolve the confusion and allocate permanent ownership by confirming royal patents or allocating land to the government, which then awarded grants. Records of original titles by the Land Commission are in the state archive, while the grants by purchase are at the Land Management Section of the Department of Land and Natural Resources, 1151 Punchbowl St., Honolulu, HI 96813. The major parts of both collections have been microfilmed. Deeds for all of the islands (1844–1900) with an index (1845–1917) have been microfilmed in 108 reels. See also Jon J. Chinen, *Original Land Titles in Hawaii* (the author, 1961), and his *The Great Mahele: Hawaii's Land Division of 1848* (Honolulu: University of Hawaii Press, 1958); Thomas Marshall Spaulding, *Crown Lands of Hawaii* (Honolulu: University of Hawaii, 1923); and Robert H. Horwitz, *Public Land Policy in Hawaii: An Historical Analysis* (Honolulu: University of Hawaii, 1969).

Idaho

Public-domain state with one principal meridian (established 1867). Of the five GLO land districts, the earliest offices opened in Boise City and Lewistown in 1867. The township plats are in the National Archives—Pacific Northwest Region in Seattle. Obtain patents from the BLM Idaho State Office, 3380 Americana Terrace, Boise, ID 83706, which also has copies of the tract books and township plats. The National Archives in Washington, D.C., has the land-entry case files as described in Inventory No. 22 and also the GLO headquarters originals of the tracts books and township plats.

Illinois

Public-domain state with three principal meridians (established 1805 and 1815). Of the ten GLO land districts, the earliest opened at Kaskaskia in 1809 and the last closed at Springfield in 1876. The records of these offices are in the state archive. The Illinois State Archives has a computer index to all federal patents in Illinois. *Illinois State Archives Index to First Purchasers in the Public Domain* is available on microfiche. For an account of its land records, see Victoria Irons and Patricia C. Brennan, *Descriptive Inventory of the Archives of the State of Illinois* (Springfield: Illinois State Archives, 1978), 549–60. The Shawneetown GLO records are indexed in Lowell M. Volkel, *Shawneetown Land District Records* (Indianapolis: Heritage House, 1978). Obtain patents from the BLM Eastern States Office, which also has copies of the tract books and township plats. The National Archives has the land-entry case files as described in Inventory No. 22. For private land claims, see the *American State Papers, Public Lands* as indexed in McMullin's *Grassroots of America*. One of the War of 1812 military reserves for bounty-land warrants was in Illinois. Its records are in the state archives and also on NARS microfilm M848, *War of 1812 Military Bounty Land Warrants, 1815–1858*, fourteen reels. House Doc. 262, 26th Congress, 1st sess., 1840, has been reprinted with an index as Lowell M. Volkel, *War of 1812 Bounty Lands in Illinois* (Thomson, Ill.: Heritage House, 1977); it identifies patentees in the military tract. See Theodore L. Carlson, *Illinois Military Tract: A Study of Land Occupation, Utilization and Tenure*, Illinois Studies in the Social Sciences, vol. 32, item 2 (Urbana: University of Illinois Press, 1951). See also Paul W. Gates, "The Disposal of the Public Domain in Illinois, 1848–1856," *Journal of Economics and Business History* 3 (1931): 216–40; James E. Wright, *The Galena Lead District: Federal Policy and Practice, 1824–1847* (Madison: State Historical Society of Wisconsin, 1966).

Indiana

Public-domain state with two principal meridians (established 1799 and 1805). Of the six GLO land districts, the earliest opened at Vincennes in 1807; the last closed at Indianapolis in 1876. The records of these local offices were transferred to the auditor of state but are now in the state archive. Obtain patents from the BLM Eastern States Office, which also has copies of the tract books and township plats. The National Archives in

Washington, D.C., has the land-entry case files as described in Inventory No. 22. The land entries for the Cincinnati land district (1801–1840) and Vincennes land district (1807–1877) are indexed in Margaret R. Water, *Indiana Land Entries*, 2 vols. (1948. Reprint. Knightstown, Ind.: Bookmark, 1977). Vincennes had been settled since 1733 and experienced a large influx of Americans after the revolution, a white enclave within Indian lands. For records on the resulting private land claims, see Leonard Lux, *The Vincennes Donation Lands,* Indiana Historical Society Publications, vol. 25, item 4 (Indianapolis: Indiana Historical Society, 1949), and also the *American State Papers, Public Lands* as indexed in McMullin's *Grassroots of America*. See also Malcolm J. Rohrbough, "The Land Office Business in Indiana, 1800–1840," in *This Land of Ours: The Acquisition and Disposition of the Public Domain* (Indianapolis: Indiana Historical Society, 1978), 39–59; Stephen Frederick Strausberg, "The Administration and Sale of Public Land in Indiana 1800–1860" (Ph.D. dissertation, Cornell University, 1970).

IOWA

Public-domain state with one principal meridian (established 1815 in Arkansas). Iowa had nine land districts, the earliest opening in 1838 in Burlington and Dubuque, the last closing at Des Moines in 1910. Their records are in the National Archives—Central Plains Region in Kansas City. Obtain patents from the BLM Eastern States Office, which also has copies of the tract books and township plats. The National Archives has the land-entry case files as described in Inventory No. 22. More than 20,000 settlers were in Iowa prior to the first land sales and thus had no legal title to their claims. To prevent speculators and latecomers from buying such improved lands at land office auctions, the settlers and speculators formed claims clubs to rig the auctions on grounds of first settlement. See Allan G. Bogue, "The Iowa Claims Clubs: Symbols and Substance," *Mississippi Valley Historical Review* 45 (1958): 231–35; Benjamin F. Shambaugh, ed., *Constitution and Records of the Claim Association of Johnson County, Iowa* (Iowa City: University of Iowa Press, 1894); Roscoe L. Lokken, *Iowa Public Land Disposal* (Iowa City: State Historical Society of Iowa, 1942); and Robert P. Swierenga, *Pioneers and Profits: Land Speculation on the Iowa Frontier* (Ames: Iowa University Press, 1968).

KANSAS

Public-domain state with one principal meridian (established 1855). Of the eleven GLO land districts, the first opened at Lecompton in 1856, and the last closed at Topeka in 1925. The Kansas GLO records are in the National Archives—Central Plains Region in Kansas City but are reportedly incomplete. Obtain patents from the BLM New Mexico State Office, P.O. Box 27115, 1474 Rodeo Rd., Santa Fe, NM 87592-0115, which also has copies of the tract books and township plats for Kansas. The National Archives in Washington, D.C., has the land-entry case files as described in Inventory No. 22 and the GLO headquarters original tract books and township plats. Significant portions of Kansas fell within railroad land grants, the land offices of the Santa Fe and the Rock Island railroads being especially important. The Kansas State Historical Society holds some of these papers. See Paul W. Gates, *Fifty Million Acres: Conflicts over Kansas Land Policy, 1854–1890* (Ithaca: Cornell University Press, 1954), and G.L. Anderson, "The Administration of Federal Land Laws in Western Kansas, 1880–1890: A

Factor in Adjustment to a New Environment," *Kansas Historical Quarterly* 20 (1952): 233–51.

KENTUCKY

State-land state surveyed in indiscriminate metes and bounds east of the Tennessee River and in townships and ranges west of it. The Kentucky Land Office Division, Capitol Building, Frankfort, KY 40601-3493, is an active department of the Office of Secretary of State and still issues an occasional new grant because the land-grant process, though rarely used, is still in effect in Kentucky for vacant, ungranted lands. Warrants, surveys, patents, and other records are in the land office, indexed and microfilmed, open to public research. In 1792, Virginia sent to Kentucky its loose land papers relevant to Kentucky along with copies of its Virginia grants to Kentucky lands.

The separate categories of Kentucky grants are:

1. Virginia Grants, 1782–1792. Sixteen volumes of 10,000 warrants issued by Virginia, including service in the French and Indian War, and transcribed in Richmond in the 1790s by order of the Kentucky legislature. See Joan E. Brookes-Smith, *Master Index: Virginia Surveys and Grants, 1774–1791* (Frankfort: Kentucky Historical Society, 1976).

2. Old Kentucky Grants, 1793–1856. Twenty volumes of military, seminary, academic, treasury warrant, and preemption grants made by Kentucky. See Kentucky Historical Society, *Index for Old Kentucky Surveys and Grants [and Tellico Surveys & Grants] Microfilmed by Kentucky Historical Society* (Frankfort: Kentucky Historical Society, 1975).

3. Grants South of Green River, 1797–1866. Eighteen volumes of non-military headrights of two hundred acres in the military reserve. These grants were first given as a relief for squatters.

4. Kentucky Land Warrants, 1816–73. Forty-three volumes covering lands east of the Tennessee River purchased from the state.

5. Tellico Grants, 1803–53. Two volumes describing 572 grants in the small Cherokee cession of 1805 in eastern Kentucky. See the *Index* listed in no. 2 above.

6. County Court Orders, 1836–1924. One hundred twenty-six volumes on warrants sold by each county court east of the Tennessee River for any vacant lands within its bounds.

7. Grants west of the Tennessee River, 1822–58. Eleven volumes surveyed in townships and ranges.

8. Grants South of Walker's Line, 1825–1923. Loose papers from Kentucky's right to grant lands in Tennessee north of 36 degrees 30 minutes, the intended state line. Walker ran the (present) line too far north. Researchers should also check the Tennessee land records for these grants. See James W. Sames III, *Four Steps West: A Documentary Concerning the First Dividing Line in America . . . Virginia, North Carolina, Kentucky, Tennessee* (Versailles, Ky.: the author, 1971).

9. Warrants for Headrights, 1827–49. One volume containing fifty-five grants that probably belong in one of the other collections but became separated.

These and some other early land records are indexed in Willard Rouse Jillson, *The Kentucky Land Grants: A Systematic Index to All of the Land Grants Recorded in the State Land Office at Frankfort, Kentucky, 1782–1924*, Filson Club Publication No. 33 (1925. Reprint. 2 vols. Baltimore: Genealogical

Publishing Co., 1994), and his *Old Kentucky Entries and Deeds: A Complete Index to All of the Earliest Land Entries, Military Warrants, Deeds and Wills of the Commonwealth of Kentucky*, Filson Club Publication No. 34 (1926. Reprint. Baltimore: Genealogical Publishing Co., 1987). These categories of land records have been summarized here because Kentucky suffered more than any other state from land-title litigation, because of the convergence of three unfortunate circumstances: liberal land-granting by Virginia in an area distant from its supervision; Kentucky's settlement during the turmoil of the revolution and its Indian wars, which meant that claims were frequently abandoned; and a tendency toward do-it-yourself rather than professional surveying. The resulting litigation produced a bonanza of depositions about first settlers, though such records are scattered in various courthouses and manuscript collections. An important collection is the microfilmed Kentucky Court of Appeals deed books, 1780 to 1909, in thirteen reels, and Hattie M. Scott, "Heirs in Court of Appeals Deeds," *Register of the Kentucky State Historical Society* 42 (1944): 6–18, 158–73, 256–62, 348–53. A Virginia Land Court sat at several Kentucky forts in 1780 to hear claims involving land north of Green River. Its transcripts appear in "Certificate Book of the Virginia Land Commission, 1779–80," *Register of the Kentucky State Historical Society* 21 (1923): 3–323. There were never any private land claims in Kentucky. The county tax lists, 1782 to ca. 1825, have been microfilmed.

See Beverley West Hathaway, *Kentucky Genealogical Research Sources* (West Jordan, Utah: Allstates Research, 1974), 25–42, 119–22; Jack F. Royce, *The Preservation of Land Office Records*, Information Bulletin 89 (Frankfort: Legislative Report Commission, 1971); Philip Fall Taylor, *A Calendar of the Warrants for Land in Kentucky, Granted for Service in the French and Indian War* (Baltimore: Genealogical Publishing Co., 1967); Samuel M. Wilson, *Catalogue of Revolutionary Soldiers and Sailors of the Commonwealth of Virginia to Whom Land Bounty Warrants Were Granted* (Baltimore: Genealogical Publishing Co., 1967), reprinted from the *Yearbook of the Society, Sons of the American Revolution in the Commonwealth of Kentucky, 1894–1913*; and George Mark Harding, "The Uncertainly of Early Kentucky Land Titles," *Genealogy* no. 64 (October 1981): 1–4.

LOUISIANA

Public-domain state with two principal meridians (established 1807 and 1819). Of the five GLO land districts, the first opened at Opelouses in 1805, and the last closed at Baton Rouge in 1927. The papers of these offices are now in the Louisiana State Land Office, Box 44124, Baton Rouge, LA 70804. Obtain patents from the BLM Eastern States Office, which also has copies of the tract books and township plats. Federal patents are indexed in the GLO Automated Records System. A CD-ROM of Louisiana land patents is available from the GLO. The National Archives has the land-entry case files as described in Inventory No. 22 and a card index to Louisiana patentees to 30 June 1908 (excluding private land claims). The French and Spanish governments of Louisiana left many pre-1804 papers, but the land grant papers seem to have suffered more losses than other categories of records. The Spanish Louisiana Cabildo judicial records (1769–1804) at the Louisiana Historical Center in New Orleans are on microfilm and are rich in land transactions. Because a fairly fluent knowledge of French and Span-

ish is required to read handwritten records, these pre-American records are beyond the average genealogist's reach. However, the Historical Records Survey transcribed in nineteen volumes the records from the District of Baton Rouge in Spanish West Florida, and these are indexed in Stanley Clisby Arthur, *Index to the Archives of Spanish West Florida, 1782–1810* (New Orleans: Polyanthos, 1975). See also NARS microfilm T1116 in seven rolls for the HRS typescripts of the Archives of the Spanish Government of West Florida, 1789 to 1816. The Historical Records Survey issued a *Survey of Federal Archives in Louisiana: Land Claims and Other Documents* (Baton Rouge: Historical Records Survey, 1940). The private land claims to 1837 are in the *American State Papers, Public Lands* as indexed in McMullin's *Grassroots of America*. Some of these materials in *American States Papers, Public Lands* were reorganized along geographical lines in Charles R. Maduell, *Federal Land Grants in the Territory of Orleans; the Delta Parishes* (New Orleans: Polyanthos, 1975). Seek deeds in the parishes, Louisiana's equivalent of counties. See also Harry L. Coles, Jr., "Applicability of the Public Land System to Louisiana," *Mississippi Valley Historical Review* 43 (1936–37): 39–58; Frances P. Burns, "The Spanish Land Laws of Louisiana," *Louisiana Historical Quarterly* 11 (1928): 557–81; Elizabeth Gaspar Brown, "Legal Systems in Conflict: Orleans Territory 1804–1812," *American Journal of Legal History* 1 (1957): 35–75; Harry L. Coles, Jr., "The Confirmation of Foreign Land Titles in Louisiana," *Louisiana Historical Quarterly* 38 (1955): 1–22; and Glenn R. Conrad, *Land Records of the Attakapas District*, vol. 1, *The Attakapas Domesday Book: Land Grants, Claims, and Confirmations in the Attakapas District, 1764–1826* (Lafayette, La.: Center for Louisiana Studies, 1990).

MAINE

State-land state surveyed in coastal areas in the usual New England towns and into townships in the backwoods areas. In the 1620s and 1630s, a number of vaguely defined large tracts were granted that overlapped each other and snarled later land titles. Then Massachusetts exploited the English Civil War to assert claims to Maine during 1652 to 1674, which further confused titles, as did the abandonment of nearly all Maine settlements during the Indian wars beginning in the 1670s.

Here is a drastic simplification of history: The Kennebec River was a dividing line, the area west (i.e., south) being in the Ferdinando Gorges proprietary (granted 1622 and 1639) that was purchased by Massachusetts in 1677, while the area east (i.e., north) of the Kennebec to the Saint Croix River was granted to James, Duke of York, in 1664. Reverting to the crown upon his overthrow, this eastern area was granted to Massachusetts in 1691 with reservation to the crown of rights to grant first titles. Thus, until the American Revolution, Massachusetts granted Maine lands west of the Kennebec as proprietor, while it granted lands east of the river only with crown confirmation. Also scattered along the coast were those large and small overlapping early grants, which land developers/speculators purchased and resurrected by many lawsuits. A fifteen-mile strip on each side of the Kennebec itself was an outstanding example as described in Gordon E. Kershaw, *The Kennebec Proprietors, 1749–1775* (Portland: Maine Historical Society, 1975). In 1783 Massachusetts created the Committee for the Sale of Eastern [i.e., Maine] Lands. The Maine State Archives considers these records to be the beginning of the Maine Land Office that is now a division of the archive in Augusta. The enabling act for Maine's 1820 statehood reserved half its public lands for disposal by Massachusetts, these lands being surveyed into blocks intermixed with Maine's half. In 1853, Maine bought Massachusetts' remaining Maine lands. The Maine Land Office, State Capitol—Station 84, Augusta, ME 04333, has essentially the records since the revolution, including microfilms of Massachusetts land sales. Both Massachusetts and Maine issued military bounty warrants, but no specific reservation was established. Revolutionary War veteran land grants are microfilmed in thirteen reels. See also Charles J. House, *Names of Soldiers of the American Revolution Who Applied for the State Bounty under Resolves of March 17, 1835, March 24, 1836 and March 20, 1836 as Appears of Record in Land Office* (Augusta: by order of the Governor and Executive Council, 1893). The various Maine and Massachusetts genealogical journals have useful lists as well. York County was created in 1640 and was Maine's only functioning county until 1760. Its deeds (1642–1737) were published as *York Deeds*, 18 vols. (Portland: John T. Hull, et al., 1887–1910). The counties of Aroostook and Oxford each have two deed-registration districts. See also James Sullivan, *History of Land Titles in Massachusetts* (Boston: I. Thomas and E.T. Andrews, 1801); *Note by the Commissioner on the Sources of Land Titles in Maine* in *Revised Statutes of Maine, 1883*; Frederick S. Allis, ed., *William Bingham's Maine Lands, 1790–1820* (Boston: Colonial Society of Massachusetts, 1954), vols. 36–37 in *Collections, Colonial Society of Massachusetts*; and the microfilm publication of papers of Bingham's estate agent, John Black, in Lawrence Donald Bridgham, "Maine Public Lands 1781–1795: Claims, Trespassers, and Sales" (Ph.D. dissertation, Boston University, 1959).

MARYLAND

State-land state surveyed in indiscriminate metes and bounds except for lots in the military tract in the extreme western end of the state. The Calverts, Lords Baltimore, were proprietors of the colony from its founding in 1634 until the American Revolution. Their political control passed into other hands from 1654 to 1660 and 1692 to 1715, but their land-granting rights did not. In 1641 a surveyor-general was appointed, in 1680 a specific land office was established, and in 1684 a land council was created to oversee disposal of land. At about the same time, the previous headright system was replaced by cash sales of proprietary lands. Those persons transported and claimed for headright grants are listed in Gust Skordas, *The Early Settlers of Maryland, an Index to Names of Immigrants Compiled from Records of Land Patents, 1633–1680* (1968. Reprint. Baltimore: Genealogical Publishing Co., 1986). The Maryland Hall of Records, Box 828, Annapolis, MD 21404, holds the land office papers, all microfilmed, including the warrants and patents from 1634. See Elizabeth Hartsook and Gust Skordas, *Land Office and Prerogative Court Records of Colonial Maryland* (1946. Reprint. Baltimore: Genealogical Publishing Co., 1989).

The Hall of Records has extensive card indexes to its land records, including the tract names of the Maryland properties; see *A Guide to the Holdings at the Hall of Records*, Bulletin No. 17 (Annapolis, Md.: Hall of Records, October 1972). Colonial deeds were recorded at the county courts but have been collected at the Hall of Records and microfilmed. The deed books are inventoried in Morris L. Radoff, et al., *The County Courthouses and Records of Maryland, Part Two: The Records* (Annapolis: Hall of Records Commission, 1963). There were also conveyances in the Provincial and the General Court of the Western Shore, all likewise at the Hall of Records.

Maryland surveyed fifty-acre lots in its western panhandle and granted them as military bounty lands to revolutionary war veterans. For details, see John M. Brewer and Lewis Mayer, *The Laws and Rules of the Land Office of Maryland* (Baltimore: Kelly, Piet, 1871) and a list of recipients in J. Thomas Scharf, *History of Western Maryland* (1882. Reprint. Baltimore: Genealogical Publishing Co., 1968). The proprietary patents stipulated a quitrent, which was payable to the proprietor, not the government. See Beverley W. Bond, "The Quitrent System in Maryland," *Maryland Historical Magazine* 5 (1910): 350–65. The manuscript rent rolls listing the tracts within each county and the debt books listing individuals and their lands are scattered, and many have been lost, but there are significant collections in the Hall of Records in Annapolis and in the Calvert Papers of the Maryland Historical Society in Baltimore. See also Clarence P. Gould, *The Land System in Maryland, 1720–1765* (Baltimore: Johns Hopkins Press, 1913); Paul H. Giddens, "Land Policies and Administration in Colonial Maryland, 1753–1769," *Maryland Historical Magazine* 28 (1933): 142–71; and Canville D. Benson, "Notes on the Preparation of Conveyances by Laymen in the Colony of Maryland," ibid. 60 (1965): 428–38.

MASSACHUSETTS

State-land state surveyed in irregular New England town bounds in the east and in more regular town rectangles in the west. Massachusetts pioneered the New England system of towns with its grants by the legislature (General Court) to groups of settlers (town proprietors) who, in turn, oversaw land distributions within their town areas. Often, the General Court had likely frontier areas surveyed into convenient town-size tracts—six-mile squares were common—and offered publicly to potential proprietors for settlement. The proprietors' system is described in John Frederick Martin, *Profits in the Wilderness: Entrepreneurship and the Founding of New England Towns in the Seventeenth Century* (Chapel Hill, N.C.: 1991).

The Massachusetts Bay colonial records of such grants are in Nathaniel B. Shurtleff, ed., *Records of the Governor and Company of the Massachusetts Bay in New England,* 5 vols. (Boston: Order of the Legislature, 1853–54), published in 6 vols. Plymouth colonial records are in Shurtleff, *Records of the Colony of Plymouth in New England,* 12 vols. (Boston: Order of the Legislature, 1855–61); vol. 12 is deeds (1620–51). The deeds for Massachusetts Bay were recorded in town records until the creation of counties around 1643, although land transactions continued to be recorded in some towns after this date. Plymouth colony was joined by charter with Massachusetts Bay in late 1691. In 1685, it had been divided into three counties that recorded conveyances. Several Massachusetts counties were later divided into deed-registration districts: Berkshire into three districts in 1788, Bristol into two in 1837, Middlesex into two districts in 1854, Essex into two in 1869, and Worcester into two in 1884, each with its own courthouse. The Salem registry of Essex County, aside from its own deeds, also has those of old Norfolk County (1637–1714) and Ipswich (including Newbury and later Rowley) town deeds (1640–1694). The important county of Suffolk (Boston) has its early deeds (1629–1697) published as *Suffolk Deeds*, 14 vols. (Boston: Rockwell and Churchill Press, 1880–1906). It should be obvious from these brief facts that you must allow for variations in where, when, and what local land records survive. Town proprietor records also often survive, and some have been published. Property valuations and taxes for 1760 to 1771 and 1780 to 1811 have been microfilmed in four and nineteen rolls respectively. See also James Sullivan, *The History of Land Titles in Massachusetts* (Boston: I. Thomas and E.T. Andrews, 1801); Mark D. Howe, "Recording of Deeds in the Colony of Massachusetts Bay," *Boston University Law Review* 28 (1948): 1–6; and William I. Davisson and Dennis J. Dugan, "Land Precedents in Essex County, Massachusetts," *Essex Institute Historical Collections* 106 (1970): 252–76.

MICHIGAN

Public-domain state with one principal meridian (established 1819). Michigan was under British jurisdiction until 1796, when the American government assumed control of Detroit. The five-to-eight-mile Toledo Strip on the Michigan-Ohio border, now in Ohio, was under Michigan jurisdiction until 1835. The earliest GLO land office opened in 1804 in Detroit, and the last closed in Marquette in 1925. The location of Michigan's eight GLO district records could not be learned, except that the BLM turned over to the Bentley Historical Library of the University of Michigan, 1150 Beal Ave., Ann Arbor, MI 48109, a set of the tract books and township plats. There are microfilms at some other Michigan libraries. Obtain patents from the BLM Eastern States Office, which also has copies of the tract books and township plats. Michigan's federal patents are indexed in the GLO Automated Records System. A CD-ROM of Michigan land patents is available for purchase from the GLO. The National Archives in Washington, D.C., has the land-entry case files as described in Inventory No. 22. For private land claims, see the *American State Papers, Public Lands* as indexed in McMullin's *Grassroots of America*. See also D. Jones, "The Survey and Sale of the Public Land in Michigan, 1815–1862" (M.A. thesis, Cornell University, 1952); LeRoy Barnett, "Milestones in Michigan Mapping," *Michigan History* 63 (September/October 1979): 34–43; 63 (November/December 1979): 29–38. Detroit property owners in 1805 are discussed in detail in Clarence M. Burton, with A. Agnes Burton, ed., *Governor and Judges Journal, Proceedings of the Land Board of Detroit* (Detroit, 1915).

MINNESOTA

Public-domain state with two principal meridians (established 1831 and, far south in Arkansas, 1815). Of the dozen GLO land districts, the earliest opened in 1848 at Falls Saint Croix River, Wisconsin, and moved to Stillwater, Minnesota, in 1849; the last closed at Cass Lake in 1933. The tract books are available at the State Archives, which is a part of the Minnesota Historical Society, and the records are housed at the Minnesota History Center, home of the Minnesota Historical Society. Obtain patents from the BLM Eastern States Office, which also has copies of the tract books and township plats. Minnesota's federal patents/deeds are indexed as part of the GLO Automated Records System. The National Archives in Washington, D.C., has the land-entry case files as described in Inventory No. 22. See Matthias N. Orfield, *Federal Land Grants to the States With Special Reference to Minnesota*, University of Min-

nesota Studies in the Social Sciences (Minneapolis: the author, 1915); C.J. Ritchey, "Claim Associations and Frontier Democracy in Early Minnesota," *Minnesota History* 9 (1928): 85–95; C.E. Worth, "The Operation of the Land Laws in the Minnesota Iron District," *Mississippi Valley Historical Review* 13 (1927): 483–98; and Gregory Kinney and Lydia Lucas, *Guide to the Records of Minnesota's Public Lands* (St. Paul: Minnesota Historical Society, Division of Archives and Manuscripts, 1985).

MISSISSIPPI

Public-domain state with five principal meridians (established 1803 to 1833). Of the eight GLO land districts between 1806 and 1925, the earliest opened in Washington in 1807, and the last closed in Jackson in 1925. The records of these offices are in the National Archives in Washington, D.C., not in Mississippi. The records of the Mississippi Land Office, a state agency, are now in the Mississippi Department of Archives and History, including some early records for the southern part of the state. Territorial land and court records (1798–1817) at the state archive have been microfilmed in five rolls. Obtain patents from the BLM Eastern States Office, which also has copies of the tract books and township plats. Mississippi's federal patents are indexed in the GLO Automated Records System. The National Archives in Washington, D.C., has the land-entry case files as described in Inventory No. 22. For private land claims, numerous along the Gulf and the Mississippi River, see the *American State Papers, Public Lands* as indexed in McMullin's *Grassroots of America*. Early land claims are also given in May Wilson McBee, *The Natchez Court Records, 1767–1805: Abstracts of Early Records* (Greenwood, Miss.: the author, 1954). It should be remembered that the area south of thirty-one degrees was part of Spanish West Florida until 1810–11; thus, West Florida archives are partly in the state archive at Tallahassee and partly in Seville, Spain. See Richard S. Lackey, "Credit Land Sales, 1811–1815: Mississippi Entries East of the Pearl" (M.A. thesis, University of Southern Mississippi, 1975); and Robert V. Haynes, "The Disposal of Lands in Mississippi Territory," *Journal of Mississippi History* 24 (1962): 226–52.

MISSOURI

Public-domain state with one principal meridian (established 1815). The earliest of the eight GLO land districts opened at Saint Louis in 1818, and the last closed in Springfield in 1922. Their records are in the state archive. See Missouri Records Management and Archives Service, "Missouri Public Domain: United States Land Sales, 1818–1922," *Archives Information Bulletin* 2 (July 1980), which summarizes Missouri's land history, gives maps of the GLO land district boundaries, and lists the land records in the state archive. Obtain patents from the BLM Eastern States Office, which also has copies of the tract books and township plats. The National Archives has the land-entry case files as described in Inventory No. 22.

The opening of the first land office was delayed by extensive private-land claims requiring adjudication, then delayed again by the New Madrid earthquakes of 1811–12. Congress in 1815 granted scrip for up to 640 acres to sufferers in such "injured lands" with claims to be processed prior to opening the federal lands to public sales. For private land claims, see the *American State Papers, Public Lands* as indexed by

McMullin's *Grassroots of America*. See also *Missouri Land Claims* (New Orleans: Polyanthos, 1976), reprint of Congressional Document, 24th Congress, 1st Session, no. 16, 1835. It is noteworthy that, by 1793, Spanish Upper Louisiana had five administrative districts, from north to south: Saint Charles, Saint Louis (the provincial capital), Sainte Genevieve, Cape Girardeau, and New Madrid (which included Arkansas). These districts became the new American counties.

In 1795, a Spanish surveyor-general was appointed for Upper Louisiana. The archives of the Spanish districts are at several localities. Those at the Missouri Historical Society have been microfilmed and include major land records. There are also several hundred rolls of microfilmed land records at the state archive. One of the War of 1812 bounty-land reserves was in Missouri, for which an index and other records are available on NARS microfilm M848, *War of 1812 Military Bounty Land Warrants, 1815–1858,* in fourteen rolls. See also Lemont K. Richardson, "Private Land Claims in Missouri," *Missouri Historical Review* 50 (1955–56): 132–44, 271–86, 387–99; and Paul W. Gates, *History of Public Land Law Development* (Washington, D.C.: Public Land Law Review Commission, 1968), 96–108.

MONTANA

Public-domain state with one principal meridian (established 1867). The earliest of the nine GLO land districts opened at Helena in 1867. The records of these offices, including pre-1908 patents, are in the National Archives—Rocky Mountain Region in Denver. Obtain post-1908 patents from the BLM Montana State Office, P.O. Box 36800, 222 N. 32nd St., Billings, MT 59107-6800, which also has copies of the tract books and township plats. The National Archives in Washington, D.C., has the land-entry case files as described in Inventory No. 22, and also the GLO headquarters original tract books and township plats. See William S. Peters and Maxine C. Johnson, *Public Lands in Montana; Their History and Current Significance*, Regional Study no. 10 (Missoula: Bureau of Business and Economic Research, 1959).

NEBRASKA

Public-domain state with one principal meridian (established 1855). Of the thirteen GLO land districts, the earliest opened in 1855 in Omaha, the last closed at Alliance in 1933. The records of these offices are in the state archive in the Nebraska State Historical Society, which has microfilmed all the tract books in fifty-three rolls and indexed some. Obtain patents from the BLM Wyoming State Office, P.O. Box 1828, 2515 Warren Ave., Cheyenne, WY 82003, which also has copies of the tract books and township plats for Nebraska. The National Archives in Washington, D.C., has the land-entry case files as described in Inventory No. 22 and the GLO headquarters original tract books and township plats. The land grant to the Union Pacific Railroad totaled a tenth of Nebraska, but its land office records were mostly destroyed in a fire. See Barry B. Combs, "The Union Pacific Railroad and the Early Settlement of Nebraska, 1868–1880," *Nebraska History* 50 (1969): 1–26; Addison Erwin Sheldon, "Land Systems and Land Policies in Nebraska," *Publications of the Nebraska State Historical Society* 22 (Lincoln: Nebraska State Historical Society, 1936): 302–15; and Homer Socolofsky, "Land Disposal in Nebraska, 1854–1906: The Homestead Story," *Nebraska History* 48 (1967): 225–48.

NEVADA

Public-domain state with one principal meridian (established 1851 in California). Nevada had four GLO land districts; the first opened in 1864 at Carson City. Obtain patents from the BLM Nevada State Office, Box 12000, 850 Harvard Way, Reno, NV 89520-0006, which also has copies of the tract books and perhaps some township plats. The National Archives in Washington, D.C., has the land-entry case files as described in Inventory No. 22 and the GLO headquarters original tract books and township plats. It also has a card index to Nevada patentees to 30 June 1908. The National Archives—Pacific Sierra Region in San Bruno, California, has the records of the Nevada GLO district offices, including the originals of the local office tract books and township plats. See John M. Townley, "Management of Nevada's State Lands, 1864–1900," *Journal of the West* 17 (1978): 62–73.

NEW HAMPSHIRE

State-land state surveyed in irregular New England town bounds along the coast and in fairly rectangular towns farther west and north. In the 1620s, John Mason was granted the land between the Merrimack and Piscataqua rivers, but he and his heirs failed to establish a successful proprietary colony. Beginning around 1641–42, Massachusetts claimed jurisdiction over the area, which fell within old Norfolk County, Massachusetts. The land records for old Norfolk are now at Salem in Essex County, Massachusetts. In 1679, New Hampshire escaped from Massachusetts control and became a royal province, while the Masonian assignees received qualified right to grant subject to local court decisions.

Prior to 1741, Massachusetts also claimed the Merrimack Valley and established several towns there until New Hampshire's authority was confirmed by royal decree in 1741. New Hampshire then began granting land west of the Connecticut River in what is now Vermont—the Hampshire Grants—but never prevailed against the competing New York claims. The state archive has the major early land records and has published *Documents and Records Relating to the Province*, also called the *New Hampshire Provincial Papers* or the *New Hampshire State Papers*. Records on the town charters are in vols. 24–25 (1894–1895), the town grants in vols. 27–28 (1895), the Masonian patent papers in vol. 29 (1896), and the Hampshire Grants in Vermont in vol. 26 (1895). Deeds from 1679 were recorded at the provincial capital until about 1771. They have all been microfilmed and are located in the state archive. The first counties were created in 1769 and took over the recording of conveyances. See Jonathan Smith, "Town Patents Under Belcher," *Massachusetts Historical Society Proceedings* 45 (1911–12): 197–210; John F. Looney, "Benning Wentworth's Land Grant Policy: A Reappraisal," *Historical New Hampshire* 23 (1968): 3–13; and Maurice H. Robinson, *A History of Taxation in New Hampshire* (New York: 1903).

NEW JERSEY

State-land state (though the state never owned the land) surveyed in indiscriminate metes and bounds, plus some New England towns south of Staten Island. Compared to the other colonies, New Jersey had complex political and land-granting jurisdictions. After the fall of New Sweden and then New Netherlands, the area was granted to James, Duke of York, who regranted it to two proprietors. After several more transfers and agreements, a 1686 West Jersey existed with its capital at Burlington while a corresponding East Jersey was governed from Perth Amboy. The dividing line between the two was poorly surveyed and caused conflicting land grants. In 1702, the proprietors surrendered governance to the crown but retained the right to grant vacant lands. From 1702 to 1738, New York and the reunified New Jersey had the same royal governor. In the late 1740s, land riots in East Jersey opposed the titles of the proprietors.

New Jersey is unique among the thirteen colonies in that its proprietors retained their rights after the Revolution to grant lands and receive escheated land. They still retain these rights. Proprietary shares pass down the generations by inheritance and purchase like any other property. Consequently, proprietary land records (warrants, surveys, and patents) remain at the proprietary offices in Burlington and Perth Amboy. The major series have been microfilmed. Since colonial deeds had also been recorded at the two Jersey capitals, the New Jersey legislature in 1795 ordered them all transferred to Trenton. They are now in the state archive and have been microfilmed in separate series. Deeds after 1785 should be in the counties. The early Jersey deeds are published in William Nelson, *Calendar of Records in the Office of the Secretary of State, 1664–1703* (Paterson: state of New Jersey, 1899), as vol. 26 in *Documents Relating to the Colonial History of the State of New Jersey* (commonly called the *New Jersey Archives*). This book has been reprinted under the title *Patents and Deeds and Other Early Records of New Jersey, 1664–1703* (Baltimore: Genealogical Publishing Co., 1976). Kenn Stryker-Rodda has noted three special problems concerning early New Jersey property conveyances: (1) only an estimated twenty-five percent of the colonial deeds were recorded; (2) Jerseymen tended to record deeds when they needed to mortgage property, hence monied people are less likely to appear in the land records than the impecunious; and (3) "No one can pretend to do research on East Jersey families without careful examination of the contents of most of the 32 boxes of Alexander papers at the New-York Historical Society, where are preserved surveys, deeds, letters concerning property, litigation, etc.; nor on West Jersey families without similar examination of the Penn and Logan papers in Philadelphia."[38] See John E. Pomfret, *The New Jersey Proprietors and Their Lands, 1664–1776* (Princeton: D. Van Nostrand, 1964); Edgar J. Fisher, "Colonial Land Conflicts in New Jersey," *Historical Society of Hudson County Papers* no. 6; Crestview Lawyers Service, *Colonial Conveyances: Provinces of East & West New Jersey*, 2 vols. (Summit, N.J.: Crestview Lawyers Service, 1974); Charles H. Winfield, *History of the Land Titles in Hudson County, N.J., 1609–1871* (New York: Wynkoop & Hallenbeck, 1872), 1–25; and James C. Connolly, "Quit Rents in Colonial New Jersey," *Union County Historical Society Proceedings* 1 (1923): 3–12.

NEW MEXICO

Public-domain state with one principal meridian (established 1855). The first of New Mexico's four GLO land districts opened at Santa Fe in 1858. Their records are in the National Archives—Rocky Mountain Region in Denver. Obtain patents from the BLM New Mexico State Office, P.O. Box 27115, 1474 Rodeo Rd., Santa Fe, NM 87502-1449, which also has copies of the tract books and township plats. The National Archives in Washington, D.C., has the land-entry case files as described in Inventory No. 22 and the GLO headquarters original tract books and township plats. The 1854 Donation Act for New Mexico seems to have been little used, for *The Guide to Genealogical Research in the National Archives,* p. 216, does not even mention this act in its section on donation lands, and the National Archives' Inventory No. 22, pp. 55–56, lists only 344 New Mexico donation patents. New Mexico private land grants are still being adjudicated and occasionally provoke violence. The large secondary literature is conveniently listed in Annabelle M. Oczon, "Land Grants in New Mexico: A Selective Bibliography," *New Mexico Historical Review* 57 (1982): 81–87. For information on the microfilm series on Spanish and Mexican archives, including land papers and private land claims, write the New Mexico State Records Center and Archives, 404 Montezuma, Santa Fe, NM 87503. See also Victor Westphall, *The Public Domain in New Mexico, 1854–1891* (Albuquerque: University of New Mexico Press, 1965); W.A. Keleher, "Law of the New Mexico Land Grant," *New Mexico Historical Review* 4 (1929): 350–71; and a series of articles collectively titled "Spanish Land Grants in New Mexico and Colorado," *Journal of the West* 19 (July 1980): 1–99.

NEW YORK

State-land state surveyed in several systems: indiscriminate metes and bounds, large manors with tenant farms, New England towns on eastern Long Island and along the Connecticut border, and large tracts in central and western New York often surveyed in townships, ranges, and lots. Very large grants were always a common feature of New York land policy, the government officials finding it convenient (and lucrative both for fees and sharing the spoils) to have entrepreneurs do the subdividing and selling or leasing in farm-size parcels. Maps locating these major tracts have been printed often. One source is J.R. Bien, *Atlas of the State of New York* (New York: J. Bien & Co., 1895).

Several mammoth tracts in the western part of the state came into the hands of Phelps-Gorham, Robert Morris, and the Holland Land Company. The original papers of the Holland Land Company are in Amsterdam, The Netherlands, but they are available in the United States on microfilm. The Holland Land Company Project at the Reed Library, State University of New York, College of Fredonia, Fredonia, NY 14063 has identified other holdings in the United States concerned with the Holland Land Company and is collecting microfilmed copies. See O(rasmus) Turner, *Pioneer History of the Holland Purchase of Western New York* (Reprint. Bowie, Md.: Heritage Books, 1991). William Wyckoff, *The Developer's Frontier: The Making of the Western New York Landscape* (New Haven, Conn.: Yale University Press, 1988) looks at the Holland Land Company as a developer. Karen E. Livsey, *Western New York Land Transactions, 1804–1824* (Baltimore: Genealogical Publishing Co., 1991) and *Western Land Transactions, 1825–1835* (Baltimore: Clearfield Co., 1996), help to locate settlers and their land and index the microfilmed records of the Holland Land Company.

The private papers of the large Hudson River manors may be necessary to complete a genealogy, since tenants who leased but did not buy land may never appear in the county conveyance records. See B. Fernow, *Documents Relating to the History and Settlement of the Towns Along the Hudson and Mohawk Rivers (With the Exception of Albany) From 1630 to 1682* (Albany: Weed, Parsons, 1881). The background history is excellently summarized in Sung Bok Kim, *Landlord and Tenant in Colonial New York: Manorial Society, 1664–1775* (Chapel Hill: University of North Carolina Press, 1978). In 1650, the Dutch government of New Netherlands recognized Connecticut's title to Long Island east of Oyster Bay, though Long Island was soon reunited with New York under the Duke of York's proprietary (1664–1689). See B. Fernow, *Documents Relating to the History of the Early Colonial Settlements Principally on Long Island* (Albany: Weed, Parsons, 1883). Deeds in these early New England towns were recorded in the town, not the county, prior to the successful extension of Suffolk County jurisdiction. This is also sometimes true of the debatable land east of the Hudson adjoining Connecticut and Massachusetts, where New Englanders settled on lands claimed by New York. (See the Vermont entry for lands granted in what is now that state by New York.)

The major land records—patents, deeds, and land grant applications—of the colonial and state government are in the state archive. They are listed in New York State Archives, *Public Records Relating to Land in New York State* (Albany: New York State Archives, 1979). They are on microfilm. Land grant applications are partly available in New York Secretary of State, *Calendar of N.Y. Colonial Manuscripts, Indorsed Land Papers, in the Office of the Secretary of State of New York, 1643–1803* (Albany: Weed, Parsons, 1864). In 1784, the Board of Commissioners of the Land Office was established to dispose of the state's remaining public lands. In 1979, the Division of Land Utilization (Office of General Services) still held the land grant applicant files from 1799.

New York allotted its revolutionary war soldiers bounty land, giving privates five hundred acres. The military reserve in the Finger Lakes region was surveyed into six hundred-acre lots so that veterans could take their one hundred-acre federal bounty alongside their state bounty in lieu of one hundred acres in Ohio. Most veterans sold their claims and never settled in the military tract. The surveyed land in this reserve was distributed by lottery drawing; hence, the title of the state's published list of recipients: New York Legislature, *The Balloting Book, and Other Documents Relating to Military Bounty Lands in the State of New York*, New York Legislature (Albany: Packard & Van Benthuysen, 1825). See Robert S. Rose, "The Military Tract of Central N.Y." (M.A. thesis, Syracuse University, 1935). An earlier military tract was established northeast of the Adirondacks, but very few accepted this poor land. For background on New York's varied land tenure and law, see Robert L. Fowler, *History of the Law of Real Property in New York* (New York: Baker, Voorhis, 1895); S.G. Nissinson, "The Development of a Land Registration System in New York," *New York History* 20 (1939): 16–21; Armand LaPotin, "The Minisink Grant: Partnerships, Patents, and Processing Fees in Eighteenth Century New York," ibid. 56 (1976): 28–50; Charles W. Spencer, "The Land System of Colonial New York," *New York State Historical Association Proceedings* 16 (1917): 150–64; Arthur E. Sutherland, "The Tenancy on the New York Manor," *Cornell Law Quarterly* 41 (1956): 620–39; and H. Gresham Toole, "The Dutch Land System of New Netherlands," Marshall Review 2 (1938): 31–39.

NORTH CAROLINA

State-land state surveyed in indiscriminate metes and bounds. By charter in 1663 (amended 1665), eight proprietors received a grant of all lands between 29 degrees and 36 degrees 30 minutes, the latter being the present North Carolina-Virginia line. In 1729, George II bought seven of the eight shares and made the Carolina proprietary a royal colony (actually three colonies—the two Carolinas and, in 1732, Georgia). The eighth share belonged to Lord Carteret, later Earl Granville, whose one-eighth part was laid off using the already surveyed Virginia line. Thus the northern half of present-day North Carolina composed the Granville District, where Earl Granville had the right to grant lands and collect quitrents, though not to govern. The boundary of the Granville District was the present southern line of the counties of Rowan-Davidson-Randolph projected east to the ocean. This Granville line was not even partially surveyed until the 1740s, when a land office was opened, only to be closed permanently about 1763. See E. Merton Coulter, *The Granville District*, James Sprunt Historical Publications, vol. 13, no. 12 (Chapel Hill: University of North Carolina, 1913), 33–56. Also see Margaret M. Hofmann's five-volume *The Granville District of North Carolina 1748–1763 Abstracts of Land Grants*. George Stevenson's introduction in vol. 1 provides important information relating to the Granville District.

The Granville grants, with an index, are in the state archive. The remaining grants from the early proprietary, the royal colony, and the state government, are also in the state archive, and there is a separate card index to them. The archive also provides MARS, a computerized finding aid for searching grants statewide. However, be alert to its peculiar arrangement, described in Margaret M. Hofmann, "Land Grants," in *North Carolina Research: Genealogy and Local History*, edited by Helen F.M. Leary (Raleigh: North Carolina Genealogical Society, 1996), pp. 313–28. Hofmann has also abstracted grants from the proprietary period in *Province of North Carolina, 1663–1729, Abstracts of Land Patents* (Weldon, N.C.: Roanoke News, 1979) and the crown colony era in *Colony of North Carolina 1735–1764: Abstracts of Land Patents Volume 1* and *Colony of North Carolina 1765–1775: Abstracts of Land Patents Volume 2*. In progress as of 1996 by Hofmann is *From the Charter to the Revolution: An Index to North Carolina Proprietary and Crown Patents and Granville District Claims*. Headrights were offered throughout the colonial period, though the requirements and acreage varied. For such stipulations, see "Land Grants in Colonial North Carolina," *Family Puzzlers* no. 653 (24 April 1980): 1–4.

Deeds were recorded in the counties, though irregularly in the earliest years. North Carolina's military bounty-land act was the most generous of the states in granting 640 acres (in Tennessee) to a private in the continental line. Researchers should read George Stevenson's description of the state's bounty-land records as given in Leary's *North Carolina Genealogy* (cited above), pp. 384–90. Also see Kenneth B. Pomeroy and James G. Yoho, *North Carolina Lands: Ownership, Use, and Management of Forest and Related Lands* (Washington, D.C.: American Forestry Association, 1964); George Henry Swathers, *The History of Land Titles in Western North Carolina* (Ashville: Miller Printing, 1938); Lawrence N. Morgan, *Land Tenure in Proprietary North Carolina*, James Sprunt Historical Publications, vol. 12, no. 2 (Chapel Hill: University of North Carolina, 1912), 41–63; Dan Lacy, "Records in the Offices of Registers of Deeds in N.C.," *North Carolina Historical Review* 14 (1937): 213–29; Jacquelyn H. Wolf, "Patents and Tithables in Proprietary North Carolina, 1663–1729," ibid. 56 (1979): 263–77; and Marvin L. Michael Kay, "The Payment of Provincial and Local Taxes in North Carolina, 1748–1771," *William and Mary Quarterly*, 3rd series, 26 (1960): 218–40.

NORTH DAKOTA

Public-domain state with one principal meridian (established 1815 in Arkansas, North Dakota being surveyed much later). The earliest of North Dakota's seven GLO land districts opened at Pembina in 1870. The bulk of their records are in the State Historical Society of North Dakota. The original township plats are at the North Dakota Water Commission, State Office Building, 900 East Blvd., Bismarck, ND 58505. Obtain patents from the BLM Montana State Office, P.O. Box 36800, 222 North 32nd St., Billings, MT 59107-6800, which also has copies of the tract books and township plats for North Dakota. The National Archives in Washington, D.C., has the land-entry case files as described in Inventory No. 22 and the GLO headquarters original tract books and township plats. See N. Thomas, "Distribution of the Public Domain in Dakota Territory" (M.A. thesis, University of South Dakota, 1944).

OHIO

Public-domain state with a complicated surveying history. Aside from the Virginia Military District's indiscriminate metes and bounds, Ohio has a dozen different township-and-range surveys, the major principal meridians being established from 1785 to 1819. Some of these surveys do not use the usual federal numbering system but have five-mile-square townships. Researchers should be alert to four different boundary jurisdictions in early Ohio:

1. The actual surveys with their meridians and baselines (or lack of same in the Virginia Military District). See C.E. Sherman, *Original Ohio Land Subdivisions*, 4 vols. (1949. Reprint. Columbus: Ohio Department of Natural Resources, 1982). Vol. 3 recounts the history of the various surveys and gives detailed maps showing the numbering of townships. This book is a must for early Ohio research.

2. The various tracts as they opened for settlement, such as the Seven Ranges, the U.S. Military District, the Congress Lands east of Scioto River, and the Congress Lands west of Miami River. A map of these tracts is frequently reproduced in Ohio how-to books and articles. See, for instance, Carol Willsey Flavell and Florence Clint, *Ohio Area Key* (Denver: Area Keys, 1977), 45.

3. The land office districts, such as Symmes's private land office at Cincinnati, the GLO's Chillicothe land office (1801–1876), and the Virginia Military District's land office, also at Chillicothe. For GLO districts, see National Archives Inventory No. 22, pp. 57–59. The National Archives and the Ohio State Land Office, 1272 S. Front St., Columbus, OH 43206, have guides to the changing GLO district boundaries.

4. The counties with their registries of deeds. See Randolph Chandler Downs, *Evolution of Ohio County Boundaries* (1927. Reprint. Columbus: Ohio Historical Society, 1970).

The state auditor of Ohio is in charge of the State Land Office. It has issued a pamphlet entitled *Ohio Lands: A Short History* (Columbus: auditor of state, 1991) by Thomas A. Burke, which helps orient the beginning researcher. The office also has an index to all Ohio patentees except the Symmes Pur-

chase and the Connecticut Western Reserve, both of which were issued as single patents. Most Symmes land papers apparently burned. The Connecticut Land Company papers are in the Litchfield Historical Society, Box 385, Litchfield, CT 06759. There are land papers for the Western Reserve, both in the Western Reserve Historical Society and in the Connecticut State Library, Hartford.

Settlers in the Western Reserve sometimes dealt through the Susquehannah Land Company and the Phelps-Gorham Land Company. See Julian P. Boyd and Robert J. Taylor, *Susquehannah Company Papers*, 11 vols. (Wilkes-Barre, Penn.: Wyoming Historical and Geological Society, and Ithaca, N.Y.: Cornell University Press, 1930–71). The original papers in the Connecticut State Archives, titled "Susquehannah Settlers, 1755–1796" and "Western Lands, 1783–1789," include many references to the Fire Lands and the Connecticut Land Company. The papers and an every-name index are microfilmed. The Phelps-Gorham papers in the New York State Archives in Albany also include numerous references to Ohio lands, such as "Vol. 145. Book of Conveyances of Lands in Ohio, 1795–1808, and Vol. 156. Book of Conveyances of Lands in Ohio, 1801–1822."

A major listing of early Ohio entrymen and patentees is Clifford Neal Smith, *Federal Land Series*, 4 vols. to date (Chicago: American Library Association, 1972–). Smith is meticulously listing the contents and indexing the name lists in various manuscript collections. While not limited to Ohio, these first volumes are heavy on Ohio entrymen because the earliest federal land sales were mostly there. Smith's introductions should be read by any genealogist working in early Ohio records.

The earliest of Ohio's nine GLO land districts opened in 1800 in Marietta and Steubenville; the last closed at Chillicothe in 1876. The records of these land offices are divided between the State Archives in the Ohio Historical Center, which has original land survey field notes, land survey plats, tract and entry books, and index cards related to federal lands and Virginia Military District lands; and the Ohio Historical Society, which holds surveys and first transfers of land. Research inquiries will be answered by the OHS Archives/Library, Ohio Historical Society, 1982 Velma Ave., Columbus, OH 43211-2497. Obtain patents from the BLM Eastern States Office, which also has copies of the tract books, township plats, and a five-volume index to Ohio patents, ca. 1800 to 1820. Ohio's federal patents are indexed in the GLO Automated Records System. A CD-ROM of Ohio land patents is available for purchase from the GLO. The National Archives in Washington has the land-entry case files as described in Inventory No. 22. The two major military reserves in Ohio for Revolutionary veterans—the Virginia Military District and the U.S. Military District—were discussed earlier in this chapter under Bounty Lands. Also see William Thomas Hutchinson, "Military Bounty Lands of the American Revolution in Ohio" (Ph.D. dissertation, University of Chicago, 1927).

The Connecticut Western Reserve was not a military reserve, nor did Connecticut grant its soldiers bounty land. Several categories of sufferers in the American Revolution were granted lands in Ohio. The inhabitants of Connecticut towns burned by British/Loyalist raiders received compensation in the Fire Lands of the Western Reserve, also called the Sufferers' Lands. Pro-independence refugees from Canada and Nova Scotia received land in the Refuge Tract. See Smith's *Federal*

Land Series, vol. 1, sources F and G, for sufferers and refugees. Tax records for 1800 to 1838 at the Ohio Historical Society are microfilmed.

See William E. Peters, "Ohio Lands and Their History," *Bulletin of the History and Philosophy Society of Ohio* 15 (1957): 340–48, and his *Ohio Lands and Their Subdivision*, 3rd ed. (Athens, Ohio: the author, 1930); his seventeen-volume typescript, "Code of Land Titles in Ohio. A Compilation from Official Records of All Charters, Indian Treaties, Grants . . ." (1935), is microfilmed and available at several major Ohio research libraries. See also Carol Willsey Bell, *Ohio Guide to Genealogical Sources* (Baltimore: Genealogical Publishing Co., 1988); Kenneth Duckett, "Ohio Land Patents," *Ohio History* 72 (1963): 51–60; and Mayburt Stephenson Riegel, *Early Ohioans' Residences From the Land Grant Records* (Mansfield, Ohio: Ohio Genealogical Society, 1976).

OKLAHOMA

Public-domain state with two principal meridians (established 1870 and 1881). Of the eleven GLO land districts, the earliest opened at Guthrie and Kingfisher in 1889, and the last closed at Guthrie in 1927. The records of these local offices are in the state archive. While it never had a unified territorial government, eastern Oklahoma was called the Indian Territory after an 1830 act of Congress. It continued until 1907, the major tribes each having their organized governments, complete with tribal capitals. Only in 1889 was present-day Oklahoma opened to the federal land disposal process operated by the GLO. What made Oklahoma settlements spectacularly different were the formal land rushes with their opening day stampedes to stake claims to already surveyed quarter sections. Those who illegally jumped the gun were called "sooners." The last major land tract was distributed by lottery rather than land rush. Obtain patents from the BLM New Mexico State Office, P.O. Box 27115, 1474 Rodeo Rd., Santa Fe, NM 87502-0115, which also has copies of the tract books and township plats for Oklahoma. The National Archives in Washington, D.C., has the entry-land case files as described in Inventory No. 22 and the GLO headquarters original tract books and township plats.

Before Indian lands were opened for white settlement, each tribal member received an individual land allotment. While there is no one repository for the Indian allotment records, the researcher should check the National Archives—Central Plains Region in Kansas City, Missouri, and the Southwest Region in Fort Worth, Texas, and also the National Archives microfilm publications. The Indian Archives Division of the Oklahoma Historical Society, Oklahoma City, holds the records of many tribes. See Jean C. Brown, *Oklahoma Research: The Twin Territories* (Sapulpa, Okla.: the author, 1975); *Guide to Genealogical Research in the National Archives* (Washington, D.C.: National Archives and Records Service, 1982), 159–70; and Berlin Basil Chapman, "Federal Management and Disposition of the Lands of Oklahoma Territory, 1866–1907" (Ph.D. dissertation, University of Wisconsin, 1932).

OREGON

Public-domain state with one principal meridian (established 1851). Of the six GLO land districts, the earliest opened in Oregon City in 1855. Obtain patents from the BLM Oregon State Office, P.O. Box 2965, 1300 N.E. 44th St., Portland, OR 97208-2965, which also has copies of the tract books and township plats. The GLO office records are in the National Archives—Pacific Northwest Region in Seattle. The National Archives in Washington, D.C., has the land-entry case files as described in Inventory No. 22 and the GLO headquarters original tract books and township plats.

Oregon's earliest white and mixed-blood settlers were entitled to free federal land under the Donation Act of 1850. An index and abstracts are on NARS microfilm M145, *Abstracts of Oregon Donation Land Claims, 1852–1903,* in six rolls, which serves as an index to the case files reproduced in NARS microfilm M815, *Oregon and Washington Donation Land Files, 1851–1903,* in 108 rolls. Because of a law forbidding their reproduction, the naturalization certificates in M815 case files were not microfilmed. The law was changed in the 1970s, so naturalization records referred to in these files can now be obtained from the National Archives. Donation case files are valuable because they should contain a statement of the date and place of birth of the entryman. See Genealogical Forum of Portland, Ore., *Genealogical Material in Oregon Donation Land Claims,* 5 vols. (Portland: Genealogical Forum of Portland, 1957–75). See also Jerry A. O'Callaghan, "The Disposition of the Public Domain in Oregon" (Ph.D. dissertation, Stanford University, 1952); and James M. Bergquist, "Oregon Donation Act and National Land Policy," *Oregon Historical Quarterly* 58 (1957): 17–35.

PENNSYLVANIA

State-land state surveyed mostly in indiscriminate metes and bounds, though the donation and depreciation lands north of Pittsburgh were surveyed in rectangular, numbered lots. William Penn, as proprietor, established a land office in 1682 that became the Division of Land Records until it merged with the archive in 1990 (Pennsylvania Historical and Museum Commission, Bureau of Archives and History, William Penn Memorial Museums and Archives Building, Box 1026, Harrisburg, PA 17108-1026). The archive holds such major land series as applications for warrants, original warrants, original surveys, patents, and military grants—all microfilmed in many hundreds of reels. There are also smaller but no less valuable collections, such as depositions (1683–1881), caveats (1699–1890), title papers (1784–1852), etc., which have also been microfilmed. Donna Bingham Munger's landmark publication, *Pennsylvania Land Records, A History and Guide for Research* (Wilmington, Del.: Scholarly Resources, 1991), is required reading on the subject.

The Penn proprietary was very businesslike in disposing of its lands at a fixed price (no headrights) as supervised by an appointed surveyor and a commission/board of property, which helps explain its wealth of records. The archive is constructing tract maps for each county and has completed these "warrantee township maps" for most of the counties. They are available for purchase. A valuable feature of many Pennsylvania grants is the tract names—at least for earlier tracts—such as "Lithuania" or Levi Andrew Levi's "Uncircumcision." Such names may give ethnic and religious clues. To the records mentioned above should be added the first nine volumes of Pennsylvania grant records, discovered in the Philadelphia City Hall in 1952 and now indexed in Allen Weinberg and Thomas E. Slattery, *Warrants and Surveys of the Province of Pennsylvania Including the Three Lower Counties, 1759* (Philadelphia: Philadelphia Department of Records, 1965). See John E. Pomfret, "The First Purchasers of Pennsylvania, 1681–1700,"

Pennsylvania Magazine of History and Biography 80 (1956): 137–63. The *Pennsylvania Archives*, 3rd series, contains William Henry Egle, *Warrantees of Land in the Several Counties of the State of Pennsylvania, 1730–1898*, vols. 24–26 (Harrisburg: State Printer, 1898–1899), vols. 24–26. The *Pennsylvania Archives*, 2nd series, vol. 19 (1893) contains minutes of the Board of Property, 1687–1732, and has been reprinted as William Henry Egle, *Early Pennsylvania Land Records* (Baltimore: Genealogical Publishing Co., 1976).

The lands north of Pittsburgh reserved for the Pennsylvania continental line were called the Donation Lands. Certificates were also issued to Pennsylvania troops entitling them to cheap lands in compensation for the ravages of inflation on their pay; these were called Depreciation Lands. The records are in the Division of Land Records, though most soldiers sold their rights rather than settle on the lands. See John E. Winner, "The Depreciation and Donation Lands," *Western Pennsylvania Historical Magazine* 8 (1925): 1–11. The Pennsylvania State Archives also has land records, such as land warrant and patent receipts (1781–1809), mortgages and valuations (1773–1793), and colonial quitrent books and rent rolls.

Pennsylvania had several major boundary controversies with its neighbors, and various colonies gave grants of their neighbors' lands. From about 1753 to 1782, Connecticut claimed and settled the upper Delaware River Valley (the Delaware Company papers are mostly lost) and the Wyoming Valley along the Susquehanna River. Its records are published in Julian P. Boyd and Robert J. Taylor, *The Susquehannah Company Papers*, 11 vols. (Wilkes-Barre, Penn.: Wyoming Historical and Geological Society, and Ithaca, N.Y.: Cornell University Press, 1930–71). The Pennsylvania Surveyor General's Office papers on Connecticut patents in seventeen townships in Luzerne County, 1785 to 1810, have been microfilmed in twenty-five reels. Also on microfilm are the *Susquehannah Settlers, 1755–96* and *Western Lands, 1783–89*. An every-name index makes these papers valuable for genealogical research, especially because many men died before their claims were satisfied, necessitating mention of heirs as well as other property details.

In southwestern Pennsylvania around the time of the Revolution were three active Virginia counties. See Raymond M. Bell, "Virginia Land Grants in Pennsylvania," *Virginia Genealogist* 7 (1963): 78–83, 103–7, 152–62, and 11 (1967): 126–27, and John F. Vallentine, "Research in Virginia's District of West Augusta," *Genealogical Journal* 4 (1975): 141–47. See also W.R. Shepherd, "The Land System of Provincial Pennsylvania," *American Historical Association Annual Report* (1895): 117–25. For early settlers living along Pennsylvania's southeastern border, be alert for possible Maryland land records.

The Holland Land Company also had lands in Pennsylvania and operated a land office in Philadelphia. Original materials are scattered, with many at the Buffalo and Erie County Historical Society, Buffalo, New York. See Walter J. McClintock, "Title Difficulties of the Holland Land Company in Northwestern Pennsylvania," *Western Pennsylvania Historical Magazine* 21 (1938): 119–38.

RHODE ISLAND

State-land state surveyed in New England towns. These towns, in the colonial period, were particularly strong relative to the colony's central government. Deeds were recorded by the towns, not the counties, although the colonial government for some time also recorded some conveyances. The earliest volume is abstracted in Dorothy Worthington, *Rhode Island Land Evidences, Vol. 1, 1648–1696, Abstracts* (Providence: Rhode Island Historical Society, 1921; no more published). These land evidence volumes are the major land record held by the state archive, though it has a few other records with land information. Information on town grants can be found in John R. Bartlett, *Records of the Colony of Rhode Island and Providence Plantations in New England*, 10 vols. (Providence: Rhode Island General Assembly, 1857–65).

SOUTH CAROLINA

State-land state surveyed in indiscriminate metes and bounds. A proprietary colony from 1670 to 1719 and a royal colony from 1719 to 1775, South Carolina's gradual separation from North Carolina was recognized by parliament in 1729 and confirmed by the partial running of their dividing line in 1735. Subsequent segments were later run ever farther west, and many settlers unexpectedly found themselves inhabitants of the neighboring colony. Each colony made some grants in the other's territory. South Carolina had headright grants, which are sometimes in council journals from the 1749 to 1773 period. See also A.S. Salley, Jr., *Warrants for Land in South Carolina, 1672–1711*, rev. ed. (Columbia: University of South Carolina Press, 1973). No other recorded land warrants survive.

The colonial and state surveys/plats and grants are in the state archive and have been microfilmed. There are separate series with indexes for the proprietary, royal, and state periods. Land office business was suspended all through the 1720s, South Carolina having expelled the proprietary government in 1719. The situation was resolved when George II bought out the proprietors in 1729. In 1731, a more regularized processing of land titles was implemented, with the proprietary titles and claims to be registered as "memorials." In 1744, this memorializing of land titles was required of all titles granted from 1731, a system that helped the government identify quitrent obligations. Five manuscript volumes of quitrents exist for the 1733-to-1774 period. See Alan D. Watson, "The Quit Rent System in Royal South Carolina," *William and Mary Quarterly*, 3rd series, 33 (1976): 182–211.

South Carolina land records created before the revolution may refer to the counties of Colleton, Craven, Berkeley, and Granville; these were nonfunctioning but useful as geographical locators. Deeds and mortgages were recorded only at Charleston until 1769–72; and until 1785, such records from local courthouses continued to be sent to and stored in Charleston. Pre-1719 records are at the state archive in Columbia. See Charles H. Lesser, *South Carolina Begins: The Records of a Proprietary Colony, 1663–1721* (Columbia: South Carolina Department of Archives and History, 1995). Also see Silas Emmett Lucas, Jr., *An Index to Deeds of the Province and State of South Carolina 1719–1785 and Charleston District 1785–1800* (Easley, S.C.: Southern Historical Press, 1977), and Clara A. Langley, *South Carolina Deed Abstracts, 1719–1772*, 4 vols. (Spartanburg, S.C.: 1983). From 1785 to 1799, there were first seven and then nine "old" districts, where conveyances were stored. About 1799 these large districts were abolished and conveyances were recorded and stored at twenty-four small "new" districts. (These districts have been called counties since

1868.) See Michael E. Stauffer, *County Formation in South Carolina* (Columbia: South Carolina Department of Archives and History, 1994). The need, until about 1769–72, to go to Charleston to record conveyances, the turmoil of the revolution from 1775 to 1783, and the loss of many "old" district records means South Carolina deeds created before 1800 are very incomplete. The original tracts in the up-country vicinity of the Broad, Tyger, and Enoree rivers have been platted and published as Union County Historical Foundation, *Land Grant Maps* (Union, S.C.: A Press, 1976). South Carolina passed a bounty-land act and established a small military reserve. See "Bounty Grants to Revolutionary Soldiers," *South Carolina Historical Magazine* 7 (1906): 173–78, 217–24. A unique land source is the state's Reconstruction attempt to buy land for black freedmen. Some records exist showing whites selling to the project and blacks buying. See Carol K. Rothrock, *The Promised Land; The History of the South Carolina Land Commission, 1869–1890* (Columbia: University of South Carolina Press, 1969). See also "Granting of Land in Colonial South Carolina," *South Carolina Historical Magazine* 77 (1976): 208–12; Robert K. Ackerman, *South Carolina Colonial Land Policies* (Columbia: University of South Carolina Press, 1977); David A. Means, "The Recording of Land Titles in South Carolina . . . ," *South Carolina Law Quarterly* 10 (1957–58): 346–419; Marion C. Chandler and Earl W. Wade, *The South Carolina Archives: A Temporary Summary Guide*, 2nd ed. (Columbia: South Carolina Department of Archives and History, 1976), 5, 8–9, 41; and Robert L. Meriwether, *The Expansion of South Carolina 1729–1765* (Kingsport, Tenn.: Southern Publishers, 1940).

South Dakota

Public-domain state with three principal meridians (established 1855 and 1878, and in Arkansas in 1815). Of South Dakota's eight GLO land districts, the earliest opened in Vermillion in 1861. The records of these offices are in the National Archives—Rocky Mountain Region in Denver. Obtain patents from the BLM Montana State Office, P.O. Box 36800, 222 N. 32nd St., Billings, MT 59107-6800, which also has copies of tract books and township plats for South Dakota. The National Archives in Washington, D.C., has the land-entry case files as described in Inventory No. 22 and the GLO headquarters original tract books and township plats. See Charles L. Green, *The Administration of the Public Domain in South Dakota* (Pierre, S.D.: Hipple Printing, 1939); and N. Thomas, "Distribution of the Public Domain in Dakota Territory" (M.A. thesis, University of South Dakota, 1944).

Tennessee

State-land state surveyed in indiscriminate metes and bounds, except the lands west of the lower Tennessee River, which were surveyed in five-mile-square townships. In 1777, North Carolina annexed its western reserve (now the state of Tennessee), established Washington County, and opened a land office there to issue purchase-warrants for lands ceded by the Indians. That office was closed in 1781. In 1783, North Carolina set aside a military reservation in what is today upper middle Tennessee, out of which bounty lands were to be issued as payment to its revolutionary war soldiers. In its "land-grab act" of 1783, North Carolina opened for entry its entire western reserve outside the military and Cherokee reservations. At a price of £10 for every one hundred acres, nearly 4 million acres were entered, mostly by speculators, and to a large extent for lands not yet relinquished by the Indians. In that same year North Carolina enacted laws permitting military warrants to be satisfied outside the reservation; and some 8 million acres of Tennessee lands eventually were taken up in this fashion, again largely by speculators who had bought up the soldiers' warrants. See Shirley Hollis Rice, *The Hidden Revolutionary War Land Grants in the Tennessee Military Reservation* (Reprint. Lawrenceburg, Tenn.: 1992).

In 1789, North Carolina ceded its western reserve to the U.S. government but continued to issue grants for lands in the area during the years of federal control (1790–1796). Disputes involving North Carolina, Tennessee, and the United States prevented Tennessee from opening offices for the sale of public lands for more than a decade after statehood. In terms reached in the Compact of 1806, the United States set aside a Congressional Reservation lying mostly west of the lower Tennessee River, on lands still claimed by the Chickasaw. The United States withheld settlement from that area and disallowed the satisfying of outstanding North Carolina warrants and entries there. Tennessee was permitted to open land offices for the sale of its own lands outside the Congressional Reservation but was required to continue honoring outstanding North Carolina warrants in those areas.

Beginning in 1806, Tennessee enacted laws that addressed and defined the rights of those who had squatted on vacant and unappropriated lands. Occupant grants sought to encourage immigration and recognize the rights of actual settlers by granting small amounts of land based on residence and improvements made to the property. The remainder of the grants issued by the state of Tennessee, representing the bulk of the total, were based on general land sales. These purchase grants eventually sold for as little as one cent per acre. The lands of West Tennessee were opened in 1818, when the Chickasaw surrendered their rights. This district was laid out on a grid system, preferential rights were given to occupants, and offices were opened for land sales. Once again, however, Tennessee was required to satisfy outstanding North Carolina warrants and entries.

The Cherokees had relinquished their rights to the lands of Tennessee in piecemeal fashion, giving up the lands along the southern boundary in 1805 and 1806. The remainder of their lands, the Cherokee Reservation, was ceded in treaties dated 1819 and 1835; the resulting Hiwassee and Ocoee districts were laid out under the GLO land system. Because this area had been exempt from military warrants and from entries under the 1783 act, it was the only section unencumbered by North Carolina claims that had caused so much confusion in the rest of the state.

Grants issued by Tennessee, as well as those North Carolina grants issued for Tennessee lands, are on microfilm along with a card file that indexes and summarizes them. Surviving warrants, entries, and surveys are available on microfilm at the Tennessee State Library and Archives Record Group 50. For further discussion of Tennessee's land history and laws, see Thomas Abernethy, *From Frontier to Plantation in Tennessee* (Chapel Hill: The University of North Carolina Press, 1932); L.D. Smith, "Land Laws of Tennessee," *Tennessee Law Review*, vols. 1–3 (Knoxville: Editorial Board of Tennessee Law Review Association, 1922–25); Daniel Dovenbarger, "Land

Registration in Middle Tennessee" (M.A. thesis, Vanderbilt University, 1981); Thomas B. Jones, "The Public Lands of Tennessee," *Tennessee Historical Quarterly* 27 (1): 13–36 (Spring 1968); and Henry D. Whitney, *The Land Laws of Tennessee* (Chattanooga: J.M. Deardorff & Sons, Printers, 1893).

TEXAS

State-land state surveyed in often rectangular metes and bounds with some large tracts subdivided into numbered blocks often a mile square. Many rivers have parallel long lots running back from the water. The first Spanish settlements in Texas were at Nacogdoches in 1716 and San Antonio in 1718; over the next 120 years approximately 26 million acres were granted by the Spanish and Mexican governments. Entrepreneurs such as Stephen Austin, Sterling Robertson, Martin de Leon, and Benjamin Milam contracted with the Mexican government to bring settlers into Texas. In return, they received large grants and established their own land offices. The Texas Constitution of 1836 validated all Spanish and Mexican land grants provided they conformed to the laws in effect at their issuance, though title disputes were heard by the state courts. Also in 1836, the Texas legislature created the Texas General Land Office, which still manages 22 million acres, including lucrative gas and oil lands. When Texas entered the Union in 1845, it retained its right to sole disposal of its public domain.

Since 1836, the Texas General Land Office has overseen the transfer of most of the public land into private ownership. Its archives, along with the county deeds, are the major Texas land source for researchers. The Texas General Land Office, Archives and Records Division, Research Room 500, 1700 N. Congress Ave., Austin, TX 78701, encourages both written queries and research in person. Here is the land office's summary of its major collections, excluding its important Spanish Archives of the pre-Republic period.[39]

Bounty grants for service in the Army of the Republic of Texas were awarded at the rate of 320 acres per three months of service.

Donation grants of 640 acres were given for special service during the Texas Revolution. Men who fought at any battle, such as the Siege of Bexar, Goliad, the Alamo, San Jacinto, etc., were eligible, and later donations were given to widows and surviving veterans.

Headrights were given to the heads of families and single men who settled in the Republic of Texas. First-class grants were given to any man who arrived in the republic before 2 March 1836. Married men received one league (4,423.4 acres) and one labor (177.1 acres), and single men received one-third of a league (1,476.1 acres). Second-class grants were given to any man who arrived in the Republic after 2 March 1836 but prior to 1 October 1837. Married men received 1,280 acres, and single men received 640 acres. Third-class grants were given to any man who arrived in the republic after 1 October 1837 but prior to 1 January 1840. Married men received 640 acres, and single men received 320 acres. Fourth-class grants were given to men who arrived in the republic after 1 January 1840 but prior to 1 January 1842. Married men received 640 acres, and single men received 320 acres.

Preemption grants (homestead or settler's claims) went to individuals who actually resided on a tract of no more than 320 acres for at least three consecutive years from 22 January 1845.

Under an act of 1854, preemptors could locate no more than 160 acres. Under an act of 1870, married men could locate no more than 160 acres and single men no more than 80 acres. The last preemption was approved in 1899.

School lands were sold to individuals under an act of 1874, and the proceeds went into the common school fund.

The land office has county maps showing the original surveys for each county and indexes by county to all grant records. A major guide is Texas General Land office, *Abstracts of All Original Texas Land Titles*, 8 vols. plus supplements (Austin: General Land Office, 1941–42), which can be purchased from the land office on microfiche. In 1855, the Texas Adjutant-General's office was destroyed along with its bounty warrants, donation records, and muster rolls, which necessitated creating a Court of Claims (1856–1860) whose records are in the land office. Two major indexes to early grants are Virginia H. Taylor, *Index to Spanish and Mexican Land Grants in Texas* (Austin: Lone Star Press, 1974); and Thomas Lloyd Miller, *Bounty and Donation Land Grants of Texas, 1835–1888* (Austin: University of Texas Press, 1967). Miller's introduction (pp. 3–56) describes these grants in detail. There are also published indexes to some of the other grant series. The land office has issued a pamphlet summarizing the history of Texas land, but the standard treatment is Thomas Lloyd Miller, *The Public Lands of Texas 1519–1970* (Norman: University of Oklahoma Press, 1972). The National Archives—Southwest Region in Fort Worth reports no GLO or private land claims records. See also Reuben McKitrick, *The Public Land System of Texas, 1823–1910* (Madison: University of Wisconsin, 1918), Bulletin no. 905; J.J. Bowden, *Spanish and Mexican Land Grants in the Chihuahuan Acquisition* (El Paso: Texas Western Press, 1971); and Florence Johnson Scott, *Royal Land Grants North of the Rio Grande, 1777–1821* (Rio Grande City: Texian Press, 1969).

UTAH

Public-domain state with two principal meridians (established 1855 and 1875). Of Utah's three GLO land districts, the earliest opened in 1869 at Salt Lake City. Obtain patents from the BLM Utah State Office, Suite 301, 324 S. State St., Salt Lake City, UT 84111-2303, which also has copies of tract books and township plats. The National Archives has the land-entry case files as described in Inventory No. 22 and the GLO headquarters original tract books and township plats. It also has a card index to all Utah patentees to 30 June 1908. The records of the local GLO land offices are in the National Archives—Rocky Mountain Region in Denver, summarized in Joel Barker, *Preliminary Inventory of the Records of the Bureau of Land Management—Utah* (Denver: Denver Archives and Records Center, 1979).

When the first Mormons settled in Utah in 1847, their church allotted lands and encouraged communal irrigation systems and living in villages rather than on farms. While these practices worked well in semi-arid Utah, they did not conform to the federal policy of having people live on 160-acre homesteads. Thus, when the first GLO land office opened in 1869 it was often necessary to have entrymen—often LDS church officials—take out homestead patents and then redeem them piecemeal to actual owners. These transactions are recorded in county deed books. See Lawrence L. Linford, "Establishing and Maintaining Land Ownership in Utah Prior to 1869," *Utah Histori-*

cal Quarterly 42 (1974): 126–43; and Lawrence B. Lee, "Homesteading in Zion," ibid. 28 (1960): 28–38.

VERMONT

State-land state surveyed in fairly rectangular New England towns. Although New Hampshire, New York, and Massachusetts all made grants in present-day Vermont, many of the settlers were from Connecticut, having migrated up the Connecticut River Valley. Any standard history of colonial Vermont will explain the New Hampshire-New York dispute of 1749 over control of Vermont, and the latter's simple solution of declaring itself independent of any jurisdiction during the 1776 to 1791 period. A brief account is in William H. Dumont, "The New York-Vermont Land Dispute, 1749–1791," *New York Genealogical and Biographical Record* 100 (1969): 91–95. The standard discussion is Matt Bushnell Jones, *Vermont in the Making* (Cambridge: Harvard University Press, 1939). Check also the Phelps-Gorham Collection at the New York State Archives, Albany, for documents relating to the Gore, a narrow strip of land along the New York-Connecticut-Vermont border.

The state's official land records are mostly in the Division of State Papers, Office of the Secretary of State, 109 State St., Montpelier, VT 05602. The Vermont secretary of state's *State Papers of Vermont* has published several volumes on land records: vol. 2, Franklin H. Dewart, *Charters Granted by the State of Vermont* (1922); and vols. 5–7, Mary Greene Nye, *Petitions for Grants of Land 1778–1811* (1939); *Sequestration, Confiscation and Sale of [Loyalist] Estates* (1941); and *New York Land Patents 1688–1786 Covering Land Now Included in the State of Vermont (Not Including Military Patents)* (1947). Vol. 2 listed above has been indexed in Jay Mack Holbrook, *Vermont's First Settlers* (Oxford, Mass.: Holbrook Research Institute, 1976). Also see Hiram A. Huse, *The New Hampshire Grants, Being Transcripts of the Charters of Townships and Other Minor Grants of Land Made by the Provincial Government of New Hampshire Within the Present Boundaries of the State of Vermont, From 1749 to 1754*, New Hampshire State Papers, vol. 26 (Concord: Edward N. Pearson, Printer, 1895); and Herbert W. Denio, "Massachusetts Land Grants in Vermont," *Publications of the Colonial Society of Massachusetts* 24 (1920–22): 35–59. Vermont deeds are recorded in the towns, surviving records being microfilmed at least to 1850. Also see Florence May Woodward, *The Town Proprietors in Vermont: New England Town Proprietorship in Decline* (New York: Columbia University Press, 1936), 2.

VIRGINIA

State-land state surveyed in indiscriminate metes and bounds. Virginia settlement began under a private stock company called the Virginia Company of London. The Crown revoked the company's charter in 1624. Only near the end of this period did the company begin granting land for private ownership, and there are a few references in surviving records to grants in the 1619 to 1624 period. The fifty-acre headright existed from 1618 to 1725, and long headright lists of transported persons survive in the early patents. They provide the most significant list of early Virginia settlers by far and are often the earliest reference to an immigrant in Virginia by several years. The researcher must be alert to clerical and transcription errors and duplicated names when using the headright lists. See Noel Currer-Briggs, "Headrights and Pitfalls," *Virginia Genealogist* 23 (1979): 45–

56, and Richard Slatten, "Interpreting Headrights in Colonial-Virginia Patents: Uses and Abuses," *National Genealogical Society Quarterly* 75 (September 1987): 169–79.

Virginia's land office records in the royal period (1624–1776) and for statehood are in the Library of Virginia at Richmond and have been microfilmed with indexes. For a survey of these holdings, see Daphne S. Gentry, *Virginia Land Office Inventory*, revised by John S. Salmon (Richmond: Virginia State Library, 1981). The first fourteen patent books (1623–1732) are abstracted in Nell Marion Nugent, *Cavaliers and Pioneers*, 3 vols. (Richmond: Virginia State Library, 1934–79; also vol. 1, reprinted Baltimore, 1963), and patent books fifteen through twenty-eight (1732–1749) by Denis Hudgins, *Cavaliers and Pioneers, 1732–41*, vols. 4 and 5 (Richmond: Virginia Genealogical Society, 1994). The introductions in these volumes offer useful explanations of these records.

The Northern Neck Proprietary of the Fairfax family, between the Potomac and Rappahannock rivers, was granting lands after 1690. Its patent books are also in the Library of Virginia and have been microfilmed with an index. The Northern Neck's southern boundary, beginning at the far southwestern tip of Maryland's panhandle and extending to the headwaters of the Rappahannock River, was in dispute in the mideighteenth century. A court case between 1746 and 1753 resulted in the headwaters of the Rappahannock being set as the present Rapidan River, the boundary being shifted southward and a significant portion of Virginia being confirmed to the Proprietary. See Gertrude E. Gray, *Northern Neck Land Grants*, 4 vols. (Baltimore: 1987–93), and Peggy Shomo Joyner, *Abstracts of Virginia's Northern Neck Warrants and Surveys*, 5 vols. (Portsmouth, Va.: 1985–95).

Virginia had entail until 1776 and primogeniture until 1786. A special complication with Virginia entail was the absence for estates worth more than £200 of a way to terminate (dock) the entail except by an act of the legislature. Dower for wives and curtesy rights for husbands are other important legal concepts relating to land ownership which the researcher must understand.

Tax records are important sources for researching Virginia land. Some eighteenth-century quitrent rolls survive. The 1704 record is in the Public Records Office in England, but it has been published several times. The most reliable readings of this 1704 list are in Louis des Cognets, Jr., *English Duplicates of Lost Virginia Records* (Princeton, N.J.: the author, 1958), 123–232, and Thomas J. Wertenbaker, *The Planters of Colonial Virginia* (New York: Russell & Russell, 1959), 183–247. The 1704 rolls only cover the area south of the Rappahannock, because the Northern Neck quitrents belonged to the Fairfax Proprietary. Some Northern Neck quitrents for fourteen counties are at the Huntington Library in San Marino (Los Angeles), California, but because the Huntington Library restricts access to its collections, genealogists must obtain these lists on microfilm. See D. Forrest, "A History of Taxation in Colonial Virginia, 1607–1775" (M.A. thesis, William and Mary College, 1931), and Mrs. G. Dice, "Lord Fairfax Rent Rolls," *National Genealogical Society Quarterly* 39 (1951): 113–18. Extensive land tax lists from 1782 to the present are in the Library of Virginia, and most created before 1850 have been microfilmed and are available on interlibrary loan. See Conley L. Edwards III, *Using Land Tax Records in the Archives*, Research Notes no. 1 (Richmond, Virginia State Library, 1993), and Frederick T. Neeley, "The Development of Virginia Taxation, 1775–1860" (Ph.D. dissertation, University of Virginia, 1956).

There are other Virginia records with some relation to land that deserve mention. A microfiche publication by Ransome B. True, *Biographical Dictionary of Early Virginia, 1607–1660* (Jamestown: The Association for the Preservation of Virginia Antiquities, 1982), lists in its 1982 edition approximately 120,000 entries for more than 33,000 persons and includes deeds (though few of Nugent's patents). The bounty-land warrants by Virginia for the French and Indian War, Dunmore's War, and especially the American Revolution are numerous (see the earlier discussion of bounty lands).

In the 1770s and 1780s, Virginia had several active counties in what is now southwestern Pennsylvania. See John F. Vallentine, "Research in Virginia's District of West Augusta," *Genealogical Journal* 4 (1975): 141–47; Raymond M. Bell, "Virginia Land Grants in Pennsylvania," *Virginia Genealogist* 7 (1963): 78–83, 103–7, 152–62; ibid. 11 (1967): 126–27. Virginia has a significant number of independent cities that keep their own conveyances; some have records from colonial times. Alice Eichholz, *Ancestry's Red Book: American State, County and Town Sources,* rev. ed. (Salt Lake City: 1989), lists Virginia's independent cities.

The secondary literature on Virginia land is extensive. For instance, see Fairfax Harrison, *Virginia Land Grants, a Study of Conveyancing in Relation to Colonial Politics* (Richmond, Va.: Old Dominion Press, 1925); W. Stitt Robinson, *Mother Earth: Land Grants in Virginia, 1607–1699* (Williamsburg, Va.: 350th Anniversary Celebration Corporation, 1957); Manning C. Voorhis, "The Land Grant Policy of Colonial Virginia, 1607–1774" (Ph.D. dissertation, University of Virginia, 1940), and his "Crown versus Council in the Virginia Land Policy," *William and Mary Quarterly,* 3rd series, 3 (1946): 499–514; Faye B. Reeder, "The Evolution of the Virginia Land Grant System in the Eighteenth Century" (Ph.D. dissertation, Ohio State University, 1937); Daphne S. Gentry, "Colonial and Commonwealth Land Records of Virginia," *Genealogical Journal* 4 (1975): 127–40; Sarah S. Hughes, *Surveyors and Statesmen: Land Measuring in Colonial Virginia* (Richmond: The Virginia Surveyors Foundation and the Virginia Association of Surveyors, 1979); William H. Seiler, "Land Processioning in Colonial Virginia," *William and Mary Quarterly,* 3rd series, 6 (1949): 416–36; and Robert Young Clay, *Virginia Genealogical Resources* (Detroit: Detroit Society for Genealogical Research, 1980), 11–12, 19–26. Additionally, Carol McGinnis, *Virginia Genealogy: Sources and Resources* (Baltimore: Genealogical Publishing Co., 1993), 65–86, includes a chapter on land and court records that is most useful as a general overview while mentioning many land records which are seldom used.

WASHINGTON

Public-domain state with one principal meridian (established 1851). Of Washington's seven GLO land districts, the earliest opened in 1855 in Olympia, and the last closed in Seattle in 1927. The records of these offices are in the National Archives—Pacific Northwest Region in Seattle. Obtain patents from the BLM Oregon State Office, P.O. Box 2965, 1300 N.E. 44th St., Portland, OR 97208-2965, which also has copies of the tract books and township plats. The National Archives in Washington, D.C., has the land-entry case files as described in Inven-

tory No. 22 and the GLO headquarters original tract books and township plats. Washington's earliest white and mixed-blood settlers were entitled to free federal land under the Donation Act of 1850. An index and abstracts are on NARS microfilm M203, *Abstracts of Washington Donation Land Claims, 1855–1902,* in one roll, which serves as an index to the case files reproduced on NARS microfilm M815, *Oregon and Washington Donation Land Files, 1851–1903,* in 108 rolls. Donation case files are valuable because they typically contain a statement of the date and place of birth of the entryman. Because of a law forbidding their reproduction, the naturalization certificates in the M815 case files were not microfilmed. They can now be obtained from the National Archives. See Frederick Jay Yonce, "Public Land Disposal in Washington" (Ph.D. dissertation, University of Washington, 1966); Roy Otto Hoover, "The Public Land Policy of Washington State: The Initial Period, 1889–1912" (Ph.D. dissertation, Washington State University, 1967); Seattle Genealogical Society, *Washington Territory Donation Land Claims: An Abstract of Information in the Land Claim Papers of Persons Who Settled in Washington Territory Before 1856* (Seattle: Seattle Genealogical Society, 1980).

WEST VIRGINIA

State-land state surveyed in indiscriminate metes and bounds. Since West Virginia was part of Virginia until 1863, its first-title grants prior to the Civil War were made by Virginia. The colonial grants are in separate series for the Virginia royal government and for the Northern Neck Proprietary. They include significant portions of present West Virginia. (For the Northern Neck boundary, see the Virginia entry, above.) West Virginia land records are at the State Auditor, Capitol Building, West Wing 231, Charleston, WV 25305. The Virginia royal/commonwealth and Northern Neck grants are in the Library of Virginia, microfilmed with indexes. The West Virginia state auditor has extensive grant records, 1754 to 1864 and 1748 to 1912, also microfilmed. Pursuant to a 1951 act of the legislature, the state auditor attempted to collect and index all identifiable grantees: Edgar B. Sims, *Sim's Index to Land Grants in West Virginia* (Charleston: Auditor's Office, 1952), with a supplement. Also see Edgar B. Sims, *Making a State: Formation of West Virginia, Including Maps, Illustrations, Plats, Grants. . . .* (Charleston: State Auditor, 1956).

Researchers doing colonial and antebellum genealogy in West Virginia must remember that they are actually working with Virginia records. Thus, the bounty-land laws for the French and Indian War, Dunmore's War, and the revolution apply to West Virginia. Likewise, the extension of Virginia counties into southwestern Pennsylvania in the 1770s and 1780s has ramifications for early West Virginia migrations—parts of those counties included West Virginia. The *Virginia Genealogist* and other Virginia genealogical and historical journals have much on early West Virginia lands.

WISCONSIN

Public-domain state with one principal meridian (established 1831). Of the nine GLO land districts, the earliest opened in 1834 at Mineral Point; the last closed in 1925 at Wausau. The local records of these districts are at the Commissioner of Public Lands, 127 W. Washington Ave., Madison, WI 53703. Obtain patents from the BLM Eastern States Office in Springfield, Virginia, which also has copies of the tract books and township plats. Wisconsin's federal patents are indexed in the GLO Automated Records System. A CD-ROM of Wisconsin land patents is available from the GLO. The National Archives has the land-entry case files as described in Inventory No. 22 and also the GLO headquarters original tract books and township plats. For private land claims, see the *American State Papers, Public Lands*, as indexed in McMullin's *Grassroots of America*.

Also see Paul W. Gates, "Frontier Land Business in Wisconsin," *Wisconsin Magazine of History* 52 (1962): 306–27; Frederick N. Trowbridge, "Confirming Land Titles in Early Wisconsin," ibid. 26 (1942): 314–22; and Michael Fox, *Maps and Atlases Showing Land Ownership in Wisconsin* (Madison: State Historical Society of Wisconsin, 1978).

WYOMING

Public-domain state with two principal meridians (established 1855 and 1875). Of Wyoming's six GLO land districts, the earliest opened in Cheyenne in 1870. The records of these offices are mostly in the National Archives—Rocky Mountain Region in Denver, though the Wyoming state archive has records for entries not brought to patent. Obtain patents from the BLM Wyoming State Office, Box 1828, 2515 Warren Ave., Cheyenne, WY 82003, which also has copies of the tract books and township plats. The National Archives has the land-entry case files as described in Inventory No. 22 and the GLO headquarters original tract books and township plats.

NOTES

1. Donald Lines Jacobus, "Connecticut," in Milton Rubincam and Kenn Stryker-Rodda, eds., *Genealogical Research Methods and Sources*, vol. 1 (Washington, D.C.: American Society of Genealogists, 1960–71), 129.

2. Indenture from William Eskridge and wife Betty to Thomas Williams, 7 May 1763, Northumberland County, Virginia, Deed Book 6, pp. 220–22, Family History Library (FHL), Salt Lake City, Utah, microfilm 032,675.

3. J. Harvey Bloom, "Seals," *Genealogists' Magazine* 13 (1959): 111.

4. Indenture from Dempsey Wood, Sr., to Hardy Wood, 31 March 1800 (recorded 21 March 1896), Montgomery County, Georgia, Deed Book 2W, pp. 404–5, FHL 218,775; Indenture from Glasingham Haney, Sr., to Dempsy [*sic*] Wood, 30 Dec. 1791 (recorded 30 July 1901), ibid., Deed Book 2U, pp. 5–6, FHL 218,779.

5. Kip Sperry, "Processioning in the Southern States," *Genealogical Journal* 4 (1955): 150–54.

6. Robert D. Mitchell, *Commercialism and Frontier: Perspectives on the Early Shenandoah Valley* (Charlottesville, Va.: University Press of Virginia, 1977), 31–33.

7. Royal Grant to Ezekiel Backler, 11 August 1774 (recorded 15 March 1773), South Carolina Royal Grants, Book 32, p. 49; FHL 022,596.

8. Grant to John Lemon, 1 July 1760 (re-recording date), Northern Neck Grants, Book K, p. 11; FHL 029,515.

9. For an absorbing narrative of how such a reconstruction can provide an intimate understanding of the evidence, see James

Franklin Sutherland, *Some Original Land Grant Surveys Along Green River in Lincoln and Casey Counties, Kentucky (1781–1836)* (Casey County Bicentennial Committee, 1975), 1–27.

10. David F. Stoddard, "Land System of the New England Colonial Colonies," *Connecticut Nutmegger* 11 (1979): 556–64. Capitalization standardized.

11. The historical summary which follows is drawn from David A. Bundy, *100 Acres More or Less: The History of the Land and People of Bow, New Hampshire* (Canaan, Conn.: Bow Town History Committee, by Phoenix Press, 1975).

12. *Brief Notes on the Public Domain* (Bureau of Land Management, 1957), 21.

13. As quoted in Lawrence L. Linford, "Establishing and Maintaining Land Ownership in Utah Prior to 1869," *Utah Historical Quarterly* 43 (1974): 139.

14. Payson Jackson Treat, *The National Land System, 1785–1820* (New York: E.B. Treat, 1910), 215.

15. *Guide to Genealogical Research in the National Archives* (Washington, D.C.: National Archives Trust Fund Board, 1983), 222.

16. Paul Gates, *History of Public Land Law Development* (Washington, D.C.: Public Land Law Review Commission, 1968), 251–57.

17. Ibid., 278.

18. James W. Oberly, "Military Bounty Land Warrants of the Mexican War," *Prologue* 14 (1982): 28.

19. Gates, *History of Public Land Law Development*, 279.

20. Treat, *The National Land System*, 252–53.

21. Ibid., 340.

22. Gates, *History of Public Land Law Development*, 256.

23. Ibid., 255.

24. Clifford Neal Smith, *Federal Land Series*, vol. 4, pt. 1 (1982).

25. Kenn Stryker-Rodda, "Limit of 18th Century Sources in New York and New Jersey," *Families* 11 (1972): 121.

26. Raymond A. Winslow, Jr., "Tax and Fiscal Records," in Helen F.M. Leary, *North Carolina Research: Genealogy and Local History*, rev. ed. (Raleigh: North Carolina Genealogical Society, 1996), 231–32.

27. Poll Tax List, 1799, Warren County, Kentucky, Tax Lists 1799, pp. 5–6, 14, 17; FHL 008,255.

28. *Laws of the State of Indiana . . . Tenth Session* (Indianapolis: Douglas and Maguire, printers, 1826), p. 68, chap. 57.

29. "Bute Co., N.C.: 1771 Tax List," *The North Carolinian* 7 (1961): 899–907; "Franklin-Warren-Vance Cos. Area Father-Son Relationships in 1771," ibid. 11 (1965): 1,499–1,515.

30. Richard LeBaron Bowen, *Early Rehoboth: Documented Historical Studies of Families and Events in this Plymouth Colony Township*, vol. 4 (Rehoboth, Mass.: the author, 1950), 143–45.

31. Edward W. Hanson and Homer Vincent Rutherford, "Genealogical Research in Massachusetts: A Survey and Bibliographical Guide," *New England Historical and Genealogical Register* 13 (1981): 177.

32. Dall W. Forsythe, *Taxation and Political Change in the Young Nation, 1781–1833* (New York City: Columbia University Press, 1977), 59.

33. William Blackstone, *Commentaries on the Laws of England* (Oxford: Clarendon Press, 1766), book 2, ch. 20, p. 315.

34. Deed of feoffment from Arthur Harris to James Heaburn, 26 March 1744 (recorded 5 April 1744), Westmoreland County, Virginia, Deeds and Wills, Book 9, pp. 347–48; FHL 034,272.

35. Deed of Release from John Tyler the Aged to Richard Taylor, 17 July 1713 (date of recording unknown), Chesapeake City, successor to Norfolk Co., Virginia, Deed Book 9, pp. 261–62; FHL 032,829; and Will of Richard Taylor, 26 Sept. 1729, proved 19 February 1730/1 (never officially recorded), Chesapeake City, Virginia, Unrecorded Wills Book 1722–26, p. 22.

36. William Thorndale, "The Lindseys of Maury County, Tennessee," typescript, in Family History Library, Salt Lake City, Utah, n.d.

37. *Guide to New England Genealogy* (Newton, Mass.: New England Family History Society, 1982), p. NE25.1.

38. Kenn Stryker-Rodda, "That Genealogical Quagmire: New Jersey," *National Genealogical Society Quarterly* 48 (1960): 62–64.

39. Andrea G. Morgan, *Land: A History of the Texas General Land Office* (Austin: Texas General Land Office, 1992).

BIBLIOGRAPHY

Akagi, Roy Hidemichi. *The Town Proprietors of the New England Colonies: A Study of Their Development, Organization, Activities and Controversies, 1620–1770.* Philadelphia: Press of the University of Pennsylvania, 1924.

Allen, David Grayson. *In English Ways: The Movement of Societies and the Transferral of English Local Law and Custom to Massachusetts Bay in the Seventeenth Century.* Chapel Hill: University of North Carolina Press, 1981.

Allen, Robert S. *Loyalist Literature: An Annotated Bibliographic Guide to the Writings on the Loyalists of the Loyalists of the American Revolution.* Toronto and Charlottetown: Dundurn Press, 1982.

Beers, Henry Putney. *Spanish & Mexican Records of the American Southwest: A Bibliographical Guide to Archive and Manuscript Sources.* Tucson: University of Arizona Press and the Tucson Corral of the Westerners, 1979.

Billington, Ray Allen, and Martin Ridge. *Western Expansion, A History of the American Frontier.* 5th ed. New York: Macmillan Publishing Co., 1982.

Bockstruck, Lloyd D. *Revolutionary War Bount Land Grants Awarded by State Governments.* Baltimore: Genealogical Publishing Co., 1996.

Bond, Beverley W., Jr. *The Quit-Rent System in the American Colonies.* New Haven: Yale University Press, 1919.

Brumbaugh, Gaius Marcus. *Revolutionary War Records . . . Virginia Army and Navy Forces With Bounty Land Warrants for Virginia Military Scrip; From Federal and State Archives.* Washington, D.C., 1936.

Bureau of Land Management. *Public Land Bibliography.* Washington, D.C.: Bureau of Land Management, 1962.

Bureau of Land Management. *Manual of Instructions for the Survey of the Public Lands of the United States.* Technical Bulletin 6. Washington, D.C.: Department of the Interior, 1973.

Coldham, Peter Wilson. *American Loyalist Claims: Abstracted From the Public Record Office, Audit Series 13, Bundles 1–35 & 37.* Washington: National Genealogical Society, 1980.

_____. *Settlers of Maryland.* 4 vols. Baltimore: Genealogical Publishing Co., 1995–96.

Department of the Interior. *Catalog of the United States Geological Survey Library.* 24 vols. plus a first supplement of 11 vols. and a second of 4. Boston: G.K. Hall, 1964, 1972–74.

Donaldson, Thomas. *The Public Domain: Its History with Statistics.* House Misc. Doc. 45 pt. 4, 47th Cong., 2nd Sess. 1884. Reprint. New York: Johnson Reprint, 1970.

Emery, Margaret Hickerson. "The Adeustone-Rogers Families of Virginia: Tracing a Colonial Lineage through Entailment and Naming Patterns." *National Genealogical Society Quarterly* 77 (2) (June 1989): 89–106.

Fox, Michael J. "The Map Collection." In *Genealogical Research: An Introduction to the Resources of the State Historical Society of Wisconsin.* Edited by James P. Danky. Madison: State Historical Society of Wisconsin, 1979.

Freund, Rudolf. "Military Bounty Land and the Origins of the Public Domain." *Agricultural History* 20 (1946): 8–18.

Fraser, Alexander, ed. *United Empire Loyalists Inquiry Into the Losses of Services in Consequence of Their Loyalty. Evidence in the Canadian Claims.* 2 vols. Toronto: The King's Printer, 1905.

Friedman, Lawrence M. *A History of American Law.* Rev. ed. New York: Simon and Schuster, 1985.

Gates, Paul W. "Private Land Claims in the South." *Journal of Southern History* 22 (1956): 183–204.

_____. *History of Public Land Law Development.* Washington: Public Land Law Review Commission, 1968.

Greenwood, Val D. *Researcher's Guide to American Genealogy.* Baltimore: Genealogical Publishing Co., 1990.

Harris, Marshall. *Origin of the Land Tenure System in the United States.* Ames: Iowa State College Press, 1953.

Hibbard, Benjamin Horace. *A History of the Public Land Policies.* New York: Peter Smith, 1939.

Hughes, Sara S. *Surveyors and Statesmen: Land Measuring in Colonial Virginia.* Richmond: Virginia Surveyors Foundation and The Virginia Association of Surveyors, 1979.

Jillson, William Rouse. *Old Kentucky Entries and Deeds: A Complete Index to All of the Earliest Land Entries, Military Warrants, Deeds and Wills of the Commonwealth of Kentucky.* Filson Club Publication No. 34. Reprint. Baltimore: Genealogical Publishing Co., 1987.

Kirkham, E. Kay. *The Land Records of America and Their Genealogical Value.* Salt Lake City: Deseret Book, 1964.

Knowlton, Clark S., ed. "Spanish and Mexican Land Grants in the Southwest: A Symposium." *Social Science Journal* 13 (October 1976): 1–63.

Leary, Helen F.M. *North Carolina Research: Genealogy and Local History.* Raleigh: North Carolina Genealogical Society, 1996.

Lee, Lawrence B. "American Public Land History: A Review Essay." *Agricultural History* 55 (1981): 284–99.

Library of Congress. *List of Geographical Atlases in the Library of Congress.* 8 vols. Washington, D.C.: Library of Congress, 1909–74.

Lutz, Paul V. "Land Grants for Service in the Revolution." *New York Historical Society Quarterly* 48 (1964): 221–35;

McKee, T. H. "Index to Reports of Committee on Private Land Claims, House of Representatives." *House Index to Committee Reports* (Y1.3:C73/2): 5–20.

McMullin, Phillip W. *Grassroots of America.* Reprint. Greenville, S.C.: Southern Historical Press, 1993.

Martin, T.P. "The Confirmation of French and Spanish Land Titles in the Louisiana Purchase." M.A. thesis, University of California, Berkeley, 1914.

Meek, W. Frank. "Federal Land Office Records." *University of Colorado Law Review* 43 (1971–72): 177–97.

Morris, Richard B. "Colonial Law Governing the Distribution and Alienation of Land." In *Studies in the History of American Law with Special Reference to the Seventeenth and Eighteenth Centuries.* New York: Columbia University Press, 1930.

National Archives. *Guide to Genealogical Research in the National Archives.* Washington, D.C.: National Archives and Records Service, 1982.

National Genealogical Society. *Index of Revolutionary War Pension Applications in the National Archives.* Washington, D.C.: National Genealogical Society, 1976.

The Newberry Library. *Checklist of Printed Maps of the Middle West to 1900.* 11 vols. Boston: G.K. Hall, 1980.

Oberly, James W. "Military Bounty Land Warrants of the Mexican War." *Prologue* 14 (1982): 25–34.

_____. *Sixty Million Acres: American Veterans and the Public Lands before the Civil War.* Kent, Ohio: Kent State University Press, 1990.

Palmer, Gregory, ed. *A Bibliography Loyalist Source Material in the United States, Canada, and Great Britain.* Westport and London: Meckler Publishing and the American Antiquarian Society, 1982.

Pelzer, Louis. "The Private Land Claims of the Old Northwest Territory." *Iowa Journal of History and Politics* 12 (1914): 363–93.

Powell, Sumner Chilton. *Puritan Village: The Formation of a New England Town.* Middletown: Wesleyan University Press, 1963.

Radoff, Morris L., et al. *The County Courthouses and Records of Maryland. Part Two: The Records.* Annapolis: Hall of Records Commission, 1963.

Reports of the Committees on Private Land Claims of the Senate and House of Representatives. 2 vols. 45th Cong., 3d sess. Misc. Doc. 81, serial 1836.

Richardson, Lemont K. "Private Land Claims in Missouri." *Missouri Historical Review* 50 (1955–56): 132–44, 271–86, 387–99.

Robbins, Roy Marvin. *Our Landed Heritage: The Public Domain, 1776–1970.* 2nd ed. Lincoln: University of Nebraska Press, 1976.

Rohrbough, Malcolm J. *The Land Office Business: The Settlement and Administration of American Public Lands, 1789–1837.* Belmont Calif.: Wadsworth Publishing Co., 1990.

Salmon, John. "Revolutionary War Records in the Archives & Records Division of the Virginia State Library." *Genealogy* 70 (July 1982): 2–10.

Salmon, Marylynn. *Women and the Law of Property in Early America.* Chapel Hill: University of North Carolina Press, 1986.

Shammas, Carole, Marylynn Salmon, and Michel Dahlin. *Inheritance in America From Colonial Times to the Present.* New Brunswick: Rutgers University Press, 1987.

Smith, Clifford Neal. "Virginia Land Grants in Kentucky and Ohio, 1784–1799." *National Genealogical Society Quarterly* 61 (1973): 16–27.

Stephenson, Richard W. *Land Ownership Maps.* Washington, D.C.: Library of Congress, 1967.

Szucs, Loretto D., and Sandra H. Luebking. *The Archives: A Guide to the National Archives Field Branches.* Salt Lake City: Ancestry, 1988.

Treat, Payson Jackson. *The National Land System, 1785–1820.* New York: E.B. Treat, 1910.

U.S. Congress. *The American State Papers, Class VIII, Public Lands* and *The American State Papers, Class IX, Claims.* Washington, D.C.: Gales and Seaton, 1832–61. Reprint. Greenville, S.C.: Southern Historical Press, 1993.

U.S. Public Land Commission. *Laws of the United States of a Local or Temporary Character and Exhibiting the Entire Legislation of Congress Upon Which the Public Land Titles in Each State and Territory Have Depended.* House Exec. Doc. no. 47, pts. 2–3, 46th Cong., 3rd sess., serial no. 1976. Washington, D.C.: Government Printing Office, 1881.

Vallentine, John F. "Histories of the American Frontier: A Series." *Genealogical Journal* 6 (1977): 200–05.

Vivian, Jean H. "Military Land Bounties During the Revolutionary and Confederation Periods." *Maryland Historical Magazine* 61 (1966): 231–56.

Yoshpe, Harry P., and Philip P. Brower. *Preliminary Inventory of the Land-Entry Papers of the General Land Office.* Preliminary Inventory 22 (Washington, D.C.: National Archives, 1949. Reprint. San Jose, Calif.: Rose Family Association, 1996).

RESEARCH IN MILITARY RECORDS
CHAPTER CONTENTS

9

RESEARCH IN MILITARY RECORDS

by Johni Cerny; revised for the current edition
by Lloyd DeWitt Bockstruck and David Thackery

The uses and value of military records in genealogical research for ancestors who were veterans are obvious, but military records can also be important to researchers whose direct ancestors were not soldiers in any war. The fathers, grandfathers, brothers, and other close relatives of an ancestor may have served in a war, and their service or pension records could contain information that will assist in further identifying the family of primary interest. Due to the amount of genealogical information contained in some military pension files, they should never be overlooked during the research process. Those records not containing specific genealogical information are of historic value and should be included in any overall research design. The wars considered in this chapter are grouped as follows:

- Colonial wars

King Philip's War	1675–76
King William's War	1689–97
Queen Anne's War	1702–13
King George's War	1744–48
French and Indian War	1754–63

- Revolutionary war and frontier conflicts   1775–1811
- Post-revolutionary wars to 1848

War of 1812	1812–15
Indian Wars	1815–58
Mexican War	1846–48

- Civil War   1861–65
- Spanish-American War   1898
- Modern wars

World War I	1917–18
World War II	1941–45
Korean War	1950–53
Vietnam War	1961–73

At least the remnants of records exist for every war that the colonies and states were involved in; but, as with other records maintained in the United States during the first centuries of its existence, there is little uniformity of content or style in those records.

This chapter will discuss the two principal categories of military records in detail: service records and records of veteran's benefits. Other record categories are referenced where they supply genealogical information.

SERVICE RECORDS

COLONIAL WARS (1607–1774)

Service records of soldiers in the colonial wars have more historical than genealogical information and usually provide only the name of the soldier and the colonial unit in which he served. They consist primarily of rosters, rolls, and lists that survived the wars and several fires. Most of these rosters and rolls have been published and can be found in genealogical and historical libraries throughout the nation (see the chapter bibliography).

Despite the scanty genealogical information these records provide, you should not ignore them. They may be sparse, but few records in general exist for that period to help locate an ancestor. The presence of a soldier in a particular unit may be a valuable clue to his place of residence as well as useful in identifying his family in other records of the same location, even though there may be problems in distinguishing between two or more soldiers with the same name.

REVOLUTIONARY WAR AND FRONTIER CONFLICTS (1775–1811)

Some of the original service records of the Revolutionary War were destroyed by fire, but those remaining are on file at the National Archives, compiled primarily from rosters and rolls of soldiers serving in the Continental Army, state lines, and militia units, with additions from correspondence and filed reports of military officers. These service records contain much more genealogical information than colonial records: name, rank, and military organization of the soldier. Included in some records are the name of the state from which the soldier served; the date that his name appears on one or more of the rolls; sometimes the date or dates of his enlistment, or the date of his appointment; and, rarely, the date of his separation from the service. His physical description, date and place of birth, residence at the time of enlistment, and other personal details are also included in some categories. For example, in the size roll for Captain Aaron Ogden's Company, 1st Regiment of New Jersey, we find these men:

> WILLIAM JONES, private, 22, 5'4"; brown [eyes], fair [hair]; taylor [tailor]; b. & res. Woodbridge, Essex Co., enl. 15 June '77.
>
> JONAS KENT, private, 32, 5'3"; black, dark; laborer; b. & res. Horse Neck, Essex Co.; enl. 7 Mar. '77.
>
> JOSEPH KING, private, 30, 5'5 1/2", bloomer; b. & res. Morris, Morris Co.; enl. 24 Dec. '76; on detail at Wyoming all of '82.
>
> WILLIAM LEGEER, private, 19, 5'9"; light, fair; laborer; b. & res. Amwell, Hunterdon Co.; enl. 15 Apr. '79.
>
> WILLIAM McMULLIN, private, 36, 5'8 1/2"; black, fair; laborer; b. Glenarm, Embrim, Ireland; res. Mendham, Morris Co.; enl. 16 Feb. '78; deserted at Morris Hutts, 18 Apr. '82, retaken 28 June '82, 100 lashes.[1]

Revolutionary war service records are indexed. Most of the indexes have been microfilmed, and many libraries have copies. The service records themselves can be searched at the National Archives and its regional archives or at the Family History Library of The Church of Jesus Christ of Latter-day Saints and its family history centers, and at other research libraries. (See appendix D for addresses.)

Genealogists who have access to the microfilmed records can search them more efficiently by following the guide in table 9-1. Those using the collection of the Family History Library in Salt Lake City or one of its family history centers should check the Military Records Register for the appropriate call numbers for the above microfilms. The collection of the Family History Library is almost as large as that of the National Archives, making these records more widely available throughout the United States, especially since the NARA interlibrary loan program for microfilmed military records has been discontinued. Copies of individual records can, however, be obtained from the National Archives and Records Administration in Washington, D.C. Patrons must use the current NATF Form 80 to request a particular record.

Three types of records are available from NARA: (1) pensions (2) bounty-land warrant applications, and (3) military service records. A search of these records cannot be completed without the full name of the veteran, his branch of service, the state from which he served, and the war in which he served. You may also use this form to request records pertaining to soldiers of other wars prior to World War II. Expect a six-to-eight week processing time before you receive the records.

Many revolutionary war roster lists and other service records have been published. For a list of titles available in many genealogical library collections, consult the chapter bibliography.

Loyalists and German Auxiliary Troops
Many American colonists retained their allegiance to the British crown. Known as Loyalists, they probably comprised about one third of the colonial population. In some areas they may have been in the majority. Some of them simply refused to support the revolutionary cause. Others took up arms against it.

With the defeat of the British, many fled to other points of the Empire, notably to what was called Canada West (Ontario) and the Canadian Maritime Provinces.

The British forces were also augmented by a large contingent of German auxiliaries imported to America to help suppress the rebellion. Inaccurately labeled mercenaries or Hessians, these troops originated not only from Hessen Kassel and Hessen Hanau, but also from Braunschweig, Ansbach-Bayreuth, Waldeck, and Anhalt-Zerbst. Perhaps as many as 7,000 of the nearly 32,000 German auxiliary troops remained in North America.

There are many printed works of genealogical value pertaining to Loyalists and German auxiliary troops in the American Revolution. Consult the relevant bibliographies at the end of this chapter.

POST-REVOLUTIONARY WARS (1812–48)

There are service records for the War of 1812, Indian Wars, and the Mexican War. The information included, similar to that in the service records of soldiers in the colonial wars and the Revolutionary War, has been indexed and microfilmed (see table 9-2). If a personal search of the microfilmed indexes at the National Archives, the Family History Library, or elsewhere is not possible, you can request a search of the indexes of the National Archives using NATF form 80.

During the Mexican War, special units came from the Indian nations, the Mormons (Mormon Battalion) and New Mexico (Santa Fe Battalion of the Missouri Mounted Volunteers). Each of these units compiled its own records.

CIVIL WAR (1861–65)

Union Service Records
Union Army records contain enlistment papers, muster rolls, prisoner-of-war papers, death reports, and others. The records are indexed by state and by military units for those units organized within a specific state. You must know the state in which a soldier served or the unit with which he served to obtain his service records. Table 9-3 summarizes Union Army indexes and service records. Note that there is a separate index for soldiers in the United States Colored Troops (USCT), which encompassed black troops from all states. For a discussion of these records, see chapter 15, Tracking African American Family History.

Enlistment papers often contain a description of the soldier and the place where he enlisted. Typically, though not necessarily, a soldier enlisted near his home. This information can be valuable in helping you pinpoint the movements of an ancestor between 1850 and 1880, when pioneers were on the move in great numbers.

The National Archives will search its index to service records if you know the branch of service and the state from which a soldier served in the Civil War. Use NATF Form 80 to request Civil War service records for the Union Army. There are microfilmed copies of the indexes at the National Archives and its regional archives, the Family History Library and its family history centers, and at various other libraries throughout the country. The actual service records are available, however, only at the National Archives.

Civil War Soldier Draft Records, 1863–65. The U.S. government enacted a draft in March 1863, creating a pool of men

Table 9-1. List of Microfilmed Military Service and Other Records, 1775-1811*

Record or Index	NARA Microfilm Number	Comments/Access
Compiled Service Records of Soldiers Who Served in the American Army During the Revolutionary War	M881	At least one jacket envelope for each soldier containing card abstracts of entries relating to that soldier from original records.
General Index to Compiled Military Service Records of Revolutionary War Soldiers	M860	Considered the most comprehensive name index to compiled service records, this lists soldiers who served in the American army during the revolutionary war. The index also contains entries for several small series of revolutionary war compiled service records of sailors, members of army staff departments, and other persons associated with the American army and navy. Each card of the index gives the name and unit of a soldier or civilian and sometimes rank, profession, or office.
Index to Compiled Service Records of Volunteer Soldiers Who Served . . . From North Carolina	M257	
Index to Compiled Service Records of Volunteer Soldiers Who Served . . . in Connecticut Organizations	M290	
Index to Compiled Service Records of Volunteer Soldiers Who Served . . . in Georgia Organizations	M1051	A name index listing the name and unit of each soldier or civilian employee and sometimes rank, profession, or office.
Card Indexes for Delaware, Maryland, Massachusetts, New Hampshire, New Jersey, New York, Pennsylvania, Rhode Island, South Carolina, Vermont, and Virginia	NA	Available only at NARA; not microfilmed.
Compiled Service Records of American Naval Personnel and Members of Departments of Quartermaster General and Commissary General of Military Stores Who Served During the Revolutionary War	M880	
Index to Compiled Service Records of Revolutionary War Naval Records, T516, 1 roll.		
Revolutionary War Rolls, List of Jackets, 1775-83	M246	Shows militia rolls, payrolls, supply lists for each regiment. These are the volumes in which the men will be listed. Most of the men will appear in more than one list, so check them all. Use M860 index, above, first.
Numbered Record Books Concerning Military Operations and Service Pay, Settlements of Accounts, Supplies, War Department Collection of Revolutionary War Records.	M853	
Miscellaneous Numbered Records (The Manuscript File) War Department Collection of Revolutionary War Records	M859	Original records, approximately 35,000 items. Includes civilians in war service; paymasters, wagons, judges, chaplains, medical officers, teamsters, and others.
Special Index to Numbered Records in the War Department Collection of Revolutionary War Records, 1775-83	M847	Indexes all or some of the names in M859 and M853.
Compiled Service Records of Volunteer Soldiers Who Served From 1784-1811	M905	Service records of soldiers who served in the various Indian campaigns, insurrections, and disturbances that occurred in the post-revolutionary period. Arranged by U.S. organization, alphabetically by state or territorial organizations, thereunder by military unit, then alphabetically by surname of soldier.
Index to Compiled Service Records of Volunteer Soldiers Who Served From 1784-1811	M694	Indexes M905.
War Department Collection of Post-Revolutionary War Manuscripts, 1784-1811	M904	Includes muster rolls.
Every-Name Card Index at NARA Only	NA	Index not on microfilm; search only at NARA.

Record or Index	NARA Microfilm Number	Comments/Access
Central Treasury Records of the Continental and Confederation Government Relating to Military Affairs, 1775-89	M1015	Includes military pay and muster rolls which can be used as evidence of service. Also included are company and account books of officers.
Papers of the Continental Congress, 1774-89	M247	Includes muster rolls, payrolls, wagoneer lists, claims for pay by revolutionary war soldiers and officers, many of whom did not live long enough to file for pension.
Miscellaneous Papers of the Continental Congress, 1774-1789	M332	Records that are not a part of the numbered sequence of Continental Congress papers reproduced in M247, including despatches and letters, reports of committees, bonds, receipts, deeds of cession of western lands, credentials of delegates to the Congress, and broadsides issued by the Congress.
John P. Butler, comp., *Index to Papers of the Continental Congress,* 5 vols. (Washington, D.C.: NARS, 1978)	NA	Published work; not on microfilm. A comprehensive personal name and major subject index to documents of the Continental Congress.

* Although only the NARA microfilm number is provided for each record or indix listed, microfilm sets of many of these records are available at the Family History Library and at other libraries with strong genealogy collections.

Sources:

National Archives Microfilm Publications in the Regional Archives System, Special List 45 (Washington, D.C.: National Archives and Records Administration, 1990).

Guide to Genealogical Research in the National Archives (Washington, D.C.: National Archives and Records Service, 1985).

Arlene Eakle and Johni Cerny, eds., *The Source: A Guidebook of American Genealogy,* 1st ed. (Salt Lake City: Ancestry, 1984).

Table 9-2. Service Records Indexes, 1812–1848

Title	NARA Microfilm Number	Comments
Index to Compiled Records of Volunteer Soldiers Who Served During the War of 1812	M602, 234 rolls	There are also microfilm records for Mississippi (M678, 22 rolls), Louisiana (M229, 3 rolls), North Carolina (M250, 5 rolls), and South Carolina (M652, 7 rolls).
Index to Compiled Service Records of Volunteer Soldiers Who Served During the Indian Wars and Disturbances, 1815–58 (encompasses all of the indexes listed in the "comments" column)	M629, 12 rolls	

		Also Available	
State	Disturbance and Date	Microfilm Publication	Number of Rolls
Alabama	Creek War, 1836-37	M244, index	2
	Cherokee removal, 1838	M243, index	1
	Florida War, 1836-38	M245, index	1
Florida	Florida War, 1836-56	M1086, service records	63
Georgia	Cherokee disturbances and removal, 1836-38	M907, index	1
Louisiana	Florida War, 1836-38	M239, index	1
	War of 1837-38	M241, index	1
Michigan	Patriot War, 1838-39	M630, index	1
New York	Patriot War, 1838	M631, index	1
North Carolina	Cherokee disturbances and removal, 1836-38	M256, index	1
Tennessee	Cherokee disturbances and removal, 1836-38	M908, index	2

Title	NARA Microfilm Number	Comments
Index to Compiled Records of Volunteer Soldiers Who Served During the Mexican War, 1846-48	M626, 41 rolls	Service records are available for Mississippi (M863, 9 rolls), Pennsylvania (M1028, 13 rolls), Tennessee (M638, 15 rolls), Texas (M278, 19 rolls), Mormon Battalion (M351, 3 rolls).

Table 9-3. Microfilmed Indexes and Compiled Service Records for Union Army Volunteers

State	Microfilm Publication Index	Compiled Military Service Records
Alabama	M263, 1 roll	M276, 10 rolls
Arizona Territory	M532, 1 roll	
Arkansas	M383, 4 rolls	M399, 60 rolls
California	M533, 7 rolls	
Colorado Territory	M534, 3 rolls	
Connecticut	M535, 17 rolls	
Dakota Territory	M536, 1 roll	
Delaware	M537, 4 rolls	
District of Columbia	M538, 3 rolls	
Florida	M264, 1 roll	M400, 11 rolls
Georgia	M385, 1 roll	M403, 1 roll
Idaho Territory (see Washington Territory)		
Illinois	M539, 101 rolls	
Indiana	M540, 86 rolls	
Iowa	M541, 29 rolls	
Kansas	M542, 10 rolls	
Kentucky	M386, 30 rolls	M397, 515 rolls
Louisiana	M387, 4 rolls	M396, 50 rolls
Maine	M543, 23 rolls	
Maryland	M388, 13 rolls	M384, 238 rolls
Massachusetts	M544, 44 rolls	
Michigan	M545, 48 rolls	
Minnesota	M546, 10 rolls	
Mississippi	M389, 1 roll	M404, 4 rolls
Missouri	M390, 51 rolls	M405, 854 rolls
Montana (see Washington Territory)		
Nebraska Territory	M547, 2 rolls	
Nevada	M548, 1 roll	
New Hampshire	M549, 13 rolls	
New Jersey	M550, 26 rolls	
New Mexico Territory	M242, 4 rolls	M427, 46 rolls
New York	M551, 159 rolls	
North Carolina	M391, 2 rolls	M401, 25 rolls
Ohio	M552, 122 rolls	
Oklahoma (see Dakota Territory)		
Oregon	M553, 1 roll	
Pennsylvania	M554, 136 rolls	
Rhode Island	M555, 7 rolls	
South Carolina	None	
Tennessee	M392, 16 rolls	M395, 220 rolls
Texas	M393, 2 rolls	M402, 13 rolls

	Microfilm Publication	
State	*Index*	*Compiled Military Service Records*
Utah Territory	M556, 1 roll	M692, 1 roll
Vermont	M557, 14 rolls	
Virginia	M394, 1 roll	M398, 7 rolls
Washington Territory	M558, 1 roll	
West Virginia	M507, 13 rolls	M508, 261 rolls
Wisconsin	M559, 33 rolls	
Wyoming (see Washington Territory)		
U.S. Colored Troops	M589, 98 rolls	
U.S. Volunteers (1st and 6th Regiments only)		M1017, 65 rolls
Veteran Reserve Corps	M636, 44 rolls	

Also see "Former Confederates Who Served in the Union Army," part of M1290 (thirty-six rolls), titled *Indexes to Compiled Service Records of Volunteer Union Soldiers Who Served in Organizations Not Raised By States or Territorie.*

Sources:

James P. Neagles, *U.S. Military Records: A Guide to Federal and State Sources, Colonial America to the Present* (Salt Lake City: Ancestry, 1994).

Guide to Genealogical Research in the National Archives (Washington, D.C.: National Archives and Records Service, 1985).

age twenty to forty-five who were subject to conscription. Assuming they were physically fit, the law affected white citizens as well as most aliens who had declared their intention to naturalize. The draft created three types of records:

1. Consolidated lists. These are the principal draft records concerning individuals. An entry for a man gives his name, place of residence, age as of 1 July 1863, occupation, marital status, state, territory, or country of birth, and the military organization (if a volunteer) of which he was a member. The records are arranged by state and thereunder by congressional or enrollment district.

2. Descriptive rolls. These rolls give additional information on men eligible for service. Although many of the entries are not completely filed out, they may give a personal description, exact place of birth, and whether accepted or rejected for service. The records are also filed by state and thereunder by congressional district.

Neither the consolidated lists nor the descriptive rolls have been microfilmed. They are part of National Archives Record Group 110 and are available only at the National Archives in Washington, D.C. To use the records you must know the number of the congressional district for the county in which a man lived. This can be determined by consulting Kenneth C. Martis, *The Historical Atlas of United States Congressional Districts 1789–1983* (New York: Free Press, 1982).

3. Case files on drafted aliens. These case files concern only aliens who were drafted and released from 1861 to 1864. The files may include name, district from which drafted, country of citizenship, age, length of time in United States, and a physical description. The files are in alphabetical order by surname in Record Group 59, available only at the National Archives.

The draft records, available for a historical period in which tracing families is sometimes very difficult, are invaluable for men living in cities. They are more complete and give important details not found in corresponding censuses. Furthermore, their alphabetical arrangement makes searching them easier.

Confederate Service Records

When Richmond was evacuated by the Confederate government in April 1865, the centralized military personnel records of the Confederate Army were taken to Charlotte, North Carolina, by the Confederate Adjutant and Inspector General, Samuel Cooper. When the Confederate civil authorities left Charlotte after agreeing to an armistice between the armies in North Carolina, President Jefferson Davis instructed Cooper to turn the records over, if necessary, to "the enemy, as essential to the history of the struggle." When General Joseph E. Johnston learned, after the armistice, that the records were at Charlotte, he turned them over to the Union Commander in North Carolina, saying, "As they will furnish valuable materials for history, I am anxious for their preservation, and doubt not that you are too."

The Confederate records surrendered or captured at the end of the war and taken to Washington, D.C., have been augmented by other records collected or copied in later years. In 1903, the War Department began to compile a service record for each soldier by copying the entries pertaining to him in these records. The result is an immense file of "compiled military service records" from which inquiries about Confederate soldiers are answered. Because of the efforts made over many years to incorporate all available information into this file, it is by far the most complete and accurate source of information about Confederate soldiers.

This file is accessed through the massive consolidated index to Confederate soldiers (NARA microfilm publication M1290), contained on 535 rolls of microfilm. If no record can be located by using this index, there is another set of Confederate records: those which were never identified as pertaining to a specific soldier or were not used in compiling the service records when the government ceased that project.

The compiled military service record of a Confederate soldier consists of one or more card abstracts and usually one or more original documents. Each card abstract entry comes from such original records as Confederate muster rolls, returns, descriptive rolls, and Union prison and parole records. If the original record of a soldier's service was complete, the card abstracts may serve to trace his service from beginning to end, but they normally do little more than account for where he was at a given time. The compiled military service record may provide the following information of genealogical interest: age, place of enlistment, places served, place of discharge or death, and often, physical description.

The original Confederate records from which the cards were made are among the holdings of the National Archives. Microfilm copies of all indexes and some records are available at the National Archives and at the Family History Library (see table 9-4). The index will provide the rank, unit, and name of the soldier, and the pertinent file can then be ordered from the National Archives.

The National Archives also compiled histories of Confederate military units and vessels (M861). They are arranged alphabetically by state and then by unit.

Because prisoner exchanges late in the Civil War were not working, approximately 28,000 Confederate soldiers, sailors, and citizens died in the North. While federal legislation from 1867 to 1873 provided for the reburial of Union soldiers in national cemeteries and for durable headstones, this early legislation made no specific provision for Confederate dead. Their graves were sometimes given thin headstones with a grave number and the soldier's name. Many of the non-Union graves, however, were marked with wooden headboards that disintegrated, although the names were often preserved in cemetery burial registers.

Finally, in 1912, a typescript register of Confederate soldiers and sailors buried in federal cemeteries was compiled in accordance with a 1906 statute, to provide for marking the graves of Confederate soldiers and sailors who died in Union prisons. This register (M918) was generally arranged alphabetically by name of prison camp, other location where the death occurred, or occasionally by cemetery name. The individual burial lists are also arranged alphabetically by the name of the deceased and generally include rank, company, regiment, date of death, and number and location of grave. Some cemeteries did not bury the dead in numbered graves. Some regimental and company designations or death dates are not entered in the register. The registers also include few entries for private Confederate citizens. Some are unknown. Other entries are for bodies "removed," "sent home," and "taken home by friends."

Table 9-4. Microfilmed Indexes and Compiled Military Service Records for Confederate Army Volunteers

| State | *Microfilm Publication* | |
	Indexes	*Compiled Military Service Records*
Alabama	M374, 49 rolls	M311, 508 rolls
Arizona Territory	M375, 1 roll	M318, 1 roll
Arkansas	M376, 26 rolls	M317, 256 rolls
Florida	M225, 9 rolls	M251, 104 rolls
Georgia	M226, 67 rolls	M266, 607 rolls
Kentucky	M377, 14 rolls	M319, 136 rolls
Louisiana	M378, 31 rolls	M320, 414 rolls
Maryland	M379, 2 rolls	M321, 22 rolls
Mississippi	M232, 45 rolls	M269, 427 rolls
Missouri	M380, 16 rolls	M322, 193 rolls
North Carolina	M230, 43 rolls	M270, 580 rolls
South Carolina	M381, 35 rolls	M267, 392 rolls
Tennessee	M231, 48 rolls	M268, 359 rolls
Texas	M227, 41 rolls	M323, 445 rolls
Virginia	M382, 62 rolls	M324, 1,075 rolls
Consolidated Index. The index (M818) and compiled service records (M258) are to Confederates who served in military organizations raised directly or otherwise formed by the Confederate government or who served in some capacity other than belonging to a unit at or below the regimental level.	M818, 26 rolls	M258, 123 rolls
General and Staff Officers		M331, 275 rolls

Also see "Former Confederates Who Served in the Union Army," part of National Archives microfilm publication M1290 (36 rolls), titled *Index to Compiled Service Records of Volunteer Union Soldiers Who Served in Organizations Not Raised by States or Territories and Compiled Service Records of Former Confederate Soldiers Who Served in the First Through Sixth U.S. Volunteer Infantry Regiments, 1864-1866,* National Archives Microfilm Publication M1017.

Source:

James C. Neagles, *U.S. Military Records: A Guide to Colonial and State Sources, Colonial America to the Present* (Salt Lake City: Ancestry, 1994).

Entries for the Green Lawn Cemetery in Indianapolis, Indiana, have been lined through and a notation added: "Remains of above removed to lot 285, sec. 32, Crown Hill Cemetery, Indianapolis, Indiana, and reinterred as unknowns on October 27, 1931." (Check other explanatory notes at the beginning or end of the burial list.) This register is now part of Record Group 92, Records of the Quartermaster General.

Record Group 92 also includes some records of the Office of the Commissioner for Marking the Graves of Confederate Dead not reproduced on M918: a two-volume 1914 register of Confederate soldiers and sailors who died in the North, the commissioner's incoming and outgoing correspondence (two of his files are in the Office of the Quartermaster General, files 128991 and 342020), Confederate burial registers, lists, and correspondence pertaining to particular cemeteries.

The War Department Collection of Confederate Records, Record Group 109, includes registers of Confederates who died in Union prisons: M598, *Selected Records of the War Department Relating to Confederate Prisoners of War 1861–1865.* Particularly useful is a two-volume series of registers of prisoner deaths compiled by the Office of the Commissary General of Prisoners (rolls 5 and 6). The volumes are alphabetically arranged by name of deceased and show the name; rank; regiment; company; place and date of capture; place, date, and cause of death; and number and locality of grave for each individual. The information in these registers may be used to supplement the information on M918, but burial information is frequently unavailable or obsolete. Rolls 10 through 12 are a five-volume series of registers of prisoner deaths compiled by the Surgeon General's Office and arranged by the states in which the deceased served. They contain most of the information described above.

State Confederate Records

The War Department Collection of Confederate Records is not complete, even though great efforts were made to assemble all official information. A soldier may have served in a state militia unit that was never mustered into the service of the Confederate government. Records of service in such units, if extant, may be in the state archive or in the custody of the state adjutant general. Since the federal government of the United States did not pay benefits to Confederates, pensions and other state benefits are recorded only in state records.

The Family History Library has the single largest collection of microfilmed state Confederate records. The call numbers for ordering the microfilms through family history centers are most easily located in the *Military Records Register, Vol. II: Civil War.* If the center does not have a copy, have the librarian request a copy from the main library in Salt Lake City.

Two additional categories of records require special mention: military academy records and Reconstruction court records. Many Confederate officers received their early training in Southern military academies. Others had attended West Point and had to choose which side to support. Consult Bvt. Major-General George W. Cullum, *Biographical Register, Officers and Graduates of the U.S. Military Academy, West Point, New York,* 3rd ed., 9 vols. (Boston: Houghton-Mifflin, 1891); Stanley P. Tozeski, *Preliminary Inventory of the Records of the U.S. Military Academy* (Washington, D.C.: National Archives and Records Service, 1976); and Jon L. Wakelyn, *Biographical Dictionary of the Confederacy* (Westport, Conn.: Green-

wood Press, 1977). Second, the confiscation of land by the Reconstruction government led to lengthy and bitter court battles. Genealogists seldom check these records, which can yield numerous details about Southern soldiers even though they are not technically military records. Also see chapter 7, Research in Court Records.

SPANISH-AMERICAN WAR THROUGH MODERN WARS, 1898 TO THE PRESENT

Service records for soldiers serving in the armed forces after the Civil War are not as readily available, even though the records of these later wars are more detailed. (See the records index list in table 9-5.)

Using records for soldiers who served within the last seventy-five years is restricted to the service person, the next of kin if the veteran is deceased, or requesters with release authorization signed by the veteran or, if deceased, by the next of kin. Many of the federal records in this category are housed at the National Personnel Records Center, 9700 Page Blvd., St. Louis, MO 63132. Records protected by privacy laws cannot be copied or viewed by the public, but some information contained in the records can be provided upon request. Use the current version of Form 180.

Documents issued to the veteran at time of discharge (or to his or her next of kin, in case of death) usually contain important genealogical information. The National Personnel Records Center candidly acknowledges that its priority is providing information on benefits, not genealogical data, and encourages contacting the veteran or next of kin. However, under the Freedom of Information Act (amended 1974), it will release an individual's age or date of birth, salary, photographs, source of commission, duty status, office telephone number, military and civilian educational level, decorations and awards (including a copy of the citation, if available), present and past duty assignments (including geographical location), future assignments which have been finalized, records of court-martial trials (unless classified), marital status, education/schooling, rank/grade, serial/service number, date of rank/grade, promotion sequence number, and dependents, including name, sex, and age.

If the identity needs to be verified, the center will also add such items as name of father and/or mother, home address, etc. This service takes several weeks; you will be billed for researching, processing, and photocopying.

On 12 July 1973, a fire on the top floor of the National Personnel Records Center in St. Louis destroyed millions of military records and damaged millions more. According to James E. Cole, Jr., acting assistant archivist for federal records centers, eighty percent of the army records for 1912 to 1959, sixty percent of the air force records for 1947 to 1963, and one percent or less of army records for personnel discharged since 1 January 1973 were destroyed.[2]

The center has since reconstructed a portion of the records of living military personnel who need the data to apply for pensions and other benefits. There are no plans at this time to reconstruct the records of deceased personnel where no benefits are owed.

Certain draft records and veterans' medical treatment records were not in the fire. World War I draft records have been microfilmed and are available for searching. See chapter

Table 9-5. Microfilmed Indexes to Service Records and Pensions, 1898-1902

Title	Microfilm Publication	Comments
General Index to Compiled Service Records of Volunteer Soldiers Who Served During the War With Spain, 1898-1901	M871 (126 rolls)	This general comprehensive index identifies the compiled service records of volunteer soldiers regardless of their military units. Each index card gives name, rank, and unit in which the soldier served.
Index to Compiled Records of Volunteer Soldiers Who Served During the Philippine Insurrection	M872 (24 rolls)	Numerous miscellaneous records are included. Files can include news clippings and printed reports as well as original documents. The personnel file for one veteran injured at Kutubic Bay, Philippines, exceeds two hundred pages.
Index to Compiled Service Records of Volunteer Soldiers Who Served During the War With Spain in Organizations From the State of Louisiana	M240 (1 roll)	
Index to Compiled Service Records of Volunteer Soldiers Who Served During the War With Spain in Organizations From the State of North Carolina	M413 (1 roll)	
General Index to Pension Files, 1861–1934	T288 (544 rolls)	Index cards are arranged alphabetically by surname of veteran and show the name of the veteran; name and class of dependent, if any; service data; application number or file number; and, for an approved claim, certificate number or file number and state from which the claim was filed.
General Index to Compiled Service Records of Volunteer Soldiers Who Served During the War With Spain, 1898-1901	M871 (126 rolls)	Separate indexes for each state and for special units of U.S. volunteers.
Index to Compiled Records of Volunteer Soldiers Who Served During the Philippine Insurrection	M872 (24 rolls)	Numerous miscellaneous records. The personnel file for one veteran injured at Kutubic Bay, Philippines, exceeds 200 pages. Files include newspaper clippings and printed reports as well as original documents.

18, Tracking Twentieth-Century Ancestors, for details. To obtain medical records information from the Department of Veterans Affairs computer database, you will need a soldier identification number. A military unit and a name are not sufficient.

Discharge Records

Each county in the United States was required to record the honorable discharge of soldiers and sailors who served in World War I. Some discharges for the Civil War and Philippine Insurrection are also on record, as well as some dishonorable and medical discharges. The records are kept in the local courthouse and usually consist of typed or handwritten transcripts of the original documents given to the soldier. Some of these discharge records from county collections have been microfilmed by the Genealogical Society of Utah, but most have not.

The records may contain the individual's name, race, rank, serial number, reason for discharge, birthplace, age at time of enlistment, occupation, and a personal description. His or her service record, sometimes included with the discharge record, gives the length of service, prior service, marital status, arms and horsemanship qualifications, advancement, battles, decorations, honors, leaves of absence, physical condition, and character evaluation.

The same requirement for recording discharges was in effect for World War II veterans. The information contained in these records is the same as that on file for veterans of World War I.

United States Merchant Marine

Records pertaining to the service of merchant marine personnel are on file with the U.S. Coast Guard. Records of discharged, deceased, and retired merchant marine personnel are in the custody of the National Personnel Records Center, Military Personnel Records, 9700 Page Blvd., St. Louis, MO 63132. Records of officers and active or reserve personnel prior to 1929 are in the custody of the Commandant of the U.S. Coast Guard, Washington, DC 20590.

Regular U.S. Army Enlistments

If a search of the relevant index or indexes does not reveal a service record for an individual, remember that there was another capacity other than that of volunteer or draftee. The veteran could have served in the Regular U.S. Army. The registers of enlistments for the period 1798 to 1914, except those for hospital stewards, quartermaster sergeants, and ordnance sergeants, have been microfilmed as NARA microfilm publication M233, forty-seven rolls. Prior to 1821, the records of officers are included as well. The records are arranged in subcategories of time blocks. The alphabetical arrangement within each subcategory varies.

RECORDS OF VETERANS BENEFITS

The provision of benefits was not widespread until after the revolutionary war, although the separate colonies sometimes provided pensions for veterans disabled by injuries incurred during their service. Fighters in Indian skirmishes and local riots submitted claims for supplies, equipment, and time spent to both legislative assemblies and county courts. These records are discussed at greater length in chapter 7. Bounties were also paid in both land and money for some military actions. (See chapter 8, Research in Land and Tax Records, for details on bounty land.)

PENSION RECORDS (1774–1811)

The first congressional legislation authorizing the payment of pensions for Revolutionary War service was dated 26 August 1776, but the government did not begin paying pension allowances until 28 July 1789; applications for pensions were made to the federal government from that date. Many of the early applications were destroyed by fire in 1800 and 1814. A partial record of the earlier pensioners is included among reports to Congress in 1792, 1794, and 1795.

Although applications for pensions were made to the U.S. government, they were initiated in the courts of the counties and towns in which the veterans lived. Note that a Pension Board refusal often led the claimant to seek relief from Congress directly. (See chapter 7 for more details.)

The pension records for the revolutionary war and later wars can contain much of genealogical value: affidavits made by the veteran and his neighbors or associates to support his claim, summaries of his service, the military organization in which he served, the dates of his service, his date and place of birth, names of heirs, relationship to others who served with him, his movements after the war, and information from family Bible records. Sometimes the Bible pages, torn out of the book, are enclosed as evidence.

For example, the revolutionary war pension file of Reuben Johnson was filed in Anderson District, South Carolina, on 19 November 1832. The file is too long to reproduce in its entirety but is illustrative even in summary. Reuben Johnson filed a sworn statement with the justice of the peace of Anderson District to apply for a pension for his revolutionary war services as a member of the Fourth Regiment of the North Carolina Line. He enlisted with Richard Phillips in 1776 at Surry County, North Carolina, and served for two and one-half years in the command of Captain Joseph Philips. On his statement he also named the marches in which he took part. After reenlisting he was present at the siege of Charleston, where he was taken prisoner by the British.

While his affidavit does not indicate his birth date or place of birth, many applications do contain that information, as well as the veteran's residences after the war.

Reuben's wife applied for a widow's pension after her husband's death. This document contains information of greater importance. Nancy Johnson's affidavit of 29 March 1843 states that she was the widow of Reuben Johnson, that they were married 20 November 1788, and that her husband died 26 January 1833. Her sister Margaret Burroughs made a sworn statement that her sister was Nancy Johnson, nee Greenlee, who had married Reuben Johnson in North Carolina many years before. Margaret was six years old when Nancy and Reuben were married and did not know the exact date of their marriage, but she knew Reuben and Nancy had moved to South Carolina with her father, Peter Greenlee, and that the two families lived on the same plantation. Peter died about forty years before her testimony. Her mother died 1 December 1842.

Reuben Johnson's file also contained a copy of his marriage record from Wilkes County, North Carolina. The documents in Reuben Johnson's file permit the researcher to outline his movements from the time of his enlistment to his death and document two generations of ancestry.

A four-volume set by Virgil D. White will prove useful in locating information from these files: *Genealogical Abstracts of Revolutionary War Pension Files* (National Historical Publishing Co., 1990–92). Also helpful are the compilations by Murtie J. Clark, including *The Pension Lists of 1792–95; With Other Revolutionary War Pension Records* (Baltimore: Genealogical Publishing Co., 1991. Reissued 1996). The National Genealogical Society's Special Publication No. 40, *Index of Revolutionary War Pension Applications in the National Archives,* indexes applicants and indicates the disposition of their applications. This last publication will identify certain applications that were rejected.

Rejection of revolutionary war pension applications did not necessarily mean that the applicant made a dishonest claim. Hundreds of applicants simply could not provide the necessary proof of service to be awarded a pension. The majority of applications were filed when Congress granted permission to all veterans in 1832. Discharges had often been lost or, in many cases, never issued. Comrades-in-arms who could have attested to service were often deceased or had moved away.

The revolutionary war pension application files have been microfilmed by the National Archives, and copies are on file at libraries throughout the country, including the Family History Library and its centers. This library has facilities for inexpensive photocopying. You may also request copies from the National Archives using NATF form 80.

The Act of 1832, mentioned earlier, required pension applications to include the birthplace, age, and residence of the applicant, and more. Applications may also include mention of a soldier substituting for another relative who was drafted into service. Once all of the applications pertaining to a veteran were received, including those of the widows and other claimants, they were combined into one file.

Bounty-Land Records

Bounty-land warrants were authorized by Congress in 1776 as a substitute for the wages it was unable to pay its soldiers. (See the section on bounty lands in chapter 8.) If the soldier was deceased, his heirs took claim to the land after the war. The number of acres granted was based upon the soldier's rank and ranged from 100 to 1,100 acres. This method of decreasing military costs worked so well that bounty-land warrants continued to be issued for post-revolutionary war service. Congress eventually authorized bounty-land warrants to be issued for military service performed prior to 1855.

The number of applicants for bounty lands far exceeded the number of persons applying for pensions, but the bounty-land warrant application file is basically the same as that of the pension application file. The application provides the veteran's name, age, residence, the military organization in which he served, and the term of his service. If his widow or other heirs made claim, their names, ages, and places of residence are given. Not all veterans actually farmed the land granted to them. Many assigned their warrants to others for a fee. Figure 9-1 shows bounty-land warrant 8057, which designates Philip van Cortlandt the assignee of Eleazar Yeomans, a soldier in the New York line. Yeoman's claim for one hundred acres was authorized by an act of Congress on 9 July 1788 and assigned to van Cortlandt on 16 July 1790.

Not all bounty-land applications were approved. The claimant had to prove his service in the war in exactly the same manner that a pensioner had to prove his service. Again, a rejected claim did not necessarily indicate that the claimant's service was never rendered, only that the claimant was not able to provide sufficient proof.

An estimated 450,000 bounty-land claims are on file in the National Archives. Some early claims were destroyed by the fires previously mentioned, but those remaining are available from the National Archives upon request using NATF form 80. In addition to land grants made by the federal government for revolutionary service, Connecticut, Georgia, Maryland, Massachusetts, New York, North Carolina, Pennsylvania, South Carolina, and Virginia chose to reward their soldiers with bounty land. Lloyd DeWitt Bockstruck has indexed the bounty-land records from these nine states in *Revolutionary War Bounty Land Grants Awarded by State Governments* (Baltimore: Genealogical Publishing Co., 1996).

PENSION RECORDS (1789–1861)

Pension records exist for the period between the end of the revolutionary war and the beginning of the Civil War, primarily dealing with the War of 1812, the Indian Wars, and the Mexican War. All of the indexes to these pension records have been published. These records are classified in three groups as the Old War Series Pension Records. These records pertain to pension applicants who were disabled or killed while serving in any war after the close of the revolutionary war and before the start of the Civil War, except for the War of 1812 pensions included in the regular War of 1812 pension application files. A few early death and disability claims of Civil War veterans prior to July 1861 are included. The original applications are located at the National Archives and can be requested in the same manner as all of the records discussed earlier. These pension applications have been indexed; the microfilmed index is available at the Family History Library.

War of 1812

Pension application files for veterans of the War of 1812 include applications of veterans still living after 1871, when Congress authorized pensions to veterans who did not later support the Confederate States of America. Applications for death, disability, regular service, widows, and other claimants are included in the same collection. A second act of Congress in 1878 authorized pensions for veterans who saw as few as fourteen days active duty. Virgil D. White's three-volume *Index to War of 1812 Pension Files* (National Historical Publishing Co., 1989)

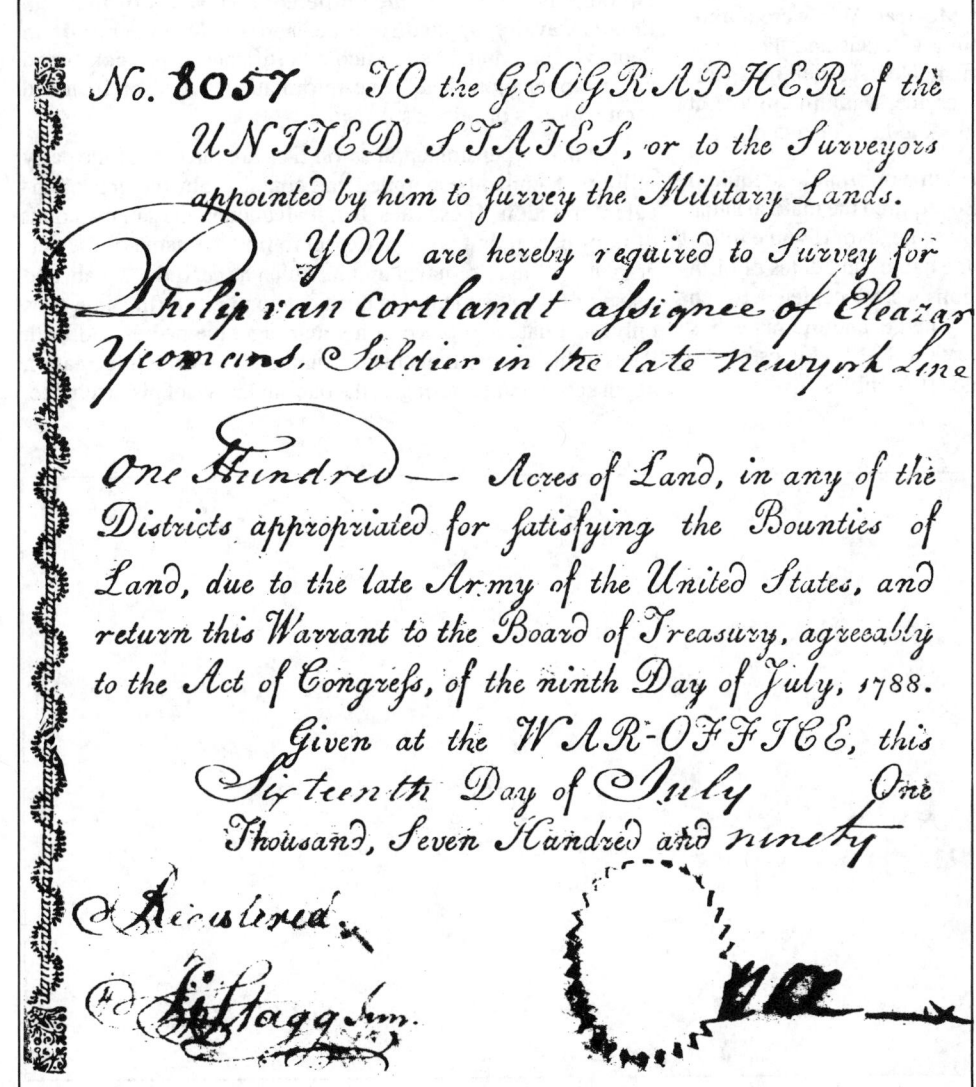

Figure 9-1. Bounty-land warrant 8057, 15 July 1790, for Philip van Cortlandt, assignee of Eleazar Yeomans. National Archives. Family History Library (hereafter FHL) 1,025,145.

indexes applicants eligible for pensions or bounty lands under these two acts.

These pension files will give you the veteran's name, age, and place of residence. If he was married, the marriage date and the maiden name of his wife are stated. The unit in which he served, the date and place of enlistment, and the date and place of discharge are also given. The widow's pension file will provide her name, age, and place of residence, their pertinent marriage information, the date and place of the veteran's death, his enlistment date and place, and the date and place of his final discharge. The pension files are available from the National Archives, but the microfilmed indexes are available in various libraries throughout the United States.

Indian Wars

There were innumerable Indian Wars between 1817 and 1858. Veterans of these wars received pensions for and claims dating from 1892 to 1926. The files are classified as Indian survivors, originals, Indian survivors' certificates, Indian widows' originals, and Indian widows' certificates. These files are indexed, and the microfilmed indexes are available at various libraries throughout the United States. The pension files are located at the National Archives.

Mexican War

Pension application files from the Mexican War were authorized by Congress in 1887, permitting veterans and their widows to file claims with the government. New restrictions specified a minimum of sixty days of service, a minimum age at application of sixty-two, or being disabled or dependent.

These files contain basically the same information required in other pension applications but also required the maiden name of the wife, the names of former wives, death or divorce information about previous wives, and the names and dates of birth of living children. Pension applications were accepted between 1887 and 1926. They are indexed by name, and the index has been microfilmed as NARA publication T317. Copies of the files can be obtained from the National Archives.

Civil War and Later Pensions Records (1861–1934)

Pension applications filed for the Civil War and later include records of Union soldiers. The files are arranged in nine categories: navy survivors, originals, navy survivors' certificates, navy widows' originals, navy widows' certificates, survivors' originals, survivors, certificates, widows' originals, widows' certificates, "C" and "XC" files.

Federal pensions were granted to veterans of the Spanish-American War of 1898, the Philippine Insurrection of 1899 to 1902, the Boxer Rebellion of 1900, and the regular establishment. Pensions based upon such service are included in the same index for Union Civil War veterans for 1861 to 1934.

Pensions of Civil War veterans, their widows, minor children, or parents have been indexed by the name of the veteran. You should not presume, however, that the actual files of a Union pensioner will be in the National Archives in Washington. While most of them are, others are still maintained in appropriate federal agencies across the nation. If the file is not in the custody of the National Archives in Washington, D.C., you will be directed to the proper agency for copies.

The indexes have been microfilmed and are available at local libraries. Figure 9-2 shows the index card of John W. Fulton, who served in three different companies of the 12th Illinois Cavalry, applied for a pension 20 November 1901 in Pennsylvania, and was granted a certificate of pension based on his application. The same information would be included for a widow's or minor's pension.

Civil War pension application files are the best of the early military documents compiled and contain valuable genealogical information. These files do not all contain the same amount of information, but one can expect to find the name of the veteran, the military or naval unit in which he served, the date and place of his enlistment, his birth date and place (in some files only), the date and place of his marriage, the names and birth dates of his children, the maiden name of his wife, information about subsequent marriages, the date and place of his discharge,

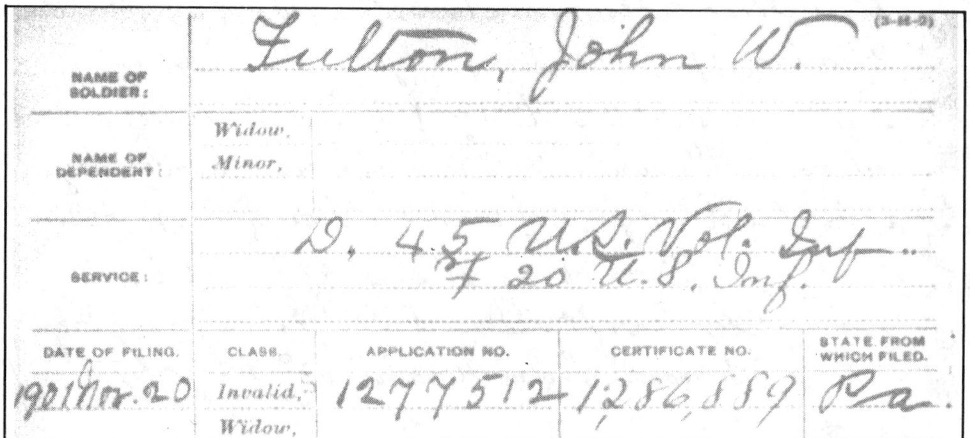
NAME OF SOLDIER: Fulton, John W.
NAME OF DEPENDENT: Widow, Minor,
SERVICE: D. 45 U.S. Vol. Inf. / F 20 U.S. Inf.
DATE OF FILING: 1901 Nov. 20
CLASS: Invalid, Widow, Minor,
APPLICATION NO.: 1277512
CERTIFICATE NO.: 1,286,559
STATE FROM WHICH FILED: Pa.
ATTORNEY: Byington & Wilson.
REMARKS:

Figure 9-2. Civil War pension index card of John W. Fulton, 20 November 1901, no. 1349885. National Archives. FHL 540,921.

physical disabilities connected with service-related injuries, and his residences since his discharge. There will also be general affidavits of individuals who could attest to his disabilities and copies of the findings of examining physicians at the time of his injury and during subsequent periodic physicals.

Each pension applicant was required to complete a Declaration for an Original Invalid Pension. Figure 9-3 is the declaration filed by James W. Reddish on 2 February 1891. In addition to most of the information noted above, his declaration also provides his physical description.

Figure 9-4 is the Declaration for a Widow's Pension filed by James's widow, Matilda Sweat, who stated that he died on 19 February 1894, that she was married on 5 January 1886 at Owensboro, Kentucky, and that both she and James were widowed at the time of their marriage. She had one minor child, Alonzo Reddish, who had been born in March 1884.

The Declaration for Dependent Pension of a Mother or Father (figure 9-5) was submitted by Polly Ann Right, the mother of Markus L. Reddish and James. She stated that Markus had died of measles while in the service at Corinth, Mississippi, on 6 July 1862. She had married his father 2 October 1836 at Daviess County, Kentucky. After her husband died 1 March 1863 at Ohio County, Kentucky, she married Amos Right, who had in turn died 5 July 1880.

Polly Ann Right had four sons in the Union Army at one time, and her husband was killed by Confederate troops as he worked on their farm. This unusual family situation is fully explained in the collected Civil War pension files of the entire family. This family's files are representative of the majority of the records on file.

Pensioners also completed periodic requests for additional information. For example, Figure 9-6 shows documentation of the maiden name of Solomon Winne's wife, the date of their marriage, and the names and dates of birth of their living children. Because she died a few months before her husband, his pension file included a copy of her death certificate. The document provides the exact date of her death, her age at the time of her death, the names and birthplaces of her parents, and where she was buried.

Winne's file also included an unusual document. His daughter Mary H. Swarthout of Kingston, New York, filed an application to be reimbursed for expenses related to his last illness. He died 20 July 1909 at the Old Soldier's Home in Bath, New York, owing $75 for his board at the time of his death. He owned no real estate, personal property, or money. Figure 9-7 is a copy of the application.

Another document in the pension file is the termination of the pension. If the cause was death—the most common reason—the death date is usually listed.

One of the most valuable contributions that a pension file can make in genealogical research is listing the veteran's residences after discharge. Westward expansion sent many families leapfrogging states between censuses in the post-Civil War years. Tracing the exact movements of individuals and families during that period is difficult at best and sometimes impossible without the assistance of the "road maps" provided in these pension files.

Because the Confederacy was dissolved after the war, no central governmental agency provided pensions for service or disability of Confederate soldiers. Some of the former Confederate states, including Alabama, Arkansas, Florida, Georgia, Kentucky, Louisiana, Mississippi, North Carolina, Oklahoma, South Carolina, Tennessee, Texas, and Virginia, authorized pensions to veterans and their widows. Each state had its own regulations which applicants had to meet. In each case, however, the pension could be paid only if the applicant continued to reside within the borders of the state. If he or she moved elsewhere, the applicant had to qualify under the regulations of the new jurisdiction. Many of these pension files are on microfilm in the Family History Library. The originals will be found with the various state archives.

Figure 9-8 illustrates the Soldier's Application for Pension from the State of Tennessee. The record lists the veteran's name, date and place of enlistment, residence, date and place of birth, injuries resulting from military service, marital status, the number and ages of his children, the age of his wife, the number of years he resided in Tennessee, and his occupation. There is no standard format for pension applications for the Confederacy, but the Tennessee application is representative of most of the others.

Tennessee also compiled a valuable but little-used record consisting of the biographical sketches of veterans of the Civil War who were still living in 1922 (figure 9-9). These records are filled with valuable genealogical information, including the veteran's name, residence, age, place of birth, occupation, the unit he served in during the war, his parents' names and birthplaces, the names of his paternal grandparents, and their residence. The residence of the veteran's father and all facts known about parents, grandparents, and great-grandparents (including when the family came to America, property owned by the veteran and his parents, education, and the general quality of the veteran's life) are included in these sketches.

Similar to the Tennessee Civil War questionnaires were censuses of pensioners taken in 1907 and 1921 in Alabama, 1911 in Arkansas, and 1911 in Louisiana.

WAR OF 1812 PRISONER-OF-WAR RECORDS

Records relating to British and American prisoners of war for 1812 to 1815 include miscellaneous correspondence and lists of prisoners sent from the Treasury Department to the Adjutant General's Office and from the Navy Department to the Adjutant General's Office. Some of these records have been microfilmed by the National Archives as M2019, *Records Relating to War of 1812 Prisoners of War* (one roll). These are indexed in M1747, *Index to War of 1812 Prisoners of War* (three rolls).

BURIAL RECORDS

Veterans of the military services have had the benefit of being buried in one of the many national and other federally administered cemeteries since 1861. The most famous of them is Arlington National Cemetery just outside of Washington, D.C. Records pertaining to almost all soldiers and veterans buried in the cemeteries under federal jurisdiction are in the custody of the Cemetery Service, National Cemetery System, Department of Veterans Affairs, 810 Vermont Ave., Washington, DC 20420. The names of the deceased are indexed, and information will be furnished on request.

Some soldiers were buried on U.S. military installations between 1807 and 1939. Records of those buried in the U.S.

Figure 9-3. Civil War pension application file of James W. Reddish, 2 February 1891, Hancock County, Kentucky. National Archives. Photocopy in the possession of Johni Cerny.

[No. 1.]

DECLARATION FOR AN ORIGINAL INVALID PENSION.

☞ This must be Executed before a Court of Record or some Officer thereof having custody of the Seal.

State of Kentucky County of Hancock, ss:

ON THIS Second day of February A. D. one thousand eight hundred and ninety one, personally appeared before me W. S. Morrison Notary Public of the County of Hancock ~~a COURT OF RECORD~~ within and for the county and State aforesaid James W. Reddish aged 52 years, who, being duly sworn according to law, declares that he is the identical James W. Reddish who was ENROLLED as a private on the 25th day of October 1861, in Company "B" of the 17th Regiment of Kentucky Infy Vols commanded by Col. McHenry, and was honorably DISCHARGED at Calhoun Ky on the 31st day of December, 1861; that his personal description is a follows: age 52 years; height 5 feet 5 inches; complexion light; hair brown; eyes gray. That while a member of the organization aforesaid, in the service and in the line of duty, at Hartford, in the State of Kentucky, on or about the latter part day of November, 1861, he, whilst on the march, was injured in the right foot by a wagon running over and crushing the same, and being thereby rendered unable to walk, he was placed on a commissary wagon to ride, from which said wagon he was thrown, with his left elbow dislocated; was thereupon taken to regimental hospital at Calhoun Ky for treatment. Whilst in said hospital contracted measles, from the effects of which he lost the sight of his left eye entirely.
(Here state the name or, nature of disease, or the location of the wound or injury. If disabled by disease state fully its cause, if by wound or injury, the precise manner in which received.)

That he was treated in hospitals, as follows: Regimental Hospital at Calhoun Ky – November and December 1861
(Here state the names or numbers, and the localities of all hospitals in which treated, and the dates of treatment.)

That he has not been employed in the military or naval service otherwise than as stated above save and except as a Home Guard from 1862 to 186[illegible]
(Here state what the service was, whether prior or subsequent to that stated above, and the dates at which it began and ended.)
That he has not been in the military or naval service of the United States since the 31st day of December 1861. That since leaving the service this applicant has resided in the Ohio Co Ky, Rockport Ind and Daviess ~~in the State of~~ & Hancock Counties Ky, and that his occupation has been that of a Farmer since Jany 1862. That prior to his entry into the service above named he was a man of good, sound physical health, being when enrolled a Farmer.
That he is now .... disabled from obtaining his subsistence by manual labor by reason of his injuries above described, received in the service of the United States; and he therefore makes this declaration for the purpose of being placed on the invalid pension roll of the United States. He hereby appoints, with full power of substitution and revocation [illegible] of Washington, D. C. his true and lawful attorney to prosecute his claim. That he has never received nor applied for a pension; that his residence is ~~No.~~ Hawesville Hancock Co — street Ky and that his post-office address is Hawesville Hancock Co Ky

Robert E. Duncan
Joe B. Vickers
(Two witnesses who can write sign here.)

James W. his + mark Reddish
(Signature of Claimant.)

Figure 9-4. Declaration for widow's pension filed by Matilda (Sweat) Raddish [*sic*], wife of James W. Reddish.

DECLARATION FOR WIDOW'S PENSION.

Under act approved June 27, 1890.

STATE OF *Kentucky* COUNTY OF *Daviess* SS.

ON THIS *4th* day of *December* A. D. one thousand eight hundred and ninety *Eight* personally appeared before me *E. G. Adams, a Notary Public* within and for the County and State aforesaid *Matilda Raddish* aged *56* years, a resident of the *city* of *Owensboro* County of *Daviess*, State of *Ky*, who, being duly sworn according to law, makes the following declaration in order to obtain the Pension provided by Acts of Congress granting Pensions to widows: That she is the widow of *James W. Raddish* who enlisted under the name of *James W. Raddish* at *Calhoun, Ky* on the *25* day of *Oct* A. D., 186*1*, in Co *F*, *17* Reg't *Ky. Inf* Vols., and served at least ninety days in the late war of the rebellion, who was *honorably discharged* on the ___ day of ___ A. D. 186_, and who died on the *19* day of *February* A. D. 18*94*.

That she was married under the name of *Matilda Sweat* to said *James W. Raddish* on the *5* day of *Jan* 188*6*, by *E. G. Adams, J.P.* at *Owensboro, Ky.*, there being no legal barrier to such marriage *Former husband died Dec. 74, Former inf. died Jan. 1. 85,* that she has to the present date remained his widow.

<small>Give date of death or divorce of former husband or wife, if any.</small>

That she is without other means of support than her daily labor; that names and dates of birth of all the children now living under sixteen years of age of the soldier are as follows:

Alonzo Raddish, born *March — 1884* , born ___ 18 .
___, born ___ 18 . ___, born ___ 18 .
___, born ___ 18 . ___, born ___ 18 .
___, born ___ 18 . ___, born 18 .
___, born ___ 18 . ___, born 18

That she has not heretofore received *nor* applied for Pension. *a claim war filed by soldier 987.165* That she makes this declaration for the purpose of being

<small>If you previously applied, so state, giving number of claim.</small>

placed on the Pension roll of the United States under the provisions of the act of June 27, 1890.

She hereby appoints, with full power of substitution and revocation,

Jas. H. Vermilya & Co., of Washington, D. C.,

her true and lawful attorneys to prosecute her claim. That her Post Office Address is *% E. G. Adams Owensboro* County of *Daviess* State of *Ky*

her
Matilda X Raddish.
mark
<small>Signature of Claimant.</small>

Nora Adams
Jno Dugan

<small>Two witnesses who can write sign here.</small>

[Stamp: PENSION BUREAU U. S. DEC 17 1898 OFFICE.]

ATTY FILED

Figure 9-5. Declaration for dependent pension of a mother or father filed by Polley [*sic*] Ann Right.

Declaration for Dependent Pension of a Mother or Father

UNDER ACT OF CONGRESS APPROVED JUNE 27, 1890.

This must be Executed before a Court of Record or some Officer thereof having Custody of the Seal.

State of Kentucky County of Ohio, ss:

ON THIS 23rd day of July, A. D. one thousand eight hundred and ninety ...., personally appeared before me a Deputy Clerk of the Ohio Co. Court, a Court of Record within and for the County and State aforesaid Polley Ann Right, aged 70 years, who, being duly sworn according to law, makes the following declaration in order to obtain the Pension provided by Act of Congress approved June 27 1890. That She (or she) is the mother (Mother or Father) of Markus D Riddish (Name of Soldier), who enlisted under the name of Markus D. Riddish, at Hartford Ky on the 10" day of Oct, A. D. 1861 in Co "F" 17" Ky Infty (Here state Company and Regiment, if in the Army; or vessel and Rank, if in the Navy.) in the war of the rebellion 1861, who was honorably discharged at .... on the day of .... 18...., and who died at Corinth Miss, on the 6" day of July, 1862 of Measles while in the united states service & without fault on his part & said Measles killed the said son & said son contracted same while in U.S. service & in line of duty

that said soldier left neither widow nor child under sixteen years of age surviving; that the said declarant was married to the father (Mother or Father.) of said son at Davies Co Ky ...., on the 2nd day of Oct, A. D. 1836, by Rubin Cotter; that She (or she) is now wholly dependent upon others not legally bound for her support; that the father (Mother or Father.) of said son died at Ohio Co Ky, on the 1st day of March A. D. 18.63

That She has .... heretofore received .... applied for pension No 252,831 (If the Mother or Father of the Soldier had previously applied, so state, giving number of claim.) and that she has remarried & married Amos Right & he died 5-Jay. (If mother's claim, here add "she has not again married.") Declarant hereby appoints, with full power of substitution and revocation, R R Wedding, of Rosine Ohio Co Ky her (His or her) true and lawful attorney, to prosecute this claim; that her residence is No. .... street .... and her Post Office address is Horton Ohio Co, Ky.

J. Raleigh
J.B. Wallace M.J.R.
(Two witnesses who can write, sign here.)

Polley Ann Right her mark
(Signature of Claimant.)

Soldiers' Home Cemetery in Washington, D.C., national cemeteries, military installations in the United States, and post cemeteries in Cuba, the Philippines, Puerto Rico, and China are also included in this collection. You must know where the soldier is buried to find the burial record. The early burial registers record primarily burials of active-duty soldiers except in the case of frontier army posts, where family members and civilian dependents were also buried in the post cemeteries.

Four volumes of records dating from 1861 to 1868 pertain to burials of soldiers at the U.S. Soldiers' Home Cemetery. The registers provide the soldier's name, military organization, date and place of burial, rank, place of residence before enlistment, name and residences of the soldier's widow or other relative, age, cause of death, and place and date of death. Each volume is indexed by the initial letter of the soldier's surname.

Three correspondence files also contain information pertaining to soldiers' burials: letters relating to buried soldiers (1864–90), quartermaster's notifications (1863–66), and reports of Arlington National Cemetery sexton (1864–67).

Applications for headstones to be placed at the graves of soldiers and veterans range in date from 1879 to 1924. The information in the applications includes the name and addresses of headstone applicant, name of the veteran, rank, years of service, place and date of burial, and sometimes the date and cause of death. Most of these applications are filed by state, then by county, then by cemetery. Applications for headstones for soldiers, sailors, and marines buried outside the United States between 1911 and 1924 are arranged by country of burial. Soldiers buried in the cemeteries of the National Home for Disabled Volunteer Soldiers for whom headstone applications were made are arranged by the name of the home.

A card file indexing applications for headstones for 1870 to 1903 has been compiled and includes the serviceman's name, military organization, date and place of death, name and location of the cemetery, and date of the application. These cards

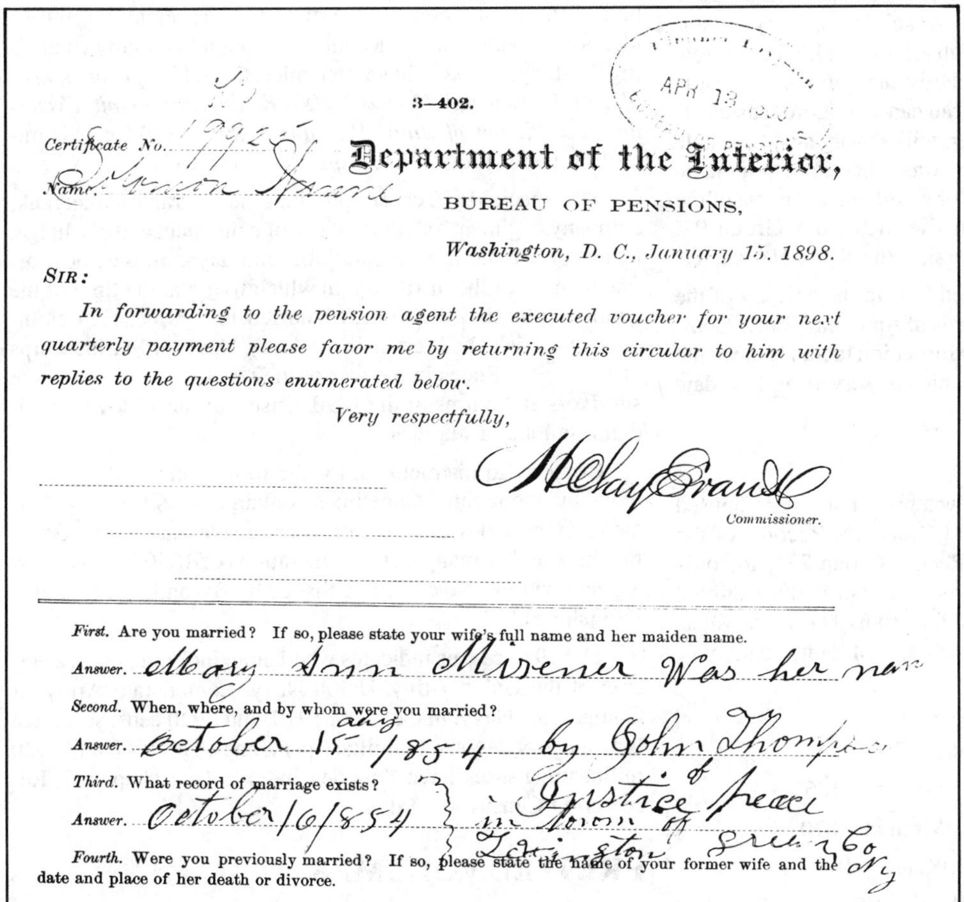
3–402.

Certificate No. 17925

Name Simon Winne

Department of the Interior,

BUREAU OF PENSIONS,

Washington, D. C., January 15, 1898.

SIR:

In forwarding to the pension agent the executed voucher for your next quarterly payment please favor me by returning this circular to him with replies to the questions enumerated below.

Very respectfully,

H. Clay Evans

Commissioner.

First. Are you married? If so, please state your wife's full name and her maiden name.

Answer. Mary Ann Mirener Was her nam

Second. When, where, and by whom were you married?

Answer. October 15 day 1854 by John Thomps

Third. What record of marriage exists?

Answer. October 16/1854 } Justice of peace in town of Lexington Green Co NY

Fourth. Were you previously married? If so, please state the name of your former wife and the date and place of her death or divorce.

Answer.

Fifth. Have you any children living? If so, please state their names and the dates of their birth.

Answer. Harvey S Born April 27/1860 Robert E May 31, 1868 Mary E June 8/1870 M Helen March 17/1874 all married } Josephine Feb 1878 } James William January 25/1880 } Eliza Jan 7 Julia Ann March 29/1870

Date of reply, , 189 (Signature.)

5301b750m1-98

Figure 9-6. Civil War pension application file of Solomon Winne, Kingston, New York, 13 April 1898. National Archives. Photocopy in the possession of Johni Cerny.

are arranged alphabetically by the surname of the soldier and include Confederate and post-Civil War veterans' applications.

The names of 228,639 Union soldiers who were buried in more than three hundred national cemeteries during the Civil War are published in *Roll of Honor: Names of Soldiers Who Died in Defense of the American Union, Interred in the National Cemeteries, Numbers I–XIX*. Originally published by the Quartermaster General's Office in 1868, the entries are arranged by name of cemetery and thereunder alphabetically by name of soldier. The date of death is shown. In 1994, the Genealogical Publishing Company of Baltimore reprinted this work. In 1995, the same company published an alphabetical list of soldiers and a comprehensive, state-by-state index to burial sites: Martha and William Remy, comps., *Index to the Roll of Honor*.

There are also card file records of World War I-era soldiers who died overseas between 1917 and 1922. These files consist mainly of grave registrations, records of American names in European chapels, and records of American soldiers who were buried in Russia. They are arranged alphabetically by surname of the soldier or name of the cemetery. The collection of grave registrations includes the name of the soldier, military organization, date of death, a statement that he was killed in action, name and address of the nearest relative or guardian, and name of the chapel. The record of American names in European chapels includes the name of the soldier, military organization, date of death, statement that the soldier was killed in action, name and address of the nearest relative or guardian, and name of the chapel. These records are all on file in Record Group 92, Records of the Quartermaster General, in the National Archives.

A list of soldiers missing in action is in the custody of the National Archives under the Records of American Battle Commission, Record Group 117. The information includes the name of the missing soldier, the unit in which he served, and the date of disappearance.

VETERANS' HOMES

Records pertaining to the federal veterans' homes are housed in the National Archives in Record Group 15, Records of the Veterans Administration, and in Record Group 231, Records of the U.S. Soldiers' Home. Below is a list of the National Homes for Disabled Volunteer Soldiers (now known as Veterans Administration Centers) and the dates of their creation:

Eastern Branch, Togus, Maine: 1866

Central Branch, Dayton, Ohio: 1867

Northwestern Branch, Wood, Wisconsin: 1867

Southern Branch, Kecoughtan, Virginia: 1870

Western Branch, Leavenworth, Kansas: 1885

Pacific Branch, Sawtelle, California: 1888

Marion Branch, Marion, Indiana: 1888

Roseburg Branch, Roseburg, Oregon: 1894

Danville Branch, Danville, Illinois: 1898

Mountain Branch, Johnson City, Tennessee: 1903

Battle Mountain Sanitarium, Hot Springs, South Dakota: 1907

Bath Branch, Bath, New York: 1894

Saint Petersburg Home, Saint Petersburg, Florida: 1930

Biloxi Home, Biloxi, Mississippi: 1930

Tuskegee Home, Tuskegee, Alabama: 1933

MILITARY CENSUS RECORDS

For a discussion of military censuses, see chapter 18, Tracking Twentieth-Century Ancestors. Census information involving military service was taken in 1840 and 1890. At the time of the 1840 federal population census, enumerators were asked to list all living pensioners of the revolutionary war or other military service. These names and the accompanying information have been published in *A Census of Pensioners for Revolutionary or Military Services; With Their Names, Ages, and Places of Residence, as Returned by the Marshals of the Several Judicial Districts Under the Act for Taking the Sixth Census* (Washington, D.C.: 1841, 1956. Reprint. Baltimore: Genealogical Books in Print, 1996). The 1840 census provides the veteran's name, age, and residence.

The schedules for the 1890 census of pensioners for (in alphabetical order) Alabama through Kansas and approximately half of those for Kentucky are missing. The remaining schedules for the latter half of Kentucky through Wyoming (including Washington, D.C.) have been microfilmed as *Special Schedules of the Eleventh Census (1890) Enumerating Union Veterans and Widows of Union Veterans of the Civil War*. This microfilm publication, M123, consists of 118 rolls.

This special 1890 census provides the veteran's name; rank; company, regiment, or vessel; dates of enlistment and discharge; length of service in years, months, and days; aliases; post office address of the institution in which living at the time of the enumeration; and disabilities incurred in service. Entries include those who had served in the Army, Navy, or Marine Corps of the United States in the war of the rebellion, and who were survivors at the time of the 1890 census, or the widows of soldiers, sailors, or marines.

Contrary to instructions, for the former states of the Confederacy, the records sometimes contain entries for Confederate veterans and widows of confederate veterans as well. Separate indexes for many state enumerations of 1890 Union veterans and widows have been published by Byron L. Dilts (Index Publishing).

The 1910 census indicates whether an individual was a veteran of the Union Army, Union Navy, Confederate Army, or Confederate Navy. In the 1900, 1910, and 1920 censuses, there is a category devoted to military personnel. The 1900 and 1920 military censuses have Soundex indexes (see chapter 5, Research in Census Records).

PRINTED VOLUMES

Hundreds of volumes pertain to the military history of the United States and to the service and pension/bounty-land applications that were granted prior to the modern wars. A recent work by James C. Neagles, *U.S. Military Records: A Guide to Federal and State Sources, Colonial America to the Present* (Salt Lake City: Ancestry, 1994), is unique in that it describes the records that are available and where they can be found. While there is no known comprehensive bibliography to printed sources, a partial list of sources is provided at the end of this chapter. A few examples of the information contained in randomly selected printed volumes are included for your study. On the page

Figure 9-7. Application for reimbursement to Mary H. Swarthout for expenses connected with the final illness of her father, Solomon Winne; in his pension file.

3—044.

APPLICATION FOR REIMBURSEMENT.

(This application, when properly executed before some officer having authority to administer oaths for general purposes, should be forwarded, together with the pension certificate and itemized bills of all expenses, to the Commissioner of Pensions, Washington, D. C.)

STATE OF *New York*

COUNTY OF *Ulster*   } ss:

On this _____*5th*_____ day of _____*August*_____, A. D. one thousand nine hundred and _____*Ten*_____, personally appeared before me, a _____*Notary Public*_____ within and for the County and State aforesaid, *Mary H. Swarthout* , aged _____*37*_____ years, a resident of _____*Kingston*_____, County of _____*Ulster*_____, State of _____*New York*_____, who, being duly sworn according to law, makes the following declaration in order to obtain reimbursement from the accrued pension for expenses paid (or obligation incurred) by claimant for the last sickness and for the burial of _____*Solomon Winne*_____, who was a pensioner of the United States by certificate No. *19925* , on account of the service of _____*Solomon Winne*_____ in _____*Company G 1st Battery New York Volunteers*_____

(Name of soldier or sailor.)

(Describe service by company and regiment, etc., if in the Army, or by the words U. S. Navy, if in the Navy.)

That pension was last paid to _____*May 4th*_____, 19*16*, by the U. S. Pension Agent at *New York*

That the answers to questions propounded below are full, complete, and truthful to the best of my knowledge, information, and belief, and that no evidence necessary to a proper adjustment of all claims against the accrued pension is suppressed or withheld.

1. What was the full name of the deceased pensioner? *Solomon Winne*

2. In what capacity was decedent pensioned? (As invalid soldier or sailor, or as a widow, minor child, dependent relative, etc.) *As Invalid Soldier*

3. If decedent was pensioned as an invalid soldier or sailor—

    (*a*) Was he ever married? (Answer yes or no.) *Yes*

    (*b*) How many times, and to whom? *Once and to Mary A. Misner*

    (*c*) If married, did his wife survive him? (Answer yes or no.) *no*

    (*d*) If so, is she still living? (Answer yes or no.) *no*

    (*e*) If not living, give full names and dates of death of all wives *March 10th 1909*

    (*f*) Was he ever divorced? (Answer yes or no.) *no*

    (*g*) If so, is the divorced wife still living? (Answer yes or no.) _____ (If living, a copy of the decree of divorce must be filed.)

    (*h*) If not living, give her full name and the date of her death _____

4. Did pensioner leave a child under 16 years of age? (Answer yes or no.) *no*

5. Is any such child still living? (Answer yes or no.) *no*

6. Was there insurance (life, accident, or health) in force on life of pensioner at time of death? (Answer yes or no.) *no*

7. If so, give the name of each company in which a policy was carried and the amount in which each policy was written

8. Who was the beneficiary named in each policy? _____

9. What was the relation of each beneficiary to the pensioner? _____

10. Were the premiums paid by the deceased pensioner? _____

11. If not paid by the deceased pensioner, state the amount of premiums paid by each person who made payment on that account _____

PENSION
U. S.
AUG 8 1910
OFFICE

6—1572

Figure 9-7 (continued)

12. Was pensioner a member of any society paying sick or death benefits? (Answer yes or no.) ...... *No*

13. Is there an executor or administrator, or will application be made for appointment of any person as administrator? ....
No

14. Did the deceased pensioner leave any money, real estate, or personal property? *No money Real Estate or ......*

15. If so, state the character and value of all such property ....

16. What was the assessed value (last assessment) of the real estate? ....

17. How was the pensioner's property disposed of? *None to dispose of*

18. Did pensioner leave an unindorsed pension check? (Answer yes or no.) ...... *no*

19. What was your relation to the deceased pensioner? ...... *Daughter*

20. Are you married? (Answer yes or no.) ...... *Yes*

21. What was the cause of pensioner's death? ...... *Senile Dementia* .... *at Home*

22. When did the pensioner's last sickness begin? *Cannot say, admitted to Hospital an arm*

23. From what date did the pensioner become so ill as to require the regular and daily attendance of another person constantly
until death? *Was at Soldiers Home, Bath, N.Y., cannot give date*

24. Give the name and post-office address of each physician who attended the pensioner during last sickness
*Attended by the Physicians at the Soldiers
Home Bath, N.Y.*

25. State the names of the persons by whom the pensioner was nursed during the period or any portion of the period of last
sickness and the period covered by such service in each instance
Nursed at the Home

26. Where did the pensioner live during last sickness? *Soldiers Home, Bath N.Y.*

27. Where did the pensioner die? *Soldiers Home, Bath, N.Y.*

28. When did the pensioner die? *July 20th 1909*

29. Where was the pensioner buried? *Bath, N.Y.*

30. Has there been paid, or will application be made for payment to you or any other person, any part of the expenses of the
pensioner's last sickness and burial by any State, County, or municipal corporation? (Answer yes or no.) *No*

31. State below the expenses of the pensioner's last sickness and burial. Write the word *none* where no charge is made in
case of any item of expense noted.

(Each charge entered below should be supported by an itemized bill of the person who rendered the service or furnished
any supplies for which reimbursement is demanded, and should show, over his signature, by whom paid, or who is held
responsible for payment, and contain the name of the pensioner for whom the expense was incurred or service rendered.)

NAMES.	NATURE OF EXPENSES.	STATE WHETHER PAID OR UNPAID.	AMOUNT.	
	Physician			
	Medicine			
	Nursing and care			
	Undertaker			
	Livery			
	Cemetery			
	Other expenses and their nature:			
	Board rc	*unpaid*	*75*	*00*
	TOTAL			

32. **Is the above a complete list of *all* the expenses of the last sickness and burial of the
deceased pensioner?** (Answer yes or no.) *Yes*

That my post-office address is No. *28* , on *Taylor* .... street,

town or city of *Kingston* , County of *Ulster* ,

State of *New York*

(When the claimant for reimbursement is a married woman, she is required to sign the application with her own full
name, not using the Christian name or the initials of her husband, and all bills should be receipted to her in her own name.)

Mary. H. Swarthout
(Claimant's signature in full.)

6—1572

Figure 9-7 (continued)

Also personally appeared *Emma Freelewich*

and *Dorothy P Booth* , persons whom I certify to be respectable and entitled to credit, and who, being by me duly sworn, say that they were present and saw *Mary H. Swarthart* , the claimant, sign *her* name (or make ____ mark) to the foregoing application, and that they know the claimant therein: that they have read all the questions, answers, and declarations in said application and believe the facts therein set forth to be true; and that they have no interest, direct or indirect, in this claim.

Emma Freelewich
171 Green & Virginia Ave,
Dorothy P Booth
121 Greenwich ___ st. N.Y.
(Signatures and post-office addresses of witnesses.)

Subscribed and sworn to before me this ____*5th*____ day of ____*August*____, A. D. 19*10*; and I certify that the contents of the foregoing application, etc., were fully made known and explained to the claimant and witnesses before swearing, including the words _____ erased and the words _____ added; and that I have no interest, direct or indirect, in the prosecution of this claim.

F. W. Freelewich
(Signature.)
Notary Public
(Official character.)
177 Green & Knph st

STATEMENT OF ATTENDING PHYSICIANS.

Give date of the pensioner's death ....

Give date of commencement of pensioner's last sickness ....

From what date did the pensioner require the regular and daily attendance of another person constantly until death?

....

During what period did you attend the pensioner? ....

State nature of disease from which pensioner died ....

....

....

Give name of each person who rendered service as nurse, and who has made or will make a charge for such service ....

....

Give name of any other physician who attended the pensioner in last sickness ....

Does your bill include a charge for all medicine furnished the pensioner during last sickness? ....

State whether you have read the questions in the foregoing application, and the claimant's answers thereto, and whether such answers are correct according to your best knowledge, information, and belief? ....

....

Mention any other facts within your knowledge which in your opinion would be helpful in adjusting this claim for reimbursement:

....

....

I certify that the foregoing statement is correct.

_____, 191___

Attending Physician.

6—1572

_____, 191___

Attending Physician.

PENSION
N
AUG
8
1910
U. S.
OFFICE.

below from the *Roster of Revolutionary Soldiers in Georgia*, note that the information included is extensive for one veteran but scant for others.

JESSE POPE, b. in Chowan Co., N.C.; d. Hancock Co., Ga, 1820. Received bounty grant of land in Ga. for his services, in N.C. Troops. Married Mary Fort.

JOHN POPE, b. 1755, Halifax Co., N.C.; d. 1819, Wilkes Co., Ga. Served as Capt., Ga Troops. Received bounty grant of land in Ga. for his services. Married Elizabeth Smith, d. 1829.

Children:

1. Huldah, mar. Henry Jossey, Jr.

2. Keturah, mar. James Mathews, Jr.

3. Mary L, mar. —Henderson.

4. Wylie.

5. Rowena.

6. Louisa.

7. Martha, mat. Rev. Wm. A. Callaway.

8. Augustine Burwell.

JOHN HENRY POPE, b. 1756; d. 1821, Wilkes Co., Ga. Received bounty land in Ga. for his services with N.C. Troops. Married Mary Burwell.

OLIVER PORTER (son of JOHN PORTER, REV. SOLDIER of Va, and Mary Anthony), b. Prince Edward Co., Va., 1763; d. Greene Co., Gal, 1838. Enlisted in the Reg. of his brother WILLIAM PORTER and was at the Siege of Yorktown. Received land in Greene Co., Ga, for his services. Married Margaret Watson, b. 171- (dau. of DOUGLASS WATSON, b. 1750 in Va.; d. 1797, Wilkes Co., Ga. Served in Va. and received bounty grant of land in Wilkes Co., Ga, for his services, and his wife Margaret Parker).

Children:

1. Ann (1793–1875); mar. 1815, Adam Goudylock Saffold (son of WILLIAM SAFFOLD, REV. SOLDIER who received land in Ga. for his services; d. in Gal; mar. Ann Goudelock).

2. Douglass Watson, mar. Annabelle Burwell (dau. of JOHN BURWELL, REV. SOLDIER, and his wife Ann Powell).

3. James, b. Greene Co., Ga.; mar. Athline (or Abijah) Cox, b. Morgan Co., Ga. (dau of John Cox and his wife Elizabeth Hyde, dau. of JAMES HYDE, REV. SOLDIER who d. from effects of wounds received in service).

Virginia Soldiers of 1776 is also rich in genealogical information:

William Brown, Midshipman.

Exec. Dept. July 23rd. 1835. The heirs of William Brown are allowed L.B. for his services as a Midshipman in the Va. State Navy, for three years. Littleton Tazewell. Gov.

Matthews Co. Court. Aug. 13, 1835. On motion of

Figure 9-8. Tennessee Civil War pension application file of L.H. Hathcock, Rutherford County, Tennessee, 3 August 1891. Tennessee Historical Library. FHL 969,942.

ACCEPTED

No. *415*

Soldier's Application for Pension.

(The Board Reserve the Right to Call for Additional Testimony if they Deem it Necessary.)

L. H. Hathcock

Filed *Augt 3. 1891*

Allow *Augt 6. 1891*

Quarter   lowance. $ *25⁰⁰*

Pension allowed from *Filing*

Rejected

Geo. N. Nunn President.

Jno. P. Kirkman Secretary.

Board Pension Examiners.

A. B. TAVEL. Printer to the State.

Figure 9-8 (continued)

SOLDIER'S APPLICATION FOR PENSION.

I, L. H. Nattcock ...., a native of the State of Tennessee,
and now a citizen of Tennessee, resident at ...., in the County of ...., in
said State of Tennessee, and who was a soldier from the State of Tennessee........................, in the war between the
United States and the Confederate States, do hereby apply for aid under the Act of General Assembly of Tennessee, entitled "An
Act for the benefit of the indigent and disabled soldiers of the late war between the States, and to fix the fees of attorneys or agents
for procuring such pensions, and fixing a penalty for the violation of the same." And I do solemnly swear ....

charge of my duty in the service of the Confederate ...... States, as a member of ....

I was wounded in the battle or battles of ....

and that, from the effects of such wound or wounds I was disabled as follows: ....

and that, by reason of such wound and disability, I am now entitled to receive the benefits of this Act. I further swear that I do not
hold any national, State or county office, nor do I receive aid or a pension from any other State, or from the United States, and that
I am not an inmate of any soldiers' home, and that I am unable to earn a reasonable support for myself and family. I do further
solemnly swear that the answers given to the following questions are true:

In what county, State and year were you born?
Ans. ....

When did you enlist, and in what command? Give the names of regimental and company officers under whom you were serving at date of wound or wounds.
Ans. ....

In what battle or battles were you wounded, and if not in battle state under what circumstances you received the injury or
injuries?
Ans. ....

What was the precise nature of your wound or wounds?
Ans. ....

What limb, if any, did you lose by reason of said wound or wounds, and if no limb, state fully the disability caused by said
wound or wounds, and is said disability permanent?
Ans. ....

Were you incapacitated for service by reason of said wound, wounds or service?
Ans. ....

Were you discharged from the army by reason of said wound, wounds or service?
Ans. ....

If discharged from the army, where were you and what did you do until the close of the war?
Ans. ....

What was the name of the surgeon that attended you?
Ans. ....

Are you married, or have you been married?
Ans. ....

READ THIS ACT BEFORE FILLING OUT APPLICATION.

CHAPTER 64, LAWS OF TENNESSEE, 1891.

AN ACT for the benefit of the indigent and disabled soldiers of the late war between the States, and to fix the fees of attorneys or agents for procuring such pensions, and fixing a penalty for the violation of the same.

SECTION 1. *Be it enacted by the General Assembly of the State of Tennessee,* That the Comptroller, Attorney-general of the State, and three ex-Confederate soldiers, to be suggested by the Tennessee Division of Confederate Veterans, appointed by the Governor, and hold their office for two years, without pay, shall constitute the "Board of Pension Examiners," who are invested with full power and authority to hear and determine all applications for pensions under the provisions of this Act, and to prescribe such rules and regulations touching such applications at such times as they may deem necessary for the proper conduct of their business as such board; and to hear evidence touching such applications, at such times and places, and in such manner, as they may desire; and to allow or refuse pensions according as justice and law may require. They are invested with full power over the entire pension roll at all times, and it is their duty to strike from the roll such names as may be improperly there, after proper notice and hearing. Their decision shall be final.

SEC. 2. *Be it further enacted,* That only disabled soldiers, Federal and Confederate, that enlisted from the State of Tennessee in Tennessee regiments, or citizens of this State at the time of their enlistment in regiments of other States, who are now residents of this State; or citizens of other States who enlisted in Tennessee or other States, but who are now and have been citizens of this State for one year, shall be entitled to the benefits of this Act; and they must be *bona fide* residents of the State at least one year before making their application for pension; and their characters as soldiers must have been free from dishonor; and it must appear that they are not pensioners entitled to pension under the laws of the Federal Government or of any other State, and that they are not already in possession of a competency—the object of this statute being to provide for the indigent and disabled.

SEC. 3. *Be it further enacted,* That the rates of pensions to be paid under this Act shall be as follows:

1. For total disability, such as the loss of both arms, both legs or both eyes, or the use of the same either in battle, skirmish or on picket, or from sickness, exposure or other injuries received during the war, in prison, or on the way home, $25 per month.

2. For partial disability, such as the loss of *one leg and one arm,* such as the loss of *one leg and one arm,* in battle, skirmish or on picket, or one of the aforesaid limbs lost in battle, or skirmish, or on picket, and the other so disabled as to since render it useless or made amputation necessary, $10 per month.

3. For smaller disability, such as the loss of one leg or one arm, or the use of the same, either in battle, skirmish or on picket, or in prison, $8.33⅓ per month.

The Board of Pension Examiners shall pass on all ap-

plications, give their approval before a pension shall be granted; when granted, the Comptroller shall issue his warrant quarterly to the pensioner for the amount of the pension, on the Treasurer, who shall pay the same out of any moneys not otherwise appropriated.

SEC. 4. *Be it further enacted,* That no pension shall be allowed to any one unless it shall clearly appear that his disabilities resulted from some injury received while engaged in the military service, and while in the line of duty, or in prison.

SEC. 5. *Be it further enacted,* That the pensions allowed under this Act shall be paid quarterly; and that no arrears shall be allowed beyond the date of making application, and in no case for more than one year. If, from inheritance or otherwise, any pensioner shall acquire a competency sufficient for his support, cease to be a resident of the State, or die, it shall be the duty of the board to strike such pensioner from the pension roll.

SEC. 6. *Be it further enacted,* That the Board of Pension Examiners shall keep a book in which shall be recorded the names of each pensioner, company and regiment, date, place, and nature of wound received, date and place where paroled or discharged, date of granting and amount of pension.

SEC. 7. *Be it further enacted,* That it shall be the duty of the board to fix the fees of attorneys prosecuting applications for pensions, which shall in no case exceed $10, which shall be paid directly to the attorney.

SEC. 8. *Be it further enacted,* That it shall be a misdemeanor punishable by a fine of not less than $500 and imprisonment not less than ten days, for any person to contract for or receive, directly or indirectly, more than the legal fees for prosecuting pension claims under this Act. The grand jury are given inquisitorial power over this offense, and the "Board of Pension Examiners" are required to investigate such matters, and have them brought before the courts.

SEC. 9. *Be it further enacted,* That the Board shall have power, with the consent of the Trustees, in case of applicants having no families, to allow them a support in the Confederate Soldier's Home in lieu of a pension.

SEC. 10. *Be it further enacted,* That it shall be the duty of the Board to withhold pension from any pensioner who may habitually waste the State's bounty in dissipation or other dishonorable manner.

SEC. 11. *Be it further enacted,* That this Act take effect from and after its passage, the public welfare requiring it; and that all former laws on the subject of pensions be and the same are hereby repealed.

Passed March 10, 1891.

THOMAS R. MYERS,
Speaker of the House of Representatives.
W. C. DISMUKES,
Speaker of the Senate.

Approved March 12, 1891.

JOHN P. BUCHANAN,
Governor.

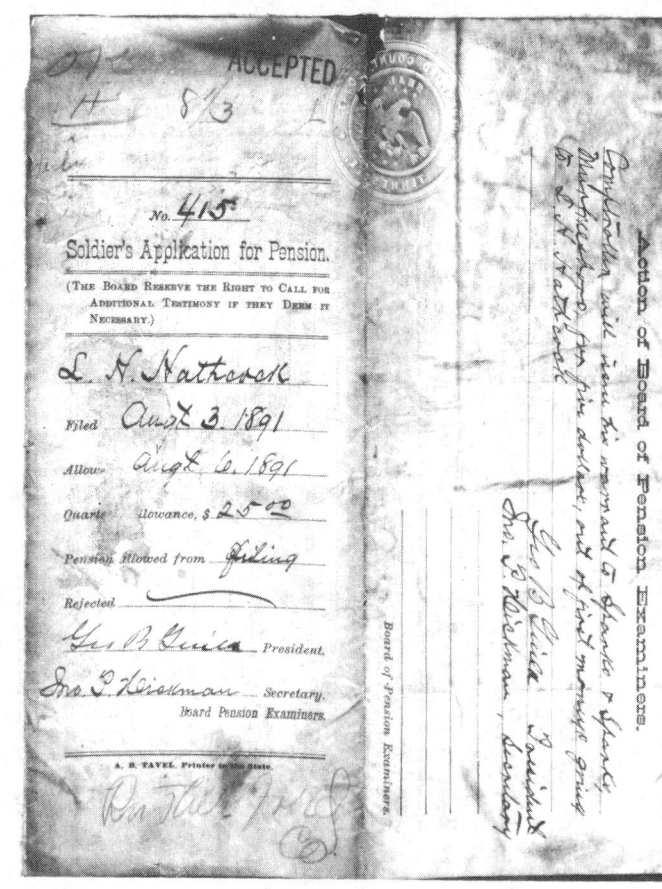

No. 415.

Soldier's Application for Pension.

(THE BOARD RESERVE THE RIGHT TO CALL FOR ADDITIONAL TESTIMONY IF THEY DEEM IT NECESSARY.)

L. H. Nattcock

Filed Aug. 3. 1891.

Allowed Aug. 6. 1891.

Quarterly Allowance, $25.00

Pension allowed from Filing

Rejected

Geo. B. Guild President.

Jno. P. Hickman Secretary.

Board Pension Examiners.

A. B. TAVEL, Printer to the State.

Figure 9-8 (continued)

If so, what is the size of your family?

Ans _____

What are the respective ages of your wife and children?

Ans _____

To what sex do your children belong?

Ans _____

In what business are you now engaged, if any; and what do you earn?

Ans _____

What estate have you in your own right, real and personal, and what is its value?

Ans _____

What estate has your wife in her own right, real and personal, and what is its value?

Ans _____

How have you derived support for yourself and family for the last five years?

Ans _____

Do you use intoxicants to any extent?

Ans _____

How long have you been an actual resident of the State of Tennessee?

Ans _____

Have you an attorney to look after this application?

Ans _____

If so, give his name and address.

Ans _____

Witness my hand, this _____ day of _____ 1891.

WITNESSES:

_____
_____
_____ Witness.
_____ Witness.

State of Tennessee, } Personally appeared before me _____
_____ County. }

Clerk of the County Court of said county, the above named _____ the applicant, with whom I am personally acquainted, and having the application read and fully explained to him, as well as the statements and answers therein made, made oath that the said statements and answers are true.

Witness my hand at office this _____ day of _____ 1891.

_____ Clerk.

State of Tennessee, } Personally appeared before me _____
_____ County. }

Clerk of the County Court of said county, the above named _____ subscribing witnesses to the foregoing application, and who is a physician of good standing, and being duly sworn, says that he has carefully and thoroughly examined _____ the applicant, and finds him laboring under the following disabilities:

_____

Witness my hand at office, this _____ day of _____ 1891.

_____ Clerk.

(If possible the two witnesses as to Character should have served with the Applicant in the Army, and if so let them, or either, state it in their oath.)

State of Tennessee, } Personally appeared before me _____
_____ County. }

Clerk of the County Court of said county, the above named _____ and _____ two of the subscribing witnesses to the foregoing application, with whom I am personally acquainted, and known to me to be citizens of veracity and standing in this community, and who make oath that they are personally acquainted with the foregoing applicant, and that the facts set forth and statements made in his application are correct and true, to the best of their knowledge and belief, and that they have no interest in this claim, and that said applicant's habits are good and free from dishonor. And _____ they further make oath to the following facts touching the applicant's service in the _____ army.

_____

Witness my hand, at office, this _____ day of _____ 1891.

_____ Clerk.

Figure 9-8 (continued)

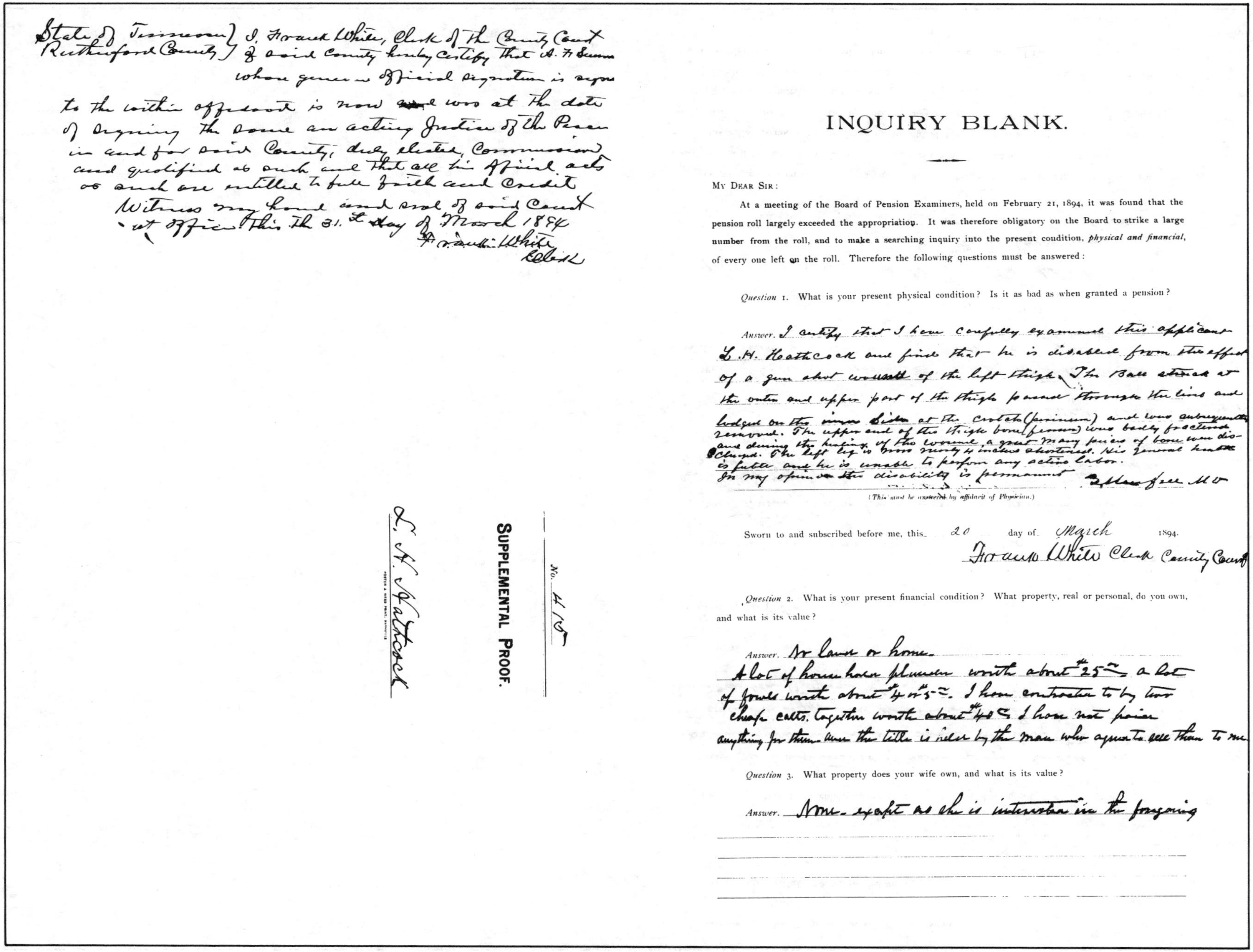

INQUIRY BLANK.

MY DEAR SIR:

At a meeting of the Board of Pension Examiners, held on February 21, 1894, it was found that the pension roll largely exceeded the appropriation. It was therefore obligatory on the Board to strike a large number from the roll, and to make a searching inquiry into the present condition, *physical and financial*, of every one left on the roll. Therefore the following questions must be answered:

Question 1. What is your present physical condition? Is it as bad as when granted a pension?

Answer. I certify that I have carefully examined this applicant L. H. Hathcock and find that he is disabled from the effect of a gun shot wound of the left thigh. The Ball struck at the outer and upper part of the thigh passed through the limb and lodged on the inner side at the crotch (perineum) and was subsequently removed. The upper end of the thigh bone (femur) was badly fractured and during the healing of the wound a great many pieces of bone were discharged. The left leg is now nearly 4 inches shortened. His general health is feeble and he is unable to perform any active labor. In my opinion the disability is permanent. [illegible] M.D.

(*This must be answered by affidavit of Physician.*)

Sworn to and subscribed before me, this 20 day of March 1894.

Frank White Clerk County Court

Question 2. What is your present financial condition? What property, real or personal, do you own, and what is its value?

Answer. No land or home.
A lot of household furniture worth about $25.00 a lot of fowls worth about $4 or $5.00. I have contracted to buy two cheap colts, together worth about $40.00 I have not paid anything for them since the title is held by the man who agreed to sell them to me

Question 3. What property does your wife own, and what is its value?

Answer. None except as she is interested in the foregoing

State of Tennessee } I, Frank White, Clerk of the County Court
Rutherford County } of said County hereby certify that A. H. Sum[illegible] whose genuine official signature is [illegible] to the within affidavit is now and was at the date of signing the same an acting Justice of the Peace in and for said County, duly elected, Commissioned and qualified as such and that all his official acts as such are entitled to full faith and Credit.
Witness my hand and seal of said Court at office this the 31st day of March 1894
Frank White
Clerk

No. 415

SUPPLEMENTAL PROOF.

L. H. Hathcock

FOSTER & WEBB PRINT, NASHVILLE

Figure 9-8 (continued)

Question 4. What is the present size of your family?

Answer. The home [whan] family

Question 5. How many children have you, and what are their ages and sex?

Answer. 2 daughters 18 & 19 years of age. the latter has been married, her husband is dead. she has two children both boys. One is 1½ years old, and the other is 3 years old. Born Dec. 18th years of age.

Question 6. Are not some of your children able to support you?

Answer. No.

Question 7. What is your present occupation, and how much do you earn thereby?

Answer. Trying to make a living by working the laws of other persons. [Natural] to mark Mr. Rington

Sworn to and subscribed before me, this 20 day of March 1894.

his
L.N. X Hadcock
mark

Squire White Clew County Court

We D. R. Summers and Jonathan Oneal and
x D. R. Summers
x Jonathan, O'Neal
know the above answers to be literally true.

Sworn to and subscribed before me, this 21st day of March 1894.

H.F. Summers
Justice of the peace

THESE questions must be answered and returned to me by the next meeting of the Board (May 21, 1894), or it will be taken for granted that you are not now in condition to draw a pension.

This action is taken by the Board on account of the meager appropriation allowed for pensions by the Legislature. The Board, at the last meeting of the Legislature, asked for an increased appropriation, but the Legislature refused to grant its request.

It is also obligatory on the Board that these questions should be answered, from time to time, by all men remaining on the pension roll. This is a positive requirement of the law. (See Section 5.)

Very respectfully,

JNO. P. HICKMAN, *Secretary*.

Figure 9-8 (continued)

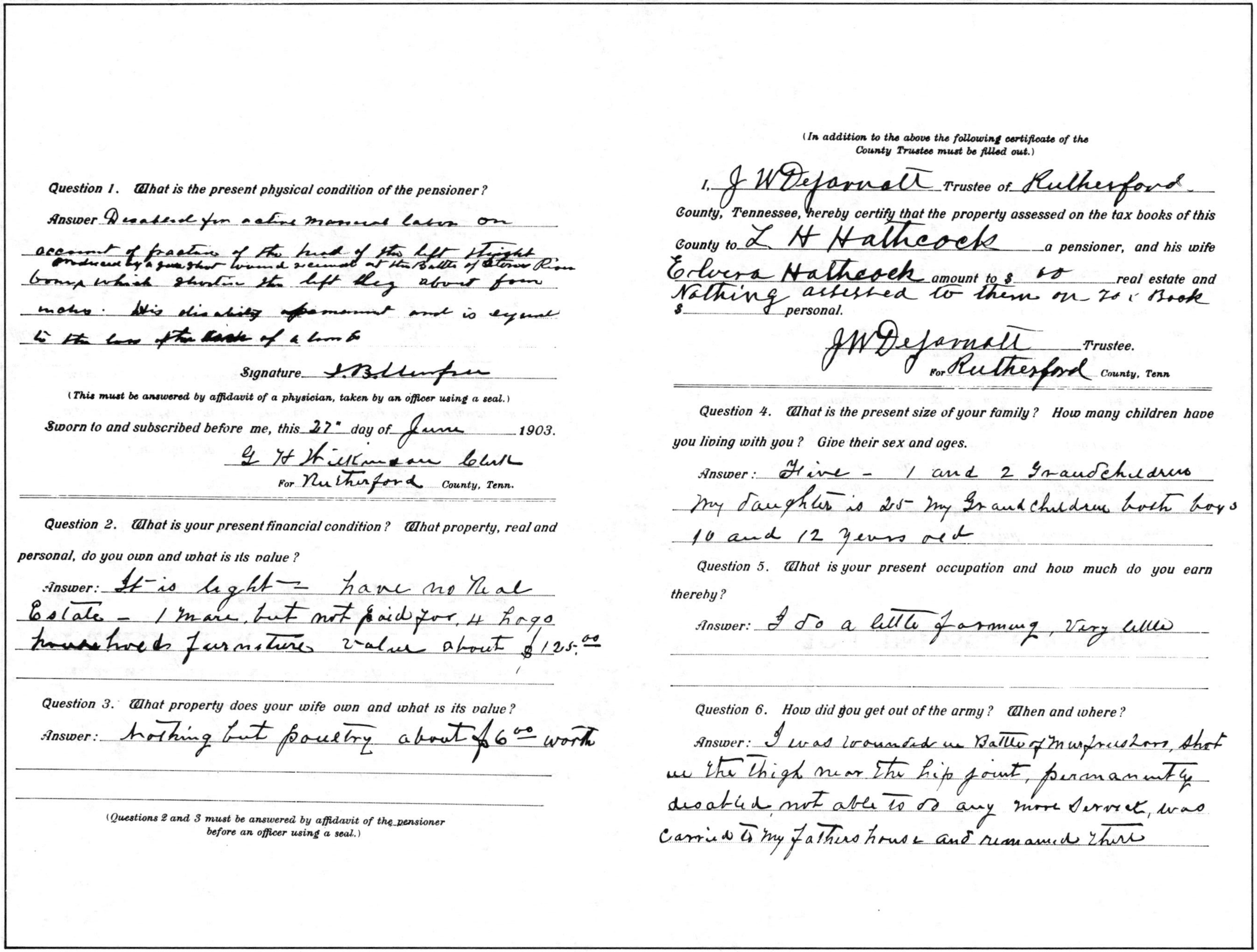

Question 1. What is the present physical condition of the pensioner?

Answer Disabled for active manual labor on account of fracture of the head of the left thigh bone produced by a gun shot wound received at the Battle of Stones River which shortens the left leg about four inches. His disability is permanent and is equal to the loss of the use of a limb

Signature J. B. Murfree

(This must be answered by affidavit of a physician, taken by an officer using a seal.)

Sworn to and subscribed before me, this 27" day of June 1903.

G H Wilkinson Clerk

For Rutherford County, Tenn.

Question 2. What is your present financial condition? What property, real and personal, do you own and what is its value?

Answer: It is light – have no Real Estate – 1 mare, but not paid for, 4 hogs household furniture value about $125.00

Question 3. What property does your wife own and what is its value?

Answer: nothing but poultry about $6.00 worth

(Questions 2 and 3 must be answered by affidavit of the pensioner before an officer using a seal.)

(In addition to the above the following certificate of the County Trustee must be filled out.)

I, J W Dejarnatt Trustee of Rutherford County, Tennessee, hereby certify that the property assessed on the tax books of this County to L. H. Hathcock a pensioner, and his wife Elvera Hathcock amount to $ 60 real estate and Nothing assessed to them on 70's Book $ personal.

J W Dejarnatt Trustee.

For Rutherford County, Tenn

Question 4. What is the present size of your family? How many children have you living with you? Give their sex and ages.

Answer: Five – 1 and 2 Grandchildren My daughter is 25 – My Grandchildren both boys 10 and 12 years old

Question 5. What is your present occupation and how much do you earn thereby?

Answer: I do a little farming, very little

Question 6. How did you get out of the army? When and where?

Answer: I was wounded in Battle of Murfreesboro, shot in the thigh near the hip joint, permanently disabled, not able to do any more service, was carried to my fathers house and remained there

Figure 9-8 (continued)

Question 7. Did you take the oath of allegiance to the U. S. Government? If so, when, where and under what circumstances?

Answer: I never did - I remained at my fathers house in a permanently crippled condition during the remainder of the war

(If the pensioner was discharged or paroled let him file the papers if he has them. If they have been lost or destroyed let him make proof by affidavit of some officer or comrade who knows the fact.)

STATE OF TENNESSEE, } ss.
__________ County.

Personally appeared before me, L. H. Hathcock a pensioner of the State of Tennessee, to me well known, who makes oath that the answers given to the questions asked him in the foregoing paper are true.

Witness
W. W. McLemore

(Signature of Pensioner) L H his x mark Hatchcock

Sworn to and subscribed before me this 24" day of June 1903.

[Seal]

G H Wilkinson Clerk
For Rutherford County, Tenn.

TO TENNESSEE PENSIONERS.

Nashville, Tenn., May _____ 1903.

The Pension Laws of the State as amended by the Legislature of 1903 require the Special Examiner to "fully investigate the pensioners now on the roll; and in case a doubt exists as to the worthiness of a pensioner, or where charges are preferred by reputable persons, to visit the said pensioner, and fully investigate his condition, both physical and financial, and make a written report of his investigation to said board."

In order that the requirements of the law may be carried out, you will at once answer the following questions under oath before an officer using a seal, and mail to the Special Examiner in the enclosed envelope.

TENNESSEE BOARD OF PENSION EXAMINERS.

By FRANK A. MOSES,
Special Examiner.

Figure 9-9. Biographical questionnaire of Civil War veteran Samuel S.M. Blankenship, Lafayette County, Tennessee, 1821. Tennessee Historical Commission. FHL 975,591.

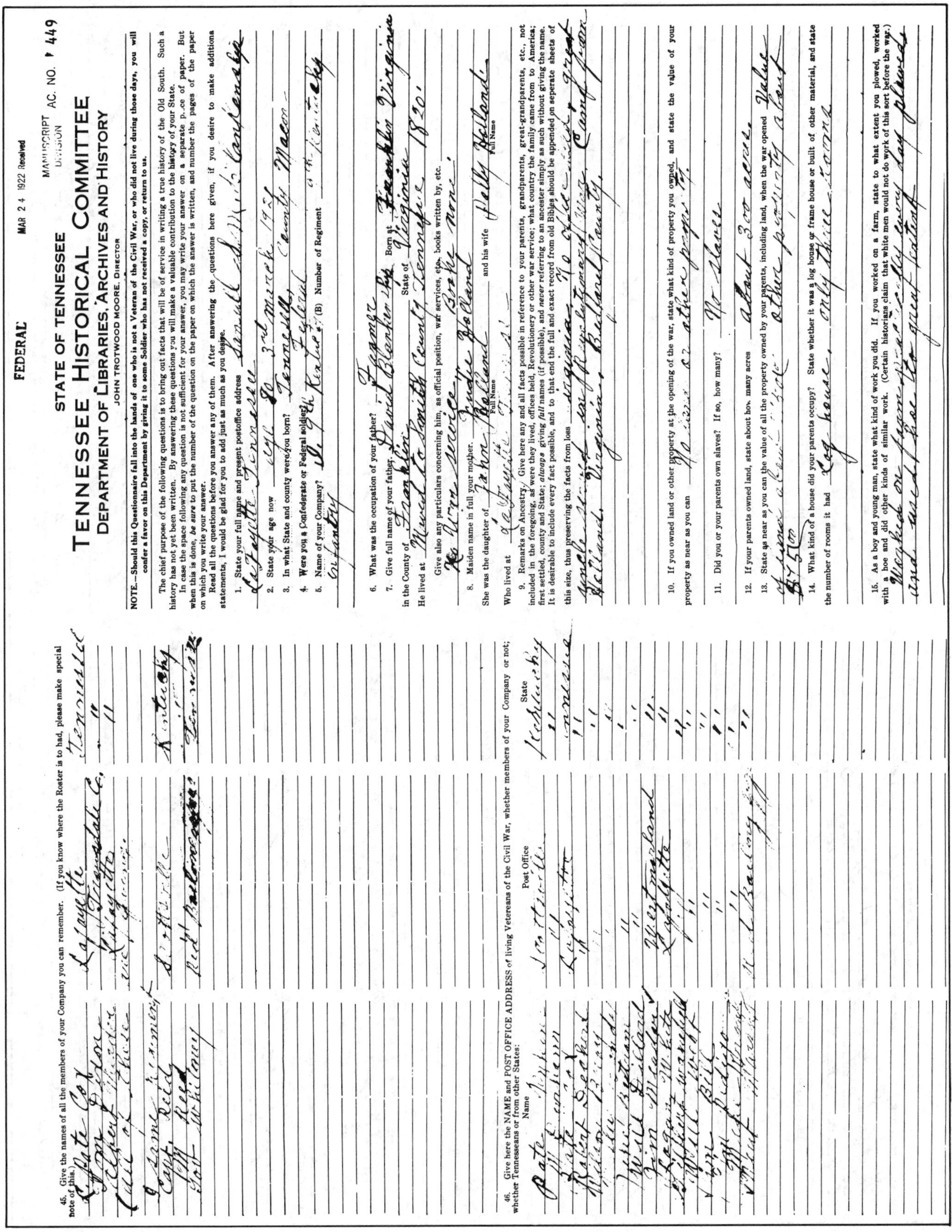

Figure 9-9 (continued)

16. State clearly what kind of work your father did, and what the duties of your mother were. State all the kinds of work done in the house as well as you can remember—that is, cooking, spinning, weaving, etc. Father worked on farm all of life. Mother did work house chores, wove and spun all the cloth to make clothing for the children, husband, and herself.

17. Did your parents keep any servants? If so, how many? None

18. How was honest toil—as plowing, hauling and other sorts of honest work of this class—regarded in your community? Was such work considered respectable and honorable? Among most classes it was considered respectable and honorable for anyone to do.

19. Did the white men in your community generally engage in such work? yes

20. To what extent were there white men in your community leading lives of idleness and having others do their work for them? practically all did their own work. very few had slaves

21. Did the men who owned slaves mingle freely with those who did not own slaves, or did slaveholders in any way show by their actions that they felt themselves better than respectable, honorable men who did not own slaves? Cant remember

22. At the churches, at the schools, at public gatherings in general, did slave-holders and non-slave-holders mingle on a footing of equality? Cant remember

23. Was there a friendly feeling between slave-holders and non-slave-holders in your community, or were they antagonistic to each other? So far as can remember they were all right to each

24. In a political contest in which one candidate owned slaves and the other did not, did the fact that one candidate owned slaves help him any in winning the contest? Cant Remember

25. Were the opportunities good in your community for a poor young man, honest and industrious, to save up enough to buy a small farm or go in business for himself? opportunities were poor unless one had a good capital of which he had helped

26. Were poor, honest, industrious young men, who were ambitious to make something of themselves, encouraged or discouraged by slaveholders? Those that depended on daily labor for their support were discouraged because of less work to do and also for smaller wages

27. What kind of school or schools did you attend? Country school

28. About how long did you go to school altogether? Lasted about three months each year, in all about 30 months

29. How far was it to the nearest school? about one mile. Roads leading to the school was rough.

30. What school or schools were in operation in your neighborhood? Only one school could have handily been reached while boarding at home.

31. Was the school in your community private or public? Most public

32. About how many months in the year did it run? about three months

33. Did the boys and girls in your community attend school pretty regularly? yes

eacher of the school you attended a man or a woman? all men teacher

5. In what year and month and at what place did you enlist in the service of the Confederacy or of the Federal Government? December 4, 1861 at Columbia Kentucky

36. After enlistment, where was your Company sent first? Glasgow Kentucky and and shortly to Nashville

37. How long after enlistment before your Company engaged in battle? 4 months

38. What was the first battle you engaged in? Battle of Shiloh engaged in this battle only one day.

39. State in your own way your experience in the War from this time on to its close. State where you went after the first battle—what you did, what other battles you engaged in, how long they lasted, what the results were; state how you lived in camp, how you were clothed, how you slept, what you had to eat, how you were exposed to cold, hunger and disease. If you were in hospital or in prison, state your experience here. Had experience which proved to be beneficial after leaving army. After battle went to Corinth Mississippi. Made preparation for battle but enemy left before any battle. Murfreesboro & [illegible] about two days, results good. Well taken care of in hospital

40. When and where were you discharged? Huntsville Alabama January 8 1865

41. Tell something of your trip home. From Huntsville we came to Nashville to Bowling Green Kentucky thence to Scottsville Kentucky and then home

42. What kind of work did you take up when you came back home? Working on farm with father.

43. Give a sketch of your life since the close of Civil War, stating what kind of business you have engaged in, where you have lived, your church relations, etc. If you have held any office or offices, state what it was. You may state here any other facts connected with your life and experience which has not been brought out by the questions. Working in farm as long as physical ability allowed me. Lived in Macon county Tennessee since I came from army. Was married to Katherine Jane White March 8 1865. 7 children were born six boys and one girl, all of whom are living except one. Four of them have taught school in Macon County. One after made a Medical doctor and also he served in the Spanish American War 1898 and in the Worlds war as first Lieutenant but did not go overseas. Another Jr M. Blankenship studied law and afterwards went to Los Angeles California. Other four are farmers. Belong to Missionary Baptist Church

44. On a separate sheet give the names of some of the great men you have known or met in your time, and tell some of the circumstances of the meeting or incidents in their lives. Also add any further personal reminiscences. (Use all the space you want).

John Borun, and by the oath of Matthias Gayle it was proved that Thomas Brown, William, Francis, Ralph, Ann, Mary and Judith Brown are the children of William Brown a Midshipman in the Rev. war. That all the children died intestate except Judith Brown and Mary (who married Robert Weston) that the said Mary and Robert Weston are both dead and that they left one child only, named, Judith Weston; that Judith Brown and Judith Weston are the only surviving heirs of Midshipman William Brown. Copy teste, Shepard G. Miller, Clerk of court.

Note. Written at the bottom of this paper is a memorandom (sic) of names: —1. Th. Brown, 2. Wm. B., 3. Ralph B. 4. Frs Brown. Whether or not these are relatives I know not.

Abstract of the will of William Brown of Gloucester Co. Parish of Kingston. "To my loving wife, Judith Brown: all my children: —Thomas, William, Francis, Ralph, Ann, Mary and Judith". Signed, 20th Oct., 1791. Witnesses. Simon Laughlin, Ann Laughlin, Dorothy Buckner.

Matthews Co., 10th Dec. 1792 the will was proven. Test, John Cary, Clerk. Copy teste, Shepard G. Miller.

Warrant 8228 for 2666-2/3 acres issued 19 Aug. 1835 to Judith Brown and Judith Weston, heirs of William Brown. Recorded, Book 3, page 9 5. Va. L. Off.

The Roster and Record of Iowa Soldiers in the War of the Rebellion shows still another approach:

Company "A"

Babcock, Charles W. (Veteran) Age 22. Residence Clayton County, nativity New York. Re-enlisted Jan. 4, 1864. Re-mustered Feb. 2, 1864 Mustered out July 6, 1865, Louisville, Ky. Transferred from company A, Third Battalion.

Baker, James H. (Veteran) Age 28. Residence Cedar Falls, nativity Pennsylvania. Re-enlisted Dec. 17, 1863. Re-mustered Dec 23, 1863 Discharged July 1, 1865, Louisville, Ky. Transferred from company A, Third Battalion.

Barrett, George W. (Veteran) Age 19. Residence Boone County, nativity New York. Re-enlisted Jan. 4, 1864. Re-mustered Feb. 2, 1864. Mustered out July 12, 1965, Louisville, Ky. Transferred from company A, Third Battalion.

Billick, Joseph. (Veteran) Age 22. Residence Columbus City, nativity Pennsylvania. Re-enlisted Jan. 4, 1864. Re-mustered Feb. 2, 1864 Mustered out July 12, 1865. Transferred from company A, Third Battalion.

STATE MILITARY RECORDS AND PRIVATE COLLECTIONS

Military records, which may be referred to as militia records, were also created and preserved by state and local jurisdictions. Their contents are much like those described above. These militia records, however, are often the first to be disposed of because local militias no longer exist. They will be found scattered through state archives, historical societies and museums, military forts (both those still active and museums for those discontinued), and among the papers in the county clerk's office. These records may sometimes be located using state and local record inventories.

Private collections of military records also exist, often housed in a records repository some distance from the location where they were created or refer to. Check the *National Union Catalog of Manuscripts Collections of the Library of Congress (NUCMC)* (see chapter 2, Databases, Indexes, and Other Finding Aids) and The National Historic Trust for Records Preservation, available in most research libraries of any size, to discover their locations.

WOMEN IN THE MILITARY

American Women and the U.S. Armed Forces: A Guide to the Records of Military Agencies in the National Archives Relating to American Women identifies records of interest to those tracing females. The introduction describes their involvement:

During the 18th and 19th centuries women had relatively little contact with military agencies. Women sought and received pensions based upon the service of male relatives. They served the Armed Forces as cooks, hospital matrons, and laundresses. A few were contract nurses and physicians, but until the Spanish-American War, most military nurses were men. Seamstresses worked for the Quartermaster making uniforms and women worked in arsenals. Welfare agencies were staffed with women both as employees and volunteers. They sometimes wrote to high-ranking government and military officials to inquire about relatives or friends in one of the services. In rare cases women ventured into the intelligence area as informants or disguised themselves as men and served as soldiers.[3]

Women also contributed much to the war efforts in a variety of roles in the twentieth century. Both mainstream and obscure records found in the National Archives are well described in the above-cited work.

SPECIAL PROJECTS

The first entry in the Civil War Soldiers System Database was made on 28 April 1993. This joint project of the National Archives, the National Park Service, the Federation of Genealogical Societies, and the Genealogical Society of Utah is utilizing the efforts of thousands of volunteers through the country. The Civil War Soldiers System will be a database of every soldier who fought in the Civil War. Each entry will identify whether the soldier was Union or Confederate, his regiment, and his rank. It will provide the location of every identified civil war soldier buried in the cemeteries operated by the National Park Service. The database will also provide information about the 7,000 regiments and units formed during the war and on many of the 10,500 battles and skirmishes. Watch the pages of *Everton's Genealogical Helper,* the FGS [Federation of Genealogical Societies] *Forum,* and the *NGS Newsletter* of the National Genealogical Society for announcements of this and other special projects.

NOTES

1. Book 75, 1782, Old Loan Records, NARA M1015, roll 4.

2. *The Office,* December 1973, p. 30, as quoted in the *Utah Genealogical Association Newsletter,* October 1974, p. 6.

3. *American Women and the U.S. Armed Forces: A Guide to the Records of Military Agencies of the National Archives Relating to American Women* (Washington, D.C.: National Archives and Records Administration, 1992), ix.

BIBLIOGRAPHY

Compiled by Lloyd DeWitt Bockstruck

SOURCES COVERING VARIOUS STATES AND TIME PERIODS

Callahan, Edward W. *List of Officers of the Navy of the United States and of the Marine Corps from 1775 to 1900. . . .* Gaithersburg, Md.: Olde Soldier Books, 1988.

Carroll, John M., and Byron Price. *Roll Call on the Little Big Horn, 28 June 1876.* Ft. Collins, Colo.: The Old Army Press, 1974.

Cullum, Bvt. Major-General George W. *Biographical Register, Officers and Graduates of the U.S. Military Academy, West Point, New York,* 3rd ed., 9 vols. Boston: Houghton-Mifflin, 1891.

Deputy, Marilyn, and Pat Barben. *Register of Federal United States Military Records, a Guide to Manuscript Sources at the Genealogical Library Salt Lake City and the National Archives in Washington, D.C.* 3 vols. Bowie, Md.: Heritage Books, 1986.

Guide to Genealogical Research in the National Archives. Washington, D.C.: National Archives Trust Fund Board, 1982.

Heitman, Francis B. *Historical Register and Dictionary of the United States Army, From Its Organization September 29, 1789, to March 2, 1903.* 2 vols. 1965. Reprint. Baltimore: Genealogical Publishing Co., 1994.

Horowitz, Lois. *A Bibliography of Military Name Lists From Pre-1675 to 1900: A Guide to Genealogical Sources.* Metuchen, N.J.: The Scarecrow Press, 1990.

Kirkham, E. Kay. *Some of the Military Records of America (Before 1900): Their Use and Values in Genealogical and Historical Research.* Salt Lake City: Deseret Book Co., 1964.

List of Pensioners on the Roll January 1, 1883 Giving the Name of Each Pensioner, the Cause for Which Pensioned, the Post Office Address, the Rate of Pension per Month, and the Date of Original Allowance as Called for by Senate Resolution of December 8, 1882. 5 vols. Baltimore: Genealogical Publishing Co., 1970.

Martis, Kenneth C. *The Historical Atlas of United States Congressional Districts 1789–1983.* New York: Free Press, 1982.

Military Service Records: A Select Catalog of National Archives Microfilm Publications. Washington, D.C.: National Archives Trust, 1985.

Neagles, James C. *U.S. Military Records: A Guide to Federal and State Sources, Colonial America to the Present.* Salt Lake City: Ancestry, 1994.

Powell, William H. *List of Officers of the Army of the United States From 1779 to 1900 Embracing a Register of All Appointments by the President of the United States in the Volunteer Service During the Civil War and of Volunteer Officers in the Service of the United States June 1, 1900.* Detroit: Gale Research Co., 1967.

Tozeski, Stanley P. *Preliminary Inventory of the Records of the U.S. Military Academy.* Washington, D.C.: National Archives and Records Service, 1976.

U.S. Veterans Administration. *Abstracts of Service Records of Naval Officers ("Records of Officers") 1798–1893.* M330, 19 rolls. Washington, D.C.: National Archives Microfilm Publications.

_____. *List of Navy Veterans for Whom There Are Navy Widows' and Other Dependents' Disapproved Pension Files ("Navy Widows' originals"), 1861–1910.* M1391, 15 microfiche. National Archives Microfiche Publications, 1985.

_____. *Registers of Enlistments in the United States Army, 1789–1914.* M233, 80 rolls. Washington, D.C.: National Archives Microfilm Publications, 1963.

White, Virgil D. *Index to Old Wars Pension Files 1815–1926.* 2 vols. Waynesboro, Tenn.: National Historical Publishing Co., 1987.

SOURCES, BY STATE, THAT COVER VARIOUS TIME PERIODS

Arizona

Akey, Elizabeth J. *Military Burials in Arizona.* Tucson, Ariz.: Arizona Genealogical Society, 1987.

Arkansas

Payne, Dorothy E. *Arkansas Pensioners 1818–1900, Records of Some Arkansas Residents Who Applied to the Federal Government for Benefits Arising From Service in Federal Military Organizations (Revolutionary War, War of 1812, Indian and Mexican Wars).* Easley, S.C.: Southern Historical Press, 1985.

Georgia

_____. *Georgia Pensioners (American Revolution, War of 1812, Mexican War).* 2 vols. McLean, Va.: Sunbelt Publishing Co., 1985–86.

North Carolina

Kearney, Timothy. *Abstracts of Letters of Resignations of Militia Officers in North Carolina 1779–1840.* Raleigh, N.C.: Waleworth Pub., n.d.

COLONIAL WARS, 1607–1774

Various States

Baker, Mary Ellen. *Bibliography of Lists of New England Soldiers.* Boston, Mass.: New England Historic Genealogical Society, 1977.

Bodge, George Madison. *Soldiers in King Philip's War. . . .* 3rd ed. Baltimore: Genealogical Publishing Co., 1976.

Clark, Murtie June. *Colonial Soldiers of the South 1732–1774.* Baltimore: Genealogical Publishing Co., 1983.

Coleman, Emma Lewis. *New England Captives Carried to Canada Between 1677 and 1760 During the French and Indian Wars.* 2 vols. Bowie, Md.: Heritage Books, 1989.

Connecticut

Andrews, Frank DeWette. *Connecticut Soldiers in the French and Indian War.* Vineland, N.J.: the compiler, 1923.

Buckingham, Thomas. *Roll and Journal of Connecticut Men in Queen Anne's War.* New Haven, Conn.: Acorn Club of Connecticut, 1916.

Jacobus, Donald Lines. *List of Officials Civil, Military, and Ecclesiastical of Connecticut Colony From March 1635 Through 11 October 1677 and of New Haven Colony Throughout Its Separate Existence Also Soldiers in the Pequot War Who Then or Subsequently Resided Within the Present Bounds of Connecticut.* Baltimore: Clearfield Co., 1989.

Rolls of Connecticut Men in the French and Indian Wars, 1755–1762. 2 vols. Hartford, Conn.: Connecticut Historical Society, 1903–05.

Shepard, James. *Connecticut Soldiers in the Pequot War of 1637, With Proof of Service, a Brief Record for Identification and References to Various Publications in Which Further Data May Be Found.* Meriden, Conn: Journal Publishing Co., 1913.

Delaware

Delaware Archives Military, vol. 1. Wilmington, Del.: Mercantile Printing Co., 1911.

Massachusetts

Donahue, Mary E. *Massachusetts Officers and Soldiers, 1702–1722: Queen Anne's War to Dummer's War.* Boston: New England Historic Genealogical Society, 1980.

Doreski, Carole. *Massachusetts Officers and Soldiers in the Seventeenth Century Conflicts.* Boston: New England Historic Genealogical Society, 1982.

Goss, K. Davis, and David Zarowin. *Massachusetts Officers and Soldiers in the French and Indian Wars 1755–1756.* Boston: New England Historic Genealogical Society, 1985.

MacKay, Robert E. *Massachusetts Soldiers in the French and Indian Wars 1744–1755.* Boston: New England Historic Genealogical Society, 1978.

Peirce, Ebenezer W. *Peirce's Colonial Lists, Civil, Military and Professional Lists of Plymouth and Rhode Island Colonies . . . 1621–1700.* Baltimore: Genealogical Publishing Co., 1968.

Roberts, Oliver A. *History of the Military Company of Massachusetts Now Called the Ancient and Honorable Artillery Company of Massachusetts 1637–1888.* 4 vols. Boston: Alfred Mudge & Son, 1895–1901.

Stachiw, Myron O, *Massachusetts Officers and Soldiers 1723–1743: Dummer's War to the War of Jenkins' Ear.* Boston: New England Historic Genealogical Society, 1979.

Voye, Nancy S. *Massachusetts Officers in the French and Indian Wars, 1748–1763.* Boston: New England Historic Genealogical Society, 1975.

Watkins, William K. *Soldiers in the Expedition to Canada in 1690 and Grantees of the Canada Townships.* Boston: the author, 1898.

New Hampshire

Hammond, Isaac W. *Rolls of the Soldiers in the Revolutionary War, 1775, to May, 1777. . . .* Vol. 14 of Provincial and State Papers of New Hampshire. Concord, N.H.: Parsons B. Cogswell, 1885. The rolls of various Indian and French wars not published in Adjutant General's report in 1866 appear on pp. 1–30.

Potter, Chandler E. *The Military History of the State of New Hampshire 1623–1861.* Part I. Baltimore: Genealogical Publishing Co., 1972.

Roll of New Hampshire Men at Louisburg, Cape Breton, 1745. Concord: Edward N. Pearson, 1896.

New York

Meyers, Carol. *Early Military Records of New York 1689–1738.* Sangus, Calif.: RAM Publishers, 1967.

Muster Rolls of New York Provincial Troops 1755–1764. Bowie, Md.: Heritage Books, 1990.

Second Annual Report of the State Historian of New York. Appendix H, "Muster Rolls of a Century from 1664 to 1760," 371–1029. Albany, N.Y.: Wynkoop Hallenbeck Crawford Co., 1897.

Third Annual Report of the State Historian of New York. Appendix M, "Colonial Muster Rolls," 437–1158. Albany, N.Y.: Wynkoop Hallenbeck Crawford Co., 1898.

Pennsylvania

Bradshaw, Audrey E. *Pennsylvania Soldiers in the Provincial Service 1746–1759.* The author, 1985.

Officers and Soldiers in the Service of the Province of Pennsylvania, 1744–1764. Pennsylvania Archives, 2nd Series, vol. 2, 417–528. Harrisburg, Pa.: Harrisburg Publishing Co., 1906.

Officers and Soldiers in the Service of the Province of Pennsylvania, 1744–1765. Pennsylvania Archives, 5th Series, vol. 1, 1–368. Harrisburg, Pa.: Harrisburg Publishing Co., 1906.

Rhode Island

Chapin, Howard Miller. *Rhode Island in the Colonial Wars. A List of Rhode Island Soldiers and Sailors in King George's War, 1740–1748.* Providence: Rhode Island Historical Society, 1920.

_____. *A List of Rhode Island Soldiers & Sailors in the old French & Indian War, 1755–1762.* Providence: Rhode Island Historical Society, 1918.

_____. *Rhode Island Privateers in King George's War, 1739–1748.* Providence: Rhode Island Historical Society, 1926.

Collins, Clarkson A. *A Muster Rolls of Newport County Troops Sent Toward Albany in 1757.* Providence: Roger Williams Press, 1961.

Niles, Samuel. *Rhode Island's Victory at Louisburg in 1745.* East Greenwich, R.I.: Society of Colonial Wars in the State of Rhode Island and Providence Plantations, 1986.

South Carolina

Draine, Tony, and John Skinner. *South Carolina Soldiers and Indian Traders, 1725–1730.* Columbia, S.C.: Congaree Publications, 1986.

Andrea, Leonardo. *South Carolina Colonial Soldiers and Patriots.* Columbia, S.C.: R.L. Bryan Co., 1952.

Warren, Mary Bondurant. *South Carolina Newspapers: The South Carolina Gazette, 1760.* Danielsville, Ga.: Heritage Papers, 1988. Rosters of French and Indian War veterans appear on pp. 75–92.

Virginia

Bockstruck, Lloyd DeWitt. *Virginia's Colonial Soldiers.* Baltimore: Genealogical Publishing Co., 1988.

Crozier, William A. *Virginia Colonial Militia, 1651–1776.* Baltimore: Genealogical Publishing Co., 1973.

Eckenrode, Hamilton J. *List of the Colonial Soldiers of Virginia.* Baltimore: Genealogical Publishing Co., 1980.

Lewis, Virgil A. *History of the Battle of Point Pleasant Fought Between White Men and Indians at the Mouth of the Great Kanawha River (Now Point Pleasant, West Virginia) Monday, October 10th, 1774, The Chief Event of Lord Dunmore's War.* Harrisonburg, Va.: C.J. Carrier Co., 1974.

_____. *The Soldiery of West Virginia in the French and Indian War; Lord Dunmore's War; the Revolution; the Later Indian Wars; the Whiskey Insurrection; the Second War With England; the War With Mexico. And Addenda Relating to West Virginians in the Civil War. The Whole Compiled From Authentic Sources.* Baltimore: Genealogical Publishing Co., 1972.

Poffenbarger, Livia Simpson. *Battle of Point Pleasant, First Battle of the American Revolution, October 10, 1774.* 4th ed. Pt. Pleasant, W. Va.: Mattox Printing Service, 1976.

Taylor, Philip F. *A Calendar of the Warrants for Land in Kentucky Granted for Service in the French and Indian War.* Baltimore: Genealogical Publishing Co., 1975.

Thwaites, Reuben Gold, and Louis Phelps Kellogg. *Documentary History of Dunmore's War 1774. . . .* Harrisonburg, W. Va.: C.J. Carrier Co., 1974.

REVOLUTIONARY WAR

Various States

Benson, Adolph B. *Sweden and the American Revolution.* Baltimore: Clearfield Co., 1926.

Bockstruck, Lloyd DeWitt. *Revolutionary War Bounty Land Grants Awarded by State Governments* (Baltimore: Genealogical Publishing Co., 1996).

A Census of Pensioners for Revolutionary or Military Services; With Their Names, Ages, and Places of Residence, as Returned by the Marshals of the Several Judicial Districts Under the Act for Taking the Sixth Census. Washington, D.C.: 1841, 1956. Reprint. Baltimore: Genealogical Books in Print, 1996. *A General Index to a Census of Pensioners for Military Service, 1840,* by the Genealogical Society of the Church of Jesus Christ of Latter-day Saints. Baltimore: Genealogical Publishing Co., 1965.

Claghorn, Charles E. *Naval Officers of the American Revolution, a Concise Biographical Dictionary.* Metuchen, N.J.: Scarecrow Press, 1988.

Clark, Murtie June. *Index to U.S. Invalid Pension Records, 1801–1815.* Baltimore: Genealogical Publishing Co., 1991.

_____. *The Pension Lists of 1792–1795, With Other Revolutionary War Pension Records.* Baltimore: Genealogical Publishing Co., 1991. Reissued 1996.

_____. *The Pension Roll of 1835.* 4 vols. Genealogical Publishing Co., 1992.

Les Combattants Francais de la Guere Americaine 1778–1783. Baltimore: Genealogical Publishing Co., 1969.

Dandridge, Danske B. *American Prisoners of the Revolution.* Baltimore: Genealogical Publishing Co., 1967.

Duncan, Louis C. *Medical Men in the American Revolution, 1775–1783.* Carlisle Barracks, Pa.: Medical Field Service School, 1931.

Gephart, Ronald M. *Revolutionary America 1763–1789, a Bibliography.* 2 vols. Washington, D.C.: Library of Congress, 1984.

Godfrey, Carlos E. *The Commander-in-Chief's Guard: Revolutionary War.* Baltimore: Genealogical Publishing Co., 1972.

Greene, Robert Ewell. *Black Courage 1775–1783, Documentation of Black Participation in the American Revolution.* Washington, D.C.: National Society Daughters of the American Revolution, 1984.

Hatcher, Patricia Law. *Abstract of Graves of Revolutionary Patriots.* 4 vols. Dallas: Pioneer Heritage Press, 1987–88.

Heitman, Francis B. *Historical Register of Officers of the Continental Army During the War of the Revolution, April 1775 to December 1783.* Baltimore: Genealogical Publishing Co., 1967.

Is That Service Right? Washington, D.C.: National Society Daughters of the American Revolution, 1986.

Kaminkow, Marion J., and Jack Kaminkow. *Mariners of the American Revolution.* Baltimore: Magna Carta Book Co., 1967.

Letter From the Secretary of War, Communicating a Transcript of the Pension List of the United States. . . . [June 1, 1813]. Washington, D.C.: A and G Way, 1813.

Letter from the Secretary of War, Transmitting a Report of the Names, Ranks, and Line of Every Person Placed on the Pension List in Pursuance of the Act of the 18th March 1818, &c. Baltimore: Southern Book Co., 1959.

McLane, Curren R. *American Chaplains of the Revolution.* Louisville, Ky.: National Society Sons of the American Revolution, 1991.

National Genealogical Society. *Index of Revolutionary War Pension Applications in the National Archives.* Bicentennial edition, rev. and enl. Washington, D.C.: National Genealogical Society, 1976.

Neagles, James C. *Summer Soldiers: A Survey and Index of*

Revolutionary War Courts-Martial. Salt Lake City: Ancestry, 1986.

Newman, Debra L. *List of Black Servicemen Compiled From the War Department Collection of Revolutionary War Records.* Washington, D.C.: National Archives, 1974.

O'Brien, Michael J. *A Hidden Phase of American History, Ireland's Struggle for Liberty.* Baltimore: Genealogical Publishing Co., 1973.

Pension List of 1820. Baltimore: Genealogical Publishing Co., 1991.

Pensioners of Revolutionary War Struck off the Roll With an Added Index to States. Baltimore: Clearfield Co., 1989.

Peterson, Clarence S. *Known Military Dead During the American Revolutionary War 1775–1783.* Baltimore, 1959.

Pierce, John. *Pierce's Register, Register of the Certificates Issued By John Pierce, Esquire, Paymaster General and Commissioner of Army Accounts for the United States to Officers and Soldiers of the Continental Army Under Act of July 4, 1783.* Baltimore: Genealogical Publishing Co., 1969.

Rejected or Suspended Applications for Revolutionary War Pensions With an Added Index to States. Baltimore: Genealogical Publishing Co., 1969.

Saffell, William T.R. *Records of the Revolutionary War. . . .* 3rd ed. Baltimore: Genealogical Publishing Co., 1969.

Schweitzer, George K. *Revolutionary War Genealogy.* Knoxville, Tenn., 1982.

Smith, Clifford Neal. *Federal Land Series, A Calendar of Archival Material on the Land Patents Issued by the United States Government, With Subject, Tract and Name Indexes.* 4 vols. in 5. Chicago: American Library Association, 1972–86.

U.S. House of Representatives. *Digested Summary and Alphabetical Index of Private Claims Which Have Been Presented to the House of Representatives From the First to the 31st Congress, Exhibiting the Action of Congress on Each Claim.* 3 vols. Baltimore: Genealogical Publishing Co., 1970.

White, J. Todd, and Charles H. Lesser. *Fighters for Independence: A Guide to Sources for Biographical Information on Soldiers of the American Revolution.* Chicago: University of Chicago Press, 1977.

White, Virgil D. *Genealogical Abstracts of Revolutionary War Pension Files.* 4 vols. Waynesboro, Tenn.: National Historical Publishing Co., 1990–. A cumulative index completes the set.

Women Patriots of the American Revolution, a Biographical Dictionary. Metuchen, N.J.: Scarecrow Press, 1991.

Connecticut
Connecticut Revolutionary Pensioners. Baltimore: Genealogical Publishing Co., 1982.

List and Returns of Connecticut Men in the Revolution, 1775–1783. Hartford: Connecticut Historical Society, 1909.

Minority Military Service Connecticut 1775–1783. Washington, D.C.: National Society Daughters of the American Revolution, 1988.

Rolls and Lists of Connecticut Men in the Revolution, 1775–1783. Hartford: Connecticut Historical Society, 1901.

Delaware
Delaware Archives. Vols. 1–3. Wilmington, Del.: Mercantile Printing Co., 1911–19.

Gooch, Eleanor B. "Delaware Signers of the Oaths of Allegiance." *National Historical Magazine* 75 (September–December 1941), 76 (January 1942).

Whiteley, William G. *The Revolutionary Soldiers of Delaware.* Wilmington: Historical Society of Delaware, 1896.

Georgia
Davis, Robert S. *Georgia Citizens and Soldiers of the American Revolution.* Easley, S.C.: Southern Historical Press, 1979.

Hemperley, Marion. *Military Certificates of Georgia 1776–1780 on File in the Surveyor General Department.* Atlanta: State Printing Office, 1983.

Houston, Martha L. *600 Revolutionary Soldiers and Widows of Revolutionary Soldiers Living in Georgia in 1827–28.* Ann Arbor, Mich.: Edwards Brothers, 1946.

Knight, Lucian L. *Georgia's Roster of the Revolution.* Baltimore: Genealogical Publishing Co., 1967.

McCall, Ettie. *Roster of Revolutionary Soldiers in Georgia.* 3 vols. Baltimore: Genealogical Publishing Co., 1968.

O'Kelley, Nicole M., and Mary B. Warren. *Georgia Revolutionary Bounty Land Records, 1783–1785.* Athens: Heritage Press, 1992.

Indiana
English, William Hayden. *Conquest of the Country Northwest of the River Ohio, 1778–1782, and Life of Gen. George Rogers Clark Volumes I and II.* New York: Arno Press, 1971. The bounty-land recipients in Clark Co., Indiana, as well as muster and pay rolls, appear on pp. 1034–1122.

List of Non-commissioned Officers and Soldiers of the Virginia Line on Continental Establishment Whose Names Appear on the Army Register and Who Have Not Received Bounty Land. Indianapolis: Ye Olde Genealogy Shoppe, n.d.

Kentucky
Harding, Margery H. *George Rogers Clark and His Men: Military Records, 1778–1784.* Frankfort, Ky.: Kentucky Historical Society, 1981.

Seineke, Katherine W. *The George Rogers Clark Adventure in the Illinois and Selected Documents of the American Revolution at the Frontier Posts.* New Orleans: Polyanthos, 1981.

Quisenberry, Anderson C. *Revolutionary Soldiers in Kentucky: Containing a Roll of the Officers of Virginia Line Who Received Land Bounties; a Roll of the Revolutionary Pensioners in Kentucky; a List of the Illinois Regiment Who Served Under George Rogers Clark in the Northwest Campaign.* Baltimore: Genealogical Publishing Co., 1974.

Louisiana
DeVille, Winston. *Louisiana Soldiers in the American Revolution.* Ville Platte, La.: Smith Books, 1991.

Maine
Fisher, Carleton E. *Soldiers, Sailors, and Patriots of the Revo-*

lutionary War: Maine. Louisville, Ky.: National Society Sons of the American Revolution, 1982.

Flagg, Charles A. *An Alphabetical Index of Revolutionary Pensioners Living in Maine.* Baltimore: Genealogical Publishing Co., 1967.

Minority Military Service 1775–1783: Maine. Washington, D.C.: National Society Daughters of the American Revolution, 1990.

House, Charles J. *Names of Soldiers of the American Revolution Who Applied for State Bounty under Resolves of March 17, 1835; March 24, 1836; and March 20, 1836 as Appears of Record in the Land Office.* Baltimore: Genealogical Publishing Co., 1967.

Maine Old Cemetery Association. *Revolutionary War Soldiers Index.* 13 microfiche.

Maryland

Brumbaugh, Gaius M. *Maryland Records: Colonial, Revolutionary, County and Church From Original Sources.* 2 vols. Baltimore: Genealogical Publishing Co., 1985.

_____. *Revolutionary Records of Maryland.* Baltimore: Genealogical Publishing Co., 1967.

Calendar of Maryland State Papers: The Red Books; the Brown Books; the Executive Miscellanea. Annapolis, Md.: Hall of Records, 1950–55.

Carothers, Bettie S. *Maryland Oaths of Fidelity.* 2 vols. The author, n.d.

Clements, S. Eugene. *Maryland Militia in the Revolutionary War.* Silver Spring, Md.: Family Line Publications, 1987.

Meyer, Mary K. "Revolutionary War Soldiers Granted Pensions by the State of Maryland." *Bulletin of the Maryland Genealogical Society* 4 (November 1963), 7 (February 1966).

Muster Rolls and Other Records of Service of Maryland Troops in the American Revolution, 1775–1783. Archives of Maryland, vol. 18. Baltimore: Genealogical Publishing Co., 1972.

Newman, Harry W. *Maryland Revolutionary Records.* Washington, D.C.: the compiler, 1938.

Papenfuse, Edward C. *An Inventory of Maryland State Papers.* Vol. 1, *The Era of the American Revolution, 1775–1783.* Annapolis, Md.: Hall of Records Commission, 1977.

Scharf, John S. *History of Western Maryland.* Philadelphia: Louis H. Everts, 1882. Bounty-land recipients appear in vol. 1, pp. 146–61.

Stewart, Rieman. *A History of the Maryland Line in the Revolutionary War, 1775–1783.* Society of the Cincinnati of Maryland, 1969.

Massachusetts

Allen, Gardner Weld. *Massachusetts Privateers of the American Revolution.* Cambridge, Mass.: Harvard University Press, 1927.

Draper, Belle. *Honor Roll of Massachusetts Patriots Heretofore Unknown, Being a List of Men and Women Who Loaned Money to the Federal Government During the Years 1777–1779.* Boston: 1899.

Hambrick-Stowe, Charles E., and Donna D. Smerlas. *Massachusetts Militia Companies and Officers in the Lexington Alarm.* Boston: New England Historic Genealogical Society, 1976.

Massachusetts Soldiers and Sailors of the Revolutionary War. 16 vols. Boston: Wright & Potter Printing Co., 1896–1908. There is a seventeen-roll microfilm supplement: Massachusetts Archives Revolutionary War Index Appendix.

Minority Military Service: Massachusetts, 1775–1783. Washington, D.C.: National Society Daughters of the American Revolution, 1989.

New Hampshire

Batchellor, Albert Sullivan. *Miscellaneous Revolutionary Documents of New Hampshire.* Manchester, N.H.: John B. Clark, 1910.

Hammond, Isaac Weare. *Rolls of the Soldiers of the Revolutionary War.* 4 vols. Concord, N.H.: Parsons B. Cogswell, 1885–89.

Minority Military Service: New Hampshire, Vermont, 1775–1783. Washington, D.C.: National Society Daughters of the American Revolution, 1989.

New Jersey

Campbell, James W.S. *Roster Officers of the New Jersey Continental Line in the Revolutionary War Who Were Eligible to Membership in the Society of the Cincinnati.* Bowie, Md.: Heritage Books, 1987.

Stryker, William S. *Official Roster of the Officers and Men of New Jersey in the Revolutionary War.* Baltimore: Genealogical Publishing Co., 1967.

Index of Official Roster of the Officers and Men of New Jersey in the Revolutionary War. Newark, N.J.: Works Progress Administration, 1941.

New York

Balloting Book and Other Documents Relating to Military Bounty Lands in the State of New York. Ovid, N.Y.: W.E. Morrison, 1983.

Fernow, Berthold. *New York in the Revolution.* Cottonport, La.: Polyanthos, 1972.

Knight, Erastus C. *New York in the Revolution as Colony and State: Supplement.* Albany, N.Y.: Oliver A. Quayle, 1901.

Mather, Frederic G. *Refugees of 1776 From Long Island to Connecticut.* Albany, N.Y.: J.B. Lyon Co., 1913.

Muster and Pay Rolls of the War of the Revolution, 1775–83. Collections of the New York Historical Society, vols. 47 and 48. New York: the society, 1916.

Roberts, James A. *New York in the Revolution as Colony and State.* 2nd ed. Albany, N.Y.: Brandow Printing Co., 1898.

North Carolina

Bailey, James D. *Commanders at Kings Mountain.* Greenville, S.C.: A Press, 1980.

Draper, Lyman. *King's Mountain and Its Heroes, History of the Battle of Kings Mountain October 7th 1780, and the*

Events Which Led to It. Baltimore: Genealogical Publishing Co., 1978.

Haun, Weynette P. *North Carolina Revolutionary Army Accountants, Secretary of State Treasurer's and Comptroller's Papers.* 3 vols. to date. Durham, N.C.: the compiler, 1988–.

Roster of Soldiers From North Carolina in the American Revolution With an Appendix Containing a Collection of Miscellaneous Records. Baltimore: Genealogical Publishing Co., 1967.

White, Katherine. *The King's Mountain Men: The Story of the Battle With Sketches of the American Soldiers Who Took Part.* Baltimore: Genealogical Publishing Co., 1970.

Ohio

Jackson, Ronald Vern. *Ohio Military Land Warrants, 1789–1801.* North Salt Lake, Utah: Accelerated Indexing Systems International, 1988.

Smith, Clifford Neal. *Grants in the Virginia Military District of Ohio.* Vol. 4 of Federal Land Series. 1 vol. in 2. Chicago: American Library Association, 1982–86.

U.S. Veterans Administration. *U.S. Revolutionary War Bounty Land Warrants Used in the U.S. Military District of Ohio and of Related Papers (Acts of 1788, 1803, and 1806).* M829, 16 rolls. Washington, D.C.: National Archives Microfilm Publications.

Pennsylvania

Cope, Harry E. *List of Soldiers and Widows of Soldiers Granted Revolutionary War Pensions by the Commonwealth of Pennsylvania.* Greeneburg, Pa.: Daughters of the American Revolution, 1976.

Egle, William H. *Journals and Diaries of the War of the Revolution With List of Officers and Soldiers, 1775–1783.* Pennsylvania Archives, 2nd Series, vol. 15. Harrisburg, Pa.: Secretary of the Commonwealth, 1892.

_____. *Muster Rolls of the Navy and Line, Militia and Rangers, 1775–1783.* Pennsylvania Archives, 3rd Series, vol. 23. Harrisburg, Pa.: Secretary of the Commonwealth, 1898.

_____. *Pennsylvania in the War of the Revolution, Associated Battalions and Militia, 1775–1783.* Pennsylvania Archives, 2nd Series, vols. 13–14. Harrisburg, Pa.: Clarence M. Busch, 1890–92.

_____. *Pennsylvania Women in the American Revolution.* New Orleans, La.: Polyanthos, 1972.

_____. *Rolls of Soldiers of the Revolution Pennsylvania Line Found in the Department of the State, Washington, D.C.* Pennsylvania Archives, 2nd Series, vol. 15, 371–560. Harrisburg, Pa.: E.K. Meyers, 1890.

_____. *Soldiers of the Pennsylvania Line Entitled to Donation Lands.* Pennsylvania Archives, 3rd Series, vol. 3, 607–57. Harrisburg, Pa.: Harrisburg Publishing Co., 1896.

Linn, John B., and William Egle. *List of Officers and Men of the Pennsylvania Navy, 1775–1781.* Pennsylvania Archives, 2nd Series, vol. 1, 243–434. Harrisburg, Pa.: Clarence M. Busch, 1896.

_____. *List of "Soldiers of the Revolution Who Received Pay for Their Services," Taken from Manuscript Record, Having Neither Date nor Title, but Under "Rangers on the Frontiers, 1778–83."* Pennsylvania Archives, 5th Series, vol. 4, 597–777. Harrisburg, Pa.: Harrisburg Publishing Co., 1906.

_____. *List of Soldiers Who Served as Rangers on the Frontier, 1778–83.* Pennsylvania Archives, 3rd Series, vol. 23, 193–356. Harrisburg, Pa.: William Stanley Ray, 1898.

_____, and William H. Egle. *Pennsylvania in the War of the Revolution, Battalions and Line, 1775–1783.* Pennsylvania Archives, 2nd Series, vols. 10–11. Harrisburg, Pa.: Secretary of the Commonwealth, 1895–96.

Muster Rolls and Papers Relative to the Associators and Militia of the Counties. Pennsylvania Archives, 5th Series, vols. 5–8 and 6th Series, vols. 1–2. Harrisburg, Pa.: Harrisburg Publishing Co., 1906.

Montgomery, Thomas L. *Muster Rolls of the Pennsylvania Navy, 1776–79.* Pennsylvania Archives, 5th Series, vol. 1, 415–609. Harrisburg, Pa.: Harrisburg Publishing Co., 1906.

Pennsylvania Historical and Museum Commission. *Guide to the Microfilm of the Records of Pennsylvania Revolutionary Governments 1775–1790.* Harrisburg, Pa.: Pennsylvania Historical and Museum Commission, 1978.

Richards, Henry M.M. *The Pennsylvania-Germans in the Revolutionary War, 1775–1783.* Baltimore: Genealogical Publishing Co., 1978.

Soldiers Who Received Depreciation Pay as per Cancelled Certificates on File in the Division of Public Records Pennsylvania State Library. Pennsylvania Archives, 5th Series, vol. 4, 105–83. Harrisburg, Pa.: Harrisburg Publishing Co., 1906.

Trussell, John B.B. *The Pennsylvania Line: Regimental Organization and Operations, 1776–1783.* Harrisburg, Pa.: Pennsylvania Historical and Museum Commission, 1977.

Rhode Island

Cowell, Benjamin. *Spirit of '76 in Rhode Island With Cowell's "Spirit of '76": An Analytical and Explanatory Index by James N. Arnold.* Baltimore: Genealogical Publishing Co., 1973.

Minority Military Service: Rhode Island, 1775–1783. Washington, D.C.: National Society Daughters of the American Revolution, 1988.

Smith, Joseph J. *Civil and Military List of Rhode Island, 1647–1800.* Providence, R.I.: Preston and Rounds Co., 1901.

South Carolina

Draine, Tony, and Edd Bannister. *Guide to South Carolina Pensions and Annuities, 1783–1869.* Columbia, S.C.: Draban Publications, 1991.

_____, and John Skinner. *Revolutionary War Bounty Land Grants in South Carolina.* Columbia, S.C.: Congaree Publications, 1986.

Ervin, Sara. *South Carolinians in the Revolution.* Baltimore: Genealogical Publishing Co., 1965.

Gilmer, Georgia, and Elmer Parker. *American Revolution Roster of Fort Sullivan, 1776–1780.* Moultrie, S.C.: Fort Sullivan Chapter, Daughters of the American Revolution, 1980.

Moss, Bobby B. *The Patriots at the Cowpens.* Greenville, S.C.: A Press, 1985.

_____. *The Patriots at King's Mountain.* Blacksburg, S.C.: Scotia-Hibernia Press, 1990.

_____. *Roster of South Carolina Patriots in the American Revolution.* Baltimore: Genealogical Publishing Co., 1983.

Revill, Janie. *Copy of the Original Index Book Showing the Revolutionary Claims Filed in South Carolina Between August 20, 1783 and August 31, 1786.* Baltimore: Genealogical Publishing Co., 1969.

Salley, Alexander S. *Audited Accounts of Revolutionary Claims Against South Carolina.* 3 vols. Columbia, S.C.: The State Company, 1935–43.

_____. *South Carolina Provincial Troops Named in Papers of the First Council of Safety of the Revolutionary Party in South Carolina, June–November, 1775.* Baltimore: Genealogical Publishing Co., 1977.

Stub Entries to Indents Issued in Payment of Claims Against South Carolina, Growing out of the Revolution. 12 vols. Columbia, S.C.: The State Company, 1919–57.

Tennessee
Bates, Lucy W. *Roster of Soldiers and Patriots of the American Revolution Buried in Tennessee.* Rev. ed. Brentwood, Tenn.: Tennessee Society, Daughters of the American Revolution, 1979.

Vermont
Crocket, Walter H. *Soldiers of the Revolutionary War Buried in Vermont.* Baltimore: Genealogical Publishing Co., 1973.

Fisher, Carleton Edward, and Sue Gray Fisher. *Soldiers, Sailors, and Patriots of the Revolutionary War—Vermont.* Camden, Maine: Picton Press, 1992.

Goodrich, John E. *Rolls of the Soldiers in the Revolutionary War, 1775 to 1783.* Rutland, Vt.: Tuttle Co., 1904.

Virginia
Abercrombie, Janice L., and Richard Slatten. *Virginia Revolutionary Publick Claims.* 3 vols. Athens, Ga.: Iberian Publishing Co., 1992.

Brown, Margie G. *Genealogical Abstracts Revolutionary War Veterans, Script Act 1852.* Decorah, Iowa: Anundsen Publishing Co., 1990.

Brumbaugh, Gaius M. *Revolutionary War Records.* Baltimore: Genealogical Publishing Co., 1967.

Burgess, Louis A. *Virginia Soldiers of 1776.* 3 vols. Spartanburg, S.C.: Reprint Co., 1973.

Church, Randolph W. *Virginia Legislative Petitions, Bibliography, Calendar, and Abstracts From Original Sources, 6 May 1776–21 June 1782.* Richmond: Virginia State Library, 1984.

Dorman, John Frederick. *Virginia Soldiers of the American Revolution.* 49 vols. to date. Washington, D.C.: John Frederick Dorman, 1958–.

Eckenrode, Hamilton J. *Virginia Soldiers of the American Revolution.* 2 vols. Richmond: Virginia State Library and Archives, 1989.

Gwathmey, John H. *Historical Register of Virginians in the Revolution: Soldiers, Sailors, Marines 1775–1783.* Baltimore: Genealogical Publishing Co., 1987.

Hopkins, William L. *Virginia Revolutionary War Land Grant Claims 1783–1850 (Rejected).* Richmond, 1988.

McAllister, Joseph T. *Virginia Militia in the Revolutionary War.* Bowie, Md;: Heritage Books, 1989.

Sanchez-Saavedra, E.M. *A Guide to Virginia Military Organizations in the American Revolution 1774–1787.* Richmond: Virginia State Library, 1978.

Stewart, Robert A. *History of Virginia's Navy of the Revolution.* Richmond, Va.: Mitchell & Hotchkiss, 1933.

U.S. Veterans Administration. *Virginia Half-Pay and Other Related Revolutionary War Pension Application Files.* M910, 18 rolls. Washington, D.C.: National Archives Microfilm Publications.

Van Schreeven, William J. *Revolutionary Virginia, the Road to Independence.* 7 vols. in 8. University Press of Virginia, 1973–83.

Virginia Revolutionary War State Pensions. Richmond: Virginia Genealogical Society, 1980.

Wardell, Patrick G. *Virginia/West Virginia Genealogical Data From Revolutionary War Pension and Bounty Land Warrant Records.* 3 vols. to date. Bowie, Md.: Heritage Books, 1988–.

Wilson, Samuel M. *Catalogue of Revolutionary Soldiers and Sailors of the Commonwealth of Virginia to Whom Bounty Warrants Were Granted by Virginia for Military Service in the War of Independence.* Baltimore: Southern Book Company, 1953.

West Virginia
Johnston, Ross. *West Virginians in the American Revolution.* Parkersburg, W. Va.: West Augusta Historical and Genealogical Society, 1959.

Reddy, Anne W. *West Virginia Revolutionary Ancestors Whose Services Were Non-Military and Whose Names, Therefore, Do not Appear in Revolutionary Indexes of Soldiers and Sailors.* Baltimore: Genealogical Publishing Co., 1963.

LOYALISTS IN THE REVOLUTIONARY WAR

Antliff, W. Bruce. *Loyalists Settlements 1783–1789: New Evidence of Canadian Loyalist Claims.* Ontario: Ministry of Citizenship and Culture, 1985.

Brown, Wallace. *The Good Americans: The Loyalists in the American Revolution.* New York: William Morrow and Co., 1969.

Bunnell, Paul L. *The New Loyalist Index.* Bowie, Md.: Heritage Books, 1989.

_____. *Research Guide to Loyalist Ancestors, A Directory to Archives Manuscripts and Published Sources.* Bowie, Md.: Heritage Books, 1990.

The Centennial of the Settlement of Upper Canada by the United Empire Loyalists, 1784–1884. Boston: Gregg Press, 1972.

Clark, Murtie J. *Loyalists in the Southern Campaign of the Revolutionary War.* 3 vols. Baltimore: Genealogical Publishing Co., 1981.

Coldham, Peter Wilson. *American Loyalist Claims.* Washington, D.C.: National Genealogical Society, 1980.

Demond, Robert O. *The Loyalists in North Carolina During the Revolution.* Hampden, Conn.: Archer Books, 1964.

Dubeau, Sharon. *New Brunswick Loyalists: A Bicentennial Tribute.* Lambertville, N.J.: Generation Press, 1983.

Dwyer, Clifford S. *Index to Series I of American Loyalists Claims.* DeFuniak Springs, Fla.: RAM Publishing, 1985.

_____. *Index to Series II of American Loyalists Claims.* DeFuniak Springs, Fla: RAM Publishing, 1985.

Fitzgerald, E. Keith. *Loyalist Lists, Over 2000 Loyalist Names and Families From the Haldimand Papers.* Ontario Genealogical Society, 1984.

Gilroy, Marion, comp. *Loyalists and Land Settlement in Nova Scotia.* Baltimore: Genealogical Publishing Co., 1980.

Hammond, Otis Grant. *Tories of New Hampshire in the War of the Revolution.* Boston: Gregg Press, 1972.

Hancock, Harold B. *The Loyalists of Revolutionary Delaware.* University of Delaware Press, 1977.

Jones, E. Alfred. *The Loyalists of Massachusetts, Their Memorials, Petitions and Claims.* London: The Saint Catherine Press, 1930.

_____. *The Loyalists of New Jersey, Their Memorials, Petitions, Claims, Etc., From English Records.* Newark: New Jersey Historical Society, 1927.

Kelby, William. *Orderly Book of the Three Battalions of Loyalists Commanded by Brigadier-General Oliver de Lancey, 7776–1778.* Baltimore: Genealogical Publishing Co., 1972.

Livinston, Mildred R. *Upper Canada Sons and Daughters of United Empire Loyalists.* Kingston, Ontario: Brown & Martin Ltd., 1981.

Maas, David E. *Divided Hearts: Massachusetts Loyalists 1765–1790. A Biographical Directory.* Boston: New England Historic Genealogical Society, 1980.

Montgomery, Thomas L. *Forfeited Estates Inventories and Sales, Pennsylvania Archives,* 6th Series, vols. 12–13. Harrisburg: Harrisburg Publishing Co., 1907.

Palmer, Gregory. *A Bibliography of Loyalist Source Material in the United States, Canada, and Great Britain.* Westport, Conn.: Meckler Publishing Co., 1982.

Paltsits, Victor Hugo. *Minutes of the Commissioners for Detecting and Defeating Conspiracies in the State of New York.* Albany County Sessions 1778–1781. 3 vols. in 2. Boston: Gregg Press, 1972.

Peterson, Jean, and Lynn Murphy. *The Loyalist Guide to Nova Scotian Loyalists and Their Documents.* Halifax, N.S.: Nova Scotia Public Archives, 1983.

Pruitt, Albert Bruce. *Abstracts of Sales of Confiscated Loyalist Land and Property in North Carolina.* The author, 1989.

Reid, William D. *The Loyalists in Ontario: Sons and Daughters of the American Loyalists of Upper Canada.* Larnbertville, N.J.: Hunterdon House, 1983.

Ryerson, Adolphus E. *The Loyalists of America: Their Times From 1620–1816.* 2 vols. Toronto: William Briggs, 1880.

Sabine, Lorenzo. *Biographical Sketches of Loyalists of the American Revolution.* 2 vols. Port Washington, N.Y.: Kennikat Press, 1966.

Siebert, Wilbur H. *Loyalists in East Florida, 1774–1785.* 2 vols. Boston: Gregg Press, 1972.

Stark, James H. *The Loyalists of Massachusetts and the Other Side of the American Revolution.* Boston: W.B. Clarke Co., 1910.

Tyler, John W. *Connecticut Loyalists: An Analysis of Loyalist Land Confiscations in Greenwich, Stamford, and Norfolk.* New Orleans, La.: Polyanthos, 1977.

Van Tyne, Claude H. *The Loyalists in the American Revolution.* Bowie, Md.: Heritage Books, 1989.

Wallace, W. Stewart. *United Empire Loyalists. A Chronicle of the Great Migration.* Boston: Gregg, 1972.

Wright, Esther C. *Loyalists of New Brunswick.* Hantsport, N.S.: the author, 1981.

Yoshpe, Harry B. *The Disposition of Loyalist Estates in the Southern District of New York.* New York: AMS Press, 1967.

GERMAN AUXILIARY TROOPS IN THE REVOLUTIONARY WAR

Burgoyne, Bruce E. *The Waldeck Soldiers of the American Revolution.* Bowie, Md.: Heritage Books, 1991.

DeMarce, Virginia E. *Mercenary Troops From Anhalt-Zerbst, Germany Who Served With the British Forces During the American Revolution.* McNeal, Ariz.: Westland Publications, 1984.

_____. *The Settlement of Former German Auxiliary Troops in Canada After the American Revolution.* Supplement. Sparta, Wis.: Joy Reisinger, 1984.

Dickore, Marie P. *Hessian Soldiers in the American Revolution, Records of Their Marriages and Baptisms of Their Children in America Performed By the Rev. G.C. Coster, 1776–1783, Chaplain of Two Hessian Regiments.* Cincinnati, Ohio: C.J. Krehbiel Co., 1959.

Dulfer, Kurt. *Hessische Truppen im amerikanischen Unabhängigkeitskrieg (Hetrina).* 6 vols. Marburg, Germany: Institut für Arachivwissenschaft, 1972–90.

Eelking, Max von. *The German Allied Troops in the North American War of Independence, 1776–1783.* Genealogical Publishing Co., 1969.

Journal of the Johannes Schwalm Historical Association 1 (1981).

Miles, Lion G. *Hessians of Lewis Miller.* Millville, Pa.: Precision Printers, 1983.

Smith, Clifford Neal. *British and German Deserters, Discharges, and Prisoners of War Who May Have Remained in Canada and the United States, 1774–1783.* McNeal, Ariz.: Westland Publications, 1988.

_____. *Brunswick Deserter Immigrants of the American Revolution.* Thomson, Ill.: Heritage House, 1973.

_____. *Deserters and Disbanded Soldiers From British, German, and Loyalist Military Units in the South, 1782.* McNeal, Ariz.: Westland Publications, 1991.

Mercenaries From Ansbach and Bayreuth, Germans Who Remained in America After the American Revolution. Thomson, Ill.: Heritage House, 1974.

_____. *Mercenaries From Hessen-Hanau Who Remained in Canada and the United States After the American Revolution.* DeKalb, Ill.; Westland Publications, 1976.

_____. *Muster Rolls and Prisoner-of-War Lists in American Archival Collections Pertaining to the German Mercenary Troops Who Served With British Forces During the American Revolution.* DeKalb, Ill.: Westland Publications, 1976.

_____. *Notes on Hessian Soldiers Who Remained in Canada and the United States after the American Revolution, 1775–1784.* McNeal, Ariz.: Westland Publications, 1992.

_____. *Some German-American Participants in the American Revolution.* McNeal, Ariz.: Westland Publications, 1990.

Städtler, Erhardt. *Die Anebach-Bayreuther Truppen im americanischen Unabhängigkeitskrieg, 1777–1783.* Nürnberg, Germany: Gesellachaft für Familienforschung in Franken, 1956.

FRONTIER CLASHES, 1784–1811

Various States
Clark, Murtie June. *American Militia in the Frontier Wars, 1790–1796.* Baltimore: Genealogical Publishing Co., 1990.

Dent, David L. *Foreign Origins, Comprising an Enumeration of Men of Foreign Birth Enlisted in the United States Army From 1798 to 1815; Together With the Dates & Places of Enlistment and Ages of the Men; the Whole Conveniently Arranged by State Alphabetically; and Identifying in the Case of Each Man With No Exception the Town or City of Birth Abroad; to Which Is Appended a Complete Index of All Names Included in the Work.* Arlington, Va.: C.M. Kent, 1981.

White, Virgil D. *Index to Volunteer Soldiers, 1784–1811.* Waynesboro, Tenn.: National Historical Publishing Co., 1987.

Indiana
Muster Rolls and Payrolls of Militia and Regular Army Organizations in the Battle of Tippecanoe, November 1811. T1085,

1 roll. Washington, D.C.: National Archives Microfilm Publications.

Virginia
Butler, Stuart L. *Virginia Soldiers in the United States Army, 1800–1815.* Athens, Ga.: Iberian Publishing Co., 1986.

WAR OF 1812

Various States
Carr, Deborah E.W. *Index to Certified Copy of List of American Prisoners of War, 1812–1815, as Recorded in General Entry Book Ottawa, Canada.* N.p., 1924.

Fredericksen, John C. *Free Trade and Sailor's Rights: A Bibliography of the War of 1812.* Westport, Conn.: Greenwood Press, 1985.

Peterson, Clarence Stewart. *Known Military Dead During the War of 1812.* Baltimore, 1955.

U.S. Veterans Administration. *War of 1812 Military Bounty Land Warrants 1815–1858.* M848, 14 rolls. Washington, D.C.: National Archives Microfilm Publication.

White, Virgil D. *Index to War of 1812 Pension Files, 1815–1926.* 3 vols. Waynesboro, Tenn.: National Historical Publishing Co., 1989.

Arizona
Christensen, Katheren. *Arkansas Military Bounty Grants (War of 1812).* Hot Springs, Ark.: Arkansas Ancestors, 1971.

Connecticut
Johnston, Henry Phelps. *Record of Service of Connecticut Men in the I. War of the Revolution; II. War of 1812; III. Mexican War.* Hartford, Conn.: Case, Lockwood & Brainard, 1889.

Delaware
Delaware Archives Military Records, vols. 4 and 5. Wilmington, Del.: Star Publishing Co., 1916.

Georgia
Kratovil, Judy Swaim. *Index to War of 1812 Service Records for Volunteer Soldiers From Georgia.* Atlanta, Ga.: the compiler, 1986.

Georgia Military Affairs, vol. 3, 1801–13, vol. 4, 1814–19.

Illinois
War of 1812 Bounty Lands in Illinois. Thomas, Ill.: Heritage House, 1977.

Elliott, Isaac H. *Record of the Services of Illinois Soldiers in the Black Hawk War, 1831–32, and in the Mexican War, 1846–8 . . . With an Appendix Giving a Record of the Services of the Illinois Militia, Rangers and Riflemen, in Protecting the Frontier From the Ravages of the Indians From 1810 to 1813.* Springfield, Ill.: H.W. Rokker, 1882.

Indiana
Franklin, Charles M. *Indiana War of 1812 Soldiers Militia.* Indianapolis: Ye Olde Genealogie Shoppe, 1984.

Kentucky
Clift, G. Glenn. *Remember the Raisin! Kentucky and Kentuckians in the Battles and Massacre at Frenchtown, Michigan Territory in the War of 1812.* Frankfort, Ky.: Kentucky Historical Society, 1961.

Kentucky Soldiers in the War of 1812. Baltimore: Genealogical Publishing Co., 1969.

Quisenberry, Anderson C. *Kentucky in the War of 1812*. Baltimore: Genealogical Publishing Co., 1969.

Louisiana
Casey, Powell A. *Louisiana in War of 1812*. Baton Rouge: 1963.

Morazan, Donald R. *Biographical Sketches of the Veterans of the Battalions of Orleans, 1814–1815*. Legacy Publishing Co., 1979.

Pierson, Marion J.B. *Louisiana Soldiers in the War of 1812*. Baton Rouge: Louisiana Genealogical and Historical Society, 1963.

Maryland
Huntsberry, Thomas V., and Joanne M. Huntsberry. *Maryland War of 1812 Privateers*. Baltimore: J. Mart, 1983.

_____. *North Point War of 1812*. N.p., 1985.

_____. *Western Maryland/Pennsylvania Virginia Militia in Defense of Maryland, 1805 to 1815*. Baltimore: 1983.

Marine, William M. *The British Invasion of Maryland, 1812–1815*. Hatboro, Pa.: Tradition Press, 1965.

Wright, F. Edward. *Maryland Militia War of 1812*. 8 vols. Silver Spring, Md.: Family Line, 1979–92.

Massachusetts
Barker, J. *Records of the Massachusetts Volunteer Militia Called Out By the Governor of Massachusetts to Suppress a Threatened Invasion During the War of 1812–14*. Boston: Wright & Potter Printing Co., 1913.

Michigan
Miller, Alice D. *Soldiers of the War of 1812 Who Died in Michigan*. Ithaca, Mich.: the author, 1962.

Mississippi
Rowland, Mrs. Dunbar. *Mississippi Territory in the War of 1812*. Publications of the Mississippi Historical Society, vol. 4. Jackson, Miss.: Mississippi Historical Society, 1921.

Missouri
Dunaway, Maxine. *Missouri Military Land Warrants, War of 1812*. Springfield, Mo.: the author, 1985.

Military Land Warrants in Missouri, 1819. Denver: The Stagecoach Library for Genealogical Research, 1988.

New Hampshire
Potter, Charles E. *Military History of the State of New Hampshire, 1623–1861*. Baltimore: Genealogical Publishing Co., 1972.

New Jersey
Records of Officers and Men of New Jersey in Wars 1791–1815. Trenton, N.J.: State Gazette Publishing Co., 1909.

New York
Index of Awards on Claims of the Soldiers of the War of 1812, New York Adjutant General's Office. Baltimore: Genealogical Publishing Co., 1969.

North Carolina
Muster Rolls of the Soldiers of the War of 1812 Detached From the Militia of North Carolina in 1812 and 1814. Baltimore: Genealogical Publishing Co., 1976.

Ohio
Garner, Grace. *Index to Roster of Ohio Soldiers, War of 1812*. Spokane, Wash.: Eastern Washington Genealogical Society, 1974.

Miller, Phyllis B. *Index to the Grave Records of Servicemen of the War of 1812, State of Ohio*. Brookville, Ohio: Dillon's Printery, 1988.

Roster of Ohio Soldiers in the War of 1812. Columbus, Ohio: The Edward T. Miller Co., 1916.

Pennsylvania
Muster Rolls of the Pennsylvania Volunteers in the War of 1812–1814. Reprinted from *Pennsylvania Archives*, 2nd Series, vol. 12. Baltimore: Genealogical Publishing Co., 1967.

Rhode Island
Smith, Joseph J. *Civil and Military List of Rhode Island, 1800–1850*. Providence, R.I.: Preston and Rounds Co., 1901.

South Carolina
Service Records: War of 1812 Records of the First, Second, and Third Regiments. 5 microfiche. South Carolina Historical Society.

Tennessee
McCown, Mary Harden, and Inez E. Burns. *Soldiers of the War of 1812 Buried in Tennessee. . . .* Johnson City, Tenn.: The Overmountain Press, 1977.

Moore, Mrs. John Trotwood. *Record of Commissions of Officers in the Tennessee Militia, 1796–1811*. Baltimore: Genealogical Publishing Co., 1977.

Sistler, Byron, and Samuel Sistler. *Tennesseans in the War of 1812*. Nashville: Byron Sistler & Associates, 1992.

Texas
Fay, Mary Smith. *War of 1812 Veterans in Texas*. New Orleans: Polyanthos, 1979.

Vermont
Roster of Soldiers in the War of 1812–14. St. Albans, Vt.: The Messenger Press, 1933.

Virginia
Butler, Stuart Lee. *A Guide to the Virginia Militia Units in the War of 1812*. Athens, Ga.: Iberian Publishing Co., 1988.

_____. *Virginia Soldiers in the United States Army, 1800–1815*. Athens, Ga.: Iberian Publishing Co., 1986.

Virginia Auditor General. *Muster Rolls of the Virginia Militia in the War of 1812*. Richmond, Va.: 1852.

_____. *Pay Rolls of Militia Entitled to Land Bounty Under the Act of Congress of 1850*. Richmond, Va.: 1851.

Indian Wars, 1815–1858

Various States
White, Virgil D. *Index to Indian War Pension Files, 1892–1926*. Waynesboro, Tenn.: National Historical Publishing Co., 1987.

U.S. Veterans Administration. *Compiled Service Records of Michigan and Illinois Volunteers Who Served During the*

Winnebago Indian Disturbances, 1827. M1505, 3 rolls. Washington, D.C.: National Archives Microfilm Publications.

Alabama

Horn, Robert C. *Creek Indian War Index to Records of Volunteer Soldiers From Alabama.* Dadeville, Ala.: The Genealogical Society of East Alabama, 1983.

_____. *Index to Compiled Service Records for Alabama Soldiers in the Florida Indian War, 1836–1838.* Auburn, Ala.: The Genealogical Society of East Alabama, 1987.

Arkansas

Morgan, James Logan. *Arkansas Volunteers of 1836–37: History and Roster of the First and Second Regiments of Arkansas Mounted Gunmen, 1837–1837, and a Roster of Captain Jesse Bean's Company of Mounted Rangers.* Newport, Ark.: Morgan Books, 1984.

Florida

Soldiers of Florida in the Seminole Indian, Civil and Spanish-American Wars. Macclenny, Fla.: R.J. Ferry, 1983.

Illinois

Whitney, Ellen M. *The Black Hawk War, 1831–1832.* Collections of the Illinois State Historical Library, vols. 25–27. Springfield, Ill.: Illinois State Historical Library, 1970–78.

Indiana

Loftus, Carrie. *Indiana Militia in the Black Hawk War.* The author, n.d.

Maine

Aroostock War. Historical Sketch and Roster of Commissioned Officers and Enlisted Men Called Into Service for the Protection of the Northeastern Frontier of Maine. From February to May 1839. Baltimore: Clearfield Co., 1989.

Texas

Stephens, Robert W. *Texas Ranger Indian War Pensions.* Quannah, Tex.: Nortex Press, 1975.

MEXICAN WAR, 1846–1848

Various States

Peterson, Clarence S. *Known Military Dead During the Mexican War, 1846–48.* Baltimore: Genealogical Publishing Co., 1957.

White, Virgil D. *Index to Mexican War Pension Files.* Waynesboro, Tenn.: National Historical Publishing Co., 1989.

Wolfe, Barbara Schull. *An Index to Mexican War Pension Applications.* Indianapolis: Heritage House, 1985.

Arizona

Allen, Desmond Walls. *Arkansas' Mexican War Soldiers.* Conway, Ark.: Arkansas Research, 1988.

Connecticut

Johnston, Henry Phelps. *Record of Service of Connecticut Men in the I. War of the Revolution II. War of 1812 III. Mexican War.* Hartford, Conn.: Case, Lockwood & Brainard, 1889.

Florida

Soldiers of Florida in the Seminole Indian, Civil and Spanish-American Wars. Macclenny, Fla.: R.J. Ferry, 1983.

Illinois

Elliott, Isaac H. *Record of the Services of Illinois Soldiers in the Black Hawk War, 1831–32, and in the Mexican War, 1846–8. . . .* Springfield, Ill.: H.W. Rokker, 1882.

Indiana

Perry, Oran. *Indiana in the Mexican War.* Indianapolis: William B. Burford, 1908.

Kentucky

Report of the Adjutant General of the State of Kentucky: Mexican War Veterans. Frankfort, Ky.: John D. Woods, 1889.

Maryland

Wells, Charles J. *Maryland and District of Columbia Volunteers in the Mexican War.* Family Line, 1991.

Michigan

Joint Documents of the Senate and House of Representatives at the Annual Session of 1848. Joint Document No. 7, pp. 31–43.

Welch, Richard. *Michigan in the Mexican War, First Regiment of Michigan Volunteers.* Durand, Mich.: 1967.

New Hampshire

Potter, Charles E. *The Military History of the State of New Hampshire, 1623–1861.* Baltimore: Genealogical Publishing Co., 1972.

New Jersey

Records of Officers and Men of New Jersey in the War With Mexico, 1846–1848.

Ohio

Reprint Edition of the Official Roster of the Soldiers of the State of Ohio in the War With Mexico, 1846–1848. Ohio Genealogical Society, 1991.

Pennsylvania

Segraves, Antoinette J. "A Guide to Pennsylvania Soldiers in the Mexican War." *The Pennsylvania Genealogical Magazine* 36 (1989–90): 55–57, 176–91, 274–84; 37 (1991–92): 22–38, 117–36, 203–18, 335–52.

Rhode Island

Smith, Joseph J. *Civil and Military List of Rhode Island, 1800–1850.* Providence, R.I.: Preston & Rounds Co., 1901.

Tennessee

Brock, Reid, Thomas Brock, and Tony Hays. *Volunteers: Tennesseans in the War With Mexico.* 2 vols. Kitchen Table Press, 1986.

Texas

Spurlin, Charles D. *Texas Veterans in the Mexican War, Muster Rolls of Texas Military Units.* The compiler, 1984.

Utah

Tyler, Daniel. *A Concise History of the Mormon Battalion in the Mexican War 1846–1848.* Glorietta, N.M.: Rio Grande Press, 1969.

CIVIL WAR, 1861–1865

Various States

Brewer, Willis. *Alabama: Her History, Resources, War Records and Public Men From 1540 to 1872.* Spartanburg, S.C.: The Reprint Co., 1975.

Groene, Bertram Hawthorne. *Tracing Your Civil War Ancestors.* Rev. ed. Winston-Salem, N.C.: John F. Blair Publisher, 1980.

Mills, Gary B. *Civil War Claims in the South: An Index of Civil War Damage Claims Filed Before the Southern Claims Commission, 1871–1880.* Laguna Hills, Calif.: Aegean Park Press, 1990.

_____. *Southern Loyalists in the Civil War: The Southern Claims Commission: A Composite Directoy of Case Files, 1871–1880.* Baltimore: Genealogical Publishing Co., 1994.

Neagles, James C. *Confederate Research Sources: A Guide to Archive Collections.* Salt Lake City: Ancestry, 1986.

Official Army Register of the Volunteer Force of the United States Army for the Years 1861, '62, '63, '64, '65. 9 vols. Gaithersburg, Md.: Ron R. Van Sickle Military Books, 1987.

Pardons by the President: Final Report of the Names of Persons Who Lived in Alabama, Virginia, West Virginia, or Georgia, Were Engaged in Rebellion and Pardoned By the President, Andrew Johnson. Bowie, Md.: Heritage Books, 1986.

Roll of Honor: Names of Soldiers Who Died in Defense of the American Union, Interred in the National Cemeteries, Numbers I–XIX. Quartermaster General's Office, 1868. Reprint. Baltimore: Genealogical Publishing Co., 1994. *Index to the Roll of Honor.* Compiled by William and Martha Remy. Baltimore: Genealogical Publishing Co., 1995.

Schweitzer, George K. *Civil War Genealogy.* Knoxville, Tenn.: 1981.

Wakelyn, Jon L. *Biographical Dictionary of the Confederacy.* Westport, Conn.: Greenwood Press, 1977.

Arizona
Allen, Desmond Walls. *Arkansas's Damned Yankees: An Index to Union Soldiers in Arkansas Regiments.* Conway, Ark.: Arkansas Research, 1987.

_____. *Index to Arkansas Confederate Soldiers.* 3 vols. Conway, Ark.: Arkansas Research, 1990.

Ingmire, Frances Terry. *Arkansas Confederate Veterans and Widows Pension Applications.* St. Louis, Mo.: 1985.

McLane, Bobbie J., and Capitola Glazner. *Arkansas 1911 Census of Confederate Veterans.* 4 vols. N.p., 1977–88.

Pickett, Connie. *Old Soldiers Home: Arkansas Confederate Soldiers and Widows.* St. Louis, Mo.: Frances T. Ingmire, 1985.

California
Orton, Richard H. *Records of California Men in the War of the Rebellion, 1861 to 1867.* Detroit: Gale Research Co., 1979.

Parker, J. Carlyle. *A Personal Name Index to Orton's Records of California Men in the War of the Rebellion, 1861 to 1867.* Detroit: Gale Research Co., 1978.

Colorado
Biennial Reports of the Adjutant General, 1861. Denver: 1866.

Connecticut
Smith, Stephen R. *Record of Service of Connecticut Men in the Army and Navy of the United States During the War of the Rebellion.* Hartford, Conn.: Case, Lockwood & Brainard Co., 1889.

North Dakota
Dakota Militia in the War of 1862. 58th Congress, 2nd Session, Senate Document No. 241. Washington, D.C., 1904.

Delaware
Scharf, John Thomas. *History of Delaware, 1609–1888.* Appendix, "Roster of Delaware Volunteers in the War of the Rebellion," vol. 1, i–xxxiii. Port Washington, N.Y.: Kennikat Press, 1972.

Florida
Soldiers of Florida in the Seminole Indian, Civil, and Spanish-American Wars. Macclenny, Fla.: R.J. Ferry, 1983.

White, Virgil D. *Register of Florida CSA Pension Applications.* Waynesboro, Tenn.: National Historical Publishing Co., 1989.

Georgia
Brightwell, Juanita S., Eunice S. Lee, and Elsie C. Fulghum. *Roster of the Confederate Soldiers of Georgia 1861–1865, Index.* Spartanburg, S.C.: The Reprint Co., 1982.

Henderson, Lillian. *Roster of the Confederate Soldiers of Georgia 1861–1865.* 6 vols. Hapeville, Ga.: Longino & Porter, 1959–64.

Illinois
Reece, J.N. *Report of the Adjutant General of the State of Illinois.* 8 vols. Springfield, Ill.: Phillips Bros., 1900–02.

Volkel, Lowell. *Illinois Soldiers and Sailors Home at Quincy, Admission of Mexican War and Civil War Veterans.* 2 vols. Thomson, Ill.: Heritage House, 1975–80.

Indiana
Terrell, William H.H. *Report of the Adjutant General of the State of Indiana.* 8 vols. Indianapolis: Alexander H. Conner, 1865–69.

Trapp, Glenda K. *Index to the Report of the Adjutant General of the State of Indiana First Volume, an Every Name Index to Volumes I, II, and III. Second Volume, an Every Name Index to Volume IV.* 2 vols. Evansville, Ind.: Trapp Publishing Service, 1986–87.

Iowa
Alexander, William L. *List of Ex-Soldiers, Sailors, and Marines Living in Iowa.* Des Moines, Iowa: 1886.

Baker, N.B. *Report of the Adjutant General and Acting Quartermaster General of the State of Iowa, January 1, 1865, to January 1, 1866.* Des Moines, Iowa: 1866.

Thrift, William H. *Roster and Record of Iowa Soldiers in the War of the Rebellion Together With Historical Sketches of Volunteer Organizations, 1861–1866.* 6 vols. Des Moines, Iowa: Emory H. English, 1908–11.

Kansas
Noble, P.S. *Report of the Adjutant General of the State of Kansas . . . 1861–1865.* 2 vols. Topeka, Kans.: Kansas State Printing Co., 1896.

Kentucky

Report of the Adjutant General of the State of Kentucky [Union]. 2 vols. Utica, Ky.: McDowell Publications, 1984–88.

Report of the Adjutant General of the State of Kentucky. Confederate Kentucky Volunteers War 1861–65. Hartford, Ky.: McDowell Publications, 1979–80.

Simpson, Alicia. *Index of Confederate Pension Applications, Commonwealth of Kentucky.* Frankfort, Ky.: Division of Archives and Records Management, 1978.

Louisiana

Booth, Andrew B. *Records of Louisiana Confederate Soldiers and Louisiana Confederate Commands.* 3 vols. Spartanburg, S.C.: The Reprint Co., 1982.

Burt, W.G. *Annual Report of the Adjutant General of the State of Louisiana for the Year Ending December 31st, 1899.* New Orleans, La.: State Papers, 1890.

Maine

Annual Report, 1861–66. Supplement: Alphabetical Index of Maine Volunteers, Etc., Mustered Into the Service of the United States During the War of 1861. Augusta, Maine: Stevens & Sayward, 1867.

Hodson, John L. *Annual Report of the Adjutant General of the State of Maine, for the Year Ending December 31, 1863.* Augusta, Maine, 1863.

_____. *Returns of Desertions, Discharges, and Deaths in Maine Regiments.* Augusta, Maine, 1864.

Maryland

Goldeborough, W.M. *Maryland Line in the Confederate Army, 1861–1865.* Gaithersburg, Md.: Butternut Press, 1983.

Hartzler, Daniel D. *Marylanders in the Confederacy.* Silver Spring, Md.: Family Line Publications, 1986.

Huntsberry, Thomas V. *Maryland in the Civil War.* 2 vols. Baltimore: J. Mart Publishers, 1985.

Reamy, Martha, and Bill Reamy. *History and Roster of Maryland Volunteers Wars of 1861–5 Index.* Westminster, Md.: Family Line Publications, 1990.

Toomey, Daniel Carroll. *Index to the Roster of the Maryland Volunteers, 1861–1865.* Harmans, Md.: Toomey Press, 1986.

Williams, L. Allison, J.H. Jarret, and George W. F. Vernon. *History and Roster of Maryland Volunteers, War of 1861–5.* Silver Spring, Md.: Family Line Publications, 1987.

Massachusetts

Massachusetts Soldiers, Sailors, and Marines in the Civil War. 8 vols. Norwood, Mass.: Norwood Press, 1931–15. Vol. 9, *Index to Army Records,* pertains to vols. 1–6 and part of 7. Boston: Wright & Potter Printing Co., 1937.

Record of the Massachusetts Volunteers, 1861–65. Boston: 1868–70.

Michigan

Alphabetical General Index to Public Library Sets of 85,271 Names of Michigan Soldiers and Sailors Individual Records. Lansing, Mich.: Wynkoop, Hallenbeck Crawford Co., 1915.

Record of Service of Michigan Volunteers in the Civil War, 1861– 1865. 46 vols. Kalamazoo, Mich.: Ihling Bros. & Everand, 1905.

Robertson, John. *Annual Report of the Adjutant General of the State of Michigan for the Year 1864.* Lansing, Mich.: 1865.

_____. *Annual Report of the Adjutant General of the State of Michigan for the Years 1865–66.* Lansing, Mich.: 1866.

_____. *Michigan in the War.* Rev. ed. Lansing, Mich: 1882.

United States Civil War Soldiers Living in Michigan in 1894. St. Johns, Wash.: The Genealogists of Clinton County Historical Society, 1988.

Minnesota

Minnesota in the Civil and Indian Wars, 1861–1865. 2 vols. St. Paul, Minn.: Pioneer Press Co., 1890.

Warming, Irene B. *Minnesotans in the Civil and Indian Wars: An Index to the Rosters in Minnesota in the Civil and Indian Wars, 1861–1865.* St. Paul, Minn.: Minnesota Historical Society, 1936.

Missouri

Confederate Roll of Honor: Missouri. Warrensburg, Mo.: West Central Missouri Genealogical Society and Library, 1989.

Simpson, Samuel P. *Annual Report of the Adjutant General of Missouri.* Jefferson City, Mo.: Emory S. Foster, 1866.

Mississippi

Rietti, J.C. *Military Annals of Mississippi. Military Organizations Which Entered the Service of the Confederate States of America from the State of Mississippi.* Spartanburg, S.C.: The Reprint Co., 1976.

Rowland, Dunbar. *Military History of Mississippi 1803–98, Taken from the Official and Statistical Register of the State of Mississippi, 1908.* Pp. 420–556. Spartanburg, S.C.: The Reprint Co., 1988.

Wiltshire, Betty Couch. *Mississippi Confederate Grave Registrations.* 2 vols. Bowie, Md.: Heritage Books, 1991.

Nebraska

Allen, John C. *Roster of Soldiers, Sailors, and Marines of the War of 1812, the Mexican War, and the War of the Rebellion Residing in Nebraska, June 1, 1893.* Lincoln, Nebr.: Jacob North & Co., 1893.

Dudley, E.S. *Roster of Nebraska Volunteers From 1861 to 1869.* Hastings, Nebr.: 1888.

History of the State of Nebraska. Vol. 1, pp. 227–318. Evansville, Ind.: Unigraphics, 1975.

Patrick, John R. *Report of the Adjutant General of the State of Nebraska.* Des Moines, Iowa: 1871.

Piper, J.A. *Roster of Soldiers, Sailors, and Marines of the War of 1812, the Mexican War, and the War of the Rebellion Residing in Nebraska, June 1, 1895.* York, Nebr.: Nebraska Newspaper Union, 1895.

Pool, Charles H. *Roster of Veterans of the Mexican, Civil, and Spanish-American Wars Residing in Nebraska, 1915.* Lincoln, Nebr.: Nebraska Secretary of State, 1915.

Nevada
Cradlebaugh, J. *Annual Report of the Adjutant General for 1865.* Carson City, Nev.: John Church, 1866.

Laughton, C.E. *Roster of Volunteers.* Biennial Report of the Adjutant-General, pp. 29–55. N.p., 1884.

Nevada Adjutant General. *Nevada Territory and State Civil War Muster Rolls and Index.* Microfilm, 2 rolls.

New Hampshire
Ayling, Augustus D. *Revised Register of the Soldiers and Sailors of New Hampshire in the War of the Rebellion, 1861–66.* Concord, N.H.: Ira C. Evans, 1895.

New Jersey
Stryker, William S. *Record of Officers and Men of New Jersey in the Civil War, 1861–1865.* 2 vols. Trenton, N.J.: John L. Murphy, 1876.

New York
Phisterer, Frederick. *New York in the War of the Rebellion, 1861 to 1865.* 3rd ed. 6 vols. Albany, N.Y.: J.B. Lyon Co., 1912.

A Record of the Commissioned and Non-Commissioned Officers and Privates of the Regiments organized in the State of New York. 4 vols. Albany, N.Y.: 1864–68.

Registers of New York Regiments in the War of the Rebellion. 46 vols. Albany, N.Y.: 1894–1906.

North Carolina
Manarin, Louis H. *North Carolina Troops 1861–1865, a Roster.* 12 vols. to date. Raleigh, N.C.: State Department of Archives and History, 1968–.

Moore, John W. *Roster of North Carolina Troops in the War Between the States During the Years 1861, 1862, 1863, 1864, and 1865.* 4 vols. Raleigh, N.C.: Ashe and Gatling, 1882.

Ohio
Official Roster of the Soldiers of the State of Ohio in the War of the Rebellion, 1861–1866. 12 vols. Akron, Ohio: The Werner Co., 1893–95. *Alphabetical Index to Official Roster of the Soldiers of the State of Ohio in the War of the Rebellion.* Works Progress Administration, 1938.

Petty, Gerald M. *Index of the Ohio Squirrel Hunters Roster.* Columbus, Ohio: Petty's Press, 1984.

Oklahoma
Oklahoma Confederate Pension Applications Submitted by Confederate Soldiers, Sailors, and Their Widows. Oklahoma City, Okla.: Oklahoma Genealogical Society, 1969.

Oregon
Reed, C.A. *Report of the Adjutant General of the State of Oregon for the Years 1865–6.* Salem, Oreg.: H.L. Pittock, 1866.

Pennsylvania
Bates, Samuel P. *History of Pennsylvania Volunteers 1861–5.* 5 vols. Harrisburg, Penn.: State Printer, 1869–71. *Alphabetical Index of Civil War Soldiers.* Microfilm, 80 rolls.

Russell, A.L. *Annual Report of the Adjutant General of Pennsylvania, 1863.* N.p., 1864.

Rhode Island
Dyer, Elisha. *Annual Report of the Adjutant General of the State of Rhode Island and Providence Plantations for the Year 1865.* Providence, R.I.: E. Freeman & Sons, 1893–95.

South Carolina
Recollections and Reminiscences, 1861–1865 Through World War I. 3 vols. to date. South Carolina Division of the United Daughters of the Confederacy, 1990–.

Salley, A.S. *South Carolina Troops in Confederate Service.* 3 vols. Columbia, S.C.: The R. L. Bryan Co., 1913.

South Dakota
Dakota Militia in the War of 1862. 58th Congress, 2nd Session, Senate Document No. 241. Washington, D.C., 1904.

Tennessee
Dyer, Gustavus W. *Tennessee Civil War Veterans Questionnaires.* 5 vols. Easley, S.C.: Southern Historical Press, 1985.

Index to Tennessee Confederate Pension Applications. Nashville: Tennessee State Library and Archives, 1964.

Tennessee's Confederate Widows and Their Families. Cleveland, Tenn.: Cleveland Public Library, 1992.

Tennesseans in the Civil War: A Military History of Confederate and Union Units With Available Rosters of Personnel. 2 vols. Nashville: University of Tennessee Press, 1985.

Texas
Kinney, John M. *Index to Applications for Texas Confederate Pensions.* Rev. ed. Austin, Tex.: Archives Division Texas State Library, 1977.

Miller, Thomas L. *Texas Confederate Script Grantees C.S.A.* N.p., 1985.

White, Virgil D. *Index to Texas CSA Pension Files.* Waynesboro, Tenn.: National Historical Publishing Co., 1989.

Vermont
Peck, Theodore S. *Revised Roster of Vermont Volunteers and Lists of Vermonters Who Served in the Army and Navy of the United States During the War of the Rebellion, 1861–66.* Montpelier, Vt.: Press of the Watchman Publishing Co., 1892.

Virginia
Virginia Regimental Histories Series. 83 vols. to date. Lynchburg, Tenn.: H.E. Howard, 1982–. The series deals with each Virginia unit and each Virginia soldier. Each volume contains a unit history and an annotated muster roll of every man who served in that unit.

West Virginia
Lang, Theodore F. *Loyal West Virginia From 1861 to 1865.* Baltimore: Deutsch Publishing Co., 1895.

Annual Report of the Adjutant General for the Year Ending December 31, 1864. Wheeling, W.Va.: John F. M'Dermot, 1865.

Annual Report of the Adjutant General for the Year Ending December 31, 1865. Wheeling, W. Va.: John Frew, 1866.

Wisconsin
Chapman, Chandler P. *Roster of Wisconsin Volunteers, War of the Rebellion, 1861–65.* Madison, Wis.: 1886.

Wisconsin Volunteers, War of the Rebellion, 1861–1865. Ar-

ranged Alphabetically. Madison, Wis.: Democrat Printing Co., 1914.

SPANISH AMERICAN WAR AND PHILIPPINE INSURRECTION, 1898–1902

Various States

Coston, William Hilary. *The Spanish American War Volunteer.* Freeport, N.Y.: Books for Libraries Press, 1971. A discussion of African American volunteers.

Arizona

Herner, Charles. *Arizona Rough Riders.* Appendix 3, "Muster-In Roll," pp. 234–44. Tucson: The University of Arizona Press, 1970.

Allen, Demond Walls. *Arkansas Spanish American War Soldiers.* Conway, Ariz.: Arkansas Research, 1988.

Connecticut

Connecticut Volunteers Who Served in the Spanish-American War, 1898–1899. Hartford, Conn.: Connecticut Adjutant General's Office, 1899.

Florida

Soldiers of Florida in the Seminole Indian, Civil and Spanish-American Wars. Macclenny, Fla.: R.J. Ferry, 1983.

Georgia

Thaxton, Carlton J. *Roster of Spanish American War Soldiers From Georgia.* Americus, Ga.: Thaxton Co., 1984.

Indiana

Gore, James K. *Record of Indiana Volunteers in the Spanish-American War, 1898–1899.* Indianapolis, Ind.: Indiana Adjutant General's office, 1900.

Kansas

Fox, S.M. *13th Biennial Report of the Adjutant General of the State of Kansas, 1901–2.* Topeka: Kansas Adjutant General's Office, 1902.

Louisiana

Wright, Nancy Lowne. *Louisiana Volunteers in the War of 1898.* Wright Shannon Pub., 1989.

Maryland

Riley, Hugh Ridgely. *Roster of the Soldiers and Sailors Who Served in Organizations From Maryland during the Span-*

ish American War. Silver Spring, Md.: Family Line Publications, 1990.

Minnesota

Eleventh Biennial Report . . . Including Military Operations . . . up to November 30, 1900. St. Paul: Minnesota Adjutant General's Department, 1901.

New Jersey

Report of the Adjutant General of New Jersey. . . . Somerville, N.J.: New Jersey Adjutant General's Office, 1899.

New York

New York in the Spanish American War, 1898. 3 vols. Albany, N.Y.: J.B. Lyon, 1902.

North Carolina

Roster of the North Carolina Volunteers in the Spanish-American War 1898–1899. Raleigh, N.C.: Press of Edwards & Broughton, 1900.

Ohio

Broglin, Jana Sloan. *Index to Official Roster of Ohio Soldiers in the War With Spain, 1898–1899.* Mansfield, Ohio: The Ohio Genealogical Society, n.d.

Hough, Benson W. *The Official Roster of Ohio Soldiers in the War With Spain, 1898–1899.* Columbus, Ohio: Edward T. Miller Co., 1916.

Oregon

Gantenbein, C.U. *The Official Records of the Oregon Volunteers in the Spanish War and Philippine Insurrection.* 2nd ed. Salem, Oreg.: Oregon Adjutant General's Office, 1903.

Pennsylvania

Stewart, Thomas J. *Record of Pennsylvania Volunteers in the Spanish-American War, 1898.* 2nd ed. Harrisburg: Pennsylvania Adjutant General's Office, 1901.

Utah

Saldana, Richard H. *Index to the Utah Spanish-American War Veterans,* 1898. A.I.S.I. Publishers, 1988.

West Virginia

Biennial Report of the Adjutant General of West Virginia, 1899–1900. Charleston, W. Va.: West Virginia Adjutant General's Office, 1900.

RESEARCH IN BUSINESS, EMPLOYMENT, AND INSTITUTIONAL RECORDS

CHAPTER CONTENTS

10

RESEARCH IN BUSINESS, EMPLOYMENT, AND INSTITUTIONAL RECORDS

Kory L. Meyerink and Johni Cerny

This chapter discusses a class of records usually overlooked by genealogists, even though they often reveal as much or more than such standard sources as censuses and death certificates. These sources are business, employment, and institutional records.

BUSINESS AND EMPLOYMENT RECORDS

Kory L. Meyerink

Businesses have employed or served our ancestors at least since the first mill was built to grind grain or saw wood, and a surprising number of employer-employee or buyer-seller records were kept and have survived. When we remember that many vital events were not recorded by some states until after 1900, the value of business and employment records which predate many standard genealogical records becomes evident. Business records are a broad and varied set of records. They include, of course, those records that a business may have kept regarding its customers or employees.

However, researchers must not overlook other records created during a business's existence, even when such records may fall into another genealogical category. These can include local licenses permitting a business to operate (government records), histories of a specific business or an industry, biographical collections (manuscript and published) of a company's officers or an industry's leaders, city directories which identify businesses and their owners and employees, and even old photographs that name the photographer. In some cases, a business created other records we use in genealogy. Newspapers and mortuary records are the products of businesses, although we seldom label them as business records. While the focus of this chapter will be the records created by businesses, other records related to the existence of a business or an industry will be noted where especially useful.

Business records can be used in three significant ways during genealogical research: (1) On occasion, they provide important genealogical information in the absence of traditional genealogical records—as, for instance, a mortuary record where a death or cemetery record cannot be found. (2) More commonly, they provide clues that may lead to other, traditional genealogical records, such as an account book that places the ancestor in a specific location at a certain date. (3) Another important use is to "flesh out" an ancestor's personal history, making him or her "come alive" as you compile a more complete family history.

A common misconception in using business records is our image of rural America as being comprised largely of farmers until the last generation or so. As evidence of this point, it is not well known that by 1880 more than half of the population were in non-farming occupations.[1] A breakdown by professions shows that agriculture was outnumbered by the combination of manufacturing and trades by 1910.[2]

As a case in point, consider the six American great-grandfathers of my own children. They included three farmers living in the western states, a painter in Chicago and western Montana, a physician in Manhattan, and a coal and grain merchant in western Massachusetts. All of them lived from about the 1850s to the 1930s. The painter Andrew Sticht (born 1860) was a classic research "dead end." A carved box that his father had made supported the tradition that the father—whose name was unknown—was a cabinet maker in New York City. This occupational clue, when used in conjunction with city directories, was enough to lead to additional records which extended the ancestry back two more generations to the immigrant ancestor.

Another great-grandfather, Francis Cromwell, was reportedly born in a town called Woodstock, but not even the state was specified. His pension application for Civil War service turned out to have false birth information. A photograph of his mother, however, included the photographer's name and town of Woodstock on the back of the photograph. This record, created by a frontier business, led to the Canadian province of Ontario, where the only Woodstock large enough to have a photographer in the 1860s was located. Francis was a farmer, not a businessman or a business employee. Thus, even for our farmer ancestors, business records can be relevant.

Business and employment records include our ancestors in at least four situations:

- As the owner of a business

- As the practitioner of a vocation (and often, therefore, an owner)

- As an employee of a business

- As a customer of a business

A researcher must pay attention to all of these situations for each ancestor. Even self-employed ancestors who kept few records and had no employees, such as farmers, can appear as customers of someone else's business. The value of employment records is especially apparent for immigrant ancestors, many of whom settled in large cities, where the nation's largest businesses were also typically located. (See chapter 19, Tracking Urban Ancestors, for information on city research.)

However, using these records can pose challenges. Business records can be very difficult to find, and those that do exist may be few and far between. To find them you must know your ancestor's location and profession. Many records no longer exist. Of those that do, some are much more complete than others, including birthplace, residence (previous and concurrent to the employment), relatives and family members, education level, and employment history. Some businesses are no longer extant, and tracking down their records becomes a challenge. Almost none of the records are indexed. Many are stored in locations that make consulting them very difficult, and many have been destroyed or lost through the years. Most business records are private, as were the businesses they bear record of. If the business is still operating, it may not allow access to its records. If the business is defunct, the records will be hard to find. Still, the kind of information and breakthrough possibilities mean that business records simply should not be overlooked.

The first step for finding and searching business records is to determine an ancestor's profession. Begin with home and family sources, obituaries and census records, and probate or perhaps property records. (See the chapters on those topics in this volume.) City directories, even in small towns, often include the employer's name in the listings. If all else fails, you should search local histories to learn what major employers were in that area for the relevant time period.

Probably your ancestor did not work for the same employer during his or her entire lifetime. Give priority to the records of the company where he or she worked the longest or to the most recent employer, because recent records are typically more complete. Other suggestions for locating pertinent records are given throughout the chapter.

Most of this chapter will deal with the specific types of records in each historical period and how to locate them, followed by a bibliography. Generally, the records fall into three time periods: colonial (to about 1780), early American (about 1780 to 1870), and modern American (about 1870 to the present). Records which fall into more than one time period are fully described under the era where they are most helpful.

COLONIAL BUSINESS AND EMPLOYMENT RECORDS

The predominance of farming as an occupation naturally limits the number of business and employment records in the colonial period. Also, the hazards of the intervening centuries limit surviving documents. But the ten to twenty percent of the colonial population involved in non-farming activities often recorded their transactions with the rest of the population. Many tradesmen had apprentices with whom they had formal written agreements, and most farmers bought some supplies or had their grain milled and lumber sawn. Often these were credit arrangements, recorded by the tradesman in an account book. Careful searching of these kinds of documents in the years before 1780 can yield important facts.

APPRENTICE RECORDS

To *indenture* is to bind one person to another for a given period of time in payment for some service. The Old World system of indenturing apprentices to learn a trade was one of the first imports to America. In colonial days most apprentices were boys in their teens, often younger than fourteen. The agreement, called an indenture, was signed by the master as well as the parent or guardian of the boy.[3] The trades were often family businesses, and many fathers formally took their sons as apprentices. (Paul Revere learned the silversmith trade from his father, and Benjamin Franklin was indentured as a printer to his brother James.)

Apprentices were usually bound until they were twenty-one, so the length of the indenture specified in the document gives an excellent indication of a boy's age. If a boy was bound to his master for twelve years and five months, for example, he was probably about eight and a half years old when the indenture was signed.

In New England it was not uncommon, especially among poorer families, for children under the age of ten to be bound out. The 1676 indenture below illustrates the kinds of genealogical and historical information available in such records:

> This Indenture witnesseth that I, Nathan Knight, sometime of Black Point, with the consent of my father-in-law, [*sic*, likely stepfather] Harry Brooken and Elend, his wife, have put myself apprentice to Samuel Whidden, of Portsmouth, in the county of Portsmouth, mason, and bound after the manner of an apprentice with him, to serve and abide the full space and term of twelve years and five months, thence next following, to be full, complete and ended; during which time the said apprentice his said master faithfully shall serve, his lawful secrets shall keep, and commands shall gladly do, damage unto his said master he shall not do, nor see to done of others, but to the best of his power shall give timely notice thereof to his said master. Fornication he shall not commit, nor contract matrimony within the said time. The goods of his said master, he shall not spend or lend. He shall not play cards, or dice, or any other unlawful game, whereby his said master may have damage in his own goods, or others, taverns, he shall not haunt, nor from his master's business absent himself by day or night, but in all things shall behave himself as a faithful apprentice ought to do. And the said master his said apprentice shall teach and instruct, or cause to be taught and instructed in the art and mystery as mason; finding unto his said apprentice during the said time meat, drink, washing, lodging, and apparel, fitting an apprentice, teaching him to read, and allowing him three months towards the latter end of his time to go to school to write, and also double the apparel at the end of said time. As witness our hands and seals, interchangeably put to two instruments of the same purpose, November the twenty-fifth, one thousand six hundred and seventy-six.[4]

If your ancestor was a tradesman, seeking out his apprenticeship could provide a wealth of information. Recently, apprenticeship records have become more available. For example, books by Kathy Ritter, *Apprentices of Connecticut 1637–1900* (Salt Lake City: Ancestry, 1986), and Harold B. Gill, Jr., *Apprentices of Virginia 1623–1800* (Salt Lake City: Ancestry, 1989), contain extracts of records long lost in archives and historical collections that identify apprentices and masters.

OTHER INDENTURE RECORDS

The most common type of indenture was probably that used to pay for passage to America. Many former prisoners from England, indentured as servants for a number of years to pay for their passage, settled in the Southern states. In most cases, children were bound out to help earn money for a family or so daughters could learn "housewifry."

An example from the Philadelphia Mayor's Office, Records of Indentures, shows several different types of indentures and the kinds of information included in each:

- Mary Stamper was to learn "Housewifry." Her mother's full name is given. Since the term of service was seven years, she was probably almost fourteen years old.

- Mary Barrett was apparently indentured to pay for passage to America, as her service lasted only one year, beginning with her arrival in America. The reference to the mayor of Cork in her indenture is a strong clue about her former residence in Ireland, a necessary fact to know before seeking her among Irish records.

- Jacob Grubb was apparently transferred from the apprenticeship of one cordwainer (shoemaker) to another.

- Mary Barbara Leichtin was bound for five years to pay a debt of twenty-one pounds, nine shillings, the cost of her passage from Rotterdam.

Indentures can also provide clues about the home or business where the person was to serve. Sometimes the original certificates of indenture still exist as well.

Less formal records of indentures are also valuable. Research on William Plaskett of Trenton, New Jersey, led to the New Jersey Archives, which has extracts of newspaper articles published between 1704 and 1780 relative to New Jersey citizens (regardless of where the paper was printed). An item extracted from the 17 September 1747 *Pennsylvania Gazette* (printed in Philadelphia) indicated that Plaskett had a bound servant named "Sarah Davis, about 27 years of age, middle stature, somewhat freckled, [who] has a small scar in her forehead, and is slow of speech." A Welshwoman, she had run away on 11 September wearing "a calico gown, a black fur hat, shagged on the upper side, with a patch on the crown, and an ozenbrigs apron."[5] This clue turned research to indenture records, which revealed that Plaskett also had another indentured servant: "Abigail Edwards (a servant from Ireland in the ship Pomona) . . . four years from Sept. 18th 1746, consideration 13L: customary dues."[6]

The fact that William Plaskett had at least two servants during the same year (1746–47) indicates his social standing. This is an example of how business records contribute important biographical information, even though no new genealogical information was located.

ACCOUNT BOOKS

Even if our ancestors did not employ others or run a business, they were dependent on other businesses for some of their daily goods. The most common and genealogically useful records of such early businesses are storekeepers' account books. The example below is from a printed account book in which the storekeeper noted family relationships to identify the individuals involved. The *d* means that the goods were delivered to that person, and *nr* means "near" or possibly "neighbor."

> Addedle (Adedle, Addle), William, June 38-Dec. 42 nr. Peter Demun of Peack; d John Brady, Andrew Jones, d to Peter Demun, Samuel Alexander, Jerry Rolandt; paid James Alexander note
>
> Adkinson, see Atkinson
>
> Ake, Jacob, Jly 35-Apr 39, son to Jerry, d to Jacob Bodine Jerry, Jly 36-Sep 39, at the Society, Peter Jarvis nr; d to Jacob Bodine
>
> Akeman (Akerman,) John, Jly 42-Jly 43, nr Samuel Alexander
>
> Akerly, Arthur, Apr. 35-May 37; & joint account with Obediah Seward[7]

Another example of the value of these records is from the set of account books of John Avery, a schoolmaster in Huntington, Long Island, from 1763 to 1779, who kept a record for each year he taught the children. Such books could be considered school records, but because most schools were privately run and the teachers paid by the students' families, these are also business records.

> Chaden. Henry: Jonathan (1770-1)
>
> Chichester. James: Jemmy (1766-7): Ephraim (1767): Sally (1767): Sarah (1767)
>
> Chichester. Joseph: schooling (betw. 1963-67)
>
> Chichester. Widow: portion of wood for schoolhouse (betw. 1963-7)
>
> Clocke. Mr. Phebe (1778)
>
> Conkline. Col. Platt: Nathaniel (1775-6)
>
> Conkline. Widow: Jacob (betw. 1763-7)
>
> Conkline. Ananias: daughter (1777)
>
> Conkling. Capt. Cornelius: Ebenezer Morgan (1767)
>
> Conkling. David: 2 children (1777): Phebe (1778): David (1778-9)
>
> Conkling. Ezekiel: Elizabeth Betsy (1776-8): Philetus (1776-8): Silas (1778)
>
> Conkling. Hubbard: Charlotte (1777): Isaac Wood (1768)
>
> Conkling. Isaac: Timothy (1767): Henry Titus (1766-7)
>
> Conkling. Jeremiah: son (1765): Jacob (1767)
>
> Conkling. John: Phebe (1770-1): Mary (1777): Sarah (1777)
>
> Conkling. Joseph: John (1768)

Conkling. Philip: Patty (1770): Bennet (1776-9):
Richard Titus (1765-6)

Conkling. Richard: Titus (1765-67)

Conkling. Richard: Jr; 2 children (1778)

Conkling. Stephen: daughter (betw. 1767)

Conkling. Thomas: Hanah (1778): Lucy (1778):
Richard Hults (1777)

Conkling. Thomas. Jr.: son (betw 1763-7): Selah
(1767-8): Esther (1767): Zophar (1767)

Conkling. Timothy: Abel (1766. 68): Ezra (1767):
Jonathan (1766-8): Timothy (1767)

Conkling. Widow. of West Neck: 2 children (1778)

Could. Ruth: 2 children (1776): Christian (1777):
William (1777)[8]

The Conkling family was a fairly large family in the Huntington area, and it is often difficult now to sort out who belongs to whom.[9] Imagine how illuminating Avery's notations about various Conkling families would be, especially since the children are linked to their parents and they can be definitely located in Huntington for the specified years. Although abstracts like these are very useful, other historical (if not genealogical) information may be found in the originals, the locations of which are mentioned in the periodical in which the abstracts appear.

OTHER RECORDS

During the colonial period, small companies were formed for various purposes, most frequently to buy land outside a township or to construct a road or a major new building within a town. These companies would formulate policy, elect officers, collect money, and delegate and supervise the work. They also kept records (usually called minutes), some of which survived and have been published. While the genealogical information in such records may be limited, they do serve to place an ancestor in a place at a particular time, and they attest to the social involvement of an ancestor. In this way they can lead to additional records for that locality.

The following examples further illustrate the wide variety of business records kept in local and state collections throughout the United States:

- The St. Louis Board of Pharmacy has preserved the records of druggists' licences from 1893 through 1909.

- The Smith-Townsend papers at the Massachusetts Historical Society include the business papers of two generations of Townsend, Massachusetts, businessmen up to 1870.

- The South Carolina Department of Archives and History has the minute book of the Carolina Narrow Gauge Railroad Company for 1872 to 1897.

- The National Archives—Pacific Sierra Region in San Bruno, California, has custom house records for the port of San Francisco.

- The Georgia Department of Archives and History has licences and bonds for selling liquor from 1850 to 1901.

- The Stevens family papers at the New Jersey Historical Society include extensive documentation on the Hoboken Land Improvement Company.

LOCATING THE RECORDS

In general, locating business records of the colonial period is less difficult than working with later records. Contact the local town clerk, librarian, or historian (through the local library or historical society) to help you determine where these records are now. Many historical societies have published detailed guides to their published and unpublished records. For example, the Historical Society of Pennsylvania has approximately five hundred volumes of business, professional, and personal account books dated as early as 1676 and covering an impressive range. These are described in *Guide to the Manuscript Collections of the Historical Society of Pennsylvania*, 2nd ed. (Philadelphia: Historical Society of Pennsylvania, 1949).

ACCOUNT BOOKS, 1676-1904. Approx. 500 vols. Presented by various persons.

Records of miscellaneous business enterprises:

Nehmiah Allen, Philadelphia merchant and cooper, account books, 1698-1736, 1 vol.

Andrews and Meredith, merchants and shippers, invoice book, 1794-95, 1 vol.

Isaac Archer, business and personal receipt book, 1795-1841, 1 Vol.

Joseph Archer, engaged in Canton silk, rice, tea trade, letter books, 1833-34, 2 vols.

William Armstrong, merchant and army contractor, receipt book, 1778, 1 vol.

William H. Ashurst, Philadelphia merchant, receipt book, 1839-44, 1 vol.

Aurora, office account book, 1822-24, 2 vols.

Backhouse, Jones and Backhouse, Philadelphia merchants, raccoon and beaver skins, ledger, 1773-75, 1 vol.

Robert and Francis Bailey, Philadelphia printers, day book, 1794-97, waste book, 1794-1829, memorandum book, 1795-1811, journal, 1799-1856, 4 vols.

Robert Bailey, Philadelphia liver oil merchant, fish and general merchandise, letter book, 1796-1807, 1 vol.

Abel Baker and William Sill, general merchants, whiskey, shoes, tobacco, muslin, ledger, 1813-15, 1 vol.

Charles H. Baker, account book, 1812, letter book, 1812-13, 2 vols.

John and Samuel Baker, receipt book, 1786-95, 1 vol.

John R. Baker, receipt book, 1824-29, 1 vol.[10]

This society also has a volume of Philadelphia Insurance Company records (item 1019 in the *Guide to the Manuscript Collections of the Historical Society of Pennsylvania*), Philadelphia Dancing Assembly Records from 1749 (item 1015), and other business records. "The Descriptive Inventory of the Archives of the City and County of Philadelphia," a loose-leaf finding aid updated regularly by the staff, is replete with references to apprenticeship and indenture records, including an indexed volume as early as 1751–87.

Almost every manuscript collection has some kind of guide to indicate its contents. If the collection has been microfilmed by the Genealogical Society of Utah, it can be found in the *Family History Library Catalog* under the locality the record concerns and is available on loan through its family history centers. Thus, indentures for Spotsylvania County, Virginia, would be found under that county in the catalog. Often, records of areas neighboring an ancestor's residence are also helpful.

In New York City, the minutes of the Civil Court Quarter Sessions contain petitions of release from apprentices whose masters have moved from the town. Indenture records of passengers to America are usually in the city where the ship landed—such port cities as Philadelphia, Baltimore, and New York.

More and more colonial business records are being published, either as books or as articles in periodicals. A diligent genealogist will search carefully through the back issues of the county, state, and regional publications for the area he or she is searching. In this regard the *Genealogical Periodical Annual Index* (*GPAI*) or *Periodical Source Index* (*PERSI*) may be helpful. See chapter 2, Databases, Indexes, and other Finding Aids, for more details.

EARLY AMERICAN BUSINESS RECORDS, 1780–1870

All of the business records discussed in the previous section carry forward into the early American time period, from 1780 to 1870. Apprenticeship continued into the twentieth century and, in some forms, up to the present. Account books are still kept today, although they are usually less helpful to the genealogist because of the abundance of other sources. Indentures became less common during the first half of the nineteenth century and rarely appear in later years.

American society remained largely agrarian in the nineteenth century, but more businesses were created, nurtured by the *laissez-faire* policy of the government; thus, more ancestors will appear in contemporary business records. Insurance companies began keeping voluminous records, simple account books evolved into credit reporting agencies, and an increasingly large professional class began generating more records. The records associated with these businesses are the major new sources in this time period.

INSURANCE RECORDS

Prior to 1843, a few attempts were made to develop life insurance programs, but only one, the Presbyterian Ministers Fund, established in 1758, continues to function. However, as more Americans left the relative security of the farm, life insurance became more popular. Other kinds of insurance societies thrived, notably fire and marine insurance. The growth of cities, however, led directly to the establishment of life insurance companies.[11] Sixteen major life insurance companies formed between 1843 and 1852 survived until at least 1942. Nineteen more had been founded by 1875. (See table 10-1.)

The nature of life insurance makes such records very interesting for a genealogist. Early insurance contracts were brief and loosely worded, but they did contain certain kinds of information about their clients. Even then, policy holders had to

provide information about their lifestyle, health, age, residence, and relatives (notably the beneficiaries). By 1865, medical information on diseases or health conditions was included, and in 1889 Mutual Life began attaching a medical examination to the policy.[12]

Because life insurance is usually paid after the death of the insured, companies need to keep their records for many years. To protect themselves legally, most companies kept their records long past the death of the insured. For many years most companies had no policy on discarding records. When one company (apparently Connecticut Mutual Life[13]) was preparing to move into a new home office around 1925, it decided to design a records retention policy. Its policy, as of 1941, suggests what materials other life insurance companies might have retained. For historical reasons, all correspondence from the company's first twenty years was kept.

- Applications, which were the basis for the insurance contract, are kept while the policy is in force. Applications not approved are destroyed after ten years, and the application of a deceased policy holder is destroyed after twenty years.

- The abstract, or history, cards are retained permanently. These cards contain a summary history of each account.

- Other records kept permanently include account or renewal cards (records of premium payments), accumulated dividend cards, canceled checks and bank statements, cash books, directors' minutes and committee records, ledgers, payrolls, and real estate records. Because older records are the most likely to be discarded, it is wise to search relevant records as soon as possible.

The application is most useful for genealogical purposes because it contains most of the personal information. Some companies keep original applications permanently or microfilm them. Even if the application is discarded, other records may be helpful in providing relevant information about residence, health, age, etc.

In 1910, one company realized it had lost contact with a considerable number of policy holders or their beneficiaries to whom large sums of money were due. It undertook systematic, often lengthy, searches to find those heirs. Their files are very valuable to the family historian who finds an ancestor or relative in them.[14]

Although most insurance companies still exist under some name or another, many are unwilling to search their large files for a family historian. However, you can offer to search yourself; be prepared to show proof of descent from the person. Most of these records are in corporate archives, and a pleasant letter to the home office may help locate the desired materials. A current agent of the company may help you gain access to old records.

Several examples of how to use life insurance records to help reconstruct families are in Duane Galles, "Using Life Insurance Policies in Genealogical Research," *Genealogical Journal* 20 (1992): 156–71.

The most common way of learning which company insured your ancestor is to contact living family members. Old insurance certificates or personal account books among family papers may also provide this information. Although these may be among the most difficult records to pursue, they are also among the most helpful.

Table 10-1. Life Insurance Companies in Business by 1876 and Still Operating in 1942

Name of Company	Home Office	Date of Commencing Business	Name of Company	Home Office	Date of Commencing Business
Presbyterian Ministers' Fund	Philadelphia	1759	Home Life Insurance Co.	New York City	1 May 1860
Mutual Life Insurance Co. of New York	New York City	1 Feb. 1843	Germania Life Insurance Co. (name changed to Guardian Life Insurance Co. of America, 1918)	New York City	16 July 1860
New England Mutual Insurance	Boston, Mass.	1 Dec. 1843			
Mutual Benefit Life Insurance Co.	Newark, N.J.	1 April 1845	John Hancock Mutual Life Insurance Co.	Boston	27 Dec. 1862
New York Life Insurance Co.	New York City	12 April 1845	Maryland Life Insurance Co.	Baltimore	12 July 1865
State Mutual Life Assurance Co.	Worcester, Mass.	1 June 1845	Provident Life and Trust Co. of Philadelphia (name changed to Provident Mutual Life Insurance Co. of Philadelphia, 1908)	Philadelphia	31 July 1865
Connecticut Mutual Life Insurance Co.	Hartford, Conn.	15 Dec. 1846			
Penn Mutual Life Insurance Co.	Philadelphia	25 May 1847			
Union Mutual Life Insurance Co.	Portland, Maine	1 Oct. 1849	Connecticut General Life Insurance Co.	Hartford, Conn.	October 1865
National Life Insurance Co.	Montpelier, Vt.	1 Feb. 1850	Travelers Insurance Co.	Hartford, Conn.	October 1865
U.S. Life Insurance Co.	New York City	4 Mar. 1850	Metropolitan Life Insurance Co.	New York City	January 1867
Aetna Life Insurance Co.	Hartford, Conn.	July 1850	Equitable Life Insurance Co. of Iowa	Des Moine, Iowa	March 1867
Manhattan Life Insurance Co.	New York City	1 Aug. 1850	Union Central Life Insurance Co.	Cincinnati	1867
Phoenix Nutual Life Insurance Co.	Hartford, Conn.	May 1851	Pacific Mutual Life Insurance Co.	Louisiana, Calif.	April 1868
Massachusetts Mutual Life Insurance Co.	Springfield, Mass.	1 Aug. 1851	Masonic Mutual Relief Association (name changed to Monumental Life Insurance Co., 1935)	Washington, D.C.	3 March 1869
Berkshire Life Insurance Co.	Pittsfield, Mass.	4 Sep. 1851			
German Mutual Life Insurance Co. (name changed to Mutual Life Insurance Co., 1919)	St. Louis	12 Apr. 1858	Mutual Life Insurance of Baltimore	Baltimore	1870
			Pennsylvania Mutual Insurance Co.	Philadelphia	1870
Northwestern Mutual Life Insurance Co.	Milwaukee	25 Nov. 1858	Life Insurance Co. of Virginia	Richmond, Va.	April 1871
Equitable Life Assurance Society of the United States	New York City	28 July 1859	Prudential Insurance Co. of America	Newark, N.J.	13 Oct. 1875

Source: Shepard B. Clough, *A Century of American Life Insurance: A History of the Mutual Life Company of New York, 1843–1943* (New York: Columbia University Press, 1946), 30, 46.

CREDIT REPORTING AGENCIES

During the nineteenth century, most businessmen and business-women purchased goods from suppliers with whom they were not personally acquainted. Credit was common, but suppliers needed to determine the credit worthiness of businesses. In 1841, the Mercantile Agency, the first commercial credit-reporting company, was launched. Later known as R. G. Dun and Company, it dominates the credit reporting field even today as Dun and Bradstreet. By the early 1850s, it employed 2,000 correspondents in the United States and Canada who sent semiannual credit reports about business people in their areas to the New York Office.

Dun's 1841–90 ledger books are deposited in Baker Library at Harvard University; they comprise 2,580 volumes arranged by county. The reports almost always indicated the subject's occupation, net worth, value of real and personal estate, and business prospects. Many reports also include age, marital status, former residence, personal character, and family background. The best information is from the 1850 to 1880 period. Usually, only those likely to apply for credit are represented. Since accuracy was vital to Dun's subscribers, the reports provide reliable data.[15]

These records are available to serious, scholarly researchers at Baker Library. The staff cannot search the files in response to inquiries, so be prepared to visit the library in person, or hire a local researcher. Some indexes may be difficult to use, but, if your ancestor was a merchant or businessman in this time period, a wealth of information may well be available. Permission from Dun and Bradstreet is necessary before publishing material from this source, but such permission is not difficult to obtain; write a letter to the company's public relations officer. For a more detailed history of early credit reporting, see James H. Madison, "The Evolution of Commercial Credit Reporting Agencies in Nineteenth Century America," *Business History Review* 48 (1974): 164–86.

THE PROFESSIONS AND TRADES

Between 1780 and 1870, more and more of our ancestors became ministers, lawyers, doctors, or other professionals; more of them also entered the various trades. Such occupations generated valuable records. (See chapter 11, Research in Directories.) Histories and directories of such occupations in a specific area are valuable sources. Compiled from several sources, they usually contain secondary information rather than primary, but they are generally carefully prepared by professional historians.

Clergy

Most ministerial records are kept by the archives of each denomination. A great deal of information may be included in these records, especially if they are relatively recent or if the minister drew a pension. Some denominations have published directories of their ministers. Old editions of directories or historical directories, such as the following example, can give important biographical and genealogical information about an ancestor who was an ordained clergyman or notable church layman.

> **Brinkman, Benjamin F., b Graafschap, Mich, May 3, 1863. WTS, 1906. Ord United Presby. Pas Second, Englewood, Chicago, Ill 1906-10; Second, Pella, Ia 1911-17; fin agt Central**

> **1917-20; pas Calvary Cleveland, 1920-21. d Cleveland, Mar 5, 1921.**

> **Breck, John Randlett, b Newbury, Vt, jun, 1831, s of Jacob R. AB, Rutgers C, 1859; NBTS, 1862. Lic Cl Passic, 1862; ord Cl Paramus, 1862. Pas West New Hempstead, N.Y. 1862-65; Spring Valley, N.Y. 1865-69; tchr 1869-71. d Marysville, Tenn Aug 7, 1872.**

> **Brocklos, Albert. Received Presby 1911; pas Ave B, NYC 1911-13; dismissed Meth Ch 1914.**

> **Brodhead, Jacob, b Marbletown, N.Y.,May 14, 1782, s of Charles W. AB. Union C, 1801; NBTS 1804; ord Cl Poughkeepsie, 1804. Pas Rhinebeck Flats, N.Y. 1804-09; Collegiate, NYC 1809-13; Crown St, Philadelphia, Pa 1813-26; Broome St, NYC 1826-37; Flatbush, Ulster Co, N.Y. 1837-41; Central, Brooklyn. N.Y. 1841-46. Pres Gen Syn, 1816-17 and 1825-26. d Springfield, Mass Jun 6, 1855.[16]**

The current edition of the annual *The Yearbook of American and Canadian Churches* (Nashville: Abingdon Press) is the most helpful source for locating the central headquarters of most denominations. (See chapter 6, Research in Church Records.) It may also help determine the present name of a church which has merged with others. It also includes lists of "Depositories of Church History Material and Sources," arranged by denomination, with an appended "Standard Guides to Church Archives."

Lawyers and Judges

Legal professionals have occupied prominent positions in our society for the last two hundred years. Since they deal with the public trust, they have long been registered in many cities and very early established the bar as a means of determining qualifications. The most easily accessed records of the law profession are, again, printed sources. In most states and many large cities and counties, books have been written on "The Bench and Bar of . . ." These books contain biographical information on those practicing law in a locality at the time of and prior to publication. *Martins's Bench and Bar of Philadelphia* (Philadelphia: Rees Welsh and Co., 1883), for example, includes reference to most attorneys who ever practiced in Philadelphia and many colonial lawyers who worked anywhere in Pennsylvania. It also includes an alphabetical list of all those admitted to practice in the courts of Philadelphia, both city and county, including death dates and ages at death for those no longer living at the time of publication (figure 10-1). Books of this type have been published since the late 1800s for most states and major cities, as well as some counties. Several statewide titles are identified in the chapter bibliography.

Another valuable source for lawyers is *Martindale-Hubbell Law Directory* (Martindale, N.J.: Martindale-Hubbell), an annual publication which lists nearly every practicing lawyer in the country. Predecessors of this directory were first published in the 1860s. While most public libraries have only recent editions, many law libraries retain the earliest copies. This source gives some biographical information, as well as residence and affiliation with a law firm.

Figure 10-1. From John Hill Martin, *Martin's Bench and Bar of Philadelphia* (Philadelphia: Rees Welsh and Co., 1883), 243.

The Philadelphia Bar.

Being a List of the names of gentlemen who have been admitted to practice, as Attorneys-at-law in the County Courts of the City and County of Philadelphia, from 1682 to 1883, with the dates of their admission.

Abbreviations—A–age at death. ADM.–for admitted to practice. ATTY-GEN.–Attorney General. B–for born. B. G. or BRIG. GEN.–for Brigadier General. C. J–Chief Justice. Co.–for county. COL. OF VOLS.–Colonel of volunteers, 1861-65. COL.–before christian name, colonel of militia. C. P.–for Common Pleas C. R.–Colonial Records. D–for died. D. C–for District Court. DIRECT'RY–for Philadelphia Directory. IN. PRAC.–for in practice J.–Judge. J. C. P.–Judge of the Common Pleas. J. O. C.–Associate Judge of the Orphans Court. M. C.–for Member of Congress. M. G.–Major General. PA.–for Pennsylvania. P. V.–Pennsylvania Volunteers, 1861-65. PA. MAG–Pennsylvania Magazine. P. J.–President Judge. Q. M. G.–for Quarter-Master-General. S. C.–for Supreme Court of Pennsylvania U. S.–for United States. U. S. C. C.–for United States Circuit Court. U. S. S. C.–for United States Supreme Court. * Name from Sheriff's Deed Book B, which is the date of admission in the Supreme Court, which I have used where an earlier date could not be found.

Abbett, Benjamin Franklin,		Jan. 25, 1868
Edwin L.,		Dec. 5, 1864
Leonidas,		Feb. 5, 1857
Abbey, William Burling,		Nov. 4, 1876
Abbott, Montelius,	*d. May 18, 1877, a. 38*	June 21, 1862
William Holloway,		July 13, 1844
Abrams (Rev.) Joseph,	*d. Mch 30, 1881, a. 69*	Nov. 2, 1839
Joseph Addison,		Nov. 30, 1878
Ackley, John Edward,		Dec. 13, 1879
Ackworth, Edmund,[1]	*Chester Co. Records*	Feb. 23, 1741
John,	*d. Dec. 14, 1744*	Before 1744
Adams, Frederick Mayhew,		Jan. 22, 1847
George Bethune,		Mch 2, 1878
John Bell,	*d. Jan. 4, 1874*	Mch 13, 1855
John,		Nov. 1, 1879
John Quincy,		May 3, 1856
Josiah Robert,		Dec. 5, 1874
Robert, Jr.,		Apl 27, 1872
Thomas Boylston,[2]	*Judge, d. 1832, a. 60*	Dec. 7, 1793

Doctors

Similar directories and biographical sketch books exist in some areas for doctors and surgeons (see the chapter bibliography). They, too, were often registered by the city; such certificates or licenses should be sought in city, county, and state archives. The Pennsylvania State Archives, for example, has medical licenses from 1894 and dental licenses from 1897. Earlier licenses are found in county archives.

The American Medical Association has been gathering information since the late 1800s on the personal and professional background of licensed medical practitioners. Its collection includes information on more than 350,000 doctors who practiced in the United States from as early as 1804 through 1969, although records prior to 1907 are incomplete. Arrangements have been made for this file to be microfilmed by the Family History Library, after which the original cards will be deposited with the National Genealogical Society. Almost 150,000 deceased doctors are listed in the two-volume *Directory of Deceased American Physicians: 1804–1929* (Chicago: American Medical Association).

Artisans

Artisans, writers, and skilled tradesmen are also the subject of biographical sketches in collective biographies. The example below of a silversmith in Staunton, Virginia, is from an excellent book-length study of local professions.

C. E. EVARD & BROTHER opened a "New Jewellery and Watch Establishment" in Staunton in June 1849. There were two persons in the silversmith and jewelry business in this vicinity who might have been the principle in this firm. Charles Eugene Evard of Winchester and Charles Edward Evard of Leesburg. This was undoubtedly the Leesburg jeweler, for the same illustration was used in the advertising in Staunton and Leesburg. The name of the brother is unknown. This firm advertised clocks, watches, and jewelry repaired, and warranted at its shop, one door above M. Cushing's Confectionery Store. On July 9, following, the firm had just received from their manufactory a large supply of "silver Table and Tea Spoons, also Dessert and Salt Spoons, Sugar Tongs, Butter Knives, all superior articles and manufactured especially to order. . . . The public generally are informed that the subscribers will sell all kinds of jewellery and spoons much lower than the Baltimore prices." How long this firm continued in business here is not definitely known, but on March 1, 1850,

C. E. Evard announced to the public of Leesburg that he had returned to and permanently located himself in Leesburg; so that the firm did business in Staunton not longer than nine months."[17]

Similar books are available for many of the early states. See the chapter bibliography for other occupational histories.

BIOGRAPHICAL DICTIONARIES

An ancestor need not have been exclusively engaged in an occupation to be included in a biographical dictionary. Many people who achieved some prominence in a vocation are profiled in biographical dictionaries. For example, Mary Q. Elliott, *Biographical Sketches of Knox County (Ohio) Writers* (Mount Vernon, Ohio: 1937), included a brief sketch of James Blair, a local farmer who wrote poems that were occasionally published in local newspapers. The sketch indicated that Blair originally came from Blairs Valley, Washington County, Maryland. Subsequent research in Blairs Valley extended the line two more generations. A variety of specialized sources are available, such as the *Biographical Directory of Railway Officials of America*, published since 1885.

Robert B. Slocum, *Biographical Dictionaries and Related Works,* 2 vols. (Detroit: Gale Research Co., 1986), lists dozens of books about authors and others distinguished by their vocations. Indeed, Slocum's entire second volume is a list of vocational collective biographies.

Many collective biographies are not specifically tied to a particular vocation. Rather, several sets profile major figures in American history. Many of these individuals were prominent businessmen. Major national collective biographies include the *Dictionary of American Biography* (first published in 1922), the *National Cyclopedia of American Biography,* and a wide variety of "who's who" publications. The *Cyclopedia* was begun in 1898 by the James T. White Company of New York to give biographical coverage to business leaders, especially young men from the West, with information supplied by the subjects themselves.

Most of these nationwide dictionaries are indexed in *Biography and Genealogy Master Index*, discussed in chapter 2. It is easy to check and is available in most research libraries.

FREEDMEN BANK RECORDS

Among the most useful sources for tracing African Americans for the period immediately after the Civil War are the records from the various branches of the *Freedman's Savings and Trust Company*. Chartered by Congress in 1865 to benefit former slaves, branches of this bank were established throughout the South and in some northern states. The branches kept registers of depositors with some personal and family information. While the information varied from branch to branch, it often included name, age, birthplace, residence, name of former master and of parents, spouse, children, and siblings. These registers have been microfilmed through 1874 by the National Archives on twenty-seven rolls of microfilm (series M816). A forty-two-volume index is available on five rolls of microfilm (series M817).

OTHER RECORDS

An ancestor need not be prominent to be included in a business record. Many people were recorded by cities because of their occupations. An 1863 register of prostitutes compiled by the Guardians of the Poor in Philadelphia is remarkable for its completeness. It includes information about these women's ages, length of time in the city, literacy, marital status, number of children, how long and why they were involved in the profession, other trades they held, parents' occupations, and when, why, and from where they emigrated. Often, parents' or siblings' names were also recorded. Despite the uniqueness of such a record, it illustrates the eclectic nature of such records. If a local government was interested in a particular occupation, there are likely to be records among the archives of that government.

A wide range of information is available on other occupations that we might not expect to find documented. For example, the Pennsylvania State Archives houses applications for teaching certificates from 1866, a Register of Pilots' Homes and Securities for 1783 to 1876, Philadelphia licenses for peddlers and hawkers from 1820 to 1838, and tavern licenses applied for and granted from 1750 to 1855.[18]

LOCATING THE RECORDS

Much of what was stated about locating colonial records applies to the 1780–1870 period. Original manuscript records are usually found in local or state archives, historical societies, and university manuscript collections. Unlike colonial records, however, very few have been published, although guides to the collections and/or the archives that house them are often available. For example, some twelve pages in *The Guide to Genealogical Sources at the Pennsylvania State Archives* describe various collections which they have designated as "occupational records."

MODERN BUSINESS AND EMPLOYMENT RECORDS, 1870–PRESENT

With the conclusion of the Civil War and the reunification of the country, American business began to grow rapidly. As businesses grew, so did their records. Only two to six ancestors may have been in the labor force around the year 1900, but odds are that half of them were either working for someone else (hence employed) or in business for themselves (thus creating their own business records). By 1880, farming involved only fifty percent of the work force, and even farming activities were more regularly documented. In difficult research problems, the records of collateral "ancestors" and siblings of an ancestor should not be overlooked.

Several topics are relevant to researching modern business records—most notably, procedures for locating such records. Corporations and governments began keeping more complete records, and several valuable new types of records were begun, including records of labor unions, railroads, schools, mortuaries, and the Social Security system.

Obviously, knowledge of an ancestor's employer is crucial to this research. Again, family members and home records are the best initial sources of information. Photographs in family records, even unidentified ones, often show owners and employees of local shops and mercantile businesses standing in front of the company sign.

Most residential directories (both city and rural) include the employer's name for each listing. It does not matter if the ancestor lived in a small town or a large city, as directories exist for most areas. The extract below from the 1922 directory of Missoula, Montana, then considered a small town, shows the kind of information you can expect.

> Sterriet George H. lab Missoula White P S Co. h rear 601 Phillips
>
> Stetson Harry E, mail carrier R F D 2
>
> Stevens Clare, appr G A Meisinger, r 1529 De Foe
>
> Stevens Harry H, driver, h 208 S 3rd W
>
> Stevens John M, carmn N O Ry, r 117 N 2n W
>
> Stevens Lyman W brkmn N P Ry, r 117 N 2n W
>
> Stevens Russell, student, r 405 S 1st W
>
> Stevenson Derrick, moved to Boxeman, Mont
>
> Stewart C Donald, clk C M & St P Ry, h 246 Edith
>
> Stewart Dee, chauf H L Haines, r 314 W Railroad
>
> Stewart Fleming K, surveyor Forest Service, r Grand Hotel
>
> Stewart Jas A, firemn N P Ry, h 402 W Cedar
>
> Stewart Leighton, formn N P Ry, h 1520 S 7th W
>
> Stewart R D, clk, h Orchard Homes R F D 1
>
> Stewart Thomas, car opr, h Orchard Homes R F D 4
>
> Stewart Wm m, mgr Traffic Service Vureau, h Rattlesnake
>
> Sticht Bert, lab Anton Vogt & Sons, h East Missoula
>
> Sticht Glenn, lab Anton Vogt & Sons, h East Missoula[19]

Note that both the occupation and employer are given. The Northern Pacific Railroad (NPR) appears to have been a major employer. Bert and Glenn Sticht are laborers for Anton Vogt and Sons. This valuable information had never been mentioned to the Sticht family historian by older members of the family.

Local history sources can also identify business firms a relative may have been associated with. Centennial histories or local scrapbooks published in special sections of the newspaper or issued separately for distribution at local celebrations often carry lists of historical businesses pursued by local families.

LABOR UNIONS

As American business grew, so did the desire of employees for better working conditions, and labor unions were created. Because the purpose of labor unions is the improvement of employment conditions, accurate membership records are vital. Many unions have preserved volumes of records which may contain information relevant to your research. A description of the potential treasures vividly suggests the possibilities: "The ITU (International Typographical Union) Headquarters Basement is comprised of a labyrinth of corridors. Each corridor is replete with shelves, filing cabinets, boxes, etc. I would imagine an archivist would be delirious with joy to be [loosed] in this musty atmosphere."[20] This description was part of an excellent 1960 survey conducted by the Society of American Archivists' Committee on Labor Records. Their findings are the result of a survey sent to 265 organizations, of which 118—forty-five percent—responded. Thus, their information represents about half of the labor organizations in the country. It is unfortunate that several major unions,

such as the United Automobile Workers, International Ladies Garment Workers, United Mine Workers, Teamsters, and most railroad and building trade unions, did not reply.

The article in which the survey was published—Paul Lewinson and Morris Rieger, Labor Union Records in the United State," *American Archivist* 25 (January 1963): 46–57—answers several questions about the unions covered and suggests what records the non-responding unions might have. Although the original survey did not ask about membership records, many of the responses mentioned such information. The earliest records and the quality of records also provide clues to the scope of their holdings.

Obviously, you need to know the union and the local to which an ancestor belonged before researching this source, but often the union can be deduced by occupation if family sources lack this information. An ancestor's residence or employer's name may be sufficient for a helpful union secretary to determine the relevant local for members working in that area, and they may know the history of the union at that company.

If your ancestor was active in one of the twentieth-century trade or labor unions, the Archives of Labor at Wayne State University in Detroit, Michigan, may have information about him or her. They hold the records of many officers and rank and file leaders who participated in the two principal collecting areas of that archive: labor history (predominately twentieth century), with special emphasis on industrial unionism and urban history, especially twentieth-century reform groups. The holdings include records of the American Federation of State, County, and Municipal Employees; American Federation of Teachers, Newspaper Guild; Union of Farm Workers; Industrial Workers of the World; and Congress of Industrial Organizations (CIO) prior to its merger with the American Federation of Labor (AFL). Consult Warner Pflug, *A Guide to the Archives of Labor History and Urban Affairs* (Detroit: Wayne State University Press, 1974) for details. Most records will be at union or local headquarters, but some may have been deposited in local archives. The Library of Congress's *National Union Catalogue of Manuscript Collections* includes labor union records, including some membership lists of union locals. (See "Locating Modern Business Records," below.)

The *National Union Catalogue of Manuscript Collections* includes labor union records, including some membership lists of union locals. (See "Locating Modern Business Records," below.)

RAILROAD EMPLOYEES

The special status of railroading in America has been recognized in several ways. Railroad workers of the twentieth century received special Social Security numbers (the first three, or area, numbers 700–729 until 1964) and their own pension plan. As many as two and a quarter million people worked for the railroad companies at their peak around 1920. Furthermore, many railroad company records are easily located.

A *Biographical Directory of Railway Officials of America* (New York: Simmons-Boardman) was issued periodically during the nineteenth century. The California State Railroad Museum Library, 111 I St., Sacramento, CA 95814, has copies for 1885, 1906, 1913, and 1922. The same library also has some fifty drawers of employment cards for the Southern Pacific Railroad dating back to 1903.

To determine which railroads merged with any other major service, consult *Moody's Transportation Manual*, issued annually by Moody's Investors Service, Inc., 99 Church St., New York, NY 10007. Current and back issues are available at most public and research libraries.

An ancestor who received a pension from certain railroad lines should be on record at the Railroad Retirement Board, 844 N. Rush St., Chicago, IL 60611-2092. The board is very helpful in answering requests for information if you can provide the employee's name, position, the railroad worked for, and where and when employed. There is a fee for a search, whether successful or not.

COLLEGES AND UNIVERSITIES

Although not usually considered business records as such, personnel and student files of colleges and universities and the records of civil and military personnel of the United States government are also of genealogical value.

There are 1,700 four-year colleges and 1,000 junior colleges in the United States today, many of them dating from before 1850; more then 1,300 of them have historical archives. Today these institutions of higher learning employ 730,000 faculty members and enroll more than 10,000,000 students. Some faculty and student records, such as the matriculation records of Harvard College from 1636, have been published.[21] For addresses and telephone numbers consult Rod Nordland, *Names and Numbers; a Journalists Guide to the Most Needed Information Sources and Contacts* (New York: John Wiley and Sons, 1978), 263–77, or the current *American Library Directory*, published biannually by R.R. Bowker Company of New York.

U.S. GOVERNMENT PERSONNEL

Personnel files retained by the federal government for employees and civil service personnel, 1860 to 1951, have surpassed 60 million. These are available for research, with some restrictions on files dealing with living persons. Some files require invoking the Freedom of Information Act for access. Claire Prechtel-Kluskens, "Documenting the Career of Federal Employees," *Prologue* 26 (Fall 1994): 180–85, explains the difficult yet potentially fruitful task of searching government personnel records.

SMALL BUSINESSES

If your ancestor owned a small business, there may be a record of the business license in the city or state where he or she did business. The application for a license should include a variety of information, such as age, birthplace, marital status, and residence, depending on when the license was applied for.

The number of employees of small businesses has typically varied greatly, but is often less than twenty and sometimes only two or three. Typically they were friends or relatives of the owner, and few, if any, personal records were kept. Payroll records, however, might have been preserved. If the business still exists, try contacting the present owner for information and records. In some cases, he or she may be a relative of the previous owner and may have been a child when the ancestor worked there. (Records of defunct businesses are discussed at the end of this chapter.)

CORPORATIONS

Big businesses employ a large portion of the labor force and typically have kept better employee records for longer periods. Also, these companies are more likely still to be in business, making it easier to locate their records. The information recorded will vary greatly, but it is more important to discuss how to locate those records than to describe what you may find. Before beginning research into a corporation's records, you should do some basic background research: read the company history (if there is one), check periodicals for articles, or request reading suggestions from its public relations office. Showing an interest in and knowledge of the company will make it easier for the company to help you.

Major U.S. companies, such as those listed in the Fortune 500 (*Fortune* magazine's annual list), have records commensurate with their size. When *Fortune* started rating companies in 1954, its "Five Hundred" employed approximately 8 million people, or approximately twelve percent of the labor force.[22] Currently, *Fortune* also rates a second five hundred, as well as separate lists of fifty top businesses in seven different service categories, leaving the first and second five hundred as industrial (not service) companies. This creates a total of 1,350 businesses ranked by *Fortune*. In 1981, they employed more than 33 million people—almost one-third of the total American work force. The complete *Fortune* listing is available in most public libraries. Many of these companies have substantial archives to house their historical records. Others have deposited their records in local libraries and historical societies. The section "Locating Modern Business Records," below, describes how to find some of these archives and collections.

PENSIONS

Most major corporations have developed pension plans, which require significant information about each employee, even after they have died. While the pension plan is primarily a twentieth-century concept, many of the persons recorded were born in the late nineteenth century, often before birth records were kept. The records should include the employee's full name, birth and death information, places of residence, parents and/or spouses, and children's names and birth information. Often, children or siblings were employed by the same corporation, especially when it was one of the major employers in a locality. Unfortunately, pension records for living persons are seldom available; if the search subject is deceased, the records may or may not be made available to researchers.

SOCIAL SECURITY

One of the largest groups of employment records in the world are those of the U.S. Social Security system. These records are fairly recent, since the Social Security Administration was formed in 1936, and records of living persons are restricted. With proof of death, you can obtain records of deceased persons, even if you are not directly related. In some situations, you can obtain information on a living person as well.

The greatest benefit of these records may be that applicants for Social Security are required to provide complete birth information. The early Social Security files include many people born in the 1850s, 1860s, 1870s, and later. This group includes naturalized citizens. The information on a person's specific birthplace may not be recorded anywhere else. This is especially true for people naturalized before 1906, when detailed birth information was not required for naturalization.

If a person lived past about 1936, he or she may have a Social Security file (some payments were made as early as 1940). Although the Social Security Administration has issued approximately 330 million numbers since 1936, the numbers have not always been as common as they are today. (Since 1988, a child more than two years of age must have a Social Security number to be claimed as a dependent on an income tax form). Until recently, government employees, some other people with separate retirement plans, and non-employed persons, including many wives, did not need Social Security numbers. These also included many self-employed persons, including farmers, into the 1960s. However, the chances are still great that a recent ancestor or relative had a Social Security number.

In order to enroll in the system, the applicant completes an "Application for Social Security Number" form, also known as an SS-5 form. This form has changed over time, but usually it required the applicant to provide his or her full name (including maiden name), complete birth date and place, parents' complete names, his or her own and employer's address when the form was filled out, and the date completed.

The Social Security Administration has microfilmed the application forms and computerized some of the information on the forms. After review of the microfilm, the forms were destroyed (by agreement with the archivist of the United States) because of the volume of the original records.

REQUESTING INFORMATION

If you provide proof of death (usually a death certificate) and the person's Social Security number (see below), you can obtain information from the SS-5 form. Most requests are answered with a printout from the computerized database. Note that the complete information from the forms was *not* entered into the database. Only the birth date, state or country of birth, place of residence, and employer were entered. However, name changes of married women appear on the printout, as do changes of residence. Therefore, be sure you request both a copy of the printout and the original SS-5 form. There is a fee for this service, but do not include money with your request; you will be billed. Many local offices of the Social Security Administration will search the computer database while you wait, but this appears to be a local office policy. Of course, they can only provide the information in the database, if any at all, so you will need to write for the SS-5 form.

Requests for information about living persons are generally restricted to that person or to someone who has the written consent of the living individual. Such requests are considered on a case-by-case basis and will require good cause. A judge's order may be necessary.

The Social Security Administration has a letter-forwarding service for use if the matter is of great importance to the person being sought. This includes notification of serious illness of a family member or if the person is due a sizeable amount of money. For such requests, write a letter to the person and place it in a plain, unstamped, unsealed envelope and send it to the Social Security Administration. The letter will be read and considered and, if appropriate, will be sent to the person's last known employer. There is no fee for letters with a humanitar-

ian purpose, but letters informing the missing person of property or money require a fee for searching the records.

No specific form is required for any request. Write a short letter that includes the name and Social Security number of the person for whom information is needed, the type of information requested, and the reason. Write to the Social Security Administration, Freedom of Information Officer, 4-H-8 Annex Building, 6401 Security Blvd., Baltimore, MD 21235. It may take several weeks to process your request, but don't give up. If the person is dead, the Freedom of Information Act gives you the right to this information. Even the Social Security number itself gives you a clue to the ancestor's residence: the first three digits of the number indicate the state where the number was applied for. For a state-by-state guide to Social Security numbers see chapter 18, Tracking Twentieth-Century Ancestors.

FINDING THE SOCIAL SECURITY NUMBER

Any requests made to the Social Security Administration should include the person's Social Security number. The death certificate is the best source of this information. The number may also appear on records held by the family, such as insurance policies, identification cards, passports, and pension and employment papers. Another excellent source is the Social Security Death Index, described in chapter 2. Ask family members if they have the number. Some local government records, such as voter lists, tax rolls, and driver's licenses, may include the number. Private companies, such as funeral homes and credit reporting agencies, often have the number. Local Social Security office personnel may be able to find the number in their computer database, but they may not share it with the public. If necessary, you can make your request without the number, but the search will cost more and may not locate the right person. In such cases you must provide identifying information for the person you seek, including the person's date and place of birth and parents' full names.

MORTUARY RECORDS

During the contemporary period, almost all of our ancestors have been recorded in one final business record: that of the local mortician. These records can be very complete and include information not found elsewhere. In the case of an Irish mining family in upstate New York, the mortuary records of two sons' burials in 1939 and 1942 provided the most important clues to their origins.

In most cases the mortician is named either on the death certificate, the sexton's burial records, or in the obituary, if not all three. To locate a particular mortuary or any mortuary in a particular town, consult *The Yellow Book of Funeral Directors* or the *National Directory of Morticians* (figure 10-2). Either of these directories should be available from your local funeral director.

If these directories are not available at the local public library, consult a local mortician. Often, if a mortuary went out of business, it was purchased by another mortuary and its records were transferred to the new company.

IDENTIFYING AND LOCATING MODERN BUSINESS RECORDS

Smaller companies may not be as difficult to locate as large ones. They are less tangled in the web of corporate ownerships and, if still in operation, probably have the same name. Usually, if an ancestor worked for a smaller company, the headquarters was probably in the same town or state where the person lived. If the business still exists, you can probably locate it in the local telephone directory or current city directory. Never underestimate the ability of a local public or university librarian to help you locate the address of a small or large company. The best guidebook is Lorna M. Daniells, *Business Information Sources,* 3rd ed. (Berkely: University of California Press, 1993). It cites hundreds of publications that provide information on today's businesses.

BUSINESS DIRECTORIES

The best method of finding records of existing businesses is to contact the business directly. Addresses for the largest compa-

nies (and hence the largest employers) are found in many sources, but there are thousands of smaller companies. Several useful books can help locate these other companies (see the chapter bibliography).

An excellent layman's guide to four hundred of the largest U.S. companies is Milton Meskowitz, *Everybody's Business: A Field Guide to the 400 Leading Companies in America* (New York: Doubleday/Currency, 1990). This book profiles each company in everyday terms rather than business jargon or technical language. Among information of interest to a genealogist would be the year of founding, the company's history, the number of employees and, most importantly, whom to contact at the home office for general information, including telephone number.

The complicated world of modern business often makes it

Figure 10-2. From *National Directory of Morticians,* Vol. KK (Youngstown, Oh.: National Directory of Morticians, 1970), 553.

Explanation of ELEMENTS OF LISTING,

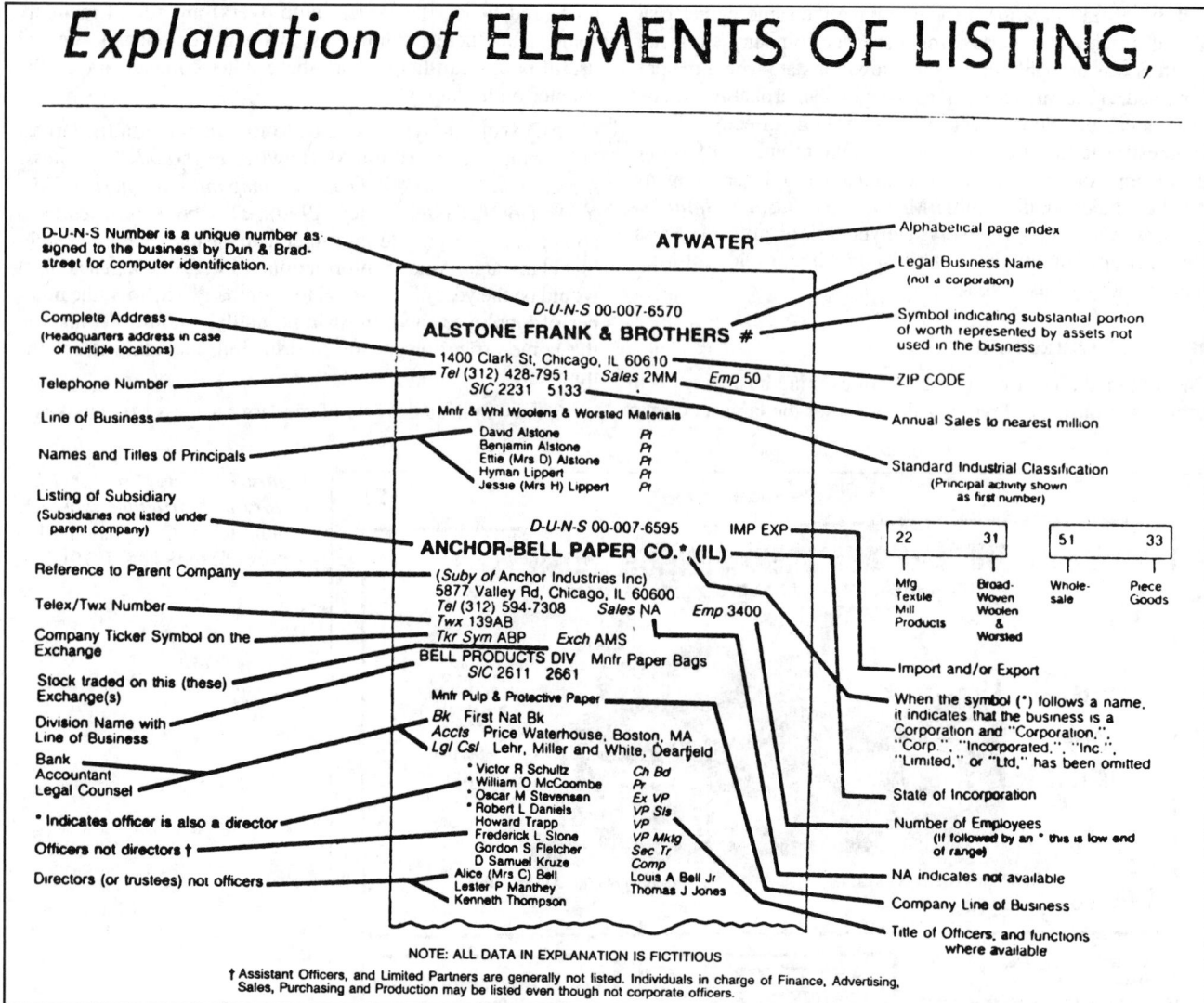

Figure 10-3. From Dun's Marketing Services, *Million Dollar Directory* (New York City: Dun and Bradstreet Corporation, 1983).

difficult to determine whether a company is independent or a subsidiary of a larger corporation. Dun and Bradstreet's annual *America's Corporate Families* (Skokie, Ill.: National Register Publishing Co.) helps to clarify the confusion. It includes the "family tree" of 11,000 U.S. parent corporations and their 60,000 subsidiaries, indicating which companies own which others. It lists the mergers, acquisitions, name changes, divisions, subsidiaries, and affiliates of most major American corporations.

Once you know the company you're looking for, you still need to know where its office is. The annual *Ward's Business Directory of U.S. Private and Public Companies* (Petaluma, Calif.: Baldwin H. Ward) is considered by many to be the best directory in its field. In it, each company is listed alphabetically, geographically, by industry, and by amount of sales. The current business address is given, including telephone numbers. This directory can help locate both large and small companies.

Another helpful tool is Dun and Bradstreet's annual *Million Dollar Directory: America's Leading Public and Private Companies,* which lists approximately 160,000 U.S. businesses with a net worth of more than $500,000 or 250 employees or

2.5 million dollars in sales. It also lists companies alphabetically and geographically. Figure 10-3 illustrates the kind of information included in each entry.

Several other sources list business firms from the past or supply the clues needed to determine what the name of a historical business was and when it was in operation. Using these records is complicated, and the process is called the "dragnet" strategy by William G. Roy in his "Collecting Data on American Business Officials in the Late Nineteenth and Early Twentieth Century," *Historical Methods* 15 (Fall 1982): 143–51. Since these materials are easily found in public and research libraries, even beginners can locate both current and historical businesses.

The biggest difficulty in locating information on specific companies is identifying them. Firms go out of business; merge to form new companies; are acquired by other, usually larger, companies; change names, directors, and even locations. The directories which keep track of these identities are modern sources. Our ancestors recorded changes with county and state officials or announced them in newspapers and trade publications.

In addition to Dun and Bradstreet's *Directory of Corporate Affiliations* and *Million Dollar Directory* is the *Robert D. Fisher Manual of Valuable and Worthless Securities* (New York: R.D. Fisher), which lists businesses reorganized, liquidated, or dissolved. Each of these directories is published annually and is available in most public and university libraries in the business/economic section.

Other directories include Poor's *Manual of Railroads* and Moody's *Manuals* with separate volumes for railroads, municipal governments, banks and finance, and public utilities. Published annually since 1900 by Moody's Investors Service, Inc., a division of Dun and Bradstreet, these directories omit some of the most important companies, such as Carnegie Steel and Standard Oil. They are also less likely to cover decentralized industries, such as books, shoes and boots, and the lumber industry.

TRADE ASSOCIATION DIRECTORIES

Members of most vocations have banded together to exchange information, learn from each other, assess competition, and provide referrals. Generally, these groups have taken the form of trade associations, most of which publish regular directories of their members. Farley's *Reference Directory of Booksellers, Stationers, and Printers in the U.S. and Canada,* published since 1886, and the *Pocket Directory of Shoe Manufacturers*, published by the *Boot and Shoe Reporter* since 1907, are examples of trade directories—although they are now, like most older directories, superceded by different directories and titles. The National Electric Light Association (1923), the National Retail Dry Goods Association (1934), and the National Fire Protection Association (1935) are some of the trade associations that publish directories of members with their specific affiliations. The publishers of trade association directories often have older copies in their offices which can be consulted to learn of older, now defunct, businesses. Current trade association directories are listed in the annual *Directories in Print* (Detroit: Gale Research Co.).

The *Encyclopedia of Associations,* published biannually by Gale Research Co., includes precise addresses, telephone numbers, titles, and frequency of bulletins and newsletters published, library information services offered, employment exchanges, and many other facts and figures for trade associations, many of which have a continuous history from the mid-nineteenth century to the present.

CORPORATE HISTORIES

Many American businesses have official corporate histories. The history of Standard Oil Company took some eighteen years to write, in part because its 35,000 boxes of records took so long to study and digest. Some years ago, the Harvard University Graduate School of Business History began to chronicle individual American business histories. Some of the titles in their series include: Ralph M. Hower, *History of Macy's of New York, 1858–1939: Chapters in the History of a Department Store* (Cambridge: Harvard, 1943), and *The History of an Advertising Agency: N. W. Ayer & Son at Work, 1869–1949* (Cambridge: Harvard, 1949); John S. Ewing and Nancy P. Norton, *Broadloom and Businessmen: A History of the Bigelow-Sanford Carpet Company, 1825–1953* (Cambridge, Mass.: Harvard, 1955); Gerald T. White, *A History of the Massachusetts Hospital Insurance Company* (Cambridge: Harvard, 1955); and George

S. Gibb, *The Whitesmiths of Taunton: A History of Reed and Barton, 1824–1943* (Cambridge, Mass.: Harvard, 1943).

For other histories, consult:

Business History, published quarterly by the Harvard Graduate School of Business History. Includes reviews and announcements of historical studies of American businesses.

Cochran, Thomas. *Railroad Leaders, 1845–1890: The Business Mind in Action.* Cambridge: Harvard University Press, 1953. Based on 100,000 letters from sixty-one railroad officials.

Daniells, Lorna M. *Studies in Enterprise.* Boston: Little, Brown, 1957. Includes a list of business histories.

Larson, Henrietta. *Guide to Business History.* Cambridge: Harvard University Press, 1948. Bibliography of histories and printed sources.

TRADE JOURNALS

Periodicals and news sheets have been published for the shipping and maritime industry, for agriculture, and for many other trades since the mid-nineteenth century. Books about an industry may include a discussion of periodicals devoted to the industry. For example, a list of agricultural journals is in Albert L. Demaree, *The American Agricultural Press, 1819–1860* (New York: Columbia University Press, 1941), pp. 393–400. Periodical sources are traditional materials to consult in checking for historical businesses of any size, and they are as close as your nearest public or research library. However, if local libraries do not have the volumes you want, check collections in libraries of those cities and towns where the industry was most common. Try Pittsburgh for the steel industry, San Francisco or Seattle for the Pacific shipping trade, and Atlanta and Savanna for the turpentine industry, for example.

LOCATING MODERN BUSINESS RECORDS

The most difficult problem facing the user of business and employment records is locating them. They may not be easily accessible or they may not include your ancestor; but if they cannot be located, your other problems are irrelevant.

Once you know the name (both former and present if still operating) of your ancestor's business or place of employment, several finding aids are available in most public and research libraries to locate business records.

Interestingly enough, the survival of historical business records may turn out to be more likely for records created before 1900 than since, for early records were kept in bound volumes, and some had subject or name indexes. Thus, customer orders were kept in order books and invoices in invoice books. Correspondence was copied into letter books and accounts were entered, transaction by transaction, into ledger books. The pre-1890 system was based on double-entry bookkeeping, which is unfamiliar to many genealogists today. After 1890, index cards became popular because data could be more easily sorted and arranged. Carbon copies came into use around 1900, and loose-leaf binders, folders, and envelope-like jackets were available by the 1920s.[23]

While the modern system is easier to understand and use, it is also more vulnerable to destruction, since loose papers tend to accumulate faster and take up more storage space than bound ledgers.

Obviously, if a company (large or small) still exists, the problem of locating its records should not be great. Someone in the home office should know were the records are, what information is in them, and how to get that information. Some companies have deposited their records in various archives, as described below.

The success or failure of your search may depend on your correspondence with the company, whether it is large or small. Remember when contacting companies that, while they may be consumer-conscious, genealogy is not their business. In the initial letter, it may help to explain that you have an interest in the company's history because of a family connection and would like to know where information such as that found in personnel and employment records is stored. Ask if there are company or corporate archives and who the archivist or librarian is. Don't expect to achieve your goal in a single letter. The first task is to locate someone who knows what you're looking for. Then you can begin to acquire the records. Remember, these are generally private records, and company policy may severely restrict access to them. A well-trained historical scholar doing a study of the business will likely have more success accessing private archives than an amateur genealogist who does not understand the business or appreciate the nature of the archives.

It may be more efficient to make an initial contact by telephone so that you can learn to whom you need to speak. Be patient, for you will probably be shuttled from department to department and put on hold several times. Many companies have a toll-free line (an 800 or 888 number) which you can call at no charge. You can determine if the company you are seeking has a toll-free number by calling 1-800-555-1212.

If you are not successful, ask for the customer relations department and briefly explain your problem. When you find the right person, be clear, courteous, and brief in your letters or conversations. Ask if the records are open to public research by someone like you or an agent representing you. If possible, offer to search the records personally, as they will probably be voluminous and unindexed. Most record custodians do not want to search such records, but some may allow you to. Always offer to pay necessary charges. Again, learning a bit about the company's background can be very helpful in opening the proper doors to the records you are seeking.

Many companies prefer to control the searches of their archives themselves, leaving it to trained staff or volunteers. For example, the Pullman Car Works established search arrangements with the South Suburban Genealogical and Historical Society for its massive file of personnel records. Research into the records of some 200,000 individuals in the collection is done only by society members who belong to the "Pullman Committee." The search fee supports the maintenance of the collection. Address requests to the South Suburban Genealogical and Historical Society, P.O. Box 96, South Holland, IL 60473-0096.

Directory of Business Archives in the United States and Canada (Chicago: Society of American Archivists, 1975). Some 2,000 corporations, private companies, and institutions, with employees were surveyed, including the *Fortune* 500. The directory describes the holdings of each of the 196 firms that responded. The major reason for this low response was that no archives had been established. Although a few companies established historical archives as early as 1925, most of them

date from 1950 as a result of the massive awareness program launched after the Second World War by the Society of American Archivists. A more recent survey in 1977 showed that some 310 business archives had been created. See Gary D. Saretsky, "North American Business Archives: Results of a Survey," *American Archivist* 40 (October 1977): 413–20.

MANUSCRIPT COLLECTIONS

In 1959, the Library of Congress began a catalog of manuscripts housed throughout the country. Known as the *National Union Catalog of Manuscript Collections* (*NUCMC*), it is issued yearly with information on more than 2,000 newly cataloged manuscript collections each year. Through the 1993 catalog, approximately 72,300 collections located in 1,406 repositories had been cataloged. Most annual catalogs are indexed, and comprehensive cumulative indexes cover 1959 to 1962, 1963 to 1966, 1967 to 1969, and every four or five years subsequent. A wealth of information on defunct and current business and employment records can be found in these indexes. For example, Joseph Stulb of Philadelphia worked for Schrack and Company, a nineteenth-century paint firm. The *NUCMC* index lists:

STULB, Joseph Jr. 72-121

SCHRACK (C.) and Company, Philadelphia, Pa 72-121

This citation means that they both appear in the collection cataloged 72-121, which was the 121st collection cataloged in 1972. The Schrack entry reads:

MS 72-121

Schrack (C) and company, Philadelphia, Pa.
  Records, 1808-1938. ca. 200,000 items.

  In Eleutherian Mills Historical Library (Greenville, Del.) (various accessions)

  Correspondence, accounts, bills and receipts, stock books, formula books (1844-1912), orders, shipping records, banking records, and other business records of a paint, varnish, and color manufacturing firm. Persons represented include Christian Schrack (ca. 1790-1854.), founder of the firm, who began business as a carriage builder; his partner, Joseph Stulb (d. 1898); Stulb's sons, Edwin H Stulb (1850-1920) and Joseph Stulb Jr.; his grandsons, Joseph Reichert Stulb (b.1883) and Edwin H. Stulb, Jr.; and Townsend Willits.

  In part, described in A guide to the Manuscripts in the Eleutherian Mills Historical Library, by John B. Riggs (1970) p.970-971.

  Gift 1966 and purchases, 1965-68.[24]

This collection is a wonderful find—approximately 200,000 items pertaining to Schrack and Company, Joseph Stulb, his sons, and his grandsons. It indicates that the collection is not in Philadelphia or even in Pennsylvania, but rather in a historical library in Delaware. *NUCMC* also includes the manuscript collections of several labor unions. The two-volume cumulative *Index to Personal Names in the National Union Catalog of Manuscript Collections, 1959–1984*, is an alphabetical arrangement of all the "personal and family names appearing in the descriptions of manuscript collections cataloged from 1959 to 1984." An even more valuable reference for business research is the three-volume companion publication, *Corporate Names Index, 1959–1984* (Alexandria, Va.: Chadwyck-Healey, 1994). This work brings together the names of corporate entities that appeared in the *NUCMC* for the years indicated. As indicated in the Schrack and Company example above, *NUCMC* locates collections that are "out of place" rather than where they might be expected to be found. This index and the *NUCMC* series are described more fully in chapter 2.

Obviously, not all manuscript collections have been cataloged in *NUCMC*. Thousands of specific archives also exist which may be affiliated with the company you are researching. National Historical Publications and Records Commission, *Directory of Archives and Manuscript Repositories in the United States* (Phoenix, Ariz.: Oryx Press, 1988) describes the manuscript holdings of 4,225 repositories and identifies 335 additional institutions. Arranged geographically, the directory also includes a list of repositories by type, including corporate archives, local historical societies, organizational archives, state and university archives, and thirteen other types of repositories. Even this list is not complete, however. The directory itself estimates that between 6,000 and 11,000 such repositories exist in the country, any number of which may contain business records.

Finally, the use of published guides to manuscript collections in larger archives cannot be overlooked. The *Guide to Genealogical Records in the Pennsylvania State Archives* was mentioned earlier as a good example. Another example is the section from the *Guide to Manuscripts Collections and Institutional Records in Ohio* (see the chapter bibliography).

HISTORICAL SOCIETY PUBLICATIONS

Numerous business records have been deposited in historical societies across the country. Most societies publish an annual report, a quarterly journal, archive inventories, and/or guides to their principal collections in which each set of records is described with dates, names of owners, types of records deposited, restrictions on use (if any), and size of collection. Sample entries from *Manuscripts of the Historical Society of Pennsylvania* follow. The collection includes both company and personal business records.

1009.

PHILADELPHIA CENTRE SQUARE WATER-WORKS. 1801-6. 1 Vol. Presented by the Jenkintown Trust Co., 1936. List of first Subscribers.

1019.

PHILADELPHIA INSURANCE COMPANY. 1814-45. 1 vol. Presented by Mrs. Howard W. Page, 1934. Minutes, accounts, names of officers, and records of general transactions.

1025.

PHILADELPHIA SUGAR REFINING COMPANY RECORDS. 1812. 1 vol. Presented by A.C. Kline, 1863. Articles of association, list of stockholders, constitution, bylaws, and other data.

108: PERSONAL and PROFESSIONAL RECORDS. 1676-1904. Approximately 500 vols.

John Q. A. McConkey, canal boat owner and shipper (Delaware and Raritan Canal), invoice book, 1877-79, 1 vol.

Mary Ann, John Q.A.., and James McConkey, canal boat transportation, boat book, 1847-80. 1 vol.

William McCorkle, advertising and periodical dealer, ledger 1804-87, 1 vol.

James McCurrah and Company, shipping agents, accounts current, 1790-96. 1 vol.: letter book, 1794-1800. 1 vol.

George Mead, shipper and general merchant, receipt book, 1784-88, 1 vol.

David Meredith, Philadelphia merchant, memorandum, and account book, 1813-17, 1 vol.

Jonathan Meredith, Philadelphia tanner, hide accounts, waste, leather, sales, bark, ledger, day, and blotter books, 1784-1800, 34 vols.[25]

SUBJECT COLLECTIONS

The most comprehensive coverage of unique library collections is Lee Ash, ed., *Subject Collections: A Guide to Special Book Collections and Subject Emphasis,* 7th ed. (Providence, N.J.: R.R. Bowker Co., 1993). It is especially valuable for special manuscript collections in public libraries which are not described in other publications. Sample entries under *Business* are:

Atlanta Public Library, Ivan Allen, Jr. Dept. of Science.

Industry & Government. Richard L. Tubesing, Head.

10 Pryor Street Atlanta, GA 30303

Vols. (15,000) Cat. Microfilms

Budget ($75,000)

Notes: This collection incl. on microform annual reports and Securities Exchange Commission 10-k reports for some 11,000 companies from 1976 to date; current and retrospective stock quotations, stock reports, corporate and industry records and directories and supporting loose-leaf services; information file on Atlanta's largest 10,000 companies from 1976 to date, with annual updates; and current plat maps for the five county Metro-Atlanta area. Atlanta and Georgia business history sections are being developed. Most material in this collection is non-circulating. Telephone ready reference service is provided.

Pomona Public Library, Special Collections

David Streeter, Libn.

625 S. Garey Avenue

Mailing Add.: P.O. Box 2271

Pomona, CA 91766

Uncat. Mss.

Notes: 165 linear feet of Pomona Valley business records incl. 16 water companies and 28 citrus companies; diaries; clubs and organizations; Laura Ingalls Wilder.

BIBLIOGRAPHIES

Special bibliographies also carry references to business archives. An annotated list of more than four hundred articles and books on business archives is in Karen M. Benedict, *A Select Bibliography on Business Archives and Records Management* (Chicago: Society of American Archivists, 1981). An example of a bibliography that includes reference to business archives is Alan M. Meckler and Ruth McMullin, comps. and eds., *Oral History Collection* (New York: R.R. Bowker Co., 1975). In it, oral history programs are listed by company, project, or person. Below are some sample entries.

> WEYERHAEUSER, C.D. with C.S. Martin, Weyerhaeuser Timber Company (98 pages, permission required) *Columbia University NY*
>
> WEYERHAEUSER, CHARLES A. Discussed in Columbia University interview with William L. Maxwell.
>
> WEYERHAEUSER, FREDERICK KING (1895-___) Industrialist. Weyerhaeuser Timber Company (1956, 167 pages, permission required) *Columbia University* NY
>
> WEYERHAEUSER, JOHN PHILIP, JR. (1899-1956) Weyerhaeuser Timber Company (41 pages, permission required) *Columbia University* NY Discussed in Columbia University interview with Albert B. Curtis
>
> WEYERHAEUSER TIMBER COMPANY Participants and pages: Volume I: A.E. Aitchison, 85; John Aram, 98; David H. Bartlett, 59; Jack Bishop, 32; Ralph Boyd, 26; Hugh B. Campbell 32; Norton Clapp, 32; R.V. Clute, 65; T.S. Durment, 45; O.D. Fisher, 73; A.N. Frederickson, 71; John H. Hauberg, 126; E.F. Heacox, C.S. Martin and C.D. Weyerhaeuser, 98; F.W. Hewitt, 66; Robert W. Hunt, 85; C.H. Ingram, 12; R.E. Irwin, 40; S.P. Johns, Jr., 46; Don Lawerence, 66; George S. Long, Jr., 46 R.R. Macartney, 44; Charles J. McGough, 66 William L. Maxwell, 112; Howard Morgan, 54; C.R. Musser, 27; Leonard H. Nygaard, 49; Harold H. Ogle, 47; Arthur Priaulx and James F. Stevens, 75; Al Raught, 54; Otto C. Schoenwerk, 40; A. O. Sheldon, 41; H.C. Shelworth, 77; Frand Tarr, 17; G. Harris Thomas, 63; David S. Troy, 36; Roy Voshmik,16; John A. Wahl, 18; Frederick K. Weyerhaeuser, 167; J. Philip Weyerhaeuser, 41; Maxwell W. Williamson, 38. Volume II: Earl R. Bullock, 32; Albert B. Curtis, 103; Wells Gilbert, 26; Roy Huffman, 68; W.K. McNair, 33; Leslie Mallory, 13 S.G. and C.D. Moon, 32; Jack Morgan, 43; J.J. O'Connell, 77; R.E. Saberson, 81; Hugo Schlenck, 113; Gaylord M. Upington and Lafayette Stephens, 75 (1956, 2981 pages, permission required,) *Columbia University NY.*

AMERICAN ARCHIVIST

Each issue of the *American Archivist,* published quarterly by the Society of American Archivists since 1936, contains reviews of new archival guides and "News and Notes" describing the transfer of business records to local archives. Keeping track of new collections made available for research requires that genealogists review every issue of the *American Archivist.* Copies are available at public and research libraries.

INCORPORATION REGISTERS AND FILES

Most businesses are required to register with a government agency. Larger businesses (and many smaller ones) are incorporated. These papers can tell you much about a business and, in particular, the principle owners of the business. They may also suggest the location of the business or its records. Check both the county and state incorporation registers where the business was located. The process of incorporation and how it has changed over time is described in George H. Evans, Jr., *Business Incorporations in the United States, 1800–1943* (Princeton: Princeton University Press, 1948). Evans also includes a useful appendix of business firms and their dates of incorporation.

Some businesses are recorded at the county level, while some are filed only with the state. Some are chartered or licensed by federal government agencies and may not be listed at the local level. This is especially true of federally chartered banks. The secretary of state (or equivalent) in most states maintains two registers: one of current companies (now accessible by computer) and one of defunct or dissolved companies. Each company in the register has a file number to locate loose documents. With this number, ask for the corporate case files which include the original charter, amendments to articles of incorporation, correspondence dealing with name changes and appointments of new directors, statement of dissolution with cause, and court proceedings or claims (if any) against the corporation or its officers.

Your initial contact can be made by telephone to determine which government agency has the records, what information you must send, and how much a search costs. Telephone numbers for state and county officials can be found in *Names and Numbers* (New York: John Wiley and Sons, 1978 and subsequent editions) or *National Directory of Addresses and Telephone Numbers* (New York: Nicholas Publishing Co., published annually).

Many county registers have been transferred to state archives and historical societies. An example is Weber County, Utah, for which corporate records include incorporation index, 1871–1959; incorporation records (including articles and by-laws), 1958–65; and affidavits of business firms and partnerships, 1913–63, with indexes. These volumes have all been deposited in the Utah State Archives in Salt Lake City. Weber County articles of incorporation from before 1958 are found in the secretary of state's (lieutenant governor's) office. The Utah lieutenant governor also maintains state incorporation records. They are located in the state offices several miles from the archive.

DEFUNCT BUSINESSES

Unfortunately, many of our ancestors worked for companies no longer in existence. However, many seemingly defunct companies have not actually disappeared but continue under a different name and/or ownership. If an ancestor worked for Victor Talking Machine, for example, you would have to learn that the name is now RCA before pursuing further research. Businesses that cease operating usually have customers who are attractive to their competitors. Therefore, the records of the old company may be transferred to another firm—often the one which bought the defunct company out. In a small city, try contacting present businesses in the same line of work for information about an ancestral company.

The defunct business might have belonged to a trade association or some other group of businesses in the same trade or locality. These types of organizations may have information on the company in question and may know where their records are. Anthony T. Kruzas and Robert C. Thomas, eds., *Business Organizations and Agencies Directory* (Detroit: Gale Research Co., 1980) lists and provides addresses of trade, business, and commercial organizations, stock exchanges, labor unions, chambers of commerce, and many other groups. Better business bureaus, as well as federal and state government agencies, are also included. It includes sixty pages of addresses of business libraries and information centers with a geographic index. Another good source book is David M. Brownstone and Gordon Carruth, *Where to Find Business Information,* 2nd ed. (New York; John Wiley and Sons, 1982), a source which can help locate agencies particular to the business you are seeking. If you are looking for employee information about a railroad company, the source finder section will refer you to several sources of information.

Information about old companies may appear in articles in various business magazines. One of the best ways to search this source is the *Business Periodicals Index,* which began in 1958 and is readily available in public libraries. Articles are listed under the industry or company name. The format is like that of the *Reader's Guide to Periodical Literature.*

If you know where a business was located you can then write to the local chamber of commerce or state archive for information on what became of it and its records. The secretary of state in each state should have incorporation records specifying the years a company was in business or if the name was changed. A local town or county historical society may also have knowledge of a business's demise. As mentioned earlier, local cities or counties may have business licenses for unincorporated businesses within their boundaries. Their records may indicate when a business folded and if the owner started a new and similar business.

To locate local historical societies which might have information about defunct businesses and record repositories, consult the *Directory of Historical Organizations in the United States and Canada,* 14th ed. (Nashville: American Association for State and Local History, 1990). It lists almost every historical society in both countries and includes a brief description of their collections and major programs. These societies are usually quite knowledgeable about history in their areas and can help determine what happened to a local business.

NOTES

1. *Information Please Almanac, Atlas, and Yearbook,* 35th ed. (New York: Simon and Schuster, 1982), 48.

2. U.S. Bureau of the Census, "Labor Force and Employment by Industry: 1800–1960," *Historical Statistics of the United States, Colonial Times to 1970,* part 1, series D (Washington, D.C.: Government Printing Office, 1975), 165–.

3. U.S. Department of Labor, *Apprenticeship Past and Present,* rev. ed. (Washington D.C.: U.S. Department of Labor, 1964).

4. Ibid.

5. William Nelson, ed., *Documents Relating to Colonial History of New Jersey,* 1st series, vol. 12 (Patterson, N.J.: Press Printing and Publishing Co., 1895), 401.

6. George W. Neible, "Account of Servants Bound and Assigned Before James Hamilton, Mayor of Philadelphia," *Pennsylvania Magazine of History and Biography* 32 (October 1908): 369.

7. Kenn Stryker-Rodda, "The Janeway Account Books 1735–1746." *Genealogical Magazine of New Jersey* 33 (January–April 1958): 4.

8. Kenneth Scott, "Some Huntington, Long Island Residents, 1763–1779," *National Genealogical Society Quarterly* 62 (September 1974): 177.

9. Conklin Mann, "The Family of Conchelyne, etc. in America," *American Genealogist* 21: 48–58, 133–47, 210, 215, 246–53; 22: 111–21, 226–36.

10. *Guide to the Manuscript Collections of the Historical Society of Pennsylvania,* 2nd ed. (Philadelphia: Historical Society of Pennsylvania, 1949), item 108.

11. Shepard B. Clough, *A Century of American Life Insurance: A History of the Mutual Life Company of New York, 1843–1943* (New York: Columbia University Press, 1946), 5.

12. Ibid., 8.

13. Harold F. Larkin, "Retention of Life Insurance Records," *The American Archivist* 5 (April 1942): 95–98.

14. Ibid.

15. James H. Madison, "The Credit Reports of R.G. Dun and Co. as Historical Sources," *Historical Methods Newsletter* 8 (September 1975): 128–30.

16. Peter N. Vandenberge, *Historical Directory of the Reformed Church of America, 1625–1965* (New Brunswick, N.J.: Reformed Church in America, 1966), 22.

17. George Berton Cutten, *The Silversmiths of Virginia From 1694 to 1850* (Richmond: Diete Press, 1952), 172.

18. Robert H. Dructor, *A Guide to Genealogical Sources at the Pennsylvania State Archives* (Harrisburg: Pennsylvania Historical and Museum Commission, 1980).

19. *Missoula City Directory* (Missoula: R. L. Polk and Co., 1922), 271; *h* means house, *r* means resides at.

20. Paul Lewinson and Morris Rieger, "Labor Union Records in the United States, *American Archivist* 25 (January 1962): 39.

21. Maynard Brickford, "Academic Archives," *American Archivist* 43 (1980): 449–60.

22. Lewinson, 39.

23. Oliver Wendell Holmes, "Evaluation and Preservation of Business Archives," *American Archivist* 1 (October 1938): 171–85.

24. *National Union Catalog of Manuscript Collections* (Washington, D.C.: Library of Congress, 1972), 20.

25. *Manuscripts of the Historical Society of Pennsylvania* (Philadelphia: the society, n.d.).

BIBLIOGRAPHY

RESEARCH AND FINDING AIDS

Ash, Lee. *Subject Collections: A Guide to Special Book Collections and Subject Emphasis.* . . . 7th ed. Providence, N.J.: R. R. Bowker Co., 1993.

Benedict, Karen M. *A Select Bibliography on Business Archives and Records Management.* Chicago: Society of American Archivists, 1981.

Brownstone, David M., and Gordon Carruth. *Where to Find Business Information.* New York: John Wiley and Sons, 1979.

Cochran, Thomas Childs. *200 Years of American Business.* New York: Basic Books, 1977.

Craumer, Lucille V., ed. *Business Periodicals Index.* New York: H. W. Wilson Co., annual since 1958.

Daniels, Lorna M. *Business Information Sources.* 3rd ed. Berkeley: University of California Press, 1993.

Moskowitz, Milton, Michael Katz, and Robert Levering, eds. *Everybody's Business: A Field Guide to the 400 Leading Companies in America.* New York: Doubleday/Currency, 1990.

Roy, William G. "Collecting Data on American Business Officials in the Late Nineteenth and Early Twentieth Century. *Historical Methods* 15 (Fall 1982): 143–51.

Slocum, Robert B. *Biographical Dictionaries and Related Works.* 2 vols. Detroit: Gale Research Co., 1986.

DIRECTORIES

The American Blue Book of Funeral Directors. New York: Kates-Boylston Publications, biennial since 1929.

Biographical Directory of the Railway Officials of America. New York: Simmons-Boardman Publishing Co., irregular since 1885. (Later editions titled *Who's Who in Railroading in North America.*)

Directories in Print. Detroit: Gale Research Co., annual.

Directory of Business Archives in the United States and Canada. Chicago: Society of American Archivists, 1975.

Directory of Corporate Affiliations. Skokie, Ill.: National Register Publishing Co., annual since 1967.

Directory of Deceased American Physicians: 1804–1929. Chicago: American Medical Association, 199(?).

Directory Historical Societies and Agencies in the United States and Canada. 14th ed. Nashville: American Association for State and Local History, 1990.

Dun's Marketing Services. *(Dun's) Million Dollar Directory.* New York: Dun and Bradstreet Corp., annual since 1963.

Encyclopedia of Associations. Detroit: Gale Research Co., biennial.

Fortune Magazine. *Fortune Double 500 Directory.* Trenton, N.J.: Fortune Magazine, annual since 1970.

Jacques, Constant H., ed. *Yearbook of American and Canadian Churches.* Nashville: Abington Press, annual since 1935.

Kruzas, Anthony T., and Robert C. Thomas, eds. *Business Organizations and Agencies Directory.* Detroit: Gale Research Co., 1980.

Martindale-Hubble Law Directory. Summit, N.J.: Martindale-Hubble, annual.

The National Directory of Morticians. Irregular. Youngstown, Ohio.: National Directory of Morticians, 1950–.

National Historical Publications and Records Commission. *Directory of Archives and Manuscript Repositories in the United States.* Phoenix, Ariz.: Uryx Press, 1988.

National Yellow Book of Funeral Directors. Youngstown, Ohio: Nomis Publications, annual.

Nordland, Rod. *Names and Numbers; A Journalists Guide to the Most Needed Information Sources and Contacts.* New York: John Wiley and Sons, 1978.

Standard and Poor's Register of Corporations, Directors and Executives. New York: Standard and Poor's Corp., annual since 1928.

Vandenberg, Peter N., ed. *Historical Directory of the Reformed Church in America 1628–1965.* New Brunswick, N.J.: Reformed Church in America, 1966.

Ward, Baldwin H., ed. *Ward's Business Directory of U.S. Private and Public Companies.* Petaluma, Calif.: Baldwin H. Ward Publications, annual.

_____, ed. *Ward's Directory of 55,000 Largest Corporations.* Petaluma, Calif.: Baldwin H. Ward Publications, annual.

TYPICAL GUIDES TO MANUSCRIPT COLLECTIONS

Dructor, Robert M. *A Guide to Genealogical Sources at the Pennsylvania State Archives.* Harrisburg: Pennsylvania Historical and Museum Commission, 1980.

Guide to the Manuscript Collections of the Historical Society of Pennsylvania. 2nd ed. Philadelphia: Historical Society of Pennsylvania, 1949.

Larson, David R., ed. *Guide to Manuscripts Collections and Institutional Records in Ohio.* N.p.: Society of Ohio Archivists, 1974.

Lovett, Robert W., and Eleanor C. Bishop, comps. *List of Business Manuscripts in Baker Library.* Boston: The Library, 1969.

The National Union Catalog of Manuscript Collections. Washington, D.C.: Library of Congress, annual since 1962.

Pflugll, Warner. *A Guide to the Archives of Labor History and Urban Affairs.* Detroit: Wayne State University Press, 1974.

EXAMPLES OF PRINTED ORIGINAL BUSINESS RECORDS

Gill, Harold B., Jr. *Apprentices of Virginia 1623–1800*. Salt Lake City: Ancestry, 1989.

Kingsbury, Susan Myra, ed. *The Records of the Virginia Company of London*. 4 vols. Washington, D.C.: U.S. Government Printing Office, 1938.

Neible, George W. "Account of Servants Bound and Assigned Before James Hamilton, Mayor of Philadelphia." *Pennsylvania Magazine of History and Biography* 32 (1908): 88–103, 237–49, 351–70.

Nelson, William, ed. *Documents Relating to the Colonial History of the State of New Jersey*. 1st series, vol. 12. Patterson, N.J.: Press Printing and Publishing Co., 1895.

Pennsylvania German Society. *Record of Indentures of Individuals Bound Out as Apprentices, etc., [in] Philadelphia . . . 1771 to 1773. . . .* Baltimore: Genealogical Publishing Co., 1973.

Ritter, Kathy. *Apprentices of Connecticut 1637–1900*. Salt Lake City: Ancestry, 1986.

Scott, Kenneth. "Some Huntington, Long Island Residents, 1763–1779." *National Genealogical Society Quarterly* 61 (September 1974): 173–77.

Severance, Frank Haywood. *The Holland Land Company and Canal Construction in Western New York*. Buffalo, N.Y.: The Buffalo Historical Society, 1910.

The Stoystown and Greensburgh Turnpike Road Company: Minutes 1815–1826. Southwest Pennsylvania Genealogical Services, 1976.

Stryker-Rodda, Kenn. "The Janeway Account Books 1735–1746." *Genealogical Magazine of New Jersey* 33 (January–April 1958): 1–4.

SELECTED VOCATIONAL COLLECTIVE BIOGRAPHIES

Barrett, Walter. *The Old Merchants of New York*. 5 vols. New York: Carleton, 1863–70.

Bell, Charles H. *The Bench and Bar of New Hampshire*. Boston: Houghton, Mifflin and Co., 1894.

The Bench and Bar of Chicago: Biographical Sketches. Chicago: American Biographical Publishing Co., n.d.

Bjerkoe, Ethel Hall. *The Cabinetmakers of America*. Garden City, N.J.: Doubleday, 1957.

Bowers, William S. *Gunsmiths of Pen-Mar-Va, 1790–1840*. Mercersburg, Pa.: Irwinton Publishers, 1979.

Burton, E. Milby. *South Carolina Silversmiths, 1690–1860*. Rutland, Vt.: Tuttle Co., 1968.

Carlisle, Lilian Baker. *Vermont Clock and Watchmakers, Silversmiths, and Jewelers, 1778–1878*. Burlington, Vt.: Stinehour Press, 1970.

Currier, Ernest M. *Marks of Early American Silversmiths*. Watkins Glen, N.Y.: American Life Foundation, 1970.

Cutten, George Barton. *The Silversmiths of North Carolina From 1696 to 1860*, 2nd rev. ed. Raleigh, N.C.: North Carolina Department of Cultural Resources, 1984.

_____. *The Silversmiths of Virginia From 1694 to 1850*. Richmond: Dietz Press, 1952.

De Voe, Shirley Spaulding. *The Tinsmiths of Connecticut*. Middletown, Conn.: Wesleyan University Press for the Connecticut Historical Society, 1968.

Drepperd, Carl William. *American Clocks & Clockmakers*. Boston: C.T. Brandord Co., 1958.

Drost, William E. *Clocks and Watches of New Jersey*. Elizabeth, N.J.: Engineering Publishers, 1966.

Eckhardt, George H. *Pennsylvania Clocks and Clockmakers*. New York: Devin-Adair Co., 1955.

Elliott, Mary Quigley. *Biographical Sketches of Knox County Writers*. Mount Vernon, Ohio, 1937.

Ensko, Stephen Guernsey Cook. *American Silversmiths and Their Marks*. 3 vols. New York, 1927–48.

Foote, Henry Stuart. *The Bench and Bar of the South and Southwest*. St. Louis: Soule, Thomas & Wentworth, 1876.

French, Hollis. *A List of Early American Silversmiths and Their Marks*. 1917. Reprint. New York: Da Capo Press, 1967.

Fried, Frederick. *Artists in Wood: American Carvers of Cigarstore Indians, Show Figures, and Circus Wagons*. New York: C.N. Potter, 1970.

Gardner, Albert Ten Eyck. *Yankee Stonecutters: The First American School of Sculpture, 1800–1850*. New York: Columbia University Press for the Metropolitan Museum of Art, 1945.

Gerstell, Vivian S. *The Silversmiths of Lancaster, Pennsylvania 1730–1850*. Lancaster, Pa.: Lancaster County Historical Society, 1972.

Gill, Harold B., Jr. *The Gunsmith in Colonial Virginia*. Williamsburg, Va.: Colonial Williamsburg Foundation, 1974.

Heisey, John W. *A Checklist of American Coverlet Weavers*. Williamsburg, Va.: Colonial Williamsburg Foundation, 1978.

Hiatt, Noble W. *The Silversmiths of Kentucky: Together With Some Watchmakers and Jewelers, 1785–1850*. Louisville, Ky.: Standard Print Co., 1954.

Hutslar, Donald A. *Gunsmiths Of Ohio 18th and 19th Centuries*. Longrifle Series. York, Pa.: George Shumway, 1973.

Kovel, Ralph M. *A Directory of American Silver, Pewter, and Silver Plate*. New York: Crown Publishers, 1961.

Langdon, John Emerson. *Canadian Silversmiths, 1700–1900*. Toronto: Stinehour Press, 1966.

Laughlin, Ledlie Irwin. *Pewter in America: Its Makers and Their Marks*. Boston: Houghton, Mifflin, 1940.

Lewis, George E. *The Bench and Bar of Colorado*. Denver: Bench and Bar Publishing Co., 1917.

Lynch, James Daniel. *The Bench and Bar of Texas*. St. Louis: Nixon-Jones Printing Co., 1885.

Martin, John Hill. *Martins Bench and Bar of Philadelphia.* Philadelphia: Rees Welsh and Co., 1883.

Miller, Stephen Francis. *The Bench and Bar of Georgia.* 2 vols. Philadelphia: J.B. Lippincott, 1858.

Palmer, John McAuley. *The Bench and Bar of Illinois*, 2 vols. Chicago: Lewis Publishing Co., 1899.

Parsons, Charles Sumner. *New Hampshire Clocks & Clockmakers.* Exeter, N.H.: Adams Brown Co., 1976.

Proctor, Lucien Brock. *The Bench and Bar of New York.* New York: Diossy, 1870.

Reed, George Irving. *The Bench and Bar of Michigan.* Chicago: Century Publishing and Engraving, 1897.

Reed, George Irving. *The Bench and Bar of Ohio*, 2 vols. Chicago: Century Publishing and Engraving, 1897.

Reed, Parker McCobb. *The Bench and Bar of Wisconsin.* Milwaukee: the compiler, 1882.

Rice, Alvin H. *The Shenandoah Pottery.* Berryville, Va.: Virginia Book Co., 1974.

Roberts, Kenneth D. *Planemakers and Other Edge Tool Enterprises in New York State in the Nineteenth Century.* Cooperstown, N.Y.: New York State Historical Association, 1970.

Sams, Conway Whittle. *The Bench and Bar of Maryland.* Chicago: Lewis Publishing Co., 1901.

Shelton, Lawrence P. *California Gunsmiths, 1846–1900.* Fair Oaks, Calif.: Far Far West Publishers, 1977.

Smart, Charles E. *The Makers of Surveying Instruments in America Since 1700.* 2 vols. Troy, N.Y.: Regal Art Press, 1962–67.

Wendell, Emory. *Wendell's History of Banking and Banks and Bankers of Michigan.* Detroit: Winn & Hammond, n.d.

Selected Historical Information About Businesses and Records

Apprenticeship Past and Present. Rev. ed. Washington, D.C.: U.S. Department of Labor, 1964.

Bailyn, Bernard. *The New England Merchants in the Seventeenth Century.* Cambridge, Mass.: Harvard University Press, 1955.

Clough, Shepard B. *A Century of American Life Insurance: A History of the Mutual Life Insurance Company of New York 1843–1943.* New York: Columbia University Press, 1946.

Cochran, Thomas. *Railroad Leaders, 1845–1890: The Business Mind in Action.* Cambridge: Harvard University Press, 1953.

Commerce, Manufactures and Resources of Buffalo and Environs: A Descriptive, Historical and Statistical Review; Industry, Development, Enterprise. Buffalo, N.Y. : Commercial Publishing Co., 1880.

Daniells, Lorna M. *Studies in Enterprise.* Boston: Little, Brown, 1957.

Dun and Bradstreet. *America's Corporate Families.* Skokie, Ill.: National Register Publishing Co., annual.

Engelhardt, George Washington. *Buffalo, New York: The Book of Its Merchants Exchange.* Buffalo, N.Y.: Matthews-Northrup Co., 1897.

Evans, George H., Jr. *Business Incorporations in the United States, 1800–1943.* Princeton: Princeton University Press, 1948.

Galles, Duane "Using Life Insurance Records in Genealogical Research." *Genealogical Journal* 20 (1992): 156–71.

Herrick, Cheesman A. *White Servitude in Pennsylvania.* 1926. Reprint. New York: Negro University Press, 1969.

Historical Statistics of the United States Colonial Times to 1970. Washington, D.C.: U.S. Department of Commerce, 1975.

The Industrial Advantages of Houston, Texas and Environs: Also a Series of Comprehensive Sketches of the City's Representative Business Enterprises. Bryan, Tex.: Fuller Printing Co., 1977.

Information Please Almanac, Atlas and Yearbook. Annual. New York: Simon and Schuster, 1947–.

Lanier, Henry Wysham. *A Century of Banking in New York, 1822–1922.* New York: Gilliss Press, 1922.

Larkin, Harold F. "Retention of Life Insurance Records." *American Archivist* 5 (April 1942): 93–99.

Larson, Henrietta. *Guide to Business History.* Cambridge: Harvard University Press, 1948.

Levitt, James H. *For Want of Trade: Shipping and the New Jersey Ports, 1680–1783.* Newark, N.J.: New Jersey Historical Society, 1981.

Lewinson, Paul, and Morris Rieger. "Labor Union Records in the United States." *American Archivist* 25 (January 1962): 39–57.

Madison, James H. "The Credit Reports of R. G. Dun and Co. as Historical Sources." *Historical Methods Newsletter* 8 (September 1975): 128–31.

_____. "The Evolution of Commercial Credit Reporting Agencies in Nineteenth Century America." *Business History Review* 48 (1974): 164–86.

Moody's Transportation Manual. New York: Moody's Investors Service, annual.

Peabody, Robert E. *Merchant Venturers of Old Salem: A History of the Commercial Voyages of a New England Family to the Indies and Elsewhere in the XVIII Century.* Boston: Houghton Mifflin, 1912.

Robert D. Fisher Manual of Valuable and Worthless Securities. . . . New York: R.D. Fisher, 1926 to present.

Salinger, Sharon V. *To Serve Well and Faithfully: Labor and Indentured Servants in Pennsylvania.* New York: Cambridge University Press, 1987.

Saretsky, Gary D. "North American Business Archives: Results of a Survey." *American Archivist* 40 (October 1977): 413–20.

SAMPLE CORPORATE HISTORIES

100 Years 100 Men, 1871–1971: A History of the Edwards & Broughton Company in Raleigh, North Carolina. Edited by Christopher Crittenden, William S. Powell, and Robert H. Woody. Raleigh, N.C.: Edwards & Broughton, n.d.

Clough, Shepard B. *A Century of American Life Insurance: A History of the Mutual Life Company of New York, 1843–1943.* New York: Columbia University Press, 1946.

Ewing, John S., and Nancy P. Norton. *Broadloom and Businessmen: A History of the Bigelow-Sanford Carpet Company, 1825–1953.* Cambridge: Harvard University Graduate School of Business History, 1955.

Gibb, George S. *The Whitesmiths of Taunton: A History of Reed and Barton, 1824–1943.* Cambridge: Harvard University Graduate School of Business History, 1943.

Hower, Ralph M. *History of Macy's of New York, 1858–1939: Chapters in the History of a Department Store.* Cambridge: Harvard University Graduate School of Business History, 1943.

_____. *The History of an Advertising Agency: N. W. Ayer & Son at Work, 1869–1949.* Cambridge: Harvard University Graduate School of Business History, 1949.

Shinn, Charles Howard. *The Story of the Mine: As Illustrated by the Great Comstock Lode of Nevada.* New York: D. Appleton, 1897.

White, Gerald T. *A History of the Massachusetts Hospital Life Insurance Company.* Cambridge: Harvard University Graduate School of Business History, 1955.

INSTITUTIONAL RECORDS

Johni Cerny

Institutional records are some of the least used but most valuable sources of genealogical information available to the researcher. School, hospital, mortuary, coroner, orphanage, and prison records require sophisticated research methods, apply to a restricted population, and are not always available to the public because some are recent and thus are protected by the laws of privacy which are discussed in chapter 1, The Foundations of Family History Research. Still, because these and earlier records contain valuable genealogical information, it is important to understand the kinds of records and their content, their availability, and special problems in their use.

Few of the records in this category have received the attention given to the major record sources, but they have developed into valuable genealogical sources during the twentieth century. Each record has existed in one form or another for nearly 150 to 200 years. Such an accumulation of information is obviously important, yet much remains to be done before the records of U.S. orphanages and prison systems, for example, become familiar tools in working genealogists' hands. The task of compiling the information available and putting it in a usable format for the researcher is beyond the scope of this work, but it must be done in the future.

PRISON RECORDS

Prisons, as they currently exist, first appeared approximately two hundred years ago. The first modern prison is believed to have been the Walnut Street Jail in Philadelphia, which was established in 1790. It was fashioned after the workhouses of London and other European cities.

Penologists saw a need for more sophisticated correctional institutions and designed what was considered a model prison at Auburn, New York, in 1825. It was followed by Eastern State Penitentiary at Cherry Hill in Philadelphia in 1829. Thousands of prisons, reformatories, correctional institutions, and related penal groups have been established since.

The early criminal judicial system was likely to convict offenders for violations less serious than those of modern offenders. Probation was instituted in the United States at about the same time the prison at Auburn, New York, was established. The purpose of probation was the same then as it is now: to provide supervision for first-time offenders who committed lesser crimes and to avoid imprisoning juveniles.

JURISDICTIONS

Early prisons were operated, as they are today, by federal, state, local, and military authorities. The correctional institutions of all four jurisdictions are listed in *Directory: Juvenile and Adult Correctional Departments, Institutions, Agencies and Paroling Authorities* (1995), a publication of the American Correctional Association, 8025 Laurel Lakes Court, Laurel, MD 20707-5075. This directory includes an organizational description of each institution. Most of the institutions listed in it were founded since the 1930s and thus are not within the time period of primary interest to most genealogists, but the list below gives the names of those functioning by 1900, plus some federal institutions that began operating after 1900. The list also includes some institutions which were once operational but are no longer functioning. Contact the correctional agency of the state to determine the exact scope of a prison's existence and the disposition of its records.

CORRECTIONAL INSTITUTIONS BEFORE 1900 AND CONTEMPORARY FEDERAL/STATE AGENCIES

Federal Agencies and Institutions

Bureau of Prisons
320 First St. N.W.
Washington, DC 20534

Mid-Atlantic Region:

Junction Business Park
10010 Junction Dr., Suite 100-N
Annapolis, MD 20701

North Central Region:

Gateway Complex Tower II
4th and State, 8th floor
Kansas, City, KS 66101-2492

Northeast Region:

U.S. Customs House, 7th floor
2nd and Chestnut Sts.
Philadelphia, PA 19106

South Central Region:

4211 Cedar Springs Rd., Suite 300
Dallas, Texas 75219

Southeast Region:

523 McDonough Blvd. S.E.
Atlanta, GA 30315

Western Region:

7950 Dublin Blvd., 3rd floor
Dublin, CA 94568

Penitentiaries and Date Established

United States Penitentiary, Atlanta, GA 30315 (1902)

United States Penitentiary, Leavenworth, KS 66048 (1906)

United States Penitentiary, Lewisburg, PA 17837 (1932)

United States Penitentiary, Marion, IL 62959 (1963)

United States Penitentiary, Terre Haute, IN 47808 (1940)

United States Penitentiary, Lompo c, CA 93436 (1959)

United States Penitentiary, Florence, CO 81226 (1994)

United States Penitentiary, White Deer, PA 17887 (1993)

Military

Commandant
U.S. Army Disciplinary Barracks
Fort Leavenworth, KS 66027-7100 (1874)

U.S. Army Confinement Facility
1st Infantry Division
Fort Riley, KS 66442 (1880)

Correctional Facility
Marine Corps Recruit Depot
Parris Island, SC 29905

State and Local Agencies and Institutions

Alabama*

State Department of Corrections
Gorden Person Building, Third Floor
50 N. Ripley St.
Montgomery, AL 36130

Alaska*

Department of Health and Social Services
Board of Parole
P.O. Box 110630
Juneau, AK 99811

Arizona*

Department of Corrections
1601 W. Jefferson
Phoenix, AZ 85007

Arkansas*

Department of Correction and Community Punishment
Box 8707
Pine Bluff, AR 71611

California

Department of Corrections
1515 S. St.
P.O. Box 942883
Sacramento, CA 94283-0001

California State Prison at San Quentin
San Quentin, CA 94964 (1852)

California State Prison at Sacramento
P.O. Box 29
Represa, CA 95671 (1992)

Colorado

State Department of Corrections
2862 S. Circle Dr., Suite 400
Colorado Springs, CO 80906-4195

Canon Correctional Facility
Box 1010
Canon City, CO 81212 (1871)

Buena Vista Correctional Facility
P.O. Box 2017
Buena Vista, CO 81211 (1892)

Connecticut

Department of Correction
340 Capitol Ave.
Hartford, CT 06106-1494

Cybulski Correctional Institution
P.O. Box 775
264 Bilton Rd.
Somers, CT 06071

Delaware*

Department of Correction
80 Monrovia Ave.
Smyrna, DE 19977-1597

Washington, D.C.*

Department of Corrections
1923 Vermont Ave. N.W.
Washington, DC 20001

Florida

Department of Correction
2601 Blair Stone Rd.
Tallahassee, FL 32399-2500

Florida State Prison
Box 747
Starke, FL 32091 (1960)

Georgia*

Department of Corrections
Floyd Building, Twin Towers E., Room 756
Martin Luther King, Jr., Dr. S.E.
Atlanta, GA 30334

Hawaii*

Department of Public Safety
919 Ala Moana Blvd.
Honolulu, HI 96814

Idaho

Department of Corrections
500 S. 10th
State-House Mail
Boise, ID 83720

Idaho State Correctional Institution
Box 14
Boise, ID 83707 (1870)

Illinois

Department of Corrections
1301 Concordia Court
P.O. Box 19277
Springfield, IL 62794-9277

Joliet Correctional Center
Box 515
Joliet, IL 60432 (1860)

Menard Correctional Center
Box 711
Menard, IL 62259 (1878)

Pontiac Correctional Center
Box 99
Pontiac, IL 61764 (1871)

Indiana

Department of Correction
Indiana Government Center South
302 W. Washington St., Room E334
Indianapolis, IN 46204-2278

Indiana State Prison
Box 41
Michigan City, IN 46360 (1859)

Indiana Boys' School
501 W. Main St.
Plainfield, IN 46168 (1867)

Iowa

Department of Corrections
Capital Annex
523 E. 12th St.
Des Moines, IA 50319-0001

The Men's Reformatory
Box B
Anamosa, IA 52205 (1872)

Iowa State Penitentiary
Box 316
Fort Madison, IA 52627 (1839)

Kansas

Department of Corrections
Landon State Office Building, 4th floor
900 S.W. Jackson
Topeka, KS 66612-1284

Hutchinson Correctional Facility
500 S. Reformatory Rd.
Box 1568
Hutchinson, KS 67504-1568 (1895)

Lansing Correctional Facility
Box 2
Lansing, KS 66043 (1864)

Kentucky

Department of Corrections
State Office Building
Frankfort, KY 40601

Kentucky State Penitentiary
Box 128
Eddyville, KY 42038-0128 (1888)

Louisiana

Department of Public Safety and Corrections
P.O. Box 94304, Capital Station
Baton Rouge, LA 70804-9304

Louisiana State Penitentiary
Angola, LA 70712 (1866)

Maine

Department of Corrections
State House Station 111
Augusta, ME 04333

Maine State Prison
Box A
Thomaston, ME 04861 (1824)

Maine Youth Center
675 Westbrook St.
South Portland, ME 04106 (1853)

Maryland

Department of Public Safety and Correctional Services
Division of Correction
6776 Reistertown Rd., Suite 311
Baltimore, MD 21215-2342

Maryland Penitentiary
954 Forrest St.
Baltimore, MD 21202 (1811)

Maryland House of Correction
Box 534
Jessup, MD 20794 (1878)

Cheltenham Youth Facility
Cheltenham, MD 20623 (1870)

Massachusetts

Executive Office of Public Safety
Department of Correction
Saltonstall Office Building
100 Cambridge St.
Boston, MA 02202

Bridgewater State Hospital
20 Administration Rd.
Bridgewater, MA 02324 (1855)

Massachusetts Correctional Institution
Box 9007
Framingham, MA 01701-9007 (1877)

Massachusetts Correctional Institution
Box 00
West Concord, MA 01742 (1878)

Michigan

Department of Corrections
Grandview Plaza Building
P.O. Box 30003
Lansing, MI 48909

Michigan Reformatory
1342 W. Main St.
Ionia, MI 48846 (1877)

Marquette Branch Prison
P.O. Box 779
Marquette, MI 49855 (1889)

State Prison of Southern Michigan
4000 Cooper St.
Jackson, MI 49201 (1839)

Adrian Training School
Box 218
Adrian, MI 49221 (1881 for juveniles)

Minnesota

Department of Corrections
300 Bigelow Building
450 N. Syndicate St.
St. Paul, MN 55104-4127

Minnesota Correctional Facility—St. Cloud
Box B
2305 Minnesota Blvd. S.E.
St. Cloud, MN 56302 (1889)

Minnesota Correctional Facility—Red Wing
1079 Hwy. 292
Red Wing, MN 55066 (1889)

Mississippi

Department of Corrections
723 N. President St.
Jackson, MS 39202-3097

Missouri

Department of Corrections
P.O. Box 236
2729 Plaza Dr.
Jefferson City, MO 65102-0236

Jefferson City Correctional Center
Box 597
Jefferson City, MO 65102 (1835)

Boonville Correctional Center
P.O. Box 379
Boonville, MO 65233 (1889)

Chillicothe Correctional Center
1500 W. 3rd
Chillicothe, MO 64601 (1889)

Montana

Department of Corrections and Human Services
Corrections Division
1539 11th Ave.
Helena, MT 59620-1301

Montana State Prison
400 Conley Lake Rd.
Deer Lodge, MT 59722 (1870)

Pine Hills School
P.O. Box 1058
Miles City, MT 59301 (1894 for juveniles)

Nebraska

Department of Correctional Services
Box 94661
Lincoln, NE 68509-4661

Nebraska State Penitentiary
Box 2500
Lincoln, NE 68502-0500 (1869)

Nevada

Department of Prisons
Box 7011
Carson City, NV 89702-7011

Nevada State Prison
Box 607
Carson City, NV 89702 (1861)

Nevada Youth Training Center
Box 469
Elko, NV 89801 (1913)

New Hampshire**

Department of Corrections
P.O. Box 769
Concord, NH 03302-0769

New Hampshire State Prison Complex
Box 14
Concord, NH 03301 (1880)

New Hampshire Youth Development Center
1056 N. River Rd.
Manchester, NH 03104-1998 (1858)

New Jersey

Department of Corrections
Whittlesey Rd., CN-863
Trenton, NJ 08625-0863

New Jersey State Prison
CN-861
Trenton, NJ 08625

New Mexico

Corrections Department
P.O. Box 27116
Santa Fe, NM 87502-0116

Penitentiary of New Mexico
Box 1059
Santa Fe, NM 87504-1059

New York

New York State Commission of Correction
Department of Correctional Services
State Office Building Campus
Albany, NY 12226

Albion Correctional Facility
3595 State School Rd.
Albion, NY 14411 (1893)

Auburn Correctional Facility
Box 618
135 State St.
Auburn, NY 13021 (1817)

Clinton Correctional Facility
P.O. Box 2000
Dannemora, NY 12929 (1845)

Elmira Correctional Facility
Box 500
Davis and Bancroft Sts.
Elmira, NY 14902 (1876)

Fishkill Correctional Facility
Box 307
Prospect St.
Beacon, NY 12508 (1892)

Sing Sing Correctional Facility
354 Hunter St.
Ossining, NY 10562-5442 (1825)

New York City

New York City Department of Corrections
60 Hudson St.
New York, NY 10013-4393

North Carolina

Department of Correction
214 W. Jones St.
Raleigh, NC 27603-1337

Division of Prisons
831 W. Morgan St.
Raleigh, NC 27603

Central Prison
1300 Western Blvd.
Raleigh, NC 27606 (1884)

North Dakota

Department of Corrections and Rehabilitation
P.O. Box 1898
Bismarck, ND 58502-1898

North Dakota State Penitentiary
Box 5521
Bismarck, ND 58502-5521 (1886)

Ohio

Department of Rehabilitation and Correction
1050 Freeway Dr. N.
Columbus, OH 43229

Mansfield Correctional Institution
1150 N. Main St.
P.O. Box 1368
Mansfield, OH 44901 (1896)

Oklahoma*

Department of Corrections
3400 Martin Luther King, Jr., Ave.
Oklahoma City, OK 73136-0400

Oregon

Department of Corrections
2575 Center St. N.E.
Salem, OR 97310-0470

Oregon State Penitentiary
2605 State St.
Salem, OR 97310-0505 (1853)

Pennsylvania

Department of Corrections
Box 598
Camp Hill, PA 17011-0598

State Correctional Institution—Huntingdon
1100 Pike St.
Huntingdon, PA 16651-1112 (1889)

State Correctional Institution and Correctional Diagnostic and Classification Center
Box 99901
Pittsburgh, PA 15233 (1826)

Philadelphia

Philadelphia Prison System
8201 State Rd.
Philadelphia, PA 19136

House of Correction
8001 State Rd.
Philadelphia, PA 19136 (1874)

Holmsburg Prison
8215 Torresdale Ave.
Philadelphia, PA 19136 (1896)

Rhode Island
Department of Corrections
40 Howard Ave.
Cranston, RI 02920

Rhode Island Training School
300 New London Ave.
Cranston, RI 02920 (1850)

South Carolina

Department of Corrections
4444 Broad River Rd.
Box 21787
Columbia, SC 29221

Wateree River Correctional Institution
P.O. Box 189
Rembert, SC 29128 (1892)

South Dakota

Department of Corrections
115 E. Dakota Ave.
Pierre, SD 57501-3216

South Dakota State Penitentiary
Box 5911
Sioux Falls, SD 57117-5911 (1882)

South Dakota Training School
Box 70
Plankinton, SD 57368-0070 (1887 for juveniles)

Tennessee

Department of Correction
Rachel Jackson State Office Building
320 Sixth Ave. N.
Nashville, TN 37243-0465

Tennessee Prison for Women
Stewarts Lane
Nashville, TN 37243-0468 (1898)

Brushy Mountain Prison
P.O. Box 1000
Petros, TN 37845 (1896)

Texas

Department of Criminal Justice—Institutional Division
Box 99
Huntsville, TX 77342-0099

Huntsville Unit
Box 99
Huntsville, TX 77342 (1849)

Jester Unit I, II, and III
Horlen Rd.
Richmond, TX 77469 (1885)

Jester Unit IV
2020 Imogene Rd.
Richmond, TX 77469

Wynne Unit
P.O. Box 99
Huntsville, TX 77342 (1899)

Utah

Department of Corrections
6100 S. 300 E.
Salt Lake City, UT 84107

South Point Facilities
Box 250
Draper, UT 84020 (1868)

Vermont*

Agency of Human Services
Department of Corrections
103 South Main St.
Waterbury, VT 05671-1001

Virginia

State Department of Corrections
Box 26963
6900 Atmore Dr.
Richmond, VA 23261-6963

Powhatan Correctional Center
State Farm, VA 23160 (1895)

Beaumont Learning Center
P.O. Box 491
Beaumont, VA 23014 (1898)

Hanover Learning Center
Hanover, VA 23069 (1898)

Washington

Department of Corrections
P.O. Box 41100
Olympia, WA 98504-1100

Washington State Penitentiary
Box 520
Walla Walla, WA 99362-1065 (1887)

West Virginia

Department of Public Safety
Division of Corrections
112 California Ave., Building 4
Charleston, WV 25305

North Correctional Center
Rd. 2, Box 1
Moundsville, WV 26041 (1866)

West Virginia Industrial School for Boys
Grafton, WV 26354 (1891)

Industrial Home for Youth
P.O. Box 7
Salem, WV 26375 (1899)

Wisconsin

Department of Corrections
Box 7925
149 E. Wilson St.
Madison, WI 53707-7925

Waupun Correctional Institution
Box 351
Waupun, WI 53963-0351 (1851)

Green Bay Correctional Institution
Box 19033
Green Bay, WI 54307-9033 (1898)

Wyoming
Department of Corrections
Herschler Building
Cheyenne, WY 82002

Wyoming State Penitentiary
Box 400
Rawlins, WY 82301 (1892)

*There are no pre-1900 correctional institutions listed in these states.

**New Hampshire has no central department of corrections.

TYPES OF RECORDS

Unfortunately, there is no complete inventory of the records maintained by each of the early correctional institutions in the United States. The types of records compiled by early Pennsylvania correctional institutions are representative of those found in other states for the same time period and include admission and discharge books, biographical registers, hospital record books, descriptive registers, convict dockets, reception descriptive books, registers of prisoners, death warrants, clemency files, pardon books, and lists of executions.

Admission and Discharge Books

Admission and discharge books contain the name of the inmate, date of admission, race, sex, health, habits (temperance), marital status, immunizations, family diseases, number of convictions, length of sentence, time in county jail, birthplace, occupation, physical and mental health at release, time in prison, and pardon information. Figure 10-4 is a page from the 1844 admissions register of the Eastern Pennsylvania State Penitentiary.

Registers of Prisoners

Registers of prisoners are similar to admission books and list the name of the prisoner, age, race, birthplace, number of convictions, county of residence, court of sentencing, date of sentencing, crime, maximum sentence, and remarks (usually about release). Figure 10-5 is a page from the Register of Prisoners, 1899 to 1901, of the Pennsylvania Industrial Reformatory.

Biographical Registers

The Biographical Register of the Pennsylvania Industrial Reformatory is a good example of the valuable information found in these registers. The information is divided into data about the inmate and data about the inmate's family (figure 10-6).

Inmate	**Family**
Name	Insanity
Date of record	Epilepsy
Crime	Dissipation
Maximum sentence	Education
Family	Pecuniary condition
Schools	Occupations
Labor	Pauper or criminal
Religion	Religion
Associations	
Physical stature	
Mental capabilities	
Moral susceptibility	
Health	
Culture	
Addresses of correspondents	

The register in figure 10-6 gives more details than called for by the form. Joseph Larkey's parents are not named in it, but the dates and causes of their deaths are noted. His living relatives were two uncles, Michael and Charles Haggerty of Philadelphia. His grandparents were not identified by name but were listed as deceased. Other records list the names of parents, grandparents, and other relatives in the space for addresses of correspondents. All of this information is, of course, helpful to a genealogical effort.

Hospital Record Books

Sometimes detailed in their information about the inmate's medical treatment while imprisoned, hospital record books may include a specific date and cause of death. They sometimes contain statistical accounts of the types of illnesses treated and the frequency of treatment.

Descriptive Registers

Descriptive registers are similar to registers of prisoners, giving the date of entry, name, age, birthplace, occupation, complexion, color of eyes, color of hair, stature, physical marks, sentence, when sentenced, number of convictions, when and

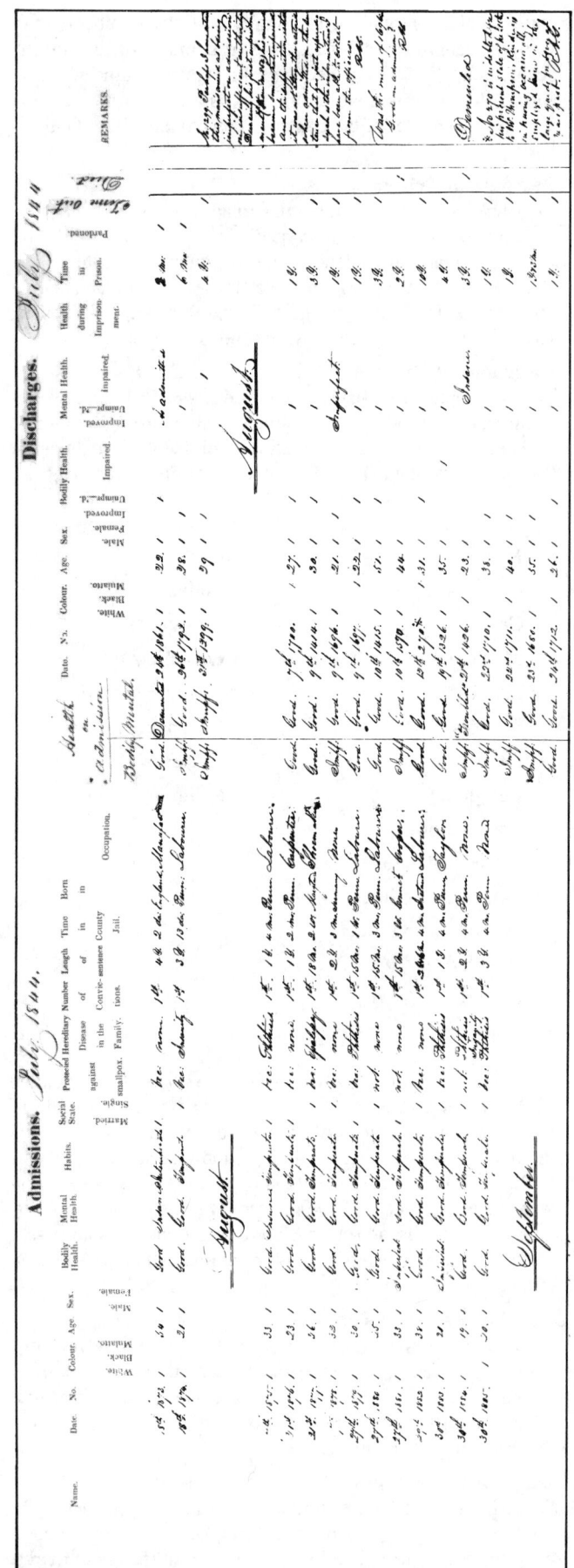

how discharged, expiration of sentence, and remarks. Figure 10-7 is the 1826 Descriptive Register of the Pennsylvania State Penitentiary.

Convict Dockets

Some of the information found in convict dockets is provided in other records, including name of inmate, crime, sentence, when sentenced, court of sentencing, name of prosecutor, date admitted, physical description, when discharged, and how. This list is part of the "A" page from the index to the 1826 Convict Docket of Western Pennsylvania State Penitentiary.

Reception Descriptive Lists of Convicts

An expanded form of early prison registers, the reception descriptive lists contain detailed information about the prison inmate. The information listed in these records includes the convict's name, age, race, crime, date of reception, date of sentence, county of conviction, occupation before and at the time of arrest, physical description, shoe size, weight, birthplace, education, occupational training, marital status, parental relations at fifteen, drinking habits, relatives in prison, cause of crime, and relative's residence.

Death Warrants

These files, which consist of the actual warrant and all the supporting documentation of the conviction, contain information of greater historical than genealogical value. The disposition of appeals for clemency and commutation are often included in the file. Figure 10-8 is the death warrant of Thomas Munley, inmate of the Pennsylvania prison system, from the records of the Pennsylvania State Board of Pardons.

Clemency Files

Clemency files contain requests to the governor for clemency in the sentence of a convict. A narrative in these files explains the circumstances involved in the commission of the crime, the reasons for clemency, and attestations to the character of the convict. The petition was signed by individuals who supported the granting of clemency. Figure 10-9 is the 1833 clemency file of Isaac F. Clarke, inmate of the Western Pennsylvania Penitentiary.

Pardon Books

These brief records attest to pardons granted to convicts by the state governor and contain little genealogical information. They do, however, include references to the place of conviction and the court of sentencing.

Lists of Executions

Some descriptive information about convicts is provided in these lists, including date and time of execution, name, age, weight, and color, name of the person murdered, and the sheriff's name.

AVAILABILITY OF RECORDS

Locating early prison records can be challenging. The records of Pennsylvania prisons, for example, have been microfilmed by the Genealogical Society of Utah, but the actual records are still on file at the prison or at the state archive. If you know the place or state of imprisonment, write to the prison itself or to the state department of corrections at the address given in the list above; request photocopies of the records available and the

Figure 10-4. July 1844 admissions from Admissions and Discharge Book, Eastern Pennsylvania State Penitentiary, vol. 1, p. 1. FHL microfilm 1,032,652, item 2.

Figure 10-5. From the Register of Prisoners, 1889–1901, Pennsylvania Industrial Reformatory, p. 1. FHL 1,032,656, item 3.

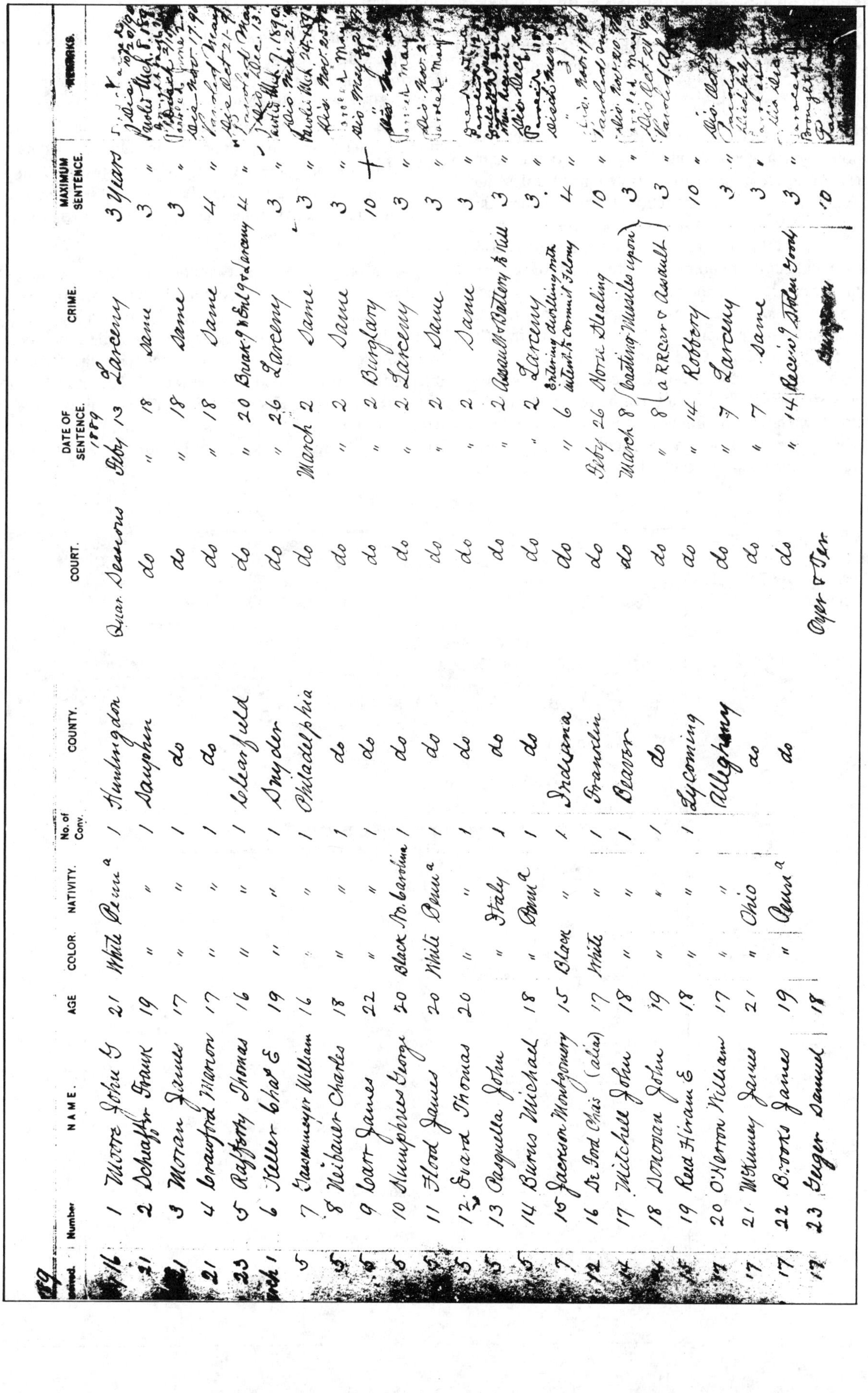

1889 eived.	Number	NAME.	AGE	COLOR.	NATIVITY.	No. of Conv.	COUNTY.	COURT.	DATE OF SENTENCE. 1889	CRIME.	MAXIMUM SENTENCE.	REMARKS.
16	1	Moore John G	21	White	Penn^a	1	Huntingdon	Quar. Sessions	Feby 13	Larceny	3 Years	Dis. 10/20/90
21	2	Schaeffer Frank	19	"	"	1	Dauphin	do	" 18	same	3 "	Parolee Mch. 8. 189[illegible]
21	3	Moran James	17	"	"	1	do	do	" 18	Same	3 "	Paroled June 2 [illegible]
21	4	Crawford Marion	17	"	"	1	do	do	" 18	Same	4 "	Paroled May [illegible] Dis Oct 21-91
23	5	Rafferty Thomas	16	"	"	1	Clearfield	do	" 20	Break'g & Ent'g & Larceny	4 "	Paroled May [illegible] Dis. Dec. 13
March 1	6	Keller Chas E	19	"	"	1	Snyder	do	" 26	Larceny	3 "	Paroled Mch. 7. 1890 Dis. Mar. 2
5	7	Gassemmeyer William	16	"	"	1	Philadelphia	do	March 2	Same	3 "	Paroled Mch 24. 189[illegible] Dis. Nov. 25. 9[illegible]
5	8	Neibauer Charles	18	"	"	1	do	do	" 2	Same	3 "	Paroled May 12 Dis. May [illegible]
5	9	Carr James	22	"	"	1	do	do	" 2	Burglary	10 +	[illegible]
5	10	Humphries George	20	Black	No. Carolina	1	do	do	" 2	Larceny	3 "	Paroled May Dis. Nov. 2[illegible]
5	11	Flood James	20	White	Penn^a	1	do	do	" 2	Same	3 "	Paroled May 12
5	12	Evard Thomas	20	"	"	1	do	do	" 2	Same	3 "	[illegible]
5	13	Pasquella John		"	Italy	1	do	do	" 2	Assault & Battery to Kill	3 "	[illegible] Dis. Dec [illegible]
5	14	Burns Michael	18	"	Penn^a	1	do	do	" 2	Larceny	3 "	Paroled [illegible] Disch Mar 6
7	15	Jackson Montgomery	15	Black	"	1	Indiana	do	" 6	Entering dwelling with intent to commit Felony	4 "	" 31
12	16	De Ford Chas (alias)	17	White	"	1	Franklin	do	Feby 26	Horse Stealing	10 "	Dis. Nov. 17. 90
14	17	Mitchell John	18	"	"	1	Beaver	do	March 8	Casting Missiles upon a RR car & Assault	3 "	Paroled [illegible] Dis. Nov. 20 9[illegible]
14	18	Donovan John	19	"	"	1	do	do	" 8		3 "	Paroled May Dis Oct 24 90
15	19	Reed Hiram E	18	"	"	1	Lycoming	do	" 14	Robbery	10 "	Paroled [illegible]
17	20	O'Herron William	17	"	"		Allegheny	do	" 7	Larceny	3 "	Dis. Oct 2[illegible]
17	21	McKinney James	21	"	Ohio		do	do	" 7	Same	3 "	Paroled [illegible] Died July [illegible]
17	22	Brooks James	19	"	Penn^a		do	do	" 14	Receiv'g Stolen Goods	3 "	Paroled [illegible]
17	23	Geiger Samuel	18					Oyer & Ter.		[illegible]	10	Brought [illegible] Paroled [illegible]

location of the records, if they are no longer maintained by the prison authorities. Requests should list the specific record desired—"the entries from the biographical register, the reception descriptive list, and the clemency file," for example—to insure receiving records of maximum genealogical value.

USE OF PRISON RECORDS

Most family genealogists do not need prison records regularly, but professional genealogists should know how to use them. The incarceration of an ancestor may go unnoticed unless the court records index a criminal conviction, the newspapers describe and report the trial, or family members remember the story. A client told me that his great-grandfather had been convicted of arson and negligent homicide in the death of his first wife. Research revealed that the ancestor had actually been married five times. The alleged homicide involved his second wife, whom he had divorced before 1880. She sued for fraudulent divorce after his third marriage. The suit was filed in Missouri, although she was a resident of Tennessee. The ancestor was reportedly so enraged by the suit that he returned to Tennessee to burn down her house, unknowingly causing her death in the fire. The court records of Greene County, Missouri, supported the information about the fraudulent divorce suit. There was, however, no record of a criminal trial, arrest, or incarceration in Missouri or Tennessee.

Because the man was a veteran of the Civil War and had received a disability pension, I requested his pension files to determine his movements after being discharged and to gain additional information about his marriages. The pension file shows that he received a periodic physical at Lansing, Kansas, in 1884, where the Kansas State Prison is located. He had been a resident of Montgomery County, Kansas, just prior to living in Lansing. A document in his file states that he misplaced his pension certificate when he was arrested at Cherryvale, Kansas, just before being taken to the prison at Lansing.

The Montgomery County records produced nothing about his arrest and trial. I requested his prison record, but officials at Lansing responded disappointingly that they had no record of him in their files. In a second letter I included the document from the pension file to assist in identifying the records. The prison officials indicated that the records had been transferred to the Kansas State Historical Society. The historical society would not provide photocopies but affirmed that the ancestor had served a three-year sentence in the Kansas State Prison at Lansing for larceny.

Figure 10-6. From the Biographical Register, Pennsylvania Industrial Reformatory, no. 670. FHL 1,032,655, item 1.

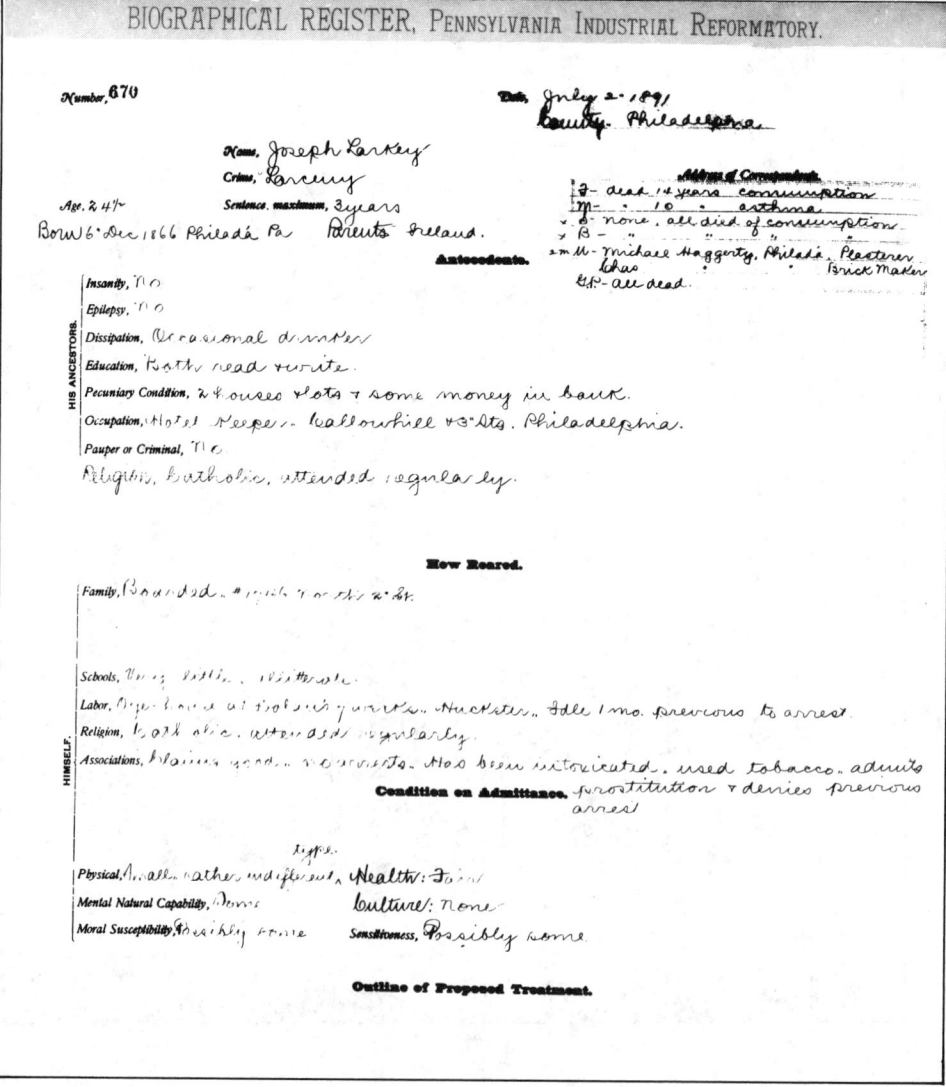

Researchers must often use a variety of records to lead them to the prison in which an ancestor was incarcerated. Once that has been determined, finding the actual prison records should be no more complicated than my own process. Obtaining the records is worth the effort, however, because they will help identify other family members. For instance, the biographical register shown in figure 10-6 contains at least five leads to follow:

1. Joseph Larkey was born in Philadelphia on 6 December 1866. The 1866 city directory should list all of the Larkey families in that city during the year of his birth, possibly giving clues to parents, grandparents, and other relatives with the same surname.

2. Joseph's father was a hotelkeeper who died fourteen years before his son's incarceration (1877). The city directory of Philadelphia should be searched specifically for a hotelkeeper named Larkey also. Later directories should list his widow.

3. Joseph Larkey named Michael and Charles Haggerty as uncles. They are probably maternal uncles, so his mother's family should be sought among the Haggerty families of Philadelphia.

4. Information gained from city directories should lead to a search of the 1870 census for a Larkey family living in Philadelphia, with both parents having been born in Ireland and the head of the household employed as a hotelkeeper.

5. Records of the Catholic church closest to Callowhill and 3rd Street in Philadelphia, where Joseph's father worked, should be examined to see if the family was in the nearest parish.

The records of the court in which a convict was sentenced should also be searched for additional historical information.

PROBLEMS IN USING PRISON RECORDS

The problems encountered in using prison records are similar to those encountered in using any other early records. Early records of the correctional institutions are sometimes difficult to locate. Modern prison records within the last seventy-two years fall under the jurisdiction of privacy laws and cannot be released. Family members may obtain the records of deceased convicts and ex-convicts under some circumstances, but you should inquire about those conditions at the prison or correctional agency by letter or telephone.

Legibility is also a problem. Early records are handwritten and can be difficult to read. Others are faded and damaged. Microfilmed copies may be unclear. When microfilmed copies are poor, it may be necessary to obtain a copy of the original.

Although prison records will only occasionally be used in the research process, they are valuable sources of genealogical and historical information. Researchers should take the time and effort to track them down. Sometimes prison records cannot be used alone and require the information included in court records, newspaper articles, coroners' records, and other sources to complete the picture of the individuals and circumstances involved in the events that led to imprisonment.

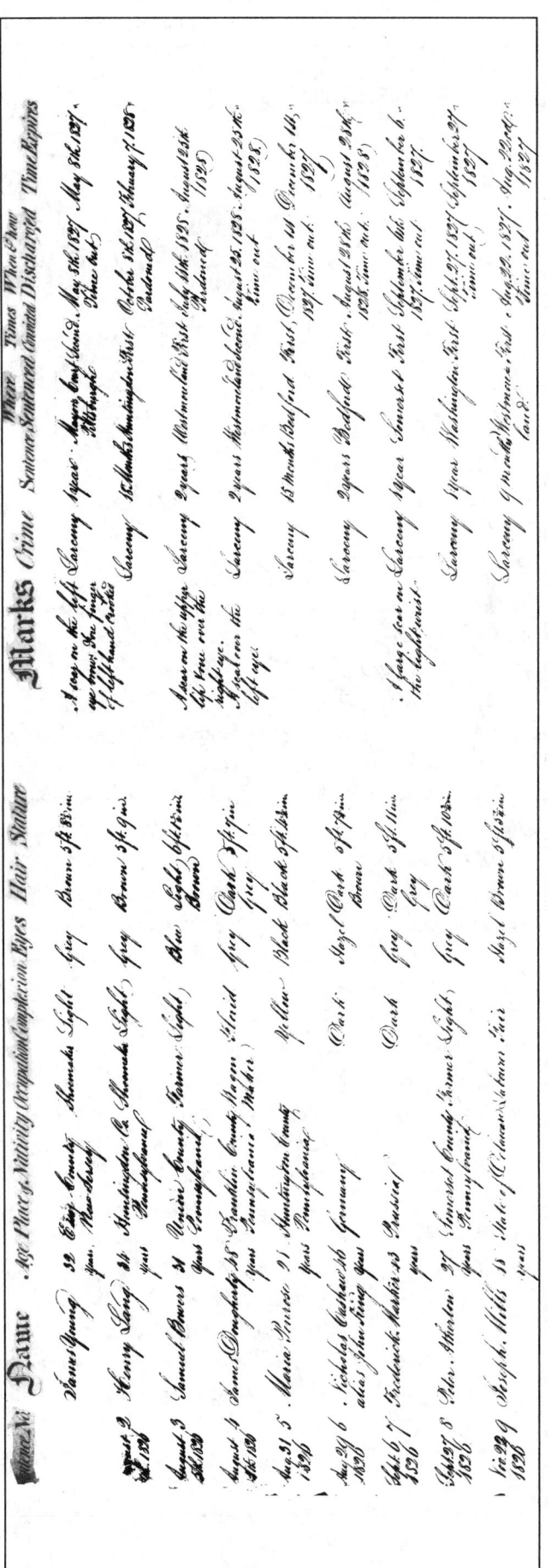

Figure 10-7. From the Descriptive Register, May 1826–February 1827, Pennsylvania Western State Penitentiary, p. 1. FHL 1,032,653, item 2.

Figure 10-8. Death warrant of Thomas Munley, 7 September 1876, Pennsylvania State Board of Pardons. FHL 1,032,659.

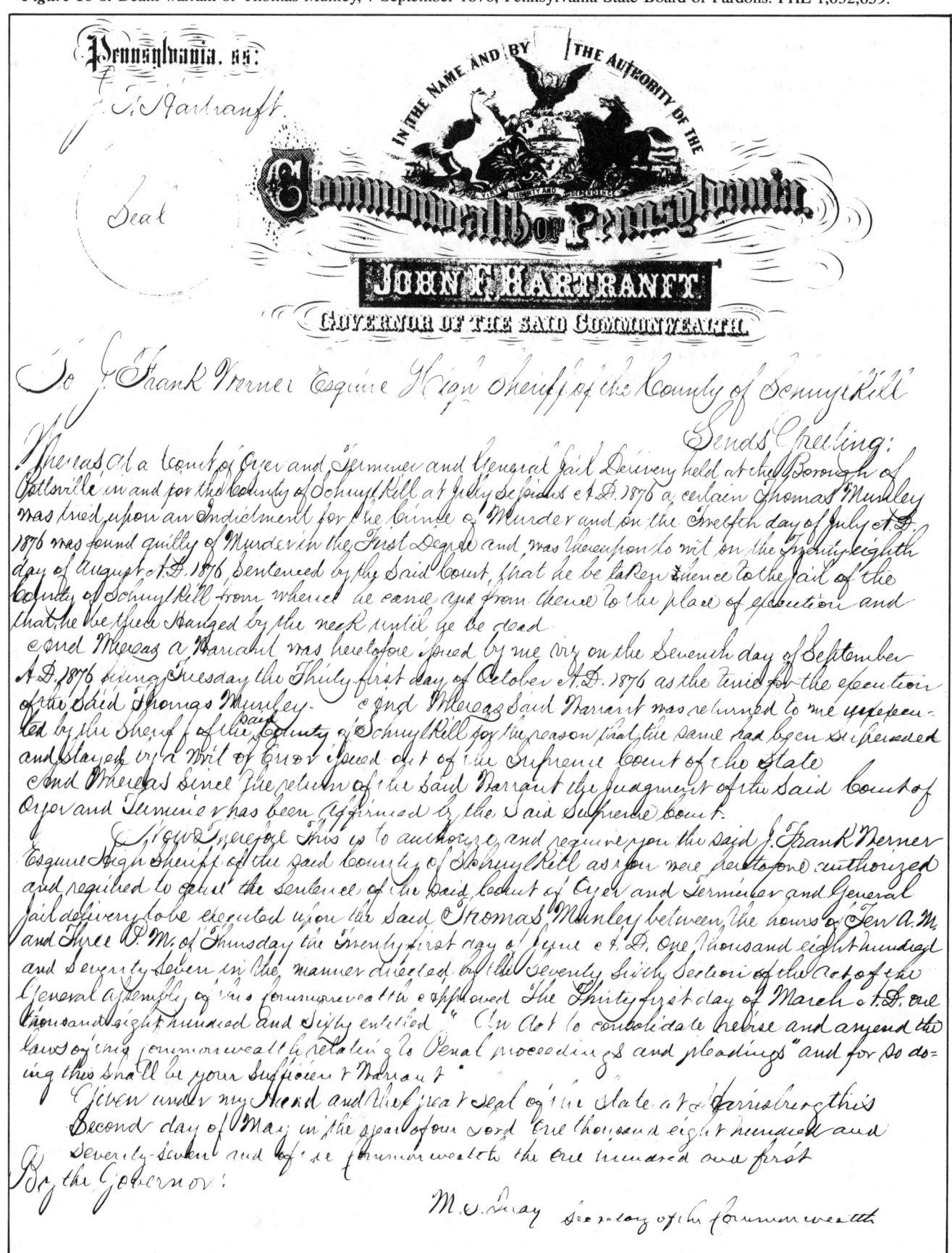

MORTUARY RECORDS

Mortuaries and funeral homes in the United States are privately owned business establishments. Many of them have maintained records for more than 125 years. The amount of genealogical information recorded in the early years of record keeping was limited compared to the amount of information compiled later; at a minimum, however, the early records list the name of the deceased, death date, place of death, cause of death, and name of the informant. Occasionally, the age, residence, occupation, birthplace, and next of kin of the deceased are included. Most early morticians' records are available to the public.

Modern morticians' records are more complete. The mortician gathers information needed to compile both the death certificate and obituary notice. These records are not available to the public, but they can be obtained by close relatives of the deceased.

Morticians' records are extremely valuable sources of information for the period before vital records were kept. The records are maintained at the mortuary and contain facts not available in other sources. Locating morticians' records is not difficult if the place of death is known. The annual *National Directory of Morticians* (Youngstown, Ohio: National Direc-

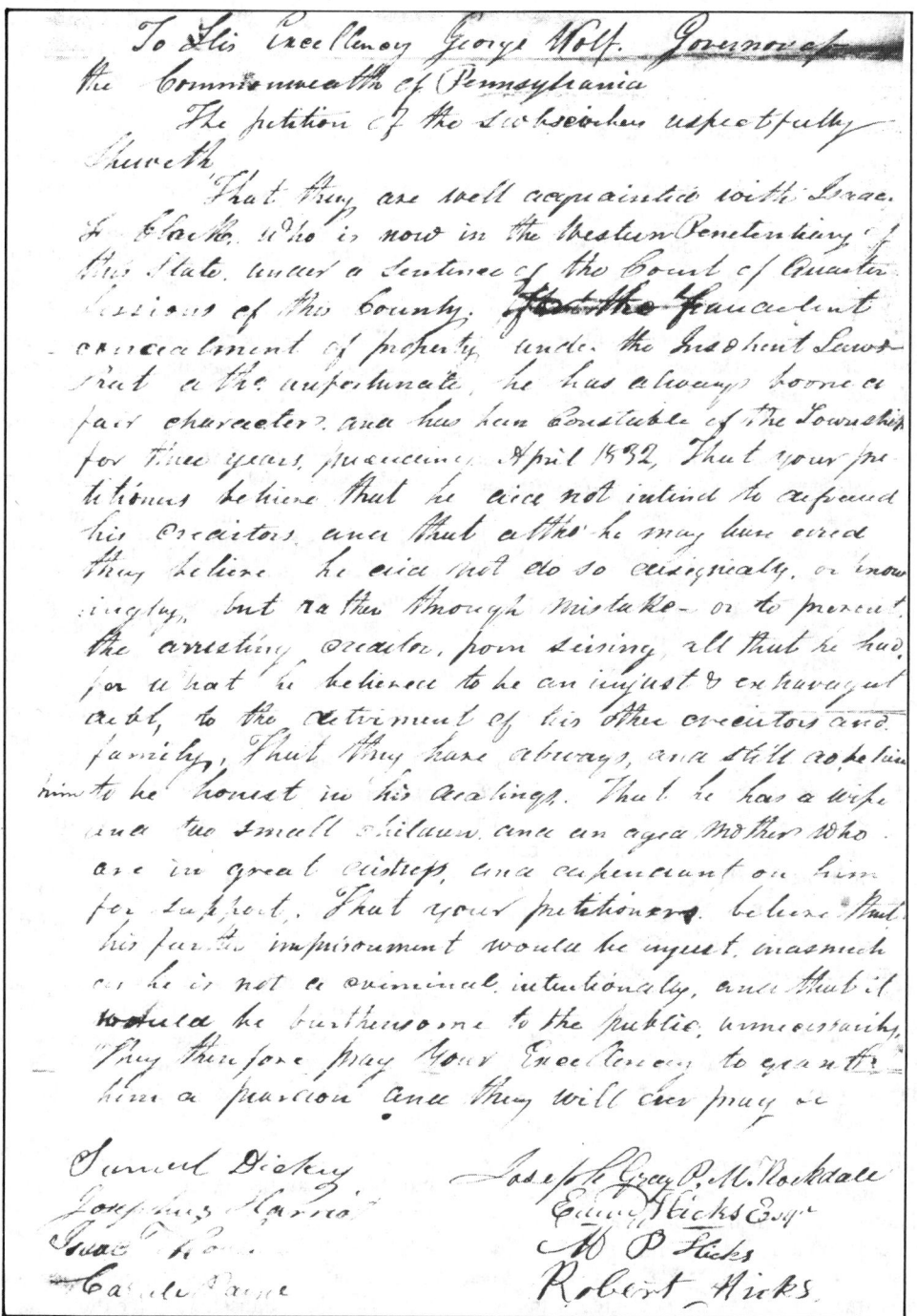

Figure 10-9. From the clemency files of Isaac F. Clarke, 1833, Department of State, Secretary of the Commonwealth of Pennsylvania. FHL 1,018,404.

tory of Morticians), which lists the names and addresses of most morticians and funeral directors in the United States, can be found in the collections of numerous genealogical libraries and in the offices of local mortuaries. Records of mortuaries and funeral homes that are no longer in operation or that have changed proprietorship can often be found in the custody of the town or county clerk, the local public library or historical society, and even university collections with a local focus. Check the *National Union Catalog of Manuscript Collections* (see chapter 2) for morticians' records deposited locally.

Once the mortician's record has been obtained, evaluate it carefully for both the information it contains and the research it suggests, such as:

1. Occupation. If the occupation of the deceased was unusual or governed by a labor union, investigate employment or union records.

2. Service in the armed forces. Request military service records if the ancestor was a veteran. The branch of service may not be listed in the morticians' records, but it may be found in the obituary notice or in the documents created by the mortician to apply for veteran's burial benefits. Department of Defense Form 214, Record of Discharge, must accompany the application for burial benefits, and a photocopy may be in the mortician's files.

3. Name and address of the informant. You may be able to contact the informant. If he or she is deceased, an heir of either the informant or the deceased may own or reside in the residence listed.

4. Hospital, nursing home, or institution where the death occurred. These establishments maintain excellent records which are discussed in detail later in this chapter.

5. Cemetery or crematory. If the deceased is buried in a family cemetery plot, cemetery records and tombstone inscriptions will provide information about other family members buried in that plot. Figure 10-10 is a form from the cemetery file, obtained after reviewing the records of mortician George F. Myers.

6. Marriage. Follow up on the marriage record to obtain details about the spouse of the deceased.

7. Church affiliation. The name and location of the church attended by the deceased may be recorded. The religion of the deceased will also be stated, if known. Church records may offer extensive information about the parents, grandparents, brothers, sisters, and children of the deceased.

8. Fraternal organizations. If the deceased was a member of the Masons, Order of the Elks, Knights of Columbus, or a similar organization, their records may provide extensive biographical information.

9. Survivors. The list of survivors usually includes residences of family members and the married names of daughters, excellent clues to other avenues of research in previously unknown locations.

Morticians' records are not without problems for the researcher. The information contained in the records is only as accurate as the knowledge and memory of the informant. Therefore, inaccuracies can be present if the informant was not closely related to the deceased or lacked detailed knowledge. When the information is fragmented or does not agree with previously known facts, you will need to conduct additional searches to clarify the discrepancies.

CORONERS' RECORDS

Coroners' records are maintained at any of three levels of government, depending upon the size and structure of state and local governments. Large metropolitan cities have established medical examiners' offices to investigate the circumstances of unusual deaths. County coroners and state medical examiners exist at higher levels for the same purpose. Some states have only a state medical examiner if the population is too small to economically maintain local or county coroners' offices.

The coroner or medical examiner creates several records in the investigation of unusual deaths, including pathology reports, necrology reports, toxicology reports, testimony offered at the inquest, and a jury report. The first three reports contain medical facts that indicate the condition of the deceased at the time of death; they offer little genealogical information. The inquest testimony may provide biographical and historical facts about the deceased. The most valuable document which may be found in a coroner's records is the death certificate, which provides some degree of genealogical information.

The coroner or medical examiner may not request an inquest if the autopsy reports indicate that the death was not caused by negligence or an act of violence, although some states have recently passed legislation requiring a coroner's report for all deaths if a doctor was not present at the time of death. Inquest testimony frequently contains sworn statements by the family and friends of the deceased. While these statements do not always contain genealogical information, they can suggest other avenues of research. (Also see chapter 7, Research in Court Records, and chapter 19, Tracking Urban Ancestors.)

Most coroners' and medical examiners' records are available to the public. Some of the early records of metropolitan cities have been microfilmed by the Genealogical Society of Utah. Figure 10-11 is the first page of a five-page entry from the Coroner's Evidence Book of Philadelphia County, Pennsylvania, recording Isadore Raimonda's fatal stabbing of Dominic Raimonda in 1876. It does not contain extensive genealogical information, stating specifically only the deceased's name, age, height, and date and cause of death, the hospital to which the deceased was taken, and the name of the attending physician. The jury's verdict is given; Isadore Raimonda was convicted of manslaughter, suggesting a search of prison records.

Modern coroners' records may contain more detailed information and they have greater historical value, so they should be used in addition to vital records.

The value of coroners' records is similar to that of morticians' records. The information found in the records should be carefully analyzed for genealogical facts and clues to other record sources that may prove helpful. The information found in figure 10-11 suggests several possibilities for additional research:

1. Names of the deceased and the defendant. Although not specifically stated, the record implies that Isadore and Dominic were cousins. Any further research should be approached with this possibility in mind.

2. Translator. The police officer interviewed the wounded Dominic with a translator, so the dying man may have been a recent immigrant. Naturalization records may show if either Dominic or Isadore had petitioned for or received citizenship.

Figure 10-10. A form from a cemetery file of the Catholic Cemeteries Associations of the diocese of Pittsburgh.

CEMETERY COPY

THE [C]ATHOLIC CEMETERIES A[S]SOCIATIONS
OF THE DIOCESE OF PITT[SBUR]GH
718 HAZELWOOD AVE., PITTSBU[RG]H 17, PA.

03177

DIVISION 2

ACCOUNT NAME Myers George — DATE 6-26- 19

ADDRESS 1437 Page St. — CITY Pgh Pa

☑ INTERMENT — DATE OF DEATH 6-25- 19

☐ REMOVAL — AGE 43

☐ RECEIVING VAULT — PLACE OF DEATH 1437 Page St.

NAME OF DECEASED Myers George — ADDRESS same

BURIAL DATE 6-29- 19 TIME 9 a.m. — CHURCH St. Gabriel — PRIEST PERMIT ☑ — UNDERTAKER Cieslak M. H.

DEED IN NAME OF Meyers Mrs Bridget — RELATIONSHIP TO DECEASED grandmother — ☐ NON-CATHOLIC ☑ CATHOLIC BURIAL

1. ☐ SINGLE GRAVE — SEC. — ROW — NO. — ☐ POOR GROUND ☐ D. P. A.
2. ☐ LOT — SEC. E — LOT 153 — GRAVES
3. ☑ OPEN GRAVE # 4 — ☑ O. D. ☐ E. D. — O. T. ☐ — ☑ ADULT ☐ CHILD — 30
4. ☑ LOWERING DEVICE AND GREENS — 30
5. ☐ TENT
6. TYPE VAULT ☐ OURS ☐ OTHERS — COMPANY P. V. cave proof — SIZE 6
7. ☐ DISINTERMENT OF — ORIGINAL INT. MADE 19 — TYPE VAULT ☐ O. D. ☐ E. D.
   FROM SEC. LOT GR. TO SEC. LOT GR.
8. REASON TO RECEIVING VAULT — TIME ALLOWED
9. OTHER SERVICES

SECTION	LOT NO	MONTH	YEAR	DAY	PRICE	FOLIO NUMBER
E	153					

NAME
Bridget Meyers

STREET — TOWN — STATE

GRAVE	BURIED	DATE	GRAVE	BURIED	DATE
1	Martin Meyers 3-20-1900 Bridget Myers 1-7-10				
2	Anna M. Meyers 1-27-36 George Meyers 5-4-51				
3	John & Ella Kane 3-20-1900				
4	Andrew Cain 12-14-03 Patrick Cain 2-17-13 removed to 602 M #2, 10-29-13				
5	George Myers 6-29-53				
6					

3. Hospital. The hospital records may still exist and should be checked for more information.

4. Verdict. The record concludes with the report that Isadore was convicted of manslaughter and sentenced, a notation made later after the appropriate court has dealt with the case. Prison records may contain additional biographical facts about Isadore Raimonda.

5. The coroner also issues death certificates. This document generally provides the deceased's name, age, sex, place of birth, race, occupation, marital status, place of death, date of death, and cause of death.

In contrast to the very full record on the fatal Raimonda quarrel is an entry in the Coroner's Evidence Book of the New York City coroner in 1862 (figure 10-12).

Most family researchers will not need coroners, and medical examiners' records to establish genealogical facts, but pro-

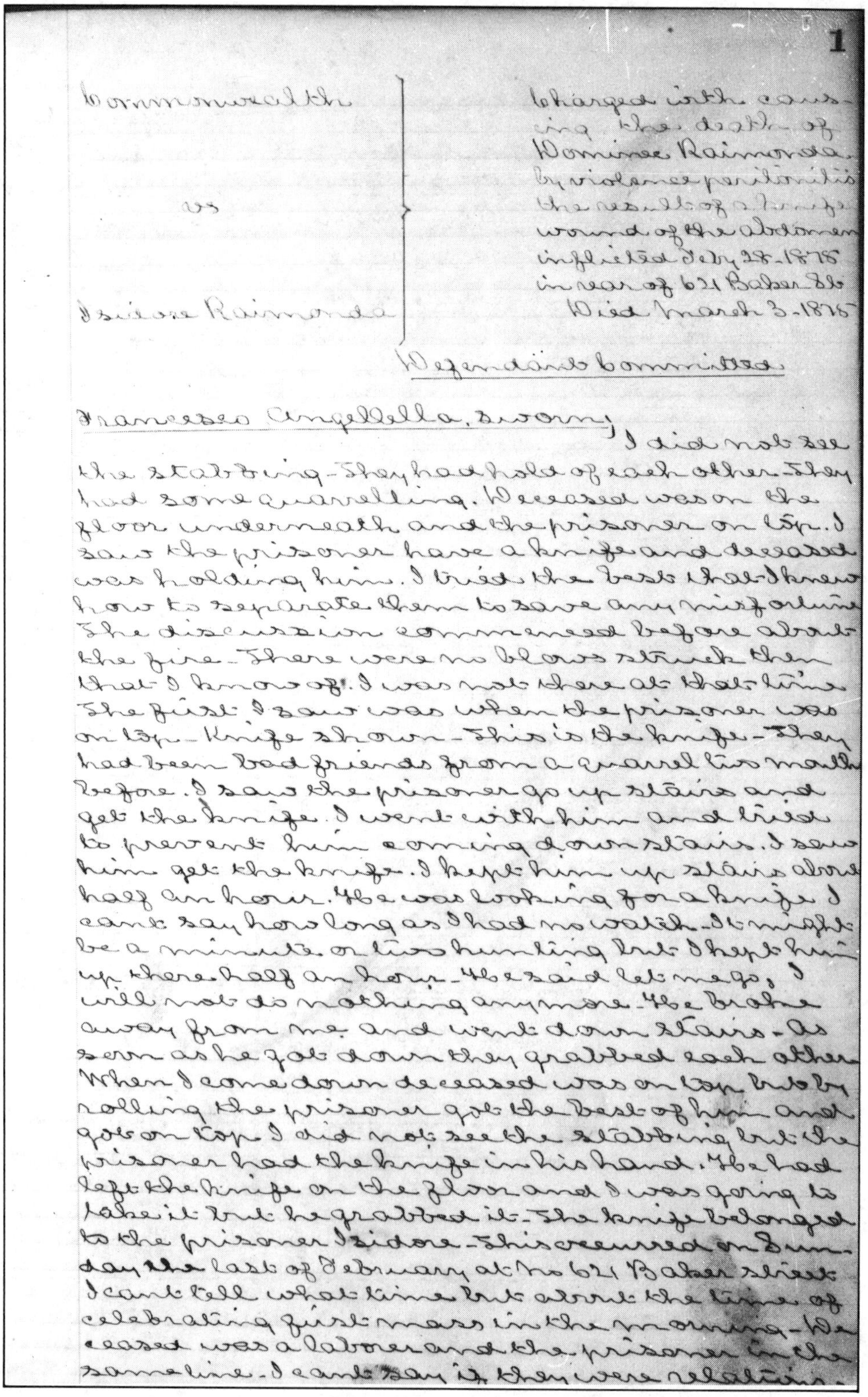

Figure 10-11. From the Commonwealth vs. Isadore Raimonda, Coroner's Evidence Book, Philadelphia County, Pennsylvania, p. 1. FHL 965,369, item 1.

fessional genealogists should find them most valuable. Usually the records are on file at the office of the coroner or medical examiner. Early records may have been transferred to the city or county clerk's office, the local historical society, or a state archive. The coroner's office will know where the old records are located. Some offices will not release the records without proof of relationship to the deceased and a statement indicating how the information in the record will be used. Family history is usually considered a valid reason.

Once you have located the records, there should be few problems in using them. However, they may have suffered deterioration over the years, making all or part of the records difficult to read. Unless the witnesses at an inquest perjured themselves, the testimony should be factual, eliminating erroneous information about the deceased. The major problem in using coroner's records is locating the old records, a process that may involve writing several letters of inquiry to various levels of government, local clerks, and historical societies. Still, despite the specialization and inconvenience involved in using coro-

ners' records, they should not be overlooked, especially when you need historical information.

SCHOOL RECORDS

The records of schools, colleges, and universities in the United States have gradually developed into valuable sources of genealogical information. Early school records lack uniformity, especially in rural primary school systems; many no longer exist. Most commonly found are school board minutes (figure 10-13). While board minutes deal primarily with administrative and financial matters involved in operating the school, they may include such potentially valuable information as the names of administrators and teachers, and reference to other records that might be valuable. For instance, these 1873 minutes from McDuffey County, Georgia, refer to a school census. Does that census still exist in the files of the county school district or the county clerk?

Salaries were set by the number of students in attendance rather than by the number of school days taught. McDuffey

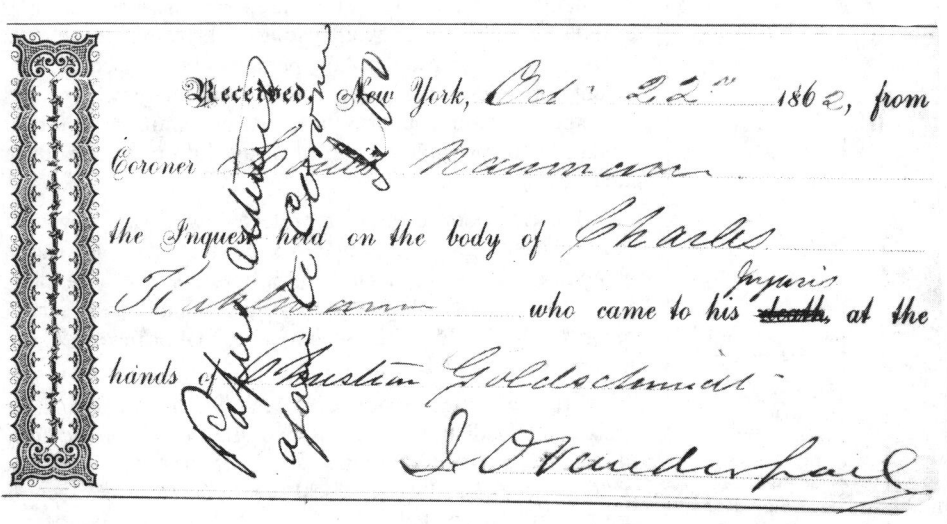

Figure 10-12. Inquest reports on Joseph P. Thompson, 2 October 1862, and Charles Kikleman [?], 22 October 1862, Coroner's Office Inquests to Deaths, New York City, 1862–64. FHL 514, 332.

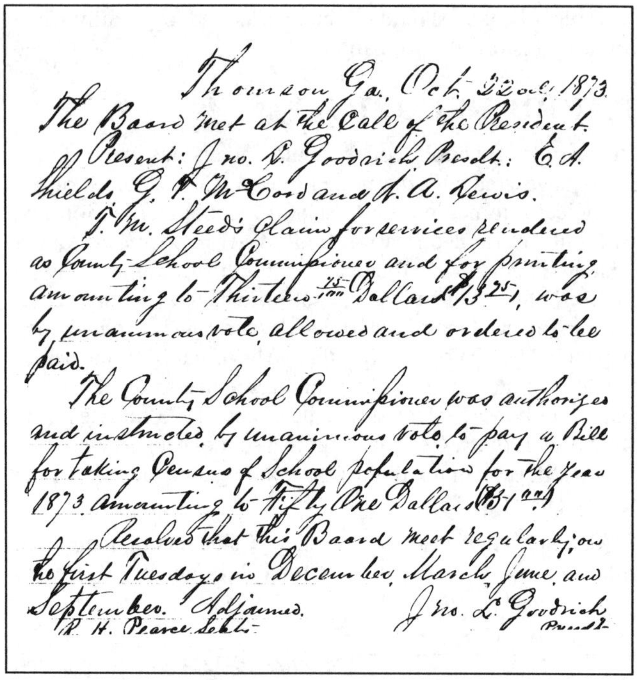

Thomson Ga. Oct. 22nd 1873.
The Board met at the Call of the President.
Present: Jno. L. Goodrich Presdt: E. A. Shields, G. F. McCord and A. A. Lewis.
T. M. Steed's Claim for services rendered as County School Commissioner and for printing amounting to Thirteen 25/100 Dollars $13.25, was by unanimous vote, allowed and ordered to be paid.
The County School Commissioner was authorized and instructed by unanimous vote, to pay a Bill for taking Census of School population for the year 1873 amounting to Fifty One Dollars ($51.00)
Resolved that this Board meet regularly on the first Tuesdays in December, March, June and September. Adjourned.
Jno. L. Goodrich Presdt.
R. H. Pearce Secty.

Figure 10-13. School board minutes, 22 October 1873, McDuffey County, Georgia, 1872–1960, p. 25. FHL 220,521, part 1.

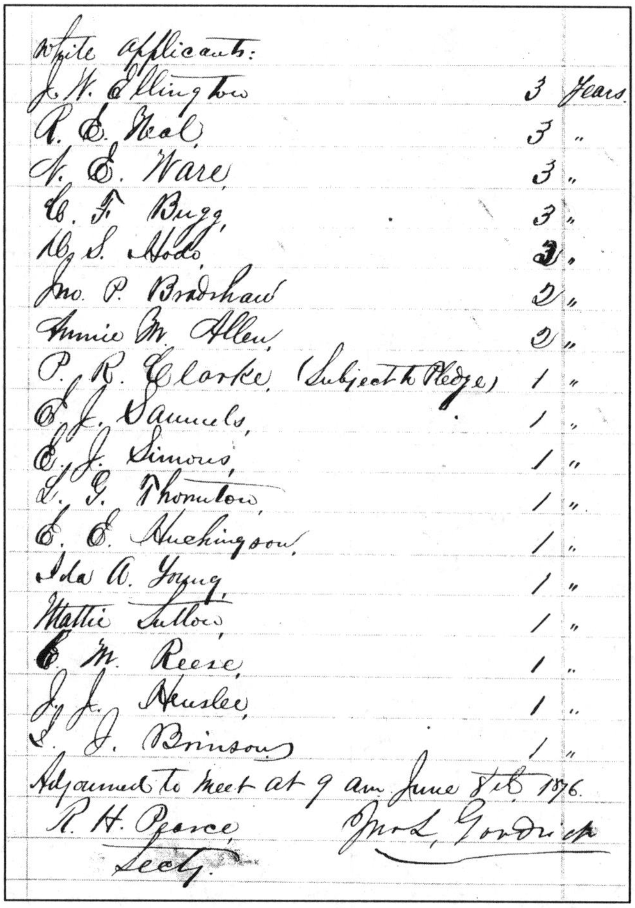

White applicants:

J. W. Ellington	3 Years
R. E. Neal	3 "
N. E. Ware	3 "
C. F. Bugg	3 "
W. S. Hood	3 "
Jno. P. Bradshaw	2 "
Annie M. Allen	2 "
P. R. Clarke (Subject to Pledge)	1 "
E. J. Samuels	1 "
E. J. Simons	1 "
L. G. Thornton	1 "
E. E. Hutchingson	1 "
Ida A. Young	1 "
Mattie Sutton	1 "
C. M. Reese	1 "
J. J. Hensley	1 "
L. J. Brinson	1 "

Adjourned to meet at 9 am June 8th 1876.
R. H. Pearce, Secty.
Jno L. Goodrich

Figure 10-14. School board minutes, 22 October 1873, McDuffey County, Georgia, p. 40.

County required licensing earlier than most rural school systems, and figure 10-14 shows the applicants who were granted licenses to teach in 1876 and the number of years for which the license was granted.

Many metropolitan and rural schools received funds from the local government to cover the cost of educating poor children. Records of children receiving an education at government expense can be found in court records, school board minutes, or town meeting records. The information—name, age, and sex of the child—is typical of all early school records.

Some of the best early primary school records were kept by private preparatory and boarding schools whose students were from the region's wealthy families. References to children's parents, residence, curriculum, and activities, as well as individual and class photographs, can more often be found in these school records.

As with most other records in the United States, school records became more comprehensive after the turn of the twentieth century. Schools maintained by the Bureau of Indian Affairs are excellent sources of information and reflect the type of information found in modern school records. These records, maintained by the federal government, have been microfilmed. Records of the Juneau Indian Agency in Alaska are housed at the National Archives—Alaska Region at Anchorage, and were microfilmed by the Genealogical Society of Utah in 1969.

The Office of Indian Affairs also compiled school censuses of Indian children taken at the town and county levels throughout the United States at one time or another but without any predictable format or consistency. The 1939–49 census of the Indian children on the Afognak, Alaska, reservation is shown in figure 10-15. (See chapter 5, Research in Census Records, for further information about school censuses.)

University and college records are excellent sources of genealogical information compared to early primary school records. Records document admission, registration, course of study, and graduation. Additionally, many alumni associations and school archivists have compiled biographies and histories of former students. Many schools have preserved applications for admission containing valuable family information. Yearbooks and annuals are on file with alumni associations and in college and university libraries.

Many colleges, universities, prep schools, and boarding schools have directories, while listings of local primary schools are difficult to locate and usually pertain only to a specific area. County histories often mention the early county schools and sometimes list students of a particular graduating year. Local or state historical societies may also have information about an area's early schools.

Modern school records are protected by privacy laws, but family members are sometimes able to obtain the information or photocopies of the documents in the files. Because state, local, and school policies govern the availability of school records, you should write to the local school of interest to determine what procedure to follow.

Early school records may be located in the archive of the present school district, in the office of the city, town, or county clerk, in local or state libraries, or in local or state archives or historical societies. Ask the local school board where records are presently deposited.

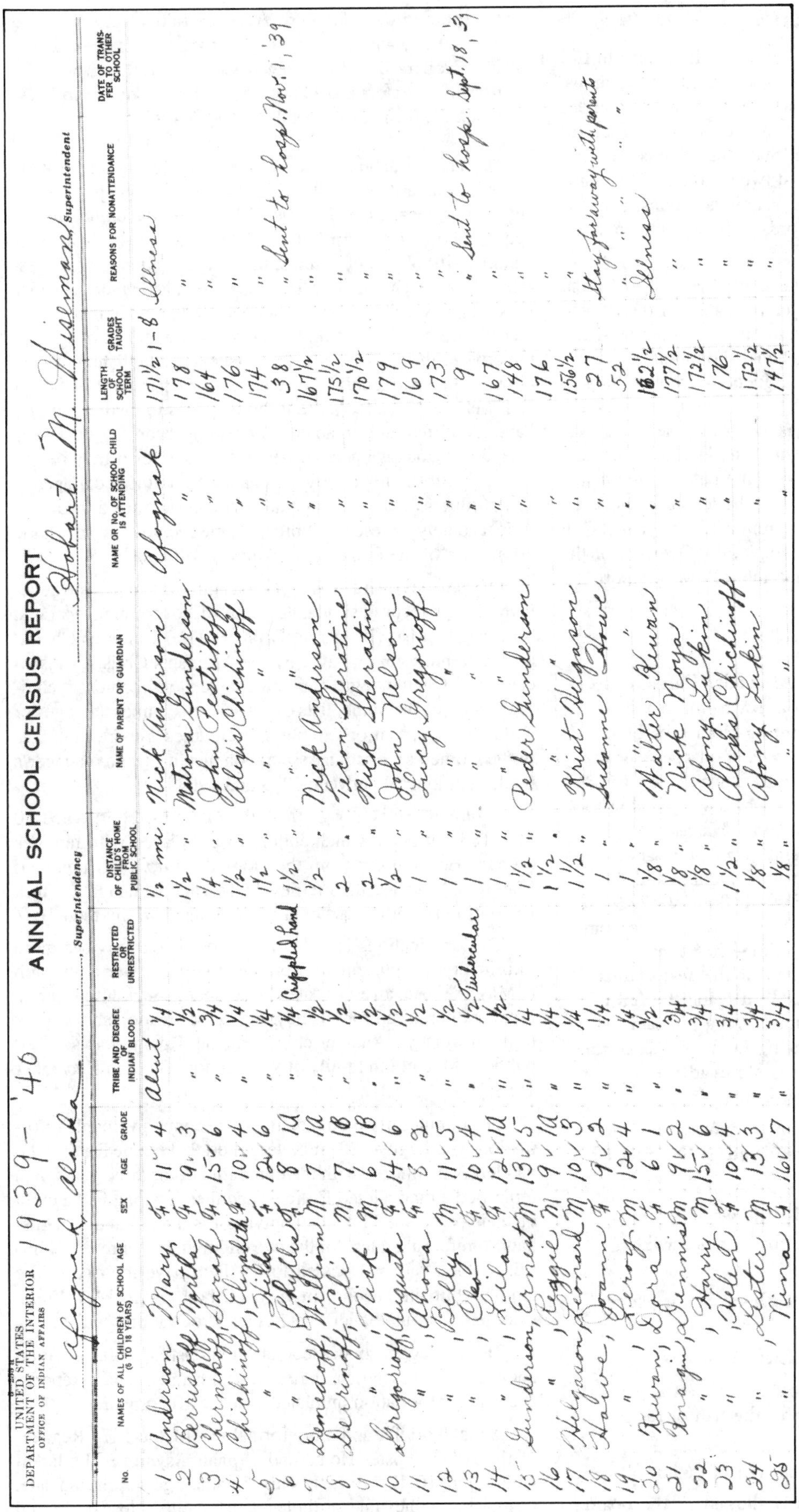

UNITED STATES
DEPARTMENT OF THE INTERIOR
OFFICE OF INDIAN AFFAIRS

1939 – '40

ANNUAL SCHOOL CENSUS REPORT

Afognak, Alaska, Superintendency

Hobart M. Wiseman, Superintendent

No.	NAMES OF ALL CHILDREN OF SCHOOL AGE (6 TO 18 YEARS)	SEX	AGE	GRADE	TRIBE AND DEGREE OF INDIAN BLOOD	RESTRICTED OR UNRESTRICTED	DISTANCE OF CHILD'S HOME FROM PUBLIC SCHOOL	NAME OF PARENT OR GUARDIAN	NAME OR No. OF SCHOOL CHILD IS ATTENDING	LENGTH OF SCHOOL TERM	GRADES TAUGHT	REASONS FOR NONATTENDANCE	DATE OF TRANSFER TO OTHER SCHOOL
1	Anderson Mary	F	11	4	Aleut 1/4		1/2 mi.	Nick Anderson	Afognak	171 1/2	1-8	Illness	
2	Berristoff Martha	F	9	3	" 1/2		1 1/2 "	Matrona Gunderson	"	178		"	
3	Chernikoff, Sarah	F	15	6	" 3/4		1/4 "	John Pestrikoff	"	164		"	
4	Chichinoff, Elizabeth	F	10	4	" 1/4		1 1/2 "	Alexis Chichinoff	"	176		"	
5	" , Hilda	F	12	6	" 1/4		1 1/2 "	" "	"	174		"	
6	" , Phyllis	F	8	1A	" 1/4	Crippled hand	1 1/2 "	" "	"	38		" Sent to hosp. Nov. 1, '39	
7	Demedoff, William	M	7	1A	" 1/2		1/2 "	Nick Anderson	"	167 1/2		"	
8	Derrinoff, Eli	M	7	1B	" 1/2		2 "	Tecon Sheratine	"	175 1/2		"	
9	" , Nick	M	6	1B	" 1/2		2 "	Nick Sheratine	"	170 1/2		"	
10	Gregorioff, Augusta	F	14	6	" 1/2		1/2 "	John Nelson	"	179		"	
11	" , Anona	F	8	2	" 1/2		1 "	Lucy Gregorioff	"	169		"	
12	" , Billy	M	11	5	" 1/2		1 "	" "	"	173		"	
13	" , Cleo	F	10	4	" 1/2	Tubercular	1 "	" "	"	9		" Sent to hosp. Sept. 18, '39	
14	" , Lila	F	12	1A	" 1/2		1 "	" "	"	167		"	
15	Gunderson, Ernest	M	13	5	" 1/4		1 1/2 "	Peder Gunderson	"	148		"	
16	" , Reggie	M	9	1A	" 1/4		1 1/2 "	" "	"	176		"	
17	Helgason, Leonard	M	10	3	" 1/4		1 1/2 "	Krist Helgason	"	156 1/2		"	
18	Howe, Joann	F	9	2	" 1/4		1 "	Susanne Howe	"	27		Stay far away with parents	
19	" , Leroy	M	12	4	" 1/4		1 "	" "	"	52		" " " " "	
20	Kewan, Dora	F	6	1	" 1/2		1/8 "	Walter Kewan	"	162 1/2		Illness	
21	Knagin, Dennis	M	9	2	" 3/4		1/8 "	Nick Noya	"	177 1/2		"	
22	" , Harry	M	15	6	" 3/4		1/8 "	Afony Lukin	"	172 1/2		"	
23	" , Helen	F	10	4	" 3/4		1 1/2 "	Alexis Chichinoff	"	176		"	
24	" , Lester	M	13	3	" 3/4		1/8 "	Afony Lukin	"	172 1/2		"	
25	" , Nina	F	16	7	" 3/4		1/8 "	" "	"	147 1/2		"	

Figure 10-15. School census of Indian children, Afognak, Alaska, 1939–49, United States Department of the Interior, Office of Indian Affairs. FHL 1,030,793.

ORPHANAGE RECORDS

Orphanages, which date from the seventeenth century in England, were originally workhouses, poorhouses, and asylums. Modern orphanages hardly resemble those depicted by Charles Dickens, but their purpose is the same: to provide refuge for orphaned and abandoned children. Such institutions have existed in the United States for at least two centuries. They have been operated by civil authorities, religious groups, and private benefactors. The types of records kept vary and are often difficult to locate.

During the early history of the United States, town and county officials appointed or elected overseers of the poor to deal with paupers and orphaned children. Local courts usually appointed guardians to care for orphans who might be heirs to property. When relatives or local residents were unwilling or unable to care for the child, he or she, if old enough, was bound out to learn a trade. If the child was too young, he or she was sent to an institution, usually maintained on a local level. County court records or probate records give the date the child was apprenticed, to whom, and the trade to be learned. These are often indexed under "orphans," "apprentices," or "paupers" in court indexes and dockets. For example, the Overseer of the Poor in Ohio County, Indiana made the following report and financial accounting in May 1827.

May Term 1827

And now at this time comes Alexander Dale Overseer of the Poor in and for Harrison Township in Ohio County and exhibits an account of Monies by him Received of Wilkerson McCarty Administrator of the Estate of Samuel McCarty Deceased, which the said Administrator States is the sum which was coming to Nancy Smith (Now a pauper of said Harrison Township) as one of the Heirs at Law of the said Decedent amounting to twenty-two Dollars and Ninety Cents #22.90. Out of which Sum of $22.90 it appears he (Dale) has paid to Eleazur Carver the Sum of Sixteen Dollars and Ninety Three 3/4 cents for keeping said pauper the Last half of the Year ending on the first Monday of May 1827 it being the full of the balance due said Carver for keeping the said pauper the year aforesaid. Leaving in the hands of the said Alexander Dale Overseer as aforesaid the Sum of Five Dollars and Ninety Seven Cents.

Aside he (Dale) also exhibits an account against the County for Services by him rendered as Overseer afsd as follows towit:

To Tending court one day with Carver $1.00

To Binding out a poor boy to the Cabinet making business 1.00

To Advertising and letting out Nancy Smith pauper aforesd for 1827 2.00

For making report of Sale to Clerk 1.00

For going to Carver's to see pauper and settling with him for keeping pauper one year, the half of his pay 1.00

Amounting in the whole to the sum of $6.00

Which account of Six Dollars is allowed by the Board

for the Services aforesaid. And the said Overseer agrees to retain and keep in his hands the aforesaid Five Dollars & Ninety Seven Cents in full satisfaction of the aforesaid Charge against the County to Six Dollars which is approved by the Board.[1]

Orphanages maintained by state and local governments were funded agencies that maintained better records than private and church agencies. Their files usually include the child's name, age or date of birth, birthplace, date of admission, names of parents, birthplaces of parents, name and residence of nearest kin, date of discharge, to whom indentured and when, whether the child was orphaned or abandoned, and any remarks. These records are available at orphanages that are still in operation. Otherwise, the records of a state-operated establishment may be with the state archivist or the state's Department of Social and Welfare Services. Write to both offices to insure that you have identified and obtained all existing records. Records of closed orphanages operated below the state level may be deposited with the town, city, or county clerk, the local agency responsible for currently operating orphanages, or a local historical society or research library. Some records may be in the possession of the families of institution officials.

Orphanages operated by religious groups and private benefactors kept records similar to those of government-operated orphanages. The Vine Street Orphan's [sic] Home of Chattanooga, Tennessee, operated by the Women's Christian Association of Chattanooga, maintained excellent records, including a diary of the home, lists of subscribers, names and ages of children there, matrons' reports, secretaries' reports, minutes of the Women's Christian Association meetings, and manager's books and journal between 1879 and 1903.

Figure 10-16 is a page from the matron's report dated 30 May 1887. It notes which children were placed with families ("Laura Henry taken from the Home by Mrs. DeGrummond May 10th") and also their retrieval ("Martha Bennett taken from Dr. Hall May 16th on account of ill useage [sic] by them").

The Applications for Children record book provides more information on placement. Sometime between her admission in May 1887 and an entry dated December 1888, Laura Henry's grandmother asked for custody, but "investigation showed her to be unworthy." Another child, Frankie Tipton, was adopted by the F. McCullum family of Wilmington, Ohio, in December 1888.

The minutes of board meetings also contain valuable information. The August 1887 minutes report that Jennie Davis, who had left two children with the home for two or three years, had remarried a man named Holmes, and that they had had a child of their own. She "intends applying for them," and her husband "prefers a request for the two children. He represents himself as their father. Decided to let them have the one in the Home," but the second, in "a good home with Mrs. Frank George . . . would be left there at least for the present."

The managers' books contain administrative information about employee salaries, statistics, health and financial reports, and other information unrelated to a specific orphan.

A much briefer and more formal record, the 1876 Register of the Jewish Foster Home and Orphan Asylum in Philadelphia (figure 10-17), gives the child's name, age, admission date, birthplace, names and birthplaces of parents, closest kin and address, date of discharge, indenturing, and trade. This register does not explain the circumstances surrounding the child's placement in the home, but most records do.

The early records of non-government-operated orphanages that are no longer in existence may be difficult to locate. If the orphanage is or was operated by a religious group, the records may be at its headquarters. The Catholic church, which operated the largest number of non-governmental orphanages in metropolitan cities, usually maintains diocesan archives. State and local historical societies may have some early orphanage records; university libraries are anxious to get them, and many are in the possession of families of institution officials. Check the *National Union Catalog of Manuscript Collections* under the name of the institution, names of officials, and localities where orphanages existed.

Problems with using orphanage records include lack of legibility and availability, damage, and determining their location. Court records can sometimes be substituted for incomplete or nonexistent orphanage records.

The information found in orphanage records can be critically important. The Vine Street matron's report of 30 May 1887 notes that Alice Moore was "taken by Mrs. Day, Ringold, Geor-

gia." Unless family records reflect her transfer to the Day household in Georgia, the researcher might spend endless hours searching Chattanooga records for her. If her name was changed to Day, it might be impossible to trace her parents without the orphanage link to Moore.

ORPHAN TRAIN

The direction of institutional care of orphans and neglected children changed course in the mid-nineteenth century. A successful trial placement of abandoned city children on farms in rural New York and nearby Connecticut proved successful, encouraging placement on a larger scale. In 1854, forty-seven boys and girls between the ages of seven and fifteen boarded a train in New York City; they were destined for a rural community in southwestern Michigan. This was the beginning of an exodus that transferred well over 100,000 homeless children from cities such as Boston, New York, and Cincinnati to entirely different lifestyles in small towns and farms in states in the Midwest, the South, and the West.

The plan, designed and implemented by the Reverend Charles Loring Brace, is believed to have been a success, some experts estimating the ninety percent of the placements re-

Figure 10-17. From the register of the Jewish Foster Home and Orphan Asylum, 1876–1911, Philadelphia, Pennsylvania, January 1876, pp. 1–2. FHL 1,013,425, item 3.

sulted in better lives for the children. Records of the transfers may be found at the city asylums which participated or in the deed books of the courthouses of the counties which received the children. Deed books were commonly used to record the adoptions of children (usually males under the age of ten and young females) or the apprenticeships (usually males ten and over). But do not overlook justice of the peace dockets, guardians records, county order records, and board of supervisors minutes, among other county records.

An indenture dated 15 December 1860 and recorded in Marion County, Illinois, is between the New York Juvenile Asylum and a farmer named Clifton R. Wills. The agreement outlines the duties of Wills, who is accepting ten-year-old Cornelius Shay as an apprentice. Wills is to instruct Shay in "the art of farming" and in "reading, writing, and arithmetic, as least as far as and including Compound Interest." Wills also agreed to "carefully watch over and guard the morals of the said apprentice, and prevent him from frequenting taverns, porterhouses, play-houses, or gaming houses of any kind."

When you have completed your research at the county of the child's rural residence, contact the Orphan Train Heritage Society of America, 4912 Trout Farm Rd., Springdale, Arkansas 72764. This organization serves as a national clearinghouse for information about persons who rode the orphan trains. They may be able to help you identify the sending organization. Possibilities, in addition to the New York Juvenile Asylum, include the New York Foundling Hospital, The New England Home for Little Wanderers (Boston), the State Charities Aid Association of New York City, and the Cincinnati, Ohio Children's Home.

HOSPITAL AND MEDICAL RECORDS

Hospital and physicians' medical records are excellent sources of genealogical information. However, as confidential documents, they are difficult to obtain and are often not available even to immediate family members. Some hospital records from the nineteenth century have been released and microfilmed by the Genealogical Society of Utah, including the early records of the St. Louis City Hospital, which are fairly representative of the content in most records of this period. Figure 10-18 is a page from the St. Louis City Hospital register, 1860.

Normally, early hospital registers will indicate the patient's name, age, birthplace, date of admission, illness or disease, and date of discharge or death. Some records, however, are less informative.

In addition to registers, hospitals maintained early death records such as those compiled by the Almshouse Hospital in Philadelphia in 1893 (figure 10-19). The information on death records varies from hospital to hospital, but almost always you can expect to find the deceased's name, death date, and cause of death.

An entire volume could—and should—be written about institutional records, possibly the most neglected genealogical sources currently available to researchers.

NOTES

1. County Commissioners' Minutes, Book B, Fayette County, Indiana. May Term 1827.

BIBLIOGRAPHY

CORONERS' RECORDS

Naanes, Ted, and Loretto Szucs. "Dead Men Do Tell Tales." *Ancestry* 12 (2) (March–April 1994): 6.

Roebuck, Haywood. "North Carolina Colonial Coroners' Inquests, 1738–75." *North Carolina Genealogical Society Journal* 1 (1975): 11–37.

HOSPITALS

Clay, Robert Y. "Patients in the Hospital at Williamsburg, 1800–37." *Virginia Genealogist* 24 (1980): 23–28, 90–94.

Gilliam, Charles Edgar. "Mount Malado." *Tyler's Quarterly* 20 (1938–39): 138–42, 250. Virginia's earliest hospital.

New York Down-State Medical Center. *History of Long Island College Hospital: Alumni Association Highlights, 1880–1955 and Biographies of Graduates, 1900–1955.* New York: New York Alumni Association, 1961.

Johns, Frank S., and Anne Page. "Chimborazo Hospital and J.B. McCaw, Surgeon in Chief." *Virginia Magazine of History and Biography* 62 (1954): 190–200. An excellent description of revolutionary war hospital records with examples and locations.

Jordan, John W. "Military Hospital at Bethlehem and Lititz during the Revolution." *Pennsylvania Magazine of History and Biography* 20 (1896): 137–57. An undocumented account with patient lists.

Kelner, Joseph. "Examination of Hospital Records." *Case and Comment* 84 (1979): 51–54. Describes access to modern records.

Larrabee, Eric. *The Benevolent and Necessary Institution: New York Hospital, 1771–1971.* Garden City, N.Y.: Doubleday, 1971.

Uppedegraff, Marie. *The Story of Stamford Hospital, 1896–1971.* Stamford, Conn.: Stamford Hospital, 1971.

Williams, William H. "The Industrious Poor and the Founding of the Pennsylvania Hospital." *Pennsylvania Magazine of History and Biography* 97 (1973): 431–43. Established 1751.

MORTICIANS

Elder, Charlotte DeVolt. "New Englanders in the Mortuary Records of Savannah, Georgia." *New England Historic and Genealogical Register* 125 (1971): 28–44. Covers 1803–22.

"Undertakers Records." *Maryland Genealogical Bulletin* 20 (1979), 21 (1980).

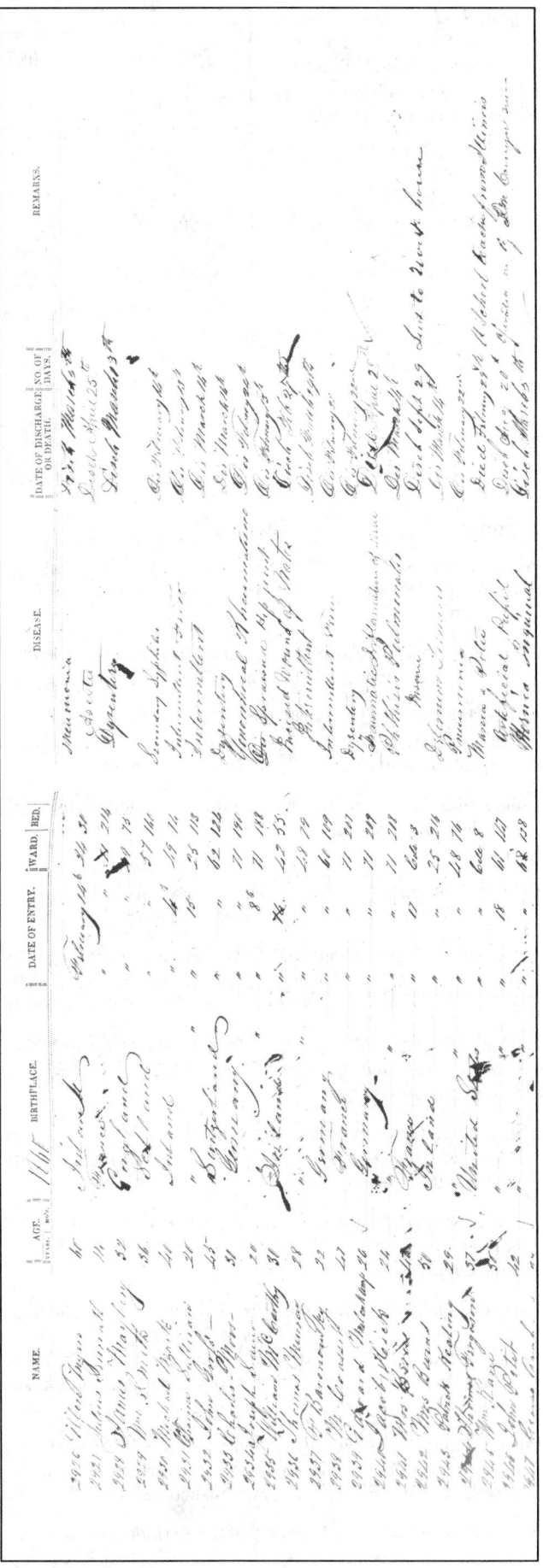

Figure 10-18. From the Register of St. Louis City Hospital, 1860. FHL 980,610.

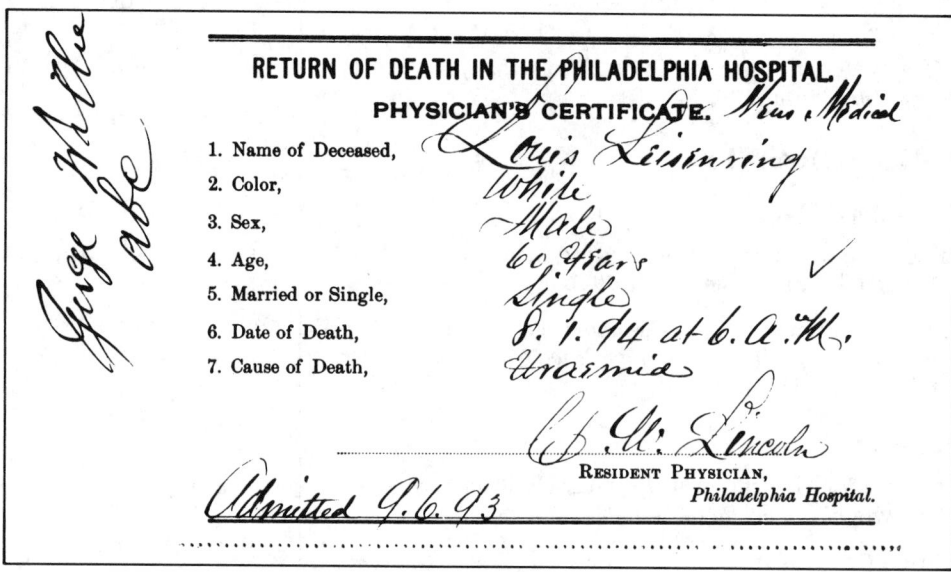

Figure 10-19. Death certificate of Annie Spence, 6 June 1894, Almshouse Hospital, Bureau of Charities, Philadelphia County, Pennsylvania, p. 1. FHL 975,748, item 1.

ORPHANAGES

Allen, Desmond Walls. "Paupers at the Turn of the Century." *Professional Genealogists of Arkansas, Inc. Newsletter* 6 (6) (November 1993).

Charlotte County (Florida) Genealogical Society. "Orphan Trains." *Geneagram* 24 (1) (June 1991): 44–46.

Coble, Janet. "They Came to Our Town: A Story of Orphan Train Children." *Illinois State Genealogical Society Quarterly* 24 (2) (Summer 1992): 102–04.

Fink, Arthur E. "Changing Philosophies and Practices in North Carolina Orphanages." *North Carolina Historical Review* 48 (1971).

Gilbert, Meredith. "Orphan Trains." *Polish Genealogical Society of Texas News* 10 (3) (Fall 1993): 26–28.

Greenwood, Peggy Thomson. "City's House of Refuge; Orphanages 1827–1870" and "Orphanages (Part 2) 1870–1900." *St. Louis Genealogical Quarterly* 24 (1) (Fall 1990).

Harland, Thomas. "Of Franklin, Whitfield, and the Orphans." *Georgia Historical Quarterly* 29 (1945): 201–16. Bethesda Orphanage in Georgia.

Illinois State Genealogical Society. *Children of Orphan Trains From NY to IL, and Beyond.* Springfield, Ill.: Illinois State Genealogical Society, 1995.

Jones, Newton B. "The Charleston Orphan House, 1860–1976." *South Carolina Historical Magazine* 62 (1961): 203–14. Organized 1790.

Langson, Miriam Z. *Children West: A History of the Placing-out System of the New York Children's Aid Society, 1853–1896.* Madison: State Historical Society of Wisconsin, 1964. Describes records for one of the most important social institutions in New York City.

Pickett, Robert S. *House of Refuge: Origins of Juvenile Reform in New York State, 1815–1857.* Syracuse, N.Y.: Syracuse University Press, 1969. Established 1825.

Rothman, David J. *The Discovery of the Asylum: Social Order and Disorder in the New Republic.* Boston: Little, Brown and Company, 1971.

Speare, Jean E., and Dorothy Paul. *Admission Record Indianapolis Asylum for Friendless Colored Children, 1871–1900.* Indianapolis: Family History and Genealogy Section, Indiana Historical Society, 1978.

Teeters, Negley K. "The Early Days of the Philadelphia House of Refuge." *Pennsylvania History* 27 (1960): 165–87. Established in 1828. Based on minutes of the Board of Inspectors, journals, and daybooks of the house.

OVERSEERS OF THE POOR AND ALMSHOUSES

Benton, Josiah Henry. *Warning Out in New England.* 1911. Reprint. Bowie, Md.: Heritage Books, 1992.

"Chautauqua County Home and Infirmary. Poor House for Chautauqua County, New York." *FGS Forum* 3 (4) (Fall 1992). Journals are being abstracted by the Chautauqua County Genealogical Society, P.O. Box 404, Fredonia, NY 14063.

Lainhart, Ann S. "Records of the Poor in Pre-Twentieth-Century New England." *New England Historical and Genealogical Register* 146 (January 1992): 80–85.

_____. "Cambridge, Massachusetts, Notifications and Warnings Out (1788 to 1797)." *New England Historical and Genealogical Register* 144 (July 1990): 215.

_____. "Weston Cautions, 1757–1803." *New England Historical and Genealogical Register* 144 (July 1990): 215.

Lucas County Infirmary Register, Vol. I, 1855–1882. Book 2, Feb 1868–Mar 1882. Toledo, Ohio: Lucas County Chapter—OGS, 1993. More than 3,500 entries which include births, deaths, indentures, and adoptions of minor children.

McLaird, Lee N. "Haven for Those in Need." *Archival Chronicle* 14 (1) (March 1995): 1–2.

Sangamon County Almshouse, Buffalo, Illinois: Inmate Record, Sangamon County Poor Farm. 3 vols. Springfield, Ill.: Sangamon County Genealogical Society, 1993.

Warren, Paula Stuart, and James W. Warren. *Ramsey County Minnesota Relief Records, 1862–1868.* St. Paul: Warren Research and Publishing, 1990.

PRISONS

Carleton, Mark T. *Politics and Punishment: The History of the Louisiana State Penal System.* Baton Rouge: Louisiana State University Press, 1971.

Carter, Kent. "The Hanging Judge's Records." *The Record* [newsletter of the National Archives and Records Administration] 1 (1) (September 1994).

Kidd, Julie. "Oregon State Penitentiary." *Bulletin of the Genealogical Forum of Oregon, Inc.* 45 (2) (December 1995): 75–78. Lists of prisoners extracted from *Report of the Superintendent Oregon State Penitentiary* (Salem, Oreg.: W.A. McPherson, State Printer, 1870).

Lewis, Orland F. *The Development of American Prisons and Prison Customs, 1776–1845.* 1922. Reprint. New York: Arno Press, 1962.

New York State Temporary State Committee of Investigation. *County Jails and Penitentiaries in New York State.* Albany, 1966.

Phelps, Richard H. *A History of Newgate [Prison] of Connecticut.* New York: Arno Press, 1969.

Shepard, William. "Records From Old Jail at Cumberland Courthouse, Virginia." *William and Mary Quarterly,* 2nd Series, 12 (1932): 39–40. Records dated 1782 to 1786.

Teeters, Negley K. "The Early Days of the Eastern State Penitentiary at Philadelphia." *Pennsylvania History* 16 (1949): 261–302.

SCHOOLS

Ambler, Charles H. "Poor Relief Education, 1818–1847." *West Virginia History* 3 (1941–42): 285–304. Based on school records transferred from the courthouse in Kanawha County to West Virginia University, Morgantown.

Andrews, Edward D. "The County Grammar Schools and Academies of Vermont." *Vermont Historical Society Proceedings* September 1936: 174ff.

Finkelstein, Barbara J. "Schooling and Schoolteachers: Selected Bibliography of Autobiographies in the Nineteenth Century." *History of Education Quarterly* 14 (19741: 293–300. An important bibliography.

Fuller, Wayne E. *The Old Country School: The Story of Rural Education in the Middle West.* Chicago: University of Chicago Press, 1982. Includes a description of the records.

Gersman, Elinor M. "A Bibliography for Historians of Education: Historical Perspectives on the Educational Experience in the United States." *History of Education Quarterly* 14 (1974): 279–92.

Hogue, Arthur R. "The Record of an Indian School District, 1837–1844." *Indian Magazine of History* 48 (1952): 185–92.

Index to Georgia Poor-School and Academy Records, 1826–1850. Atlanta: R.J. Taylor, Jr., Foundation, 1980. Records include lists of children with names, ages, school attendance, records of parents, and tuition payments.

McMahon, Clara R.P. "A Note on the Free School Idea in Colonial Maryland." *Maryland Historical Magazine* 54 (1959): 149–52.

Morison, Samuel Eliot. *The Founding of Harvard College.* Cambridge: Harvard University Press, 1935. An excellent description of the records kept by a university. Alumni registers for many original universities in the United States have been published and will be found in major research libraries.

"Records of Pennsylvania School Children, 1802–1809." *National Genealogical Society Quarterly* 50 (1962): 78. Tax lists included school-age children with their ages.

Sloane, Eric. *The Little Red Schoolhouse: A Sketchbook of Early American Education.* Garden City, N.Y.: Doubleday, 1972.

Staubo, Merete. *History of the Council of School Superintendents, Cities and Villages of the State of New York, 1883–1967.* Ithaca, N.Y.: Cornell University Press, 1971.

Szucs, Loretto Dennis. "Education Records." *Ancestry* 13 (1): (January–February 1995): 20.

RESEARCH IN DIRECTORIES
CHAPTER CONTENTS

11

RESEARCH IN DIRECTORIES

Gordon Lewis Remington

DIRECTORY: A Book containing one or more alphabetical lists of the inhabitants of any locality, with their addresses and occupations; also a similar compilation dealing with the members of a particular profession, trade, or association, as a Clerical or Medical Directory, etc.[1]

While a directory can often in itself be a source of interesting genealogical and biographical information, its chief value lies in its use as an aid to locating a person in place and time. One type of directory groups people by a common residence. The second groups them by a common association or attribute. In addition, many directories cover organizations rather than individuals and are sometimes called registers, catalogs, annuals, yearbooks, or guides. Whatever its title, contents, or method, a directory will always list and locate members of a group. This chapter gives a history of directories, describes the limitations and resources of seven kinds of directories, and provides numerous examples of how to use them.

Gale Research Company, of Detroit, publishes the most comprehensive guides to existing directories. These are *Directories in Print,* 13th edition, 1996 (Detroit, 1996); *City and State Directories in Print,* 1st edition, 1990–91 (Detroit, 1989); and *International Directories in Print,* 1st edition, 1989–90 (Detroit, 1988). These periodic publications, which succeed the *Directory of Directories* first published by Information Enterprises in 1980, are available at most public and university libraries. The current editions will, however, cover only those directories in publication as of their own respective dates of publication. Their chief value for genealogical research is to provide current addresses and telephone numbers of publishing companies with directory libraries and the names and addresses of organizations for which directories may have been published in the past.

The Oxford English Dictionary cites J. Brown's *The Directory or List of Principal Traders in London* (1732) as the earliest use of the word *"directory"* as defined above. Lists of inhabitants or associates are extant from at least two hundred years earlier. Dorothea N. Spear, in the introduction to her *Bibliography of American Directories Through 1860,* gives a concise account of the history of directories in the United States:

Although as early as 1665 in New York a grouping of residents by streets was shown in the Records of the Dutch Magistrates, the first directory-type listing of the inhabitants of an American city of which we have knowledge is a Baltimore broadside. It is entitled *The Following Lists of Families, And Other Persons Residing in the Town of Baltimore, Was Taken in the Year 1752, By a Lady of Respectability,* and is believed to have been printed between 1830 and 1840 by Joseph Townsend (1756–1841) from the original manuscript in the Maryland Historical Society. Next came the two Charleston directory lists of 1782 and 1785 printed in the *South Carolina and Georgia Almanack* for those years, owned by the Charleston Library Society and reprinted in 1951. Philadelphia has the honor of having produced the first separately printed directories in this country, two rivals issued in 1785, the earlier being *MacPherson's Directory for the City and Suburbs of Philadelphia,* first issued on 16 November 1785, and the second, *The Philadelphia Directory,* by Francis White, first issued on 29 November 1785. The John MacPherson edition is to be found in the Philadelphia Free Library and in the Historical Society of Pennsylvania, while the White volume is owned by the Philadelphia libraries and the American Antiquarian Society . . . New York quickly followed Philadelphia with *The New-York Directory* of 1786, by David Franks, which was frequently reprinted in later years. The New York Historical Society and the New York Public Library own original copies of this directory. Following the lead of the most progressive cities, many others throughout the country began to issue directories in rapid succession. . . . The compilation of the early directories was usually a side issue rather than the principal line of the compiler's work. Therefore it is natural to find that some of the authors combined the listing with their duties as letter carriers, postmasters, county constables, school principals, teachers, and brokers. Often the modest compiler's own name and address were not even included in the alphabetical listing. The majority of these publications, however, were issued by newspaper offices. From the mid-nineteenth century we find separate directory publishers such as the well-known firms of George Adams and of Damrell & Moore of Boston, C.S. Williams of Cincinnati, and the John F. Trow and John Doggett Companies of New York, William H. Boyd, who had offices in New York, Philadelphia, and Washington, and many others. Boyd advertised in 1859 that he owned the largest collection of directories in the world and was prepared to publish the directory of any city or state. We know that he issued directories for many of the eastern and mid-western cities. Then came the R.L. Polk Company of New York and Detroit, with numerous branch offices. It presumably became the largest directory publisher and so continues today. The price of directories ranged from twenty-five cents to four dollars by the end of the 1850s, whereas the comprehensive Polk publications of today cost us fifty dollars a copy. It is true that the earliest attempts were quite crude, often with the names sorted only under each letter but not completely alphabetized. In the early volumes there were no house numbers, so e locations given were quite general; sometimes the millers and merchants were located merely "next the bridge" or "opposite the town hall."[2]

Originally, the two basic types of directories (residence and attribute) were more or less combined. The business orientation of the early directories influenced their development and content. Just as the census was designed primarily for congressional apportionment and not for genealogical purposes, so the directory is limited as a genealogical source by the intent of its compilers.

The early English directories listed "principal traders" and "gentleman of accompte." It is doubtful that the "Lady of Respectability," who compiled the *List of Families, and Other Persons* in Baltimore, 1752, included in her list those families and "other persons" who weren't "respectable." Although such economic and class distinctions became less apparent later, it was not until the second half of the nineteenth century that directories included common laborers with any regularity, and even then they usually left out transient residents.

As cities grew in the nineteenth century, directories became more detailed. They included special sections devoted to businesses, organizations, churches, and even steamship lists along with the list of general inhabitants. These special sections eventually evolved into nongeographic directories by the late 1800s. The directories considered in this chapter are:

1. City directories
2. Telephone Directories
3. County and regional business directories
4. Professional directories
5. Organizational directories
6. Religious directories
7. Post office and street directories

Finding a directory, the first step in using one, is also the most difficult step, particularly for researchers far from major record centers. Before attempting to locate a directory, you should be aware that the directory you want might not exist. It may be that a directory was never published for a particular place or group in the year of interest or that no copies of a directory known to have existed have survived. The law that requires copyrighted material to be deposited in the Library of Congress dates only from 1870. Some directories were originally published for short-term use and were disposed of when they became obsolete. In addition, libraries may gradually dispose of their directory collections due to lack of space or low demand.

Another major consequence of publication for short-term use is low-quality paper. Individual pages may deteriorate badly.

A binding can always be replaced, but when segments of the printed page tear off and are swept up at the end of the day by the library custodian, they are gone forever. Microform reproduction has helped to preserve older directories, but, in many cases, image reduction and poor exposure make the microfilm or microfiche copies hard to read.

LOCATING DIRECTORIES

CITY DIRECTORIES

Surprisingly, access is not a great problem with city directories. You can find city directories in almost every local library in the country, though larger libraries might have a greater variety. Go first to the public library nearest the place you are researching; if you can't travel there, telephone its reference desk. The reference librarian may be willing to photocopy the pages you need and send them to you or give you the desired information verbally. Reference staffs are quite busy, however, so a letter may be better if you're not in a hurry.

Most libraries, historical societies, and archives at the state level have fairly extensive collections of in-state directories and may also have directories from major out-of-state cities. On the national level, the Library of Congress in Washington, D.C., and the American Antiquarian Society in Worcester, Massachusetts, contain major collections of directories. If you can't travel to a state or national repository, consider employing a record searcher to search the directories for you. If you have someone do a directory search for you, be sure to specify the parameters—for instance, if you do not want all entries of the surname Smith, ask for those on a certain street, at a certain address, or for those with particular first names.

If you can't locate the directory you want through any of the above places, you may need to write the directory publishing company. The following are the three main directory publishing companies in business in the United States today:

Haines & Company, Inc.
8050 Freedom Ave., N.W.
North Canton, OH 44720-6985
(216) 494-9111
Fax (216) 494-6859

Hill-Donnelly Cross Reference Directories
2602 S. MacDill Ave.
Tampa, FL 33629-7289
(813) 837-1009
Fax (813) 839-8420

R.L. Polk & Company
1155 Brewery Park Blvd.
Detroit, MI 48207-2602
(313) 393-0880
Fax (313) 393-2862

Gale Research's *City and State Directories in Print* lists the cities that the Haines and Hill-Donnelly directories cover in a special subject index under "Cross-reference directories." R.L. Polk directories are also listed under "Cross-reference directories" in the subject index, but simply as "Polk's City Directories [name of state]." The specific cities Polk publishes are listed under "Polk's City Directories" in each state section, not under the name of the city itself. These companies may have directory libraries for their own publications dating back several years, and R.L. Polk has branch offices in many cities. To find the nearest branch office that may have directories of interest, call the main office listed above. These companies probably do not have copies of directories published by other, now defunct companies. Fortunately for researchers, the older directories of many American cities are available in microform through the efforts of Research Publications (a division of Primary Source Media), which completed the first part of a four-phase project early in 1967 by recording on microfiche city directories through 1860 listed in Spear's bibliography. The pre-1861 collection of the American Antiquarian Society, which contains almost two-thirds of Spear's titles, was microfiched in its entirety, and almost one hundred libraries contributed one or more additional directories. Of Spear's almost 1,600 titles, all but forty-five were microfilmed, a completion rate of better than ninety-seven percent.

Positive response to phase I encouraged microfilming of city directories from 1861 to 1881 (phase II). To keep the project manageable, it was limited to the fifty largest cities of the period, with some others added for regional representation. Research Publications used the collection of the American Antiquarian Society, created its own bibliography, and arranged for microfilming.

Phase III covers the same cities and uses the same format but extends coverage from 1882 to 1901. The editors note that "During the period included, and running through the years covered by Segment 3 [phase III], the city directories were printed on very poor paper. Many of the directories are literally falling to pieces. The microfilm collection will insure continued availability and access to this important research source."[3]

Phase IV includes directories for fifty-three cities for the years 1902 to 1935. As cities like New York grew more populous, the frequency with which directories were published diminished, so directory representation may not be complete for every year in this last phase. Phase V, covering the years 1936 to 1965, will be released in 1996.

These microform reproductions are available for purchase individually or in segments. The Library of Congress has the entire set, while state and local libraries may choose only to purchase directories of interest in their areas. The Family History Library of The Church of Jesus Christ of Latter-day Saints in Salt Lake City has most of phase I (those directories that it didn't already have in its collection) and almost all of phases II, III, and IV of the Research Publications series in its collection. In order to obtain a catalog or the microform directories themselves write or call:

Primary Source Media
Research Publications Dept.
12 Lunar Dr.
Woodbridge, CT 06525-2398
(203) 397-2600
(800) 444-0799
Fax (203) 397-3893

Two finding aids specifically designed for genealogists seeking information in nineteenth-century directories have been published by Gale Research in its Genealogy and Local History Series: vol. 10, Nathan C. Parker, *Personal Name Index to the 1856 City Directories of California* (Detroit: 1980), and vol. 13, Elsie L. Sopp, *Personal Name Index to the 1856 City Directories of Iowa* (Detroit: 1980). These indexes can be used in conjunction with the Research Publications microfiche for the pre-1861 period.

Some early directories are being reprinted. The New England Historic Genealogical Society has published, under the editorship of Ann Smith Lainhart, the *First Boston City Directory (1789) Including Extensive Annotations by John Haven Dexter (1791–1876)*. This volume is unusual, as Dexter made a hobby of studying the people listed in the directory, and his annotations are quite useful for genealogical purposes.

Table 11-1 shows the cities available in the Research Publications series, with inclusive dates for all segments. It should be noted that there are occasions when a directory was not published or has not survived for a year within the inclusive dates. If a city does not appear in the chart, check the local and regional repositories mentioned above in order to determine the existence of any directories.

TELEPHONE DIRECTORIES

Telephone directories are classic examples of publications made of low-quality paper for short-term use. Whether obsolete telephone directories are retained by local and state libraries may depend on space considerations and the physical condition of the older directories. The Library of Congress has some telephone directories. Access to current telephone directories, both in microform and by computer, is more fully discussed in chapter 18, Tracking Twentieth-Century Ancestors.

BUSINESS DIRECTORIES

Business directories can be found in most of the repositories mentioned above. Both the Library of Congress and the Family History Library have such directories, but the collection of the Library of Congress is more comprehensive. A list of the Library of Congress's directories as of 1931 was printed in *The American Genealogist* 13: 51–53 and reprinted in Colleen Neal, *Lest We Forget: A Guide to Genealogical Research in the Nation's Capital* (Annandale, Va.: 1982). These business directories were often published by the same companies that published city directories, so private directory libraries should also be consulted.

LAW DIRECTORIES

Every law library should have at least one current law directory. How many—if any—back issues are kept and for how far back depends on the individual library and its storage capabilities. Even if the library has kept old directories, access to them may be limited. Large public libraries often keep back issues for reference. You might also find law directories through local and state bar associations. Again, whether they have back issues may depend on their space limitations. The American Bar Association has not kept past directories since 1981.

The Library of Congress has a complete set of the Martindale-Hubbell Directory from 1931 on. The library has only sporadic copies of earlier directories, the earliest Hubbell

Table 11-1. Directories on Microform

This table serves two purposes. The first is to list those cities in each state for which Research Publications has microform directories and for which years. Those segments of years marked with an asterisk (*) are not currently (August 1995) available at the Family History Library. In these cases, the years given are those for the particular phase; consequently, directories may not exist for all years in that phase.

The second purpose is to show compatibility with the 1910 census by showing whether Soundex or Miracode indexes exist for a city or if there is an enumeration district map or street index for a city. Those cities and states that are not included in the Research Publications microform series, but for which 1910 finding aids exist, are bracketed.

State/City	Date/1910 Census Compatibility
Alabama:	Soundex (entire state)
Birmingham	1902-35/Soundex (Alabama Cities)
Greene County	1855/56, 1862-1935*
Mobile	1837-1935/Soundex (Alabama Cities)
Montgomery	1882-1901,* 1902-35/Soundex (Alabama Cities)
Arizona:	
Phoenix	1903-35/Street Index
Tucson	1902-35
Arkansas:	Miracode (entire state)
Little Rock	1871-1901
Texarkana	1904-34
California:	Miracode (entire state)
Bakersfield	1915-35
Fresno	1926-35
Long Beach	1907-35/Street Index
Los Angeles	1873-1935/Street Index
Marysville	1853-58
Nevada City	1856
Oakland	1869-81, 1902-35
Sacramento	1851-81, 1902-35
San Diego	1903-35/Street Index
San Francisco	1850-1934/Street Index
Stockton	1852-56, 1902-35
Tuolumne Co.	1856
Colorado:	
Colorado Springs	1902-35
Denver	1859-1935/Street Index
Grand Junction	1902-35
Leadville	1882-1901*
Connecticut:	
Regional	1849-58
Ansonia	1902-35
Bristol	1902-35
Bridgeport	1855-81, 1902-35/Election District Map
Danbury	1882-1901,* 1902-35
Hartford	1799-1935/Election District Map
Meriden	1872-81
Middletown	1868-81, 1882-1901,* 1902-31
New Haven	1840-1935/Election District Map
New London	1855-60, 1902-35
Norwich	1846-60, 1881-1901,*1902-35

State/City	Date/1910 Census Compatibility
Stamford	1882-1901,* 1902-33
Southington	1882-1901,* 1902-35*
[Waterbury]	Election District Map
Delaware:	
Regional	1859/60
Wilmington	1814-1901, 1902-35*
District of Columbia:	
Washington	1822-1935/ Street Index
Florida:	Miracode (entire state)
Jacksonville	1902-35
Miami	1916-35
Orlando	1902-35*
Pensacola	1903-34
St. Petersburg	1914-35
Tampa	1903-35/Street Index
Georgia:	Soundex (entire state)
Regional	1850
Atlanta	1859-1935/Soundex (Georgia Cities)/Street Index
Augusta	1841-59/Soundex (Georgia Cities)
Columbus	1859/60, 1906-34
Savannah	1848-1934/Soundex (Georgia Cities)
Hawaii:	AISI Index
Honolulu	1902-36
Idaho:	Idaho G.S. Index
Boise	1901-35
Pocatello	1902-35
Illinois:	Miracode (entire state)
Regional	1847-60
Alton	1858
Belleville	1860, 1901-35
Bureau County	1858/59
Chicago	1839-1929/Street Index
Evanston	1902-35
Galena	1854-59
Joliet	1872-1935
Kane County	1857-60
Moline	1855-59, 1901-35
Peoria	1844-1935/Street Index
Quincy	1855-60
Randolph County	
Rockford	1857-60, 1902-35
Rock Island	1855-59, 1902-35

State/City	Date/1910 Census Compatibility	State/City	Date/1910 Census Compatibility
Springfield	1855-60, 1901-35	Saco	1849, 1902-34 (with Biddeford)
Will County	1859/60	Westbrook	1902-34
Indiana:		**Maryland:**	
Regional	1858-61	Baltimore	1752/1796-1930/Street Index
Evansville	1858-1934/Election District Map	Frederick	1859/60
Fort Wayne	1858-81, 1902-35/Street Index	**Massachusetts:**	
Gary	1908-35/Street Index	Regional	1849-59
Indianapolis	1855-1935/ Street Index	Boston	1789-1935/Election District Map/ Street Index (FHL)
Jefferson County	1859	Brockton	1874-80, 1882-1901,* 1915-35/ Election District Map
Lafayette	1858-59, 1901-35	Brighton	1850
Lawrenceburg	1859/60	Brookline	1868-81
Logansport	1859/60	Cambridge	1847-81, 1882-1901,* 1902-31/ Election District Map
Madison	1859-60	Charlestown	1831-74
New Albany	1856-60, 1903-36	Chelsea	1847-80, 1902-35
Richmond	1857-61, 1901-35	Clinton	1856, 1902-35
Shelbyville	1860/61	Dorchester	1850
[South Bend]	Street Index	East Boston	1848-52
Terre Haute	1858-60/Election District Map	Fall River	1853-1935/Election District Map
Iowa:		Fitchburg	1847-60
Regional/State	1846, 1902-23	Gloucester	1860, 1882-1935
Burlington	1856-59, 1902-35	Haverhill	1853-61, 1902-35
Davenport	1853-81	Holyoke	1882-1901,* 1902-35/Election District Map
Des Moines	1866-1935/Election District Map/ Street Index (FHL)	Lawrence	1847-61/Election District Map
Dubuque	1856-81, 1882-1901*	Leominster	1882-1935
Henry County	1859/60	Lowell	1832-1935/Election District Map
Iowa City	1857, 1919-34	Lunenburg	1834
Keokuk	1854-60	Lynn	1832-80, 1902-35/Election District Map
Muscatine	1856-60	Malden	1868-81
Sioux City	1902-35*	Medford	1849, 1902-30
Kansas:	Miracode (entire state)	Milford	1856, 1901-34
Atchison	1859-61	New Bedford	1836-82, 1902-34/Election District Map
Emporia	1902-35	Newburyport	1849-60, 1902-36
[Kansas City]	Street Index	Pittsfield	1859/60
Leavenwoth	1860-61, 1902-34	Plymouth	1846-60
Ottawa	1903-33	Quincy	1868-81
Topeka	1868-80, 1902-35	Roxbury	1847-60
[Wichita]	Street Index	Salem	1837-81, 1902-35
Kentucky:	Miracode (entire state)	Somerville	1851/Election District Map
Regional	1859/60	South Boston	1852
Covington	1861-87, 1902-32	Southbridge	1854
Lexington	1806-82, 1902-35	Springfield	1845-81/Election District Map
Louisville	1832-1935	Taunton	1850-59, 1902-35
Louisiana:	Soundex (entire state)	Woburn	1868-77
New Orleans	1805-1935/Miracode (Louisiana Cities)	Worcester	1828-1935/Election District Map
Maine:		**Michigan:**	Miracode (entire state)
Regional	1849-56	Regional	1856-60
Augusta	1861-81,* 1902-35	Ann Arbor	1902-35
Bangor	1834-59	Battle Creek	1901-35
Biddeford	1856-57, 1902-34		
Portland	1823-1935/ Election District Map		

State/City	Date/1910 Census Compatibility
Coldwater	1902-23
Detroit	1837-1934/Street Index
Grand Rapids	1856-1935/Street Index
Kalamazoo	1902-35
Petoskey	1903-35
Minnesota:	
Duluth	1881-1901,* 1902-35/Election District Map
Minneapolis	1865-1935/Election District Map/Street Index (FHL)
St. Anthony	1859/60
St. Paul	1856-1935/Election District Map
Mississippi:	Soundex (entire state)
Jackson	1860
Vicksburg	1860
Missouri:	Miracode (entire state)
Regional	1860
Kansas City	1859-1921
St. Joseph	1905-33
St. Louis	1821-1935
Montana:	
Territory	1868-80
Billings	1902-35
Butte	1902-34
Great Falls	1903-35
Livingston	1904-35
Nebraska:	
Hastings	1903-34
Omaha	1866-1935/Street Index
Nevada:	
Territory	1862-81
New Hampshire:	
Regional	1849
Concord	1830-61, 1902-35
Dover	1830-81, 1902-35
Great Falls	1848
Keene	1827-31, 1871-80, 1902-35
Manchester	1844-1935/Election District Map
Nashua	1841-82, 1902-35
New Ipswich	1858
Peterborough	1830
Portsmouth	1817-61, 1903-34
New Jersey:	
Regional	1850/51
Atlantic City	1902-35
[Bayonne]	Election District Map
Camden	1860, 1863-81, 1882-1901,* 1902-31/Election District Map
Elizabeth	1865-81, 1882-1901,* 1902-35/Street Index/Election District Map
Essex County	1859
Hoboken (with Jersey City)	Election District Map

State/City	Date/1910 Census Compatibility
Jersey City	1849-1901/Election District Map
Newark	1835-1935/Street Index/Election District Map
New Brunswick	1855-61
Passaic	Election District Map
Paterson	1855-1935/Street Index/Election District Map
Trenton	1844-81, 1902-35/Election District Map
New Mexico:	
Albuquerque	1905-35
New York:	
Regional	1850-59
Albany	1813-1935/Election District Map
Auburn	1857-60, 1861-81, 1902-35
Binghamton	1857-60, 1909-24
[Bronx]	Street Index (w/Manhattan)
Brooklyn	1822-1934/Street Index
Buffalo	1828-1935/Election District Map
Cortland	1902-35
Elmira	1857-81, 1882-1901,* 1902-35*
Geneva	1857, 1902-35
Greenpoint	1854
Hudson	1851-57, 1902-35
Ithaca	1882-1901,* 1903-35
Kingston	1857-58, 1902-35
Long Island	check phase one
Middletown	1857/58, 1905-35
Morrisania	1853
Newburgh	1856-76, 1902-35
New York City	1786-1934/Street Index (Manhattan)
Ogdensburg	1857
Oswego	1852-59, 1902-35
Poughkeepsie	1843-61, 1902-35
[Queens]	Street Index(FHL)/Election District Map
Rochester	1827-1935/ Election District Map
Rome	1857-60, 1903-34
Schenectady	1841-61, 1902-35/ Election District Map
[Staten Island]	Street Index
Syracuse	1844-1935/Election District Map
Troy	1829-1935
Utica	1817-1935/Election District Map
Watertown	1840-55
Westchester Co.	1860/61
Williamsburg	1847-54
Yonkers	1859/60, 1902-31/Election District Map
North Carolina:	Miracode (entire state)
Asheville	1902-24
[Charlotte]	Street Index
Greensboro	1903-35
Raleigh	1903-35

State/City	Date/1910 Census Compatibility
North Dakota:	
Fargo	1902-34
Ohio:	Miracode (entire state)
Regional	1853-61
Akron	1859-60/ Street Index
[Canton]	Street Index
Chillicothe	1855-61, 1902-34
Cincinnati	1819-1935/Street Index
Circleville	1859
Cleveland	1837-1935
Columbus	1843-1935
Dayton	1850-1935/Street Index
Delaware	1859-60, 1902-35*
Hamilton	1858-59
Mansfield	1858/59, 1902-35
Marietta	1860/61, 1902-35
Mt. Vernon	1858/59
Portsmouth	1858-59, 1908-35
Sandusky	1855-78, 1902-35
Springfield	1852-60, 1902-35
Steubenville	1856/57, 1902-35
Toledo	1858-1935
[Youngstown]	Street Index
Zanesville	1851-61, 1902-36
Oklahoma:	Miracode (entire state)
Enid	1905-35
Oklahoma City	1902-35*/Street Index
Tulsa	1909-35/Street Index
Oregon:	
Astoria	1902-34
Portland	1863-1935/Election District Map
Pennsylvania:	Miracode (entire state)
Regional	1844-60
Carnegie	1902-35*
Chester	1859/60, 1902-31
Erie	1853-1935/Street Index
Erie County	1859/60
Harrisburg	1839-1935
Lancaster	1843-60, 1903-35
Lancaster Co.	1843-60
Monongahela V.	1859
Norristown	1860/61, 1902-35
Philadelphia	1785-1860,* 1861-1935/Miracode (City)/Street Index
Pittsburgh	1813-60,* 1861-1935
Reading	1806/56-1935/Street Index
Scranton	1861-1935
Wilkes-Barre	1882-1901,* 1902-19
Williamsport	1866-81, 1882-1901,* 1902-34
West Chester	1857
Rhode Island:	
Regional	1849

State/City	Date/1910 Census Compatibility
East Providence	1902-35
Newport	1856-58
Pawtucket	1857/58, 1902-35*/Election District Map
Providence	1824-1935/Election District Map
Westerly	1902-35*
South Carolina:	Soundex (entire state)
Camden	1816/24
Charleston	1782-1935*
Columbia	1859-60, 1903-35
South Dakota:	
Sioux Falls	1902-35
Tennessee:	Soundex (entire state)
Regional	1860/61
Chattanooga	1871-81, 1902-35/Soundex (Tennessee Cities)
Clarksville	1859/60
Knoxville	1869-81, 1882-1901,* 1902-35/Soundex (Tennessee Cities)
Memphis	1849-1935/Soundex (Tennessee Cities)
Nashville	1853-1935/Soundex (Tennessee Cities)
Texas:	Soundex (entire state)
Amarillo	1903-35
Austin	1857, 1903-35
Beaumont	1903-35
Dallas	1875-1935
Fort Worth	1877-79, 1902-36
Galveston	1856-1935
Houston	1882-1901,* 1902-35
San Antonio	1877-1935/Street Index
Waco	1882-1901,* 1902-34
Utah:	
Logan	1904-35
Ogden	1882-1901,* 1902-35
Salt Lake City	1867-1935/Election District Map/Street Index (FHL)
Vermont:	
Regional	1849-60
Barre	1902-35
Brattleboro	1902-35
Burlington	1865-1910, 1911-35*
Virginia:	Soundex (entire state)
Regional	1852
Norfolk	1801/51-1935
Petersburg	1859, 1902-35
Richmond	1819-1935/Street Index
Wythe County	1857
Washington:	
Bellingham	1902-35
Everett	1902-35
Seattle	1872-1935/Street Index
[Spokane]	Election District Map

State/City	Date/1910 Census Compatibility
[Tacoma]	Election District Map
West Virginia:	Soundex (entire state)
Clarksburg	1905-35*
Wheeling	1839-60, 1861-1901,* 1903-34
Wisconsin:	
Regional	1857-59
Appleton	1882-1901,* 1904-34
Beloit	1858
Fond du Lac	1857-57, 1903-34
Green Bay	1903-29
Janesville	1858-60
Kenosha	1858, 1903-35
Madison	1851-81, 1903-35
Milwaukee	1847-1935/Election District Map
Mineral Point	1849

State/City	Date/1910 Census Compatibility
Oshkosh	1857, 1861-81, 1903-28
Racine	1850-59, 1902-35
Rock County	1857-58
Watertown	1902-35
Waukesha	1858
Whitewater	1858
Wyoming:	
Laramie	1908-35
Regional:	
The East	1846
Mississippi	1844
New England	1849-60
The South	1854
The West	1837
Western Reserve	1852

directory being from 1871 and the earliest Martindale-Hubbell directory being from 1885.

The publishing companies themselves maintain libraries, but access is a problem. The best approach is a specific written request. The addresses of the two oldest law list compilers are:

Martindale-Hubbell, Inc.
Reed Reference Publishing
P.O. Box 1001
Summit, NJ 07902-1001
(908) 464-6800
(800) 526-4902 (customer service)
Fax (908) 464-3553

Campbell's List, Inc.
P.O. Box 428
Maitland, FL 32751
(407) 644-8298

MEDICAL DIRECTORIES

Medical school libraries should have the most current edition of the *American Medical Directory* readily available. Your access to back issues may depend on the individual library's policy. The Eccles Health Science Library at the University of Utah medical school keeps a complete collection of the directory available to the general public. Local and state medical associations may also maintain old directories, including those published on a regional level.

R.L. Polk published a *Medical and Surgical Register of the United States and Canada,* which was in its fifth edition by 1898. You may have a hard time finding early issues of this register; the Library of Congress does not seem to have any.

The Library of Congress maintains a complete collection of the *American Medical Directory.* If you can't get to a large medical library, consider sending a letter to the American Medical Association, which publishes the directory. Its library and archive will also provide biographical details from its database on physicians from 1878 to 1969 for a small fee. Contact:

AMA Library and Archives
P.O. Box 109050
Chicago, IL 60610-9050
(312) 464-5000
Fax (312) 645-4184

CIVIL AND MILITARY SERVICE DIRECTORIES

According to an 1816 act of Congress providing for a biennial register of the civil and military service of the United States, twenty-five copies of the register were to be deposited in the Library of Congress. In 1851, a provision was added that allowed for a copy to be sent to the secretary of state of each state. Presumably, the Library of Congress and state libraries and archives contain copies today.

The Library of Congress has apparently transferred the older registers to the National Archives, but you should check both repositories. State libraries and archives may not have kept all of the registers from each year, so there may be gaps. States in the former Confederacy may not have copies of the registers for 1861 to 1865.

PROFESSIONAL DIRECTORIES

The Library of Congress and local and state archives will probably have some directories relevant to their areas of interest. If you can find a publisher of pre-twentieth-century professional directories that is still in business today, see if it maintains a directory library. *Directories in Print* can aid in this task. The addresses of the publishers of the two professional directories of special interest to genealogists are:

The American Blue Book of Funeral Directors
Kates-Boylston Publications
1501 Broadway
New York, NY 10036-5503
(212) 398-9266

American Cemetery Association Membership Directory and Buyer's Guide
American Cemetery Association
5201 Leesburg Pike, Suite 1111
Falls Church, VA 22041-3203
(703) 379-5838
(800) 654-7700
Fax (703) 998-0162

RELIGIOUS DIRECTORIES

Access is the major problem in locating religious directories. Common designations such as "Baptist" and "Methodist" may comprise several distinct denominations. You will therefore need to research the ancestor's exact religion to find the appropriate directory. Also, the denomination as it existed in the nineteenth century may be defunct or have merged with another group. In such a case, lack of a modern directory showing church locations may limit your access to the original records.

The best way to determine the existence and location of a directory for the denomination of interest is to look for a church archive for the particular denomination. Such archives may have back issues of these directories, as well as information on where to find the records of modern churches. Also, check the seminary or training college libraries for the denomination.

Among public repositories, check the Library of Congress, state and local libraries, and general university libraries (particularly those that were once denominational), but don't stop there. The Library of Congress, for example, has *The Official Catholic Directory* only as early as 1886, although it has been published since 1817. In such a case contact the publisher:

> P.J. Kenedy and Sons
> Reed Reference Publishing
> P.O. Box 31
> New Providence, NJ 07974
> (800) 521-8110

POST OFFICE DIRECTORIES

Most research libraries of any size should have the Gale Research reprint (discussed below) available in their reference sections. The Library of Congress and the Family History Library have copies. The Library of Congress should also have other back issues of post office directories.

COMPREHENSIVENESS OF DIRECTORIES

When consulting any directory, keep in mind why it was compiled. If an individual was not at home when the city directory agent called, his or her name may not appear for that particular year. Even today, the general population must cooperate to put together a city directory. The agent or compiler usually leaves a notice on the door if the resident is not home, and not everyone will take the time or trouble to respond. The compiler may not follow up if it is too costly. Methods in the nineteenth century may have been considerably more primitive. Business and professional directories may have required a fee for inclusion. If you can't find an ancestor in the alphabetical sequence of a directory, be sure to check the beginning for listings "received too late to be included."

City directories, however, seem to lack the most for their subject matter, if only for their scope. In some cities, early directories were published in the same year by competing companies, and they did not always include the same people. If an ancestor is not listed in a directory but should be, check for misplaced letter spellings—Tohmson instead of Thomson, for example. Names may also be spelled differently. Early New York City directories often contained lists of variant name spell-

ings. Pittsburgh city directories listed the names Meyers, Meyer, Myers, and Myer together until the 1860s. Some early directories grouped names with the same initial letter but did not list them in strict alphabetical sequence. Consider the type style when using early directories, particularly those from the eighteenth century. Don't misread the old double-ess character (ƒ) as ƒ.

The date on the title page of a directory is usually that of publication and does not necessarily indicate when the information was compiled. Often, a directory will state that it is for the "year ending" on a particular day. Remember that many city dwellers rented rather than owned their residences and may not have stayed at one address for long; this fact does have an impact on using the directory for census searches (see discussion below). While it refers to a non-urban area, the following excerpt from the foreword to the *Alaska Directory and Gazetteer for 1934–1935* helps to explain the difficulties of listing people constantly on the move:

> This Second Biennial Edition of the Alaska Directory and Gazetteer represents a complete new compilation of the residents and business houses of the Territory of Alaska. . . . Extreme care has been taken to secure the most complete and accurate information possible but the publishers cannot assume responsibility for any accuracies [*sic*] or omissions. A frontier country, one-fifth the size of the United States, with its approximately 29,000 white population distributed among more than 400 widely scattered towns and settlements, present[s] difficulties which subscribers will appreciate. The shift of population from point to point in the Territory by seasonal occupation and winter vacationing in the States offer further problems of reporting proper locations of many residents. In order to meet these situations, the issuing of supplements from time to time prior to publication of the next directory proper will be continued. Also, all purchasers are entitled to two years reference, inquiry and tracing service.[4]

CITY DIRECTORIES

City directories are primarily useful for locating people in a particular place and time. They can tell you generally where an ancestor lived and give an exact location for census years. They are also useful for linkage with sources other than censuses.

There are usually several parts to a city directory. The section of most interest to the genealogist, of course, is the alphabetical listing of names, for it is there that you may find your ancestor. The other parts of a directory are equally important, however, as they will help you utilize the information contained in the alphabetical listings more efficiently. Street directories and ward boundary descriptions will be discussed in detail below. There are also sections listing government offices, churches, civic and fraternal organizations, and businesses. These sections may be separated or combined.

Whenever you use a directory, however, it is important to refer to the page showing abbreviations used in the alphabetical section of the directory, usually following the name in each entry. Some abbreviations are quite common, such as *h* for home or *r,* indicating residence. There may even be a subtle distinction between *r* for residents who are related to the homeowner and *b* for boarders who are not related.

Some city directories list adult children who lived with their parents but were working or going to school. Look for persons of the same surname residing at the same address. If analyzed and interpreted properly, these annual directories can tell you (by implication) which children belong to which household, when they married and started families of their own, and when they established themselves in business. In cases where a specific occupation is given, you can search records pertinent to that occupation.

There may be a page at the beginning of the alphabetical section that gives changes, additions, and deletions—usually due to removals, but sometimes due to death. Some city directories also give special facts—separate listings for African Americans or places of birth and death, for example, but such notations are usually for one year only and are not the norm

Beginning in the late nineteenth century, but more regularly in the twentieth century, city directories have often contained a "reverse" street directory, listing streets alphabetically and then the names of the people residing at each address. This is an important tool for identifying persons of different surnames residing at the same address. Another kind of "reverse" directory—by telephone number—has also become part of twentieth-century directories.

Once an ancestor has been found in a city directory, there are several ways the information can be used to gain access to, or link with, such sources as censuses, death and probate records, church records, naturalization records, and land records.

USING CENSUS RECORDS WITH DIRECTORIES

The usefulness of city directories for gaining access to census records of urban areas cannot be overstated. Even where census indexes exist, there is always the possibility that the census taker or the indexer erred in the spelling or coding of the surname. In such cases, it is just as difficult to find someone in an indexed urban area as it is in an unindexed urban area, and the methodology for doing so is the same.

Census indexes currently exist for every state for the years 1790 through 1850. The 1860 census is indexed for almost every state, and the indexing of the 1870 census is following closely. The 1880 census is Soundexed only for those families with children under ten, the 1900 and 1920 censuses are soundexed for every family in every state, while the 1910 census is soundexed or Miracoded only for certain states. Most state censuses are as yet unindexed. For those federal censuses as yet unavailable to the general public (from 1930 on), the census bureau will conduct a search in an urban area only if a precise address for the census year is known.

The federal census for most urban areas is divided into at least wards. Beginning with the 1880 census, wards are further subdivided into enumeration districts. Some state censuses for urban areas are divided into election districts or other sub-ward designations. For a city directory to be useful in making a census search, you must know the correct ward or enumeration district of a particular address for the census year desired. There are several aids to locating the correct ward or enumeration district.

STREET DIRECTORIES

Street directories vary depending on the publisher of the city directory and the date of publication. At best, they will give you the exact ward or wards through which a street runs, as well as cross streets. At worst, they will simply list the names of the streets in alphabetical order. Even such a limited listing can be valuable if notations of name changes are included.

If a street runs through several wards, checking the cross street nearest to the street address for the ancestor will help to determine the correct ward to search. The 1910 street directory for Rochester, New York (figure 11-1), shows that Portland Avenue runs through wards 8, 16, 18, and 22. Suppose the ancestor lived at 1100 Portland Avenue. The closest cross street is Pomeroy Street, which lies entirely within Ward 22. Ward 22 is therefore the proper ward to search.

The one problem that you might encounter when using street directories to determine the correct ward is if the street of interest forms the boundary between wards. In such a case, you need to determine which side of the street the address of interest lies on and, depending on whether the address number is even or odd, you should be able to determine in which ward it lies. While the even and odd numbering of streets may now be standardized, it cannot be assumed that there was any consistency in the nineteenth century. You may have to use maps in conjunction with the street directory, however, to make this determination.

MAPS

If the street directories alone cannot provide the proper ward, or if identification of a specific enumeration district is desired, maps can be utilized to find the appropriate census subdivision. There are basically three kinds of maps: those created with ward or enumeration district boundaries, those without boundaries, and those with boundaries added after publication.

Maps created with boundaries are the most useful. Many city directories were published with maps showing ward boundaries that can be used in conjunction with the street directories. City maps showing ward boundaries were also created independently of city directories for other reasons—for guides or for insurance purposes, for instance. The Library of Congress has an excellent collection of city maps created from 1840 to 1900 showing ward boundaries. This collection has been acquired by the Family History Library, adding to an already good city map collection. (See chapter 19, Tracking Urban Ancestors, for more information on city maps.)

There are also maps with census enumeration district boundaries for the 1880, 1900, 1910, and 1920 censuses. These maps are available at the Washington National Records Service, 4205 Suitland Rd., Suitland, Maryland; or they can be ordered from the Cartographic and Architectural Branch (NNSC), National Archives, Washington, DC 20408. The Family History Library has microfiche copies of these maps for forty-seven major cities in 1910. The appropriate call numbers can be found in the Family History Library's *1910 Census Register.*

Maps without boundaries will help you if you can find a description of the ward or enumeration district boundaries. There will sometimes be a description of ward boundaries in the city directory itself, even if there is no map and the street directory does not contain ward designations. In this case, you

Figure 11-1. From a 1910 street directory for Rochester, New York.

42   ROCHESTER STREET DIRECTORY.

Left.	Rt.	
—	—	Plymouth Park
	ch.	Church Immaculate Conception
270	271	Glasgow
278		Greig
	287	Santiago
318	317	Winter
	335	Caledonia av.
342		Clarissa
354		Aiken alley
—	—	Penn. R. R.
	363	Frost avenue
	367	Emmanuel Presbyterian ch.
	377	Bartlett
386		Edith
400		Doran
	408	Columbia avenue
410		Ethel
428		Violetta
	455	Schell place
458		Fenwick
	465	Colbert court
480	488	Flint
	525	Fuller place
528		Mt. Pleasant pk.
542	541	Magnolia
	605	Jefferson avenue
604	605	Cottage
	651	Barton
—	—	Penn. R. R.
	745	Brooks avenue
—	—	Grandview ter.

Plymouth Avenue, N., from 96 Main West, north, to 207 Commercial; wards 1, 2

Left.	Rt.	
1	2	Main West
	40	Central church
	44	Church
75		United Pres. ch.
99		Pullman court
107	108	Allen
—	—	N. Y. C. R. R.
—	—	Commercial

Plymouth Terrace, fr. 225 Plymouth avenue, west; ward 3

Poco, fr. 8 Caledonia av., east, to Hemlock alley; ward 3

Pomeroy, from 1106 Portland avenue, near city line, east; ward 22

Poplar, from 77 Gregory, south, to 140 Linden; ward 14

Left.	Rt.	
2	1	Gregory
52	53	Sanford
104	103	Cypress
140	139	Linden

Portage, across 1484 Clifford avenue, north, to 217 Jennings; ward 22

Porter, fr. Breck, south, ward 18

Portland Avenue, from 484 North, northeast, to city line; wards 8, 16, 18, 22

Left.	Rt.	
	2	North
81		Bingle alley
87		Wesley
146		Syracuse
190		Central park
206		Draper
	400	Day
212		Merrimac
	402	Cuper
241		Baynes

Left.	Rt.	
	354	Irondequoit
	898	Council
417		Lansing
	488	Lochner place
523	526	Clifford avenue
541		Carter
	560	Aebersold
	620	Jennings
625		Kintz place
	786	DeWitt
798		Holbrooke
881	888	Lux
857		Folsom place
	886	Randolph
897		Durnan
	924	Oneida
951		Barbara
	974	Grafton
995		Urquhart
	1026	Chapin
1047		Mohawk
	1068	Jackson
1079		Furlong
	1106	Pomeroy
1113		Turpin
	1142	Sylvester
1145		Dickinson
1175	1176	Norton (city line)

Portsmouth Terrace, fr. 821 East avenue, northeast, to 809 University avenue; ward 6

Post, from 425 Chili avenue, south, to Arnett; ward 19

Left.	Rt.	
	2	1 Chili avenue
	61	Ringle place
	109	Hobson
—	—	Arnett

Powers, from 984 North Goodman, east, to Winterroth; ward 18

Priem, from 284 Monroe avenue, north and east, to 225 Alexander; wd. 12

Primrose, fr. 308 Flower City park, north, to Ridgeway av.; ward 10

Prince, from 226 East av., northeast, to Champeney terrace; wards 6, 16

Left.	Rt.	
1	2	East avenue
29	30	University av.
	57	Erion crescent
	64	College avenue
69	70	Main East
83		Kenilworth ter.
—	—	Champeney ter.

Princeton, from 86 Oakman, north, to 108 Scrantom; ward 5

Probert, from 620 East avenue, north, to railroad; ward 21

Prospect, from 177 West avenue, south, to 242 Adams; ward 11

Left.	Rt.	
2	1	West avenue
18		Strable
29	31	Troup
	47	Clifton
	57	Melody
72	73	Atkinson
92	91	Babbitt place
108	101	Adams

Pryor, from 340 Joseph avenue, east, to 73 Hanover; ward 8		

Pulaski, fr. St. Casimir, east, to 1059 Hudson avenue; ward 17

Pullman Court, from 99 Plymouth avenue North, west, to Scott place; ward 1

Putnam, fr. 29 Cleveland, south, to 28 Helena; ward 8

Quincy, from 1550 Main East, north, to 645 Garson avenue; ward 18

Left.	Rt.	
1	2	Main East
123	124	Federal
145	146	R. & S. B. R. R.
165	166	Garson avenue

Race, from 10 Aqueduct, east, to Graves; ward 1

Railroad, from 1040 Main East, northwest, to Public Market; ward 18

Left.	Rt.	
1	2	Main East
	94	Fourth
—	—	Public Market

Raines Park, fr. 34 Lake View park, north, to 337 Flower City park; ward 10

Rainier, from 234 Glenwood avenue, north, to 243 Lexington avenue; ward 10

Randolph, from 886 Portland avenue near Durnan, east; ward 22

Rano Alley, across 211 Gibbs, west, to Schlitzer; ward 16

Rau Place, from 341 St. Paul, west; ward 5

Rauber, from 664 Clinton avenue North, east, to 27 Widman; ward 8

Left.	Rt.	
2	1	Clinton av. N.
174	173	Joseph avenue
242	241	Widman

Ravine Avenue, from Hastings, west, to Erie canal; ward 10

Left.	Rt.	
1	2	Hastings
9	10	Clarkson
39	40	Lake avenue
69	70	Leavenworth
97	100	Fulton avenue
127	122	Malvern
	155	Aldern place
161		Salter place
	210	Tacoma
	339	Maryland
373	374	Dewey avenue
	416	Finch
419	428	Erie canal

Raymond, from 1147 Clinton avenue South, southwest, to Howard, at city line; ward 14

Redfield, from Freeman, south; ward 5

Regent Place, from 181 Milburn, south; ward 12

Remington, fr. 490 Clifford avenue, north, to Norton; ward 17		

Left.	Rt.	
	2	Clifford avenue
39		LaForce
	46	DeJonge
65		Mead
	78	Boston
93		Carl
	118	Langham
139		Avenue A
	156	Wilkins
171		Ketchum
201		Morrill
	218	Terhaar
238		Bloomingdale
263	264	Avenue D
	298	Pardee
—	—	Farbridge
329		Kohlman
	364	Leo
373		Ereth
	390	Zimbrich
399		Oscar
	422	Weaver
441		Borchard
485	484	Lang
551	552	Norton (city line)

Renfrew Place, fr. 395 Troup, south; ward 11

Renwood, fr. 1852 Clifford avenue, north, to 135 Jennings; ward 22

Reservoir Avenue, from 922 Mt. Hope avenue, east, to Highland Park; ward 14

Reynolds, from 281 West avenue, south, to 435 Seward; wards 11, 19

Left.	Rt.	
2	1	West avenue
6		Rice alley
	7	Lapey place
18	19	Troup
40	39	Clifton
60		Atkinson
88	87	Adams
102	101	Knowles alley
116	117	Tremont
	129	Penn
144	145	Bronson avenue
170	171	Cady
190		Faxon alley
198	199	Champlain
212	211	Ruff alley
226	225	Frost avenue
238	237	Whittlesey alley
250	255	Bartlett
278	277	Columbia avenue
294	293	Hawley
312	313	Flint
336	337	Seward

Rhine, from 74 Hanover, east, to 331 Hudson avenue; ward 8

Rhona Place, from 233 Sanford, south; ward 14

Rice Alley, from 288 Troup, north and west, to 6 Reynolds; ward 11

Rice Place, from 20 Lyell avenue, north; wd. 9

Richard, from 210 Meigs, easterly, across Wilcox; ward 12

Left.	Rt.	
2	1	Meigs
20		Edmonds
32	33	South Goodman
50		Rising place
58		Boardman
76		Sumner park
100		Wilcox

can draw the ward boundaries on a map, but be sure to use a map that was published near the date of the directory.

Enumeration district descriptions exist for 1880, 1900, 1910, and 1920. These descriptions indicate the boundaries of each district. They constitute National Archives Microfilm Publication T1224 and are available at the main and regional archives of the National Archives as well as the Family History Library.

Drawing ward and enumeration district boundaries on a map without boundaries can be a time-consuming process, but it is sometimes necessary in cases where such maps do not exist or are inaccessible to the researcher intent on locating an ancestor in the census.

Maps with boundaries added after publication are time-savers, but take care that such maps have been drawn correctly, or you will have to search a long time to find the right entries. The Newberry Library in Chicago has constructed a 1900 atlas for the city of Chicago from the enumeration district maps. This atlas is especially valuable for finding alleys, courts, and other short streets. The Family History Library is adding ward and enumeration district boundaries to maps already in its collection. Another general source of city maps is E. Kay Kirkham, *A Handy Guide to Record Searching in the Larger Cities of the United States* (Logan, Utah: The Everton Publishers, 1974). The maps included street indexes, so Kirkham's is a useful compilation. Take care, however, as this book does not cover all of the major cities for which such maps are available, nor do the maps always cover every census year. In addition, most of the maps are taken from atlases dated 1855, 1866, and 1878; the ward boundaries may not correspond to those existing in the closest census years.

STREET INDEXES

The 1910 census is not indexed for many of the major urban areas of the country. Microfiche street indexes compiled by the Census Bureau for thirty-nine major cities were distributed to all National Archives branches under the auspices of the NARA (National Archives and Records Administration) Gift Fund of the Federation of Genealogical Societies. The Family History Library also has this microfiche collection and has added indexes for five more cities. See table 11-1 for a list of cities with street indexes. The street indexes generally break each street down by address number and indicate the enumeration district in which the number can be found.

The New York City Municipal Archives has specialized street indexes for the 1905, 1915, and 1925 state censuses of New York City (Manhattan and the Bronx). The Family History Library has these indexes and has also compiled its own street index for the 1915 state census of Manhattan. Other libraries and societies may have compiled street indexes for their particular urban areas or may have purchased the microfiche mentioned above.

SPECIAL FINDING AIDS

Many local libraries and societies have created their own aids to finding the correct ward or enumeration district for a particular address. The Family History Library has created an enumeration district index for all states for which there are no 1910 Soundex or Miracode indexes. (See chapter 5, Research in Census Records.) Other examples of privately compiled finding aids are Mary Lou Craver Mariner and Patricia Roughan

Bellows, *A Research Aid for the Massachusetts 1910 Federal Census* (Sudbury, Mass.: Computerized Assistance, 1988), and Barbara Hillman, *Guide to the Use of the United States. Census Office. 10th Census 1880 New York City* (New York: New York Public Library, 1963). Mariner and Bellows list the 1910 census enumeration districts for wards of various Massachusetts cities, and Hillman actually uses contemporary assembly and election district maps and corresponds them to the proper enumeration district for the 1880 census of New York City. In both cases, you must have a street address for your ancestor in order to locate him or her; this information can be obtained from the city directory corresponding to the census year.

It would be impossible to list all of the specialized guides available for particular cities and particular censuses. The best rule of thumb before searching the census of an urban area is to call the local library or genealogical society for the city to determine if a street index or finding aid does exist.

METHODOLOGY

The basic methodology for locating an ancestor in the census using city directories is to find the street address of that ancestor in a directory for the year of or close to the date of the census. Keep in mind that an ancestor might have moved between the date of the census and the compilation of the directory for the same year, so it is always a good idea to check the directories for either side of a census year in order to be certain of all possible addresses. If a member of the family in question was born, married, or died in the census year and vital records were kept by the city in that year, then the address that appears on the vital record may be a more accurate locator. Once an address is found, the next step is to determine the ward or enumeration district in which that address was located. It should be possible to do this using the finding aids mentioned above. Once the proper ward or enumeration district is determined, then it is a matter of reading the district.

Prior to 1880, few cities were divided below the ward level in the census. New York and Philadelphia were among those that were. Fortunately, there are two census enumerations in those years for these cities, the second of which lists the exact street address for each family. If an ancestor can be located in the second enumeration (which often contains a minimal amount of information, as it was basically a recount), then a corresponding entry can be found in the first enumeration using not only the ward number but the subdistrict designation. For most other cities, you may have to search through an entire ward, but narrowing down to one reel of film is a considerable time saver. Eventually, the 1870 census will be indexed in its entirety, leaving the address and ward method of searching pre-1880 censuses to cases involving error by the census taker or indexer.

Beginning in 1880, the name of the street is usually listed in the margin of the census page, and the house number is listed along with the visitation numbers (dwelling and family). When a ward and enumeration district have been located for a post-1880 census using one of the finding aids mentioned above, the family can usually be found by looking for the street name and then house number.

The following examples illustrate two different ways to find an ancestor in the 1910 census for two unindexed cities: Rochester, New York, and Baltimore, Maryland.

The 1910 city directory for Rochester, New York, showed

that Harvey F. Remington had a home at 7 Reservoir Avenue (figure 11-2). The street directory for Rochester showed that Reservoir Avenue was contained entirely in the 14th Ward (figure 11-1). The index to enumeration districts for the 1910 census showed that the 14th Ward of Rochester consisted of enumeration districts 138 to 144. A 1910 enumeration district map does exist for Rochester, but it was unavailable for consultation at the time the search was made. Fortunately, the 1910 city directory for Rochester had a map showing ward boundaries (figure 11-3). Using the enumeration district descriptions, it was determined that Reservoir Avenue lay in the 141st Enumeration District (figure 11-4). It was then simply a matter of reading that enumeration district—but in this case looking for the street name was useless, as the name of the street was not given in the margin for this particular address. By reading each family entry, the Harvey F. Remington family was found on sheet 11B, line 72.[5]

There is no 1910 directory for Baltimore, Maryland, in the Research Publications microfilm collection, but there is one for 1911. John L. Alcock, a lumber exporter, had a home at 2742 St. Paul Street (figure 11-5). The street directory in 1911 did not give ward designations; it stated only the streetcar line that served a particular address (figure 11-6). Fortunately, Baltimore is one of the thirty-nine cities for which a census bureau street index exists.

Reference to the street index showed that even-numbered addresses on St. Paul Street from 2600 to 2800 were in enumeration district 191 (figure 11-7). By searching this enumeration district, the John L. Alcock family was found on sheet 9B, line 72.[6]

The 1910 census will likely remain unindexed longer than the pre-1880 censuses. For this reason, existing enumeration district maps and street indexes for the major cities are listed in table 11-1. It should be stressed that similar finding aids exist for the other post-1870 censuses, and they can be utilized in the same manner as illustrated above when searching the Soundex fails.

USING DEATH AND PROBATE RECORDS WITH DIRECTORIES

When you know that an ancestor died in a large city, you can use his or her presence in a directory to approximate the date of death. This makes voluminous city death and probate records much easier to search. It is often easier, however, to estimate the date of a man's death because, unlike a recently widowed woman, a widower will not be designated as such. Take care with this method: an individual's nonappearance in a directory does not always indicate death. Sometimes a person will disappear for a year or so and then mysteriously reappear at the same address. More likely than not, the ancestor was there all the time. Remember how the source was compiled. It is best, therefore, to check directories for several years after an individual's first disappearance: to determine if that ancestor died or moved away. Beginning in the twentieth century, however, some directories will list a date of death for an individual who had died since the last directory was compiled if that information was provided to the publisher, usually by a related person residing at the same address.

Unless a death date is provided or a man appears in one

directory at a particular street address and his widow appears at the same address in the year following, you should not assume that you will find a death or probate record in the year immediately following his disappearance. This is especially true where older individuals (particularly widows) are involved. They may still be alive and living with children. It is also possible that a "widow" was actually a divorcee—particularly in the nineteenth century—and that her husband's death will not be found prior to her appearance as such in the directory. Nevertheless, even a date with which to begin a death or probate search is valuable.

METHODOLOGY

James Renwick and Ellen/Helen Gibson were married in Scotland in 1814. They had three known children: Andrew, born 1815; Alexander, born 1818; and Marion, born 1820. Sometime between 1820 and 1833 they immigrated to New York City (Manhattan). We first found James in the 1833–34 New York City Directory at 406 Washington Street.[7] In the 1850 Manhattan census, Ellen was living alone, presumably as a widow.[8] A search of *Doggett's New York City Directories 1845–46* and *1846–47* revealed the following entries:

1845-46	1846-47
Renwick, Alexander, stonecutter, 400 Washington	Renwick, Ellen, widow James, boarding, 400 Washington
Renwick, James, boarding 400 Washington[9]	

In 1845–46 there was also a James Renwick, professor, living at another address. We can draw several conclusions from these entries. Additional research showed that Alexander, the son, was a mason by trade. The Alexander Renwick who appears at 400 Washington Street was a stonecutter. Thus, it is

Remington Alvah C physician 576 West av
    Charles W laborer 438 Exchange bds 2
      Johnson   [993 do
    Clifford E florist 1023 South av house
    Edith F cashier 201 Powers bldg bds
      192 N Union
    Elizabeth Miss bds 175 Rosedale
    Eva P Mrs teacher East High School h
      44 Quincy
    Frederic remd to New York city
    Frederick carpenter bds 130 Main W
    Frederick B instructor (at Industry) h
      409 Linden
    Genevieve Miss bds 389 Brown
    Harvey F lawyer 911 Wilder bldg h 7
      Reservoir av   [1Reservoir av
    Janet stenographer 23 City Hall house
    Louise A widow Edward C house 656
      Lake av   .[Union
    Margaret A widow Charles E h 192 N
    Stanley D salesman 612 Granite bldg b
      580 Averill av
    Typewriter Co 44 East av
    Walter C (*Barnard, Porter & Viall*) 17
      N Water bds 656 Lake av
    William B clerk 64 Trust bldg bds 7
      Reservoir av
    Willis S steward Roch State Hospital
      house do   [der

Figure 11-2. Entry for Harvey F. Remington in the 1910 street directory for Rochester, New York.

Figure 11-3. Portion of a map of the city of Rochester, New York, 1910, from the street directory.

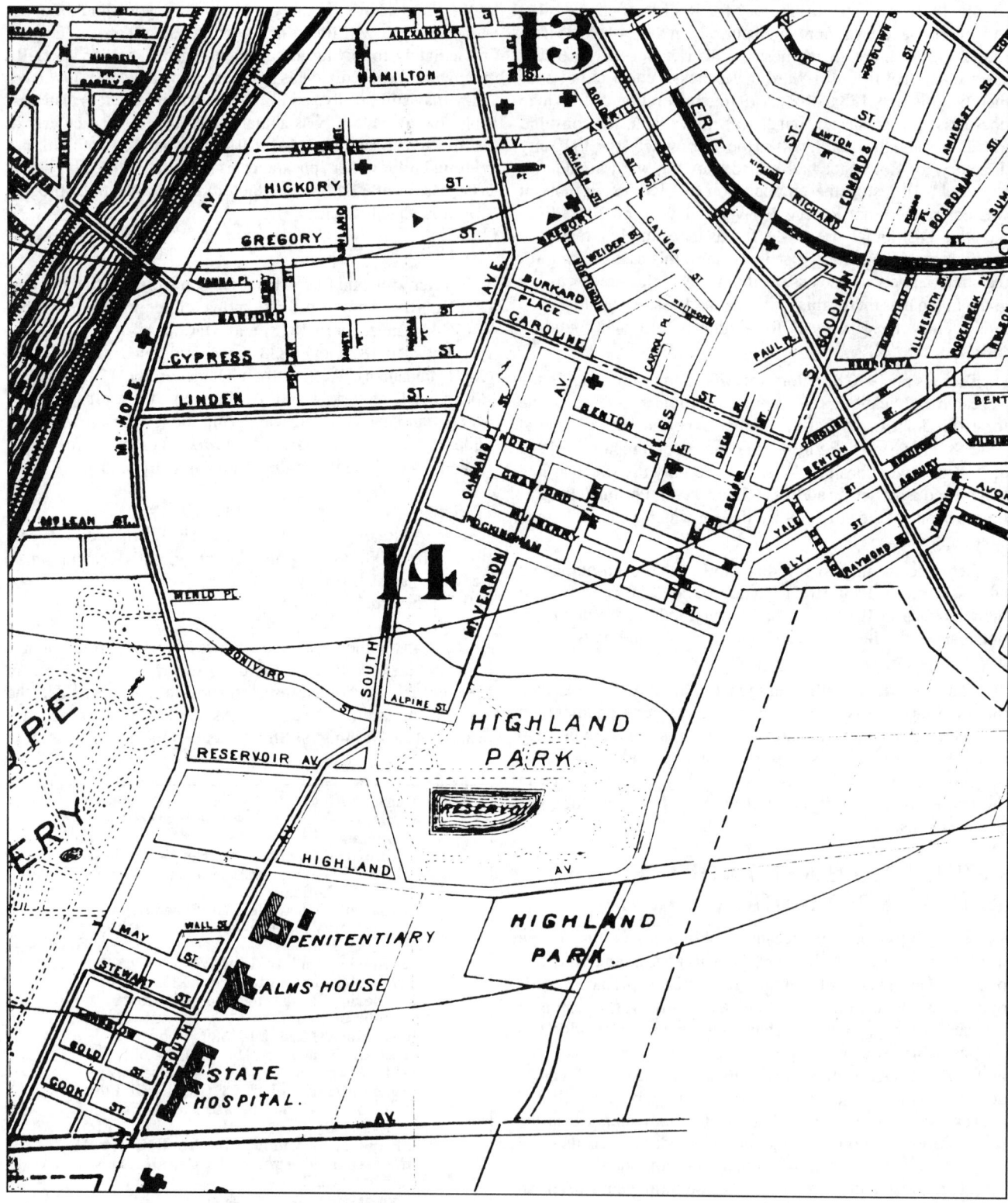

probable that the James Renwick also residing at that address is the ancestor. We verified this conclusion with the 1846–47 directory. Although neither Alexander nor James appears, the entry for "Renwick, Ellen, widow James, boarding 400 Washington" indicated that James had died sometime between 1845 and 1846. We knew from previous research that Alexander had moved to Pittsburgh by this time.

Manhattan death registers also exist for this time period. These records are arranged alphabetically by the first letter of each surname for each year. To search the entire 1840–50 decade would have been tedious and time consuming. A search in the 1845 death registers quickly yielded this entry:

5 June 1845
James Renwick, age 59
400 Washington St.
Disease of Heart
Place of burial: Scotch Presbyterian Cemetery
Sexton: C.A. Stewart[10]

As it turned out, this record quickly and efficiently provided the only mention of James Renwick's age at a given date.

USING CHURCH RECORDS WITH DIRECTORIES

You can use city directories to gain access to church records. In most major cities, civil marriage records have existed longer than in rural areas. In Philadelphia, for example, civil marriages have been recorded since 1860, while, in the rest of Pennsylvania, the normal starting date is 1885. Similarly, Pittsburgh records begin in 1875. Since there was little governmental apparatus to record marriages effectively, it was up to the clergyman who performed the service to return the information to the city authorities. In states where marriages were recorded at the county level, large cities benefitted from this registration by being included on that level.

Whatever the circumstances under which marriages were recorded, the information given is very similar: the names of the bride and groom, the license date, the marriage date, sometimes names of witnesses, and almost always the name of the clergyman or magistrate who performed the marriage.

METHODOLOGY

According to Philadelphia's 1900 census, Christian and Sophia Hochwald had been married for thirty-eight years.[11] Christian had lived in Philadelphia before this date, so a check in the marriage registers might determine Sophia Hochwald's maiden name. The microfilm copy of the Board of Health marriage registers for 1862 was extremely faded but was clear enough to find a possible marriage entry on 3 May 1862.[12]

Reverend G. Wiehle performed the marriage, and his address was 531 St. John Street. The Philadelphia city directories showed that this man was the pastor of the Salem German Reformed Church on St. John Street.[13] Now a check in church records can be made for this couple's marriage, membership, and children's baptisms. See the sections on telephone and religious directories for information on how to locate such records.

USING NATURALIZATION AND LAND RECORDS WITH DIRECTORIES

It may seem odd to group naturalization and land records, but methodologically they are very similar. They both reflect the parameters of residence in an area. If a person owned a home in a city, there should be some record of its purchase when the family moved into the city and its sale when the family changed residences or moved out of the city. Finding the first and last years of residence narrows down the search for these land records, which, in a city like New York or Boston, can be voluminous.

Similarly, finding an immigrant's first year of residence in a city narrows down the naturalization records you'll have to search. In cases where these records are indexed, knowing that one of two naturalized immigrants of the same name lived in the city before the other may differentiate the two.

METHODOLOGY

James Renwick appeared in the city directories of New York beginning in 1833. He made his declaration of intention on 3 February 1835.[14] During that time period, declarations were usually filed after three years of residence; the information in James Renwick's case corresponds nicely with his residence in New York City. He may have arrived too late in 1832 to be included in that year's directory.

Renwick is an uncommon name, but this method, for both land and naturalization records, works well when the surname is more common and differentiation using auxiliary sources is necessary.

TELEPHONE DIRECTORIES

Telephone directories are the descendants of city directories, with the criterion for inclusion simply being subscription to the phone service. Telephone directories are useful as locators in place and time—but primarily for twentieth-century research. However, they won't include such useful information as occupation or the names of spouses and children—unless the sub-

```
140. Ward 14 (part of) Election district 3
         Bounded by Caroline
                    So. Goodman
                    Rockingham
                    South Ave.

141. Ward 14 (part of) Election district 4
     excluding State Hospital for Insane.
         Bounded by North boundary of Mt.Hope Cemetery
                    Mt.Hope Ave.,Bonivard,South Ave.
                    Mt.Vernon, Rockingham
                    So. Goodman, Highland Ave., City
                       line, Elmwood, Lehigh Valley R.R
                    Westfall Road
                    Genesee River

142. Ward 14 (part of) Election district 5 (part of)
         Bounded by Averill Ave.extended, Averill Ave.
                    South Ave., Hickory, Ashland
                    Gregory, Mt.Hope Ave., Clarissa
                    Genesee River
```

Figure 11-4. Descriptions of the enumeration districts of the sixteenth supervisor's district of New York. Bureau of the Census, thirteenth census. National Archives microfilm T1224, roll 35; FHL 1374008.

Figure 11-5. From R.L. Polk and Co. 1911 city directory for Baltimore, Maryland.

216   ALB   1911   R. L. POLK & CO'S   ALE

Albright Jas, lab, 216 s Duncan
Albright Jesse, driver, 1159 Columbia av
Albright Jesse jr, lab, 1159 Columbia av
Albright Jesse P, brklyr, 731 Columbia av
Albright John A, stonectr, 404 n Mount
Albright Jos, carp, 1121 Aisquith
Albright Louis A, agt, h 1034 n Milton av
Albright Perry W, carp, h 1704 Lamont
Albright Stephen, lab, 1502 n Durham
Alburn Mary C, tchr, 1901 e Lafayette av
Alcalay Henry, eng, 775 St Peter
Alcalay Ghisela, notions, 657 w Conway, h 775 St Peter
Alcarese Eleodro, shoemkr, 1302½ w Franklin, h 813 Low
Alcarese Josephine, confr, 712 e Balto
Alcazar The, moving pictures, 121 n Howard
Alchimowicz Peter, tailor, 413 s Central
Alchine Harry C, clk, 949 w Lexington
Alchine Minnie, confr, 949 w Lexington
Alcock John L (John L Alcock & Co), h 2742 St Paul
ALCOCK JOHN L & CO (John L Alcock), Lumber and Log Exporters, 1 s Gay, C & P Tel St Paul 2754
Alcock Kath L, h 638 n Fremont av
Alcock Nathl M (Nathl M Alcock & Co), 638 n Fremont av
Alcock Nathl M & Co (Nathl M Alcock), printers, 932 w Balto
Alcocke Norwood L, com trav 36 Hopkins pl
Alcorn Wm N, timekpr, h 2303 n Calvert
Alcovitch Morris, tailor, 20 s High
Alden Loyal R, electr eng, Pimlico av c Linwood
Alder Chas A, brakeman, 1723 Jackson
Alder Chas B, mach, 209 Prospect av, R P
Alder Chas F, clk, 2025 Woodberry av
Alder Chas H, molder, h 209 Prospect av
Alder Chester A, horseshr, 209 Prospect av, R P
Alder Danl S, police, h 2821 n Fulton av
Alder Frank C, clk, 2025 Woodberry av
Alder Georgianna Mrs, 2025 Woodberry av
Alder Geo, condtr, 721 w 35th n
Alder Harvey A, lab, h 322 w 29th n
Alder Ida Mrs, h 322 w 29th n
Alder Saml, lab, h 104 s Duncan
Alder Tena Mrs, h 2025 Woodberry av
Alder Thos T, fireman, h 1730 Jackson
Alder Victor, condtr, h 1723 Jackson
Alder Victor, millhd, 3359 Falls rd
Alder Wm, lab, h 3359 Falls rd
Alder Wm jr, fireman, h 3212 Cedar av
Alderman Leroy V, bkkpr, 721 w Fayette
Alderson Anne B, grocer, 1719 Riggs av
Alderson Chas I, molder, h 1009 Brentwood av
Alderson Ella J, h 1009 Brentwood
Alderson Frank, fireman, 1009 Brentwood
Alderson Geo, molder, 1009 Brentwood av
Alderson Wallace W, slsmn, 1719 Riggs
ALDRED J EDWARD, President Consolidated Gas Electric Light and Power Company, Residence New York
Aldrich Alfred, printer, h 540 e 23d n
Aldrich Arthur, draftsman, 540 e 23d n
Aldrich Denton B, carp, 2538 Woodbrook
Aldrich Elmer E, grocer, 2201 Preston pl
Aldrich Geo W, carp, 2538 Woodbrook
Aldrich Herbert, clk, 540 e 23d n
Aldridge Albert Z, student, 3005 Baker
Aldridge Arthur, confr, 2103 Homewood
Aldridge Elizab, nurse, 1100 n Stricker
Aldridge Elmira, boarding, 2538 Woodbrook av
Aldridge Harry L, clk, 1214 Fdk av ext
Aldridge J Edwd, student, Hotel Condon
Aldridge Jas E, bkkpr, 618 w Lee
Aldridge John W, condtr, h 1313 Light
Aldridge Laura V, cook, 901 w Fayette
Aldridge Nicholas A, condtr, h 3005 Baker

Aldridge Rachael J Mrs, M E Ch Home
Aldridge Roscoe H, dentist, 1514 w Fayette, h do
Aldridge Wm S R, bkkpr, 1818 Park av
Ale Myra, stenogr, 209 e 24th n
Ale Sara Z, engraver, 209 e 24th n
Aler Edwd P, sec, 412 w Saratoga
Aler Edwd V, auditor, 20 n Gilmor
Aler Emanuel V, jobber, h 20 n Gilmor
Aler Howard C, clk, h 1916 n Payson
Aler John E, mngr, 835 w Fayette
Aler Margt Mrs, h 412 n Saratoga
Aler Wallace N, shirtctr, h 926 w 34th n
Aler Washington Z, h 416 Mulberry
Aler Willis W, dentist, 412 w Saratoga
Alert Volunteer Fire Co, Belgravia
Ales Frank J, teas, 2139 Jefferson, h do
Aleshire Denver F, clk, 3645 Cedar av
Aleshire Jas E, carp, h 3645 Cedar av
Alexander Alfred L, clk, h 801 n Bdway
Alexander Andw D, clk, 533 n Calhoun
Alexander Annie F, tchr, 19 n Carrollton
Alexander Caroline K Mrs, h 111 n Carrollton av
Alexander Chas, driver, h 616 w Hamburg
*Alexander Chas, lab, 1128 Etting
Alexander Chas jr, driver, 616 w Hamburg
Alexander Chas E, moving picture opr, 1926 e Lanvale
Alexander Chas H, ice, h 510 w Hamburg
Alexander Chas N, barber, 2941 Hudson
Alexander David, tailor, 1004 Low
*Alexander Della, h 421 St Mary
*Alexander Edgar B, porter, 1432 Division
Alexander Edwd, 1941 Ridgewood av
Alexander Edwd, eng, h 27 Ash
Alexander Edwd, soldier, Ft McHenry
Alexander Ethel D Mrs, 720 n Carey
Alexander Frank, condtr, 2222 e Chase
Alexander Frank, lab, 1537 Ludlow
Alexander Frank J, fireman, 104 Greene
Alexander Geo, lab, h 1537 Ludlow
Alexander Geo B, clk, h 125 w Conway
Alexander Geo W, mngr, h 1018 Brantly
Alexander Geo W, printer, 427 n Carey
Alexander Hannah Mrs, h 2104 Brookfield
Alexander Harry E, clk, Garrison av nr Palatka
Alexander Harry W, metermkr, h 245 Hickory av
Alexander Henry W, lab, 1105 William
Alexander Isadore, tailor, 1830 Greenmt av, h 1532 Orleans
Alexander Jas, chemist, h 2208 Callaway
*Alexander Jas, porter, 1432 Division
Alexander Jas M, prod, Belair rd, Gardenville
*Alexander Jas W, eating, h 407 Druid Hill av
*Alexander John, lab, 514 Druid Hill av
*Alexander John, lab, 1342 Druid Hill av
Alexander John, lab, 336 Norris al
Alexander John, mach, h 2224 Eager pl
*Alexander John, porter, 1342 Druid Hill
Alexander John J, ins, 1113 Forrest
Alexander John J M, exp messr, h 1926 e Lanvale
Alexander Jos, mariner, h 41 e Fort av
Alexander Julia C Mrs, h 19 n Carrollton
*Alexander Lafayette, waiter, h 1354 n Stockton
*Alexander Levi, waiter, 216 s Sharp
Alexander Mary E, boarding, 110 w Saratoga
Alexander Maurice B, student, St Mary's Seminary
Alexander Max, hauling, 1236 e Lexington
Alexander Milton O, off sec, Y M C A
Alexander Morris, tailor, 1115 e Lombard
Alexander Nathan E, lumber inspr, h Garrison av nr Palatka
Alexander Nathan J, baker, 1605 Madison
*Alexander Paul, lab, 650 w Hoffman

Figure 11-6. From R.L. Polk and Co. 1911 city directory for Baltimore.

58	BALTIMORE CITY		

ROCHE'S LA, W fm Pimlico av N of Ridgely av

ROCK No 1, N fm 39th W of Rogers, Woodberry ......Q

ROCK No 2, N fm Lexington E of Poppleton ....E

ROCKDALE (village) adjoining Hampden.R

ROGERS, N fm 39th W of Gambrill, Woodberry ......Q

ROGERS AL (See Factory al)

ROGERS AV, N fm 1100 e Baltimore
1 Laurel ....M
101 Fayette ....O
201 Lexington .....F
301 Low ....G
— Gay ....G
401 Ensor ....G
501 Hillen ....E
527 Front ....E

ROGERS AV, N E and S W fm Pimlico boul W of Hayward av X3

ROGNEL HEIGHTS, N fm Edmondson av ext W of Collins X

ROLAND AV, (formerly Central av n), N and S fm 36th E of Hickory av ....R

ROLAND PARK, between Falls rd and Md and Pa R R, N of Cold Spring la...R

ROLAND HEIGHTS Av, Heathbrook Park X5

ROLLING RD, N fm Edmondson av N W of Catonsville X

ROOK CT, W fm 214 s Castle ....D

ROOKWOOD AV, S fm Hayward av E of Charles-st av..X8

ROPEWALK LA, E and W fm Charles S of West ....B

ROSE, n w (See Camel al)

ROSE N, fm 2520 e Baltimore
1 Baltimore .....F
101 F irm't av .....F
201 Fayette ......E
401 Orleans ....E
501 Jefferson .....E
601 McElderry ...X7
1201 Biddle ....W

ROSE S, fm 2523 Eastern av
501 Eastern av.....R
601 Fleet ......B
701 Foster av.....A
801 Fait av........B
825 Hudson ....A

ROSE AV, S fm Arlington av n E of Old York rd ....Y

ROSE CT (See Bud ct)

ROSEBANK AV, E fm Bellona av N of Lyman av ....T

ROSEDALE, w (village), S of Frederick av one-half mile W of Carroll.W

ROSEDALE, e (village), 5 miles on Philadelphia rd....Z

ROSEDALE, N and S fm Edmondson av W of Longwood X

ROSEDALE PL, W fm 1904 n Longwood ....N

ROSEKEMP AV, E fm Harford rd S of Southern av ....B

ROSELAND AV (See Gittings)

ROSEMARY AV, N fm Wisteria av E of Harford rd......H

ROSLYN AV, N fm Windsor Mill rd W of Liberty rd.....N

ROSSBACH CT, S fm 13 e Hughes .....O

ROSSITER AV, E fm York rd N of Radnor av ....T

ROXBURY PL, Mt Washington ......Q

ROYAL OAK AV, Gwynn Oak Uplands ....Q

ROYER HILL, bet Falls rd and Oak N of 36th ....K

RUECKERT AV, E fm Harford rd N of Ailsa av ....H

RUSK AV, N fm Rogers av, W of Pimlico av ....Q

RUSKIN AV, S W fm 3000 Evergreen ter.X3

RUSSELL, S W fm 812 s Fremont av.X1
901 Fremont av....X1
1001 Hamburg X1
1101 Cross ....J
1201 West ....J
1301 Stockholm ....J
— Ostend.........J
1401 Carey ....J
1631 Bayard ....J

RUSSELL CT, (See McAleer al) ....G

RUSSELL TER (See Hillock al)

RUTLAND AV, N fm Monument E of Bdway
701 Monument ....E
801 Madison ....E
901 Ashland av E & A
— Barnes ....E & A
1001 Eager .....E & A
1101 Chase ....E & A
1201 Biddle ....G
— Gay ....G
1221 Preston ......G
Not opened up from Preston to Oliver
1501 Oliver ....G & N
1601 Federal ...G & N
1701 Lanvale ...G & N
1841 North av...G & N

RUTTER, N W fm Dolphin W of Mt Royal av ....J

RUXTON (village), on N C Ry 8½ miles fm Baltimore.X5

RUXTON AV, S fm North W of Smallwood ....N

RYAN, W fm 315 Otterbein
701 Otterbein ....J
801 Scott ....J
901 Poppleton .....J

S

SABINA AV, E fm Mattfeldt av N of Belvidere av ......Q

SACK AV, S W fm Grindon la W of Harford rd.......H

SADLER, S fm Winder E of Henry.B

ST AGNES AV, S W fm Dukeland S of Industrial av .....W

ST ANDREWS AL, fm 914 Watson ....P

ST ANN AV, S E fm Montebello av N of Gutman av.........Y

ST BARNABAS CT, N fm Biddle W of Pa av ....N

ST BENEDICT, W fm Millington av S of Louden av

ST CHARLES AV, an extension of Charles rd X3

ST CLAIR LA (See Sinclair la)

ST DENIS (village), 9 miles on W Br B & O R R ....J

ST ELIZABETH CT, W fm Hargrove al N of Saratoga .....E

ST GEORGE AV, N fm Arlington av n, E of Ready av ....T

ST HELENA (village), 7½ miles on Baltimore and Sparrows Point R R..S

ST JAMES, W fm 814 n Central av...H

ST JAMES CT (See Lewis)

ST JOHN'S AL, W fm 878 McKim ....Y

ST JOHN'S RD, W fm Roland av N of Beechdale rd......R

ST JOSEPH, e (See Ellsworth)

ST JOSEPH, w, S of Wesley av W of Dorsey la, Irvington ....T

ST LUKE LA, N E fm Windsor Mill rd W of Gwynn's Falls.N

ST MARY, S W fm intersection of Madison av and Eutaw
401 Madison av.....M
501 Druid Hill av...D
589 Penna av.......P

ST MARY AV (See Rectory la)

ST MARY CT (See Seminary ct)

ST MARY CT No 2 (See Fruit ct)

ST MATTHEW, E fm Aisquith N of Fayette ....O

ST PAUL, N fm 100 e Baltimore
1 Baltimore C
101 Fayette C
201 Lexington C
301 Saratoga C
401 Mulberry C
501 Franklin C
601 Centre C
701 Monument C
801 Madison C
901 Read C
1001 Eager C
1101 Chase C
1201 Biddle C
1301 Preston C
— Hoffman C
1601 Federal C
1701 Lanvale C
1801 Lafayette av...C
1901 North av......C
2001 20th C
2101 21st C
2201 22d C
2301 23d C
2401 24th C
2501 25th C
2601 26th C
2701 27th C
2801 28th C
2901 29th C
3001 30th C
3047 31st C

ST PAUL BOULEVARD, St Paul ex..R

ST PAUL CT (See St Elizabeth ct)

ST PETER, W fm Paca S of Columbia av.........J

ST PETER AL (See Nanticoke)

ST THOMAS CT, E fm 531 Colvin......Y

SALEM, N fm 1512 Retreat ....D

SALISBURY AL, E and W fm 23 s Exeter ....P

SALISBURY CT (See Temple)

SAMUEL READY PL, S E fm 2201 Harford rd

SANDERS, E fm 1203 Riverside av.......O

SAPP, N fm Jefferson E of Aisquith, also N fm rear 1208 e North av ....H

SARAH ANN, W fm Pearl N of Saratoga
601 Pearl X
701 Myrtle av......X
801 Fremont av.....X
901 Poppleton X
1001 Schroeder ...X & W
1101 Arlington av...X
1135 Carrollton av.X
1601 Gilmor X

SARATOGA E, fm 300 n Charles
1 Charles ....E
101 St Paul........E
201 Calvert C
301 Guilford av ...C
401 Holliday C
425 Gay ....G

SARATOGA W, fm 300 n Charles
1 Charles ....E
101 Liberty ....E
— Cathedral ......E
201 Park av........E
301 Howard ....E
401 Eutaw X
501 Paca X
601 Greene X
701 Pine X
801 Fremont av.....X
901 Poppleton X
929 Amity..........X
1001 Schroeder X
1101 Arlington av...X
1201 Carrollton av..X
1301 Carey X
1401 Calhoun X
1501 Stricker X
1601 Gilmor X
1701 Mount X
1801 Fulton av......X
1839 Monroe X

SARATOGA CT (See Melrose al)

SARGEANT, S W fm Stockholm N of Columbia av
1101 Cross ....J
1201 Stockholm .....J
1301 Carey ....J

SASSAFRAS CT, S fm 119 e Hamburg.O

SCAMMEL, S W fm Monroe S of Steuben ....W

SCHAEFFER CT, rear of 217 Hanover...........R

SCHAFFER AV, E fm Harford rd S of White av.........H

SCHOOL, W fm 2100 Pa av
601 Pa av.........P
701 Carey ....B
1401 Calhoun .....B

SCHOTT NO 1 (See Orange ct)

SCHOTT No 2, N fm 26 Gould la .....B

SCHROEDER N, fm 1000 w Baltimore
1 Baltimore ......G
101 Fayette ....B
201 Lexington .....B
301 Saratoga ......W
401 Mulberry ......W

scriber has requested and paid for this information to be included. Moreover, there are always unlisted numbers and persons who do not wish their address or given name to be printed even if their phone number is. The use of telephone directories for the genealogist is, therefore, somewhat limited.

Nevertheless, a book "with no plot, but a cast of thousands" can't be all bad. When used in conjunction with other sources, telephone directories can help to locate living distant relatives or modern successors to nineteenth-century churches and funeral homes.

METHODOLOGY

I was contacted by a man from Australia who was seeking his father—an American sailor who had been stationed there in the closing days of World War II. The client had only his father's name and that of the ship on which he had served. Through naval muster rolls available at the National Archives, it was determined that his father had enlisted in a certain Midwestern city. City directories for that city in 1945 and 1946 showed the client's father living with his parents and a brother who was also in the navy, but their names disappeared from the city directories in the 1950s without a clue as to where they had gone. The Social Security Death Index revealed the death of the brother on the West Coast in the early 1970s, at which time the client's father was living in New England—but no one of that name listed with a New England address in PhoneDisk USA, a nationwide computer telephone database (see chapter 18, Tracking Twentieth-Century Ancestors), was the right man.

While the surname was not as common as Smith, for example, and the given names were relatively uncommon, dozens of entries for the names of the client's father were found in PhoneDisk USA. Nevertheless, letters and self-addressed, stamped envelopes were sent to each of the addresses. Some were returned as undeliverable—the individual had moved or died—and many were returned by the addressees, indicating no knowledge of the persons named in the letter, which had been carefully worded to avoid a negative response if the client's father did not wish to be found.

At last, a response was received from the client's father. He was among those listed in PhoneDisk USA and was living in a Southern state. Without this current nationwide telephone directory, locating the client's father would have been like looking for a needle in a haystack.

COUNTY AND REGIONAL BUSINESS DIRECTORIES

The business directory, as a distinct entity, evolved partly from special sections in city directories and partly from the needs of people in sparsely populated rural areas to communicate their services to one another. Because the rural economy often centered on the county seat, these early business directories were usually organized by county or region. In addition to the names of farmers and businessmen, they contained advertisements of goods and services; and although they were primarily business oriented, they also served as general directories in those rural areas. Much like a modern almanac, they often included other useful information.

A regional (multi-county, state, or market area) business directory combines a city directory's specialized business sections with a county directory's wide geographic market coverage. As communications developed, nineteenth-century manufacturers, farmers, and service-oriented businesses found that directories covering more than their own county were quite useful and even necessary. These regional business directories varied in comprehensiveness. The earlier ones, often called "advertising directories," mentioned only those businesses that could afford to be included. By the late 1800s, however, statewide business directories listed nearly every place and a variety of businesses, from farms to pharmacies. County directories can also be found in nineteenth and early twentieth century county histories and atlases.

Information obtained from county or regional business directories helps locate people in place and time. County business directories that include farmers, like city directories, narrow census searches to specific

STREETS	HOUSE NOS.	E. D.
St Joseph West	(outside city)	---
St. Luke Lane	(outside city)	---
St. Mary	---	155;280
St. Mary Avenue	(see Rectory Lane)	---
St. Mary Court	(see Seminary Court)	---
St. Mary Court No. 2	(see Fruit Court)	---
St. Matthew	---	52;51;76
St. Paul	(0-99) odd	47
	(0-99) even	37
	(100-200)	47
	(300-400)	46
	(500)	159
	(600) odd	160
	(600) even	159
	(700)	160;159
	(800-1000) odd	160
	(800-1000) even	161
	(1100) odd	174
	(1100) even	161
	(1200-1400)	174
	(1500-1600)	175
	(1900) odd	178
	(1700) even	179
	(1800)	178
	(1900) odd	180
	(1900) even	181
	(2000-2100)	181
	(2200-2300)	184
	(2400-2500) odd	187
	(2400-2500) even	188
	(2600-2800) odd	192
	(2600-2800) even	191
	(2900) odd	192
	(2900) even	193
	(3000-3200)	193
	(3300-end)	195

Figure 11-7. From a 1910 street index for Baltimore; FHL 6331480, pt. 3.

townships. This is especially useful when the ancestor married someone from another township in the same county, and the marriage record doesn't state which township. Some county business directories also contain dates and places of birth, dates of marriage, length of residence in the town, names of children, and other biographical details on their subjects as well as names.

You can use regional business directories in the same way. A region can be defined as an entire state or a geographic area, such as a valley or a coast. If you know which state an ancestor lived in but not the exact place, regional directories can help, although they are less likely to give such extensive biographical information, and their coverage may be limited.

HOW TO USE COUNTY AND REGIONAL BUSINESS DIRECTORIES

The Gazetteer and Business Directory of Monroe County, New York for 1869–1870 is a typical county business directory. On the page displayed (figure 11-8), the residents of the rural town of Henrietta are listed alphabetically. The information following each name, when properly interpreted, is very enlightening. For example, the entry for Alvy Remington indicates that his post office was in West Henrietta; thus, it was the closest settlement as well. His land was in lot 10, range 6, according to the survey of the land company that originally owned the land. By occupation he was a farmer and owned ninety-five acres. If he had leased his land, it would have been indicated.

There are three other Remingtons in Henrietta in this directory: George T., Seth W., and William T. Without knowing anything about the family, one could conclude that there is some relationship between Alvy, Seth, and William on the basis of the lot and range information. In fact, William and Seth were Alvah (the correct spelling) Remington's sons. William had fifty-seven acres, the directory tells us, while Seth had only one. A bit of family history provides a gloss on the directory information. Thomas Remington, Alvah's father, originally purchased lot 10, range 6, in the 1820s from a consortium of Dutch land speculators. Alvah bought out his brothers and sisters and then distributed the land among his own children. The fact that Seth had only one acre in 1870 helps explain the relationship between father and son: when Alvah died in 1888, he

left nothing to Seth's children because Seth had been unable to pay back a debt to his father before he had died in 1885.

One of the earliest regional directories is *The American Advertising Directory: Manufacturers and Dealers in American Goods for the Year 1831*. Most of the listings are in the Northeast manufacturing area, but places as far (in 1831) from the East Coast as Nashville, Tennessee, had at least one listing. This contrasts starkly with the *New Mexico Business Directory* for 1907–08, which mentions every city, town, and village in New Mexico as well as El Paso, Texas, and Denver, Colorado. The town of Central had 450 inhabitants, but only fifteen entries were given:

CENTRAL

Postoffice and important town in Grant county, 9 miles east of Silver City, the most convenient railroad point. Mining, stockraising, farming and fruitgrowing the principal industries. Population 450.

Bayard Smelting & Mining Co, W D Murray mgr.
Crowley J, postmaster, justice peace, drugs.
GOULD BROS, general merchandise.
Hamilton A, mines and mining
Helde Mrs. G W, millinery and dressmaker.
Link B T, fruitgrower and dairy.
McMillen Geo, mines and mining.
MURRAY BROS, general merchandise.
MONTGOMERY & DALRYMPLE, meat market.
Reed Mrs W, restaurant.
Rendall L G, notary public.
Rodgers Clark, fruitgrower.
Stephens Chas, fruitgrower.
SWEENEY W H, general merchandise.
Wiley J A, saloon.[15]

Note that the postmaster was also the justice of the peace and pharmacist for the town. The directory does not list the men who worked on the fruit farms and in the mines. This 1912 directory is, however, more detailed and for a smaller region than the 1831 directory cited above.

Quirk, Mathew, (Brighton,) lot 11, R. 6, farmer 72.
Raas, Frederick, (West Henrietta,) lot 25, R. 5, farmer 23.
Raynor, Leonard, (West Henrietta,) lot 12, R. 6, farmer leases 90.
REEVE, JOHN, (Henrietta,)(*with Thomas*,) lot 22, R. 1, farmer 340.
Reeve, Thomas, (Henrietta,) (*with John*,) lot 22, R. 1, farmer 340.
Reeves, George, (West Brighton,) lot 1, R. 3, farmer 1½.
Remington, Alvy, (West Henrietta,) lot 10, R. 6, farmer 95.
Remington, George T., (Henrietta,) lot 22, R. 1, farmer 11.
Remington, Seth W., (West Henrietta,) lot 10, R. 6, farmer 1.
Remington, William T., (West Henrietta,) lot 10, R. 6, farmer 57.
Renner, John, (West Brighton,) lot 3, R. 5, farmer 21.
Richardson, David H., (Henrietta,) lot 10, R. 3, farmer 180.
Roberts, George M. C., (Henrietta,) lot 11, R. 3, farmer leases 116.

Sherman, Oliver B., (West Henrietta,) lot 25, R. 4, farmer 100.
Shilling, Frederick, (West Henrietta,) lot 23, R. 6, farmer 35.
Sholts, Henry, (West Brighton,) lot 4, R. 5, farmer 65.
Short, Andrew, (Henrietta,) lot 15, R. 3, farmer 34.
Sibbey, Elisha, (Henrietta,) lot 16, R. 1, farmer 99.
SIBLEY, ELISHA, (North Rush,) lot 18, Scott Tract, farmer 106.
SIMMONS, EDWARD, (Henrietta,) lot 16, R. 3.
Sipperly, John, (Henrietta,) lot 19, R. 2, farmer 50.
Skilton, William, (Henrietta,) lot 17, R. 1, farmer 30.
Slade, Hannah Mrs., (Henrietta,) lot 15, farmer 50.
Slow, Jacob, (West Henrietta,) lot 22, R. 5, wagon maker.
Smith, Charles J., (West Henrietta,) lot 31, R. 4, farmer 80.
Smith, David, (Henrietta,) lot 2, R. 3, retired farmer 80.

Figure 11-8. From Hamilton Child, *The Gazetteer and Business Directory of Monroe County, New York for 1869–1870* (Rochester, N.Y.: Erastus Darrow, 1870), 195.

SPECIAL PROBLEMS

Business directories are limited in that the editor selected which businesses to include, sometimes based on subscription. If your ancestor was a businessman, but was not mentioned, it doesn't mean that he wasn't there.

Another problem with regional directories is availability. These directories seem to have been published much less regularly than the yearly city directories; consequently, they may be harder to find.

PROFESSIONAL DIRECTORIES

The late nineteenth-century business directory, as might be expected, coincided with a proliferation of specialized professions. As the *Directories in Print* (cited earlier) confirms, the number of professional directories at present is astounding. Refer to that work for information on twentieth-century professional directories. In this section we will consider only law, medicine, civil and military service, and a category called miscellaneous. We will consider each of these professions separately due to the different circumstances under which each directory was published.

LAW

The description of law directories in the original *Directory of Directories* is representative of the history of professional directories and the criteria by which they are compiled:

> Background: 'Law Lists' refers to a group of directories which provide varying amounts of information about lawyers, and which were formerly certified by a committee of the American Bar Association as being ethically appropriate sources in which lawyers could make known their availability for consultation. As a result of the United States Supreme Court decision in 1977 governing advertising by lawyers and subsequent actions by the ABA, the Standing Committee on Law Lists no longer certifies law lists, state or national, as being in compliance with any rules or standard. (In response to requests for guidance from some states the committee prepared proposed guidelines for state regulation of law lists which were submitted to committees of the ABA and reported to the ABA house of delegates in August 1979.) About sixty law lists were formerly certified by the committee and described in the 'Directory Information Service.' These listings, revised as needed, are continued in this volume. The law list which has operated longest under a single title is 'Campbell's List,' established in 1879. 'Martindale-Hubbell Law Directory,' resulted from a merger of 'Martindale's American Law Directory,' founded in 1868, and 'Hubbell's Legal Directory,' founded in 1870; it is currently the largest of the law lists and among the most highly regarded. Covers: Martindale-Hubbell, a national list, and the state and regional directories published by the Legal Directories Publishing Company, Inc., are the only comprehensive law lists which include every attorney nationally or in an area. There are no law lists which attempt to include every attorney in a special field. In fact, the essence of the appeal of law lists is exclusivity: all lists charge fees for inclusion (usually based on the population of the area where a given attorney practices, and ranging to $600 or more), except [that] comprehensive lists include a minimum listing without a fee; many lists operate on the basis of 'exclusive representation,' i.e., they list only one firm in a given locality. A few, such as the 'Rand McNally List of Bank-Recommended Attorneys,' operate on the basis of recommendations or sponsorships. Some lists use rating systems, and firms listed are coded for ability, diligence, etc., as evaluated by peers. Entries include: Even within a single law list, entries may run from a brief name-and-address notation to one or two pages or more, depending upon the size of the firm and how much it is willing to spend for its listing. In a typical full entry, a firm name, address, and phone will be given along with names and backgrounds of partners and names of typical clients; associates may also be listed. Many lists include uniformly less data. Arrangement: The most frequent use of a law list is in finding a lawyer in a location where the user has no contacts. Therefore, nearly all law lists are geographical in arrangement. Indexes: Alphabetical indexes by personal name may or may not be provided. Price: Part of the service provided by law list publishers is the free distribution of their lists to lawyers listed and to others who can be assumed to be users of the services of lawyers listed. There is no ethical restriction on the sale of law lists, but it was the experience of the DOD staff in compiling law list material that many publishers are not anxious to give laypersons information about their publications to promote commercial sales; whether this lack of cooperation resulted from a desire to enhance the exclusive image of their lists or for other reasons is not clear.[16]

Law directories are generally arranged by state and are frequently not indexed. In the past, law directories could generally be found on the local and state level. In areas where such regional directories are not available prior to the advent of the national directories in the 1870s, you can usually find lawyers in general business directories. Most law directories today are national-level directories, but there are some on the state and local levels, particularly in large metropolitan areas.

Law directories locate an individual in place and time for the purposes of gaining access to, or linking with, other sources, including other directories. Other significant data may include the law school graduated from, or, in cases where law was read the state in which the lawyer was first admitted to the bar. You may also find other biographical information that will help you trace the individual lawyer's career and suggest other records to search.

MEDICINE

The *American Medical Directory,* published under the auspices of the American Medical Association, has existed only since 1906. Unlike law directories, it is published intermittently, so a complete collection may not cover every year since 1906. The directory is arranged by state, and the later editions also contain alphabetical listings. Before 1906, medical directories were published by private companies or by local and state medical associations. Some city directories contained separate lists for doctors, and doctors were listed in general business directories as well.

The *American Medical Directory* presently contains the following information: name, address, year licensed, medical school, type of practice, primary and secondary specialties, and board certifications. Some of the earlier editions also contain year of birth and year graduated from medical school.

Medical directories will help you locate a person in place and time and will provide links with other sources.

CIVIL AND MILITARY SERVICE

In 1816, Congress passed a bill providing for the biennial publication of a register "containing correct lists of all the officers and agents, civil, military, and naval, in the service of the United States." This list contained the individual's name and office, pay, place of birth, and place of residence. The resolution further provided that the registers should be current as of 30 September the year preceding the publication date. Thus, the civil register for 1864 would reflect information collected in 1863. In 1851, the state from which the person was appointed was added.[17]

Although the main register of government civil servants contained the names of military and naval officers, separate registers for these two services were also eventually published. These registers are considerably more detailed than the general register. They contain the date of enlistment or entry into the service and the date the most recent rank was achieved. In addition, the state of birth and state from which the soldier was appointed are invaluable as links to other sources when military service records are not readily available.

These army and navy registers include officers only. Army and navy registers accounted for regular (career) service only. Therefore, an ancestor known to have been an officer in the Civil war may not be listed if he was part of the volunteer army. Directories of army and navy officers might also be found in directories for graduates of the appropriate service academies.

The general register is arranged alphabetically. The army register is arranged by regiment, with a name index and a list of where each regiment was stationed in the year of publication. The Navy register is arranged by ship rather than regiment and includes the location of each ship. The Marine Corps is listed in the navy register.

The government of the United States has probably generated more paper than any single organization in the history of this country. If an ancestor worked for the government, there should be a record of it somewhere. These registers can connect you with those records when information more specific than "he worked for the government" or "he was an army officer" is unavailable.

MISCELLANEOUS PROFESSIONS

Early directories exist for a number of professions. R.L. Polk published the following directories before 1920:

Dental Register of the United States

Architects and Builders' Directory of the United States

Marine Directory of the Great Lakes

Ohio Architects and Builders' Directory

Pennsylvania Architects and Builders' Directory

Western New York Architects and Builders' Directory

The Library of Congress has these early professional directories: *The Dentist Register* (1879); *Banker's Almanac and Year Book* (1844); *Rand McNally Banker's Blue Book* (1872); *Polk's World Bank Directory* (1895). Perhaps the best way to find out whether an early professional directory exists is to find that profession in the *Directory of Directories* and contact the publisher.

One directory that has been published only since 1932 is nevertheless relevant to earlier genealogical research: *The American Blue Book of Funeral Directors,* published every two years. Any professional directory will locate an ancestor in time and place, but the funeral director's blue book will let you trace a funeral home to the present day and, if it has gone out of business, perhaps determine the successor and thus where the records might be. A funeral home in business in 1932 may have existed for fifty years. In a given community, its records could almost substitute for death registers.

Similarly, the *American Cemetery Association Membership Directory and Buyer's Guide* can help in locating cemeteries where your ancestors might be buried, especially if the name or ownership of the cemetery has changed.

HOW TO USE PROFESSIONAL DIRECTORIES

Below are two hypothetical examples relevant to our use of various professional directories:

The ancestor in question is known to have been a doctor in the greater New York City area about 1910, but whether in Manhattan, Brooklyn, Queens, the Bronx, Staten Island, Long Island, Westchester County, Connecticut, or New Jersey is unknown. The *American Medical Directory* for 1909 had an alphabetical listing, and Lucy Criddle Jones was easily located in its New York City section (figure 11-9).

This listing indicates that Lucy Criddle Jones was born in 1872, that she graduated from Syracuse University Medical School in 1898, and that in 1909 she lived at 212 East 53rd Street. (Office addresses are indicated separately from home addresses.) From this information, positive identification can be made using Manhattan city directories and subsequently the census, and medical school records can be consulted.

Robert Nelson Eagle was known to have been a lieutenant in the U.S. Army before the Civil War, and family lore held that he had served with Robert E. Lee. Eagle was listed in the Army Register for 1860 (figure 11-10) as serving with the Second Regiment of Cavalry, of which Robert E. Lee was lieutenant colonel. Eagle had entered the service as a first lieutenant on 3 March 1855. He was born in New York but appointed from Texas. Since the register also gave the location of the Second Regiment in 1860, the census for that year as well as military records could be consulted.

ORGANIZATIONAL DIRECTORIES

Like professional directories, organizational directories are highly specialized and suited to the needs of a particular organization. Two examples of such directories are university alumni directories and fraternity directories. If your ancestor belonged to some other organization, you can consult Directories in Print to see if a directory for that organization currently exists and, if so, contact the organization and determine if it has any earlier directories.

These sorts of directories, however, may not be published annually, and so may not appear in *Directories in Print.* You may even have to consult the *Encyclopedia of Associations* (published annually by Gale Research) to find a specific directory for the particular organization in which you are interested. In some cases, an organizational directory will not tell you the names of its members but may provide the addresses of various branches to which you can write. This would be helpful in cases where an ancestor belonged to an organization in the 1800s that is no longer active and for which you must locate records. The kind of information given in an organizational directory can range from a mere address to dates of transfer or membership, or even of birth and death.

How to Use Organizational Directories

Here is a hypothetical example of the joint use of two organizational directories. A modern descendant of the Weed family discovers an old fraternity pin in the attic bearing the Greek letters Alpha Delta Phi. On the back of the pin, the initials H.A.W. are inscribed. Some time ago, this family had moved to the West Coast from New York and had lost all touch with the family in the East. In fact, Grandpa Weed had been reluctant to talk about his ancestors beyond the information that "they came from New York."

Seizing upon this artifact as a potential key to the Weed family mysteries, the modern Weed tries to locate information on H.A.W. His best approach would be to find some list of past fraternity members, but there was none listed in *Directories in Print* at the local library. There was, however, a listing for *Baird's Manual of American College Fraternities.* Upon calling the publisher (the local library did not have this source), the modern Weed encounters a typical problem for genealogists: the publisher would rather sell him the book than provide, free of charge, the address of the Alpha Delta Phi Fraternity Alumni Association. Fortunately, Weed's library did have the *Encyclopedia of Associations,* which provided him—free of charge—with the information he desired. After Weed sends a request for information, the Alumni Association sends him a copy of the following page from the 1966 *Catalogue of the Alpha Delta Phi,* the listing for the chapter at Columbia University:

1836

Hillyer, Giles Mumford
Hobart, John Henry
Jay, John
McVickar, Henry
Ward, Henry, Jr.
Waters, George Gilfert
Weed, Harvey Augustus

1837

Aldis, Charles
Blatchford, Samuel
Chittenden, Nathaniel William
Fessenden, Henry Partridge
Galsey, Anthony
Leggett, William Henry
MacMullen, John
Tucker, John Ireland
Vanderbilt, John, Jr.
Whitlock, Samuel H.[18]

A letter accompanying the page indicates that this is the only Weed with the initials H.A. in the general index to the catalogue, which also listed him as deceased.

This information led Weed to examine the *Columbia University Alumni Register,* which revealed that, although Harvey Augustus Weed did indeed graduate in 1836, he went on to receive a higher degree in 1839.

Weed, Edgar Theodore MD 1881, 39 W 87 NYC

Weed, Edwin Dunning AB 1894, 2218 E 1 Duluth Minn, Clergy

Weed, Eleanor Hill (see Sharp, Elearnor Weed)

Weed, Ethel Georgine AM 1906, Maplewood NJ

Weed, G B ent 1834 P&S, decd.

Weed, Harvey Augustus AB 1836, AM 1839 C, d. 1872

JONES, CATESBY ⊕—Md.1,'93; 7 E. 32d St.; 9-1, 4-5.
JONES, CHAS. NOALE DIXON ⊕—N.Y.1,'83; 601 W. 179th St.; 8-10, 6-7; Or.
JONES, DAVID H. (b 1874) ⊕—N.Y.5,'97; 215 W. 101st St.; 12-1, 4-7:30.
Jones, Henry Woodward (b 1847)—Mich.7,'74; 301 W. 107th St.
Jones, Horace Loomis—Pa.2,'81; 126 W. 127th St.; 7-9, 6-8.
JONES, ISRAEL C. ⊕—O.9,'74; Home for Incurables, Fordham; until 10.
Jones, Leonard W.—Ont.5,'02; office, Manhattan Eye and Ear Hospital.
JONES, LUCY CRIDDLE (b 1872) ⊕—N.Y.15,'98; 212 E. 53d St.; 12-1:30, 6-7.
Jones, Robt. Mortimer—H—N.Y.9,'90 130 Madison Ave.; 11-1, 5-6; AI.R.
Jones, Roland D.—Pa.1,'81; 56 E. 59th St.; 9-1.
JONES, S. BEACH—N.Y.1,'72; Park Ave. and 62d St.; 12-1; N.
Jones, Walter Hastings—H—N.Y.9,'86; The Ansonia, 73d St. and Broadway; 9-10, 1-2, 5-6.
Jones, Wm. Fredk.—Vt.2,'83; 323 W. 19th St.; 8-9, 1-2, 6-8.
JONES, WM. J., Jr.—N.Y.20,'99; 238 W. 118th St.; 5-7.

Figure 11-9. From *American Medical Directory, 1909,* 3rd ed. (Chicago: American Medical Association Press, 1909), 799.

Figure 11-10. From *Adjutant General's Office, Official Army Register for 1860* (Washington, D.C.: Government Press, 1860), 16.

16   SECOND REGIMENT OF CAVALRY.

NAME.	Rank in the Reg't.	Rank in the Army.	Original entry into service.		Born in.	
Colonel.						
Albert S. Johnston,	3 Mar. 55	B. G. bvt.	18 Nov. 57	(d) Bvt. 2 lt. 2 inf. 1 July, 26	Ky.	T
Lieutenant Colonel.						
Robert E. Lee,	3 Mar. 55	Col. bvt.	13 Sept. 47	Bvt. 2 lt. eng. 1 July, 29	Va.	V
Majors.						
William J. Hardee,	3 Mar. 55	L. C. bvt. Comm't cadets, M. A. with loc. rank of L. C.	20 Aug. 47	2 lt. 2 drag. 1 July, 38	Ga.	Ge
George H. Thomas,	12 May, 55	Bvt.	23 Feb. 47	2 lt. 3 art. 1 July, 40	Va.	Va
Captains.						
Earl Van Dorn,	3 Mar. 55	M. bvt.	20 Aug. 47	Bvt. 2 lt. 7 inf. 1 July, 42	Miss.	Mi
Edmund K. Smith,	3 Mar.	Bvt.	20 Aug.	Bvt. 2 lt. 5 inf. 1 July, 45	Fla.	Fl
James Oakes,	3 Mar.	Bvt.	8 Sept.	Bvt. 2 lt. 2 drag. 1 July, 46	Pa.	Pa
Innis N. Palmer,	3 Mar.	Bvt.	13 Sept.	Bvt. 2 lt. m. rifles, 1 July,	N. Y.	N.
George Stoneman,	3 Mar.			Bvt. 2 lt. 1 drag. 1 July,	N. Y.	N.
William R. Bradfute,*	3 Mar.			Capt. 3 Mar. 55	Tenn.	Te
Albert G. Brackett,*	3 Mar.			Capt. 3 Mar.	N. Y.	In
Charles J. Whiting,	3 Mar.			(e) Bvt. 2 lt. 2 art. 1 July, 35	Mass.	Ca
Nathan G. Evans,	1 May, 56			Bvt. 2 lt. 1 drag. 1 July, 48	S. C.	S.
Richard W. Johnson,	1 Dec.			Bvt. 2 lt. 6 inf. 1 July, 49	Ky.	Ky
First Lieutenants.						
Joseph H. McArthur,	3 Mar. 55			Bvt. 2 lt. 2 inf. 1 July, 49	Mo.	Mo
Charles W. Field,	3 Mar.			Bvt. 2 lt. 2 drag. 1 July,	Ky.	Ky
Kenner Garrard,	3 Mar.			Bvt. 2 lt. 4 art. 1 July, 51	Ky.	Oh
Walter H. Jenifer,*	3 Mar.			(f) 1 lt. 3 drag. 9 Apr. 47	Md.	Mc
William B. Royall,*	3 Mar.			1 lt. 3 Mar. 55	Va.	Mc
William P. Chambliss,*	3 Mar.			1 lt. 3 Mar.	Va.	Te
Robert Nelson Eagle,*	3 Mar.			1 lt. 3 Mar.	N. Y.	Te
John T. Shaaff,	1 May, 56			Bvt. 2 lt. 6 inf. 1 July, 51	D. C.	D.
George B. Cosby,	1 May,			Bvt. 2 lt. m. rifles, 1 July, 52	Ky.	Ky
William W. Lowe,	1 Dec.	Adjt.	31 May, 58	Bvt. 2 lt. 2 drag. 1 July, 53	Ind.	Io
John B. Hood,	18 Aug. 58			Bvt. 2 lt. 4 inf. 1 July,	Ky.	K

Weed, John Went 1819 P&S, decd.

Weed, John Waring LLB 1868, d. Nov 7, 1915

Weed, Lowry Albert AB 1916 (cl 1914). Internat'l Composition Co 25 Broadway NYC[19]

The register also indicated that Harvey Augustus Weed died in 1872. Without knowing his exact date of birth, the modern Weed estimates, based on the date of Harvey's first degree, that Harvey was in his late forties when he died. Grandpa Weed had been born in 1870; perhaps this was the reason he knew little of his past. With the information from the *Alumni Register*, the modern Weed checks Columbia University's records, and these allow him to extend the line by linking them with other sources.

SPECIAL PROBLEMS

Locating directories is the major problem. Since many of them are published after the fact—that is, they are really books that contain membership lists since the organization's inception—more recent copies may be just as valuable as earlier copies. Some directories, however, may prune earlier membership lists.

Check the organization itself and the Library of Congress first, then go to major university and public libraries in the area where the school is located.

RELIGIOUS DIRECTORIES

Religious directories began as books containing directions for the order of public or private worship. As time passed, some denominational directories began to include lists of clergy and/or churches. Eventually the listings outweighed the direction, and these books became directories in the modern sense. Some denominational directories have dropped all statements of creed, such as *The Official Catholic Directory,* first published in 1817. Religious directories may also be called registers, annuals, and yearbooks. The information they include differs from denomination to denomination, the minimum amount being the name and address of the church and its pastor.

The information contained in religious directories is significant in two ways. If the ancestor was a clergyman, such directories can guide you to the places of service. This is especially true in the case of itinerant ministers; religious directories narrow down these ministers' assigned working areas. Also, like funeral and cemetery directories, religious directories may suggest where to find the contemporary records of the church where the ancestor worshipped.

Figure 11-11. From J. Lansing Burrows, ed., *American Baptist Register for 1852* (Philadelphia: American Baptist Publication Society, 1853), 237.

New York Association.

CHURCHES.	CONST.	COUNTIES.	PASTORS.	BAPT.	MEMBERS
First Church, N. Y.,	1762	New York,	S. H. Cone, D. D.,	15	557
First Church, Staten Island,	1785	Richmond,	Samuel White,	2	177
Middletown,	1792	Rockland,	J. W. Griffiths,		56
Abyssinian, N. Y.,	1808	New York,	J. T. Raymond,	8	373
North Beriah, N. Y.,	1809	New York,	J. S. Backus,	26	235
Ebenezer, N. Y.,	1825	New York,	G. L. Marsh,	2	98
Greenport, L. I.,	1832	Suffolk,	C. J. Hopkins,		151
Zion, N. Y.,	1832	New York,	Thomas Henson,		378
Newburgh,	1833	Orange,	James Scott,	5	103
Sixteenth St., N. Y.,	1833	New York,	J. W. Taggart,	54	714
Berean, N. Y.,	1838	New York,	J. R. Stone,	20	420
Sag Harbor, L. I.,	1844	Suffolk,	E. W. Bliss,	9	137
Welsh, N. Y.,	1833	New York,	Thomas H. Davies,		167
Monticello,	1836	Sullivan,	————		49
Piermont, First,	1839	Rockland,	————	1	48
Bethesda, N. Y.,	1841	New York,	N. B. Baldwin,	16	130
Middletown, First,	1842	Orange,	S. S. Barrett,	4	62
Hempstead,	1842	Rockland,	E. J. Williams,		21
Cold Spring, L. I.,	1842	Suffolk,	W. B. Harris,		40
Bloomingdale, N. Y.,	1843	New York,	S. Wilkins.	3	130
Parksville,		Sullivan,	Wm. W. Murphy,		67
First Mariner's,	1843	New York,	J. R. Steward,	11	122
Providence, N. Y.,	1845	New York,	————	1	66
Newtown, L. I.,		Queens,			15
Central, Brooklyn,	1847	Kings,	J. W. Sarles,	11	172
West, Staten Island,.	1848	Richmond,	William Pike,	5	31
Olive Branch, N. Y.,	1849	New York,	————	19	183
Oyster Bay, L. I.,	1724	Suffolk	Marmaduke Earle.		39
East Marion, L. I.,	1847	Kings,	Erastus Denison,	4	35
Hastings, First,	1850	West Chester,	Henry F. Smith,	9	28
Shiloh, Newburg,	1848	Orange,	Elisha Hawkins,	14	27
			Total,	239	4582

HOW TO USE RELIGIOUS DIRECTORIES

Suppose the ancestor was a Baptist in Rochester, New York, in the first half of the nineteenth century. *The American Baptist Register* for 1852 shows four Baptist churches in Rochester, the two earliest having been established in 1818 and 1834.[20] We know the ancestor lived in Rochester before 1834, so he probably belonged to the First Baptist Church. A check of Baptist churches in modern Rochester shows that the First Baptist Church still exists. We write to its pastor, requesting a check in early records for mention of our ancestor.

In another hypothetical example, suppose it is known that the ancestor was a Baptist minister named Henry Smith and that he lived somewhere in New York around 1850. A check of all of the Baptist associations in New York revealed only one Henry Smith, who preached at Hastings, Westchester County (figure 11-11). With this information we don't need to check all of the Henry Smiths in the 1850 census index of New York; we can zero in on the relevant one.

POST OFFICE AND STREET DIRECTORIES

Post office and street directories were originally published by the government to help deliver the mail correctly before zip codes. Post office directories list all active post offices in the year of publication. For instance, *The Street Directory of the Principal Cities of the United States . . . to April 1908*, 5th ed.

(1908. Reprint. Detroit: Gale Research Co., 1973), contains the names of streets and the cities with streets by those names. This was necessary in cases where the sender listed only a street address, no city of addressee, and no return address. The directory was published mainly for the use of the Division of Dead Letters and should not be confused with the street directories discussed with city directories.

HOW TO USE POST OFFICE AND STREET DIRECTORIES

You can use both of these types of directories with old family letters. If you have a letter that bears only the name of a "town.. and state and this "town" cannot be found in any modern gazetteer, it may no longer exist, or the name may have been changed. A post office directory from the right period will give you the location. If the letter bears only the address on Religious Street and the date of 13 January 1908, the original envelope having been lost, the street directory can help. A 1908 directory shows:

Reliance Place
  Flushing, N.Y.
    (Elmhurst)
Relic Alley
  Pittsburg, Pa.

Relief
 Oil City, Pa., 1-20
Relief Alley
 Allegheny, Pa.
 Pittsburg, Pa.
Relief Ave.
 Poplar Bluff, Mo., 200-600
Religious
 New Orleans, La., 1400-1999
Rellis
 Saginaw, Mich., 200
Relyea Place
 New Rochelle, N.Y., 1-20
Rembert
 Memphis, Tenn., N.

 61-662 S.[21]

Thus, in 1908, Religious Street existed only in New Orleans. If, however, the name is Relief, you would have more cities to consider. This method can be used with any stray street address, including photographer's addresses on the backs of old photographs.

NOTES

1. *The Oxford English Dictionary* (Oxford: Clarendon Press, 1961), 393.

2. Dorothea N. Spear, *Bibliography of American Directories Through 1860* (Worcester, Mass.: American Antiquarian Society, 1961), 5–10.

3. 1982 information brochure supplied by Research Publications, Inc., 12 Lunar Drive, Woodbridge, CT, 06525.

4. *Alaska Directory and Gazetteer 1934–1935* (Seattle: Alaska Directory Co., 1935), foreword.

5. 1910 U.S. Census, Rochester, Monroe County, New York, Vol. 145, E.D. 141, sheet llB, line 72; NARA Microfilm Publications T624, Roll 991 (FHL 1375004).

6. 1910 U.S. Census, Baltimore, Baltimore County, Maryland, Vol. 24, E.D. 191, sheet 9B, line 72; NARA Microfilm Publications T624, Roll 556 (FHL 1374569).

7. *Doggett's New York Directory 1833–1834* (New York: John Doggett, Jr., 1834), 505.

8. 1850 U.S. Census, New York City, New York County, New York, Ward 5, folio 125, dwelling 937, family 1837; NARA Microfilm Publications M432, Roll 537.

9. *Doggett's New York City Directories 1845–46* and *1846–47* (New York: John Doggett, Jr.), 302, 326.

10. Entry for James Renwick, 5 June 1845, Manhattan Death Register, Volume 14 (1844–1845) (FHL 447550).

11. 1900 U.S.Census, Philadelphia, Philadelphia County, Pennsylvania, Vol. 167, E.D. 412, sheet 7, line 24; NARA T623, Roll 1461 (FHL 1241461).

12. Marriage Record of Christian [Hochwald?] and [illegible], 3 May 1862, Philadelphia Board of Health Marriage Registers, 1860–1863, p. 193 (FHL 978997).

13. *McElroy's Philadelphia City Directory 1862* (Philadelphia: E.C. and J. Biddle, 1862), 862.

14. Declaration of Intention of James Renwick to Become a Naturalized Citizen of the United States, New York Co., N.Y., Naturalization Records Court of Common-Pleas, Bundle 26, No. 69, 3 November 1840 (FHL 901057).

15. *New Mexico Business Directory . . . 1907–1908* (Denver: The Gazetteer Publishing Co., 1907, 217).

16. James M. Ethridge, ed., *The Directory of Directories* (Detroit: Information Enterprises, 1908), 245; reprinted by permission.

17. Adjutant General's Office, *Register of Officers and Agents, Civil, Military and Naval in the Service of the United States 30 Sept. 1863* (Washington, D.C.: Government Printing Office, 1864), notes.

18. Executive Council of the Alpha Delta Phi, *Catalogue of the Alpha Delta Phi, 1832–1866* (New York: Alpha Delta Phi, 1966), 101.

19. The Committee on [the] General Catalogue, *Columbia UniversityAlumni Register, 1754–1931* (New York: Columbia University Press, 1932), 931.

20. J. Lansing Burrows, ed., *American Baptist Register for 1852* (Philadelphia: American Baptist Publication Society, 1853), 236.

21. *Street Directory of the Principal Cities of the United States Embracing Letter-Carrier Offices Established to April 30, 1908* (Washington, D.C.: Postmaster General, 1908), 637.

BIBLIOGRAPHY

Burton, Robert E. "City Directories in the United States, 1784–1820: A Bibliography with Historical Notes." M.S. thesis, University of Michigan, 1956. Gives locations of directories.

Catalog of City, County, and State Directories Published in North America. New York: North American Directory Publishers, 1967. May help to identify and locate directories no longer in print.

City and State Directories in Print, 1990–1991, 1st ed. Detroit: Gale Research Co., 1989.

City Directories of the United States Pre 1860 Through 1901: Guide to the Microfilm Collection. Woodbridge, Conn.: Research Publications, 1983.

Davis, Marjorie V. *Guide to American Business Directories.* Washington, D.C.: Public Affairs Press, 1948. May help to identify and locate directories no longer in print.

Directories in Print, 1992. 9th ed. Detroit: Gale Research Co., 1991.

"Directories in the Library of Congress." *The American Genealogist* 13 (1937): 46–53; 27 (1951): 142.

Hillman, Barbara. *Guide to the Use of the United States. Census Office. 10th Census 1880 New York City.* New York: New York Public Library, 1963.

Hofstetter, Eleanore O., and Harold C. Livesay. "Pre-Civil War Directories Sources in American History." *RQ* 8 (1968): 174–76.

Kirkham, E. Kay. *A Handy Guide to Record Searching in the Larger Cities of the United States.* Logan, Utah: The Everton Publishers, 1974.

Klein, Bernard. *Guide to American Directories.* 5th ed. Englewood Cliffs, N.J.: Prentice-Hall, 1962.

Knights, Peter R. "The Plain People of Boston." *Scientific American* (November 1981). Includes a perceptive appendix on directories.

Mariner, Mary Lou Craver, and Patricia Roughan Bellows. *A Research Aid for the Massachusetts 1910 Federal Census.* Sudbury, Mass.: Computerized Assistance, 1988.

Moriarty, John H. "Directory Information Materials for New York City Residents, 1626–1786: A Bibliographic Study." *Bulletin New York Public Library* (October 1942).

Neal, Colleen. *Lest We Forget: A Guide to Genealogical Research in the Nation's Capital.* Annandale, Va.: 1982.

Parker, Nathan C. *Personal Name Index to the 1856 City Directories of California.* Genealogy and Local History Series, vol. 10. Detroit: Gale Research Co., 1980.

Sopp, Elsie L. *Personal Name Index to the 1856 City Directories of Iowa.* Genealogy and Local History Series, vol. 13. Detroit: Gale Research Co., 1980.

Spear, Dorothea N. *Bibliography of American Directories Through 1860.* Worcester, Mass.: American Antiquarian Society, 1961.

The Street Directory of the Principal Cities of the United States . . . to April 1908. 5th ed. 1908. Reprint. Detroit: Gale Research Co., 1973.

RESEARCH IN NEWSPAPERS
CHAPTER CONTENTS

12

RESEARCH IN NEWSPAPERS

James L. Hansen

*T*he *Wall Street Journal* once advertised itself as the "daily diary of the American dream." That statement, like much advertising copy, may have been somewhat overblown, but it does encapsulate much of the importance of newspapers to the genealogical researcher. Newspapers are, for those who become proficient in their use, the day-to-day (or week-to-week) diaries of local community events. They are thus excellent sources for family history, giving accounts of events from a contemporary point of view and often including details recorded nowhere else. The genealogist who overlooks newspapers misses a great mass of potentially valuable material.

Newspapers are intended for general readers, usually serve a geographic region, and may also be oriented toward a particular ethnic, cultural, social, or political group. Because newspapers preserve the collected thoughts of many minds, they reflect moral, cultural, educational, and political development more broadly than do the isolated thoughts of an individual's correspondence or diary. Nowhere can a clearer idea be gained of public sentiment than in the American newspaper.

While records of birth, marriage, and death are the most commonly sought and the most consistently helpful, only the genealogist's imagination and resourcefulness limit the newspaper's usefulness in supplying clues about historical events, local news items, probate court and legal notices, real estate transactions, political biographies, announcements, notices of new and terminated partnerships, business advertisements, and notices for settling debts.

Newspapers can provide at least a partial substitute for nonexistent civil records. For example, an obituary may have appeared in a newspaper even when civil death records did not exist. And newspapers are an important source of marriage records, particularly in those states, such as Pennsylvania and South Carolina, where the civil recording of marriages was essentially nonexistent until the twentieth century.

Newspapers take on added importance where official public records have been destroyed. All Cook County, Illinois, official records, for example, were destroyed in the Great Chicago Fire of 1871. Newspapers consequently become even more critical in reconstructing the history of the city and tracing the roots of its settlers.

Because newspapers are unofficial sources, even when they merely supplement the public records, they can provide much incidental information that is simply not recorded anywhere else. Also, because of their unofficial nature, they are not bound by the regulations and forms used by more "official" sources. A newspaper account of a marriage might, for example, indicate that it took place at the home of the bride's parents, perhaps even naming them; it might list the occupation of the groom, or indicate that the ceremony was part of a double wedding in which the bride's sister was also being married. None of these details is likely to appear in the marriage record at the courthouse.

Unlike official records, newspapers are not limited to a particular geographical area. They can include reports of the weddings of local citizens, even when they occurred in a neighboring county or another state. They can report visits of geographically distant relatives or the return visits of local residents to them. They can publish death notices of individuals who had left the area long before but who still had local family or friends. In each case the newspaper account can identify the date and place of an event, thus opening the possibility of turning up additional documentation in other sources.

THE EVOLUTION OF NEWSPAPERS

The newspapers we know and take for granted today are the products of some three centuries of development, and they are quite different from their colonial predecessors. Except for an abortive, single-issue attempt in 1690, the first regularly published newspaper in what is now the United States was the *Boston News-Letter,* which was begun in 1704. Its basic format—four pages, content concentrating on international news and "literary" matter, and wealth of advertising and legal notices—remained generally standard for newspapers for the next century and a half. The early newspaper was very much a local product, designed to convey news of the wider world to the citizens of a particular community. Little attention was given to local news which everyone presumably knew already.

Three nineteenth-century developments changed the newspaper dramatically: the invention of the power printing press, the development of the railroads (which allowed much wider distribution of a paper), and the increasing demand for news, particularly during the Civil War. The major city dailies, with their telegraphic news gathering, large steam presses, and railroad-based distribution systems, co-opted the international, national, and state news reporting functions. Papers in smaller communities had to concentrate on local news if they were to survive and prosper.

Metropolitan dailies were (and are) primarily concerned with international, national, and state affairs. Municipal events were often given only general coverage. Little, if any, attention was given to the activities of ordinary people, except for advertisements. Metropolitan papers would also occasionally pick up items from distant or rural areas which had news appeal outside their own communities. In contrast, small country or community newspapers were concerned with local people and their immediate surroundings. Genealogically, these small papers are especially valuable.

WHAT CAN BE FOUND

Not all newspaper records are "vital records." In many cases, newspapers chronicled fairly mundane events in peoples' lives— graduations, anniversaries, first communions, reunions, card parties, charivaris, illnesses, and visits from family to family—but accounts of any of those activities can individually or cumulatively provide genealogical detail and clues.

VITAL STATISTICS

One of the most useful genealogical applications of newspapers is for vital statistics—as substitutes for or supplements to civil or other sources for birth, marriage, and death information. In older newspapers, notices of births, deaths, and marriages appeared almost anywhere in the publication. Because of their brevity they made good filler items—to fill in a few lines at the end of a column or a page. Unless you read every page thoroughly, you may miss a notice. Column headings can be misleading too. An unsuspecting researcher looking for the death notice or obituary of an ancestor who had died in a construction accident might miss the article headed "Blown to Eternity" if the search is concentrated on a personal name. A twentieth-century attitude toward newspapers will not be of much help in reading an eighteenth-century publication.

Deaths
When many genealogical researchers think of newspapers, they immediately think of obituaries—a natural and understandable connection. The wealth of genealogical and biographical information to be found in an informative obituary certainly makes the effort of searching for one worthwhile. For many of our ancestors (and relatives), the obituary is the only "biographical sketch" that was ever devoted to that individual. In addition to names, dates, and places of birth, marriage, and death, the obituary often identifies relationships of the deceased as child, sibling, parent, grandparent, etc., to numerous other individuals. Obituaries may even suggest other documentation of an individual's death—a death certificate in another county because the hospital was located there; church or cemetery records (by identifying the place of burial or the officiating minister); or records of a coroner's inquest because the death was sudden or unexpected. And, of course, the wealth of detail in an informative obituary may open up many research avenues (figure 12-1).

The amount of information on deaths found in newspapers will not be consistent over the years. Practices also varied in different parts of the country, and individual papers and editors had differing attitudes toward obituaries. Very early obituaries tended to limit the account to one or two lines. A typical early nineteenth-century entry stated the name of the deceased, perhaps an age or estimated age, the date of death, and the late residence; mention of the funeral was sometimes included. Further details of the death may have been given, but rarely were survivors named. The fact that a husband or wife "is left with ten children to mourn the loss" may be the extent of the help provided in such a notice. Parents' names were rarely given except in the case of a child, and even these may merely say: "Baby Mary departed this life to live with the angels."

As the nineteenth century progressed, an increasing amount of information was furnished. It is not uncommon to find biographical accounts that include birth dates, marriage dates and places, and children's and grandchildren's names. While the small-town newspaper could afford space to print details on the deaths of even common people, this policy was not practical for the metropolitan press. Large dailies printed lengthy obituaries only of the prominent, the powerful, the wealthy— those for whom a fee was paid to laud their lives or whose passing was considered newsworthy. In short, there are no set rules on the amount of information which can be expected.

In an obituary search, it is necessary to investigate the files of all likely newspapers. It is impossible to know beforehand which, if any, paper is going to have the best or fullest obituary. Today even the largest cities often have only one or two daily newspapers, but a century ago that city may have had eight or ten, any one of which might have carried the death notice of your ancestor. Even comparatively small communities had at least two papers—usually, one Democratic and one Republican. Also, unlike today's papers, which often share a printing plant or even editorial staff, older papers were often fiercely competitive, and each paper had its own strengths of coverage.

When searching for an obituary, don't just search for the obituary itself. Begin your search of a weekly paper at least two weeks before the date of death. Your ancestor may have been in a final illness, family members rushing to the bedside— all reported in the paper. Don't assume that the death notice you found in the paper three days after the individual's death is all there is. The news of the death may have reached the paper shortly before the printing deadline, a fuller obituary following later. Also, be sure to check the locals columns for mention of out-of-town family members coming for the funeral. In a weekly paper, check four to six weeks after the date of death before concluding there is no obituary to be found—in that paper; in a daily paper, check seven to ten days after the date of death.

If an obituary was to appear in the newspaper, someone had to write it, and that someone may not have gotten around to it until things had settled down a bit. Perhaps the saddest news to the genealogical researcher is the announcement of the "obituary next week" that never appeared because no one got around to writing it. In some areas, particularly around the turn of the century, professional obituary writers were in vogue. The family would provide the basic biographical information, which the writer would turn into a properly flowery tribute.

The circumstances of the death will often determine where information appears within the newspaper itself. Accidental deaths, murders, and suicides were news items and were therefore placed in attention-getting spots but might not be mentioned in other notices. These news items often mention that an inquest was held; thus, you might find more information from a coroner's records or from other court proceedings. The word *suddenly* is a clue that the death was unnatural and that an inquest may have been held, even if it was not reported.

When considering possible obituary sources, don't just check in the community where the individual died—also check the community (or communities) where the individual lived. Many people in their later years went to live with children and often died far from where they had spent most of their adult lives. But, if they still had connections with the home community, there is a good chance that an obituary will appear there, perhaps a more detailed one than will be found in the community of death, where that person was just a new or temporary resident. However, the opposite may also be true, depending on the policies of the individual papers or whether or not it was a slow news week in a particular community.

The obituary is not the only record of death that can be found in the newspaper. Other possibilities are death or funeral notices, burial permit lists, and death lists. They may not have the immediate payoff of obituaries, but they can provide important documentation of deaths.

Death or funeral notices were paid announcements. Unlike the obituary, the notice usually stated only the name of the decedent, when and where the death occurred, and, occasionally, the name of a survivor. An example might be: "Dyer, Harry, 26th inst., funeral from St. James at 1 pm, thence by carriage to Greenwood Cemetery." Even this simple statement can provide needed clue's to continue research. Many ancestors will not be found in paid announcements because survivors either did not deem them necessary or couldn't afford them. In hard economic times, such as the Great Depression, there were noticeably fewer paid announcements.

Official lists of the dead are commonly found in newspapers. This kind of list gives the meager information supplied to the newspaper from city or county records and was included as a free service to the readers. Also providing needed death dates or places are lists of war dead, disaster victims, and deceased members of fraternal organizations. Names of policemen and firemen who died within the year are often published periodically. Sometimes all of the area deaths are noted simultaneously at the end of the year, or as part of the summary of the previous year in a January issue.

Marriages

Marriage information, like death information, varies considerably, both over time and from one paper to another. The listings range from brief announcements or lists of licenses to full, detailed accounts of the wedding ceremony itself, occasionally including even a list of wedding gifts.

OBITUARY

MRS. CAROLINE GREER

Caroline Coombs, daughter of Edward Pindell and Nancy Hickman Coombs, was born at Hurricane Corners, Lancaster township, Wisconsin, December 2, 1842. She was the youngest daughter of a family of seven daughters and three sons. She died at her home in Bloomington, Wis., November 26, 1933, at the age of 90 years, 11 months and 24 days.

The Coombs and Hickman families are descended from Colonial and Revolutionary ancestors, many of whom were prominent in the development of the colonies, the Revolutionary war, and the formation of our government. Mrs. Greer's father was a soldier in the war of 1812, thus making her a real Daughter, and she was so honored by the Illinois Society, U. S. Daughters of 1812. Her mother's father, Jacob Hickman, also was a soldier in the War of 1812.

Her grandfather, John Coombs, served in the Revolutionary war, as did also her great-grandfather, Captain Philip Pindell, father of her grandmother, Rachel Pindell Coombs, Captain Philip Pindell served in the Maryland militia for more than 30 years. He was a friend of George Washington, and served with him during the French and Indian War in the ill-fated Braddock expedition, as well as at Fort Duquesne. Later he served, throughout the American Revolution. Her great-grandmother, Rachel Shelby, married Capt. Philip Pindell. Her father, Evan Shelby Sr., came from Glamorganshire, Wales, shortly after 1730. Her brother was Gen. Evan Shelby, and Gov. Isaac Shelby, first governor of Kentucky, also a general in the Revolution, was her nephew. From this family many towns and counties in the United States have derived their names. The Pindell family came to America about 1680, to Maryland, the first being Thomas, his son Thomas, and then Capt. Philip.

In 1836 Mrs. Greer's parents, with five young children and several neighbor families, left their home town, Uniontown, Penn., on a large flatboat, drifting down the Ohio river to the Mississippi. At St. Louis they boarded one of the famous early river steamboats, and ascended the Mississippi river to Cassville, then a straggling young settlement. On board the steamer was Black Hawk, the noted Indian chief, who in 1832 had waged an unsuccessful war against the onrushing tide of white pioneers. This voyage around by the rivers was the great event in the life of these pioneers.

Mrs. Greer was a member of the Congregational church, the Order of the Eastern Star, the Daughters of the American Revolution, and the Daughters of 1812.

She was a woman of splendid character and right principles, and intellectually was bright and cultured, keeping pace with the rapidly changing march of events. She was possessed of an amiable, even-tempered disposition, which with a splendid physical inheritance no doubt assisted in the atainment of her great span of life—nearly 91 years. The cares, troubles and disappointments incident to the times through which she lived served only to intensify and develop her lovable qualities. A kind and generous friend and neighbor, and a great lover of little children, she endeared herself to all. She was ever ready to respond to the call for assistance, or to serve in any position that she was called upon to fill. Outliving her generation, she readily made friends with and adopted the customs of the new. She was devoutly religious without ostentation. The following verse, which she possessed for many years, embodied her attitude:

"I do not fear to tread the path
That those before have long since trod;
I do not fear to pass the gates,
And stand beside the living God.
In this world's fight, I've done my part;
If God be God, He knows it well;
He will not turn his back on me,
And send me down to blackest hell,
Because I have not prayed aloud
And shouted in the market place.
'Tis what we do, not what we say,
That makes us worthy of His grace."

In her declining years Mrs. Greer's life was made pleasant and happy by the devotion of her children, one or more of whom were at her home frequently. Every attention and comfort were bestowed with tender and loving solicitude. This was a welcome reward for her life of boundless love and service. A FRIEND.

Funeral services for Mrs. Greer were held from the home to the Congregational church November 29, the Rev. C. C. Richardson officiating, Interment was made in the family lot in the Bloomington cemetery. A large congregation of relatives, old friends and neighbors attended, to pay a last tribute to a good woman.

Card of Thanks.

To our neighbors and other friends, for their many kindnesses to our dear mother and grandmother, during the past years, and expressions of sympathy at the end of her life, we express our heartfelt thanks.—The Greer Family.

LANCASTER

(Continued from First Page)

Wolfe of Rockville, Dec. 9; one to Mr. and Mrs. Leo Duve of Lancaster, Dec. 24, and one to Mr. and Mrs. Sylvester Pleumer of Potosi, Dec. 10th. Dr. Houghton reports a baby girl at

Figure 12-1. An obituary from the Bloomington, Wisconsin, *Bloomington Record,* 13 December 1933.

Marriage license notices appear frequently in both city and rural newspapers. Often, these were posted weekly and in many instances noted the age of the bride and groom as well as their places of residence. The *Central Illinois Gazette* of West Urbana ran this fairly typical notice on 12 May 1858:

> **The following marriage licenses have been issued since our last report:**
>
> P. Haynes to Temps Green,
>
> J.R. Thomas to M.J. Stacy,
>
> W.I. Traywick to Willella Gray,
>
> J.Y. Pearce to Cora Pearce
>
> COLORED
>
> Charley Weathers to Van King

Again, the best sources for engagement and marriage information are local papers. Generally only the socially and politically elite were newsworthy enough to get coverage in metropolitan dailies. Because couples getting married frequently traveled to the place of marriage—perhaps they eloped or went to the bride's home town, or went to another state where there was no waiting period—newspaper accounts can frequently provide the clues leading to an otherwise elusive record. And that account might appear in a paper wherever the bride or groom was known.

Wedding anniversaries celebrating twenty-five, fifty, or more years of marriage were of special interest in local papers. For example, the golden wedding of Mr. and Mrs. Joseph V. Parkinson merited two full columns on the front page, including a complete review of their fifty years together, in the *Rensselaer Semi-Weekly Republican,* Jasper County, Indiana, in 1901 (figure 12-2). Consider the interesting account below from the *Nashville Banner,* 6 October 1897.

DISAPPOINTED IN LOVE

> Clarkeville, October 11, Disappointment in love is the reason assigned for J.C. Northington, a well-known planter of Fort Royal, becoming demented. He was brought here yesterday but was refused admission into the county jail without proper papers. Miss Olive Sockett married Walter Nayler, of this place, several days ago. A license had been issued for her and Northington, but she changed her mind at the last moment.

Few eyes would miss this bit of sensational gossip. For the genealogist, however, perplexed by a Sockett-Northington wedding license, this little item provides a much-needed explanation.

Births

Even prior to the time that birth registration was required by law, birth announcements, though uncommon, could be found in certain papers. Notices of births may appear in the society column several days, weeks, or even months after the event. Birth notices tended to be brief and often uninformative, frequently omitting the name or even the sex of the child. For example, the *Green Bay* (Wisconsin) *Advocate* of 21 March

1896 reported that "A 10 pound telegraph line repairer came to the home of Henry McConnell last Friday."

LOCAL NEWS

The weekly editions of community newspapers give a personal glimpse of people found nowhere else. Country papers would allow plenty of space for a column prepared by a local resident to tell of recent births, upcoming or recent marriages, illnesses, visitors to the community, former residents vacationing with relatives in their old home, and news of a more personal nature. A common example of the kind of clues to be found is one which reads, "Miss Marjorie Dyer of our town is visiting her cousin Miss Margaret Howley in Fort Wayne." This example gives another location of family members and possibly a surname previously unknown. These columns also note anniversaries, parties, reunions, and achievements such as a promotion or a school award. Newcomers to a community often received the attention of the columnist, and former residents were naturally included.

School news might include awards won and detailed coverage of a graduation, complete with a class picture or even individual photographs of the graduates. School board minutes, lists of teachers and pupils, and other school events are also frequently recorded. A social event for which the guest list is printed, like this 12 May 1858 report in the *Central Illinois Gazette* of a masquerade party, is a genuine find:

> **The young people did themselves proud last Friday night in the masquerade party at Mr. R.H. Carter's. It was the first of the kind they had gotten up for some time and the occasion was looked too [sic] with considerable interest. A large number of both ladies and gentlemen were en-masque, while there were many who attended that did not conform to the rules of the entertainment, but appeared in their customary dress. The following are the parties who were en-masque and the characters represented:**
> Miss Cora Townes .... Flower Girl
>   "   Lena Hawkins .... Dinah
> [the list continues]

Local news columns are one of the most important sources for data on women and children—two groups of people who rarely appear in other records in their own right. Local columns also provide clues leading to other records. If great-grandmother belonged to a Methodist charitable organization or a sewing circle sponsored by a church, it is a clear indication of church membership. If the religious affiliation was previously unknown, the researcher has a valuable lead.

BIOGRAPHICAL SKETCHES

Newspapers carry biographical sketches in a variety of guises—birthday announcements, testimonials, feature articles, and other items. Sometimes these items are indexed; sometimes they can only be found by searching page by page. An example with a touch of humor is this obviously muckraking letter to the editor of the *Central Illinois Gazette* in West Urbana, Illinois, 12 February 1858, passed on by the addressee, John G. Oiler:

> Dear Sir:—I am requested by many good citizens (Hodges, McLaurie & Co., we suppose) of our Town

to enquire of you concerning the one Dr. Scroggs who is said to have lived for some time in your town. Scroggs came here about a year ago and he is making himself a great nuisance. He proposes to be a great temperance man and officiously seeks to enlighten the Barbarians out here as he calls them. I am told you can give some light on his true character. We wish to know whether Scroggs ever carried on a Drug Store in your place or rather a dram shop. Did he sell whiskey to back door customers? Did he keep a station on the underground R.R.? Was your neighborhood glad when he left? Was he a man of integrity, of good moral character, was he a notorious s–t-as or a gentleman?

If you will please answer the above inquiries and give his true character to us you will much oblige many good citizens of our Town who think him a great bore. Answer soon.

Very truly, J.S. Jones

N.H. Tell us especially whether he traded in liquor.

Loyally, Scroggs's friends replied on 1 April 1858 from Harveyeburg, Ohio:

We whose names are hereunto annexed do certify that we have known J.W. Scroggs for some years past–known him as a physician, and as one who kept a drug store–do not think he would or ever did sell whiskey to any persons who were in the habit of drinking to excess; and our understanding was, that he did not sell whiskey or any other kind of spirituous liquors, except for medical purposes, and always looked upon him as one of our best Temperance men. He always took part in favor of Temperance when any occasion offered in our place.

Ausahem Antram, M.T. Macy, A.L. Antram, A.T. Sabia, Samuel G. Welch, Joshua Garwood, John Howe, S.O. Garwood, B.D. Gaddis, David Mason, M.D., C. Sikes, F.D. Harian, Jos. T. Mistletoe, Jabes H. Crew, Ephraim Mills, Nathan Macy, John D. Abbott, Thomas Wilson, Joseph Williamson, Wm. Macy, Christian Ilirey, Mark Haynes, E.L. Macy, Jesse Randall, James Astram, Wm. Randall, Joseph Nedery, Thos. Wilson, Jr., Joseph Lippincott, Finey Ham, G.W. Ham

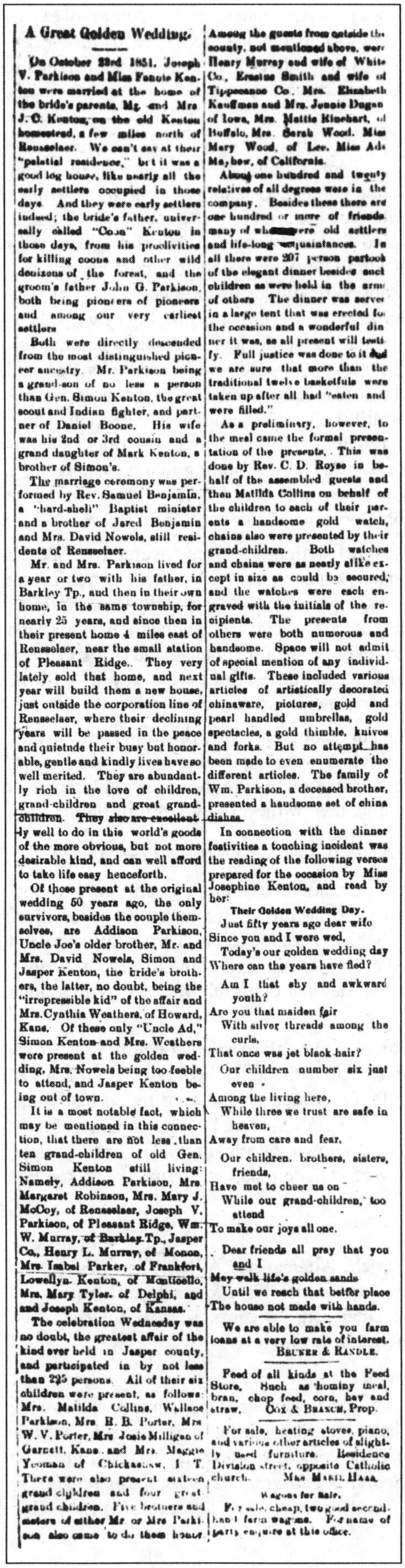

A Great Golden Wedding.

On October 23rd 1851, Joseph V. Parkison and Miss Fannie Kenton were married at the home of the bride's parents, Mr. and Mrs J. C. Kenton, on the old Kenton homestead, a few miles north of Rensselaer. We can't say at their "palatial residence," but it was a good log house, like nearly all the early settlers occupied in those days. And they were early settlers indeed; the bride's father, universally called "Coon" Kenton in those days, from his proclivities for killing coons and other wild denizens of the forest, and the groom's father John G. Parkison, both being pioneers of pioneers and among our very earliest settlers.

Both were directly descended from the most distinguished pioneer ancestry. Mr. Parkison being a grand-son of no less a person than Gen. Simon Kenton, the great scout and Indian fighter, and partner of Daniel Boone. His wife was his 2nd or 3rd cousin and a grand daughter of Mark Kenton, a brother of Simon's.

The marriage ceremony was performed by Rev. Samuel Benjamin, a "hard-shell" Baptist minister and a brother of Jared Benjamin and Mrs. David Nowels, still residents of Rensselaer.

Mr. and Mrs. Parkison lived for a year or two with his father, in Barkley Tp., and then in their own home, in the same township, for nearly 25 years, and since then in their present home 4 miles east of Rensselaer, near the small station of Pleasant Ridge. They very lately sold that home, and next year will build them a new house, just outside the corporation line of Rensselaer, where their declining years will be passed in the peace and quietude their busy but honorable, gentle and kindly lives have so well merited. They are abundantly rich in the love of children, grand-children and great grand-children. They also are excellently well to do in this world's goods of the more obvious, but not more desirable kind, and can well afford to take life easy henceforth.

Of those present at the original wedding 50 years ago, the only survivors, besides the couple themselves, are Addison Parkison, Uncle Joe's older brother, Mr. and Mrs. David Nowels, Simon and Jasper Kenton, the bride's brothers, the latter, no doubt, being the "irrepressible kid" of the affair and Mrs. Cynthia Weathers, of Howard, Kans. Of these only "Uncle Ad," Simon Kenton and Mrs. Weathers were present at the golden wedding, Mrs. Nowels being too feeble to attend, and Jasper Kenton being out of town.

It is a most notable fact, which may be mentioned in this connection, that there are not less than ten grand-children of old Gen. Simon Kenton still living: Namely, Addison Parkison, Mrs. Margaret Robinson, Mrs. Mary J. McCoy, of Rensselaer, Joseph V. Parkison, of Pleasant Ridge, Wm. W. Murray, of Barkley Tp., Jasper Co., Henry L. Murray, of Monon, Mrs. Isabel Parker, of Frankfort, Lewellyn Kenton, of Monticello, Mrs. Mary Tyler, of Delphi, and and Joseph Kenton, of Kansas.

The celebration Wednesday was no doubt, the greatest affair of the kind ever held in Jasper county, and participated in by not less than 225 persons. All of their six children were present, as follows: Mrs. Matilda Collins, Wallace Parkison, Mrs H. B. Porter, Mrs W. V. Porter, Mrs Josie Milligan of Garnett, Kans. and Mrs. Maggie Yeoman of Chickasaw, I. T. There were also present sixteen grand children and four great grand children. Five brothers and sisters of either Mr. or Mrs Parkison also came to do them honor. Among the guests from outside the county, not mentioned above, were Henry Murray and wife of White Co., Erastus Smith and wife of Tippecanoe Co., Mrs. Elizabeth Kauffman and Mrs. Jennie Dugan of Iowa, Mrs. Mattie Rinehart, of Buffalo, Mrs. Sarah Wood, Miss Mary Wood, of Lee, Miss Ada Mayhew, of California.

About one hundred and twenty relatives of all degrees were in the company. Besides these there are one hundred or more of friends many of wh[illegible]ere old settlers and life-long acquaintances. In all there were 207 person partook of the elegant dinner besides such children as were held in the arms of others. The dinner was served in a large tent that was erected for the occasion and a wonderful dinner it was, as all present will testify. Full justice was done to it and we are sure that more than the traditional twelve basketfuls were taken up after all had "eaten and were filled."

As a preliminary, however, to the meal came the formal presentation of the presents. This was done by Rev. C. D. Royse in behalf of the assembled guests and then Matilda Collins on behalf of the children to each of their parents a handsome gold watch, chains also were presented by their grand-children. Both watches and chains were as nearly alike except in size as could be secured; and the watches were each engraved with the initials of the recipients. The presents from others were both numerous and handsome. Space will not admit of special mention of any individual gifts. These included various articles of artistically decorated chinaware, pictures, gold and pearl handled umbrellas, gold spectacles, a gold thimble, knives and forks. But no attempt has been made to even enumerate the different articles. The family of Wm. Parkison, a deceased brother, presented a handsome set of china dishes.

In connection with the dinner festivities a touching incident was the reading of the following verses prepared for the occasion by Miss Josephine Kenton, and read by her:

Their Golden Wedding Day.

Just fifty years ago dear wife
Since you and I were wed,
Today's our golden wedding day
Where can the years have fled?

Am I that shy and awkward youth?
Are you that maiden fair
With silver threads among the curls,
That once was jet black hair?

Our children number six just even
Among the living here,
While three we trust are safe in heaven,
Away from care and fear.

Our children, brothers, sisters, friends,
Have met to cheer us on
While our grand-children, too attend
To make our joys all one.

Dear friends all pray that you and I
May walk life's golden sands
Until we reach that better place
The house not made with hands.

We are able to make you farm loans at a very low rate of interest.
BRUNER & RANDLE.

Feed of all kinds at the Feed Store, Such as hominy meal, bran, chop feed, corn, hay and straw. COX & BRANCH, Prop.

For sale, heating stoves, piano, and various other articles of slightly used furniture. Residence Division street, opposite Catholic church. MRS MABEL HAAS.

Wagons for Sale.

For sale, cheap, two good second-hand farm wagons. For name of party enquire at this office.

Figure 12-2. Newspaper article titled "A Great Golden Wedding." *Rensselaer Semi-Weekly Republican,* 25 October 1901, p. 1.

Membership lists, printed minutes, and summaries of events for fraternal organizations, benevolent associations, lists of retirees, political groups, musicians, firemen, and policemen are common. You will sometimes be able to find group photographs.

LEGAL NOTICES

The requirement that some judicial actions (in cases including more persons than the principals) cannot be concluded without public notice carries side benefits for the genealogist. Legislatures either provided for and supported an official county or community publication, or they designated existing newspapers for these purposes. Examples include land sales for payment of taxes, administration in probate, proving of wills, heirship determination and the settlement of estates, pending divorce proceedings, sales of properties of insolvent estates, and more. When court records are not available for any reason, these public notices can fill the gap. Or, a legal notice spotted in a newspaper search might direct the researcher to otherwise unknown court records. The chance spotting in a newspaper of a court docket might be the only clue leading to a divorce case that solves a perplexing genealogical problem (figure 12-3).

In larger cities, this function was often covered by a special kind of professional newspaper, devoted entirely to publishing legal notices. For example, the *Chicago Daily Law Bulletin,* which began publication in 1854, has calendars, reports, and public notices from every court for Chicago and Cook County. For the genealogist, these entries can be the key to locating original case files and other court records.

Actually, any legal record could be printed in a newspaper, wherever local authorities were required to make public a specific set of facts or where they felt it to be in the public interest to do so. For example, review the 1764 tax roll in figure 12-4.

PUBLIC ANNOUNCEMENTS AND ADVERTISEMENTS

Paid advertisements, common from the beginning of newspaper publication, chronicle the products, housing, transportation, dress, and reading habits of our ancestors. Particularly relevant for the genealogist are advertisements about insolvent debtors, forced land sales, educational opportunities, and professional services.

Early newspapers frequently carried touching advertisements from worried relatives who had lost contact with loved ones. These ads often provided the missing individual's personal description, clothing description, last known whereabouts, and the destination, if known, of a lost traveler. For example, *Sower's Newspaper* of Philadelphia, on 22 June 1759, ran this notice:

> Nicholas Emrich, Allemangel, Albany Township, Berks County, inquires for his two sons, and one daughter. The older son, Valentin, is married; the other son Friedrich, is single.

These notices were particularly common in papers that were directed to a particular immigrant group. For example, the New England Historic Genealogical Society has issued four stout volumes of *The Search for Missing Friends; Irish Immigrant Advertisements Placed in the Boston Pilot,* covering the period from 1831 to 1860.

Common, too, were notices that horses and other property had been lost or stolen, claims against estates, and even announcements by irate husbands like this one in 1776:

> Whereas the Wife of Joseph Cartwright having eloped from him sundry times, he requests all persons not to trust her, as he will not pay any debts she may contract.
>
> Joseph Cartwright

One wife defended herself vigorously in the *Boston Evening Post* in 1762:

> I find in your last Monday's Papers that my husband informed the Publick That I have eloped—and that I run him into Debt, and has given a Caution not to Trust me on his Account. Although I am very sensible that neither he or I are of much Importance to the Publick, for he has no Estate to entitle me to any Credit on his account; yet I desire you to be so kind to me, as to let the Publick know That I never run him in Debt in my Life, nor never eloped, unless it was to Day Labour, to support me and the Children, which I am of necessity Obliged to do; and shall be ever glad to do my Duty to him, and wish he would for the future behave to me in such a Manner that I may do it with more Ease than heretofore.
>
> Her
>
> Mary X. Wellington
>
> Mark

A fascinating background to an eighteenth-century marriage comes from a protest advertisement paid for by the groom (figure 12-5).

IMMIGRATION, MIGRATION, AND SHIPPING INFORMATION

Newspapers are especially helpful in tracing migrations from one place to another. In the personal and local news columns, we can trace trips to see distant relatives, farewell parties for families about to move, and visits back home from those who had moved away. Sometimes letters back home were published in the newspaper, especially those that reported on the destination. Announcements, letters to the editor, and "Marine Intelligence" include such useful entries as lists, names of ships docking or cleared for departure, letters of gratitude for a safe journey, or descriptions of the ocean voyage.

When mail and packages sent general delivery were not called for or when the addressee had moved without leaving a forwarding address, local papers frequently printed letter lists. Below is a partial list first printed in the *Western Bugle* of Council Bluffs, Iowa, 16 June 1852, then picked up by the *Deseret News* in Salt Lake City, Utah. (Many Mormons living in Winter Quarters completed their migration to Utah in 1852.)

Anderson, James M.

Anthony, John

Atherton, Joseph

Anderson, Hiram

Alcock, Robert

Armstrong, A.

Ashley, Thomas

Alexander, N.B.

Adams, A.J.

Armstrong, John A.

The list continues through several hundred names. It is important to remember that these were lists of those who had not picked up their mail—people who should have been in a particular locality but for some reason were not.

It was customary for individuals setting up business in a new community to announce the fact in the local paper. In the 1760s, the *South Carolina Gazette* was filled with such notices. Robert Catherwood, "surgeon to the hospitals and garrisons in East Florida" (16 February 1767), opened a practice with an announcement, and a Mrs. Grant proposed "to practice midwifery having studied that art regularly and practiced it afterwards at Edinburgh: Certificates of which she can produce from the Gentlemen whose lectures she attended, and likewise from the professors of Anatomy and Practice of Physick in that city. . . ." (29 December 1768).

ANNOUNCEMENTS REGARDING RUNAWAY SLAVES OR INDENTURED SERVANTS

Early American newspapers are full of announcements from masters about their slaves or servants. Notices offered slaves for sale or hire, listed runaways, reported captures, and sought the return of runaways, indentured servants, and apprentices. Physical descriptions and descriptions of clothing are usually very detailed.

Newspapers are important sources for tracing blacks before the Civil War. Announcements of sales, with complete physical descriptions, can be combined with probate files, slave census schedules, cemetery inscriptions, church records, and other resources to provide as complete a record as possible for a slave or a free black family. For blacks involved in rebellions or accused of local crimes, the news accounts can be combined with court and coroner's records to round out information.

HISTORICAL ITEMS

Not all useful newspaper information was published immediately after an event. Historical features, columns, and features that describe events of the same date ten, twenty, or fifty years previously can all provide useful information. Frequently, papers published special historical issues to commemorate both community milestones and notable anniversaries of the paper itself. These special issues frequently contain a wealth of historical information gathered from many sources. For some communities, they represent the only published history.

Just as useful may be the regular historical column published over several years by a dedicated local historian. These columns, which often range widely, frequently contain biographical and historical information recorded nowhere else. Sometimes local libraries or historical societies, recognizing the importance of such a series, will have clipped the columns and organized them in scrapbooks; sometimes they have been gathered and published in books or pamphlets. When using these columns from a secondary source, it is wise to check the newspaper files to be sure all of the columns were included.

The "ten, twenty, or fifty years ago" columns are also worth keeping an eye on. In addition to providing reference to otherwise unconsidered events, they sometimes preserve information from newspaper files that may have later been lost.

HOW TO FIND NEWSPAPERS

Locating local newspapers of the past can be difficult. The first step in the search is to identify papers which served the area of interest and which have survived. The same basic reference tools that help us in using periodicals guide the intelligent use of newspapers. The three most needed tools are bibliographies (What was published?), inventories of library and depository holdings (Where is it?), and indexes (How do I find what I want in it?).

County histories are a good starting point to learn what newspapers were published in a county. In them, newspapers are often accorded lengthy treatment, from the earliest in the county until the publication date of the history. If a newspaper is still being published, the *Gale Directory of Publications and Broadcast Media* will provide a location and correct title. The predecessor of this directory began publishing in 1869, so newspapers that have ceased publication since that time can be identified in earlier volumes. Newspapers are listed by state and community of publication.

Union lists—catalogs that describe the holdings of multiple libraries—are also helpful in locating newspaper files: Clarence Brigham, *History and Bibliography of American Newspapers, 1690–1820*, 2 vols. (Worcester, Mass.: American Antiquarian Society, 1947); Winifred Gregory, *American Newspapers, 1821–1936: A Union List of Files Available in the United States and Canada* (1937. Reprint. New York: Kraus, 1967); and the U.S. Library of Congress, *Newspapers in Microform: United States, 1848–1983*, 2 vols. (Washington, D.C.: Library of Congress, 1984), are essential. For most states, other union lists exist. Usually arranged by state and community, union lists give information on specific libraries, historical societies, newspaper offices, and private collections where these newspaper files have been located. They also tell the time period covered by each newspaper and its frequency of publication. Reference departments in most public and university libraries will hold the national lists and the union lists necessary for their areas. For specific titles, see the chapter bibliography.

When trying to identify the newspapers that covered a particular area, it is important to remember that the coverage area of a particular paper was controlled more by the competition than by any civil boundaries. If there were no newspapers published in a particular community of interest, a nearby town may have been the news center serving the area. The area served might include another county or even a county across a state line. Make a careful study of maps for clues of area coverage. Also, change must be considered. Just because a particular newspaper was the choice for recording an 1890 event does not mean it would have been the choice for an event in 1930. It

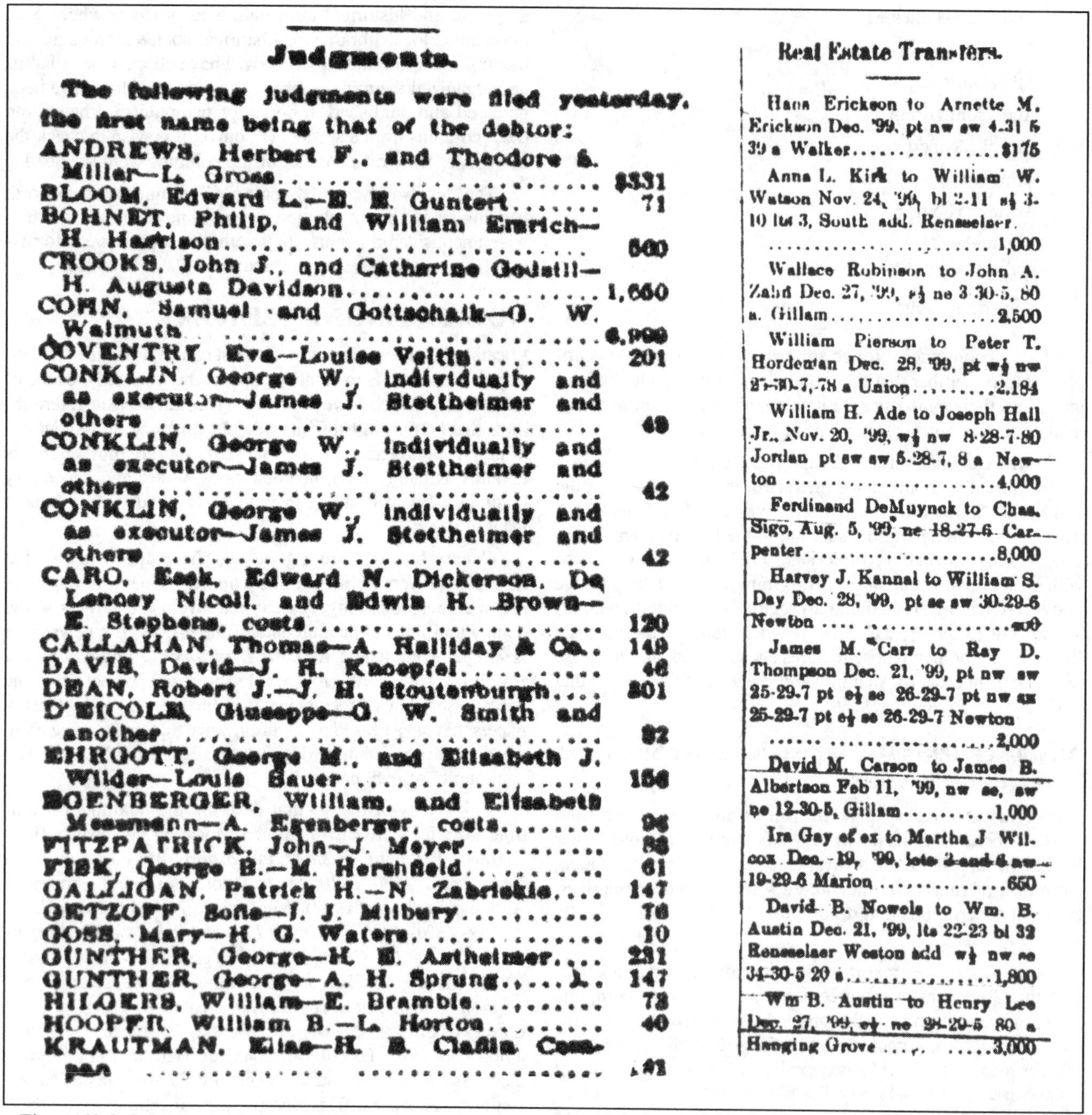

Judgments.

The following judgments were filed yesterday, the first name being that of the debtor:

ANDREWS, Herbert F., and Theodore &. Miller—L. Gross.......................... $331
BLOOM, Edward L.—B. E. Guntert....... 71
BOHNET, Philip, and William Emrich—H. Harrison........................... 500
CROOKS, John J., and Catharine Godstill—H. Augusta Davidson.................. 1,650
COHN, Samuel and Gottschalk—O. W. Walmuth 6,900
COVENTRY, Eva—Louise Veitis......... 201
CONKLIN, George W., individually and as executor—James J. Stettheimer and others 49
CONKLIN, George W., individually and as executor—James J. Stettheimer and others 42
CONKLIN, George W., individually and as executor—James J. Stettheimer and others 42
CARO, Eask, Edward N. Dickerson, De Lancey Nicoll, and Edwin H. Brown—E. Stephens, costs...................... 120
CALLAHAN, Thomas—A. Halliday & Co.. 149
DAVIS, David—J. H. Knoepfel.......... 46
DEAN, Robert J.—J. H. Stoutenburgh.... 801
D'NICOLA, Giuseppe—G. W. Smith and another 92
EHRGOTT, George M., and Elizabeth J. Wilder—Louis Bauer................. 158
EGENBERGER, William, and Elizabeth Messmann—A. Egenberger, costs....... 96
FITZPATRICK, John—J. Meyer.......... 88
FISK, George B.—M. Hershfield.......... 61
GALLIGAN, Patrick H.—N. Zabriskie.... 147
GETZOFF, Sofie—J. J. Milbury........... 76
GOSS, Mary—H. G. Waters............... 10
GUNTHER, George—H. E. Astheimer.... 231
GUNTHER, George—A. H. Sprung....... 147
HILGERS, William—E. Bramble.......... 73
HOOPER, William B.—L. Horton......... 40
KRAUTMAN, Elias—H. B. Claflin Company 41

Real Estate Transfers.

Hans Erickson to Arnette M. Erickson Dec. '99, pt nw sw 4-31 5 39 a Walker......................$175

Anna L. Kirk to William W. Watson Nov. 24, '99, bl 2-11 s½ 3-10 lts 3, South add. Rensselaer. 1,000

Wallace Robinson to John A. Zabi Dec. 27, '99, s½ ne 3-30-5, 80 a. Gillam..........................2,500

William Pierson to Peter T. Hordeman Dec. 28, '99, pt w½ nw 27-30-7, 78 a Union.........2,184

William H. Ade to Joseph Hall Jr., Nov. 20, '99, w½ nw 8-28-7-80 Jordan pt sw sw 5-28-7, 8 a Newton 4,000

Ferdinand DeMuynck to Chas. Sigo, Aug. 5, '99, ne 18-27-6 Carpenter..........................8,000

Harvey J. Kannal to William S. Day Dec. 28, '99, pt se sw 30-29-6 Newton ....[illegible]

James M. Carr to Ray D. Thompson Dec. 21, '99, pt nw sw 25-29-7 pt e½ se 26-29-7 pt nw sw 25-29-7 pt e½ se 26-29-7 Newton 2,000

David M. Carson to James B. Albertson Feb 11, '99, nw se, sw ne 12-30-5, Gillam...........1,000

Ira Gay et ox to Martha J Willcox Dec. 19, '99, lots 3 and 6 nw 19-29-6 Marion 650

David B. Nowels to Wm. B. Austin Dec. 21, '99, lts 22-23 bl 32 Rensselaer Weston add w½ nw se 34-30-5 20 a..................1,800

Wm B. Austin to Henry Lee Dec. 27, '99, e½ ne 34-29-5 80 a Hanging Grove 3,000

Figure 12-3. Judgements, the *New York Times,* 3 January 1900. Real estate transfers, *Rennselaer Semi-Weekly Republican,* Jasper County, Indiana, 9 January 1900. Notice, *Hocking Sentinel,* Logan, Ohio, 16 April 1845.

may have changed editors or political orientation; other papers may have appeared in the area, perhaps in communities that had had no newspaper at all forty years earlier.

If a paper of interest can be identified and its files located in one or more libraries, consider the possibility of obtaining microfilm reproductions of the paper through interlibrary loan. If it is not available on loan or the paper has not been microfilmed, it may be possible to write to the holding institution and request a search for a specific item, if the date and place of the event are known. Many libraries will undertake a brief search (usually of one paper) if sufficient identifying information can be provided. Be willing to pay any necessary search and copy charges. Search policies vary widely from one library to another and are subject to change. More extensive searching may require a personal visit or the services of a professional researcher.

United States Newspaper Program

Since the publication of Gregory's *American Newspapers* (cited earlier), which covered the period from 1821 to 1936, historians and librarians have been interested in bringing it up to date and making it more complete. State historical societies, state libraries, university libraries, archives, and many state library consortia have become involved. The result is that nearly every state has some kind of newspaper identification, cataloging, and microfilming program, and many institutions have published lists of their specific holdings or union lists covering

Notice.

The State of Ohio, ⎱ Court of Com Pleas
Hocking county SS ⎰ March Term 1845

NOTICE is hereby given that the following Executors and Administra-
tors filed their accounts current and vouch-
ers for inspection and settlement at the next
term of said court, to wit:

Alexander White, Administrator of John
Campbell, deceased.

Joseph Whipple, Executor of Samuel
Moore, deceased.

Jeremiah Rose, Administrator of William Rose, deceased.

David Shultz, Administrator of Joseph
Funk, deceased.

John S. Hawk, Administrator of Jesse Dowd, deceased.

David Young, Administrator of Henry
Hedlebaugh, deceased.

Attest,   C. W. JAMES, Cl'k.

Robert Smith, ⎱ Hocking Common Pleas,
       vs   ⎰
Mary Smith, ⎰   Petition for Divorce.

The defendant is hereby notified that the
above named Robert Smith did, on the 18th
day of March, A. D. 1845, file in the Clerks
office in this Court his petition therein al-
ledging that she has been wilfully absent
from him more than three years, that she
has been guilty of Adultery, and guilty of
gross neglect of duty, and praying to be divorced for these causes, and that said petition will be for hearing before said court
at its next May term.

       C. W. JAMES, Clerk.
March 25, 1845.   6w35

multiple repositories (see the chapter bibliography). These projects have always been somewhat limited in scope and haphazard in execution. For some states, the increasingly outdated *American Newspapers* was still the best newspaper identification and location guide.

Far and away the most comprehensive program directed at updating Gregory's bibliography began in 1973. The Organization of American Historians, with the support of funds from the National Endowment for the Humanities (NEH), began planning for what is now known as the United States Newspaper Program. Within a few years, as a result of this effort, American genealogists will have access, in one form or another, to almost every extant newspaper file in the United States.

Iowa was chosen as the pilot state, because it did not then have a statewide newspaper bibliography and because it had an average number of newspapers and repositories. The project, known as the Iowa Pilot Project, was completed in 1979. The outcome of the project was the listing of Iowa newspapers in both an automated catalog and a published list (cited in the chapter bibliography), thus demonstrating that a national project was feasible.

In 1981, the Online Computer Library Center (OCLC) in Dublin, Ohio, agreed to accept newspaper records into its database, thereby acting as the computer network for the project. In 1982 and 1983, respectively, the Library of Congress and six national newspaper repositories began to catalog (or re-catalog) their holdings and enter the data into the OCLC database. The holdings of the national repositories, some 35,000 titles from all fifty states, provided the bibliographic foundation for projects by the various states' projects, testing the guides and procedures developed for the national plan.

In the fall of 1982, NEH invited universities, libraries, archives, and historical societies to submit applications for grants covering their own states. In July 1983, the first awards were made, and the United States Newspaper Project was up and running. Altogether, the project has involved forty-six states and two territories in planning and/or implementation of projects. In addition, eight national newspaper repositories (plus the Library of Congress) have also participated in the program.

The ultimate goal of the project is to identify, catalog, reproduce on microform, and make available to researchers every extant U.S. newspaper published since 13 September 1690. Together, the completed and current projects are expected to produce bibliographic records for approximately 193,000 newspaper titles and microfilm some 49 million pages of newsprint. The NEH expects to conclude the project by 2002, but each project has committed to maintain the database and continue microfilming of current or newly discovered publications.

Newspapers cataloged through the project can be identified on OCLC, but it does not provide detailed holdings. For example, a library may be identified as holding a particular newspaper when, in fact, it holds only a single issue. Every several years, the program also issues the *United States Newspaper Program National Union List* (4th ed., 1993) on microfiche. It provides more detailed holdings information. Several states have also published union lists based on project data.

Newspapers on Microfilm

Very few researchers are likely to view old newspapers in their original format. With the development of microfilming technology in the 1940s and 1950s, newspapers, because of the high acid content of newsprint, their considerable bulk, and the difficulties of proper storage, were seen as natural candidates for extensive microfilming. That microfilming, by commercial firms and newspaper repositories themselves, has been continuing steadily ever since. This, in turn, makes newspapers one of the most accessible sources genealogists have. Many libraries and historical societies will loan microfilm at a nominal cost. It is usually unnecessary to contact the original publisher or its successor, because most historical papers are now in public repositories.

Early American Newspapers

Researchers interested in early newspapers have been particularly well served. Papers published between 1690 and 1820 are thoroughly described in Brigham's *History and Bibliography*

The Proprietors of that Part of

Coxhall so called, in the County of York, purchased by *Roger Haskins* and 36 others, of *Harvinshindint Symonds*, are hereby notified that at their Meeting by Adjournment at *Ipswich*, May 13. 1763. they agreed upon and ordered a Tax of 12*f* to be laid on each 100 Acre Right in said Tract, and at a further Adjournment on the 6th Day of October last, they agreed upon and ordered a further Tax of 6*f* on each 100 Acre Lot in that Tract, making in the whole 18*f.* on each 100 Acre Right, and in that Proportion, for defreying the common Charges which have already arisen, or may hereafter arise in bringing forward a Settlement of said Lands, and to be paid to Capt. *Francis Goodhue*, of *Ipswich*, their Treasurer. The Purchasers subject to said Taxes are as follows, viz.

	Acres.		Acres.
Roger Haskins	200	Richard Walker	300
Edward Bishop	200	John Brownfarmer	300
William Baker	200	Nathaniel Brown	300
George Herrick	100	Zechariah Herrick	100
Thomas Edwards	100	Thomas Higginson	100
Samuel Ingalls, jun.	200	John Staniford	200
John Low, jun.	200	Thomas Low	200
William Dixee	200	Samuel Ingalls	100
Thomas Shepherd	200	Robert Lord, jun.	100
William Goodhue	500	Robert Bradford	100
Samuel Giddings	200	Nicholas Woodbery	100
Barnard Thorn	100	Mark Haskell	100
Michael Farlow	200	William Haskell	100
Michack Farlow	200	William Cleaves	100
Molin Brishira	200	John Harris	600
Matthew Perkins	200	John Busnam	600
John Giddings	200	Nathaniel Rust	200
Paul Thorndike	200	Andrew Elliot	100
Isaac Fellows	300		

And the said Proprietors are hereby notified, that if they fail to make such Payment within the Time limited by Law for Payment thereof, so much of their common Land belonging to such delinquent Rights will be sold, as will be necessary for Payment thereof according to an Act of this Province, made in the 26th Year of the Reign of King *George* the Second, intitled 'An Act in Addition to an Act intitled An Act directing how Meetings of Proprietors of Lands lying in common may be called.'

Ipswich, March 26. 1764.

Figure 12-4. From the *Boston Gazette and Country Journal,* 21 May 1764, p. 3.

of American Newspapers, 1690–1820 (cited earlier). The Readex Corporation, of New Canaan, Connecticut, in conjunction with the American Antiquarian Society, has for many years sponsored the Early American Newspapers Project to make available in microform all of the newspapers described by Brigham. The project gathers volumes and issues from various holding libraries to make the files as complete as possible, then microfilms them for distribution to libraries. They were originally issued on a proprietary medium called Microprint (similar to a large microcard), which required special readers and copiers, but they are now available on microfilm. The series, which is continuing, will most often be found in larger research libraries. Also, many of the libraries holding files of pre-1820 newspapers have microfilmed those files and made them available to the larger research community.

SEARCH STRATEGIES

Once a file of the newspaper from the ancestor's time and location has been procured, what information can you find in it?

Just look and see. There really is no better way to learn about old newspapers than to spend some time reading them.

There are two sorts of newspaper research: searching at or around a particular date for obituaries, etc.; and searching issue by issue over a period of time for whatever of interest might turn up. Certainly, when the exact or approximate date of a potentially newsworthy event is known, a search of the likely paper or papers is necessary. However, particularly if the researcher has an entire family or several families active in an area, a search of the papers for that area for several years will almost certainly turn up unique bits of useful information.

An issue-by-issue search does not have to be a hopeless, tedious task. Because a particular newspaper usually follows a fairly standard pattern, the researcher does not have to read every word of every issue. The national and international news, the patent medicine ads, the serialized novel can safely be ignored. Concentrate on the local news and the columns describing who visited whom. When a search rhythm has been established, it is possible to search a year's issues of a small-town weekly or a month of a daily in an hour or two.

When items of interest are found, carefully note them (and photocopy them, if possible), as few researchers are likely to go back to perform this search again. In fact, you should have a good overall view of the family (or families) of interest before tackling a sizable newspaper file; this is a strategy for the difficult problem, not a beginning research approach.

To fully tap their potential, begin at the front page of the first issue available in the time period of your search and proceed issue by issue, page by page, through the entire publication. Obviously, the size of large metropolitan papers makes this approach impossible. In these larger papers, narrow your search to specific dates determined by other sources.

Indexes and Abstracts

Because newspapers are such a voluminous and time-consuming resource, the researcher needs to use whatever shortcuts may be available. Fortunately, a surprising number of newspapers have some indexes available. In addition, many researchers have abstracted items of genealogical interest from newspaper files. Some of these indexes and abstracts have been published and are widely available; others may be available only at a particular repository.

Betty Jarboe, *Obituaries: A Guide to Sources,* 2nd ed. (Boston: G.K. Hall, 1989), is a good state-by-state directory for obituary indexes. Anita Milner, *Newspaper Indexes: A Location and Subject Guide for Researchers,* 3 vols. (Metuchen, N.J.: Scarecrow Press, 1977–82), identifies and locates unpublished indexes and card files. Wherever you are searching, it is worth asking about any available indexes, particularly unpublished ones. They are often not listed (or not easily found) in library catalogs. About half of all current newspaper indexes were begun in the 1970s.

The most commonly used newspaper index in American libraries is the *New York Times Index,* because of the tremendous volume of material it covers and because both the index and the microfilm edition of the paper are available in so many public, college, and university libraries. Coverage of the *New York Times Index* now extends back to 1851 (with variations in coverage). This index covers published articles by subject matter and indexes names as well. Since most metropolitan newspapers report important events at approximately the same time, the *Times* index serves as an index to other newspapers for the same subjects. For example, the *New York Times Index* identifies major battles of the Civil War and includes some casualty lists. Once the date of a particular battle has been identified, you can check other newspapers for similar lists of local men killed or wounded in the same engagement. The index is especially valuable when the casualty lists were issued weeks or even months after the battle was fought.

There is also a separately published *New York Times Obituaries Index* with 390,000 entries covering 1858 to 1968 and a supplement covering 1969 to 1978. Official death lists and casualty lists are not indexed. References for casualty lists may appear in the *New York Times Index* under subject headings such as "Philippine Insurrection, casualty lists . . . ," etc.

The researcher no longer needs to search even the annual volumes of the *New York Times Index* for a particular name of interest. The personal names listed in the *New York Times Index* from 1851 to 1989 have been gathered in the *Personal Name Index to the New York Times Index 1851–1974* and its 1975–1989 supplement. The *Personal Name Index* includes only those names listed in the *New York Times Index,* not every name mentioned in the individual issues of the *New York Times.*

Numerous major-city daily newspapers have been indexed in recent years, in much the same fashion as the *New York Times.* Most of these indexes are of relatively little use to genealogists because they are intended to index major news, not the "minor" items the genealogist most needs to find. Not even the *New York Times Index,* which normally fills several shelves in a library's reference section, includes every name. Of more genealogical utility are those indexes that were created by genealogists (or local historians) or at least were created to index newspaper items of genealogical interest.

The American Antiquarian Society, of Worcester, Massachusetts, pioneered the indexing of many early newspapers. The society indexed marriages and deaths that appeared in the *Columbian Sentinel* of Boston from 1784 to 1840, a major achievement because this newspaper printed marriage and death notices from all over the country and included 80,000 names. Other indexing projects of the society have been a death index to the *Christian Intelligencer* of the Reformed Dutch Church, 1830 to 1871, an index to marriages and deaths in the *New York Weekly Museum,* 1788 to 1817, and an index of obituary notices of the *Boston Transcript,* 1875 to 1930. Copies of these newspaper indexes have been deposited in the Library of Congress, the New York Public Library, and the New England Historic Genealogical Society.

The *Index of Obituaries of Boston Newspapers 1704–1800,* 3 vols. (Boston: G.K. Hall, 1968) abstracts deaths within Boston (1704–1800) and outside of Boston (1704–95). Brent Holcomb, *Marriage and Death Notices From Baptist Newspapers of South Carolina, 1835–1865* (Spartanburg, S.C.: Reprint Co., 1981), has abstracted and indexed the marriages and deaths that were reported in numerous South Carolina newspapers. Kenneth Scott (see the chapter bibliography) has compiled vital records and other genealogical information printed in the *New York Post-Boy* and other eighteenth-century New York and Philadelphia papers.

Most of these indexes are included in Betty Jarboe, *Obituaries: A Guide to Sources* (cited earlier). Many more partial indexes and abstracts have been published in genealogical society newsletters and publications, and can best be approached through the *Periodical Source Index (PERSI)* published by the Allen County Public Library of Fort Wayne, Indiana.

Newspaper indexing projects are popular among the hundreds of genealogical societies across the nation. The Chicago Genealogical Society has published *Index to Vital Records From Chicago Newspapers,* which covers 1833 to 1848 in seven volumes. Many of these indexes are known only to the compilers and those who may be familiar with local library collections. The ambitious and imaginative researcher should make inquiries about the existence of such tools.

From 1896 to 1941, the *Boston Transcript* published a regular column of genealogical queries and answers, containing in those issues a cumulative file of genealogical information of significant value. But what researcher will search forty-five years of a newspaper on the possibility that something might

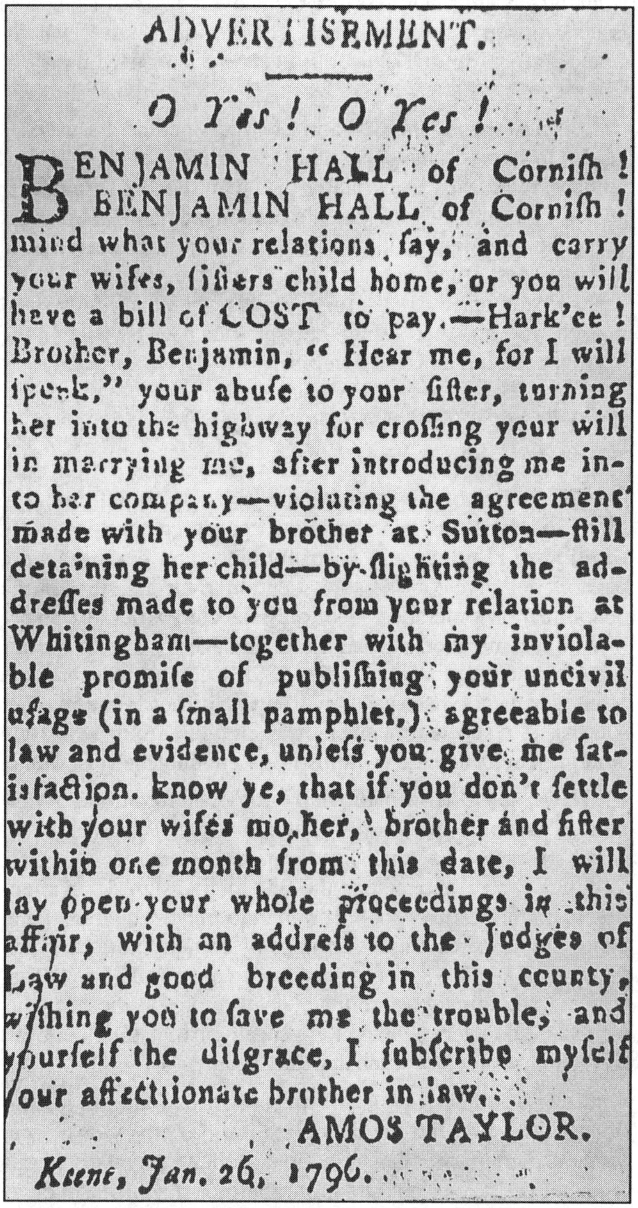
ADVERTISEMENT.

O Yes! O Yes!

BENJAMIN HALL of Cornish! BENJAMIN HALL of Cornish! mind what your relations say, and carry your wifes, sisters child home, or you will have a bill of COST to pay.—Hark'ee! Brother, Benjamin, "Hear me, for I will speak," your abuse to your sister, turning her into the highway for crossing your will in marrying me, after introducing me into her company—violating the agreement made with your brother at Sutton—still detaining her child—by slighting the addresses made to you from your relation at Whitingham—together with my inviolable promise of publishing your uncivil usage (in a small pamphlet,) agreeable to law and evidence, unless you give me satisfaction. know ye, that if you don't settle with your wifes mother, brother and sister within one month from this date, I will lay open your whole proceedings in this affair, with an address to the Judges of Law and good breeding in this county, wishing you to save me the trouble, and yourself the disgrace, I subscribe myself your affectionate brother in law,

AMOS TAYLOR.

Keene, Jan. 26, 1796.

Figure 12-5. Advertisement in the *New Hampshire Gazette,* 26 January 1796.

turn up? Fortunately, the genealogical columns of the *Transcript* have been indexed in the *American Genealogical-Biographical Index,* published by the Godfrey Memorial Library of Middletown, Connecticut. The columns themselves are available on microfiche in many genealogical libraries.

The *Boston Transcript* may have published the best-known genealogical column, but it was by no means the only one. Numerous papers today have genealogical columns, best found through Anita Cheek Milner, *Newspaper Genealogical Column Directory,* 5th ed. (Bowie, Md.: Heritage Books, 1992). Current columns can be useful sources of genealogical news, notes of new publications, and queries devoted to a particular area.

In the 1930s, the Work Projects Administration (WPA) and related programs compiled, among other projects, numerous newspaper indexes. Some were published, and others remain in manuscript form. They are notable because they tended to cover large time spans. The *General Index to Contents of Savannah Georgia Newspapers,* which covers 1763 to 1830, was issued in twenty-seven volumes. The *Virginia Gazette* was indexed from 1736 to 1780. Both indexes are in the Library of Congress.

All newspaper indexes and abstracts should be used as guides to items in the papers, not substitutes for them. Comprehensive indexes are virtually unknown. Few indexes cover gossip columns, advertisements, announcements, passenger lists, and other equally important items. For these, search page by page. A shortcut of sorts is to check the vital records indexes first to narrow down time periods when the family lived in each area, and then search these periods page by page in the local papers, covering all columns.

RELIGIOUS NEWSPAPERS

The general interest newspaper as we know it is not the only possible source of biographical and genealogical information. Many religious denominations have sponsored newspapers. In addition to religious and doctrinal news and features, these papers often give considerable attention to the activities of the denomination's members—not only the clergy, but also many of its other members. If you know an ancestor's religious affiliation, the effort to find copies of the religious newspaper is often worthwhile because they offer details not found in other sources. A respected member of a religious group will often command more attention within that community than elsewhere.

Newspapers can be particularly important for those denominations, such as the various Methodist and Baptist groups, which otherwise have rather poor genealogical records. Also, religious papers were among the first to give significant attention to obituaries. It is not uncommon to find a denominational paper in the 1830s with a full page of obituary notices, when the typical secular paper at best ran two or three brief death notices. Sometimes the obituary dwelt more on the religious history of the deceased than the genealogical history, but even then significant clues often appear (figure 12-6).

Religious newspapers will most often be found in institutions connected with the denomination—archives, historical societies, seminary or denominational college/university libraries—but don't overlook the more traditional sources, such as state historical libraries and archives or the libraries of public colleges and universities with significant newspaper collections. Also, because the distinction between a denominational newspaper and a denominational journal was often a fine one, a search of periodical bibliographies is often necessary. The vagaries of bibliographical description often place what, by format, are clearly newspapers among the periodicals. For example, the various editions of the *Christian Advocate,* an important Methodist newspaper, are listed in the *Union List of Serials,* not in Gregory's *American Newspapers.*

Because religious papers include only a segment of an area's population, they are spread more thinly than secular papers. There may well be only a single newspaper for a particular denomination covering an entire state or region, or for smaller denominations, covering the entire United States. Like secular papers, religious papers have come and gone. A particular state in the 1830s may have been covered only by a distant regional paper; by the 1870s it may have had its own publication.

In one case, I searched all existing daily papers printed in Chicago at the time of my subject's death. Each paper noted his death, age, and last known address. Only a few of the papers provided funeral information. However, the weekly Catholic diocesan newspaper included his town of origin in Europe, the year he emigrated to the United States, the year he arrived in Chicago, the year he became a member of the parish, the date of his marriage, the maiden name of his wife, the names of their children, and those of their children's spouses. The flowery eulogy that one expects to find in a turn-of-the-century publication was also provided, along with the names of the clergy in attendance at the funeral service.

FOREIGN-LANGUAGE NEWSPAPERS

Immigrants arrived in the United States with their own culture, customs, and language. They were all hungry for news from their homelands, where most had left relatives and friends. The foreign-language press opened a natural channel of communication to bridge the Old World and the new environment.

As in religious communities, in foreign communities a person had a better opportunity to be recognized. Where the local English-language newspaper glosses over or carries one-line death notices of persons of foreign birth and tongue, the person often received detailed notice in his or her ethnic newspaper. If you don't read the language, broad searches in a foreign-language paper may not be possible, but an obituary reads like an obituary in virtually any language. If an item can be located, perhaps by recognizing your ancestor's name, it can usually be copied and translated later, either through the word-by-word dictionary method or through the services of someone who does read the language.

Ethnic organizations are still numerous throughout the United States, and most of them publish their own foreign-language newspapers. Large collections can be found in the Immigration History Research Center at the University of Minnesota in St. Paul, the Balch Institute for Ethnic Studies in Philadelphia, and the State Historical Society of Wisconsin. All of these centers seek and preserve immigrant materials for all groups. More specialized collections, concentrating on a particular group, include the Swenson Swedish Immigration Research Center at Augustana College in Rock Island, Illinois, and the Balzekas Museum of Lithuanian Culture in Chicago.

(For more details see chapter 13, Immigration: Finding Immigrant Origins.)

College and university libraries frequently have significant collections of foreign-language newspapers. Some of these are extracted and indexed (see the chapter bibliography). If you have a problem locating your specific immigrant group, a foreign consulate can often provide help. Also consult public libraries and museums for newspaper collections and special, local indexes.

CURRENT NEWSPAPERS

Current newspapers are especially useful in locating unknown relatives. Distant relatives may still be living in old hometowns though the direct ancestor moved away. A well-prepared advertisement, placed in a local paper with sufficient identifying information, will sometimes open the door to assistance from descendants of a common ancestor. It works especially well in smaller communities. Consult Vincent L. Jones, et al., *Family History for Fun and Profit* (Salt Lake City: The Genealogical Institute, 1972) for sample advertisements and how to place them.

Current newspapers at least occasionally feature historical articles about the community and its people, particularly in conjunction with centennials, sesquicentennials, etc., of either the community or the newspaper. These articles may also provide useful leads.

The quality of information found in newspapers varies greatly. Genealogists, like historians, must be cautious. The hurried nature of news-gathering—then, as now—has often led to error. Not everything found in print is to be taken without question. Two accounts will always be better than one. However, newspaper accounts may often be the only available records of a particular event. In general, since the newspaper account was drawn from contemporary sources, we can hope for accuracy and appreciate anew the flavor of the times.

BIBLIOGRAPHY

The following lists of works related to newspapers are extensive but by no means exhaustive. Some of the works cited are only a few pages in a periodical, while other works are comprehensive or multi-volumed. The bibliography includes research aids, identifying and locating specific newspapers with content descriptions and suggestions on use where appropriate, as well as abstracts of newspaper data.

Not every newspaper has survived the ravages of time and neglect, and not all those that have survived (at least to the present) are available for research. Those identified in the various bibliographies are those that have (in most cases) been stored in research institutions. It is entirely possible that the newspaper file you need is still sitting on a shelf (or attic) in a newspaper office, in a shed of the former editor's grandson, or is uncataloged in the basement of a library, museum, or historical society. Original research to track down those elusive resources may be necessary, but check the available bibliographic resources to be sure it is necessary.

As this chapter is concerned with American newspapers, no reference is made to British or non-U.S. foreign newspapers, American newspapers in England and elsewhere, or English-language newspapers elsewhere in the world.

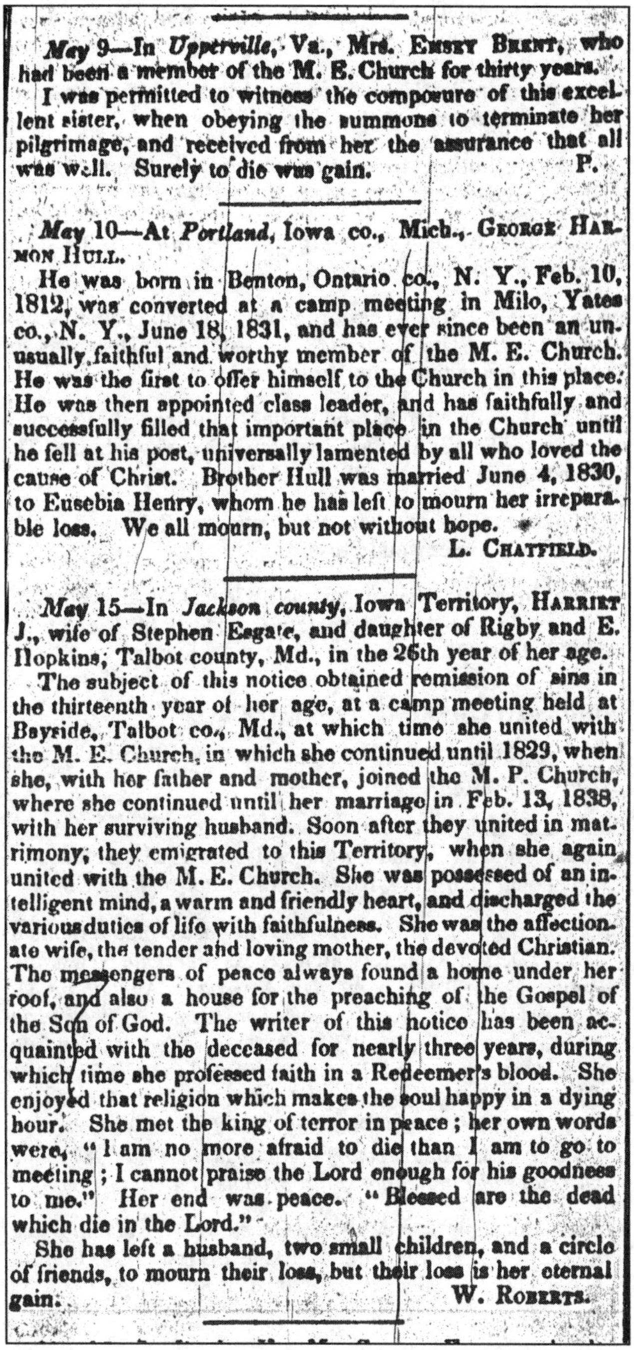

Figure 12-6. Obituaries from the *Christian Advocate and Journal* (New York) of the Methodist Episcopal Church, 6 July 1842, p. 188.

HOW-TOS, ANALYTICAL STUDIES

Clark, Thomas D. "The Country Newspaper as a Source of Social History." *Indiana Magazine of History* 48 (1952): 217–32.

Eakle, Arlene H. *Were Your Ancestors Front-Page News?* Salt Lake City: The Genealogical Institute, 1974.

Golembiewski, Thomas. *The Study of Obituaries as a Source for Polish Genealogical Research.* Chicago: Polish Genealogical Society, 1983.

Hosman, C. Lloyd. *Newspaper Research.* Indianapolis: Heritage House, 1985.

Lantz, Herman R. "Use of the Local Press in Historical Research." *Mid-America* 38 (1956): 172–79.

Mott, Frank Luther. *American Journalism, a History: 1690–1960.* 3rd ed. New York: Macmillan, 1971.

Park, Robert Ezra. *The Immigrant Press and Its Control.* Westport, Conn.: Greenwood, 1970.

Pease, Janet K. "Your Ancestors and How to Find Them: Newspapers." *Tri-State Trader* (28 August 1982). Discusses indexing, abstracting, copying newspapers.

Randall, Barbara Nichols, and Walter Cybulski. "Using Newspapers for Family History Research in New York State." *The Bookmark* 49 (Spring 1991): 164–75.

Schwarzlose, Richard Allen. *Newspapers, a Reference Guide.* New York: Greenwood Press, 1987.

Sniffen, Irene G. "Newspapers as a Genealogical Resource." *National Genealogical Society Quarterly* 68 (September 1980): 179–87.

Guides to Current Newspapers

American Newspaper Directory (annual), 1869–1908. New York: George P. Rowell and Co.

Editor and Publisher. *International Year Book* (annual) 1921–. New York: Editor and Publisher. Issued 1921–1958 as "International Year Book Number" of *Editor and Publisher.*

Gale Directory of Publications and Broadcast Media (annual) 1880–. Detroit: Gale Research Co. As *American Newspaper Annual* (1880–1909); *American Newspaper Annual and Directory* (1910–29); *N. W. Ayer & Sons Directory of Newspapers and Periodicals* (1930–69); *Ayer Directory, Newspapers, Magazines, and Trade Publications* (1970–71); *Ayer Directory of Publications* (1972–82); *IMS . . . Ayer Directory of Publications* (1983–85); *IMS Directory of Publications* (1986); *Gale Directory of Publications* (1987–89); *Gale Directory of Publications and Broadcast Media* (1990–).

Milner, Anita Cheek. *Newspaper Genealogical Column Directory.* 5th ed. Bowie, Md.: Heritage Books, 1992. Preliminary ed. 1975; 1st ed. 1979; 2nd ed. 1985; 3rd ed. 1987; 4th ed. 1989.

Parch, Grace D. *Directory of Newspaper Libraries in the U.S. and Canada.* New York: Special Libraries Association, 1976.

Working Press of the Nation (annual), 1945–. Burlington, Iowa: National Research Bureau.

National Bibliographies

Barnes, Timothy M. "Loyalist Newspapers of the American Revolution, 1763–1783; a Bibliography." *Proceedings of the American Antiquarian Society* 83 (1973): 217–83.

Brigham, Clarence S. *History and Bibliography of American Newspapers, 1690–1820.* 2 vols. Worcester, Mass.: American Antiquarian Society, 1947. Brigham's "Additions and Corrections to History and Bibliography of American Newspapers" appeared in the *Proceedings of the American Antiquarian Society* 72 (1971): 15–62.

Center For Research Libraries. *The Center For Research Libraries Catalogue: Newspapers.* 2nd ed. Chicago: the center, 1978.

Chicago Historical Society. *A Checklist of the Kellogg Collection of "Patent Inside" Newspapers of 1876.* Chicago: Historical Records Survey, 1939.

Gregory, Winifred. *American Newspapers, 1821–1936: A Union List of Files Available in the United States and Canada.* 1937. Reprint. New York: Kraus, 1967. Clarke, Avis G. *An Alphabetical Index to the Titles in American Newspapers. . . .* Oxford, Mass: 1958. Clarke is particularly useful when the title of a paper, but not the place of publication, is known.

Griswold, Ada Tyng. *Annotated Catalogue of Newspaper Files in the Library of the State Historical Society of Wisconsin.* 2nd ed. Madison: State Historical Society of Wisconsin, 1911. *Supplementary Catalogue of Newspaper Files in the Wisconsin Historical Library Listing the Papers Acquired During the Years 1911–1917,* by Lillian J. Beecroft and Marguerite Jenison, was published by the Society in 1918 as its Bulletin of Information No. 93.

Guide to Microforms in Print (annual), 1961–. Munich: K.G. Saur. Cumulative annual catalog of microform titles, including newspapers.

Haskell, Daniel C. *Checklist of Newspapers and Official Gazettes in the New York Public Library.* New York: New York Public Library, 1915. Reprinted from *NYPL Bulletin,* July–December 1914.

Hoornstra, Jean, and Trudy Heath. *American Periodicals, 1741–1900: An Index to the Microfilm Collections—American Periodicals 18th Century, American Periodicals, 1800–1850, American Periodicals, 1850–1900, Civil War and Reconstruction.* Ann Arbor, Mich.: University Microfilms International, 1979.

Kellerman, Lydia Suzanne. *Index to Readex Microopaque Collections of Early American Newspapers.* Harrisburg, Pa.: State Library of Pennsylvania, 1990.

Lathem, Edward Connery. *Chronological Tables of American Newspapers, 1690–1820; Being a Tabular Guide to Holdings of Newspapers Published in America Through the Year 1820.* Worcester, Mass.: American Antiquarian Society, 1972. Companion to Brigham, above.

New York Metropolitan Reference and Research Library Agency. *Union List of Selected Microforms in Libraries in the New York Metropolitan Area.* 3rd ed. New York: the agency, 1980.

Newspapers in the State Historical Society of Wisconsin: A Bibliography With Holdings. New York: Norman Ross Pub., 1993.

Serials and Newspapers in Microform (annual). Ann Arbor, Mich.: University Microfilms International. Annual catalog of microfilmed newspapers available for sale.

Union List of Serials in Libraries of the United States and Canada. 3rd ed. 5 vols. New York: H. W. Wilson, 1965. Although it excludes general-interest newspapers, the *Union List of Serials* does include listings for many religious and special-interest publications that appeared in newspaper format and often contained obituaries and other materials of interest to the genealogical researcher.

U.S. Library of Congress. Catalog Management and Publication Division. *Newspapers in Microform: United States, 1848–1983*. 2 vols. Washington, D.C.: Library of Congress, 1984.

United States Newspaper Program National Union List. 4th ed. Dublin, Ohio: OCLC, 1993. Microfiche.

University of Chicago. *Newspapers in Libraries of Chicago, a Joint Check List*. Chicago: University of Chicago Libraries, Document Section, 1936.

RELIGIOUS NEWSPAPERS

Allbaugh, Gaylord P. *History and Annotated Bibliography of American Religious Periodicals and Newspapers Established From 1730 Through 1830*. 2 vols. Worcester, Mass.: American Antiquarian Society, 1994.

Ames, Charlotte. *Directory of Roman Catholic Newspapers on Microfilm—United States*. Notre Dame, Ind.: Memorial Library, University of Notre Dame, 1982.

Batsel, John D., and Lyda K. Batsel. *Union List of United Methodist Serials, 1773–1973*. Evanston, Ill.: Garrett Theological Seminary, 1974. Prepared in cooperation with the Commission on Archives and History of the United Methodist Church, United Methodist Librarians' Fellowship and Garrett Theological Seminary.

Flake, Chad S. *A Mormon Bibliography, 1830–1930*. Salt Lake City: University of Utah Press, 1978. *Ten Year Supplement*. Salt Lake City: University of Utah Press, 1989. *Indexes to A Mormon Bibliography and Ten Year Supplement*. Salt Lake City: University of Utah Press, 1992.

Microfilm Catalog of Baptist Historical Materials. Nashville: Historical Commission, Southern Baptist Convention, 1984. Supplement published in 1989.

Hebrew Union College—Jewish Institute of Religion. American Jewish Periodical Center. *Jewish Newspapers and Periodicals on Microfilm, Available at the American Jewish Periodical Center*. Cincinnati: the center, 1984.

Norton, Wesley. *Religious Newspapers in the Old Northwest to 1861: A History, Bibliography, and Record of Opinion*. Athens, Ohio: Ohio University Press, 1977.

Spencer, Claude E. *Periodicals of the Disciples of Christ and Related Religious Groups*. Canton, Mo.: Disciples of Christ Historical Society, 1943.

Stroupe, Henry S. *The Religious Press in the South Atlantic States, 1802–1865*. Durham, N. C.: Duke University Press, 1956.

Willging, Eugene P., and Herta Hatzfeld. *Catholic Serials of the 19th Century in the United States; a Descriptive Bibliography and Union List*. 1st series, 2 vols. 2nd series, 15 vols. Washington, D.C.: Catholic University of America Press, 1959–68. The 1st series, which covered those states with a smaller publication history, first appeared in the *Records of the American Catholic Historical Society of Philadelphia*, September 1954–December 1963.

ETHNIC NEWSPAPERS

Arndt, Karl J. R., and Mary E. Olson. *The German Language Press of the Americas*. 3rd rev. ed. 3 vols. Munich: K. G. Saur, 1976–1980.

Balys, Jonas. *Lithuanian Periodicals in American Libraries: A Union List*. Washington: Library of Congress, 1982.

Campbell, Georgetta Merritt. *Extant Collections of Early Black Newspapers: A Research Guide to the Black Press, 1880–1915, With an Index to the* Boston Guardian, *1902–1904*. Troy, N.Y.: Whitston Publishing Co., 1981.

Danky, James P., ed. *Native American Periodicals and Newspapers, 1828–1982; Bibliography, Publishing Record, and Holdings*. Westport, Conn.: Greenwood Press, 1984.

Edelman, Hendrik. *The Dutch Language Press in America*. Nieuwkoop: De Graaf Publishers, 1986.

Ethnic Serials at Selected University of California Libraries: A Union List. Los Angeles: University of California, 1977. A useful source for Asian-American, Hispanic, and African American publications.

Grose, Charles William. *Black Newspapers in Texas, 1868–1970*. Thesis. University of Texas at Austin, 1972.

Henritze, Barbara K. *Bibliographic Checklist of African American Newspapers*. Baltimore: Genealogical Publishing Co., 1995.

Hoerder, Dirk. *The Immigrant Labor Press in North America, 1840s–1970s; an Annotated Bibliography*. New York: Greenwood Press, 1987. Vol. 1: migrants from northern Europe; vol. 2: migrants from eastern and southeastern Europe; vol. 3: migrants from southern and western Europe.

Hoglund, A. William. *Union List of Finnish Newspapers Published by Finns in the United States and Canada, 1876–1985*. Minneapolis: Finnish-American Newspapers Microfilm Project, 1985.

Hovde, Oivind M., and Martha E. Henzler. *Norwegian American Newspapers in Luther College Library*. Decorah, Iowa: Luther College Press, 1975.

Kestercanek, Nada. *Croatian Newspapers and Calendars in the United States*. Scranton, Pa.: Marywood College, 1952. Reprint. San Francisco: R. & E. Research Associates, 1971.

Marzolf, Marion. *The Danish-Language Press in America*. New York: Arno Press, 1979.

Saar, Amanda. *Black Arkansas Newspapers, 1869–1975: A Checklist*. Fayetteville, Ark.: David W. Mullins Library, University of Arkansas, 1976.

Setterdahl, Lilly. *Swedish American Newspapers: A Guide to the Microfilms Held By the Swenson Swedish Immigration Research Center, Augustana College, Rock Island, Illinois*. Rock Island: Augustana College Library, 1981.

University of Minnesota. Immigration History Research Center. *The Newspaper and Serial Holdings of the Immigration History Research Center, University of Minnesota*. St. Paul: the center, 1984–. Part 1: Ukrainian American periodicals; part 2: Italian-American periodicals; part 3: Finnish-American periodicals, Baltic-American periodicals, West Slavic-American periodicals, East Slavic-American periodicals.

Wepsiec, Jan. *Polish American Serial Publications, 1842–1966; An Annotated Bibliography.* Chicago: 1968.

Wynar, Lubomyr R., and Anna T. Wynar. *Encyclopedic Directory of Ethnic Newspapers and Periodicals in the United States.* 2nd ed. Littleton, Colo.: Libraries Unlimited, 1976. Lists "current" publications.

Zeps, Valdis J. *Lettica in Microform; a Subject Guide.* Madison, Wis.: Association for the Advancement of Baltic Studies, 1982.

SPECIALTY NEWSPAPERS

Dornbusch, Charles E. *Stars and Stripes: Check List of the Several Editions.* New York: New York Public Library, 1948. "Reprinted From the Bulletin of the New York Public Library of July 1948." Supplement, New York: New York Public Library, 1949. "Reprinted From the *Bulletin* of the New York Public Library of July 1949."

Labor Papers on Microfilm: A Combined List. Madison: State Historical Society of Wisconsin, 1965.

Lutz, Earle. "Soldier Newspapers of the Civil War." *Papers of the Bibliographical Society of America* 46 (1952): 373–86.

Rudeen, Marlys. *The Civilian Conservation Corps Camp Papers: A Guide.* Chicago: Center for Research Libraries, 1991.

The Walter S. and Esther Dougherty Collection of Military Newspapers: A Guide to the Microfilm Edition. Ann Arbor, Mich.: University Microforms International, 1993.

NEWSPAPER SOURCES BY STATE

Alabama

Alabama State Department of History and Archives. *Checklist of Newspapers and Periodical Files in the Department of Archives and History.* Montgomery: Brown Printing Co., 1904.

Alabama. University. Library. *Alabama Newspapers in the University of Alabama Library.* University, Ala.: the library, 1951.

Ellison, Rhoda C. *History and Bibliography of Alabama Newspapers in the 19th Century.* Birmingham: University of Alabama Press, 1954.

Owen, Thomas M. "Alabama Newspapers and Periodicals." In *Alabama Official and Statistical Register.* 1915. Reprint. Sheffield, Ala.: Jump Fast Copy Service, 1991.

Alaska

Davis, Phyllis. *A Guide to Alaska's Newspapers.* Compiled for the Alaska Division of State Libraries and Museums. Juneau: Gastineau Channel Centennial Association, 1976.

Arizona

Arizona Newspapers on Microfilm. Phoenix: Department of Library, Archives and Public Records, 1989.

Lutrell, Estelle. "Newspapers and Periodicals of Arizona, 1859–1911." *University of Arizona Bulletin* 20 (3) (July 1949) [*General Bulletin* No. 15].

Arkansas

Arkansas Union List of Newspapers. Fayetteville: University of Arkansas Libraries, 1993.

Historical Records Survey. *Union List of Arkansas Newspapers, 1942. A Partial Inventory of Arkansas Newspaper Files Available in the Offices of Publishers, Libraries, and Private Collections.* Little Rock, Ark.: Historical Records Survey, 1942.

Hudson, John A., and Robert L. Peterson. "Arkansas Newspapers in the University of Texas Newspaper Collection." *Arkansas Historical Quarterly* 14 (1955): 207–24.

California

Budenz, Justine, Paul Jordan Smith, and J. H. Young. *Early Newspapers and Periodicals of California and the West.* San Francisco: Warren R. Howell, 1970.

Dawson, Muir. *History and Bibliography of Southern California Newspapers, 1851–1876.* Los Angeles: Dawson's Bookshop, 1950.

Leach, Marianne. *Newspaper Holdings of the California State Library.* Sacramento: California State Library Foundation, 1986.

Union List of Newspapers in the Libraries of San Diego and Imperial Counties. 3rd ed. San Diego: Serra Cooperative Library System, 1990.

Union List of Newspapers in Microforms in the California State University and College Libraries. 2nd ed. Fullerton: California State University, Fullerton, 1975.

Colorado

Oehlerts, Donald E. *Guide to Colorado Newspapers, 1859–1963.* Denver: Rocky Mountain Bibliographic Center, 1964.

Rex, Wallace H. *Colorado Newspaper Bibliography, 1859–1933.* Denver: Bibliographical Center for Research, Rocky Mountain Region, 1939.

Connecticut

Gustafson, Don. *A Preliminary Checklist of Connecticut Newspapers, 1755–1975.* 2 vols. Hartford, Conn.: Connecticut State Library, 1978.

Delaware

Union List of Newspapers in Delaware. Newark, Del.: Delaware Newspaper Project, University of Delaware Library, 1990.

District of Columbia

Millington, Yale O. "A List of Newspapers Published in the District of Columbia, 1820–1850." *Papers of the Bibliographical Society of America* 19 (1925): 43–65.

Florida

Emig, Elmer J. "A Check-List of Extant Florida Newspapers, 1845–1846." *Florida Historical Society Quarterly* 11 (1932): 77–87.

Florida Newspapers, 1885–1898. Jacksonville, Fla.: Historical Records Survey, 1937.

Knauss, James O. "List of Florida Newspapers Published Before July 1845." In *Territorial Florida Journalism,* 86–128. Deland, Fla.: 1926.

Georgia

Flanders, Ralph B. "Newspapers and Periodicals in the Washington Memorial Library, Macon, Georgia." *North Carolina Historical Review* 7 (1930): 220–23.

Georgia Newspapers on Microfilm at the UGA Libraries. Athens: University of Georgia Libraries, 1977.

Hawaii

Hawaii. State Archives. *Hawaii Newspapers and Periodicals on Microfilm: A Union List of Holdings in Libraries of Honolulu.* Honolulu: Hawaiiana Section, Hawaii Library Association, 1977.

Hawaii Newspaper Project. *Hawaii Newspapers: A Union List.* Dublin, Ohio: OCLC, Inc., 1987.

Mookini, Esther K. *The Hawaiian Newspapers.* Honolulu: Topgallant Pub. Co., 1974.

Idaho

University of Idaho Newspaper Holdings as of July 1, 1975. Moscow: University of Idaho Library, 1975.

Illinois

Bibliography of Foreign Language Newspapers and Periodicals Published in Chicago. Chicago Public Library Omnibus Project, 1942.

James, Edmund J. *A Bibliography of Newspapers Published in Illinois Prior to 1860.* Illinois State Historical Society Publications, no. 1. Springfield, Ill.: Phillips Bros., 1899. Appendix A: Chronological List of Missouri and Illinois Newspapers 1808–1897, in the Saint Louis Mercantile Library. Appendix B: List of County Histories of Illinois.

Mabbott, Thomas O., and Philip D. Jordan. *A Catalog of Illinois Newspapers in the New York Historical Society.* Springfield: Journal Printing Co., 1931. Reprinted from *Illinois State Historical Society Journal* 24 (1931): 187–242.

Newspapers in the Historical Library. Illinois State Library, Special Report Series, vol. 1, issue 1. Springfield: Illinois State Library, 1994.

Pease, Margaret J. *Checklist of Newspapers in the Illinois Historical Survey.* Urbana: Illinois Historical Survey, 1953.

Scott, Franklin W. *Newspapers and Periodicals of Illinois, 1814–1879.* Collections of the ISHS Library, vol. 6. Rev. and enl. Springfield: Trustees of the Illinois State Historical Society, 1910.

University of Chicago. *Newspapers in the Libraries of Chicago.* Chicago: University of Chicago Library, 1936.

Wrone, D. R. "Newspapers of DeWitt County, Illinois, 1854–1960; a Bibliography and Checklist." *Illinois Libraries* 46 (May 1964): 367–92.

Indiana

Miller, John W. *Indiana Newspaper Bibliography: Historical Accounts of All Indiana Newspapers Published From 1804–1980 and Locational Information for All Available Copies, Both Original and Microfilm.* Indianapolis: Indiana Historical Society, 1982.

Iowa

Cheever, L.O. *Newspaper Collection of the State Historical Society of Iowa.* Iowa City: State Historical Society of Iowa, 1969.

Iowa Pilot Project of the Organization of American Historians. The Library of Congress, United States Newspaper Project. *A Bibliography of Iowa Newspapers, 1836–1976.* Iowa City: Iowa State Historical Department, 1979.

Iowa Union List of Newspapers. Dublin, Ohio: OCLC, 1994.

Pittman, Edward F. *Index to Bound Newspapers in Iowa State Department of History and Archives.* Des Moines: State of Iowa, 1947.

Kansas

Anderson, Aileen. *Kansas Newspapers: A Directory of Newspaper Holdings in Kansas.* Topeka: Kansas Library Network Board, 1984.

Haury, David A. *Guide to the Microfilm Collection of the Kansas State Historical Society.* Topeka: Kansas State Historical Society, 1991. Supplement, 1993–.

Kentucky

Evans, Herndon J. *The Newspaper Press in Kentucky.* Lexington: University of Kentucky, 1975.

Henry, Edward A. "The Durrett Collection [of Kentucky Newspapers] Now in the University of Chicago." *Papers of the Bibliographical Society of America* 8 (1914): 57–94.

Jillson, Willard R. *Newspapers and Periodicals of Frankfort, Kentucky, 1795–1945.* Lexington: Kentucky State Historical Society, 1945.

Kinkead, Ludie, and T. D. Clark. *Checklist of Kentucky Newspapers Contained in Kentucky Libraries.* Lexington, 1935.

Rawlings, Kenneth W. "Trial List of Titles of Kentucky Newspapers and Periodicals Before 1860." *Kentucky Historical Society Register* 36 (1938): 263–87.

Louisiana

Historical Records Survey. *Louisiana Newspapers, 1794–1940. List of Louisiana Newspaper Files in Offices of Publishers, Libraries, and Private Collections in Louisiana.* Baton Rouge: Louisiana State Library, 1941.

Louisiana Newspaper Project Printout, April 1990. Baton Rouge: Louisiana Newspaper Project, LSU Libraries, 1990.

McMullen, T.N., ed. *Louisiana Newspapers, 1794–1969; a Union List of Louisiana Newspaper Files Available in Public, College, and University Libraries in Louisiana.* Baton Rouge: Louisiana State University and Agricultural and Mechanical Library, 1965.

McMurtrie, Douglas C. *Early Printing in New Orleans, 1774–1810, With a Bibliography of the Issues of the Louisiana Press.* New Orleans: Searcy & Pfaff, 1929.

———. "The French Press of Louisiana. Notes in Supplement for Edward Laroque Tinker's Bibliography of French Newspapers and Periodicals of Louisiana." *Louisiana Historical Quarterly* 18 (1935): 947–65.

Tinker, Edward L. "Bibliography of French Newspapers and Periodicals of Louisiana." *Proceedings of the American Antiquarian Society* 26 (October 1932): 247–370.

Maryland

Hofstetter, E. O., and Marcella S. Eustis. *Newspapers in Maryland Libraries: A Union List*. Baltimore: State Department of Education, Division of Library Services, 1977.

Keidel, George C. "Early Maryland Newspapers: a List of Titles." *Maryland Historical Magazine* 28 (1933); 29 (1934); 30 (1935).

Maryland Newspaper Project. *A Guide to Newspapers and Newspaper Holdings in Maryland*. Baltimore: Maryland State Department of Education, Division of Library Development and Services, 1991.

White, Les, et al. *Newspapers of Maryland: A Guide to the Microfilm Collection of Newspapers at the Maryland State Archives*. Annapolis: Maryland State Archives, 1990.

Massachusetts

Ayer, Mary Farwell. *Check-list of Boston Newspapers, 1704–1780*. Boston: Colonial Society of Massachusetts, 1907.

Boston Public Library. *A List of Periodicals, Newspapers in Principal Libraries of Boston and Vicinity*. Boston: Trustees of the Library, 1897.

Michigan

Brown, Elizabeth Read. *A Union List of Newspapers Published in Michigan Based on the Principal Newspaper Collections in the State With Notes Concerning Papers Not Located*. Ann Arbor: University of Michigan, Department of Library Science, 1954.

Hathaway, Richard. *Ethnic Newspapers and Periodicals in Michigan: A Checklist*. Ann Arbor: Michigan Archival Association, 1978.

Leasher, Mary. *Newspapers on Microfilm; Holdings of the Clarke Historical Library, September 1987*. Mt. Pleasant: Clarke Historical Library, 1987.

McMurtrie, Douglas C. "Newspaper Record of Michigan Newspapers, 1796–1850." In *Early Printing in Michigan, With a Bibliography of the Michigan Press*, 227–320. Chicago: John Calhoun Club, 1931.

Michigan State Library. *Michigan Newspapers, Preliminary Bibliography, a Partial List of Michigan Newspapers Based Upon a Survey of Public Libraries and Newspaper Offices in the State of Michigan*. Lansing: State Department of Education, 1966.

Michigan Newspapers on Microfilm. 7th ed. Lansing: Michigan State Board of Education, State Library Service, 1985.

Sullivan, H. A., and T. Friedes. *Newspaper Resources of Metropolitan Detroit Libraries*. Detroit: Wayne State University Press, 1965.

Minnesota

Hage, George S. *Newspapers on the Minnesota Frontier, 1849–1860*. St. Paul: Minnesota Historical Society, 1967.

South-Central Minnesota Inter-Library Exchange (SMILE). *Newspapers in the Region Nine Area: A Listing of All Newspapers Published in Blue Earth, Brown, Faribault, LeSueur, Martin, Nicollet, Sibley, Waseca, and Watonwan Counties*. Mankato, Minn.: SMILE, 1976.

University of Minnesota Library, Newspaper and Microform Division. *Newspapers in the University of Minnesota Library: A Complete List of Holdings*. Minneapolis: University of Minnesota Press, 1964.

Mississippi

Historical Records Survey. *Mississippi Newspapers, 1805–1904*. Jackson, Miss.: Works Progress Administration, 1942.

Mitchell Memorial Library, Mississippi State University. *Union List of Newspapers*. Mississippiana, vol. 2. Jackson: Mississippi Library Commission, 1971.

Missouri

Newspapers in Missouri, a Union List, 1994. 3 vols. Kansas City, Mo.: University Libraries, University of Missouri-Kansas City, 1994.

Organ, Minnie. "Old Newspaper Files in the State Historical Society at Columbia." *Missouri Historical Review* 5 (1910–11): 34–42.

St. Louis Mercantile Association. *Missouri and Illinois Newspapers, 1808–1897*. St. Louis: the association, 1897.

Taft, William H. *Missouri Newspapers, When and Where, 1803–1963*. Columbia: State Historical Society of Missouri, 1964.

Montana

Montana Historical Society Newspaper Project. *A Union List of Montana Newspapers in Montana Repositories*. Dublin, Ohio: OCLC, Inc., 1986.

Nebraska

Diffendal, Anne P. *A Guide to the Newspaper Collection of the State Archives, Nebraska State Historical Society*. Rev. ed. Lincoln: Nebraska State Historical Society, 1977.

Nevada

Folkes, John Gregg. *Nevada's Newspapers: A Bibliography . . . 1854–1964*. Reno: University of Nevada Press, 1964.

Lingenfelter, Richard E., and Karen R. Gash. *The Newspapers of Nevada: A History and Bibliography, 1854–1979*. Reno: University of Nevada Press, 1984.

New Jersey

Wright, William C., and Paul A. Stellhorn. *Directory of New Jersey Newspapers, 1765–1970*. Trenton: New Jersey Historical Commission, 1977.

New Mexico

Gonzales, Joanne, and Anita Lopez. *New Mexico State Library Newspaper Holdings, 1983*. Santa Fe: New Mexico State Library, 1983.

Grove, Pearce S., et al. *New Mexico Newspapers; a Comprehensive Guide to Bibliographical Entries and Locations*. Albuquerque: University of New Mexico Press, 1975.

Stratton, Porter A. *The Territorial Press of New Mexico, 1834–1912*. Albuquerque: University of New Mexico Press, 1969.

New York

A Bibliography of Newspapers in Two New York State Counties. 2 vols. Fredonia: State University of New York, College at Fredonia, 1975 (?). Installment 1 (Chautauqua Co.); installment 2 (Cattaraugus Co.).

Chautauqua County Historical Society. *A Guide to Newspapers in Microform in Chautauqua County, New York.* Westfield, N.Y.: the society, 1982. Part 1, Guide; part 2, Microfilm Index.

Faibisoff, Sylvia G. *Bibliography of Newspapers in Fourteen New York Counties.* Cooperstown: South Central Research Library Council, New York State Library Association, 1978. Covers Allegany, Broome, Cayuga, Chemung, Chenango, Cortland, Delaware, Otsego, Schuyler, Seneca, Steuben, Tioga, Tompkins, and Yates counties.

Fox, Louis H. "New York City Newspapers, 1820–1850; a Bibliography." *Papers of the Bibliographical Society of America* 21 (1927): 1–131.

Mercer, Paul. *Bibliographies and Lists of New York State Newspapers: An Annotated Guide.* Albany: New York State Library, 1981.

New York State Library. *A Checklist of Newspapers in Microform in the New York State Library, the University of the State of New York, State Education Department.* Albany: New York State Library, 1979.

Newspapers on Microfilm: A Listing of Newspapers on Microfilm in Allegheny, Chemung, Schuyler, Steuben, and Yates Counties. Corning, N.Y.: Southern Tier Library System, 1981.

Rochester Public Library. *Union List of Serials in the Libraries of Rochester, Including Periodicals, Newspapers, Annuals, Publications of Societies, and Other Books Published at Intervals.* Rochester: Rochester Public Library, 1917.

Severance, Frank H. "Contributions Towards a Bibliography of Buffalo and the Niagara Region. The Periodical Press of Buffalo, 1811–1915." *Publications of the Buffalo Historical Society,* 19 (1915): 177–312.

Shultes, Dorothea. *Newspapers on Microfilm in Syracuse University Libraries.* Syracuse, N.Y.: Syracuse University Press, 1971.

North Carolina

Jones, H. G., and Julius H. Avant. *Union List of North Carolina Newspapers, 1751–1900.* Raleigh: State Department of Archives and History, 1963.

Jones, Roger C. *Guide to North Carolina Newspapers on Microfilm: North Carolina Newspapers Available on Microfilm From the Division of Archives and History.* 6th rev. ed. Raleigh: North Carolina Division of Archives and History, 1984.

North Dakota

Kolar, Carol K. *Union List of North Dakota Newspapers, 1864–1976.* Fargo: North Dakota Institute for Regional Studies, 1981.

Ohio

Galbreath, C. B. *Newspapers and Periodicals in Ohio State Library, Other Libraries of the State, and Lists of Ohio Newspapers in the Library of Congress, and the Library of the State Historical Society of Wisconsin.* Columbus: Fred J. Heer, 1902.

Gutgesell, Stephen. *Guide to Ohio Newspapers, 1793–1973: Union Bibliography of Ohio Newspapers Available in Ohio Libraries.* Columbus: Ohio Historical Society, 1976.

Levinson, Marilyn. *Guide to Newspaper Holdings at the Center for Archival Collections.* 3rd ed. Bowling Green, Ohio: Center for Archival Collections, Bowling Green University, 1991.

Ohio Newspaper Catalog: 1991 Microfiche Edition. Columbus: Ohio Historical Society, 1991. 5 microfiche.

Oklahoma

Foreman, Carolyn T. *Oklahoma Imprints, 1835–1907; a History of Printing in Oklahoma Before Statehood.* Norman, Okla.: University of Oklahoma Press, 1936.

Ray, Grace E. *Early Oklahoma Newspapers: History and Description of Publications From Earliest Beginnings to 1889.* University of Oklahoma Bulletin, new series, No. 407, Studies No. 28. Norman: University of Oklahoma Press, 1928.

Stewart, John, and Kenny Franks. *State Records, Manuscripts, and Newspapers at the Oklahoma State Archives and Oklahoma Historical Society.* Oklahoma City: Oklahoma Historical Society, 1975.

Oregon

Oregon Newspapers—Holdings of: Library Association of Portland, Oregon Historical Society Library, Oregon State Library, University of Oregon Library. Salem: Oregon State Library, 1963.

Turnball, G. S. *History of Oregon Newspapers.* Portland: Binsfords, 1939.

University of Oregon. Library. *Oregon Newspapers on Microfilm.* Portland: Genealogical Council of Oregon, 1991.

Pennsylvania

Columbia County Historical Society. *A Checklist of Newspapers Available in and for the Counties of Columbia, Luzerne, Lycoming, Montour, Northumberland, Schuylkill and Sullivan, Pennsylvania.* Bloomburg, Pa.: Bloomburg State College, 1972.

Nolan, James B. *Newspapers of Berks County, Pennsylvania, 1789–1900.* Reading: Historical Society of Berks County, 1951.

Pennsylvania Historical Survey. *A Checklist of Pennsylvania Newspapers.* Harrisburg: Pennsylvania Historical Commission, 1944. Vol. 1 (all published), Philadelphia County.

Newspapers on Microform, Pattee Library, Pennsylvania State University. New ed. University Park: Pennsylvania State University Library, 1978.

Pennsylvania Newspapers and Selected Out-of-State Newspapers. Harrisburg: State Library of Pennsylvania, 1976.

Rossell, Glenora E. *Pennsylvania Newspapers: A Bibliography and Union List.* 2nd ed. Pittsburgh: Pennsylvania Library Association, 1978.

Rhode Island

Chudacoff, Nancy F. *Providence Newspapers on Microfilm, 1762 to the Present; a Bibliography and Subject Guide.* Providence, R.I.: 1974.

South Carolina

Moore, John Hammond. *South Carolina Newspapers.* Columbia: University of South Carolina Press, 1988.

South Dakota

Checklist of South Dakota Newspapers in the South Dakota Historical Society and the Historical Resource Center at Pierre. Pierre, S.D.: South Dakota Historical Society, 1976.

"Newspapers of South Dakota." *South Dakota Historical Society.* Historical Collections 11 (1922): 411–518.

Tennessee

John Willard Brister Library. *Newspapers on Microforms.* Memphis: Memphis State University, 1975.

Tennessee State Library and Archives. State Library Division. *Tennessee Newspapers: A Cumulative List of Microfilmed Tennessee Newspapers in the Tennessee State Library.* Nashville: Tennessee State Library, 1978.

Texas

HARLiC Union List of Newspapers. Houston: Houston Area Research Library Consortium, 1992.

Historical Records Survey. *A Union List of Texas Newspapers, 1831–1939.* San Jacinto, Tex.: Museum of History Association, 1941.

Jackson, Lynnell. *True Witnesses: A Check List of Newspapers, 1845–1861.* Austin: Department of Journalism Development Program, University of Texas, 1966.

Murphy, Virginia B. *Newspaper Resources of District V, Texas Library Association: A Union List.* Houston: University of Houston Library, 1968.

_____. *Newspaper Resources of Southeast Texas.* Houston: University of Houston Libraries, 1971.

Sibley, Maralyn McAdams. *Lone Stars and State Gazettes: Texas Newspapers Before the Civil War.* College Station, Tex.: Texas A & M University Press, 1983.

Texas State Library, Austin, Information Services Division. *Newspapers on Microfilm.* Austin: Public Services Department, 1978.

Wallace, John Melton. *Gaceta to Gazette: A Check List of Texas Newspapers, 1813–1846.* Austin, Tex.: Department of Journalism Development Program, University of Texas, 1966.

Wittenmyer, M. O. *Union List of Newspapers on the Libraries of Fort Worth-Dallas Major Resource Centers.* Fort Worth: Texas Christian University Library, 1969.

Utah

Thatcher, Linda. *Guide to Newspapers Located in the Utah State Historical Society Library.* Salt Lake City: Utah State Historical Society, 1985.

Vermont

Forbes, Charles S. "History of Vermont Newspapers." *The Vermonter,* August 1905.

Virgin Islands

Gregg, Kathleen. *Virgin Island Newspapers, 1770–1983.* Charlotte Amalie, St. Thomas, U.S.V.I.: Department of Conservation and Cultural Affairs, 1984.

Virginia

Cappon, Lester J. *Virginia Newspapers, 1821–1935: A Bibliography With Historical Introduction and Notes.* New York: Appleton-Century, 1936.

Minor, Kate P., and Susie B. Harrison. *A List of Newspapers in the Virginia State Library, Confederate Museum, and Valentine Museum.* Richmond: Virginia State Library Bulletin 5 (1912): 285–425.

"Virginia Newspapers in Public Libraries: Annotated List of Virginia Newspapers in the Library of Congress." *Virginia Magazine of History and Biography* 8 (1900–01); 9 (1901–02); 10 (1902–03).

Washington

Hamilton, Katryn S. *Newspapers on Microfilm in the Washington State Library.* Olympia: Washington State Library, 1980.

"Newspapers of Washington Territory to 1890." *Washington Historical Quarterly* 13 (1922): 181–195, 251–268; 14 (1923): 21–29, 100–07, 186–200, 269–90; 26 (1935): 34–64, 129–43.

Palmer, Gayle L. *Washington State Union List of Newspapers on Microfilm.* Olympia: Washington State Library, 1991.

West Virginia

Norona, Delf, and Charles Shetler. *West Virginia Imprints, 1790–1863. A Checklist of Books, Newspapers, Periodicals, and Broadsides.* Moundville: West Virginia Library Association, 1958.

Mertins, Barbara. *Newspapers in the West Virginia University Library.* Morgantown: West Virginia University Library, 1973.

West Virginia Newspapers: A Union List by Place of Publication. Dublin, Ohio: OCLC, Inc., 1987.

Wisconsin

Hansen, James L. *Wisconsin Newspapers, 1833–1850: An Analytical Bibliography.* Madison: State Historical Society of Wisconsin, 1979.

Oehlerts, Donald E. *Guide to Wisconsin Newspapers, 1833–1957.* Madison: State Historical Society of Wisconsin, 1958.

Wyoming

Homsher, Lola. *Guide to Wyoming Newspapers, 1867–1967.* Cheyenne: Wyoming State Library, 1971.

Keen, Elizabeth. "Guide to Wyoming Frontier Newspapers." *Annals of Wyoming* 33 (1961): 135–68; 34 (1962): 218–133; 35 (1963): 88–101.

GUIDES TO INDEXES AND ABSTRACTS

Brayer, Herbert O. "Preliminary Guide to Indexed Newspapers in the United States, 1850–1900." *Mississippi Valley Historical Review* 33 (1946): 237–58.

Jarboe, Betty M. *Obituaries: A Guide to Sources.* 2nd ed. Boston: G.K. Hall, 1989.

Milner, Anita Cheek. *Newspaper Indexes: A Location and Subject Guide for Researchers.* 3 vols. Metuchen, N.J.: Scarecrow Press, 1977–82. Includes unpublished indexes and card indexes.

Morse, Grant W. *Guide to the Incomparable New York Times Index.* New York: Fleet Academic Editions, 1980.

New England Library Association. Bibliography Committee. *A Guide to Newspaper Indexes in New England*. Holden, Mass.: New England Library Association, 1978.

Periodical Source Index (PERSI). 16 vols. Fort Wayne, Ind.: Allen County Public Library, 1986–. Sixteen volumes covering 1847–1985 and annual supplements.

Sell, Kenneth D. "Checklist of Published Indexes to Current American Daily Newspapers." *RQ* 17 (1977): 13–16.

GENERAL INDEXES AND ABSTRACTS

Abajian, James. *Blacks in Selected Newspapers, Censuses and Other Sources: An Index to Names and Subjects*. 3 vols. Boston: G. K. Hall, 1977.

Anastas, Walter, and Maria Woroby. *A Select Index to "Svoboda," Official Publication of the Ukrainian National Association, Inc., a Fraternal Association*. St. Paul, Minn.: Immigration History Research Center, University of Minnesota, 1990–. Vol. 1: 1893–99; vol. 2: 1900–07.

Falk, Byron A., and Valerie R. Falk. *Personal Name Index to "The New York Times Index" 1851–1974*. 22 vols. Succasunna, N.J.: Roxbury Data Interface, 1976–1983. 1975–1989 Supplement. 5 vols. Verdi, Nev.: Roxbury Data Interface, 1990–1991. Single alphabetical index to millions of personal names buried in the *New York Times* indexes. Poor coverage of ca. 1905-to-1912 period because of weakness of original indexes. An excellent source for identifying an individual's "fifteen minutes of fame."

Haller, Dolores, and Marilyn Robinson. *Gleanings From the* Christian Advocate and Journal *and* Zion's Herald, *September 1827–August 1831*. Bowie, Md.: Heritage Books, 1987.

Hayward, Elizabeth. *American Vital Records From the* Baptist Register, *1824–1829, and the* New York Baptist Register, *1829–1834*. Mt. Airy, Md.: Pipe Creek Pubs., 1991.

Holloway, Lizabeth M., et al. *Medical Obituaries: American Physicians' Biographical Notices in Selected Medical Journals Before 1907*. New York: Garland Publishing Co., 1981.

Index of Obituaries of Boston Newspapers 1704–1800. 3 vols. Boston: G.K. Hall, 1968.

Manning, Barbara. *Genealogical Abstracts From Newspapers of the German Reformed Church, 1830–1839*. Bowie, Md.: Heritage Books, 1992.

Martin, George A. *Marriage and Death Notices From the* National Intelligencer, *Washington, D.C., 1800–1850*. Washington, D.C.: National Genealogical Society, 1976. 3 reels of microfilm.

New York Times. *Index*. 1851–present. Published annually since 1913. 1851–1912 covered by indexes originally printed for use by *New York Times* staff, as well as newly prepared indexes.

New York Times Obituaries Index, 1858–1968. New York: New York Times, 1970. Supplement, 1969–78. New York: New York Times, 1980. Contains more than 390,000 listings compiled from the *New York Times Index*. Alphabetically arranged list of names giving year of death and reference to the obituary in the *New York Times*.

Unrau, Ruth. *Index to Obituaries in the* Mennonite Weekly Review, *1924–1990*. North Newton, Kan.: Bethel College, 1991.

Ware, Lowry. *Associated Reformed Presbyterian Death and Marriage Notices From the* Christian Magazine of the South, the Erskine Miscellany, *and the* Due West Telescope, *1843–1863*. Columbia, S.C.: South Carolina Magazine of Ancestral Research, 1993.

Waters, Margaret, Dorothy Riker, and Doris Leistner. *Abstracts of Obituaries in the* Western Christian Advocate, *1834–1850*. Indianapolis: Indiana Historical Society, 1988.

Young, David C., and Robert L. Taylor. *Death Notices From Freewill Baptist Publications, 1811–1851*. Bowie, Md.: Heritage Books, 1985.

INDEXES AND ABSTRACTS BY STATE

The listings for the states are only a sample of those available. Some states have had very few indexes and abstracts published, others could have their lists extended almost indefinitely. Many more are held in typescript, printout, or microform at a limited number of research institutions.

Alabama
Foley, Helen S. *Marriage and Death Notices From Alabama Newspapers and Family Records, 1819–1890*. Easley, S.C.: Southern Historical Press, 1981.

——. *Obituaries From Barbour County, Alabama, Newspapers, 1890–1905*. Easley, S.C.: Southern Historical Press, 1981.

Gandrud, Pauline Jones. *Marriage, Death, and Legal Notices From Early Alabama Newspapers, 1819–1893*. Easley, S.C.: Southern Historical Press, 1981.

Wellden, Eulalia Yancey. *Death Notices From Limestone County, Alabama, Newspapers, 1828–1891*. N.p., 1986.

Alaska
DeArmond, Robert N. *Subject Index to* The Alaskan, *1885–1907, a Sitka Newspaper*. Juneau: Alaska Division of State Libraries, 1974.

Hales, David A. *An Index to the Early History of Alaska as Reported in the 1903–1907 Fairbanks Newspapers:* Fairbanks News, *September 1903–May 1905;* Fairbanks Evening News, *May 1905–June 1907*. Fairbanks: Elmer E. Rasmuson Library, University of Alaska, 1980.

Stallings, Mike. *Index to the* Seward Gateway, *a Newspaper, 1904–1910*. Seward, Alaska: Seward Community Library, 1983.

Arizona
Underhill, Lonnie E. *Index to the Tombstone, Arizona,* Daily Nugget. Tucson: Roan Horse Press, 1984.

Arkansas
Martin, James Logan. *Arkansas Newspaper Index, 1819–1845*. Newport, Ark.: Morgan Books, 1981.

California
Alaworth, Mary Dean. *Gleanings From Alta California: Marriages and Deaths Reported in the First Newspaper Pub-*

lished in California, 1846 Through 1850. Rancho Cordova, Calif.: Dean Publications, 1980.

_____. *More Gleanings From Alta California: Vital Records Published in California's First Newspaper, Year—1851.* Rancho Cordova, Calif.: Dean Publications, 1982.

Gold Rush Days: Vital Statistics Copies From Early Newspapers of Stockton, California. 6 vols. Stockton, Calif.: San Joaquin Genealogical Society, 1958–1989. Covers 1850–66.

Purdy, Tim I. *Index to Birth and Death Notices of the Lassen Advocate Newspaper of Susanville, California, 1868–1899.* Susanville, Calif.: Lahontan Images, 1986.

Colorado

Griffin, Walter R., and Jay L. Rasmussen. "A Comprehensive Guide to the Location of Published and Unpublished Newspaper Indexes in Colorado Repositories." *The Colorado Magazine* 49 (Fall 1972): 326–39.

Connecticut

Gingras, Raymond. *Quelques francos au Connecticut: notes, références, et index des nécrologies parties dans des journeaux de 1963 à 1975.* Quebec: the author, 1976.

Ireland, Norma Olin, and Winifred Irving. *Index to* Hartford Times *"Genealogical Gleanings," 1912–1916.* Fallbrook, Calif.: Ireland Indexing Service, 1974.

Scott, Kenneth, and Roseanne Conway. *Genealogical Data From Colonial New Haven Newspapers.* Baltimore: Genealogical Publishing Co., 1979.

Delaware

Wright, F. Edward. *Delaware Newspaper Abstracts.* Silver Spring, Md.: Family Line Publications, 1984. Vol. 1, 1786–95.

District of Columbia

Wright, F. Edward. *Abstracts of the Newspapers of Georgetown and the Federal City, 1798–1799.* Silver Spring, Md.: Family Line Publications, 1986.

Georgia

Colket, Meredith B., Jr. "Indexes to Savannah, Georgia, Newspapers." *National Genealogical Society Quarterly* 69 (September 1981): 181–83.

Hartz, Fred R., and Emily K. Hartz. *Genealogical Abstracts From the "Georgia Journal" (Milledgeville) Newspaper.* Vidalia, Ga: Gwendolyn Press, 1990–. Vol. 1, 1809–18; vol. 2, 1819–23.

Huxford, Folks. *Genealogical Material From Legal Notices in Early Georgia Newspapers.* Easley, S.C.: Southern Historical Press, 1989.

LeMaster, Elizabeth T. *Abstracts of Georgia Death Notices From the* Southern Recorder, *1830–1855.* Orange, Calif.: Orange County Genealogical Society, 1971.

_____. *Abstracts of Georgia Marriage Notices From the* Southern Recorder, *1830–1855.* Orange, Calif.: Orange County Genealogical Society, 1971.

Warren, Mary Bondurant. *Marriages and Deaths, Abstracted From Extant Georgia Newspapers.* 2 vols. Danielsville, Ga.:

Heritage Papers, 1968–1972. Vol. 1: 1763–1820; vol. 2: 1820–30.

Hawaii

McKinzie, Edith Kowelohea. *Hawaiian Genealogies: Extracted From Hawaiian Language Newspapers.* 2 vols. Laie, Hi.: Institute for Polynesian Studies, 1983–85.

Illinois

Chicago Genealogical Society. *Vital Records From Chicago Newspapers.* 7 vols. Chicago: Chicago Genealogical Society, 1971–80. Covers 1833–48.

Helge, Jan, and Paula Malak. *The Greater Roseland Area of Chicago; Newspaper Extracts, 1882–1894.* South Holland, Ill.: South Suburban Genealogical and Historical Society, 1992.

Koss, David. "Chicago Obituaries in Der Christliche Botschafter, 1844–1871." *Chicago Genealogist* 11 (Summer 1979): 5–11.

Indiana

Beeson, Cecil. *Newspaper Items From the* Hartford City Telegram, *Hartford City, Indiana.* Fort Wayne, Public Library, 1972.

Capt. Jacob Warrick Chapter, NSDAR. *Warrick County, Indiana Newspapers, Standard and Enquirer of Boonesville.* Owensboro, Ky.: McDowell Publications, 1981.

Cox, Carroll O., and Gloria M. Cox. *New Harmony, Indiana, Newspaper Gleanings, 1825–1844.* Owensboro, Ky.: McDowell Publications, 1980.

Fort Wayne and Allen County Public Library. *Index to Obituary Records as Found in the* "Journal Gazette," *Fort Wayne, Indiana.* Fort Wayne, Ind.: the library, 1973–76. Vol. 1: 1900–18; vol. 2: 1938–49; vol. 3: 1971–75.

Smith, W. W. *Newspaper Abstracts of Owensville and Gibson County, Indiana, 1872–1915, Being a Reprint of the Information Contained in the Several Editions of a True Record.* Evansville, Ind.: Tri-State Genealogical Society, 1978.

Wilke, Katherine. *Newspaper Gleanings, Union City, Randolph County.* Union City: the author, 1969. Vol. 1: 1873–83.

Iowa

Newspaper Abstracts. 4 vols. Jamaica, Iowa: Guthrie County Genealogical Society, 1984. Vol. 1, *Panora Weekly Umpire,* Panora, Iowa, January–December 1888; vol. 2, *The Guthrian,* 1903–1904; vol. 3, *Umpire-Vedette,* Panora, Iowa, January–December 1889; vol. 4, *Vedette,* Panora, Iowa, January–December 1891.

Kansas

Branigar, Tom. *Birth and Death Notices From Early Chapman Newspapers, 1884–1901.* Abilene, Kans.: Dickinson County Historical Society, 1981.

Herrick, James L. *Death Notices as Listed in* Neosho Valley/ Hartford Times, *and Burials in Hartford Cemetery, Lyon County, Kansas (Tombstone Inscriptions and Sexton's Records): Supplemented With Information From the* Hartford Call. Topeka, Kans.: Topeka Genealogical Society, 1978.

Pantle, Alberta. "Death Notices From Kansas Territorial Newspapers, 1854–1861." *Kansas Historical Quarterly* 18 (1950): 302–23.

Kentucky

Clift, G. Glenn. *Kentucky Obituaries, 1787–1854*. Baltimore: Genealogical Publishing Co., 1984. Reprinted from a series originally published in the *Register of the Kentucky Historical Society*.

Green, Karen Mauer. *The Kentucky Gazette, 1787–1800: Genealogical and Historical Abstracts*. Galveston, Tex.: Frontier Press, 1983.

_____. *The Kentucky Gazette, 1800–1820: Genealogical and Historical Abstracts*. Galveston, Tex.: Frontier Press, 1985.

Smith, Pearl O. *Genealogical Excerpts From Ohio County, Kentucky Newspapers, 1881–1899*. Owensboro, Ky.: McDowell Publications, 1980.

Louisiana

Chauvin, Philip, Jr. *Houma Newspaper Deaths, 1855–1981*. Houma, La.: Terrebonne Genealogical Society, 1988.

Mayers, Brenda LaGroue, and Gloria Lambert Kerns. *Death Notices From Louisiana Newspapers*. 6 vols. Baker, La.: Folk Finders, 1984–85. Vol. 1, 1811–19; vol. 2, 1822–1914; vol. 3, 1833–1917; vol. 4, 1847–93; vol. 5, 1824–87; vol. 6, 1836–77.

Maine

Labonte, Youville. *Necrologies of Franco-Americans Taken From Maine's Newspapers*. Auburn, Me.: the author, 1977. Vol. 1, 1966–1976.

Young, David. *Index of Selected Obituaries:* Kennebec Journal, *1825–1354,* Oxford Observer, *1826–1828,* Oxford Democrat, *1833–1855*. Farmington, Me.: Mantor, Library, University of Maine at Farmington, 1977.

_____, and Elizabeth Keene Young. *Vital Records From Maine Newspapers, 1785–1820*. 2 vols. Bowie, Md.: Heritage Books, 1993.

Maryland

Arps, Walter E., Jr. *Before the Fire, Genealogical Gleanings From the* Cambridge *(MD)* Chronicle, *1830–1855*. Lutherville, Md.: Bettie Carothers, 1978.

Barnes, Bobert. *Gleanings From Maryland Newspapers, 1727–1795*. 3 vols. Lutherville, Md.: Bettie Carothers, 1975–76.

_____. *Marriages and Deaths From Baltimore Newspapers, 1796–1816*. Baltimore: Genealogical Publishing Co., 1978.

_____. *Marriages and Deaths From the Maryland Gazette, 1727–1839*. Baltimore, Genealogical Publishing Co., 1973.

Green, Karen Mauer. T*he Maryland Gazette, 1727–1761; Genealogical and Historical Abstracts*. Galveston, Tex.: Frontier Press, 1989.

Hollowak, Thomas L. *Index of Marriages and Deaths in the (Baltimore)* Sun, *1837–1850*. Baltimore: Genealogical Publishing Co., 1978.

_____. *Index to Marriages and Deaths in the (Baltimore)* Sun, *1851–1860*. Baltimore: Genealogical Publishing Co., 1978.

_____. *Indices of the Obituaries in the* Jednosc-Polonia. Chicago: Polish Genealogical Society, 1983. The most important Polish newspaper in Baltimore.

Wright, F. Edward. *Marriages and Deaths of the Lower Delmarva, 1835–1840: From Newspapers of Dorchester, Somerset and Worcester Counties, Maryland*. Silver Spring, Md.: Family Line Publications, 1987.

_____. *Newspaper Abstracts of Cecil and Harford Counties, 1822–1830*. Silver Spring, Md.: Family Line Publications, 1984.

_____. *Western Maryland Newspaper Abstracts, 1786–1810*. 3 vols. Silver Spring, Md.: Family Line Publications, 1985–87.

_____, and I. Harper. *Maryland Eastern Shore Newspaper Abstracts*. 8 vols. (1790–1834). Silver Spring, Md.: Family Line Publications, 1981–87.

Massachusetts

American Antiquarian Society. *Index of Marriages in the* Massachusetts Centinel *and the* Columbian Sentinel, *1784–1840*. 4 vols. Boston: G.K. Hall, 1961.

Codman, Ogden. *Index of Obituaries in Boston Newspapers, 1704–1800*. 3 vols. Boston: G.K. Hall, 1968. The index is in two parts: deaths within Boston, 1704–1800; deaths outside Boston, 1704–95.

Harris, Ruth-Ann M., and Donald Jacobs. *The Search for Missing Friends; Irish Immigrant Advertisements Placed in the* Boston Pilot. Boston: New England Historic Genealogical Society, 1989–. Vol. 1, 1831–50; vol. 2, 1851–53; vol. 3, 1854–56; vol. 4, 1857–60.

Historical Records Survey. *Index to Local News in the* Hampshire Gazette, *1786–1937*. 3 vols. Boston: Historical Records Survey, 1937.

Michigan

Cowles, Jane A., et al. *Condensed Transcripts of Obituaries in the Region of Southeast Isabella County, Michigan and Surrounding Area*. Owensboro, Ky.: McDowell Publications, 1980.

DeZeeuw, Donald J. *Death and Marriage Items Abstracted From the* Lansing State Republican, *1861–1871, and Some Divorces and Name Changes Noted in the Michigan Territorial and State Laws*. Lansing: Mid-Michigan Genealogical Society.

Minnesota

Anoka County Newspapers: Marriage Records, 1863–1870; Death Records, 1863–1870. Anoka, Minn.: Anoka County Genealogical Society, 198(?).

The White Bear Press—A Genealogical Index, January 1, 1911 to 27 August 31, 1988. White Bear Lake, Minn.: White Bear Lake Genealogical Society, 1988.

Mississippi

Mississippi Genealogical Society. *Newspaper Notices of Mississippians, 1820–1860*. Jackson: Mississippi Historical Society, 1960. Reprinted from *Journal of Mississippi History*, vols. 18–21 (1956–59).

Wiltshire, Betty Couch. *Marriages and Deaths From Mississippi Newspapers*. 4 vols. Bowie, Md.: Heritage Books,

1987–89. Vol. 1: 1837–63; vol. 2: 1801–50; vol. 3, 1813–50; vol. 4, 1850–61.

Missouri

Jackson, Vivian Poe, and Wanda Poe Fitzpatrick. *Genealogical Gleanings From Cape Girardeau, Mo. Newspapers.* 2 vols. (1849–62). Cape Girardeau, Mo.: the authors, ca. 1988.

McManus, Thelma S. *Ripley County (Missouri) Records: Obituaries, 1874–1910.* Doniphan: the author, 1979. 259 pp.

Rising, Marsha Hoffman. *Genealogical Data From Southwest Missouri Newspapers, 1850–1860.* Springfield, Mo.: the author, 1985.

_____. *Genealogical Data From Southwest Missouri Newspapers, 1860–1870.* Springfield, Mo.: the author, 1987.

_____. The Springfield Advertiser, *Freene County, Missouri, 1844–1850.* Springfield, Mo.: the author, 1984.

Stanley, Lois, and Maryhelen Wilson. "Death and Estate Notices, Missouri Gazette, 1808–1822." *National Genealogical Society Quarterly* 65 (September 1977): 226–233; 67 (September 1979): 193–201.

Stanley, Lois, George F. Wilson, and Maryhelen Wilson. *Death Records From Missouri Newspapers: The Civil War Years, Jan. 1861–Dec. 1865.* St. Louis: the authors, 1983.

Nebraska

Heil, Leila R. *Genealogical Abstracts From the* Tecumseh Chieftan, *Johnson County, Nebraska, Official Newspaper, 1873–1900.* N.p., 1970.

New Hampshire

Evans, Helen F. *Index of References to American Women in Colonial Newspapers Through 1800.* Bedford, N. H.: the bibliographer, 1979–87. Vol. 1: New Hampshire, 1756–70; vol. 2: New Hampshire, 1771–85.

Hammond, Otis G. *Death and Marriage Notices From the* New Hampshire Gazette, *1765–1800.* Lambertville, N.J.: Hunterdon House, 1970.

New Jersey

Lupp, Robert E. *New Jersey Obituaries Index, 1974–1983.* Trenton, N.J.: Division of State Library, New Jersey State Department of Education, 1983.

Nelson, William. "Extracts From American Newspapers Relating to New Jersey, 1704–1775." *New Jersey Archives,* series 1, vols. 11–12, 19–20, 24–29, 31.

Wilson, Thomas B. *Notices From New Jersey Newspapers, 1781–1790.* Lambertville, N.J.: Hunterdon House, 1988.

New York

Gottesman, Rita S. *The Arts and Crafts in New York: Advertisements and News Items From New York City Newspapers.* 3 vols. New York: New York Historical Society, 1938–49. Reprinted from the society's *Collections,* 1936, 1948, 1949. Vol. 1: 1726–76; vol. 2: 1777–99; vol. 3: 1800–04.

Hoff, Henry B. "Marriage and Death Notices in New York City Newspapers." *NYG&B Newsletter* 2 (1991): 3–5. A listing of available indexes and abstracts, both published and manuscript.

Hoff, Henry B. "Marriage and Death Notices in Long Island Newspapers." *NYG&B Newsletter* 2 (1991): 20–21. A listing of available indexes and abstracts, both published and manuscript.

Losee, John, and Clara Losee. *Death Notices, Dutchess and Columbia County, New York, 1859–1918, From Red Hook Newspapers.* Rhinebeck, N.Y.: Kinship, 1991.

New York Daily Tribune Index, 1875–1906. 31 vols. New York: Tribune Association, 1876–1907.

Scott, Kenneth. *Genealogical Data From Colonial New York Newspapers: A Consolidation of Articles From the New York Genealogical and Biographical Record.* Baltimore: Genealogical Publishing Co., 1977.

_____. *Genealogical Abstracts From the* American Weekly, *1719–1746.* Baltimore: Genealogical Publishing Co., 1974.

_____. *Genealogical Data From the* New York Post Boy, *1743–1773.* Washington, D.C.: National Genealogical Society, 1973.

_____. *Rivington's New York Newspaper: Excerpts From a Loyalist Press, 1773–1783.* New York: New York Historical Society, 1973.

Smith, Mrs. Edwin P. *Deaths, Births, and Marriages From Newspapers Published in Hamilton, Madison County, N.Y., 1818–1886.* 1958. Reprint. Mt. Airy, Md.: Pipe Creek Pub., 1991.

North Carolina

Broughton, Carrie L. *Marriage and Death Notices From* "Raleigh Register" *and* "North Carolina State Gazette," *1799–1825.* 1945. Reprint. Baltimore: Genealogical Publishing Co., 1975.

_____. *Marriage and Death Notices in* "Raleigh Register" *and* "North Carolina State Gazette," *1826–1845.* 1947. Reprint. Baltimore: Genealogical Publishing Co., 1968.

_____. *Marriage and Death Notices in the* "Raleigh Register" *and* "North Carolina State Gazette," *1846–1867.* 1949–50. Reprint. Baltimore: Genealogical Publishing Co., 1975.

Topkins, Robert M. *Marriage and Death Notices From Extant Asheville Newspapers, 1830–1870: An Index.* Raleigh: North Carolina Genealogical Society, 1977.

_____. *Marriage and Death Notices From the* "Western Carolinian" *(Salisbury, N.C.) 1820–1842: An Indexed Abstract.* 1975. Reprint. Spartanburg, S.C.: Reprint Co., 1982.

Ohio

Green, Karen Mauer. *Pioneer Ohio Newspapers, 1793–1810: Genealogical and Historical Abstracts.* Galveston, Frontier Press, 1986.

_____. *Pioneer Ohio Newspapers, 1802–1818: Genealogical and Historical Abstracts.* Galveston: Frontier Press, 1988.

Herbert, Jeffrey G. *Index of Death Notices and Marriage Notices Appearing in the* Cincinnati Daily Gazette, *1827–1881.* Bowie, Md.: Heritage Books, 1993.

Wilke, Katherine. *Newspaper Death Records, Darke County, Ohio.* 4 vols. Union City, Ind.: 1968. Vol. 1: 1850–80; vol. 2, 1880–85; vol. 3, 1886–91; vol. 4, 1892–98.

Oklahoma

Bogle, Dixie. *Cherokee Nation Births and Deaths, 1884–1901.* Venita: Northeast Oklahoma Genealogical Society, 1980.

_____, and Dorthy Nix. *Cherokee Nation Marriages, 1884–1901.* Venita, Okla.: Abraham Coryell Chapter, DAR, 1980.

Mauldin, Dorothy Tincup. *Cherokee Advocate Newspaper Abstracts.* Tulsa: Oklahoma Yesterday Pubs., 1991–. Vol. 1: 1845–77; vol. 2: 1877–80; vol. 3: 1880–83; vol. 4: 1883–93.

Parker, Doris Whitehall. *Footprints on the Osage Reservation.* 2 vols. Pawhuska, Okla.: the author, 1984. Covers 1894–1907.

Vanpool, Fern P. *Obituaries and Death Notices Printed in* Miami Daily News-Record, *Miami, Oklahoma.* Genealogical Records Committee, Oklahoma Society, DAR, n.d.

Pennsylvania

Hawbaker, Gary T. *Runaways, Rascals and Rogues; Abstracts From Lancaster County, Pennsylvania Newspapers.* Hershey, Pa.: the author, 1987. Vol. 1: "Lancaster Journal," 1794–1810.

Heilman, Robert A. *Deaths Reported in* "Der Libanon Demokrat," *a German-Language Newspaper Published at Lebanon, Pennsylvania, 1832–1864.* Bowie, Md.: Heritage Books, 1990.

Hocker, Edward W. *Genealogical Data Relating to the German Settlers of Pennsylvania and Adjacent Territory: From Advertisements in German Newspapers Published in Germantown, 1743–1800.* Baltimore: Genealogical Publishing Co., 1980.

Meier, Judith A. H. *Elopements and Other Miscreant Deeds of Women, as Advertized in the Pennsylvania Gazette, 1730–1789.* Norristown, Pa.: J.A.H. Maier, 1986.

Rentmeister, Jean R. *Marriage and Death Notices Extracted From the Genius of Liberty and Fayette Advertiser of Uniontown, Pa., 1805–1854.* Apollo, Pa.: Closson Press, 1981.

Scott, Kenneth. *Abstracts From Ben Franklin's* Pennsylvania Gazette, *1728–1748.* Baltimore: Genealogical Publishing Co., 1975.

_____, and Janet R. Clarke. *Abstracts From the* "Pennsylvania Gazette," *1748–1755.* Baltimore: Genealogical Publishing Co., 1977.

_____. *Genealogical Abstracts From the* "American Weekly Mercury," *1719–1746.* Baltimore: Genealogical Publishing Co., 1974.

_____. *Genealogical Data From the* Pennsylvania Chronicle, *1767–1774.* Washington, D.C.: National Genealogical Society, 1980.

South Carolina

Elliott, Colleen M. *Marriage and Death Notices From the* Keowee Courier, *1849–1883.* Easley, S.C.: Southern Historical Press, 1979.

Holcomb, Brent H. *Marriage and Death Notices From Baptist Newspapers of South Carolina, 1835–1865.* Spartanburg, S.C.: Reprint Co., 1981.

_____. *Marriage and Death Notices From Camden, South Carolina Newspapers, 1816–1865.* Easley, S.C.: Southern Historical Press, 1978.

_____. *Marriage and Death Notices From the Up-country of South Carolina: As Taken From Greenville Newspapers, 1826–1863.* Columbia, S.C.: South Carolina Magazine of Ancestral Research, 1983.

_____. *Marriage and Death Notices From Columbia, South Carolina Newspapers, 1792–1839.* Easley, S.C.: Southern Historical Press, 1982.

_____. *Marriage and Death Notices From the* "Pendleton (South Carolina) Messenger," *1807–1851.* 1977. Reprint. Easley, S.C.: Southern Historical Press, 1979.

_____. *Marriage and Death Notices From the* "Lutheran Observer," *1831–1861; Southern Lutheran, 1861–1865.* Easley, S.C.: Southern Historical Press, 1979.

_____. *Marriage and Death Notices From the* "Southern Christian Advocate." Easley, S.C.: Southern Historical Press, 1979–1980. Vol. 1: 1837–60; vol. 2: 1861–67.

_____. *Marriage and Death Notices From Upper South Carolina Newspapers, 1843–1865.* Easley, S.C.: Southern Historical Press, 1977.

Revill, Janie. *Marriage and Death Notices Abstracted From Newspapers Published in Camden, South Carolina, 1822–1842.* Columbia, S.C., 1936.

Salley, Alexander S. *Marriage Notices in* "Charleston Courier," *1803–1808.* 1919. Reprint. Baltimore: Genealogical Publishing Co., 1976.

_____. *Marriage Notices in the* "South Carolina" *and* "American General Gazette," *1766–1781;* "The Royal Gazette," *1781–1782.* 1914. Reprint. Baltimore: Genealogical Publishing Co., 1976.

Wilkinson, Tom C. *Early Anderson County, South Carolina Newspapers Marriages and Obituaries, 1841–1882.* Easley, S.C.: Southern Historical Press, 1978.

Wilson, Teresa E., and Janice L. Grimes. *Marriage and Death Notices From the* Southern Patriot. Easley, S.C.: Southern Historical Press, 1982–86. Vol. 1: 1815–30; vol. 2: 1831–48.

South Dakota

Ferris, Edna M. *Jones County in Memory.* Pierre, S.D.: the author, 1989. Collection of obituaries and memorials from newspapers and funeral homes.

Johnson, Linda. *Newspaper Extracts From Java, South Dakota, 1903–1918.* Seattle: the author, 1991.

Tennessee

Baker, Russell P. *Marriages and Obituaries From the* "Tennessee Baptist," *1844–1862.* Easley, S.C.: Southern Historical Press, 1879.

Eddlemon, Sherida K. *Genealogical Abstracts From Tennessee Newspapers, 1791–1808.* Bowie, Md.: Heritage Books, 1988.

_____. *Genealogical Abstracts From Tennessee Newspapers, 1803–1812.* Bowie, Md.: Heritage Books, 1989.

_____. *Genealogical Abstracts From Tennessee Newspapers, 1821–1828.* Bowie, Md.: Heritage Books, 1991.

Garrett, Jill K. *Obituaries From Tennessee Newspapers, 1851–1899.* Easley, S.C.: Southern Historical Press, 1980.

Lucas, Silas Emmett, Jr. *Marriages From Early Tennessee Newspapers, 1794–1851.* Easley, S.C.: Southern Historical Press, 1978.

_____. *Obituaries From Early Tennessee Newspapers, 1794–1851.* Easley, S.C.: Southern Historical Press, 1978.

Scoggins, Margaret B. Banner of Peace *and* Cumberland Presbyterian Advocate; *Abstracts of Marriage, Death, and other Notices, 1843–1853.* Poplar Bluff, Mo.: the author, 1988.

Texas
Cawthon, Juanita Davis. *Marriage and Death Notices, Marion County, Texas and Environs, 1853–1927.* Shreveport, La.: the author, 1980.

El Paso Genealogical Society. *Births, Deaths, and Marriages From El Paso Newspapers Through 1885 for Arizona, Texas, New Mexico, Oklahoma and Indian Territory.* Easley, S.C.: Southern Historical Press, 1982.

Lu, Helen Mason. *Texas Methodist Newspaper Abstracts, 17 April 1850–17 Sept. 1881.* 4 vols. Dallas, Tex.: the author, 1987.

Swenson, Helen S. *Early Texas News, 1831–1848; Abstracts From Early Texas Newspapers.* St. Louis: F.T. Ingmire, 1984.

Utah
Historical and Genealogical Register of Indexes to Corinne, Utah Newspapers, 1869–1875. Brigham City, Utah: Golden Spike Chapter, Utah Genealogical Association, 1975.

Vermont
Historical Records Survey, Vermont. *Index to the* Burlington Free Press *in The Billings Library, University of Vermont.* 10 vols. Burlington: University of Vermont, 1940–42. Covers 1848–70.

Virginia
Cappon, Lester J., and Stella F. Duff. Virginia Gazette *Index.* 2 vols. (1736–1780). Williamsburg: Institute of Early American Culture, 1950.

Headley, Robert K. *Genealogical Abstracts From 18th-Century Virginia Newspapers.* Baltimore: Genealogical Publishing Co., 1987.

Hodge, Robert Allen. *Death Notices,* Virginia Herald, *Fredericksburg, Virginia, 1788–1836.* Fredericksburg, Va.: the author, 1981.

McIlwaine, H.R. *Index to Obituary Notices,* "Richmond Enquirer," *May 9, 1824–1829;* "Richmond Whig," *1824–1838.* 1923. Reprint. Baltimore: Genealogical Publishing Co., 1979.

Obituary Notices From the Alexandria Gazette, *1784–1915.* Compiled by the staff of Lloyd House, Alexandria Library. Bowie, Md.: Heritage Books, 1987.

Washington
McNeill, Ruby Simonson. *Lewis County, Washington, Newspaper Abstracts.* 5 vols. Spokane: the author, 1978. Vol. 1: 1884–86; vol. 2: 1887–89; vol. 3: 1890–93; vol. 4: 1894–96; vol. 5: 1897–99.

Townsend, Homer. *Obituaries From the* Skamania County Pioneer *Newspaper, Skamania County, Washington, 1900–1929.* Goldendale, Wash.: the author, 1985.

West Virginia
Hassig, Carol. *Wetzel County, WV, Obituary Book, 1870–1940.* 2 vols. New Martinsville, W.V.: Wetzel County Genealogical Society, 1981–92.

Hodge, Robert Allen. *An Index for the* Martinsburg Gazette, *Martinsburg (West) Virginia.* Fredericksburg, Va.: the author, 1973–74. Vol. 1: 1810–15; vol. 2: 1823–33; vol. 3: 1834–39; vol. 4: 1839–48; vol. 5: 1851–55.

Wisconsin
Albertz, Sally P. *Fond du Lac Comonwealth Newspaper: Genealogical Items Extracted From Newspapers Dated January 1863 Through December 1870.* Fond du Lac, Wisc.: the author, 1988.

Gee, Patricia, and Wilma Foley. *Marriages and Deaths in the* "Depere News," *1871–1883.* Dearborn, Mich.: the authors, 1976.

_____. *Deaths in the* "Green Bay Advocate," *1870–1880.* Dearborn, Mich: the authors, 1976.

_____. *Marriages in the* "Green Bay Advocate," *1870–1880.* Dearborn, Mich.: the authors, 1976.

Noonan, Barry C. *Index to Green Bay Newspapers, 1833–1840.* Monroe, Wis.: Wisconsin State Genealogical Society, 1987.

Obituary Index, 1939–1971, the New North, Rhinelander Daily News; *Obituary Index, 1972–1975,* Rhinelander Daily News. N.p., 1983. 2 microfilm reels.

Obituary Index: Stevens Point Journal. Stevens Point, Wis: Stevens Point Area Genealogical Society, 1987. Vol. 1: 1881–1952. 28 microfiche.

IMMIGRATION: FINDING IMMIGRANT ORIGINS
CHAPTER CONTENTS

13

IMMIGRATION: FINDING IMMIGRANT ORIGINS

Kory L. Meyerink and Loretto Dennis Szucs

We are all descended from immigrants. Whether they came to America in prehistoric times via the Bering Strait or later on ships, or airplanes, at some point in history, every person's ancestors came from somewhere else. And almost everyone has a strong desire to know why, when, and from where their ancestors emigrated. Most of us begin with the simple goal of finding "Old Country" origins. Yet, the quest usually does not end when that discovery is made. Once we begin tracking ancestors back in time and across continents, we are often drawn so deeply into the story that it's difficult to stop searching. There are always a few more relationships to be proved and details to be learned. And when finally discovered, the ancestor's homeland takes on a fascination of its own. We find ourselves intrigued with histories and cultures, wanting to know as much as possible about "our people." Scarcely any phase of family history research is as fascinating as tracking immigrant origins—and scarcely any phase is as challenging.

Knowing the immigrant's birthplace or last place of residence before emigrating is essential to finding more information in the native land. Yet, unless the ancestors arrived relatively recently in the United States, family origins may have been forgotten. Because most foreign records are kept at the town level, discovering the name of a native town, county, or parish is an important goal. Without that information, it is impossible to know where to conduct research in the country of origin.

Every American hoping to link generations and reach back in time will ultimately be faced with immigration questions. The three-fold purpose of this chapter is to facilitate the search for immigrant origins by (1) identifying the principles of immigration research, (2) describing a vast body of American sources that document immigration, and (3) briefly outlining some foreign emigration sources that are immediately available and extremely useful in identifying immigrants and their homelands.

PRINCIPLES OF IMMIGRATION RESEARCH

There is no "universal" record source that can be counted upon to provide the name of the immigrant's ancestral home. Rather, there are dozens of records that may, depending on the time period and ethnic nature of the family, provide the necessary information. Therefore, it is important to follow certain principles when researching an immigrant ancestor. These principles include:

- Clearly identifying the immigrant
- Learning the historical background
- Using the right research approaches
- Searching American records thoroughly first
- Knowing the process of immigration

IDENTIFYING THE IMMIGRANT

The likelihood of tracing individuals and families successfully is greatly enhanced if the work is begun by making every effort to learn everything possible about the immigrant or family using U.S. record sources. An immediate concern should be to learn the full name of the immigrant and the names of as many other family members as possible. It is sometimes necessary to trace the lives of all the person's children in order to obtain the critical clues that will tell exactly where the immigrant was born.

Biographical Information

To clearly identify an immigrant in records of the country from which the person came, you must know:

The full name: Given names and surnames (last names) are necessary. It is useful to learn all of the immigrant's given names, such as Johann Wilhelm Karl Hummel. Some individuals went by a second name, a confirmation name, or a nickname. Not only will learning the full name help to identify a person in the records of the country of origin; sometimes the name alone, or part of the name, can be a clue to the immigrant's original country or region.

A date: A birth date is preferable, but a date of marriage, a record of a religious event, military release, or other such information may substitute for a birth date, as long as the event took place in the native country. A complete date (day, month, and year) should be sought, but it is sometimes possible to identify an individual with only the year of an event.

A place of origin: Eventually, you must determine the specific place (town or parish) where the immigrant was born or lived before coming to the United States. This is the focus of immigrant origin research for most researchers. Sometimes it is possible to learn the specific town from records in the native country, but you should try to determine it from American records.

A relative: Family relationships—especially parentage—are important. The more you know about a family as a whole, the easier it is to correctly identify the immigrant in records of his or her native country. If it is not possible to discover the father's name, seek the mother's name or the name of a spouse, brother, sister, or other close relative (uncle, aunt) as a substitute. Not only will this information help identify the person in native records, but you may be able to learn more about a brother's or son's place of origin than that of the ancestor who is the subject of your search. Many of the sources discussed in this chapter might name the native towns of some family members, yet not include your immediate ancestor.

While the minimum identification discussed above should allow you to recognize the ancestor in the records of the native country, you should also seek additional information that could provide clues to the town or county of origin or confirm that you have found the correct family. While some records might not indicate specifically where the person came from, they might provide clues that will lead to others until you find a record which finally shows the town of origin. If at all possible, learn the following about the immigrant:

Family stories, traditions, and heirlooms: Surprising clues may survive in family traditions, letters, diaries, journals, religious records, postcards, photographs, scrapbooks, and mementos that have been saved over the years. One researcher, for example, was able to discover the area in Germany from which her family had emigrated because of a photograph in which her grandmother appeared in a lace cap. As she learned from reading about the country, the particular lace was a distinctive part of the costume worn in a specific region of Germany. An African American was able to determine the tribe from which his family had come through oral tradition and the distinctive pattern in a cloth that had been handed down in the family. Yet another family learned of its origins in France because of a medallion passed down through the generations. A watchmaker's descendant learned the precise town of the family's origin when she investigated the origin of the timepiece she had inherited. Songs, dances, food, recipes, costumes, memorabilia, and many other things can provide important clues in finding ethnic origins. While many family traditions are exaggerated, especially regarding the immigrant's importance in the old country, there are usually some accurate facts that will serve as a basis to begin research. Yet these clues will mean nothing unless one has an understanding of the customs, geography, and history of an ethnic group. Linked with a basic knowledge of the immigrant's homeland—including the leading industry of the native district, common occupations, names of nearby towns, rivers, mountains, and other features of the area—a family story, a tradition, or an heirloom could provide the breakthrough that will identify the exact immigrant origins.

Friends and neighbors: Many immigrants traveled together or settled among friends from their native land. Your search may need to include them.

Religion: Records created by religious organizations comprise a likely source of information in the country of origin. By learning the immigrant's religion, you can further identify him or her, limit your searches to records most likely to include the immigrant, and gain clues to more-specific geographical origins. For example, a Protestant German ancestor was more likely to have come from northern Germany than from a southern area. Often, entire religious colonies traveled together and are documented in religious literature. Knowing, for example, that an immigrant Englishman was a Quaker can significantly change your research approach. (See chapter 6, Research in Church Records.)

Ethnicity: The natural security of living among people who speak the same language and have the same cultural or religious background is the bonding force that has traditionally kept ethnic communities together. Immigrants, particularly those who did not speak English, tended to settle in enclaves within cities and to cluster in specific regions of the United States. It was common for immigrants arriving in large numbers as a result of difficulties in their home countries to settle together on this side of the ocean, and then to migrate *en masse* within the United States. Many immigrants felt a need to transplant and preserve, as much as possible, their culture and lifestyle as it existed in their native lands. Immigrant groups frequently founded their own churches, schools, banks, boarding houses, and other institutions. They also had their own academic, athletic, charitable, fraternal, occupational, and social organizations. Volumes have been written about virtually every ethnic group. Ethnic presses generated newspapers and histories that focused on specific communities. Many ethnic publications survive that could be invaluable for those who want to learn more about the lives and times of their immigrant ancestors. Biographical sketches of Mrs. Isabella Atlanta Anderson and Jonas Anton Anderson, published in Algot E. Strand, *A History of the Norwegians in Illinois* (Chicago: J. Anderson Publishing Co., 1905) (figure 13-1), are typical of those found in ethnic publications. In most cases, birthplace, names of parents, spouse, and children, and details of the family or individual's arrival in the United States and other interesting information is revealed in these historical sources. To learn what motives your ancestor may have had in coming to the United State, which groups came in what time period, where large concentrations of national groups typically settled, and other important information about settlement patterns, consult one or more of the works that focus on the specific ethnic group. (A bibliography at the end of this chapter lists sources for groups that immigrated to the United States in the largest numbers. Other chapters provide more detail for African American, Hispanic, Native American, and Jewish research.)

Name changes: The immigrant's name often changed around the time he or she arrived in the United States. Sometimes this change was the result of a conscious choice to become Americanized, but usually it simply evolved during years of life in a new culture that used a language foreign to the immigrant. Therefore, name changes are most common among foreign-speaking immigrants. Some preliminary reading can be interesting and will almost always enhance the potential for success in the long run. (Several useful titles are identified in the chapter bibliography.)

Where to Look for Immigration Information

There are advantages to beginning a search with at least some knowledge about the immigrant's voyage. Certain tactics used to learn the place of origin require knowing as much as possible about when and where the immigrant arrived in America, and from where in the native country he or she came. Try to calculate the date of immigration as closely as possible. Know-

Figure 13-1. Biographical sketches such as these, from Algot E. Strand, *A History of the Norwegians of Illinois* (Chicago: J. Anderson Publishing Co., 1905), often provide immigration information that is not available elsewhere.

---

264   A HISTORY OF THE NORWEGIANS OF ILLINOIS

His father died in Norway in 1860. His mother is still living in Eidegaarden, Vestre Aker, Norway.

Mr. Anderson's machine shop, which will be referred to in another part of this history, is at 147 Fulton street. The family resides at 470 Austin avenue.

MRS. ISABELLA ATLANTA ANDERSON

Divides the distinction of having been born on the Atlantic Ocean with the renowned "Sloop

Mrs. Isabella Anderson.

Girl," Mrs. Atwater, mentioned in the first part of this volume. This fact also explains her somewhat unusual middle name Atlanta.

Mrs. Anderson was born on board the Norwegian steamer "Norge," May 21, 1861, while her parents were on their way to America. Her father is Mr. K. B. Olson, a well known manufacturing tailor, of this city, and her mother's maiden name was Miss Susan Stene.

Mrs. Anderson received her education in the Chicago public schools and was confirmed in the first Norwegian Lutheran church on the North side by Rev. Mikkelsen.

When twenty years of age she was joined in holy wedlock to Mr. Hans Ludvig Anderson, May 24, 1881. Her husband hailed from Fossen, Norway, and became a very prominent business man in Chicago, being engaged in the wholesale booth and shoe business, at his death, which occurred Feb. 4, 1903, leaving his family amply provided for.

This marital union was blessed with three children: one son and two daughters: Cyrus A., born March 4, 1884; Irene Harriet, Febr. 3, 1888, and Grace Susette, Febr. 17, 1892.

Mrs. Anderson's mother departed this life on July 19, 1906, but her father is still living and active in business.

Mrs. Anderson has never cared much about social clubs or distinctions, her inclinations having been more toward the duties of a good housewife and mother. When it came to charitable work, she has, however, been very much interested. She was one of the first two lady members on the board of directors of the Norwegian Old People's Home Society, on which she has served for a number of years. She has also been interested in the Norwegian Lutheran Children's Home Society and other charitable work among her countrymen.

With her family Mrs. Anderson attends the Wicker Park English Lutheran Church and resides in her own home at 98 Fowler street.

JONAS ANTON ANDERSON.

The manufacturer of cameras and photographic specialties at 65 E. Indiana street, Chicago, was born Nov. 28, 1840, to Peter and Margrette Anderson, of Christiania, Norway. The parents came to America, with the subject of our sketch, in 1852, locating in Detroit, Mich., where they landed in July. Jonas had attended school in Norway and for some time went to school in Detroit, but at the age of 14 he was apprenticed to learn the carpenter trade. After five years in Detroit he came to Chicago, in 1857. Here he continued to work at his trade until 1862, when he engaged in the building business on his own account. In 1869 he started the making of cameras and other

ing the name of the ship that brought the individual or family to the United States is desirable, but it is not entirely impossible to discover that specific information at some later point in the project.

Date of immigration: If the approximate date of immigration can be determined, it is usually possible to locate passenger lists and records of ethnic or religious groups. Census records are particularly useful for learning this information. The 1900, 1910, and 1920 U.S. censuses usually provide the approximate year of arrival, though census information is not entirely reliable. Children's birthplaces in the 1850 through 1880 censuses can also help determine the year of arrival.

Once the date of immigration has been established, it is easier to determine the location of other important records, including naturalization papers. A date of immigration may also suggest when the immigrant was granted a release from military service in the native country.

Place of departure: If American records document the port or city the immigrant left, a number of records from the country of departure should indicate the name of the home town. These include emigration lists (departure lists) and indexes as well as newspapers, church records, and other records at the port of departure. From these, it may be possible to learn the date of immigration as well as the ship's name, which may be necessary to locate them in U.S. arrival records.

Port or city of arrival: Immigrants often stayed in the city of arrival for months or years before moving on. If you learn the place they arrived in America, it may be possible to find applications for naturalization, church records, and government vital records, including marriage, death, and birth records. Any of these are likely to provide more clues about the ancestral home.

Name of the ship: The name of an immigrant's ship is more than an interesting biographical footnote. It may be needed to find passenger lists, place of departure and arrival, and the names of other immigrants in the group. Sometimes the name of the ship that brought an immigrant ancestor to America will be remembered and handed down as the only clue to native origins.

Reason for immigrating: Biographical and family sources often imply why the immigrant came to America. In some cases, knowing why a person immigrated can help in locating ethnic or religious group records, the date of immigration, or the places of departure and arrival.

Immigrant's original country or region: Sometimes knowing the country or region a person left is enough to begin a search in the records of that area, and it might imply the place of departure.

HISTORICAL BACKGROUND

Since 1607, some 57 million immigrants have come to America from other lands. Approximately 10 million passed through on their way to some other place or returned to their original homelands, leaving a net gain of more than 47 million people:

1607–1790:	900,000
1790–1819:	250,000
1820–1860:	5,000,000

1861–1880:	5,100,000
1881–1920:	23,400,000
1921–1960:	8,200,000
1961–1990:	14,000,000

In 1907, immigration peaked at 1,285,349.[1] (See figures 13-2 and 13-3.)

Between 1607 and 1790, early European immigration was mostly from Britain (England, Scotland, Ulster Ireland, Southern Ireland, Wales) and Germany. However, the largest number of immigrants were the forced immigrants from Africa, who accounted for approximately forty percent of the colonial immigrants to the future United States. Based on a careful review of current demographic studies by immigration historians, the approximate distribution of immigrants before 1790 was as follows (see figure 13-4):[2]

Africa	360,000
England	230,000
Ulster	135,000
Germany	103,000
Scotland	48,500
Ireland	8,000
Netherlands	6,000
Wales	4,000
France	3,000
Jews	2,000
Sweden/Finland	500

Before 1790, North America's population was confined to the area east of the Appalachian Mountains, with only a scattering of Americans over the line along the frontiers. However, as the numbers of immigrants continued to climb, the frontiers simply had to be constantly pushed back, eventually bringing the immigrants to the Rocky Mountains and northern plains states. During the last two hundred years of immigration to the United States, the numbers of immigrants have risen and fallen in response to conditions in America as well as abroad.

The ethnicity of immigrants also changed considerably over time (table 13-1). Between 1820 and 1855, Ireland contributed the largest single group of immigrants. Germany, especially Prussia, contributed twenty percent of the immigrants during those years. A smattering from other parts of Europe and an introduction of people from China and Mexico rounded out the population.[3]

Irish flowed into New York and Boston to build canals and railroads, and the Europeans answered the call for settlement on vacant lands in the Midwest. The discovery of gold in California brought an American population to the West Coast practically overnight.

Before 1885, most European immigrants originated north of the Alps and west of the Elbe River. After 1885, the so-called New Immigration came from southern and eastern Europe, with the largest number of immigrants from Italy and Russia (mostly Jews). These immigrants concentrated in urban centers where jobs were available and where churches,

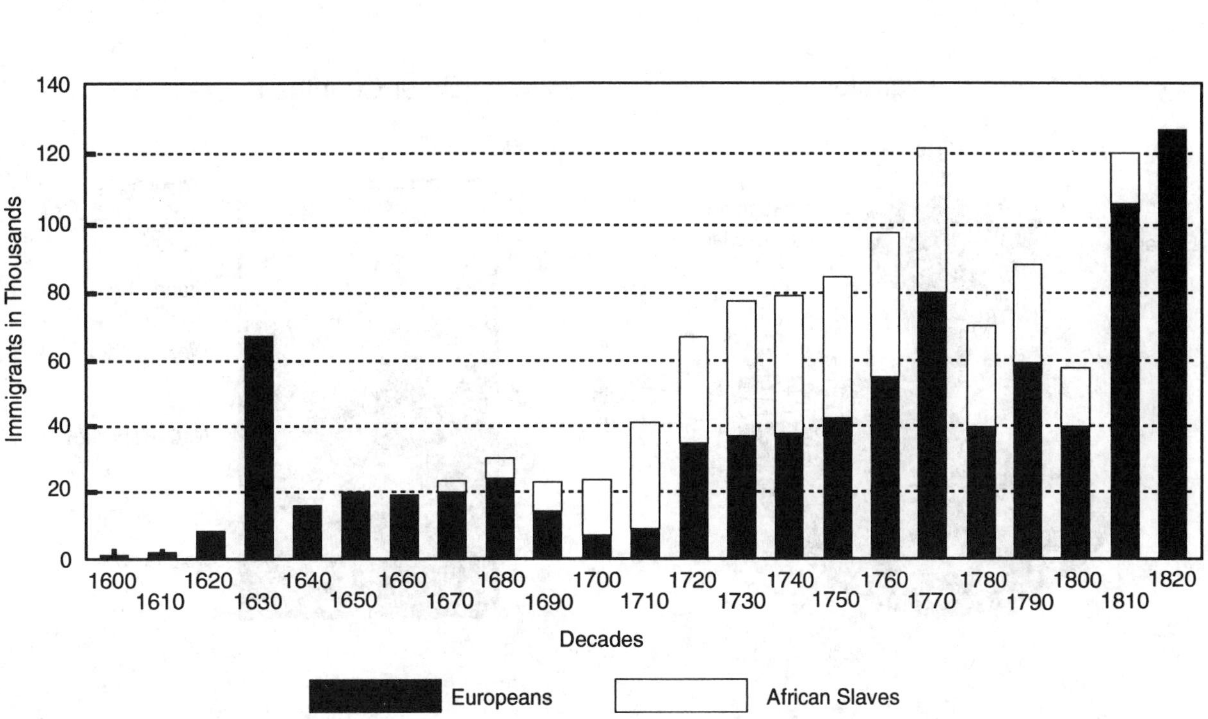

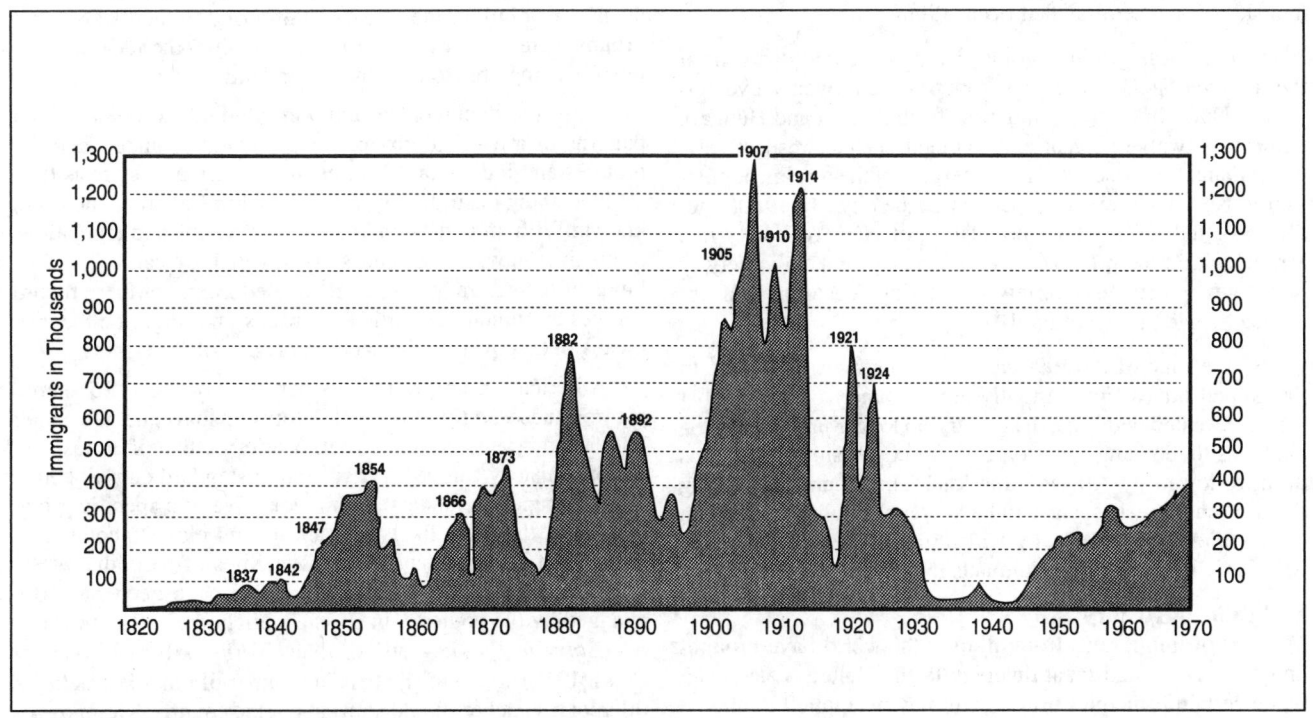

Figure 13-2. Pre-1820 Immigration to the United States.

Figure 13-3. Immigration to the United States From 1820 to 1970.

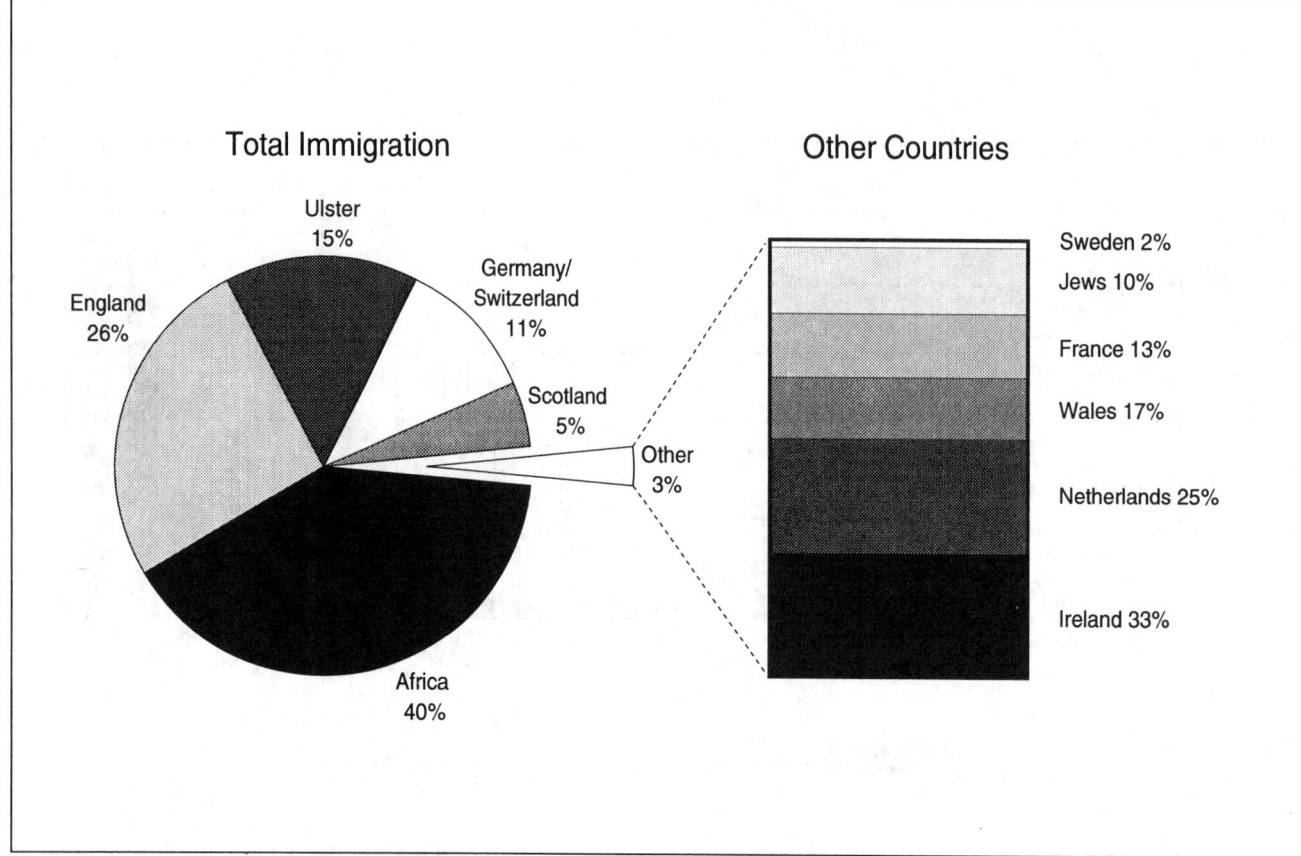

Total Immigration

Ulster 15%

Germany/ Switzerland 11%

England 26%

Scotland 5%

Other 3%

Africa 40%

Other Countries

Sweden 2%

Jews 10%

France 13%

Wales 17%

Netherlands 25%

Ireland 33%

Figure 13-4. Total immigration to the United States to 1790.

neighbors, and immigrant aid societies cushioned the immigrant experience. Most of these families were too poor to buy land when they arrived in America, and many heads of family had skilled and semi-skilled occupations.[4]

In 1910, Russian immigrants comprised twenty percent of the foreign population of New York State and twenty-five percent of New York City; immigrants from Austria and Hungary comprised twelve percent and fourteen percent, respectively; and Italians comprised seventeen percent of the foreign population in New York, eighteen percent in the city. By 1910, one-fourth of the foreign-born population of New York City had arrived within the previous five years; they spoke a variety of languages, practiced a variety of religious customs, and demanded a wide range of food.[5]

By the time of the 1990 census, immigrants had come to the United States from virtually every country on earth. That census revealed that English ancestry no longer prevailed. German was the leading ancestry, followed by Irish; English was third, followed by African American. The others comprising the top ten were Hispanic, Italian, French, Polish, American Indian, and Dutch. Table 13-1 identifies each ancestry group with more than 1 million claimants in 1990.

The Value of History
Millions of immigrants from all over the world have brought unique customs and great diversity to the United States. And while certain principles of research may be applied to almost any country, there comes a time in every investigation when something of the specific history and the customs of the place

from which our ancestors emigrated must be understood. Immigrants' experiences were not isolated. Groups were forced to leave by religious oppression, famine, agricultural and industrial revolution, the threat of conscription, and war. Other groups were lured by the American dream—the idea of commoners being able to own their own land.

From the documented and well-studied experiences and patterns of a national group, we can begin to understand the motives and individual histories of our own ancestors as they molded their destinies by leaving behind all that they had known. With an understanding of the customs and regulations of the time in which our ancestors traveled, we can know what kinds of records may have been created. Some of these record sources are unique to particular groups and might be the sole means of discovering the specific origins of ancestors.

America's immigration history is two-sided. To search records successfully, it is most helpful to study the newcomer both as emigrant and immigrant. A brief outline of almost any nation's history can be gleaned from a standard encyclopedia, but the deeper the understanding you have of a specific group of people, the more likely you are to find clues to continue a search and to understand the personalities of individuals. For example, how might an ancestor's life have been radically changed by the pogroms in Russia? Nicholas V. Riasanovsky, *A History of Russia,* 2nd ed. (New York: Oxford University Press, 1969) addresses that and a number of other issues that a diligent researcher should know about the country. Riasanovsky describes and illustrates the cultural, economic, geographical, and social aspects of "Russia before the Russians," "Appa-

Table 13-1. Top U.S. Ancestry Groups in 1790 and 1990

1790 U.S. Ancestry[6] *(Based on Evaluated 1790 Census Figures)*			*1990 U.S. Ancestry* *(1990 U.S. Census)*		
Ancestry Group	Number (1790 Estimate)	Percentage of Total	Ancestry Group	Number	Percentage of Total
English	1,900,000	47.5	German	57,981,710	23.3
African	750,000	19.0	Irish	38,735,539	15.6
Scotch-Irish	320,000	8.0	English	32,651,788	13.1
German	280,000	7.0	African American	23,777,098	9.6
Irish	200,000	5.0	Hispanic*	17,418,496	7.0
Scottish	160,000	4.0	Italian	14,664,550	5.9
Welsh	120,000	3.0	Franco-American*	13,176,333	5.3
Dutch	100,000	2.5	Polish	9,366,106	3.8
French	80,000	2.0	Native American	8,708,220	3.5
Native American	50,000	1.0	Dutch	6,227,089	2.5
Spanish	20,000	0.5	Scotch-Irish	5,617,773	2.3
Swedish and other	20,000	0.5	Scottish	5,393,581	2.2
			Swedish	4,680,863	1.9
			Norwegian	3,869,395	1.6
			Russian	2,952,987	1.2
Total U.S. population	4,000,000	100	Total U.S. population	248,708,823	100

* Hispanic comprises Spanish, Mexicans, and other Latin Americans of Spanish ancestry; Franco-American comprises French (except Basque), French Canadian, and Acadian/Cajun (Bureau of the Census 1993, table 1).

nage Russia," "Muscovite Russia," "Imperial Russia," and "Soviet Russia."

If you want to know more about living conditions and concerns of your British grandparents from 1830 to 1902, for example, a book like G.M. Young, *Victorian England: Portrait of an Age* (New York: Oxford University Press, 1964) will provide an unusual degree of detail. Histories of this sort abound, and they provide not only the necessary background information for the researcher, but they also enhance appreciation of the lives of ancestors who lived in times very different from our own.

Besides learning something of the history of an ancestor's national group, it is beneficial for the family historian to understand what occurred after an immigrant arrived in the United States. Were entrance records kept on this side of the ocean? Where might an immigrant have chosen to live immediately after his or her arrival? Where did others of the same nationality settle, and what kinds of documents survive from ethnic communities? Was the immigrant likely to have been naturalized? If so, where and when?

From important immigration sources such as Philip Taylor, *The Distant Magnet: European Emigration to the U.S.A.* (New York: Harper and Row, 1971) and Oscar Handlin, *Immigration as a Factor in American History* (Englewood Cliffs, N.J.: Prentice Hall, 1959), which cover the emigration experience and its broadest implications, to the histories of particular groups, such as James G. Leyburn, *The Scotch-Irish: A Social History* (Chapel Hill: The University of North Carolina Press, 1962); Rowland Tappan Berthoff, *British Immigrants in Industrial America, 1790–1950* (Cambridge, Mass.: Harvard University Press, 1953. Reprint. New York: Russell and Russell, 1968); Andrzej Brozek, *Polonia Amerykaska: The American*

Polonia (Warsaw, Poland: Interpress Publications, 1980); Albert Camarillo, *Chicanos in a Changing Society: From Mexican Pueblo to American Barrios in Santa Barbara and Southern California, 1848–1930* (Cambridge, Mass.: Harvard University Press, 1979); and Jay P. Dolan, *The Immigrant Church: New York's Irish and German Catholics* (Baltimore: Johns Hopkins University Press, 1975), there is a rich storehouse of printed material to expedite immigration research.

History journals and dissertations often provide even more detailed discussions of why people emigrated, when and how they traveled, what they did when they got to the United States, and what kinds of records will divulge their individual names and personal facts. Not only do writings such as Oliver MacDonagh, "The Irish Famine Emigration to the United States," *Perspectives in American History* 10 (1976): 357–446; Robert Swierenga, "Dutch Immigrant Demography, 1820–1880," as it appeared in *Journal of Family History* 5 (Winter 1980): 390–405; or Paula Kaye Benkart, "Religion, Family, and Community Among Hungarians Migrating to American Cities, 1880–1930" (Ph.D. dissertation, Johns Hopkins University, 1975), provide critical insights in themselves, but they will usually point to original and often obscure records used by the authors to prove their theses.

Ethnic and Religious Groups

It would be impossible to cite all of the sources valuable for immigration research, but the determined researcher will find an abundance of published material on specific ethnic and religious groups available in or through public, university, and private libraries. Because every national and religious group of people can be considered an ethnic group, "ethnic" is an important subject heading to consider when searching any library catalog.

Probably one of the most definitive and useful background sources for all ethnic groups is Stephen Thernstrom, *Harvard Encyclopedia of American Ethnic Groups* (Cambridge, Mass.: The Belknap Press of Harvard University Press, 1980). This reference work, found in most large libraries, includes the basic information about the multitude of people who make up the population of the United States. It is a succinct, authoritative treatment of the origins and histories of 106 ethnic groups; it includes twenty-nine thematic essays, eighty-seven maps, and a critical bibliography for each section. Among the many important points made by the *Encyclopedia* is the fact that few ethnic groups are evenly distributed throughout all regions of the United States. There is a definite tendency for ethnic groups to concentrate in some areas and to avoid others. This reference work provides a lengthy discussion of this and many other aspects of the immigrant experience. Though somewhat dated, the depth and scope of the work and the many specialized bibliographies make the *Encyclopedia* a very useful source for ethnic research.

If religion was a catalyst that sent many an immigrant from his or her homeland, it was also the glue that bound ethnic communities together in the new country. The immigrant church and synagogue were extensions of Old World traditions and provided forms of assistance that were often an integral part of immigrants' lives. Records kept by religious institutions can be among the most useful in tracing immigrant origins. It is not uncommon for immigrant church registers to note the foreign birthplaces of those baptized, married, confirmed, transferring in or out of a church, or buried. Native towns or parishes are sometimes listed for sponsors or witnesses of religious events as well. The records of religious organizations, such as schools, orders, newspapers, orphanages, hospitals, old people's homes, and fraternal organizations, are yet other sources for biographical information that may be otherwise hard to find for an immigrant. Methods and sources for finding immigrant church records are discussed in chapter 6, and Jewish records are discussed in chapter 17, Tracking Jewish-American Family History.

RESEARCH APPROACHES

In their eagerness to find the town or city that was home to their ancestors, researchers frequently spend too much time and energy looking in the wrong places—or in the right places but in the wrong sequence. For example, as novices, many are tempted to begin immigrant research with a search of passenger lists.

Most researchers have a strong desire to find detailed documentation of the ship on which their ancestors came to America. Such a passage, after all, is a seminal event in the history of any family. From a passenger list, we hope to learn exactly where an immigrant ancestor came from, how old he or she was at the time, what occupation he or she claimed, the ports of departure and arrival, and anything possible about the journey. But getting answers to these questions depends on when and where an ancestor arrived in the United States. Until the 1880s, a typical passenger list gave only the name, age, sex, occupation, country of origin, and destination of the passenger. The native town was seldom named.

Is the port of the ancestor's arrival known with certainty? Are passenger arrival lists indexed for the port of entry and for the right time period? If there is an index for the port, will the person of interest appear in the index, or can he or she be identified in the long list of frequently misspelled names? If the surname is a common one, how will the person be distinguished from others? While many individuals traveled in groups, making them easier to find, a larger number came to the United States on their own. Unless you are fairly certain of the date and port of arrival, or unless you can quickly and surely identify the immigrant by name, age, occupation, or traveling companions, it may be better to postpone a passenger list search until other sources have been investigated.

Family and Home Sources

In many cases, the *only* evidence of a family's origins will be found in personal possessions. For more information, see chapter 1, The Foundations of Family History Research.

Organizing and Evaluating Material for Clues

A particularly useful way to organize information and clues is to keep a summary of the people the immigrant came in contact with—potential relatives (father-in-law, spouses of children, brothers-in-law) and traveling companions. After you have tracked the individual through life, make a summary of contact points: sponsors and godparents for children, witnesses for deeds and wills, fellow soldiers or officers in military units, neighbors who settled near each other, business partners, surnames of those marrying into the family, and those who worshipped in the same religion, or those in the same cemetery lot.

Previous Research

After reviewing home and family sources, look for research that has been completed by others. Begin with large collections of compiled records before original records, because they usually are easy to search and often provide important clues. You may find that someone else has already identified the immigrant's place of origin. Even if you do not find the place of origin, you will probably uncover important clues that will lead to this information. As you work through these records, seek information for both the immigrant ancestor and other members of the family.

Local Resources

Libraries, archives, and societies in the area where an immigrant settled may have collected previous research about local people. For example, local genealogies, biographies, town or county histories, and genealogical and historical periodicals may furnish place-of-origin information. Seek compiled works done at the town, county, state, or provincial level. Also look for local genealogical or historical societies that may publish periodicals or have research registration programs which could provide valuable information.

Because there is no single source that always indicates the place of origin, it is crucial to thoroughly search all available original records for several reasons. First, searching all records increases your chances of finding the place of origin. Second, you may learn additional identification facts about the immigrant. Also, you can develop a fuller biography and better family group records for the immigrant. Such full information often provides circumstantial evidence such as the date of arrival, which will help you search for a native town.

Among local records, first seek records related to the immigrant's death. These include church records, vital records, obituaries, cemetery records, and probate records. These may give the immigrant's date and place of birth, or the names of parents and other relatives or friends. They can also provide

Major Settlements, Immigration, and Naturalization: A Chronology, 1562-1990[7]

1562: French Huguenots established a colony on Parris Island near Beaufort, South Carolina, but abandoned it within two years.

1565: The earliest Hispanic settlers within the area of the United States settled Saint Augustine, Florida in 1565.

1598: Hispanics settled in New Mexico.

1607: Jamestown, Virginia, was founded by English colonists.

1614: The first major Dutch settlement was founded near Albany, New York.

1619: The first black slaves arrived at Jamestown.

1620: The *Mayflower,* carrying Pilgrims, arrived in Massachusetts.

1623: New Netherland (Hudson River Valley) was settled as a trading post by the Dutch West India Company.

1629–40: The Puritans migrated to New England.

1634: Lord Baltimore founded Maryland as a refuge for English Catholics.

1642: The outbreak of civil war in England brought a decrease in Puritan migration.

1648: The treaty ending the Thirty Years' War stipulated that only the Catholic, Lutheran, and Reformed religions would be tolerated in Germany henceforth. Religious intolerance motivated large numbers of Germans belonging to small sects, such as Baptist Brethren (Dunkers), to leave for America.

1649: Passage of Maryland Toleration Act opened the door to any professing trinitarian Christianity.

1654: North America's first Jewish immigrants fled Portuguese persecution in Brazil, arriving at New Amsterdam.

1660: Acting on mercantilist doctrine that the wealth of a country depends on the number of its inhabitants, Charles II officially discouraged emigration from England.

1670: English courtiers settled the Carolinas.

1681: Quakers founded Pennsylvania based on William Penn's "holy experiment" in universal philanthropy and brotherhood.

1683: The first German settlers (Mennonites) arrived in Pennsylvania.

1685: Huguenots fleeing religious intolerance in France and the Revocation of the Edict of Nantes by Louis XIV settled in South Carolina.

1697: The slave trade monopoly of the Royal African Company ended and the slave trade expanded rapidly, especially among New Englanders.

1707: A new era of Scottish migration began as a result of the Act of Union between England and Scotland. Scots settled in colonial seaports. Lowland artisans and laborers left Glasgow to become indentured servants in tobacco colonies and New York.

1709: In the wake of devastation caused by wars of Louis XIV, German Palatines settled in the Hudson Valley and Pennsylvania.

1717: The English Parliament legalized transportation to American colonies as punishment; contractors began regular shipments from jails, mostly to Virginia and Maryland.

1718: Discontent with the land system: absentee landlords, high rents, and short leases in the homeland motivated large numbers of Scotch-Irish to emigrate. Most settled first in New England, then in Maryland and Pennsylvania.

1730: Germans and Scotch Irish from Pennsylvania colonized Virginia valley and the Carolina back country.

1732: James Oglethorpe settled Georgia as a buffer against Spanish and French attack, as a producer of raw silk, and as a haven for imprisoned debtors.

1740: The English Parliament enacted the Naturalization Act, which conferred British citizenship on alien colonial immigrants in an attempt to encourage Jewish immigration.

1745: Scottish rebels were transported to America after a Jacobite attempt to put Stuarts back on the throne failed.

1755: French Acadians were expelled from Nova Scotia on suspicion of disloyalty. The survivors settled in Louisiana.

1771–73: Severe crop failure and depression in the Ulster linen trade brought a new influx of Scotch-Irish to the American colonies.

1775: The outbreak of hostilities in American colonies caused the British government to suspend emigration.

1783: The revolutionary war ended with the Treaty of Paris. Immigration to America resumed, with especially large numbers of Scotch-Irish.

1789: The outbreak of the French Revolution prompted the emigration of aristocrats and royalist sympathizers.

1790: The first federal activity in an area previously under the control of the individual colonies: An act of 26 March 1790 attempted to establish a uniform rule for naturalization by setting the residence requirement at two years. Children of naturalized citizens were considered to be citizens (1 Stat. 103).

1791: After a slave revolt in Santo Domingo, 10,000 to 20,000 French exiles took refuge in the United States, principally in towns on the Atlantic seaboard.

1793: As a result of the French Revolution, Girondists and Jacobins threatened by guillotine fled to the United States.

1795: Provisions of a naturalization act of 29 January 1795 included the following: free white aliens of good moral character; five-year residency with one year in state; declaration of intention to be filed after two years; petition to be filed three years after the declaration (1 Stat. 414).

1798: An unsuccessful Irish rebellion sent rebels to the United States. Distressed artisans, yeoman farmers, and agricultural laborers affected by bad harvests and low prices joined the rebels in emigrating.

U.S. Alien and Sedition Acts gave the president powers to seize and expel resident aliens suspected of engaging in subversive activities.

Naturalization requirements were changed to require fourteen years' residency; the declaration of intention was to be filed five years before citizenship (1 Stat. 566).

Aliens considered to be dangerous to the peace and safety of the United States were to be removed; passenger lists were to be given to the collector of customs (1 Stat. 570).

1802: Residency requirements of the 1795 act were reasserted; children of naturalized citizens were considered to be citizens (2 Stat. 153).

1803: War between England and France resumed. As a result, transatlantic trade was interrupted and emigration from continental Europe became practically impossible.

Irish emigration was curtailed by the British Passenger Act, which limited the numbers to be carried by emigrant ships.

1807: Congress prohibited the importing of black slaves into the country. Individual states previously prohibited importation of slaves: Delaware in 1776; Virginia, 1778; Maryland, 1783; South Carolina, 1787; North Carolina, 1794; Georgia, 1798. South Carolina reopened importation of slaves in 1803.

1812: The War of 1812 between Britain and the United States brought immigration to a halt.

1814: The War of 1812 ended with the Treaty of Ghent.

1815: The first great wave of immigration to the United States brings 5 million immigrants between 1815 and 1860.

1818: Liverpool became the most-used port of departure for Irish and British immigrants, as well as considerable numbers of Germans and other Europeans as the Black Ball Line of sailing packets began regular Liverpool-New York service.

1819: The first significant federal legislation relating to immigration: passenger lists to be given to the collector of customs; reporting of immigration to the United States on a regular basis; specific sustenance rules for passengers of ships leaving U.S. ports for Europe (3 Stat. 489).

1820: The U.S. population was at 9,638,453. One hundred and fifty-one thousand new immigrants arrived in 1820 alone.

The government of Prussia attempted to halt emigration by making it a crime to urge anyone to emigrate.

1824: Alien minors were naturalized upon reaching twenty-one years of age if they had lived in the United States for five years (4 Stat. 69).

1825: Great Britain officially recognized the view that England was overpopulated and repealed laws prohibiting emigration.

The first group of Norwegian immigrants arrives from their overpopulated homeland.

1830: Public land in Illinois was allotted by Congress to Polish revolutionary refugees.

1837: Financial panic. Nativists claimed that immigration lowered wage levels, contributed to the decline of the apprenticeship system, and generally depressed the condition of labor.

1840: The Cunard Line began passenger transportation between Europe and the United States, opening the steamship era.

1845: The Native American party, precursor of the nativist, anti-immigrant Know-Nothing party, was founded.

1846: Crop failures in Europe. Mortgage foreclosures sent tens of thousands of dispossessed to United States.

1846–47: Irish of all classes emigrated to the United States as a result of the potato famine.

1848: Failure of German revolution resulted in the emigration of political refugees to America.

1855: Castle Garden immigration receiving station opened in New York City to accommodate mass immigration.

Alien women married to U.S. citizens were considered to be citizens (10 Stat. 604).

1856: The Know-Nothing movement was defeated in the presidential election. An Albany convention to promote Irish rural colonization in the United States was strongly opposed by Eastern bishops and thus unsuccessful.

1860: New York became "the largest Irish city in the world." Of its 805,651 residents, 203,760 were Irish-born.

1861–65: The Civil War caused a significant drop in the number of foreigners entering the United States. Large numbers of immigrants serve on both sides during the Civil War.

1862: Aliens who received honorable discharges from the U.S. Army were not required to file declarations (12 Stat. 597).

The Homestead Act encouraged naturalization by granting citizens title to 160 acres, provided that the land was tilled for five years.

1864: Congress centralized control of immigration with a commissioner under the secretary of state. In an attempt to meet the labor crisis caused by the Civil War, Congress legalized the importation of contract laborers.

1875: The first direct federal regulation of immigration was established by prohibiting entry of prostitutes and convicts. Residency permits were required of Asians (18 Stat. 477).

1880: The U.S. population was 50,155,783. More than 5.2 million immigrants entered the country between 1880 and 1890.

1882: The Chinese exclusion law was established, curbing Chinese immigration. Further exclusions: persons convicted of political offenses, "lunatics," "idiots," and persons likely to become public charges. A head tax of fifty cents was placed on each immigrant.

A sharp rise in Jewish emigration to the United States was prompted by the outbreak of anti-Semitism in Russia.

1883: In an effort to alleviate a labor shortage caused by the freeing of slaves, the Southern Immigration Association was founded to promote immigration to the South.

1885: Contract laborers were denied admission to United States by the Foran Act. However, skilled laborers, artists, actors, lecturers, and domestic servants were not barred. Individuals in the United States were not to be prevented from assisting the immigration of relatives and personal friends.

1886: The Statue of Liberty was dedicated.

1888: The first act since 1798 providing for the expulsion of aliens became law.

1890: New York had the distinction of being home to as many Germans as Hamburg, Germany.

1891: The Bureau of Immigration was established under the Treasury Department to federally administer all immigration laws (except the Chinese Exclusion Act). Congress added health qualifications to immigration restrictions. Classes of persons denied the right to immigrate to the United States included the insane, paupers, persons with contagious diseases, persons convicted of felonies or misdemeanors of moral turpitude, and polygamists (26 Stat. 1084).

Pogroms in Russia caused large numbers of Jews to immigrate to the United States.

1892: Ellis Island replaced Castle Garden as the reception center for immigrants.

Immigration of Chinese to the United States was prohibited for ten years; Chinese illegally in the United States could be removed (27 Stat. 25).

1893: Chinese legally in the United States were required to apply to collectors of internal revenue for certificates of residence or be removed (28 Stat. 7).

Economic depression brought dramatic strength to the anti-Catholic American Protective Association.

1894: Congress created the Bureau of Immigration. The Immigration Restriction League was organized to lead the restrictionist movement for the next twenty-five years. The league emphasized the distinction between "old" (northern and western European) and "new" (southern and eastern European) immigrants.

Aliens who received honorable discharges from the U.S. Navy and U.S. Marine Corps were not required to file declarations (28 Stat. 124).

1894–96: To escape Moslem massacres, Armenian Christians began emigrating to the United States.

1897: President Cleveland vetoed literacy tests for immigrants.

1900: The U.S. Population at 75,994,575. More than 3,687,000 immigrants were admitted in the previous ten years.

1903: Extensive codification of existing immigration law. Added to the exclusion list were polygamists and political radicals (anarchists or persons believing in the overthrow by force or violence of the government of the United States or any government, or in the assassination of public officials—a result of President McKinley's assassination by an anarchist).

1905: As a protest against the influx of Asian laborers, the Japanese and Korean Exclusion League was formed by organized labor.

1906: The Bureau of Immigration and Naturalization was established. The purpose of the act of 29 June 1906 (32 Stat. 596) was to provide for a uniform rule for the naturalization of aliens throughout the United States. The law, effective 27 September 1906, was designed to provide "dignity, uniformity, and regularity" to the naturalization procedure. It established procedural safeguards and called for specific and uniform information regarding applicants and recipients of citizenship status. Rule Nine of the code required that all blank forms and records be obtained from and controlled by the Bureau of Immigration, "Those alone being official forms. No other forms shall be used." As a consequence of the act, the agency controlled the number of courts able to naturalize. Knowledge of English became a basic requirement for citizenship.

1907: An increased head tax on immigrants was enacted. People with physical or mental defects or tuberculosis and children unaccompanied by parents were added to the exclusion list. Japanese immigration was restricted.

1907–08: A Japanese government agreement to deny passports to laborers going directly from Japan to the United States failed to satisfy West Coast exclusionists.

1910: The Mexican Revolution sent thousands to the United States seeking employment.

1913: The Alien Land Law passed by California effectively barred Japanese, as "aliens ineligible for citizenship," from owning agricultural land in the state.

1914–18: World War I halted a period of mass migration to the United States.

1917: To the exclusion list were added illiterates, persons of "psychopathic inferiority," men and women entering for immoral purposes, alcoholics, stowaways, and vagrants.

The Jones Act made Puerto Ricans U.S. citizens and eligible for the draft.

1919: Anti-foreign prejudice was transferred from German Americans to alien revolutionaries and radicals in the Big Red Scare. Thousands of aliens were seized in the Palmer raids, and hundreds were deported.

1921: The first quantitative immigration law set temporary annual quotas according to nationality. The emergency immigration quotas heavily favored natives of northern and western Europe and all but closed the door to southern and eastern Europeans. An immediate drop in immigration followed.

1922: Alien wives of U.S. citizens were allowed to file for citizenship after one year of residency. The citizenship status of native-born American women was removed if they were married to aliens not eligible for citizenship (42 Stat. 1021).

1923: A strong anti-immigrant movement spearheaded by the Ku Klux Klan reached peak strength.

1924: The National Origins Act, the first permanent immigration quota law, established a discriminatory quota system, nonquota status, and a consular control system. The Border Patrol was established (49 Stat. 153).

1929: The National Origins Act came into effect. The stock market crash and economic crisis prompted demands for further immigration reductions. The Hoover administration ordered rigorous enforcement of a prohibition against the admission of persons liable to be public charges.

1930: The U.S. population was 123,203,000. Only 528,000 new immigrants arrived in the previous decade, the lowest number since the 1830s.

1933: As Hitler's anti-Semitic campaign began, Jewish refugees from Nazi Germany emigrated.

1934: Filipino immigration was restricted to an annual quota of fifty by the Philippine Independence Act.

1936: American women who had lost their citizenship because they married aliens are allowed to regain citizenship by taking oaths of allegiance to the United States (49 Stat. 1917).

1939: World War II began.

1940: The Alien Registration Act, also known as the Smith Act, called for registration and fingerprinting of all aliens. Approximately 5 million aliens were registered.

1941: Immigrant groups supported the united war effort as the United States entered World War II.

1942: Japanese-Americans were evacuated from their homes and moved to detention camps.

Through the Bracero Program, Mexican laborers were strongly encouraged to come to the United States to ease the shortage of farm workers brought on by World War II.

1943: Legislation provided for the importation of agricultural workers from North, South, and Central America—the basis of the "Bracero Program."

The Chinese exclusion laws were repealed.

1945: Thousands of Puerto Ricans emigrated to escape poverty. Many settled in New York.

1946: The War Brides Act facilitated the immigration of foreign-born wives, fiancé(e)s, husbands, and children of U.S. armed forces personnel.

1948: The Displaced Persons Act, the first U.S. policy for admitting persons fleeing persecution, allowed 400,000 refugees to enter the United States during a four-year period.

1950: Increased grounds for exclusion and deportation of subversives were enacted. All aliens were required to report their addresses annually.

1952: The Immigration and Naturalization Act brought into one comprehensive statute the multiple laws which governed immigration and naturalization to date: reaffirmed the national origins quota system; limited immigration from the Eastern Hemisphere while leaving the Western Hemisphere unrestricted; established preferences for skilled workers and relatives of U.S. citizens and permanent resident aliens; tightened security and screening standards and procedures; and lowered the age requirement for naturalization to eighteen years (66 Stat. 163).

The McCarren-Walter Immigration and Naturalization Act extended token immigration quotas to Asian countries.

1953–56: The Refugee Relief Act admitted more than 200,000 refugees beyond existing quotas.

Visas were granted to some 5,000 Hungarians after the 1956 revolt. President Eisenhower invited 30,000 more to come on a parole basis.

1954: Ellis Island closed, marking an end to mass immigration.

1957: Special legislation admitted Hungarian refugees.

1959: Castro's successful revolution in Cuba began the emigration of refugees.

1960: The United States paroled Cuban refugees.

1962: The United States granted special permission for the admission of refugees from Hong Kong.

1965: The National Origins Quota System was abolished, but the principle of numerical restriction by establishing 170,000 hemispheric and 20,000 per-country ceilings and a seven-category preference system (favoring close relatives of U.S. citizens and permanent resident aliens, those with needed occupational skills, and refugees) for the Eastern Hemisphere and a separate 120,000 ceiling for the Western Hemisphere was maintained (79 Stat. 911).

The Cuban refugee airlift program admitted Cubans to the United States under special quotas for the next eight years.

1970: The Immigration Act of 1965 was amended by President Nixon, further liberalizing admission to the United States.

1972: Congress passed the Ethnic Heritage Studies Bill, encouraging bilingual education and programs pertaining to ethnic culture.

1976: The 20,000-per-country immigration ceilings and the system of preference system for Western Hemisphere countries was applied, and separate hemispheric ceilings were maintained.

1978: The separate ceilings for Eastern and Western Hemisphere immigration were combined into one worldwide limit of 290,000.

1979: Congress appropriated more than $334 million for the rescue and resettlement of Vietnamese "boat people."

1980: The Refugee Act removed refugees as a preference category and established clear criteria and procedures for their admission, reducing the worldwide ceiling for immigrants from 290,000 to 270,000.

The so-called "Freedom Flotilla" of Cuban refugees came to the United States.

1986: Comprehensive immigration legislation legalized aliens who had resided in the United States in an unlawful status since 1 January 1982; established sanctions prohibiting employers from hiring, recruiting, or referring for a fee aliens known to be unauthorized to work in the United States; created a new classification of temporary agricultural worker and provided for the legalization of certain such workers; and established a visa waiver pilot program allowing the admission of certain nonimmigrants without visas.

Separate legislation stipulated that aliens deriving their immigrant status based on a marriage of less than two years apply within ninety days after their second-year anniversary to remove conditional status.

1989: Adjustment from temporary to permanent status of certain nonimmigrants who were employed in the United States as registered nurses for at least three years and met established certification standards.

1990: Comprehensive immigration legislation increased total immigration under an overall flexible cap of 675,000 immigrants beginning in fiscal year 1995, preceded by a 700,000 level during fiscal years 1992 through 1994; created separate admission categories for family-sponsored, employment-based, and diversity immigrants; revised all grounds for exclusion and deportation, significantly rewriting the political and ideological grounds and repealing some grounds for exclusion; authorized the attorney general to grant temporary protected status to undocumented alien nationals of designated countries subject to armed conflict or natural disasters, and designated such status for Salvadorans; revised and established new non-immigrant admission categories; revised and extended through fiscal year 1994 the Visa Waiver Program; revised naturalization authority and requirements; and revised enforcement activities.

important clues about religion, naturalization, length of residence, arrival and property in the old country.

After death records, seek out the records of other vital events such as the immigrant's marriage and births of children. Vital record entries for marriages and births were kept by both church and civil authorities. Other local original records include a wide variety of record types. Use census records, court records, and land and property records to establish where an immigrant settled, his or her occupation, neighbors, and other information.

Voter registrations are not available for every city or county in the United States, but when they are, they can be valuable sources of immigration information. Typically the registrations (usually in list form) are kept at the county level and provide the full name, address, birth date, birthplace, and, for naturalized citizens, the naturalization court and date (figure 13-5). Many lists will note the number of years the voter was a resident of the state and county.

Employment files and voters' registration records may give the date and court of naturalization, port and date of arrival, ship, and country of birth. These records are created as a result of residence in the United States.

By studying a combination of records it is usually possible to estimate an immigrant's year of arrival in the United States. Even when an immigrant's census or naturalization records do not provide a specific arrival date, noting the dates and places of birth of the immigrant's children in census records, or tracking urban dwellers in city directories may help determine the immigration date. Look for clues to these dates in places the individual or family first settled and in land purchases.

Immigration Sources

After the above-mentioned sources have been investigated, a search of immigration and naturalization records is in order. Citizenship papers, passenger lists, and immigrant aid society records fall into this category. Passports and oaths of allegiance are other valuable sources. Some records, though created for other purposes, will provide evidence of citizenship status. If the immigrant served in the U.S. military, there may be special naturalization papers connected with that service. Local and federal courts usually record military naturalizations in separate ledgers, and these may be indexed with other naturalizations in that jurisdiction. Some religious denominations kept separate lists of immigrant families as they arrived, reporting on their arrival, place of origin, and where they settled.

Passenger arrival lists for many ports and time periods are indexed, so approximate dates may be sufficient to begin a search. Unfortunately, some ports, such as New York City (from 1846 to 1897), are only partially indexed. Lists of ship arrivals may be useful in determining possible arrival dates if an approximate arrival date or a ship name is known. Note, however, that a ship may have arrived in North America several times in a year.

While none of the records mentioned should be overlooked, most American immigration and naturalization records before

Figure 13-5. Page from an 1892 poll list of Chicago voters that was recently found in the Cook County, Illinois, County Recorder's Office. The records have since been microfilmed and are available through the Illinois State Archives and through several microfilm rental libraries.

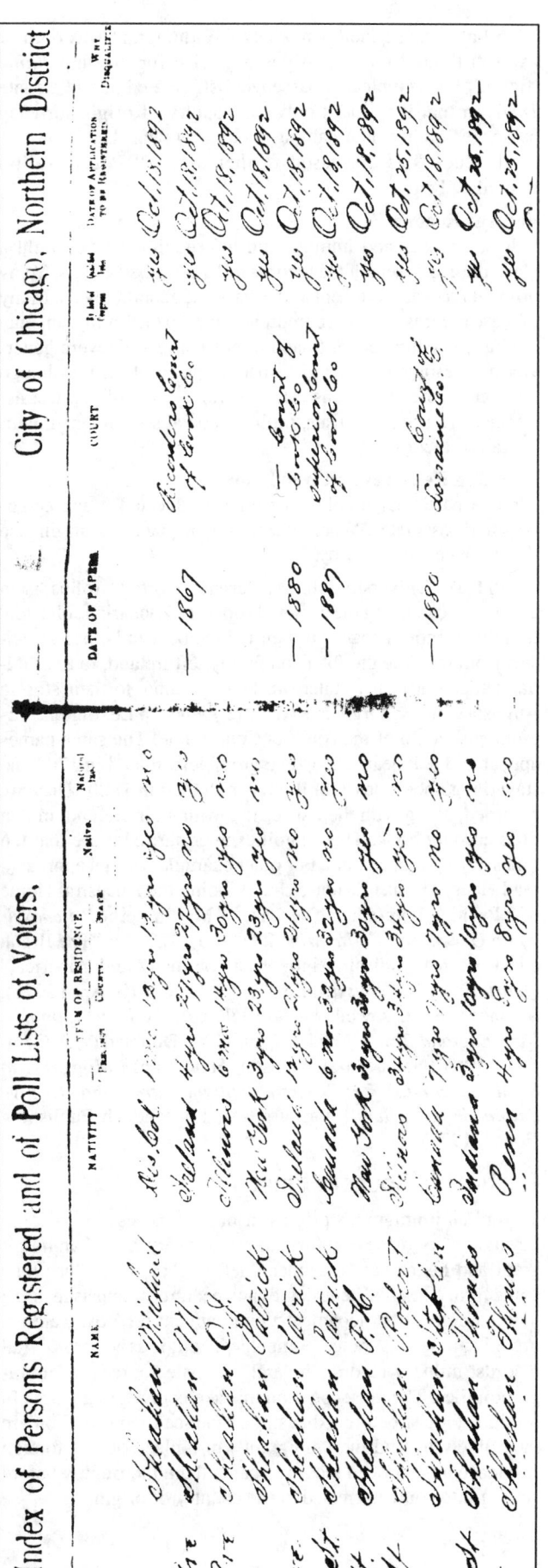

1906 fail to name the town where the immigrant was born or lived in the old country. A passenger list for the ship *Rhine* (figure 13-6) is typical of passenger lists created before the late 1880s in that it includes only the country of origin for each passenger, rather than naming a city or town. The nature of these records is discussed further under "Naturalization Records," below.

Federal Records

If local records and immigration information do not yield a place of origin, search the records of larger jurisdictions. Many original records were kept at the state and federal levels. Many of these records were not comprehensive, so the immigrant may not have been included. In addition, such records were generally not designed to record a specific place of origin, though there are some exceptions. The federal records of greatest assistance are usually census, military, social security, and naturalization records.

Tracking Relatives and Neighbors

When a particular immigrant cannot be located, track neighbors and associates. When you find their places of origin, see if your ancestor is nearby.

In Duke University Library, Durham, North Carolina, is an account book among the personal papers of Zachariah Johnston. It includes money loaned to family members and close associates from the time the Johnston family left Ireland, to their initial settlement near Bethlehem, Pennsylvania, to their stop in Augusta County, Virginia, to their residence in Lexington, Virginia, just south of the Augusta County line. The same names appear and reappear. The whole group left Ireland in 1709 and stayed together at least until Zachariah died in 1800. They are recorded, along with their specific townland in Ireland, in that little account book. These families intermarried more that ten times during that century. For other examples of this approach, read Henry (Hank) Z. Jones, Jr., "Finding the Ancestral Home of a Palatine Forefather: The Case of Martin Zerbe," *Pennsylvania Genealogical Magazine* 29 (1975): 129–32; "The Braun and Loesch Families: Neighbors in Germany and America," *Quarterly of the Pennsylvania German Society* 10 (April 1976); Sumner Chilton Powell, *Puritan Village: The Formation of a New England Town* (Garden City, N.Y.: Doubleday & Company, 1965); and Jean Stephenson, *Scotch-Irish Migration to South Carolina, 1772: Reverend William Martin and His Five Shiploads of Settlers* (Strasburg, Va.: Shenandoah Publishing House, 1971).

USING U.S. SOURCES FIRST

To find an immigrant's origins, it may be necessary to comb through every piece of information and every record an immigrant and his or her descendants left in America. Clues may come from compiled genealogies and pedigrees; census records; land records; court documents; employment records; fraternal organizations; insurance companies; religious records; vital records; military records; federal and state sources; or immigration files. The most common mistake is to begin a search in foreign sources before exhausting American records. You are most likely to find the immigrant's birthplace or last foreign residence in American records: search them thoroughly before getting into sources created in the country of origin.

THE IMMIGRATION PROCESS

Immigration Patterns

Once you have exhausted American records, consider immigration patterns. Some immigrants came directly to the United States from their places of birth. Many, however, came via other countries where they may have stayed for months, years, or even generations. Some French Huguenots stayed for extended periods in Germany, Switzerland, Holland, England, or some other place before coming to America. The Palatines who immigrated in 1709 to New York came via England and Ireland. English, Irish, French and several other nationalities may have made Canada their home before coming to the United States. Some Germans went to Russia, Lithuania, or Brazil before establishing residency in America. Australia, the Carribean, and South America were stopping places for many groups before they came here. The researcher who is unaware of these possibilities may miss births, marriages, or records of deaths of parents or spouses in the temporary residences.

Another overlooked fact is that immigrants did not always stay in the United States. Many came as adventurers or looking for temporary jobs that would enable them to return to their homelands with their savings. Some immigrant groups traveled back and forth across the ocean as work opportunities presented themselves. Some researchers have documented two or more generations settling in this country and then been puzzled by the sudden disappearance of one or more of the family members. In some cases the fathers or both parents, and in other cases the children, became disenchanted with the American lifestyle and returned to the home country permanently. When a family or individual tracked in American records suddenly disappears, it is easy to assume that there was a death or a move within the U.S. In these less-than-common circumstances, it sometimes pays to look back into the records of the country of origin.

Tickets

The purchase of tickets and travel accommodations was usually done through an emigration agent. Early agents were appointed by church or emigrant groups to secure the best price and to insure that fellow travelers were not cheated. These agents, some of whom were pastors or church clerks, traveled with the group to their destination. Later agents worked for shipping lines to fill steerages so the trip was profitable for the company. They were licensed by local authorities and paid on commission or percentage, some by the length of the journey and some by the total cost of the ticket and provisions. For a more detailed description of how these agents operated, see R.J. Dickson, *Ulster Emigration to Colonial America, 1718–1775* (London: Routledge and Kegan Paul, 1966), Norman McDonald, *Canada: Immigration and Colonization, 1841–1903* (Toronto: Macmillan of Canada, 1976); and Clifford Neal Smith and Anna P. Smith, *American Genealogical Resources in German Archives* (New York: R.R. Bowker, 1977).

Indentures

Emigrants too poor to pay their own way could agree to sell themselves into service for the cost of their passage. Those who contracted through an emigrant agent before they left their country of origin were referred to as indentured servants. They carried a copy of the contract with them, knowing in advance how much time they owed. These contracts would be sold to employers in the New World. Those who did not negotiate con-

Figure 13-6. Passenger lists created before the late 1880s, such as this one for the ship *Rhine,* which sailed from London on 9 August 1873, rarely indicate a precise birthplace.

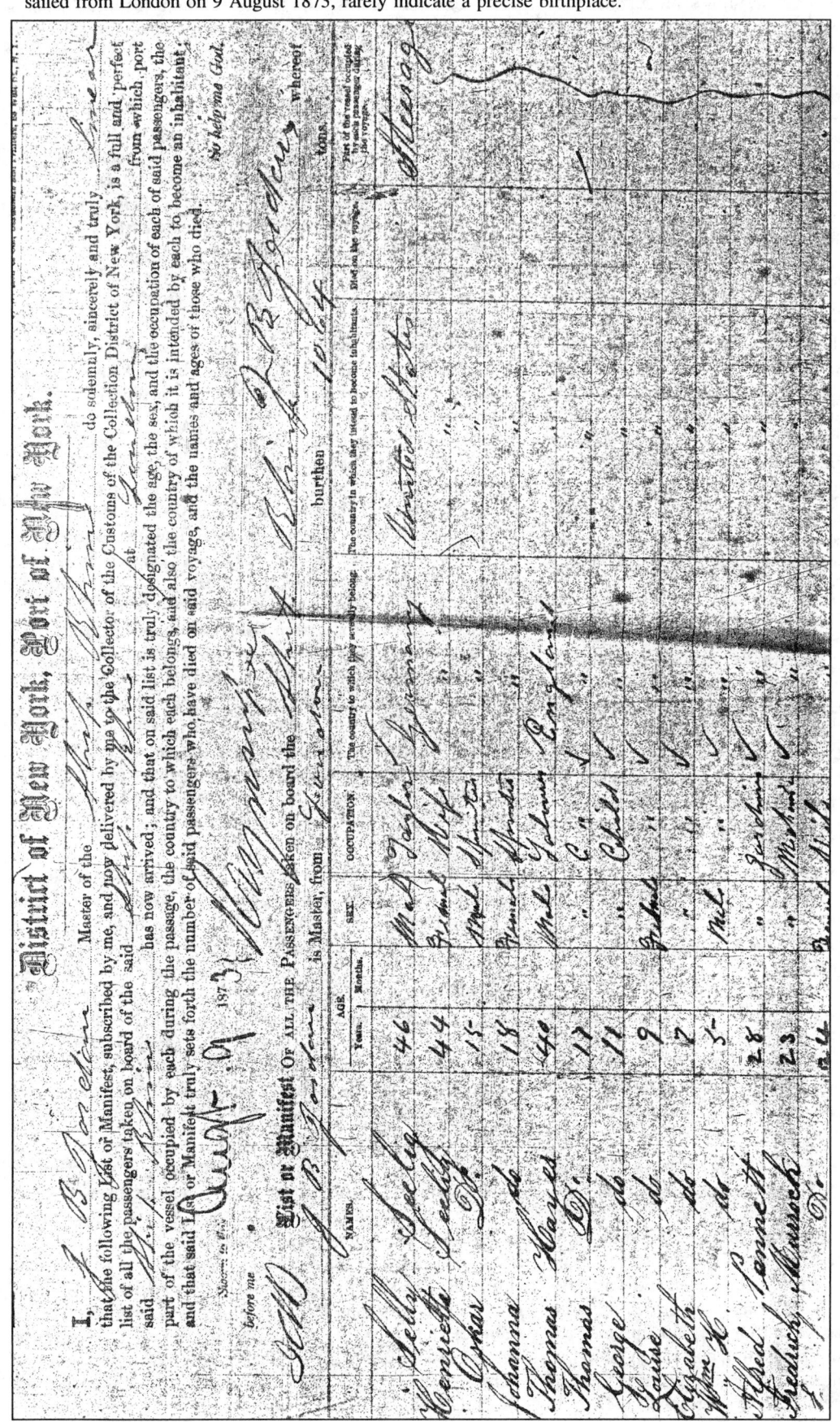

tracts before they left redeemed the cost of their passage and provisions by selling themselves to the highest bidder once they arrived in America. They were called redemptioners. English emigrants were most often indentured with articles signed before a magistrate; Germans usually redeemed their passages at auction. Richard B. Morris, *Government and Labor in Early America* (New York: Harper and Row, 1965) is the classic work on the subject. Other studies examine servitude in individual colonies—for example, Warren B. Smith, *White Servitude in Colonial South Carolina* (Danielsville, Ga.: Heritage Papers, 1972). A list of these local studies is included in Barbara Bigham, "Colonists in Bondage: Indentured Servants in America," *Early American Life* 10 (1979): 30–33, 83–84.

The Journey

Conditions on the immigrants' voyage changed and improved over time, especially with the advent of steamships in the mid-1800s which considerably shortened the journey. Also, as early as the 1810s, some foreign governments established rules and regulations regarding the number of immigrants a ship could carry, based on its size. Because much of the interest in the nature of the voyage pertains to colonial immigrants, the following descriptions will provide a general picture.

Emigrants traveling from German principalities to Pennsylvania faced a long, three-part journey. The first stage was the trip down the Rhine to Rotterdam or Amsterdam. Wrote one 1750 voyager:

> This journey lasts from the beginning of May to the end of October, fully half a year, amid such hardships as no one is able to describe adequately with their misery. The cause is because the Rhine boats from Heilbronn to Holland have to pass by 26 custom houses, at all of which the ships are examined, which is done when it suits the convenience of the custom-house officials. In the meantime the ships with the people are detained long, so that the passengers have to spend much money. The trip down the Rhine lasts therefore four, five, and even six weeks. When the ships come to Holland, they are detained there likewise five to six weeks. Because things are very dear there, the poor people have to spend nearly all they have during that time.[8]

The second stage was from Rotterdam to the English port of Cowes on the Isle of Wight, then the principal port for immigrant traffic, although ships also stopped at Dover, Plymouth, London, and other ports. Here was another delay while ships awaited customs clearance, provisioning, and favorable winds. This phase took fourteen to twenty-one days.

The final stage of the journey was the seven-to-twelve week ocean crossing, later shortened by steam to fewer than fourteen days. The passengers were densely packed into the steerage decks below the ship's waterline. Shipping companies, to increase profits and cut expenses, often filled the cargo spaces with people too, rather than carry adequate food and water. By the mid-nineteenth century, government authorities required minimum rations of food and water from the ships' provisions; but earlier travelers risked disease, storm, and a high mortality rate. For a detailed description of the ocean voyage, see Philip Taylor, *The Distant Magnet: European Emigration to the U.S.A.* (London: Eyre and Spottiswoode, 1971).

The process of arrival in the new country generated another series of records. The Reverend Henry M. Muehlenberg described the arrival process in a report to his superiors in Halle, Germany, in 1769:

> After much delay one ship after another arrives in the harbor of Philadelphia, when the rough and severe winter is before the door. One or more merchants receive the lists of the freights and the agreement which the emigrants have signed with their own hand in Holland, together with the bills for their travel down the Rhine and the advances of the "newlanders" for provisions, which they received on the ships on account. Formerly the freight for a single person was six to ten louis d'ors, but now it amounts to fourteen to seventeen louis d'ors [one louis d'ors equalled about $4.50]. Before the ship is allowed to cast anchor at the harbor front, the passengers are all examined, according to the law in force, by a physician, as to whether any contagious disease exists among them. Then the arrivals are led in procession to the City Hall and there they must render the oath of allegiance to the king of Great Britain. After that they are brought back to the ship. Then announcements are printed in the newspapers, stating how many of the new arrivals are to be sold. Those who have money are released. Whoever has well-to-do friends seeks a loan from them to pay the passage, but there are only a few who succeed. The ship becomes the market-place. The buyers make their choice among the arrivals and bargain with them for a certain number of years and days. They then take them to the merchant, pay their passage and their other debts and receive from the government authorities a written document, which makes the newcomers their property for a definite period.[9]

Some aspects of the immigrant experience were traumatic—selling all they owned, traveling for weeks to reach a new land, watching loved ones sicken and die away from the rest of the family. Many immigrants cushioned the shock by living, at least temporarily, with family and friends who had already immigrated. When searching census records, it is sometimes helpful to record the names of all boarders listed in a multiple-family dwelling, because they are often related to the head of house even if the surname is different. As the family head of house acquired work and earned some income, the family moved into its own residence, often rented, sometimes owned.

Immigrants of the same background tended to cluster in particular areas so that language would be less of a problem. These immigrant clusters have been plotted on maps by historians. If your ancestor does not appear in a city directory right away, check these immigrant maps. Examples include Leo F. Schnore, *The New Urban History* (Princeton, N.J.: Princeton University Press, 1973), which shows the locations of German, Irish, native-born, and mixed populations in the city of Milwaukee; and Donald B. Cole, *Immigration City: Lawrence, Massachusetts, 1845–1921* (Chapel Hill, N.C.: University of North Carolina Press, 1963). Within one mile of the local textile mills, immigrants representing fifty-one different countries settled.

AMERICAN SOURCES FOR DOCUMENTING IMMIGRANTS

FAMILY HISTORIES

Published genealogies and family histories comprise one of the most significant compiled sources. These genealogies, generally compiled by family members, sometimes include biographies, pictures, maps, timelines, and heraldry, and some are documented. Often they go back to the original immigrant with information concerning ethnic and geographical beginnings. They generally tend to show all that was known about the family at the time it was written. Technological advances of the past few years have facilitated research, publication, and the distribution of thousands of genealogies and family histories. In some cases, nearby or distant relatives have completed well-documented genealogies and their work can spare you hours of work and frustration. It may be that someone else has identified your immigrant ancestor's place of origin in a published work. Keep in mind, however, that it always pays to double-check the accuracy of any such research.

Two useful finding aids for locating published genealogies are the Family History Library surname catalog, which identifies approximately 60,000 North American genealogies; and the catalogs of the Library of Congress. Among them is Marion J. Kaminkow, ed., *Genealogies in the Library of Congress: A Bibliography*, 2 vols. and 2 supplements (Baltimore: Magna Carta Book Co., 1972, 1977, 1987) and *Genealogies Cataloged by the Library of Congress Since 1986* (Washington, D.C.: Library of Congress Cataloging Distribution Services Center, 1991). Most archives, historical societies, and genealogical societies have special collections and indexes of genealogies of value to immigrant origin researchers. Search as many library catalogs and indexes as possible. Collections vary from one library to another, and the ever-growing number of published family histories increases the potential for finding information on one or more of your immigrant ancestors as time goes by.

DATABASES

A growing number of genealogical databases (both electronic and manual) are available. They are easy to search and often include immigrant ancestors. Many appropriate databases are described in chapter 2, Databases, Indexes, and Other Finding Aids. Many of these records have a worldwide focus and can be searched strictly by surname, so only a vague idea of place of origin is needed to search them. Two of the most important databases are the Family History Library's Ancestral File, which links millions of computerized names into families and pedigrees (many lines extend back to the country of origin, and it can also help to find other researchers on your lines); and the Family Group Records Collection (available on microfilm from the Family History Library), which includes millions of family group sheets arranged alphabetically by the father's name. Many lines are followed back to the emigrant's place of origin. The International Genealogical Index, also discussed in chapter 2, is another significant database to search. Important to keep in mind is the fact that European borders have changed with relative frequency. For example, the geography of twentieth-century Germany has changed radically several times since the sixteenth century (figure 13-7).

International Genealogical Index

This well-known index is actually a database of births and deaths and lists hundreds of millions of names by country or state. It serves as a partial index to church births and marriages, and is one of the most helpful tools for finding specific individuals or localizing where surnames were most common.

Early in your research check the International Genealogical Index (IGI) at the Family History Library, one of its family history centers, or at one of selected libraries across the United States. It is the largest genealogical database in the world; there are 200 million entries in the 1993 edition. It indexes and abstracts births and marriages in civil and church records with some other records for some countries. The index is easy to check because it is available on microfiche or on CD-ROM and combines spelling variants in one alphabetized sequence. Most countries can be searched by county, or by searching the entire country. For more information on the IGI, see chapter 2.

Emigrant/Immigrant Databases

A number of computer projects concerned with immigrants have been underway for many years. Mostly supported by public grants to universities, they enter the public domain when they are complete. Inquiries can be addressed to such a project directly in care of the sponsoring university or institution. Below are some examples of databases that specifically concern immigrants.

Don Yoder, a retired folklife professor of University of Pennsylvania and former editor of *Pennsylvania Folklife*, began a project to link Pennsylvania German emigrant lists with Ameri-

Figure 13-7. Sixteenth-century Germany. From Lee C. Hopple, "European Religious and Spatial Origins of the Pennsylvania Dutch," *Pennsylvania Folklife* (Autumn 1979): 2–11.

can church records and other local sources in Pennsylvania, thus bridging the Atlantic. Under his editorship, *Pennsylvania Folklife* published several lists that he translated from the German. See Arlene H. Eakle, "Emigrant Sources for Tracing Pennsylvania German Ancestors," *APG Newsletter* 3 (May 1981): 8–13, for titles.

Dr. Richard Vann, professor of history and letters at Wesleyan University, has created a database of 35,000 English Quakers. Taken from alphabetized registers in the England's Public Record Office, his project includes data on Quakers who immigrated to the colonies before the American Revolution.

Ulf Beijbom, director of the House of Emigrants at the Emigrant Institute, Växjö, Sweden, is indexing all the Swedish-American church records, while the University in Umeå is creating a computerized index to all Swedish church records. Meanwhile, the Emigrant Register in Karlstad has created a database of more than 1 million names covering all of Sweden. For each emigrant, a special questionnaire was prepared that included information from church registers, remaining relatives, returning emigrants and even newspapers.

The Balch Institute at Temple University is using the U.S. customs passenger lists created from 1850 to 1892 to study immigration in a variety of aspects. Data input from the passenger lists is coded and then published in several series based on ethnic groups by Scholarly Resources of Wilmington, Delaware. See, for example, *Germans to America* and *Italians to America*. An earlier compilation of Irish arrivals, *Famine Immigrants*, was published by the Genealogical Publishing Company of Baltimore, Maryland.

GENEALOGICAL COMPENDIA

Collected lineages are often published in genealogical dictionaries and periodicals; they are especially useful if the indexes are good. An outstanding example of a compendium that includes places of origin is Hank Z. Jones, *The Palatine Families of New York: A Study of the German Immigrants Who Arrived in Colonial New York in 1710* (Universal City, Calif.: the author, 1985), which focuses on the Germans who arrived in New York in 1710. His extensive research into the origins of these early colonists is a model for others to follow. Also see Hank Z. Jones, *More Palatine Families: Some Immigrants to the Middle Colonies 1717–1776 and Their European Origins Plus New Discoveries on German Families Who Arrived in Colonial New York in 1710* (Universal City, Calif.: the author, 1991). For a number of years, the Genealogical Publishing Company has reprinted journal articles identifying the origins of early colonists and has published them as sets. The chapter bibliographies identify the current titles.

LOCAL HISTORIES AND BIOGRAPHIES

Published histories of towns, counties, or regions in which an ancestor lived are often the key to identifying the national and ethnic origin of an immigrant. Histories of a locality's churches, schools, or businesses for a locality may also mention the immigrant. If an ancestor is included with the area's founding families or was a prominent citizen, a local history may include an account of his or her life.

Despite their tendency to focus on society's most prominent citizens, state and local histories, biographies, and biographical encyclopedias can be useful for tracking down some

immigrants' origins. State, county and local histories were especially popular during the late nineteenth century and the first twenty or thirty years of the twentieth century. Many were produced on a subscription basis and biographical sketches of the subscribers formed a substantial part of each history. Centennial publications of various institutions, organizations, churches, cities and towns were frequently financed and formatted in a similar manner. If the subject of the biographical sketch was an immigrant, the exact birthplace might have been noted in such a source. Even the foreign birthplace of the subject's parents may be mentioned in a published history. If an immigrant or his parents did not make it into the pages of a biographical work, there is always a chance that the accomplishments of a sibling, or one or more descendants will appear somewhere in print.

Local histories often mention less prominent immigrants as well. Common folk become especially important if they were among an area's original settlers. Immigrants often considered it a mark of success to be included in the typical local histories of the nineteenth century, even if they had to pay to be included. If an immigrant was willing to spend the necessary money, the publisher would include him, no mater how obscure. Often, the names of immigrants are included in lists of early settlers as members of a founding church, as original town settlers, landholders, school teachers, or in cemetery and sexton records. Bibliographies of local histories and biographical sources are available for most countries, states, and provinces where immigrants settled.

Histories are also available for many ethnic and religious groups. Examples include Martin Ulvestad, *Nordmændene i Amerika* [Norwegians in America], 2 vols. (Minneapolis: History Book Company's Forlag, 1907–10) and Rose Rosicky, *A History of Czechs (Bohemians) in Nebraska* (Omaha: Czech Historical Society of Nebraska, 1929).

Some of the best sources of information about a given group or individual originate in the ethnic community itself. Immigrant groups clung together to sustain their memories, culture, and communication with the old country. Every ethnic organization in the United States has played a role in preserving and perpetuating group identity and national pride. Hundreds of ethnic organizations have flourished and published periodicals, newspapers, and historical and biographical albums—frequently in their native tongue. Histories produced by ethnic presses may focus on the national, state or local level. A typical volume reviews the history of the group from its earliest involvement in American history, extols the group's contributions to the development of the United States, and pays tribute to members of the ethnic group who had become prominent for one reason or another. Biographical sketches in these volumes tend to describe group members in only the most glowing terms, but frequently the degree of detail is very useful. Many a genealogical breakthrough can be attributed to an ethnic biographical sketch. *Chicago und sein Deutschthum* (Chicago: German Press Club, 1902) is one such example. Among the volume's biographical sketches are many that give a specific date and place of birth of the subject as well as date of immigration, former places of residence, arrival date in the country and the city, educational and occupational history, and names of parents, spouse, and children. The reader must be proficient in German, however, because this Chicago source is printed in that language.

Histories also exist for most religious groups, such as Henry R. Holsinger, *History of the Dunkers and the Brethren Church. . . .* (North Manchester, Ind.: L.W. Shultz, 1962). Even histories of larger ethnic and religious groups, such as Germans or Episcopalians, can provide valuable background information about migration and settlement patterns.

In addition to local and group histories, biographical sketches are often found in local and national collective biographical works. These were very common in the last half of the nineteenth century. Many other biographical records have been published and can be located in local libraries. An excellent bibliography listing more than 16,000 national and international collective biographies from around the world is Robert C. Slocum, *Biographical Dictionaries and Related Works*, 2 vols., 2nd ed. (Detroit: Gale Research Co., 1986).

Mirana C. Herbert and Barbara McNeil, *Biography Genealogy Master Index* (Detroit: Gale Research Co., 1980–), is one of several published biographical references described in chapter 2. This index includes more than 8 million references to 3 million individuals profiled in approximately 1,500 histories, blue books, and "who's who" compilations. Like any other index, it is not all inclusive, but it will tease the imagination and point to other potential sources. Even if the subject of your interest is not found in one of these volumes, there is always a strong possibility that a biographical sketch of another member of the family or of the same ethnic or religious group will provide some important clues for immigrant research. This index gives the name of the subject of the biographical sketch, birth and death years, and cites the source for the sketch. By following through to cited sources, it is sometimes possible to find the foreign origins of a family.

CENSUS RECORDS

Census records from as early as 1850 indicate birthplaces for individuals and possible dates of immigration. Later census records provide more specific information on individuals as well as their parents. U.S. federal census records are widely available on microfilm in many large libraries and archives. (See chapter 5, Research in Census Records.)

While U.S. census records rarely indicate the exact birthplace of an individual, significant immigration facts can be gleaned from the federal enumerations, especially in later years. From 1850 to 1870, every person's country or state of birth was shown. Censuses from 1880 to 1920 asked for birthplaces of both parents as well. Because the country of birth was asked for on the census, responses such as Hannover, Baden, or Cassel invariably refer to the German state, not the city of the same name.

Because almost all states are indexed for almost all years, the census is a logical starting point for determining family origins. Judging from ages and birthplaces, it is usually possible to estimate the date of arrival in the United States, even in earlier enumerations. Beginning with the 1900 census, more detailed immigration information was required. The 1920 census asked for specific birthplaces (state, province, or city) of foreigners who had been born in a country whose boundaries had been changed in World War I (the German, Austrian, Russian, and Ottoman empires). Approximately half of the enumerators complied with this requirement. Other clues in the 1920 census, such as mother tongue, may provide additional insights.

Even if you are unable to find your own ancestor's country of origin in census records, the discovery of another relative's origins or those of others of the same surname may prove helpful. Since there are many printed index books and Soundex microfilms available, it may prove useful to survey the occurrence of a given surname in a statewide index. Frequently individuals of the same family settled in close proximity. Concentrations of an unusual surname will provide a starting place to search for additional information.

State censuses can also be useful in tracking family origins. In addition to the standard questions asked by federal censuses, the 1925 Iowa State Census, for example, asked for the names of parents, mother's maiden name, nativity of parents, place of parent's marriage, military service, occupation and religion.

It should be remembered that, while census records are extremely useful in immigration research, the information provided in them is not entirely reliable. An individual might not have remembered his or her age exactly. Sometimes, foreigners fearing problems with a strange new government, did not answer questions honestly, especially those that related to citizenship status. Sometimes immigrants could not remember accurately the date of their arrival in the U.S. or the date of their naturalization, but when they did, and when it was recorded correctly, these dates will facilitate naturalization and passenger list searches (see chapter 5).

SOCIETIES

Many historical, lineage, genealogical, fraternal, and ethnic societies may have records concerning immigrants. Such societies often collect records, such as family and local histories, oral histories, church records, newspapers, cemetery collections, passenger lists, manuscripts, organization membership applications, early settler indexes, military records, directories, and other records which may help with your search. Genealogical and historical societies are organized for almost every geographic locality. Historical societies for most ethnic and religious groups also exist—for example, the American Historical Society of Germans from Russia. Also search for pioneer or old settler societies. Contact these various kinds of societies to learn about their services and hours. They are usually very cooperative and can help locate good local researchers. Genealogical and historical societies should be approached early in most searches.

Publications of genealogical and historical societies are especially rich and unique sources of local information. Some genealogical societies, libraries, and archives maintain surname registries that have proved useful in linking individuals with similar research interests. These organizations tend to focus on the ethnic groups prominent in their respective areas, and this will be reflected in their publications. Newsletters and quarterlies published by societies can be especially rich sources of information on immigrant groups. There are also single-ethnic genealogical and historical societies that have been organized for the purpose of promoting study and preservation of specific national and religious groups.

Mary K. Meyer, *Directory of Genealogical Societies in the U.S.A. and Canada*, 10th ed. (Maryland: the compiler, 1994), is a listing of names and addresses of genealogical societies in the two countries, including in many cases, information submitted by the organizations regarding their membership fees, publications and collection and project objectives.

Historical Societies

In Pennsylvania, for example, several county historical societies have "family reports" with information previously collected and filed by family name. Some societies will send photocopies of the materials they have on hand for a fee. When requesting information, write or call ahead to be sure of the particular society's research policy. Some of these files are also available on microfilm at the Family History Library and its family history centers throughout the United States.

Immigrant Societies

The records of societies an immigrant may have joined during his or her life may be hard to locate. Arriving foreigners often received financial and other assistance from immigrant aid societies which helped them settle in their new home. An immigrant may have sent money back to his or her family or brought relatives from the old country through an immigrant aid society. These societies were usually associated with ethnic, religious, or community organizations. The most famous is the Hebrew Immigrant Aid Society. Ask local and ethnic historical societies for addresses of immigrant aid societies which operated in their area.

Immigrant aid societies sprang up to supply information on lodgings, work opportunities, and local resources; to provide credit references and sometimes cash or food where needed; to advise and caution immigrants against the unscrupulous; to collect and forward mail; to coordinate group insurance and benefits for living family members; and to aid in burial of loved ones and with legal transactions unfamiliar to new immigrants. These societies kept some invaluable records. See G.A. Dobbert, "An On-Line System for Processing Loosely Structured Records," *Historical Methods* 15 (Winter 1982): 16–22, for the use of 1,700 obituaries clipped by the German Immigrant Society of Cincinnati, Ohio; and John Guertler and Adele Newburger, *Records of Baltimore's Private Organizations: A Guide to Archival Resources* (New York: Garland Press, 1981) for ethnic and immigrant societies in the city of Baltimore. The YWCA operated institutes for women to help them adjust, learn English, and care adequately for their families. See Nicholas V. Montalto, *The International Institute Movement: A Guide to Records of Immigrant Society Agencies in the United States* (St. Paul: Immigration History Research Center, 1978) for a state-by-state listing of aid societies for women immigrants. Erna Risch's important work, "Immigrant Aid Societies Before 1820," *Pennsylvania History* 3 (January 1936): 15–32, discusses societies for Germans, Scots, Irish, and others throughout the American colonies. Also useful is Bradford Luckingham, "Benevolence in Emergent San Francisco: A Note on Immigrant Life in the Urban Far West," *Southern California Quarterly* 55 (1973): 431–44, which describes societies for French, Germans, Catholics, Protestants, seamen, ladies, Hebrews, and others.

Fraternal Organizations

After the immigrant settled, he or she may have sought the company of people with similar interests and joined an ethnic or fraternal organization like the Veterans of Foreign Wars, a Jewish Landsmanschaft, the Grange, a Masonic lodge, Knights of Columbus, etc. Although they may be difficult to locate, ethnic and fraternal society records sometimes provide crucial

immigration information. A book which helps locate some of these societies is the *Encyclopedia of Associations: Regional, State, and Local Organizations* (annual; Detroit: Gale Research Co., 25th ed. in 1991).

Public libraries normally have guides to help locate these organizations. Particularly useful for locating societies dealing with immigrants is Lubomyr R. Wynar, *Encyclopedic Directory of Ethnic Organizations in the United States* (Littleton, Colo.: Libraries Unlimited, 1975).

PERIODICALS

Genealogical, lineage society, religious, and historical periodicals are most helpful when you know the area in which an immigrant settled, and his or her ethnic group. Genealogical and historical societies usually publish periodicals about the people in the geographic area or ethnic group they cover. Family organizations often publish newsletters with immigrant information.

Periodicals often reprint a wide variety of material, including abstracts from original sources that discuss immigrants. Periodicals may include:

- Passenger list abstracts
- Naturalization list abstracts
- Sketches about early pioneers
- Ethnic group background information
- Genealogical sketches
- Pedigrees and *ahnentafels*

Periodicals published by genealogical societies are good places to publish queries asking for information about immigrant ancestors. There are sometimes fees for this service (especially for non-members). Also check indexes for previous queries and answers. There are approximately 230 ethnic societies listed separately under "Special Interests" in the 1994 *Meyer's Directory of Genealogical Societies in the U.S.A. and Canada*.

Genealogical and historical societies in the United States have been churning out publications for more than 150 years. One of the quickest and most efficient ways to locate articles that relate to an ethnic group is to consult one of the periodical source indexes discussed in chapter 2. One of the largest compilations is the *PERiodical Source Index (PERSI)* (Allen County Public Library Genealogy Department, 1987–; annual volumes published since 1986), a comprehensive place, subject, and surname index to current genealogical and local history periodicals. The Foreign Places section of *PERSI*, for example, can be particularly helpful in immigration research; it is arranged first by country, then by record type. European locations may contain current smaller political subdivisions; for example, Great Britain may include materials of a regional nature; Germany includes entries for German provinces, as well as pre-unification East and West Germany, Prussia, etc.; U.S.S.R. includes articles pertaining to the Ukraine, Latvia, Lithuania, and other countries once part of the Soviet Union.

LIBRARY AND ARCHIVE COLLECTIONS

Libraries, archives, and societies in the area where an immigrant settled may have collected previous research about local people. For example, local genealogy collections, vertical files, scrapbooks, school records, newspapers, obituaries, and histories of organizations, towns, and counties are sources that may reveal an immigrant's origins.

A growing number of organizations are devoted exclusively to collecting and preserving materials for specific immigrant or ethnic groups. An example of a repository dedicated to a particular ethnic group is the Swenson Swedish Immigration Center (Augustana College, 639 38th Street, Rock Island, IL 61201-2296). See listings for other single-nationality collections listed under the appropriate ethnic groups listed at the end of this chapter.

Look for catalogs, inventories, guides, or periodicals that describe the holdings of archives and libraries, then study these guides before visiting the repository. An example of a helpful guide is Suzanna Moody and Joel Wurl, eds. *The Immigration History Research Center: A Guide to Collections* (New York: Greenwood Press, 1991).

Foreign Collections in American Libraries and Archives
Researchers commonly make the mistake of looking in foreign archives for documents that are available in U.S. libraries and archives in original, photocopy, or microfilm form. For example, the Huntington Library in San Marino, California, has the original manuscripts of the Hastings family of Great Britain. These 50,000 manuscript items of one of the most important noble families cover from the 1100s to 1892. They cannot be searched in Great Britain, for they exist only in America. The Family History Library has several thousand reels of microfilmed emigration registers available to all genealogists. The library also has microfilm copies of original records pertaining to the Jews in Poland; they are available at Hebrew University in Jerusalem as well. Although these records are written in Polish, their accessibility in Poland today is limited. In America they are available to anyone within driving distance of an LDS family history center.

VITAL RECORDS

The amount of information provided in vital records varies from county to county and from year to year. As a rule, vital records are limited in their usefulness as clues to immigrant origins, but it is always worth seeking out every vital record available for every member of the family if immigrant origins are being sought. In most instances, birth, marriage, and death records provide only the country of birth and not the hoped-for native town.

In vital records, first seek records related to the immigrant's death. These may give the immigrant's birth place and date, or the names of parents, relatives or friends. They can also provide important clues regarding religion, naturalization, length of residence, arrival and property in the old country.

After death records, seek out the records of other vital events, such as the immigrant's marriage and his children's births. Vital record entries for marriages and births of the immigrant's children kept by civil authorities can also provide important clues. Generally, records of later periods contain more information than earlier ones. While indication of birthplace is rare, it does sometimes appear. This illustrates the importance of locating every possible record, even when the likelihood of immigration information is slight.

As in every other aspect of genealogical research, the records of siblings, aunts and uncles, and even distant relatives can be very important. For example, an Irish family tracing its ancestry documented events and activities of their father's,

grandfather's, and great-grandfather's lives back to the immigrant's arrival in the United States in 1836. To their great disappointment, other than the census and death records noting Ireland as the birthplace, nothing in any of the records provided clues to specific origins. At the suggestion of a professional researcher, the family began to collect information on all the other children of the immigrant. Fortunately, on the death certificate of the eighth of the immigrant's twelve children, more specific information appeared. The father's birthplace was listed as Wexford, and the mother's as Queenstown. Had the research not been extended to include the great uncles and aunts, it is doubtful that the project could have progressed.

For a complete discussion of vital records, see chapter 3, Research in Birth, Death, and Cemetery Records, and chapter 4, Research in Marriage and Divorce Records.

ECCLESIASTICAL RECORDS

A local religious congregation could alleviate "culture shock." The church was a haven that offered services in a familiar tongue, and its officials and members were often known to the immigrant. The formality of christening a child born enroute or solemnizing a marriage begun as a shipboard romance provided a ritual sanction for the move. In some denominations, letters of recommendation for church membership were surrendered shortly after arrival. Loose documents kept by individual immigrants have seldom survived, but some religious denominations kept records of recommendations and removals.

Whenever possible study immigrant church registers; patterns sometimes emerge that will point to the foreign emigration point for an entire group. For example, while searching for a certain immigrant in Catholic church records in a small Indiana town, a genealogist searched baptism and marriage entries in several ledgers. The native towns were noted in the church registers for many of those receiving the sacraments, as well as for the witnesses and sponsors. Unfortunately, there was no such notation identifying the birthplace of the subject of interest. The astute genealogist did not give up there, however. Knowing that sponsors and witnesses are frequently close relatives and friends, he noted the names of all the towns mentioned in the registers during the time the family resided in the parish. Next, he took a detailed map of the area near a recognizable city mentioned in the church register. Some towns were not on the map, but most were located, though their names had been misspelled in the registers. This study revealed that a large number of towns cited were within a thirty-mile radius of the central city on the detailed map. Once the Indiana genealogist focused on a specific area in Germany, another genealogist specializing in German research was able to find emigration records for the family of interest.

The records of many ethnic American church records are easily available for searching. For example, many Swedish-American church records have been microfilmed by the Emigration Institute in Växjö, Sweden. They are listed in *Svensk-Amerikansha Kyrkoarkiv Med Canada* (Växjö, Sweden: Emigrantinstitutet, 1979). For more information on church records, see chapter 6.

CEMETERIES

Surviving cemetery and mortuary records are important sources for immigrant research. Sometimes the only recording of an original name or the exact birthplace is on a tombstone. For example, one family historian had literally reached a "dead end" in researching the Doner name in New York. After many tries at locating cemetery records, it was discovered that the original cemetery deed had been recorded under the name Dooner. Once alerted to the original spelling, the researcher was able to determine when family members changed the name spelling, and to continue researching the correct spelling in older records.

Often, children and other relatives of immigrants honored the memory of their deceased ancestors by noting the person's birthplace on his or her tombstone. Ethnic cemeteries, ethnic sections of larger cemeteries, and family burial plots of immigrants can be veritable gold mines for determining ethnic origins. Whenever possible, visit cemeteries personally to inspect and photograph monuments.

MORTUARIES

For immigrants, especially those living in cities or ethnic clusters, it was most common to conduct business with those who came from the same or similar backgrounds. The undertaker with Irish origins would best understand the needs and wants of his fellow countrymen when it came time for a wake and burial; likewise, a Jewish undertaker was best qualified to handle religious burial rituals for members of the Jewish community. Over the years, the undertaking establishments begun by immigrants have frequently changed in one way or another or have disappeared completely. Whether changes came about because of a shift in ethnic makeup of a neighborhood, the transfer of the business to another generation, or the complete shutdown of the undertaking company, it is frequently difficult to discover what has become of mortuary or undertaker's records. Contacting currently operating cemeteries and mortuaries of the same ethnic or religious background may be the best method of tracking down the records of older mortuaries. Genealogical and historical societies, especially those with an ethnic focus, are also good sources of information because a typical goal for that kind of an organization is to preserve and publish information with historical and genealogical value.

NEWSPAPERS

Newspapers provide a variety immigration information. Search both the local newspapers where the immigrant settled and the ethnic newspapers in the immigrant's language or for the cultural group. In addition to obituaries (described below), newspapers from the immigrant's lifetime may also give the following kinds of information to help find an immigrant's place of origin:

- Lists of passengers or new arrivals
- Immigrants treated in a local hospital
- Lists of immigrants who came as indentured servants or apprentices
- Missing relative or friend queries
- Marriage announcements
- Notices of probates of estates

Many of the immigrants had relatives and friends who had already come to America and frequently tried to locate them with newspaper advertisements. About ten German-language newspapers served German immigrants in or near Philadelphia by 1776. In addition, there were the English-language papers.

Examples of extracts of inquiries and advertisements include Anita L. Eyster, "Notices by German and Swiss Settlers Seeking Information of Members of their Families, Kindred, and Friends Inserted Between 1742–1761 in *Pennsylvania Berichte* and 1762–1779 in the *Pennsylvania Staatsbote*," *Pennsylvania German Folklore Society* 3 (1938): 32–41; and Edward Hocker, *Genealogical Data Relating to the German Settlers of Pennsylvania From Advertisements in German Newspapers Published in Philadelphia and Germantown, 1743–1800* (Baltimore: Genealogical Publishing Co., 1981).

Many Irish who settled in Boston used the newspapers to seek friends and relatives who arrived earlier. Often, their queries indicated where in Ireland the person they were seeking came from. Abstracts of thousands of notices from 1831 to 1856 have been gathered by Ruth-Ann Harris and Donald M. Jacobs, *The Search for Missing Friends: Irish Immigrant Advertisements Placed in the Boston Pilot* (Boston: New England Historic Genealogical Society, 1989–93).

Immigrants often had to redeem the cost of their passage by indenture. Announcements of new arrivals to be sold into indentureship were printed in newspapers, with dates of auction. After the negotiations were over, the results were also printed in newspapers.

Newspapers carry more than indentures or letters and announcements. They also publish probate processes originating in Europe and obituaries of family members who died in Europe. Be sure to research both the original papers, often available on microfilm through interlibrary loan, and the abstracts published in the local newspaper. Indeed, immigrants can appear in newspapers for a variety of reasons, as this excerpt shows:

Philadelphia, September 17. 1747.

Run away, on the 11th of this instant September, at night, from William Plaskett, of Trenton, a Welsh servant woman, named Sarah Davis, about 27 years of age, middle stature, somewhat freckled, has a small scar in her forehead, and is slow of speech: Had on when she went away, a callicoe gown, a black fur hat, shagged on the under side, with a patch on the crown, and an ozenbrigs apron. Whoever takes up and secures said servant woman, so as her master may have her again, shall have Twenty Shillings reward, and reasonable charges, paid by William Plaskett.[10]

Ethnic newspapers can be particularly helpful. According to Lubomyr R. and Anna T. Wynar, *Encyclopedic Directory of Ethnic Newspapers and Periodicals in the United States,* 2nd ed. (Littleton, Colo.: Libraries Unlimited, 1976), "The major function of the ethnic press lies in its role as the principal agent by which the identity, cohesiveness, and structure of an ethnic community are preserved and perpetuated." Unusual or special events in the lives of working-class immigrants that were routinely unnoticed by major daily newspapers often warranted lengthy articles in ethnic and religious newspapers. Birth, marriage, anniversary, and death notices and articles in ethnic newspapers can be invaluable sources for discovering immigrant origins. Even mention of an individual's running for public office, a promotion, or a trip to visit family in the native country may provide personal details that will not be found elsewhere.

Obituaries

Obituaries are excellent sources for biographical information about immigrants. In addition to the name and death date of the immigrant, surviving family members, church affiliation, spouses, parents, occupations, burial places, and most importantly, the native town in the old country may be noted. For many an immigrant, an obituary may have been the only "biographical sketch" ever written for him or her.

For example, research on Carl Schultz, a Mecklenburg immigrant to Wisconsin, was stymied because of his common name and the lack of good biographical information. His obituary, while not providing the town of origin, gave the year of immigration. This information then made it possible to identify him in the Hamburg passenger lists which indicated his native town.

Obituaries were usually published in local and church newspapers. Some also appear in church, professional, company, and school periodicals. Although brief death notices appeared in the earliest newspapers, traditional obituaries are most common after the mid-1800s. You are most likely to find obituaries of immigrants who lived in rural areas rather than in large cities.

Search smaller, local newspapers that focus on community news, such as weekly newspapers. Many such newspapers are available on microfilm. Public libraries can usually obtain copies via interlibrary loan. Local historical societies and libraries where the newspaper is published may also have copies. Many North American newspapers are listed in *Newspapers in Microform: United States,* 2 vols. (Washington, D.C.: Library of Congress, 1984). Also see chapter 12, Research in Newspapers.

CITY DIRECTORIES

City directories are among the best sources for tracking an immigrant through the years (see chapter 11, Research in Directories, and chapter 19, Tracking Urban Ancestors). Immigrants have typically settled in cities in the United States, especially in Eastern Seaboard cities, until they could find better opportunities in rural areas. City directories generally provide the names, occupations, and addresses of working adults in any given household, and are an important means of tracking individuals from year to year. While directories of residents may date back to a city's earliest days, no directory is all-inclusive. Unfortunately, foreigners, especially those who did not speak English, were those most frequently excluded or overlooked as city directories were those compiled. Some groups, such as the Poles in Chicago, independently published city or community directories in their own language to compensate. Ethnic and local historical societies have frequently microfilmed or reprinted these special directories.

While city directories seldom, if ever, name the town or even country the immigrant came from, they can provide other important information. From a directory you may learn, within a year or two, when the immigrant arrived. Carefully tracking the addresses of others with the same surname may reveal unknown siblings or children. City directories can also help you determine which church of the family's preferred denomination was nearest the family residence.

IMMIGRATION RECORDS

Passenger Lists

Passenger arrival lists can be among the most valuable sources for documenting our ancestors' immigration. Unfortunately, however, lists were not kept for every ship, some lists have been lost, and many are not indexed. The content of passenger lists has also changed significantly over the years. Passenger lists created before the 1880s rarely indicate the immigrant's town of origin. In earlier years of record-keeping, lists typically showed only the immigrant's name, age, and country of origin or the ship's last port of call. The formats of lists in the 1880s gradually evolved to include more detailed information, including the place of origin.

The vast majority of immigration records are the passenger arrival lists kept by the U.S. federal government (after 1820) or by other authorities (cities, states, port officials and shipping lines). However, there are several other significant record sources for immigrants. They exist in published or manuscript form and include naturalization records, records of border crossings, passports, records of immigrant societies, alien registration, consular records and others.

While at least some passenger lists have been indexed for virtually every U.S. port, a large number remain unindexed. And, as with all indexes, there are errors—especially errors of omission. In addition to the problem of simply missing names in transcription, individuals who departed from a country illegally may not have been recorded at all. Children who emigrated with their parents were often not included on early lists. Even if you find the name you are looking for in the index, in many cases it will be impossible to identify that person with a great degree of certainty. Illegible handwriting on passenger lists, combined with misspelled names, incorrect ages, and only a vague name of the country or region of origin, give passenger lists the distinction of being the most difficult-to-use immigration sources. What's more, you may not know if the immigrant traveled alone, or with other family members or friends. In other words, how will you know if John Miller, age twenty-three, laborer, is the right one if there are several others of the same name and similar description? Very often, one or more of the family would travel to America, get a feel for the new land, establish residency, and then send for other family members. Sometimes parents left their children with relatives at home until they were able to bring them over. Sometimes the father was the solitary pioneer, sending for the family after establishing himself in America. Often, young, unmarried adults set out alone to find a new life in a new world.

As with other government documents, passenger lists were not intended to be genealogical documents, but rather were a means of monitoring immigrant arrivals. There were, historically, up to seven different passenger lists created and perhaps more for some groups of passengers. These include lists made and filed with (1) the port of embarkation, (2) ports of call along the route, (3) the port of arrival, (4) newspapers at the port of departure, (5) newspapers at cities of arrival, (6) a copy kept with or as part of the ship's manifest (see figure 13-8), and (7) notations of passengers in the ship's log. In addition, some travelers recorded their fellow passengers in diaries, journals, and letters home. If the group was chartered by a government agency, a specific church, or an emigrant aid society (see figure 13-9), a list may have been kept with the official archives

Figure 13-8. Report and Manifest of the *Langdon Cheves,* Philadelphia to New York via St. Thomas, 1824; Port of Philadelphia Passenger Lists, 1820–54; FHL microfilm 419,614.

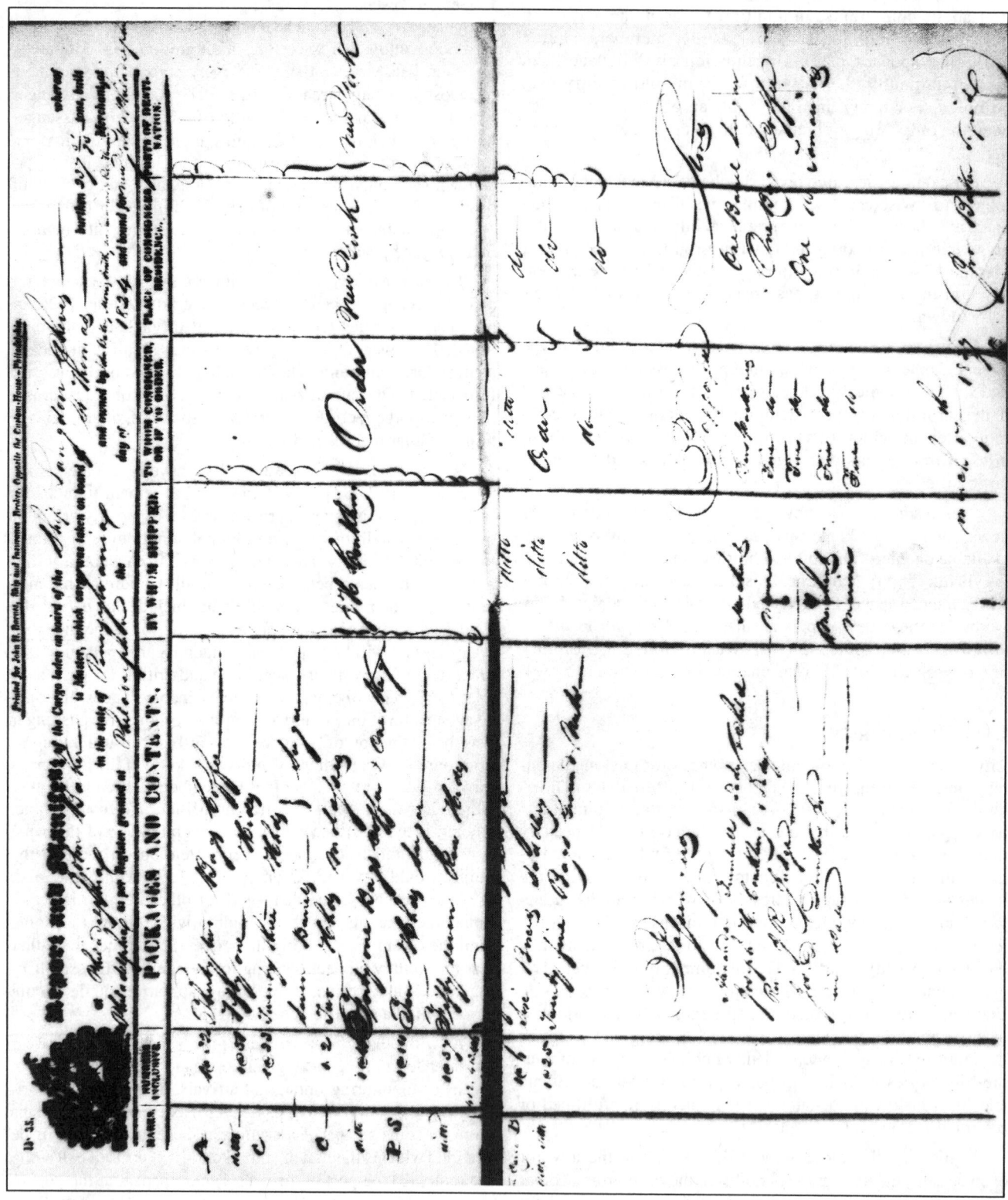

of the project. If the ship was quarantined for disease, a copy of the list was attached to medical reports. Germans arriving in Pennsylvania from 1727 to 1808 were required to take an oath of allegiance and an oath of abjuration when they landed in Philadelphia. All able-bodied heads of families were taken immediately before a magistrate when they arrived.

Some of these passenger lists are official lists that were required by law; others were private recordings. For family historians, the fact that multiple copies were sometimes made improves the chances that at least one survived for most immigrants. The main problem is in finding the lists.

Official U.S. government passenger lists are available from 1820 through 1945 for most of the ports in the United States with customs houses. Those available in the National Archives on microfilm are tabulated in *Immigration and Passenger Arrivals: A Select Catalog of National Archives Microfilms,* rev. ed. (Washington, D.C.: National Archives Trust Fund, 1991). They are divided into customs passenger lists (original lists, copies, or abstracts) and immigration passenger lists (State Department transcripts, lists) with pertinent indexes (table 13-2). Microfilm publication call numbers are given where appropriate. Copies are also available for searching at the Family History Library and its family history centers located throughout the United States. Selected passenger lists are available at some public libraries. The Allen County Public Library in Fort Wayne, Indiana, for example, has a large collection of passenger list microfilms.

No official records exist until those of the late nineteenth century for persons entering the United States through Canada or Mexico (see "Border Crossings" below). Lists for the Pacific Coast ports are in the possession of the Customs Service in those ports or have been transferred to National Archives regional archives on the West Coast. The National Archives has recently microfilmed available records for these ports. There are a few passenger lists for San Francisco at the National Archives—Pacific Sierra Region, in San Bruno, California. Other official lists were destroyed by fire in 1851 and 1940. Reconstructed lists are indexed in P. William Filby with Mary K. Meyer, *Passenger and Immigration Lists Index* (Detroit: Gale Research Co., 1981–).

In addition to the passenger lists kept by the state and federal governments, there are some city lists. The Baltimore City Passenger Lists, 1833 to 1866, have a Soundex index. The originals are in the Baltimore City archive, and the Family History Library has microfilm copies that can be borrowed from LDS family history centers.

For pre-1820 official lists, researchers must rely on surviving ship cargo manifests. Many colonial and U.S. ports kept copies of manifests filed as a requirement of clearance. Extant manifests have been scattered among archives, museums, and other historical agencies, but most have been published and are indexed in *Passenger and Immigration Lists Index.*

The amount of literature included for each passenger varies from one list to another. Some lists give the names of ship and passengers, country of origin, and port of arrival only. Others also include sex, age, occupation, and place of residence when ticket was purchased. On some lists, the passengers are grouped into family units, on some they are listed by tickets, on some they are arranged in alphabetical order, and on others they are arranged in the order which the passengers boarded the ship. The name of the ship's master and dates of departure and arrival will be found on some. Later lists, like those for Hamburg, give date and place of birth, date and parish of confirmation, marital status, and state or city of destination.

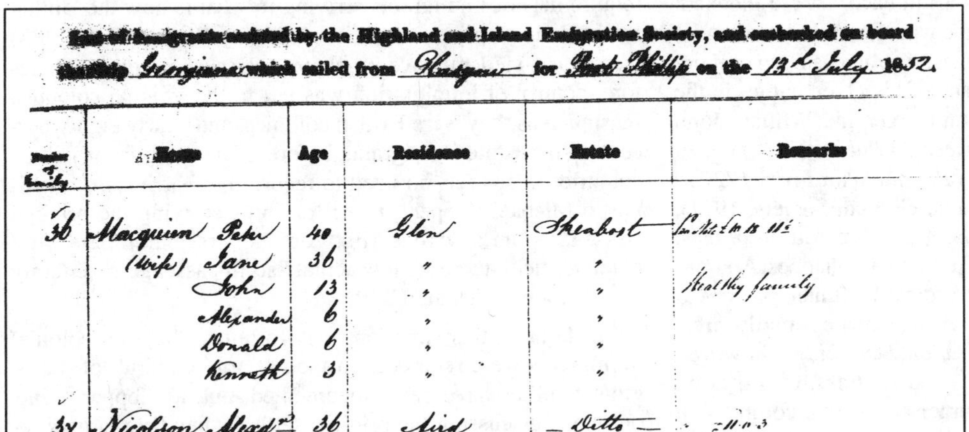

Figure 13-9. List of emigrants, 1852–57, assisted by the Highland and Emigration Society; FHL 404,437.

Passenger lists created after 1820 are usually separate documents if the ship was a passenger liner. If the ship was a cargo vessel which also carried passengers, they were listed on the ship's manifest with the master, crew, and cargo. Some ancestors were actually shipped by the pound as if they were trunks of books or bales of wool. Before 1820, most immigrants were not declared as passengers, and many were landed in harbors where customs houses had not been established.

Masters who landed passengers without permission, however, could be forced to return them or give security to customs officials by bond to cover costs of removal for illegal entry. Some ports required the payment of a head tax and issued certificates or permits to land. When the federal government began to regulate immigration in 1820, each ship was required by law to submit an official list of passengers carried. Masters who failed to comply could be fined and denied port clearance.

Federal control brought about the creation of three types of passenger arrival records: customs passenger lists, immigration passenger lists, and customs lists of aliens. All of them are available for searching, with some restrictions. A thorough discussion of the nature and history of U.S. passenger lists is Michael Tepper, *American Passenger Arrival Records* (Baltimore: Genealogical Publishing Co., 1988). A succinct guide to using those lists and the available indexes is John P. Colletta, *They Came in Ships: A Guide to Finding Your Immigrant Ancestor's Arrival Record,* rev. ed. (Salt Lake City: Ancestry, 1993).

Published Lists and Indexes

One of the most significant developments in genealogy in the past fifteen years is the publication of indexes to immigration lists. The largest project is the *Passenger and Immigration Lists Index* (cited above), which contains more than 2 million entries for immigrants from the British Isles and Europe (see figure 13-10). In this source, all names in each list are indexed: where maiden names are found, the women are indexed under both their married and maiden names; if a man has two or more given names, he is listed under each of his given names in the source. By contrast, Ralph B. Strassburger and William John Hinke, *Pennsylvania German Pioneers: A Publication of Original Lists of Arrivals in the Port of Philadelphia From 1727 to 1808* (Norristown, Pa.: Pennsylvania German Society, 1934), include Johannes Andreas Hoffman from three different lists. All three lists, however, are indexed under Johannes Andreas only. Thus, if you were looking for Andreas Hoffman, you would find only two entries in the index, when there are actually three. In Filby's *Passenger and Immigration Lists Index*, however, he is indexed under both Johannes and Andreas, thus making him retrievable from the Strassburger and Hinke compilation as well.

In Filby's index, each immigrant is identified by name (spelled as it appeared in the source), age (if given), place of arrival, year of arrival, source code, and page number. All persons traveling together are listed with the head of the household as a group and cross-referenced to all family members who immigrated together.

The *Passenger and Immigration Lists Index* covers only lists that have been printed. It does not include entries from the original passenger arrival records. As these materials are published, however, they will be indexed in future *Index* volumes. The list of sources appears in two forms: a

short title with key and a full bibliographic entry. It is easy to photocopy the short title list on four pages and keep it with your research notes.

An important aid to the series is P. William Filby, comp., *Passenger and Immigration Lists Bibliography, 1538–1900,* 2nd ed. (Detroit: Gale Research Co., 1988). This bibliography updates Harold Lancour's original *Bibliography of Passenger Lists* (New York: New York Public Library, 1937), which was revised and enlarged by Richard Wolfe (New York: New York Public Library, 1963) and expands it from 262 titles to more than 2,550. Each source listed is cited in full with a descriptive annotation of contents, coverage, and related immigration lists (see figure 13-11). For the sources that have been reprinted, the facts of publication for the reprint are given. This bibliography will continue to expand as Filby adds new sources to the index. It is the "master list" from which sources to be included in the *Passenger and Immigration Index* are selected. As of 1994, over 2,200 of the sources had been indexed. Each annual index adds approximately one hundred sources to total number indexed each year. However, sources continue to be published, so there is no apparent end to this indexing project.

Of the original 262 lists described in Lancour's bibliography drawn from printed sources, thirty percent are emigrant lists recorded at the port of embarkation, eight percent are passenger lists recorded at the port of arrival, four percent are ships' lists, and approximately fifteen percent are compiled works on settlers in specific localities drawn from church records, convict and pauper lists, naturalizations, customs lists, legal papers and petitions, county histories, oaths of allegiance, and other records. Filby's bibliography continues this broad coverage.

Colonial Lists

Before 1820, the American colonies made virtually no effort to require lists of immigrants arriving in what is now the United States. Indeed, prior to the Revolutionary War (1775 to 1783) there was no federal government to make such a request. Therefore, control of immigration was left to the original colonies. Inasmuch as they were British colonies, and nearly eighty percent of the white immigrants before 1790 came from British countries, there was no need to record these arrivals. According to Michael Tepper, "Even for ships carrying the original colonists—the so-called first comers, first purchasers, first planters, etc.—there are few actual lists of passengers, certainly few that are undisputed."[11]

In light of this situation, it is fortunate that any colonial immigrants were recorded. In fact, a large majority of immigrant families have been documented, but, as Tepper points out when discussing the original settlers, they "are largely recorded—where they are recorded at all—in ancillary records and documents."[12] Use of such "ancillary records," including lists of departure from British countries, is a great boon to colonial immigration studies. They allow identification of at least some members of an immigrant's family (usually the head) for upwards of seventy to eighty percent of the colonial white immigrants. The vast majority of these records have been published over the past few decades, with the happy result that virtually all of them are indexed in Filby's *Passenger and Immigration Lists Index*.

Because of the great interest in, and availability of, the colonial Pennsylvania lists, some discussion is warranted here.

Beginning in 1727, Pennsylvania required that non-British immigrants (essentially Germans) be identified. Three passenger lists compiled for these Pennsylvania German immigrants: (1) the captain's lists made on board the ship by the ship's mate from the manifest; (2) lists of oaths of allegiance to the king of Great Britain that were signed by all male immigrants over age sixteen who were well enough to march in procession to a magistrate (these two lists were submitted to the Pennsylvania government on large, loose sheets of paper and not all of them have survived); and (3) lists of signers of the oath of fidelity and abjuration (see figure 13-12.) The oath was a renunciation of claims to the throne of England by "pretenders" and a denial of the right of the pope to outlaw a Protestant monarch. Those males over age sixteen who were well enough to walk to the courthouse also signed these renunciations in a series of bound ledger volumes that have survived intact. The editors of *Pennsylvania German Pioneers*, Strassburger and Hinke, estimated that only two out of five passengers are recorded on the signed lists (figure 13-12).

The original order of the names on the lists is important. The first signatures are often those of the leaders, for the Palatines (immigrants from the Rhine River Valley of Germany—the Palatinate) came in groups. The names themselves are significant, for they may represent a whole church group or a group of related families. For these reasons, copy the whole passenger list where the ancestor appears and study the names carefully. The lists serve as a check to identify the correct ancestor in church registers, census lists, news announcements, and other records.

The spelling of names on the captains' lists is often inaccurate and different from the way the names appear on the other two. The mate wrote what he heard, while the signatures represent the way the person spelled his or her own name. When you compare the two, you can often determine how the name was originally pronounced. For example, Johann Herman Ekell (as spelled in his signature) is listed on the captain's list as Johann Harmon Akel. In Pennsylvania and Maryland, where

Figure 13-10. Sample from P. William Filby, *Passenger and Immigration Lists.* Reproduced from a promotional brochure issued by Gale Research Co., 1982.

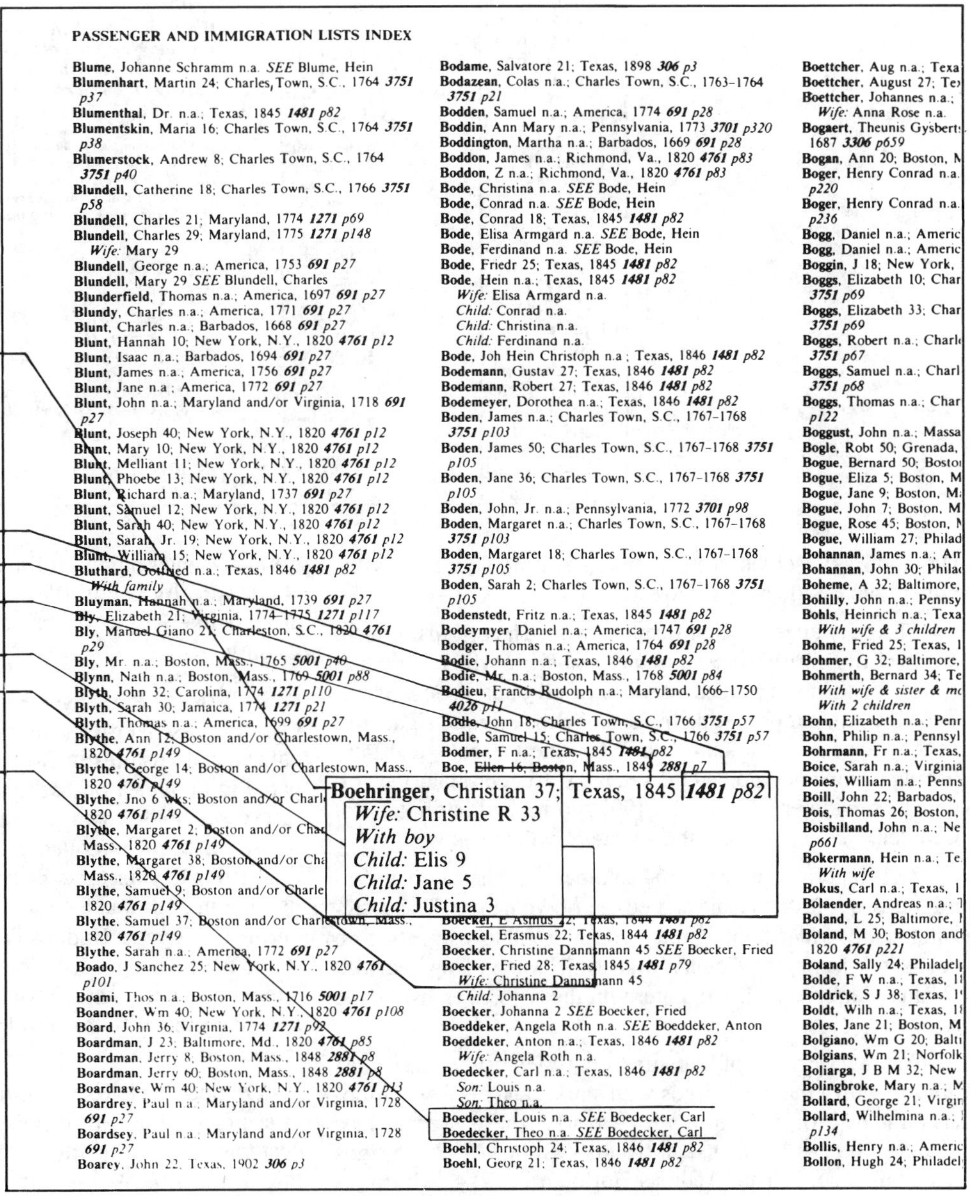
Name of passenger
Specific source containing arrival record (and possible additional information). No need for endless and perhaps fruitless search through many different books, magazines, and manuscripts.
Date of arrival
Port of arrival
Accompanying dependents or relatives
Ages
Special Feature: "See" references guides users to family entries.
PASSENGER AND IMMIGRATION LISTS INDEX
Boehringer, Christian 37; Texas, 1845 1481 p82
Wife: Christine R 33
With boy
Child: Elis 9
Child: Jane 5
Child: Justina 3

Figure 13-11. Samples from P. William Filby, *Passenger and Immigration Lists Bibliography, 1538–1900* (Detroit: Gale Research Co., 1981).

Page 149	Passenger and Immigration Lists Bibliography	In

Australia, Germans to
  1800s 1858
  1825-1846 5085
  1835-1854 3474
  1847-1886 4460
  1850-1903 3914
  Hamburg ships
  1850 ....
  Poles (Old Luth
  1835-1854 ....
  Wends to, 19th
Austria, Salzburg
  1734-1739 .....
Austrians
  arrivals, 1850-1
  from Guessing,
  from Imperial (
  1843-1877 ...
  to Georgia, 173
  to Texas, 1858-

B

Bacon, Anthony,
  1740 ....
Baden, Duchy of,
  Germans from,
  Germans from,
  Germans from I
Baden-Durlach, G
  1710-1815 ....
  1738 ....
  1749 ....
  1749-1751 ....
  1749-1755 ....
  1751 ....
  1752 ....
  1753 ....
Baden-Wuerttemb
  1727-1775 ....
  18th, 19th c ...
Baltimore
  arrivals
    from Bremen
    from the Netl
  Central and Eas
  Dutch to, 1847
  Germans to, fro
  Germans to, fro
  1873-1876 ..

Baltimore County, Md., servants to,
  1772-1774 1
Baptismal records, French in "New
  France," 1621-1700 6
Baptist Herald, obituaries of Germans
  from Russia, 1800s to 1950s 6

2765-2768   **Passenger and Immigration Lists Bibliography**

2765-2768
GREAT REGISTER, TULARE CO. [CALIFORNIA], 1888, NATURALIZATION DATA. In *Sequoia Genealogical Society Newsletter.*
2765
---Vol. 1:1 (Jan. 1975), p. 4; vol. 1:2 (Feb. 1975), p. 3; vol. 1:3 (Mar. 1975), p. 4; vol. 1:4 (Apr. 1975), p. 4; vol. 1:5 (May 1975), p. 4.
2766
---Vol. 2:1 (Sept. 1975), p. 3; vol. 2:2 (Oct. 1975), p. 4; vol. 2:3 (Nov. 1975), p. 4 vol. 2:4 (Jan. 1976), p. 4; vol. 2:5 (Feb. 1976), p. 4; vol. 2:6 (Mar. 1976), p. 4; vol. 2:7 (Apr. 1976), p. 4; v
2767
---Vol. 3:1 (S
3:3 (Nov. 197
(Feb. 1977),
1977), p. 4; v
2768
---Vol. 4:1 (S
vol. 4:4 (Jan.
vol. 4:6 (Mar
vol. 4:8 (May

From vol.
of Tulare (
of arrival (
tries. Cove
the years
1890. This
1978 issue

2772
GREER, GI
grants, 1623-
Co., 1912, 37
Co., Baltimo

Includes 25
Office. Ex
published

2802
GRUCHALLA, ROBER
der Personen, welche mit
nach Quebec zur Auswan
engagirt sind." In *Bism
Genealogical Society [Ne
pp. 8-24.

A list of persons emigrat
Hamburg to Quebec, 186
in Minnesota, and their d
area of North Dakota. F

Page 57	Passenger and Immigration

2960
HAYNES, EMMA SCHWABENLAND. "Arrival Dates in New York of Steamships Given in *Work Papers* 9 Through 14." In *Journal of the American Historical Society of Germans from Russia,* vol. 3:1 (Spring 1980), pp. 60-61.

Gives date of departure from Hamburg and date of arrival in New York between 1873 and 1878 of the ships mentioned in *Work Papers* 9 through 14, all by Gwen Pritzkau, nos. 6920-6925. Included in this article are a few names omitted from the lists in *Work Papers* 9 through 14.

*   *   *

2966
HAYNES, EMMA S. "Passenger Lists." In *Journal of the American Historical Society of Germans from Russia,* vol. 1:1 (Spring 1978), pp. 76-78.

Names 400 German passengers, most from Bremen to New York, 1875-1876, and one to Baltimore, 1875.

*   *   *

2969

Harmon Eakle settled, the surname is still pronounced Ay-kle rather than Ee-kle as in the West.

The signatures are significant as well. The original printed volumes of *Pennsylvania German Pioneers* in which these lists appear contain the printed versions of all three lists, with the second volume reproducing in facsimile the original signatures as they appear on the third list. When the Genealogical Publishing Company reprinted the set, it did not reproduce the volume of signatures. However, a 1992 reprint by Picton Press of Camden, Maine, includes the signature volume as well.

The majority—a surprising number—of the German immigrants were literate and signed their own names. These signatures are evidence of identity. Harmon Eakle's signature on deeds in Washington County, Maryland, when compared with Johann Herman Ekell's signature on the passenger list, is the same.

Andrew Hoffman of Dauphin County, Pennsylvania, signed his will with a mark, his deeds with marks, and his Revolutionary War oath of allegiance with a mark. The passenger lists include Andreas Hofman, age twenty-two in 1730, who signs his own name; Johann Andreas Hoffman in 1754, who signs his name; and Andrew Hoffman in 1772, who signs with a mark. While identity is not proved with this evidence, the first two are less likely to be the same man as the Andrew in Dauphin County.

U.S. Customs Passenger Lists (1820–1905)

Custom passenger lists were filed by the shipmasters with the collector of customs in each port. The original lists were prepared in duplicate on board ship and signed by the master of the vessel (under oath) and the customs authority. One copy was filed with the collector of customs; the other copy was returned to the master to be kept with the ships' papers. On the list, the master was also required to record births and deaths during the voyage. Under a British/American law of 1855, copies of the passenger lists for British ships were also given to the British consuls in the American port. Some may have been filed with the British consuls as early as 1829, when federal regulation began.

Original lists are extant for seven U.S. ports only. Copies or abstracts of the original lists were made by the collectors of customs and sent quarterly to the secretary of state. In them, the information was usually abbreviated, and copying errors were undoubtedly made. Transcriptions were also made for 1819 to 1832 lists from the copies sent to the Department of State. These are arranged by name of district or port, name of vessel, and name of passenger. The transcripts are third-generation copies and, as such, contain many errors.

Customs officials were also responsible to see that each ship entering and leaving port was licensed and registered. They also recorded ships' manifests listing crew, passengers, and cargo; ships' logs with statements on the conditions of the passengers, and births, marriages, and deaths at sea; payroll accounts with signatures for seamen; ships' accounts for provisions advanced to emigrants; and miscellaneous documents that related to the ship itself. These documents, sometimes called shipping records, sometimes referred to as customs records, can be found either in the possession of the shipping company, the customs house, or in local and federal archives.

Immigration Passenger Lists (1883–1945)

As the result of an act of 1882 (22 Stat. 214), immigrants arriving in the United States were to be recorded by federal immigration officials. The resulting lists date from 1891 for most ports and from 1883 for the port of Philadelphia. The National Archives has microfilmed these lists, which contain the following information: name of master, name of vessel, ports of arrival and embarkation, date of arrival, and, for each passenger, name, place of birth, last legal residence, age, occupation, sex, and remarks (figure 13-13).

With the introduction of standard federal forms in 1893,

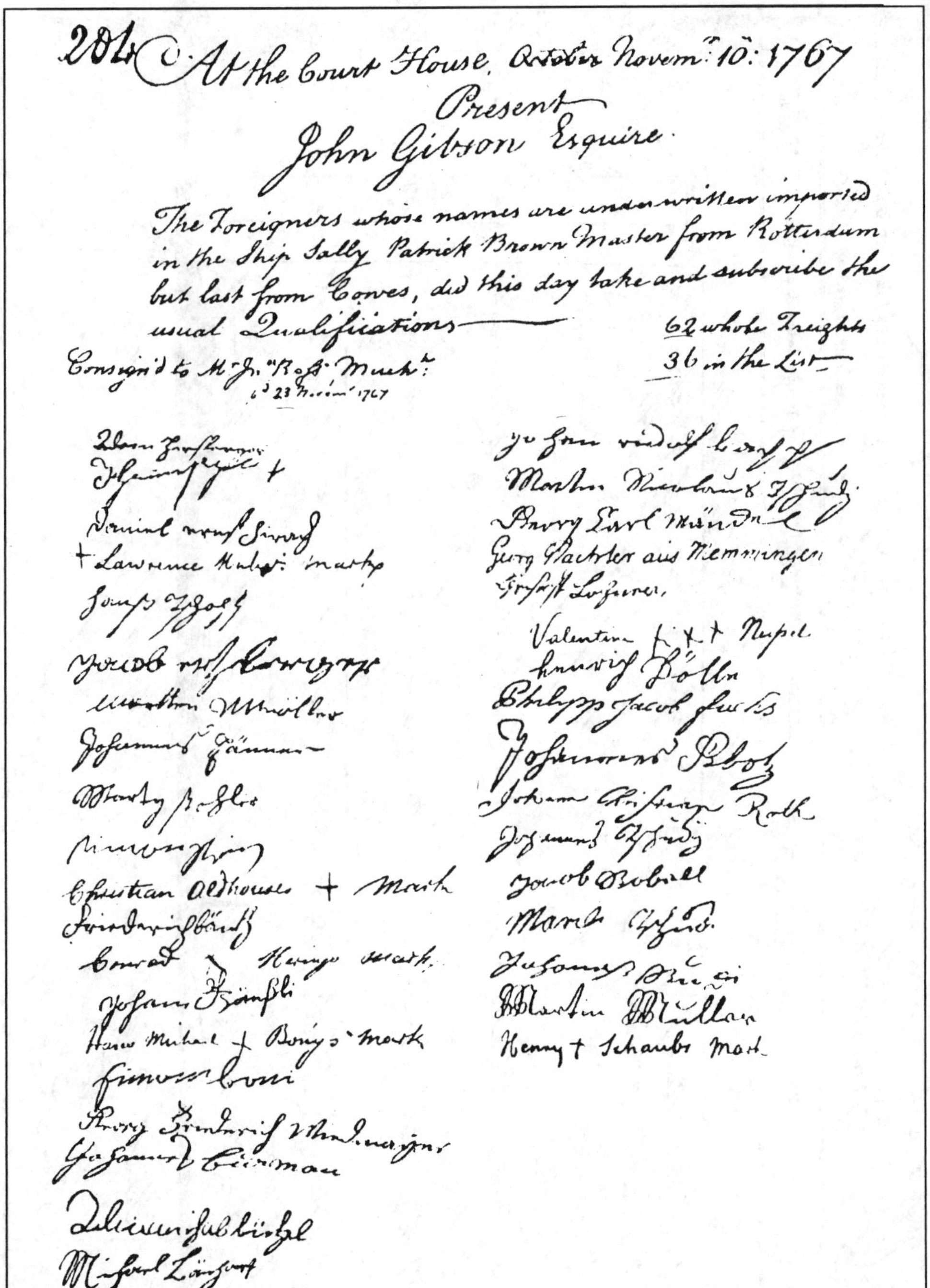
204 At the Court House, October Novem.r 10: 1767
Present
John Gibson Esquire.

The Foreigners whose names are underwritten imported in the Ship Sally Patrick Brown Master from Rotterdam but last from Cowes, did this day take and subscribe the usual Qualifications—

62 whole Freights
36 in the List

Christian Oldhouse + mark
Philipp Jacob Fuchs
Martin Müller
Henry + Schaub mark

Figure 13-12. From Ralph B. Strassburger with William J. Hinke, *Pennsylvania German Pioneers,* 3 vols. (Norristown, Pa.: Pennsylvania German Society, 1934), 2: 829.

Figure 13-13. A page from the passenger list of the SS *Nevada,* which sailed from Liverpool and Queenstown in January 1892.

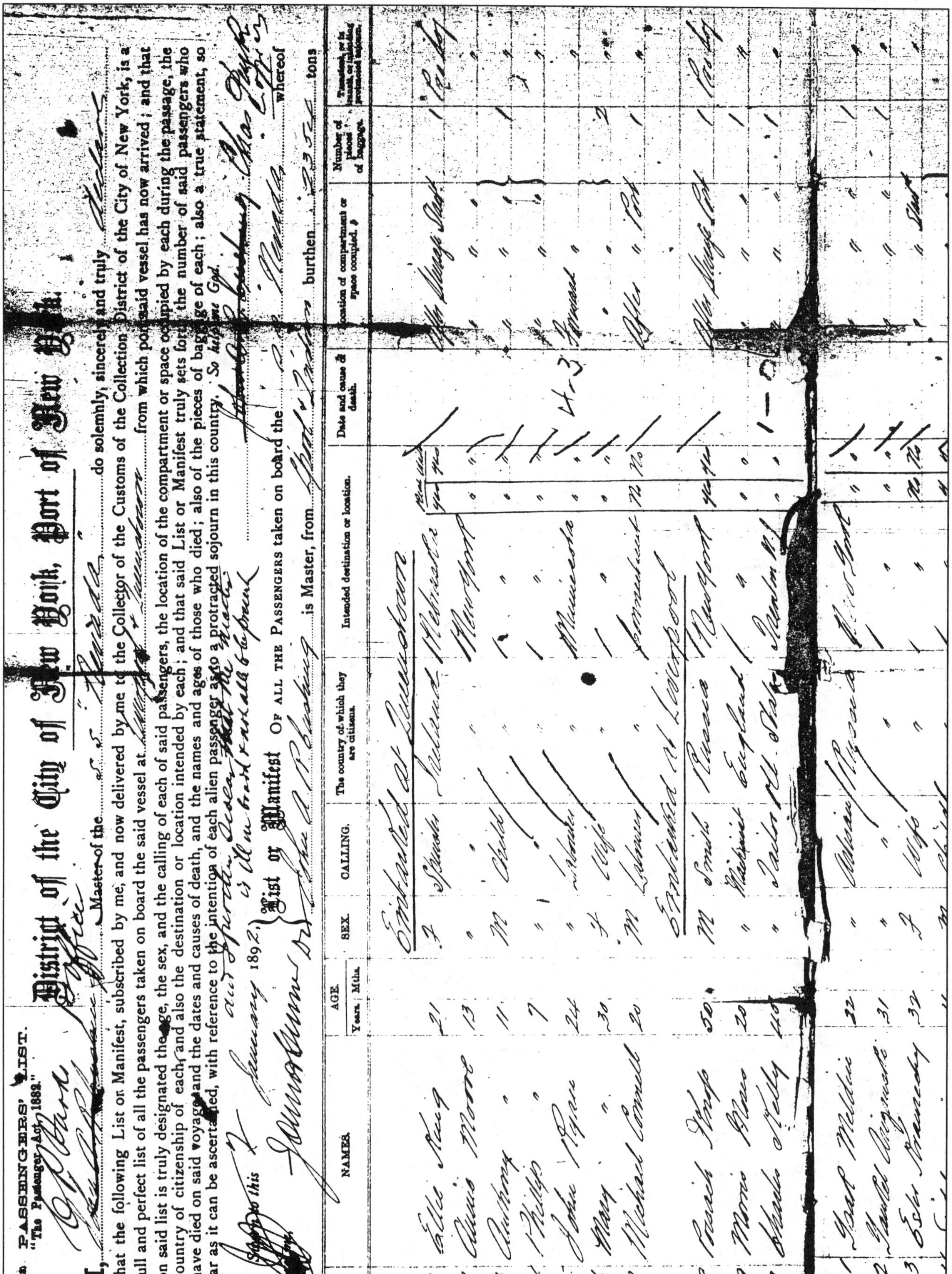

PASSENGERS' LIST.
"The Passenger Act, 1882."

District of the City of New York, Port of New York.

I, ... Master of the .... do solemnly, sincerely and truly .... that the following List or Manifest, subscribed by me, and now delivered by me to the Collector of the Customs of the Collection District of the City of New York, is a full and perfect list of all the passengers taken on board the said vessel at .... from which port said vessel has now arrived; and that on said list is truly designated the age, the sex, and the calling of each of said passengers, the location of the compartment or space occupied by each during the passage, the country of citizenship of each, and also the destination or location intended by each; and that said List or Manifest truly sets forth the number of said passengers who have died on said voyage, and the dates and causes of death, and the names and ages of those who died; also of the pieces of baggage of each; also a true statement, so far as it can be ascertained, with reference to the intention of each alien passenger as to a protracted sojourn in this country. So help me God.

Sworn to this .... 1892, before me

List or Manifest Of all the Passengers taken on board the .... whereof .... is Master, from .... burthen .... tons

No.	NAMES.	AGE Years.	AGE Mths.	SEX.	CALLING.	The country of which they are citizens.	Intended destination or location.	Date and cause of death.	Location of compartment or space occupied.	Number of pieces of baggage.	Transient, or in transit, or intending protracted sojourn.

passenger list information was changed to include the following: name of shipmaster, name of vessel, ports of arrival and embarkation, date of arrival, and the following information for each passenger: full name; age; sex; marital status; occupation; nationality; last residence; final destination; whether in the United States before and, if so, when and where; whether going to join a relative and, if so, the relative's name, address, and relationship to the passenger. Other revisions of the format included race (1903); personal description and birthplace (1906); and name and address of the nearest relative in the immigrant's home country (1907). It should be noted that these lists include not only names of immigrants but also of visitors and Americans returning from abroad. Passenger lists are arranged by port and thereunder chronologically. Records of a few ports have been indexed, some for limited years.

Border Crossings

The National Archives of the United States has several collections of arrival indexes and manifests for persons crossing the border between the United States and Canada. Most of these are listed as records of the St. Albans District, but they are not limited to those who actually came through St. Albans. Rather, the district encompassed most of the U.S.-Canadian border. The records begin in 1895 and cover arrivals as late as 1954. The microfilmed collections, most of which are also available through the Family History Library and its centers, include:

St. Albans District Manifest Records of Aliens Arriving from Foreign Contiguous Territory. These 1,169 rolls of microfilm that include Soundex cards and original manifests giving detailed information pertaining to border crossings. All crossings (from Maine to Washington) are included between 1895 and 1915. Beginning in 1915, the records are limited to border crossing in the New York-Vermont region. However, this includes major eastern Canadian seaports where U.S. officials processed ship passengers bound for the United States. This collection includes:

Soundex Index to Canadian Border Entries Through the St. Albans, Vt. District, 1895–1924. These four hundred rolls of index cards give complete geographic coverage to 1915. Some of these index cards are the actual records of crossing; in those cases there is no original manifest.

Soundex Index to Entries into the St. Albans, Vermont District Through Canadian Pacific and Atlantic Ports, 1924–1952. The ninety-eight rolls of index cards in this set pertain to border crossing in the New York-Vermont area.

Manifests of Passengers Arriving in the St. Albans, Vermont District Through Canadian Pacific and Atlantic Ports, 1895–1954. These six hundred and forty rolls are the ship lists of arrivals indexed by the above Soundex cards.

Manifests of Passengers Arriving in the St. Albans, Vermont District Through Canadian Pacific Ports, 1929–1949. These twenty-five rolls of microfilm supplement the above passenger lists.

St. Albans District Manifest Records of Aliens Arriving from Foreign Contiguous Territory, 1895–1924. These six rolls of microfilm are of card indexes of arrivals at small ports in Vermont. Each port is arranged alphabetically. This is especially useful for identifying Canadians who settled in New England.

Detroit District Manifest Records of Aliens Arriving from Foreign Contiguous Territory. This collection includes one

hundred and seventeen rolls of microfilm of the original card manifests, arranged alphabetically, for persons entering the United States through Detroit, and some other Michigan ports from 1906 to 1954. An additional twenty-three rolls include passenger and alien crew lists of vessels arriving at Detroit, 1946 to 1957.

Recently, the National Archives has begun microfilming border crossings for later years in western Canada and for arrivals across the Mexican border. Information on these records is sketchy but will undoubtedly be described in genealogical periodicals as the records become available.

New York City—Castle Garden and Ellis Island

New York City was the port of entry for by far the largest number of immigrants. Of the 5,400,000 people who arrived between 1820 and 1860, more than two-thirds entered at New York. By the 1850s, New York was receiving more than three-quarters of the national total of immigrants, and by the 1890s more than four-fifths.[13]

In 1855, Castle Garden, an old fort on the lower tip of Manhattan, was designated as an immigrant station under state supervision. When a new federal law excluding paupers and others was passed in 1882, Castle Garden continued to operate under contract to the U.S. government. But by 1890 its facilities had long since proved to be inadequate for the ever-increasing number of immigrant arrivals. After a government survey of potential locations, Ellis Island was the site chosen to establish an entirely new United States immigration station. Several Manhattan sites were rejected because earlier immigrants had been ruthlessly exploited as they left Castle Garden. On the island, immigrants could be screened, protected and filtered more slowly into the new culture. The Ellis Island Immigration Center was officially dedicated on New Year's Day in 1892.

Information on passengers who arrived at the Port of New York is available principally from the passenger lists microfilmed by the National Archives. Indexes for the New York City port are available only for the years 1820 to 1846; 1897 to 1902; 1902 to 1943; and 1944 to 1948. While far from complete, a monumental effort is underway to index ship passenger lists for the port of New York for the years between 1846 and 1897. The significant interest level and advances in computer technology should make the long-awaited project a reality.

Indexed Ports

In addition to the above-mentioned indexes for the Port of New York, the following major ports have been indexed:

Baltimore: 1820 to 1897 and 1897 to 1952.

Boston: 1848 to 1891; 1902 to 1906; 1906 to 1920; and 1899 to 1940

New Orleans: 1853 to 1899; and 1900 to 1952

Philadelphia: 1800 to 1906; and 1883 to 1948

When Passenger Lists Are Not Indexed

As noted in the very detailed description of passenger lists in *Guide to Genealogical Research in the National Archives,* rev. ed. (Washington D.C.: National Archives Trust Fund board, 1991), p. 41, the lists were "written by many different hands over many years and conditions of their preservation before

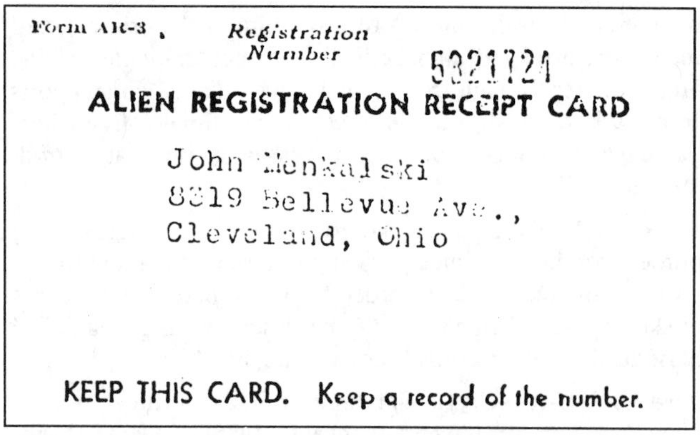

Form AR-3 , *Registration Number* 5321724

ALIEN REGISTRATION RECEIPT CARD

John Menkalski
8319 Bellevue Ave.,
Cleveland, Ohio

KEEP THIS CARD. Keep a record of the number.

Figure 13-14. Alien registration card of John Menkalski.

they were placed in the National Archives were not ideal." Many lists are difficult to read; some brittle pages have broken away, and smeared ink has blurred words beyond recognition. Unless an immigrant's name can be found in an index, or unless the exact date and port of arrival are known, searching through voluminous and hard-to-read passenger lists can be exhaustive and futile work. After microfilming the records, the National Archives transferred them to the Balch Institute at Temple University in Philadelphia, so originals are no longer available for inspection.

For the Port of New York, there are some potentially helpful finding aids. On twenty-seven rolls of National Archives microfilm (M1066) is *Registers of Vessels Arriving at the Port of New York from Foreign Ports, 1789–1919.* The volumes, most of which identify ships by name, country of origin, type of rig, date of entry, master's name, and last port of embarkation, are arranged in chronological order of arrival. If a researcher can eliminate some vessels because of port of embarkation or date, the search may be more manageable. More readily available to most is Bradley W. Steuart, *Passenger Ships Arriving in New York Harbor (1820–1850)* (Bountiful, Utah: Precision Indexing, 1991). The latter covers unindexed peak immigration years. A volume that has been in use for years is *The Morton Allan Directory of European Passenger Steamship Arrivals* (Immigrant Information Bureau, 1931). The *Morton Allan Directory* includes information on vessels arriving at New York (1890 to 1930) and at Baltimore, Boston, and Philadelphia (1904 to 1926).

Alien Registration

Registration of aliens with a local court of record was required from 1802 to 1828. (Customs officers in Salem and Beverly, Massachusetts, recorded passenger lists with aliens clearly marked, 1798–1800. These records are in the National Archives.) Enforcing this law during the War of 1812 has given us some valuable data for persons immigrating after 1800. Many of these are indexed in the *Passenger and Immigration Lists Index* (cited earlier).

Under the 1929 Alien Registration Act, aliens were again required to register their current residence and place of employment annually with the federal government. Immigrant identification cards, certificates of registry, certificates of lawful entry, certificates of arrival, and alien registration cards (figure 13-14) are forms of identification. All aliens were required to carry one of these identification cards with them to be considered legal aliens. Any alien without one of these could be deported without a hearing. These cards or certificates will usually be preserved among home sources.

Passports

Some immigrants returned to visit family and relatives in the native country. Often, they applied for U.S. passports. These records will usually indicate their birth place or the destination for the visit, which is likely near the native town.

More than 2,150 microfilms of U.S. passport records from the National Archives and Department of State have been released for research. These records from the U.S. Passport Office are travel documents "attesting to the citizenship and identity of the bearer." People of all walks of life used passports. The first extant passport given to an individual is dated July 1796. Passports generally became more popular in the late 1840s, but until the outbreak of World War I in 1914, American citizens were generally permitted to travel abroad without passports. Naturally, the requirement to carry a passport caused a significant increase in the numbers issued. By 1930, the U.S. government had issued more than 2.5 million passports.

To receive a U.S. passport, a person had to submit some proof of U.S. citizenship. This was usually in the form of a letter, affidavits of witnesses, and certificates from clerks or notaries. By 1888 there were separate application forms for native citizens, naturalized citizens, and derivative citizens. Passport applications often include information regarding an applicant's family status, date and place of birth, residence, naturalization (if foreign born), and other biographical information. Twentieth-century applications often include marriage and family information as well as dates, places, and names of ships used for travel.

The microfilmed passport records, registers, and indexes are available from the earliest dates to about 1925. They are arranged in several sets; each passport application series is arranged chronologically. A number is assigned to most applications. For some years there are registers but no actual applications. You must use the registers and indexes to determine an application's date (and number, where applicable) in order to locate a particular application.

Applications for 1925 and later are in the custody of the Passport Office, Department of State, 1425 K St. N.W., Washington, DC 20520. Microfilm copies are available from the LDS Family History Library and through its family history centers.

Naturalization Records

Naturalization is the legal procedure by which an alien becomes a citizen of a state or country. Every nation has different sets of rules that determine citizenship. While citizenship documents are sought by family historians, both for their sentimental and for their informational value, probably no other records are more difficult to fully understand or locate. Complex and ever-changing naturalization laws and interpretations of laws have resulted in the dissemination of a great deal of incorrect information in this area of research. Unfortunately, many inaccuracies have found their way into genealogical publications.

Sometimes, naturalization documentation cannot be found simply because an immigrant was not naturalized. Historically, the number of non-naturalized aliens in the United States has been significant. Tabulations of the 1890 through 1930 censuses indicate that 25.7 percent of the foreign-born population was not naturalized or had filed only declarations of intention. As John Newman points out in *American Naturalization Processes and Procedures 1790–1985,* "Many aliens lived their lives as positive contributors to their community and new nation without formally acquiring citizenship."[14] He further notes that the constitutions of some states allowed aliens who had filed only declarations of intention to vote, and, except for certain periods when full citizenship was required, to own land. Another important point made by Newman is the fact that many individuals believed themselves to be citizens by derivation from parent or spouse.

Naturalization During the American Colonial Period
The naturalization process in what is now the United States has been an important issue since the seventeenth century. American colonists, subject to the British Crown, considered themselves only "inhabitants" of the colonies, and therefore assumed protection of the laws of Great Britain. According to the practice in England, aliens could acquire citizenship either by letters of denization or by naturalization through an act of Parliament. Denization, though not requiring an oath of loyalty, allowed the transfer of properties and real estate to heirs. Aliens wishing to qualify for public office, to vote, to own a ship, and, in most cases, to own land, had to become naturalized British citizens. Only through parliamentary action could an alien obtain full citizenship status. Finding it necessary to attract immigrants, the American colonies made citizenship and land available. Most of the citizenship records surviving from the American colonial period consist only of lists of oaths of allegiance signed by individuals as they disembarked from the immigrant ships.[15]

In 1740, Parliament enacted new laws that allowed the colonies to naturalize aliens without having to obtain a special act in London. These laws failed to end disputes over the jurisdiction and authority of colonial governments that overrode English law with their own acts. In 1773, the crown disallowed naturalization acts from Pennsylvania and New Jersey, and through an order-in-council instructed colonial governors to cease assenting to such statutes. The strict policy prompted the charge in the Declaration of Independence that George III had endeavored to limit the population growth of the United States by "obstructing the laws for the naturalization of foreigners."

The Continental Congress had resolved on 6 June 1776 "that all persons abiding within any of the United Colonies and deriving protection from the laws of the same owe allegiance to the said laws, and are members of such colony."[16] No oath was required from members of the Continental Congress nor from soldiers enlisting in the American army. Those enlisting during the revolution were sworn to be true to the United States of America and to serve them honestly and faithfully. Congress later required an oath for all officers in Continental service and for all holding civil office from Congress. For a detailed discussion of the naturalization process during the Revolutionary Period, see Frank George Franklin, *The Legislative History of Naturalization in the United States* (New York: Arno Press and the *New York Times,* 1969).

Passed by Congress on 26 March 1790, the first naturalization act (1 Stat. 103) provided that any free white persons who had resided for at least two years in the United States might be admitted to citizenship on application to any common law court in any state where they had resided for at least one year. Citizenship was granted to those who satisfied the court that they were of good character and who took an oath of allegiance to the Constitution. Their children under age twenty-one also became citizens.

On 29 January 1795, Congress repealed the 1790 act and passed a more stringent law (1 Stat. 414) which provided that free white aliens might be admitted to citizenship under certain conditions. It required applicants to declare in court their intention to become citizens of the United States and to renounce any allegiance to a foreign prince, potentate, state, or sovereignty three years before admission as citizens. It increased the period of residence required for citizenship from two to five years. The act also required one year's residence in the state in which the court was held and to which application was made. Aliens who had "borne any hereditary title, or been of any of the orders of nobility" were required to renounce that status. These actions could be taken before the supreme, superior, district, or circuit court of any state or of the territories, or before a circuit or district court of the United States. As with the 1790 act, citizenship was automatically granted to the minor children of those naturalized.

From 1798 to 1800, during the undeclared war with France, Federalist leaders pushed through Congress four alien and sedition acts curbing freedom of speech and of the press and curtailing the rights of foreigners in the United States. One of the statutes, approved 18 June 1798 (1 Stat. 566), required the filing of a declaration of intention at least five years before admission to citizenship, and residence of fourteen years in the United States and five years in the state or territory where the court was held. Condemned for its severity, the law was replaced with a new naturalization law (2 Stat. 153) reasserting the basic provisions of the 1795 act. The act of 1802 specified that free white aliens might be admitted to citizenship provided they: (1) declared their intention to become citizens before a competent state, territorial, or federal court at least three years before admission to citizenship, (2) took an oath of allegiance to the United States, (3) had resided at least five years in the United States and at least one year within the state or territory where the court was held, (4) renounced allegiance to any foreign prince, potentate, state, or sovereignty, and (5) satisfied the court that they were of good moral character and attached to the principles of the Constitution. While generally poor sources for biographical detail, some naturalization documents survive as evidence of citizenship status (figure 13-15).

The 1802 legislation was the last major act affecting the basic nature of naturalization until 1906. Revisions during this period simply altered or clarified details of evidence and certification.

With the ratification of the Fourteenth Amendment to the Constitution on 28 July 1868, "All persons born or naturalized in the United States and subject to the jurisdiction thereof are citizens of the United States and the state in which they reside."

New States and Territories
As the United States acquired territory by treaty or purchase, it also acquired jurisdiction over people living on that land at the time. Acquisitions included Louisiana in 1803, Florida—including Mississippi and Alabama—in 1819, and Alaska in 1867. By joint resolution of Congress, Texas residents were granted

Figure 13-15. Certificate of naturalization of Wyrick Seltzer, 10 April 1765, Pennsylvania Supreme Court. From Earl W. Ibach, *Hub of the Tulpehocken* (Womelsdorf, Pa.: the author, 1975), 52. Used with permission.

Pennsylvania, ii.

I *Edward Shippen Junr* Prothonotary of the Supream Court of the Province of *Pennsylvania,* DO hereby certify, That at a Supream Court held at *Philadelphia,* for the Province of *Pennsylvania,* before *William Allen, William Coleman and Alexander Stedman* Esquires, Judges of the said Court, the *Tenth* Day of *April* in the Year of our Lord, *One Thousand Seven Hundred* and *Sixty five* between the Hours of Nine and Twelve of the Clock in the Forenoon of the same Day, *Wyrick Seltzer* of *Tolpohocken* in the County of *Berks* being a Foreigner, and having inhabited and resided for the Space of Seven Years in his Majesty's Colonies in *America,* and not having been absent out of some of the said Colonies for a longer Space than Two Months at any one Time during the said Seven Years. And being one of the People who conscientiously scruple and refuse the taking an Oath, did take and subscribe the Affirmations and Declarations, according to the Directions of an Act of Parliament, made in the thirteenth Year of the Reign of his late Majesty King *G E O R G E,* the Second, intituled, *An Act for naturalizing such foreign Protestants, and others, therein mentioned, as are settled, or shall settle, in any of his Majesty's Colonies in* America, and according to an Act of General Assembly of this Province of *Pennsylvania,* made in the sixteenth Year of his said late Majesty, intituled, *An Act for naturalizing such foreign Protestants, as are settled, or shall settle within this Province, who not being of the People called* Quakers, *do conscientiously refuse the taking of any Oath,* and thereupon was admitted to be his Majesty's natural born Subject of the Kingdom of *Great Britain,* and, of this Province, pursuant to the Direction and Intention of the said Act of Parliament, and Act of Assembly *In Testimony* whereof I have hereunto set my Hand, and affixed the Seal of the Supream Court, the *Tenth* Day of *April* in the Year first above-mentioned.

Edward Shippen Junr

citizenship in 1845. By acts of Congress, citizenship was conferred upon residents of Hawaii in 1900, of Puerto Rico in 1917, and of the Virgin Islands in 1927.

The United States has always agreed to validate property titles of persons who become citizens because they lived on newly acquired territories. To validate the title, however, a private land claim had to be filed, and these claims can be very valuable. The current land owner must document claim to the title, and if the grant was originally given to a father or grandfather, the claimant had also to prove descent. Some such files contain four to seven generations of genealogical proof through family Bible pages, original land transactions, genealogy charts, and affidavits and testimony of neighbors and relatives. See the *Guide to Genealogical Research in the National Archives* (cited earlier).

Significant Changes in 1906

By the beginning of the twentieth century, the steadily increasing number of immigrants entering the United States prompted significant procedural changes to ease the workload of clerks of courts, who did most of the work relating to naturalizations. The creation of the Bureau of Immigration and Naturalization under the act of 29 June 1906 (32 Stat. 596 sec. 3) provided the first uniform rule for the naturalization of aliens throughout the United States. After September 1906, naturalization forms could be obtained exclusively from the Bureau of Immigration and Naturalization. The new forms were expanded to include each applicant's age, occupation, personal description, date and place of birth, citizenship, present and last foreign addresses, ports of embarkation and entry, name of vessel or other means of conveyance, and date of arrival in the United States; also included were spouse's and children's full names with their respective dates and places of birth, and residence at the date of the document. The declaration of intention of famous physicist Enrico Fermi (figure 13-16) was filed in the Common Pleas Court of Bergen County, New Jersey, on a standard federal form in 1939. Typical of many would-be U.S. citizens, Fermi began the naturalization process in a court near the place where he arrived in the United States and finalized the procedure in another county and state where he took up permanent residency. In this case, the final papers were taken out in Chicago. Fermi's declaration of intention is filed together with his petition at the National Archives—Great Lakes Region in Chicago, where citizenship documentation is also available for his wife, Laura.

Women and Children

An act of 10 February 1855 granted citizenship to alien wives of citizens if they "might lawfully be naturalized under the existing laws" (10 Stat. 604). Prior to 1922, women and children automatically became U.S. citizens when the husband/father did. While it was definitely the exception rather than the rule, some women, especially single adults, found it necessary or desirable to become naturalized citizens themselves (figure 13-17). The names of individuals given citizenship by legislative act were often omitted, and the group may be referred to as a whole. An act of 22 September 1922 (42 Stat. 1021) had significant effects on the status of women. By this act a woman could not become a citizen by virtue of her marriage to a citizen, but, if eligible, might be naturalized by compliance with the naturalization laws. No declaration of intention was required. The act specifically provided that "any woman citizen who marries an alien ineligible to citizenship shall cease to be a citizen" (section 3). Further, no woman whose husband was not eligible to become a citizen was to be naturalized during the marriage (section 5). Figure 13-18 is an example of the thousands of documents created when American-born women who had lost their citizenship because of marriage to a foreigner sought to reclaim their citizenship. An act of 3 March 1931 repealed section 5 of the 1922 law, and section 3 was amended so that citizenship was not to be lost by a woman solely through marriage (46 Stat. 1511).

Military Service

Aliens who served in the U.S. military and had received honorable discharge were given special consideration. An act of 17 July 1862 (12 Stat. 597) stated that:

> Any alien, of the age of twenty-one years and upwards, who has enlisted, or may enlist in the armies of the United States, either the regular or the volunteer forces, and has been, or may be hereafter, honorably discharged, shall be admitted to become a citizen of the United States, upon his petition, without any previous declaration of intention to become such; and he shall not be required to prove more than one year's residence.

Designed to encourage aliens to enlist for the Civil War, this legislation applied to later wars as well. Many individuals have misunderstood this law and reported it to mean that those serving in the military gained automatic citizenship. It should be emphasized that this was not the case. With the length of residency shortened and the declaration of intention waived, the process was expedited. Instead of naturalization "first papers," some courts may have filed military discharges for some individuals. Frequently, military papers were filed independently, making it necessary to consult a separate military index. Military naturalization records were, however, included in the WPA-created indexes described later in this section. It should be noted that, when the WPA indexes were microfilmed, the reverse sides of normally blank cards were sometimes missed. An index card for William C. Wilson (figure 13-19) illustrates the importance of a thorough search.

An act of 26 July 1894 (28 Stat. 124) extended naturalization privileges to those who had "served five consecutive years in the United States Navy or one enlistment in the United States Marine Corps" so long as they had received an "honorable discharge."

Another modification regarding the naturalization of soldiers, sailors, and veterans came about because of World War I. An act of 9 May 1918 (40 Stat. 542) consolidated military naturalization laws and stated that: "Any alien serving in the military or naval service of the United States during the time this country is engaged in the present war may file his petition for naturalization without making the preliminary declaration of intention and without proof of the required five years residence within the United States." The act provided for immediate naturalization of alien soldiers, waiving the required declaration of intention or first papers, the certificate of arrival, and a proof of residence. Members of the armed forces were naturalized at military posts and nearby courts instead of at their legal residences.

African Americans and Native Americans

A law approved on 14 July 1870 opened the naturalization process to persons of African nativity or descent (16 Stat. 256). In the early years, American Indians were admitted to citizenship through treaty provisions and under special statutes. Prior to 1924, the most important law relating to Indian citizenship was the Allotment Act of 8 February 1887 (24 Stat. 387). This statute conferred citizenship on (1) every Indian born in the United States to whom allotments were made by this act or any law or treaty and (2) every Indian born in the United States who had voluntarily taken up within its limits a residence that was "separate and apart from any tribe of Indians" and had "adopted the habits of civilized life." By an act of 9 August 1888, every Native American woman who was a member of a tribe and married to a U.S. citizen was declared to be a citizen (25 Stat. 392). The act of 2 June 1924 provided that all Indians born in the United States were to be citizens (43 Stat. 253).

Genealogical Information in Naturalization Documents

A great number of alien residents never became naturalized, for various reasons; therefore, citizenship documentation for

Figure 13-16. In 1939, Enrico Fermi declared his intention to become a citizen of the United States in Bergen County, New Jersey. Information on Fermi's declaration of intention is typical of that found on naturalization documents of the era. The original declaration is at the National Archives—Great Lakes Region in Chicago.

these individuals is nonexistent. Also, some individuals did not decide to become naturalized citizens until they had been residents of this country for many years. Extreme examples have been found—some men and women did not become citizens for seventy or eighty years after immigration—but most people began naturalization proceedings within five years of their arrival in the United States.

A most important fact to remember is that the format and content of naturalization records varied dramatically from county to county, from state to state, and from year to year *prior to 1906* when the Bureau of Immigration and Naturaliza-

tion was established. After September 1906, when the new law went into effect, uniform naturalization forms were required by all courts involved in naturalizing.

Before 1906, state, county, and other courts printed various naturalization forms and certificate formats. Some courts, following directions of the 14 April 1802 Act (2 Stat. 153), were careful to record the name, birthplace, age, nation and allegiance, country from which emigrated, and the intended place of settlement of each registering alien. For example, the declaration of intention for Patrick Loyd (figure 13-20) provides the kind of detail sought by all family historians but rarely found

---

State of New-York, }
KINGS COUNTY,
CITY OF BROOKLYN. } ss.

BE IT REMEMBERED,

That on *This 8th* day of *December* in the year of our Lord, one thousand eight hundred and sixty *nine*

Mary E. Ryburn

at present of *Brooklyn*   appeared in the CITY COURT OF BROOKLYN, in said County of Kings, (the said Court being a Court of Record, having Common Law jurisdiction, Clerk and seal,) and applied to the said Court to be admitted to become a CITIZEN OF THE UNITED STATES OF AMERICA, pursuant to the directions of the Act of Congress of the United States of America, entitled an "Act to establish an Uniform Rule of Naturalization, and to repeal the Acts heretofore passed on that subject," and also an Act entitled an "Act in addition to an Act entitled an Act to establish an Uniform Rule of Naturalization, and to repeal the Acts heretofore passed on that subject," and the "Act relative to evidence in cases of Naturalization," passed 22d March, 1816; and the Act entitled an "Act in further addition to an Act to establish an Uniform Rule of Naturalization, and to repeal the Acts heretofore passed on that subject," passed May 26th, 1824; and an Act entitled an "Act to amend the Acts concerning Naturalization," passed May 24th, 1828; and an "Act to define the pay and emoluments of certain Officers of the Army and for other purposes," passed July 17th, 1862; and the said

Mary E. Ryburn

having thereupon produced to the Court such evidence, made such Declaration and renunciation, and taken such oaths as are by said Acts required:

Thereupon it was ordered by the said Court, that the said

Mary E. Ryburn

be admitted, and she was accordingly admitted by the said Court to be a CITIZEN OF THE UNITED STATES OF AMERICA.

In Testimony Whereof, the Seal of the said Court is hereunto affixed, this *8th* day of *Dec* in the *94th* year of the Independence of the United States.

Figure 13-17. Before 1922, the vast majority of alien women derived citizenship from their husbands or fathers who were already American citizens. However, the example of Mary E. Pyburn, naturalized in a Brooklyn, New York, court in 1869, points to the possibility of exceptions to the rule. Indexes to naturalizations should be searched for all family names.

Figure 13-18. Thousands of U.S.-born women lost their American citizenship when they married foreigners. This record for Myrits Ellen Roberts, first filed in U.S. District Court in Milwaukee, is now at the National Archives—Great Lakes Region. Similar documents survive in courts across the country, and many are preserved in various regional archives of the National Archives.

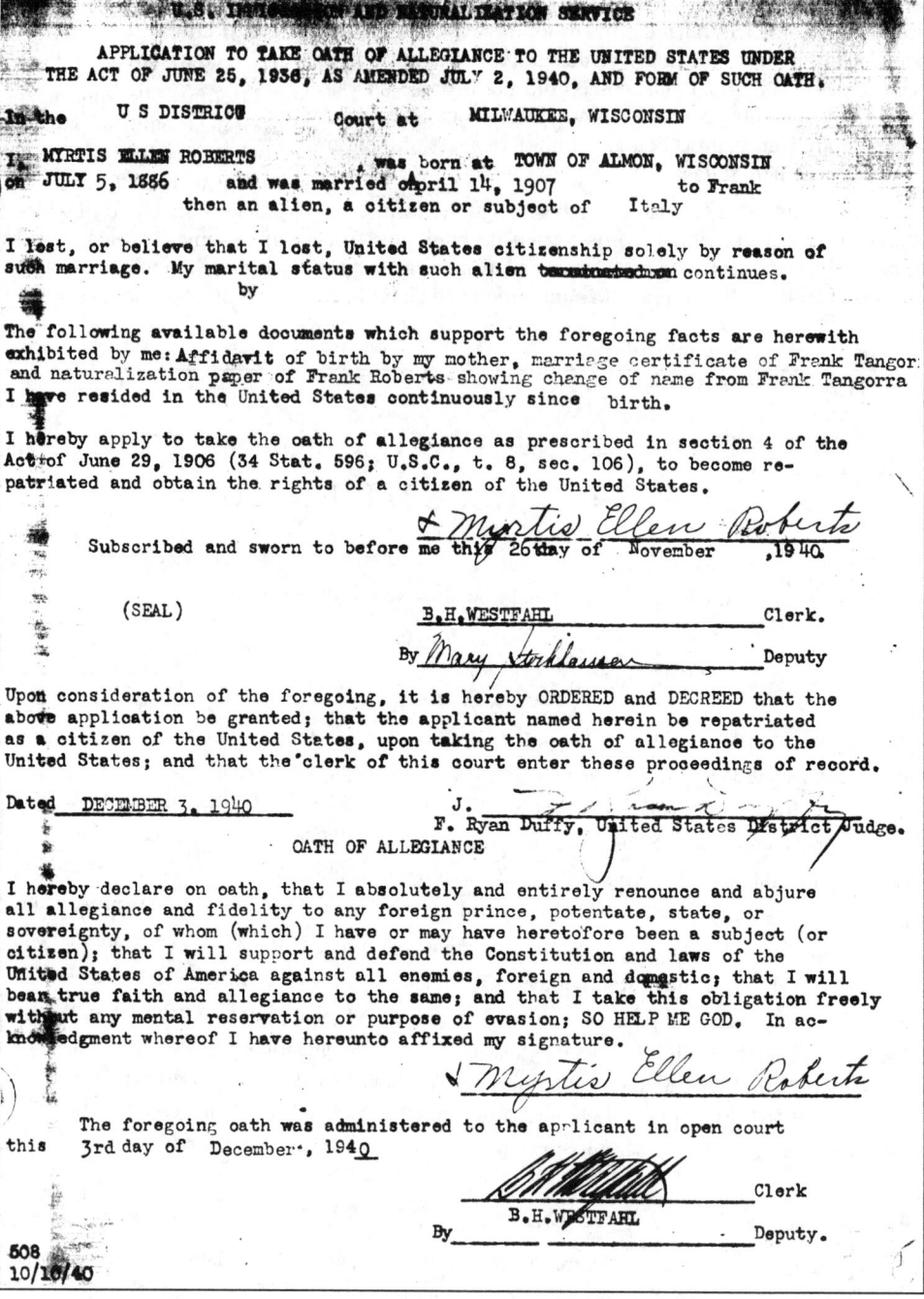

in naturalization documents created before 1906. Unfortunately, the great majority of the pre-1906 records do not reflect the directions of the 1802 Act. A typical naturalization record for this time period will provide only the name and location of the naturalizing court, the name of the person seeking naturalization, a statement renouncing allegiance and fidelity to any foreign prince, potentate, state or sovereignty (naming country of origin), and the date of the event (declaration of intention, petition, or final certificate). If the individual being naturalized could write, a signature on citizenship documents may be worth all the effort of the search. An examination of a large number of these records suggests that many immigrants could not write; thus, their marks may be the only confirmation of their desire to become American citizens. Another disappointing fact is that

many naturalization documents were copied onto forms in ledger books by county clerks. Often, the clerk's handwriting is mistakenly accepted as the petitioner's signature. Scanning other naturalization entries in a particular volume will usually make it possible to determine whether or not the signature is that of the clerk or the petitioner. Many of the earlier records contain little information that is of genealogical value, but significant exceptions in some states and counties make it advisable to conduct a thorough search of all potential naturalization documentation for the person or persons of interest. Figures 13-21 and 13-22, from courts in Oneida County, New York; Wood County, Ohio; and Cook County, Illinois, are representative of the variety of forms used by local courts before 1906. Usually, very little biographical information is offered in these early records.

Becoming a Citizen: The Process and the Records

The first Naturalization Act provided that an alien who wished to become a citizen could apply to "any common law court of record, in any of the states wherein he shall have resided for the term of one year at least."

Aliens interested in becoming citizens of the United States generally took the following steps:

Declaration of Intention (First Papers): Usually, the declaration of intention was the first step in the naturalization process. Normally, the first papers were completed soon after arrival in the United States, depending on the laws in effect at the time. (See the "Major Settlements, Immigration, and Naturalization: A Chronology" section, above.) Certain groups, such as women and children, were exempt in early years. After 1862, those who were honorably discharged from U.S. military service were excused from this initial procedure. Until 1906, the content of forms for declarations of intention varied dramatically from county to county and court to court. A large percentage of the first papers created before 1906 contain very little biographical information. Declarations of intention produced after 25 September 1906 generally contain the following information: name, address, occupation, birthplace, nationality, country from which emigrated, birth date or age, personal description, date of intention, marital status, last foreign residence, port of entry,

name of ship, date of entry, and date of document. Declarations of intention, affidavits, petitions, and oaths of allegiance were generally filed together in the court in which the final steps to citizenship were taken. Affidavits and final oaths were not always recorded on separate forms, depending on the court and the year. When they do exist as individual papers, they are usually filed with the final papers, as in the case of Patrick Lynch, who was naturalized in the United States Court in Cuyahoga County (Cleveland), Ohio. See figures 13-23, 13-24, 13-25, and 13-26.

Petition (Second or Final Papers): Naturalization petitions were formal applications submitted to the court by individuals who had met the residency requirements and who had declared their intention to become citizens. As with the declarations of intention, informational content varied dramatically from court to court. Most petitions created before 1906 offer very little in terms of personal information. After 1906, the following information might be found: name, address, occupation, date emigrated, birthplace, country from which emigrated, birth date or age, time in the United States, date of intention, name and age of spouse, names of children, ages of children, last foreign residence, port and mode of entry, name of ship, date of entry, names of witnesses, date of document, address of spouse, and photograph (after 1940).

W-425

Family name **WILSON.**	Given name or names **WILLIAM C.**
Address **"0"**	
Certificate no. (or vol. and page) **V.C.P. 64. SOLDIER.**	(CAMBRIDGE, ILL) Title and location of court **CIRCUIT COURT, HENRY CO.**
Country of birth or allegiance **NORWAY.**	When born (or age) **"0"**
Date and port of arrival in U.S. **1854—14Yrs in U.S.**	Date of naturalization **FEBRUARY—4—1868**
Names and addresses of witnesses **J.S.SHAWALTER. "0"**	
PHILLIP EMMERT. "0" (OVER)	

U.S. Department of Labor, Immigration and Naturalization Service.   Form No. 1-IP.

ADDITIONAL INFORMATION IN COURT RECORD

Certificate canceled (date and court) _____

Why canceled _____

Expatriated _____   Deceased _____

Other facts of record **WILLIAM C. WILSON-ENLISTED IN THE U.S. ARMY,IN Co.H.13th REG'T ILL'S VOL.**

DISCHARGED—MAY-15-1866.

Figure 13-19. Both sides of a WPA-created index card which indicates the military service of William C. Wilson. The original card is from The Soundex Index to Naturalization Petitions for the United States District and Circuit Courts, Northern District of Illinois and Immigration and Naturalization Service District 9, 1840–1950, at the National Archives—Great Lakes Region, Chicago.

Figure 13-20. Naturalization papers for Patrick Loyd were originally filed in the U.S. Court for the Eastern District of Michigan. They are now preserved at the National Archives—Great Lakes Region.

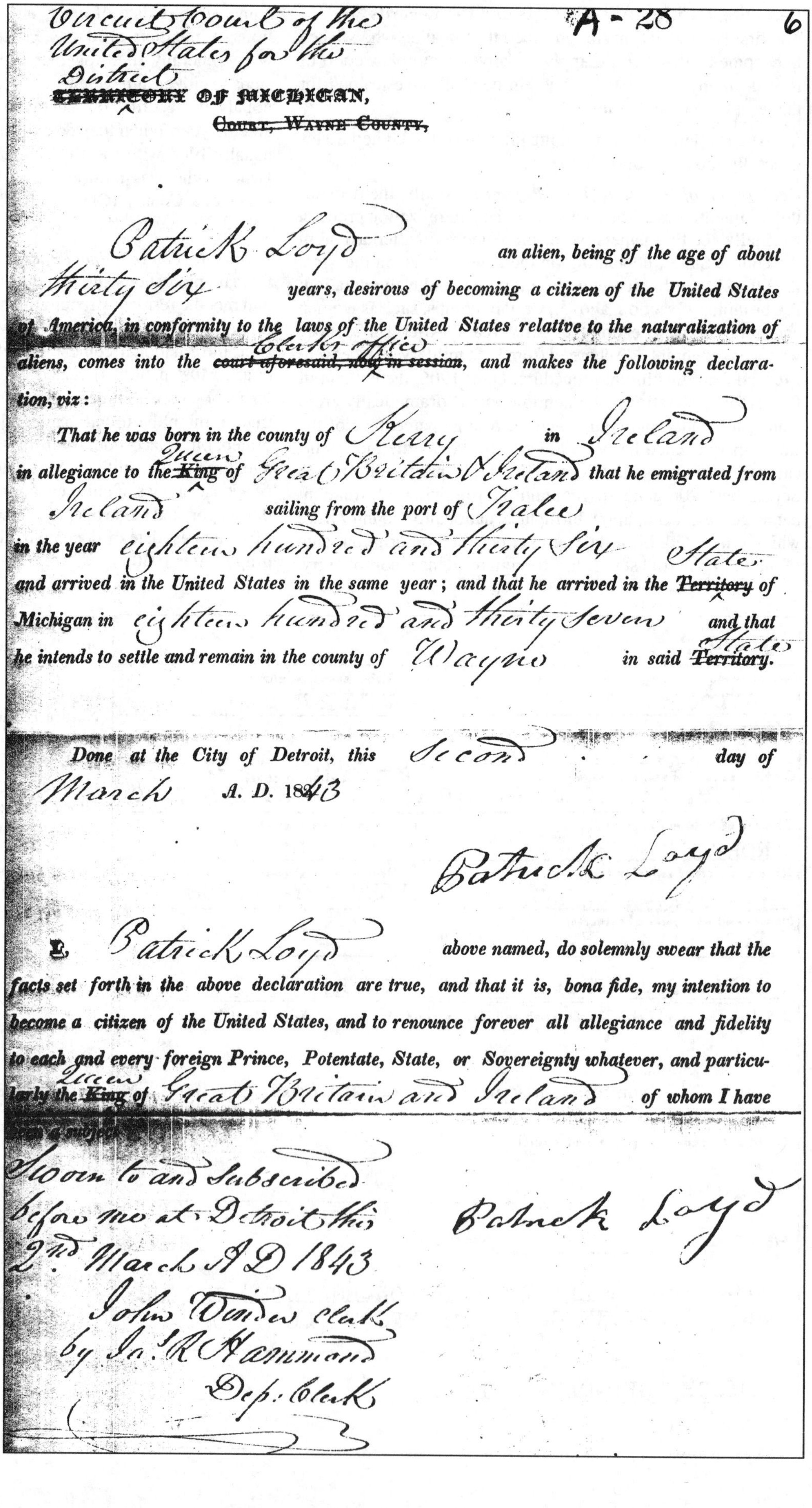

Circuit Court of the United States for the District

~~TERRITORY OF MICHIGAN,~~
~~Court, Wayne County,~~

A - 28   6

Patrick Loyd an alien, being of the age of about *thirty Six* years, desirous of becoming a citizen of the United States of America, in conformity to the laws of the United States relative to the naturalization of aliens, comes into the ~~court aforesaid, now in session~~ *Clerks office*, and makes the following declaration, viz :

That he was born in the county of *Kerry* in *Ireland* in allegiance to the ~~King~~ *Queen* of *Great Britain & Ireland* that he emigrated from *Ireland* sailing from the port of *Tralee* in the year *eighteen hundred and thirty Six State* and arrived in the United States in the same year; and that he arrived in the ~~Territory~~ *State* of Michigan in *eighteen hundred and thirty Seven* and that he intends to settle and remain in the county of *Wayne* in said ~~Territory~~ *State*.

Done at the City of Detroit, this *Second* day of *March* A. D. 18*43*

Patrick Loyd

I, *Patrick Loyd* above named, do solemnly swear that the facts set forth in the above declaration are true, and that it is, bona fide, my intention to become a citizen of the United States, and to renounce forever all allegiance and fidelity to each and every foreign Prince, Potentate, State, or Sovereignty whatever, and particularly the ~~King~~ *Queen* of *Great Britain and Ireland* of whom I have

Sworn to and Subscribed before me at Detroit this 2nd March AD 1843

Patrick Loyd

John Winder clerk by Jno R Hammond Dep: Clerk

Certificate of Naturalization: Most certificates contain only the name of the individual and the name of the court and the date of issue. Certificates were issued to the naturalized citizens upon completion of all citizenship requirements. As in the cases of the declarations of intention and the petitions, the amount of information provided on the certificate may vary greatly from court to court and from year to year. In some cases, the certificate will provide the name; address; birthplace or nationality; country from which emigrated; birth date or age; personal description; marital status; name of spouse; names, ages, and addresses of children; and date of document.

Naturalization Certificate Stubs: Generally, the court did not retain copies of certificates issued to new citizens, but certificates were usually issued from bound volumes. Typical volumes were designed in a check book fashion, with the certificate to the right side of the page, and a stub to the left to be kept as a permanent record of the person to whom the certificate was issued. These "naturalization stub books," as they are sometimes called, vary in content from court to court and from year to year, but they sometimes contain much genealogical information. Some court officials regarded stub books as a duplication of records that occupied needed space and ordered them destroyed. If certificate stubs have survived, they may be found in the creating courts, archives, and historical agencies. See, for example, figure 13-27, a page from a stub book for the U.S. District Court, Northern District of Ohio, for Julius August Behnke. It shows his age, when and where he declared his in-

tention to become a citizen, names, ages, and places of residences of his wife and children, and the date of issue of the certificate of naturalization.

Certificates of Arrival: Aliens arriving in the United States after 29 June 1906 were issued a certificate of arrival which verified their presence in the United States. The certificates were then filed with subsequent citizenship papers. Figure 13-28 is such a certificate for Solomon Brain, who arrived at the port of Detroit, Michigan, on 1 April 1910.

Where to Search for Naturalization Documents

Prior to 1906 an alien could be naturalized in any court of record. In most cases it is best to begin a search for naturalization documents in courts in the county where the immigrant is known to have resided. It is not uncommon to discover that immigrants, anxious to become citizens, began the citizenship process by taking out first papers in the county in which they first arrived in this country. One may have started the process somewhere on Eastern Seaboard, for example, and then completed the requirements in the county or state when final residency was established in the Midwest.

In addition to county and federal courts, there may have been city or municipal courts, marine courts, criminal courts, police courts, or other courts having authority to naturalize in the area where the immigrant lived. Often it was a matter of the alien simply choosing to travel to the most conveniently located court—and the court house in an adjoining county might

Figure 13-21. Declaration of intention for Francis O'Connor, filed in Utica, Oneida County, New York, on 27 March 1851.

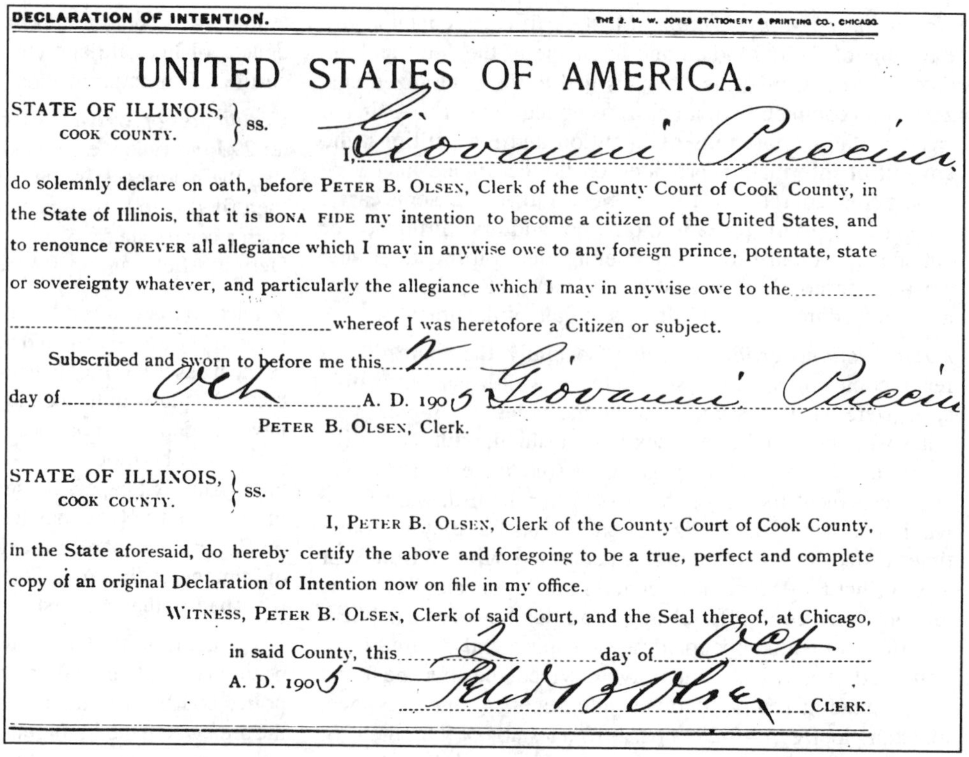

Figure 13-22. Declaration of intention for Giovanni Puccini, filed in the County Court of Cook County, Illinois, on 2 October 1905.

have been more convenient than the court house in the county of residence.

While all naturalization records are supposed to be permanent records and kept indefinitely by the courts, major and minor situations have caused records to be lost, destroyed, or moved from their creating agencies. Floods, fires, carelessness, politics, and other acts of humans and nature have destroyed some records and made others unaccessible. Over the years some long-forgotten naturalization records have been rediscovered in warehouses, attics, and basements. Still others collections have been carefully maintained by museums, libraries, and historical and genealogical societies. State archives and historical agencies typically strive to preserve and catalog these historical records. If a record is not immediately found at the county level, an investigation of any such records kept at the state level may be in order.

Some courts will have master naturalization indexes, but many will have separately indexed volumes of naturalization records that will need to be examined book-by-book. Frequently, the naturalizations of military personnel and of minors are in separate volumes and may be easily overlooked. It is not unheard of to find naturalization records intermingled with other court records; some have even been found among land records. An excellent source for locating courts and naturalization records is Alice Eichholz, ed., *Ancestry's Red Book: American State, County and Town Sources*, rev. ed. (Salt Lake City: Ancestry, 1992).

Millions of naturalization records from counties all over the United States have been microfilmed by the Genealogical Society of Utah and are available at the LDS Family History Library in Salt Lake City. Copies of the microfilm may be borrowed through LDS family history centers. In some cases, it may be more convenient to access naturalization indexes and files through the Family History Library if the records have been microfilmed.

WPA Indexes

During the 1930s and 1940s, most states participated in a nationwide project, sponsored by the U.S. Department of Justice and carried out by the Work Projects Administration (WPA), to locate and photograph naturalization records predating 27 September 1906. Although all photostatic copies were to be deposited with the Immigration and Naturalization Service, few of the states or districts were completed when the WPA was disbanded in 1942.

There are several enormous naturalization indexes that should be consulted initially if the alien of interest lived in one of the areas covered by these compilations. One of the largest is: *Index to Naturalization Petitions of the United States District Court for the Eastern District of New York 1865–1957*, described in a pamphlet of the same title (National Archives Trust Fund Board, 1991). The records which have been microfilmed consist of approximately 650,000 three- by five-inch cards that index bound and unbound naturalization petitions. The cards are arranged in three groups covering the periods July 1865 to September 1906, October 1906 to November 1925, and November 1925 to December 1957. The cards within each group are arranged alphabetically by the name of the person naturalized.

Index cards for the first group include the name of the naturalized individual, the date of naturalization, and the volume and record number of the naturalization petition. These cards may also contain such information as the address, occupation, birth date or age, former nationality, and port and date of arrival of the person naturalized, and the name of the witness to the naturalization.

The cards for the second and third groups show the name and the petition and certificate numbers of the person natural-

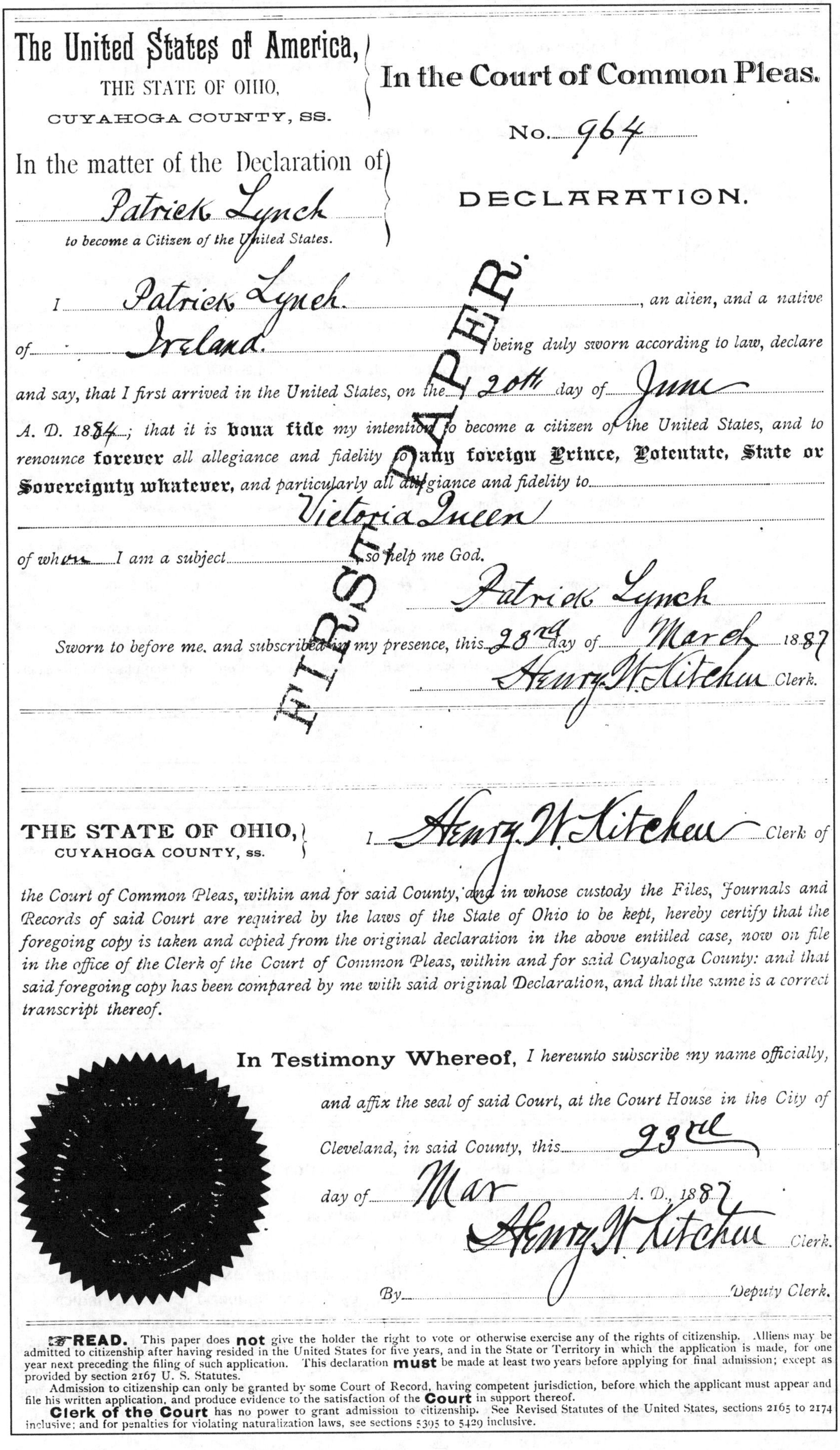

The United States of America,

THE STATE OF OHIO,

CUYAHOGA COUNTY, SS.

In the matter of the Declaration of

Patrick Lynch

to become a Citizen of the United States.

In the Court of Common Pleas.

No. *964*

DECLARATION.

I *Patrick Lynch*, an alien, and a native

of *Ireland* being duly sworn according to law, declare

and say, that I first arrived in the United States, on the *20th* day of *June*

A. D. 18*54*; that it is **bona fide** my intention to become a citizen of the United States, and to

renounce **forever** all allegiance and fidelity to **any foreign Prince, Potentate, State or**

Sovereignty whatever, and particularly all allegiance and fidelity to

Victoria Queen

of whom I am a subject so help me God.

Patrick Lynch

Sworn to before me, and subscribed in my presence, this *23rd* day of *March* 18*87*

Henry W. Kitchen Clerk.

FIRST PAPER.

THE STATE OF OHIO,

CUYAHOGA COUNTY, ss.

I *Henry W. Kitchen* Clerk of

the Court of Common Pleas, within and for said County, and in whose custody the Files, Journals and
Records of said Court are required by the laws of the State of Ohio to be kept, hereby certify that the
foregoing copy is taken and copied from the original declaration in the above entitled case, now on file
in the office of the Clerk of the Court of Common Pleas, within and for said Cuyahoga County: and that
said foregoing copy has been compared by me with said original Declaration, and that the same is a correct
transcript thereof.

In Testimony Whereof, I hereunto subscribe my name officially,

and affix the seal of said Court, at the Court House in the City of

Cleveland, in said County, this *23rd*

day of *Mar* A. D., 18*87*

Henry W. Kitchen Clerk.

By Deputy Clerk.

☞READ. This paper does **not** give the holder the right to vote or otherwise exercise any of the rights of citizenship. Alliens may be
admitted to citizenship after having resided in the United States for five years, and in the State or Territory in which the application is made, for one
year next preceding the filing of such application. This declaration **must** be made at least two years before applying for final admission; except as
provided by section 2167 U. S. Statutes.
   Admission to citizenship can only be granted by some Court of Record, having competent jurisdiction, before which the applicant must appear and
file his written application, and produce evidence to the satisfaction of the **Court** in support thereof.
   Clerk of the Court has no power to grant admission to citizenship. See Revised Statutes of the United States, sections 2165 to 2174
inclusive; and for penalties for violating naturalization laws, see sections 5395 to 5429 inclusive.

Figure 13-23. Declaration of Intention for Patrick Lynch, filed in the U.S. Court in Cleveland, Ohio. It is now preserved at the National Archives—Great Lakes Region in Chicago.

Figure 13-24. Affidavit of Patrick Lynch, from the U.S. Court in Cleveland, Ohio. It is now preserved at the National Archives—Great Lakes Region.

United States of America, NORTHERN DISTRICT OF OHIO, ss. } In the District Court of the United States for the Northern District of Ohio. EASTERN DIVISION.

In the matter of the Application of Patrick Lynch For Admission to Citizenship of the United States of America.

AFFIDAVIT.

Martin McCarthy (143 Mason St) of lawful age, being duly sworn according to law, says: That he is by occupation a Laborer and resides in the City of Cleveland, in the County of Cuyahoga and State of Ohio, that for more than five years last past he has been personally acquainted with the above named applicant Patrick Lynch who now resides in the City of Cleveland, in said county and State; that said applicant has been a **Bona Fide** resident of the United States, for the five years immediately preceding the filing of his petition in this cause, and for the year last past he has been a **Bona Fide** resident of the State of Ohio; that during that time he has behaved as a man of good moral character, attached to the principles of the Constitution of the United States, and well disposed to the good order and happiness of the same.

and further this deponent saith not.

Martin McCarthy

Sworn to before me and subscribed in my presence, by the said Patrick Lynch this 21st day of October 18[illegible]

O. C. Beatty

UNITED STATES COMMISSIONER, Northern District of Ohio.

ized and generally include the address, age, and date of admission to citizenship.

The petitions to which these microfilmed index cards relate are in the National Archives—Northeast Region. They have not yet been microfilmed.

Petitions for the period from July 1865 to September 1906 are arranged in bound volumes. The information on each petition varies. Petitions dated 1 July 1865 to 5 July 1895 indicate the city of residence, former nationality of petitioner, name of witness, dates of petition, and admission to citizenship. Petitions dated from 5 July 1895 through 26 September 1906 may also contain information on the petitioner's occupation, date and place of birth, and port and date of arrival in the United States; the name, address, and occupation of the witness; and the signature of the alien.

Petitions filed after September 1906 are unbound and are arranged numerically by petition number. They usually indicate the occupation, place of embarkation, and date and port of arrival of the petitioner; name of the vessel or other means of conveyance into the United States; the court in which the alien's declaration of intention was filed and filing date; marital status; name and place of residence of each of the applicant's children; date of the beginning of the alien's continuous U.S. residence; length of residence in the United States; names, occupations, and addresses of witnesses; and signatures of alien and witnesses.

A caveat in the descriptive pamphlet states:

> The index reproduced on this microfilm publication refers only to those aliens who sought naturalization in the U.S. District Court for the Eastern District of New York, located in Kings County, New York. An alien, however, could become a naturalized citizen through any court of record, making it possible for those living in any of the five counties that make up the eastern district to seek naturalization through the city or county courts in the counties in this district. This index, therefore, does not contain the names of all individuals naturalized in the counties of Kings, Queens, Richmond, Suffolk, and Nassau. The clerks of these county courts will, as a rule, have custody of the naturalization records of aliens who became citizens in their courts.

The National Archives—Great Lakes Region in Chicago has in its custody the Soundex index to more than 1.5 million naturalization petitions from northern Illinois, northwestern In-

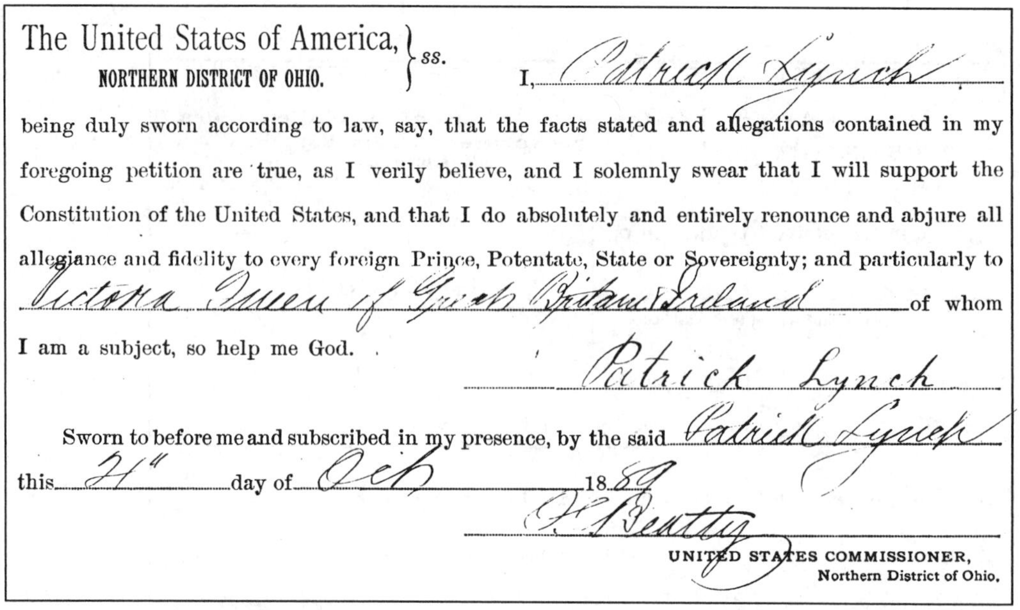

The United States of America, } ss.
NORTHERN DISTRICT OF OHIO.

I, Patrick Lynch being duly sworn according to law, say, that the facts stated and allegations contained in my foregoing petition are true, as I verily believe, and I solemnly swear that I will support the Constitution of the United States, and that I do absolutely and entirely renounce and abjure all allegiance and fidelity to every foreign Prince, Potentate, State or Sovereignty; and particularly to Victoria Queen of Great Britain & Ireland of whom I am a subject, so help me God.

Patrick Lynch

Sworn to before me and subscribed in my presence, by the said Patrick Lynch this 21st day of Oct 1889

F. A. Beatty
UNITED STATES COMMISSIONER,
Northern District of Ohio.

Figure 13-26. Final oath of Patrick Lynch, from the U.S. Court in Cleveland, Ohio. It is now preserved at the National Archives—Great Lakes Region.

diana, southern and eastern Wisconsin, and eastern Iowa. The microfilmed records are described in a pamphlet titled *Soundex Index to Naturalization Petitions for the United States District and Circuit Courts, Northern District of Illinois, and Immigration and Naturalization Service District 9, 1840–1950* (National Archives Trust Fund Board, 1991). The index consists of 162 cubic feet of three- by five-inch cards arranged in Russell-Soundex order and thereafter alphabetically by given name. The index includes civil and military petitions.

While the Soundex index includes references to naturalizations that took place in Illinois, Indiana, Wisconsin, and Iowa, a great portion of the records cited in the index are not physically located at the National Archives (see figure 13-29). Naturalization records in the custody of the National Archives—Great Lakes Region, with one exception, consist of records for persons naturalized in certain federal (not county or state) courts. The one exception is copies (not originals) of county naturalization records for 1871 through 1906 for Chicago/Cook County, Illinois. A sampling of the Soundex index described above (figure 13-30) illustrates the standard format used for the cards and the kind of information about the individual that may or may not be included. Besides the name of the naturalized citizen, it is especially important to note the name of the court in which the naturalization took place and the petition number (when it is included on the card) when following through with a search for the actual naturalization documents. Normally, all biographical information recorded in the original document was copied to the Soundex card. If the spaces on the card for date of birth, birthplace, date and place of arrival in the United States, etc., are blank, it is likely that the original naturalization documents did not include that information.

While there is no comprehensive index to other naturalizations in its custody, the National Archives—Great Lakes Region also has naturalization documents for other federal courts in Illinois, Indiana, Michigan, Minnesota, Ohio, and Wisconsin for certain years.

The National Archives—New England Region has original copies of naturalization records of the federal courts for the six New England states. Individuals were also naturalized in state, county, and local courts. The branch has copies (dexographs—white-on-black photographs) of such court records between 1790 and 1906 for Maine, Massachusetts, Rhode Island, Vermont, and New Hampshire. For Connecticut there are originals of some state, county, and local naturalizations for the years 1790 to 1974. An index to naturalization documents filed in courts in Connecticut, Maine, Massachusetts, New Hampshire, and Rhode Island is also at the National Archives—New England Region. The index contains some cards for New York and Vermont as well, but the records to which they refer are not among the photocopies at that regional archive. The New England WPA index consists of three- by five-inch cards arranged by name of petitioner and by the Soundex system. The index refers to the name and location of the court that granted citizenship and to the volume and page number of the naturalization record.

For a listing of naturalization records and indexes available for research in the regions of the National Archives, see Loretto Dennis Szucs and Sandra Hargreaves Luebking, *The Archives: A Guide to the National Archives Field Branches* (Salt Lake City: Ancestry, 1988).

Naturalizations After 1906

The Immigration and Naturalization Service, 425 Eye St. N.W., Washington, DC 20536, maintains a duplicate file of naturalizations that took place after 27 September 1906.

Other Federal Records

In addition to the many records in the United States already discussed, some other federal records may identify the immigrant's place of origin. These records are usually used later in the research process because the records already discussed are more likely to provide the name of the native town. However, on occasion, military records, Social Security records, or others may provide information about the immigrant found nowhere else.

Military Records

Military records are among the most important and most extensive U.S. records of genealogical value. Because the military needed to fully identify the soldiers who fought and the veterans who received pensions, birth information is common in military records. Immigrants were often ready recruits for the military, especially when they had few relatives in America. Many were willing to fight for their adopted country, including, paradoxically, those who left their native countries to avoid military service. As with most other genealogical records, the more recent records include more information. Indeed, records of revolutionary war service seldom identify the birthplace of the soldier, let alone his home in the native country. By the time of the Civil War, however, enlistment records usually indicated at least the country where an immigrant was born, and sometimes the town. Although immigration decreased during the Civil War, a surprisingly large number of immigrants who arrived in the early years of the war enlisted in the army. To receive a Civil War pension, veterans did not have to require proof of birth; however, the birthplace of the veteran was often included on pension application forms.

By the end of the nineteenth century, military enlistment records almost invariably indicated the town of birth. Any significant military record created during the twentieth century will aid most researchers seeking the native towns of immigrants born after 1875. World War I draft records documented virtually every adult male between the ages of eighteen and forty-five in the years 1918 to 1920. World War II draft records have recently become available for some states, and they are found in some regions of the National Archives. They would include virtually any immigrant born between 1875 and 1900, whether they had been naturalized or not. For more information on these and other military records, see chapter 9, Research in Military Records.

Social Security Records

Beginning in the 1930s, the federal government made Social Security benefits available for an increasingly large number of U.S. citizens. To apply for these benefits, the individual had to file an application for a social security number. This application, called an SS no. 5 form, required a specific statement about the person's date and place (town) of birth. By the 1940s, many citizens had obtained Social Security numbers. They could include virtually any immigrant born in the last third of the nineteenth century. These records are discussed in greater detail in chapter 18, Tracking Twentieth-Century Ancestors.

Homestead Records

Homestead records can also offer valuable clues. Much of the great prairie lands of the United States and Canada were settled by immigrants. Immigrants were required to have at least filed a declaration of intent to be naturalized before applying for homestead land, and the application often called for specific birth information. Indeed, the immigrant ancestor may have had any number of dealings with the federal government, even including federal court cases. Any such records will be important in documenting the immigrant's life and, if the records date from after the Civil War (1865), they very likely will provide significant information about the immigrant's foreign origins.

FOREIGN SOURCES AND STRATEGIES

If, after carefully searching American sources, a reference to the town from which the immigrant left is still undiscovered, it is sometimes possible to use foreign sources to determine immigrant origins. When searching records in the country of origin, the general process is to search nationwide records first. Next, search other records that will narrow the possible locations until the right one is found. The foundation for such a search lies in the information located in American records. The sections below will facilitate systematic searches of records in the country of origin. As new information is gathered, consider which tactic to apply next.

Name etymologies can help identify the region a name

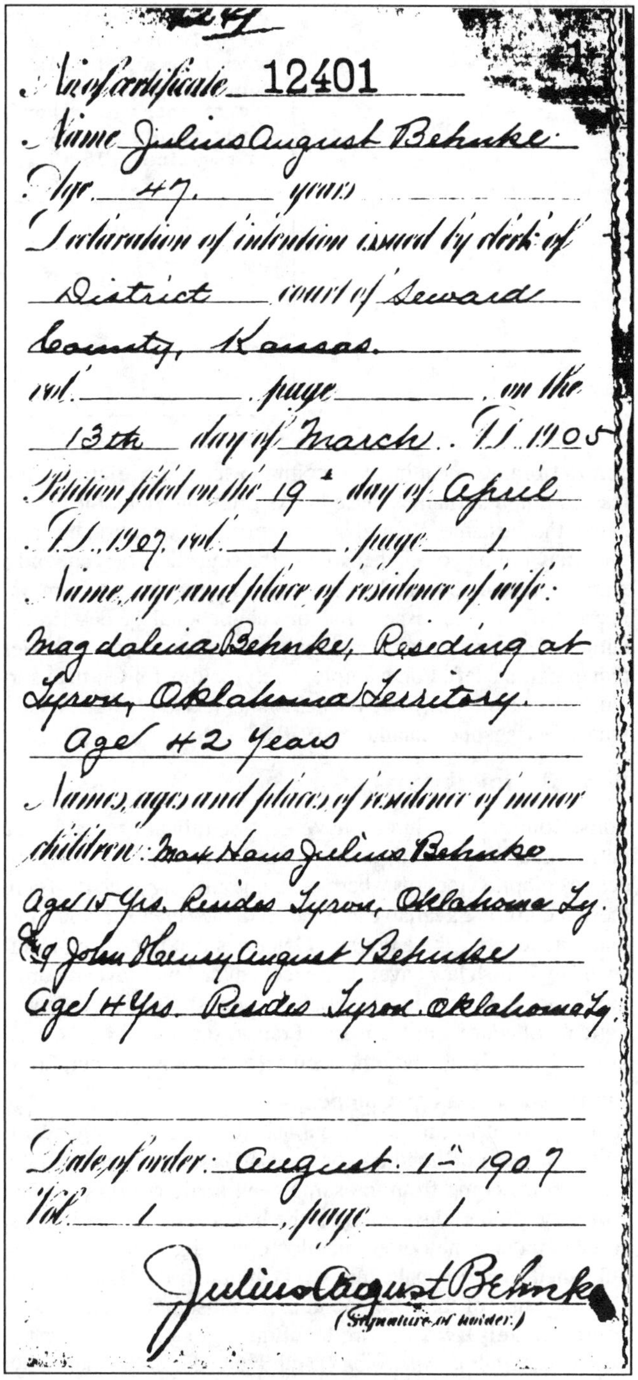

No. of certificate 12401
Name Julius August Behnke
Age 47 years
Declaration of intention issued by clerk of District court of Seward County, Kansas.
vol. ______ page ______ on the 13th day of March A.D. 1905
Petition filed on the 19th day of April A.D. 1907 vol. 1 page 1
Name, age and place of residence of wife: Magdalena Behnke, Residing at Tyrone, Oklahoma Territory. Age 42 Years
Names, ages and places of residence of minor children: Max Hans Julius Behnke Age 15 Yrs. Resides Tyrone, Oklahoma Ty. John Henry August Behnke Age 4 Yrs. Resides Tyrone, Oklahoma Ty.
Date of order: August 1st 1907
Vol. 1 page 1
Julius August Behnke
(Signature of holder.)

Figure 13-27. From a stub book for naturalization certificates. This one was issued to Julius August Behnke in the U.S. Court, Northern District of Ohio, Cleveland. The original stub book is now preserved at the National Archives—Great Lakes Region in Chicago.

Figure 13-28. This certificate of arrival for Solomon Brain is filed with his petition for naturalization at the National Archives— Great Lakes Region.

```
Form 526-B

            CERTIFICATE OF ARRIVAL--FOR NATURALIZATION PURPOSES
        (For use of aliens arriving in the United States after June
        29, 1906. To be issued immediately prior to petitioning for
        naturalization.)

        U. S. DEPARTMENT OF LABOR---IMMIGRATION SERVICE

            OFFICE        The Commissioner
            AT            Montreal, Canada              APR 24 1930

            The immigration records at this station show that the alien named below
        was duly examined and found admissible to the United States under the immigra-
        tion laws and furnished with a certificate entitling him to admission for
        permanent residence at a Canadian border port of entry. While no actual rec-
        ord of entry at a border port exists, this Service is satisfied from the evi-
        dence furnished that said certificate was used by the applicant to gain entry
        at the time, place, and manner stated below:

            PORT OF ENTRY   Detroit, Michigan ON  April 1, 1910
            NAME              Solomon Brain

            MANNER OF ENTRY        CP
            (Name of vessel, railroad, or other means of conveyance)

    VS/hm                                           H. R. LANDIS
                                               U. S. Commissioner of Immigration

                                           (TITLE)        In Charge, Statistical Division
```

comes from, its meaning, and common spelling variations. For less-common surnames these books often provide clues to localize the surname. Regard such sources with caution because they may not be comprehensive in the sources surveyed, and a name's presence in one location does not preclude it from appearing elsewhere, especially for occupational or descriptive names. Surname etymologies exist for most major countries that emigrants left. For example, an etymology for German surnames is Hans Bahlow, *Deutsches Namenlexikon* (Munich, Germany: Verlagsbuchhandlung, 1972).

NATIONWIDE RECORDS

Some countries in Europe have kept significant records at a nationwide level. Also, many countries have many fully indexed compiled records where the emigrant may appear. Where these records are available and indexed, they are excellent tools that may identify the emigrant. Countries that have been influenced by British law have some excellent national-level records, more and more of which are being indexed. Published genealogical collections in Germany, France, the Netherlands, Belgium, Switzerland, and other countries may also be helpful.

Published Genealogy Compendia

In many countries, books are published which collect genealogies (lineages) of hundreds or thousands of families. Usually the families come from the same geographic region or social rank. The higher classes tend to be better represented in most compendia and they often mention emigrants. They are often published as periodicals. Indexes are published only occasionally for many of these compendia. An outstanding series with approximately two hundred volumes for Germany is the *Deutsches Geschlechterbuch* (Limburg an der Lahn, Germany: C. A. Starke, 1889–).

Indexes and Bibliographies

Many countries have bibliographies of published family histories with alphabetical indexes to the major surnames included in the books and articles cited. Periodical indexes may also help locate emigrant families. The comprehensiveness of these sources varies by country. The genealogies cited in these bibliographies or indexes often mention emigrants. The chapter bibliography identifies some of the most significant of these.

Foreign Researchers and Collections

It is often possible to find a person researching your immigrant's surname in the very country the immigrant left. You can place queries in local genealogical periodicals or ask local genealogical societies in the foreign country for a list of researchers. A particularly useful publication for immigrant research is Keith A. Johnson and Malcolm R. Sainty, *Genealogical Research Directory* (Washington, D.C.: Johnson and Sainty, 1985–), an annual volume identifying researchers and the families they are working on. Each annual edition includes thousands of new listings from many countries throughout the world. There are many private researchers in Europe who keep a file of emigrants, often culled from newspaper announcements and government records.

Societies

Genealogical and historical societies in the immigrant's home country can provide help in finding the origin of an ancestor. They are usually helpful if the request takes into account the limited services, budget and time that the staff, usually volunteers, have. Through a society, you may find living relatives, others who are searching the same family, and records or indexes that might provide the place of origin of an ancestor.

Some societies, such as the Institut fuer pfaelzische Geschichte und Volkskunde (Benzinoring 6, 67651 Kaiserslautern, Germany) maintain files of emigrants from their specific area of interests. For societies in Germany, see Ernest Thode, *Address Book for Germanic Genealogy*, 5th ed. (Baltimore: Genealogical Publishing Co., 1994).

Figure 13-29. Counties outlined in bold are those included in the Soundex index to naturalizations.

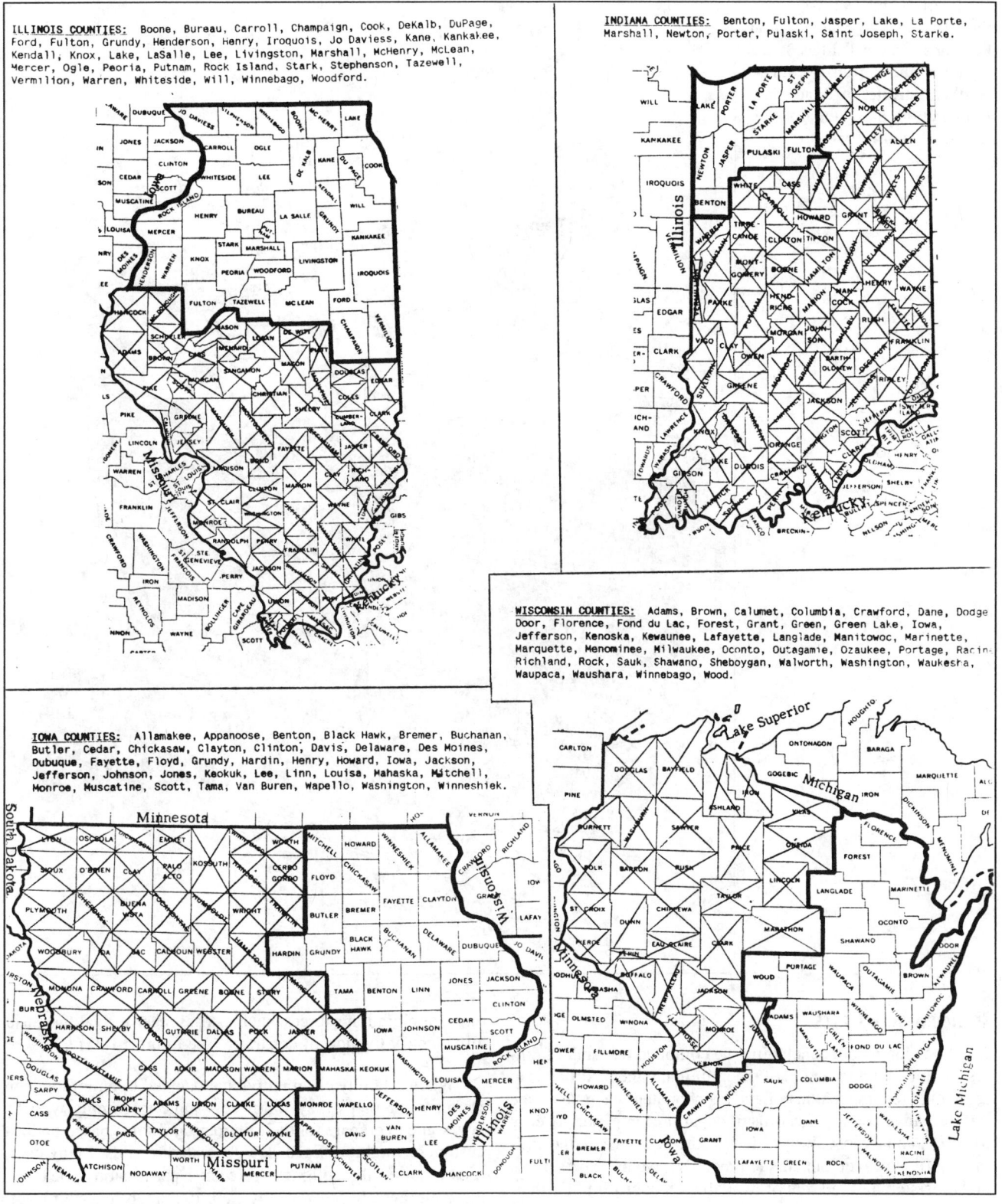

ILLINOIS COUNTIES: Boone, Bureau, Carroll, Champaign, Cook, DeKalb, DuPage, Ford, Fulton, Grundy, Henderson, Henry, Iroquois, Jo Daviess, Kane, Kankakee, Kendall, Knox, Lake, LaSalle, Lee, Livingston, Marshall, McHenry, McLean, Mercer, Ogle, Peoria, Putnam, Rock Island, Stark, Stephenson, Tazewell, Vermilion, Warren, Whiteside, Will, Winnebago, Woodford.

INDIANA COUNTIES: Benton, Fulton, Jasper, Lake, La Porte, Marshall, Newton, Porter, Pulaski, Saint Joseph, Starke.

WISCONSIN COUNTIES: Adams, Brown, Calumet, Columbia, Crawford, Dane, Dodge, Door, Florence, Fond du Lac, Forest, Grant, Green, Green Lake, Iowa, Jefferson, Kenoska, Kewaunee, Lafayette, Langlade, Manitowoc, Marinette, Marquette, Menominee, Milwaukee, Oconto, Outagamie, Ozaukee, Portage, Racine, Richland, Rock, Sauk, Shawano, Sheboygan, Walworth, Washington, Waukesha, Waupaca, Waushara, Winnebago, Wood.

IOWA COUNTIES: Allamakee, Appanoose, Benton, Black Hawk, Bremer, Buchanan, Butler, Cedar, Chickasaw, Clayton, Clinton, Davis, Delaware, Des Moines, Dubuque, Fayette, Floyd, Grundy, Hardin, Henry, Howard, Iowa, Jackson, Jefferson, Johnson, Jones, Keokuk, Lee, Linn, Louisa, Mahaska, Mitchell, Monroe, Muscatine, Scott, Tama, Van Buren, Wapello, Washington, Winneshiek.

Figure 13-30. A sampling of cards from the WPA-created Soundex Index to Naturalization Petitions for the United States District and Circuit Courts, Northern District of Illinois and Immigration and Naturalization District 9, 1840–1950.

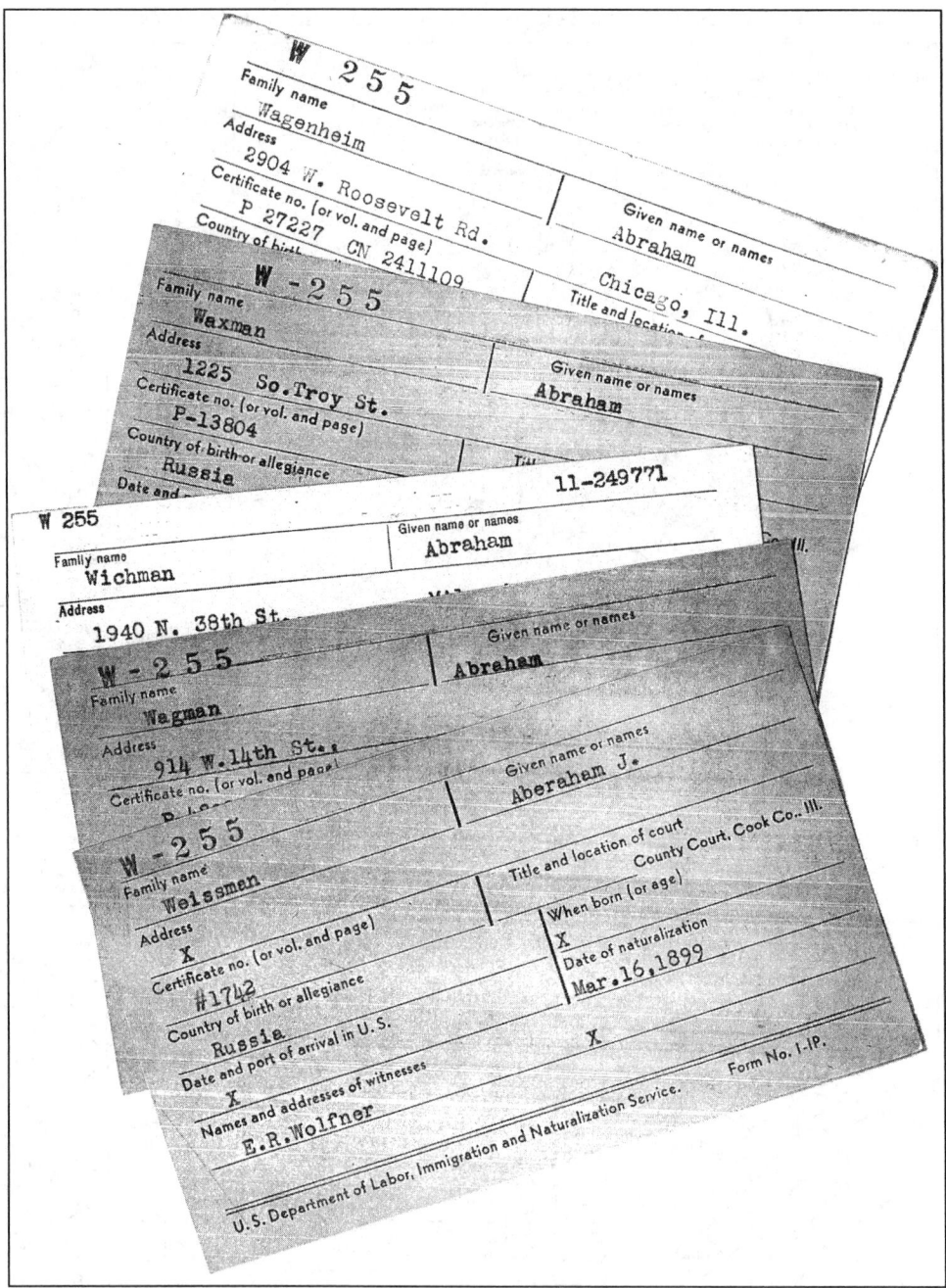

EMIGRATION LISTS

If nationwide records, including the compiled research of others, do not include mention of the immigrant, the next step is to search the records that may have been created when he or she left the native country. Records of departure are generally easy to access and almost always identify the place where the emigrant left. However, not all such records have been preserved, and others are not indexed or available on microfilm. Furthermore, some emigration was illegal. In such cases, there will be few, if any, records of departure.

The country of departure is generally not hard to discover from other sources; the district is more difficult to determine. For this reason, learn as much as possible about the emigrant, including the state or area of residence and the port of depar-

ture. Immigration sources, such as passenger arrival lists, usually identify the port of departure (see figure 13-31).

When a family or an individual decided to emigrate, there were several steps they followed—some to comply with the law, some to prepare for their journey, and some based on local custom or tradition. Each step generated records. Many countries required the emigrant to receive permission to leave. If the emigrant obeyed this law (approximately one-third emigrated without permission), there may be an application to leave or a passport. Emigrants also had to book passage and board a vessel for the new country. Each of these steps potentially saw the creation of a new record. Records of departure in the country of origin are called emigration records. Most of them give the name, age, close relatives or traveling companions, and usually the last place of residence (sometimes the birthplace) of the emigrant.

Departure records are generally kept under the jurisdiction of the port city (such as passenger departure lists) or by the state or national government where the emigrant lived, such as permissions to emigrate. To use such lists, you should know the emigrant's state or region of residence, and/or the port of departure. Sometimes knowing only the country of origin allows access to these records. You also need to know when the emigrant left that country or port. These sources may be difficult to use; however, a growing number are indexed. The archives in some countries and provinces, in order to better document emigration, have prepared indexes of emigrants from particular regions. In other cases, private authors have compiled or indexed specific emigration records. The following discussion describes many of these records.

The emigration/immigration process generated a wealth of records, both personal and administrative, to keep track of who emigrated, where they were going, the status of their personal affairs at the time they left, and their ability to care for their own needs on arrival. Some have been indexed and abstracted by government order or by genealogists who need faster access. Many more are available on microfilm through the National Archives and its regional archives system and through the Family History Library and its family history centers.

Some important projects to publish emigration lists are ongoing. For example: In the first half of the twentieth century, Germans accounted for twenty percent of this new growth of the immigrant population in the United States. Close to 1 million of these Germans made applications to emigrate at Wuerttemberg. To date, Trudy Schenk and Ruth Froelke have transcribed handwritten lists and indexed the names of 72,000 individuals who emigrated from Wuerttemberg from 1750 to 1900 in *The Wuerttemberg Emigration Index,* 6 vols. to date (Salt Lake City: Ancestry, 1986–). Table 13-2 outlines the availability of European emigrant lists.

Letters of Manumission
If the head of the house was tied to the soil on which he lived

Figure 13-31. Major European ports of departure.

Table 13-2. Availability of European Emigrant Lists

Port or Jurisdiction	Document	Dates Covered	Index	Originals	Copies	Comments
Australia Victoria	Passenger lists (outward)	1852–1924	Not indexed	Australian Archives, Outer Crescent, Middle Brighton, Melbourne, Victoria 3186	Family History Library (FHL), 121 reels, microfilm 35983, pts. 1–121	
Belgium Antwerp	Passport applications	1854–55	Not indexed	Stadsarchief Venustraat II, Antwerp, Belgium	"Passenger Lists," FHL, 3 reels, microfilm 392,910–12	Many immigrants from Austria-Hungary, Italy, Switzerland, through Antwerp
Denmark Copenhagen		1868–1911	Indexed alphabetically by year	Landsarkivet Sjaelland, Copenhagen, Denmark	FHL, 35 reels of microfilm, 898, 564–622; 1868–1911	Separate register for Mormons only, 1872–94
England London	Lists	1709		Public Record Office, Chancery Lane, London WC2A 1LR England #C.O. 388/76 No. 56, 56i, 56ii, 64, 68–70	Microfilm copies available from Public Record Office, London	
All shires	Licenses to pass beyond the seas	Elizabeth I to 1677		Public Record Office E.157 (Exchequer), 2 boxes	Printed in John C. Hotten, *Original Lists of Persons of Quality* (Reprint, Baltimore: Genealogical Publishing Co., 1974)	Indexed in Filby, *Passenger and Immigration Lists Index*
Liverpool	"Settlers"	1817–76	Not indexed	Public Record Office, Original correspondence. Settlers (C.O. 384/14–18)		Applications from intending immigrants
British Mission (LDS)	Emigration records	1849–1923	Alphabetical index	LDS Church Historical Department, Salt Lake City, Utah	FHL, 15 reels microfilm.	Church leaders acted as licensed emigration agents
France Le Havre		ca. 1750–1850		Archives de la Chambre de Commerce et d'Industrie du Havre, Place Leon-Meyer (B.P. 1410) 76600 Le Havre, France		Many Italians came through Le Havre
La Rochelle	Lists of passengers embarking in Louisiana for France	1732–33, 1737, 1748–49, 1752, 1754, 1758, 1765	Not indexed	Archives Nationales de la France, 60 rue des Francs-Bourgeois, Paris Cedex, France	Library of Congress (LC), microfilm copy. French Archives Nationales; colonie Serie F5B, Selected Transcripts. Vol. 34.	Includes lists from other French ports as well as La Rochelle
	Lists of soldiers and passengers embarking for Louisiana	1717–20	Not indexed		Same, vol. 39	
Germany Braunschweig	German emigration index				FHL 1,125,001	Names from periodicals, compiled 1976
Baden	Emigration index	1866–1911	Cards arranged alphabetically	Badisches Generallandsarchiv Nordl, Jiedapromenade 2, 7500 Karlsruhe, Germany	FHL, 38 reels microfilm	Copies of emigrant lists sent from district offices to central government. Fee charged to search originals. Index called Baden-Württemberg, but Württemberg not included.
Bremen	Emigration lists			Destroyed during World War II	LC, 3 reels microfilm: Bremen, Germany. Archive der Handel-Skammer, A.I.I. Auswanderer, 1841–75.	Many Austria-Hungary emigrants went through Bremen

Port or Jurisdiction	Document	Dates Covered	Index	Originals	Copies	Comments
Hamburg	Emigration lists	1850–1934	Indexed alphabetically in sections		LC microfilm. 1850–72; FHL, 361 reels of microfilm 1850–1934; includes index	Thirty percent of all European emigrants passed through Hamburg, including Russians and Austrians. See "Hamburg Passenger Lists," research paper C-30 (Salt Lake City: Genealogical Society of Utah, 1976)
Hessen	Emigration lists	1800–1900	Indexed alphabetically in sections		FHL, 5 reels microfilm	
Westfalen	List of emigrants				Printed in *Beitrage zur Westfalischen Familien forschung,* vols. 22–24 (Münster, Germany: Verlag Aschendorff, 1966)	
Alsace	Passport applications	1817–66	Indexed alphabetically		FHL, 6 reels microfilm. Includes Bas-Rhin, Haut-Rhin	
Trier	Emigration lists	19th century	Indexed alphabetically		Josef Jergen, "Emigration to America from District of Trier," typescript, 5 vols. FHL 298,106	
Ireland Antrim				Public Record Office, Northern Ireland		
Netherlands	Emigration register	1847–77	Indexed alphabetically		Computer listing, FHL 1,181,553	
	Dutch nationals on U.S. passenger lists	1820–80	Indexed alphabetically		Computer listing, 4 vols.	Copy at FHL 973/W25W. See also Robert P. Swierenga, *Dutch Immigrants in United States Ship Passenger Manifests, 1820–1880,* 2 vols. (Wilmington, Del.: Scholarly Resources, 1983)
	Emigration naar American en andere landen	1831–77		Algemeen Provincial Archive, Loosduinseweg 17, The Hague 2028 Netherlands	FHL, 12 reels microfilm 487, 360–371	
Rotterdam	Embarkation lists	1709		Public Record Office, T1/119: 6–10, 19–26, 58–65, 68–72, 79–82		German Palatines to New York only. Rotterdam lists reportedly destroyed
Netherland Mission (LDS)	List of emigrants	1904-14		LDS Church Historical Department	FHL 6,186	
Norway Bergen		1874–1924	Indexed		FHL, 78 microfiche; microfilm 357,704	
Kristiansand		1873–1901			FHL 365,931	
Nedenes Amt		1873–1901			FHL, 1 reel microfilm	
Oslo		1867–1902	Indexed		FHL, 18 reels microfilm 353,081–98	
Trondheim		1867–1900	Not indexed		FHL, 3 reels microfilm 362,609–11	
Tromsö		1850–1900		Statsarkivkontoret 1 Tromsö Petersborggata 21-24 9000 Tromsö		
Portugal Lisbon				Reparticäo Do Arquivo E Bibliotéca Do Ministeria Dos Negócios Estrangeiros, Palácio das Necessiodades, Lisboa 3		

Port or Jurisdiction	Document	Dates Covered	Index	Originals	Copies	Comments
Scotland	Treasury papers	1715–1820		Public Record Office, Chancery Lane, London WC2A 1LR England Treasury Papers. T.47. Emigration Registers, 23 vols.	Portion published in *New England Historical and Genealogical Register* (1911)	
				Misc. 12. 1773–1776 Lists from Scottish Ports: Greenock, Kirkaldy, Wigtown, Kirkwall, Stornaway, Stranraer, Lerwick, Glasgow. Misc. 1: 500, 231–35. Scots Highlanders to America, 1774. Misc. 1: 338. Scots Highlanders to America, 1776		Formerly "misc. Refugees, Carolina, 6 (1)"
Spain	Asientos de pasajeros	1509–1701		Archivo General de Indias, Seccion de Contración, Sevilla, Spain	FHL, 11 rolls microfilm. 1,223,690–700	Passengers to the New World
Sweden Göteborg	Emigration lists	1869–1951	Indexed for 1869–93	Göteborg Provincial Archives, Götegborgs Arkivkontar Box 2258 403 14 Göteborg, Sweden. 143 vols.		Provincial archives one of centers indexing emigrants. Many indexes are under way. Göteborg is the principal port for Sweden
Helsingborg		1907–64	Göteborg Provincial Archives			
Kalmar City	Emigrant contracts	1880–92	Göteborg Provincial Archives			
Karlstad	Emigrant index			Emigrantregistret i Karlstad Box 331, S-651 05 Karlstad, Sweden		100,000 emigrants from Värmland
Malmö		1874–1939	Indexed for 1874–1891	Malmö City Archives Stadsarkivet 1 Malmo S:t Petrigatan 7 A 211 22 Malmö, Sweden	FHL, 3 reels microfilm. 1,043,345–347	
Swedish Mission (LDS)	Emigrants lists	1904–32		LDS Church Historical Department	FHL, 025,700	
Norrkoping		1859–1919	Indexed	Göteborg Provincial Archives, 1 vol.		
Stockholm	Emigration lists	1869–1944	Indexed for 1869–86; 1883–86 (incomplete)	Stockholm City Archives Stockholms Stadsarkiv Kungsklippan 6 Box 22063 104 22 Stockholm 22	FHL, 402,933; 1869–1904 only	Includes some immigrants from Finland
	Passport journals	1737–1879		Göteborg Provincial Archives	On microfilm at FHL	
	Passport journals (Navy Pension Fund Departure Lists)	1798–1851	Indexed for 1817–50	Royal Swedish Military Record Office, Fack, 100 26 Stockholm 34	FHL, 275 reels microfilm	Cataloged by city
Värmland				Emigrantregistret for Värmland Drottninggatan 1 A 652 24 Karlstad, Sweden.		Collections on emigration from Varmland
				Index only at Goteborg Provincial Archives		
Broderne Larrson & Co.	Emigration agency records	1873–1913	Not indexed	Göteborg Provincial Archives	FHL, 9 reels microfilm. 479,331; 479, 587–479, 605	Central and southern Sweden. Includes letters, ticket stubs. Gives destinations

Port or Jurisdiction	Document	Dates Covered	Index	Originals	Copies	Comments
	Emigration extracts	1851 to present.	Indexed for 1851–60	[National Central Bureau of Statistics] Statistiska Centralbyräns Arkiv Karlavägen 100,115 26 Stockholm, Sweden	FHL, 567 reels microfilm, 1851–1940	From Swedish parish register. Some by county, some by parish. From 1865 uniform schedules of emigrants extracted
West Indies Santo Domingo	Passports	1799–1801				Printed in Nellis H. Fowler, *National Genealogical Society Quarterly* 56 (1968): 263–75

by medieval serf-lord commitments, the first step was to obtain a letter of manumission. This document freed him, usually with payment of a fee, from these obligations.

Sale of Property

If the head of the house owned property, he would advertise it for sale or dispose of it among family members who stayed behind. Some emigrants left their property in the care of relatives or friends and returned to sell it after they were sure they could make a success of their move to America. These documents are duly recorded with the proper authorities, often with direct statements of intent to emigrate or precise locations in the New World.

Letters of Recommendation

Letters of recommendation from local church authorities stating that the emigrant was a member of the congregation in good standing were often obtained by would-be emigrants. With these documents in hand, the emigrant could approach local authorities for permission to leave.

Permit to Emigrate

The permit to emigrate certified that the emigrant's bills were paid, affairs in the community were settled, and that he or she was free to leave. The passport allowed the emigrant to cross country, provincial and district boundaries. In some countries, the permit to emigrate and the passport were combined in a single exit visa issued by district or provincial authorities. These identification papers were carried on the person of the emigrant, and copies may still be in the family's possession.

Shipping Company Records

An invaluable tool for English research is P. Mathias and A.W.H. Pearsall, *Shipping: A Survey of Historical Records* (Newton Abbot, England: David and Charles, 1980). The survey is in two parts: (1) shipping companies and their record holdings and (2) shipping records in county and other record offices. There is an index of named ships, an index of persons and firms, and an index of places and principal trades and there are separate entries for dozens of shipping firms. Often, passenger lists retained by these shipping companies can be substituted for official lists missing for English ports. Where lists exist in United States or European ports, they can be compared for details. Included among the collections are pictures of ships sailing of each line.

Port of Departure Lists

Some ports made lists of passengers as they departed. These included such information as age, occupation and last place of residence or birthplace, which can be of particular value in determining an ancestor's place of origin. While some of these records have not been preserved, many others are now on microfilm. Where available, these are excellent sources for determining the emigrant's origin. Many of the existing departure lists are available at the Family History Library and other research libraries that specialize in emigration records. Of particular interest are the records of the Scandinavian ports and those of Hamburg. Unfortunately, the records of Europeans who emigrated through other ports, such as Bremen, LeHavre, Amsterdam, Rotterdam, and Antwerp, have either been destroyed or lost. There are also published transcripts and indexes for some ports and countries. Significant published departure lists for Europe and Great Britain are noted in the chapter bibliography.

Hamburg Passenger Lists

The Hamburg passenger lists comprise the most significant collection of port of departure lists for immigration research. They contain the names of millions of Europeans who emigrated through Hamburg between 1850 and 1934 (except 1915 through 1919). Nearly one-third of the people who emigrated from central and eastern Europe during this time are included on these lists. If your ancestors emigrated from these areas, the Hamburg passenger lists could provide important information about them, including their native towns. Extensive indexes make these records easier to use than most other passenger lists and emigration records. These lists and indexes are on 486 rolls of microfilm at the Family History Library. (Articles in genealogical periodicals have touted a search service in Hamburg that provides information on emigrants from this port. This service uses the same records any researcher can use at the Family History Library or one of its family history centers.)

The Hamburg passenger lists are made up of two sections: The direct lists include passengers who left Hamburg and sailed directly to their destination without stopping at other European ports. The indirect lists identify passengers who stopped at other European ports before sailing to their final destination. About twenty percent of the immigrants leaving Europe took indirect routes.

Most of the Hamburg passenger lists have been indexed. The only ones not indexed are those from 1850 to 1854, which are arranged alphabetically. There are two sets of indexes: the Fifteen-year Index to the Direct Hamburg Passenger Lists, 1856–1871, and the regular indexes.

The fifteen-year card index arranges all the names on the direct lists from 1856 to 1871 in one alphabetical index. Though it is convenient to use, this index is not complete. After checking the index, you may still need to use the regular index for the same time period. The regular indexes are more complete, but they are more difficult to use.

The regular indexes, for both the direct passenger lists and the indirect list, are divided into segments that cover one year or part of a year. The direct indexes begin with 1854 lists and end with 1934 lists. The indirect indexes begin in 1854 and end in 1910. To use the index, you must find the year the emigrant departed and the initial letter of the ancestor's surname. Names are arranged by the first letter of the surname only, so you may need to search the entire section to find the person you are looking for. Sometimes the index pages for one letter were continued on blank pages under another letter. Usually a notation will refer you to the proper letter for the continuation. An index entry contains the name of the ship, the departure date, the passenger's name, the ship's captain, the destination port, and the page on the actual passenger lists with this information.

For more information on the Hamburg Passenger Lists and how to use them, see *The Hamburg Passenger Lists* (Salt Lake City: Genealogical Society of Utah, 1984).

LOCALIZING THE SURNAME

When departure records are not available, or if the state or region of residence is not known, it may be possible to narrow the search by determining the general region or area where the family came from or where the surname is most common. After the surname has been localized, there may be local emigration indexes or other sources available which cover only specific regions or localities.

Records exist at all levels of jurisdiction. Some emigration and even vital records are kept on a national, regional, provincial, county, or local level. The more closely a residence is determined, the more levels of records you can search.

Directories

To localize a specific, uncommon, surname, it is often useful to check city and telephone directories. Computerized telephone directories are available for Germany and the Netherlands on CD-ROM and in France through Minitel computer services. Expect similar sources to become available for other major countries within the next few years. With such tools, you can search for a name for the entire country. While this approach locates currently living persons with the surname, you may find relatives of the emigrant or other persons interested in your research. Often, families with the same surname (if it is not a common surname) know the area where the family originated.

Several research libraries have good collections of city directories of the nineteenth century from major cities of several countries. These directories may identify the emigrant, if he or she lived in a city. They also serve to indicate how common the surname was in the region where the city was located. To use older directories to localize a surname, search all available city directories for the country where the immigrant was born. Note the number of occurrences of the surname compared to the total names (or pages) in the directory. You will usually find that uncommon surnames are more strongly represented in one or two cities. This indicates the region where the name was most common.

Local Records

Eventually it will be necessary to search local foreign records. Ideally, it will be possible to search them after identifying the town of origin through earlier searches. However, even church records and civil registration in the areas where the emigrant is thought to have come from may be successfully searched if the native town is not known. In such circumstances it is necessary to begin with a very limited area from which you believe the immigrant came. Then begin the tedious, but often successful, process of searching the records of every town or parish in that area.

Local Histories

Many early emigrants (especially before the 1850s) left from small areas within the old country and settled together in the same area of the new country. Local histories of these areas in the native country often include lists of local inhabitants who emigrated or indicate places they settled in America. They are an easily searched source and even when they do not name emigrants, they include the names of many local families, which can help further narrow the locality of the surname. Obviously some idea of an area where the immigrant came from is needed before such histories can be used. Particularly useful local histories include the Norwegian Bygdboker and German Ortssippenbücher (especially for Baden). Because they are easier to search than most other local records, several local histories from a region can be easily checked, once the region is established.

Combining information from North American sources with European history to establish a region of origin and then using local histories can be very fruitful. For example, if U.S. sources identify an ethnic German or Austrian in different sources as coming from both Hungary and Yugoslavia, this is a strong suggestion that the family came from a region known as the Banat in the former Kingdom of Hungary which was colonized (in part) by Germans. Several local histories are available for this area (usually published in German although that was not the "official" language) that identify towns where Germans lived. A specific example of a particularly useful local or ethnic history dealing with Germans who lived in Russia is Karl Stumpp, *The Emigration from Germany to Russia in the Years 1763–1862* (Reprint. Lincoln, Neb.: American Historical Society of Germans from Russia, 1978). This source identifies which families lived in which German settlements.

READING THE PLACE NAME

The final principle to consider when tracking an immigrant's origin is the necessity of reading the place name after it is correctly located. There is nothing more frustrating to an immigration researcher than finding the long-sought place name and then learning that such a town does not exist in the native country!

Some sources are more likely to give an accurate place of origin than others. When a place name is found in the records, use gazetteers and other reference tools to evaluate the information. After information about an immigrant's place of origin is discovered, interpret the findings. To accurately read the place name you have found, you need to understand foreign spellings and then evaluate if you have found the place name. One genealogical society apparently did the best it could with unfamiliar ethnic names and tombstones ravaged by time and weather, but the results of their work were found to be unreliable. In the society's cemetery inscription publication, *Qui Riposo* (Here Rests) was listed as the name of one individual, and *geborenen* 1843 (born 1843) as the German birthplace and birth date of another.

Terminology

Foreign terms can be easily mistaken for place names. The phrase Koenigreich Preussen, for example, means the "Kingdom of Prussia"; it does not refer to a town called Koenigreich in Prussia. Examples of foreign terms that may confuse researchers include:

Bezerk	district (German)
arrondissement	district (French)
estância	estate, ranch (Portuguese)
województwo	province (Polish)
megye	county (Hungarian)
sogn	parish (Danish)
gemeente	town (Dutch)

Place Name Changes

Many places have been known by more than one name historically. Place names have changed when other countries occupied weaker countries. Bratislava in Slovenia was known as Pressburg under German rule. Some changes were for political reasons; Kitchener, Ontario, was Berlin before World War I. Other changes have evolved over time. Oxfordshire, England, is still sometimes referred to as Oxon, its old name, while Hants is the common abbreviation for the English county of Hampshire. Examples of similar name changes include:

Christiania	Oslo
Hindenburg	Zabrze
Königsberg	Kaliningrad
Tilsit	Sovetsk
Chemnitz	Karl-Marx-Stadt
Lemburg	L'vov, now L'wow
Schneidemühl	Pia

Spelling

Foreign place names have often been misspelled in American records because the clerks who wrote it did not know the foreign spelling. And often the spelling was not standardized in the foreign location itself, so many variations may exist. Such errors in spelling can sometimes make it very difficult to interpret the correct locality. Spelling errors can be of several types:

Phonetic spelling: Some letters have a different sound in other languages. For example, in many languages *J* is pronounced like the English *I* or *Y*; *J* in French is pronounced like *Zi* in English. In Polish, *X* is often used for the *ks* sound. The Swedish *å* is often written in English as *o*.

Misreading: Handwritten or gothic printed letters can be misinterpreted either by you or by a previous reader. Example: The German handwritten letter *W* can be confused with *M* and the letter *K* often looks like *R*. The German *ss* is written like the Greek letter beta (*β*) and is often misread as a capital B. Also, the German practice of capitalizing all nouns may make many words appear as a proper place name.

Special characters: Many languages use special symbols, often called diacritics, that indicate changes in sound, and sometimes alphabetical order of the letters. Sometimes these characters are eliminated in the new language. The German umlaut

(¨) may be translated as the letter *e* following another vowel; therefore, the German *ü* often (but not always) becomes the English *ue*. The Czech *š* may have become *sh* or *sch*. The Dutch *ij* is usually translated as *y*.

English versions: The proper spelling of a town name in English may be quite different than the spelling in the native language. In such cases, you may find the native spelling of a town, but not recognize it because it is not the spelling used in English. This is usually only a problem with larger cities that are well known in North America, such as:

Antwerp	Anvers or Antwerpen
Geneva	Genève, Genf, or Ginevra
Ratisbone	Regensburg
Brunswick	Braunschweig
Cassel	Kassel
Prague	Praha
Posnania	Posen or Poznan
Gothenburg	Göteborg
Prussia	Borussua (Latin)
Colonge	Köln
Vienna	Wien
Nuremberg	Nürnberg
Venice	Venezia
The Hague	s'Gravenhage

Multiple Places With the Same Name

Once you have found an actual town name, it may still be difficult to identify the town. Often there was more than one town in a country with the same or similar names. For example, there are ninety-six places named Newton or New Town in Great Britain and at least ten towns (and dozens of hamlets) named Lindenberg in Germany. Scotland has four Kildonans. While the city of Hoorn is well known in the Netherlands, there are also six villages and hamlets with that name, while another town and two hamlets are named Horn. This is why it is so important to know more about the area the immigrant came from, such as the name of the state, province, or county. It is also helpful to know of nearby cities.

Place Names That Are Not Towns of Origin

By far the most common mistake that researchers make is in assuming that the place name they have found in their research is that of the very town where the immigrant lived. In many cases, they have found a legitimate foreign location, but it is not the immigrant's home. It may be the name of the country, state or region where the immigrant lived, but the researcher is not familiar enough with the country to identify it as such. In other cases, it may be the name of a city that is not the immigrant's home. Often, the nearest large city or the port of departure was recorded as the home. In other cases the name of the city is also the name of the state or province. Here are some examples of these problems.

Country, state, regional, and provincial names: Many genealogical sources about immigrants only give the name of the country, region, or province. Foreign names of states, counties, provinces, or regions are unfamiliar to many researchers. Beware of place names, such as the following, that are not town names:

Deutschland	Germany
Österreich	Austria
Bayern	Bavaria
Franconia	Franken
Norge	Norway
Cechy	Bohemia
Eire	Republic of Ireland
Piedmont	region in northwestern Italy
Fyn	Danish island
Silesia	Southwestern Poland
Burgundy	region in eastern France
Schwaben	old German Duchy in southern Germany
Valencia	region in eastern Spain
Wessex	southern counties in England
Erz	Mountain range on German-Czech border
Holland	Two provinces in the Netherlands
Siebenburgen	Transylvania region in Romania

City and county share the same name: Many states or provinces have a major or capitol city with the same name as the state. If you find the names Baden, Hannover, Kassel, Luxembourg, Bern, Utrecht, Derby, or similar names in censuses or some other records, they likely apply to the county or state with that name and not the specific cities of those names. The name of the city Darmstadt often applied to the entire portion of Hesse that was ruled from the city of Darmstadt. Even the name Lüneburg in Germany can apply to the city or to the extensive region around the city. In fact, in many countries, districts are named after the chief city. Often the immigrant came from the district of that name, not the city.

Nearby large city: If you find the name of a large or well-known city, the ancestor is probably not from the city itself, but rather from some smaller, lesser-known place nearby. While some immigrants were from large cities, most were from rural areas. In fact, the same forces also encouraged many persons to migrate to the larger cities, where jobs were more plentiful. Because most people in North America were unfamiliar with small localities, immigrants often referred to their homes by the name of some significant, well-known city nearby. Thus, while many immigrants claimed to have come from London or Berlin, in reality the person was usually from a smaller town near London or Berlin. In some cases, the immigrant came from a place much further away and there seems to be no valid reason for citing the big city. One "Berlin" emigrant was finally found in Cottbus, some eighty miles away. It is also possible that the immigrant traveled through the big city or lived there for a short period before leaving the old country.

If the records say that the immigrant came from a large city, look for clues that he or she actually came from a small town. A person who indicated to have been from a large city would not likely have had an occupation which is associated with small-town life, such as farming or fishing. Family traditions regarding trips to the market or traveling several miles to

church are also clues that the immigrant came from a small town.

Port cities: Sometimes the place name found is really the port where the immigrant left the old country. However, the chances that he actually lived in the port city are slim. The major and many minor port cities for emigrants included Amsterdam, Antwerp, Bremen, Copenhagen, Cork, Danzig, Genoa, Gothenberg, Hamburg, Hull, Le Havre, Liverpool, Londonderry, Marseilles, Naples, Odessa, Oslo, Queenstown, Rotterdam, Southampton, Stockholm, Trieste, and others. Of course, such a city could be an important clue because departure records exist for some cities, and local police records in others may document the immigrant.

Geographic Tools

The best way to overcome these and many other problems in reading the place name is to make extensive use of gazetteers, maps, and other geographic tools. Be very cautious when using maps of foreign countries. Most maps do not list every town, and many are not well indexed. Relying only on a few maps will likely cause you to overlook the town you are looking for, as it may be quite small. A comprehensive gazetteer, however, should identify all possible towns that may correspond with the spelling you have found. Detailed gazetteers exist for virtually every country and most foreign states and provinces; they can identify the specific jurisdictions for the towns in question, leading to the records needed to prove you have found the immigrant. It is also very useful to become familiar with spelling rules, phonetics, and handwriting of the immigrant's home country.

ACKNOWLEDGMENTS

The authors wish to acknowledge the original version of this chapter, which was written by Arlene Eakle and published in 1984. Several important concepts from that chapter were retained here. Some of the concepts presented in this chapter first found their way into print in *Tracing Immigrant Origins Research Outline* (Salt Lake City: Family History Library, 1992). The appearance of similar concepts here in no way implies the endorsement of this chapter or book by the Family History Library or The Church of Jesus Christ of Latter-day Saints. Rather, it is due to the common author. Indeed, much of the 1992 outline is based on the authors' previous instructional presentations in genealogical classes and seminars.

NOTES

1. *An Immigrant Nation: United States Regulation of Immigration, 1798–1991* (Washington, D.C.: U.S. Department of Justice, 1991), 34.

2. Meyerink compiled these numbers based on a careful reading of the works of major American immigration historians, including: Bernard Bailyn, *Voyagers to the West* (New York, Knopf, 1986); David Cressy, *Coming Over: Migration and Communication between England and New England in the Seventeenth Century* (New York: Cambridge University Press, 1987); Roger Daniels, *Coming to America* (New York: Harper Collins, 1990); Marcus Lee Hansen, *The Atlantic Migration, 1607–1860* (New York: Harper & Row, 1940); and Maldwyn Allen Jones, *American Immigration* (Chicago: University of Chicago Press, 1960).

3. John F. Vallentine, "Tracing the Immigrant Ancestor," *Genealogical Journal* 3 (1974): 5.

4. Peter Roberts, *The New Immigration: A Study of the Industrial and Social Life of East Europeans in America* (Reprint. New York: Arno Press, 1970).

5. Philip Taylor, *The Distant Magnet: European Emigration to the U.S.A.* (New York: Harper and Row, 1971).

6. Meyerink based this table largely on the analysis of 1790 census data by Thomas L. Purvis in "The European Ancestry of the United States Population, 1790," *William & Mary Quarterly*, 3rd series, 41 (1): 85–. There has been much discussion about the ethnic stock of colonial America as various scholars have tried to use the 1790 census to arrive at precise figures. This cannot be done precisely, as the method depends on assigning *every 1790 head of household to one, and only one, ancestry* based on the presumed origin of the surname. American ancestry, even in 1790, was not always from only one race or nation. At that time many Americans already had five to seven generations in America, including ancestors from different countries.

Purvis and others have been criticized for their methodology in determining these figures (e.g.: Akenson, same issue, p. 102–), but this is the best estimate available and is defended by Purvis (same issue). While not specifically accurate, the numbers are surely close. However, Purvis and earlier studies focused only on the white population in 1790. Meyerink has rounded Purvis's figures to the nearest percent (to account for the lack of precision), then adjusted them (to the nearest half-percent) to include the non-white (i.e.: African and limited [eastern] Native American) population. The actual census count (including African Americans) for the area enumerated was 3,929,625, but did not include the Northwest Territory and areas under French or Spanish control (upwards of 50,000 people), nor most Indian tribes. Hence the rounded figure of 4 million.

Earlier studies attempting to discern America's colonial "ethnic stock" include: American Council of Learned Societies, "Report of the Committee on Linguistic and National Stocks in the Population of the United States," *Annual Report of the American Historical Association, 1931*, vol. 1 (Washington, D.C.: 1932), as well as *A Century of Population Growth, 1790–1900* (Washington, D.C.: Government Printing Office, 1909).

7. Donald J. Bogue, *The Population of the United States: Historical Trends and Future Projections* (New York: The Free Press, a Division of Macmillan, Inc., 1985); Mary Kupies Cayton, Elliott J. Gorn, and Peter W. Williams, eds., *Encyclopedia of American Social History*, 3 vols. (New York: Scribner, 1993); *INS Fact Book: Summary of Recent Immigration Data* (U.S. Department of Justice, Immigration and Naturalization Service Statistics Division, July 1993); Stephanie Bernardo Johns, *The Ethnic Almanac* (Garden City, N.Y.: Doubleday, 1981); John F. Kennedy, *A Nation of Immigrants* (New York: Harper and Row, 1964); George Thomas Kurian, *Datapedia of the United States 1790–2000: America Year by Year* (Lanham, Md.: Bernan Press, 1994).

8. Gottlieb Mittelberger, "Journey to Pennsylvania in the Year 1750," translated by Carl T. Eben, in Strassburger with Hinke, *Pennsylvania German Pioneers* 1: xxxiii.

9. Ibid., xxxvii.

10. William Nelson, ed., *Documents relating to Colonial History of New Jersey,* 1st series, vol. 12 (Patterson, N.J.: Press Printing and Publishing Co., 1895), 401–02.

11. Michael Tepper, *American Passenger Arrival Records* (Baltimore: Genealogical Publishing Co., 1988), 16.

12. Ibid.

13. Maldwyn A. Jones, *Destination America* (New York: Holt, Rinehart and Winston, 1976), 78.

14. John J. Newman, *American Naturalization Processes and Procedures 1790–1985* (Indianapolis: Indiana Historical Society, 1985).

15. Linda R. Green, "Citizenship and Naturalization in Colonial America from Pre-Revolutionary Times to the United States Constitution," *Illinois State Genealogical Society Quarterly* 14 (3) (Fall 1992).

16. *Journals of Congress*, II, 16 January 1777.

GENERAL IMMIGRATION SOURCES AND SOURCES FOR SELECTED ETHNIC GROUPS

Once the national origins of an individual have been discovered, there is a great and ever-increasing assortment of background materials that are worth pursuing. A public library is a logical place to begin research. Most collections will include a basic history for any given ethnic group. Through computer networking, libraries can track down even the most obscure materials that will facilitate the search and add to the enjoyment of any research project. Many large public libraries and university and college libraries have special ethnic collections, as do some private libraries. The overwhelming amount of information currently available on ethnic groups and immigration in general makes it impossible to outline all of it in this chapter. While every effort has been made here to present an up-to-date list of ethnic organizations and publications, the field is changing rapidly; new sources and avenues are constantly being opened for research.

SELECTED RESEARCH CENTERS FOR IMMIGRATION STUDIES

Balch Institute for Ethnic Studies

Center for Immigration Research
Temple University
18 S. Seventh Street
Philadelphia, PA 19106
215-925-8090

The Balch Institute, dedicated to documenting and interpreting America's multicultural heritage, has a unique collection relating to more than one hundred ethnic groups. The institute's research library collections consist of books, newspapers on microfilm, photographs, posters, tape and phonograph recordings, sheet music, and more than 2,400 linear feet of manuscripts. Donna Potter Phillips, "Using the Balch Institute for Ethnic Studies," *Ancestry Newsletter* 6 (3) (May–June 1988): 1–2, provides an overview of the institute's history, a brief description of the types of materials available, and research policies.

The Balch Institute is conducting demographic and genealogical research on the origins of the American people. As part of the project, an important database is being constructed from eleven tons of ship passenger lists that were transferred from the National Archives. The original lists contain the names of some 35 million immigrants who arrived at the Port of New York from 1847 to 1896.

American Museum of Immigration

Statue of Liberty/Ellis Island National Monument

Library

Ellis Island

New York, NY 10004

(212) 363-7620

Ellis Island has a small library containing limited records that focus primarily on Ellis Island and Liberty Island history, with minor emphasis on immigration in general, ethnic groups, and genealogical material (excluding passenger lists). The library has a collection of rare books, unpublished manuscripts, periodicals, films and video, and many photographs. It is open only by appointment and special arrangement. See Barbara Benton, *Ellis Island: A Pictorial History* (New York: Facts on File, 1985); August C. Bolino, *The Ellis Island Source Book* (Washington, D.C.: Kensington Historical Press, 1985); E. Wade Hone, "A Present from the Past: An Ellis Island Experience," *Ancestry* 13 (1): 14–15; Ted Naanes, "Ellis Island: Doorway to Dreams," *Ancestry* 13 (1): 11–13; Loretto Dennis Szucs, *Ellis Island: Gateway to America* (Salt Lake City: Ancestry, 1986); George Thurston, "Ellis Island Records on Computer," *Genealogical Computing* 13 (4): 1, 22–23; Jayare Roberts, "Ellis Island and the Making of America," *Journal of Genealogy* 23 (1995): 51–139.

Family History Library of The Church of Jesus Christ of Latter-day Saints

35 North West Temple

Salt Lake City, UT 84150

801-240-2331

No library in the United States has an immigration collection surpassing that of the Family History Library in Salt Lake City. The key to finding records in the library is the *Family History Library Catalog*. The catalog describes the library's records and provides the call numbers. Copies of the catalog on microfiche are at the Family History Library and at most of the family history centers that are located all over the United States. Additionally, the catalog is available at some large public and private libraries in various parts of the country. See appendix D and Johni Cerny and Wendy Elliott, eds., *The Library: A Guide to the LDS Family History Library* (Salt Lake City: Ancestry, 1988).

Immigration History Research Center

University of Minnesota

826 Berry St.

St. Paul, MN 55114

612-627-4208

The Immigration History Research Center was founded at the University of Minnesota in 1965 to encourage study of the role of immigration and ethnicity in shaping the society and culture of the United States and to collect the records of twenty-four American ethnic groups originating from eastern, central, and southern Europe and the Near East. Working closely with eth-

nic communities, the Research Center has preserved and made available for research priceless documents of immigrant America, including personal papers, newspapers, books, periodicals, and the records of churches and cultural, fraternal, and political organizations. Ethnic collections include those for Albanians, Armenians, Bulgarians, Byelorussians, Carpatho-Ruthenians, Croatians, Czechs, Estonians, Finns, Greeks, Hungarians, Italians, Jews (Eastern European), Latvians, Lithuanians, Macedonians, Poles, Romanians, Russians, Serbs, Slovaks, Slovenes, and Ukrainians, and people from the Near East.

The Library of Congress

Local History and Genealogy Reading Room

Thomas Jefferson Annex

10 First St. S.E.

Washington, DC 20540

202-287-5537

The Library of Congress has a large collection of immigration- and ethnic-related publications. Chapter 7, Immigrant Ancestors, in James C. Neagles, *The Library of Congress: A Guide to Genealogical and Historical Research* (Salt Lake City: Ancestry, 1990), provides an overview of the rich materials available in the national library.

Steamship Historical Society of America, Inc.

University of Baltimore Library

1420 Maryland Ave.

Baltimore, MD 21201

The Steamship Historical Society Photo Bank files contain more than 50,000 alphabetically arranged ship photographs. Photo Bank files may be inspected at the University of Baltimore Library (address above). Appointments may be made in advance so that a library staff member familiar with the Photo Bank will be on hand to assist in locating. Pictures can be ordered by mail as follows: Send a list of ships of which pictures are wanted, alphabetically arranged (on a separate sheet—not within the body of a letter). Identify each vessel as fully as possible (there are often several ships of the same name). Library personnel will search files for all reasonable requests, but unduly long lists will be subject to special search fees. The library staff will return the list marked to show which pictures are available and the cost of copies. See Michael J. Anuta, *Ships of Our Ancestors,* 2nd ed. (Baltimore: Genealogical Publishing Co., 1993).

Texas Seaport Museum

2016 Strand

Galveston, TX 77550

409-763-1877

From 1840 until 1954, Galveston served as an immigration port and a gateway for settlement of the Southwest. The Seaport Museum features a database, a project of the Galveston Historical Foundation and the U.S. Immigration and Naturalization Service. Constructed from passenger lists in the National Archives, the database, when completed, is expected to include the names of 150,000 passengers. (The database will not be a complete record of passengers disembarking at Galveston because lists for 1871 to 1894 are missing.)

IMMIGRATION BACKGROUND SOURCES

Adamic, Louis. *From Many Lands*. New York: Harper and Bros., 1940.

Agueros, Jack, et al., eds. *The Immigrant Experience*. New York: Dial Press, 1971.

Allen, James Paul, and Eugene James Turner. *We the People: An Atlas of America's Diversity*. New York: McMillan, 1988. Atlas focused on ethnic settlement in the United States. Includes maps showing the distribution of ethnic groups in America and a discussion of immigration and migration of ethnic groups within the United States.

Anuta, Michael J. *Ships of Our Ancestors*. 2nd ed. Baltimore: Genealogical Publishing Co., 1993.

Appel, John J. *The New Immigration*. New York: Pitman Publishers, 1971.

_____. *Immigrant Historical Societies in the USA*. New York: Arno Press, 1980.

Auerbach, Frank L. *Immigration Laws of the United States*. Indianapolis: Bobbs-Merrill, 1961.

Bahr, Howard M., and Bruce A. Chadwick, eds. *American Ethnicity*. Lexington, Mass.: Heath, 1979.

Barton, Josef J. *Peasants and Strangers*. Cambridge: Harvard University Press, 1975.

Benton, Barbara. *Ellis Island: A Pictorial History*. New York: Facts on File, 1985.

Bernard, Richard. *The Melting Pot and the Altar*. Minneapolis: University of Minnesota Press, 1980.

Bernardo, Stephanie. *The Ethnic Almanac*. Garden City, N.Y.: Dolphin Books, Doubleday and Co., 1981.

Bigham, Barbara. "Colonists in Bondage: Indentured Servants in America." *Early American Life* 10 (1979): 30–33, 83–84.

Bodnar, John. *The Transplanted: A History of Immigrants in Urban America*. Bloomington: Indiana University Press, 1987.

Bogue, Donald J. *The Population of the United States: Historical Trends and Future Projections*. New York: Macmillan, 1985.

Bolino, August C. *The Ellis Island Source Book*. Washington, D.C.: Kensington Historical Press, 1985. In addition to a history of Ellis Island, this volume provides an exhaustive immigration bibliography.

Boorstin, Daniel J. *The Americans: The Democratic Experience*. New York: Random House, 1973.

Brye, David L. *European Immigration and Ethnicity in the United States and Canada: A Historical Bibliography*. Santa Barbara, Calif.: ABC-Clio Information Services, 1982.

Buenker, John D., Nicholas C. Burckel, and Rudolph J. Vecoli. *Immigration and Ethnicity: A Guide to Information Sources*. Detroit: Gale Research Co., 1977. Contains more than 1,500 annotated bibliographic entries. African Americans and Native Americans are not included in this work; foreign-language materials, which at least equal in volume those in English, are seldom cited; and only a sampling of thousands of doctoral dissertations devoted to immigration and ethnic topics appears in the guide. As the compilers note, to have included those categories of materials would have made this a multivolume work, and to "attempt a bibliography of immigration and ethnicity literature is like taking a snapshot of an avalanche."

Carpenter, Niles. *Immigrants and Their Children 1920: A Study Based on Census Statistics Relative to the Foreign Born and the Native White of Foreign or Mixed Parentage*. Census Monographs VII. Washington, D.C.: Department of Commerce, Bureau of the Census, 1927.

Cayton, Mary Kupies, Elliott J. Gorn, and Peter W. Williams, eds. *Encyclopedia of American Social History*. 3 vols. New York: Scribner, 1993.

Cerny, Johni, and Wendy Elliott, eds. *The Library: A Guide to the LDS Family History Library*. Salt Lake City: Ancestry, 1988.

The Church of Jesus Christ of Latter-day Saints. *Research Outline: Tracing Immigrant Origins*. Salt Lake City: The Church of Jesus Christ of Latter-day Saints, Family History Library, 1992.

Cole, Donald B. *Immigration City: Lawrence, Massachusetts, 1845–1921*. Chapel Hill, N.C.: University of North Carolina Press, 1963.

Commager, Henry Steele, ed. *Immigration and American History*. Minneapolis: University of Minnesota Press, 1961.

Cordasco, Francesco, ed. *A Bibliography of American Immigration History*. Fairfield, N.J.: Augustus M. Kelly Publishers, 1978.

_____. *The Immigrant Woman in North America: An Annotated Bibliography of Selected References*. Metuchen, N.J.: Scarecrow Press, 1985.

_____. *The New American Immigration: Evolving Patterns of Legal and Illegal Emigration: A Bibliography of Selected References*. New York: Garland, 1987.

Cutler, Carl C. *Queens of the Western Ocean: The Story of America's Mail and Passenger Sailing Lines*. Annapolis, Md.: U.S. Naval Institute, 1961.

Dashefsky, Arnold, ed. *Ethnic Identity in Society*. Chicago: Rand McNally, 1976.

Dinnerstein, Leonard, and David M. Reimers. *Ethnic Americans: A History of Immigration*. New York: Harper and Row, 1987.

Directory of Historical Organizations in the United States and Canada. Nashville, Tenn.: American Association for State and Local History, 1994. This biennial lists addresses, telephone numbers, and other important information for state historical societies and agencies as well as those for local and specialized collections.

Eichholz, Alice, ed. *Ancestry's Red Book: American State, County and Town Sources*. Rev ed. Salt Lake City: Ancestry, 1992. An expansive guide to the most useful resources in each of the states and the District of Columbia. Every state's chapter includes a brief historical background discussion, including settlement patterns that will be useful background information for ethnic research. Each state chapter concludes with a section titled "Special Focus Category," in which ethnic sources specific to the particular state are described. Under the *Red Book*'s section on Pennsylvania, for example, are such references as John E. Bodnar, Ethnic History in Pennsylvania: A Selected Bibliography (Harrisburg, Pa.: Pennsylvania Historical and Museum Commission, 1974). Also useful is David E. Washburn, comp. and ed., *The Peoples of Pennsylvania: An Annotated Bibliography of Resource Materials* (Pittsburg: University for International Studies, University of Pittsburgh, 1981). Individual ethnic groups included in the Pennsylvania ethnic bibliography section are the Quakers, Germans, Amish, Scotch-Irish, Swiss, and Welsh. Its relatively recent publication gives the *Red Book* a distinct advantage: It cites a great number of works not yet published when other major ethnic reference sources were released. The *Red Book* also provides names, addresses, origins, and jurisdictions of county courts to facilitate naturalization research.

Eldridge, Grant J., ed. *Encyclopedia of Associations: Regional, State, and Local Organizations.* 4th ed. 5 vols. Detroit: Gale Research Co., 1994.

Erickson, Charlotte, ed. *Emigration from Europe, 1815–1914: Select Documents.* London: Adam and Charles Black, 1976.

Ethnographic Bibliography of North America. 4th ed. 5 vols. Behavior Science Bibliographies. New Haven, Conn.: Human Relations Area Files, 1975. Supplement (3 vols.) added in 1990. A nearly complete listing of serious published accounts of North American cultures.

Fermi, Laura. *Illustrious Immigrants: The Intellectual Migration from Europe, 1930–1941.* Chicago: University of Chicago Press, 1968.

Fleming, Thomas J. *The Golden Door.* New York: W.W. Horton, 1970.

Genealogies Cataloged by the Library of Congress Since 1986. Washington, D.C.: Library of Congress Cataloging Distribution Services Center, 1991.

Glazer, Nathan, and Daniel P. Moynihan, eds. *Ethnicity: Theory and Experience.* Cambridge, Mass.: Harvard University Press, 1975.

Greeley, Andrew M., and Gregory Baum, eds. *Ethnicity.* New York: Seabury Press, 1977.

Guide to Genealogical Research in the National Archives. Rev. ed. Washington D.C.: National Archives Trust Fund board, 1991.

Guillet, Edwin C. *The Great Migration: The Atlantic Crossing by Sailing Ship Since 1770.* Rev. ed. Toronto: University Press, 1963.

Handlin, Oscar. *The Uprooted: The Epic Story of the Great Migrations That Made the American People.* New York: Grosset and Dunlap, 1951.

_____. *Immigration as a Factor in American History.* Englewood Cliffs, N.J.: Prentice Hall, 1959.

_____. *The American People in the Twentieth Century.* Cambridge, Mass.: Harvard University Press, 1954.

Hansen, Marcus L. *The Atlantic Migration, 1607–1860.* New York: Harper, 1961.

Harkness, George E. *The Church and the Immigrant.* New York: Doran, 1921.

Heaps, Willard A. *The Story of Ellis Island.* New York: Seabury Press, 1967.

Heaton, Elizabeth Putnam. *Steerage.* New York: L. Heaton, 1919.

Herbert, Mirana C., and Barbara McNeil. *Biography Genealogy Master Index.* Detroit: Gale Research Co., 1980–.

History of the Immigration and Naturalization Service. Washington, D.C.: Government Printing Office, 1980.

Hodges, Patrick, and Flavia Hodges. *A Dictionary of Surnames.* New York: Oxford University Press, 1988.

Hoglund, A. William. *Immigrants and Their Children in the United States: A Bibliography of Doctoral Dissertations, 1885–1982.* New York: Garland, 1986.

Holli, Melvin G., and Peter d'A. Jones, eds. *The Ethnic Frontier.* Grand Rapids, Mich.: Eerdmans Publishers, 1977.

Hone, E. Wade. "A Present from the Past: An Ellis Island Experience." *Ancestry* 13 (1): 14–15.

Hutchinson, E.P. *Legislative History of American Immigration Policy, 1798–1965.* Philadelphia: University of Philadelphia Press, 1981.

Immigration and Naturalization Service. *Foreign Versions, Variations, and Diminutives of English Names, Foreign Equivalents of United States Military and Civilian Titles.* Washington, D.C.: Government Printing Office, 1970. This oversize publication is divided into two parts: The first section has tables of twenty-three foreign versions of common English given names; the second section defines equivalents for military and civilian titles. It is very useful for translating given names.

Johns, Stephanie Bernardo. *The Ethnic Almanac.* Garden City, N.Y.: Doubleday, 1981.

Johnson, Keith A., and Malcolm R. Sainty. *Genealogical Research Directory.* Washington, D.C.: the authors, 1985–.

Jones, Maldwyn. *American Immigration.* New York: Holt, Rinehart and Winston, 1960.

_____. *Destination America.* New York: Holt, Rinehart and Winston, 1976.

Kaminkow, Marion J., ed. *Genealogies in the Library of Congress: A Bibliography.* 2 vols. Baltimore: Magna Carta Book Co., 1972, 1977, 1987.

Kennedy, John F. *A Nation of Immigrants.* New York: Harper and Row, 1964.

Kludas, Arnold. *Great Passenger Ships of the World.* Translated by Charles Hodges. 6 vols. Cambridge, England: Patrick Stephens, Ltd., 1975–86.

Kraut, Alan M. *The Huddled Masses: The Immigrant in American Society, 1880–1921.* Arlington Heights, Ill.: Harlan Davidson, 1982.

Kurian, George Thomas. *Datapedia of the United States 1790–2000: America Year by Year.* Lanham, Md.: Bernan Press, 1994.

Lieberson, Stanley. *Ethnic Patterns in American Cities.* New York: Free Press, 1963.

Lind, Marilyn. *Immigration, Migration and Settlement in the United States: A Genealogical Guidebook.* Cloquet, Minn.: The Linden Tree, 1985.

Luckingham, Bradford. "Benevolence in Emergent San Francisco: A Note on Immigrant Life in the Urban Far West." *Southern California Quarterly* 55 (1973): 431–44.

Makower, Joel, ed. *The American History Source Book.* New York: Prentice Hall, 1987.

Marden, Charles F., and Gladys Meyer. *Minorities in American Society*, 4th ed. New York: D. Van Nostrand, 1973.

Meyer, Mary K. *Meyer's Directory of Genealogical Societies in the U.S.A. and Canada.* 10th ed. Mt. Airy, Md.: 1994.

Miller, Sally M. *Ethnic Press in the United States: A Historical Analysis and Handbook.* New York: Greenwood Press, 1987.

Miller, Wayne Charles, et al. *A Comprehensive Bibliography for the Study of American Minorities.* New York: New York University Press, 1976. Contains more than 29,000 entries; essays on ethnic groups with extensive bibliographies for each; exhaustive though dated bibliography. Divided into sections on the geographic areas from which immigrants came: Africa, Europe, Eastern Europe and the Balkans, Asia, Puerto Rico and Cuba, Mexico, and America (Native Americans). American minority groups are discussed from various perspectives. Each section follows essentially the same format. Under "The Arab-American Experience," for example, is a brief history of Arabs in the United States, followed by Bibliographies of Bibliographies, Periodicals, Essays and Indexes Dealing with Periodicals, Periodicals in English, Periodicals in Arabic, History and Sociology, Education and Language, Religion, Biography and Autobiography, Literature, Literary Criticism, Folklore, and the Arts.

The researcher who does not consider European ancestors as "minorities" might overlook this source, thereby missing some rather obscure yet important ethnic sources listed under the section "From Europe," which has subsections on the French, German, Spanish, Portuguese, Irish, Jewish, Greek, Swedish, Norwegian, Danish, Icelandic, Finnish, and Scandinavians as groups.

In the subsection titled "German Americans: A Guide to the German American Experience," the *Comprehensive Bibliography* provides a historical sketch of the first permanent German settlement (1683) in Germantown, Pennsylvania, to World War I and what is probably the most extensive German-American bibliography published as of 1976.

Montalto, Nicholas V. *The International Institute Movement: A Guide to Records of Immigrant Society Agencies in the United States.* St. Paul: Immigration History Research Center, 1978.

Moody, Suzanna, and Joel Wurl, eds. *The Immigration History Research Center: A Guide to Collections.* New York: Greenwood Press, 1991.

Morris, Richard B. *Government and Labor in Early America.* New York: Harper and Row, 1965.

Morrison, Joan, and Charlotte Fox Zabusky. *American Mosaic: The Immigrant Experience in the Words of Those Who Lived It.* 2nd ed. Pittsburg: University of Pittsburg Press, 1993.

Naanes, Ted. "Ellis Island: Doorway to Dreams." *Ancestry* 13 (1) 11–13.

National Historical Publications and Records Commission. *Directory of Archives and Manuscript Repositories in the United States.* 3rd ed. Phoenix: Oryx Press, 1990.

Neagles, James C. "Immigrant Ancestors." In *The Library of Congress: A Guide to Genealogical and Historical Research.* Salt Lake City: Ancestry, 1990.

Newspapers in Microform: United States. 2 vols. Washington, D.C.: Library of Congress, 1984.

Novotny, Ann. *Strangers at the Door.* Riverside, Conn.: The Chatham Press, 1971.

Periodical Source Index (PERSI). Fort Wayne, Ind.: Allen County Public Library Genealogy Department, 1987–. Annual volumes published since 1986. PERSI is a locality, subject, and surname index to genealogical and historical journals. A section in PERSI for Foreign Places, for example, can be particularly helpful in ethnic research, as it is arranged first by country, then by record type. European locations may contain current smaller political subdivisions; for example, Great Britain may include materials of a regional nature; Germany includes entries for German provinces, as well as pre-unification East and West Germany, Prussia, etc.; U.S.S.R. includes articles pertaining to the Ukraine, Latvia, Lithuania, and other countries once part of the Soviet Republic. PERSI is just one of the finding aids discussed in chapter 2.

Phillips, Donna Potter. "Using the Balch Institute for Ethnic Studies." *Ancestry Newsletter* 6 (3) (May–June 1988): 1–2.

Powell, Sumner Chilton. *Puritan Village: The Formation of a New England Town.* Garden City, N.Y.: Doubleday & Company, 1965.

Reimers, David M. *Still the Golden Door: The Third World Comes to America.* New York: Columbia University Press, 1985.

_____. *The Immigrant Experience.* New York: Chelsea House Publishers, 1989.

Rosen, Philip. *The Neglected Dimension: Ethnicity in American Life.* South Bend, Ind.: Notre Dame Press, 1980.

Schnore, Leo F. *The New Urban History.* Princeton, N.J.: Princeton University Press, 1973.

Scott, Franklin D. *The Peopling of America: Perspectives on Immigration.* Washington, D.C.: American Historical Society Association, 1972.

Slocum, Robert C. *Biographical Dictionaries and Related Works.* 2 vols. 2nd ed. Detroit: Gale Research Co., 1986.

Smith, Eugene W. *Passenger Ships of the World, Past and Present.* Boston: George H. Dean, 1978.

Smith, Jessie C., ed. *Ethnic Genealogy: A Research Guide.* Westport, Conn.: Greenwood Press, 1983.

Smith, Warren B. *White Servitude in Colonial South Carolina.* Danielsville, Ga.: Heritage Papers, 1972.

Sowell, Thomas. *Ethnic America: A History.* New York: Basic Books, 1981.

Szucs, Loretto Dennis. *Ellis Island: Gateway to America.* Salt Lake City: Ancestry, 1986.

_____, and Sandra Hargreaves Luebking. *The Archives: A Guide to the National Archives Field Branches.* Salt Lake City: Ancestry, 1988.

Taylor, Philip. *The Distant Magnet: European Emigration to the U.S.A.* New York: Harper and Row, 1971.

Thernstrom, Stephan. *Harvard Encyclopedia of American Ethnic Groups.* Cambridge, Mass.: The Belknap Press of Harvard University Press, 1980. This work is one of the most definitive and useful background sources for almost every ethnic group. It brings together the basic information about the multitude of people who make up the population of the United States. It is a succinct, authoritative synthesis of the origins and histories of 106 ethnic groups, containing twenty-nine thematic essays, eighty-seven maps, and a critical bibliography for each section.

Tift, Wilton, and Thomas Dunne. *Ellis Island.* New York: W.W. Norton, 1971.

Vecoli, Rudolph J., and Suzanne M. Sinke, eds. *A Century of European Migrations, 1830–1930.* Chicago: University of Illinois Press, 1991.

Wasserman, Paul, and Alice E. Kennington. *Ethnic Information Sources of the United States: A Guide to Organizations, Agencies, Foundations, Institutions, Media, Commercial and Trade Bodies, Government Programs, Research Institutes, Libraries and Museums, Religious Organizations, Banking Firms, Festivals and Fairs, Travel and Tourist Offices, Airlines and Ship lines, Bookdealers and Publishers' Representatives, and Books, Pamphlets, and Audiovisuals on Specific Ethnic Groups.* 2nd ed. 2 vols. Detroit: Gale Research Co., 1983. This work brings together information about the various ethnic groups that comprise the U.S. populace. Topics and resources covering standard ethnic sources and research institutions, as well as more obscure information on embassies, ethnic fraternal organizations, ethnic newspaper collections, ethnic bookdealers, and ethnic museums, may be especially useful for genealogists.

Wittke, Carl F. *We Who Built America: The Saga of the Immigrant.* Cleveland: Western Reserve University Press, 1964.

Wynar, Lubomyr R. *Encyclopedic Directory of Ethnic Organizations in the United States.* Littleton, Colo.: Libraries Unlimited, 1976. As Wynar states in the preface to this work, "The historian, sociologist, political scientist, or any other researcher studying American ethnicity must closely scrutinize the phenomenon of ethnic organized life as it reflected in the objectives of various ethnic organizations. For the researcher, ethnic organizations serve as 'primary sources' since they reflect the social structure of the ethnic group." The objective of the *Encyclopedic Directory* was to provide addresses for some 1,475 major ethnic organizations represent-

ing seventy-three ethnic groups, and to briefly describe the nature of their holdings, which include, in most cases, references to printed ethnic sources held by each organization.

_____, and Anna T. Wynar. *The Encyclopedic Directory of Ethnic Newspapers and Periodicals in the United States.* Littleton, Colo.: Libraries Unlimited, 1976. A dated but valuable source of information on printed ethnic publications.

Published Passenger and Emigration Lists and Sources for Locating Ships

Baca, Leo. *Czech Immigration Passenger Lists.* 4 vols. Richardson, Tex.: the compiler, 1983–91.

Boyer, Carl, III. *Ship Passenger Lists.* 4 vols. Newhall, Calif.: 1977–80.

Burgert, Annette K. *Eighteenth-Century Emigrants From German-Speaking Lands to North America.* Breinigsville, Pa.: The Pennsylvania German Society, 1983–.

Cassady, Michael. *New York Passenger Arrivals, 1849–1868.* Papillion, Nebr.: Nimmo, 1983. Contains approximately 10,200 names from selected passenger lists.

Coldham, Peter Wilson. *The Complete Book of Bonded Passengers to America.* 9 vols. Baltimore: Genealogical Publishing Co., 1983–85.

Colletta, John P. *They Came in Ships: A Guide to Finding Your Immigrant Ancestor's Arrival Record.* Rev. and enl. ed. Salt Lake City: Ancestry, 1993.

Ferguson, Laraine K. "Hamburg, Germany, Gateway to Ancestral Home." *German Genealogical Digest* 2 (1) (first quarter 1986): 10–14.

Filby, P. William, Mary K. Meyer, and Dorothy M. Lower. *Passenger and Immigration Lists Index.* Detroit: Gale Research Co., 1981– (including supplements).

_____, and Mary K. Meyer, eds. *Passenger and Immigration Lists Index: A Guide to Published Arrival Records of More Than 1,775,000 Passengers Who Came to the New World Between the Sixteenth, Seventeenth, and Eighteenth Centuries.* Detroit: Gale Research Co., 1981. Supplements 1982–.

_____, *Passenger and Immigration Lists Bibliography, 1538–1900: Being a Guide to Published Lists of Arrivals in the United States and Canada.* 2nd ed. Detroit: Gale Research Co., 1988.

_____, and Mary K. Meyer, eds. *Passenger and Immigration Lists of Arrivals in the United States and Canada in the Seventeenth, Eighteenth and Nineteenth Centuries.* 3 vols. Detroit: Gale Research Co., 1981. Supplements 1982–.

Glazier, Ira A., and Michael Tepper, eds. *The Famine Immigrants: Lists of Irish Immigrants Arriving at U.S. Ports 1850–1855.* 7 vols. Baltimore: Genealogical Publishing Co., 1983–87.

_____, and P. William Filby, eds. *Germans to America: Lists of Passengers Arriving at U.S. Ports, 1850–1855.* Wilmington, Del.: Scholarly Resources, 1988– (28 volumes to date).

_____. *Italians to America: Lists of Passengers Arriving at*

U.S. Ports, 1880–1899. 2 vols. to date. Wilmington, Del.: Scholarly Resources, 1992–.

Hall, Charles M. *Antwerp Emigration Index.* Salt Lake City: Heritage International, 1986.

Haury, David A., ed. *Index to Mennonite Immigrants on U.S. Passenger Lists, 1872–1904.* North Newton, Kans.: Mennonite Library and Archives, 1986.

Immigration Information Bureau. *Morton Allen Directory of European Passenger Steamship Arrivals.* 1931. Reprint. Baltimore: Genealogical Publishing Co., 1993.

Jones, Hank Z., Jr. *More Palatine Families: Some Immigrants to the Middle Colonies, 1717–1776, and Their European Origins.* San Diego: the author, 1991.

Lancour, Harold. *Bibliography of Passenger Lists.* New York: New York Public Library, 1937.

McManus, J. *Comal County, Texas, and New Braunfels, Texas German Immigrant Ships, 1845–1846.* St. Louis: F.T. Ingmire, 1985.

Mathias, P., and A.W.H. Pearsall. *Shipping: A Survey of Historical Records.* Newton Abbot, England: David and Charles, 1980.

Mitchell, Brian, comp. *Irish Passenger Lists 1847–1871.* Genealogical Publishing Co., 1988.

The Morton Allan Directory of European Passenger Steamship Arrivals. Immigrant Information Bureau, 1931.

National Archives Trust Fund Board. *Immigrant and Passenger Arrivals: A Select Catalog of National Archives Publications.* Revised. Washington, D.C., 1992.

Olsson, Nils William. *Swedish Passenger Arrivals in New York, 1820–1850.* Chicago: Swedish Pioneer Historical Society, 1967.

Owen, Robert Edward, ed. *Luxemburgers in the New World.* 2 vols. Esch-sur-Alzette, Luxembourg: Editions Reliures Schortgen, 1987.

"Passenger Arrivals at Salem and Beverly, Massachusetts, 1798–1800. *New England Historical Genealogical Register* 106 (1952): 203–09.

Potter, Constance. "St. Albans Passenger Arrival Records." *Prologue: Journal of the National Archives* 22 (1) (Spring 1990): 90–93.

Prins, Edward. *Dutch and German Ships.* Holland, Mich.: the compiler, 1972.

Rasmussen, Louis J. *San Francisco Ship Passenger Lists.* 4 vols. Baltimore: Genealogical Publishing Co., 1978.

Register and Guide to the Hamburg Passenger Lists, 1850–1934. Research Paper Series C., no. 30. Salt Lake City: Genealogical Department of The Church of Jesus Christ of Latter-day Saints.

Reider, Milton P., and Norma Gaudet Rieder, eds. *New Orleans Ship Lists.* 2 vols. Metairie, La., 1966–68.

Risch, Erna. "Immigrant Aid Societies Before 1820." *Pennsylvania History* 3 (January 1936): 15–32.

Rockett, Charles Whitlock. *Some Shipboard Passengers of Captain John Rockett (1828–1841).* Mission Viejo, Calif.: the compiler, 1983.

Schenk, Trudy, Ruth Froelke, and Inge Bork. *The Wuerttemberg Emigration Index.* 6 vols. to date. Salt Lake City: Ancestry, 1988–.

Schrader-Muggenthaler, Cornelia. *Alsace Emigration Book.* 2 vols. Apollo, Pa.: Closson Press, 1989–91.

_____. *Baden Emigration Book.* Apollo, Pa.: Closson Press, 1992.

Smith, Clifford Neal. *Reconstructed Passenger Lists for 1850: Hamburg to Australia, Brazil, Canada, Chile, and the United States.* 4 vols. McNeal, Ariz.: Westland Publications, 1980.

Ships Passenger Lists, Port of Galveston, Texas, 1846–1871. Easley, S.C.: Southern Historical Press, 1984.

Steuart, Bradley W. *Passenger Ships Arriving in New York Harbor (1820–1850).* Bountiful, Utah: Precision Indexing, 1991.

Strassburger, Ralph Beaver, comp., and William John Hinke, ed. *Pennsylvania German Pioneers: A Publication of the Original Lists of Arrivals in the Port of Philadelphia from 1727 to 1808.* 3 vols. Norristown, Pa.: Pennsylvania German Society, 1934.

Sweiringa, Robert P., comp. *Dutch Immigrants in U.S. Ship Passenger Manifests, 1820–1880: An Alphabetical Listing by Household Heads and Independent Persons.* 2 vols. Wilmington, Del.: Scholarly Resources, 1983.

Tepper, Michael. *American Passenger Arrival Records: A Guide to the Records of Immigrants Arriving at American Ports by Sail and Steam.* 2nd ed. Baltimore: Genealogical Publishing Co., 1993.

_____, ed. *Emigrants to Pennsylvania, 1641–1819: A Consolidation of Ship Passenger Lists from Pennsylvania Magazine of History and Biography.* Baltimore: Genealogical Publishing Co., 1978.

_____. *Immigrants to the Middle Colonies.* Baltimore: Genealogical Publishing Co., 1978.

_____. *New World Immigrants: A Consolidation of Ship Passenger Lists from Periodical Literature.* 2 vols. Baltimore: Genealogical Publishing Co., 1988.

_____. *Passenger Arrivals at the Port of Baltimore, 1820–1834, From Customs Passenger Lists.* Baltimore: Genealogical Publishing Co., 1982.

_____. *Passenger Arrivals at the Port of Philadelphia, 1800–1819: The Philadelphia Baggage Lists.* Baltimore: Genealogical Publishing Co., 1986.

Wolfe, Richard. *Bibliography of Passenger Lists.* New York: New York Public Library, 1963.

Yoder, Don, ed. *Pennsylvania German Immigrants, 1709–1786: Lists Consolidated from Yearbooks of the Pennsylvania German Folklore Society.* 1984. Reprint. Baltimore: Genealogical Publishing Co., 1989.

Zimmerman, Gary J., and Marion Wolfert. *German Immigrants:*

Lists of Passengers Bound From Bremen to New York. 3 vols. Baltimore: Genealogical Publishing Co., 1988.

NATURALIZATION

Eichholz, Alice, ed. Ancestry's *Red Book: American State, County and Town Sources.* Rev. ed. Salt Lake City: Ancestry, 1992.

Filby, P. William. *Philadelphia Naturalization Records.* Detroit: Gale Research Co., 1982.

Franklin, Frank George. *The Legislative History of Naturalization in the United States.* New York: Arno Press and the New York Times, 1969.

Holcomb, Brent H. *South Carolina Naturalizations, 1783–1850.* Baltimore: Genealogical Publishing Co., 1985.

Journals of Congress, II, 16 January 1777.

National Archives Trust Fund Board. *Index to Naturalization Petitions of the United States District Court for the Eastern District of New York 1865–1957.* Washington, D.C.: National Archives and Records Administration, 1991.

Newman, John. *Naturalization Processes and Procedures, 1790–1985.* Indianapolis: Indiana Historical Society, 1985.

Soundex Index to Naturalization Petitions for the United States District and Circuit Courts, Northern District of Illinois, and Immigration and Naturalization Service District 9, 1840–1950. National Archives Trust Fund Board, 1991.

Scott, Kenneth. *Early New York Naturalizations, 1790–1840.* Baltimore: Genealogical Publishing Co., 1981.

Szucs, Loretto Dennis, and Sandra Hargreaves Luebking. *The Archives: A Guide to the National Archives Field Branches.* Salt Lake City: Ancestry, 1988.

Wolfe, Richard J. "The Colonial Naturalization Act of 1740; With a List of Persons Naturalized in New York Colony, 1740–1769." *New York Genealogical and Biographical Record* 94 (1963): 132–47.

Wyand, Jeffrey A., and Florence L. Wyand. *Colonial Maryland Naturalizations.* Baltimore: Genealogical Publishing Co., 1986.

ADDITIONAL SOURCES FOR SELECTED ETHNIC GROUPS

Addresses (and telephone numbers, if available) of selected ethnic organizations are included in this section. Chosen for listing here are those organizations that publish newsletters or quarterlies, or have particularly valuable libraries.

Albanian

The Albanian in America: The First Arrivals. Boston: Society Fatbardnesia of Katundi, 1960.

Armenian

Armenian American Almanac: A Guide to Organizations, Churches, Newspapers. Glendale, Calif. Armenian Reference Books Co., 1990 (annual).

Avakian, Arra. *The Armenians in America.* Minneapolis, Minn.: Lerner Publications Co., 1977.

Der Nersessian, Sirarpie. *The Armenians.* New York: Praeger, 1970.

Kulhanjian, Gary A. *An Abstract of the Historical and Sociological Aspects of Armenian Immigration to the United States, 1890–1930.* San Francisco: R & E Research Associates, 1975.

Mirak, Robert. "The Armenian Orthodox and Armenian Protestant Churches in the New World to 1915." In *Immigrants and Religion in Urban America.* Edited by Randall M. Miller and Thomas D. Marzik. Philadelphia: Temple University Press, 1977.

Tashjian, James H. *The Armenians of the U.S. and Canada.* Boston: Armenian Youth Federation, 1947.

Vartan, Malcolm M. *The Armenians in America.* Boston: The Pilgrim Press, 1919.

Waldstreicher, David. *The Armenians in America.* New York: Chelsea House, 1989.

Wertsman, Vladimir. *The Armenians in America, 1618–1976.* Dobbs Ferry, N.Y.: Oceana Publications, 1978.

Asian

Hoyt, Edwin Palmer. *Asians in the West.* Monograph. Nashville, Tenn.: T. Nelson, 1974.

Kim, Hyung-Chan, ed. *The Dictionary of Asian-American History.* Westport, Conn.: Greenwood Press, 1986. Has entries on the various groups from Asia and Pacific Isles: individuals, events, places, terms and other data applicable to Asian-Americans.

Melendy, Howard Brett. *The Oriental Americans.* New York: Hippocrene Books, 1972.

Perrin, Linda. *Coming to America: Immigrants from the Far East.* Monograph. New York: Delacorte Press, 1980; Dell Publishing Co., 1981.

Takaki, Ronald T. *Strangers From a Different Shore: A History of Asian Americans.* Boston, Mass.: Brown, 1989.

Tong, Te-kong. *The Third Americans: A Select Bibliography on Asians in America.* Oak Park, Ill: CHCUS, 1980.

Wong, James I. *A Selected Bibliography on the Asians in America.* Palo Alto, Calif.: R & E Research Associates, 1981.

British

Krans-Buckland Family Association
P.O. Box 1025
North Highlands, CA 95660-1025

Publishes *The English Researcher*

Baxter, Angus. *In Search of Your British and Irish Roots: A Complete Guide to Tracing Your English, Welsh, Scottish and Irish Ancestors.* Baltimore: Genealogical Publishing Co., 1991.

Berthoff, Rowland Tappan. *British Immigrants in Industrial America, 1790–1950.* Cambridge, Mass.: Harvard University Press, 1953. Reprint. New York: Russell & Russell, 1968.

Coldham, Peter W. *The Complete Book of Emigrants in Bondage, 1607–1640.* Baltimore: Genealogical Publishing Co., 1988.

_____. *The Complete Book of Emigrants 1607–1776.* 4 vols. Baltimore: Genealogical Publishing Co., 1990–93.

_____. *Emigrants in Chains.* Baltimore: Genealogical Publishing Co., 1992.

Cressy, David. *Coming Over: Migration and Communication Between England and New England in the Seventeenth Century.* New York: Cambridge University Press, 1987.

Erickson, Charlotte. *Invisible Immigrants: The Adaptation of English and Scottish Immigrants in Nineteenth-Century America.* Coral Gables, Fla.: University of Miami Press, 1972.

Filby, P. William. *American and British Genealogy and Heraldry: A Selected List of Books.* 3rd ed. Boston: New England Historic Genealogical Society, 1983. 1982–85 supplement, 1987.

_____. *American and British Genealogy and Heraldry: 1982–1985 Supplement.* Boston: New England Historic Genealogical Society, 1987. This supplement contains 2,817 entries divided geographically—United States, Latin America, Canada, England, Ireland, Scotland, Wales, and former British dominions.

Foster, Janet. *British Archives: A Guide to Archives Resources in the United Kingdom.* 2nd ed. New York: Stockton Press, 1989.

Irvine, Sherry. *Your English Ancestry: A Guide for North Americans.* Salt Lake City: Ancestry, 1994.

Jones, Maldwyn A. "The Background to Emigration From Great Britain in the Nineteenth Century." *Perspectives in American History* 7 (1973): 3–92.

Lines, Kenneth. *British and Canadian Immigration to the United States Since 1920.* Monograph. San Francisco: R & E Research Associates, 1981.

Moulton, Joy Wade. *Genealogical Resources in English Repositories.* Columbus, Ohio: Hampton House, 1988. Information on the principal repositories of England and their holdings.

Norton, Mary Beth. *The British Americans: The Loyalist Exiles in England, 1774–1789.* Boston: Little, Brown, 1972.

Roberts, Gary B. *English Origins of New England Families: From the New England Historic Genealogical Register.* 3 vols. Baltimore: Genealogical Publishing Co., 1984.

Young, G.M. *Victorian England: Portrait of an Age.* New York: Oxford University Press, 1964.

Canadian

American-Canadian Genealogical Society
P.O. Box 668
Manchester, NH 03105-0668
603-622-1554

Baxter, Angus. *In Search of Your Canadian Roots: Tracing Your Family Tree in Canada.* Baltimore: Genealogical Publishing Co., 1989. An updated edition of Baxter's earlier guide titled *In Search of Your Roots: A Guide for Canadians Seeking Their Ancestors.* Includes addresses, sources, and repositories for all provinces.

Elliot, Noel M. *The French Canadians 1600–1900: An Alphabetized Directory of the People, Places and Vital Dates.* 3 vols. Toronto: Genealogical Research Library, 1993.

Jonasson, Eric. *The Canadian Genealogical Handbook: A Comprehensive Guide to Finding Your Ancestors in Canada.* 2nd ed. Winnipeg, Manitoba: Wheatfield Press, 1978. Although out of print and somewhat dated, this remains a useful handbook for determining what resources are available in each of the provinces and the territories. Addresses should be double-checked as many have changed since its publication.

Kennedy, Patricia, and Janine Roy. *Tracing Your Ancestors in Canada.* Ottawa: Public Archives of Canada, 1987. Write the Canadian National Archives for this free pamphlet outlining repository addresses and an overview of holdings. The address is Public Archives of Canada, 395 Wellington St., Ottawa, Ontario K1A ON3.

Lebel, Gerard. *Our French Canadian Ancestors.* Translated by Thomas J. Laforest. Palm Harbor, Fla.: the translator, 1983.

Merriman, Brenda Dougall. *Genealogy in Ontario: Searching the Records.* Ontario: Ontario Genealogical Society, 1984.

McDonald, Norman. *Canada: Immigration and Colonization, 1841–1903.* Toronto: Macmillan of Canada, 1976.

Punch, Terrence M., ed. *Genealogist's Handbook for Atlantic Canada Research.* Boston: New England Historical Society, 1989. Covers the history and resources available for Prince Edward Island, Newfoundland, New Brunswick, Labrador, and "Acadia," and Nova Scotia.

Roy, Janine. *Tracing Your Ancestors in Canada.* 11th rev. ed. Ottawa: National Archives of Canada, 1993.

Woodcock, George. *The Century That Made Us: Canada 1814–1914.* Toronto: Oxford University Press, 1989.

Chinese

Archer, Jules. *The Chinese and the Americans.* New York: Hawthorn Books, 1976.

Barth, Gunther. *Bitter Strength: A History of the Chinese in the United States, 1850–70.* Cambridge: Harvard University Press, 1964.

Chen, Jack. *The Chinese of America: From the Beginnings to the Present.* New York: Harper and Row, 1981.

Hoobler, Dorothy, and Thomas Hoobler. *Chinese American Family Album.* New York: Oxford University Press, 1994.

Hsu, Francis L. *The Challenge of the American Dream: The Chinese in the United States.* Belmont, Calif.: Wadsworth Publishing Co., 1971.

Lee, Rose Hum. *The Chinese in the United States of America.* Hong Kong: Hong Kong University Press, 1960.

Lee Sung, Betty. *Mountain of Gold: The Story of Chinese in America.* New York: Macmillan, 1967. A Historical look at Chinese immigration and life of the Chinese in America.

Lyman, S.M. *Chinese Americans.* New York: Random House, 1974.

Miller, Stuart C. *Unwelcome Immigrant: The Image of the Chinese, 1785–1882.* Berkeley: University of California, 1969.

Cornish

Rowe, John. *The Hand-Rock Men: Cornish Immigrants and the North American Mining Frontier.* New York: Barnes and Noble, 1974.

Rowse, Alfred Leslie. *Cousin Jacks: The Cornish in America.* New York: Scribner, 1966.

Croatian

Kraljic, Frances. "Croatian Migration To and From the United States Between 1900 and 1914." Ph.D. dissertation, New York University, 1975.

Preveden, Francis R. *A History of the Croatian People.* 2 vols. New York: Philosophical Library, vol. 1, 1956; vol. 2, 1962.

Prpic, George J. *The Croatian Immigrants in America.* New York: Philosophical Library, 1971.

Czech

Czecho-Slovak Genealogical Society
P.O. Box 16225
St. Paul, MN 55116

Baca, Leonard. *Czech Immigration Passenger Lists.* Hallettsville, Tex.: Old Homestead, 1983–.

Capek, T. *Czechoslovak Immigration.* New York: Service Bureau for Intercultural Education, 1938.

_____. *The Czechs (Bohemians) in America: A Study of Their National, Cultural, Political, Social, Economic, and Religious Life.* 1920. Reprint. New York: Arno Press, 1969.

Dvornik, E. *Czech Contributions to the Growth of the United States.* Chicago: Benedictine Abbey Press, 1962.

Laska, V. *The Czechs in America, 1633–1977.* Dobbs Ferry, N.Y.: Oceana Publications, 1978.

Miller, K.D. *The Czechoslovaks in America.* New York: Doran, 1922.

Psencik, L.F. *Czech Contributions to American Culture.* Austin: Texas Education Agency, 1970.

Rechcigl, E. *Directory of the Members of the Czechoslovak Society of Arts and Sciences in America.* New York: Czechoslovak Society of Arts and Sciences in America, 1969.

Rosicky, Rose. *A History of Czechs (Bohemians) in Nebraska.* Omaha, Nebr.: Czech Historical Society, 1929.

Roucek, Joseph S. *The Czechs and Slovaks in America.* Minneapolis: Lerner Publications, 1967.

Schlyter, Daniel M. *Czechoslovakia: A Handbook of Czechoslovak Genealogical Research.* Buffalo Grove, Ill.: Genun, 1985.

Danes

Bille, J. H. *A History of the Danes in America.* 1896. Reprint. San Francisco: R & E Research Associates, 1971.

Danus, E. *Danish American Journey.* Franklin, Massachusetts: Gauntlet, 1971.

Hvidt, Kristian. *Flight to America: The Social Background of 300,000 Danish Emigrants.* New York: Academic Press, 1975.

Mortensen, Enok. *Danish American Life.* Arno, 1978.

Nielsen, Alfred. *Life in American Denmark.* Arno, 1978.

Dutch

Bertus, Harry Wabeke. *Dutch Emigration to America, 1624–1860.* New York: Arno Press, 1944.

Currer-Briggs, Noel. *Colonial Settlers and English Adventurers.* Genealogical Publishing Co., 1971.

De Jong, G.F. *The Dutch in America, 1609–1974.* Boston: Twayne, 1975.

Doezma, Linda Pegman. *Dutch-Americans: A Guide to Manuscript Sources.* Detroit: Gale Research Co., 1979.

Fernow, Berthold. *Records of New Amsterdam, 1653–1674.* Reprint. Baltimore, Md.: Genealogical Publishing Co., 1978.

Fiske, John. *The Dutch and Quaker Colonies in America.* Houghton Mifflin Co., 1899.

Franklin, Charles M. *Dutch Genealogical Research.* Indianapolis, Ind.: Ye Olde Genealogie Shoppe, 1982.

Lucas, Henry S. *Netherlands in America: Dutch Immigration to the United States and Canada, 1789–1950.* Ann Arbor: University of Michigan Press, 1955.

_____, ed. *Dutch Immigrant Memoirs and Related Writings.* Assen, Netherlands: Van Gorcum & Co., 1955.

Rupp, I. Daniel. *A Collection of Upwards of 30,000 Names of German, Swiss, Dutch French and Other Immigrants in Pennsylvania from 1726 to 1776.* 2nd ed.. Philadelphia: Leary, Steward, 1927.

Smit, J.W. *The Dutch in America, 1609–1970.* Dobbs Ferry, N.Y.: Oceana Publications, 1972.

Swierenga, Robert P. *Dutch Emigrants to the United States, South Africa, South America, and Southeast Asia, 1835–1880.* Wilmington, Del.: Scholarly Resources, 1983.

_____. *Dutch Immigrants in the U.S. Passenger Manifests 1820–1880.* Wilmington, Del.: Scholarly Resources. 1983.

_____. "Dutch Immigrant Demography, 1820–1880." *Journal of Family History* 5 (Winter 1980): 390–405.

_____. *Dutch Immigrants in Federal Population Censuses, 1850, 1860, 1870, 1900.* Kent, Ohio: Kent State University, 1992.

_____, comp. *Dutch Households in U.S. Population Censuses, 1850, 1860, 1870: An Alphabetical Listing by Household Heads and Independent Persons.* 3 vols. Wilmington, Del.: Scholarly Resources, 1987.

_____. *Dutch Emigrants to the United States , South Africa, South America, and Southeast Asia, 1835–1880.* Wilmington, Del.: Scholarly Resources, 1983.

_____. *Dutch Immigrants in U.S. Ship Passenger Manifests, 1820–1880: An Alphabetical Listing by Household Heads and Independent Persons.* Wilmington, Del.: Scholarly Resources, 1983.

_____. *The Forerunners: Dutch Jewry in the North American Diaspora.* Detroit: Wayne State University Press, 1994.

Estonian

Pennar, Jaan. *The Estonians in America, 1627–1975.* Dobbs Ferry, N.Y.: Oceana Publications, 1975.

Filipino

Kim, Hyung-Chan. *The Filipinos in America, 1898–1974.* Dobbs Ferry, N.Y.: Oceana Publications, 1976.

Munoz, Alfredo. *The Filipinos in America.* Los Angeles: Mountainview Publishers, 1971.

Finnish

Hoglund, William. *Finnish Immigrants in America, 1880–1920.* Madison: University of Wisconsin Press, 1960.

Jalkanen, Ralph J. *The Finns in North America.* Hancock: Michigan University Press, 1969.

Karni, Michael, ed. *Finnish Diaspora II: United States.* Toronto: Multicultural History Society of Ontario, 1981.

Kolehmainen, John Ilmari. *The Finns in America: A Bibliographical Guide to Their History.* Hancock, Mich.: Teachers College, 1968.

Louhi, E. A. *The Delaware Finns: Or The First Permanent Settlements in Pennsylvania, Delaware, West New Jersey, and Eastern Part of Maryland.* New York: Humanity Press, 1925.

Ross, Carl D., and K. Marianne Wargelin Brown, eds. *Women Who Dared: The History of Finnish American Women.* St. Paul, Minn.: Immigration History Research Center, University of Minnesota, 1986.

Vincent, Timothy Laitila, and Rick Tapio. *Finnish Genealogical Research.* New Brighton, Minn.: Sampo Publishing, 1994.

Wargelin, John. *The Americanization of the Finns.* Hancock: The Finnish Lutheran Book Concern, 1924.

Wuorinen, J.H. *The Finns on the Delaware, 1638–1655.* 1938. Reprint. New York: Arno Press, 1966.

French

American-Canadian Genealogical Society
P.O. Box 668
Manchester, NH 03105-0668

Publishes *American-Canadian Genealogist,* including significant information on French subjects.

Boudreau, Rev. Dennis M. *Beginning Franco American Genealogy.* Pawtucket, R.I.: American French Genealogical Society, 1986.

Eccles, William J. *France in America.* New York: Harper & Row, 1972.

Fecteau, Edward. *French Contributions to America.* Methuen, Mass.: Soucy Press, 1945.

Hirsch, Arthur H. *The Huguenots of Colonial South Carolina.* Hamden, Conn.: Shoe String, 1973.

Kunz, Virginia B. *The French in America.* Minneapolis: Lerner Publications, 1966.

Morgan, T. *On Becoming American.* Boston: Houghton Mifflin, 1978. A former French Count, Sanche de Gramont,

became an American citizen in 1977, shedding his title and his old name.

Pula, James S. *The French in America 1488–1974.* Dobbs Ferry, N.Y.: Oceana Publications, 1975.

Ronciere, Charles De La. *What the French Have Done in America.* Paris: Typographie Lon-Nourrit et Cie, 1915.

Rupp, I. Daniel. *A Collection of Upwards of 30,000 Names of German Swiss, Dutch, French, and Other Immigrants in Pennsylvania From 1726–1776.* 2nd ed., rev. and enl. Philadelphia: Leary, Steward, 1927.

Thwaites, Reuben G. *France in America, 1497–1763.* New York: Cooper Square, 1968.

Zoltvany, Yves F. *The French in America.* Columbia: University of South Carolina Press, 1969.

German

Germanic Genealogy Society
P.O. Box 16312
St. Paul, MN 55116-0312

Publishes a newsletter

Immigrant Genealogical Society
Immigrant Library
1310 B West Magnolia Blvd.
P.O. Box 7369
Burbank, CA 91510-7369
(818) 848-3122

Publishes *German American Genealogy*

Arndt, Karl J. R. *German-American Newspapers and Periodicals, 1732–1955.* New York: Johnson Reprint, 1985.

Baxter, Angus. *In Search of Your German Roots.* 3rd ed. Baltimore: Genealogical Publishing Co., 1994.

Bahlow, Hans. *Deutsches Namenlexikon.* Munich, Germany: Verlagsbuchhandlung, 1972.

Billigmeier, Robert Henry. *Americans From Germany: A Study in Cultural Diversity.* Belmont, Calif.: Wadsworth Publishing, 1974.

Bittinger, Lucy F. *The Germans in Colonial Times.* Philadelphia: Lippincott, 1901; New York: Russell & Russell, 1901. Reissued 1968.

Bosse, Georg von. *German Achievements in America.* New York: Steiger, 1916.

Boyers, Robert, ed. *The Legacy of the German Refugee Intellectuals.* New York: Schocken, 1972.

Bruncken, Ernest. *German Political Refugees in the United States During the Period From 1815–1860.* Chicago: Deutsch-Amerikanische Geschichtsblatter, 1904. Reprint. San Francisco: R & E Research Associates, 1970.

Chicago und sein Deutschthum. Chicago: German Press Club, 1902.

The Church of Jesus Christ of Latter-day Saints. *Resource Guide: The Hamburg Passenger Lists, 1850–1934.* Salt Lake

City: The Church of Jesus Christ of Latter-day Saints Family History Library, 1992.

Coster, G.C. *Hessian Soldiers in the American Revolution: Records of Their Marriages, and Baptisms of Their Children in America Performed by the Reverend G.C.Coster, 1776–1783, Chaplain of Two Hessian Regiments.* Translated and abstracted by Marie Dickore. Cincinnati, Ohio: 1959.

Deutsches Geschlechterbuch. Limburg an der Lahn, Germany: C. A. Starke, 1889–.

Eakle, Arlene H. "Emigrant Sources for Tracing Pennsylvania German Ancestors." *APG Newsletter* 3 (May 1981): 8–13.

Eyster, Anita L. "Notices by German and Swiss Settlers Seeking Information of Members of Their Families, Kindred, and Friends Inserted Between 1742–1761 in *Pennsylvania Berichte* and 1762–1779 in the *Pennsylvania Staatsbote.*" *Pennsylvania German Folklore Society* 3 (1938): 32–41.

Frank, W. *Deutchland in Amerika.* San Francisco: R & E Research Associates, 1970.

Fredericks, Heinz F. *How to Find My German Ancestors and Relatives.* Newstadt, Germany: Verlag Degener & Co., 1985.

Furer, Howard. *The Germans in America, 1607–1970: A Chronology and Fact Book.* Dobbs Ferry, N.Y.: Oceana Publications, 1973.

Glazier, Ira, and P. William Filby. *Germans to America: Lists of Passengers Arriving at U.S. Ports, 1850–1893.* Wilmington, Del.: Scholarly Resources, 1992–.

The Hamburg Passenger Lists. Salt Lake City: Genealogical Society of Utah, 1984.

Hawgood, John Arkas. *The Tragedy of German-America: The Germans in the United States of America During the Nineteenth Century—and After.* New York: Putnam's, 1940. Reprint. New York: Arno, 1970.

Hinke, W.J., and J.B. Stoudt, eds. "A List of German Immigrants to the American Colonies From Zweibruecken in the Palatinate." *Pennsylvania-German Folklore Society, Yearbook,* 1 (1936): 101–24.

Hocker, Edward. *Genealogical Data Relating to the German Settlers of Pennsylvania From Advertisements in German Newspapers Published in Philadelphia and Germantown, 1743–1800.* Baltimore: Genealogical Publishing Co., 1981.

Holsinger, Henry R. *History of the Dunkers and the Brethren Church. . . .* North Manchester, Ind.: L.W. Shultz, 1962.

Jones, Henry (Hank) Z. "The Braun and Loesch Families: Neighbors in Germany and America." *Quarterly of the Pennsylvania German Society* 10 (April 1976).

_____. "Finding the Ancestral Home of a Palatine Forefather: The Case of Martin Zerbe." *Pennsylvania Genealogical Magazine* 29 (1975): 129–32.

_____. *More Palatine Families: Some Immigrants to the Middle Colonies 1717–1776 and Their European Origins Plus New Discoveries on German Families Who Arrived in Colonial New York in 1710.* Universal City, Calif.: the author, 1991.

_____. *The Palatine Families of New York: A Study of the German Immigrants Who Arrived in Colonial New York in 1710.* Universal City, Calif.: the author, 1985.

Kamphoefner, Walter D., Wolfgang Helbich, and Ulrike Sommer. *News From the Land of Freedom: German Immigrants Write Home.* New York: Cornell University Press, n.d. A broad cross-section of 350 German immigrant letters.

Keresztesi, Michael, and Gary R. Cocozzoli. *German-American History and Life: A Guide to Information Sources, 1980.* Detroit: Gale Research Co., 1980. Annotated.

Kloss, Heinz. *Atlas of German American Settlements.* Marburg, Germany: N.G. Elwert, 1974.

Kollmann, Wolfgang, and Peter Marschalack. "German Emigration to the United States." Translated by Thomas C. Childers. *Perspectives in American History* 7 (1973): 499–554.

Miller, Daniel. *Early German-American Newspapers.* Lancaster: Pennsylvania German Society, 1911.

O'Connor, Richard. *The German Americans, An Informal History.* New York: Little, Brown & Co., 1946.

Pochmann, Henry August. *Bibliography of German Culture in America to 1940.* Rev. and corr. Madison: University of Wisconsin Press, 1982. Contains 18,500 entries.

Rippley, La Vern J. *The German Americans.* Boston: Twayne Publishers, 1976.

_____. *Of German Ways.* New York: Barnes & Noble Books, 1980.

Rothan, Emmet. *The German Catholic Immigrant in the United States, 1830–1860.* Washington, D.C.: Catholic University Press, 1946.

Rupp, I. Daniel. *A Collection of Upwards of 30,000 Names of German, Swiss, Dutch, French, and Other Immigrants in Pennsylvania from 1726 to 1776.* Rev. and enl. Reprint. Philadelphia: Leary, Stewart, 1994.

Sallet, Richard. *The Russian German Settlements in the United States.* Translated by J. Rippley and Armand Bauer. Fargo, N.D.: Institute for Regional Studies, 1974.

Schenk, Trudy, Ruth Froelke, and Inge Bork. *The Wuerttemberg Emigration Index.* 6 vols. to date. Salt Lake City: Ancestry, 1986–.

Schweitzer, George K. *German Genealogical Research.* The author, 1992.

Smelser, Ronald M. *Finding Your German Ancestors.* Salt Lake City: Ancestry, 1991.

Smith, Clifford Neal, and Anna Piszezan-Czaja Smith. *American Genealogical Resources in German Archives.* Munich, Germany: Verlag Documentation, 1977.

Strassburger, Ralph B., and William John Hinke. *Pennsylvania German Pioneers: A Publication of Original Lists of Arrivals in the Port of Philadelphia From 1727 to 1808.* Norristown, Pa.: Pennsylvania German Society, 1934.

Stumpp, Karl. *The Emigration From Germany to Russia in the*

Years 1763–1862. Reprint, Lincoln, Neb.: American Historical Society of Germans from Russia, 1978.

Thode, Ernest. *Address Book for Germanic Genealogy.* 5th ed. Baltimore: Genealogical Publishing Co., 1994.

_____. *German-English Genealogical Dictionary.* Baltimore: Genealogical Publishing Co., 1992.

Tolzmann, Don Heinrich. *German Americans: A Bibliography.* Metuchen, N.J.: Scarecrow Press, 1975.

Walker, Mack. *Germany and the Emigration, 1816–1885.* Cambridge, Mass.: Harvard University Press, 1964.

Wellauer, M. *German Immigration to America in the Nineteenth Century: A Genealogist's Guide.* Milwaukee: the author, 1985.

_____. *Family History Research in the German Democratic Republic.* Milwaukee: the author, 1987.

_____. *Record Keeping and Archives in West Germany.* Milwaukee: the author, 1987.

Wittke, Carl F. *German-Language Press in America.* Louisville: University of Kentucky Press, 1957.

Wood, Ralph, ed. *The Pennsylvania Germans.* Princeton, N.J.: Princeton University Press, 1942.

Wolfert, Marion, comp. *German Immigrants: Lists of Passengers Bound From Bremen to New York, 1868–1871, With Places of Origin.* Vol. 4. Baltimore: Genealogical Publishing Co., 1993.

Wust, Klaus. *The Virginia Germans.* Charlottesville: University of Virginia Press, 1969.

Yoder, Don, ed. *Pennsylvania German Immigrants, 1709–1786.* Baltimore: Genealogical Publishing Co., 1989.

Zimmermann, Gary J., and Marion Wolfert, comp. *German Immigrants: Lists of Passengers Bound From Bremen to New York, 1847–1867, With Places of Origin.* 3 vols. Baltimore: Genealogical Publishing Co., 1985–88.

Germans From Russia

Miller, Michael M., comp. *Researching the Germans From Russia: Annotated Bibliography of the Germans From Russia Heritage Collection.* Fargo: North Dakota Institute for Regional Studies, North Dakota State University, 1987.

Greeks

Adamic, Louis. "Americans from Greece." In *A Nation of Nations.* New York: Harper, 1945.

Burgess, T. *Greeks in America.* 1913. Reprint. New York: Arno Press, 1975.

Cutsumbis, Michael. *A Bibliographic Guide to Materials on Greeks in the United States, 1890–1968.* New York: Center for Migration Studies, 1970.

Fenton, Heike, and Melvin Heckler. *The Greeks in America, 1528–1977.* Dobbs Ferry, N.Y.: Oceana Publications, 1978.

Holden, David. *Greece Without Columns: The Making of Modern Greece.* Philadelphia: J.B. Lippincott Co., 1972.

Saloutos, Theodore. *The Greeks in the United States.* Cambridge: Harvard University Press, 1964.

_____. *They Remember America: The Story of the Repatriated Greek-Americans.* Berkeley: University of California Press, 1956.

Woodhouse, C.M. *A Short History of Modern Greece.* New York: Praeger Publishers, 1968.

Xenides, J.P. *The Greeks in America.* New York: George H. Doran Co., 1922.

Zotos, Stephanos. *Hellenic Presence in America.* Wheaton, Ill: Pilgrimage, 1976.

Hispanic (also see Mexican and Puerto Rican)

The Society of Hispanic Historical and Ancestral Research (SHHAR)
P.O. Box 5394
Fullerton, CA 92635

Beers, Henry Putney. *Spanish and Mexican Records of the American Southwest.* Tucson: University of Arizona Press, 1979.

De Platt, Lyman. "Hispanic-American Records and Research." In *Ethnic Genealogy: A Research Guide.* Edited by Jessie Carney Smith. Westport, Conn.: Greenwood Press, 1983.

Flores, Norma, and Patsy Ludwig. *A Beginner's Guide to Hispanic Genealogy: Introduccion a la Investigacion Genealogica Latino Americana.* San Mateo, Calif.: 1993.

Ryskamp, George. *Tracing Your Hispanic Heritage.* Hispanic Family History Research, 1984.

Hungarian

Babo, Elemer. *Guide to Hungarian Studies. A Bibliography.* 2 vols. Stanford: Hoover Institute Press, 1973.

Benkart, Paula Kaye. "Religion, Family, and Community Among Hungarians Migrating to American Cities, 1880–1930." Ph.D. dissertation, Johns Hopkins University, 1975.

Gunda, Bela. "The Ethno-Sociological Structure of the Hungarian Extended Family." *Journal of Family History* 7 (Spring 1982): 40–51.

Gracza, Rezsoe, and Margaret Gracza. *The Hungarians in America.* Minneapolis: Lerner Publications Co., 1969.

Hanzell, Victor E. *The Hungarians.* Human Relations Area Files. New Haven, Conn.: Yale University, 1955.

Hungarians in the U.S.A.: An Immigration Study. St. Louis: The American Hungarian Review, 1967.

Korosfoy, John. *Hungarians in America.* Cleveland: Szabadsag, 1941.

Lengyel, Emil. *Americans from Hungary.* Westport: Greenwood Press, 1975.

Puskas, Julianna. *From Hungary to the United States, 1880–1914.* Budapest: Akademiai Kiado, 1982.

Szeplaki, Joseph. *The Hungarians in America, 1583–1974.* Oceana Publications, 1975.

Vardy, Steven Bela. *The Hungarian Americans.* New York: Chelsea House Publishing, 1990.

Icelandic

Stefansson, V. *Iceland: The First American Republic.* 1939. Reprint. Westport, Conn.: Greenwood Press, 1971.

Irish

American Irish Historical Society
991 Fifth Ave.
New York, NY 10028
212-288-2263

Publishes *The Recorder*

Irish Family Names Society
P.O. Box 2095
La Mesa, CA 92041
619-466-8739

Publishes a newsletter

The Irish at Home and Abroad
P.O. Box 521806
Salt Lake City, UT 84152
Fax: 801-467-6507

Publishes *The Irish at Home and Abroad*

Adams, W.F. *Ireland and Irish Emigration to the New World: From 1815 to the Famine.* New Haven, Conn., 1932.

Begley, D.F. *Irish Genealogy: A Record Finder.* Dublin: Heraldic Artists, 1981.

Betit, Kyle J., and Dwight A. Radford. *Ireland: A Genealogical Guide for North Americans.* 2nd ed. Salt Lake City: The Irish at Home and Abroad, 1995.

Blessing, Patrick J. *The Irish in America: A Guide to the Literature and Manuscript Collections.* Washington, D.C.: Catholic University of America Press, 1992.

Byrne, Stephen. *Irish Emigration to the United States.* New York: Arno Press, 1969.

Clark, Dennis. *Hibernia America: The Irish and Regional Cultures.* Westport, Conn.: Greenwood Press, 1986.

Cooper, Brian E., ed. *The Irish American Almanac and Green Pages.* Rev. and enl. New York: Harper and Row, 1990.

Crawford, E. Margaret. *Famine: The Irish Experience 900–1900.* Edinburgh: John Donald Publishers, 1989.

Curtis, Edmund. *A History of Ireland.* London: Methuen, 1968.

Delaney, Mary. *Of Irish Ways.* Minneapolis: Dillon Press, 1973.

Dickson, R.J. *Ulster Emigration to Colonial America, 1718–1775.* London: Routledge and Kegan Paul, 1966.

Diner, Hasia R. *Erin's Daughters in America.* Baltimore: Johns Hopkins University Press, 1983.

Dolan, Jay P. *The Immigrant Church: New York Irish and German Catholics.* Baltimore: Johns Hopkins University Press, 1975.

Doyle, David N. "The Regional Bibliography of Irish America, 1800–1930; Selected Readings, A Review and Addendum." *Irish Historical Studies* 23 (1983): 254–83.

_____. *Irish Americans, Native Rights, and National Empires.* New York: Arno Press, 1976.

Drudy, P.J., ed. *The Irish in America: Emigration, Assimilation and Impact.* London: Cambridge University Press, 1985.

Duff, John B. *Irish in the United States.* Belmont, Calif.: Wadsworth, 1971.

Falley, Margaret Dickson. *Irish and Scotch-Irish Ancestral Research.* 2 vols. Evanston, Ill.: Reprint. Baltimore: Genealogical Publishing Co., 1984.

Fallows, Marjorie. *Irish Americans: Identity and Assimilation.* Englewood Cliffs, N.J.: Prentice-Hall, 1977.

Fitzgerald, Margaret E., and Joseph A. King. *The Uncounted Irish in Canada and the United States.* Toronto: P.D. Meany Publishers, 1990.

Glazer, Michael A., and Michael Tepper, eds. *The Famine Immigrants: Lists of Irish Immigrants Arriving at the Port of New York 1846–1851.* 7 vols. Baltimore: Genealogical Publishing Co., 1983–87.

Greeley, Andrew M. *The Irish Americans: The Rise to Money and Power.* New York: Harper and Row, 1981.

_____. *That Most Distressful Nation: The Taming of the American Irish.* Chicago: Quadrangle Books, 1972.

Greenham, John. *Tracing Your Irish Ancestors.* Dublin: Gill and Macmillan, 1992.

Griffin, William D., comp. *The Irish in America.* Dobbs Ferry, N.Y.: 1973.

_____. *A Portrait of the Irish in America.* New York: Charles Scribner's Sons, 1981.

Harris, Ruth Ann M. "The Nearest Place Which Wasn't Ireland: A Study of Pre-Famine Irish Circular Migration to Britain." Ph.D. dissertation, Tufts University, 1980.

_____, and Donald M. Jacobs, eds. *The Search for Missing Friends: Irish Immigrant Advertisements Placed in the Boston Pilot.* 3 vols. Boston: New England Historic Genealogical Society, 1989–94.

Hoobler, Dorothy, and Thomas Hoobler. *The Irish American Family Album.* New York: Oxford University Press, 1994.

Kennedy, Robert E. *The Irish: Emigration, Marriage and Fertility.* Berkeley: University of California Press, 1973.

Lees, Lynn Hollen. *Exiles of Erin: Irish Migrants in Victorian London.* Ithaca, N.Y.: Cornell University Press, 1979.

MacDonagh, Oliver. "The Irish Famine Emigration to the United States." *Perspectives in American History* 10 (1976): 357–446.

Maclysaght, Edward. *Irish Families: Their Names, Arms, and Origins.* New York: Crown, 1972.

Maguire, John Francis. *The Irish in America.* New York: Arno Press, 1969.

McCaffrey, Lawrence. *The Irish Diaspora in America.* Bloomington: Indiana University, 1978.

Metress, Seamus P. *The American Irish and Irish Nationalism: A Sociohistorical Introduction.* Lanham, Md.: Scarecrow Press, 1995.

_____. *A Regional Guide to Informational Sources on the Irish in the United States and Canada.* Monticello, Ill: Vance Bibliographies, 1986.

Miller, Kerby. *Emigrants and Exiles: Ireland and the Irish Exodus in North America.* New York and London: Oxford University Press, 1985.

Mitchell, Brian. *Pocket Guide to Irish Genealogy.* Baltimore: Clearfield Co., 1991.

O'Day, Edward J. "Tracking Irish Immigrant Ancestors." *Illinois State Genealogical Society Quarterly* 16 (4) (Winter 1984): 192–97; 17 (1) (Spring 1985): 31–32.

O'Grady, J.P. *Irish-Americans and Anglo-American Relations, 1880–1888.* New York: Arno Press, 1976.

O'Grady, Joseph P. *How the Irish Became Americans.* New York: Twayne, 1973.

Rugg, John D. "Brighter Skies Forecast for Irish Researchers." *Ancestry Newsletter* 6 (5) (September–October 1988): 4–6.

Ryan, James G. *Irish Records: Sources for Family and Local History.* Salt Lake City: Ancestry, 1988.

_____, ed. *Irish Church Records: Their History, Availability and Use in Family and Local History Research.* Dublin, Ireland: Flyleaf Press, 1992.

_____. *A Guide to Tracing Your Dublin Ancestors.* Dublin, Ireland: Flyleaf Press, 1988.

Schrier, Arnold. *Ireland and the American Immigration, 1850–1900.* 1958. Reprint. New York: Russell and Russell, 1970.

Shannon, William V. *The American Irish: A Political and Social Portrait.* Rev. ed. 1967. Reprint. New York, 1974.

Wittke, Carl F. *The Irish in America.* New York: Russell and Russell, 1956. Reprint. Louisiana State University Press, 1970.

_____. "Erin Research: It Takes More Than the Luck o' the Irish."

Ancestry Newsletter 6 (5) (September–October 1988): 1–2.

_____. *A Guide to Tracing Your Dublin Ancestors.* Dublin: Flyleaf Press, 1988.

Yurdan, Marilyn. *Irish Family History.* Baltimore: Genealogical Publishing Co., 1990.

Italian

Italian Genealogical Group

7 Grayson Dr.

Dix Hills, NY 11746

POINT (Pursuing Our Italian Names Together)

P.O. Box 2977

Palos Verdes Peninsula, CA 90274

Barzini, Luigi. *The Italians.* New York: Atheneum, 1964.

Briggs, John W. *An Italian Passage: Immigrants to Three American Cities, 1890–1930.* New Haven, Conn.: Yale University Press, 1978.

Cole, Trafford R. *Italian Genealogical Records: How to Use Italian Civil, Ecclesiastical, and Other Records in Family History Research.* Salt Lake City: Ancestry, 1995.

Cordasco, Francesco. *A Bibliographic Guide to the Bollettino Dell'Emigrazione, 1902–1927.* Totowa, N.J.: Rowen and Littlefield, 1979.

_____, ed. *Studies in Italian American Social History.* Totowa, N.J.: Rowman and Littlefield, 1975.

_____, ed. *Italian Immigrants Abroad: A Bibliography.* Detroit: Blaine Ethridge, 1979.

_____. *Italian Americans: A Guide to Information Sources.* Detroit: Gale Research Co., 1978.

_____, and Eugene Bucchioni, eds. *The Italians: Social Backgrounds of an American Group.* Clifton, N.J.: Augustus Kelley Publishers, 1974.

DeConde, Alexander. *Half Bitter, Half Sweet: An Excursion into Italian-American History.* New York: Charles Scribner's Sons, 1971.

De Angelis, Priscilla G. "A Look at Italian-American Research Sources." *Ancestry Newsletter* 8 (1) (January–February 1990): 3–9.

Dore, Grazia. *Bibliografia Per la Storia Dell'Emigrazione Italiano in America.* Rome, 1956.

Foerster, Robert F. *The Italian Emigration of Our Times.* Cambridge, Mass.: Harvard University Press, 1919.

Gallo, Patrick J. *Old Bread, New Wine: A Portrait of the Italian Americans.* Chicago: Nelson-Hall, 1982.

Gabaccia, Donna R. *From Italy to Elizabeth Street.* Albany: SUNY Press, 1983.

Gli Italiani Negli Stati-Uniti d'America 1906 [Italians in the United States in 1906]. Italian-American Directory Col., 1906.

_____. *Italian Americans: A Guide to Information Sources.* Chicago: Gale Research Co., 1978.

Hoobler, Dorothy, and Thomas Hoobler. *The Italian American Family Album.* Oxford University Press, 1994.

Italians in the United States: A Repository of Rare Tracts and Miscellanea. New York: Arno Press, 1975.

Lo Gatto, A.F. *The Italians in America.* Dobbs Ferry, N.Y.: Oceana Publications, 1972.

Moquin, W., and D. Van Doren. *A Documentary History of the Italian-Americans.* New York: Praeger, 1974.

Null, G., and C. Stone. *The Italian Americans.* Harrisburg, Pa.: Stackpole Books, 1976.

Pisani, L.F. *The Italian in America.* New York: Exposition Press, 1957.

Rolle, Andrew F. *The American Italians: Their History and Culture.* Belmont, Calif.: Wadsworth Publishing Co., 1972.

Salvadori, Massimo. *Italy.* Englewood Cliffs, N.J.: Prentice-Hall, 1965.

Schiavo, G. *Four Centuries of Italian American History.* New York: Vigo, 1958.

Schiavo, Giovanni Ermenegildo. *The Italians in America Before the Civil War.* New York: Arno Press, 1975.

Smith, Denis Mack. *Italy: A Modern History.* Ann Arbor: University of Michigan Press, 1969.

Tomasi, Silvano, and Madeline Engel, eds. *The Italian Experience in the United States.* New York: Center for Migration Studies, 1970.

Trevelyan, J.P. *A Short History of the Italian People: From the Barbarian Invasions to the Present Day.* New York: Pitman Publishing, 1956.

Japanese
Ichihashi, Yamato. *Japanese in the United States.* New York: Arno Press, 1969.

Kitano, Harry. *Japanese-Americans: The Evolution of a Subculture.* Englewood Cliffs, N.J.: Prentice-Hall, 1969.

Masako, H. *The Japanese in America, 1843–1973.* Dobbs Ferry, N.Y.: Oceana Publications, 1974.

Peterson, William. *Japanese Americans: Oppression and Success.* New York: Random House, 1971.

Wakatsuki, Yasuo. "The Japanese Emigration to the United States, 1866–1924: A Monograph." *Perspectives in American History* 12 (1979): 389–516.

Latvian
Akmentins, O. *Latvians in Bicentennial America.* Latvju Gramata, 1976.

Karklis, M., et al. *The Latvians in America, 1640–1973.* Dobbs Ferry, N.Y.: Oceana Publications, 1974.

Lebanese and Syrian
Hitti, Philip K. *Syrians in America.* New York: George H. Doran Co., 1924.

Kayal, Joseph. *The Syrian Lebanese in America.* Boston: Twayne, 1975.

Wakin, Edward. *The Lebanese and Syrians in America.* Chicago: Claretian, 1971.

Lithuanian
Balys, J. *Lithuania and Lithuanians: A Selected Bibliography.* New York: Praeger, 1961.

Daraska, Jessie L. "The Immigration History and Genealogy Department of the Balzekas Museum of Lithuanian Culture." *Illinois Libraries* 74 (5) (November 1992).

Budreckis, A.M. *The Lithuanians in America, 1651–1975: A Chronology and Fact Book.* Dobbs Ferry, N.Y.: Oceana Publications, 1976.

Kucas, A. *Lithuanians in America.* San Francisco: R & E Research Associates, n.d.

Roucek, J.S. *American Lithuanians.* New York: Lithuanian Alliance of America, 1940.

Mexican
Camarillo, Albert. *Chicanos in a Changing Society: From Mexican Pueblos to American Barrios in Santa Barbara and Southern California, 1848–1930.* Cambridge, Mass.: Harvard University Press, 1979.

Cardosa, Lawrence. *Mexican Emigration to the United States, 1897–1931.* Tucson: University of Arizona Press, 1980.

Cortes, Carlos, ed. *The Mexican American: Mexican American Bibliographies.* New York: Arno Press, 1974.

Corwin, Arthur F. "Causes of Mexican Emigration to the United States: A Summary View." *Perspectives in American History* 7 (1973): 557–635.

Gamino, Manuel. *El Immigrante Mexicano: La Historia de su Vida.* Mexico City: Universidad Nacional Autonoma de Mexico, 1969.

Garcia, Richard A. *The Chicanos in America, 1540–1974.* Dobbs Ferry, N.Y.: Oceana Publications, 1977.

Hoobler, Dorothy, and Thomas Hoobler. *The Mexican American Family Album.* New York: Oxford University Press, 1994.

Martinez, J. *Mexican Emigration to the U.S.* San Francisco: R & E Research Associates, 1971.

McWilliams, Carey. *North From Mexico: The Spanish Speaking People of the United States.* Contributions in American History, no. 140. Rev. ed. New York: Greenwood Press, 1990.

Meier, Matt S. *Bibliography of Mexican American History.* Westport, Conn.: Greenwood Press, 1984.

_____. *The Chicanos: A History of Mexican-Americans.* New York: Hill and Wang, 1972.

_____, and Feliciano Rivera. *The Dictionary of Mexican-American History.* Westport, Conn.: Greenwood Press, 1981.

Pinchot, J. *The Mexicans in America.* Minneapolis: Lerner Publications, 1973.

Rosales, Francisco A. "Mexican Immigration to the Urban Midwest During the 1920s." Ph.D. dissertation, Indiana University, 1978.

Prago, Albert. *Strangers in Their Own Land: A History of Mexican-Americans.* New York: Four Winds Press, 1973.

Steiner, Stan. *La Raza: The Mexican Americans.* New York: Harper & Row, 1968.

Norwegian
Anderson, Arlow William. *The Norwegian-Americans.* Boston: Twayne, 1975.

Bergmann, Leola N. *Americans From Norway.* Philadelphia: J.B. Lippincott Co., 1950.

Blegen, Theodore Christian. *The Norwegian Migration to America. 1891–1969.* 2 vols. New York: Arno Press, 1969.

Moen, Margaret. "Information Wanted and Norwegian Genealogy." *Ancestry Newsletter* 7 (2) (March–April 1989): 7–10.

Morgan, Freeman E. "An Overview of Norwegian Naming Practices and the Extensive Changes Circa 1900." *Ancestry Newsletter* 5 (6) (November–December 1987).

Qualey, Carlton Chester. *Norwegian Settlement in the United States.* New York: Arno Press, 1970.

Smith, Frank, and Finn A. Thomsen. *Genealogical Guidebook and Atlas of Norway.* Logan, Utah: The Everton Publishers, 1979.

Ulvestad, Martin. *Nordmændene i Amerika* [Norwegians in America]. 2 vols. Minneapolis: History Book Company's Forlag, 1907–10.

Wellauer, Maralyn A. *Tracing Your Norwegian Roots.* Milwaukee: the author, 1979.

Polish

Baker, T. Lindsay. *The First Polish Americans.* College Station, Tex.: A & M University Press, 1979.

Bolek, F., and L.J. Siekaniec. *Polish American Encyclopedia.* Buffalo: Polish American Encyclopedia Committee, 1954.

Bolek, F. *Who's Who in Polish America.* 1943. Reprint. New York: Arno Press, 1970.

Brozek, Andrzej. *Polonia Amerykaska: The American Polonia.* Warsaw, Poland: Interpress Publications, 1980.

Bukowczyk, John J. *And My Children Did Not Know Me.* Bloomington: Indiana University Press, 1987. A history of the Polish experience in America.

Chorzempa, Rosemary A. *Korzenie Polskie: Polish Roots.* Baltimore: Genealogical Publishing Co., 1993.

Janowska, Halina. "An Introductory Outline of the Mass Movement of Polish Emigrants: Their Directions and Problems, 1870–1945." In *Employment-Seeking Emigration of the Poles World Wide, XIX and XX Centuries.* Edited by Celina Bobinska and Andrzej Pilch. Krakow, Poland: Panstowe Wydawni Naukowe, 1975.

Hoskins, Janina W. *Polish Genealogy and Heraldry: An Introduction to Research.* New York: Hippocrene Books, 1990.

Lopata, H. Z. *Polish Americans.* Englewood Cliffs, N.J.: Prentice-Hall, 1976.

_____. *Poland and the Poles in America.* Chicago: Polish American Congress, 1971.

Murdzek, Benjamin P. *Emigration in Polish Social-Political Thought, 1870–1914.* New York: Columbia University Press, 1977.

Obal, Thaddeus J. *A Bibliography for Genealogical Research Involving Polish Ancestry.* Hillsdale, N.J.: the author, 1978.

Ortell, Gerald A. *Polish Parish Records of the Roman Catholic Church: Their Use and Understanding in Genealogical Research.* Buffalo Grove, Ill.: Genun Publishers, 1979.

Renkiewicz, F.A. *The Poles in America, 1608–1972.* Dobbs Ferry, N.Y.: Oceana Publications, 1973.

Rosicky, Rose. *A History of Czechs (Bohemians) in Nebraska.* Omaha: Czech Historical Society of Nebraska, 1929.

Thomas, William I., and Florian Znaniecki. *The Polish Peasant in Europe and America.* New York: Dover Publications, 1958.

Toor, Rachel. *The Polish Americans.* New York: Chelsea House, 1988.

Wandycz, D.S. *Register of Polish American Scholars, Scientists, Writers, and Artists.* New York: Polish Institute of Arts and Sciences in America, 1969.

Wellauer, Malalyn A. *Tracing Your Polish Roots.* Milwaukee: the author, 1979.

Wieczerzak, J.W. *A Polish Chapter in Civil War America.* New York: Twayne, 1967.

Wytrwal, Joseph Anthony. *America's Polish Heritage.* Detroit: Endurance Press, 1961.

_____. *The Poles in America.* Minneapolis: Lerner, 1969.

Zurawski, Joseph W. *Polish American History and Culture: A Classified Bibliography.* Chicago: Polish Museum of America, 1975.

Portuguese

Bertao, David E. "Portuguese Parish Registers: A Genealogical and Historical Examination." *Ancestry Newsletter* 6 (3) (May–June 1988): 8–9.

Cardozo, Manoel DaSilveira Soares. *The Portuguese in America, 590 B.C.–1974.* Dobbs Ferry, N.Y.: Oceana Publications, 1976.

DosPassos, John. *The Portugal Story: Three Centuries of Exploration and Discovery.* New York: Doubleday & Co., 1969.

Ley, Charles David. "Portuguese in America." *Literary Digest* 63 (22 November 1919).

Livermore, H.V. *A Short History of Portugal.* Chicago: Aldine Publishing Co., 1973.

Tuohy, Frank, and Graham Finlayson. *Portugal.* New York: Viking Press, 1970.

Puerto Rican

Cordasco, Francesco. *The Puerto Ricans, 1493–1973.* Dobbs Ferry, N.Y.: Oceana Publications, 1973.

Larsen, Ronald J. *The Puerto Ricans in America.* Minneapolis: Lerner, 1973.

Romanian

Galitzi, Christine Avghi. *A Study of Assimilation Among the Roumanians of the United States.* Columbia Press, 1929.

Tigan, Joseph R. "Romanian-American Resources," *Ancestry Newsletter* 7 (4) (July–August 1990): 13–14.

Wertsman, Vladimir. *The Romanians in America, 1748–1974.* Dobbs Ferry, N.Y.: Oceana Publications, 1975.

Russian

David, J. *The Russian Immigrant.* 1922. Reprint. New York: Macmillan, 1969.

Glazier, Ira A. *Migration From the Russian Empire: Lists of*

Passengers Arriving at the Port of New York. Baltimore: Genealogical Publishing Co., 1995–.

Eubank, N. *The Russians in America.* Minneapolis: Lerner Publications, 1973.

Hutchinson, E.P. *Immigrants and Their Children: 1850–1950.* New York: John Wiley and Sons, 1956.

Riasanovsky, Nicholas V. *A History of Russia.* 2nd ed. New York: Oxford University Press, 1969.

Sack, Sallyann Amdur, and Suzan Fishl Wynne. *The Russian Consular Records Index and Catalog.* New York: Garland Publishing, 1987.

Wertsman, V. *The Russians in America: A Chronology and Fact Book.* Dobbs Ferry, N.Y.: Oceana Publications, 1977.

Scandinavian

Fonkalsrud, Alfred O. *The Scandinavian-American.* San Francisco: R & E Research Associates, 1973.

Furer, Howard B. *The Scandinavian in America, 986–1970.* Dobbs Ferry, N.Y.: Oceana Publications, 1972.

Malmberg, Carl. *American Is Also Scandinavian.* New York: Putnam, 1970.

Nelson, O.N. *History of the Scandinavians and Successful Scandinavians in the U.S.A.* 1904. Reprint. New York: Haskell House, 1969.

Scotch-Irish

Campbell, R.G. *Scotch Irish Family Research Made Simple.* Munroe Falls, Ohio: Summit Publications, 1974.

Dickson, R.J. *Ulster Emigration to Colonial America, 1718–1775.* London: Routledge and Kegan Paul, 1966.

Ford, Henry Jones. *The Scotch Irish in America.* 1915. Reprint. New York: Arno Press, 1969.

Johnson, James E. *Scots and Scotch Irish in America.* Minneapolis: Lerner, 1966.

Leyburn, James G. *The Scotch-Irish: A Social History.* Chapel Hill: The University of North Carolina Press, 1962.

Reid, Whitelaw. *The Scot in America and the Ulster Scot.* San Francisco: R & E Research Associates, 1970 (reprint of 1911 address).

The Scotch-Irish in America. Proceedings and Addresses. Cincinnati: R. Clark and Co., 1889–1901.

Stephenson, Jean. *Scotch-Irish Migration to South Carolina, 1772: Reverend William Martin and His Five Shiploads of Settlers.* Strasburg, Va.: Shenandoah Publishing House, 1971.

Scottish

Black, G.F. *Scotland's Mark on America.* 1921. Reprint. San Francisco: R & E Research Associates, 1972.

Black, George F. *The Surnames of Scotland.* New York: New York Public Library, 1946.

Cory, Kathleen B. *Tracing Your Scottish Ancestry.* Edinburgh, 1990.

James, Alwyn. *Scottish Roots: A Step-by-Step Guide for Ancestor-hunters.* Gretna, La.: Pelican Publishing Co., 1981.

Erickson, Charlotte, *Invisible Immigrants: The Adaptation of English and Scottish Immigrants in Nineteenth-Century America.* Coral Gables, Fla.: University of Miami Press, 1972.

Ferguson, Joan P.S. *Scottish Family Histories Held in Scottish Libraries.* Edinburgh: Scottish Central Library, 1960.

Gray, Malcolm. "Scottish Emigration: The Social Impact of Agrarian Change in the Rural Lowlands, 1775–1875." *Perspectives in American History* 7 (1973): 95–174.

Lamont-Brown, Raymond. "A Quick Guide to Tracing Your Scottish Forbears." *Ancestry Newsletter* 9 (1) (January–February 1991): 10–12.

Slavic

Balch, Emily. *Our Slavic Fellow Citizens.* New York: Arno Press, 1969.

Gimbutas, Marija. *The Slavs.* New York: Praeger, 1971.

Pehotsky, Bessie Olga. *The Slavic Woman.* San Francisco: R & E Research Associates, 1974.

Portal, Roger. *The Slavs.* New York: Harper & Row, 1969.

Roucek, Joseph S. *Slavonic Encyclopedia.* 1949. Reprint. Port Washington: Kennikat Press, 1969.

_____. *American Slavs: A Bibliography.* New York: Bureau of Intercultural Education, 1944. Reprint. The author, 1970.

Slovak

Bogatyrev, Petr. *The Functions of Folk Costume in Moravian Slovakia.* The Hague, The Netherlands: Mouton, 1971.

Miller, K.D. *The Czecho-Slovaks in America.* New York: Doran, 1922.

Roucek, J. S. *The Czechs and Slovaks in America.* Minneapolis: Lerner Publications, 1967.

Stasko, J. *Slovaks in the United States of America.* Cambridge: Dobra Kniha, 1974.

Stolarik, M. Mark. *The Slovak Americans.* New York: Chelsea House, 1988.

Slovenian

Prisland, Marie. *From Slovenia in America.* Chicago: Slovenian Women's Union of America, 1968.

Prpic, George P. *On South Slav Immigrants in America and Their Historical Background.* Cleveland: John Carroll University, 1972.

Swedish

American Swedish Historical Foundation
1900 Pattison Ave.
Philadelphia, PA 19145
215-389-1776

Publishes a newsletter

National Council of the Swedish Cultural Society in America
1123 South Courtland Ave.
Park Ridge, IL 60068
708-825-8408

Publishes *Swedish Heritage*

Swedish American Genealogist
P.O. Box 2186
Winter Park, FL 32790

Publishes *Swedish American Genealogist*

Swedish Historical Society
404 S. Third St.
Rockford, IL 61104
815-963-5559

Publishes *Swedish Heritage*

Swedish Pioneer Historical Society
5125 N. Spaulding Ave.
Chicago, IL 60625
312-583-5722

Publishes *Swedish Pioneer Historical Quarterly*

Swenson Swedish Immigration Research Center
Augustana College
3520 Seventh Ave.
P.O. Box 175
Rock Island, IL 61201
309-794-7204

Publishes *Swenson Center News*. The Swenson Swedish Immigration Research Center also has Swedish church records on microfilm.

Beijbom, Ulf. *Swedes in Chicago: A Demographic and Social Study of the 1946–1880 Immigration*. Stockholm: Laromedelsforlagen and Chicago Historical Society, 1971.

Benson, Adolph B., and Naboth Hedin. *Americans From Sweden*. Philadelphia: Lippincott, 1950.

Hasselmo, Nils. *Swedish America: An Introduction*. New York: Swedish Information Service, 1976.

Janson, Florence E. *The Background of Swedish Immigration*. Chicago: University of Chicago Press, 1931.

Johansson, Carl-Erik. *Cradled in Sweden*. Logan, Utah: The Everton Publishers, 1979.

Johnson, Timothy J. "Swedish-American Genealogy and the Archives at North Park College." *Illinois Libraries* 74 (5) (November 1992): 446–48.

Kastrup, Allan. *The Swedish Heritage in America*. Minneapolis: Swedish Council of America, 1975.

Lindberg, John S. *The Background of Swedish Emigration to the United States*. Minneapolis: University of Minnesota Press, 1930.

Lorenzen, Lilly. *Of Swedish Ways*. New York: Barnes & Noble Books, 1964.

Nelson, Helge. *The Swedes and Swedish Settlements in North America*. 2 vols. New York: 1943.

Nilsson, Fred. *Emigration fran Stockholm till Nordamerika 1880–1893*. Stockholm, Sweden: Studia Historica Upsaliensia, 1970.

Olsson, Nils William. *Tracing Your Swedish Ancestry*. Sweden: Swedish Institute, 1982.

Runblom, Harold, and Hans Norman. *From Sweden to America: A History of the Migration*. Minneapolis: University of Minnesota Press and Uppsala: Acta Universitatis Upsaliensis, 1976.

Svensk-Amerikansha Kyrkoarkiv Med Canada. Växjö, Sweden: Emigrantinstitutet, 1979.

Westman, E. *The Swedish Element in America*. Biograph Society, 1931.

Westerberg, Kermit B. "Genealogical Research and Resources at the Swenson Swedish Immigration Research Center." *Illinois Libraries* 74 (5) (November 1992): 443–46.

Swiss

Eyster, Anita L. "Notices by German and Swiss Settlers Seeking Information of Members of their Families, Kindred, and Friends Inserted between 1742–1761 in *Pennsylvania Berichte* and 1762–1779 in the *Pennsylvania Staatsbote*." *Pennsylvania German Folklore Society* 3 (1938): 32–41.

Kuhns, L. *German and Swiss Settlements of Colonial America*. Holt, 1901.

Rupp, I. Daniel. *A Collection of Upwards of 30,000 Names of German, Swiss, Dutch, French, and Other Immigrants in Pennsylvania From 1726 to 1776*. Rev. and enl. Reprint. Philadelphia: Leary, Stewart, 1994.

Schelberd, Lev. *Swiss Migration to America*. Arno, 1981.

Von Grueningen, John. *Swiss in the United States*. Swiss Historical Society, 1940.

Wellauer, Maralyn M. *Tracing Your Swiss Roots*. Milwaukee: the author, 1979.

Ukrainian

Chyz, Yaroslaw J. *The Ukrainian Immigrants in the United States*. Scranton, Pa.: Ukrainian Workingmen's Association, 1940.

Halich, Wasyl. *Ukrainians in the United States*. New York: Arno Press, 1970.

Kubijovic, Volodymyr. *Ukraine: A Concise Encyclopedia*. Toronto: University of Toronto Press, 1963.

Kuropas, M. *Ukrainians in America*. Minneapolis: Lerner Publications, 1972.

Shtohryn, D.M. *Ukrainians in North America: A Biographical Directory of Noteworthy Men and Women of Ukrainian Origin in the United States and Canada*. Champaign: Association for the Advancement of Ukrainian Studies, 1975.

Wrestman V. *The Ukrainians in America, 1608–1975. A*

Chronology and Fact Book. Dobbs Ferry, N.Y.: Oceana Publications, n.d.

Welsh

Conway, Alan. "The Welsh Emigration to the United States." *Perspectives in American History* 7 (1973): 177–271.

Yugoslavian

Colakovic, Branko Mita. *Yugoslav Migrations to America.* San Francisco: R & E Research Associates, 1973.

Eterovich, A.S. *A Guide and Bibliography to Research on Yugoslavs in the United States and Canada.* San Francisco: R & E Research Associates, 1973.

Some U.S. Passenger Arrival Lists Available on Microfilm

The following list was adapted from *Immigrant and Passenger Arrivals: A Select Catalog of National Archives Microfilm Publications,* 2nd ed. (Washington, D.C.: National Archives Trust Fund Board, National Archives Records Administration, 1991).

Indexes exist for years marked by asterisks. For some ports, indexes cover a longer time period than do the microfilmed passenger lists. In other instances, such as New York, indexes have not been created for all years for which passenger lists are available. There are time gaps in some cases, usually because lists are missing for those years. Date overlaps for some ports on this list generally mean that more than one set of passenger lists are available, and that the lists and/or indexes were created by different agencies. Some lists are incomplete, as indicated by the notation "(gaps)." Some small ports included on this list have been indexed and microfilmed together in a series titled *A Supplemental Index to Passenger Lists of Vessels Arriving at Atlantic and Gulf Coast Ports (Excluding New York), 1820-1874.*

This list is intended to provide a quick reference for determining ports and time frames for which passenger lists have been microfilmed and indexed. For further details see *Immigrant and Passenger Arrivals: A Select Catalog.*

Alexandria, Virginia 1820-65*

Annapolis, Maryland 1849*

Baltimore, Maryland 1820-1909, 1820-97*, 1897-1952*, 1954-57

Bangor, Maine 1848*

Barnstable, Maine 1820-26*

Bath, Maine 1825, 1827, 1832, 1867*

Beaufort, North Carolina 1865*

Belfast, Maine 1820-51*

Boston, Massachusetts 1820-91*, 1899-1940*, 1891-1943*

Bridgeport, Connecticut 1870*

Bristol and Warren, Rhode Island 1820-71*

Cape May, New Jersey 1828*

Charleston, South Carolina 1820-28*

Darien, Georgia 1823, 1825*

Detroit, Michigan 1906-54*, 1946-57

Dighton, Massachusetts 1820-36* (gaps)

East River, Virginia 1830*

Edenton, North Carolina 1820*

Edgartown, Massachusetts 1820-70*

Fairfield, Connecticut 1820-21*

Fall River, Massachusetts 1837-65* (gaps)

Frenchman's Bay, Maine 1821, 1826-27* (gaps)

Galveston, Texas 1846-71*, 1896-1906*, 1896-1951

Georgetown, D.C. 1820-21*

Gloucester, Massachusetts 1820, 1832-39, 1867-68, 1870*

Gulfport, Mississippi 1904-54

Hampton, Virginia 1820-21*

Hartford, Connecticut 1837*

Havre de Grace, Maryland 1820*

Hingham, Massachusetts 1852*

Kennebunk, Maine 1820-72*

Key West, Florida 1837-68*, 1898-1945*

Little Egg Harbor, New Jersey 1831*

Marblehead, Massachusetts 1820-36, 1849*

Mobile, Alabama 1832-52*

Nantucket, Massachusetts 1820-51, 1857-62*

Newark, New Jersey 1836*

New Bedford, Massachusetts 1826-52* (gaps), 1902-42*

New Bern, North Carolina 1820-45*, 1865*

Newburyport, Massachusetts 1821-39* (gaps)

New Haven, Connecticut 1820-73*

New London, Connecticut 1820-47*

New Orleans, Louisiana 1820-1903, 1820-50*, 1853-99*, 1900-52*

Newport, Rhode Island 1820-75* (gaps)

New York, New York 1820-97, 1820-46*, 1897-1957, 1897-1902*, 1902-43*, 1906-42*, 1944-48*

Norfolk and Portsmouth, Virginia 1820-57*

Oswegatchie, New York 1821-23*

Pascagoula, Mississippi 1903-35*

Passamaquoddy, Maine 1820-59*

Penobscot, Maine 1851*

Perth Amboy, New Jersey 1801-37* (gaps)

Petersburg, Virginia 1820-21*

Philadelphia, Pennsylvania 1800-82, 1800-1906*, 1883-1945, 1906-26*, 1883-1948*

Plymouth, Massachusetts 1821-36*, 1846*

Plymouth, North Carolina 1820, 1825, 1840*

Portland and Falmouth, Maine 1820-68* (gaps)

Portland, Maine 1893-1943, 1893-1954*

Port Royal, South Carolina 1865*

Portsmouth, New Hampshire 1820-61* (gaps)

Providence, Rhode Island 1820-67* (gaps), 1911-43, 1911-54*

Provincetown, Massachusetts 1887-89, 1893, 1895-96

Richmond, Virginia 1820-44* (gaps)

Rochester, New York 1866*

St. Albans, Vermont 1895-1952*, and Canadian entries through small ports in Vermont 1895-1924*

St. Augustine, Florida 1821-22*, 1824*, 1827*, 1870*

St. Johns, Florida 1865*

Sag Harbor, New York 1829*, 1832*, 1834*

Salem, Massachusetts 1865-66*

San Francisco, California 1893-1934*, 1893-1953, 1954-57

Sandusky, Ohio 1820*

Savannah, Georgia 1820-68*, 1906-45

Saybrook, Connecticut 1820*

Seattle, Washington, and other Washington ports 1882-1916, 1890-1957

Waldeboro, Maine 1820-21*, 1833*

Washington, North Carolina 1820-48* (gaps)

Wilmington, Delaware 1820-48*

Yarmouth, Maine 1820*

TRACKING NATIVE AMERICAN FAMILY HISTORY

CHAPTER CONTENTS

14

TRACKING NATIVE AMERICAN FAMILY HISTORY

Curt B. Witcher and George J. Nixon

INTRODUCTION

Curt B. Witcher

Native American genealogical research is among the most challenging and rewarding of historical research endeavors. Interest in the life patterns, religions, migration and settlement patterns—indeed, in the entire culture of these earliest inhabitants of the North American continent—remains high. There are numerous fundamental differences between the Native American and the European American cultures, and it is these differences that present the greatest challenge to the genealogist.

In beginning Native American genealogical research, it is important to employ a fundamentally sound research methodology—the same methodology that would be used in compiling any family history. Initially, family sources should be consulted for information about previous generations. These sources include all living relatives, family papers and scrapbooks, daybooks, photograph albums, and diaries (see chapter 1, The Foundations of Family History Research). Considering the very strong oral tradition among Native American peoples, special attention should be given to conducting thorough interviews of all relatives.

Sound research methodology mandates that one research from the present into the past, from more recent times to more distant times, building a solid case based on primary and excellent secondary sources. The temptation to begin with the records of a particular tribe and prove forward to a more contemporary ancestor should be avoided. Not only is proving forward more difficult, it does not afford one the opportunity to investigate the widest range of records. Further, it tempts one to make assumptions that are clearly not based on the preponderance of evidence.

Maintaining extensive and accurate records is essential for any genealogical endeavor, but especially so for Native American research. All places, dates, and other data associated with a potential ancestor should be recorded with appropriate documentation even if their relevance is unknown or unclear at the time. No piece of data about a potential ancestor is inconsequential.

Adhering to a defined series of research strategies is the most productive way to engage in Native American genealogical research. The researcher must be willing to employ research strategies in a sequence which gathers useful general material first, tribe-specific data second, and, finally, individual (person-specific) data and records. A successful research strategy could be outlined in a manner similar to the following:

1. Thoroughly investigate the areas where ancestral research is being considered for the identities, histories, and cultural attributes of the native peoples.

2. Employ a carefully constructed and consistently applied methodology for locating the greatest number of research documents and data on the tribe of the potential ancestor.

3. Work through all of the materials relating to a particular tribe or nation to obtain the fullest understanding of its peoples and the most complete individual-specific group of records.

This chapter details a number of sources which the Native American genealogical researcher may want to investigate in the process of establishing and documenting a family history.

GENERAL HISTORIES AND RECORDS

More so than in any other area of genealogical research, knowledge of general history is a crucial factor for the researcher of Native American family history. A good working knowledge of general history will ground one's research in the proper time period, identify a more defined geographic area in which to conduct research, maximize all potential record possibilities, greatly assist in establishing tribal affiliations, and lead to a fuller understanding of the Native American culture. Because Native American naming patterns, kinship terms, and intertribal relations typically were quite different from those experienced by European Americans, it is essential to place one's Native American research in a historical context. Only in the proper historical context, devoid of assumptions and stereotypes, can truly effective Native American genealogical research be conducted.

There are many bibliographies of Native American historical works that should be consulted by the researcher endeavoring to gather general and tribe-specific histories. These bibliographies are useful because they are numerous, rather widely available, and greatly assist the researcher in striving to gather a comprehensive collection of documents. Annotated bibliographies compiled by academic institutions and experts in the fields of Native American history, archaeology, culture, etc., often provide a more complete list of sources and easier methods of accessing the specific information. An example of such a work is one by Katherine M. Weist and Susan R. Sharrock, *An Annotated Bibliography of North Plains Ethnohistory* (Missoula: University of Montana, 1985). Besides the descriptive annotations provided in this work, many title entries contain a section entitled "other subjects" in which tribes covered by the particular work are listed, as well as major topics and subjects the author(s) encountered.

Establishing tribal affiliation should be a primary objective in the initial stages of Native American research. Determining the tribe of a potential ancestor is essential to continued research because the vast majority of records are grouped, published, and accessed by tribe, clan, or nation. There are several approaches the researcher may need to take in determining tribal affiliation. First, critically evaluate oral traditions and stories preserved and communicated through generations of family members. It is important to remember that recollections of actual events, people, and places tend to fade over time and may be changed or embellished to make individuals appear more favorable than they actually were or to hide less-than-honorable deeds.

Another approach is to engage in a survey of the general histories of a large geographic region or the continent, as well as general histories of the native peoples. Both dated and more recently published histories are useful. These general histories typically provide significant data on village locations and settlement patterns, hunting and gathering areas, and migration patterns. They assist the researcher in beginning to determine the tribe of a potential ancestor.

A remarkable compilation in the realm of general histories which details Native American life at the beginning of the twentieth century in words and photographs is Edward S. Curtis, *The North American Indian, Being a Series of Volumes Picturing and Describing the Indians of the United States and Alaska* (Cambridge, Mass.: The University Press, 1907–30). The twenty volumes of descriptive text and photographic plates are complemented by twenty folios of additional photographic images. This work has been reprinted and is available in microform formats.

Some of the classic works of Americana pertaining to early travel and the native peoples provide valuable background data that is essential to exploring all of the record possibilities for Native American research. Henry R. Schoolcraft, *Historical and Statistical Information Respecting the History, Conditions and Prospects of the Indian Tribes of the United States: Collected and Prepared under the Direction of the Bureau of Indian Affairs, per Act of Congress of March 3, 1847* (Philadelphia: Lippencott, Grambo & Company, 1851), published in six parts, is an excellent general history covering a variety of topics for numerous tribes including national and tribal histories, antiquities, geography, government, languages, biography, and art. This work has been reprinted several times and is available at many university and large public libraries.

A host of general histories published more recently provide the genealogical researcher with good background data. Eleanor Burke Leacock and Nancy Oestreich Lurie, *North American Indians in Historical Perspective* (Prospect Heights, Ill.: Waveland Press, 1971) is such a work. Its nearly five hundred heavily noted pages detail the history of the major native tribes and clans of North America. Placing the historical past of particular Native American groups into a more general historical context provides a research context more suitable for capitalizing on the record possibilities. General footnote sections, biographical notes, and references all provide the researcher with access to primary and documented secondary source materials. The origins of tribes are traced, with these historical recountings giving the researcher information on the groups who interacted with particular tribes. Most general histories can be located in both automated and traditional library catalogs under terms such as "Native Americans," "North American Indians," and "Indians of North America."

A third approach to establishing tribal affiliation is to engage in a thorough study of maps and atlases that place indigenous peoples in particular geographic areas (figure 14-1). These works are often valuable for determining not only the specific tribe of a potential ancestor but also migration and commerce routes, names and sites of villages, and locations of intertribal confrontations. Helen Hornbeck Tanner, ed., *Atlas of Great Lakes Indian History* (Norman: University of Oklahoma Press, 1987), is a remarkable example of such a historical atlas. Time lines assist in setting Native American events in context of the encroaching European settlement; narratives complement the detail provided by the numerous maps; and a selected bibliography provides the researcher with hundreds of additional sources of information.

Finally, assistance in determining tribal affiliation can be provided by published local and community histories. Nearly every community has some accounting of its early days, and the compiled histories of cities and towns often contain pages about the earliest inhabitants of the areas. While typically not filled with large amounts of documented data, these works can provide information useful in determining the identity of the native peoples of a specific geographic area.

TRIBE-SPECIFIC DATA

Once a reasonable hypothesis has established the tribe of a potential ancestor, a host of new sources become available for the researcher to gather information about particular Native Americans. Learning as many specific details about the clan or tribe as possible continues to be of paramount importance, and locating and accessing specific records will increasingly become the focus of research endeavors.

The history of a potential ancestor's tribe is critical to continuing research. It is important to know where and when the tribe existed, the customs of the tribe-especially those customs relating to naming patterns, marriage and burial practices, and other important life events. Emmet Starr, *History of the Cherokee Indians and Their Legends and Folk Lore* (Oklahoma City, Okla.: The Warden Company, 1921. Reprint. Millwood, N.Y.: Kraus Reprint Company, 1977), is an extraordinary example of a tribe/nation history containing excellent general data and significant genealogical information. Six chapters of more than one hundred and fifty pages are devoted to "Old Families and Their Genealogy." Other lists include council members and nearly two hundred pages of biographical sketches. Woven through the entire work is a serious treatment of the customs and legends of the Cherokees.

Though customs varied from one tribe to another, scholars

have found that Native Americans generally used two types of names: personal names and honorary names. In some tribes, one or the other of these names was considered sacred. Personal names may have been given or changed at birth, adolescence, the first hunting or war expedition, some notable feat, or the attainment of chieftainship. Tracking and documenting these name changes for any given Native American can be a formidable challenge. To these Native American names, Europeans often added a third, English, name. A transitional record is one that indicates both a Native American name and the English name of a potential ancestor. Such records are a great boon to furthering research, but they are somewhat rare.

Kinship terms have varying meanings among many Native Americans. For example, "father" does not always denote the natural parent. Many tribes are organized matriarchally rather than patriarchally, with lines of descent and property being passed down through the mother's line. The following excerpt is from a classic work of reprinted ethnology reports titled *The North American Indian* (New York: Garland Publishing, 1985). From "An Iroquois Source Book, Volume 1, Political and Social Organization," it indicates how complex such an organization can be for the genealogical researcher, describing some of the laws of descent of the Iroquois league, which was comprised of five nations: Onondaga, Cayuga, Oneida, Mohawk, and Seneca.

In each of the five nations who composed the original league, there were eight tribes, named as follows: Wolf, Bear, Beaver, and Turtle; Deer, Snipe, Heron, and Hawk. . . . In effect, the Wolf tribe was divided into five parts, and one fifth of it placed in each of the five nations. The remaining tribes were subject to the same division and distribution. . . . The Mohawk of the Turtle tribe recognized the Seneca of the Turtle tribe as a relative, and between them existed the bond of kindred blood. . . . A cross-relationship existed between the several tribes of each nation and the tribes of corresponding name in each of the other nations, which bound them together in the league with indissoluble bonds. . . .

Originally, with reference to marriage, the four tribes first named were not allowed to intermarry; neither were the last four. In their own mode of expressing the idea, each four were brother tribes to each other, and cousins to the other four. . . . At no time in the history of the Iroquois could a man marry a woman of his own tribe, even in another nation. . . . Husband and wife, therefore, were in every case of different tribes. The children were of the tribe of the mother. . . . As all titles, as well as property, descended in the female line, and were hereditary in the tribe, the son could never succeed to his father's title of sachem, nor inherit even his tomahawk. . . .

. . . The mother, her children, and the descendants of her daughters in the female line, would, in perpetuity, be linked with the fortunes of her own tribe; while the father, his brothers and sisters, and the descendants in the female line of his sisters, would be united to another tribe, and held by its affinities.

The next feature of importance in their system of

descent was the breaking up of the collateral line. . . . Thus a mother and her sisters stood equally in the relation of mothers to the children of each other; the grandmother and her sisters were equally grandmothers, and so up in the ascending series. . . . Thus the children of two sisters were brothers and sisters to each other; they were all of the same tribe. So also were the children of two brothers, although they might be of different tribes.

Knowledge of the individuals and groups which interacted with Native Americans is important for successful Native American genealogical research because most native peoples had few written records. Indeed, most Native American languages have a written history of only approximately one hundred years, making the researcher dependent almost exclusively upon the records of individuals who interacted directly with the tribes or clans. Understanding the collection development policies and record retention schedules of local, state, and national archives and societies is vital to successfully locating these primary source accounts and documents. Indeed, understanding the basics of what might be called an *information hierarchy* will greatly assist research endeavors. Figure 14-2 is a record of the Charles Poupart family, created by the Lac Du Flambeau Agency, Wisconsin.

At the local level, city and county historical societies tend to collect the manuscript or primary source documents as well as very early imprints or first editions, while local public libraries tend to collect published accounts and secondary source materials. Local archives tend to collect official governmental papers as well as those records not kept in the local courthouse which deal with sale and transfer of property, tax records, and other locally generated documents. State historical societies tend to collect primary source documents that concern multi-county areas of a state or those primary sources which local historical societies do not or cannot maintain in their collections. State libraries typically attempt to collect all consequential secondary source materials for their particular states. Indeed, special state-named collections can be found in many state libraries. In many areas, these special collections are rather comprehensive. Some larger academic libraries contain substantial historical collections, and in very rare cases even function as the archive for a county.

Combining knowledge of the information hierarchy, the geographic area historically and contemporarily inhabited by a particular tribe or clan, and the various individuals and organizations that interacted with specific native peoples will maximize record possibilities. Local and state historical societies and libraries contain many record possibilities which must be explored when collecting Native American data.

Extraordinary record possibilities may also be explored at federal records centers and National Archives regional archives. Because the federal government interacted frequently with the Native American tribes and nations during the United States' settlement period, one can expect to find many useful records in repositories that contain federal documents. Edward Hill, comp., *Guide to Records in the National Archives of the United States Relating to American Indians* (Washington, D.C.: National Archives and Records Administration, 1981), describes thousands of feet of manuscript collections and many important microform collections. Genealogists can also glean many

Figure 14-1. Indian tribes, reservations, and settlements in the United States, 1939. From the Bureau of Indian Affairs, RG75, National Archives—Central Plains Region

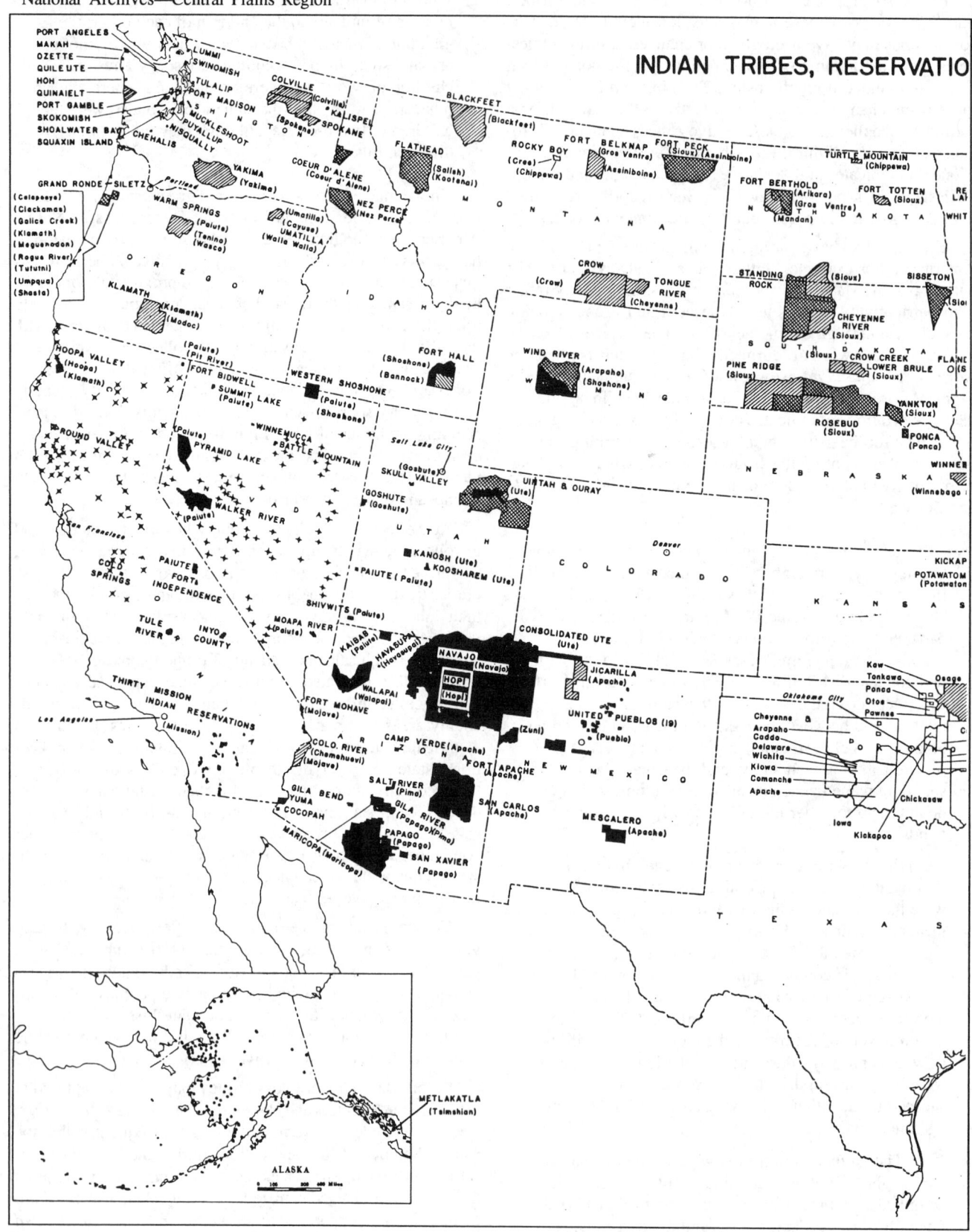

NS AND SETTLEMENTS IN THE UNITED STATES

1939

DEPARTMENT OF THE INTERIOR
HAROLD L. ICKES, SECRETARY
OFFICE OF INDIAN AFFAIRS
JOHN COLLIER, COMMISSIONER
FLOYD W. LA ROUCHE
DIRECTOR OF INFORMATION

The principal Indian tribes and many small
bands of Indians in the United States are
located on reservations, rancherias and other
communities, as shown here. In addition there
are 29,983 Eskimos and Indians in Alaska.

L E G E N D

Reservations allotted in part.

Reservations allotted and open.

Tribal lands.

Colonies in Nevada.

Rancherias in California.

Compiled and drawn by
Sam Attahvich   Comanche

Figure 14-2. A record of the Charles Poupart family, created by the Lac Du Flambeau Agency, Wisconsin. The original is at the National Archives—Great Lakes Region.

Lac du Flambeau Agency, Wisconsin.

Charles Poupart.

Photo

Allotment No.   Age   Degree   Status   Family
  3 00   56   ½   Comp.   Wife, Mother, and 8 children.

Main street in Town, about ¾ mile from Agency..7 rooms, 13 windows, 2
doors, cellar. Pump. Outhouse.
     Barn, chicken house, cow shed, boathouse.
     Team, cow, 25 chickens, 3 ponies.
     7 boats.

1866 Husband   A very successful guide. Cuts ice and wood in season. Hunts,
                  fishes, traps.
1883 Wife   Always busy with large family. Makes moccasins and beadwork.

     2 children by first wife and 6 by present wife.
1895 Dau.   Marie Poupart Buffalo is married and has own home.
1898 Son   Benjamin Poupart is a guide Is now working at fish hatchery.
1904 Son   Paul Poupart is a student at Haskell School.
1907 Son   Charles A. Poupart attends Public School.
1909 Son   Celia Poupart   "
1911 Son   Louis Poupart   "
1912 Dau.   Sarah Poupart   "
1914 Son   William Poupart   "

1844 Aged Mother, a widow lives with this family.(78 years)
     Charles and Louis are in the Potato Club. Celia raises chickens.

Reimbursable Funds...

Date of Survey.......May 13, 1922.

useful tips from Loretto Dennis Szucs and Sandra Hargreaves Luebking, *The Archives: A Guide to the National Archives Field Branches* (Salt Lake City: Ancestry, 1988).

There are several fine groups of sources for researchers seeking to obtain more tribe-specific information. These include dictionaries and encyclopedias, guides, detailed histories of tribes, federal government documents, and special transcriptions or methodology publications. The more successful researcher of Native American genealogy will pay attention to the finer details of a particular tribe's life and culture—details that may provide valuable clues and additional sources of data.

The Harvard Encyclopedia of American Ethnic Groups (Cambridge, Mass.: Belknap Press of Harvard University, 1980) devotes more than sixty pages to both a general and tribe-specific treatment of the Native American experience. While it might be considered dated, the information provided in it is concise and accurate. The maps indicating Native American tribes circa 1600 and the primary locations of 173 Native American groups in 1970 are particularly useful. *The Reference Encyclopedia of the American Indian,* 6th ed. (New York: Todd Publications, 1993), contains significant sections devoted to directory data, a bibliography of works accessible by tribe, and biographies of Native Americans. Particularly useful are the lists of reservations, tribal councils, associations, and government agencies.

Important information can be found in many dictionaries and handbooks dealing with the native peoples of North America. Such sources often contain references to other, more detailed, works. The *Dictionary of Indian Tribes of the Americas,* 2nd ed. (Newport Beach, Calif.: American Indian Publishers, 1993), contains significant tribe-specific historical details, variant spellings of tribal and clan names, and noteworthy individuals belonging to the Native American group. The various maps are useful, as is the subject and title index. Frederick W. Hodge, *Handbook of American Indians North of Mexico,* Smithsonian Institution, Bureau of American Ethnology, Bulletin 302, 2 parts (Washington, D.C.: Government Printing Office, 1912), is a classic work. Organized in a dictionary format, it has long been recognized for providing useful data about various tribes, clans, and nations of Native Americans. In it can be found significant information about Native American tools, well-known individuals, geographic locations, arts and customs, institutions, and language. Another exemplary work is John R. Swanton, *The Indian Tribes of North America,* Smithsonian Institution, Bureau of American Ethnology, Bulletin 145 (Washington, D.C.: Smithsonian Institution Press, 1984). Its dictionary format makes the more than seven hundred pages of information readily accessible.

As oral histories and interviews are used to assist in establishing tribal affiliation, they can also be used to gather more specific details about particular Native American groups, bands, or tribes. Commonly called narratives or firsthand narrative accounts, these materials often represent some of the earliest accounts concerning particular groups of Native Americans. These early accounts were typically by European Americans, such as missionaries, trappers, fur traders, and government agents. Firsthand accounts can provide citations to sources that are also narrative or firsthand accounts, well-documented works, or contemporary works that might not be so well known.

Firsthand accounts can also contain the writings of Native Americans as well as those individuals who first interacted with them. A fine example is *American Indian Women: Telling Their Lives* (Lincoln, Nebr.: University of Nebraska Press, 1984). This work contains more than fifty pages of notes and bibliography—excellent for leading the researcher to additional sources.

Late twentieth-century firsthand accounts can provide much useful historical and cultural information about particular tribes or groups of Native Americans. These sources are frequently overlooked by researchers who are too focused on individual-specific records. *Wisdomkeepers: Meetings With Native American Spiritual Elders* (Hillsboro, Oreg.: Beyond Words Publishing, 1990) is a collection of eighteen interviews with Native Americans from thirteen different tribes or confederacies. In this work, the careful reader can learn the native names for particular ancestral homelands, locations and identities of sacred places, important historical details pertaining to little-known and non-federally recognized tribes, and rough sketches of family narratives, which easily form the core around which family histories can be developed. John Gattuso, *Circle of Nations: Voices and Visions of American Indians* (Hillsboro, Oreg.: Beyond Words Publishing, 1993), is another richly illustrated collection of contemporary firsthand accounts that provide documentary assistance to the historical researcher interested in a fuller understanding of particular Native American cultures.

Careful researchers should necessarily be concerned about the objectivity of firsthand narrative accounts. It is significant to note through whose eyes the events were being seen. The usefulness of these accounts, though, in providing geographical data and kinship and cultural information, as well as actual names of some Native Americans, cannot be discounted. Larger academic and public libraries, as well as some special libraries, have such works.

Federal government documents are some of the most potentially useful records for obtaining significant data about particular Native American tribes. Two factors contributing to their significance are the frequency of federal government interactions with the native peoples during the settlement of many areas and the large number of documents produced by the Government Printing Office. Additionally, the availability of federal government documents is quite good because there are numerous repositories in most states.

While federal government documents are plentiful, their use may be challenging for the beginning researcher. The documents have their own classification system, which is designed more for archiving large bodies of material than for accessing those materials. This classification system, commonly known in library circles as the SUDOC system, groups materials by the issuing government agency regardless of subject matter. Native American records may be found filed under "I" for Department of the Interior, "LC" for the Library of Congress, "SI" for Smithsonian Institution, "W" for the Department of War, and "Y" for Congress, etc.

Having access to a good, comprehensive index is important; that one does not exist for federal government documents is problematic. There are a number of keys, though, to unlocking the rich amounts of information in documents published by the Government Printing Office (see figure 14-3). First, always seek the assistance of the government documents librarian or information professional. For almost every document collec-

386	CHEROKEES BY BLOOD		
Name.	**Roll No.**	**Name.**	**Roll No.**
Sittingdown, Nancy	2136	Sixkilller, Samuel	20061
Sittingdown, William	25634	Sixkiller, Bluford	20267
Sittingdown, Stephen	26362	Sixkiller, Annie	20268
Sittingdown, James	26363	Sixkiller, Maud	23599
Sittingdown, Thadius	26364	Sixkiller, Lola	23600
Sittingdown, Minnie	26365	Sixkiller, Blanche	23601
Sittingdown, Agnes	26366	Sixkiller, Mabel	23602
Sittingdown, Edgar	26367	Sixkiller, Henry	23603
Sittingdown, Ella	29820	Sixkiller, Mary A.	23604
Sitsler, George W.	30135	Sixkiller, Linnie	25562
Sitsler, James Lewis	30136	Sixkiller, Young Wolfe	25563
Sitten, Naomi A.	31698	Sixkiller, Mintie	25763
Sitten, Theodore L.	31699	Sixkiller, Hattie	26937
Sixkiller, Glover	768	Sixkiller, John B.	27220
Sixkiller, Nancy	1357	Sixkiller, Cicero	27221
Sixkiller, Sam	2316	Sixkiller, Dora	27222
Sixkiller, Nancy	2317	Sixkiller, Joseph	27470
Sixkiller, Lynch	2318	Sixkiller, Lucy	27471
Sixkiller, George	2319	Sixkiller, Gracie	27472
Sixkiller, Emma	2320	Sixkiller, Bertha	28556
Sixkiller, Ned	2321	Sixkiller, Carrie B.	28730
Sixkiller, Delia	2322	Sixkiller, Jennie	29721
Sixkiller, Walter	2323	Sixkiller, Peggie	29722
Sixkiller, Julia	2324	Sixkiller, Henry	32313
Sixkiller, Martha	2325	Six, John W.	6368
Sixkiller, Henry	2326	Six, Ida	17773
Sixkiller, Narcissa	2327	Six, Enoch	17772
Sixkiller, Frank	2328	Six, John	17807
Sixkiller, Stella	2329	Six, Groundhog	30551
Sixkiller, Arch	2418	Six, Humphrey	30552
Sixkiller, Walter R.	2330	Six, Tincup	30553
Sixkiller, Joshua	2547	Skaggs, Myrtle A.	11457
Sixkiller, Johnie	2548	Skaggs, Roy	11458
Sixkiller, Luke	7397	Skaloll, James	21290
Sixkiller, Emma	7398	Skelley, Cora	32247
Sixkiller, James	10732	Skelley, Charles	32248
Sixkiller, Nancy	10733	Skelley, Joseph	32249
Sixkiller, Carrie	10734	Skinner, Thomas F.	7545
Sixkiller, Pearl	10735	Skinner, Morgan D.	7546
Sixkiller, Joseph	10736	Skinner, Galuga T.	7547
Sixkiller, Henry	11223	Skinner, Bettie A.	7548
Sixkiller, Linnie M.	11224	Skinneer, Mary A.	7549
Sixkiller, William F.	11225	Skinner, Laura C.	26558
Sixkiller, Artemecie M.	11226	Skinner, John	28810
Sixkiller, Charles	12339	Skinner, Ray N.	28811
Sixkiller, Martin	12340	Skillman, Sarah E.	9210
Sixkiller, Hooley	12885	Skillman, Bessie D.	9211
Sixkiller, Jesse M.	12886	Skillman, John O.	9212
Sixkiller, James T.	13397	Skitt, Patsey	19663
Sixkiller, Claude L.	13398	Skitt, Martha	20137
Sixkiller, Robert M.	13399	Skitt, Sam	20138
Sixkiller, Ida M.	13400	Skitt, Nancy	20139
Sixkiller, Pleasant T.	13401	Skitt, Ben	20140
Sixkiller, Jesse	14348	Skitt, Ella	20141
Sixkiller, Sarah	14349	Skitt, Alice	20142
Sixkiller, Katie	14350	Skitt, Mattie	20143
Sixkiller, Ethel	14351	Skitt, Calvin	20144
Sixkiller, Josie	14967	Skitt, Margaret	22788
Sixkiller, Fannie	16040	Skitt, Lucy	25821
Sixkiller, Samuel R.	16877	Skidmore, Annie F.	21764
Sixkiller, Sallie	18313	Skidmore, Eugene O.	21765
Sixkiller, Charlie	18605	Skidmore, Otis T.	21766
Sixkiller, Eliza	18606	Skidmore, Elizabeth A.	21767
Sixkiller, Rufus	18607	Skidmore, Henry C.	21768
Sixkiller, Sampson	18608	Skidmore, Letitia F.	21769
Sixkiller, Charlotte	18913	Skidmore, Benjamin F.	21770
Sixkiller, George	18914	Sleeper, Cricket N.	15249
Sixkiller, Sam	18915	Sleeper, Nannie I.	15250
Sixkiller, Annie	19002	Sleeper, Minnie	17352
Sixkiller, John	19067	Sleeper, Julia	17353
Sixkiller, Winnie	19068	Sleeper, Gideon D., Jr.	17354
Sixkiller, Ora	19069	Sleeper, Walter J.	17355
Sixkiller, Nannie	19070	Sleeper, Mattie	17356
Sixkiller, Gafford	19245	Slack, Olive A.	31499
Sixkiller, Susie	19246	Slack, Edith	31500
Sixkiller, Nellie	19248	Slagle, Minnie H.	24377
Sixkiller, Laura	19249	Slagle, Gordon	24378
Sixkiller, Abraham	19666	Slagle, Dennis	24379
Sixkiller, Margaret	19667	Slagle, Hattie F.	24380
Sixkiller, Dennis	19668	Slagle, Ellsworth	24381
Sixkiller, Sarah	19669	Sloan, Mary E.	887
Sixkiller, Kate	19670	Sloan, Alexander G.	5116
Sixkiller, Lincoln	19671	Sloan, Nora C.	5117
Sixkiller, Retta			

Figure 14-3. From The Commission and Commissioner to the Five Civilized Tribes, "Index to the Final Roll of Citizens and Freedmen of the Five Civilized Tribes in Indian Territory" (Washington, D.C.: Government Printing Office, 1907), 386; FHL 962,366.

tion there is at least one person who is expert in its use and committed to assisting others in gaining access to the myriad of data contained in it.

Second, make use of the standard indexes available for accessing government documents, particularly the *Monthly Catalog of United States Government Publications* (Washington, D.C.: Government Printing Office, 1895-). The *Monthly Catalog* is the official index to published government documents. Having been published since 1895, it is the most comprehensive source for document location. Because federal government documents are cataloged by the authoring federal agencies, knowing the possible government agency of publication is helpful in locating documents more quickly. Access to government documents published after 1976 is enhanced by a number of CD-ROM databases that are currently available in most larger government document repositories.

Other standard indexes are listed below by general time period covered. It is imperative to consult these indexes when endeavoring to use federal government documents for any type of historical research, most especially for those time periods before 1895.

A Descriptive Catalogue of the Government Publications of the United States, September 5, 1774–March 4, 1881. Washington, D.C.: Government Printing Office, 1885.

Comprehensive Index of Publications of United States Government, 1881–93. Washington, D.C.: Government Printing Office, 1890.

United States Government Publications, A Monthly Catalog, 10 vols. Washington, D.C.: Lowdermilk & Company, 1885–94. 10 volumes.

Checklist of United States Public Documents, 1789–1909. Washington, D.C.: Government Printing Office, 1911.

Cumulative Subject Index to the Monthly Catalog of United States Government Publications, 1900–1971, 15 vols. Washington, D.C.: Carrollton Press, 1973–75.

Third, continually look for special guides, finding aids, and explanatory publications. As increasing numbers of individuals become aware of the vast amounts of information contained in government documents, new finding aids are developed to complement those which already exist. Documents librarians or local information professionals can assist in locating such guides. A useful contemporary work for the researcher seeking to become more familiar with government documents is the *Introduction to United States Government Information Sources,* 4th ed. (Englewood, Colo.: Libraries Unlimited, 1993). This work will inform you not only how to access federal documents but also of the existence of such specific titles as the *United States Statutes at Large,* which contain the text of Native American treaties from 1778 to 1842 in volume 7.

The richness of materials contained in federal government document collections can scarcely be overemphasized. Histories of tribes; laws relating to allotments, patents, alienation, citizenship, and cessation of tribal relations; reports of various territorial governors dealing with Native Americans; and tribal council resolutions can all be found in government documents. The second volume of Charles J. Kappler, *Indian Affairs: Laws and Treaties* (Washington, D.C.: Government Printing Office, 1904), is devoted entirely to eighteenth- and nineteenth-century treaties with Native American tribes. Thousands of individual names are included in its more than one thousand pages.

Major microform publishers, such as University Publications of America, make significant document collections pertaining to Native Americans available for research. These collections can include copies of major council meetings, documents from the Office of Indian Affairs, and records of the U.S. Indian Claims Commission. Large public libraries and major universities may include such records in their collections.

Almanacs and ethnic-specific encyclopedias are excellent sources of data for tribe-specific information, lists of primary and secondary source materials, supplemental historical data, and addresses of institutions and organizations that researchers may contact for specific information. Duane Champagne, ed., *The Native North American Almanac: A Reference Work on Native North Americans in the United States and Canada* (Detroit: Gale Research Co., 1994), is an excellent example of such a work. Among its nearly 1,300 pages are a general bibliography coupled with extensive chapter-specific references and maps indicating locations of tribes and bands. This encyclopedic work covers in some depth nearly every aspect of Native American life. The sections devoted to chronology, research centers and organizations, demography, and major culture areas assist the researcher both in determining tribal affiliation and in gathering substantial quantities of significant works pertaining to a particular tribe or nation. Chapters on law and legislation, languages, religion, and non-reservation populations provide vital tribe- or nation-specific details which enable a researcher to find and access a larger body of records.

INDIVIDUAL-SPECIFIC DATA

As you continue Native American genealogical research, working from general Native American materials and documents into more tribe-specific accounts and information, focus increasingly on obtaining individual (person-specific) details. As with other stages in the research process, there are a number of records at this level that are useful to genealogists. Annual Indian census lists, for example, became required in 1884. An example is figure 14-4, a census card and application of Ephraim Thorne, Talequah District, Cherokee Nation. These census records are contained on several hundred rolls of National Archives microfilm. Transitional census records, which indicate both Native American and English names, are most useful. Be careful in the use of the census materials, however: being listed in the census does not mean that a person was of the particular tribe; there were many mixed-tribe marriages. Only persons on enrollment lists are actually considered tribal members, or enrolled members.

Enrollment records are often called the "official census records" for any given tribe or nation. Typically they contain the name of the Indian tribe and date of validity, roll number, name (including given name, birth name, and married names), sex, date of death (if applicable), probate number (if applicable), blood degree (degree of Native American blood), names of both parents, and blood degree of parents. If a person or family was denied enrollment, a suit was often filed in court. Significant data may be available in court proceedings of the federal district courts.

Allotment records detail the allotment of land parcels among adult Native Americans who were of at least one-half Native American blood. They are often referred to as "heirship records" because ownership of the land would pass to the allottee's heirs upon death. Will and probate cases carry extra importance for the Native American researcher when they relate to allotted land. Normally, probate material is found in local courthouses. However, when allotted lands on reservation tracts are involved, federal records need to be consulted. Still other property records available for the Native American researcher are land claims. The land claims system enabled native tribes to file claims against the government for monies owed them for lands taken and not adequately paid for during treaty eras.

Many significant census and enrollment lists are being reprinted in indexed or transcribed form, making the information more widely accessible for today's researchers. *A Complete Roll of All Choctaw Claimants and Their Heirs Existing Under the Treaties Between the United States and the Choctaw Nation* (Conway, Ark.: Oldbuck Press, n.d.) provides a complete alphabetical list, including aliases and English names (where known). Bob Blankenship's series *Cherokee Roots* (Cherokee, N.C.: the compiler, 1992) lists the names from nearly a dozen official lists. These types of publications contribute significantly to the accessibility of Native American historical and genealogical data and should be sought by the family historian.

A number of other works published as monographs contribute substantially to the body of data available to researchers seeking individual-specific records. A more contemporary example, Toni Jollay Prevost, *The Delaware & Shawnee Admitted to Cherokee Citizenship and the Related Wyandotte & Moravian Delaware* (Bowie, Md.: Heritage Books, 1993), provides many lists, including signers of treaties, property owners, children enrolled in mission schools, and partial citizenship lists. Divided into fourteen sections, it provides many names, dates, and places to assist directly in developing ancestor charts and ancestral proof.

A number of Indian schools were operated as part of the process of attempting to assimilate Native Americans. Records of these schools, which had agricultural, industrial, or missionary focuses, may provide the researcher with plentiful details about a potential ancestor, including such facts as tribal affiliation, degree of Native American blood, names of parents, home address, dates of arrival and departure, attendance records, health cards, and letters to parents and social workers.

An abundance of tribe-specific and individual-specific records can be found in periodical literature. The historical and genealogical periodicals that cover the geographic areas where Native American tribes historically lived, as well as areas of removal and contemporary settlement, should be considered

Figure 14-4. "Dawes" census card and application. Courtesy of National Archives—Southwest Region.

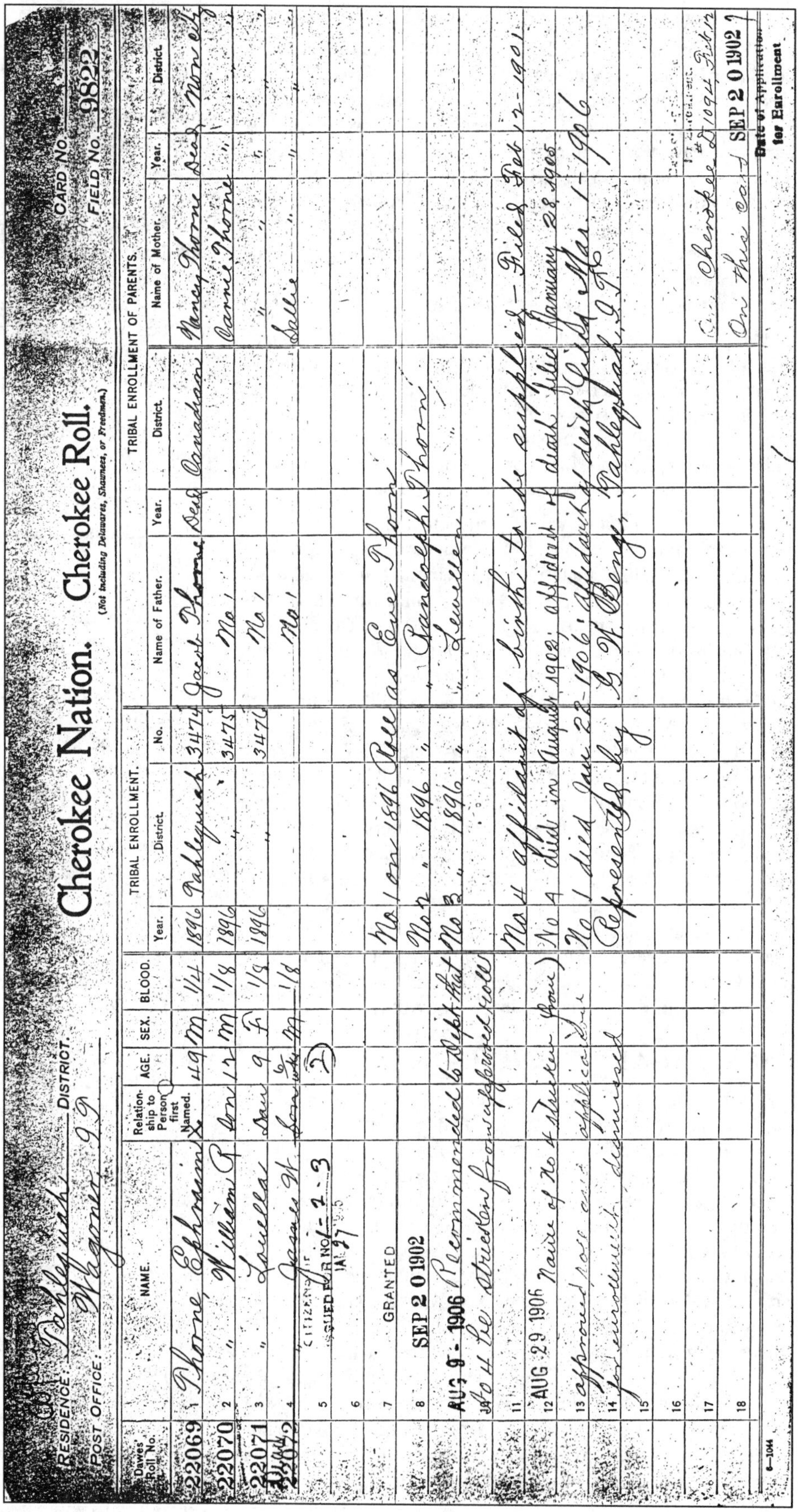

RESIDENCE: Tahlequah DISTRICT.
POST OFFICE: Wagoner, I.T.

Cherokee Nation. Cherokee Roll.

(Not including Delawares, Shawnees, or Freedmen.)

CARD No.
FIELD No. 9822

Dawes' Roll No.		NAME.	Relationship to Person first Named.	AGE.	SEX.	BLOOD.	Tribal Enrollment Year.	Tribal Enrollment District.	Tribal Enrollment No.	Name of Father.	Year.	District.	Name of Mother.	Year.	District.
22069	1	Thorne, Ephraim	X	49	M	1/4	1896	Tahlequah	3474	Jacob Thorne	Dead	Canadian	Nancy Thorne	Dead	Non citz
22070	2	" William R	Son	12	M	1/8	1896	"	3475	No 1			Carrie Thorne	"	"
22071	3	" Louella	Dau	9	F	1/8	1896	"	3476	No 1			" "	"	"
~~22072~~ Dead	4	~~" James W.~~	~~Son~~	~~6wks~~	~~M~~	~~1/8~~				No 1			Sallie "	"	"
	5	CITIZENSHIP ISSUED FOR No 1-2-3 JAN 27 1905		(2)											
	6														
	7	GRANTED					No 1 on 1896 Roll as Eve Thorn								
	8	SEP 20 1902					No 2 " 1896 " " Randolph Thorn								
	9	AUG 9 - 1906 Recommended to Dept that					No 3 " 1896 " " Lewellen								
	10	No 4 be stricken from approved roll													
	11						No 4 affidavit of birth to be supplied — Filed Feb 12-1901								
	12	AUG 29 1906 Name of No 4 stricken from					No 4 died in August 1902; affidavit of death filed January 28 1905								
	13	approved roll and application					No 1 died Jan 22-1906; affidavit of death filed Mar 1-1906								
	14	for enrollment dismissed					Represented by G. W. Benge, Tahlequah, I.T.								
	15														
	16														
	17												Cherokee D 1094 Feb 12		
	18												On this card SEP 20 1902		

Date of Application for Enrollment

6—1044

by the serious researcher. Every type of record that can be found in manuscript collections or published in monographs may be available in indexed, abstracted, transcribed, or reprinted form in periodical literature. One of the best subject indexes to these quarterlies and newsletters is the *PERiodical Source Index (PERSI)* (Fort Wayne, Ind.: Allen County Public Library, 1986–), which indexes more than four thousand periodical titles. Another source of access to this material is the *Genealogical Periodical Annual Index (GPAI)* (Bowie, Md.: Heritage Books, 1962–). (See chapter 2, Databases, Indexes, and Other Finding Aids.)

Some of the more notable geographically oriented periodicals include the *Oklahoma Genealogical Society Quarterly* (Oklahoma City: Oklahoma Genealogical Society, 1961–), *Stirpes* (Cleburne, Tex.: Texas State Genealogical Society, 1961–), and the *Topeka Genealogical Society Quarterly* (Topeka, Kans.: Topeka Genealogical Society, 1971). These journals contain indexes to and transcriptions of numerous Native American records. They can also provide leads to individuals and institutions that might be contacted for further historical and genealogical data. Other fine periodicals worthy of note cover both general Native American history and tribe- and nation-specific details. *The American Indian Quarterly* (Lincoln: University of Nebraska Press, 1974–) provides excellent information about the many sides of Native American life and assists the researcher in the same manner as do general histories; a recently published cumulative index to this quarterly makes accessing this information quite easy. Donna Williams, *Cherokee Family Researcher* (Mesa, Ariz.: 1988–) and the *Journal of Cherokee Studies* (Cherokee, N.C.: Museum of the Cherokee Indian, 1976–) are examples of tribe-specific periodical publications that can provide specific records of genealogical value as well as detailed historical data on particular tribes.

The Bureau of Indian Affairs, its regional offices, and specific tribal offices are rich sources of genealogical information. In fact, they contain the richest collections of individual-specific data for Native Americans. Guides to these collections and offices are available in some major libraries and by contacting the Bureau of Indian Affairs offices in Washington, D.C. Contact the bureau or its organizations directly for both general information and individual-specific requests.

Employment of sound research methodology, fine attention to detail with complete and accurate recording of all relevant and associated data, and a willingness to search for all possible data from a multiplicity of information sources—these are the keys to successful Native American genealogical research. The following sections provide numerous vital details useful for identifying extant records, becoming familiar with the historical and genealogical data included in those records, and accessing the specific materials needed to further research endeavors.

BIBLIOGRAPHY

American Indian Women: Telling Their Lives. Lincoln, Nebr.: University of Nebraska Press, 1984.

Blankenship, Bob. *Cherokee Roots.* Cherokee, N.C.: the compiler, 1992.

Champagne, Duane, ed. *The Native North American Almanac:*

A Reference Work on Native North Americans in the United States and Canada. Detroit: Gale Research Co., 1994.

A Complete Roll of All Choctaw Claimants and Their Heirs Existing Under the Treaties Between the United States and the Choctaw Nation. Conway, Ark.: Oldbuck Press, n.d.

Curtis, Edward S. *The North American Indian, Being a Series of Volumes Picturing and Describing the Indians of the United States and Alaska.* Cambridge, Mass.: The University Press, 1907–30.

Dictionary of Indian Tribes of the Americas. 2nd ed. Newport Beach, Calif.: American Indian Publishers, 1993.

Gattuso, John. *Circle of Nations: Voices and Visions of American Indians.* Hillsboro, Oreg.: Beyond Words Publishing, 1993.

Introduction to United States Government Information Sources. 4th ed. Englewood, Colo.: Libraries Unlimited, 1993.

The Harvard Encyclopedia of American Ethnic Groups. Cambridge, Mass.: Belknap Press of Harvard University, 1980.

Hill, Edward, comp. *Guide to Records in the National Archives of the United States Relating to American Indians.* Washington, D.C.: National Archives and Records Administration, 1981.

Hodge, Frederick W. *Handbook of American Indians North of Mexico.* Smithsonian Institution, Bureau of American Ethnology, Bulletin 30. 2 parts. Washington, D.C.: Government Printing Office, 1912.

Kappler, Charles J. *Indian Affairs: Laws and Treaties.* Washington, D.C.: Government Printing Office, 1904.

Leacock, Eleanor Burke, and Nancy Oestreich Lurie. *North American Indians in Historical Perspective.* Prospect Heights, Ill.: Waveland Press, 1971.

Monthly Catalog of United States Government Publications. Washington, D.C.: Government Printing Office, 1895–.

The North American Indian. New York: Garland Publishing, 1985.

Prevost, Toni Jollay. *The Delaware & Shawnee Admitted to Cherokee Citizenship and the Related Wyandotte & Moravian Delaware.* Bowie, Md.: Heritage Books, 1993.

The Reference Encyclopedia of the American Indian. 6th ed. New York: Todd Publications, 1993.

Schoolcraft, Henry R. *Historical and Statistical Information Respecting the History, Conditions and Prospects of the Indian Tribes of the United States: Collected and Prepared Under the Direction of the Bureau of Indian Affairs, per Act of Congress of March 3, 1847.* Philadelphia: Lippencott, Grambo & Company, 1851.

Starr, Emmet. *History of the Cherokee Indians and Their Legends and Folk Lore.* Oklahoma City, Okla.: The Warden Company, 1921. Reprint. Millwood, N.Y.: Kraus Reprint Company, 1977.

Swanton, John R. *The Indian Tribes of North America.* Smithsonian Institution, Bureau of American Ethnology, Bulletin 145. Washington, D.C.: Smithsonian Institution Press, 1984.

Szucs, Loretto Dennis, and Sandra Hargreaves Luebking. *The Archives: A Guide to the National Archives Field Branches*. Salt Lake City: Ancestry, 1988.

Tanner, Helen Hornbeck, ed. *Atlas of Great Lakes Indian History*. Norman: University of Oklahoma Press, 1987.

Weist, Katherine M., and Susan R. Sharrock. *An Annotated Bibliography of North Plains Ethnohistory*. Missoula: University of Montana, 1985.

Wisdomkeepers: Meetings With Native American Spiritual Elders. Hillsboro, Oreg: Beyond Words Publishing, 1990.

RECORDS RELATING TO NATIVE AMERICAN RESEARCH IN OKLAHOMA

George J. Nixon

Interest in Native American genealogy has increased greatly since the 1980s, and access to records of genealogical and historical importance has become easier through microfilming projects undertaken by various federal, state, and privately funded institutions. Because of the interest in Indian tribes of Oklahoma, this section focuses on records available to the genealogist and historian for those tribes (see figure 14-5).

The majority of the records cited in this chapter are available from the Oklahoma Historical Society in Oklahoma City, the Western History Collection at the University of Oklahoma in Norman, Oklahoma, the National Archives—Southwest Region in Fort Worth, Texas, the National Archives in Washington, D.C., the Family History Library of The Church of Jesus Christ of Latter-day Saints in Salt Lake City, or the American Genealogical Lending Library in Bountiful, Utah.

INDIAN REMOVAL

During the administration of President Andrew Jackson (1829 to 1837), the removal of Indians in the East to Indian territory west of the Mississippi River became an explicit policy. As early as 1803, with the Louisiana Purchase, such removals were officially encouraged, and some Indians did voluntarily move west.

Under Jackson, however, treaties were negotiated which traded tribal lands in the East for land in the unorganized territory west of the Mississippi River. An act of 28 May 1830 (4 Stat. 411) specifically authorized the president to exchange these lands. The actual removals were conducted between 1830 and 1836 by the Office of the Commissary General of Subsistence and were supervised by the military. Some Indians, however, were allowed to move by themselves, and individual Indians who wished to remain in the east could accept a "reservation" of land in fee simple and remain as citizens, giving up all rights of tribal membership. The removal process was largely complete by the late 1840s.

The removal was not without problems, most of which concerned reservations granted to Indians in the East and the compensation of Indians for losses. The three most troublesome treaties were the treaty of 29 December 1835 with the Cherokees, the treaty of 29 September 1830 with the Choctaws, and the treaty of 24 March 1832 with the Creeks.

Numerous treatments of the removal policy are available, among them Annie H. Abel, *The History of Events Resulting in Indian Consolidation West of the Mississippi*, Annual Report of the American Historical Association, 1906 (Washington, D.C.: Government Printing Office, 1908), and Grant Foreman, *Indian Removal* (Norman: University of Oklahoma Press, 1932).

CHEROKEE REMOVAL RECORDS

Cherokee removal records include a register of Cherokees who wished to remain in the East, 1817–19; applications for reservations, 1819; eastern Cherokee census rolls, 1835–84; emigration rolls, 1817–36; and miscellaneous Cherokee removal records, 1820–54.

Four commissions were appointed successively in an attempt to settle different kinds of claims arising from the Cherokee Treaty of 1835.

Records of the First Board of Cherokee Commissioners, 1836–1839

Records of the First Board of Cherokee Commissioners include letters sent, 1835–39; property valuations, 1835–39; changes in assignment of property valuations, 1837–38; reservation claims, 1837–39; reservation claim papers, 1837–39; record of judgements against Cherokee Indians, 1837; decisions on claims of attorneys against the Cherokee Nation, 1837–39; certificate stubs, 1838; and a general abstract of valuations and spoliation allowed and of balances due, 1839.

Records of the Second and Third Board of Cherokee Commissioners, 1842–45

Records of the Second and Third Board of Cherokee Commissioners include letters sent, 1842–45; proceedings of the Second Board, 1843; schedule of claims adjudicated by the Second Board, 1843; claim papers of the Second and Third Boards, 1842–45; claims presented in the west, 1845; and register of payments, 1837–45.

Records of the Fourth Board of Cherokee Commissioners, 1846–1847

Records of the Fourth Board of Cherokee Commissioners include letters sent, 1846–47; minutes, 1846–47; claim papers, 1846–47; and register of payments, 1847.

CHICKASAW REMOVAL RECORDS

Chickasaw removal records include a census roll of 1831, alphabetical list of Choctaw reserves, census roll of 1846, emigration lists, 1831–57; register of claims for reservations, 1834–36; reports concerning claims for reservations, 1836–41; statements concerning sales of Choctaw orphan lands, 1838–83; statements and schedules, 1831–1906; and miscellaneous Choctaw removals, 1825–58.

CREEK REMOVAL RECORDS

Creek removal records include a census roll of 1833, index to Creek reserves (not dated), land location registers, 1834–1886; location registers and certificates of contracts, 1834–1836; abstracts of Creek contracts, 1836; abstracts of approved contracts for sales of reservations, 1839–1842; reports concerning land of deceased reservees, 1844; miscellaneous records

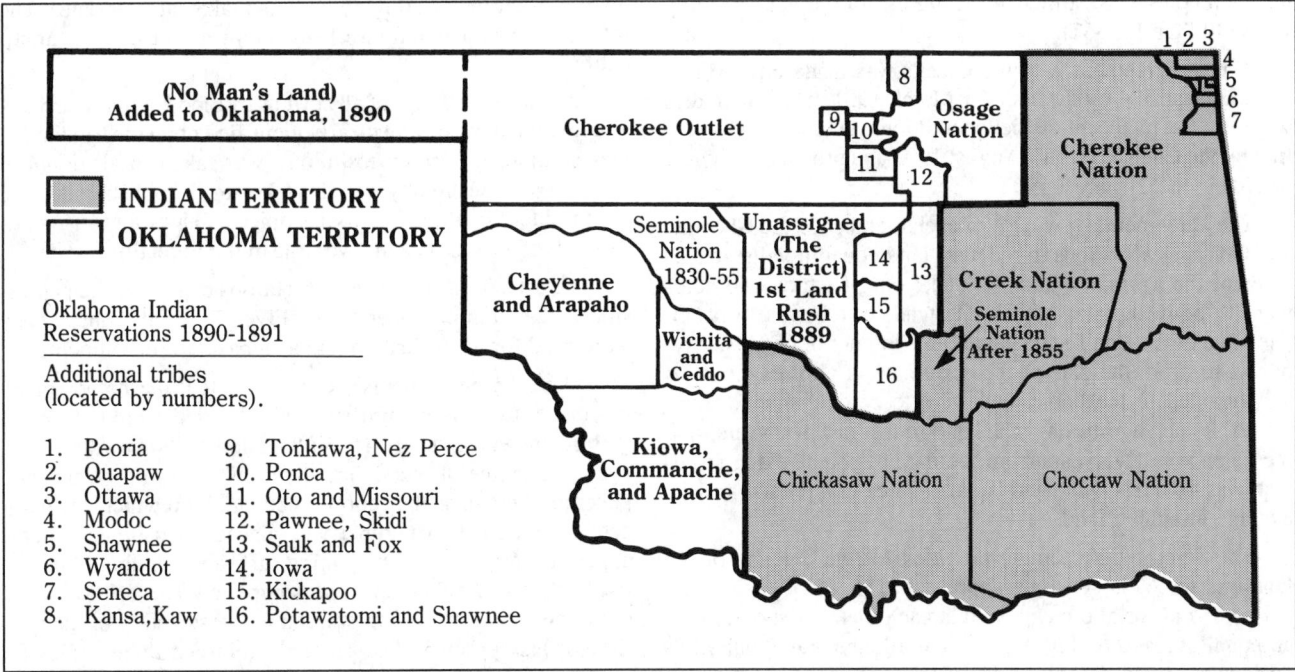

Figure 14-5. Based on Muriel Wright, *A Guide to the Indians of Oklahoma* (Norman: University of Oklahoma Press, 1971), and John Morris, et al., *Historical Atlas of Oklahoma* (Norman: University of Oklahoma Press, 1976). The Choctaws arrived west of the Mississippi in 1820; the other four Civilized Tribes soon followed. After the Civil War, other Indian tribes migrated into the nations, settling primarily in the western sections and along the Arkansas, Missouri, and Kansas borders. In 1889, the area was divided into Indian Territory (eastern part) and Oklahoma Territory (western part) as a prelude to non-Indian settlement. Specific reservations and allotments were assigned in 1890–91. By 1907, counties were formed throughout Oklahoma and the reservation boundaries disappeared.

concerning contracts, 1833–57; emigration lists, 1836–38; and miscellaneous Creek removal records, 1827–59.

APALACHICOLA, SEMINOLE, KICKAPOO, OTTAWA, POTAWATOMI, QUAPAW, AND WYANDOT REMOVAL RECORDS

Other removal records include five volumes of miscellaneous muster rolls of 1832 to 1836 that record removals for Apalachicolas and Seminoles, Kickapoos, Ottawas, Potawatomis, Quapaws, and Wyandots.

THE COMMISSION TO THE FIVE CIVILIZED TRIBES (THE DAWES COMMISSION)[1]

The Five Civilized Tribes—the Cherokee, Choctaw, Chickasaw, Creek, and Seminole—were so called by the U.S. government because they were more advanced (literate) than many others and had adopted systems of government patterned after those of the United States.

An act approved by Congress on 3 March 1893 (27 Stat. L., 645) provided for the appointment of three commissioners to negotiate with the Five Civilized Tribes for the extinguishment of the tribal title and the allotment of lands in severalty. This commission was generally known as the Dawes Commission for ex-Senator Dawes of Massachusetts, who was appointed chairman. The commission reported directly to the secretary of the interior. In 1895, the number of members was increased to five. At that time, the work of the commission was

limited to two fields: a change in the method of land ownership and the abolition of the tribal governments. The commission experienced little success in these endeavors, and on 10 June 1896 (29 Stat. L., 339) the scope of the commission's work was enlarged by an authorization and direction to "hear and determine the application of all persons who may apply to them for citizenship in any of said nations," and the commission was required to file the list of tribal members with the commissioner of Indian Affairs "for use as the final judgement of the duly constituted authorities."

On 28 June 1898 (30 Stat. L., 495), a law generally known as the Curtis Act was approved. The Curtis Act is the basis of all later legislation relating to the affairs of the Five Civilized Tribes. The main features of this act were: (1) the allotment of land in severalty; (2) leasing of tribal lands by the secretary of the interior; (3) the incorporation of cities and towns, the survey of town sites, and the sale of town lots to the lessees at half their appraised value; (4) the prohibition of any payment to tribal governments, and provision for making per-capita payments directly to individuals; (5) provision for the payments of all rents and royalties into the Treasury of the United States to the credit of the tribe; and (6) the enlargement of the power of the U.S. courts and the abolition of tribal courts.

Agreements had been made with the Choctaws and Chickasaws on 23 April 1897, with the Creeks on 27 September 1897, and with the Seminoles on 16 December 1897. The Choctaw-Chickasaw and the Creek agreements were embodied in the Curtis Act of 1898. The agreement was confirmed on 24 August 1898, but the Creeks rejected it. The agreement with the Seminoles was ratified by Congress in the act of 1 July 1898 (30 Stat. L., 567).

A new agreement with the Creeks was made on 8 March 1900 and ratified by the act of 1 March 1901. The Cherokees were the last to accept the new conditions, but an act was ratified by the Cherokees on 7 August 1902 and proclaimed by the president on 12 August 1902.

The agreements provided for each member of the Choctaw and Chickasaw Nations to receive "land equal in value to 320 acres of the average allottable land," out of which 160 acres were to be designated as a homestead, which was to be inalienable during the life of the allottee but not beyond twenty-one years from the date of the certificate of allotment. Lands not included in the homestead were to be alienable for one-fourth the acreage in one year, one-fourth in three years, and the balance in five years from the date of patent. Each freedman was to be allotted "land equal in value to forty acres of the average allottable land."[2]

The Seminole agreement provided for the division of the land into three classes to be appraised at $5, $2.50, and $1.25 per acre, and for allotments so that each member should have an equal average of 120 acres. Each allottee was required to designate a tract of forty acres, which was "made inalienable and nontaxable as a homestead in perpetuity."[3]

In the Cherokee Nation, the allotments were to be 110 acres of the average allottable land on the basis of the appraisal to be made by the Dawes Commission. Provision was made for a homestead of forty acres, which was to be inalienable and nontaxable during the lifetime of the allottee but not longer than twenty-one years. In the Seminole, Creek, and Cherokee nations, the freedmen (former black slaves of Indian slaveholders) received the same allotments as the Indians by blood.

The closing of the tribal affairs of the Five Civilized Tribes involved, among other tasks, the preparation of a correct tribal roll and division of the land among the members according to the varying provisions of the separate agreements. Applications for enrollment were received from approximately 250,000 people in all parts of the United States, but the final rolls contained the names of approximately 101,000, of whom approximately one-fourth were full blooded.

The enrollment records consist of the application made for enrollment together with all of the records, evidence, and papers filed in connection with the decision of the commissioner.[4]

During the early stages of enrollment, appointments were made by the commission at various places in the different nations at which the Indians and freedmen appeared to apply for enrollment. At that time the applicants were sworn before a notary public, but their testimony was taken orally and placed upon a card, with the exception of Cherokees. Written testimony was taken in all Cherokee cases. In a great majority of the early enrollments, except Cherokee cases, the only records shown are the statements that were taken from the applicants personally and placed on the cards, which constitute the enrollment record, together with any other evidence that may have been obtained. In a great many instances, where there was doubt as to the rights of the applicants to enrollment and the applicant could not be identified from the tribal rolls, the written testimony of the applicants was taken and made a part of the

record. Additional testimony was also taken at later dates. The information shown in figure 14-6 is typical of Cherokee applications.

After the enrollment of all citizens by blood or intermarriage, and freedmen, who were clearly identified upon the tribal rolls, was completed, written testimony was taken in all doubtful cases. Written testimony was also taken in all applications made for the identification of Mississippi Choctaws and in practically all other cases as the work neared completion.

The tribal rolls of the various nations came into the possession of the commissioner to the Five Civilized Tribes. They were used for identification and as a basis for enrollment.

When the enrollments were completed, the names of all persons whom the commission had decided were entitled to enrollment were placed on the rolls. These rolls show the name, age, sex, degree of blood, and the number of the census card, generally known as the "enrollment card," on which each citizen was enrolled. A number was placed opposite each name appearing on this roll, beginning at 1 and running consecutively until the final number was completed. This roll was made out in quintuplicate and forwarded to the secretary of the interior for his approval. The secretary returned three copies for the files of the commissioner to the Five Civilized Tribes. The roll thus approved was known as the "approval roll" and was used as the basis for allotments, except in the cases of a large number of Creeks, to whom allotments were made before the approval of their enrollment. These allotments were subsequently confirmed by Congress.

The enrollment records consist of: (1) the "census card"—the card on which the applicant was listed for enrollment (in the early enrollment, some persons were listed on what is known as a "doubtful card," and later on the names appearing on the doubtful cards were transferred to regular census cards); (2) all testimony taken in the matter of the application at various times prior to rendition of the decision granting the application; (3) birth affidavits, affidavits of death, and other evidence and papers filed in connection with the application made for enrollment; and (4) the enrollment as shown on the approved roll.

Many of the records of the Dawes Commission are still in the custody of the Muskogee Area Office of the Bureau of Indian Affairs in Muskogee, Oklahoma. Others have been deposited with the Oklahoma Historical Society in Oklahoma City. The majority of these records have been reproduced on microfilm and are available at the Oklahoma Historical Society; the National Archives records center in Fort Worth; the University of Oklahoma in Norman, Oklahoma; and the Family History Library in Salt Lake City.[5]

GENERAL RECORDS OF THE COMMISSION TO THE FIVE CIVILIZED TRIBES

Most of the correspondence received prior to 1901 and copies of letters sent prior to 1906 are in the custody of the Oklahoma Historical Society. This correspondence can also be found in the records of the Indian Division of the Office of the Secretary of the Interior (Record Group 48) and also the Bureau of Indian Affairs (Record Group 75).

Index to Letters Received From the Department of Interior, 1907–1914

This index is divided into chronological segments: 1907 to 1908,

1909 to 1910, 1911 to 1912, and 1913 to 1914. Entries are arranged alphabetically by subject and thereunder chronologically by the date the letter was written. Information given for each letter includes the date it was written, the file number assigned, and a short summary of the subject.

Register of Letters Received From the Department of Interior ("Special Index"), 1903–1914

Arranged chronologically by date of receipt. Information given for each letter includes the date written, the date received, the name of the sender, the file number assigned, and a short summary of the subject.

Letters Received From the Department of Interior ("Departmental Letters"), 1901–1914

Arranged numerically by file number assigned chronologically by date of receipt within each fiscal year. The letters relate to all phases of the commission's activities, including administration, enrollment, allotment, the leasing and sale of allotted and unallotted land, and the establishment of town sites.

Instructions Received From the Department of Interior, 1900

Carbon copies of letters received from the Department of Interior relating to enrollment and enrollment procedures, the leasing of allotted land, and the removal of non-Indians from allotted land; arranged chronologically by date of receipt and indexed by subject. Many letters transmit opinions of the assistant attorney general on legal issues relating to enrollment and allotment.

Index to Letters Received, 1897–1913

The index is divided into yearly segments. Within each segment, entries are arranged alphabetically by the first two letters of the sender's surname. Information given includes the name of the sender, the date the letter was written, the file number assigned, and a brief summary of the subject.

Registers of Letters Received, 1908–1914

Arranged chronologically by date of receipt. The information given for each letter includes the name and address of the sender, the date the letter was written, the date received, the file number assigned, a brief summary of the subject, and, occasionally, remarks about actions taken.

Registers of Letters Received From the Union Agency, 1906–1909

Arranged chronologically by date of receipt. The information given for each letter includes the date it was written, the date received, the file number assigned, and a brief summary of the subject.

Letters Received ("General Office Letters"), 1900–1914

Original letters and telegrams received from the U.S. Indian inspector for Indian Territory, the Union Agency, other Indian agencies, field offices of the Dawes Commission, including the land offices maintained for each tribe, officials of tribal governments, and the general public. The letters relate to all phases of the commission's activities. Arranged numerically by file number assigned chronologically by date of receipt within each fiscal year.

Letters Received By Commissioner Bixby, 1897–1906

Arranged alphabetically by name of sender until 1901 and thereafter numerically by file number assigned chronologically by date of receipt. The letters relate to the status of applications for enrollment or allotment, the sale and leasing of land, and

applications for employment. Many of the books are marked "personal and confidential."

Letters Sent to the Secretary of Interior, 1906–1914

Press copies of letters sent to the secretary of the interior through the commissioner of Indian affairs. Arranged chronologically by date sent and indexed by subject.

Letters Sent to the Commissioner of Indian Affairs, 1907–1911

Arranged in rough chronological order and indexed by subject.

Letters Sent ("Miscellaneous Letters"), 1895–1914

Press copies of letters sent to the U.S. Indian inspector for Indian territory, the Union Agency, other Indian agencies, field offices of the Dawes Commission, officials of tribal governments, and the general public. Arranged chronologically by date sent.

Letters Sent By Commissioner Bixby, 1902–1907

Press copies of letters sent by Commissioner Bixby from Washington, D.C., to Commissioner in Charge T.B. Needles in Muskogee and letters sent by Bixby from Muskogee to the secretary of the interior, the commissioner of Indian affairs, and members of Congress. Arranged chronologically by date sent.

Annual Narrative Reports, 1894–1914

Printed copies of the annual reports of the commission's activities submitted to the secretary of the interior. The reports provide detailed information about the activities of the commission. Arranged chronologically by date of report (no reports for 1897, 1899 to 1903).

Index to Reference Documents

The index provides the category and file number of each document. The categories used are: A—Cherokee and Delaware; B—Choctaw and Chickasaw; C—Creek; D—Enrollment; E—Leases; F—Reports; and G—Miscellaneous. Arranged alphabetically by subject.

Reference Documents ("Miscellaneous Documents"), 1896–1904.

Correspondence, printed Congressional documents, copies of agreements with tribal governments, rules and instructions issued by the secretary of the interior or the commission, receipts for rolls and other papers supplied by tribal governments, copies of documents filed in cases heard by the U.S. Supreme Court and other federal courts, and lists of persons admitted to tribal citizenship by U.S. Courts. There are also transcripts of hearings in citizenship cases. Arranged in three groups. Within each group, documents are arranged numerically by a file number assigned by the commission.

RECORDS RELATING TO ALL TRIBES

Index to Enrollment Cards, 1899–1907

Arranged by tribe and thereunder by enrollment category. Entries within each volume are arranged alphabetically by the first two letters of the applicant's surname. Generally, the index provides only the number of the card on which the applicant's name appears, but some volumes also provide the individual's enrollment number. Many of the volumes include the names of persons listed on "doubtful" and "rejected" cards.

Index and Final Rolls, 1914

The index and final rolls are contained in separate volumes. Entries in the index are arranged by tribe, thereunder by enrollment category, and thereunder in roughly alphabetical order by

Figure 14-6. A typical application for Cherokee citizenship.

Application for Citizenship in the Cherokee Nation of Indians.

To The Hon. Dawes Commission: Now comes your petitioners, Mark Tiger Smith and wife Mary Smith and seven children, and makes application to be admitted and enrolled as citizens or members of the Cherokee Nation or Tribe of Indians in the Indian Territory; *and in support of said application respectfully allege* and states as follows: Your applicants are Cherokee Indians by blood; and that I (Mark Tiger Smith) is enrolled on the Hester roll taken in 1882, as a member of the Cherokee Tribe or Band of Cherokee Indians residing in the State of North Carolina; and that I am the son of one Henry Smith who is enrolled on the Treaty roll of 1836, Mullay roll of 1848, Siler roll of 1851 and 1852 and Hester roll of 1882, and who is a member of the Cherokee Band of Indians residing in North Carolina, and an Indian by blood, recognized and enrolled as a member of the Cherokee Tribe of Indians.

And that my wife Mary Smith is enrolled on the Hester roll made in 1882, and who is a member of the Cherokee Tribe or Band of Cherokee Indians residing in the State of North Carolina, and that she is the daughter of one David Murphy,(Indian) and Caroline ~~Murphy~~, (white), said David Murphy being enrolled on the Treaty roll of 1836, Mullay roll of 1848, Sila roll of 1851 & 1852 and Hester roll of 1882, who is a member of the Cherokee Tribe of Indians and an Indian by blood, recognized and enrolled as a member of the Cherokee Tribe of Indians.

And that we have seven children the names and ages stated herein, for whom as parents and natural guardian, which we also ask to be admitted and enrolled as members and citizens of the Cherokee Tribe or Nation of Indians in the Indian Territory.

That they are Cherokee Indians by blood by reason being sons and daughters of your applicants, who are Cherokee Indians by blood as herein set forth; and that the said children live with me.

Our names and ages are as follows:

Mark Tiger Smith *father* 42 years,

Mary Smith *Mother* 42 years,

Media Olivan Smith *daughter* 19 years,

James David Smith *Son* 17 years,

Duffy Theorphus Smith ' ' ' 15 years,

Noah Smith ' ' ' ' 12 years,

Francis Elwood Smith · · · 10 years,

Faith Lew Smith *daughter* 6 years,

Oliver Smith *Son* 0 years, 10 months.

and my Post Office address is Birdtown, North Carolina.

Wherefore your applicants pray that we be by you adjudged to be Cherokee Indians by blood and entitled to and admitted as members or citizens of the Cherokee Tribe or Nation of Indians in the Indian Territory.

And the said Dawes Commission enroll us as members or citizens of the Cherokee Tribe or Nation of Indians in the Indian Territory.

Respectfully submitted,

Mark. Tiger. Smith

State of North Carolina }
County of Swain } (Affidavit)

On this ___ day of September, 1896, personally appeared before me *S.R. Suwen*, Clerk of Superior Court within county and state afore said, Mark Tiger Smith, a resident of Birdtown N.C. and who being duly sworn according to law, declare and say: I am the identical person who maketh application for citizenship, by the name of Mark Tiger Smith, and that I have

the first two letters of the surname. Entries in the final rolls are arranged by tribe, thereunder by enrollment category, and thereunder numerically by the enrollment number assigned by the Dawes Commission.

Enrollment Cards ("Census Cards"), 1899–1907

They are original fourteen- by seven-inch printed cards annotated with information about persons applying for enrollment. Cards were prepared for each "family group" and used by enrollment parties traveling throughout Indian Territory to record information about the applicants and actions taken by the commission. The information given for each applicant generally includes name, enrollment number, age, sex, degree of Indian blood, relationship to the head of the family group, references to enrollment on earlier tribal rolls used by the Commission to verify eligibility, and parents' names. The cards often include notations about an applicant's birth or death, changes in marital status, references to related enrollment cards, and actions taken by the commission or the secretary of the interior. The cards relating to applicants as "freedmen" also contain the name of the person who owned the applicant as a slave and the owner of the applicant's parents. These cards have been microfilmed. Arranged by tribe and thereunder by enrollment category. Within each category there are generally three groups: "straight" (persons who were enrolled), "doubtful," and "rejected." Within each group, the cards are arranged numerically by a number assigned by the commission.

Duplicate Enrollment Cards, 1918–1919

Duplicate paper copies of the cards were prepared to reduce the use of the original cards and contain all of the information recorded on the original. There are no copies of Creek-, Seminole-, or Cherokee-by-blood cards. Arranged by tribe, thereunder by enrollment category, and thereunder by type of card ("straight," "doubtful," or "rejected"). Within each type, the cards are arranged numerically by a number assigned by the Dawes Commission.

Letters Sent Transmitting Enrollment Schedules, 1901–1907

Press copies of letters sent to the secretary of the interior through the commissioner of Indian affairs transmitting schedules of the names of persons recommended for enrollment and press copies of the schedules. The information given in the schedules includes the person's name, enrollment number, tribal district of residence, and the tribal roll used to verify eligibility. There are occasional remarks about relationships to other persons listed in the schedule. Arranged by tribe and thereunder by enrollment category. Within each volume, the letters are arranged chronologically by date sent.

Enrollment Schedules, 1900–1907

Carbon copies of typed schedules of the names of persons recommended for enrollment. The schedules were submitted to the secretary of the interior in triplicate for approval, and one copy was returned to the commission for reference. The information given for each person includes name, age, sex, degree of blood, and enrollment number. The schedules for the Seminoles also include the band name and a reference to an 1897 Seminole census roll. Arranged by tribal enrollment category. Names within the schedule are arranged numerically by enrollment number.

Report on Enrollment, 1909

A press copy of a report prepared by Joseph W. Howell on the enrollment of the Five Civilized Tribes which was submitted to the secretary of the interior. The report provides a detailed description of the enrollment procedures, controversial decisions, and difficulties of obtaining records from the tribal governments. There are several appendixes which provide lists of tribal rolls used by the commission.

List of Claimants, 1907

A typed "Departmental List of Persons Who Claim to be Entitled to Enrollment as Citizens and Freedmen of the Five Civilized Tribes Prepared With a View to Remedial Legislation." The list contains the names of 741 persons and includes the tribal affiliation claimed by each and a summary of the facts in each case. Names within the list are arranged alphabetically by surname.

Index to Citizenship Docket

Index to an unidentified citizenship docket which provides only a case number for each claimant under the heading "Nation Number." Arranged alphabetically by the first letter of the claimant's surname.

RECORDS OF THE DAWES COMMISSION RELATING TO CHEROKEE CITIZENSHIP

List of Rejected Claimants, 1878–1880

A handwritten copy of a list of persons whose claim to citizenship was rejected by the Cherokee Commission on Citizenship. The only information given for each claimant is the case number and the reason for rejection (by decree, by default, or withdrawn). Arranged chronologically by court term and thereunder by the reason for rejection and thereunder by case number.

List of Persons Admitted to Citizenship

A printed "List of persons admitted and re-admitted to Cherokee citizenship by the National Council and Commissions on Citizenship in the year 1880, and since that year." The list covers the period from 1880 to 1899 and appears to have been printed for use by the Commission. The only information given is the person's name and the date admitted. Arranged (roughly) in alphabetical order by surname.

Cherokee Citizenship Commission Dockets, 1880–1984, 1887–1889

A record of actions taken by the tribal commission on applications for citizenship. Each docket entry generally includes the applicant's name, age, sex, names of attorneys, the text of the application, a summary of the proceedings held, and the text of the commission's decision. Arranged numerically by case number assigned chronologically by the date the case was opened and indexed by name of applicant.

Record of Births, 1897

A record of children born from 1895 to 1897. The list appears to have been completed in 1897 and contains the child's name, date of birth, and parent's names. Most of the children listed were born in 1897. Arranged by districts of the Cherokee Nation.

Dawes Commission Dockets, 1902

A record of actions taken by the Dawes Commission on applications for citizenship. The information given for each application includes the date filed, the names of the persons covered by the application, the date the attorneys for the Cherokee filed an answer, the commission's decision, the date of appeal to the U.S. court, and the court's decision. Arranged numerically by case number assigned chronologically by the date the case was opened.

Docket of Cases Appealed, 1896–1899

A record of actions taken by the U.S. Court for the Northern District of Indian Territory on appeals from decisions of the Dawes Commission on applications under the act of 1896. The information given for each case includes the names of the parties and their attorneys, a summary of proceedings and motions filed, and the decision of the court. Arranged numerically by case number assigned chronologically by the date the case was opened. Indexed by name of applicant.

Lists of Applicants, 1902

Typed lists of persons admitted or rejected for citizenship by the U.S. courts for the northern and southern districts of Indian Territory. There are lists for the following actions: applicants admitted by the Dawes Commission and affirmed by the courts, applicants admitted by the court for the Southern District who had been rejected by the commission, applicants denied by the court for the Northern District who had been admitted by the commission, and applicants admitted by the court for the Northern District who had been denied by the commission. The information given for each applicant generally includes the Dawes Commission case number, U.S. court docket number, and Dawes Commission enrollment card number. There are separate lists for admitted and rejected applicants. Within each list, names are arranged alphabetically by surname.

Decisions of the U.S. Court, 1897–1899

Press copies of decisions of Judge William M. Springer of the U.S. Court for the Northern District of Indian Territory on appeals of decisions of the Dawes Commission on applications for enrollment under the act of 1896. The decision of the judge often includes a report on the case prepared by a "special master" appointed by the court. Arranged in roughly chronological order by the date of the decision. Each volume is indexed by the name of the applicant involved in the decision.

Records Relating to Appeals, 1897–1898

Bonds for appeals to the U.S. Supreme Court from decisions of the U.S. Court for the Northern District of Indian Territory, petitions for appeals, and assignments of errors. These records appear to be copies which were filed with the court and subsequently given to the Dawes Commission for reference. Arranged by case number assigned by the date the case was opened.

Lists of Applicants as Freedmen, 1897

Lists of applicants for participation in an award by the U.S. Court of Claims to Cherokee Freedmen who had not been included in the roll prepared for payment of the award. The lists include each applicant's name, roll number from the 1880 Cherokee census, roll number from the Wallace Roll of Cherokee freedmen, an exhibit number which corresponds to the exhibit number in the Applications for Enrollment as Freedmen, district of residence within the Cherokee Nation, and, occasionally, remarks about other enrollments. These lists were submitted as evidence to the Dawes Commission by the Cherokee National Council in enrollment proceedings. Names within each list are arranged in roughly alphabetical order by applicants' surnames.

Applications for Enrollment as Freedmen, 1897

Notarized applications prepared on printed forms submitted by persons claiming a share of a payment made to Cherokee freedmen in accordance with an award of the U.S. Court of Claims in the case of Moses Whitmire, Trustee, vs. the Cherokee Nation. The applications and supporting material were submitted by James M. Keys to the commissioner of Indian affairs between 10 May and 30 June 1897 and may have been a part of the general correspondence of the bureau. It appears that the records were returned to the Dawes Commission for use in enrollment proceedings. The application provides the applicant's name, age, and district of residence in the Cherokee Nation and the names and ages of other family members. Some letters from claimants and officials of the Cherokee tribal government are included with the application forms. Arranged numerically by exhibit number assigned in roughly chronological order by date of application.

Index to Applications for Enrollment Through Intermarriage

A handwritten index to the applications for enrollment through intermarriage. The only information given is the application number. Arranged alphabetically by the first letter of the applicant's surname.

Applications for Enrollment Through Intermarriage

Original applications submitted to the Dawes Commission for enrollment, which required any person married to a Cherokee citizen to apply for themselves and their children. The applications or petitions are notarized and provide the name, age, sex, and address of each child and information in support of the claim to citizenship, such as date of marriage and enrollment on other tribal rolls. In addition to the applications, there are occasionally copies of marriage licenses, statements of witnesses to the marriage, notice of service of a copy of the application on the chief of the Cherokee tribe, and the answer of the tribal government generally rejecting the claim. The Dawes Commission held hearings on the applications at Fort Gibson, but no records of the hearings have been located. Arranged numerically by application number assigned in roughly alphabetical order by the first letter of the applicant's surname.

Dockets to Rejected and Doubtful Applications, 1904–1905

There is one docket for Cherokees by blood and one for freedmen. Within each docket there are separate sections for "doubtful" and "rejected" applications. Within each section, entries are arranged numerically by case number assigned chronologically by the date the case was opened. Each docket contains an index to names of applicants. A record of actions taken on applications classified by the commission as "doubtful" and "rejected." The information for each application includes the names of the applicants and their attorneys, the decision of the commission, the date prepared, date forwarded to the commissioner of Indian affairs, and date approved by the secretary of the interior. Many of the "doubtful" and some of the "rejected" applications were eventually enrolled, and there are references to enrollment card numbers. The case numbers in these dockets match the application numbers in the applications for enrollment and enrollment card numbers in the enrollment cards ("census cards").

Applications for Enrollment, 1898–1907

Original applications for enrollment and supporting evidence submitted to the Dawes Commission. The records include carbon copies of the testimony taken at hearings held by the commission, notices and letters sent to the applicants and the attorneys for both the applicants and the Cherokee tribe, correspondence with the secretary of the interior about the applications, and copies of the commission's decisions. There are applications only for the following categories: doubtful citizens by blood, rejected citizens by blood, doubtful freedmen, rejected freedmen, and new born freedmen. There are also some "memorandum cases" which contain applications rejected under an act of Congress that restricted the commission's jurisdiction. Applications for the bulk of the Cherokee categories are still in the custody of the Bureau of Indian Affairs and have been microfilmed. Arranged by enrollment category and thereunder numerically by application number assigned chronologically by date of application. There are numerous gaps in the applications, and some applications are missing.

Transcripts of Testimony of Applicants, 1910

Carbon copies of transcripts of testimony taken at hearings held by the commission. The majority of the applications relate to children of persons previously enrolled by the commission and persons listed on a roll of "Eastern Cherokees" who were not enrolled. Arranged numerically by application number assigned chronologically by date of application.

Record of Decisions, 1901–1902

A record of actions taken by the commission on applications for enrollment. The information given for each action includes the names of the applicants, names of attorneys for the applicants and the Cherokee tribe, the nature of the decision, and a reference to the enrollment cards. Arranged chronologically by date of decision and indexed by applicant.

Index to the Cherokee Final Rolls

Two indexes to names appearing on the "Final Roll of the Cherokees." One index is contained in a single volume, and the second index is divided into two volumes (*A* through *K* and *L* through *Z*). The only information given in the index is the enrollee's Dawes enrollment number. Arranged alphabetically by the first two letters of the enrollee's surname.

Records Relating to Choctaw and Chickasaw Citizenship

Acts of the Choctaw National Council, 1893–1895

Handwritten copies of "Acts of the General Council Admitting Parties to Citizenship." The text of the acts includes the names of persons and the authority for admission. Arranged chronologically by date of passage.

Lists of Applicants for Choctaw Citizenship, 1902

A typed list of persons who applied for Choctaw citizenship. The information given for each applicant includes the Dawes Commission case number and a reference to the enrollment cards. The list is annotated with an "A" for persons who were admitted and a "D" for persons who were denied. Arranged alphabetically by applicants' surnames.

Lists of Persons Involved in Appeals to U.S. Courts, 1900

Lists of applicants for citizenship whose cases were appealed to the U.S. Court for the Central District of Indian Territory at South McAlester or the Southern District at Ardmore. There are lists for persons admitted by the court, persons admitted by the court who were previously denied by the Dawes Commission, and persons denied by the court who had been previously admitted by the Commission. The information given for each person generally includes the Dawes Commission case number, the U.S. court docket number, and references to the Choctaw-Chickasaw Citizenship Court case number. There are

also two lists of cases heard by the U.S. Court for the Central District. One is arranged numerically by case number and the other alphabetically by the name of the first person listed in the appeal. Arranged by type of action taken by the court. The names within each list are arranged in rough alphabetical order by surname.

Indexes to Applicants, 1900–1906

Indexes to applications for enrollment under various acts of Congress, including Choctaws applying under the act of 31 May 1900; Choctaw and Chickasaw Freedmen testifying at Atoka and Colbert between 4 and 16 June 1900; Choctaw and Chickasaw applicants under the act of 1 July 1902; Choctaw children applying after 25 September 1902; Choctaws also enrolled as Cherokees; Choctaw and Chickasaw applicants listed on "rejected" and "doubtful" enrollment cards; and Choctaws and Chickasaws found on earlier rolls who had not applied for enrollment. Each index generally provides only a reference to the enrollment cards. Arranged by type of application. Entries within each index are arranged alphabetically by surname.

Lists of Chickasaw Applicants, 1899–1902

Lists of applicants for enrollment by the Dawes Commission as Chickasaws, persons listed on tribal rolls who had not applied for enrollment, persons admitted by U.S. courts, and persons denied by the Dawes Commission. There are a few copies of marriage certificates and other documents submitted as evidence in enrollment proceedings. Some of the lists are annotated with enrollment numbers. Arranged in rough chronological order by the date compiled.

Lists of Choctaw Applicants, 1899–1902

Lists of applicants or potential applicants for enrollment by the Dawes Commission as Choctaws. There are lists of "Choctaws on the 1896 roll—unenrolled by the Dawes Commission," "Choctaws not having appeared before the Dawes Commission by 28 October 1899," "applicants admitted by the Dawes Commission," and "parties on Choctaw cards who may be on Cherokee Cards." The information given in the lists generally includes the person's name, Dawes Commission enrollment number, and a reference to one of the earlier Choctaw rolls used to determine eligibility for enrollment. Arranged in rough chronological order by the date compiled.

Lists of Pending Applications, 1902–1905

Lists of names of applicants whose applications were pending at the time the lists were compiled. The information given for each applicant includes name, age, sex, and enrollment card number. There are separate lists for Choctaws by blood, Chickasaws by blood, Choctaw freedmen, and Chickasaw freedmen. Within each list the names are arranged numerically by enrollment card number.

Dockets of Special Enrollment Cases, 1905–1907

There is a separate docket for each type of case. Entries within each docket are arranged numerically by case number assigned chronologically by the date the case was opened. The information given for each case includes the names of all applicants, names of attorneys, a chronological summary of papers filed and proceedings held, the decision of the commission, actions taken by the secretary of the interior, and references to related cases.

Record of Decisions, 1902–1904, 1906–1907

A record of decisions on enrollment applications made by the Commission and forwarded to the secretary of the interior for approval. The information given for each decision includes the names of the applicants, enrollment card number, date of decision, action taken by the secretary of the interior, and date of notification to the applicant. There are separate volumes for Choctaws and Chickasaws. Within each volume, entries are in rough chronological order by date of decision.

RECORDS OF THE CHOCTAW-CHICKASAW CITIZENSHIP COURT

Section 31 of an act of Congress of 1 July 1902 (32 Stat. 641) established a Choctaw-Chickasaw Citizenship Court and authorized either tribe to file a bill of equity in the Citizenship Court to seek the annulment of the decisions made by the U.S. courts in Indian territory under the act of 10 June 1896. Persons involved in those judgements were required to institute proceedings in the Choctaw-Chickasaw Citizenship Court to regain enrollment. Cases originating in the U.S. Court for the Central District of Indian Territory were heard by the Citizenship Court at South McAlester, and cases from the Southern District were heard at Tishomingo.

The Citizenship Court heard 256 cases involving more that 3,400 people and admitted 161 to citizenship. The case files of the court are still in the custody of the Muskogee Area Office of the Bureau of Indian Affairs.

Lists of Claimants, 1902

The information given for each person claiming citizenship includes name, sex, age, degree of Indian blood, Dawes enrollment card number, and some remarks relating to decisions of the Citizenship Court. Some of the lists described under "Lists of Persons Involved in Appeals to U.S. Courts, 1900" have been annotated with case numbers from the Citizenship Court. There are separate lists for Choctaws and Chickasaws. Within each list, the names are arranged alphabetically by surname.

Index to Dockets, 1903

There is one index to the South McAlester docket, one index to the Tishomingo docket, and one consolidated index to both dockets. The information given for each person involved in a case before the Citizenship Court is the case number and the Dawes enrollment card number.

General Dockets, 1903–1904

There is one docket for cases heard at South McAlester and one docket for cases heard at Tishomingo. Entries within each docket are arranged numerically by case number assigned chronologically by the date the case was opened; indexed by surname of principal party. Information given for each case includes the names of all parties involved, names of attorneys, nature of the case, and a chronological summary of papers filed and proceedings held.

Appearance Dockets, 1902–1904

There is a separate docket for cases heard at South McAlester and Tishomingo. Entries within each docket are arranged numerically by case number assigned chronologically by the date the case was opened; indexed by the surname of the principal party. Information given for each case includes the names of all parties involved, the names of attorneys, and a summary of the orders, writs, and other documents filed with the court. The summaries in these dockets are more detailed than the summaries contained in the dockets described above under "General Dockets, 1903–1904."

Case Files, 1902–1904

Original papers filed in proceedings held by the Citizenship Court including briefs, memorandums of argument submitted by attorneys for the Choctaw and Chickasaw nations, and opinions of the court. The majority of the cases were heard at South McAlester. Arranged by docket number assigned in chronological order by the date the case was opened.

RECORDS RELATING TO THE IDENTIFICATION OF MISSISSIPPI CHOCTAWS

The Dawes Commission was required by an act of Congress to investigate the right of the Mississippi Choctaws to enrollment and allotment. The commission received 24,634 applications from all over the United States before the deadline of 25 March 1903.

Lists of Claimants Under the Treaty of 1830

Manuscript copies of lists of persons who remained in Mississippi under article 14 of the treaty of 1830 and claimed land. Each list generally includes the claimant's name, date of application, and the legal description of the land claimed. Some lists have been annotated with Dawes enrollment numbers and enrollment card numbers. Arranged alphabetically by surname.

Index and Record of Testimony, 1899

Copies of an index to Mississippi Choctaw applicants who appeared before the commission in 1899 in Carthage, Philadelphia, and Decatur, Mississippi and typed transcripts of the testimony given by the applicants. Arranged alphabetically by surname of the applicant.

Indexes to Field Cards

Index to enrollment cards. The only information provided is the "field number" of the applicant's enrollment card. Arranged alphabetically by surname of applicant.

Indexes to Applicants, 1902–1906

Indexes to applicants for enrollment under various acts of Congress. The indexes include the following categories: identified and rejected; rejected and reviewed by the secretary of the interior; decisions during the year ending 30 June 1903; applications for children whose parents were rejected; newborn and minor children. The indexes generally provide only a reference to the applicant's enrollment card number and occasionally an enrollment number. Arranged alphabetically by surname of applicant.

Decisions of the Commission, 1902–1904

Decisions of the commission on applications for identification as Mississippi Choctaws. The decision generally reviews the facts of the application. Arranged chronologically by date of decision. The first volume contains an index to all applicants covered by the decisions.

Roll of Identified Mississippi Choctaws, 1905

List of persons who were identified as Mississippi Choctaws. The information provided for each person includes enrollment number and enrollment card number. The names on the roll are arranged by enrollment card number; indexed by surname.

Lists of Identified Full-Blood Mississippi Choctaws

Information given for each person includes enrollment card number, age, sex, post office address, county or parish of residence, and date of removal to the Choctaw Nation. The lists have been annotated to indicate persons who were removed at government expense, refused to remove, could not be located, or died prior to removal to the Choctaw Nation. Arranged alphabetically by surname.

Lists of Persons Removed, 1904

List of persons identified as Mississippi Choctaws who were removed from Mississippi and Louisiana at government expense, and a list of persons who were identified but refused to remove. The information given for each person includes age, sex, post office address, county or parish of residence, and date of removal or identification. Names of persons who removed are arranged alphabetically. Names of persons who refused to remove are arranged numerically by identified roll number.

RECORDS RELATING TO CREEK CITIZENSHIP

List of Applicants, 1895–1896

List of applicants considered by the Creek Citizenship Commission in 1895 and 1896. The information given for each applicant includes type of citizenship claimed, date of application, date of judgement, decision rendered, and a reference to a "Record Book." The list has been annotated with the field numbers of Dawes enrollment cards. Arranged alphabetically by surname.

Citizenship Commission Docket, 1895

A record of cases heard by the Citizenship Commission. The information given for each case includes the names of all persons involved and occasionally a reference to the action taken by the Citizenship Commission. Arranged numerically by case number assigned chronologically by the date the case was opened and indexed by surname of applicant.

Record Books, 1885–1888, 1895–1896

Record of actions taken by the tribal Citizenship Commission on applications for citizenship. The information given for each case generally includes the text of the application, transcripts of testimony, and the commission's recommendation. There are occasional references to the docket described under "Citizenship Commission Docket, 1895." Part of the record was prepared on unbound printed forms ("Census of the Non-Citizens of the Muskogee Nation"). There is a list of persons which contains the person's age and a description of his or her property. Arranged in rough numerical order by case number assigned in chronological order by the date the case opened.

Lists of Admitted Applicants, 1902

Lists of persons admitted to citizenship by the Dawes Commission or the U.S. Court for the Northern District of Indian Territory. The list gives only the person's name and Dawes Commission case number. Some of the lists have been annotated with field numbers of Dawes enrollment cards. Arranged alphabetically by surname of applicant.

Indexes to Unenrolled Creeks, 1900

Creeks on the authenticated roll of 1890 and Creeks on the authenticated roll of 1895 who had not been enrolled by the Dawes Commission as of 15 August 1900. Information given for each person includes town of residence and the roll numbers from the 1890 and 1895 rolls. Arranged alphabetically by surname.

List of Unenrolled Creeks

A list of the names of Creeks who appeared on various tribal rolls but had not been enrolled by the Dawes Commission. The only information given is the person's name.

Miscellaneous Indexes, 1902–1906

Indexes to various enrollment categories, including citizens by blood, freedmen, minors, and newborns. The indexes generally provide only the enrollee's enrollment number or enrollment card number. Arranged alphabetically by surname of enrollee.

Lists of Applicants, 1900–1907

Lists of Creeks whose names appear on various tribal rolls and applicants for whom birth or death affidavits were submitted. Some of the lists have been annotated with enrollment card numbers. Arranged alphabetically by surname.

Index to Freedmen Enrollment Cards, 1898

Index to the "Old Series" of Freedmen enrollment cards. Arranged alphabetically by surname of enrollee.

Enrollment Cards ("Old Series Cards"), 1898

Original enrollment cards prepared from the authenticated 1895 Creek census. Each card contains the names of the members of a family group and each person's age, sex, degree of Indian blood, post office address, district or town of residence, 1895 payroll number, and relationship to the head of the family group. The card also includes remarks about names used on earlier rolls and actions taken by the Dawes Commission and references to the field numbers of the enrollment cards. Arranged numerically by card number.

Record of Enrollment

A record prepared on a printed paper form similar to the enrollment cards. The form contains the names of all members of a family group and remarks about actions taken by the Dawes Commission. The field numbers on these cards do not match the numbers on the enrollment cards. Arranged numerically by a field number.

RECORDS RELATING TO SEMINOLE CITIZENSHIP

Index to Newborns, 1905

Persons enrolled under the act of Congress of 3 March 1905. The only information given is the person's enrollment number and enrollment card number. Arranged alphabetically by enrollee's surname.

Enrollment Schedules, 1900

Schedules prepared on printed forms of the names of persons enrolled as Seminole Citizens by Blood and Seminole Freedmen. The information given for each person includes age, sex, band name, roll number from the 1897 Seminole census, post office address, and parents' names and 1897 enrollment numbers. Arranged numerically by enrollment card number.

INDIAN CENSUS ROLLS, 1885–1940

These are census rolls usually submitted each year by agents or superintendents in charge of Indian reservations, as required by an act of 4 July 1884 (23 Stat. 98). The data on the rolls varies to some extent, but usually includes the Indian and/or English name of the person, roll number, age or date of birth, sex, and relationship to head of family. Beginning in 1930, the rolls also show the degree of Indian blood, marital status, ward status, place of residence, and sometimes other information. For certain years—including 1935, 1936, 1938 and 1939—only supplemental rolls of additions and deletions were compiled.

There is not a census for every reservation or group of Indians for every year. Only persons who maintained a formal affiliation with a tribe under federal supervision are listed on these census rolls.[6]

The researcher will find many census rolls listed under particular agencies, and some of these are duplicates of census records found in this group. Often, however, the agent retained a "working copy" of a census roll upon which he penciled-in comments concerning a particular individual or family. It is worth the extra time to consult the agency copy and the copy which was sent to the Bureau in Washington, D.C.

MUSKOGEE AREA OFFICE

The Muskogee Area Office was established in 1948 to administer Bureau of Indian Affairs business concerning the Cherokee (including Delaware and Shawnee), Chickasaw, Choctaw, Creek, and Seminole Indians of Oklahoma. Until 1874 there had been agencies for the individual tribes (the agencies for the Choctaws and Chickasaws, however, were consolidated). The Union Agency was established in 1874 for all five tribes. Until 1898 the tribes largely governed themselves. In 1893 the Commission to the Five Civilized Tribes (Dawes Commission) was established. The Curtis Act of 1898 provided for the preparation of tribal rolls and the making of allotments by the commission. The act also created the positions of inspector for Indian Territory and superintendent of schools. In 1905 the commission was reduced to a single commissioner, and in 1907 the position of inspector was combined with that of commissioner. The Union Agency and the commission were combined in 1914 to form the Five Civilized Tribes Agency, which was absorbed by the Muskogee Area Office in 1948.

The records, 1835 to 1952, include letters sent by the Choctaw and Chickasaw Agency, 1867 and 1870 to 1873; account books of the Union Agency, 1876 to 1878, Choctaw national treasurer, 1868 to 1877, and Creek Nation, 1905 to 1911; journals of the House of Kings, Creek Nation, 1895 to 1897 and 1899; general records of the Union Agency and Five Civilized Tribes Agency; records of the tribal enrollments; census rolls dating from 1852; and case files for individual Indians. Fiscal records include money files for individual Indians, accounts current and other accounts, applications for per-capita payments, and annuity and other payrolls.[7]

The Muskogee Area Office at Anadarko, Oklahoma, administers Bureau of Indian Affairs programs for the following agencies: Ardmore, Okmulgee, Osage, Miami, Tahlequah, Talihina, and Wewoka.[8]

ARDMORE AGENCY RECORDS

Census Reports on Living Enrollees, 1908–1945
A record prepared on printed forms of "Living Members of the Five Civilized Tribes Owning Restricted Indian Allotted Land, 30 June 1927." The information contained on the form includes the Indian's name, Dawes enrollment number, tribe, degree of blood, age, sex, ability to read and write English, schools attended, marital status, health, occupation, legal description of land owned, and an opinion as to the person's competency. There are also some census reports compiled as of 30 June 1926 and in 1930 which provide similar information. The records include some correspondence between the agency and the field clerk pertaining to the completion of the forms and some photographs of Indians and their homes. The reports appear to include only Indians living in Carter, Garvin, Love, and Murray counties. Arranged alphabetically by first letter of the enrollee's surname.

RECORDS OF THE OFFICE AT VINITA

Census Reports on Living Enrollees, 1927–1930
A record prepared on printed forms of "Living Members of the Five Civilized Tribes Owning Restricted Indian Allotted Land, 30 June 1927." The information contained on the form includes the Indian's name, Dawes enrollment number, tribe, degree of blood, age, sex, ability to read and write English, schools attended, marital status, health, occupation, legal description of land owned, and an opinion as to the person's competency. Arranged alphabetically by first letter of the enrollee's surname.

CHICKASAW NATION RECORDS[9]

An agreement between the Chickasaws and Choctaws signed at Doaksville on 17 January 1837 (11 Stat., 573) permitted the Chickasaws to settle in the Choctaw Nation with all the rights of Choctaw citizens. A further provision created an area to be set aside as the Chickasaw District, the land to be held in common by the two tribes. Residents of the district were to have equal representation in the Choctaw General Council and were to be governed by the laws of the Choctaw Nation.

This arrangement proved to be unsatisfactory for the Chickasaws. In 1855 another treaty was signed (11 Stat., 611) giving the Chickasaws the unrestricted right of self-government and defining the boundaries of the Chickasaw Nation. In 1856 and 1857 constitutions were adopted, the government being organized into three departments. The executive authority was vested in the office of governor and the legislative in a senate and house of representatives. A supreme court was established as well as district and county courts. This form of government was retained until the advent of statehood for Oklahoma.

The original counties of the Chickasaw District were Panola, Wichita, Caddo, and Perry. When the Chickasaw Nation proper was organized under the treaty of 1855, the country was again divided into four counties called Panola, Pickens, Tishomingo, and Pontotoc.

On 23 April 1897 the Chickasaws, under the Atoka Agreement, consented to the provisions of allotment of their lands in severalty.

Chickasaw Annuity Roll, 1878
List of Chickasaws registered in Panola, Pickens, Pontotoc, and Tishomingo Counties in Chickasaw Nation and Masholatubby and Pushmatahal Districts in Choctaw Nation for the annuity payment of 1878. Contains names of head of family, indication of wife, number of children, total number in family, and name of person receiving payment. Arranged by consecutive numbers.

Chickasaw Annuity Roll, 1878
List of persons registered in Masholatubby District for Chickasaw Annuity of 1878 resulting from the Leased District claim. Contains unidentified number, name, number of men, women, and children, and total number in family. Arranged alphabetically by county and thereafter alphabetically by surname.

Chickasaw Census Roll, 1890
Census rolls of Pickens and Pontotoc counties, Chickasaw

Nation. Contains names of heads of families, indication of wives, post office address, age of head of family, number of male and female children, Chickasaw or Choctaw by blood or marriage, whether U.S. citizen, state Negro, Indian Negro, or intruder, and total number in family. Arranged by county, thereafter not arranged.

Chickasaw Payroll, 1893
Payroll of individuals in Chickasaw Nation. Includes Maytubby's roll of 1893 and Iishatubby's roll of 1893. Includes family number, names, ages, number in family, and Checkmark for payment. Notations include Dawes card number, dead, full payment, and dates. One list is arranged consecutively by family groups. Another list is arranged alphabetically by surname.

Chickasaw Census, 1896
List of Chickasaw in the Chickasaw Nation and residing in Choctaw Nation. Contains names of head of family (both parents) and children, ages, sex, whether Chickasaw by blood or intermarriage, date of intermarriage, and remarks. Remarks consist primarily of "married to . . ."

Chickasaw Census Index, 1897
Contains name and page number in census roll. Arranged alphabetically by individual's surname, thereafter by county.

Chickasaw Census, 1897
List of Chickasaws registered within Chickasaw and Choctaw Nations. Separate lists for intermarried whites and doubtful citizens within each county. List of names from 1893 Chickasaw roll but not on the 1896 Chickasaw roll. Contains name and census card number. Arranged alphabetically by county, numerically by district in Choctaw Nation.

Census and Citizenship Records
Documents concerning census, 1896; letters and documents concerning citizenship, 1861–1907; 1818 census; 1890 census of Pickens County and Tishomingo County; Choctaws in the Chickasaw Nation, 1896; journals of the Citizenship Committee and Court of Claims, 1889–95; proceedings of Investigation Committee, 1893; records of the Chickasaw Commission, 1896; Dawes Commission citizenship cases, 1896–1904; incompetent record and list of original claimants, 1839–90; journal of the Commission on Incompetent Funds, 1889–90; incompetent fund records, 1889–1890; evidence book, 1889–90; competent and incompetent roll; Chickasaw per capita, 1889–90.

Records of the Executive Department, Senate and House of Representatives
Constitutions, acts and laws, 1848–1901; senate journals, 1860–1902; house of representatives, 1866–94; journals of the house of representatives, 1894–1909; lists of national, district, and county officers, 1856–1905; official and unofficial papers of the Executive Department; Chickasaw tribal officers, Cyrus Harris and D.H. Johnston, 1856–1936.

Court Records
Panola County, 1878–94; Pickens and Wichita counties, 1849–81; Pickins County, 1864–1906; Pontotoc County, 1884–1904; District Court, unidentified county, 1891–92; Tishimingo County, 1866–1906; Supreme Court, District Court, Attorney Generals' Reports and other records, 1856–1907.

School Records
Reports and minutes of the School Committee, 1872–1905; at-tendance and financial records, 1890–1902; letters and documents concerning academies, 1867–1928.

Permit Records
Permits to non-citizens, 1868–97; taxes, permits to non-citizens, 1874–1906; Chickasaw permits, 1878–1904; traders, 1889–1902; doctors, 1894–1902.

Financial Records
National treasurer and auditor, 1858–1902; financial records of the national treasurer and auditor, 1884–98.

Land Use and Revenue
Taxes, special national agent, land, agricultural leases, cattle, hay, timber, minerals, roads, railroads, ferries, telephones and townsites, 1878–1909.

Letters Sent and Received and Other Documents, 1873–1919

OKMULGEE AGENCY—CREEK

The Creek Nation in Indian Territory was composed of the Upper and Lower Creek divisions, which were not fully united until 1867, when the "Muskogee Nation" was established with a written constitution and code of laws which remained in force until 1906. Under the constitution, a principal chief and a second chief were elected by popular vote every four years. The legislature, called the National Council, consisted of the House of Kings and the House of Warriors. These bodies met each year in regular session at the national capital. The judicial system included a Supreme Court and courts for each of the nation's six districts. The districts were Coweta, Muskogee (originally called Arkansas District), Eufaula, Wewoka, Deep Fork, and Okmulgee.

There was considerable opposition to allotment in severalty among the Creeks, and an agreement concluded with the Dawes Commission on 27 September 1897 was opposed by the chief and rejected by the National Council. This agreement was amended and in 1897 became Section 30 of the Curtis Act. A further agreement was reached providing for the allotment of 160 acres to every tribe member, including freedmen, and for the dissolution of the tribal government on or before 4 March 1906.[10]

CREEK NATION RECORDS[11]

Creek Old Settlers Roll, 1857
Contains the name of the head of each household and the names of the other members, the amount each received, the total amount paid to the family, and the payee's mark. Arranged by town and thereunder by family group.

Creek Payrolls, 1858–1859
Contains the name of the head of the family and the names of the other family members, the amount each received, and some remarks. Arranged by town and thereunder by family.

Creek Payroll, 1867
Arranged by town and thereunder by family group. Contains payee's name, amount received, and mark.

Index to Creek Freedmen, 1869
The index provides a page reference to an unidentified volume. The page numbers do not match the copy of the Dunn Roll of 1869. Arranged alphabetically by surname.

Payroll of Creek Freedmen and Index (Dunn Roll), 1869
The payroll contains the payee's name, amount received, and

mark. The index contains the payee's roll number. Arranged by District. Index is arranged alphabetically by given name.

Creek Census, 1890

Census rolls of the following towns compiled during 1890: Arbeka (Deep Fork), Arkansas (doubtful), Kialachee, Arbeka (doubtful), Northfork (colored), Tuckabache (partial); typed lists for Arbeka, Alabama, Cussetah, Coweta, North Fork (colored), Concharty, Hutcherchuppa, Tucabache, Cussetah, Thlopthlocco, Tuckabatchee, and Weogufke. The rolls contain only an individual's name and, in a few cases, an amount of money received (presumably in 1891). Arranged by town and thereunder by family group.

Annuity Roll, 1891

Receipt roll for a per-capita payment in 1891. Contains payee's name, amount received, mark, signature of witnesses, and date of payment. The roll has been annotated with Dawes enrollment card numbers. Arranged alphabetically by town and thereunder by family group.

Supplemental Annuity Roll

Contains payee's name, amount received, mark, names of witnesses, and date of payment. The roll has been annotated with Dawes enrollment card numbers. Arranged alphabetically by town and thereunder by family group.

Creek Census Roll (Omitted Roll), 1891

The roll contains individual's name, roll number, and the notation "O" for omitted and "NB" for newborn. Arranged roughly alphabetically by town and thereunder by family group.

Creek Census Roll, 1891

A manuscript list of "Citizens Not Enrolled and their Respective Towns" that was apparently prepared by the clerk of the Special Committee of the National Council, which was established to identify individuals who did not participate in the 1891 per-capita payment and children born after 3 April 1891. The roll contains an individual's name, the notation "omitted" or "newborn," and, occasionally, remarks concerning actions of the Special Committee. Arranged by town.

Creek Census, 1893

A manuscript of individuals who apparently were not citizens of the Creek Nation but were living in the nation. The list, which is on a printed form titled "Census of the Non-Citizens of the Muskogee Nation Under Act of Council, 6 Nov. 1893," is incomplete. Arranged by family group.

Creek Census, 1895

Manuscript census rolls submitted by the Special Committee on Census Rolls to the National Council for approval between 31 May and 6 June 1895. There are rolls for the following towns: Alabama, Arbeka, Arbeka (Deep Fork), Arkansas ("colored"), Artussce, Big Spring, Canadian ("colored"), Coweta, Cussehta, Conchart, Euchee, Eufaula (Canadian), Eufaula (Deep Fork), Fish Pond, Greenleaf, Hickory Ground, Hillabee (Canadian), Hitchite, Hutchechuppa, Kechapataka, Kialigee, Little River Tulsa, Lochapoka, North Fork ("colored"), Okchiye, Okfuskee (Deep Fork), Okfusky (Canadian), Osoche, Pukken, Tallehassee, Quassarty no. 1 and no. 2, Thlewaithle, Thlopthlocco, Tokpofke, Tuckabatchee, Tullahassochee, Tulmochusee, Tulsa (Canadian), Tulwathlocco, Tuskegee, Weogufkee, Wewoka, Doubtful. Arranged by town.

Creek Census, 1895

A manuscript census roll of Creek citizens. The roll contains

an individual's name and roll number. The roll has been annotated with card numbers of Dawes enrollment cards. Arranged by town.

Creek Census (Supplemental Roll), 1895

A list of persons who were omitted from the 1895 payroll and "newborns." The list was apparently prepared by the Special Committee of the National Council. The roll contains an individual's name, the name of the individual's mother and her 1895 roll number, and the designation "New Born" or "Omitted." Arranged by town.

Creek Census (Omitted Roll), 1895

List of individuals who were omitted from the 1895 payroll and "newborns" which was submitted to the National Council by the Special Committee on Census Rolls on 4 December 1895. The roll contains an individual's name, the name of the individual's mother and father, 1895 census roll number, and the designation "New Born" or "Omitted." The roll numbers in these rolls match the roll numbers in the supplemental roll. Arranged by town.

Creek Payrolls, 1895

Payrolls for a per-capita payment based on the 1895 census. There are payrolls for the following towns: Alabama, Arbeka, Arbeka (Deep Fork), Arbekoche, Arkansas, Artussee, Big Springs, Broken Arrow, Canadian ("colored"), Cheyaha, Coweta, Cussehta, Concharte, Euchee, Eufaula (Deep Fork), Hitchette, Hutchechuppa, Kechopatake, Kialigee, Lochapoka, North Fork ("colored"), Nutaka, Okchiye, Okfuske (Canadian), Okfuske (Deep Fork), Osoche, Pukon, Tulahassee, Quassarte no. 1 and no. 2, Thlewarthlee, Thlopthlocco, Tokpafka, Tuckabatchee, Tuladegee, Tulahassoche, Tulmochussee, Tulwathlocco, Tuskegee, Weogufkee, Wewoka. The roll contains each payee's name, amount received, signature of payee and witnesses, and date of payment. The roll has been annotated with field numbers of Dawes enrollment cards and card numbers of the "old series" of Dawes enrollment cards. Arranged by town.

Colbert Census Roll of Creek Nation, 1896

Census rolls submitted by the Special Committee on Census Rolls to the National Council. There are rolls for the following towns: Arbeka (North Fork), Arbekochee, Arkansas (colored), Artussee, Big Spring, Canadian ("colored"), Concharty, Cussehta, Euchee, Eufaula (Canadian), Eufaula (Deep Fork), Fish Pond, Greenleaf, Hickory Ground, Kialigee, Little River Tulsa, Nuyaka, Okchiye, Okfuskee (Deep Forks), Osoche, Pakkon Tallahasse, Quassarte no. 1 and no. 2, Tallahassoche, Thlewathle, Thlopthlocco, Tokpofka, Tuckabache, Tulladegee, Tuskegee, Weogufke, Wewoka. Arranged by town.

Loyal Creek Payment Roll, 1904
Citizenship Commission Docket Book, 1895

Arranged by case number; includes an alphabetical index.

List of Applicants for Creek Citizenship, 1895–1896
Census and Citizenship Records

Letters and documents concerning census, 1832–1900; Okmulgee District, enrollment of Shawnee Indians, undated; census of non-citizens, undated; creek reservations under the treaty of 24 March 1832, entries 1–2,000; pension list, Muskogee Nation, 1872–73; 1892 census roll, Arkansas District; census of the town of Wagoner, 1894; list of non-citizen cattlemen and roll of Shawnee Indians, Deep Fork District, 1897; letters and documents concerning citizenship, 1874–

1910; permit lists and citizenship records, 1880–1906; permit lists; citizenship applications; Creek freedmen; Creek per-capita payments, 1869–1904; letters and documents pertaining to per-capita payments, 1870–88; list of Civil War officers and record of issues to indigent refugee Creeks in the Chickasaw Nation, 1862–65; annuity payroll of Creeks who were orphans in 1832 or their heirs, 1883–89.

Records of the Creek National Council, House of Kings and House of Warriors

Journal of the House of Warriors, 1868–1903; journal of the House of Kings, 1882–95; records of the General Council, Creek Agency, 1861–62; acts and resolutions of the National Council, 1873–92; appropriation acts of the National Council, 1895–99; constitution and laws; undated and Creek miscellaneous documents, 1883–1909.

Supreme Court Records, 1870–1897

Court record book, 1884–98; records and documents, 1868–99; United States courts, 1871–1909; North Fork, Deep Fork, and Arkansas district courts, 1874.

District Court Records

Arkansas district courts, 1870–95; Muskogee District courts, 1876–98; Coweta District courts, 1877–95; Deep Fork District courts, 1872–96; Eufaula District courts, 1882–98; North Fork District courts, 1868–73; Okmulgee District courts, 1884–98; Wewoka District courts, 1871–97.

OSAGE AGENCY—OSAGE

The first historical notice of the Osages appears to have been by the French explorer Marquette, who located them on his map of 1673 on the Osage River. They were a warlike people, viewed with terror by the surrounding tribes, especially the Caddoans.

Under treaties of 1808, 1818, and 1825, the Osages ceded to the United States much of their land in Arkansas and all lands west of the Missouri River. Subsequent treaties further reduced their lands until their present reservation was established in the northeastern part of Oklahoma in 1870.[12]

RECORDS OF THE OSAGE INDIANS

Osage Annuity Rolls, 1878–1909

Includes name of band, individual's name, relationship, age, sex.

MIAMI AGENCY

The Miami Agency, located at Miami, Oklahoma, has jurisdiction over the Shawnee, Miami, Seneca-Cayuga, Quapaw, and Ottawa tribes.[13]

Shawnee

The Shawnees were a leading tribe with settlements in South Carolina, Tennessee, Pennsylvania, and Ohio.

The Shawnees became known around 1670. At that time they lived in two main bodies at a considerable distance from each other—one in the Cumberland region of Tennessee and the other on the Savannah River in South Carolina. During the late eighteenth century, the two main bodies united in Ohio. For about forty years, until the Treaty of Greenville in 1795, the Shawnees were almost constantly at war with the British and the Anglo-Americans. After the death of Tecumseh, their most famous war chief, they lost their taste for war and began

to move to their present locations. One group settled on a reservation in Kansas; another went to Texas to join a band of Cherokees. A third group settled on the Canadian River in Indian Territory, just south of the Quapaw Reserve, and are today known as the Absentee-Shawnee Tribe of Oklahoma. Another band that settled in eastern Oklahoma is today known as the Eastern Shawnee Tribe.[14]

Miami

The earliest recorded notice of this tribe was in 1658 by Gabriel Druillette, who called them Oumanik. Then living around the mouth of Green Bay, Wisconsin, they withdrew into the Mississippi Valley and were established there from 1657 to 1676. The French came into contact with them in 1668. Around 1671, the Miamis formed new settlements at the south end of Lake Michigan, where missions were established late in the seventeenth century, and on the Kalamazoo River in Michigan. The extent of territory they occupied a few years later suggests that when the whites first heard of them, the Miami Indians in Wisconsin formed but a part of the tribe, with other bodies already established in northeast Illinois and Indiana. Encroachments by the Potawatomi, Kickapoo, and other northern tribes drove the Miami out to the east, and they formed settlements on the Miami River in Ohio. They held this country until the peace of 1763, when they retired to Indiana. They took part in all the Indian wars in the Ohio Valley until the close of the War of 1812. Soon after, they began to sell their lands. By 1827, they had disposed of most of their holdings in Indiana and had agreed to move to Kansas. They later moved to Indian Territory, where the remnant still resides.[15]

Ottawa

A large party of Ottawas was first met by Champlain in 1615 near the mouth of the French River, Georgian Bay Region, Canada, which seems to have been the original location of the tribe in the historic period. They were generally counted as allies of the Huron and the French during the French and Indian War. As a result of conflicts with the Iroquois in the seventeenth century, the Ottawas emigrated westward and southwest, their location being on Lake Huron between Detroit and Saginaw Bay from around 1700.

Between 1785 and 1862, the Ottawas signed twenty-three different treaties with the United States. In 1833, they ceded all their land on the west shore of Lake Michigan and accepted a reservation in northeastern Kansas. Several bands of the Ottawa Tribe living in Ohio had ceded their lands to the government and moved to the Kansas reservation in 1832. After the Quapaw Treaty of 1857, they moved to Indian Territory. The main portion of Ottawa remained in scattered settlements in southern Michigan, though another portion continued to live in Canada with the Chippewa. The noted chief Pontiac was an Ottawa, and one of the principal events in the tribe's history was known as Pontiac's War, waged near Detroit in 1763.[16]

Quapaw

The Quapaws are a southwestern tribe. By a treaty signed in St. Louis, Missouri, 24 August 1818, the Quapaws ceded their lands south of the Arkansas River, except for a small territory between Arkansas Post and Little Rock extending inland to the Saline River. In 1824, the Quapaws signed a treaty ceding the rest of their land to the United States, and the tribe agreed to move to the country of the Caddo, where they were assigned a tract on the south side of the Red River. The river frequently overflowed its banks, destroying Quapaw crops. Soon the tribe was drifting back to its old country, now settled by whites. Finally, a treaty signed 13 May 1833 conveyed to the Quapaws 150 sections of land in the extreme southeastern part of Kansas and the northeastern part of Indian Territory, to which they agreed to move. On 23 February 1867, they ceded their lands in Kansas and the northern part of their lands in Indian Territory to the United States. Under the Allotment Act of 1887, the Quapaws objected to federal plans to allot each tribe member only eighty acres. They established their own program and allotted two hundred acres to each of the 247 members. This action was ratified by Congress in 1895.[17]

In 1865, a special agent was stationed on the river in northeastern Oklahoma, then Indian Territory, to care for the affairs of the Indian tribes living on their reservations east of the Neosho River and north of the Cherokee Nation. Some tribes had been residents since 1832. The Neosho Agency was the main agency and was located in Montgomery County, Kansas. In 1871 the Neosho Agency and the sub-agency were separated jurisdictionally, the latter being named the Quapaw Agency.[18]

Seneca-Cayuga[19]

The Senecas of the Quapaw Agency were formerly called the Seneca of Sandusky. Under treaty provisions with the United States in 1817, the Seneca of Sandusky were granted 40,000 acres on the east side of the Sandusky River in Ohio. By 1830, they had improved farms, schools for their children, and were generally well advanced. Following the policy of removing the eastern Indians to the West, the government induced them to sell their Ohio lands and accept a new reserve north of the Cherokee Nation.

A band of the Seneca of Sandusky joined the Shawnee of Ohio, who had settled near Louistown in the latter part of the eighteenth century. At that time they were known as the mixed band of Seneca and Shawnee. By a treaty of 1831, the government induced them to sell their Ohio lands and accept a new reserve adjoining the Seneca of Sandusky in Indian Territory. Both the Seneca of Sandusky and the mixed Senecas and Shawnees moved to their new country in 1832. Like the other eastern tribes, they suffered many hardships during their journey. Protesting that the lands first assigned them were unfit for cultivation, they entered into a new treaty a short time after their arrival at the Seneca Agency. By the terms of the treaty, they were assigned a permanent reservation, beginning at the northeast corner of the Cherokee cession of 1828 and situated between the Neosho River and the Missouri boundary south of the Quapaw country. In 1881, a band of more than one hundred Cayugas from Canada and New York came to join their kin in Oklahoma.

RECORDS OF THE SHAWNEE INDIANS

Shawnee-Cherokee census, 1896–1904.

RECORDS OF THE MIAMI INDIANS

Census of Miami Indians in Indiana and elsewhere, 1881.

Annuity payment roll of Miami Indians of Indiana, 1895.

RECORDS OF THE QUAPAW AGENCY[20]

Census Records

Letters and documents, 1877–97; census and lists for the Ca-

yuga, Miami, Modoc, New York, Nez Perce, Ottawa, Confederated Peoria, Potawatomi, Quapaw, Seneca, Eastern Shawnee, and Wyandot.

Vital Statistics and Related Material

Letters received and other documents, 1864–1901; allotments, births, citizenship, deaths, divorce, estates, guardianship, adoption of Indian children, indigent, insane, issues, marriages, pensions, per capita, police book, family relations, vital statistics, and civil war.

Letters received, 1880–98.

Letterpress book, 1879–84.

Letters Sent and Received and Other Documents

Cayuga, 1871–98; Chippewa, Munsee, or Christian, 1872–1901; Citizen Potowatomi, 1863–89; Delaware, 1871–86; Kansas or Kaw, 1877–78; Miami, 1848–1908; New York Indians, 1874–88; Nez Perce, 1878–79; Oneida, 1876; Modoc Indians, 1873–86; Ottawa Indians, 1871–1901; Peoria and confederated tribes, 1854–1901; Ponca Indians, 1877–97; Seneca Indians, 1872–1901; Shawnee Indians, 1870–1901; Tonkawa Indians, 1883–84; and miscellaneous.

Schools and Churches

Miscellaneous schools, 1871–1908; churches, 1876–89.

TAHLEQUAH AGENCY—CHEROKEE

In 1782, a group of Cherokees who had fought on the British side during the American Revolution petitioned the Spanish governor at New Orleans for permission to settle on the west side of the Mississippi within the Spanish territory. Permission was granted in 1794, and a group of Cherokees settled in the St. Francis River valley in what is now southeastern Missouri. More Cherokees joined them over time.

During the winter of 1811–1812, the Cherokees moved en masse to the Arkansas region. Other Cherokees who decided to emigrate from the old nation periodically joined them in small groups.

With the treaty signed 8 July 1817 at Turkey Town, these emigrants received title to their lands. Under this treaty, the Cherokees ceded two large tracts of land and two smaller tracts of land east of the Mississippi River for an area of equal value in the West between the Arkansas and White rivers. As encouragement for others to remove, the treaty promised "to give all poor warriors who remove a rifle, ammunition, blanket, and brass kettle or beaver trap each, as full compensation for improvements left by them." The treaty further promised to compensate them for improvements, provide transportation, and provide subsistence for those who would agree to remove. Consequently, more than 1,100 Cherokees emigrated from the east to the west during 1818 and 1819.

By a treaty signed 6 May 1828, the Cherokees ceded their lands in present Arkansas for land in the present state of Oklahoma. No record exists of the estimated 2,000 Cherokees who emigrated before 1817, but the rolls for those who removed under the treaties of 1817 and 1828 are available. These records include a register of Cherokees who wished to remain in the East, 1817 to 1819 (two volumes), emigration registers of Indians who wished to migrate, 1817 to 1838 (eighteen volumes), and applications for reservations, 1819.

The Treaty of New Echota, 29 December 1835, represented the final cession of all Cherokee lands east of the Mississippi

River and the beginning of the forced migration of those remaining tribal members west on the "Trail of Tears." Cherokees who had emigrated prior to 1835 became known as the Old Settler Cherokees.

ROLLS OF CHEROKEES RESIDING WEST OF THE MISSISSIPPI IN INDIAN TERRITORY

The 1851 Old Settler Roll
The 1851 Old Settler Roll lists each individual by district and his or her children unless the mother was an emigrant Cherokee. In this case, the children were listed with their mother on the annuity roll taken by John Drennen in 1851. Forty-four family groups are listed as non-residents. No other information is given.

Drennen Roll, 1852
A receipt roll for a per-capita payment made to Cherokees living in the west who removed as a result of and after the Treaty of 1835. The roll was prepared by John Drennen and contains the payee's name, amount received by the head of each household, and the name of the witness. Arranged by Cherokee District and thereunder by family group.

Drennen Roll Index, 1852
This index contains the individual's surname, given name, and a page number reference to the receipt roll. Arranged alphabetically by first two letters of the name.

Complete List of Names of Emigrant Cherokees Who Drew Emigrant Money in 1852
Flint, Sequoyah, and Illinois districts.

Tompkins Roll of 1867
A census roll of Cherokees residing in the Cherokee Nation taken by H. Tompkins. The census roll provides the name, age, and sex of the individual. It also indicates if the individual is "White," "Half-breed," or "Colored." Arranged by Cherokee District.

Tompkins Roll Freedmen Indices, 1897
Indexes of the freedmen listed by H. Tompkins in 1867. One index is alphabetical by surname and the other is alphabetical by given name. The indices provide the name, page number of the roll, and the district of residence. Arranged alphabetically by the first two letters of the name.

Receipt Roll for Per-Capita Payment, 1874
Lists head of household, family members, total in family, amount paid, to whom paid, and name of witness.

Lists of Delaware, Shawnee, and North Carolina Cherokees, 1867–1881

Lists of Rejected Claimants, 1878–1880
Arranged by type of decision and thereunder by case number. List of persons who appeared before the Cherokee Commission on Citizenship and whose claims were rejected. The list provides the name of the claimant and the decision rendered by the commission. The notation "Colored" exists in the margin preceding some of the names.

Wallace Roll of Cherokee Freedmen, Including Orphan Roll, 1880

Cherokee Census of 1880
On 3 December 1879, the Cherokee National Council authorized a census and a per-capita payment for purchase of "bread stuffs." This census later became very important to the Dawes Commission in preparing the final rolls. Any Indian or inter-married white listed on this census was accepted without challenge by the Dawes Commission. A notation on the census cards prepared by the commission showed the individuals' locations and the name by which each was enrolled on the 1880 census.

The census was arranged by district within the Cherokee Nation and thereunder by six schedules: (1) Cherokee citizens, including native, adopted white, Shawnee, Delaware, and freedmen; (2) orphans under age sixteen; (3) those rejected; (4) those whose citizenship claims were pending; (5) "intruders" (unauthorized white squatters on Cherokee land); and (6) those living in the Cherokee Nation by permit granted by the Cherokee Council. Each schedule gives the individual's name by family group, age, race, occupation, sex, and roll number.

Cherokee Census Index, 1880
A printed index to the 1880 Cherokee Census, which contains the name, roll number, nativity, age, and sex of each individual. The volume also includes lists of Shawnee and Delaware who were residing in the Cherokee Nation, North Carolina Cherokee who removed to Cherokee Nation, and persons admitted or readmitted to citizenship by the Cherokee National Council. There is also an "Orphan Roll." Arranged by Cherokee District and thereunder roughly alphabetically.

Lipe Receipt Roll, 1880
A per-capita receipt roll by D.W. Lipe. The roll provides the name of the payee, number in the family, total amount paid to the family, name of the person receiving the payment, and the name of the witness. Arranged by Cherokee district and thereunder by roll number.

Receipt Roll of Per-Capita Payment, 1881
Lists head of household and family members, nationality, and remarks.

Lists of North Carolina Cherokees Who Removed to the Cherokee Nation West, 1881
Lists roll number, family number, English name, Cherokee name (in Cherokee), age, sex, nationality, residence (in Cherokee), and remarks.

Roll of North Carolina Immigrants Allowed Per-Capita Payment, 1881
Lists name of head of household and family members.

Payroll By Right of Cherokee Blood, 1883
Lists roll number, name of head of household and family members, age, and remarks.

Lists of North Carolina Cherokees, 1882–1883
Lists name of head of household, family members, nationality, and age.

The Cherokee Census of 1883 and 1886
On 19 May 1883, the Cherokee National Council authorized another census upon which to base a per-capita payment of monies received from leased land. This census is arranged by districts like the 1880 census and includes an orphan's roll, those in nation prisons, and a supplemental roll that shows the name and age of each individual.

A receipt roll shows the individual's name and roll number, the total number in the household, the total amount paid each household, the name of the person receiving the payment, and the name of a witness to the payment.

More money was made available from the same source in 1886 and was distributed after another census. In addition to the information given in the 1883 payment roll, the 1886 roll identifies individuals by their relationship to the head of household.

Supplemental Roll of Those Left Off the Rolls of 1880 Per-Capita Payment, 1884
Lists heads of household, family members, and remarks.

Citizenship Commission Docket Book, 1880–1884
Docket of the Citizenship Commission of the Cherokee Nation which contains the names of claimants, nature of the claim, and the decision of the commission.

The 1890 Cherokee Census
This census contains the most complete information of any census for the Cherokee Nation. It is arranged by district and includes six schedules: (1) native Cherokees and adopted whites, Shawnees, and Delawares; (2) orphans under age sixteen; (3) those denied citizenship by the Cherokee authorities; (4) those whose claims to citizenship were pending; (5) "intruders"; and (6) whites living in the Cherokee Nation by permit. The 1890 census's 105 columns include such detailed information as farm improvements, products, livestock, etc.

The 1893 Cherokee Census
This census distinguishes Cherokee citizens by blood, adopted whites, freedmen, Shawnees, Delawares, intermarried persons, and Creeks. Arranged by district, this census provides the individuals's name, age, sex, admission reference, name of guardian, place of residence, and name of person providing identification.

The Wallace Roll of Cherokee Freedmen, 1890–1893
A copy of a Cherokee Freedmen census made in 1890 of those eligible to receive a per-capita payment. The roll was prepared by Special Agent John Wallace and was based on an 1883 census of Cherokee freedmen. The roll includes lists of authenticated freedmen who appear on the 1883 roll, individuals who died between 1883 and 1890, individuals admitted by Wallace, and "Free Negroes." The volume also contains a list of individuals whose rights were questioned by the commissioner of Indian affairs and supplemental lists of individuals who were admitted by the secretary of the interior. The roll contains the individual's name, age, sex, and residence. The entries have been annotated with the enrollment numbers from the Clifton Roll of Cherokee Freedmen made in 1896 and, in some cases, with the enrollment numbers from the Dawes roll of 1907. The Wallace roll was set aside as "fraudulent" by a decree of 8 May 1895 of the United States Court of Claims and was never recognized by the Cherokee Nation. Arranged by enrollment number.

Cherokee Freedmen Roll Index, 1893
The index lists the individual's surname, given name, and district of residence. The index contains page number references to an 1893 roll. Arranged alphabetically by the first two letters of the surname.

Cherokee Freedmen Roll Index, 1890–1893
An index to the Wallace roll of Cherokee freedmen. The index lists the individual's roll number, district of residence, and a page number reference to the 1890 roll. Arranged alphabetically by last name.

The Starr Roll (1894)
On 3 March 1893, Congress passed an act that resulted in the sale of the Cherokee Outlet (land to the west of Cherokee Nation to which the Cherokees had claim before the organization

of Oklahoma Territory) to the United States. A per-capita payment of $365.70 was made. E.E. Starr, treasurer of the Cherokee Nation, prepared the receipt roll, arranged by district and thereunder by enrollment number. It contains the name of the head of household, the name of the person receiving payment, and the name of a witness to the transaction. An orphans roll is also included.

Cherokee Payroll Index, 1894 (Authenticated Roll of 1894)
Arranged alphabetically by surname. This index lists the individual's name, roll number, and district of residence. It also contains page number references to the 1894 receipt roll (Starr roll). The roll number and names also correspond with the names and roll numbers on the 1894 Cherokee census roll.

Cherokee Census Roll, 1894
A census of the Cherokee Nation made in 1897. The roll is based on the 1894 payroll. The roll contains the individual's enrollment number, name, age, and sex. Under "remarks", the names of deceased parents and other names used on previous enrollments are listed. Arranged by Cherokee District and thereunder by enrollment number.

Lists of Cherokee Children, 1895–1897
These lists contain the names of children born between 1895 and 1897, their dates of birth, and parent's names. Arranged by Cherokee district.

Old Settlers Roll, 1896
A receipt roll for a per-capita payment based on the 1851 old settler roll of the western Cherokee (those removing prior to the Treaty of New Echota). The names of persons who were still living at the time of the payment are listed first, followed by the names of those who were deceased and the names of their heirs who were paid. This payment resulted from a decision of the U.S. Court of Claims made on 6 June 1893. The roll contains each payee's name, 1851 roll number, agency pay number, age, sex, amount received, post office address, signature, date of payment, and names of witnesses. The relations of heirs to the original payee is given. Information regarding guardianship, related correspondence files, and correction of names is provided under "remarks." There are also three versions of a supplemental list of original enrollees from the 1851 roll whose shares were not claimed. One version lists just the names of the heirs of the enrollees; the second version lists the names of the heirs of the individuals and the amount of payment they received; and the third version is a working copy. Arranged numerically by agency pay number.

Cherokee Census Roll, 1896
This census roll of citizens of the Cherokee Nation contains the individual's name, roll number, age, sex, precinct, proportion of blood or nativity, and place of birth. Arranged by Cherokee District and thereunder by roll number.

The 1896 Payment Roll (Lipe Roll)
This payroll is based on the 1851 old settler roll and is of major genealogical importance. The names of those still living in 1896 are listed first, followed by those who had died and their heirs and each heir's relationship. The payroll lists each payee's 1851 roll number, name, agency pay number, age, sex, amount received, and post office address.

Shawnee-Cherokee Census, 1896
This roll contains the names of Cherokee Shawnee who were

entitled to participate in the distribution of funds to equalize a per-capita payment. The roll contains the individual's name, roll number, "Cherokee number," age, sex, address, and names used on previous rolls. A notation was made after the names of individuals who were deceased. The roll includes two supplemental lists of Cherokee Shawnee entitled to funds and a list of persons "Omitted from Government Pay Rolls of the Cherokee Shawnee Tribe of Indians." Arranged roughly alphabetically by name.

Cherokee Freedmen Roll (Clifton Roll), 1896

List of Cherokee freedmen and their descendants prepared by a commission appointed by the secretary of the interior. The roll was based on testimony taken by the commission in the Cherokee Nation between 4 May and 10 August 1897. The list contains the individual's name, relationship to the head of the household, sex, age, and district of residence. There is a supplemental list of individuals whose claims to citizenship were rejected by the Cherokee Nation but approved by the Commission. Arranged numerically by roll number.

Delaware Payroll, 1896

A list of persons entitled to funds to equalize a per-capita payment. The information given for each person includes name, "census number," payroll number, age, amounts received in payments made in 1896, 1890, and 1894, name of person receiving payment, and names of witnesses. There are some remarks about deaths and relations to others on the list, and some names have been annotated with Dawes Commission enrollment numbers. Arranged alphabetically by first letter of surname.

Payment to Destitute Cherokees, 1902

Payment to Intermarried Whites, Cherokee Nation, 1909–1910

Cherokee Equalization Payment Rolls, 1910–1915

Cherokee Per Capita Payroll, 1912

Cherokee Citizenship

Lists of Rejected Claimants, 1878–1880

List of persons who appeared before the Cherokee Commission on Citizenship and whose claims were rejected. The list provides the name of the claimant and the decision rendered by the commission. The notation "Colored" exists in the margin preceding some of the names. Arranged by type of decision and thereunder by case number.

Cherokee Citizenship Commission Docket Book, 1880–1884 and 1887–1889

List of Applicants Admitted to Citizenship, 1896

List of names of applicants admitted to citizenship in the Cherokee Nation by the Dawes Commission. The list contains the applicant's name, references to case numbers from the United States Court in Indian Territory, Dawes Commission file and card numbers, other names used by the applicant, and notations concerning applicants living outside Indian Territory. Arranged alphabetically by name.

Lists of Applicants for Cherokee Citizenship, 1896

This volume contains a list of names of applicants for citizenship in the Cherokee Nation under an act of congress of 10 June 1896. There are lists of applicants admitted to citizenship by the Dawes Commission, applicants rejected by the Dawes Commission but admitted by the U.S. courts in Indian terri-

tory, and applicants admitted by the Dawes Commission but rejected by the U.S. courts. The information given in each list varies but generally includes the applicant's name, a reference to a Dawes case number, and a court case number. Arranged alphabetically by name.

District Records[21]

Canadian District
Court records, 1867–98.

Cooweescoowee District
Marriages, permits, wills and estates, 1858–98; Cherokee marriages, 1868–97; district estate records, 1875–97; permits to non-citizens, 1893–99; land records and estray property records, 1875–1914; Cherokee town sites, 1876–98; district circuit and supreme court records, 1868–95; Cherokee courts, 1857–98; divorce, 1890.

Delaware District
Marriages, 1867–1896; Delaware district permits, 1868–95; Cherokee permits, 1886; district estates, 1867–98; district circuit and supreme court records, 1868–95; divorce, 1902; improvements, 1859–98; marks and brands, 1876–98; estray property, 1875–95.

Flint District
Estates, 1876–1893; estray property, 1876–1898; marks and brands, 1876–1897; improvements, 1881–1892; district supreme, circuit, and district court records, 1877–1897; marriages, 1893.

Going Snake District
Marriages, 1880–98; estates, 1868–1904; improvements and estray property, 1880–98; district supreme, circuit, and district court records, 1876–98.

Illinois District
Marriages, estates, and permits, 1859–97; estates, 1876–98; permits, 1895–96; improvements, marks, and brands, estray property, district supreme, circuit, and district court records, 1865–98.

Saline District
Marriages, estates, permits, property improvements, estray property, and marks and brands, 1866–98; permits, 1876–97; district supreme, circuit, and district court records, 1872–98.

Sequoyah District
Marriages, estates, estray property, and property improvements, 1874–98; district supreme, circuit, and district court records, 1876–98.

Tahlequah District
Marriages, estates, and permits, 1856–98; property improvements, estray property, and marks and brands, 1872–98; district supreme, circuit, and district court records, 1865–1904.

Documents Pertaining to Determination of Tribal Membership, 1870–1909

Cherokee Citizenship, 1841–1911

Letters Sent and Letters Received and other Documents, 1829–1914

Unique Records Relating to the Cherokee Indians

Records Relating the Enrollment of Eastern Cherokees
These records deserve special attention. They are often referred

to as the Guion Miller rolls. Guion Miller was appointed by the United States Court of Claims to determine who was eligible to participate in a fund awarded to persons who were Eastern Cherokees at the time of the treaties of 1835–36 and 1845 or their descendants. While the majority of this group were residing in Indian Territory at the time of Miller's commission, many were also residing in North Carolina. The title of this record group is misleading in that the researcher is led to believe that the records pertain only to the Eastern Cherokee Tribe of North Carolina. Miller submitted his report and roll on 28 May 1909 and a supplementary report in 1910.

The "Guion Miller Report and Exhibits, 1908–1910," in twenty-nine volumes, consists of ten volumes of transcripts of testimony, arranged chronologically; a report dated 5 January 1910 concerning exceptions to findings; a printed copy of the completed roll with two 1910 supplements; and copies of the Drennen, Chapman, and "Old Settlers" rolls of 1851–52, with a consolidated index for the Chapman and Drennen rolls and a separate index for the old settlers roll. The volumes are arranged numerically as parts of classified file "33931-11-053 Cherokee Nation," which also contains other pertinent records.

Between 1906 and 1909, more than 45,000 claimants submitted applications providing detailed information of their families. A typical application includes the applicant's English name, Indian name (if any), residence, date and place of birth, marriage status, name of husband or wife, parents' names, their places of birth and residence in 1851, and dates of death; names and dates of birth and death of brothers and sisters; names of paternal and maternal grandparents and their children, their places of birth and residence in 1851, and the name of the ancestor from whom they claimed to have descended.

TAHILINA AGENCY—CHOCTAW

The Choctaw Nation in Indian Territory maintained its own constitutional government and records for many years in the nineteenth century, and in limited form after 1906 and Oklahoma statehood. The Choctaw National Constitution was adopted on 3 June 1834. The government consisted of a principal chief, a general council composed of a senate and house of representatives, and a court system consisting of a supreme court and district courts. The nation was divided into three geographical and political districts. District One, Masholatubbe, consisted of Tobucksy, Gaines, Sans Bois, Skullyville, and Sugar Loaf counties. District Two, Apuckshunnubbee, consisted of Cedar, Nashoba, Towson, Boktuklo, Eagle, Wade, and Red River counties. District Three, Pushmataha, consisted of Atoka, Jacks Fork, Blue, Jackson and Kiamichi counties. The district capitols were at Gaines, Alichi and Mayhew. The national capitol was at Tushkahomma for most of the years of the nation's existence.

RECORDS OF THE CHOCTAW INDIANS[22]

Choctaws Paid by Chickasaws, Treaty of 22 June 1855

Contains names of individuals, their marks, identification of the individual as man, woman, or child, total number in the family, the amount of the individual share, and the total dollar amount per family. There are tallies in the middle and the bottom of each page and at the end of the county list and district list. The orphans list contains the names of individuals, names of the representatives for orphans, marks, the amount received per representative, the total amount received per orphan, and

remarks. Remarks are primarily confined to "death after 4th installment." There are tallies on each page and at the end of the list.

Index to 1885 Choctaw Census

Contains individual's name, county of residence, age, number in census book for county.

Choctaw Census, 1885

A census of Choctaw citizens living in Atoka, Blue, Boktoklo, Cedar, Eagle, Gains, Jacks Fork, Kiomitia, Nashoba, Red River, San Bios, Sckullyville, sugar Loaf, Towson, Tobuksko, and Wade counties of the Choctaw Nation. The information given for each person includes name, age, sex, race ("White," "Indian," "Colored"), occupation, and agricultural schedule. Arranged by county.

Choctaw-Chickasaw Freedmen Rolls, 1885

Contains names of persons admitted to citizenship, heads of families and children, sex and age group, nationality of parents, whether a previous owner of freed slaves, number of livestock, and acres of land in cultivation. Arranged by first, second, and third Choctaw districts and thereafter consecutively by family group.

Choctaw Pay Roll, 1893

Manuscript list of individuals (Choctaw by blood) receiving annuity payments. Contains names of citizens by blood, name and sex of children, individual receiving payment, amount of payment, and remarks. Remarks primarily confined to identification of orphans. Arranged alphabetically by county, thereafter alphabetically by individual's name.

Census of Choctaw Nation, 1896

Contains names of adults, names and sex of children, age, relationship, and remarks. Remarks include whether the wife of an intermarried citizen, orphan, widow, stricken from roll, child of a Choctaw, deceased, or transferred to other rolls. Arranged numerically by district, thereinafter alphabetically by the last names of individuals living within a particular county or Chickasaw district.

Census Roll of Freedmen, 1896

Contains consecutive numbers, notation if Chickasaw, name, age, county of residence, and other notations. Other notations consist primarily of "dead", parents' names, and Dawes numbers. Arranged alphabetically.

Unpaid Choctaw Townsite Payment, 1904

Choctaw-Chickasaw Townsite Fund Pay Roll, 1906

Choctaw $20 Payment Roll, 1908

Choctaw $50 Payment Roll, 1911

Choctaw $300 Payment Roll, 1916

Choctaw $100 Payment Roll, 1917

Census and Citizenship Records

Mississippi Choctaw census and citizenship, 1830–99; census records and lists, 1830–96; census of Choctaws by blood and intermarried citizens, 1868–96; residents of the Chickasaw Nation, 1896; restricted Choctaws, 1929; Choctaw citizenship, 1897–1930; Choctaw citizenship, 1897–1930; undated, 1884–1904; Choctaw citizenship cases, 1896–1904; rejected cases, First District, 1896–97; census and citizenship, Choctaw freedmen, 1885–97.

Records of the General Council, Senate and House of Representatives

General Council and House of Representatives, 1855, 1867, and 1899; Laws of the Choctaw Nation, 1886–1906

Permit Records, 1898–1906

County Court Records

Atoka County courts, 1886–1906; Blue County courts, 1868–1906; Boktuklo County courts, 1858–1905; Cedar County courts, 1875–1905; Eagle County courts, 1889–1906; Gaines County courts, 1859–1906; Jacks County courts, 1860–1906; Jackson County courts, 1887–1906; Kiamichi County courts, 1888–1905; Nashoba County courts, 1856–1905; Red River County courts, 1866–1905; Sans Bois County courts, 1888–1906; Skullyville County courts, 1868–1906; Sugar Loaf County courts, 1874–1906; Tobucksy County courts, 1867–1906; Towson County courts, 1881–1906; Wade County courts, 1858–1906.

District, Circuit, and Chancery Records

First District (Masholatubbe), 1848–1905; Second District (Apuckshunnabbee), 1871–1905; Third District (Pushmataha), 1859–1906.

Records of the Supreme Court and Tribal Officers, 1857–1906

Letters Sent and Received and Other Documents, 1859–1907

WEWOKA AGENCY—SEMINOLE[23]

Seminole Payment and Census rolls, 1868, 1895–1897

Includes payee's name; annotated with Dawes Enrollment Card number. Arranged by band and thereunder by family.

Seminole Payment Rolls, 1895–1896

The roll contains each payee's name and amounts of money listed under columns labeled "Wewoka," "Sasakwa," and "Balance." Wewoka was the capital of the Seminole Nation and Sasakwa was the place of business of the principal chief. Arranged by band and thereunder by family group.

Seminole Payment Rolls, 1895–1897

Copies of an 1895 and 1897 "Head Right" payment roll. The 1895 payment roll is not an exact copy but contains most of the same names and amounts. Arranged by band and thereunder by family group.

Allotment Schedules for 1901 and 1902

National Council, federal relations, and per-capita laws and acts of National Council, 1886–1905; federal relations, 1900; per-capita payments, 1898–1907; Seminole miscellaneous papers.

Financial and School Records

Financial records, 1893–1907; miscellaneous documents, 1866–1923; school financial records, 1906.

Mekusukey Acadamy, 1910–1929

Student applications, rosters, progress cards, letters sent and received by the superintendent, medical and other records.

ANADARKO AREA OFFICE

The Anadarko Area Office, established in 1948, is essentially a continuation of the Kiowa Agency, which was created in 1864 and permanently located in Indian Territory in 1869.[24]

Located at Anadarko, Oklahoma, the Anadarko Area Office administers Bureau of Indian Affairs programs for regions of Oklahoma, Kansas, and Missouri and is responsible for the following agencies in Oklahoma: Anadarko, Concho, Pawnee, Shawnee, Concho Indian School, Riverside Indian School, Fort Sill Maintenance and Security Detachment, and the Chilocco Maintenance and Security Detachment.

The records, 1881–1952, include general correspondence and correspondence concerning lands, heirship, town sites, and schools; accounts and case files for individual Indians; land transactions files; annuity payrolls; annual reports; student records; and records of employees.[25]

ANADARKO AGENCY

The Anadarko Agency, located at Anadarko, Oklahoma, has jurisdiction over the Apache, Kiowa, Comanche, Caddo, Delaware, and Wichita tribes.[26]

Apache

The Apaches of Oklahoma are also called the Prairie Apache, a name applied to them through error on the assumption that they were the same as the Apache people of Arizona. They have no political connection with the Apache tribes of the Southwest, however. They came from the north as a component part of the Kiowa. More recent authorities, however, believe that the Apaches did divide somewhere in Montana, the main body going southward on the west side of the mountains and a smaller body going northward to become allied on the east side of the mountains with the Kiowas. Whichever theory is correct, the Apaches have a distinct language and call themselves Nadishdewa, or "our people." The Pawnees and early French explorers and settlers called them Gattacka or Gataka, and these names appeared on the first treaty they signed with the United States.[27]

Caddo

The Caddos were first known to have been in the Louisiana Territory and were referred to in the chronicles of the DeSoto expedition in 1541. Soon after the United States purchased the Louisiana Territory, a peace treaty was made in which the Caddos ceded all their Louisiana lands and agreed to move to the Indian Territory, settling on the Washita River in what is now Caddo County. The present Caddo tribe also includes remnants of the Anadarko tribe.[28]

Comanche

The Comanches were one of the southern tribes of the Shoshonean stock and the only one to live entirely on the Plains. They are a comparatively recent offshoot of the Shoshonis of Wyoming and, until recently, kept in continual friendly communication with them.

For nearly two centuries they were at war with the Spaniards in Mexico and raided Mexican settlements as far south as Durango and Zacatecas. Generally friendly to the Americans, they were bitter enemies of the Texans, who had dispossessed them of their best hunting grounds, and they waged relentless war against them for almost forty years. Around 1795, they became close confederates of the Kiowas and also allied themselves with the Apaches.

Several treaties were consummated between the United States and the Comanche Tribe between 1834 and 1875. In the Treaty of Medicine Lodge in 1867, the Comanche, Apache, and Kiowa tribes were assigned a tract of land in Oklahoma, which they still share.[29]

Delaware

The Delawares call themselves Lenape, meaning "real men," or Leni Lenape, meaning "men of our nation." The English name Delaware was given to the tribe from the Delaware River, the valley of which was the tribal center in earliest colonial times. The valley extends from southeastern New York into Pennsylvania through New Jersey and Delaware. The early traditional history of the Delaware is contained in the nation legend, the Walam Olum.

The Delawares were once one of the larger tribes of the eastern woodland people. Gradually they moved west and were located in at least ten different states during this migration. At present, two groups of Delawares live in Oklahoma. The main part of the tribe, known as "Registered Delaware," came from their reservation in Kansas in 1867 and settled with the Cherokees and were allotted land with them. The other group, still a district Delaware tribe, was associated with the Caddo and Wichita tribes in Texas and came to the Washita River in Indian Territory in 1859. A number of Delaware moved and associated with other tribes in the north and northwestern country. Approximately 750 Delawares are called Absentee Delawares.[30]

Fort Sill Apache

The Fort Sill Apaches are composed of members of the Warm Springs Band of Apache and the Chiricahua Apache. This small group of Indians is often referred to as Chief Geronimo's Band of Apache. According to older members of this group, Victorio, chief of the Apache, led a group of forty warriors in protesting the tribe's being moved from their New Mexico reservation to one located at San Carlos, Arizona. Upon Victorio's death at the hands of a band of Mexicans in Chihuahua state in Mexico, Geronimo assumed leadership of the group. He carried on warfare until August 1886, when Gen. Nelson A. Miles forced him to surrender. Geronimo and all of his band were taken as prisoners of war to Fort Marion, Florida, near St. Augustine. Because of many deaths and much sickness in the tribe, the government removed them to Mount Vernon Barracks, Alabama, where they were kept prisoner for seven years. On 4 October 1894, Geronimo and the remnants of his band, then about 296 in all, were moved from Alabama to Fort Sill, Oklahoma. They remained at the Fort Sill Military Reservation as nominal prisoners of war until 1913, when the government arranged to allot an eighty-acre tract of land to each member who desired to remain in Oklahoma. Those who wished to move to the Mescalero Reservation in New Mexico could do so, and only eighty-seven stayed in Oklahoma and were given allotments of land in or near what is now the town of Apache.[31]

Kiowa

The Kiowa are believed to have migrated from the mountain regions at the source of the Yellowstone and Missouri rivers in what is now western Montana. According to tradition, they left this region because of a dispute with another tribe over hunting spoils and moved to the Black Hills in present-day South Dakota. Toward the end of the eighteenth century, the Kiowa were driven south by the Sioux, finally settling in the area of present western Oklahoma and the panhandle of north Texas and west into part of New Mexico.

Early in their history, they formed an alliance with a small band of Apache which continues today in Oklahoma. In 1790,

having made peace with their one-time enemies, the Comanches, they established control of the area from the Arkansas River to the headwaters of the Red River, and the two tribes became masters of the southern Plains. This alliance appears to be the basis for both the Kiowa-Apache-Comanche alliance of today and also the Kiowa-Comanche Reservation in Oklahoma, where the two tribes were settled by the United States. In 1840 the Kiowas made a permanent peace with the Cheyenne and their allies, the Arapahos, and became friendly with the Wichitas.

Throughout the nineteenth century the Kiowas continually resisted white immigration along the overland trails. With the Comanche, they attacked Texas frontier settlements, extending their raids far south into Mexico. Treaties with the U.S. government beginning in 1837 had little effect, and the tribe continued fighting. After the Battle of Washita in 1868, the Kiowas, Apaches, and Comanches were forced onto a reservation near Fort Sill, Oklahoma. Their defiance continued, however, and only military defeat and the disappearance of the buffalo ended their resistance.[32]

The treaty of Medicine Lodge Creek, Kansas (15 Stat., 581 and 15 Stat., 589), concluded on 21 October 1868 between the United States and the Kiowas, Comanche, and Kiowa-Apache, provided for a reservation in Indian Territory to be located between the Washita and Red rivers. This was a modification and reduction of a reservation established by a treaty of 18 October 1865 (Stat. L, xiv, 717) with the Comanche and Kiowa.

In 1868 an agent was sent to Indian Territory to bring together the Kiowas, Comanches, and Apaches who wished to abide by their treaty commitments. Progress was made, and the following year a new agent arrived at the agency headquarters near Fort Sill. When he assumed control on 1 July 1869, he found himself in charge of the Wichita Agency as well. That agency had been established in July of 1859 on the south side of the Washita River near Sugar Creek in an area long claimed by the Wichita. The agency served the Kiowa, Caddo, and Kichai. Later Waco, Tawakoni, Anadarko, Ionie (Hainai), Tonkawa, some Penateka Comanche, Delaware, and Shawnee groups became part of this agency. During a brief interval in the 1870s, some of the Pawnees from Nebraska made their home at this agency before moving to their new reservation.

In 1870 the agency, properly called the Caddo, Wichita, and Affiliated Bands Agency, became independent. Although some of the tribes had long resided in the region, it was not until 19 October 1872 that an agreement (never ratified) established a reservation for Wichitas and affiliated bands between the Washita and Canadian rivers, northeast and adjacent to the Kiowa, Comanche, and Apache reservation.

In the decade following 1868, the Kiowa-Comanche Agency remained in operation near Fort Sill. On 1 September 1878 that agency and the Wichita Agency were again consolidated. At that time instructions were given to move the agency from Fort Sill to the Wichita Agency near the present town of Anadarko. The office at Fort Sill served as a subagency for a number of years.

In 1894, Geronimo and a group of Chiricahua Apache prisoners of war who had formerly been at Fort Marion, Florida, and Mount Vernon Barracks, Alabama, were brought to Fort Sill. In 1913, eighty-seven of them elected to remain in Oklahoma rather than return to the Mescalero Apache reservation in New Mexico. They were allotted land near the town of Apache.

The allotment of the Kiowas, Comanches, and Apaches was completed in 1901 after several years of their attempting to prevent the dissolution of their reservation and eventual use of surplus land for white settlement. The Wichita and other tribes of the original Wichita agency group were allotted lands before 6 August 1901, when their surplus lands as well as those of the Kiowas, Comanches, and Apaches were opened for white settlement.[33]

Wichita

Tradition indicates that the Wichita tribe migrated southward from the north and east. In 1850, the Wichitas had moved from near the Red River into the Wichita Mountains region with their main village a short distance from what is now Fort Sill, Oklahoma. In 1859, the Wichita moved to a permanent site south of the Canadian River near the present Caddo-Grady county line. A reservation consisting of 743,610 acres and known as the Wichita-Caddo Reservation was established in 1872.[34]

KIOWA AGENCY RECORDS[35]

Census Records
Letters sent and received, 1872–1920; undated census lists, worksheets, and miscellaneous undated census lists; census lists for the Apache, Comanche, Kiowa, Wichita, Waco, Tawakoni, Caddo, Kichai, and Delaware, 1869–1922.

Letterpress Books, 1869–1900

Federal Relations
Letters sent and received, 1864–1933.

Federal, State, and Local Court Relations, 1865–1925

Foreign Relations
Letters sent and received, 1866–1929.

Military Relations and Affairs, 1869–1925

Indian History, Culture, and Acculturation, 1860–1926

CONCHO AGENCY—CHEYENNE AND ARAPAHOE

The earliest known evidence of the Cheyenne and Arapaho tribes dates from 1600 and places the Arapaho east of the headwaters of the Mississippi River in Minnesota and the Cheyenne in southwestern and northern Minnesota. The two tribes have long been associated, having wandered in the same direction and fought jointly for defense; yet they were separate tribes and were politically independent. With the westward push of settlers, the Cheyenne and Arapaho moved west and adopted a lifestyle that evolved into the culture of the Plains Indians. Their wandering led them to North and South Dakota, Wyoming, Montana, Nebraska, Kansas, and Colorado. In about 1835, portions separated from the main body became known as the Southern Cheyenne and Southern Arapaho. In 1869, the Cheyenne and Arapaho were assigned a reservation in Oklahoma, and the Darlington Agency was established in 1870 to serve them.[36]

A treaty between the United States and the Cheyenne and Arapaho tribes, 28 October 1867 (Stat. L., xv, 593), provided for a reservation in what is now Oklahoma for the Southern Cheyenne and Southern Arapaho Indians. In 1869, a temporary agency was established at Camp Supply, Indian Territory. The location of the reservation was altered by executive order

on 10 August 1869, and in May 1879 the agency was moved to a site five miles northwest of the present town of El Reno.

From 1869 through 1874 this agency, called the Upper Arkansas Agency, was under the Central Superintendency, Office of Indian Affairs. In 1875 its name was changed to the Cheyenne and Arapaho Agency. This designation has remained to the present day.

In 1877, several bands of Northern Cheyenne numbering 927 people were brought to Darlington in Indian Territory. Another contingent of approximately two hundred reached Darlington in 1878. In 1881, Little Chief's band was allowed to move to Pine Ridge Agency in Dakota Territory. In September 1883 the last of the Northern Cheyenne wishing to remove to their old home arrived at Pine Ridge Agency. The records of these Northern Cheyenne for the time they were at the southern agency remain in the files of the Cheyenne and Arapaho Agency. On 30 November 1902 a "subagency" was established at Cantonment in Indian Territory. Part of the agency's affairs came under the supervision of the head of the Cantonment Indian Training School, with headquarters at the school three miles northwest of Canton. Another portion was assigned to the superintendent of Seger Indian Training School located at Colony. The remainder of the agency was under the direction of the Cheyenne and Arapaho School superintendent at the old agency headquarters at Darlington. By December 1909 a further division created the Red Moon Agency located at the Red Moon School at Hammon.

In March 1910, the removal of the Darlington Agency to Caddo Springs was authorized. The move was completed in May 1915 and the agency's name changed to the Concho Agency. On 9 April 1917 the consolidation of the Red Moon Agency with the Seger Agency was accomplished. The next reorganization took place in 1927. At that time the Seger Agency was abolished, and the Cantonment Agency became part of the Cheyenne and Arapaho Agency at Cantonment.[37]

CHEYENNE-ARAPAHOE AGENCY RECORDS[38]

Census Records
Letters sent and letters received, 1876–1931; enrollment, 1878–1914; enrollment lists and census rolls, 1870–1928.

Letterpress Books, 1876–1891

Letters Sent and Received and Other Documents, 1868–1933

Indian History, Culture, and Acculturation, 1871–1933

PAWNEE AGENCY

The Pawnee Agency, located at Pawnee, Oklahoma, has jurisdiction over the Kaw, Pawnee, Ponca, Otoe-Missouria, and Tonkawa tribes.[39]

The Pawnee Agency was the last name given the agency responsible for the affairs of the various tribes listed below from 1870-to-1930 period. The agencies and subagencies which had jurisdiction over the several tribes through the years changed locations and names and are as follows: Osage Agency; Kaw Agency; Kaw Subagency; Pawnee Agency; Pawnee Subagency; Ponca, Otoe and Oakland Agency; Ponca, Pawnee, Oakland and Otoe Agency; Ponca Subagency; Otoe Subagency; Tonkawa Subagency; and reservation schools whose superintendents were placed in charge of school and tribal affairs.[40]

Kaw

According to tradition, the Kaws, Osages, Poncas, Omahas, and Quapaws were one people who lived along the Wabash River and far up the Ohio. Pushed westward by the encroachment of superior forces, they split at the mouth of the Ohio River. Those going down the Mississippi River took the name Quapaw, or "Downstream People." They later divided into four tribes: Kaw, Osage, Ponca, and Omaha. By terms of the treaties with the United States from 1820 to 1846, the Kaws relinquished their claims to several million acres in Kansas and Nebraska. A new reservation was assigned to them in 1846 at Council Grove on the Neosho River in Kansas. These lands were finally overrun by white settlers. In 1872, the tract was sold and a new reserve was purchased for the tribe near the Osages in Indian Territory. In 1902, that reservation was allotted under law to the tribal membership.[41]

The Kaw (Kansas) Reservation was established by act of Congress on 5 June 1872 (Stat. L., xvii, 228) and consisted of 100,141 acres of the Osage reserve located to the west of that reservation, east of the Arkansas River and adjoining the Kansas border. In July 1874, the affairs of the 523 Kaws were handled by the Osage Agency. Living on their own reservation, they continued under this supervision until 1876, when the superintendent of the Central Superintendency said that the Kaw Agency was a district agency but that the Osage agent handled its affairs. In 1879 the Osage Agency title was changed to Osage and Kaw Agency. The name was changed the next year to the Osage Agency and continued as such until 1886, when the tribal affairs were managed by two agencies again, with the Kaws under the supervision of the superintendent of the Kaw School. In 1887–88, the title was changed to the Kaw Subagency; a clerk-in-charge supervised its business. By an act of Congress ratified on 1 July 1902 (Stat. 32, 636), the tribe agreed to allotment of its reservation.

In 1904, the Kaw Reservation and agency were completely separated from the Osage Agency and placed under a bonded superintendent. In 1912, Kaw affairs were transferred to the management of the Ponca School superintendent. In 1913–14, the Kaw farmer (a government employee who lived on the reservation and assisted the Indians in their farming) reported on Kaw Agency affairs. The Kaw School was abolished in 1915, and in 1922 tribal affairs supervision was given to the Pawnee School superintendent at the Pawnee Agency at Pawnee.[42]

Otoe-Missouria

According to tradition, the people later known as the Otoes, along with their relatives the Winnebagos and the Iowas, once lived in the Great Lakes region. In a prehistoric migration southwest in search of buffalo, they separated. The division that reached the mouth of the Grand River, a branch of the Missouri, called themselves Niutachi and soon separated into two bands because of a quarrel between two of their chiefs. One band went up the Missouri and became known as the Otoe, and the other band stayed near the first settlement and was called the Missouria. From 1817 to 1841, the Otoes lived near the mouth of the Platte River. Since 1829, the Missourias have been absorbed by the Otoes, and the two are now indistinguishable.

On 15 March 1854, the Otoe-Missourias signed a treaty ceding all their lands except for a strip ten miles wide and twenty-five miles long on the waters of Big Blue River, but when it was found that there was no timber on this tract, it was exchanged for another tract taken from the Kaws (Kansa). In a treaty signed 15 August 1876 and amended 3 March 1879, they agreed to sell 120,000 acres of the western end of the reserve. Finally, a treaty signed on 3 March 1881 provided for the sale of all the rest of their lands in Kansas and Nebraska and for the selection of a new reservation. Consent to the treaty was recorded on 4 May and the tribe moved the following year to the new reservation, which was in Indian Territory.[43]

The Otoe Reservation was established by act of Congress on 3 March 1881 (Stat. L. xxi, 381) and consisted of 129,113 acres west of the Pawnee Reservation and south of the Ponca Reservation in Indian Territory. The tribes were removed from the Great Nemaha Agency in Nebraska to the Otoe Agency in 1882 and later placed under the consolidated Ponca, Pawnee and Otoe Agency in 1883. The Missouri Indians had been a separate tribe until 1829, when many of them joined the Otoes. By 1885 only forty individuals were designated as Missouri. The Absentee Otoes were a group who refused to live at the new agency and went to live at the Sac and Fox Agency for some years. In 1886, the main agency's name was changed to the Ponca, Pawnee, Otoe and Oakland Agency, and the Otoes and Missouris were under its supervision for many years. Their subagency was on the Otoe Reservation.

In the 1890s the tribes resisted allotment; it was completed slowly, often with arbitrary assignment of land by the allotting agent. In 1896 the allotment schedule was in the secretary of the interior's office, unapproved. In 1897 the allotment process was repeated, with continued opposition from tribal members. In 1904 additional allotments were made (Stat. 33, 218). In 1902 the Pawnee Agency was separated from the Ponca, Pawnee, Otoe and Oakland Agency, and the Otoe superintendent became responsible for the Otoe School and tribal affairs. In 1904 the Otoe and Missouri Agency was segregated from the Ponca Agency and the Otoe Reservation lines abolished. The two eastern townships became part of Pawnee County, and the balance of the reservation area became Noble County. Later the tribe became part of the Ponca Agency.[44]

Pawnee

The prehistoric origins of the Pawnees are still largely a mystery. Archeological studies indicate that the tribe moved northward around 1400 from an original homeland beyond the Rio Grande to the Red River near the Wichita Mountains, and then to the Arkansas River in southern Kansas or northern Oklahoma. From there, the Skidi Pawnee continued northward into southwestern Nebraska, while the Southern (or Black) Pawnee remained.

Until 1770, the Southern Pawnee, aided by weapons and supplies from French traders, stayed in the Arkansas River region. As French trade lessened, they migrated northward to join the Skidis in what is now Nebraska near the Platte, Loup, and Republican rivers. The move gave the tribe renewed outlets for trade as well as good buffalo hunting south of the Platte.

The opening of the frontier brought disaster to the Pawnees. Three treaties (1833, 1848, and 1857) provided for the cession of all Pawnee lands to the United States, with the exception of a reservation thirty miles long and fifteen miles wide along both banks of the Loup River, centering near present-day Fullerton, Nebraska. In 1876 this tract was also surrendered to the United States, and the entire tribe was relocated to a new reservation in Oklahoma in a difficult exodus that caused many deaths. Under an agreement with the United States dated 23 November 1892, the Pawnees gave up certain lands for a perpetual annuity payment of $30,000 per year, to be divided equally among tribal members. This annuity, which breaks down to just a few dollars for each tribe member, is still provided. The only other tribe still to receive such payments is the Oneida.[45]

The Pawnee Reservation was established by an act of 10 April 1875 (Stat. L, xix, 28) and consisted of 230,014 acres purchased from the Cherokee and 53,006 acres from the Creek Nations. It was located between the Cimarron and Arkansas rivers, west of the Creek Nation and north of the Sac and Fox Reservation in Indian Territory. The Pawnee removal from Nebraska began around 1873, when small groups left their reservation near Genoa, Nebraska, and moved to the Wichita Reservation by invitation of that tribe, their linguistic kinsmen. The majority of the tribe migrated to their new reservation from Nebraska in the winter of 1875.

In 1883 Pawnee affairs were handled by an agent at the Ponca, Pawnee and Otoe Agency located on the Ponca Reservation. A clerk-in-charge was stationed at the Pawnee Subagency. The agency's name was changed to the Ponca, Pawnee, Otoe and Oakland Agency in 1886, with the Pawnee Subagency continuing to function.

In 23 November 1892 the Pawnees consented to accept allotments in severalty and ceded their reservation (Stat. L., xxvii, 644, ratified 3 March 1893). Allotments were made to 820 persons, and in 1896 the surplus 169,320 acres were opened to settlement. At that time Pawnee affairs were handled by the Pawnee superintendent, who was responsible for school and tribal affairs administration during the decade.[46]

Ponca

In 1673, the Poncas were living on the Niobrara River; later they moved to southwestern Minnesota and the Black Hills of South Dakota. In 1877 they were evicted from their lands by the United States, which caused such hardship among the tribe that it became the subject of a public investigation ordered by President Hayes. In a settlement, approximately a third of the tribe returned to their lands on the Niobrara in 1880, while the rest moved to new lands set aside for them in Oklahoma. A small group of Poncas known as the Northern Ponca live in Nebraska.[47]

A 3 March 1877 act of Congress provided for Ponca removal to Indian Territory "without regard to their consent." Under this act they were temporarily located at the Quapaw Agency. The act of 27 May 1878 provided for their removal to their own reservation, which was established by this act. It was located west of the Osage Reservation and the Arkansas River and northwest of the Pawnee Reservation. Six hundred and ninety-three Poncas were moved from the Quapaw to the Ponca Reservation in July 1878. The new agency was located on the Salt Fork River. It was not until 3 March 1881 (Stat. L, xxi, 422) that an appropriation was made to purchase that tract from the Cherokees.

The Poncas were under the supervision of the Ponca, Pawnee and Otoe Agency, which was responsible also for the Pawnees, Otoes, Missouris, and Nez Perce. In 1886 it became the Ponca, Otoe and Oakland Agency. This agency, established for the Nez Perce, became the home of the Tonkawa Indians in 1885. The Poncas strongly resisted allotment of their lands in

severalty, and not until 6 April 1895 could the secretary of the interior approve the allotment of 100,734 acres to 782 individuals. However, one group did not accept allotment until 1899, and in 1904 additional allotments were made (Stat. 33, 218). In 1899 a superintendent was placed in charge of the Ponca School and tribal affairs. In 1901 the Pawnee Agency separated from the Ponca, Otoe and Oakland Agency, which became known as the Ponca, Otoe and Oakland Agency located at White Eagle.

In 1904, a further separation left the agency serving only the Poncas and Tonkawas. The Ponca superintendent continued to be responsible for the tribe into the 1920s. In 1927 the Ponca Subagency fell under the jurisdiction of the Pawnee Agency, and Otoe and Missouri affairs were transferred to this agency.[48]

Tonkawa

During the eighteenth and nineteenth centuries, the Tonkawas lived in central Texas. In 1884, they moved from Texas to Indian Territory and were assigned 91,000 acres of land previously assigned to the Nez Perce in Kay County, Oklahoma.[49]

The Tonkawas and a small group of associated Lipan Apaches came to the Oakland Agency from the Sac and Fox Agency, where ninety-two tribespeople had arrived from Fort Griffin, Texas, on 23 October 1884. They were placed on the Iowa Reservation of the agency, were they remained until June 1885, when they were transferred to the Oakland Reservation, which had just been vacated by the Nez Perce the month before. A subagency was created for them, with the main agency at the Ponca, Pawnee, Otoe and Oakland Agency on the Ponca Reservation. In an agreement concluded on 21 October 1891, the Tonkawas ceded this reservation to the United States, and allotments were subsequently made to them. In 1896 the surplus lands were opened for settlement. In 1900 the subagency had a farmer-in-charge. The tribe's affairs continued under the Ponca, Otoe and Oakland Agency in 1901 and under the Ponca School superintendent in 1904. The Lipan Apaches, counted as part of the Tonkawas, had apparently been with them since their arrival in Indian Territory from Fort Griffin. This small remnant were often called Tonkawa and soon lost their identity. The combined group continued under this agency's supervision until 1928, when the Pawnee Agency became the main agency for all of the above tribes.[50]

PAWNEE AGENCY RECORDS[51]

Census Records

Letters sent and received, 1894–1927; census and lists for the Nez Perce, Kaw, Tonkawa, Pawnee and Oto and Missouri, 1880–1926; census and lists for the Ponca and Tonkawa, undated and 1926.

Letterpress Books, 1870–1903

RECORDS OF THE PAWNEE AGENCY AND SUBAGENCIES[52]

Federal, State, and Local Courts and Other Relations

Letters Sent and Received and Other Documents, 1894–1902.

KAW AGENCY RECORDS[53]

Letterpress Books, 1894–1908

PONCA, PAWNEE, OTOE AND OAKLAND AGENCY RECORDS

Letterpress Books, 1894–1908

OTOE AGENCY RECORDS

Letterpress Books, 1880–1908

PONCA AGENCY RECORDS[54]

Letterpress Books, 1879–1911

TONKAWA AGENCY RECORDS[55]

Letterpress Books, 1877–1918

SHAWNEE AGENCY

The Shawnee Agency, located at Shawnee, Oklahoma, has jurisdiction over the Iowa, Kickapoo, Citizen Potawatomi, Sac and Fox, and Absentee-Shawnee Tribes.[56]

The Shawnee Agency was originally known as the Sac and Fox Agency. It operated under the Central Superintendency. It was located about six miles south of the present town of Stroud, Oklahoma. The agent also had under his jurisdiction 467 Absentee Shawnees who were living thirty miles southwest of the Sac and Fox Agency. They were located on lands they had occupied before the Civil War. Many had remained loyal to the Union and had sought shelter in the North. After the war they returned to their old territory and were later joined by the Black Bob Band of Shawnees from Kansas.

In a series of agreements in 1890 that resulted from implementation of the Dawes Act, all of the tribes within the Sac and Fox Agency (except the Kickapoos) ceded their lands to the United States and accepted allotments in severalty. The Sac and Fox, Iowa, Potawatomi, and Shawnee lands were opened to non-Indian settlement on 22 September 1891. The agency site at that time became a part of Oklahoma Territory. The Kickapoos were allotted later, and their lands were opened to settlement on 23 May 1895. In April 1896, a special agent was appointed to handle the affairs of the band of Mexican Kickapoos known as the "Kicking" Kickapoos. The special agent assumed charge of the "Progressive" Kickapoos and the Big Jim Band of Absentee Shawnee a year or so later through an agency office located near the town of Shawnee.

In 1901 the Sac and Fox Agency was divided. The Sac and Fox Agency itself remained at the old site near Stroud with jurisdiction over the Sac and Fox and the Iowas. The Shawnee, Potawatomi and Kickapoo Agency (sometimes called the Shawnee Agency) was established about two miles south of Shawnee, Oklahoma. The agencies continued their separate existence until 1919, when they were merged, becoming the Shawnee Agency.[57]

Besides the resident tribes' records, there are files of other tribes' records brought from the Sac and Fox Agency in Kansas. They are listed below with the name of the tribe and years covered by the correspondence and records.

Chippewas of Swan Creek and Black River, and Muncie (Munsee) Indians, 1854–1901

Christian Indians, 1858–1864

Oneida Indians, 1902

Otoe Indians, 1880–1921

Ottawa Indians, 1838–1908

The majority of the Otoes listed in table 14-1 resided on the Otoe reservation under the Otoe Agency. Later they were under the jurisdiction of the Pawnee and Ponca Agencies. Some intermarried among the Iowas and others at the Sac and Fox Agency. This file refers to them and the earlier group that came from the Great Nemaha Agency in Nebraska.[58]

Absentee-Shawnee
See Eastern Shawnee.[59]

Citizen Band Potawatomi
Before 1700, the Potawatomis lived near the upper Lake Huron territory and on the islands of Green Bay, Wisconsin. They were later located near what is now Chicago and Milwaukee. During the French and Indian War they were close allies of the French until the peace of 1763. They were also allied with Ottawa Chief Pontiac against the British and white settlers. During the revolutionary war, however, they fought with the British against the American colonies, and hostilities continued until the Treaty of Greenville of 1795 brought peace between the former colonies and the Potawatomis.

In 1833 the Potawatomis, together with the Ottawas and Chippewas, signed the Chicago Treaty, ceding all their lands in Illinois and along the western shore of Lake Michigan and agreeing to move to Iowa within three years. They were in Iowa only briefly before the government moved them to Kansas. Today, in Kansas, the Prairie Band of Potawatomis is descended mainly from Indiana, Illinois, and Michigan Potawatomis.

The Citizen Band of Potawatomi tribe of Oklahoma is so called because certain Prairie Band members applied for citizenship papers in the 1860s, having been granted that right by treaty. Many sold their fee patent land in Kansas; landless and destitute, they removed to Indian Territory. Reservation land was provided for them there; however, because they were citizens, legal questions arose as to their right to live on it. Today there is no Potawatomi reservation in Oklahoma.[60]

Under a treaty of 15 November 1861 (12 Stat. 1191), the Potawatomis had received allotments in severalty in Kansas. A number accepted allotments and became citizens of the United States, then becoming known as Citizen Potawatomi. Many of them soon sold their allotments and began to plan the purchase of a new reservation in Indian Territory. A treaty of 27 February 1867 (15 Stat. 531) provided for this purchase. A thirty-square-mile reservation was selected west of the Seminole Nation between the North and South Canadian rivers, and 250 Citizen Potawatomis moved into the area. The Potawatomi lands selected encroached on those of the Absentee Shawnees' prewar settlement claims. To right this situation, Congress passed an act (Stat. L, xvii, 159) on 23 May 1872 permitting the Absentee Shawnees to select allotments on the Potawatomi Reserve. There was considerable opposition, and Sam Warrior's Band, comprising approximately one-third of the tribe, moved to an area west of the Kickapoos.[61]

Iowa
The earliest known Iowa settlement is believed to have been along the Upper Iowa River. Later, the Iowas moved into the northwestern part of the present state of Iowa. In the latter part of the eighteenth century, the Iowas moved to the Missouri River and settled south of the spot where Council Bluffs, Iowa, now stands on the east side of the river. Around 1760 they moved east and came to live along the Mississippi between the Iowa and Des Moines rivers. Early in the nineteenth century, part of

the tribe moved farther up the Des Moines River, while others established themselves on the Grand and Platte rivers in Missouri. In 1814 they were allotted lands in what was known as the Platte Purchase, extending from the Platte River of Missouri through western Iowa to the Dakota country. By treaties signed on 4 August 1824, 15 July 1830, 17 September 1836, and 23 November 1867, the Iowas ceded all their lands in Missouri and Iowa to the United States. On 19 August 1825, they also ceded lands in Minnesota. The treaty of 1836 assigned part of the tribe to a reservation along the Great Nemeha River in present-day Nebraska and Kansas. The remainder were moved to central Oklahoma in 1883.[62]

Kickapoo

The Kickapoos moved into the Wisconsin area in the early part of the seventeenth Century. They later moved into Illinois near the present-day city of Peoria. During the War of 1812 they were allied with Tecumseh against the United States. In 1809 and 1819, the Kickapoos ceded their lands in Illinois to the United States and moved to Missouri and then Kansas. Around 1852, a large number of the Kickapoos and some Potawatomis went to Texas and then to Mexico, where they became known as Mexican Kickapoos. Another dissatisfied band joined them in 1863. Ten years later, part of this band was induced to return to Indian Territory. Those who chose to remain in Mexico were granted a reservation on the Sabinas River about twelve to fifteen miles from the town of Musquiz in the state of Coahuila.[63]

After the cession of their homeland in Illinois in 1819, the Kickapoo bands separated and migrated to different areas, some going to Texas and others to Mexico. The Texas bands came to Indian Territory before the Civil War in two groups, one settling on Creek and the other on Choctaw lands. Later, many of them joined the Kickapoos living in Mexico. An effort was made under the acts of 15 July 1870, 3 March 1871, and 22 June 1874 to move the Mexican Kickapoos and others on the borders of Texas to a reservation which would be established for them in Indian Territory. A commission was appointed which succeeded in getting some three hundred to four hundred to consent to move. By 1873 these Mexican Kickapoos had begun to arrive at the Sac and Fox Agency. Their reservation was located between the South Canadian and Deep Fork rivers west of the Sac and Fox Reservation.[64]

Sac and Fox

Originally separate and independent tribes, the Sac (or Sauk) and Fox tribes have long been affiliated and allied. The original homeland of the Sac and Fox was in the Great Lakes region, where the Sac inhabited the Upper Michigan Peninsula and the Fox the south shore of Lake Superior. By 1667, when Father Allouez made the first recorded white contact with the two tribes, Iroquois and French pressure on the Sac and Chippewa pressure on the Fox had pushed both groups to the vicinity of present-day Green Bay, Wisconsin. French attacks on the Sac and Fox in the eighteenth century, attributed to Indians, strengthened the alliance of the two tribes, which amounted to a confederation. Forced to migrate south, they attacked the Illinois and forced them from their lands along the Mississippi in the present-day states of Illinois, Iowa, and Wisconsin. Those groups that stayed near the Mississippi River became known as the Sac and Fox of the Mississippi to distinguish them from the Sac and Fox of the Missouri, a large band that settled farther south along the Missouri River.

In 1804, the chiefs of the Missouri band were persuaded to sign a treaty ceding to the United States all Sac and Fox lands east of the Mississippi River, as well as some hunting grounds to the west of it. Government efforts several years later to enforce the treaty embittered the Sac and Fox, most of whom knew about the treaty. Attempts to remove the Sac and Fox caused a split in the confederation. The majority of the tribe followed the conciliatory Sac Chief Keokuk, who agreed to move. The remainder supported the rival Black Hawk, a Sac warrior who bitterly opposed the treaty and led his "British Band" into revolt (the Black Hawk War). With the Treaty of Fort Armstrong in 1832, Sac and Fox power on the frontier came to an end. In 1833, the tribe was moved to Iowa, where they lived for only thirteen years before being moved again, this time to the Osage River Reservation in Kansas. In 1869, the Sac and Fox were again moved, this time to Oklahoma. Keokuk, and later his son, Moses, continued to lead the conciliatory faction of the tribes, but many of the Fox opposed the many cessions of land to the United States and returned to Iowa in 1859 to join a smaller number who had steadfastly refused to be moved.[65]

Under terms of a treaty with the United States concluded on 18 February 1867 (15 Stat. 495), the Sac and Fox of the Mississippi ceded approximately 157,000 acres of their land in Kansas in exchange for a new reservation of 750 square miles in Indian Territory between the Cimarron and North Canadian rivers west of the Creek Nation. On 25 November 1869, 387 tribal members began the move to their new home, arriving nineteen days later. One band under Chief Mo-ho-ko-ho remained in Kansas, and the Sac and Fox of Missouri continued to live at the Great Nemaha Agency in Nebraska near the Iowas, with whom they had been associated for many years.[66]

SAC AND FOX-SHAWNEE AGENCY RECORDS[67]

Census Records

Letters and documents received, 1865–1924; census and lists for the Iowa, Mexican Kickapoo, and Otoe, 1881–1920; census and lists for the Citizen Potawatomi, 1883–1921; Sac and Fox and Absentee Shawnee census, 1850–1923.

Letterpress Books

Iowa letters sent, 1840–47; account and letter book, Sac and Fox Agency, Kansas, 1849–61; letters sent, 1874–1902.

Federal and State Relations, 1854–1918

Federal, State, and Local Relations, 1851–1928

Military Relations and Affairs, 1853–1924

Indian History, Culture, and Acculturation, 1867–1923

Land Ownership and Use, 1847–1917

Agents and Agency, 1849–1927

FLORIDA SUPERINTENDENCY

The Florida Superintendency was formally established in 1822, but officials had been assigned to Florida the previous year. Until the establishment of the Bureau of Indian Affairs in 1824, the superintendency was under the direct supervision of the secretary of war. The territorial governor, who resided permanently in Tallahassee beginning in 1824, acted as *ex officio* superintendent throughout the existence of the superintendency. The principal Indian tribe in Florida was the Seminole.

A subagent for Indians in Florida, appointed on 21 March 1821, reported to the newly appointed provisional governor, Andrew Jackson. In September of the same year a temporary agent was appointed to handle Indian affairs during the absence of the governor, and the subagent was made accountable to him. In 1822 an agent and a subagent were authorized to serve under the governor. In 1826 an additional subagent was appointed for the Indians on the Apalachicola River.

With the contemplated removal of the Indians from Florida, the superintendency and the subagencies were abolished on 30 June 1834. In 1835, control of Indians in Florida was entrusted to the army. However, there were some Bureau of Indian Affairs officials on the Apalachicola River until 1839, and in 1849 there was a short-lived subagency for the Seminoles still in Florida.

SELECT LIST OF TRIBES

The following should not be considered a comprehensive list of the numerous tribes, bands, and sub-bands mentioned in the records of the Bureau of Indian Affairs in the custody of the National Archives. Researchers can consult John R. Swanton, *The Indian Tribes of North America* (Smithsonian Institution Press), for information about specific tribes.

This table includes only the names of the agencies which had primary responsibility for a tribe. If any of the pre-1800 correspondence from that agency to the Commissioner of Indian Affairs is available on National Archives microfilm publication M234, there is a citation to the appropriate rolls. If there are any census rolls for the tribe among those taken from 1885 to 1940, there is a reference to the appropriate roll numbers of microfilm publication M595.

Select List of Tribes

Tribe	Agency	Location of Original Records*	Pre–1880 Correspondence M234 Roll No.	Post–1885 Census Records M595 Roll No.
Absentee Shawnee	See Shawnee			
Adai	Red River Agency, 1824–30	DC	727	
Adopted Delaware/ Shawnee	Muskogee Area Office, 1890–1960	FTW		
Alabama	Caddo Agency, 1824–42	DC	231	
Alleghany	New York Agency, 1838–49	DC	583–97	290–300
Anadarko	Anadarko Area Office, 1881–1962	FTW		
	Texas Agency, 1847–59	DC	858–61	
	Wichita Agency, 1859	DC	928	
Apache	Kiowa Agency, 1881–1962	FTW		211–23
	Fort Apache Agency, 1875–1955	DC/LA		
	Phoenix Area Office, 1928–37	DC/LA		344–46
	Truxton Canyon Agency, 1895–1951	LA		581
	San Carlos Agency, 1900–52	LA		461–70
Apache–Jicarilla	See Jicarilla			
Apache, Kiowa	Upper Platte Agency 1846–55	DC	889–96	
Apache, Kiowa	Upper Arkansas Agency, 1855–67	DC	878–82	
Apache, Kiowa	Kiowa Agency/Anadarko, 1864–80	DC/FTW	375–86	211–23
Apache–Mescalero	See Mescalero			
Apache–Mojave	Camp McDowell (Pima) Agency, 1901–51	DC		15
Apache, White Mountain	Fort Apache Agency, 1875–1955	DC/LA		118–25
Apalachee	Caddo and Red River Agencies, 1824–42	DC	31, 727	
Arapaho	Upper Platte Agency, 1855–74	DC	889–96	
	Upper Arkansas Agency, 1855–74	DC	878–82	
	Cheyenne and Arapahoe Agency, 1875–	DC/FTW	119–26	27–32
	Red Cloud (Pine Ridge) Agency, 1871–1961	DC/KC	715–26	
	Cantonment Agency, 1903–27	DC/FTW		16–17
	Wind River Agency, 1873–1952	DEN		663
	Seger School, 1903–12, 1914–27	DC		479
	Shoshoni Agency, 1885–1937, with gaps	DC/DEN		498–504
Arikaree	See Arikara			
Arikara	Fort Berthold Agency, 1867–70	DC	292–99	132–36
	Upper Missouri Agency, 1824–66	DC	883–88	
Assiniboin	Upper Missouri Agency 1824–66	DC	883–88	
	Fort Berthold Agency, 1867–70	DC	292–99	
	Fort Belknap Agency, 1877–1952	SEA		126–31
	Fort Peck Agency, 1877–1952	SEA		151–60
Bannock	Wind River Agency, 1873–1952	DC/DEN		11
	Fort Hall Agency, 1889–1963	DC/SEA		138–44
	Lemhi (Fort Hall) Agency, 1889–1963	SEA		248

Tribe	Agency	Location of Original Records*	Pre–1880 Correspondence M234 Roll No.	Post–1885 Census Records M595 Roll No.
Biloxi	Red River and Caddo Agencies, 1824–42	DC	31, 727	
Blackfeet	Blackfeet Agency, 1873–1927	DC/DEN	30	3–11
	Blackfeet Agency, 1875–1952	DC/SEA	30	
	Cheyenne River/Standing Rock, 1862–1957	DC/KC	127–31, 846–52	3–11
	Upper Missouri and Upper Platte, 1824–74	DC	883–96	
Blood	Blackfeet Agency, 1855–59	DC	30	11
Brotherton	Green Bay (Menominee) Agency, 1824–1961	DC/CHI	315–36	
	Six Nations Agency, 1824–34	DC	832	
Brule Sioux	Upper Platte/Missouri (Crow Creek), 1824–74	DC	883–96	427–30
	Lower Brule/Whetstone (Rosebud), 1875–1966	DC/KC	401,925–27	427–30
	Spotted Tail (Rosebud)/Grand River, 1875–1966	DC/KC	840–45,305–06	427–45
Caddo	Anadarko Area Office, 1881–1962	FTW		211–23
	Red River Agency, 1824–30	DC	727	
	Caddo Agency, 1824–42	DC	31	
	Wichita Agency, 1859–78	DC	928–30	211–23
	Kiowa Agency, 1864–1962	DC/FTW	375–86	
Capote Ute	Abiquiu and Cimarron Agencies, 1869–1882	DEN		
	Colorado Superintendency, 1877–80	DC	197–214	
Cayuga	New York Agency, 1838–49	DC	583–97	290–300
	Miami Agency, 1870–1952	DC/FTW		
	Oregon and Washington Sup., 1842–80	DC	607–30, 907–20	616–20
Chastacosta	Oregon Superintendency, 1842–80	DC	607–30	
Chehalis	Taholah Indian Agency, 1878–1952	SEA		93, 302, 407–09, 564–69
Chemehuevi	Colorado River Agency, 1867–1955	LA		
Cherokee	Cherokee Agency, 1824–80	DC	71–118	
	Union Agency, 1875–1914	DC/FTW	865–77	
	Five Civilized Tribes Agency/Muskogee, 1914–60	FTW		
Cherokee, North Carolina	Cherokee Indian Agency, 1886–1952	ATL		22
Cheyenne	Cheyenne and Arapahoe Agency, 1824–1952	FTW	119–26	11, 16–17, 27–32, 362–67, 425, 478–79, 574–79
	Upper Arkansas Agency, 1855–74	DC	878–82	
	Upper Missouri Agency, 1824–46	DC	883–88	
	Upper Platte Agency, 1846–70	DC	889–96	
	Red Cloud (Pine Ridge), 1867–1961	KC	715–26	362–69
	Red Moon Census, 1909–12,1914–16	FTW		425
	Cantonment Agency, 1903–27	FTW		16–17
	Seger School (Concho Agency), 1891–1952	FTW		479
Cheyenne, Northern	Northern Cheyenne Agency, 1884–1952	SEA		
	Tongue River, 1886–1939	DC		574–79
Chickasaw	Chickasaw Agency, 1824–70	DC	135–48	
	Choctaw Agency, 1855–74	DC	169–96	
	Muskogee Area Office, 1870–1952	FTW		
	Union Agency, 1875–1914	DC/FTW	865–77	
Chilkat	Washington and Oregon Sup., 1842–80	DC	907–20, 607–30	
Chippewa	Red Lake Agency, 1894–1961	DC/KC		417–24
Chippewa (Pembina)	Turtle Mountain Agency, 1869–1955	DC/KC		595–607
Chippewa, Boise Fort	Nett Lake Sub–Agency, 1908–18	DC/KC		287
Chippewa, Consolidated	Minn. (Consol. Chippewa) Agency, 1890–1953	DC/KC		57–62
Chippewa, Kansas	Potawatomi Agency, ca. 1876	DC/KC	678–95	2, 11, 57–76, 94–97, 117, 167, 170–71, 180
	Osage River Agency to 1851	DC	642–51	181, 140–47, 187, 229–32, 253, 392–95
	Ottawa Agency, 1863–64	DC	656–58	417, 595–607, 628, 649–62
	Sac and Fox Agency, 1851–63, 1864–69	DC/CHI	728–44	
Chippewa, L. Superior/MN	Chippewa Agency, 1851–53	DC/CHI	149–68	
Chippewa, Lake Superior	La Pointe Agency, 1831–50	DC	387–400	
	Mackinac Agency, 1853–54	DC	402–16	

Tribe	Agency	Location of Original Records*	Pre–1880 Correspondence M234 Roll No.	Post–1885 Census Records M595 Roll No.
Chippewa, L. Superior/MS	Sandy Lake Subagency, 1850–51	DC	767	
Chippewa, Michigan	Mackinac Agency, 1903–27	DC/CHI	402–16	253
Chippewa, Mississippi	Winnebago Agency, 1848–1947	DC/KC	931–47	
Chippewa, United Band	Chicago and Green Bay, East, 1824–80	CHI	132–34, 315–36	
	Council Bluffs Agency, 1837–47	DC	215–18	
Chippewa, Wisconsin	Great Lakes Consol. Agency, 1875–1952	CHI		170–71
	Lac du Flambeau Agency/School, 1896–1932	CHI		229–32
	Red Cliff Agency and School, 1901–22	CHI		417
	Tomah Indian School and Agency, 1908–34	CHI		
Chippewa	Devil's Lake–Fort Totten, 1890–1950	KC	281–84	94–97
	La Pointe Agency, 1886–1922	CHI	387–400	234–42
	Leech Lake Agency, 1899–1922	KC		243–47
	White Earth Agency, 1892–1929	KC		649–62
Chiricahua Apache	Arizona Superintendency, 1863–80	DC	3–28	
Choctaw	Choctaw Agency, 1824–76	DC	169–96	
	Jones Academy, Hartshorne, 1901–53	FTW		
	Union Agency–Muskogee Area, 1875–80	DC/FTW	865–77	685
Choctaw, Mississippi	Choctaw, Philadelphia, Miss., 1926–39	DC		15, 41–42
Christian	See Stockbridge and Munsee			
Citizen Potawatomi	Shawnee Agency, 1890–1952	FTW		490–96
	Sac and Fox Agency, Oklahoma, 1889–1919, with gaps	FTW		453–55
Clallam	Puyallup Agency, 1885–1920	SEA		93, 407–09, 584–93
Cocopa	Colorado River Agency, 1867–1955	LA		
Coeur d'Alene	Colville Agency, 1865–1952	SEA		43–45, 49–56, 302
Comanche	Anadarko Area Office, 1881–1962	FTW		211–23
	Upper Platte Agency, 1846–55	DC	889–96	211–23
	Upper Arkansas Agency, 1855–64	DC	878–82	211–23
	Kiowa Agency, 1864–80	FTW	375–86	211–23
Concow	Round Valley Agency, 1893–1920	SF		12, 447–49
Coyotero Apache	New Mexico Superintendency to 1877	DC	546–82	
	Arizona Superintendency, 1877–80	DC	3–28	
Cree	Upper Missouri Agency, 1824–74	DC	883–88	11
Creek	Creek Agency, 1824–66	DC		
	Union Agency, 1875–1914	DC/FTW	865–77	
	Eufala Boarding School, 1925–52	FTW		
	Muskogee Area Office, 1890–1960	FTW		
Crow	Crow Agency, 1874–1952	SEA		79–86
	Upper Missouri Agency, 1824–66	DC	883–88	79–86
	Fort Berthold Agency, 1867–70	DC	292	79–86
Cuthead Sioux	Upper Missouri Agency, 1824–66	DC	883–88	
Delaware	Anadarko Area Office, 1881–1962	FTW		218–223
Delaware, Kansas	Fort Leavenworth Agency, 1824–51	DC	300–03	
	Kansas Agency 1851–55	DC	364–70	
	Delaware Agency, 1855–73	DC	274–80	
Delaware, Indian Terr.	Cherokee Agency, 1867–74	DC	101–12	
	Union Agency, 1875–80	DC	865–77	
Digger	Digger Agency, 1916–20	SF		
	Greenville School and Agency, 1897–1921	SF		
Dwamish	Oregon and Washington Sup., 1842–80	DC	607–30, 907–20	
Eastern Cherokee	Cherokee Indian Agency, 1886–1952	ATL		
	See Shawnee			
Flathead	Montana Superintendency, 1864–80	DC	488–518	
	Flathead Agency, 1875–1952	SEA		107–16
Fox	See Sac and Fox			
Grande Ronde	Roseburg Agency, 1912–18	SF		
Grosventre	Blackfeet Agency, 1875–1952	SEA		
	Fort Berthold, 1867–80	DEN/KC/SEA	292–99	11, 126–36

Tribe	Agency	Location of Original Records*	Pre-1880 Correspondence M234 Roll No.	Post-1885 Census Records M595 Roll No.
	Fort Belknap, 1885–1939	SEA		126–31
	Montana Superintendency, 1864–80	DC	488–518	
	Upper Missouri, 1824–66	DC	883–88	
Havasupai	Colorado River Agency, 1867–1955	LA		178, 580–81
	Truxton Canon Agency, 1895–1951	LA		580–81
Hoa	Neah Bay (Tahola) Agency, 1878–1950	SEA		282–86
Hoopa	Hoopa Valley Agency and School, 1891–1929	SF		
	California Superintendency	DC	32–52	12
Hopi	Hopi Agency, 1910–56	LA		188–95
	Western Navajo Agency, 1902–17	LA		640–45
	California Superintendency, 1849–80	DC	32–52	12, 182–87
Iowa	Shawnee Agency, 1890–1952	FTW		176, 210, 392–95, 453–55, 491–96
Iowa	Horton (Potawatomi) Agency, 1851–1963	KC		
Iroquois	Six Nations Agency, 1824–34	DC	832	
	Seneca, New York, 1824–32	DC	808	
	New York Agency, 1835–80	DC	583–97	
Jicarilla Apache	Abiquiu and Cimarron Agencies, 1869–82	DEN		543–45
	Jicarilla Agency, 1890–1952	DEN		197–98
	Mescalero Agency, 1874–1942	DEN		
Kansa (Kaw)	Pawnee Agency, 1871–1964	FTW	659–68	199, 317–28, 337–43
Kansa (Kaw), Kansas	Ft. Leavenworth Agency, 1824–47	DC	300–03	
	Osage River Agency, 1847–51	DC	642–51	
	Potawatomi Agency, 1851–55	DC	678–95	
	Kansas Agency, 1855–76	DC	364–70	
Kansa (Kaw), Ind. Terr.	Osage Agency, 1874–80	DC/FTW	633–41	
Kaskaskia	Miami Agency, 1870–1952	FTW		
Kaw	See Kansa			
Kichai	Wichita/Kiowa Agencies, 1857–80	DC	383–86, 928–30	
Kickapoo	Shawnee Agency, 1890–1952	FTW		210, 392–95
Kickapoo, Kansas	Ft. Leavenworth Agency, 1824–51	DC	300–03	
	Great Nemaha, 1851–55	DC	307–14	
	Kickapoo Agency, 1855–76	DC	371–74	
	Horton (Potawatomi) Agency, 1874–1963	DC/KC	691–95	176, 210, 392–95
Kickapoo, Mexican	Kickapoo Agency, 1873–75	DC	373–74	
	Sac and Fox Agency, 1874–80	DC/CHI	740–44	
	Shawnee Agency, 1890–1952	FTW		
Kiowa	Upper Platte Agency, 1846–55	DC	889	
	Upper Arkansas Agency, 1855–64	FTW	878	
	Kiowa Agency, 1864–1962	FTW	375–86	211–23
Kiowa Apache	See Apache			
Klamath	Hoopa Valley Agency, 1891–1929	SF		12, 182–87, 224–27
Klamath, Lower	Greenville School/Agency, 1897–1921	SF		
	Roseburg Agency, 1913–18	SF		446
Klamath	Klamath Indian Agency, 1865–1952	SEA		12, 182–87, 224–27
Kutenai	Montana Superintendency, 1864–80	DC	488–518	107–108, 302
Lake	Coleville Agency, 1874–1964	SEA		49–56
Lipan, Apache	Texas Agency, 1847–59	DC	858–861	
	Central Superintendency, 1876–80	DC	67–70	

Tribe	Agency	Location of Original Records*	Pre-1880 Correspondence M234 Roll No.	Post-1885 Census Records M595 Roll No.
Little Lake Valley	Round Valley Agency	SF		447–449
Lower Brule, Sioux	Upper Missouri Agency to 1874	DC	883–888	
	Crow Creek Agency, 1874–1955	DC/KC	249	87–92
	Lower Brule Agency, 1875–76	DC/KC	401	87–92, 252
Lummi	Tulalip Agency, 1854–1952	SEA		582–93
Makah	Neah Bay (Tahola) Agency, 1878–1952	SEA		282–86
Mandan	Bismarck Indian School, 1904–38	KC		
	Upper Missouri Agency, 1824–66	DC	883–88	
	Fort Berthold, 1889–1939	KC	292–99	132–36
Maricopa	Pima Agency, 1901–51	LA	669	347–61
Mdewakanton Sioux	Birch Cooley (Pipestone), 1895–1954	KC		2, 35, 385
Menominee	Green Bay and Keshena, 1865–1959	CHI	325–36	172–74, 200–09
Menominee	Menominee Agency, 1865–1959	CHI		
Mescalero Apache	Mescalero Agency, 1874–1946	DEN		254–56
Mexican Kickapoo	See Kickapoo			
Miami	Miami Agency, Oklahoma, 1870–1952	FTW		487–89
Miami, Ohio	Fort Wayne and Indiana, 1824–50	DC	304, 354–60	11
Miami, Kansas	Osage River Agency, to 1871	DC	642–51	411–16
	Shawnee Agency, 1871	FTW	820–23	488–89
Miami, Indian Terr.	Quapaw Agency, 1871–80	FTW	703–14	410–12, 416
Mimbreno Apache	New Mexico Superintendency, to 1877	DC	546–82	
	Arizona Superintendency, 1877–80	DC	3–28	
Miniconjou Sioux	Upper Missouri and Upper Platte, 1824–74	DC	883–96	
	Cheyenne River Agency, 1869–1956	KC		
Mission	Mission Tule River Agency, 1920–53	LA		15, 41–42, 258–60, 267
Mission	Camp McDowell (Pima Agency), 1901–51	DC/LA		15
	Pala Subagency, 1905–07,1916–20	LA		335
Missouri	Upper Missouri Agency, 1824–37	DC	883–88	
	Council Bluffs Agency, 1837–56	DC	215–18	
	Otoe and Ponca Agencies, 1856–1964	DC/FTW	652–55	329, 386–91
	Nebraska Agencies, 1876–80	DC	519–29	
Moache Ute	Abiquiu and Cimarron Agencies, 1869–82	DEN		
Modoc	Digger Agency, 1916–20	SF		224–28
	Quapaw and Seneca Agencies, 1873–80	DC/FTW	703–13	410–12, 487–89
Mogollon Apache	New Mexico Superintendency, to 1877	DC	546–72	
	Arizona Superintendency, 1877–80	DC	3–28	
Mojave	Colorado River Agency, 1867–1955	LA		46–48
	San Carlos Agency, 1900–52	LA		460–69
Mojave-Apache	Camp McDowell (Pima Agency), 1901–51	LA		15
	Phoenix Area Office, 1907–74	LA		344–45
Mono	California Superintendency, 1849–80	DC	32–52	13
Moqui Pueblo	Moqui Pueblo Agency, 1906–23	DC		268–72
Muckleshoot	Tulalip Agency, 1854–1952	SEA		93, 582–93
Munsee	Potawatomi Agency, 1851–1902	DC/FTW	678–95	392
Munsee, East	Green Bay and Menominee, 1865–1959	CHI	325–36	
Munsee, Kansas	Ft. Leavenworth Agency, 1839–51	DC	301–03	
	Kansas Agency, 1851–55	DC	364	
	Delaware Agency, 1855–59	DC	274–75	
	Sac and Fox Agency, 1859–69	DC	734–38	

Tribe	Agency	Location of Original Records*	Pre-1880 Correspondence M234 Roll No.	Post-1885 Census Records M595 Roll No.
Munsee, Kansas	Ottawa Agency, 1863–64	DC	656	
	Potawatomi Agency, ca.1876–80	DC	692–95	
Navajo (East, North, South)	Navajo Agency, 1881–1936	DEN/LA		303–07, 405–06, 471, 518–31, 640–48
Navajo	Santa Fe Agency, 1890–1935	DEN		98–103, 190–95, 249, 273–82
	Pueblo Bonito, 1909–26	DC		401–06
Navajo, Northern	Northern Navajo and Shiprock, 1903–35	LA		303–07
Navajo, Western	Western Navajo Agency, 1902–17	LA		640–45
Navajo	Albuquerque School, 1890–1960	DEN/FTW		1
	Leupp Training School, 1915–35	DEN		249–51
Nez Perce	Ponca and Quapaw Agencies, Okla., 1878–79		675–77, 707–13	301
	Northern Idaho Agency, 1875–1952	SEA		11, 45, 49–56
	Fort Lapwai, 1902–33	DC		145–48
	Winnebago Agency, 1869–1947	KC		
Nez Perce, Joseph's Band	Colville Agency, 1865–1952	SEA		
Nisqualli	Puyallup Agency, 1888–1909	SEA		93, 302, 407–09
	Taholah Agency, 1915–39 with gaps	SEA		564–69
Nomelaki	Round Valley Agency, 1893–1920	SF		12, 447–49
Oglala Sioux	Upper Missouri/Upper Platte, 1824–74	DC	883–96	
	Red Cloud/Whetstone/Spotted Tail, 1871–80	DC	715–26, 925–27, 840–45	
	Grand River (Standing Rock), 1871–1957	DC/KC	305–06	
	Pine Ridge Agency, 1913–43 with gaps	KC		370–84
Omaha	Upper Missouri Agency, 1824–37	DC	883–88	
	Council Bluffs Agency, 1837–56	DC	215–18	
	Omaha (Winnebago) Agency, 1867–1946	DC/KC	604–06	311–14, 663–70
	Nebraska Agencies, 1876–80	DC	519–29	
Oneida	Keshena Agency, 1920–39	CHI		202–07
	Tomah Agency, 1897–1923	CHI		315–16, 572–73
Oneida, New York	Six Nations and New York, 1824–80	DC	832, 583–97	290–300
Oneida, Wisconsin	Oneida and Greenbay, 1897–1927	CHI		172–74
Onondaga	New York Agency, 1835–80	DC	583–97	290–300
Oreilles	La Pointe Agency, 1886–89	DC/CHI		234–40
Osage	Osage Agency, 1824–51, 1874–1961	DC/FTW	631–41	317–28, 530–37, 631–41
	Neosho Agency, 1851–74	DC	530–37	
Otoe	Upper Missouri Agency, 1824–37	DC	883–88	
	Council Bluffs Agency, 1837–56	DC	215–18	
	Otoe Agency, 1856–76	DC	652–55	329
	Ponca Agency, 1886–1927	DC/FTW		386–91
	Nebraska Agencies, 1876–80	DC	519–29	
Ottawa	Mackinac Agency, 1903–27	CHI		
	Miami (Quapaw) Agency, Okla., 1870–1952	DC/FTW	703–13	410–416
	Seneca Agency, 1901–7, 1910–21	DC		487–89
Ottawa, East	Green Bay and Chicago, 1824–1961	DC/CHI	132–34, 315–36	
Ottawa, Iowa	Council Bluffs Agency, 1837–47	DC	215–18	
Ottawa, Kansas	Osage River Agency, 1837–51	DC	642–51	
	Sac and Fox Agency, 1851–63	DC/CHI	733–44	
	Ottawa Agency, 1863–73	DC	656–58	
Ottawa, Indian Terr.	Neosho Agency, 1867–71	DC	530–37	

Tribe	Agency	Location of Original Records*	Pre-1880 Correspondence M234 Roll No.	Post-1885 Census Records M595 Roll No.
Ozette	Neah Bay Agency, 1878–1950	SEA		282–86
Pahvant	Utah Superintendency, 1849–80	DC	897–906	167
Paiute	Fort Bidwell Agency, 1910–31	SF		224–28, 330–34, 640–45
	Nevada Agency, 1886–1905	SF		288
	Western Navajo Agency, 1902–17	LA		12, 18–19, 104, 137, 149, 167, 199, 227–28, 252, 268, 288–89, 330–34, 410, 460, 615, 629–48
	Bishop Agency, 1916	DC		2
	Fallon (Lovelocks) School, 1909–24	SF		104, 252
Papago	Pima Agency, 1901–51	DC/LA		347–61, 478,480–85
Pawnee	Upper Missouri Agency, 1824–37	DC	883–88	386–91
	Council Bluffs Agency, 1837–56	KC	215–18	
	Pawnee (Ponca) Agency, 1859–1964	DC/FTW	659–68, 670–77	336–43, 386–91
Pembina Chippewa	Chippewa Agency, 1923–36	DC/CHI		57–76
Pend d'Oreille	Flathead Agency, 1875–1960	SEA		107–08
Peoria	Miami (Quapaw) Agency, 1870–1952	DC/FTW	703–13	410–16
	Seneca Agency, 1901–7, 1910–21	DC		487–89
Peoria, Kansas	Ft. Leavenworth/Osage River, 1824–71	DC	300–03, 642–51	48
Piankeshaw, Confederated	Miami (Quapaw) Agency, 1870–1952	DC/FTW	703–13	
Piankeshaw, Kansas	Ft. Leavenworth/Osage River, 1824–71	DC	300–03, 642–51	
Piankeshaw, Indian Terr.	Neosho Agency, 1867–71	DC	530–37	
Piegon	Blackfeet Agency, 1855–69	SEA/DEN		
Pillager Chippewa	Leech Lake/Chippewa Agency, 1908–31	KC		57–76
Pima	Pima Agency, 1901–51	LA		344–45, 347–61
Pit River	Fort Bidwell Agency, 1910–31	SF		12, 137
	Round Valley Agency, 1893–1917	SF		224, 446–49
Ponca	Upper Missouri Agency, 1824–59	DC	883–88	
	Pawnee (Ponca) Agency, 1871–1964	DC/FTW	659–68, 670–77	338–43, 385–91, 668–70
	Santee Sioux (Flandreau), 1892–1957	KC		475–77, 683–88
Potawatomi	Carter and Laona Agencies, 1911–27	CHI		22, 230–23
	Grand Rapids Agency, 1900–26	CHI		
	Great Lakes Consolidated, 1875–1952	CHI		170–71, 176
Potawatomi, East	Fort Wayne and Indiana, 1824–50	DC	304, 354–61	230–33
	Green Bay/Chicago/Mackinac, 1824–80	DC/CHI	132–34, 315–36, 402–15	
	Winnebago Agency, 1864–1965	DC/KC	931–47	
Potawatomi, Iowa	Council Bluffs Agency, 1837–47	DC	215–18	
Potawatomi, Kansas	Osage River Agency, 1837–47	DC	642–51	
	Ft. Leavenworth Agency, 1847–51	DC	300–03	
	Horton (Potawatomi) Agency 1851–80	KC		210, 392–95
	Great Nemaha and Kickapoo, 1837–80	DC/KC	307–14, 371–74	
Potawatomi, Indian Terr.	Quapaw/Shawnee/Sac and Fox, 1871–1952	DC/FTW	703–13	453–54, 490–96
Potter	Round Valley Agency	SF		447–49
Pueblo	Pueblo and Jicarilla Agencies, 1874–1900	DEN		396–406
	Pueblo Agency and Day School, 1912–22	DEN		1, 403–06
	Santa Fe Agency	DEN		471–74, 532–42, 624–27

Tribe	Agency	Location of Original Records*	Pre-1880 Correspondence M234 Roll No.	Post-1885 Census Records M595 Roll No.
Pueblo	Albuquerque Indian School, 1886–1954	DEN		
	Cimarron and Abiquiu Agencies, 1869–1883	DEN		
	Laguna Sanatorium, 1926–33	DEN		
	Moqui Pueblo, 1906,1908–16,1918–23	DC		268–72
	Northern Pueblo Agency, 1904–36	DEN		308–10
	Southern Pueblo Agency, 1911–35	DEN		532–42
Pueblo, Moqui	Hopi Agency, 1910–56	LA		268–72
Pueblos, United	United Pueblos Agency, 1935–52	DEN		
Puyallup	Tulalip Agency, 1854–1952	SEA		302, 407–09
	Puyallup Agency, 1855–1920	SEA		407–09
Quapaw	Caddo and Red River Agencies	DC	31, 727	
	Miami (Quapaw) Agency, 1870–1952	DC/FTW	703–13	411–16
	Neosho Agency, 1831–71	DC	530–37	
	Osage Agency, 1879–80	DC/FTW	633–41	317
	Seneca Agency, 1901–07,1910–21	DC		487–89
Queet	Cushman School (Puyallup), 1885–1920	SEA		93
Quileute	Taholah Agency, 1878–1950	SEA		565–69
	Neah Bay Agency, 1885–28	SEA		282–85
Quinaielt	Puyallup Agency, 1888–1909	SEA		93, 407–09, 417
	Taholah Agency, 1915–39 with gaps	SEA		564–69
Red Lake Chippewa	Red Lake Agency, 1894–1952	KC		230–42, 418–25
Redwood	Round Valley Agency	SF		2, 447–49
Sac and Fox	See Sac and Fox			
San Carlos Apache	San Carlos Agency, 1900–52	LA		461–70
Sans Arcs Sioux	Up. Missouri/Platte/Spotted Tail, 1824–74	DC	840–45, 883–96	
	Grand River/Cheyenne River, 1871–80	DC/KC	127–31, 305–06	
Santee Sioux	Saint Peters Agency, to 1870	DC	757–66	
	Santee Sioux Agency, 1871–76	DC/KC	768–69	474–77
	Nebraska Agencies, 1876–80	DC	518–29	
	Flandreau School, 1873–1951	DC/KC	285	105–06
	Winnebago and Yankton, 1867–1955	DC/KC	930–47, 959–62	660–70, 684–88
Sac and Fox, Iowa	Sac and Fox Agency and Schools, 1896–1947	CHI		449–52
Sac and Fox, Mississippi	Sac and Fox Agency, 1824–80	DC	728–44	
	Raccoon River Agency, 1843–45	DC	714	
	Osage River Agency, 1847–51	DC	643–44	
	Prairie du Chien Agency, 1824–42	DC	696–702	
Sac and Fox, Missouri	Ioway Subagency, 1829–34	DC	362	
	Upper Missouri Agency, 1835–37	DC	883–88	
	Great Nemaha Agency, 1837–76	DC	307–14	
	Nebraska Agencies, 1876–80	DC	518–29	
Sac and Fox, Missouri and Oklahoma	Shawnee Agency, 1890–1952	DC/FTW		210, 393, 453–55
Seminole	Seminole Agency, 1824–76	DC	799–807	
	Union Agency, 1875–80	DC	864–77	
Seminole, Florida	Seminole Agency Dania, 1934–52	ATL		486–87
Seneca, Indian Terr.	Miami (Quapaw) Agency, 1870–1952	DC/FTW	702–13	410–16, 487–89
Seneca, N.Y.	Six Nations Agency, 1824–34	DC	582–97	290–300, 488–89
Seneca, Ohio	Piqua and Ohio Agencies, 1831–43	DC	600–03	
Seneca, Indian Terr.	Neosho Agency, 1837–71	DC	529–37	

Tribe	Agency	Location of Original Records*	Pre-1880 Correspondence M234 Roll No.	Post-1885 Census Records M595 Roll No.
Shasta	Roseburg Agency, 1912–18	SF		446
Shawnee, Indian Terr.	Shawnee Agency, 1890–1952	FTW		
Shawnee, Ohio	Piqua and Ohio Agencies, 1831–43	DC	600–03	
Shawnee, Kansas	Fort Leavenworth Agency, 1824–51	DC	299–303	
	Kansas Agency, 1851–55	DC	363–70	
	Shawnee Agency, 1855–76	DC	808–23	
Shawnee, Kansas—Indian Territory	Union Agency, 1875–80	DC	864–77	
Shawnee, Eastern	Neosho Agency, 1867–71	DC	534–37	
	Quapaw Agency, 1885–1939	DC/FTW		410–16
	Seneca Agency, 1901–7, 1910–21	DC		487–89
Shawnee, Absentee	Wichita Agency, 1859–67	DC	927–30	
	Sac and Fox Agency, ca. 1869–80	CHI		
	Shawnee Agency, 1890–1952	DC/FTW		490–96
Sheepeater	Lemhi Agency, 1885,1887–1906	SEA		248
Shoshoni	Wind River Agency, 1873–1952	DEN		167, 498–504, 631, 663
	Carson School, 1909–39	SF		18–21
	Fort Hall, 1885–87, 1890–91, 1894–1939	SEA		138–44, 498–504
	Lemhi Agency, 1885, 1887–1906	SEA		248
Shoshoni, Western	Western Shoshone Agency, 1897–1916	SF		646–48
Sioux	Fort Peck Agency, 1885–1939	SEA		11, 150–60
Sioux, Mississippi	Saint Peters Agency, 1824–70	DC	756–66	
	Prairie du Chien and Winnebago Agencies	DC/KC	695–702, 930–47	
Sioux, Missouri/Platte River	Upper Missouri Agency, 1824–74	DC	883–88	
	Upper Platte Agency, 1846–70	DC	889–96	
	Yankton Agency, 1859–76	DC	959–62	
	Upper Arkansas Agency, 1855–74	DC	878–82	
	Whetstone Agency, 1871–74	DC	925–27	
	Spotted Tail Agency, 1875–80	DC	840–45	
	Red Cloud Agency, 1871–80	DC	715–26	
	Grand River Agency, 1871–75	DC	305–06	
	Standing Rock Agency, 1871–80	DC	846–52	
	Crow Creek Agency, 1871–76	DC	249	
	Lower Brule Agency, 1875–76	DC	401	
Sioux—Fort Totten	Fort Totten Agency, 1875–1950	KC		161–64
Sioux—Cheyenne River	Cheyenne River Agency, 1869–1956	DC/KC		33–40
Sioux—Oglala	Pine Ridge Agency, 1886–1943	DC/KC		361–84
Sioux—Spotted Tail	Rosebud Agency, 1860–1966	KC/DEN		427–45
Sioux—Standing Rock	Standing Rock Agency, 1885–1939	DC/KC	845–52	547–63
Sioux—Sisseton	Saint Peters Agency, 1824–70	DC	756–66	507–17
	Devil's Lake Agency, 1871–80	DC/KC	280–84	
	Devil's Lake Agency, 1885–90,1892–1905	DC/KC		94–97
	Sisseton Agency, 1886–1929 with gaps	KC		507–17
Skallam	Puyallup Agency, 1885–1920	SEA		302
Skokomish	Cushman School (Puyallup), 1885–1920	SEA		93, 302, 407–09, 564–69
	Taholah Agency, 1878–1950	SEA		564–69
Snake	See Shoshoni			225–26
Spokan	Spokane Agency, 1885–1950	SEA		49–56, 546
	Colville Agency, 1865–1952	SEA		
Squaxon	Puyallup Agency, 1885–1920	SEA		302, 407–09
	Taholah Agency, 1878–1950	SEA		564–69
Stockbridge	Keshena Agency, 1909–19	CHI		200–01

Tribe	Agency	Location of Original Records*	Pre-1880 Correspondence M234 Roll No.	Post-1885 Census Records M595 Roll No.
Stockbridge, New York	Six Nations Agency, 1824–34	DC	832	
Stockbridge, Wisconsin	Green Bay Agency, 1885–1908	CHI		172–74
	Tomah Indian School and Agency, 1908–34	CHI		573
Stockbridge, Kansas	Fort Leavenworth Agency, 1839–51	DC	299–303	
	Kansas Agency, 1851–55	DC	363–70	
	Delaware Agency, 1855–59	DC	274–80	
Swinomish	Tulalip Agency, 1854–1952	SEA		582–93
Tabaquache Ute	New Mexico Superintendency, to 1861	DC		
Tawakoni	Texas Agency, 1847–59	DC	857–61	
	Wichita Agency, 1859–78	DC	927–30	
	Kiowa Agency, 1878–80	DC/FTW	383–86	
Tenino	Warm Springs Agency	SEA		11, 635–38
Tonkowa	Pawnee Agency, 1871–1964	DC/FTW	661–68	338–43, 386–91
	Texas Agency, 1847–59	DC	857–61	
	Wichita Agency, 1859–1878	DC	927–30	
Tulalip	Tulalip Agency, 1854–1950	SEA		582–93
Tule	Tule River Agency	SF		12, 594
	Sacramento Agency	SF		456–57
	Pala Superintendency, 1903–21	LA		
Tuscarora	Six Nations Agency, 1824–34	DC	832	
	New York Agency, 1835–80	DC	582–97	
	Michigan Superintendency, 1832–34	DC	418–27	
Uinta Ute	Uintah and Ouray Agency, 1897–1952	DEN		608–15
Umatilla	Umatilla Indian Agency, 1854–1952	SEA		616–22
Uncompahgre Ute	Uintah and Ouray Agencies, 1897–1952	Den		608–12
United Pueblos	See Pueblos			
Ute	Santa Fe Agency	DC	767	
	Paiute Agency, 1928–39	DEN		330–34
	Uintah and Ouray Agency, 1897–1952	DEN		608–15, 628
Ute, Consolidated	Consolidated Ute Agency, 1878–1952	DEN		77–78, 628
Ute, Southern	Southern Ute and Consolidated Ute	DEN		543–545, 628
Waco	Texas Agency, 1847–59	DC	857–61	
	Wichita Agency, 1859–78	DC	927–30	
	Kiowa Agency, 1878–80	DC/FTW	383–86	
Wahkepute Sioux	See Sisseton Sioux			
Wailaki	Round Valley Agency	SF		447–49
Walapai	Colorado River Agency 1867–1955	LA		46, 196
	Truxton Canon Agency, 1895–1951	LA		580–81
Wallawalla	Uintah and Ouray Agency, 1897–1952	DEN		616–22
Warm Springs	Warm Springs Agency, 1861–1952	SEA		635–39
Wasco	Oregon Superintendency, 1842–80	DC	607–30	
	Utah and Nevada Superintendencies	DC	896–906, 538–45	
	Walker River Agency	SF		631
Wea	Miami (Quapaw) Agency, 1870–1952	DC/FTW	703–13	
Wea, Indiana	Fort Wayne and Indiana Agencies	DC	304, 354–61	
Wea, Kansas	Fort Leavenworth Agency, 1824–37	DC	300–03	
	Osage River Agency, 1837–71	DC	642–51	
Wea, Indian Territory	Neosho Agency, 1867–71	DC	534–37	
Whilkut	California Superintendency, 1849–80	DC	32–52	
Wichita, Indian Territory, Oklahoma	Kiowa Agency, 1878–1962	DC/FTW	383–86	211–23

Tribe	Agency	Location of Original Records*	Pre-1880 Correspondence M234 Roll No.	Post-1885 Census Records M595 Roll No.
Wichita	Texas Agency,1847–59	DC	858–61	
	Wichita Agency 1857–78	DC	928–30	
Wikchamni	California Superintendency	DC	32–52	
Wiminuche Ute	See Ute			
Winnebago	Wind River Agency, 1898–1955	DEN		663–71
	Prairie du Chien Agency, 1824–42	DC	696–702	
	Turkey River Subagency, 1842–46	DC	862–64	
	Winnebago Agency, 1826–76	DC	931–47	
	Nebraska Agencies, 1876–80	DC	519–29	
	Grand Rapids Agency, 1900–26	CHI		168
	Omaha (Winnebago) Agency, 1861–1955	KC		311–13
Winnebago, Wisconsin	Tomah Indian School and Agency, 1908–34	CHI		570–73
	Wittenberg Indian School, 1905–10	DC		671
Wyandot	Quapaw Agency, 1871–1952	DC/FTW		410–16
Wyandot, Ohio/Michigan	Piqua Agency, 1824–30	DC		
	Ohio Agency, 1831–43	DC	601–03	
	Saginaw Subagency, 1824–50	DC	745–46	
Wyandot, Kansas	Wyandot Agency, 1843–51, 1870–72	DC	950–52	
	Kansas Agency, 1851–55	DC	364–70	
	Shawnee Agency, 1855–63	DC	809–13	
	Delaware Agency, 1863–69	DC	276–80	
Wyandot, Indian Terr.	Neosho Agency, 1867–71	DC	534–36	
	Quapaw Agency, 1871–80	DC/FTW	703–13	411–16, 488–89
Yakima	Yakima Indian Agency, 1859–1952	SEA		671–79
Yamel	Oregon Superintendency, 1842–80	DC	607–30	
Yampa Ute	Colorado Superindentency, 1861–80	DC	197–214	
Yankton Sioux	Upper Missouri Agency to 1859	DC	883–88	
	Yankton Agency, 1859–76	DC/KC	959–62	680–88
	Fort Peck Agency, 1877–1959	SEA		151–60
Yanktonai Sioux	Upper Missouri Agency, 1824–74	DC	883–88	
	Grand River Agency, 1871–75	DC	305–06	
	Upper Platte Agency, 1846–70	DC	889–96	
	Standing Rock Agency, 1875–1957	DC/KC	846–52	
	Crow Creek Agency, 1874–1922	DC/KC		89–92
Yatasi	Red River Agency, 1824–30	DC	727	
Yavapai	Arizona Superintendency, 1863–80	DC	3–28	
Yokaia	Truxton Canyon Agency, 1895–1951	LA/DC		581
Yuki	Round Valley Agency	SF		12, 447–49
Yuma	Colorado River Agency, 1867–1955	LA		14, 48
	Fort Yuma Agency, 1907–51	LA		165–66
	San Carlos Agency, 1900–52	LA		460–69
Yupu	California Superintendency, 1849–80	DC	32–52	
Zuni	Zuni Agency, 1899–1935	DEN		689–92

* ATL: National Archives—Southeast Region, Atlanta, Georgia
CHI: National Archives—Great Lakes Region, Chicago, Illinois
DEN: National Archives—Rocky Mountain Region, Denver, Colorado
DC: National Archives, Washington, D.C.
FTW: National Archives—Southwest Region, Fort Worth, Texas
KC: National Archives—Central Plains Region, Kansas City, Missouri
LA: National Archives—Pacific Southwest Region, Laguna Niguel, California
SEA: National Archives—Pacific Northwest Region, Seattle, Washington
SF: National Archives—Pacific Sierra Region, San Bruno, California

NOTES

1. Laurence F. Schmeckebier, *The Office of Indian Affairs, Its History, Activities, and Organization* (Baltimore: The Johns Hopkins Press, 1927), 131–35.

2. Ibid.

3. Ibid.

4. Felix S. Cohen, *Handbook of Federal Indian Law* (Albuquerque: University of New Mexico Press), 433–44.

5. Kent Carter, comp., *Preliminary Inventory of the Records of the Muskogee Area Office and The Five Civilized Tribes* (1982).

6. *American Indians. A Select Catalog of National Archives Microfilm Publications* (Washington, D.C.: National Archives Trust Fund Board, U.S. Central Services Administration, 1984). Records Relating to Census Rolls and Other Enrollments. Bureau of Indian Affairs (Record Group 75), p. 32.

7. Edward E. Hill, *Guide to Records in the National Archives of the United States Relating to American Indians* (Washington, D.C.: National Archives and Records Service, General Services Administration, n.d.), 168–70.

8. Barry T. Klein, *Reference Encyclopedia of the American Indian,* 2nd ed., 2 vols. (Rye, N.Y.: Todd Publishing, 1973), 91.

9. *Notes and Documents: Catalogue of Microfilmed Publications of the Archives and Manuscript Division,* The Chronicles of Oklahoma, vol. 60, part 2 (Oklahoma City: Oklahoma Historical Society), 222–24.

10. *Records of the Creek Nation,* introduction, reel CRN-1, (Indian Archives Division, Oklahoma Historical Society).

11. *Notes and Documents,* vol. 60, part 2, 218–22.

12. The Confederation of American Indians, comp., *Indian Reservations: A State and Federal Handbook* (Jefferson, N.C., and London: McFarland & Co., n.d.), 213.

13. Klein, 91.

14. Confederation of American Indians, *Indian Reservations,* 223.

15. Ibid., 228.

16. Ibid., 234.

17. Ibid., 237.

18. *Records of the Quapaw Agency,* introduction, reel QA-1 (Indian Archives Division, Oklahoma Historical Society).

19. Confederation of American Indians, *Indian Reservations,* 241.

20. *Notes and Documents,* vol. 60, part 4, 473–75.

21. Ibid., part 1, 79–87.

22. Ibid., part 2, 225–29.

23. Ibid., 231.

24. Hill, *Guide to Records in the National Archives of the United States Relating to American Indians,* 6, 148.

25. Klein, 91.

26. Ibid.

27. Confederation of American Indians, *Indian Reservations,* 213.

28. Ibid., 214.

29. Ibid., 222.

30. Ibid.

31. Ibid., 223–34.

32. Ibid., 227.

33. *Records of the Kiowa Agency,* introduction, reel KA-1 (Indian Archives Division, Oklahoma Historical Society).

34. Confederation of American Indians, *Indian Reservations,* 242.

35. *Notes and Documents,* vol. 60, part 3, 351–55.

36. *Records of the Cheyenne and Arapaho Agency,* introduction, reel CAA-1 (Indian Archives Division, Oklahoma Historical Society).

37. Ibid.

38. *Notes and Documents,* vol. 60, part 3, 348–51.

39. Klein, 92.

40. *Records of the Pawnee Agency,* introduction, reel PA-1 (Indian Archives Division, Oklahoma Historical Society).

41. Confederation of American Indians, *Indian Reservations,* 225.

42. *Records of the Pawnee Agency,* introduction, reel PA-1 (Indian Archives Division, Oklahoma Historical Society).

43. Confederation of American Indians, *Indian Reservations,* 233.

44. *Records of the Pawnee Agency,* introduction, reel PA-1 (Indian Archives Division, Oklahoma Historical Society).

45. Confederation of American Indians, *Indian Reservations,* 234.

46. *Records of the Pawnee Agency,* introduction, reel PA-1 (Indian Archives Division, Oklahoma Historical Society).

47. Confederation of American Indians, *Indian Reservations,* 236.

48. *Records of the Pawnee Agency,* introduction, reel PA-1 (Indian Archives Division, Oklahoma Historical Society).

49. Confederation of American Indians, *Indian Reservations,* 242.

50. *Records of the Pawnee Agency,* introduction, reel PA-1 (Indian Archives Division, Oklahoma Historical Society).

51. *Notes and Documents,* vol. 60, part 3, 355–56.

52. Ibid., 358–59.

53. Ibid., 357.

54. Ibid., 356–57.

55. Ibid., 357.

56. Klein, 92.

57. *Records of the Sac and Fox-Shawnee Agency,* introduction, reel SFSA-1 (Indian Archives Division, Oklahoma Historical Society).

58. Ibid.

59. Confederation of American Indians, *Indian Reservations,* 212.

60. Ibid., 219.

61. *Records of the Sac and Fox-Shawnee Agency,* introduction,

reel SFSA-1 (Indian Archives Division, Oklahoma Historical Society).

62. Confederation of American Indians, *Indian Reservations,* 224–25.

63. Ibid., 226.

64. *Records of the Sac and Fox-Shawnee Agency,* introduction, reel SFSA-1 (Indian Archives Division, Oklahoma Historical Society).

65. Confederation of American Indians, *Indian Reservations,* 234.

66. *Records of the Sac and Fox-Shawnee Agency,* introduction, reel SFSA-1 (Indian Archives Division, Oklahoma Historical Society).

67. *Notes and Documents,* vol. 60, part 4, 476–79.

BIBLIOGRAPHY

Bantin, Philip C. *Guide to Catholic Indian Mission and School Records in Midwest Repositories.* Milwaukee: Marquette University Libraries, Department of Special Collections and University Archives, 1984.

Boyd, Stephen G. *Indian Local Names With Their Interpretations.* York, Penn.: the author, 1885.

Brandon, William. *Indians.* Boston: Houghton Mifflin Co., 1989.

Byers, Paula K., ed. *Native American Genealogical Sourcebook.* Detroit, Mich.: Gale Research, 1995.

Carpenter, Cecelia Swinth. *How to Research American Indian Blood Lines.* South Prairie, Wash.: Meico Associates, 1984.

Carter, Kent. "Wantabes and Outalucks: Searching for Indian Ancestors in Federal Records." *Ancestry Newsletter* 5 (6) (November–December 1987): 1–6.

Chepesiuk, Ron, and Arnold Shankman. *American Indian Archival Material: Guide to the Holdings in the Southeast.* Westport, Conn.: Greenwood Press, 1982. Includes bibliographic references and index.

Cohen, Felix. *Handbook of Federal Indian Law, with Reference Tables and Index.* Washington, D.C.: Government Printing Office, 1942. Reprint, with added foreword, biography, and bibliography. University of New Mexico Press, Albuquerque, 1971.

Dewitt, Donald L. *American Indian Resource Materials in the Western History Collections, University of Oklahoma.* Norman: University of Oklahoma Press, 1990. Includes bibliographic references and index.

Dictionary of Indian Tribes of the Americas. 4 vols. Newport Beach, Calif.: American Indian Publishing, 1980.

Driver, Harold E. *Indians of North America.* Chicago: University of Chicago Press, 1961. Includes bibliography.

Fixico, Donald L. *Termination and Relocation: Federal Indian Policy, 1945–1960.* Albuquerque: University of New Mexico Press, 1986. Includes index and bibliography.

Foreman, Grant. *Indian Removal.* The Emigration of the Five Civilized Tribes of Indians. Norman: University of Oklahoma Press, 1932. Includes bibliography.

Freeman, John F. *A Guide to Manuscripts Relating to the American Indian in the Library of the American Philosophical Society.* Vol. 65, *Memoirs of the American Philosophical Society.* Philadelphia: American Philosophical Society, 1966. Includes bibliography.

Galluso, John, ed. *Native America: Insight.* Singapore: APA, 1989.

Gannett, Henry. *A Gazetteer of Indian Territory.* Washington, D.C.: Government Printing Office, 1905.

Gideon, D.C. *Indian Territory—Descriptive, Biographical and Genealogical, Including the Landed Estates, County Seats, With General History of the Territory.* Chicago: The Lewis Publishing Co., 1901.

Hill, Edward E. *Guide to Records in the National Archives of the United States Relating to American Indians.* Washington, D.C.: National Archives and Records Services Administration, 1981.

_____. *The Office of Indian Affairs, 1824–1880: Historical Sketches.* New York: Clearwater Publishing Co., 1974.

Hodge, Frederick Webb. *Handbook of American Indians North of Mexico.* 2 vols. Bulletin (Smithsonian Institution. Bureau of American Ethnology); Washington, D.C.: 1907–1910. Reprint. New York, 1959; Rowman and Littlefield, Totawa, N.J., 1975. Vol. 1: A–M, vol. 2: N–Z. Includes bibliography.

Hodge, William H. *A Bibliography of Contemporary North American Indians.* New York: Interland Publishing, 1976. Includes index.

Hoover, Herbert T. *The Sioux: A Critical Bibliography.* Bibliographical series (Newberry Library Center for the History of the American Indian). Bloomington: Indiana University Press, for the Newberry Library, 1979. Includes bibliography.

Hoxie, Frederick E., and Harvey Markowitz. *Native Americans: An Annotated Bibliography.* D'Arcey McNickle Center for the History of the American Indian. Pasadena, Calif.: Salem Press, 1991. Includes index.

Huntington, Henry E., Library and Art Gallery. *Guide to American Historical Manuscripts in the Huntington Library.* San Marino, Calif.: Kingsport Press for the Huntington Library, 1979. Includes index.

Index to the Final Rolls of Citizens and Freedmen of the Five Civilized Tribes in Indian Territory. Washington, D.C.: Government Printing Office, 1961.

Jackson, Curtis E., and Marcia J. Galli. *A History of the Bureau of Indian Affairs and its Activities Among the Indians.* San Francisco: R & E Research Associates, 1977. Includes bibliography.

Johnson, Steven L. *Guide to American Indian Documents in the Congressional Serial Set, 1817–1899.* A project of the Institute for the Development of Indian Law. New York: Clearwater Publishing Co., 1977. Includes index.

Kappler, Charles J. *Indian Affairs: Laws and Treaties.* 6 vols.

Washington, D.C.: Government Printing Office, 1903. Includes indexes.

Kirkham, E. Kay. *Our Native Americans and Their Records of Genealogical Value.* Logan, Utah: The Everton Publishers, 1980.

Klein, Barry T. *Reference Encyclopedia of the American Indian.* 5th ed. West Nyack, N.Y.: Todd Publications, 1990.

Leitch, Barbara. *A Concise Dictionary of Indian Tribes of North America.* Algonac, Mich.: Reference Publications, 1979.

Lipps, Oscar Hiram. *Laws and Regulations Relating to Indians and Their Lands.* Lewiston, Idaho: Lewiston Printing and Binding Co., 1913.

McDonnell, Janet A. *The Dispossession of the American Indian, 1887–1834.* Bloomington: Indiana University Press, 1991. Includes bibliographic references and indexes.

McReynolds, Edwin C. *The Seminoles.* The Civilization of the American Indian Series, vol. 47. Norman: University of Oklahoma Press, 1957. Includes bibliography.

Native American Periodicals and Newspapers, 1828–1982: Bibliography, Publishing Record, and Holdings. Westport, Conn.: Greenwood Press, 1984.

O'Brien, Sharon. *American Indian Tribal Governments.* 1st ed. The Civilization of the American Indian Series, vol. 192. Norman: University of Oklahoma Press, 1989. Includes bibliography and index.

Otis, D.S. *The Dawes Act and the Allotment of Indian Land.* The Civilization of the American Indian Series, vol. 123. Norman: University of Oklahoma Press, 1973. Includes bibliographic references.

Prucha, Francis Paul. *Documents of United States Indian Policy.* Lincoln: University of Nebraska Press, 1975. Includes bibliography and index.

Prucha, Francis Paul. *The Great Father: The United States Government and the American Indians.* 2 vols. Lincoln: University of Nebraska Press, 1984. Includes bibliography and index.

Schmeckebier, Laurence F. *The Office of Indian Affairs, Its History, Activities, and Organization.* Service monographs of the United States government; no. 48. Baltimore: Johns Hopkins Press, 1927. Reprint. AMS Press, New York, 1972. Includes bibliography.

Spindel, Donna. *Introductory Guide to Indian-Related Records (to 1876) in the North Carolina State Archives.* Raleigh: North Carolina Division of Archives and History, 1977.

Smith, Jessie Carney, ed. *Ethnic Genealogy.* Westport, Conn.: Greenwood Press, 1983.

Sturtevant, William C. *Handbook of North American Indians.* 20 vols. Washington, D.C.: Smithsonian Institution, 1978–. Includes bibliographies and indexes.

Svoboda, Joseph G. *A Guide to American Indian Resource Materials in Great Plains Repositories.* Lincoln: Center for Great Plains Studies, University of Nebraska, 1983.

Swanton, John R. *Indian Tribes of North America.* Classics of Smithsonian Anthropology. Originally published as the Bureau of American Ethnology Bulletin no. 145, reprint edition 1969. Reprint. Washington, D.C.: Smithsonian Institution Press, 1984. Includes bibliography and index.

Szucs, Loretto Dennis, and Sandra Hargreaves Luebking. *The Archives: A Guide to the Field Branches of the National Archives.* Salt Lake City: Ancestry, 1988.

U.S. Department of the Interior Library. *Bibliographic and Historical Index of American Indians and Persons Involved in Indian Affairs.* 8 vols. Boston: G.K. Hall, 1966.

Wissler, Clark. *Indians of the United States.* New York: Anchor Books, 1989.

Witcher, Curt Bryan. *A Bibliography of Sources for Native American Family History.* Fort Wayne, Ind.; Allen County Public Library, 1988.

Wright, Muriel H. *A Guide to the Indian Tribes of Oklahoma.* The Civilization of the American Indian Series, vol. 33. Norman: University of Oklahoma Press, 1951. Includes bibliography.

Yenne, Bill. *The Encyclopedia of North American Indian Tribes.* Greenwich, Conn.: Brompton Books, 1986.

TRACKING AFRICAN AMERICAN FAMILY HISTORY

Chapter Contents

TRACKING AFRICAN AMERICAN FAMILY HISTORY

David T. Thackery

Few areas of American genealogy pose as much challenge as the search for African American ancestry prior to the Civil War—yet few areas contain as much unrealized potential. Despite great strides within the last two decades, the basic outlines of the field are only now being clarified. While the difficulties of African American genealogical research are not to be discounted, these difficulties are not always insurmountable. As time goes on, the publication and indexing of pertinent genealogical source material may make success more often the rule than the exception. It is also to be hoped that, as more African Americans publish their findings, their research will contribute to the success of others, thus eventually forming a body of mutually supporting secondary literature. What helps one will ultimately help all.

Generally speaking, many of the basic tools of American genealogical research can be successfully applied to the investigation of an African American lineage going back to the Civil War. These include vital records, the federal censuses, cemetery records and inscriptions, etc. Researchers should be aware, however, that many marriage, birth, and death records in the old slave states were, until the recent past, maintained in separate ledgers by local governments. The publication of vital records by local genealogical societies sometimes reflects this division. With the publication in recent years of indexes to the 1870 federal census enumerations, especially those for Southern states, it has become increasingly feasible for researchers of African American genealogy to trace a given line to that very important year in which ex-slaves were first enumerated as free people.

FREE BLACKS

At least one out of ten African Americans was already free when the first shots were fired on Fort Sumter. They were a diverse group. As with those who were enslaved, free African Americans could have racially mixed backgrounds encompassing African, Caucasian, and American Indian ancestry. Many of them came from families that had been free for several generations, perhaps stemming from the manumission of an ancestor or a liaison between an indentured white woman and a slave. Others were runaways who lived uncertain existences in the Northern states. Although not usually thought of in the category of "free black," one group enjoyed an essentially free status in affiliation with the Seminole Indians, while others

formed elites in Charleston and Louisiana, where many were themselves slaveowners. They were farmers, servants, artisans, and sailors in the Northeast, in many instances descended from the slave populations which existed there when slavery was found above the Mason-Dixon line. (In the state of New York, for example, slavery was not completely abolished until 1827. Approximately ten thousand enslaved blacks were enumerated there in the 1820 census.) In parts of Ohio and Indiana, their presence was due largely to the efforts of North Carolina Quakers who manumitted their slaves and settled them in those areas. In the Border states, especially in Maryland, they made up a substantial proportion of the total black population, while in much of the Deep South they were only a tiny minority who occupied a precarious position, at best.

African American researchers must be open to the possibility of encountering an antebellum free black ancestor; at the same time, however, they should not expect to find one in a time or place where the free black population was small. For example, the chances would be much higher for having such an ancestor in Virginia than in Mississippi. As with any genealogical research, knowledge of the historical context is critical to success.

In many instances, the records that are of genealogical value in the study of antebellum free blacks will not differ substantially from the records of whites. For example, the census enumerated all free people, black or white, on the same schedules.

On the other hand, the United States was a "house divided." In many states free blacks were required to register proof of their status with the county government. Such documentation could take the form of copies of manumission papers or of affidavits attesting birth to a free woman. Without such proof, free blacks risked abduction and enslavement, even in the North. These registers were also common in the upper South and Border states, where they not only provided protection for free blacks but also helped to prevent slaves from passing as free people. The free black registers of Virginia counties have been increasingly finding their way into print.[1] In one such register is the following noteworthy example:

I William Moss Clerk of the County Court of Fairfax do hereby certify that the bearer hereof Levi Richardson a light coloured black boy about twenty one years of Age five feet seven Inches high, large nose thin visage . . . a scar on the left side of his head is the son of Sally Richardson a free woman emancipated by Genl. George Washington deceased as appears by an Original Register heretofore granted by the County Court of Fairfax and this day surrendered. Whereupon at the request of the said Levi Richardson I have caused him to be Registered in my office according to law. Given under my hand this 19th day of November 1834.[2]

Similar documentation can also be found in the courthouses of many Midwestern counties. For example, Wright State University microfilmed such records for the counties of Greene, Logan, Miami, and Montgomery in Ohio.[3] More were transcribed by Joan Turpin in *Register of Black, Mulatto and Poor Persons in Four Ohio Counties 1791–1861* (Bowie, Md.: Heritage Books, 1985). If such records, whether in the South, the Midwest, or the Northeast, are indeed extant, they are not likely to be among the easier documents to locate in the county courthouse; however, more are likely to surface with the passage of time, and they will perhaps be indexed and published as well. Many have also been microfilmed by the Genealogical Society of Utah.

UNDERGROUND RAILROAD

From 1786 on, fugitive slaves could escape northward on the Underground Railroad, which covered fourteen northern states by 1830 (figure 15-1). From 1840 to 1860, some 50,000 slaves travelled it to settle in the North or in Canada. The Federal Fugitive Slave Law of 1793 was countered by the "Personal Liberty Laws" of many northern states.

More than 15,000 free African Americans returned to Africa between 1821 and 1860. The colony of Liberia was established by the American Colonization Society in 1822 and became independent in 1847.

THE TRANSITION FROM SLAVERY TO FREEDOM

At the time of the Civil War, the vast majority of African Americans were, of course, slaves. As such, they had no legal rights and could not even claim a legally recognized state of matrimony. Although records generated after emancipation can be very revealing, genealogically useful records documenting slave families which were contemporary to slavery are usually records, both private and public, concerned primarily with their owners. The researcher of slave genealogy therefore must know the identity of a slave's owner in order to research the slave. Slaveowning families—their migrations, births, deaths, and marital alliances—must therefore be the focus of research before any success can be achieved in tracing the lives of their slaves.

The search for the last slaveowner prior to emancipation then becomes the most important task. A common supposition is that emancipated slaves assumed the surnames of their last owners. If this had been the case in all instances, this critical stage of slave genealogy would be a less difficult one than it generally is; however, the truth is more complex, making research more problematic. Although there were many instances when the common assumption held true, there is ample evidence for slaves maintaining their own surname traditions, regardless of who their owners might have been.[4] Following emancipation, a slave did not necessarily "assume" a surname, but instead may have taken a name which had been in his or her family for several generations. A different surname than that of the last owner could, for example, be that of the owner of a grandparent, so such a name might be a valuable clue for future research.

More studies are still needed, but it is possible that there were regional patterns in this regard. For example, a study of a West Virginia county found no instances of ex-slaves with the surnames of their final owners,[5] while studies of Texas and South Carolina freed people indicate approximately a quarter to one third had the surnames of their last owners.[6] The signature books of the Freedman's Savings and Trust (discussed in greater detail later in this chapter) also provide evidence of the often confusing and unpredictable reality behind the surnames of ex-slaves. For example, one record from the Vicksburg, Mississippi, branch names the parents of one Jesse Taylor as Robert and Nancy Page. A brother is listed as Simpson Roberts.[7] The complex nature of the "surname problem" should be kept in mind as the sources for African American genealogy are considered.

THE FEDERAL CENSUSES

It has already been noted that African Americans were enumerated as all other U.S. residents from 1870 (the first census year following the Civil War and emancipation) onward. Prior to 1870, however, the situation was far different. Although free African Americans were enumerated by name in 1850 and 1860, slaves were consigned to special, far less informative, schedules in which they were listed anonymously under the names of their owners. The only personal information provided was usually that of age, gender, and racial identity (either black or mulatto). As in the free schedules, there was a column in which certain physical or mental infirmities could be noted. In some instances the census takers noted an occupation, usually carpenter or blacksmith, in this column. Slaves aged one hundred years or more were given special treatment; their names were noted, and sometimes a short biographical sketch was included. In at least one instance, that of 1860 Hampshire County, Virginia, the names of all slaves were included on the schedules, but this happy exception may be the only instance when the instructions were not followed.

Sometimes the listings for large slaveholdings appear to take the form of family groupings, but in most cases slaves are listed from eldest to youngest with no apparent effort to portray family structure. In any event, the slave schedules themselves almost never provide conclusive evidence for the presence of a specific slave in the household or plantation of a particular slaveowner. At best, a census slave schedule can provide supporting evidence for a hypothesis derived from other sources.[8] Prior to 1850 there were no special slave schedules for the manuscript census, as slave data was recorded as part of the general population schedules, in which only the heads of household were enumerated by name.

In the absence of any contradictory information, it might be assumed that a family of freed people enumerated in the 1870 census was living not far from its last owner, whose surname they also bore. There would, of course, be reasons to dispute both assumptions. (Knowledge of the Civil War history of a locality could come into play here; for example, such

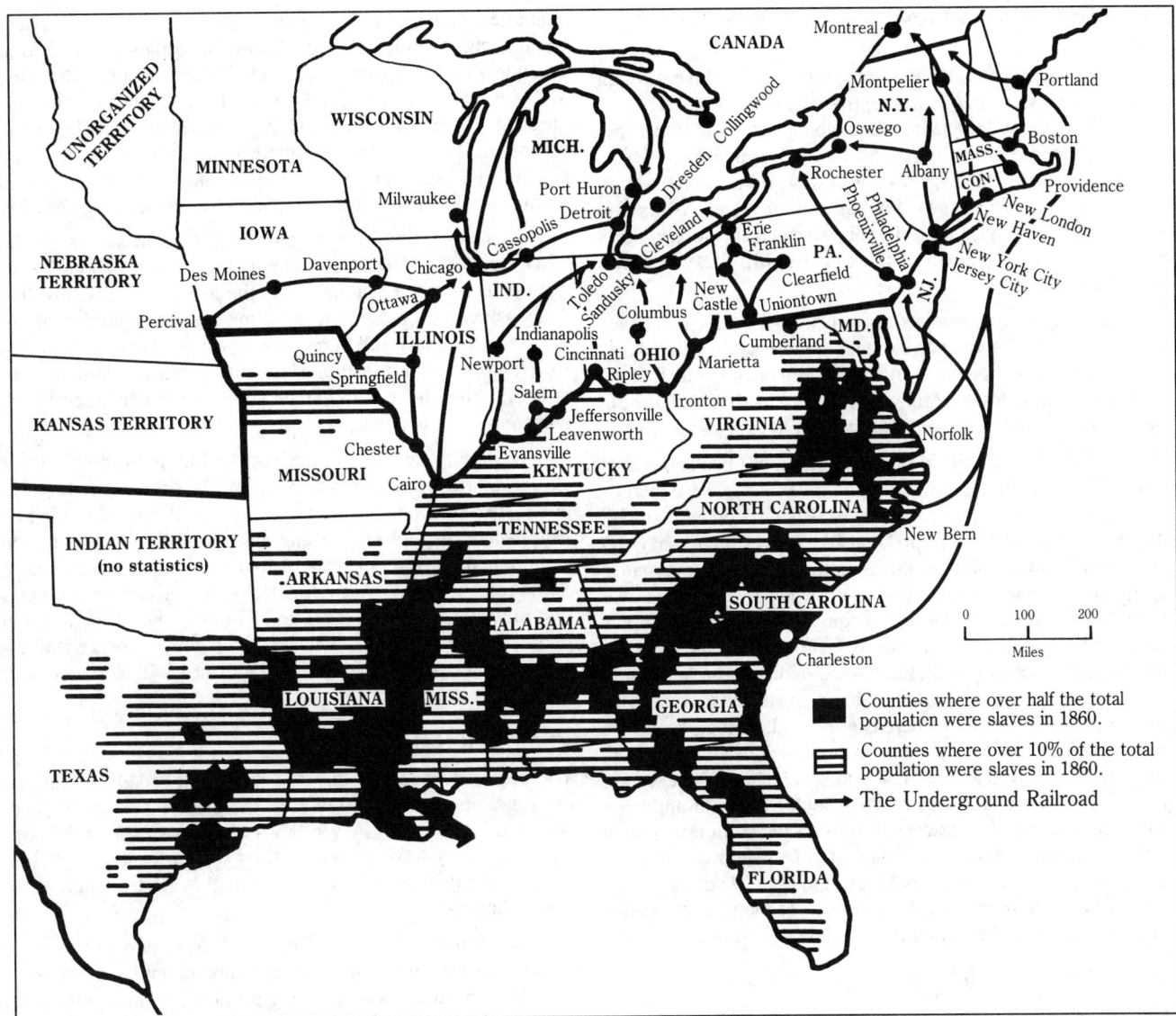

Figure 15-1. The Underground Railroad, 1786-1860.

relative stability would not have existed in a Georgia county that was in the path of Sherman's march to the sea.) Even so, this assumption represents one of the more obvious exploratory lines of research, especially in the absence of any other options. The first step in testing the hypothesis would be to search for slaveowners of the same surname in the 1860 slave schedules of the county in which the African American family resided in 1870.

Starting in 1850, another supplemental schedule, the mortality schedule (discussed in chapter 5, Research in Census Records), listed all deaths within a year before the regular census enumeration. The deaths of blacks and mulattoes, both free and slave, are recorded in them, even though their names have not been included in many of the indexes to these schedules.[9] The deaths of slaves were generally enumerated in four fashions: unnamed (as in the slave schedules), but perhaps with the owner identified; by first name only; by first name and surname; and by first name with the owner noted. The distinction between the last two categories is sometimes unclear.

PROBATE RECORDS

Slaves were property. As distasteful as we find it today, this unfortunate fact is the all-encompassing reality that informs slave genealogical research. And so the focus of research must always to some extent be on the slaveowner. Probate records are important tools in this process. As valued parts of an estate, slaves were sometimes mentioned by name or may have been referred to as having been inherited from another family member or else purchased from a particular party.

For example, one David C. Moore of Duplin County, North Carolina, died in late 1863 or early 1864, leaving to his son Thomas "one half of that portion of my negroes known as Megee Negroes including Martha & her three children excepting those that I purchased from Thomas H. Megee namely Aaron, Mary & three children."[10] Note that slaves were specifically identified only insofar as the identification served the purposes of the testator. Therefore, slaves can be identified in a will by name and by family—or else can be subsumed as simply an anonymous portion of a slaveholding. Generally speaking, the smaller the number of slaves in an estate, the more likely there will be some sort of identifying language in the will.

It is sometimes possible to trace a particular slave through two or more wills. For example, the will of Thomas Byrd, of Somerset County, Maryland, was probated on 16 March 1757, leaving "a negro girl called Nice" to his daughter Mary Byrd, later wife of Paul Dulany, whose will was probated on 6 March 1773, leaving "one negro woman named Nice" to his son Henry.[11] Interestingly, the reference to Nice in the two wills also provides evidence for relationship between the slaveowners.

Other probate documents may also be helpful, such as estate inventories drawn up to execute the terms of a will. Slaves are sometimes mentioned by name in such documents. Bills of sale may also be found amongst probate documents if, for example, slaves had to be sold in order to pay an estate's debts.

The location of wills in the slave states has been considerably aided in several instances by the indexing of these records on a statewide basis. Many such indexes have been published.[12] The Genealogical Society of Utah has microfilmed early extant wills for many of the counties in the Southern slave states, while at least one state, North Carolina, has instituted its own microfilming program. Thus, the consultation of these important documents will not necessarily be confined to viewing the originals in a county courthouse, although the researcher should do so whenever possible. In addition, abstracts or transcriptions of county wills are increasingly finding their way into print. In many of the more recent publications in this genre, references to slaves are retained and special slave indexes are included. The researcher of slave genealogy should approach such published will abstracts carefully. If the compiler of such a book has not included slave data, that fact should be readily apparent after a few minutes of examination. The researcher should then attempt to access microfilm of the records or else plan a genealogical research trip to view the originals.

DEEDS AND OTHER LOCAL RECORDS

As with any genealogical research, the quest for African American ancestry requires one to become familiar with the records and record-keeping practices of the state and county in which one is conducting investigations. It may be discovered that references to slaves exist in a variety of local record groups. County deed books may contain, in addition to real estate transactions, documentation of slave sales. For example, in Deed Book F-6 of Warren County, Kentucky, one finds certification of a bill of sale, dated 15 July 1813, of $1,500 from Upshaw R. Massey to Jesse Kerby for four slaves: a man named Moses, a woman named Milly, and two boys named Aaron and Robert, Massey and his wife to "reserve use of said slaves until their own deaths."[13] But caution should be exercised in interpreting some deed records, particularly deeds in or of trust. If a slave is named in such a deed, it does not necessarily mean that there was a change in ownership. In such instances the slave was used as collateral. If the debt for which the slave acted as collateral was eventually discharged, then he or she would remain the property of the original owner.

Court records in the antebellum slave states could document any number of situations involving slaves and their owners, some mundane, others revealing, if not tragic. The circuit court records of Estill County, Kentucky, contain the following examples: the record of an inquisition on the body of Stephen, a slave who had died as a result of mistreatment, described in great detail by his owner, William P. Noland; a suit by the same William Noland in 1837 against one Joseph Cox over the purchase of "a negro boy named Henry" for $200, in which Noland asserts that the slave had rheumatism and was subject to fits; a case in 1846 in which there is testimony of a married white woman giving birth to a child fathered by a slave named Mark.[14]

Tax records can also contain references to slaves. In the 1787 "census" of Virginia—actually tax records viewed by genealogists as a "replacement" for the lost 1790 census of that state—slaves are referred to by name together with their owners in Mecklenburg and Surry counties.[15] The books of tithables for Norfolk County, Virginia, provide another example, containing named listings of slaves with owners for much of the eighteenth century.[16]

As shown, documentation for the buying and selling of slaves can be found in a variety of official sources on the local level. Such documentation can, of course, also be found in private papers. A pilot project attempting to bring together such documentation from an array of sources was the Slave Bills of Sale Project of the African-American Family History Association in Atlanta, Georgia. This project transcribed, indexed, and published two volumes of these documents.[17] The genealogical community can hope that similar efforts will be undertaken throughout the South.

PLANTATION RECORDS

The personal papers of any slaveholder are likely to contain information on slaves, assuming the greater portion of them survived. Such papers may still be in the possession of the family or else may have been deposited with a local or state historical society. Many records have also been deposited at research libraries.

As a genre of personal records, so-called "plantation records" are often voluminous and unpredictable. As often as not, those portions which have genealogical value will make up a small portion of the whole and may be difficult to pinpoint. Yet we can gain some sense of the possibilities of these records for slave genealogy if we consider their context. They are business records which were usually kept with personal and family papers for the simple reason that the plantation was essentially a family business—a complex and often extensive enterprise which could become even more complex and extensive with new holdings added from dowries and inheritances. Accounts needed to be kept for any number of things—the price of cotton needed to be monitored; the yield of a given acreage needed to be recorded; both needed to be considered in the context of the weather conditions from day to day and week to week. Loans and mortgages were a frequent concern, and so were the affairs of tenants.

Intertwined with these concerns was the presence of slave labor on the plantation. Records of slaves can be found in several contexts. Clothes, blankets, or simply lengths of cloth were often issued on a regular basis to all slaves, and careful records were kept of these distributions. Field hands were issued tools and implements and presumably held accountable for them. A plantation owner's "day book" may contain a variety of entries recording observations on the weather, livestock, and crops. It might also note the daily tasks undertaken on the plantation and which slaves were dispatched to fix a fence or deepen an irrigation channel. As property, slaves could also be mortgaged or rented (sometimes they were even insured)—and careful records obviously had to be kept regarding such matters.

A child born of a slave mother became the property of the mother's owner, so it was in the owner's best interest to maintain a record of that birth in the absence of an official vital record. Therefore, in most cases the slaveowner's records may be the only place where slave birth records can be found. Deaths may also be recorded, although the reasons for doing so were less compelling. Many plantation owners maintained records outlining slave family groups, although, in some instances, one may find only a mother listed with her children. In such cases the identification of a slave father on a large plantation may be difficult.

These manuscript collections may also contain diaries and letters. The chance that important information concerning slaves would be contained in such items is admittedly slim, but not impossible. In letters and diaries, often written in faded and difficult-to-read handwriting, the mention of slaves by name may occur very infrequently, if at all. And if they are mentioned, their mention will not stand out in any appreciable fashion from the rest of the letter or diary. The whole letter or diary must be read with only a very limited realistic expectation of finding any information of genealogical value.

The researcher should also bear in mind that a collection of papers will not necessarily be limited to one person, one generation, or even to a family of the same surname. As the plantation, or parts of it, were sold or transferred or willed to relations and in-laws, the records could also be transferred with the property. Thus, accumulations of plantation records could have a wide familial and geographical scope.

But how can the researcher examine these records? How can it be determined whether they exist? If they have been deposited in a library or historical society—and many of them have—there is a good chance that they have been registered in the *National Union Catalog of Manuscript Collections* (*NUCMC*), a serial reference work that first appeared in 1959 and has been for the most part published by the Library of Congress. *NUCMC* contains descriptions of manuscript collections held by hundreds of libraries throughout the country. It has also become far more user friendly with the publication of *Index to Personal Names in the National Union Catalog of Manuscript Collections 1959–1984* (Alexandria, Virginia: Chadwyk-Healey, 1988). The researcher of slave genealogy who has focused on a particular slaveholding family should consult the index to see if there are any listings in *NUCMC* for the papers of members of that family. Such a listing will indicate the repository at which they are held. (Also see chapter 2, Databases, Indexes, and Other Finding Aids.)

There is also the possibility that records of interest have been microfilmed as part of the extensive microfilm series *Records of Ante-Bellum Southern Plantations From the Revolution Through the Civil War* (Frederick, Md.: University Publications of America, 1985–), edited by the noted historian Kenneth Stampp. This ongoing series is available at many research libraries and is accompanied by very thorough descriptions and reel guides for the component collections. The reel guides will reveal the likelihood of there being any records of interest in these collections, as well as their exact location in the microfilm.

OTHER RECORDS OF SLAVE BIRTHS AND DEATHS

During the antebellum period, the keeping of vital records had not yet been mandated by many state governments. For that simple reason, in many of the states official vital records do not exist for slaves—or for anyone else—prior to the Civil War. Yet, as always, there are exceptions. For example, Kentucky, in 1852, enacted legislation (repealed in 1862) requiring birth and death registrations in all counties. The birth records were to include children born to slave mothers, indicating date and place of birth, sex, and name of owner. A year later similar legislation was passed in Virginia. It has been noted that slaveowners may have been more intent on registering slave births than the births of their own children, a motivation likely arising from the need to protect their property by an act of official registration.[18]

Similar motivations may have spurred the baptism of slaves by their owners. Such baptism records are often just as detailed as those for whites. The majority of such records, at least those which are extant, appear to be from Anglican/Episcopalian churches. Unfortunately, many of these registers have probably been lost, especially those of Virginia.[19] The situation is much better in South Carolina, where the records of a number of Low Country churches survive, many extending well into the colonial era. These contain extensive slave baptismal records, some including the names of both slave parents as well as of owners. The South Carolina Historical Society has microfilmed many of these records and made them available on microfiche.

It has already noted that the personal papers of slaveowners can contain records of slave births and deaths. At this juncture should also be mentioned the possibility of slave births and deaths being noted in the slaveowner's Bible, together with those of his own family. To be sure, this was not a typical practice; however, when it did occur it likely reflected a small slaveholding, perhaps one or two slave families who had been in the possession of their owners for several decades.[20]

RUNAWAY SLAVES

Slaves sometimes attempted to escape from their owners. Some succeeded; most did not. Runaway slave advertisements, which usually contain physical descriptions and, occasionally, biographical information, can be of interest to the genealogist. In most cases, however, the identity of an ancestor's owner would have to be known for such an advertisement to be useful in compiling a family history. Many of these advertisements have been transcribed and published, most notably in Lathan A. Windley, *Runaway Slave Advertisements: A Documentary History From the 1730s to 1790,* 4 vols. (Westport, Conn.: Greenwood, 1983), which covers the states of Virginia, North Carolina, Maryland, South Carolina, and Georgia. Robert K. Headley, *Genealogical Abstracts From the 18th Century Virginia Newspapers* (Baltimore: Genealogical Publishing Co., 1987), also contains runaway advertisements. Advertisements from eighteenth-century Pennsylvania are found in Gary T. Hawbaker, *Runaways, Rascals, and Rogues: Missing Spouses, Servants and Slaves. Abstracts from Lancaster County Pennsylvania Newspapers* (Hershey, Penn.: the author, 1987), and in Billy G. Smith and Richard Wojtowicz, *Blacks Who Stole*

Themselves: Advertisements for Runaways in the Pennsylvania Gazette 1728–1790 (Philadelphia: University of Pennsylvania, 1989). Also of interest is Helen Cox Tregillis, *River Roads to Freedom: Fugitive Slave Notices and Sheriff Notices Found in Illinois Sources* (Bowie, Md.: Heritage, 1988).

THE BUREAU OF REFUGEES, FREEDMEN AND ABANDONED LANDS

The Bureau of Refugees, Freedmen and Abandoned Lands, usually referred to simply as the Freedmen's Bureau, was established by the federal government in 1865. The bureau was primarily concerned with assisting ex-slaves in their transition to life after slavery, although it also aided indigent whites shortly after the close of the war to some extent as well. Its activities among freed people were varied, including drawing up and enforcing labor contracts, feeding the hungry, conducting marriages, leasing abandoned land, providing transportation, and, in general, presiding over Reconstruction policy. The bureau's records hold great genealogical potential; however, their contents elude a concise description.

Records from bureau headquarters in Washington, D.C., have been microfilmed but are not of much genealogical value. The next level down is that of the assistant commissioners, each one of whom presided over bureau activities in a given state, the only exception being the assistant commissioner for the District of Columbia. The following assistant commissioners' records have been microfilmed by the National Archives, in whose care they reside: Alabama (M809), Arkansas (M979), District of Columbia (M1055), Georgia (M798), Louisiana (M1027), Mississippi (M826), North Carolina (M843), South Carolina (M869), Tennessee (M999), Texas (M821), and Virginia (M1053).

Because of differences in record-keeping procedures and possibly in the division of responsibility of record retention and storage between state headquarters and the field offices, their contents are by no means uniform. It also reflects a difference in the experiences of the state districts as well as the probability that more records survived from some states than from others.

The first fact the genealogist must understand is that the Freedmen's Bureau was not founded to create genealogically useful documents, and the same must be said for the microfilming of these records. Indeed, the records of the assistant commissioner for a given state may generally be without great genealogical utility. To get a sense of the contents of the records for a given district, consult *Black Studies: A Select Catalog of National Archives Microfilm Publications* (Washington, D.C.: National Archives, 1984). All of the district records contain correspondence and telegrams, as well as indexes to these documents. Much of these are intra-bureau or intra-government communications, so, as record groups, they hold little genealogical potential. The assistant commissioners' records will also contain various reports from the district field offices. Again, many of these will hold little of genealogical interest, although those reporting "outrages" (lynchings and other assaults upon African Americans) could be especially interesting, albeit somewhat chilling, to the genealogist. It should be noted that such reports, though generally a constant in district records, do not list a great many incidents.

Of all the assistant commissioners' records, those for Mis-sissippi hold the greatest genealogical potential. Only in Mississippi were local marriage registers included with the state district records. These are from Vicksburg, Davis Bend (just below Vicksburg), Natchez, and Meridian, although there are very few records from the last. These are among the most informative—and among the most poignant—of any American marriage records. Covering the years 1865 and 1866, these registers record the validation of "slave marriages" that occurred before emancipation and also record the marriages of men and women who were just beginning life together following the war. Although the names of parents are not provided, the racial identity of the bride and groom and their parents is one of the categories of information included. Often this description can be quite specific (for example, fraction of negro blood). Residence is also included, many of the men being Union soldiers, in which case a unit is indicated.

But probably the most important documents among the Mississippi assistant commissioner's records are the labor contracts. Most of these were implemented in 1865, the remainder being drawn up between 1866 and 1868. These agreements were primarily between ex-slaves and plantation owners throughout the state, although not every county is represented. Given the facts that all members of a freedman's family are usually mentioned by name and the possibility that the contracts were executed with their former owners, the importance of these documents cannot be exaggerated. Many of the laborers are identified by given name and surname, although the majority are still represented only by a first name. The arrangement on microfilm of this extensive collection of documents will strike the researcher as haphazard; searching them is problematic. The arrangement is chronological, with instances of records for a given county being "clumped" together. The Mississippi Department of Archives and History has developed a microfiche index to these records.

Labor contracts are also found in the assistant commissioners' records for Arkansas and Tennessee, again ranging from 1865 to 1868. In the former the arrangement is by year and alphabetically thereunder by name of employer; in the latter the contracts are arranged in two subseries, the first containing contracts in which the contracting parties were from Tennessee, with the arrangement being alphabetical by county and thereunder chronological. The second—and smaller—subseries pertains to contracts with out-of-state employers.

Another useful source is the collection of transportation records from the assistant commissioner for the District of Columbia. Following the Civil War, many ex-slaves were attempting to reunite with family members separated by circumstances of slavery or war, and many were assisted by the bureau. The extensive records for transportation assistance from Washington, D.C., provide evidence for journeys to places as far away as Wisconsin.

The researcher who is contemplating the use of the Freedmen's Bureau records should always take into account the possible mobility of the people under study. Many freed people from Virginia and Maryland received transportation out of Washington, just as, for example, many ex-slaves from the Louisiana side of the Mississippi River were married in Vicksburg, Davis Bend, and Natchez, Mississippi.

The next level below that of the assistant commissioners' records is that of the field offices. With the exceptions of the records of the Arkansas field offices and portions of the field office records from Louisiana and Tennessee, these materials have not been microfilmed and exist only in the form of the original documents stored at the National Archives. A final description of these records has yet to be published; however, a preliminary inventory was generated in 1973 and can be found in some genealogical libraries.[21] As with the state records, the contents of the field office records can vary considerably. It is probable that the proportion of genealogically useful records is much higher in the field office records than in the records of the assistant commissioners. If at all possible, the researcher should consult the preliminary inventory to determine, first of all, whether there are any field records for the localities under consideration and whether the records being described would have any genealogical potential. For example, any labor contracts or records of apprenticeship or marriage should be of interest.

THE FREEDMAN'S SAVINGS AND TRUST

The Freedman's Savings and Trust Company was incorporated in 1865 by act of Congress as a banking system for ex-slaves. Although it eventually failed in 1874, it had by that time established thirty-three branches, mostly in Southern and Border states. The National Archives has microfilmed two record groups generated by the Freedman's Savings and Trust, although both are incomplete. Table 15-1 shows the contents of these two record groups.

Of the two record groups, the so-called signature records (National Archives microfilm publication M816) hold the most interest for the genealogist (figure 15-2). These records were completed upon opening an account. The forms provided for a thorough identification of the depositor as well as the identification of family members in the event of the depositor's death. Their format varied among branches, and differing formats can also be found within the records of some individual branches. The extent to which the forms were filled out also varies.

Nevertheless, these records often provide information not easily found elsewhere, if at all. For example, a seamstress and washerwoman named Nancy Patterson is shown to have established an account in the Louisville branch on 15 September 1865. In the final "remarks" portion of the signature record it is noted that she "formerly belonged to Bob Smith, was bot [*sic*] by her mother upon the block in 1854 or 5."[22] No relatives were noted in her record; however, it is not unusual to find three generations chronicled in a single instance. Typical of such an entry is that for Elias Webb, who held an account in the Vicksburg, Mississippi, branch. His record states that he was born and raised in Anderson District, South Carolina, and was currently residing in Port Gibson, Mississippi. His father was Moses, his mother Rachel. He had four brothers, listed as Green Webb, Jeremiah Webb, Marcus Webb, and Scipio Lewis. His sisters were listed as Emeline, Mary, and Amanda Webb.[23] It was not unusual for people to cross a county line to make a deposit in a branch office. Therefore, while the number of cities with branches was limited, those branches served more than just the immediate vicinity. The signature records indicate that significant numbers of ex-slaves from at least ten Mississippi counties and three Louisiana parishes opened accounts at the Vicksburg branch.

Many of the signature record forms contained space to indicate regiment and company, evidence of the fact that soldiers of the United States Colored Troops were especially encour-

aged to set aside portions of their pay in Freedman's Savings and Trust accounts. Many did, and several instances of deposits made by soldiers on garrison duty in 1865 and 1866 can be found. Veterans continued to provide this information for many years after they had been mustered out.

The other partial record group which has been microfilmed is the index to the deposit ledgers (National Archives microfilm M817). Unfortunately, the deposit ledgers themselves have apparently not survived. An examination of the deposit ledger index may provide evidence of a signature record for a given individual in a particular branch; however, the signature records themselves are incomplete for many branches. The deposit ledger indexes are sometimes misidentified as indexes to the signature records; indeed, occasionally the deposit ledger number is the same as the signature register number. Even so, this happy coincidence cannot be relied upon, and the researcher who is interested in the signature records should resign himself or herself to a frame-by-frame examination of the microfilm.

MILITARY RECORDS

There are many documented instances of African Americans serving the revolutionary cause during the American Revolution.[24] For example, compiled service record files can also be found, often simply under a given name, for slaves whose services as teamsters had been donated by their owners during the War of 1812. But the most important military records for African American genealogy are those created as a result of Civil War service. Along with the records of the Freedmen's Bureau and the Freedman's Savings and Trust, the service and pension records of African Americans who served in Union regiments focus on the most critical period for African American genealogy: the Civil War and Reconstruction. As such, they often hold important information concerning the experience of an individual or family during the final years of slavery.

Americans have recently become more aware of the role played by African American soldiers in the Civil War. The renowned 54th Massachusetts Volunteer Infantry was raised by that state and maintained its state numerical designation; however, the vast majority of regiments, eventually containing more than 170,000 African Americans, were recruited as federal regiments in the United States Colored Troops (USCT). Some regiments were raised under state sponsorship but were eventually integrated into the USCT system and given USCT numerical designations. Recruits for these regiments came from a variety of circumstances. Some were free blacks who joined regiments raised in the North. Others were slaves from Border states which had not seceded. Under these circumstances their owners "volunteered" their services in exchange for the bounty which would normally have gone to the recruit. A third group comprised those who joined USCT regiments in the South after abandoning their former owners in areas under Union control.

As military service and pension records are covered elsewhere in this volume, they are not discussed in great detail here; however, some special considerations are worth mentioning. There is an index to the Civil War service records of USCT and other African American servicemen (National Archives Microfilm Publication M589). For many researchers this source will be critical in identifying veteran ancestors and in requesting their service and pension records. In most instances, especially when dealing with a common name, it will be helpful to consult Frederick H. Dyer, *Compendium of the War of the Rebellion* (Reprint. Dayton, Ohio: Morningside, 1978), which contains brief histories of all Union regiments, stating where they were organized and where they served. This information will often enable the researcher to identify an ancestor's regiment. For example, if the researcher had an ancestor from Tennessee and it was discovered that three soldiers with his name were on the rolls of three separate regiments, consulting Dyer's work might indicate that only one of those regiments was raised in Tennessee. The researcher would then be able to request the correct records from the National Archives.

PUBLISHED ROSTERS AND INDEXES FOR AFRICAN AMERICAN REGIMENTS IN THE CIVIL WAR

There is no published roster series for all USCT regiments; however, many rosters have been printed, usually as part of state roster publications. When taken together, they probably account for close to forty percent of all African Americans who served the Union cause. These are noted below; they may serve as an additional aid in identifying an ancestor's regiment.

Connecticut
See *Catalogue of Connecticut Volunteer Organizations* (Hartford, Conn.: Adjutant General, 1869) for rosters of the 29th Connecticut Volunteer Infantry and the 30th Connecticut Volunteer Infantry (later the 31st United State Colored Infantry).

Illinois
See Illinois Adjutant General's *Report,* vol. 8 (Springfield, Ill.: Adjutant General, 1886), for a roster of the 29th United States Colored Infantry.

Indiana
See Indiana Adjutant General's *Report,* vol. 7 (Indianapolis:

Table 15-1. Microfilmed Records of the Freedman's Savings and Trust Company

Roll No.	State	Branch	Dates Covered
1	Alabama	Huntsville	28 Nov. 1865-21 Aug. 1874
2	Alabama	Mobile	18 June 1867-29 June 1874
3	Arkansas	Little Rock	27 Feb. 1871-15 July 1874
4	Washington, D.C.	Washington	11 July 1865-30 Dec. 1871
5	Washington, D.C.	Washington	24 May 1872-22 July 1874
5	Florida	Tallahassee	25 Aug. 1866-15 Jan. 1872
6	Georgia	Atlanta	15 Jan. 1870-15 July 1872
7	Georgia	Augusta	23 Nov. 1870-29 June 1874
8	Georgia	Savannah	10 Jan. 1866-17 Dec. 1870
9	Georgia	Savannah	17 Dec. 1870-22 Oct. 1872
10	Georgia	Savannah	22 Oct. 1872-1 Sept. 1874
11	Kentucky	Lexington	21 March 1870-3 July 1874
11	Kentucky	Louisville	15 Sept. 1865-8 July 1874
12	Louisiana	New Orleans	20 June 1866-29 June 1874
12	Louisiana	Shreveport	11 Feb. 1871-29 June 1874
13	Maryland	Baltimore	3 May 1866-23 June 1874
14	Mississippi	Columbus	1 Aug 1870-16 June 1874
14	Mississippi	Natchez	29 March 1870-18 June 1874
15	Mississippi	Vicksburg	28 July 1868-29 June 1874
16	Missouri	St. Louis	6 April 1869-8 Oct. 1869
17	New York	New York City	20 Feb. 1871-6 July 1874
18	North Carolina	New Bern	2 Nov. 1869-25 July 1874
18	North Carolina	Raleigh	9 April 1868-20 April 1868
18	North Carolina	Wilmington	3 Sept. 1869-30 Oct. 1869
19	Pennsylvania	Philadelphia	7 Jan. 1870-26 June 1874
20	South Carolina	Beaufort	20 June 1868-3 July 1874
21	South Carolina	Charleston	19 Dec. 1865-2 Dec 1869
22	South Carolina	Charleston	4 Dec. 1869-25 Feb. 1871
23	South Carolina	Charleston	25 Feb. 1871-2 July 1872
24	Tennessee	Memphis	28 Dec. 1865-1 July 1874
25	Tennessee	Nashville	23 Dec. 1871-23 June 1874
26	Virginia	Lynchburg	8 July 1871-22 Aug. 1871
26	Virginia	Norfolk	4 Dec. 1871-29 June 1874
27	Virginia	Richmond	21 June 1870-29 June 1874

Figure 15-2. From the Register of Signatures of depositors in branches of the Freedman's Savings and Trust Company, Savannah, Georgia.

No. 9963 RECORD for *Peggy Haley*

Date, *Nov 5 1872*

Where born, *~~Don't Know~~ S Sawton Place S.C*

Where brought up, *Savannah*

Residence, *Bryan Row*

Age, *23 years* Complexion, *Dark*

Occupation, *Opens Oysters & Does work.*

Works for

Wife or Husband, *Wm H.*

Children, *Isaac 10 yrs Patsey 5. Patience 3 yrs Adaline & Wm dead*

Father, *Hector Brightley dead*

Mother, *Scilla do. Rahn Place*

Brothers and Sisters, *Hector & Peter & Francis & Solomon Brightley Nancy Jenkins, Sarah Ferguson, Phebe Brown, Elsie Polite.*

REMARKS:

Signature, *Peggy + Haley*
her mark

Adjutant General, 1865–1869), for a roster of the 28th United States Colored Infantry.

Iowa
See *Roster and Record of Iowa Soldiers in the War of the Rebellion Together With Historical Sketches of Volunteer Organizations 1861–1866* (Des Moines, Iowa: Emory English, state printer, 1911), for the First Regiment of Iowa African Infantry, later the 60th United States Colored Infantry.

Kansas
See Kansas Adjutant General's *Report* (Reprint. Topeka, Kansas: Hudson, 1896) for rosters of the 1st and 2nd Kansas Colored Volunteer Infantry (later the 79th and 83rd United States Colored Infantry, respectively), the 1st, 2nd, and 3rd Kansas Colored Light Artillery, and the Independent Colored Kansas Battery.

Kentucky
See the *Report of the Adjutant General of the State of Kentucky,* vol. 2 (Frankfort, Ken.: Adjutant General, 1867), for rosters of the 5th and 6th United States Colored Cavalry; the 100th, 107th, 108th, 109th, 114th, 115th, 116th, 117th, 118th, 119th, 122nd, 123rd, 124th, and 125th United States Colored Infantry regiments; and the 8th, 12th, and 13th United States Colored Heavy Artillery.

Maryland
See L. Allison Wilmer, et al., *History and Roster of Maryland Volunteers, War of 1861–5,* vol. 2 (Reprint. Silver Spring, Maryland: Family Line Publications in conjunction with Toomey Press, 1987), for rosters of the 4th, 7th, 9th, 19th, 30th, and 39th United States Colored Infantry regiments.

Massachusetts
See *Massachusetts Soldiers, Sailors and Marines in the Civil War,* vol. 4 (Brookline, Mass.: Adjutant General, 1931–1935), for rosters of the 54th and 55th Massachusetts Volunteer Infantry regiments; and vol. 6 for a roster of the 5th Massachusetts Volunteer Cavalry.

Michigan
See Record of Service of Michigan Volunteers in the Civil War, vol. 46, for a roster of the 1st Michigan Colored Infantry (later the 102nd United States Colored Infantry).

North Carolina
See A.H. Stein, *History of the Thirty-Seventh Regiment United States Colored Infantry* (Philadelphia: King and Baird, 1866), for a roster of this regiment, originally designated the 3rd North Carolina Colored Infantry.

Ohio
See the *Official Roster of the Soldiers of the State of Ohio in the War of the Rebellion* for rosters of the 127th Ohio Volunteer Infantry (later the 5th United States Colored Infantry) and the 27th United States Colored Infantry.

Pennsylvania
See Samuel P. Bates, *History of Pennsylvania Volunteers,* for rosters of the 3rd, 6th, 8th, 22nd, 24th, 25th, 32nd, 41st, 43rd, 45th, and 127th United States Colored Infantry regiments.

Rhode Island
See *Adjutant General's Report* (Providence, Rhode Island: Adjutant General, 1866) for a roster of the 14th Rhode Island Heavy Artillery (later the 8th and then the 11th United States Colored Heavy Artillery).

Tennessee
See *Tennesseans in the Civil War* (Nashville, Tenn.: Civil War Commission, 1965), which indexes troops in all Tennessee federal regiments, including the 11th (new), 12th, 13th, 14th, 15th, 16th, 17th, 40th, 42nd, 44th, 59th, 61st, 88th (new), and 101st United States Colored Infantry regiments, as well as batteries of the 2nd United States Colored Light Infantry and the 1st, 2nd, and 3rd United States Colored Heavy Artillery.

OTHER MILITARY SOURCES

As noted previously, slaveowners in the Border states sometimes collected bounties when their slaves joined USCT regiments. Records for this bounty may be found in the soldier's service record, hence making the service record far more valuable than is usually the case.

Civil War veterans often submitted affidavits for their comrades in support of pension claims. The writing of affidavits was often a reciprocal affair, and a network of veterans from the same company often wrote affidavits for one another. Taken as a totality, the pension affidavits can on occasion reveal a common background for the pension applicants. This could be particularly important in the research of USCT veterans, as such an approach could uncover veterans from the same locality or even the same plantation who enlisted together. Obtaining the pension files of the fellow veterans who supplied affidavits for an ancestor's application may be costly but could in the end be very revealing.

Just prior to the end of the Civil War, the Confederate government adopted a policy for the use of slave soldiers; however, the policy change came too late for meaningful enactment, and no African Americans actually served as soldiers for the Southern cause. Even so, many slaves acted as body servants to their owners or to the sons of their owners when they entered Confederate service. Such service often qualified the servants for pensions paid to Southern veterans by the former states of the Confederacy. Some were even able to find a place in retirement homes for Confederate veterans.

Many slaves were drafted by the Confederate government for manual labor, perhaps with compensation for their owners. Documentation for such labor arrangements is not centralized but does occasionally surface in private papers or government archives. Similar documentation may also be found from the Union side, such as the recent publication of a list of slaves impressed for work on the Nashville and North Western Railroad in October 1863.[25] These particular records are especially important because they supply the name of owner together with the residence and a physical description of the slave.

CONCLUSION

In a general way, the major sources for African American genealogical research have been considered in this chapter. There are others, many of them specific to particular states or localities. Again, the researcher must become thoroughly familiar with the records of a locality or state in order to fully exploit them.

Many major indexing and publication projects are needed in this field. Until they are accomplished, the researcher of African American genealogy will often need to call upon deep reserves of patience and perseverance. The continued publication of county records holds great potential, but that potential could be squandered if the importance of such records to African American genealogy is ignored or overlooked. The clearest example discussed here is the transcription of the names of slaves mentioned in wills. Unfortunately, though, many local publishing programs systematically exclude African Americans from the records being published. Books or series purporting to record the cemeteries, the postbellum marriages, school censuses, and even the census schedules for a given county have appeared within the last fifteen years in a "whites only" format. The researcher of African American genealogy must be aware of this possibility, both to evaluate what is published and, perhaps, to exert pressure to see that such omissions are rectified.

This chapter has demonstrated the often surprising richness of many research sources for African American genealogy. It is hoped that, by so doing, more people will be encouraged to begin their research in this field, fully aware of the problems yet at least a little heartened by the fact that the African American historical experience can be documented—at times in great detail—through the lives of the ancestors of present-day African Americans.

NOTES

1. Among them the following: Dorothy A. Boyd-Rush, *Register of Free Blacks, Rockingham County, Virginia, 1807–1859* (Bowie, Md.: Heritage, 1992); Katherine G. Bushman, *Registers of Free Blacks, 1810–1864, Augusta County, Virginia and Staunton, Virginia* (Verona, Va.: Mid-Valley Press, 1989); Richard B. Dickinson, *Entitled! Free Papers in Appalachia Concerning Antebellum Freeborn Negroes and Emancipated Blacks in Montgomery County, Virginia* (Washington, D.C.: National Genealogical Society, 1981); Frances B. Latimer, *The Register of Free Negroes: Northampton County, Virginia, 1853 to 1861* (Bowie, Md.: Heritage, 1992); Dorothy S. Provine, *Alexandria County, Virginia Free Negro Registers 1797–1861* (Bowie, Md.: Heritage, 1990); and Donald Sweig, *Registrations of Free Negroes Commencing September Court 1822. . . .* (Fairfax, Va.: Fairfax County History Commission, 1977).

2. Transcribed in Sweig, 97.

3. Wright State University, *Records of Black and Mulatto Persons. . . .* A printed abstract of these records entitled *Register of Blacks in the Miami Valley: A Name Abstract (1804–1857)* was compiled by Stephen Haller and Robert Smith.

4. See Herbert G. Gutman, *The Black Family in Slavery and Freedom, 1750–1925* (New York: Vintage Books, 1976), 230–56.

5. David T. Thackery, "Crossing the Divide: A Census Study of Slaves Before and After Freedom," *Origins* (Newberry Library) 2 (March 1989).

6. Gutman, 245.

7. *Freedman's Savings and Trust Signature Books* (National Archives Microfilm Publication M816). Vicksburg, Mississippi, branch, record no. 1288.

8. The use of the slave schedules as supporting documentation is amply demonstrated in David H. Streets, *Slave Genealogy: A Research Guide With Case Studies* (Bowie, Md.: Heritage, 1986), although, not surprisingly, their use is confined to small slaveholdings.

9. A notable exception is found in Jonnie B. Arnold, *Index to 1860 Mortality Schedule of South Carolina* (Greenville, S.C.: the author, 1982). On the other hand, many of the indexes appearing on the National Archives microfilm publications of these schedules, as well as those published by Accelerated Indexing, should be treated with caution.

10. The abstract of this will (Duplin County will book, vol. 3, entry 85) can be found in William L. Murphy, *Genealogical Abstracts: Duplin County Wills, 1730–1860* (Rose Hill, N.C.: Duplin County, Historical Society, 1982), 120.

11. Wills, Maryland State Archives. Liber 30, folio 351, and liber 39, folio 521, respectively. I am indebted to my colleague Tony Hoskins for bringing this interesting example to my attention.

12. Among such published indexes: Jeannette Holland Austin, *Index to Georgia Wills* (Baltimore, Md.: Genealogical Publishing Co., 1985); Thornton W. Mitchell, *North Carolina Wills: A Testator Index 1665–1900,* "corrected and revised edition" (Baltimore: Genealogical Publishing Co., 1992); Byron and Barbara Sistler, *Index to Tennessee Wills & Administrations 1779–1861* (Nashville, Tenn.: Sistler, 1990); Clayton Torrence, *Virginia Wills and Administrations 1632–1800: An Index* (Richmond, Va.: National Society of Colonial Dames of America, 1930); Betty Couch Wiltshire, *Mississippi Index of Wills* (Bowie, Md.: Heritage, 1989).

13. Abstracted in Joyce Martin Murray, *Deed Abstracts of Warren County, Kentucky 1812–1821* (Dallas, Tex.: Murray, 1986), 12.

14. Abstracted by Ellen and Diane Rogers, *Estill County, Kentucky, Circuit Court Records* (Irvine, Kent.: the compilers, 1984), vol. 1, pp. 3, 7; vol. 2, p. 240.

15. Transcribed in Nettie Schreiner-Yentis, *The 1787 Census of Virginia* (Springfield, Va.: Genealogical Books in Print, 1987).

16. See Elizabeth N. and W. Bruce Wingo, *Norfolk County, Virginia Tithables 1730–1750* (Norfolk, Va.: the compilers, 1979), and *Norfolk County, Virginia Tithables 1751–1765* (Norfolk, Va.: the compilers, 1981).

17. *Slave Bills of Sale Project* (Atlanta, Ga.: African-American Family History Association, 1986).

18. Johni Cerny, "Black Ancestral Research" in *The Source: A Guidebook of American Genealogy,* 1st ed. (Salt Lake City: Ancestry, 1984), 582.

19. One which has survived and which contains extensive slave birth and baptism listings was transcribed and published in 1897 and was reprinted recently: *The Parish Register of Christ Church, Middlesex County, Va. From 1653 to 1812* (Easley, S.C.: Southern Historical Society, 1988).

20. For example, see Hugh Buckner Johnston, Jr., "Some Bible and Other Family Records," *North Carolina Genealogical Society Journal* 7 (4) (November 1981).

21. *Preliminary Inventory of the Records of the Field Offices of the Bureau of Refugees, Freedmen and Abandoned Lands* (Washington, D.C.: National Archives and Records Service, 1973). For a sense of the potential found in many of these more local records, the researcher may wish to consult an essay by Barry Crouch and Larry Madras: "Reconstructing Black Families: Perspectives From the Texas Freedmen's Bureau Records," in *Our Family, Our Town: Essays on Family and Local His-*

tory Sources in the National Archives (Washington, D.C.: National Archives and Records Service, 1987).

22. *Freedman's Savings and Trust Signature Books.* Louisville, Kentucky, branch, record no. 1.

23. Ibid., Vicksburg, Mississippi branch, record no. 1186.

24. See Robert Ewell Greene, *Black Courage 1775–1783: Documentation of Black Participation in the American Revolution* (Washington, D.C.: National Society of the Daughters of the American Revolution, 1984).

25. Gale Williams Bamman, "African-Americans Impressed for Service on the Nashville and North Western Railroad, October 1863," *National Genealogical Society Quarterly* 80 (3) (September 1992). Although this particular record is found in the Tennessee State Library and Archives, Bamman notes that similar records can be found in National Archives Record Groups 92 (Quartermaster General's Office), 94 (Adjutant General's Office), and 109 (Captured Confederate Records).

BIBLIOGRAPHY

HISTORICAL BACKGROUND

Berlin, Ira. *Slaves Without Masters: The Free Negro in the Antebellum South.* New York: Oxford University Press, 1976.

Berlin, Ira, et al., eds. *Freedom: A Documentary History of Emancipation 1861–1867 Selected From the Holdings of the National Archives of the United States.* New York: Cambridge University Press, 1982–.

Cornish, Dudley Taylor. *The Sable Arm: Black Troops in the Union Army, 1861–1865.* Lawrence: University Press of Kansas, 1956.

Foner, Eric. *Reconstruction: America's Unfinished Revolution, 1863–1877.* New York: Harper & Row, 1988.

Gray, Deborah. *Ar'n't I a Woman? Female Slaves in the Plantation South.* New York: W.W. Norton, 1985.

Grossman, James R. *Land of Hope: Chicago, Black Southerners, and the Great Migration.* Chicago: University of Chicago Press, 1989.

Hawbaker, Gary T. *Runaways, Rascals, and Rogues: Missing Spouses, Servants and Slaves. Abstracts From Lancaster County Pennsylvania Newspapers.* Hershey, Pa.: the author, 1987.

Gutman, Herbert. *The Black Family in Slavery and Freedom, 1750–1925.* New York: Vintage Books, 1976.

Litwack, Leon F. *North of Slavery: The Negro in the Free States 1790–1860.* Chicago: University of Chicago Press, 1961.

Smith, Billy G., and Richard Wojtowicz. *Blacks Who Stole Themselves: Advertisements for Runaways in the Pennsylvania Gazette 1728–1790.* Philadelphia: University of Pennsylvania, 1989.

Windley, Lathan A. *Runaway Slave Advertisements: A Documentary History From the 1730s to 1790.* 4 vols. Westport, Conn.: Greenwood, 1983.

GUIDES AND BIBLIOGRAPHIES

Black Studies: A Select Catalog of National Archives Microfilm Publications. Washington, D.C.: National Archives, 1984.

Cerny, Johni, and Arlene Eakle. *Ancestry's Guide to Research: Case Studies in American Genealogy.* Salt Lake City: Ancestry, 1985. One of the case studies is African American.

Dyer, Frederick H. *Compendium of the War of the Rebellion.* Reprint. Dayton, Ohio: Morningside, 1978.

Headley, Robert K. *Genealogical Abstracts From the 18th Century Virginia Newspapers.* Baltimore: Genealogical Publishing Co., 1987.

Index to Personal Names in the National Union Catalog of Manuscript Collections 1959–1984. Alexandria, Virginia: Chadwyk-Healey, 1988.

Records of Ante-Bellum Southern Plantations From the Revolution Through the Civil War. Frederick, Md.: University Publications of America, 1985–.

Rose, James, and Alice Eichholz. *Black Genesis.* Detroit: Gale Research Co., 1978.

Streets, David H. *Slave Genealogy: A Research Guide with Case Studies.* Bowie, Md.: Heritage, 1986.

Thackery, David T. *A Bibliography of African American Family History at the Newberry Library.* Chicago: The Newberry Library, 1993.

_____, and Dee Woodtor. *Case Studies in Afro-American Genealogy.* Chicago: The Newberry Library, 1989.

Tregillis, Helen Cox. *River Roads to Freedom: Fugitive Slave Notices and Sheriff Notices Found in Illinois Sources.* Bowie, Md.: Heritage, 1988.

Turpin, Joan. *Register of Black, Mulatto and Poor Person in Four Ohio Counties 1791–1861.* Bowie, Md.: Heritage Books, 1985.

REPRESENTATIVE GENEALOGIES AND FAMILY HISTORIES

Johnson, Michael P., and James L. Roark. *Black Masters: A Free Family of Color in the Old South.* New York: W.W. Norton, 1984.

Lucas, Ernestine Grant. *From Paris to Springfield: The Slave Connection Basye-Basey.* Decorah, Iowa: Anundsen, 1983.

Madden, T.O., Jr., and Ann L. Miller. *We Were Always Free. The Maddens of Culpeper County, Virginia: A 200-Year Family History.* New York: Norton, 1992.

Patterson, Ruth Polk. *The Seed of Sally Good'n: A Black Family of Arkansas 1833–1953.* Lexington: University Press of Kentucky, 1985.

Pinkard, Ophelia Taylor. *Taylors of Northumberland County, Virginia.* Washington, D.C.: Pinkard, 1987.

Redford, Dorothy Spruill. *Somerset Homecoming: Recovering a Lost Heritage.* New York: Doubleday, 1988.

White, Barnetta McGhee. *In Search of Kith and Kin: The History of a Southern Black Family.* Baltimore: Gateway, 1986.

TRACKING HISPANIC FAMILY HISTORY
Chapter Contents

TRACKING HISPANIC FAMILY HISTORY

George Ryskamp

Hispanic immigration to the United States has been much more extensive than is generally recognized. Spaniards settled the Caribbean islands and Mexico more than a century before the English settled Jamestown in 1607. The earliest Hispanic settlers within the area of the United States were those who settled Saint Augustine, Florida, on the eastern end of the continent in 1565 and New Mexico, on the western end, in 1598.

The Spanish colonial period represents only the beginning. Immigration continues to this day as hundreds of thousands of Mexicans, Central Americans, and South Americans, as well as Cubans, Puerto Ricans, and others from the Caribbean islands continue to come to the United States. Many of them could ultimately trace their roots through those American countries to Spain. Others would find that their roots beyond those countries are not Spanish but Native American, French, German, Eastern European, Italian, African, and Portuguese. For just as the United States has been a melting pot, so have been the countries of Central and South America.

Before the end of the colonial period (around 1820), an estimated 12 million Spaniards emigrated, primarily to Mexico and Central and South America. The immigration that followed in the next century, however, was considerably greater. Of a total of 54 million people who emigrated from Europe to the American continents between 1820 and 1920, 20 million went to Latin America—primarily to Argentina, Brazil, Cuba, and Uruguay. Large numbers of them came from Italy, Spain, and Portugal. The flow of immigration did not stop with the Great Depression. From 1946 to 1957, 1.75 million immigrants traveled to Latin America, primarily from Italy and Spain. Spanish immigration was not, of course, entirely to Latin America. Many Spanish, among them large numbers of Galicians, Basques, and Andalucians, came directly to the United States. Still others never reached the Americas and found themselves settling in Australia.

These immigration patterns are particularly interesting because immigration from South America to the United States continues to this day. From 1820 to 1906, approximately 20,000 legal immigrants arrived from South America, and from 1907 to 1926, 77,000 more arrived. It is estimated that from 1951 to 1975, 421,000 South Americans came to the United States. These numbers do not include the extensive immigration from Cuba, Puerto Rico, Mexico, and Central America. Mexico alone is estimated to have contributed, between 1900 and 1930, 2 to 3 million immigrants, half of whom entered the United States illegally. In the 1980s, Cubans, Salvadorans, and others fleeing from political oppression and civil war streamed across the border with the larger flow of Mexicans and others who came for economic reasons.

Often, a search for Hispanic ancestry leads ultimately to Spain, but it is equally likely that one, two, or more generations settled in the countries of Central America, South America, or the Caribbean. Some authorities include Portuguese within the Hispanic population. There have been extensive migrations from Portugal to the United States as well as, of course, to Brazil and the Azores and from the Azores and Brazil to the United States.

Unless his or her Hispanic immigrant ancestors came to the United States within living memory, the greatest challenge to the family historian often is identifying the place of origin in the mother country. Fortunately, there are many good records available to Hispanics that can reveal such a place. Nothing is more exciting than a discovery that ancestry leads back to Mexico or bridges the ocean back to Spain. Whether the mother country is Argentina, Cuba, Mexico, Spain, or another Latin American or European country, the types of records to be searched and the process of searching those records remain basically the same. The emphasis of this chapter is on Spanish-language records available in the United States. For a complete understanding of this process, English-language records are briefly discussed where appropriate.

KEYS TO SUCCESS: BASIC RESEARCH CONCEPTS

THOROUGHNESS

Because clues to the place of origin are not frequently encountered, especially in records created in the United States, it is extremely important (as in any other aspect of family history research) that the researcher be thorough. Search for all information about the individual, about the family of the individual, about the surname, and about the friends of the individual.

BEGIN WITH THE KNOWN—MOVE TO THE UNKNOWN

Many researchers make the time-consuming and frequently unproductive mistake of attempting to locate a link with Spain or Mexico by searching in one or the other country first. The researcher should always begin in the United States, and even in his or her own home, because the best records for identifying the place of origin in the mother country are to be found at the destination of the immigrant. With one or two exceptions, the records that yield information about the place of origin in the mother country are the same records that have been used throughout the research process.

START WITH A THOROUGH PRELIMINARY SURVEY

Once again, following basic rules of good research is important. As new information, such as the name of a new family member, a new surname, the port or vessel of arrival, a possible place of origin or at least a former residence, is found, follow the steps of the survey phase. Those steps, as they relate to tracing the Hispanic immigrant, are discussed below.

LEARN SPECIFIC EMIGRATION-IMMIGRATION PATTERNS

In most areas throughout the world there have been basic patterns of immigration, as people moved from a particular region or country to another. An awareness of the patterns unique to the particular time period and area where your ancestors settled can help identify the region and, in some cases, even the place of origin.

Some migration patterns are generally true for a region over an extended period of time. A good example of this type of pattern is the movement of the Spanish colonial frontier in Mexico into what is now the southwestern United States. Most such migrants to early California came from Baja California, or Sonora, Sinaloa, and Nayarit in Mexico. Those for Texas came from central Mexico up through the Coahuila area. Coupled with an awareness of these patterns is an awareness that current political units and even the international boundaries may not reflect original patterns of migration and settlement. For example, two regions of Texas have different migration patterns than the central pattern just described. El Paso, Texas, traditionally was part of the New Mexico area, and its settlement pattern comes up through Chihuahua and into the El Paso region and on north into New Mexico. Likewise, the portion of Texas between the Nueces and Rio Grande rivers was, until 1848, politically part of the province of Nuevo Santander. Hence, its migratory patterns relate to the development of that part of northeastern Mexico rather than the development of central Texas.

Similarly, large migration patterns can exist in specific time periods from an origin country into specific countries or regions. Nearly all migrants from the northern Spanish ports of the Basque countries during the last quarter of the nineteenth century were destined for the island of Cuba. Early twentieth century immigration from Galicia centered extensively on the Rio de la Plata area of South America as well as Brazil, where the commonality between the Gallego language and Portuguese assisted the new immigrants. Within the recent past, Italians and southern Germans migrated to those same areas.

In addition to broad migration patterns, there have been numerous specific migrations of groups or more limited repetitive patterns. For example, many Spaniards, primarily from the Andalucia and Valencia regions of Spain, migrated to Hawaii after being recruited to work on sugar plantations there. They and the next generation of their descendants then migrated primarily to the western United States. Similarly, a great number of Basques from the Spanish and French Basque regions sought work during the same period as sheepherders and farm- and ranchhands in California and Nevada. Today their descendants can be found throughout the western United States, and the largest collection of Basque historical and cultural materials in the United States is housed at the University of Nevada at Reno.

In some cases the research pattern is even more specific: an entire group moved from one area to settle a specific region. Such was the case in the Canary Island migration to found the City of San Antonio in 1730 and also for a series of Canary Island settlements in the Louisiana area between 1766 and 1800. Similarly, and even more specific, a group of colonists was recruited in Guadalajara in 1797 and brought from the port of San Blas to Alta California.

The key for the researcher is to identify immigration patterns to determine whether or not they can help to determine the place of origin of an immigrant ancestor and to understand the background for that ancestor's life. The broad patterns of migration discussed above can be found in general history books of a regional nature. For example, information concerning migration patterns in settling the Spanish borderlands area of the United States can be found in David J. Weber, *The Spanish Frontier in North America* (New Haven: Yale University Press, 1992). Books of a broader nature that deal with immigration are also available. One is Peter Boyd Bowman, *Indice geobiografico de mas de 56 mil pobladores de la America hispana* (vol. 1, 1493 to 1519; vol. 2, 1520 to 1539), which deals with the earliest immigration into the Spanish colonies. Another, Carlos Sixerei Paredes, *A Emigracion,* is an excellent historical analysis of emigration from Galicia from the seventeenth to the twentieth centuries.

The bibliography at the end of this chapter is illustrative of the kinds of books which can be used as a starting point to identify areas and periods of research. The catalogs of major university collections, many of which are available at local universities or major public libraries through computerized search systems and interlibrary loan, are a logical next source. Items of interest may also be found in local libraries in the area in which an immigrant ancestor settled in the United States. In addition, an occasional perusal of the *Family History Library Catalog*—the catalog of the Family History Library of The Church of Jesus Christ of Latter-day Saints (LDS church) in Salt Lake City—may yield a new acquisition of particular relevance (see chapter 2, Databases, Indexes, and Other Finding Aids). There may also be articles published in major historical and genealogical periodicals which could relate to the immigration patterns for a particular locality or time period.

As these searches are done, the researcher should check each index under migration, emigration, and immigration, as well as the specific localities, both in the United States and in the prospective country and, ideally, the region of origin. For example, someone whose ancestor is known to have come from Spain to Cuba and from there to the United States might identify a family tradition that the ancestor came from northern Spain in the late 1800s. The individual would then check under Spain, as well as the regional names for the northern Spanish provinces: Galicia, Asturia, Santander, and the Basque provinces, as well as Cuba. Such a search would lead the researcher to find books such as Juan Carlos de la Madrid Alvarez, *El Viaje de los emigrantes Asturianos a América* (Gijon, Spain: Biblioteca Historica Asturiana, 1989) and Maria Pilar Pildain Salazar, *Ir a América: La Emigracion Vasca a América (Guipúzcoa 1840–1870)* (San Sebastian, Spain: Donostia, 1984), both of which provide detailed information concerning migration patterns from these areas in the late 1800s. The first book specifically emphasizes migration to Cuba as the principal migration pattern. The latter book presents a list of immigrants from the Basque province of Guipúzcoa, giving their home parishes taken from passenger lists and other documents from that Spanish province. Once again, the search for the immigrant ancestor is most likely to be rewarded by continued and thorough research, including not only normal genealogical sources but broader historical reference sources.

BE CREATIVE WITH CONNECTION IDEAS

As the researcher gains experience and becomes a good family history researcher, he or she develops an intuitive sense about small details that can connect to other records which may reveal the place of origin of the family. For example, a reference to a Cuban ancestor in a newspaper stating that he served his adopted country in war and in peace might lead a researcher to check military records. Another researcher, finding that an ancestor served in the military prior to 1832 in Puerto Rico or 1820 in Mexico and that the word "Don" appears before the ancestor's name, would then want to search nobility records. Finding the term *doctor* or *bachiller* in a reference to an ancestor, another researcher might ask what university the ancestor possibly attended. In each case, two steps take place: first, the researcher has recognized a small detail or fact in a known record and questioned what that detail could mean; second, the researcher has determined what records might substantiate, expand, or verify that detail in the ancestor's life. The creative connections cannot be taught, but knowing how to analyze people's lives and then asking what type of records may exist can be learned.

GENERAL INFORMATION

A great uniformity exists in Spanish-language records, because the basic principles of record-keeping in Spain and the types of records used there were transmitted to Spain's colonies during the colonial period—even the areas of the United States once under Spanish or Mexican dominion. For general information on working with records in Latin America and for a discussion of immigration patterns there, as well as for detailed information on specific Latin American countries, consult Lyman D. Platt, *Una guía genealógico-histórico de latinoamérica* (Salt Lake City: Acoma, 1977), or the English version, *A Genealogical Historical Guide to Latin America* (Detroit: Gale Research Co., 1978). While there is no similar volume for Spanish American research in the United States, George Ryskamp, *Tracing Your Hispanic Heritage* (Riverside, Calif.: Hispanic Family Research, 1984), will guide the researcher in using Spanish-language records found in the United States. In many cases, the Spanish American researcher will, of course, need to use U.S. records which are not Spanish or Mexican in origin.

One of the major challenges facing the genealogist in any language is learning to use and understand older language forms and handwriting styles. Of great assistance to the beginner is *Spanish Records Extraction* (Salt Lake City: The Church of Jesus Christ of Latter-day Saints, 1981), published by the LDS church. It was designed to train record extractors, many of whom spoke no Spanish, how to read Spanish-language Catholic parish records, and its workbook approach is an excellent way to learn to read those records.

The ability to read early records develops slowly and can only be obtained through actual experience. Do not try to absorb, in a single reading, all of the material written in the old script or unfamiliar Spanish. It is necessary, instead, to have available one or two of the reference works described while attempting to read an early record until an instinctive knowledge of the techniques develops.

You can compensate for any deficiency in formal Spanish instruction by study, patience, and a determination to understand the records. Consulting a good beginning grammar book (and possibly one of the quick introductory Spanish courses) and always having a dictionary at hand will also help to compensate for any deficiency. Do not be discouraged from performing research by a lack of formal training in the Spanish language.

PRELIMINARY SURVEY

A detailed preliminary survey, particularly for those whose ancestors immigrated during the twentieth century, is extremely important. In many, if not most, cases, the place of origin of the immigrant ancestor will be found in this phase. As new information is discovered about the immigrant ancestor, family, friends, and surname, the researcher will return to this phase and repeat the third and fourth steps discussed below.

The preliminary survey has a two-fold objective: first, to learn all that one's relatives know about the history of the family; and second, to identify all of the research that has already been done on the family. The preliminary survey is accomplished in four steps:

1. Check all home and family sources.

2. Interview other family members.

3. Check for information about family history research done on the family in the records of the Genealogical Department of the LDS church.

4. Check for any printed biographies or histories dealing with the family or its individual members.

CHECK HOME AND FAMILY SOURCES

The beginning researcher is frequently unaware of the wealth of genealogical and family history material in his or her own home. Search in basements, attics, and garages for anything about the family and its early members—at the bottom of that old trunk upstairs may be a letter from a great-grandfather in Spain to his son in Uruguay. You might also find there copies of military papers showing that a grandfather fought in the Mexican army during the Mexican Revolution of 1911; or perhaps the long-forgotten birth certificate of one's mother will reveal the name of the small town in Cuba where she was born. Especially significant would be photographs, clothing, or tools which had belonged to an ancestor that would give a greater reality to one's understanding and knowledge of that person. After the beginning researcher's own home has been thoroughly searched and all of the various sources, documents, and personal objects of the family are gathered together in a single place, a similar search in the homes of parents, grandparents, aunts and uncles, and even cousins will offer further family source material.

The following list of home and family sources which a person of Hispanic ancestry may encounter will guide the beginning genealogist in searching through his or her home, as well as in asking others to search theirs. Because lifestyles vary from one nation to another, this list includes sources that might be found not only in an Anglo-American home but also in the home of a family from Latin America or Spain.

Vital Records

This category includes government or church records of major life events, such as birth or baptism, marriage, and death. While, in some cases, such certificates were issued at the time of the event, usually the copies to be found in the home are certificates issued by civil or religious authorities years afterward when they were requested to prove the facts that surrounded an event. For example, in requesting a passport, a person may have had to show a certificate of birth to prove his or her citizenship. Once the passport was issued, the certificate of birth was returned to its owners, who could have filed it away among important but frequently forgotten documents. Birth and baptism certificates are most commonly found because a variety of situations require such proof—for example, obtaining a passport or visa, getting married, or requesting Social Security benefits. Naturally, a certified copy of the birth or baptismal record is the most valid proof. Likewise, death or marriage records may have been obtained to settle an estate or to make a claim for a pension. If the family has come from one of many Spanish-speaking countries in recent decades or is currently living in one, a copy of the *libro de familia* (family book) may also be found in the home. The *libro de familia* and other vital records are described in chapters 9 and 11 of Ryskamp, *Tracing Your Hispanic Heritage* (cited earlier).

Vital records are particularly valuable because they usually identify the specific place from which the ancestor came and give an exact date from which research can be begun in the records of the country of origin. By providing names of parents and, usually, in the case of birth or baptismal records, the names of grandparents, a single certificate may give the researcher a small pedigree from which to begin research.

Vital records in the adopted country should be read carefully for clues as to another country of origin. For example, one Spanish immigrant to the United States was later married there. The record of his son's birth indicated that the father was from Barcelona, Spain, and that the mother was from Cuba. While not clearly identifying whether this referred to the city of Barcelona or the province, it at least narrowed down the area of the search to locate his place of origin in Spain.

Photographs

Photographs are a particularly important home source. Perhaps more than any single source, photographs make family members come to life. Photographs that are labeled with names and dates can be of great assistance in locating the whereabouts of the ancestor who is pictured. Older photographs frequently have the name of the photographer and the address of the studio. In this way you may also identify the area of ancestral origin.

Photographs can be found in the homes of people of all income and social levels. For example, a local history project of the California State University at Fresno which attempted to reconstruct Hispanic local history in the San Joaquin Valley located and identified photographs from the homes of descendants of early migrant farm workers that showed people, places, and details of daily life among Hispanic migrant farm families in the early twentieth century.

Printed Materials

Most families have printed, in limited quantities, a wide variety of formal papers for distribution to friends and relatives. The most common of these are wedding invitations. Death announcements were also widely distributed in the past and can frequently be spotted by their black borders. In Catholic Hispanic countries, baptisms and communions were often announced by formal printed invitations or announcements.

Other printed materials commonly found among the effects of Hispanic ancestors are *relaciones de meritos* (records of merit) and *hojas de servicio* (service sheets). Similar to modern resumes, they were used in search of work or to list the qualifications of an individual to perform an act in a certain capacity. They usually include a variety of interesting biographical material regarding the individual being described. In addition to these types of printed materials, you may find business or personal calling cards, which are very commonly used in Hispanic countries, even by poorer people and students.

Passports, Visas, Work Permits, and Citizenship or Naturalization Papers

These documents relate to the process whereby a person leaves the country of birth or citizenship, immigrates to a second country, and attempts to become a citizen of that country. Passports are now issued by the national governments and/or by the civil governors in the provinces of many Hispanic countries, including Spain and Mexico (figure 16-1). Unfortunately, the use of passports as a necessary requirement for leaving most countries was not adopted until the twentieth century. A variety of policies and systems governing exit were used in the nineteenth century and earlier. The most popular involved merely going to a port and embarking on a ship. In most such cases, documents proving that a man had already served in the armed forces and had left no debts were the only ones needed to emigrate. In some cases, such as for the migrant workers coming into the southwestern United States, a work permit issued at the border was necessary to obtain work in the United States. Look for such documents preserved among the important papers of the immigrant. They may provide clues as to place of origin in the mother country.

Once in the country of destination, some type of action was necessary to achieve citizenship. In the United States before 1868, this meant first becoming a citizen of one of the states. The process was rarely extensive and frequently required nothing more than swearing an oath of allegiance to the state. Therefore, from this early period there will probably be few, if any, citizenship or naturalization documents in existence.

Nevertheless, the ancestor who immigrated during the twentieth century would most certainly have had some type of immigration, residency, or naturalization papers. For those ancestors who immigrated prior to 1906, naturalization documen-

Figure 16-1. Passport issued by the Mexican state of Aguascalientes in 1919 and found in the California home of this immigrant's descendant.

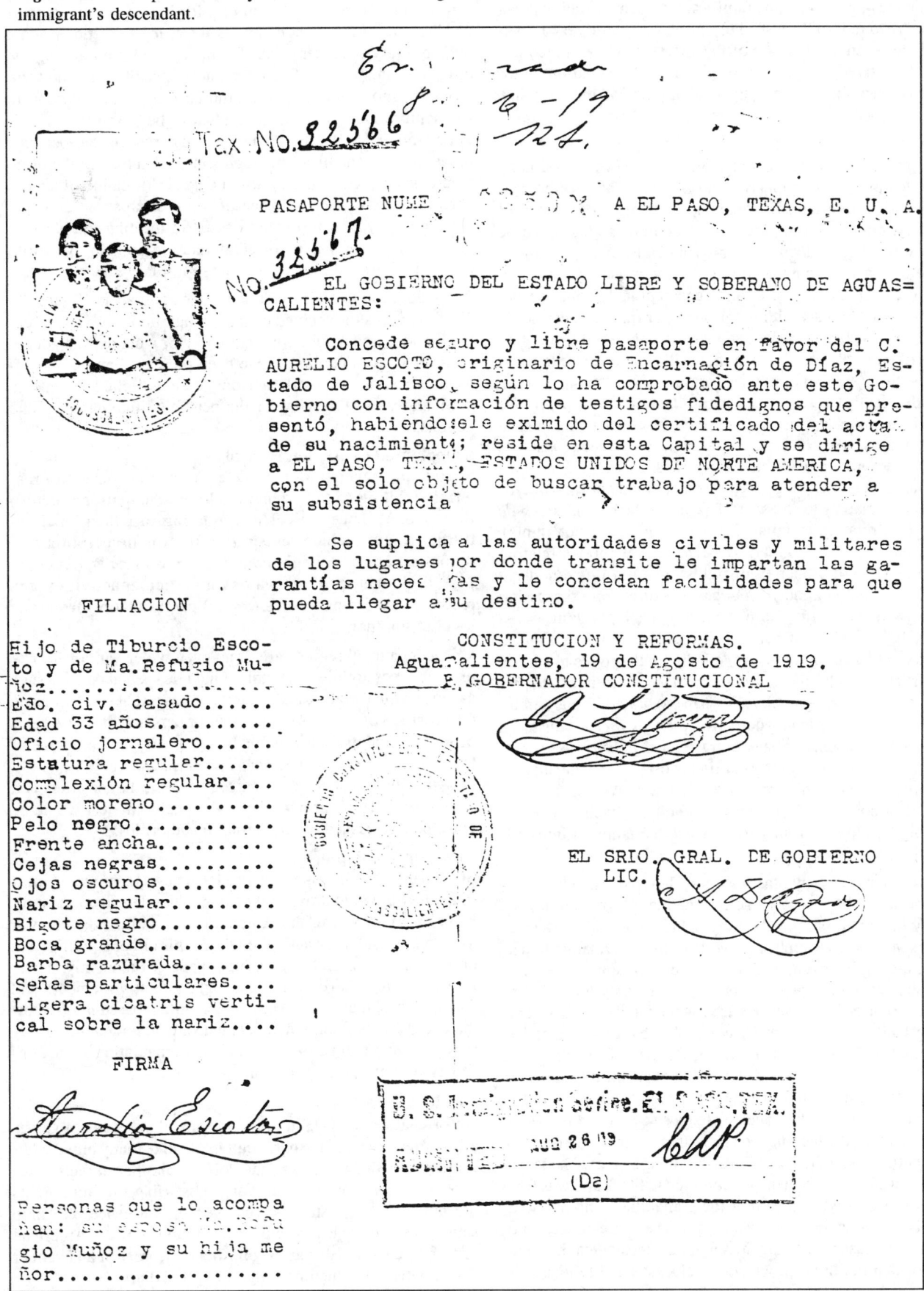

Tax No. 22566

PASAPORTE NUM.   A EL PASO, TEXAS, E. U. A.

No. 32567

EL GOBIERNO DEL ESTADO LIBRE Y SOBERANO DE AGUAS= CALIENTES:

Concede seguro y libre pasaporte en favor del C. AURELIO ESCOTO, originario de Encarnación de Díaz, Estado de Jalisco, según lo ha comprobado ante este Gobierno con información de testigos fidedignos que presentó, habiéndosele eximido del certificado del acta de su nacimiento; reside en esta Capital y se dirige a EL PASO, TEX., ESTADOS UNIDOS DE NORTE AMERICA, con el solo objeto de buscar trabajo para atender a su subsistencia

Se suplica a las autoridades civiles y militares de los lugares por donde transite le impartan las garantías necesarias y le concedan facilidades para que pueda llegar a su destino.

CONSTITUCION Y REFORMAS.
Aguascalientes, 19 de Agosto de 1919.
EL GOBERNADOR CONSTITUCIONAL

EL SRIO. GRAL. DE GOBIERNO
LIC.

FILIACION

Hijo de Tiburcio Escoto y de Ma. Refugio Muñoz........
Edo. civ. casado......
Edad 33 años..........
Oficio jornalero.......
Estatura regular......
Complexión regular....
Color moreno..........
Pelo negro............
Frente ancha..........
Cejas negras..........
Ojos oscuros..........
Nariz regular.........
Bigote negro..........
Boca grande...........
Barba razurada........
Señas particulares....
Ligera cicatris vertical sobre la nariz....

FIRMA

U. S. Immigration Office. EL PASO, TEX.
ADMITTED   AUG 26 '19
(Da)

Personas que lo acompañan: su esposa Ma. Refugio Muñoz y su hija menor..................

tation is less likely, although some records relating to immigration may be found in the family sources. Immigration documents, if found, will most likely provide certain very important facts, such as the name of the ancestor as it was recorded when he arrived, the place of origin or port of departure in the home country, and, perhaps, the date of birth and the town and/or province of birth.

Legal Papers

Legal papers encompass a wide variety of records that usually relate to financial or property transactions. They were originally written to establish ownership or transfer ownership of property, both real and personal, or contract rights. Because they were official documents proving right of ownership to specific property or contract rights, they were usually very carefully preserved, even for several generations beyond the period of actual contact with the property or rights. These documents can usually be recognized and distinguished from other kinds of papers by the fact that they will have been written and witnessed by a notary and/or carry an official stamp or seal. Included in this category are *capitulaciones matrimoniales* (marriage contracts), *actos de cesion* (cession acts, relating to the relinquishment of a particular right or power), *actos de cambio* (acts relating to a change or transfer), *actos de compra* (the papers relating to the purchase of a property or right), *actos de venta* (relating to the sale of property or right), *actos de donacion* (relating to gifts of property or powers or rights), *testamentos* (wills), *cuadernos particionales* (books relating to the division of properties or rights), *contratos de alquileres* (lease or rental contracts), *derechos de sucesión* (succession rights), *inventarios* (inventories, usually relating to some transfer, sale, or devise of property or rights), *declaración de herederos* (declaration of heirs, relating to the rights to certain properties given by the courts to the heirs of an intestate person), and *tutorias* (guardianship papers). In addition, similar papers of a less official nature would be *extractos bancarios* (financial statements or bank extracts) and *polizas de seguros* (insurance policies). For the family historian, these documents can provide much information about the activities, interests, and social position of the ancestral family, as well as perhaps the only link to the locality from which the family originated.

Letters

Perhaps more than any other category, letters written by members of the family can provide fascinating information for the family historian. Frequently, biographical notes about the activities of a family member, as well as opinions relating to personal, family, local, and national events, will appear in letters. For the genealogist, such letters may be the only link with the mother country. Such was the case for one family that had come to the United States from Uruguay. A great-grandfather had remained in Spain and had written a series of letters over a twenty-five-year period to a son in Uruguay. Sixty years later, as the great-granddaughter began her search for her family's origin in Spain, the only clues were those contained in the letters. In addition to naming localities, the letters gave important information about the activities of family members. The last of the letters was written on paper bordered in black and was from a cousin; it related the death of the grandfather who had written all of the previous correspondence. The entire collection of letters is a treasure of family history and genealogical information for that family; it provided the clues needed to locate the parish of origin in Spain.

Military Records and Decorations

Since compulsory military conscription has been a regular part of Hispanic life in most countries for at least a century and a half, military documents can frequently be found among the effects of an ancestor. Such documents usually take the form of papers showing release from military service, as these were frequently required for an individual to be permitted to emigrate (figure 16-2). The document may indicate the person's name, the rank attained, the regiment served in, and the place where he enlisted, and may also include information of a more personal nature, such as place of birth, occupation, and age. Not only may this information assist in locating the place of origin, but it can also be of great value in knowing where to look for additional records relating to military service.

In addition to enlistment and discharge papers (figure 16-3), if the ancestor received certain recognition, such as promotions or decorations for combat service or wounds, such documents will most certainly have been preserved among his effects. These may provide not only research clues but also a particularly exciting view of the person's life, character, and actions.

School and Occupation Records

School and occupation records cover a wide variety of materials relating to the educational and occupational activities of one's ancestors. Those relating to educational activities might include registration information from a particular school or college (*colegio o universidad*), exam papers, diplomas or titles, awards for particular activities, and records concerning grades (*notas*) or graduation from one level to another.

Occupational records are of an even wider variety. To cite just a few possibilities, they might include special permits such as those which were issued to street vendors, bakers, and many other classes of workers in the cities, or personal business cards or advertisements such as might be sent out by a tailor, or membership documents for the *gremios* or *sindicatos* (unions, guilds, or syndicates) that were organized in some larger cities and among some rural farm workers. Of special interest would be work permits issued by immigration authorities.

Newspaper Clippings

In the native country, mention in a local newspaper would most likely be limited to those of the upper class. However, an individual who arrived in the Americas may well have achieved local status, and information relating to his or her activities and origins may be found in local newspapers. Frequently, newspaper clippings have been preserved by family members and friends. Since these would have been written based upon information given by family members who are no longer alive, they may provide a unique source of information relating to the family, its activities, and its origin.

Diaries

Unfortunately, the keeping of a personal diary was not generally characteristic of Hispanic culture. Unlike many nineteenth-century Americans who, at one point or another in their lives, kept some form of personal diary, most Hispanic immigrants did not. In some instances, however, the influence of Anglo society or a unique position as the founder of an American branch of the family or as the unofficial recorder of an event or trip may have led the immigrant to keep a diary.

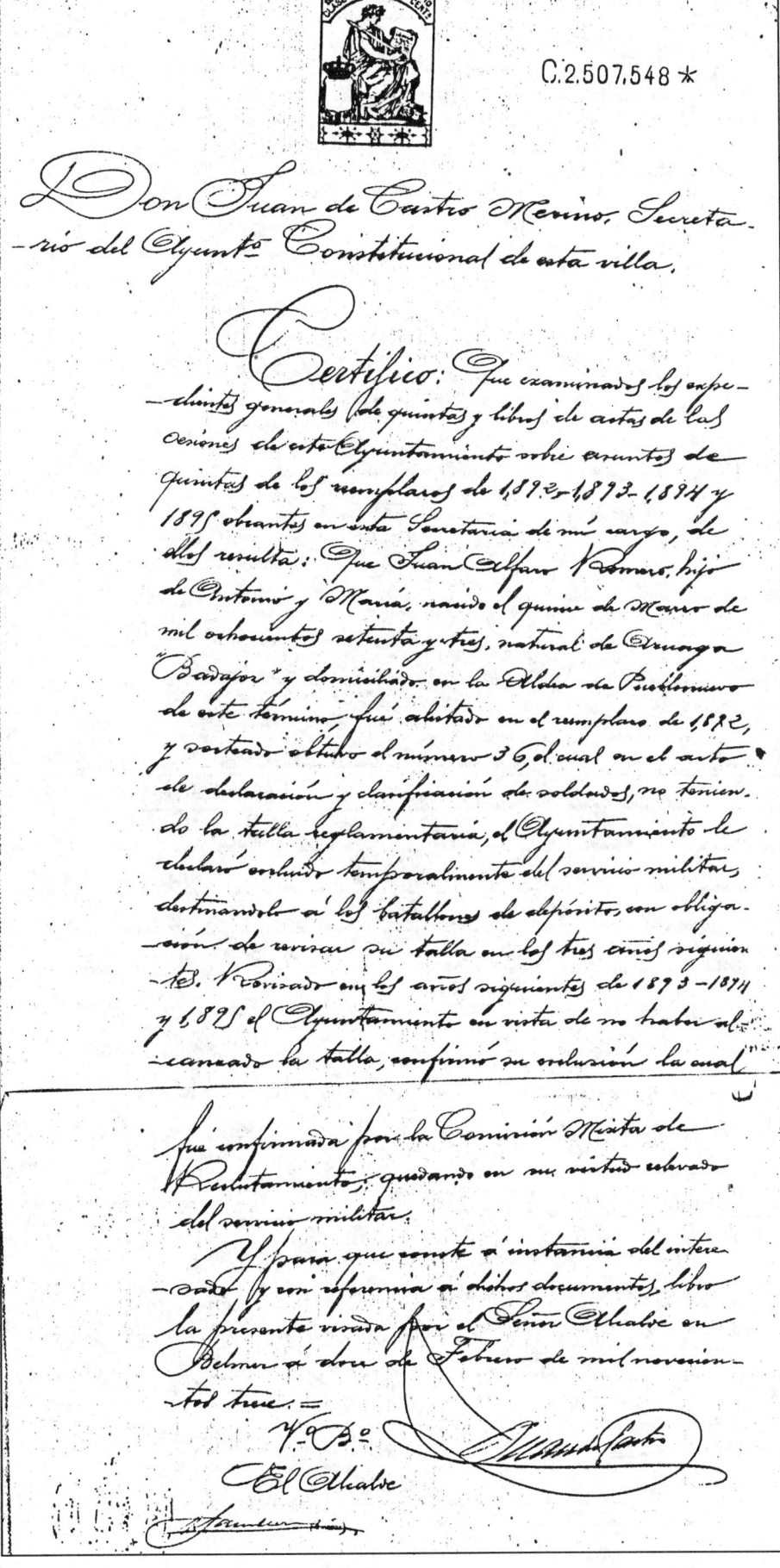

Figure 16-2. Certificate of fulfillment of military obligation by standing unsuccessfully for the draft in four consecutive years; issued by the municipal clerk of Belmez, Córdoba, Spain, in 1913 and found in the Massachusetts home of a descendant.

Figure 16-3. Military discharge issued at Córdoba, Spain, in 1892; found in the home of a descendant.

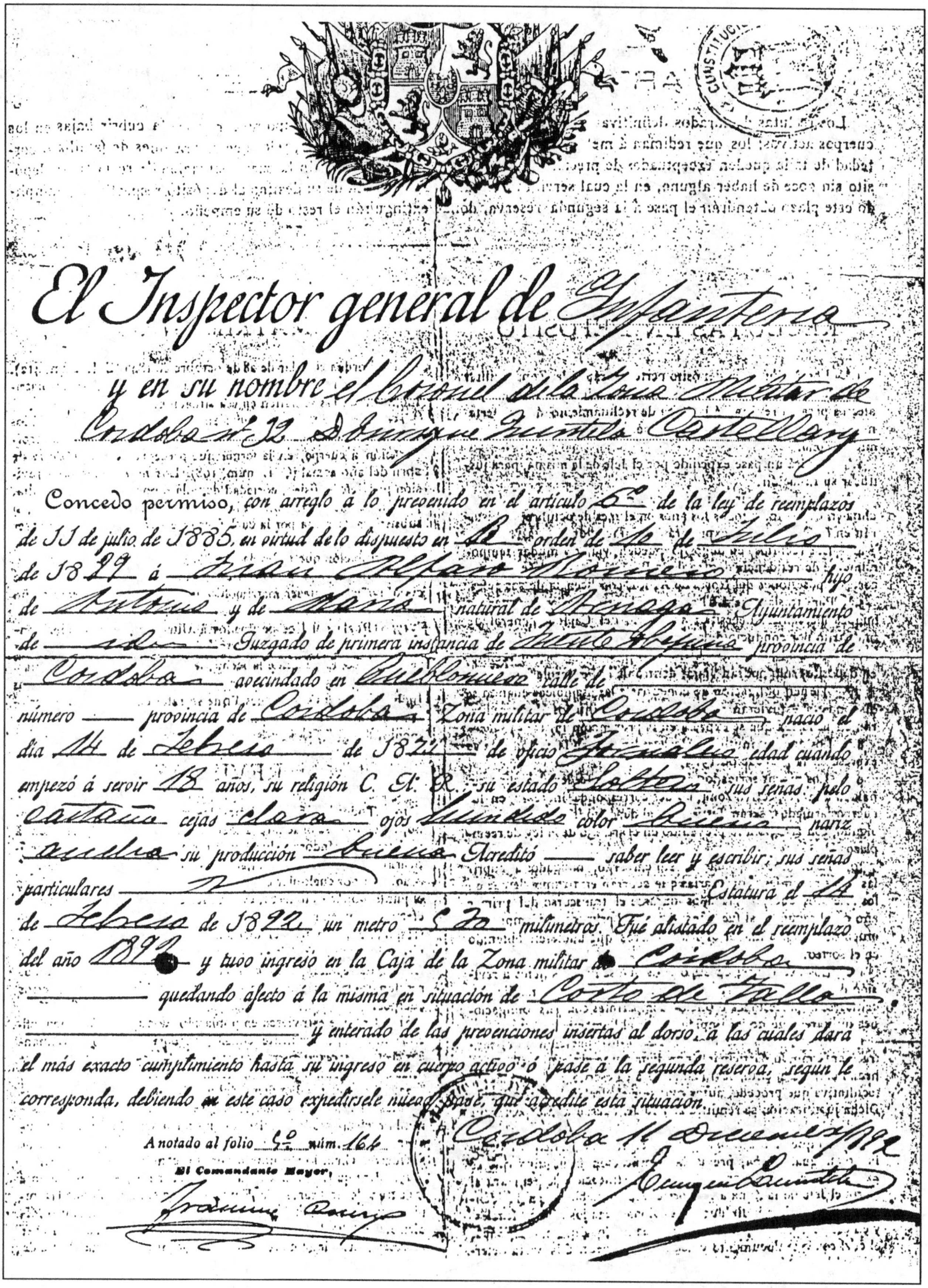

Documento Nacional de Identidad o Cedula Personal (National Identity Document or Personal Document)

In most Hispanic countries, beginning in the late nineteenth century or early twentieth century, laws were passed relating to the issuance of a personal document (*cedula personal*) which all citizens were required to carry. Locating such a document among the personal effects of an ancestor can be significant, because the point of issuance would probably be the civil register of the district in which the family resided at the time.

Memberships in Private Clubs, Civic or Nobility Organizations, and Political Parties

There appears to be inherent in the Spanish temperament—perhaps in that of everyone—a desire to belong to an organization, particularly elite organizations. A wide variety of organizations have been available to Spaniards at different points in history. Among those available to the noble families were the *ordenes militares* (military orders), *reales maestranzas* (royal riding clubs), and the *cofradias nobles* (noble fraternities). For the past century and a half, following the initial seizure of power by those of more liberal political orientation, other types of organizations appeared which were less restrictive about membership. Among these were Masonic orders, political parties, and debating clubs (*ateneos*) which appeared in most major cities. In addition, many local parishes had *cofradias* which were open to both nobles and commoners, although frequently on a hereditary basis. Membership, and especially offices held in any of the above organizations, may have been certified by a diploma, certificate, or other type of document which may be found in the collection of family sources within one's home. Such documents can be particularly significant, not only because they offer a glimpse of the active social life of an individual ancestor, but also because they can lead to more extensive records kept by such organizations. Records of this type are kept in such a wide variety of locations that the only reasonable clue to locating an individual's membership may be in finding some mention of it among home and family sources.

Honorary Distinctions

Honorary distinctions are usually limited to the upper classes in Spain. They include such distinctions as honorary doctorates or political awards issued by certification of the universities or cities which made the awards. Military decorations (mentioned above) could also be included in this category, as well as documents relating to particular literary, artistic, or scientific awards. Also noteworthy, although of a more concrete and less honorary nature, are certificates for the register of industrial and intellectual property. These are equivalents of patents or copyrights for literary, scientific, or artistic works.

Biographies or Autobiographies

Biographies are most commonly found in Hispanic cultures for the nobility or for people of political or artistic renown. However, the move to a new country and the resulting new position in society, as well as the distance from family origins in the mother country, may have prompted a Spanish immigrant or those around one to record information about his or her life or the lives of immediate ancestors.

Written Family Histories (Published and Unpublished)

Written family histories are much more common among the nobility of Hispanic countries than in the lower classes. However, as with biographies, immigration to another country may have spurred an individual to record his or her family origins in a family history. Because many of these were of interest only to the family, they will be found in manuscript form (not published).

Medical Records

Documents in this category will probably be found only for more recent ancestors. Medical record cards, x-rays, medical analyses, and dental and eyeglass prescriptions can all contribute to a knowledge of the ancestor and how he looked. Naturally, such information is most likely limited to the twentieth century due to the more extensive availability of doctors during this century.

CONTACT OTHER FAMILY MEMBERS

The second step in a preliminary survey, after a thorough search for home sources, is to check with other family members. There are two purposes in doing this. The first is to make a record of memories and feelings about the family and its ancestors. It is very likely that older family members, such as grandparents, great-aunts and uncles, or cousins from a different branch of the family, have memories that have not been passed on. Frequently, memories of other family members add new dimensions to knowledge of the lives and personalities of direct-line ancestors, and also may provide clues for finding the town of origin in the mother country.

The second purpose in making contact with other family members is to ask them to search in their homes for the same sources checked for in the researcher's home. Often, original documents from the immigrant ancestor will have passed through a different branch of the family and may not be in the hands of even immediate cousins.

Contact with other family members can be accomplished in three different ways: by questionnaire, through a personal letter, or by a personal visit. The questionnaire is basically a form letter with a series of questions relating to the family, such as: "Do you remember your grandfather, Juan Garcia? Do you have any idea where he came from in Mexico? Do you have or know someone who has any old documents relating to Juan Garcia? What memories do you have of your parents talking about Juan Garcia? Would you be interested in learning more about Juan Garcia and your other Mexican ancestors?" A space can be left for short answers at the end of each of the questions on the questionnaire.

The questionnaire is the least desirable approach in contacting other family members, since it is the least personal and less likely to get an interested response from a relative. This survey approach can best be used to reach a large number of relatives and identify those who have documents or are interested in developing a history of the family.

A second and better approach is to write a personal letter to each of the relatives. This letter could include many of the same questions as the questionnaire and should follow the basic principles of writing letters to relatives outlined in chapter 1, The Foundations of Family History Research. Ideally, the letter would be an initial contact that could be followed up by a personal visit with those who show interest.

The most effective form of contacting family members is a personal visit. Through contact with other family members, you will collect a variety of material for use in compiling an interesting and human family history. Some of the most fascinating material will be family traditions gathered through oral interviews. Exercise caution, though, in relying on family traditions, such as descent from royalty or the ancestor who "accompanied Cortez in the conquest of Mexico." Frequently, the natural desire to improve upon the prestige of the family will cause many traditions, while based on fact, to be exaggerated. Family traditions may help to locate a place of origin in the mother country or even pinpoint the original family home, or in other ways further the genealogical search, but all such family traditions should be verified by documentation before they are accepted as true.

CHECK GENEALOGICAL RECORDS AND INDEXES OF THE LDS CHURCH FOR RESEARCH PREVIOUSLY DONE ON THE FAMILY

After a thorough search of sources available within one's own family has been completed, the researcher should evaluate, as the third step of the preliminary survey, what others have done while tracing family histories and genealogies which could tie in directly with the family. In working with sources outside the family, most family history researchers first check the indexes and records gathered and prepared by the LDS church. Two of these indexes and record sources are of specific interest to the Hispanic researcher: the International Genealogical Index and the Ancestral File.

The International Genealogical Index (IGI) is an index of genealogical data from a wide variety of records, though primarily from vital records, wills, and censuses, from more than ninety countries. The IGI includes individual events, such as birth, christening, marriage, or appearance on a census. These entries are arranged by country (for Mexico and the United States, by state) and then alphabetically, first by surname and then by given name. Cross-indexing allows for a variety of pronunciations and spellings of names. Entries are not linked from one generation to another, nor are there connections between entries for a person's birth and later marriage or appearance as the parent of a child.

The IGI has been printed and published on microfiche and on CD-ROM for distribution to the family history centers found in LDS churches throughout the world. Any researcher can search the IGI at these locations without charge.

The Ancestral File contains millions of names submitted since 1978 to the LDS church specifically to be included in this computer file. Unlike the IGI, which identifies individual events such as birth and marriage without attempting to link even the events of a single persons's life together, this computerized file links families and generations. A search is made for a specific name. All persons in the index by the requested name are then listed on the computer screen. From this point it is possible to request detailed information on any individual listed, a family group record and ancestral and/or descendant charts for that person.

Unfortunately for the Hispanic researcher, the number of Hispanic references in the Ancestral File is limited. The primary source for this index is submissions by members of the LDS church of data about their ancestors during the last 150 years, although those who are not members of the church are encouraged to submit their genealogical research as well. As a growing number of people submit Hispanic ancestral lines, the significance of the Ancestral File for the Hispanic researcher

will increase. See chapter 2, Databases, Indexes, and Other Finding Aids, for more information on these two sources.

CHECK FOR PRINTED FAMILY HISTORIES AND BIOGRAPHIES

The fourth and last step in the preliminary survey is to find out what printed genealogies or biographies are available on the family or family members. This step involves two separate kinds of searches: (1) searching for family surnames and/or family members in biographical dictionaries and genealogical encyclopedias, and (2) searching for monograph histories of one's family or a collateral branch of it. The first of these can easily be accomplished nearly anywhere in the world. A wide variety of biographical and genealogical encyclopedias and dictionaries is available for Spanish surnames. Perhaps the most famous and extensive, published by Garcia-Carrafa in Madrid, is the *Enciclopedia Heraldica y Genealogica Hispano-Americana.* It was begun in 1920, and the last volume was published in 1963. There are currently eighty-eight volumes covering the letters *AA* through *URR.* The first two volumes of this series contain a study of the science of heraldry, and the remainder of the volumes contain an alphabetical list of noble and seminoble families from throughout Spain and her former American colonies. Brief accounts of the history of each family are arranged by surname and trace the family's most notable noble member. Most entries also include illustrations of coats of arms, and frequently there is a limited bibliography which can lead to more extended monographic family histories.

Although these are noble families, and while the nobility of Spain was very widespread, many families will never trace any of their family lines to Spanish nobility. The right to use the coats of arms associated with each of these surnames is limited to those who have direct ancestral ties with a family, and in many cases is limited to the direct male descendants of a family. Therefore, a person of a particular surname should not assume that the family coat of arms listed for that surname belongs to him or her.

A more modern approach is in Victor Herrero Mediavila and Lolita Rosa Aquayo Hayle, *Indice Biográfico de España, Portugal e Ibero-América,* 4 vols. (New York: K.G. Saur, 1990). This index identifies approximately 200,000 historically significant individuals from Roman times to the early twentieth century, compiled from 306 biographical encyclopedias, dictionaries, and collective works covering seven hundred original volumes published from the seventeenth to the early twentieth century from Spain, Portugal, and Latin America. Those works were copied and all of the references from all seven hundred volumes were separated and arranged in alphabetical order. That collection was then microfilmed on 1,070 microfiche and is available through the family history centers of the LDS church (microfiche sets 6002170-6002172).

Automated Archives, Inc., of Orem, Utah, has published on computer disks a set of 1,000 surname histories: Lyman D. Platt, *Spanish Surname Histories* (Orem, Utah: Automated Archives, 1984). These histories, with a heavy Spanish American emphasis, originally appeared in *Vista* magazine. Each provides a brief history of the surname, its etymology and a series of references to individuals of the surname who have been famous or found in Spanish American regional sources.

Almost every Hispanic country has national and regional

dictionaries and encyclopedias, which can often be of even greater value to the researcher because they include many families and surnames which are not noble in origin. Some of these, although by no means all, are listed in the chapter bibliography. Typical of one type of regional book from Spain is *El Solar Catalan, Valenciana y Balear* (San Sebastian, Spain: Garcia Carrafa, 1967), which follows the same pattern as the *Enciclopedea heraldica y genealogica Hispano-Americana,* referred to above, but is limited to families (once again primarily noble families) which come from a particular region or country, in this case from Cataluna, Valencia, and the Balearic Islands.

Another type of regional series is typified by Jaime de Querexeta, *Diccionario onamastico y heraldico basco.* This six-volume series lists, in alphabetical order, nearly all of the Basque names which can be found. While it does not give a family history for most of them, it indicates if the name is unique to a particular region and it may be useful in helping to locate the particular area which should be searched.

The second type of printed information that should be searched in completing the preliminary survey is articles and books that may have been published about the family, giving its history and usually including a list of living members of the family at the time of publication. Once again, these are found primarily for noble families and for families which have achieved some particular status in Spanish or Hispano-American society. Lyman D. Platt, *Latin American Family Histories* (Salt Lake City: Instituto Genealógico Histórico Latinoamericano, 1991), is the single best list of these. Others appear as articles in periodicals such as *Hidalguía* (Madrid, Spain) and *The Americas: A Journal of Latin American History.* The LDS Family History Library, as well as most large university and public libraries in the United States and Latin America, has significant numbers of monograph Hispanic family histories.

In summary, the preliminary survey brings together all that the researcher and his or her family know about the family and determines if anyone outside of the immediate or known family has done research on the family lines. At this point you can organize and evaluate the information from all of these sources to determine objectives and begin doing substantial research in original records to trace the family lines back into the country of origin.

CATHOLIC CHURCH RECORDS

The records of the Roman Catholic church represent the single best Spanish-language source for finding the family's place of origin. Most important are those found in the local parish. Parish records, which contain a rich collection of materials of interest to the family and local historian, can be divided into two major categories—sacramental records and non-sacramental records. Sacramental records are baptisms, marriages, death or burial records, and confirmations. Non-sacramental records include fraternal order books, account books, censuses, individual documents, and local history materials.

Sacramental records in Hispanic Catholic parishes are generally divided between three books or sets of books: one for baptisms, another for marriages, and a third for deaths. Frequently, confirmations are also recorded in the baptismal books, although, during some periods, and especially in larger parishes, a separate book for confirmations may have been maintained. Particularly valuable are marriage records, in which the place of origin is frequently given for the bride and groom and/or their parents. The marriage entries from Catholic parish records in Florence, Arizona (1886) (figure 16-4), and in Hidalgo del Parral, Chihuahua, Mexico (1759) (figure 16-5), and a printed page of extracts of marriages from the Saint Louis Cathedral, New Orleans, Louisiana (1786) (figure 16-6), are examples of marriage records that identify the place of origin of the bride and/or the groom as Mexico or Spain. Even in the United States, many Catholic parishes in Spanish-speaking areas continued to maintain parish records in Spanish well into the twentieth century. Always check for these records in their original form; extracts often omit the very details about place of origin that the researcher seeks.

Before a marriage, the standard procedure was for the parties involved to file a marriage petition *(expediente matrimonial, información matrimonial, aplicación matrimonial)* with the parish priest. This petition would contain the proof of good standing in the Catholic church (usually the baptismal certificates of the bride and groom), written permission from the parents if the bride or groom was under twenty-one (though this age did vary), and the priest's permission for the marriage to take place. In addition, if the groom was from another parish, there would be a statement by the priest of his parish that the three admonitions had been read or posted there on three consecutive Sundays or holy days. If the father of the bride or groom, whose consent was normally required, was dead, then the death record or date of death of that father would also be included in the marriage petition. In many parishes, such petitions have been conserved and are of particular interest if the groom is from a parish other than the one in which the marriage took place, since the petition may even provide a copy of his baptismal certificate. In American parishes, if the groom was from Spain, statements from witnesses who could testify as to his good character and Catholic standing might substitute for the other documents. Often, these witnesses were immigrants like the groom or bride and knew one or more of them in the country of origin.

The marriage petition would also include any special dispensations required from a bishop or the pope for the marriage to take place. In addition to references to *dispensas de consanguinidad,* which were granted to permit marriages between relatives in the fourth degree of blood relationship, marriage entries may offer other interesting information about the bride and groom. If either the bride or the groom lived extensively outside the diocese in which the parish was located, there is usually mention of a special *dispensa,* or note from the bishopric authorizing the marriage. All such information should be noted as the parish research is done because it may provide clues for further research in the diocesan archives.

U.S. PASSENGER LISTS AND BORDER CROSSING RECORDS

The best records for identifying the place of origin of the immigrant ancestor, aside from naturalization and citizenship records, are the passenger lists. A passenger list is a list of individuals who arrived at or left a port on a ship. It was generally created by the captain of the ship and submitted to the port authorities upon arrival or before sailing. Such lists usually

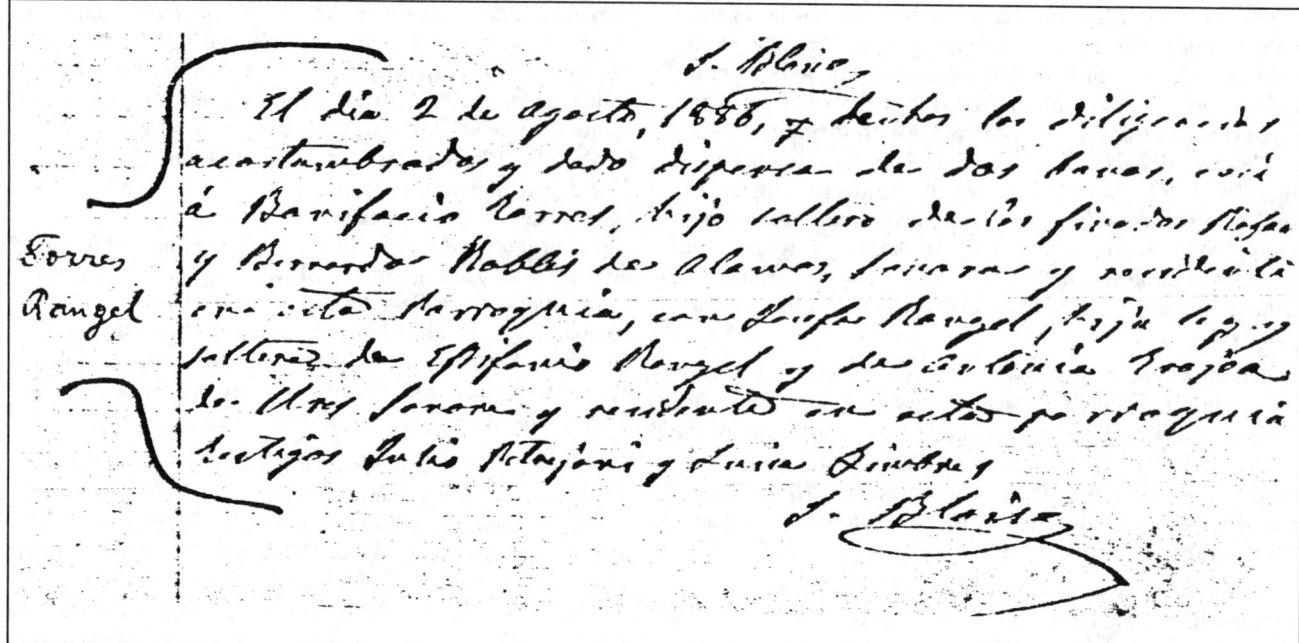

Figure 16-4. Marriage entry, 2 August 1886, from records of the Roman Catholic parish of The Assumption of the Blessed Virgin Mary, Florence, Arizona.

contain at least the name of the head of the family and the number of individuals in the family, but some list all passengers individually, the port of embarkation in Europe, or the destination, and their places of origin. Obviously, if the last is given, a good part of the work of identifying the place of origin is complete. If, for arrival lists, only the port of embarkation is given, it may then be necessary to check records in the place of embarkation, such as port records (where available) or municipal census records for the port city, as the family may have lived there for a period of time before their voyage.

Few passenger lists created before 1820 exist in the United States. However, extensive post-1820 passenger and shipping records have been preserved. Most of these are now on file at the National Archives in Washington, D.C. Those for the ports of Boston, New York, Philadelphia, Baltimore, and New Orleans, for the period 1819 to 1976, are available on microfilm through the LDS church's Family History Library. Other ports of particular interest for the Hispanic are those in Florida, Texas, and California. Chapter 2 of the *Guide to Genealogical Research in the National Archives* (Washington, D.C.: National Archives Trust Fund Board, 1983) contains an excellent discussion of U.S. passenger lists and their availability on a port-by-port basis. *Index of Spanish Citizens Entering the Port of New Orleans Between January, 1840 and December, 1865* (New Orleans: Charles Mudrell, n.d.), and its companion volume, which covers the period 1819 to 1839, provide an index of all persons with Spanish surnames who passed through the port of New Orleans during this period.

The border between the United States and Mexico was open, with few customs restrictions, until the early part of the twentieth century, so there are few records available for Mexican border immigration into the southwestern United States during that period. For the period from 1903 to 1953, approximately 1,500,000 individual records from the Immigration and Naturalization Service office in El Paso, Texas, are available on

microfilm from the National Archives. They are for non-U.S. citizens who were granted legal border-crossing privileges along the border with Mexico from California to Texas. There are also records of U.S. citizens living in Mexico.

MAJOR SPANISH COLONIAL RECORDS

Sometimes, searching the records of the American country to which the ancestor immigrated will not yield the place of origin. This is particularly true if the immigrant ancestor arrived during the colonial period (1492–1821), for which there may be no records preserved in America that could indicate the place of origin in Spain. Only when you have exhausted all possible sources in the new country, or when a Latin American or U.S. source has provided a clue as to a specific type of record in Spain that should be searched, should you search in Spanish archives.

Records relating to specific individuals and families who resided in the Americas can be found throughout the archives of Spain. When all possible American sources have been exhausted, check all potential Spanish archival sources for information to connect ancestors with a specific parish in Spain. In spite of the wide variety of archives that contain such material, the vast majority of documents relating to the Spanish colonies and colonial governments are to be found in only three archives: the Archivo General de las Indias in Seville, the Archivo Historico Nacional in Madrid, and the Archivo de Simancas in the province of Valladolid.

The Spanish colonies were divided politically into fourteen regions called *audiencias:* the thirteen *audiencias* of Latin America and that of the Philippines. Those in existence in 1800 were the following:[1]

1. Buenos Aires
2. Cuba
3. Chile
4. Philippines

Figure 16-5. Marriage entry, 22 de Julio 1759, Parroquia de San Jose, Hidalgo del Parral, Chihuahua, Mexico. FHL 0162556.

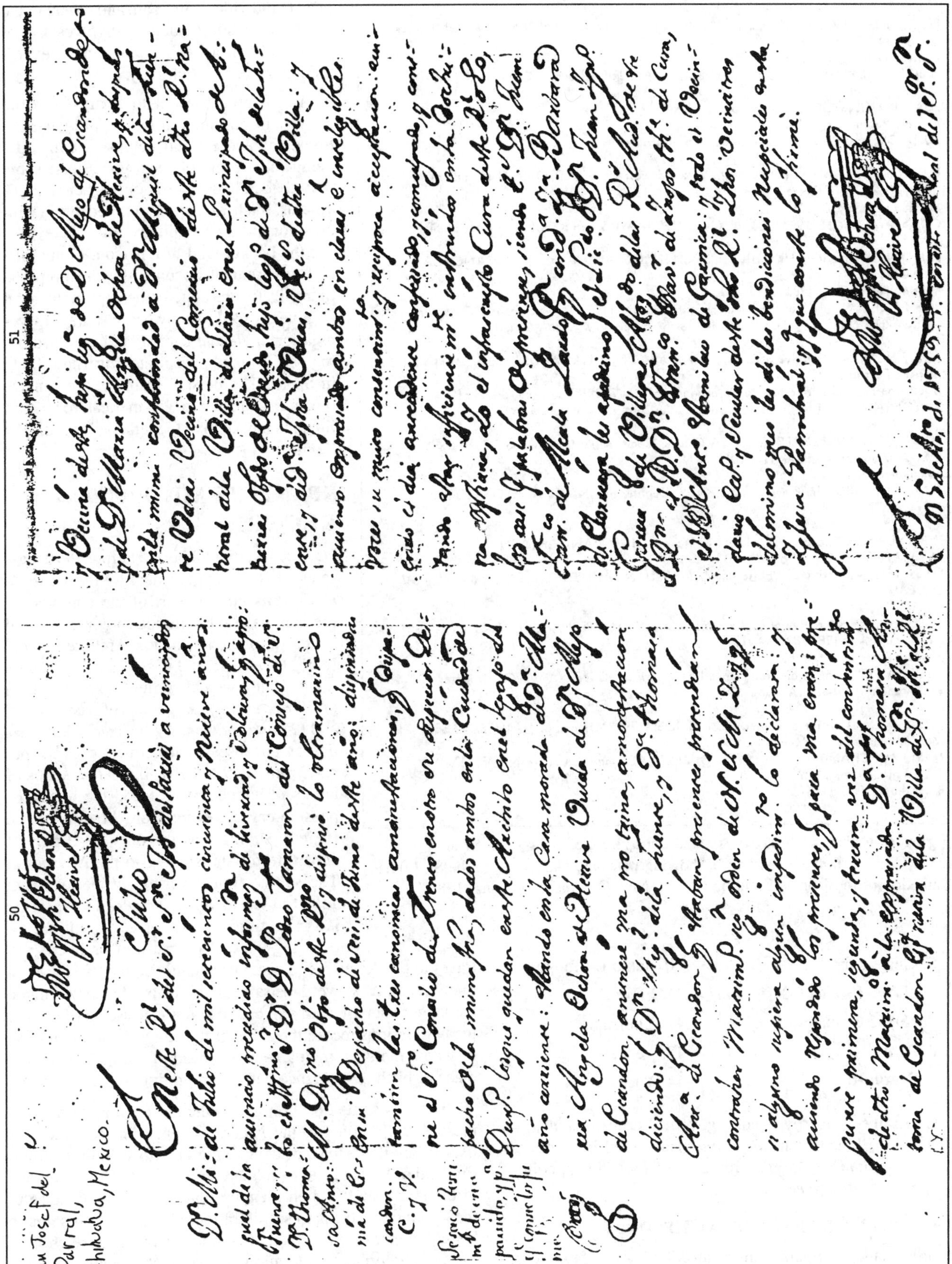

```
                           PAGE 46

PEDRO JOSEF MONTANER native of Palma in Mallorca son of SEBASTIAN MONTANER
and of MAGDALENA PERYA
Married February 5, 1786
FELICITE DURIEAU daughter of JUAN BAUTISTA DURIEAU and of CATARINA DAVID.

JUAN BAUTISTA CONET native of . . . . . . . .
Married February 6, 1786
JULIA ORET native of . . . . . . . . (record deteriorated)

PEDRO JOSEF LAMBERT native of the Arkansas Post son of PEDRO LAMBERT and of
CATARINA LANDRONY
Married February 7, 1786
CONSTANZA WILS daughter of JUAN BAUTISTA WILS and of SUSANA LANGLISE.

LUIS ANDRAVY native Marseille son of SANTIAGO ANDRAVY and of FRANCISCA
LAMBERTE
Married February 9, 1786
JOSEFA OSTEN native of the Imperial States daughter of JUAN LUIS DAUTEN and of
MARGARITA BENEVEL, she was married to the deceased Mr. BLAIGNAT.

JOSEF FERNANDES native of Lucena son of ANTONIO FERNANDES and of MARIA NIETO
Married February 19, 1786
MARIA de PRESAS native this Parish daughter of GREGORIO de PRESAS and of MARIA
ANTONIA native of Santiago de Meangos, Jurisdiction of Betanses in Galicia.

JUAN BAUTISTA BERNARD native St. Charles Coast of the Germans son of ANDRES
BERNARD and of MARGARITA AIDELAMAR
Married February 21, 1786
MARGARITA AIDELMAR native same Parish daughter of ANDRES AIDELEMAR and of
MARGARITA ALBERT.

HUGO DANIEL CREPS son of HUGO CREPS and of MARIANA CHOVIN
Married February 21, 1786
LUISA LEFLEAU native of Mobile daughter of JUAN BAUTISTA LEFLEAU and of MARIANA
LEFLEAU.

JOSEF de la PENA native of Cadiz, widow of MICAELA PERES, son of ANDRES de la PENA
and of MARIA ESTEFANIA BRAVO
Married February 22, 1786
ROSALIA VIERA native of Grand Canaries, widow of JOSEF NAVARRO, daughter of JUAN
VIERA and of DOMINGA ROMERO.

JOSEF TRICAUT native of Bordeaux son of JOSEF TRICAUT and of MARIA BARGUERY
Married March 26, 1786
MARIA MARCHAND daughter of PEDRO MARCHAND and of CATARINA BERNARD.
Groom died February 29, 1834
Bride died July 29, 1842

                               16
```

Figure 16-6. Page 46 from *Louisiana Marriages: I,* edited by Alice Daly Forsyth (New Orleans: Polyanthos, 1977), showing marriage extracts from the St. Louis Cathedral of the Roman Catholic church, New Orleans, Louisiana, 1786.

5. Guatemala

6. Nueva España (Mexico)

7. Nueva Granada

8. Peru

9. Puerto Rico

10. Santo Domingo

11. Florida

12. Louisiana

13. Venezuela

14. Yucatan

Generally, a viceroy (*virrey*) governed each *audiencia* on behalf of the king. Each *audiencia* also served in a military role as a *capitania general,* with the viceroy or his appointee serving as *capitan general.*

LOCATING SPANISH COLONIAL RECORDS

Records relating to Spain's American colonies are of two types: (1) purely local records that were sent to Spain for various administrative purposes and (2) records involving transactions between Spain and her colonies or between private individuals in Spain and others in the colonies. This last category involves a wide variety of transactions: commercial, governmental, travel, and military.

Local records sent to Spain from the American colonies are extremely varied. Some involve explicit details of daily life, being the reports of local governors; some include detailed records on particular individuals, such as those compiled by the Inquisition and by the military orders in reviewing the background of a person. Many official government documents were prepared in triplicate, one copy being kept in the local archives, a second copy being sent to a viceregal or *audiencia* capital, and the third being sent to the appropriate governing body in Spain. The most valuable and extensive repository of such local American records in Spain is the Archivo General de las Indias in Seville.

SPANISH EMIGRATION RECORDS

During the colonial period before 1790, passenger lists were generated by the *Casa de la Contratación* as part of the commercial regulations of the American colonies. Found in the third section of the Archives of the Indies in Seville, the passenger lists can be divided into two categories: (1) *listas* (lists) or *libros de pasajeros* (books of passengers); and (2) *informaciones y licencias* (information and licenses). The former cover the period from 1509 to 1701; they are a series of books in which are recorded the names of passengers traveling from Seville to the Indies. (Seville was the only legal port of departure for ships going to the Americas.) The sub-section covering the period from 1534 to 1790 for *informaciones* and *licencias* is a collection of loose copies of petitions requesting special permission or license to travel to the Americas to settle or conduct certain business; in many cases, these were the same individuals who appear in the passenger lists. In nearly all cases, both the passenger lists and the permissions record the name of the emigrant or, in the case of whole families, the name of the head of the family and his place of birth or residence before emigrating to the Americas.

There is some question as to whether even a majority of those actually going to the Americas appear in the passenger lists at Seville. It was, of course, possible to travel by ship to England or France, and from there to go to the colonies on one of the many ships which illegally transported merchandise to them (contrary to Spain's prohibition of non-Spanish ships in her colonies). It is also likely that many captains were willing, for an appropriate fee, to allow a passenger to embark for the colonies without prior legal approval. Recording was even less complete beginning in the last half of the eighteenth century, following a policy of liberalization which allowed commerce between the colonies and the ports of Seville, Alicante, Malaga, Cartagena, Barcelona, and La Coruna. After 1778, even more liberal policies that allowed trade with any ports in Spain and with many of the non-Spanish ports of Europe and the Americas contributed further to the lack of records. Peter Boyd-Bowman, in the introduction to *Indice biogeografico de cuarenta mil Pobladores espanoles de America en el Siglo XVI* (Bogota: Instituto Caro y Cuervo, 1964), expresses a belief that passenger lists reflect only about twenty percent of those who actually went to the Americas during at least the first sixty-year period. Others put the number as high as eighty percent. No matter which estimate is correct, there are two important things to remember: (1) the passenger lists at Seville are extremely valuable because, for those names that do appear, they are a key to finding a specific locality of origin in Spain; (2) if the immigrant ancestor does not appear, it does not mean that he or she did not emigrate during that time period but merely is an indication that he or she may have been among that percentage of individuals who did not follow the procedures to obtain official approval for immigration to the Americas. (Note that the rich as well as the poor evaded such restrictions for a variety of reasons; failure to follow official procedures is no indication as to the character or financial state of the person involved.)

The staff of the Archives of the Indies at Seville have been developing an index to the entire section of passenger lists, including both the *listas y libros de pasajeros* and the *informaciones y licencias*. Seven volumes of the Catalogo de pasajeros a Indias are now available in printed form. They cover the years 1509 to 1599 (and 1600 to 1607 via the Internet). The entries are arranged by date, with an alphabetical index by surname in the back of the volume. Each entry contains the name of the individual, parents' names (when known), and residence or place of birth in Spain (figure 16-7). This work is further supplemented by Peter Boyd-Bowman, *Indice geobiografico de 56 mil pobladores de America*, 2 vols. (Mexico: Fondo de Cultura Economica, 1985). These two volumes cover the period from 1493 to 1539, which includes nearly all of the 15,000 entries in the first two volumes of the Catalogo de pasajeros a India and, in addition, draws extensively from archives throughout Spain and the Americas to arrive at the 56,000 individuals contained in the index. For the period from 1600 until 1790, the archive's staff have been compiling a massive card index of all of the individuals who appear in the archive's passenger list section.

For the nineteenth century (unlike for the period before 1790), there are no passenger lists available in a single major archive. During the first years following the end of the colonial period there was little emigration from Spain. However, as the political and social situation stabilized in the former colonies, in Spain the pressure of population increase, agricultural limitations, political unrest, mandatory military service (begin-

ning in 1835), and civil war resulted in increased emigration, so that by 1840 governors of the coastal provinces in northern Spain and, by 1853, the national government, were sufficiently concerned that regulations controlling emigration were issued. The required documentation, which varied from one province to another and over time, included:

1. Provincial passport.

2. *Fianza* (bond).

3. Statement from the *alcalde* (local mayor) or corresponding local official as to the person's good conduct and legitimate reasons to travel and that there are no outstanding obligations, financial or military.

4. *La obligación de paga de reales* (contract for payment of passage).

5. *Licencia de los padres o de esposo* (permission of parents or spouse).

6. *Contrata de embarque* (boarding contract).

The challenge to the researcher is in locating these documents. Provincial passport registers are found in the provincial

---

Farfán y de Luisa de Marmolejo, a Nueva España.—24 de abril.

I - 492 v.°

4253. DIEGO BECERRA, natural de Sevilla, hijo de Diego Becerra y de Isabel Tomé, con su mujer Ana de Guido, natural de Sevilla, hija de Martín Sánchez y de Ana de Guido, y con sus hijos Diego, Isabel y María, a Nueva España, como chapinero.—24 de abril.

I - 492 v.°

4254. CATALINA DE HUERTA, natural de Segovia, hija de Alonso de la Huerta y de Isabel del Castillo, a Nueva España, donde está su marido Diego Muñoz de Montoro, llevando consigo a Catalina Muñoz, su hija.—26 de abril.

I - 492 v.°

4255. ANTON PEREZ, natural de Puertollano, soltero, hijo de Juan Pérez y de Leonor Muñoz, a Nueva España.—26 de abril.

I - 492 v.°

4256. DOÑA LEONOR SERON, natural de Sevilla, soltera, hija de Sebastián de Porras y de doña Leonor Serón, a Nicaragua, en compañia de Juan /Moreno/ Alvarez de Toledo, su primo.—27 de abril.

I - 492 v.°

4257. FRANCISCO RODRIGUEZ, natural de Cubillos, soltero, hijo de García Rodríguez y de Mayor Alvarez, a Nicaragua, como criado de Juan Moreno Alvarez de Toledo.—27 de abril.

I - 493

4258. JUAN MENDEZ, natural de Segovia, soltero, hijo de Diego Méndez y de Agueda de Espinosa, a Nicaragua, como criado de Juan Moreno Alvarez de Toledo.—27 de abril.

I - 493

4259. MARIA DE OTALORA, natural de Segovia, hija de Juan

616

Figure 16-7. Page 616 of vol. 5 of *Catálogo de pasajeros a Indias durante los Siglos XVI, XVII, y XVIII,* compiled by Luis Romera Iruela and Maria del Carmen Galbis Diez (Madrid, Spain: Ministerio de Cultura, 1980), showing extracts from April 1577.

otorgó y firmó siendo testigos D. Ramon Gonzz. Orbon D. Jose Blanco y D. Antonio Garcia de esta vecindad. Conozco la otorgante y de haber pasado asi yo Escno. doy fe =

Dolores Vazquez de Sobrado
to. Ramon Gonzz. Orbon
to. Antonio Garcia
Antemi Simon de Barañano
Libre la primera copia dho. dia
en dos hojas del sello tercero doy fé =
    Barañano»

Archivo Histórico Provincial de Oviedo, *Protocolos de Avilés*, cja 728, año 1859, fols. 196-197.

DOC. 6.

Contrata de los pasajeros del bergantín *Rápido* para viaje a La Habana.

«En Aviles a veinte y nueve de Noviembre de mil ochocientos cincuenta y nueve, antemi Escribano de su numero y testigos, presentes Don Tomas de Alvaré y Don Luis Folgueras vecinos y del comercio de esta villa dijeron: Que por Real orden de seis de Agosto ultimo dirigida por el Ministerior de la Gobernacion y comunicada por el Gobierno Civil de la Provincia al Alcalde de esta villa en diez y siete del mismo, se les dispensó el deposito pecuniario prevenido por Real orden de treinta y uno de Diciembre de mil ochocientos cincuenta y siete en la presente espedicion a la Ysla de Cuba con pasagente de sobrecarga en el Bergantin Rapido de su propiedad, con solo la obligacion de prestar en su equivalencia fianza a satisfaccion del mismo Gobierno de esta Provincia suficiente a responder de las reclamaciones que puedan hacer los pasageros por la falta de cumplimiento de sus contratos. En su consequencia como tales dueños y armadores de dicho buque, su Capitan Don Bernardino Fernandez Muñiz, declaran ambos: que tienen contratados doce pasageros de camara, veinte cuatro de antecamara, ciento cinquenta (y nueve) de sollado, total ciento ochenta y seis de conduccion a la citada Ysla de Cuba en el mencionado Bergantin a cuya carrera le tienen destinado su porte ciento ochenta y seis toneladas y cinco centimos segun las dimensiones del mismo Buque, al precio los siete primeros al contado de cin-

cuenta y cinco pesos fuertes, y los cinco a plazo de año, de cincuenta y ocho idem: de los segundos al contado nueve a cuarenta duros; y los otros quince de plazo de año a cuarenta y dos idem: Y de los terceros treinta y uno al contado a veinte y ocho pesos fuertes, y los ciento diez y nueve a plazo de año a treinta duros = Y para el esacto cumplimiento por su parte de lo que se previene especialmente en la Real orden de siete de Diciembre de mil ochocientos cincuenta y seis; por el tenor de la presente otorgan: Que desde luego se obligan bajo su responsavilidad y demas garantias que están acordadas, a cumplir estrictamente con lo prometido al tiempo del ajuste que han hecho con los indicados pasageros, dando a estos por los pertenecientes al trato y manutencion de los de sollado por la mañana aguardiente o café con su racion de galleta, y otras veces sopa; al medio dia un rancho abundante de carne y tocino con patatas, arroz, abichuela, o garbanzos, alternando estas especies, y por la noche el mismo rancho alternando con vacalao compuesto con las mismas menestras; y a los de camara y antecamara por la mañana cafe, chocolate o te a su eleccion o alternando; al medio dia un puchero abundante de carne, garbanzos, y demas con sus sopas de arroz y pasta variando un principio y algunos dias dos para los de camara, postres y vino, con mas a los de proa vino dos veces a la semana. A los mismos de camara y antecamara por la noche una menestra alternando con ensalada de legumbres de las especies para ellos mencionadas, un principio de vacalao o carne, y las mas veces dos de cualquiera de estas dos clases, con sus correspondientes postres de queso o frutas - y a unos y otros el pan abundante a la mañana, medio dia y noche acostumbrado en los Buques de esta clase de espediciones suficiente a cada uno y todo bien acondicionado y de buena calidad, bastante a su manutencion, lo mismo que el agua en cantidad tambien suficiente para el gasto diario de cada pasagero. Tambien responden de que sus contratas son unicamente de puro pasage por la espresada retribucion, sin que dichos pasageros esten sugetos ni vayan obligados a trabajar durante la navegacion personalmente por cuenta de los otorgantes ni de otra persona que de ellos dependa, estando en plena libertad tan pronto como lleguen a la referida Isla, y se proceda a su desembarque, para dedicarse a lo que tengan por conveniente haciendo uso de sus personas segun mejor le acomode; los cuales con espresion de sus concejos, nombres apellidos y Parroquias de sus vecindades, son los siguientes: = Camara al costado = Concejo de Castrillon = Don Bernardo Arias Garcia, vecino de la Parroquia de Pillarno = Sa-

Figure 16-8. Transcript of a boarding contract (*contrata de embarque*) reproduced from pages 180–182 of *El viaje de los emigrantes asturianos a América* by Juan Carlos de la Madrid Alvarez (Gijon, Spain: Biblioteca Historica Asturiana, 1989).

historical archive of the issuing province (usually the province of embarkation). It is likely that the statement of good conduct, the parents' permission, and possibly the bond will have been prepared and signed before the notary of the hometown. Unfortunately, this information is not of value in locating the place of origin. These documents, however, may be found among home sources.

The boarding contract, the passage payment contract, and sometimes the bond are likely to be found in the notarial records of the port city of embarkation. If that port has been identified, a search in its notarial records for the time period could provide these crucial documents. Unfortunately, these documents are not indexed or segregated from the other notarial documents, so a personal search among them would be necessary. See chapter 12 of Ryskamp, *Tracing Your Hispanic Heritage,* for a description of this process.

The *contrata de embarque* is in reality a full passenger list in many cases. A transcript of the initial three pages from one of these is reproduced in figure 16-8. Spanish historians' recent interest in these documents has resulted in the identification and indexing of two sets of these. They are published in the following books: Maria Pilar Pildain Salazar, *Ir A América: La emigracion Vasca a América (Guipúzcoa 1840–1870)*; and

Juan Carlos de la Madrid Alvarez, *El Viaje de los emigrantes Asturianos a América* (both cited earlier). Check the *Family History Library Catalog* and other library catalogs for similar books.

Although national passports only came into use around 1920 in Spain, passports have been in use for a much longer period in Latin America. In addition, in the nineteenth century, certain Spanish maritime provinces required passports, and these are recorded in the provincial historical archives. Unfortunately, there are no published indexes to these records, and generally there are no internal archive indexes. Figure 16-9 is a page from the register of provincial passports issued in Santander, Spain, in 1855.

GOVERNMENT SERVICE RECORDS

While the exact nature of government service records is as diverse as the government entities themselves, there are three primary types of records of interest to the family historian: *nombramientos or empleos, hojas de servicio* and *relaciones de meritos y servicios,* and *pensiones.*

NOMBRAMIENTOS OR EMPLEOS

Of special interest are those documents relating to the appoint-

las: Valentín Fernandez Casona, de Cornellana = Soto del Barco: Manuel Pulido, de la Corrada = Pravia: Bernardino Gonzalez Villazón, de Muros = Avilés: Juan Antonio Menendez, de Vidriero = Carreño: Celestino Muñiz y Perán, de Candás = Avilés: Manuel Diaz y Arias, de San Nicolás = Estos siete a cincuenta y cinco pesos = Camara a plazo = Gozón: José Segundo Solís, de Trasona = Castrillón: Eugenio Fernandez Espinosa, de Naveces = Aviles: Fernando Arias Carbajal, de San Nicolas = Cudillero: Rosa Fernandez Rozas, de Ballota = Ramona Alvarez, de idem = Estos cinco a plazo = Antecamara al contado = Concejo de Cudillero = Dn. Manuel Alvarez y Marinez, de Ballota = Ylario Diaz y Fernandez, de idem = Rita Miranda, de idem = Rosendo Arrojo Valdes, de idem = Avilés: Francisco Rodriguez Maribona, de Vidriero = Manuel Rodriguez y Fernandez, de idem = Antonio Gutierrez de idem, Jose de Bango, de Llaranes = Castrillon: José Gonzalez Carbajal, de Laspra = Estos nueve al contado = Antecamara a plazo = Castrillon: José Alvarez y Garcia, de Laspra = Agustín Fernandez Eres, de Naveces = Grado: Ramon Suarez, de Salcedo = Ramón Garcia, de idem = José Alvarez, de idem = Somiedo = Agustín Gabriel Garcia, de Saliencia = Corbera: José Maria Menendez y Fernandez, de Cancienes = Soto del Barco = Manuel Antonio Garcia, de Riveras = Aviles = Mr. Lasserre Francés, de San Nicolás = Ramon Menendez Ybarra, de idem = Corbera: José Ramon Suarez, de Trasona = Salas: Manuel Lopez, de Cornellana = Manuel Villademoro y Martinez, de Villazón = Rufino Garcia y Llana, de Cornellana = Pravia: José Cuerbo Vallín, de Forcines = Estos quince a plazo = Pasageros de sollado = Al contado = Concejo de Aviles D. Pedro de la Campa, de San Cristobal = Juan de la Campa, de Miranda = José Diaz y Lopez, de la Madalena = Angel Garcia Pola, de San Nicolas = Jose María del Valle, de idem = Victoriano Suarez, de Sabugo = Antonio de la Campa, de San Cristobal = José Garcia Alonso, de San Nicolas = Manuel Cuerbo y Leon, de idem = Castrillon: Santos Menendez y Gutierrez, de Laspra = Juan Alvarez de la Campa de Bayas = Celestino Fernandez Espinosa, de Santiago del Monte = Juan Suarez, de Bayas = José Gutierrez, de Santiago = Manuel Antonio Fernandez Lopez, de Villar = Gumersindo Rodriguez, de Santiago = José Feyto, de San Miguel = Jose Galan, de idem = Alejandro Fernandez, de idem = Manuel Garcia y Gonzalez, de Bayas = Antonio Alonso, de idem = José Solís y Lopez, de San Miguel = Agustin Fernandez Eres, de Naveces = José Gonzalez Orbón y Alvarez,

ment of government officials in the Americas. Because these records deal with specific places in the Americas and also a specific place in Spain, they can be very valuable in linking an immigrant ancestor with a place of origin in the mother country.

The *nombramientos* or *empleos* is an order or decree which names the person to a particular job or promotion. Such documents may provide the name of the person, date and place of birth, and parents' names, as well as whether or not he or she is married, and perhaps other personal information. If you are searching in the archives of Spain for government service records, check *Catalogo xx del Archivo General de Simancas, Titulos de Indias* (Valladolid, Spain: Patronato Nacional de Archivos Historicos, 1954). It indexes records from the *Seccion General del Tesoro* (General Treasury Section), which paid the colonial officials for their work. Although most who held government positions in the colonial period were of the nobility, there were also, in the colonial areas especially, many individuals who were not.

HOJAS DE SERVICIO AND RELACCIONES DE MERITOS Y SERVICIOS

These were formal documents prepared, and frequently printed, for individuals who were involved in the civil service. In many cases, several copies were filed with the appropriate authorities for use as they saw fit in petitions for promotion or other activities. In some cases, these are listed in published indexes. An example of this is Ramon Paz, *Indice de Relaciones de Méritos y Servicios Conservados en la Sección de Consejos* (Madrid, Spain: Cuerpol de Archiveros, 1943), which sets forth the printed *relaciones de meritos* found in the records of the *consejo real* (royal counsel) in the Archivo Historico Nacional in Madrid.

PENSIONES (PENSIONS)

This last category can be of the greatest interest to the genealogist because of the extensive information that may be provided in proving the relationship to a deceased government worker of the widow, orphans, or other persons who had a right to the pension. A request for a pension is likely to set forth the name of the spouse of the deceased government worker, the names of his or her children, and, frequently, those of his or her parents. It will also very likely set forth the dates and places where he served in government service. In many cases, it will also include copies of his baptismal or birth certificate, death certificate, marriage certificate, and will. It may also include the same type of records for his spouse and children. Unfortunately, published indexes for these types of records are not extensive, but often the original collections are alphabetically arranged. In exceptional cases where indexes exist, they can be very valuable. An example of this type of index is Antonio Matilla Tascon, *Indice de Expedientes de Funcionarios Publicos, Viudedad y Orfandad, 1763–1872* (Madrid, Spain: Hidalguía, 1962), which sets forth the pensions granted by the Seccion Montepios (Welfare Section).

MISCELLANEOUS LEGAL, COURT, AND LAND RECORDS

Never overlook legal documents. It is always possible, both in court transactions and in others of a legal nature, that the immigrant ancestor may have had to state his place of birth. Check the indexes to all local court records, and check the grantor and grantee land records indexes. In Hispanic countries, private legal documents were prepared by notaries. Copies are preserved in bound volumes called *protocolos* that can be found in the local archives of the country of origin.

SPANISH NOBILITY RECORDS

Spanish nobles were divided into two major categories: titled and untitled. The status of untitled nobility was called *hidalguía*. *Hidalgo,* or *hijodalgo* (one of the untitled nobility), which, literally translated, means "son of something," is defined in the fundamental thirteenth century legislation Siete Partidas (Partida Segunds, Titulo XXI) as the nobility that comes to men by lineage. To have the full rights and privileges of an *hidalgo* from that time forward, it was necessary to prove *hidalguía* in a person's lineage running back to at least his or her *bisabuelos* (great-grandparents). *Hidalguía* might be considered a general pool of nobility. Nearly every national archive in Spain has at least one or two sections relating to *hidalgos*. These archives were usually a depository for records which originated from those proving *hidalguía* as a means of entering a particular institution. The decision to search in such records will generally

Figure 16-9. Page from a Provincial Passport Register, Santander, Spain, May 1855. Archivo Histórico Provincial de Santander, Sección de Diputación Provincial, Sub-sección Pasaportes.

Número *189*	Señas generales.	*Dia 11 Mayo/55.*
SEÑAS PARTICULARES.	Edad *15 años*	
	Estatura *baja*	Se espidió pasaporte á D. *Ygnacio M.ᵉᶜ Sierra*
	Pelo *negro*	*y Ruiz, vecino de nal de Castroveca* para
	Ojos *pardos*	pasar á *Buenos Ayres en el B.ᵗᵃ*
	Nariz *reg.*	*"Amistad" (p.ᵗ Bilbao) á dedi-*
	Barba — . —	*carse al comercio*
	Cara *redonda*	
	Color *bueno*	

Número *190*	Señas generales.	*Mayo 12.*
SEÑAS PARTICULARES.	Edad *14*	
	Estatura *regular*	Se espidió pasaporte á D. *Gregorio de la Sierra*
	Pelo *castaño*	*Martinez, nat.ᵈ vecino de Penagos* — para
	Ojos *garzos* —	pasar á *la Habana en la*
	Nariz *regular*	*corbeta "Maria Luisa"*
	Barba *naciente*	
	Cara *regular*	
	Color *bueno*	

Número *191*	Señas generales.	*Dho dia*
SEÑAS PARTICULARES.	Edad *22 años*	
	Estatura *cort.ᵃ*	Se espidió pasaporte á D.ⁿ *Florentino de*
	Pelo	*Rubalcava, nat.ᵈ vecino de Pámanes* — para
	Ojos	*Mégico por la Habana*
	Nariz *neg.*	pasar á *California en la*
	Barba	*corbeta "M.ᵃ Luisa"*
	Cara *regular*	
	Color *bueno*	

Número *192*	Señas generales.	*Dho dia.*
SEÑAS PARTICULARES.	Edad *18 años*	
	Estatura *regular*	Se espidió pasaporte á D. *Anselin Al-*
	Pelo *castaño.*	*lagon, nat.ᵈ vecino de esta Ciudad* para
	Ojos *pardos*	pasar á *la Habana en la*
	Nariz *regular*	*fragata "Maria la Paz"*
	Barba *naciente*	
	Cara *regular*	
	Color *bueno*	

result from finding that an ancestor was involved with the particular institution that generated the nobility records.

Hidalguía records that are found in local Spanish and some Latin American national archives generally constitute two types: (1) censuses of the nobility and (2) prepared genealogies, known as *informaciones genealógicas* (genealogical investigation reports) or *limpiezas de sangre* (purity-of-blood records). These types of records are commonly found in the *ayuntamiento* (city hall). The censuses of the nobility were used extensively as a means of proving the nobility of one's ancestors, and in many proofs of *Hidalguía* there will be citations from these. These census documents can be found under several different names, including *padrón de hijos dalgo* (census of *hidalgos*) and *lista del estado de los vecinos* (list of the status of the heads of families). In many cases, these lists were compiled as the exceptions to the *impuesto de pechos* (commoner's tax) and to the *quintas* (military conscriptions), as those who had *hidalgo* status were exempted from both of them. *Informaciones genealógicas* were presented also to join a military or civil order and to marry after having joined the order, wherein the *hidalguía* of the bride was proved.

MILITARY SERVICE RECORDS

The number of peninsular troops stationed in a colony and the extent of the organization of provincial units varied depending on the time period and the colony. Study the history of the military in a colony to better understand an ancestor's involvement in the military.

SERVICE SHEETS (HOJAS DE SERVICIOS)

These military service records are found in all Hispanic military organizations. Generally, the name of the officer or soldier, the date and place of birth, and the names of his parents are at the top of the sheet. The body of the record is a detailed, date-by-date list of the various assignments and ranks of the soldier's military service. This may be brief and may occupy only single page, as in figure 16-10, a service sheet for a Spanish officer who served in Louisiana in 1792, or it may contain many pages.

PERSONAL FILES OR PETITIONS (EXPEDIENTES PERSONALES)

These were generally petitions compiled for a specific purpose, such as to request permission to marry or to request and prove worthiness for a special promotion or pension. In many archives, these *expedientes personales* may be arranged in special sections, such as *expedientes de academia* (academy files), *expedientes matrimoniales* (marriage files), or *expedientes de pension* (pension files), or they may be arranged alphabetically with the various petitions for a particular soldier or officer filed together under his name.

MILITARY PARISH RECORDS

The various units of the Spanish army, being overwhelmingly Catholic, had their own *capellanes* (chaplains). These military priests performed sacraments for officers and soldiers and their families, and they recorded those sacraments in special parish registers. A soldier had the option of having the sacraments for himself and his family performed by the military chaplain or the local ecclesiastical authorities. It is possible, therefore, to find for a single family within the same generation some baptisms, marriages, and last rites performed by local priests and others by military chaplains.

In Spain, access to the military parish records kept by the Vicariato General Castrense in Madrid requires permission from military and ecclesiastical authorities. Inquiries concerning consultation of these records should be addressed to the Vicario General, Secretaria General del Ejercito, Alcala 9, Madrid, España. This collection covers not only records for Spain itself but also those for colonial military units in Cuba, the Philippines, and Puerto Rico.

PUBLISHED TRANSFERS AND PROMOTIONS

It was customary in the Spanish army to maintain promotion lists in accordance with tenure as an officer. In addition, at least annually, the official promotion lists were given in published form as orders, which were distributed throughout the military. These lists have been bound into books and are available in several of the military archives. Generally, these apply to the nineteenth century and include officers serving in the military in the colonies as well as in Spain (figure 16-11).

ENLISTMENTS (FILIACIONES)

These are the individual listings (in some cases on separate sheets called *hojas de filiación*) of the soldiers in the army, as distinguished from the officers. This is the record that is more likely to exist for the common soldier, while the *hoja de servicios* and/or the *expediente personal* is more likely to exist for the officer. Generally, *filiaciones* have the names of the soldier, his parents, his birthplace, place of residence, religion, whether or not he is married, and a physical description. In some cases, it will also contain information, such as the *hoja de servicio*, which shows the various places where he served. Unfortunately, unless arranged alphabetically as part of the initial filing, these *filiaciones* are much less likely to be indexed and therefore are not easily accessible to the researcher. For this reason, when dealing with a non-officer, it is important to note any information concerning military service found in local or family records. The location of enlistment or the regiment in which a particular soldier served may be the key to finding his record.

CENSUSES (PADRONES) AND REVIEW LISTS (LISTAS DE REVISTAS)

Frequently, especially in outlying areas, censuses were taken of military personnel and their families, both officers and enlisted men, serving at particular posts. In addition, it was common to review all the members of a unit in frontier areas, such as in the southwestern United States, where censuses of the *presidios* (frontier posts) frequently included all of the citizens under the responsibility and protection of the unit, as well as the soldiers. Such censuses are found not only in military archives but also in national archives housing government records of the colonial period.

Locating the records of ancestors who served in the military may require some diligence but is well worth the effort. The major difficulty in searching for a military record is that the records tend to have been preserved in archives that correspond to the type of military service. The records of those who served in colonial areas in the Spanish regular army or who

Figure 16-10. Military service record of Felipe Treviño, 1792, Louisiana. Archivo de Simancas, Secretaria de Guerra, Hojas de Servicio en America, Legajo 7291, VIII, 3. FHL 1156353.

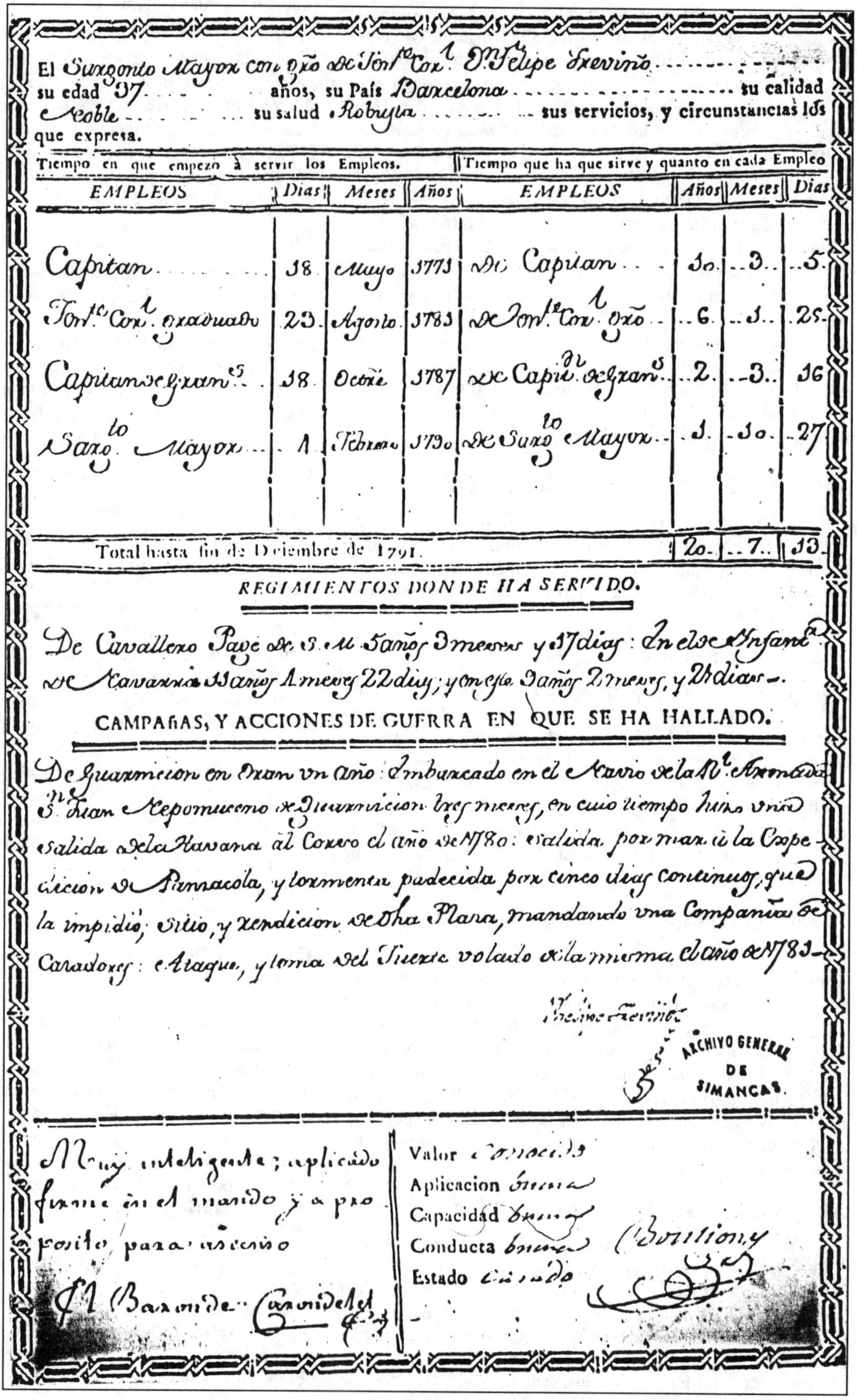

El Sargento Mayor con grado de Ten.te Cor.l D.n Felipe Treviño .... su edad 37 ...... años, su País Barcelona .... su calidad Noble .... su salud Robusta .... sus servicios, y circunstancias los que expresa.

Tiempo en que empezó à servir los Empleos.				Tiempo que ha que sirve y quanto en cada Empleo			
EMPLEOS	Dias	Meses	Años	EMPLEOS	Años	Meses	Dias
Capitan	18	Mayo	1773	De Capitan ...	10	3	5
Ten.te Cor.l graduado	23	Agosto	1783	de Ten.te Cor.l grad.o	6	1	25
Capitan de Gran.s	18	Octe	1787	de Capit.n de Gran.s	2	3	16
Sarg.to Mayor ...	1	Febrero	1790	de Sarg.to Mayor ..	1	10	27
Total hasta fin de Diciembre de 1791.					20	7	13

REGIMIENTOS DONDE HA SERVIDO.

De Cavallero Page de S. M. 5 años 3 meses y 17 dias: En el de Infant.a de Navarra 13 años 1 meses 22 dias; y en este 3 años 2 meses, y 24 dias.

CAMPAÑAS, Y ACCIONES DE GUERRA EN QUE SE HA HALLADO.

De Guarnicion en Oran un año: Embarcado en el Navio de la R.l Armada S.n Juan Nepomuceno de Guarnicion tres meses, en cuio tiempo hizo una salida de la Havana al Corso el año de 1780: salida por mar à la Expedicion de Panzacola, y tormenta padecida por cinco dias continuos, que la impidió; sitio, y rendicion de dha Plaza, mandando una Compañía de Cazadores: Ataque, y toma del Fuerte volado de la misma el año de 1781.

Felipe Treviño

ARCHIVO GENERAL DE SIMANCAS

Muy inteligente; aplicado firme en el mando y a propósito para ascenso

El Baron de Carondelet

Valor Conocido
Aplicacion buena
Capacidad buena
Conducta buena
Estado casado

Bouligny

Figure 16-11. Published order transferring Spanish soldiers to overseas colonies, Madrid, 1 March 1871. *Ordenes y circulares, año 1871,* pp. 470–71. Servicio Histórico Militar, Madrid.

*Direccion general de Infanteria.—7.° Negociado.—Circular número 253.—*Cumpliendo con lo prescrito en el reglamento de 1.° de Marzo de 1867 en lo relativo al pase y ascenso de los Jefes y Ociales de infantería y caballería de los ejércitos de Ultramar, han sido alta y baja en las escalas respectivas durante el segundo trimestre del presente año, los que figuran en la adjunta relacion por los motivos que en la misma se manifiestan.

Lo que he dispuesto se publique en el Memorial del arma para su conocimiento, el de los interesados, y en cumplimiento de lo mandado en el mencionado reglamento.—Dios guarde á V..... muchos años.—Madrid 1.° de Julio de 1871.—CÓRDOVA.

— 471 —

RELACION QUE SE CITA.

ALTA Y BAJA *ocurrida en las escalas de aspirantes para pasar en su empleo y con ascenso á los diferentes Ejércitos de Ultramar, durante el segundo trimestre del año actual.*

ALTAS.

PROCEDEN-CIA.	Clases	NOMBRES.	Ejército á que solicitan pasar.	Concepto de su pase.
Reemplazo	T. C.	D. Antonio Jimenez Fajardo	Filipinas.	
Idem	Com.	D. Benito Gutierrez Gomez	Id.	En su emp.°
Córdoba 10	Id.	D. Angel Pazos Vela–Hidalgo	Id.	
Reemplazo	Id.	D. Joaquin Rama Garcia	Id.	
Navarra 25	Id.	D. Ventura Lopez Nuño	Cuba.	Con ascenso
C.ª Mérida	Cap.	D. Joaquin Aymerich Villamil	Filipinas.	En su emp.°
Bailen 24	Id.	D. Antonio Nuñez de Prado	Id.	
Rey 1	Id.	D. Luis Lopez Garcia	Id.	
A. de Torm	Ten.	D. Diego Bordalonga Ros	Id.	
Idem	Id.	D. Manuel Seco y Shelly	Id.	
Iberia 30	Id.	D. Demetrio Camiñas Garcia	Id.	
Princesa 4.	Id.	D. Benito Saez Madruga	Id.	Con ascenso
Reemplazo	Id.	D. Rafael Perez Briz	Id.	
Zaragoza	Id.	D. Ramon Suarez Rodriguez	F.° y P.° R.°	
Bailen 24.	Id.	D. Ricardo Rubalcabar Villareal.	Pto. Rico.	
C.ª Santan.	Id.	D. José Cabello Noguera	Ultramar	
Castilla 16.	Id.	D. Ricardo Alonso Serrano	Cuba.	
Mallorca.	Id.	D. Gaspar Machado Aisa	Pto.-Rico	
Reemplazo	Id.	D. Meliton Garcia Trejo Moreno	Filipinas.	En su emp.°
Idem	Alf.	D. José Blanco Calvo	Id.	
Infante 5.	Id.	D. Gabriel Castro Castro	Id.	
Valencia	Id.	D. Juan Verdié Escalona	Cuba.	
Castilla 16.	Id.	D. Juan Fraga Silva	Id.	
Reina 2.	Id.	D. Pedro Rodriguez Sopeña	Id.	
Idem	Id.	D. José Argüelles Cortina	Id.	
Reemplazo	Id.	D. Juan Vazquez Pestana	Id.	
Reemplazo	Id.	D. Juan Zabalinchaurreta Goitia.	Id.	
Caz. Fig.	Id.	D. Antonio Rocol Rocel	Pto.-Rico	
Cantábria.	Id.	D. Manuel Rodriguez Gutierrez	Id.	
Sevilla 33.	Id.	D. Rafael Cerdan Serra	Filipinas.	
Idem	Id.	D. José Cluet Abadal	Id.	
Caz. Mad.	Id.	D. Leandro Ciria Roble	Id.	
Córdoba 10	Id.	D. Manuel Zamora Veguez	Id.	Con ascenso
Caz. Mad.	Id.	D. Agustin Guia Gomez	Id.	
Astúrias	Id.	D. Antonio Perea Lopez	Id. ó P. R.	
Res.ª Mad.	Id.	D. José Gonzalez Huelga	C.ª ó P.-R.	
Reemplazo	Id.	D. Manuel Mendoza Sainz	Filipinas.	
C.ª Santan.	Id.	D. Gerardo Moran Loredo Braña.	Id.	
Caz. Barc.	Sg. 1.°	D. Francisco Madain Celestino	Cuba.	
Leon 38.	Id.	D. Laureano Alvarez Garcia	Id.	
Bon. Prov.	Id.	D. José Alfaro Servan	Filipinas.	
Iberia 30.	Id.	D. Luis Pró Trugillo	Id.	
Res.ª Bad.	Id.	D. Arturo de la Guardia Baeza.	Cuba.	
Astúrias.	Id.	D. Pedro Valduque Ferrer	Id.	

served as officers in the provincial or militia units are likely to be found in the archives of Spain. For enlisted personnel in colonial regiments and for national armies after independence, as well as for all military units in some cases, the records will be found in national archives other than those of Spain. In addition, those for militia units may be found in provincial or state municipal archives.

Military census records, reports, promotion lists, and other administrative records were frequently prepared in duplicate or triplicate during the colonial period. One copy was kept locally, a second was sent to the regional *capitania general,* and the last one was sent to colonial administrators in Spain. This pattern, while making it somewhat difficult to determine with certainty in what archives the records may be filed, has proved very fortunate in areas where local archives have been destroyed. Some Latin American military records that were primarily local in nature can be found in Spanish national archives. Excellent examples are the military records of the Spanish American Southwest, which are preserved in the Archivo General de las Indias in Seville.

NEWSPAPERS

Newspapers have existed for many years in Hispanic countries, even in smaller towns. Many have been microfilmed, and references to them can be located either on microfilm or hard copy in the following:

1. Newspapers in Microform: Foreign Countries.

2. Catalog of the Library of Congress.

3. Many university library catalogs (identify these through the Inter-library Loan Service).

4. Catalogs of the *bibliotecas, hermotecas* (newspaper archives) or *archivos nacionales* of the country and *archivos estatales* of the state or province of interest.

Although obituaries are more common in small-town newspapers in the United States than in Latin American countries, the Hispanic researcher should carefully search all local newspapers in the area where his or her ancestors died for a published obituary.

CENSUS RECORDS

Generally, both in the United States and in Latin American countries, the census records have a column to indicate the country of birth. Fortunately, the census records of Spain and Latin America (especially those of the colonial era) sometimes indicate a specific province or parish in the country where the ancestor was born. There are many exceptions, however, particularly in the U.S. federal census records from the Southwest, where frequent and close association with the various Mexican states created an atmosphere in which the census taker would record the name of the Mexican state in response to the census question regarding the state or country in which the person was born. Census records ought to be carefully consulted, therefore, even though they may not ordinarily yield anything more than the country of origin.

Later censuses in many countries, such as the 1920 federal census in the United States, also indicate whether or not the individual was a naturalized citizen, and how long he or she had been in the country. This information indicates the time period in which the person entered the country and whether or not there may be naturalization and citizenship records.

One researcher knew only that his ancestors, Bonifacio Torres and Josefa Rangel, lived in Arizona about the turn of the century. A search for them in the Soundex index for Arizona for the 1900 census resulted in finding the census page reproduced in figure 16-12. From this the researcher learned his ancestors' ages, the year they came to the United States, and that they lived in Florence, Arizona. From the census, the researcher deduced that Josefa Rangel had not been married when she came to this country. He then wrote the Catholic parish church in Florence, asking if there was a marriage record for Bonifacio Torres and Josefa Rangel before 1900. In response, he received a certificate that gave him a marriage date but nothing about their place of origin in Mexico. He then wrote a second letter asking for a verbatim copy of the marriage entry, as he should have done originally. He received a photocopy of the original marriage entry reproduced in figure 16-4. It states that Bonifacio Torres and his family were from Alamos, Sonora, Mexico, and that Josefa Rangel and her family were from Ures, Sonora, Mexico.

ECCLESIASTICAL GUIDES AND DIRECTORIES

Many Catholic dioceses and some national church offices that serve several dioceses publish directories listing the various parishes, seminaries, and convents which make up the diocese. These directories always include the names of local parishes and the priests who serve there. They also may contain maps and other aids and interesting, pertinent information about local history, including even local jurisdictional changes. If the name given is that of an ecclesiastical subdivision, especially a parish, then these ecclesiastical guides can be particularly valuable. Many of these can be found in the *Family History Library Catalog* or in *CIDOC Collection: The History of Religiosity in Latin America ca. 1830–1870 on Microfiche,* which contains more than 30,000 volumes on microfiche. It is available in may large libraries.

LOCAL HISTORIES

As the name implies, these are histories that deal entirely with a particular town or region. Obviously, they are of no value in helping to locate exact places, but they can be extremely valuable in helping to understand the history of that locality, and especially to trace its jurisdictional changes.

RECORDS ANALYSIS

What records might an ancestor have generated? Think of the many questions that can be asked about each ancestor. Where was he born? Did she move? Did he go to school? Whom did she marry? Was he in the military? Did she have a trade or profession? The list goes on and on.

Beyond these specific questions about the individual and his or her immediate family, look at the broad historical context in which the ancestor lived. Was there any event, such as a war, drought, revolution, or social upheaval, which might have had a particular impact upon the ancestor's life? To be able to answer this last question, the researcher may need to acquire a better understanding of the history of the country from which his or her ancestors came. This can be acquired by reading some of the many histories available even in local libraries concerning Hispanic countries and their regional areas. Such broad reading should be supplemented with local or specific time period histories, where these can be identified.

List and analyze each of these questions with the answers, where possible. Eventually, file a copy of the analysis in the permanent file containing information about that particular ancestor as a guide for future research. As new information is obtained, ask additional questions and/or answer questions already asked.

What records are available for a particular locality? By considering what records each event in the life of the immigrant ancestor may have generated, a list of potential records can be made. After identifying the particular locality of ancestral origin, the question can only be answered by writing or actually going to the local archives.

NOTES

1. Angel de la Plaza Barras, *Guia del Investigador del Archivo de Simancas* (Madrid, Spain: Ministerio de Cultura, 1980), 198–200.

BIBLIOGRAPHY

American Geographical Society. *Index to the Map of Hispanic America.* Washington, D.C.: American Geographical Society, 1945.

Atlas Grafico de España. 16 vols. Madrid, Spain: Aguilar, 1969.

Archivo de Simancas. *Secretaria de Guerra, Hojas de Servicios de América.* Valladolid, Spain: Patronato Nacional de Archivos Historicos, 1958.

Atienza, Julio de. *El Diccionario heráldico de appellidos españoles y títulos nobiliarios.* Madrid, Spain: M. Aguilar, 1948.

Bannon, John F. *Spanish Borderlands Frontier, 1513–1821.* Albuquerque: University of New Mexico Press, 1974.

Basanta de la Riva, Alfredo. *Sala de los Hijosdalgo, Catálogo de todos los plietos y expedientes y probanzas.* 2nd ed. Madrid, Spain: Hidalguía, 1956.

Bermudez Plata, Cristobal. *Catálogo de Pasajeros a Indias.* Vol. 1: 1509–1534; vol. 2: 1535–1538; vol. 3: 1539–1559. Seville, Spain: Imprenta Editorial de la Gavidia, 1940.

Bancroft, Hubert H. *California Pioneer Register and Index, 1542–1848.* Baltimore: Genealogical Publishing Co., 1964.

Boyd-Bowman, Peter. *Indice biogeografico de cuarenta mil*

Figure 16-12. 1900 U.S. census schedule, Pinal County, Florence Township, Arizona Territory, p. 202. FHL 1240047.

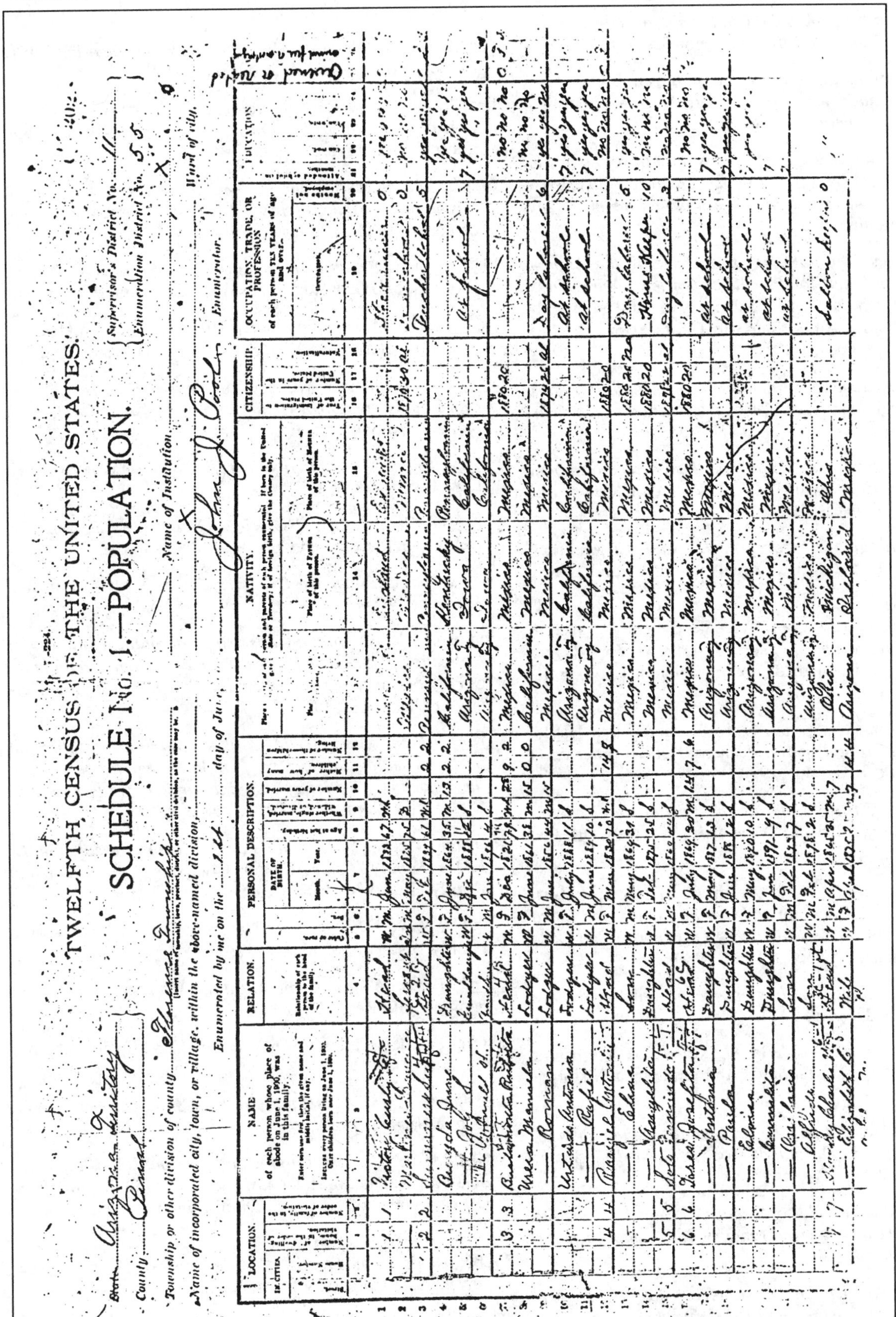

TWELFTH CENSUS OF THE UNITED STATES.

SCHEDULE No. 1.—POPULATION.

State Arizona Territory

County Pinal

Township or other division of county Florence

Enumerated by me on the ... day of June, 1900, John J. Pool, Enumerator.

Supervisor's District No. 11

Enumeration District No. 55

Pobladores espanoles de America en el Siglo XVI. Bogota: Instituto Caro y Cuervo, 1964.

_____. *Indice geo-biografico de 56 mil pobladores de América.* Mexico: D.F.: Fondo de Cultura Económica, 1985.

_____. *Indice bio-geográfico de cuarenta mil Pobladores españoles de América en el Siglo XVI.* Bogota, Colombia: Instituto Cara y Cuervo, 1964.

Cadenas y Vicent, Vicente de. *Archivos militares y civiles en donde se conservan fondos de caracter castrense relacionados con expedientes personales de militares.* Madrid: Hidalguía, 1975.

Chapman, Charles E. *Catalogue of Materials in the Archivo General de las Indias for the History of the Pacific Coast and the American Southwest.* University of California, Publications in History, vol. 8. Glendale, Calif.: Arthur H. Clark Co., 1927.

Catalogo xx del Archivo General de Simancas, Titulos de Indias. Valladolid, Spain: Patronato Nacional de Archivos Historicos, 1954.

Guía de fuentes para la historia de Ibero-América conservados en España. 2 vols. Madrid, Spain: Direccion General de Archivos y Bibliotecas, 1966.

Guide to Genealogical Research in the National Archives. Washington, D.C.: National Archives Trust Fund Board, 1983.

Heredero Roura, Federico, and Vicente Cadenas y Vicent. *Archivo General Militar de Segovia: Indice de Expedientes Personales.* 9 vols. Madrid, Spain: Ediciones Hidalguía, 1959–63.

Herrero Mediavila, Victor, and Lolita Rosa Aquayo Hayle. *Indice Biográfico de España, Portugal e Ibero-América.* 4 vols. New York: K.G. Saur, 1990.

Index of Spanish Citizens Entering the Port of New Orleans Between January, 1840 and December, 1865. New Orleans: Charles Mudrell, n.d.

Lo Buglio, Rudecinda. "The Archives of Northwestern Mexico." In *Latin American and Iberian Family and Local History.* Vol. 9 of *World Conference on Records.* Salt Lake City: Genealogical Society of Utah, 1980.

Lohman Villena, Guillermo. *Los americanos en las ordenes militares.* Madrid, Spain, 1947.

Madrid Alvarez, Juan Carlos de la. *El Viaje de los emigrantes Asturianos a América.* Gijon, Spain: Biblioteca Historica Asturiana, 1989.

Matilla Tascon, Antonio. *Indice de Expedientes de Funcionarios Publicos, Viudedad y Orfandad, 1763–1872.* Madrid, Spain: Hidalguía, 1962.

Maduell, Charles R., Jr. *Index of Spanish Citizens Entering the Port of New Orleans Between January, 1840 and December, 1865.* New Orleans: n.d.

_____. *Index of Spanish Citizens Entering the Port of New Orleans Between January, 1819 to December, 1839.* New Orleans: n.d.

Nichols, Elizabeth L. "The International Genealogical Index." *New England Historical and Genealogical Register* 137 (July 1983).

Paz, Julian. *Catálogo de Manuscritos de las Américas en la Biblioteca Nacional.* Madrid, Spain, 1933.

Paz, Ramon. *Indice de Relaciones de Méritos y Servicios Conservados en la Sección de Consejos.* Madrid, Spain: Cuerpo de Archiveros, 1943.

Pildain Salazar, Maria Pilar. *Ir a América: La emigracion Vasca a América (Guipúzcoa 1840–1870).* San Sebastian, Spain: Donostia, 1984.

Platt, Lyman D. *Latin American Census Records.* Salt Lake City: Instituto Genealógico Histórico Latinoamericano, 1987.

_____. *Latin American Family Histories.* Salt Lake City: Instituto Genealógico Histórico Latinoamericano, 1991.

_____. "The Mexican Military." In *Latin American and Iberian Family and Local History.* Vol. 9 of *World Conference on Records.* Salt Lake City: 1980.

_____. *Una guía genealógico-histórico de latinoamérica.* Salt Lake City: Acoma, 1977.

_____. *A Genealogical Historical Guide to Latin America.* Detroit: Gale Research Co., 1978.

_____. *Spanish Surname Histories.* Orem, Utah: Automated Archives, 1984.

Robinson, David J. *Finding Aids to the Microfilmed Manuscript Collection of the Genealogical Society of Utah: Preliminary Survey of the Mexican Collection.* Salt Lake City: University of Utah Press, 1978.

_____. *Finding Aids to the Microfilmed Manuscript Collection of the Genealogical Society of Utah: Research Inventory of the Mexican Collection of Colonial Parish Records.* Salt Lake City: University of Utah Press, 1980.

Ryskamp, George R. *Hispanic Family History Research in the L.D.S. Family History Center.* Riverside, Calif.: Hispanic Family History Research, 1989.

_____. *Spanish Military Records.* Riverside, Calif.: Hispanic Family History Research, 1987.

_____. *Tracing Your Hispanic Heritage.* Riverside, Calif.: Hispanic Family Research, 1984.

Sixerei Paredes, Carlos. *A Emigracion.* Vigo, Spain: Editorial Galaxia, 1988.

El Solar Catalan, Valenciana y Balear. San Sebastian, Spain: Garcia Carrafa, 1967.

Walsh, Micheline. *Irish Knights and the Spanish Military Orders.* Vol. 1. Dublin, Ireland: Government Publication Sales Office, 1960. Vols. 2 and 3. Dublin: Irish University Press, 1970.

Weber, David J. *The Spanish Frontier in North America.* New Haven: Yale University Press, 1992.

The Americas: A Journal of Latin American History.

A significant new research tool has become available: Victor

Herrero Mediavila and Lolita Rosa Aquayo Hayle, *Indice Biográfico de España, Portugal e IberoAmérica* (New York: K.G. Saur, 1990). This four-volume index identifies approximately 200,000 historical individuals from Roman times to the early twentieth century, compiled from 306 biographical encyclopedias, dictionaries, and collective works covering seven hundred original volumes published from the seventeenth to the early twentieth centuries from Spain, Portugal, and Latin America. Those works were copied and all of the references from all seven hundred volumes were separated and arranged alphabetically. That collection was then microfilmed on 1,070 microfiche and is available through the family history centers of the LDS church (microfiche sets 6002170-6002172). Note that this refers to the general sets; specific microfiche must be selected using the *Family History Library Catalog*.

TRACKING JEWISH-AMERICAN
FAMILY HISTORY
Chapter Contents

17

TRACKING JEWISH-AMERICAN FAMILY HISTORY

Gary Mokotoff

After the destruction of the First and Second Temples in Jerusalem, Jews were dispersed throughout their known world. This dispersion became known as the Diaspora (Greek for dispersion). Although Jews had the common bond of their religion, they developed separate cultures in different geographic areas.

JEWS OF THE DIASPORA

Those Jews who migrated to medieval France and Germany became known as Ashkenazic Jews (*ashkenaz* is the Hebrew word for Germany). They subsequently spread eastward to Poland and Russia and south to today's Austria, Czech Republic, Slovakia, Hungary, and Romania. Most Jewish-Americans are descended from the Ashkenazic Jews of central and eastern Europe. Those settling in the medieval Iberian peninsula became known as Sephardic Jews (*sepharad* is the Hebrew word for Spain). Their culture thrived from the twelfth to the fifteenth centuries but came to an abrupt end in Spain with the expulsion of the Jews in 1492. They fled throughout the Mediterranean rim, Holland, and other countries. Almost all Jewish-Americans are either Ashkenazic or Sephardic Jews.

Jews who settled in the Middle East in what are now Yemen, Iraq, and Iran are often categorized as Sephardic Jews. However, they actually belong to a separate group known as Oriental Jews. As the Far East was opened to Western civilization in the fourteenth century, Jews traveled eastward to settle in India and China. Probably the best-known Indian Jew today is Zubin Mehta, conductor of the New York Philharmonic, Israel Philharmonic, and other orchestras. There are no longer Chinese Jews, though they existed as late as the 1920s in Kaipheng, China. The Ethiopian Jews comprise another group that developed independently. Their origins are unknown; they claim to be descendants of King Solomon and the Queen of Sheba. Anthropologists state that they are black Africans who converted to Judaism some 1,500 years ago. Most live in Israel today, having been rescued from religious persecution in the 1980s.

NAMING PATTERNS

A cultural factor of interest to genealogists is the way children of Ashkenazic and Sephardic Jews acquire given names. Ashkenazic Jews normally name their children after deceased relatives—quite often recently deceased relatives. This rule is often the first clue as to the names of ancestors for whom there is no documentation. For example, if several male children within an extended family born in the same year were given the name Abraham, it usually shows that some common relative with the given name Abraham died shortly before the birth of the children. Two Ashkenazic Jewish genealogists who suspect they might be related will often go through the ritual of comparing given names in their families, looking for a pattern of similar given names.

Unfortunately, this naming practice has declined drastically in recent years. Israelis of Ashkenazic descent have virtually abandoned the practice, and it is becoming less common among Ashkenazic Jews in the Diaspora. But for persons who were born before 1950, these naming rules usually apply.

Sephardic Jews who follow the tradition name their children according to the following pattern: the firstborn son is named after the father's father; the firstborn daughter is named after the mother's mother; second son after the mother's father; and the second daughter after the father's mother.

ORIGIN OF SURNAMES

To this day, Jewish culture has not required hereditary surnames. In the Jewish religion, a person is known by his or her religious given name followed by "son" or "daughter" of the father's given name—for example, Gad son of Jacob or Sarah Malcah daughter of Jacob. Consequently, before the nineteenth century, most Ashkenazic Jews did not have hereditary surnames. Through a series of edicts, surnames were forced upon them by the three major empires of the period—Prussia, Russia, and Austria-Hungary—which wanted a unique way of identifying their Jewish citizens. Most chose occupation names, the names of towns, or kept to patronymics (figure 17-1). Sephardic surnames had an equally undistinguished origin. They date from the fifteenth century, when Jews were voluntarily or forcibly baptized as Roman Catholics and assumed the surnames of their sponsors. Many Jews who did not convert but had dealings with Christians assumed surnames to disguise their Jewishness.

RECORD-KEEPING

Historically, Jews have kept notoriously poor records of vital events. This has been because there is no requirement in the

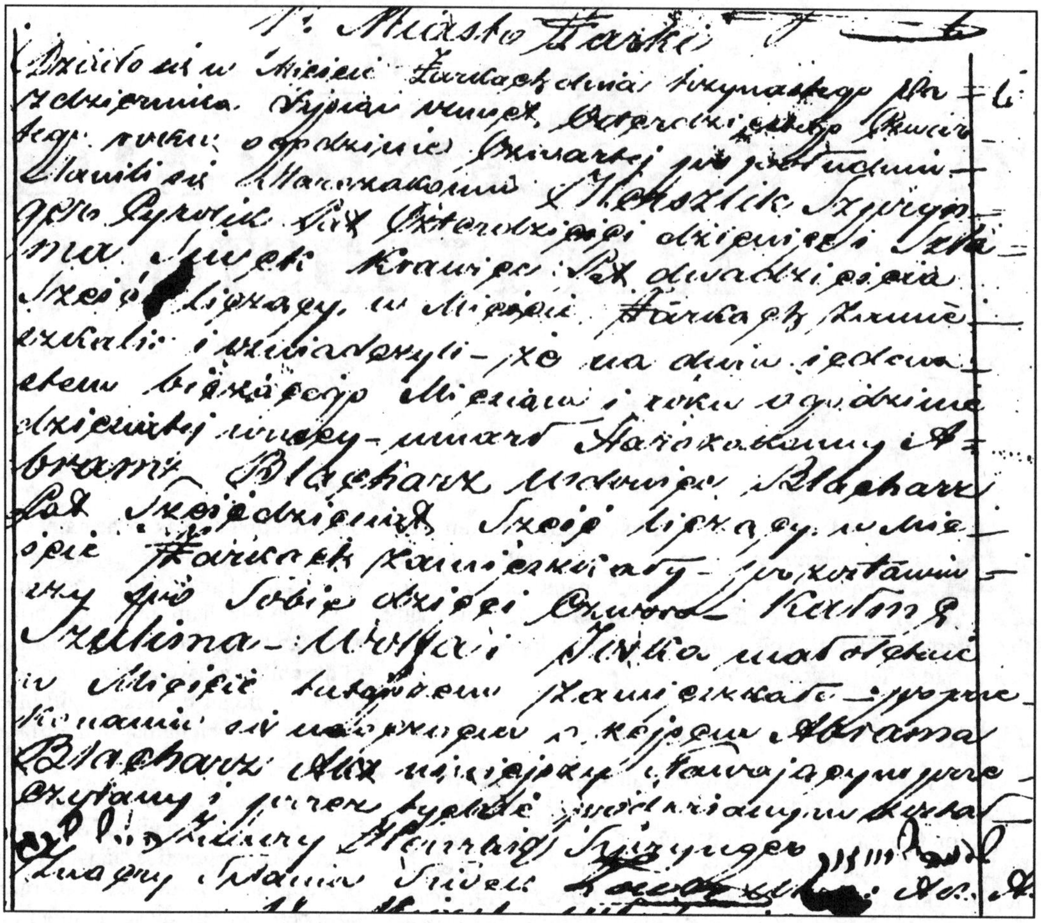

Figure 17-1. The death record of Abram Blacharz, 1844, Zarki, Poland. It indicates that his occupation was that of *blacharz,* Polish for "tinker."

religion to keep such records and because such records, if kept accurately, were used as the basis for discrimination by the Christian governments under which the Jews were ruled. The major exception, however, concerns the rabbinic dynasties. To be descended from a famous rabbi is considered a mark of honor, and famous rabbis have documented their pedigrees (*yichus* in Hebrew) to show their Jewish "blue blood." There are even alleged ascents of famous rabbis back to King David.

CASTES

The Jewish religion has a significant caste system that sometimes helps in tracing ancestry. It is a hereditary, paternal caste passed down from father to sons (there are some exceptions). There are three castes: Cohanim, Leviim, and Israelites. Members of the highest caste, Cohanim, are the descendants of Biblical Aaron. Members of this caste were the high priests of the temples (when the temples existed). Persons with the surnames Cohen, Kagan, Kogan, Kahn, Kahan, Katz, Kaplan, and Rapoport are invariably Cohanim. Members of the middle caste, Leviim, are descendants of the Biblical Levi. They served as the keepers of the temples. Persons with the surnames Levy, Levin, Segal, Landau, Horowitz, and Epstein are invariably Leviim. Most Jews belong to the lowest caste, the Israelites. These hereditary titles can be used as evidence that two men are not related. For example, a man born to the Cohanim caste cannot be related through paternal lines to a man born to the Leviim or Israelite castes. They could be related, however, through maternal lines.

JEWISH MIGRATION TO THE UNITED STATES

Jewish migration to the United States is divisible into periods. For each there are sources of information for doing genealogical research.

Dates	Period	Number of Immigrants
1654–1838	Colonial/federal	Fewer than 15,000
1838–80	German emigration	250,000
1881–1924	Eastern European emigration	2,000,000
1924–44	Pre-Holocaust	100,000
1945–60	Holocaust survivors	250,000
Present	Russian Jews and others	Up to 50,000 per year

COLONIAL PERIOD (1654–1838)

The first Jews to come to North America arrived in 1654 at the Dutch colony of New Amsterdam (renamed New York in 1664). Most were refugees from the Dutch colony of Recife, Brazil, which was conquered by the Portuguese that year. The Jews, fearing persecution from the Portuguese Inquisition, left with plans to go to Holland, the home of many Sephardic Jews who had fled the Spanish Inquisition 150 years earlier. However, they ran out of money and were forced to land at the Dutch colony.

Because Jews in the New World were allowed to practice their religion in a relatively nondiscriminatory environment, record books of American synagogues exist back to colonial times. Besides New York, early Jewish settlements were founded in Savannah, Georgia (1733), Philadelphia (1745), Charleston, South Carolina (1749), Newport, Rhode Island (1763), and Richmond, Virginia (1789).

There are records for this period at the American Jewish Historical Society (10 Thornton Dr., Waltham MA 02154) and the American Jewish Archives (3101 Clifton Ave., Cincinnati, OH 45220), as well as at the synagogue archives themselves.

The definitive genealogical work, now in its third revision, is Rabbi Malcolm H. Stern, FASG, *First American Jewish Families* (Baltimore: Ottenheimer Publishers, 1991). It contains the genealogies (descendants) of every Jewish person known to the author who arrived in the United States before 1838. Some 50,000 persons are identified in it.

German Emigration (1838–1880)

Much information about this group can be found using conventional American genealogical resources; little is available through synagogue records. Family historians who have attempted to do German emigration research, Jewish or Christian, know about the paucity of information available for tracing ancestry back to Germany. Ship's manifests and citizenship papers provide no clue as to ancestral towns in Germany, so genealogists must dig for information. Family records or death records may hold clues. For example, Jewish immigrants who arrived in the nineteenth century are among the most difficult of Jewish ancestors to document; however, Jewish tombstones of German immigrants have been known to indicate the town of birth (figure 17-2). Check census records as well; census takers sometimes wrote down the town of birth rather than the country of birth on the census record.

Most German Jews left through the ports of Hamburg and Bremen. Emigration lists from Hamburg for the years 1850 to 1934 have survived and are available on microfilm through the Family History Library of The Church of Jesus Christ of Latter-day Saints in Salt Lake City, Utah. Two separate indexes exist, both arranged by year. One, called the direct index, lists ships that sailed directly to the United States. The other, the indirect index, lists ships that stopped at other ports prior to coming across the Atlantic. Virtually no lists from Bremen exist today. Those not destroyed in periodic purgings were destroyed in Bremen by bombing raids during World War II. (See chapter 13, Immigration: Finding Immigrant Origins.)

East European Emigration (1881–1924)

In 1881, Czar Alexander II was assassinated, and the Russians blamed it on the Jews. Decades of pogroms against the Jewish population followed.

This anti-Semitism and deplorable economic conditions drove millions of Jews from Eastern Europe; 2 million went to the United States. Most Jewish-Americans are descended from these persons, and there is a wealth of genealogical information about them.

Passenger Arrival Lists

To learn more about this wave of immigrants (Jewish and others), the U.S. government began documenting them more carefully during the 1890s. Passenger arrival records included age, occupation, nationality, town of last residence, final destination, and other data. Starting in 1906, place of birth was added, and in 1907 name and address of the nearest relative in the immigrant's native country were added. The National Archives in Washington, D.C., has on microfilm the ships' manifests and

Figure 17-2. This tombstone, located in a San Francisco cemetery, provides invaluable information. Inscribed is the statement "In memory of Esther Lewis, a native of Wannbach, Bavaria, died March 7, 1885, aged 81 years, arrived in U.S. 1828." On the side of the tombstone, inscribed in Hebrew, additional information indicates that she was the daughter of David Sachs. (Photograph courtesy of Robert Griffin.)

indexes to these lists. Copies of these microfilms are available through the Family History Library and regional branches of the National Archives. If access to any of these facilities is difficult, you can write to the National Archives, Washington, DC 20408, for copies. The process for obtaining copies by mail through the National Archives is time consuming, however, and may take up to six months. An alternative is to retain a professional genealogist in Washington, D.C., or Salt Lake City. For a nominal sum (usually less than twenty-five dollars), a professional genealogist can provide you with a copy in about one week.

Citizenship Papers

Most Jewish immigrants became citizens of the United States. Even those who did not usually went through the first step of applying and filled out a declaration of intention. The declarations of intention asked a number of questions, including date of birth, date of marriage, arrival date, name of ship, current address, and, in certain years, name at time of arrival in the United States. Consequently, it is a valuable resource for Jewish-American research. Because the submitter was the immigrant ancestor him- or herself, it is not unusual to find more accurate information, such as birth dates, in citizenship papers. The location of these papers depends on which court naturalized the individual. If the certificate of naturalization, thought by many to be the "citizenship papers," is in the family's possession, it will show the county, state, or federal court in which the citizen was naturalized. Contact the court to learn the current location of the records.

Another way to determine the court of naturalization is through voter registration records. Immigrants had to prove their citizenship, and these records often indicate the court where naturalized. Contact the board of elections where the immigrant lived to determine if the records still exist. Otherwise, the long (six months to one year) route must be taken: contact the U.S. Immigration and Naturalization Service, Washington, DC 20530. Some naturalization records have been microfilmed by the Family History Library. For more information on naturalization records, see chapter 13.

Town Societies

Jewish immigrants formed societies based on their towns of origin; these were called *landsmanshaftn* societies. Membership in such a group invariably means that the person came from the town or a neighboring town. One function of these groups was to buy land in a Jewish cemetery. Even if it cannot be determined that an ancestor was a member of a *landsmanshaftn* society, burial in a plot owned by such a group implies that the ancestor came from that town. (The burial societies also sold burial plots to outsiders, however, so such evidence is not conclusive.) The archives of the YIVO Institute for Jewish Research, 555 W. 57th St., New York, NY 10019, has a large number of records of these societies. The institute has published its holdings in *A Guide to YIVO's Landsmanshaftn Archive* (New York: YIVO Institute for Jewish Research, n.d.).

Pre-Holocaust Period (1924–1944)

Because this period is contemporary, a principal source of information is the individuals themselves or their children. A wealth of twentieth-century documentation on Americans described elsewhere in this book can be used as well (see chapter 18, Tracking Twentieth-Century Ancestors).

Holocaust Survivors (1945–1960)

Friends and neighbors of Holocaust victims can often provide valuable information. The *National Registry of Jewish Holocaust Survivors* contains the names of some 80,000 survivors and their families living in the United States and Canada. The book is available in many Holocaust centers and major libraries. The organization that created the registry will forward letters to survivors. Write to the American Gathering/Federation of Jewish Holocaust Survivors, 122 W. 30th St., New York, NY 10001.

HOLOCAUST RESEARCH

Most Jewish-Americans are descended from Ashkenazic Jews who did not have surnames before the nineteenth century. Consequently, it is unusual to trace a Jewish ancestry back more than two hundred years. In fact, most Jewish-Americans do not trace their ancestry as much as they document their families; that is, they identify their most ancient ancestor and then trace forward to document all descendants of this ancestor—rarely more than ten generations. Because fifty percent of European Jewry was killed in the Holocaust (ninety-one percent of Polish Jewry), virtually every Jewish-American has relatives who were victims of the Holocaust. (I have documented more than 250 descendants of my great-great-great-grandfather who were murdered—fewer than thirty survivors are known).

Although many Holocaust victims had no surviving immediate family members, there are persons who have remembered them. These remembrances are documented in two of the most important sources of information about Holocaust victims: *yizkor* books and pages of testimony.

Yizkor Books

After World War II, the survivors of the Holocaust published books that memorialized the destroyed Jewish communities of Europe. Called *yizkor* books (*yizkor* means "memorial" or "remembrance" in Hebrew), they commemorate not only the victims but the Jewish communities themselves. To date, more than 1,000 towns have been commemorated in this manner.

Although each book was written independently of the others, *yizkor* books have a typical structure. The first section describes the history of the Jewish community in the town or city from its inception, sometimes hundreds of years ago, to the events of the Holocaust, which invariably culminated in the destruction of all Jewish religious property (synagogues, cemeteries, etc.) and the immediate murder of the Jewish population or their deportation to labor or extermination camps. For the genealogist, this overview section provides much material about Jewish community life in the town.

The next section of a *yizkor* book is a group of stories that are the personal remembrances of survivors about their families. These usually contain a wealth of information about the particular family. The following section is devoted to families from which there were no survivors. The descriptions are usually brief—one or two paragraphs headed by the names of the father and mother, as well as the names of the children. Where the name of a parent could not be remembered, it is left blank. If the children's names were not remembered, the notation might be "three children" or "two sons and a daughter." The final section is a necrology—a list of all the victims from the town.

The most complete list of towns for which yizkor books have been published is in Sallyann Amdur Sack, *A Guide to Jewish Genealogical Research in Israel* (Bergenfield, N.J.: Avotaynu, 1995). Major *yizkor* book collections are at the YIVO Institute in New York and the Library of Congress in Washington, D.C. Many public and university libraries with Judaica collections have acquired a good number of these books.

PAGES OF TESTIMONY

The major archive and documentation center for the Holocaust is Yad Vashem, P.O. Box 3477, 91034 Jerusalem, Israel. Since 1955, Yad Vashem has been attempting to document each of the 6 million Jews who were killed in the Holocaust on documents called pages of testimony. To date, 3 million Holocaust victims have been documented. Yad Vashem has requested persons to come forward and submit on these preprinted forms a host of information about victims, including name; place and year of birth; place, date, and circumstances of death; name of mother, father, and spouse; and, in some cases, name and age of children (figure 17-3). Each submitter must sign the page of testimony and indicate his or her name, address, and relationship to the deceased. Not only do pages of testimony provide lineage-linked information about Holocaust victims, they provide a connection to the present through the submitter of the document. If the submitter can be located, he or she can often provide firsthand information about the family. Unfortunately, most pages of testimony were written in the late 1950s, some forty-five years ago, and many of the submitters are no longer alive; however, their children can often provide additional information. Fortunately, the vast majority of the contributors of pages of testimony are Israelis, and a mechanism exists to find the person or his or her descendants: the Search Bureau for Missing Relatives.

SEARCH BUREAU FOR MISSING RELATIVES

Shortly after World War II, the Jewish Agency, an international Jewish help organization, established a division to aid Holocaust survivors in locating relatives. Located in Jerusalem, it is known as the Search Bureau for Missing Relatives (P.O. Box 92, Jerusalem, Israel). This department would be destined for obscurity were it not for the individual who comprises its one-person operation—Batya Unterschatz. Batya, a native of Vilnius, Lithuania, immigrated to Israel in 1971. She joined the Search Bureau in 1972. Her warm personality, dedication to her job, knowledge of seven languages, and access to Israeli government records have made her a legend in locating persons living in Israel. If you provide the Search Bureau with a copy of a page of testimony, there is a good likelihood that the bureau will find the person who submitted the document or the person's descendants.

GERMAN WAR RECORDS

The extermination of Jews, gypsies, and other "undesirables" during World War II is well documented. The level of documentation falls into three categories: (1) those events for which information about individuals involved was recorded, (2) those events for which the names of the individuals involved were not recorded, (3) and those events for which there is no documentation. Those persons who were sent to concentration camps or labor camps and were assigned to forced labor were documented. Rosters have survived which show the individual's name, place of birth, birth date, and tattooed identification number. Some of these documents, captured by U.S. and British forces, have been made available to American genealogists through the National Archives (Record Group 238). They include registers from Buchenwald and Dachau concentration camps. Others, captured by the Soviets, are only today being made available to the public. Where deaths from disease, starvation, and abuse did not occur on a massive basis, even individual deaths were recorded.

In the category of documented events for which the specific names of the individuals were not recorded, the records of the *einsatzgruppen* provide the death dates of more than 1 million Jews. After Germany invaded Russia in 1942, these special squads of the German SS had the responsibility of killing every Jew, gypsy, and Bolshevik in the towns captured by the regular German army. Consequently, their reports provide the death dates for the Jews of each town.

In the category for which there is no documentation fall the millions of people who were immediately gassed at the various extermination camps. No attempts were made to document these people. However, in specific instances, deportation lists exist today that provide useful information to the genealogist. The best known of these lists were published in Serge Klarsfeld, *Memorial to the Jews Deported From France*. For more than 70,000 individuals it lists the name, place of birth, and birth date. Because it is organized by train convoy and date of departure from France, it is possible to learn the arrival date at Auschwitz and consequently the death dates of individuals who fell into the category of those immediately gassed—children less than fourteen years of age, elderly over fifty, and mothers with children under fourteen. Similar books exist for Belgium and Germany.

VITAL RECORDS

Although everything Jewish was destroyed in the Holocaust, government records quite often were not. Most countries allow access to birth records after one hundred years. As the Holocaust recedes into history, more and more Holocaust victims fall into the category of these who were born more than one hundred years ago. Therefore, it is possible, if the town of birth is known, to get the birth and marriage records of these individuals from government archives.

HOLOCAUST CENTERS

Holocaust education centers exist throughout the world. Exhibits depict events during this period, and many have libraries containing literature about the Holocaust. Write to the Holocaust Resource Center, Queensborough Community College, 222-05 56th Ave., Bayside, NY 11364, for a catalog of these centers.

The archive at Yad Vashem contains considerable source material on the Holocaust. The holdings, arranged by town, are documented in *Guide to the Unpublished Material on the Holocaust,* vols. 3–6 (1975–81). Censuses of Jews taken before and during World War II are being discovered as well. Recently available at the Family History Library, for example, are portions of a 1938 census of Jews living in Germany. Records of Hungarian Jews are just becoming known. The

Figure 17-3. A Page of Testimony from Yad Vashem in Jerusalem. This is one for Abram Waingarten, son of Gempil and Frimet. It indicates that he was born in 1888 in Pilica, Poland, resided in Sosnowiec, and died at Auschwitz. Also identified are his wife, Sarah Leib Deidler, and two of his six children—Yehoshua, age twelve, and Chaim Schmuel, age sixteen. The person who testified to the named circumstances was Waingarten's daughter, Mindeleh Zeitman, of Kiryat Motkin, Israel.

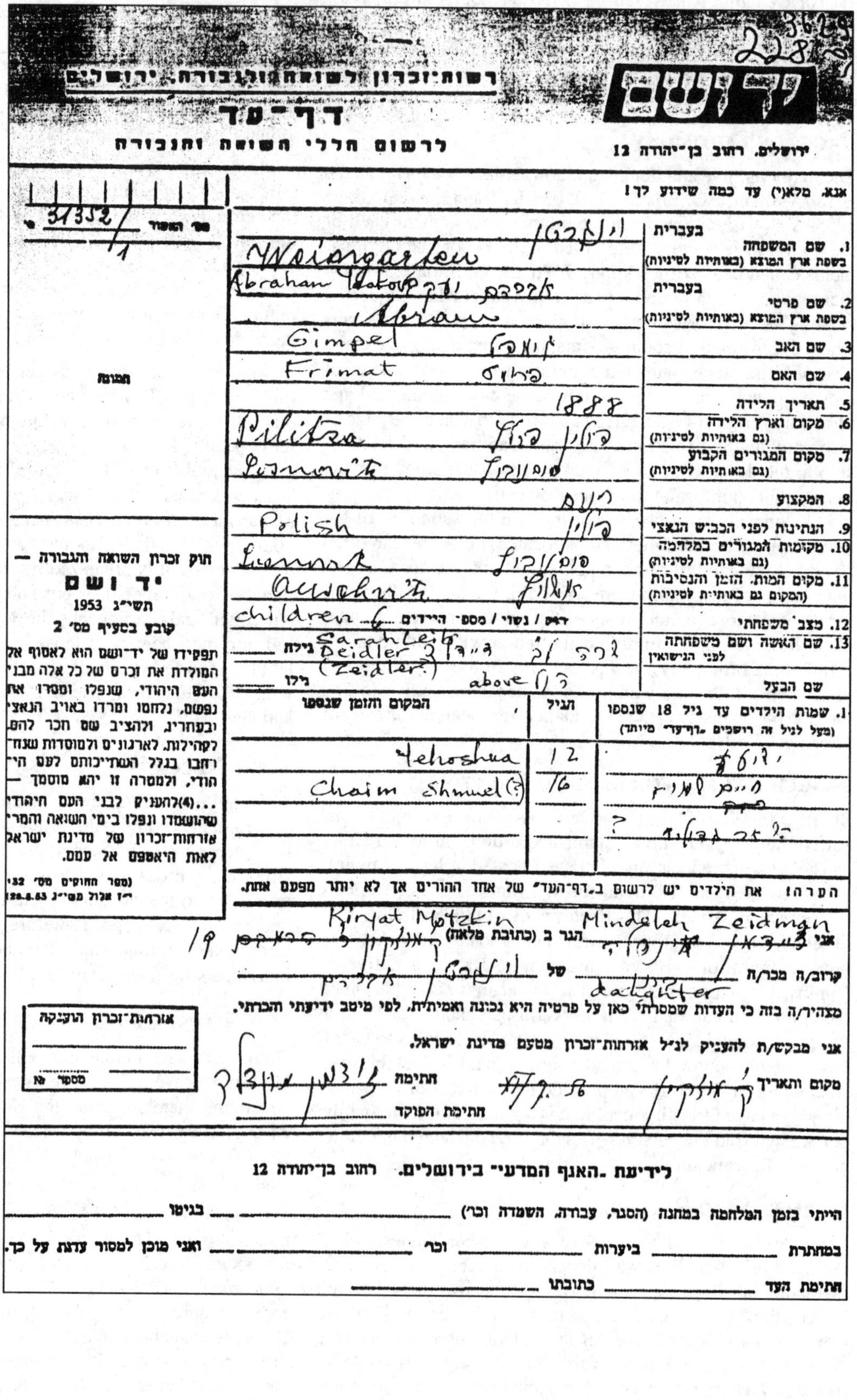

יד ושם
רשות־זכרון לשואה ולגבורה, ירושלים
דף־עד
לרשום חללי השואה והגבורה
ירושלים, רחוב בן־יהודה 12

אנא, מלא(י) עד כמה שידוע לך!

מס' הספור 31332/1

1. שם המשפחה בעברית / בשפת ארץ המוצא (באותיות לטיניות): וינגרטן / Waingarten
2. שם פרטי בעברית / בשפת ארץ המוצא (באותיות לטיניות): Abraham Abram
3. שם האב: Gimpel
4. שם האם: Frimat
5. תאריך הלידה: 1888
6. מקום וארץ הלידה (גם באותיות לטיניות): Pilitsa
7. מקום המגורים הקבוע (גם באותיות לטיניות): Sosnovitz
8. המקצוע
9. הנתינות לפני הכבוש הנאצי: Polish
10. מקומות המגורים במלחמה (גם באותיות לטיניות): Sosnovitz
11. מקום המות, הזמן והנסיבות (המקום גם באותיות לטיניות): Auschwitz
12. מצב משפחתי: children 6
13. שם האשה ושם משפחתה לפני הנישואין: Sarah Leib Deidler (Zeidler)
שם הבעל: above

תמונה

1. שמות הילדים עד גיל 18 שנספו (מעל לגיל זה רושמים «דף־עד» מיוחד) | הגיל | המקום והזמן שנספו
Yehoshua | 12
Chaim Shmuel | 16

הערה! את הילדים יש לרשום ב«דף־העד» של אחד ההורים אך לא יותר מפעם אחת.

אני Mindeleh Zeidman הגר ב (כתובת מלאה) Kiryat Motzkin
קרובה/ה מכר/ת daughter של
מצהיר/ה בזה כי העדות שמסרתי כאן על פרטיה היא נכונה ואמיתית, לפי מיטב ידיעתי והכרתי.
אני מבקש/ת להעניק לנ"ל אזרחות־זכרון מטעם מדינת ישראל.
מקום ותאריך — חתימה
חתימת הפוקד

חוק זכרון השואה והגבורה — יד ושם תשי"ג 1953
קובע בסעיף מס' 2
תפקידו של יד־ושם הוא לאסוף אל המולדת את זכרם של כל אלה מבני העם היהודי, שנפלו ומסרו את נפשם, נלחמו ומרדו באויב הנאצי ובעוזריו, ולהציב שם וזכר להם, לקהילות, לארגונים ולמוסדות שנחרבו בגלל השתייכותם לעם היהודי, ולמטרה זו יהא מוסמך — ...(4) להעניק לבני העם היהודי שהושמדו ונפלו בימי השואה והמרי אזרחות־זכרון של מדינת ישראל לאות היאספם אל עמם.

אזרחות־זכרון הוענקה
מספר

לידיעת «האגף המדעי» בירושלים. רחוב בן־יהודה 12
הייתי בזמן המלחמה במחנה (הסגר, עבודה, השמדה וכו') ______ בגיטו ______
במחתרת ______ ביערות ______ וכו' ______ ואני מוכן למסור עדות על כך.
חתימת העד ______ כתובתי ______

German census shows name (including maiden name of married women), address, and date and place of birth of the individuals. Concentration camp records are also being found. In fact, the Holocaust has been called the most documented event in Western history. Tens of thousands of books have been written on the subject. A comprehensive bibliography on the topic is *Bibliography on Holocaust Literature,* 2 vols. (Boulder, Colo.: Westview Press, 1986). This work identifies more than 14,500 books on the Holocaust.

SOURCES INDEPENDENT OF TIME PERIOD

JEWISH HISTORICAL SOCIETIES

A number of Jewish historical societies in the United States and Canada have documented the history of the Jewish presence in their locales. Many have made this information available in book form. To determine if there is a Jewish historical society in your area, write to the American Jewish Historical Society, 10 Thornton Dr., Waltham, MA 02154.

JEWISH IMMIGRANT AID SOCIETIES

For some one hundred years, Jewish immigrants have been assisted by social welfare organizations that helped them settle in the New World. The most comprehensive and oldest is the Hebrew Immigrant Aid Society, 333 Seventh Ave., New York, NY 10001, which has branches in New York, Philadelphia, Boston, and Baltimore. The society has case files on each person or family it has helped. The Canadian equivalent is the Jewish Immigrant Aid Society, 4600 Bathurst St., Suite 325, Willowdale, Ontario M2R 3V3, Canada.

GETTING RECORDS FROM THE COUNTRY OF ANCESTRY

The ancestors of most Jewish-Americans came to North America less than 150 years ago. This means that research of periods before the twentieth century invariably leads to research in central and eastern Europe. The collapse of communism has been a blessing for genealogists with roots in this area. In many countries, archives and records offices previously off-limits to inquiries are now open, and capitalist entrepreneurs offer genealogical services. Many immigrants in the United States maintain contacts with friends in their former countries who can provide access to information. The Family History Library, previously spurned by East Bloc governments, is now microfilming or negotiating to microfilm documents in most countries. Record collections thought destroyed during World War II have been found in other countries or stored in warehouses. Eastern Europeans whose relatives immigrated to the United States at the beginning of this century are reestablishing ties and creating additional sources of information. Unrestricted travel now is possible in many countries.

While the general direction is toward the positive, there are also negative elements. Some archives and record offices previously accessible to the public have been restricted as archivists realize that they have valuable, saleable records. Some "researchers" charge outlandish fees or request "deposits," never to be heard from again.

There is a variety of ways to access records. These are discussed, for the various countries, in the sections that follow.

1. Write to repositories.
2. Hire a record searcher to do the research.
3. Go to the country.
4. Use microfilm collections of the Family History Library.

Consult the latest issue of *Everton's Genealogical Helper* (The Everton Publishers, P.O. Box 368, Logan, UT 84321) for a list of U.S. and Canadian genealogical societies with interests in these countries.

The accessibility of records in each country changes by the year, usually for the better but sometimes for the worse. Consult recent issues of *Avotaynu: The International Review of Jewish Genealogy* (P.O. Box 900, Teaneck, NJ 07666) for the latest information. Outlined below is the status by location as of 1994.

BELARUS

There are no known reliable genealogical services in Belarus, but people traveling there find the population friendly and access to local archives possible. Use a record search firm or write to the Central State Historical Archive of Belarus; u. Kozlova 26; 220038 Minsk, Belarus. The Family History Library recently started microfilming records in Belarus. Also see the comments below under "Former Soviet Union."

CZECH REPUBLIC

The Bohemia and Moravia regions of Czechoslovakia split from Slovakia to become the Czech Republic in 1993. The "Velvet Revolution" of November 1989, which brought down the communist regime, brought access to the archives. Before this event, most inquiries went unanswered. Write to Stani Ustredni Archiv v. Praze; Malastrana, Karmelitska 2; 118 01 Praha 1, Czech Republic. Many genealogists have traveled to this area in recent years and find easy access to records.

ESTONIA

The author does not know of anyone who has traveled to Estonia or made inquiries by mail. The Family History Library is microfilming records there, however.

HUNGARY

Records are accessible in Hungary and professional researchers there are competent. Travel to Hungary is routine, and Americans going there have not reported any negative events in the area of freedom of travel or records access. A professional genealogical group which has produced mixed results is Hungarogens; Jzeef krt. 50; H-1085 Budapest, Hungary. The Family History Library is microfilming records at the state archives and at regional archives.

LATVIA

The author does not know of anyone who has traveled to Latvia or made inquiries by mail. Use a record search firm or write to the Central State Historical Archive; Slokas iela 16; 226007 Riga, Latvia.

LITHUANIA

The first American genealogists to travel to newly independent Lithuania found archivists cordial and access easy—but this was before the Lithuanian government realized the value of their records. It has since made access more difficult and raised the fees. The Family History Library has begun microfilming there on a limited basis. Use a record search firm or write to the Main Archival Administration; Mindaogo 8; Vilnius, Lithuania.

MOLDOVA

Moldova has no established genealogical services and has not encouraged tourism. Yet some of the earliest post-Soviet Union inquiries have yielded results. Use a record search firm or write to the Central State Archive; qtr. Dzerzhinskii 67; 277028 Kishinev, Moldova. See the comments below under "Former Soviet Union."

POLAND

Polish records have been accessible to Westerners for many years. Poland's government was the first among the former East Bloc countries to recognize that hard currency is more valuable than secrecy. The Family History Library has been microfilming Polish records for decades, and millions of records are available through it. Inquiries to the Central Archives in Warsaw receive prompt responses—in Polish. However, only two Polish words must be known: *nie* (not) means that the archive does not have the records, and *dolares* (dollars) means that it has them.

The Polish Archives is a total service organization. The staff will search for specific records (for example, the birth record of a specific person) and will accept research assignments at an hourly rate (for example, a search of one or more towns for all records containing a particular surname). Recent results demonstrate that the quality of the archive's work is excellent. Write to Naczelna Dyrekcja Archiwow Panstowowych; ul. Dluga 6; SKR Poczt 1005; 00-950 Warszawa, Poland.

ROMANIA

Conditions in Romania are still very fluid, and, to date, inquiries to the Romanian government go unanswered. One local researcher falls into the category of those who request fifty dollars and are never heard from again. However, some genealogists traveling to Romania have accessed records from local archives.

RUSSIA

Initial microfilming by the Family History Library has been in the cities of Ostrakan, Tula, and Saint Petersburg, areas with small nineteenth-century Jewish populations. Saint Petersburg, however, is a major archival center in Russia. See the comments below under "Former Soviet Union." Use a record search firm or write to the central State Archives; u. Bolshaia Pirogovkaia 17; 119817 Moscow, Russia.

FORMER SOVIET UNION

Certain considerations apply to the republics that made up the former Soviet Union, namely Belarus, Estonia, Latvia, Lithuania, Moldova, Russia, and the Ukraine. Because public access to records in these republics is a relatively new concept, the information below is an overview of the situation as of mid-1995. Consult *Avotaynu: The International Review of Jewish Genealogy* (cited earlier) for current information.

Citizens of countries that comprised the former Soviet Union have been burdened with totalitarianism for hundreds of years. The consequence has been a tremendous amount of documentation about its citizens—vital records, police records, general and specific censuses, military records (primarily of officers), and others. Unfortunately, many archivists in the area have never needed detailed inventories of these records. In fact, the term "finding aid" has only recently been added to the Russian vocabulary. Consequently, the records exist, but locating specific information is time consuming.

As of 1995, the best way to access records in the republics of Belarus, Moldova, Russia, and the Ukraine is to use a record search firm. Such a firm will provide personalized attention that minimizes the risk of incomplete research. Its efforts may produce results in as little as ninety days; other searches have been known to take more than a year. These firms regularly advertise or are mentioned in *Avotaynu*. Magazines of the various ethnic genealogical societies also carry articles and advertisements about these groups. If at all possible, use a firm recommended by someone you know; otherwise, ask the firm for references from customers in your area. If the firm cannot provide a local client, it may mean that it has done only limited work. Current rates are around six dollars per hour. Do not ask for specific records; instead, request research of any records from a specific town about specific persons or a surname. The evidence is a wealth of information that exists in the former Soviet Union but not necessarily the vital statistic or census records. Police records might be an excellent source of information. Other potential sources are tax rolls; land records; religious records; university and school rolls; newspaper collections; draft board records; merchant guild records; miscellaneous records at local town halls, libraries, and museums; and genealogies of Russian nobility.

SLOVAKIA

The "Velvet Revolution" of November 1989, which brought down the communist regime of Czechoslovakia, opened access to the archives of this recently formed country. Before that event, most inquiries went unanswered. Today, access is available in many ways. Write to the State Archives; Statny Ustredny Archiv; Cesta 42, Bratislava, Slovakia. People traveling to Slovakia have had access to record offices and find the local population friendly and accommodating. The Family History Library is microfilming there.

UKRAINE

The Ukraine is beginning to recognize that genealogical inquiries yield hard currency. People traveling to the Ukraine find the population friendly and access to local archives possible with nominal fees for records. As of mid-1995, travel and tourist conditions outside the major cities are primitive. It is recommended that a record search firm or the central archive be used for inquiries. Write to the Central State Historical Archive; u. Solomenskaya 24; 252601 Kiev, Ukraine. (See the comments above under "Former Soviet Union.")

FORMER YUGOSLAVIA

The Family History Library is microfilming in Slovenia and Croatia. Thomas Kemp, *International Vital Records Handbook* (Baltimore: Genealogical Publishing Co., 1990), states that civil registration began in 1946, but earlier records exist in churches.

The book lists addresses of archives in the various republics that are today independent or soon-to-be-independent countries.

U.S. RESOURCES

Do not overlook potential resources in the United States. Information of genealogical value that appears in published books is likely to be found in major American libraries, such as the Library of Congress, New York Public Library, major university libraries, and special interest libraries. Examples are Russian business directories from the turn of the century at the Library of Congress and other libraries; an 1898 directory (found at the Library of Congress) of Vilna Guberniya, a former province located primarily in modern Lithuania, that lists many institutions, tradesmen, and professionals from that area; a 1920 Warsaw city directory at the Family History Library; and many others.

JEWISH-AMERICAN GENEALOGY TODAY

Today, Jewish genealogy in the United States and Canada is highly organized. There are some sixty Jewish genealogical societies under an umbrella group: the Association of Jewish Genealogical Societies (AJGS), P.O. Box 50245, Palo Alto, CA 94303. They are in alliance with societies located in other countries, among them Australia, Brazil, England, France, Holland, Israel, Russia, South Africa, and Switzerland. For a list of societies, send a self-addressed, stamped envelope to the AJGS. All societies hold meetings regularly, usually monthly, with a lecture on some topic of interest to Jewish family historians. More significantly, membership provides an opportunity to share information that will enhance research efforts. In recent years, many have begun holding beginners' workshops to encourage other Jewish-Americans to trace their ancestry. Most societies publish their own newsletters as well.

Special interest groups have been formed for specific regions of ancestry. As of 1993, there were special interest groups for the Suwalki-Lomza region of Poland/Lithuania, Hungary, Lithuania, Romania, Germany, and Galicia. A complete list of special interest groups is available from the AJGS.

Avotaynu: The International Review of Jewish Genealogy (cited earlier) is published quarterly and includes articles from an international group of contributing editors. It makes readers aware of the latest resources available to Jewish genealogists in various parts of the world and includes background articles about the history of Jews in particular areas.

Annual conferences, currently sponsored by AJGS, have been held since 1982. The 1996 conference in Boston attracted seven hundred attendees. The 1997 conference will be held in Paris; 1998 in Los Angeles; 1999 in New York; and 2000 in Salt Lake City.

Several databases have been developed to help in Jewish genealogical research. They have been reproduced on microfiche and are available for use by genealogical society members at regular meetings. A list of these databases is included at the end of this chapter. The most notable is the Jewish Genealogical Family Finder—a database of ancestral surnames and towns being researched by more than 2,500 Jewish genealogists throughout the world. It currently has more than 35,000 entries. Using this list, family historians can learn if other persons are researching their surnames or ancestral towns and can contact these individuals to share their knowledge. The Jewish Genealogical Family Finder is also available on computer bulletin boards. For a list of bulletin boards, write to the AJGS at the address above.

A wealth of books of interest to Jewish genealogists have appeared in recent years. Some are listed in the chapter bibliography.

BIBLIOGRAPHY

MANUALS AND SOURCE BOOKS

Baxter, Angus. *In Search of Your European Roots: A Complete Guide to Tracing Your Ancestors in Every Country in Europe.* Baltimore: Genealogical Publishing Co., 1985. A country-by-country description of resources (now outdated for Eastern Europe). It includes a chapter on Jewish sources in Europe and Israel.

Beider, Alexander. *A Dictionary of Jewish Surnames From the Kingdom of Poland.* Teaneck, N.J.: Avotaynu, 1996.

_____. *A Dictionary of Jewish Surnames From the Russian Empire.* Teaneck, N.J.: Avotaynu, 1993. A compilation of 50,000 Jewish surnames from turn-of-the-century Russia showing etymology, where within the empire the names existed, and variants of names. A ninety-four-page introduction describes the origins and evolution of Jewish surnames in Russia.

Cohen, Chester G. *Shtetl Finder Gazetteer.* Bowie, Md.: Heritage Books: 1989. Locates, with varied spellings, many of the Jewish communities of Eastern Europe, and identifies by name some prominent citizens of each. (Also see Mokotoff-Sack, below.)

Gorr, Rabbi Shmuel. *Jewish Personal Names: Their Origin, Derivation and Diminutive Forms.* Teaneck, N.J.: Avotaynu, 1992. Some 1,200 Jewish given names are listed, not in alphabetic order but by root name. Most variants of root names are annotated to show how the name evolved.

A Guide to YIVO's Landsmanshaftn Archive. New York: YIVO Institute for Jewish Research, n.d.

Guzik, Estelle M., ed. *Genealogical Resources in the New York Metropolitan Area.* New York: Jewish Genealogical Society, 1989. A detailed guide to every agency between Albany, New York, and Trenton, New Jersey, that could provide data of use in Jewish genealogical research, including many specific records, hours of operation, public transportation, finding aids, fees, and restrictions. Appendices include bibliography and locations of *yizkor* books, vital record application forms, Soundex codes, available foreign telephone directories, U.S. city directories, newspapers, and Jewish cemeteries. Indexed.

Kemp, Thomas. *International Vital Records Handbook.* Baltimore: Genealogical Publishing Co., 1995.

Kurzweil, Arthur. *From Generation to Generation: How to Trace Your Jewish Genealogy and Personal History.* New York: Harper-Collins, 1994. A very personal approach to each step of the research process.

_____, and Miriam Weiner, eds. *The Encyclopedia of Jewish*

Genealogy. Vol. 1, *Sources in the United States and Canada.* Northvale, N.J.: Jason Aronson, 1991. An up-to-date finding aid for sources of Jewish genealogical information.

Mokotoff, Gary, and Sallyann Amdur Sack. *Where Once We Walked: A Guide to the Jewish Communities Destroyed in the Holocaust.* Teaneck, N.J.: Avotaynu, 1991. A gazetteer of 21,000 central and eastern European localities, arranged alphabetically and indexed phonetically under the Daitch-Mokotoff Soundex System so that various spellings can be readily found.

Pinkassim HaKehillot [Encyclopedae of Towns]. 14 vols. Jerusalem: Yad Vashem, 1984–92. Now fourteen volumes with more planned. A detailed history of Jewish communities in many areas of central and eastern Europe; there are five volumes for Poland alone.

Rottenberg, Dan. *Finding Our Fathers: A Guidebook to Jewish Genealogy.* Baltimore: Genealogical Publishing Co., 1986. A softcover reprint of the 1977 edition. The pioneer "how-to" guide with a list of every Jewish surname appearing in a variety of sources.

Sack, Sallyann Amdur. *A Guide to Jewish Genealogical Research in Israel.* Bergenfield, N.J.: Avotaynu, 1995. A detailed guide to the accessibility and holdings of each agency. Appendices include *yizkor* books and *landsmanshaftn* listed at Yad Vashem Library and a list of towns represented at the 1981 World Gathering of Holocaust Survivors.

Zubatsky, David S., and Irwin M. Berent. *Sourcebook for Jewish Genealogies and Family Histories.* Teaneck, N.J.: Avotaynu, 1996. A finding aid to published and manuscript genealogies in many Jewish archives and libraries for more than 10,000 surnames.

HOLOCAUST RESEARCH

Bibliography on Holocaust Literature. 2 vols. Boulder, Colo.: Westview Press, 1986. This work identifies more than 14,500 works on the Holocaust.

Yizkor books. More than 1,000 memorial books of towns in Eastern Europe where Jews once lived. Most written in Yiddish and Hebrew. Consult Sack, *A Guide to Jewish Genealogical Research in Israel,* for a list of towns that have *yizkor* books. The largest collections in the United States are at the YIVO Institute in New York and the Library of Congress in Washington. Large collections also exist at major Jewish, public, and university libraries throughout the United States and Canada.

Gedenkbuch. 2 vols. Koblenz, Germany: 1987. Compiled by the Bundesarchiv, Koblenz, Germany, and the International Tracing Service, Arolsen, Germany, with the cooperation of Yad Vashem, Jerusalem. Lists 128,000 Jewish victims of Nazis in Germany, 1933 to 1945, citing last place of residence, birth date, death date, and circumstances of death, if known.

Gilbert, Martin. *Atlas of the Holocaust.* Oxford: Pergamon Press, 1988. Maps depict the events of the Holocaust.

Hilberg, Raoul. *Destruction of European Jewry.* New York: Holmes & Meier, 1985. A good historical overview of the events of the Holocaust.

Klarefeld, Serge. *Memorial to Jews Deported From France.* New York: Klarefeld Foundation, 1983. Contains information about some 70,000 Jews deported from France to concentration camps, primarily Auschwitz. Gives name, birth date, and place of birth.

Mogilanski, Roman. *Ghetto Anthology.* Los Angeles: American Congress of Jews From Poland and Survivors of Concentration Camps, 1985. A description of events at most concentration camps and labor camps as well as some cities.

Mokotoff, Gary. *How to Document Victims and Locate Survivors of the Holocaust.* Bergenfield, N.J.: Avotaynu, 1995. A step-by-step guide to the various ways of locating information about Holocaust victims and survivors. Includes descriptions of the holdings of major repositories that have information and how to contact them.

MICROFICHE COLLECTIONS

These collections are available at any Jewish Genealogical Society meeting and through the Family History Library or can be purchased through Avotaynu, P.O. Box 900, Teaneck, NJ 07666.

Jewish Genealogical Family Finder. A database of ancestral towns and surnames being researched by some 2,500 Jewish genealogists throughout the world. Indexed by town name and surname.

Jewish Genealogical People Finder. A database of more than 300,000 individuals who appear on family trees of Jewish genealogists.

Jewish Genealogical Consolidated Surname Index. A list of more than 100,000 unique surnames showing in which of ten different databases each appears: Jewish Genealogical Family Finder, Jewish Genealogical People Finder, Russian Consular Records, Palestine Gazette, Emergency Passports, Memorial to Jews Deported From France, First American Jewish Families, U.S. State Department Records, Refusniks and Gedenkbuch.

Palestine Gazette. A list of more than 28,000 persons, mostly Jews, who legally changed their names while living in Palestine during the British Mandate from 1921 to 1948.

OTHER COLLECTIONS

Jewish Vital Statistics Records in Slovakian Archives.

Index to the 1784 Census of the Jews of Alsace.

Jewish Residents of Canada Extracted From Canadian Censuses of 1861–1901.

Index to Russian Consular Records.

Publications of the Jewish Genealogical Societies—1977 to 1990.

Index to Department of State Records Found in U.S. National Archives.

Galician Towns and Administrative Districts (a list of 6,000 Galician towns and the administrative districts to which they belong).

Gazetteer of Central and Eastern Europe. A consolidated listing of 350,000 place names in Austria, Bulgaria, Belarus,

Czechoslovakia, Estonia, Germany, Hungary, Latvia, Lithuania, Moldova, Poland, Romania, and the Ukraine.

Black Book of Localities Whose Jewish Population Was Exterminated By the Nazis (32,000 communities in Eastern Europe where Jews lived before the Holocaust).

Index to *Memorial to the Jews Deported From France* (a finding aid for the book cited above).

Index to Burials in Two Jewish Cemeteries in Washington, D.C.

SEPHARDIC GENEALOGY

Resources for Sephardic and Oriental genealogy are not as clearly defined as those for Ashkenazic. Below are some resources.

The American Sephardi Federation (ASF), 305 Seventh Ave., New York, N.Y. 10001, is an excellent source for finding Sephardic associations organized by nationality, such as the Turkish-Jewish Society, the Bulgarian-Jewish Association, the Syrian-Jewish Association, or any other oriental or Sephardic Jewish group. The ASF has lists of organizations in the United States and abroad.

The American Society of Sephardic Studies, 2815 Ocean Parkway, Brooklyn, NY 11235, is the New York center of Sephardic Jewry, especially Syrian.

Los Angeles has more Sephardic synagogues per square mile than almost any other city, except perhaps New York. Jewish Los Angeles, published by the Jewish Federation Council of Greater Los Angeles, 6505 Wilshire Blvd., Los Angeles, CA 90048, lists Sephardic synagogues by nationality. Write to the synagogue of interest for names of genealogists or contacts from that ethnic group.

In Spain, contact the Sephardic Museum in Toledo or the Ministry of Culture, Ministerio de Cultura, Museo Sefari, Toledo, Sinagoga del Transito, Ministerior de Cultura, No. I.P.O. 301-89-001. The Association of Friends of the Sephardic Museum in Spain is restoring the buildings and researching genealogy. For information about Beit Sefardi (Sephardic House) in Cordoba, Spain, or for Sephardic-interest publishers in Madrid, subscribe to *Raices,* a Spanish-language Sephardic magazine published by Sefarad Editores, Apartado 2021, 28080 Madrid. Inquire also about the church in Majorca that has the names of seventeenth-century New Christian conversos (Jews who were forced to convert to Christianity or face death or expulsion) engraved upon it.

Deposited in the Archives of the Indies in Seville, Spain, are 9 million maps, drawings, letters, and church records (and New Christian/Hebrew/converso church records). Many of the Spaniards who colonized the New World were, in fact, secret Jews. Large numbers settled in New Mexico and Mexico City. Spain warehoused all the documents generated from New Spain in the archive in Seville. Included are records of conversions, births, marriages, deaths, etc.

These records have been computerized to make them more easily available to researchers. The records were enhanced in the process of being digitized to eliminate water stains and deterioration, making them much more readable. In the United States, these records can be obtained through the Huntington Library in San Marino, California. The library's computer terminal is linked with Seville's main database via satellite. One can, for example, simply go to the Huntington Library, type in the name of an ancestor, and request a search for available records. If the name is in the database the computer will list all records (and dates) in which it appears. For example: Sebastian Cardoso, Mexico City, 1596–1649.

To locate European Sephardic genealogists, write to *Los Muestros (The Voice of Sephardim)* magazine, c/o Moises Rahmani, publisher, 25 Rue Dodonee, -B-, 1180 Brussels, Belgium. The subscription rate for the sixty-two-plus-page magazine is around thirty-five dollars yearly.

COLLECTED GENEALOGIES

Rosenstein, Neil. *The Unbroken Chain: Biographical Sketches and Genealogy of Illustrious Jewish Families From the 15th–20th Century.* 2 vols. Elizabeth, N.J.: The Computer Center for Jewish Genealogy, 1990. An enlarged revision of the 1977 edition. Includes descendants of the Katzenellenbogen family—Hassidic and other rabbis, Mendelssohn, Martin Buber, Karl Marx, Helena Rubinstein. Index of surnames only. Available from the Computer Center for Jewish Genealogy, 654 Westfield Ave., Elizabeth, NJ 07208.

Sackheim, George I. *Scattered Seeds.* 2 vols. Skokie, Ill.: R. Sackheim Publishing co. Chronicles 13,000 descendants of Rabbi Israel, one of the two martyrs of Rozanoi (Ruzhany), Byelorussia. He was executed after a blood libel of 1659. Indexed. Available from R. Sackheim Publishing Co., 9151 Crawford Ave., Skokie, IL 60076.

Stern, Malcolm H. *First American Jewish Families.* Baltimore: Ottenheimer Publishers, 1991. Reprint of a 1978 edition with an added update section. Contains genealogies of all available Jewish families settled in America prior to 1840, traced where possible to the present. 50,000-name index. Available from Ottenheimer Publishers, Inc., 300 Reisterstown Rd., Baltimore, MD 21208.

PERIODICALS

Avotaynu: The International Review of Jewish Genealogy. 1985–. Edited by Sallyann Amdur Sack and Gary Mokotoff. Quarterly. (P.O. Box 900, Teaneck, NJ 07666). Articles and data of general Jewish genealogical interest written by an international group of authors.

RESEARCH ARCHIVES AND LIBRARIES

These facilities are not staffed sufficiently to conduct research for individuals, but they will inform you of books or manuscripts on specific topics. (With any genealogical query, always enclose a self-addressed, stamped envelope.)

American Jewish Archives, 3101 Clifton Ave., Cincinnati, OH 45220 (on the campus of Hebrew Union College). Specializes in data on Jews in the western hemisphere. Contains many genealogies, vital records, biographies, organizational and congregational records, and newspaper indexes. Finding aids: James W. Clasper and M. Carolyn Dellenbach, *Guide to the Holdings of the American Jewish Archives* (Cincinnati: 1979). Also see Zubatsky and Berent, above.

American Jewish Historical Society, 2 Thornton Rd., Waltham, MA 02154 (on the campus of Brandeis University). All areas of American Jewish history, including organizational and institutional records, as well as family documents.

LDS Family History Library, 35 North West Temple, Salt Lake City, UT 84150. The world's most complete and technologically current genealogical library. Open to all researchers. Books and microfilms include Jewish records from many countries, notably Poland, Germany, and Hungary. Microfilms may be obtained through interlibrary loan at local LDS family history centers. Computerized and microfiche catalogs are available at branch libraries. Finding aid: Johni Cerny and Wendy Elliott, eds., *The Library: A Guide to the LDS Family History Library* (Salt Lake City: Ancestry, 1988). Separate chapters are devoted to records for each region of the United States and countries abroad.

Leo Baeck Institute, 129 E. 73rd St., New York, NY 10021. Library and archive of surviving records of Jews from German-speaking lands.

Library of Congress. Jefferson (main) Building, housing the Genealogy and Local History, Independence Ave. between 1st and 2nd St. S.W., Washington, D.C. Contains every book submitted for U.S. copyright, city directories, maps, gazetteers, Hebraic Division. Finding aid: James C. Neagles, *The Library of Congress: A Guide to Genealogical and Historical Research* (Salt Lake City: Ancestry 1990). The Hebraic section is located in the John Adams building.

National Archives and Records Administration, 8th and Pennsylvania Ave. N.W., Washington, DC 20408. The research room has federal censuses 1790 to 1920, passenger arrival records, eighteenth- and nineteenth-century military records, some naturalizations, land records. Holocaust-related documents from captured German records. Regional branches have microfilmed copies and regional records. Finding aids: *Guide to Genealogical Research in the National Archives,* rev. ed. (Washington, D.C.: National Archives and Records Administration, 1991) and Loretto Dennis Szucs and Sandra Hargreaves Luebking, *The Archives: A Guide to the National Archives Field Branches* (Salt Lake City: Ancestry, 1988).

U.S. Holocaust Museum, 100 Raoul Wallenberg Place S.W., Washington, DC 20024. This newest genealogical resource opened in July 1993. It has a library and archive that include many unique records concerning the Holocaust. As it acquires more material, it is expected to become the principal Holocaust research center in the United States.

YIVO Institute for Jewish Research, 555 W. 57th St., New York, NY 10019. Library and archive of data from Yiddish-speaking lands. Finding aid: Guzik, *Genealogical Resources in the New York Metropolitan Area* (cited earlier).

SOCIETIES

There are more than sixty Jewish genealogical societies worldwide. For a list, send a self-addressed, stamped envelope to the Association of Jewish Genealogical Societies, P.O. Box 50245, Palo Alto, CA 94303.

TRACKING TWENTIETH-CENTURY ANCESTORS
CHAPTER CONTENTS

18

TRACKING TWENTIETH-CENTURY ANCESTORS

Kathleen W. Hinckley

All genealogists must begin research in the twentieth century if they adhere to the rule "start with yourself and work backward," but there are many other reasons to focus attention in the twentieth century: searching for birth families (adoption); locating missing heirs, relatives, or friends; planning family, class, or military reunions; or locating descendants while compiling a family history.

Research methodology to achieve the above goals is similar to other time periods, especially when using the traditional sources, such as cemetery, census, church, court, land, newspaper, military, and vital records. The challenge of twentieth-century research lies in coping with privacy laws, record destruction, the overwhelming volume of records, the high mobility of the population, and keeping current with computer databases.

Research in this century allows interviews with relatives, friends, and neighbors, and thus access to information not usually found in public records—a bonus not enjoyed when researching earlier time periods. Twentieth-century research also includes records and databases that are unique to this time period, such as Social Security applications or driver and vehicle records.

When conducting twentieth-century research, begin with the most common and readily available record types. These sources will give the most information and build a solid base upon which to continue the research. The more specialized records can then be utilized, depending upon what type of additional information is needed. Listed below are the common and specialized sources discussed in this chapter:

Common sources of information are:

- Vital records
- Censuses
- Directories
- Probate records
- Newspaper obituaries
- Funeral home records
- Cemetery records
- Social Security records
- Military records

- Voter registration records
- School and university records
- Personal advertisements and bulletin boards

Specialized sources of information:

- Biographical indexes and databases
- Employment records
- U.S. Postal Service records
- Criminal records
- Insurance records
- Medical records
- Motor vehicle records
- Immigration and naturalization records
- "Orphan Train" records
- American Red Cross
- Salvation Army
- Information brokers

PRIVACY VERSUS ACCESS

The Freedom of Information Act (Public Law 5 USC 552A), which went into effect 4 July 1967, and the Privacy Act of 1974 (5 USC 552B) affect access to twentieth-century records. Genealogists will always encounter the conflict between rights of privacy and rights of access. Simply stated, the following general rules apply to most federal and state records:[1]

- There are no restrictions on records that concern the requester him- or herself.

- Information may be obtained about other living persons with written, notarized permission from the individual.

- Information may be obtained about a deceased person by providing proof of death—for example, a death certificate. Relationship to the deceased is sometimes required, depending upon the type of record.

- There are no restrictions on records created seventy-five to one hundred years ago. There are exceptions, such as the seventy-two-year restriction on census records. Some records of the Immigration and Naturalization Service are restricted for twenty-five to fifty years.

- Some agencies may require "just cause" to open the records—medical or legal considerations, for example.

- Records containing information on adoption, illegitimacy, or mental health remain closed indefinitely, except by court order.

- The Freedom of Information Act of 1974 requires federal government agencies and the armed forces to release records to the public on request unless the information is exempted by the Privacy Act or for national security reasons.

Many states create their own privacy laws, so their records may not be bound by the rules above; however, similar rules may apply. Private records are not subject to these laws. Access to these records will depend upon policies of each agency.

VITAL RECORDS

Birth, marriage, divorce, and death records are invaluable in twentieth-century research; however, information gleaned from these certificates needs supporting documentation because errors and omissions appear even in "official" records. It is not unusual, for example, for the names of an individual's parents to vary between a death certificate and a Social Security application.

STANDARD POLICIES AND LAWS

Access to birth and death records is subject to privacy laws and may be difficult to obtain. Laws pertaining to birth records are more stringent for two major reasons: (1) they can reveal illegitimacy, and (2) they are sometimes fraudulently used to establish a new identity. Marriage and divorce records, on the other hand, are public records in most states and are more accessible. A few states, such as New York, open divorce records only to the parties involved.

Registration of vital events is a state function governed by state law, regulations, and policy. Thus, states' policies regarding the releasing of certificates to genealogists vary. Statewide registration of birth and death records was required by law in the early 1900s for most states. When a state reached ninety-percent registration of births or deaths, it was required to enter the National Registration Area. A study of the time gap between these two events indicated that an average of 21.9 years elapsed after a law was passed before ninety percent or more of a state's population was included in the records. This gap may explain why a birth or death record cannot be located in an area or time period in which the law required registration of birth or death.[2]

The Model State Vital Statistics Act and Regulations (MSVSA)[3] serves as a guideline to states when legislators consider revision of vital statistic laws. More than thirty states have enacted portions of the model act; none have adopted it in its entirety. The first model act was developed in 1907, and there have been several revisions since—the most recent in 1977 and 1993. The 1977 model proposed that when one hundred years have elapsed after the date of birth, or fifty years have elapsed after the date of death, marriage, or divorce, the records shall become public and made available in accordance with other regulations. During the 1993 revision process, the revision committee considered reducing the span before which a death record becomes public from fifty to twenty-five years, but later changed its decision, realizing that some individuals' right to privacy could be violated, and to prevent fraudulent use of these records.

Other points covered in this model include delayed registration of birth or death; new certificates of birth following adoption, legitimation, paternity determination, and paternity acknowledgment; and regulations regarding the amendment of vital records.

A change in the 1993 model from the 1977 version recommends that family members doing genealogical research and genealogists representing family members to be allowed to obtain copies of records needed for their research. The 1993 model also recommends that, unless the registrant is deceased, appropriate authorizations be obtained from the registrant or relevant family members.

ACCESS TO VITAL RECORDS

Thomas Jay Kemp, *International Vital Records Handbook,* 3rd ed. (Baltimore: Genealogical Publishing Co., 1994), includes copies of application forms (which you may photocopy and use) for every state and provides addresses, telephone numbers, fees, and dates for which birth, marriage, and death records are available. This handbook is current as of the date of publication only; therefore, it is advisable to telephone the state health department to verify the fee and address before ordering a certificate. Current fees and addresses of all states are also available from the vital records section of the health department of each state.

There are currently 110 state and local government offices in forty-seven states that will process telephone orders for vital certificates through Visa or MasterCard. The cost of the certificate ordered, the overnight fee (if requested), and a service fee will appear on your Visa or MasterCard statement.

VitalChek Network, Inc. (1-800-255-2414), can provide the correct telephone number to place your order directly. This nationwide list of telephone numbers has also been distributed to more than five thousand post offices that process passport applications.

FOREIGN BIRTHS AND DEATHS

Births and deaths of U.S. citizens in foreign countries are reported to the nearest U.S. consulate or embassy. The U.S. Department of State issues certified copies of these foreign births only to the subject, the subject's parents or legal guardian, or a person who submits written authorization from the subject. To request copies of the Consular Report of Birth (DS-1350), write to Passport Services, Correspondence Branch, U.S. Department of State, 1425 K St. N.W., Room 386, Washington, DC 20522-1705. To determine the current fee and information required to order the birth record, consult *Where to Write for Vital Records: Births, Deaths, Marriages, and Divorces* (Hyattsville, Md.: U.S. Department of Health and Human Services Publication No. [PHS] 93-1142).

Deaths of U.S. citizens in foreign countries may be reported to the nearest U.S. consular office. If reported, and if a copy of the local death certificate and evidence of U.S. citizenship are presented, the consul prepares the official Report of the Death of an American Citizen Abroad (form OF-180). A copy of the report is then filed permanently with the U.S. Department of State (with the exception of military personnel).

To obtain a copy of a non-military death report filed in 1960 or after, write to Passport Services, Correspondence Branch, U.S. Department of State, Washington, DC 20522-1705. For reports of non-military deaths filed before 1960, write to the

National Archives and Records Service, Diplomatic Records Branch, Washington, DC 20408.

For reports of overseas military deaths (U.S. Army, U.S. Navy, U.S. Marines, U.S. Air Force, and U.S. Coast Guard) or civilian employees of the Department of Defense, write to the National Personnel Records Center (Military Personnel Records), 9700 Page Blvd., St. Louis, MO 63132-5100.

Refer to Kemp's *International Vital Records Handbook* for addresses and forms to use when ordering a vital record directly from a country.

Birth records of alien children adopted by U.S. citizens and lawfully admitted to the United States are filed within the state of adoption, but they may also be on file with the Immigration and Naturalization Services, U.S. Department of Justice, Washington, DC 20536. Requests must be submitted on INS Form G-641, which can be obtained from any INS office.

When a birth or death occurs in international territory, whether on an aircraft or a seagoing vessel, the record is filed based on the direction in which the mode of transportation was moving when the event occurred:

- If the vessel or aircraft was outbound or had docked or landed in a foreign destination, requests for copies of the record should be made to the U.S. Department of State, Washington, DC 20522-1705.

- If the vessel or aircraft was inbound and the first port of entry was in the United States, write to the registration authority in the city where the vessel or aircraft docked or landed in the United States.

- If a vessel was of U.S. registry, contact the U.S. Coast Guard facility at the port of entry and/or search the vessel logs at the U.S. Coast Guard facility at the vessel's final port of call for that voyage.

- Deaths that occur on airplanes or trains crossing the continental United States are filed in the county where the first stop is made. Births, however, are filed in the county where the mother and child disembark from the plane or train, even when several stops are made along the way.

BIRTH CERTIFICATES

Official birth certificates were not issued by most states until 1910 or later. Privacy laws make them the most difficult vital records to obtain. Some states will issue a birth certificate if a copy of the death certificate is attached to the application. Three types of birth certificates exist:

- Original: the record filed at birth.

- Amended: a revised birth record with additional or corrected information, such as names of birth parents changed to names of adoptive parents; or name of birth father added; or correction given on spelling of names, etc.

- Delayed: a certificate issued several years after a birth because an original birth certificate was not filed. Many delayed birth certificates were issued in the early 1940s as proof of age for Social Security applicants. To obtain a delayed certificate, applicants submit an affidavit by an individual who was present at birth or baptismal, Bible, school, or census records to document their age.

The Family History Library of The Church of Jesus Christ of Latter-day Saints in Salt Lake City has the statewide birth indexes listed in table 18-1; more may become available in the future.

Table 18-1. Statewide Birth Indexes at the Family History Library

Alabama	1917–19
Delaware	1861–1913
Hawaii	1909–49
Iowa	1880–1934
Kentucky	1911–54
Maine	1892–1922
Massachusetts	1841–1971; delayed and corrected, 1893–1970
New Jersey	1901–23 (not at Family History Library; located at New Jersey State Archives)
New York City	1881–1965
Pennsylvania	Philadelphia birth corrections 1872–1915, 1967–81
Tennessee	1908–12
Texas	1900–45
Vermont	1871–1908
Washington	1907–59; delayed, 1936–53
Wisconsin	1852–1907

MARRIAGE CERTIFICATES

Marriage records are usually filed at the county or town level, rather than the state office of vital statistics. The statewide marriage indexes listed in table 18-2 are available at the appropriate state vital records departments; copies held by the Family History Library are noted. Additional information concerning these indexes (and the divorce indexes) can be found in Alice Eichholz, ed., *Ancestry's Red Book: American State, County and Town Sources,* rev. ed. (Salt Lake City: Ancestry, 1992).

DIVORCE RECORDS

Although divorce records are technically court records, they are discussed here because they are related to marriage records.

Divorce records may reveal dates of birth (or ages) of both parties, state or country of birth of both parties, date and place of marriage, names and ages (or birth dates) of minor children, occupations, residence addresses (and changes of address), property owned, military service (if receiving pension or benefit), maiden name of wife, grounds for the divorce, and Social Security numbers.

The original divorce case files are often in the county where the divorce was granted. Some states require a copy of the final divorce decree to be filed with the state department of vital statistics, thereby creating a statewide index. Statewide divorce indexes known to exist are listed in table 18-2.

DEATH CERTIFICATES

Death certificates are easier to obtain than other vital records because a person's right to privacy ends upon death. However,

Table 18-2. Statewide Marriage and Divorce Indexes Held by State Health Departments

State	Marriage	Divorce	State	Marriage	Divorce
Alabama		1908–37 (FHL)	Missouri		July 1948–
Alaska		1950–	Montana		July 1943–
Arkansas	1917–	1923–	Nevada	1968– (Clark County [Las Vegas] has index, 1907–68; FHL has index, 1968–91)	1968–
California	1949–85 (FHL has indexes, 1960–1985)	1962–			
Colorado	1900–39 (FHL); groom index only	1900–39, 1975–	New Hampshire		Pre-1968 (FHL)
Connecticut		1947–	New York	1881–1917 (excludes New York City)	
District of Columbia	1811–1921		New York City	1888–1937 (FHL)	
Florida	1927–69 (FHL)		North Carolina	1962–	
Hawaii	1909–44 (FHL)	1951–	North Dakota	1925–	1949–
Idaho	1947–	1947–	Ohio	1949–	
Illinois	1962–	1962–	Oregon	1906–24, 1946–59, 1966–89	1946–60, 1966–89
Indiana	1958–		Rhode Island		1962–
Kansas	1913–	1951–	South Dakota	1905–	1905–
Kentucky	1958–	1958–	Tennessee	1945–	1945–
Maine	Brides, 1892– (FHL, 1895–1953); grooms, 1956–		Texas	1966–	1968–
			Vermont	1871–1908 (FHL); 1909–41, 1942–54	1861–1968
Maryland	June 1951–				
Massachusetts	1841–1971 (FHL)	1952– (FHL, 1952–70)	Washington	1968–	1968–
			West Virginia	1921–	
Michigan	1872–1921*		Wisconsin	1852–1907 (FHL); 1973–84	1965–84 (FHL)
Minnesota	1958–	1970–			
Mississippi	Pre-1926 (FHL); grooms only		Wyoming	1941–	1941–

* This microfilmed index is available at the Library of Michigan, State Archives of Michigan, the Burton Historical Collection of the Detroit Public Library, and the Allen County Public Library in Fort Wayne, Indiana.

some state health departments refuse to release death certificates to genealogists, while others will issue uncertified copies. The statewide death indexes listed in table 18-3 are currently available through the Family History Library. Indexes available through other libraries are noted as well.

CENSUS RECORDS

FEDERAL CENSUS RECORDS

Federal census enumerations made from 1790 to 1920 are a major source for genealogists and are discussed in depth in chapter 5, Research in Census Records. The federal census enumerations made from 1930 through 1990 are confidential, but it is possible to obtain information about a deceased relative or a living individual with written permission from the person or proof of death. To request a search, submit form BC-600 (Application for Search of Census Records) to the U.S. Department of Commerce, P.O. Box 1545, Jefferson, IN 47131. The bureau will provide a transcript of the census information, not a full copy. For its basic fee, the bureau will report the county, name, relationship, age, place of birth, race, citizenship, and occupation. For an additional sum, a "full schedule" giving information from each column on the census schedule will be supplied. A full schedule covers only one individual; other members of the same household are not included.

STATE CENSUS RECORDS

The twentieth-century state census enumerations listed in table 18-4 are available. (Also see chapter 5.)

DIRECTORIES

CITY DIRECTORIES

City directories comprise one of the most useful tools in twentieth-century research because they track an individual's residence, occupation, and place of employment. Analysis of directory information may provide clues about changes of residence, marriage, and death. Some directories include names of minor children with years of birth or ages, dates of death, or place of removal (a move to another city or state).

Directories also provide information on names of churches, cemeteries, fraternal organizations, hospitals, and businesses within a community. Refer to chapter 11, Research in Directories, for additional information about locating and using all types of directories.

Repositories with large collections of city directories include the Family History Library, the Library of Congress, the American Antiquarian Society (Worcester, Massachusetts), the New England Historic Genealogical Society (Boston), the Allen County Public Library (Fort Wayne, Indiana), the Newberry

Library (Chicago), and the New York Public Library. Large cities, such as New York City, Los Angeles, and Chicago, stopped publishing city directories in the 1920s and 1930s; telephone directories are the only available similar source.

HOUSEHOLDER DIRECTORIES

Identifying and locating neighbors of an individual is an important information-gathering step. Interviewing a neighbor may uncover clues not found in public records, such as the reason a neighbor moved, where they moved, names of children, name of employers, and colleges attended by children. Householder directories (also known as criss-cross directories) list neighborhoods by address, thereby providing names of neighbors. Some city directories include a householder section; other cities publish them as separate volumes.

CROSS-REFERENCE DIRECTORIES

Cross-reference directories are published annually for major cities in the United States and Canada and are typically available in the business or real estate divisions of large libraries. Although cross-reference directories list households by address, they also indicate the year in which each property was purchased, a better clue to locating neighbors who might have known the individual being researched. A number of firms publish these guides, each one covering different cities or states. The major publishers of cross-reference directories are Cole Publications, Division of Metromail and R.R. Donnelley Co., Lincoln, Nebraska; and Haines & Co., 29410 Union City Blvd., Union City, California. The Cole directories cover markets in Arizona, Arkansas, Colorado, Idaho, Iowa, Kansas, Louisiana, Massachusetts, Minnesota, Missouri, Montana, Nebraska, New York, Oklahoma, Oregon, Pennsylvania, Rhode Island, South Dakota, Tennessee, Texas, Utah, Washington, West Virginia, and Wyoming. The Haines directories cover markets in California, District of Columbia, Georgia, Illinois, Indiana, Kentucky, Louisiana, Missouri, New York, and Ohio.

TELEPHONE DIRECTORIES

Telephone directories exist for every community in the United States, thereby providing a tremendous research tool for tracking individuals. Unfortunately, it is difficult to locate collections of outdated telephone books. They are often discarded, and only current editions are available at libraries. Telephone companies usually archive outdated telephone books, but even this practice is being discontinued as their volume becomes unmanageable. Some telephone companies are beginning to deposit their archived collections with public repositories, but continued retention is questionable. You can order a current telephone directory for any city in the United States through your local telephone company.

Use the telephone book in the same manner as a city directory, checking every year. Some individuals will appear in a telephone directory a few years after dropping from a city directory, usually when they begin residing in a retirement community or nursing home.

Current telephone directories are available on microfiche ("phonefiche") at many public and university libraries. Some libraries purchase regional portions of the collection; others have the microfiche for the entire United States. The accompanying *Community Cross-Reference Guide to Phonefiche* (Wooster, Ohio: Newspaper Indexing Center, Micro Photo Di-

Table 18-3. Statewide Death Indexes at the Family History Library

State	Years
Alabama	1917–19
California	1905–88, 1940–90
Delaware	1855–1910
Florida	1877–1969 (by year)
Hawaii	1909–49
Idaho	1911–32
Illinois	1916–38 (certificates, 1916–45, excluding Chicago); Cook County clerk index, 1871–1916; Cook County Board of Health, 1871–1933, Cook County out of town, 1909–15
Indiana	Some county death indexes available through 1920
Kentucky	1911–86
Maine	1892–1922 (New England Historic Genealogical Society has a Maine death index through 1970)
Massachusetts	1844–1971*
Michigan	1867–1914**
Minnesota	ca. 1866–1915
New Jersey	1901–40 (not in Family History Library; located at New Jersey State Archives)
New York City	1868–1965 (actual death certificates through 1948 available at NYC Municipal Archives)
North Carolina	1901–67 (certificates, 1906–94)
Ohio	1913–32; veterans, 1941–64 (death records from 20 Dec. 1908 through 31 Dec. 1936 [and respective indexes] are located at the State Archives of Ohio, Ohio Historical Society)
Oregon	1903–70 (deaths, 1903–39, are available at Oregon State Archives, Oregon State Library, and Oregon Historical Society)
Pennsylvania (Philadelphia only)	1904–15
Rhode Island	1901–43
Tennessee	1914–42 (by county)
Texas	1900–45***
Vermont	1871–1908
Washington	1907–79
Wisconsin	1959–84

* The New England Historic Genealogical Society (NEHGS), 101 Newbury Street, Boston, MA 02116, has the statewide death index (in book form), 1901–76.

** This index is not in the FHL. It is available at the Library of Michigan, State Archives of Michigan, the Burton Historical Collection of the Detroit Public Library, and the Allen County Public Library, Fort Wayne, Indiana.

*** The genealogy collection of the Texas State Library has the following Texas Bureau of Vital Statistics indexes: births, 1903–76; marriages, 1966–94; divorces, 1968–94; deaths, 1903–94.

Table 18-4. Twentieth-Century State Census Enumerations

State	Years
Alabama	1907, Confederate veterans; 1921, Confederate pensioners
Alaska	(St. Paul and St. George islands) 1904, 1905, 1906–07, 1914, 1917
Arizona	Great registers of voters (vary by county)
Arkansas	1911, Confederate veterans
California	Some cities and towns have special twentieth-century censuses. The California State Archives has a complete listing
Connecticut	1917 military census
Florida	1935, 1945
Indiana	Jackson Township, Washington County, 1901; Henry County, 1913; Jackson Township, Ripley County, 1919; Center Township, Starke County, 1919; Henry County, 1931
Iowa	1905, 1915, 1925
Kansas	1905, 1915, 1925
Maine	1906 (York County only)
Minnesota	1905
Nebraska	School censuses available at Nebraska State: Buffalo County, 1902–04; Cass County, 1860–1977; Chase County, 1910–77; Clay County, 1872–1912; Lancaster County, 1875–1912; York County, 1905–73; various years available for Burt, Butler, Dawson, Gage, Hall, Harlan, Jefferson, Johnson, Kearney, Madison, Nuckolls, Otoe, Saunders, Sherman, and Washington counties
New Jersey	1905, 1915
New Mexico	Weed, Pinon, Avis, and McDonald Flats, 1904; Columbus, Luna County, 1913; Belen, 1918; Los Lunas, 1928
New York	1905, 1915, 1925
North Dakota	1915, 1925
Oklahoma	1907 (Seminole County only)
Oregon	1905 (Baker, Linn, Lane, and Marion counties)
Rhode Island	1905, 1915, 1925, 1935
South Dakota	1905, 1915, 1925, 1935, 1945
Wisconsin	1905

vision, Bell & Howell Co.) assists researchers in determining which communities are covered in a given telephone directory. For example, this guide would advise that the community of Heidelberg, Mississippi, is in the Laurel, Mississippi, telephone directory.

Nationwide telephone directories are becoming available on CD-ROM from several companies, such as ProCD, Inc., American Business Information, Digital Directory Assistance, and Parsons Technology. These telephone directories are available at most retail computer stores and range in price from $20 to $150. The databases vary slightly, as each company compiles information from different mailing lists, voter registrations, or telephone directories. None of the commercial telephone CD-ROMs are official telephone directories. Some products can only be searched by name; others have reverse searches that allow you to search or sort by address, telephone number, zip code, or name.

The telephone companies are beginning to compete with this market by selling their official telephone books on CD-ROM. Check with your local telephone company to determine availability and price. The Family History Library and many public libraries have one or more of these telephone CD-ROMs available for research.

PROBATE RECORDS

Never assume an individual did not own enough property to require probate action. Probate is common in the twentieth-century; therefore, always search testate and intestate indexes. Some probate clerks will check their indexes through a telephone request; others require written requests.

Examine all papers within a probate file to gather changes of address and other seemingly minor details that may prove important. If ordering photocopies by telephone, be very specific about which documents you need, because the cost often exceeds $1.00 per page. The more important documents in a probate file include the application for adjudication of intestacy, the will, the petition for probate of will, letters testamentary, the inventory, and the final report. The final report gives details of estate distribution to heirs, legatees, and devisees with complete name and address as well as relationship to the deceased. Death certificates are often found within a probate file, which can be extremely valuable when vital records are difficult to access.

Guardianship or conservatorship files may also exist for an individual prior to his or her death. These files are located in the probate office and are not always referenced within the probate file. Adoptions can also appear in the probate clerk's files, but they are usually sealed.

OBITUARIES AND FUNERAL NOTICES

Obituaries often provide important clues or direct information. A good obituary can save hours of research and frustration by providing information such as the deceased's date and place of birth, date and place of marriage, other lifetime residences, military service, employment, civic activities, and religious affiliation. A newspaper obituary or funeral notice that lists survivors with their current cities and states of residence is often the breakthrough that solves the problem of finding living descendants.

Individual obituaries are sometimes printed in more than one newspaper, and the content and completeness may vary among the newspapers. The newspapers may be within the same city, but the obituary will have been edited by one newspaper, as in the example below.

From the *Rocky Mountain News,* Denver, Colorado, 13 October 1959, p. 59:

> Col. Thomas N. Gimperling
>
> Funeral services for Col. Thomas N. Gimperling will be at 10 a.m. Tuesday, in Olinger Mortuary, Speer blvd. Burial will be in Arlington National Cemetery.
>
> Col. Gimperling died Sunday in St. Luke's Hospital after a short illness. He was 79.
>
> Born June 5, 1880, in Dayton, Ohio, he was reared

and educated there and *enlisted in the Army at 17 during the Spanish-American War*. He was graduated from West Point in 1904.

He married Miss Helen Campbell in 1909 at Annapolis, Md.

Col. Gimperling served with the 30th Division in France during World War I and with the 103d Division in Denver as recruiting officer during World War II.

Col. Gimperling was a member of the Denver Club and the Denver Country Club. He lived at 605 E. Ninth ave.

Surviving, in addition to his wife, is a daughter, Mrs. Gretchen T. Singles of Alexandria, Va., and a grandson, *Cadet Gordon Singles of West Point.*

From *The Denver Post*, Denver, Colorado, 14 October 1959, p. 40:

T.N. Gimperling

Services for Thomas N. Gimperling, 79, of 605 E. 9th Ave., a retired U.S. Army colonel, were held Tuesday at the Olinger Mortuary, Speer Blvd. and Sherman St. Interment will be Thursday at Arlington National Cemetery, Arlington, Va.

Gimperling died in St. Luke's Hospital Sunday.

He was born and reared in Dayton, Ohio, attended public schools there, and was graduated from U.S. Military Academy, West Point, N.Y., in 1904.

He married the former Helen Campbell at Annapolis, Md., in 1909.

Gimperling served with the 30th Infantry Division in France during World War I and as an enlistment and recruiting officer with 103rd Division in Denver during World War II.

He was a member of the Denver Club and the Denver Country Club.

Survivors in addition to his wife include a daughter, Mrs. Gretchen *Tritch* Singles, Alexandria, and a grandson.

Note the difference between the two obituaries. The first one includes information about service in the Spanish-American War and the complete name of the grandson. The second obituary gives a middle name (perhaps a family surname) for the daughter.

Obituaries may also appear in hometown newspapers. This occurs when a death is reported to friends or relatives in places of former residence, where it is then published.

Ethnic newspapers and trade journals also publish obituaries. These specialized publications may be found in historical societies and libraries. Refer to chapter 12, Research in Newspapers, for more information about locating newspapers and repositories that maintain newspaper collections. Some newspapers are available through interlibrary loan.

Local libraries often maintain current obituary indexes and will search for and photocopy an obituary upon request. Keep in mind the difference between an obituary and a funeral notice, as some libraries do not index both. A funeral notice announces the date and place of a funeral and may include names of survivors; an obituary is a more complete biographical sketch of the individual. The local historical society, archive, or genealogical society may also maintain newspaper obituary indexes. Examples of libraries that have obituary indexes are Alabama's Birmingham Public Library, which has maintained a file of obituaries from the *Birmingham News* and the *Birmingham Post Herald* since 1978; the Denver Public Library, which has indexes for obituaries from the *Denver Post* and the *Rocky Mountain News* since 1940; Indiana's South Bend Public Library, which has a card index to obituaries from the *South Bend Tribune* from 1940 to the present; and the Cleveland Public Library, which collects death notices from Cleveland newspapers, 1833 to the present.

Betty Jarboe, *Obituaries: A Guide to Sources*, 2nd ed. (Boston: G.K. Hall, 1989), is an excellent bibliography of references to books or articles that index or abstract obituaries. It is impossible to have a complete and current bibliography, of course, but this reference may save time in determining the location of publication of obituaries within specific time periods or places.

For research concerning a nationally prominent individual, *The New York Times Obituaries Index, 1858–1968* (New York: New York Times, 1970) and *The New York Times Obituary Index II, 1969–1978* (New York: New York Times, 1980) are important sources to consider. The first volume is from September 1858 through December 1968 and includes more than 353,000 names. The second volume added more than 36,000 names from the period 1969 to 1978.

Haverford College, *Quaker Necrology Index of Haverford College*, 2 vols. (Boston: G.K. Hall, 1961), includes approximately 59,000 entries from four Quaker periodicals between 1828 and 1960 and is a good example of published obituary references. Another example is the *Alaska Times Obituaries Index 1915–1980*, available on microfiche at the Family History Library.

FUNERAL HOME RECORDS

Funeral directors gather information about deceased persons from their families; consequently, they sometimes have information not included on the death certificate or obituary, such as complete addresses of survivors, names of pallbearers, insurance information, and financial arrangements.

Funeral home records are not public; therefore, release of information from them is a matter of individual policy. They are maintained by the funeral home owner. When the business is sold, the new owners usually keep the old records. Sometimes, however, the original owner does not relinquish the records and they end up stored in a basement or attic. A few of these valuable records are eventually recovered by family members and deposited at public libraries and museums. Sometimes—to the horror of genealogists—the records are destroyed when the business is sold. When trying to determine the location of a defunct funeral home's records, write to the local historical society. The staff may know the name of the current owner and/or the disposition of the records.

Some funeral home records have been microfilmed and are

available through the Family History Library; look under "state-county (or city)-business records and commerce" or "funeral" in the *Family History Library Catalog* (see chapter 2, Databases, Indexes, and Other Finding Aids). For example, the following funeral home records are available:

CALIFORNIA

San Francisco: J.C. O'Conner & Co. Undertakers, 1882–1919.

COLORADO

Colorado Springs: Beyle Brothers Undertakers, 1897–1940; Nolan Funeral Home, 1922–37.

ILLINOIS

Chicago: Carlson Funeral Home, ca. 1938–74; Otto Funeral Home, 1912–49; Phillips-Peterson Funeral Home, 1937–73.

PENNSYLVANIA

Philadelphia: Undertaker records of William F. Cushing, 1901–20.

Funeral home records are often abstracted and published in genealogical society journals. Use the *PERiodical Source Index (PERSI)* as a finding tool (see chapter 2).

Record-keeping styles vary among funeral homes from annual to cumulative surname indexes. If the funeral home maintains annual indexes, the request must be very specific.

The annual *National Yellow Book, Funeral Directors and Suppliers* (Youngstown, Ohio: Nomis Publication), is a helpful resource for determining the name of a likely funeral home (also published as Green Book, Red Book, and Blue Book by other companies). A current edition that lists directors with their addresses and telephone numbers is in many large libraries and most local mortuaries. A city or state directory will also list names of funeral homes, as will, of course, the yellow pages of a telephone directory.

CEMETERY RECORDS

Many cemetery offices maintain comprehensive indexes to all burials (cremations may be in a separate index). A quick search of such an index may solve many research headaches. Privacy policies vary, of course, depending upon the type of cemetery. Information about the deceased should be readily available; however, there may be problems obtaining facts about living descendants of the deceased. The cemetery can also provide the name of the funeral home.

Determining if there is a family burial plot may reveal valuable information, as may visiting the cemetery and noting information on the tombstone and names of persons buried nearby. The cemetery office should have the name of the individual who purchased the plot, as well as the current owner.

See chapter 3, Research in Birth, Death, and Cemetery Records, for a state-by-state list of local cemetery surveys and major collections of published tombstone readings. Deborah M. Burek, ed., *Cemeteries of the U.S.: A Guide to Contact Information for U.S. Cemeteries and Their Records* (Detroit: Gale Research, 1994), is helpful to locate names of cemeteries in a specific area.

SOCIAL SECURITY RECORDS

An individual's Social Security number can be helpful in gaining access to some twentieth-century records, but the number must first, of course, be known. If family papers do not supply one, it can sometimes be obtained from a voter registration card, military papers, driver's license, credit report, tax lien, divorce file, or death certificate. At many workplaces the corporate identification number issued an employee is the same as his or her Social Security number. On 1 July 1969, the U.S. Army and U.S. Air Force began using the Social Security number as the military service number. The U.S. Navy and U.S. Marine Corps initiated the same policy on 1 July 1972, and the U.S. Coast Guard on 1 October 1974. The Department of Veterans Affairs uses a patient's Social Security number as a hospital admission number and for other record-keeping purposes.

Since Social Security was begun in 1937, more than 350 million numbers have been issued, and each year another 5 million are added. The first three digits of the Social Security number comprise the area number, which indicates (with some exceptions) one of two things: where the person applied (in applications made before 1972) or where the person resided at the time of the application (for those after 1972); it does not necessarily represent the place of birth. The Social Security Administration occasionally assigns another three-digit area number to a state; therefore, some states are listed more than once in the list below. These area numbers are effective as of October 1995.

001–003	New Hampshire
004–007	Maine
008–009	Vermont
010–034	Massachusetts
035–039	Rhode Island
040–049	Connecticut
050–134	New York
135–158	New Jersey
159–211	Pennsylvania
212–220	Maryland
221–222	Delaware
223–231	Virginia
232–236	West Virginia
237–246	North Carolina
247–251	South Carolina
252–260	Georgia
261–267	Florida
268–302	Ohio
303–317	Indiana
318–361	Illinois
362–386	Michigan
387–399	Wisconsin
400–407	Kentucky
408–415	Tennessee
416–424	Alabama

425–428	Mississippi
429–432	Arkansas
433–439	Louisiana
440–448	Oklahoma
449–467	Texas
468–477	Minnesota
478–485	Iowa
486–500	Missouri
501–502	North Dakota
503–504	South Dakota
505–508	Nebraska
509–515	Kansas
516–517	Montana
518–519	Idaho
520	Wyoming
521–524	Colorado
525	New Mexico
526–527	Arizona
528–529	Utah
530	Nevada
531–539	Washington
540–544	Oregon
545–573	California
574	Alaska
574SE	Asian refugees between April 1975 and November 1979
575–576	Hawaii
577–579	District of Columbia
580	Virgin Islands
580–584	Puerto Rico
585	New Mexico
586SE	Asian refugees between April 1975 and November 1979
586	American Samoa, Philippine Islands, Guam
587–588	Mississippi
589–595	Florida
596–599	Puerto Rico
600–601	Arizona
602–626	California
627–645	Texas
646–647	Utah
648–649	New Mexico
700–728	Railroad Retirement Board; used through 1963, then discontinued
900–999	Not valid, but used for program purposes when state aid to the aged, blind, and disabled was converted to a federal program administered by the Social Security Administration

The middle two digits in a Social Security number are a code to identify fraudulent numbers. The final four digits are randomly assigned.

SOCIAL SECURITY ADMINISTRATION LETTER-FORWARDING SERVICE

Disclosure of information by the Social Security Administration (SSA) is regulated by the Freedom of Information Act, the Privacy Act of 1974, and the Tax Reform Act of 1976. Information about a living person cannot be released to a third party unless the subject has signed a written authorization (except in the case of the Parent Locator Service—a service for locating a parent who has failed to make child support payments).

However, the SSA does maintain a letter-forwarding service through which a researcher may write a letter to the holder of a specific Social Security number. There must be a humanitarian purpose—the death of a parent, medical urgency, or legal proceedings, etc. Place the letter in an unsealed, unstamped envelope and include a request that the SSA relay it via the individual's employer. Direct your request to the Location Services Department, Social Security Administration, 6401 Security Blvd., Baltimore, MD 21234. If the Social Security number is unknown, provide as much identifying information as possible. The SSA examines each letter and determines whether there is a justifiable reason to forward it. If the SSA feels the letter could be embarrassing to the individual involved, it may not be forwarded.

INTERNAL REVENUE SERVICE LETTER-FORWARDING SERVICE

The Internal Revenue Service will also forward letters to individuals for humane reasons (letters regarding debt collection will not be forwarded). Send the following to the Internal Revenue Service Center, Kansas City, MO 64999: a letter to the IRS giving the name, Social Security number (if known), any information you may have about the person and the reason you want the information you are seeking. Enclose your letter to the individual you are trying to reach in a stamped envelope with the name clearly written on the envelope and your return address. If the IRS is convinced that your letter is worthwhile, they will fill in the address and send it to the individual. The IRS will not reveal the individual's address.

Ted L. Gunderson, in *How to Locate Anyone Anywhere Without Leaving Home,* states: "The IRS will provide the date of the last return of a private individual or a business, which includes the address to which the return was sent."[4] However, according to the IRS, this is absolutely *incorrect* unless the return is your own or you have written permission from the taxpayer or a power of attorney.

SOCIAL SECURITY DEATH INDEX

The Social Security Death Index from the U.S. Department of Health and Human Services of the SSA has been made available through the Freedom of Information Act. Rights of privacy do not apply because the index includes only deceased persons.

The total number of deaths in the United States from 1962 to September 1991 is estimated at 58.2 million. Of that number, 42.5 million (seventy-three percent) are found in the Death Master File. Figure 18-1 sets forth the percentages on a yearly basis. Beginning at a low of 17 percent in 1962, the percentage included increased steadily until it peaked at 92.3 percent in 1980. Since than it has tapered off to slightly under eighty percent in the early 1990s.[5]

The percentage of individuals included in the Death Master File varies greatly by age groups (figure 18-2). The under-age-forty-five group increases from approximately ten percent in 1962 to fifty-eight percent in 1977 but now stands at around thirty-six percent. For the age forty-five-to-sixty-five group there is a more dramatic rise from twenty-four percent in the early 1960s to almost one hundred percent in the late 1970s; this has since declined to around fifty percent. The percentages for the two older groups are much more stable: the sixty-five-to-eighty-four group increases from forty-four percent in the early 1960s to almost one hundred percent from 1975 to 1985 but has since fallen to around ninety-two percent. The oldest age group follows the same pattern, increasing from thirty to ninety percent and then back down to seventy-eight percent.[6]

The year 1962 was a watershed for the availability of data on electronic media. The number of 1962 deaths on the Death Master File increased three-fold from the previous year. The next major increase occurred in 1966, when the Freedom of Information Act was enacted. The improvement in the percentage of data included from 1966 to 1980 may be attributable to increased computerization and the inclusion of other vital sta-

tistics sources. The reversal of this trend in 1981 is the result of restricting the $255 death payment to spouses and dependent children only. There is no apparent reason for the sudden, one-time drop in 1987. The tapering off of the percentage included in the last few years is mainly in the lower ages and is most likely attributable to the stricter qualifications for disability benefits. Table 18-5 is an estimate of the probability of finding a decedent in the Death Master File.[7]

The Family History Library and most of its branches have this index on CD-ROM as part of FamilySearch ™ (see chapter 2). Cambridge Statistical Research Associates, Inc., 53 Wellesley, Irvine, CA 92612, can also supply this index, known as the Social Security Death Master File. Most genealogical vendors sell the Social Security Death Index on CD-ROM. When an updated version becomes available, the older version usually drops in price.

The Family History Library's version is updated annually and currently includes more than 40 million deceased persons, mainly covering deaths reported to the SSA beginning in 1962; however, some records are from as early as 1937. Cambridge Statistical Research Associates updates its index quarterly and also offers more search options. For example, it can do a combination search using the year of birth and given name only (helpful when searching for females) or using the birth year and surname only.

The index held by the Family History Library does not have software to accomplish such refined searches. It does, however, have two search options: similar surname search or exact surname search. The similar surname search retrieves surnames that sound alike but are spelled differently; however, it may be necessary to conduct additional searches using different spellings because it is not a phonetic search—some names that sound alike may be overlooked. To conduct a search using a given name, the exact spelling of the given name must be used; if the name is spelled differently from the name entered, it will not be retrieved. The search may also be filtered to a state of issuance for the Social Security number or a state of residence upon death.

The Social Security Death Index will report the name of the deceased (middle name or initials not included), birth date, Social Security number, state where the Social Security number was obtained, month and year of death, state of residence and zip code at death, and state and zip code where the death benefit was sent.

The Social Security Death Index:

- Is not a complete death index. If a person is not included in this index, it may be because a Social Security number was never issued; the survivors may not have reported the death to the SSA; the death may have been reported before computerization began; or the information was simply not included.

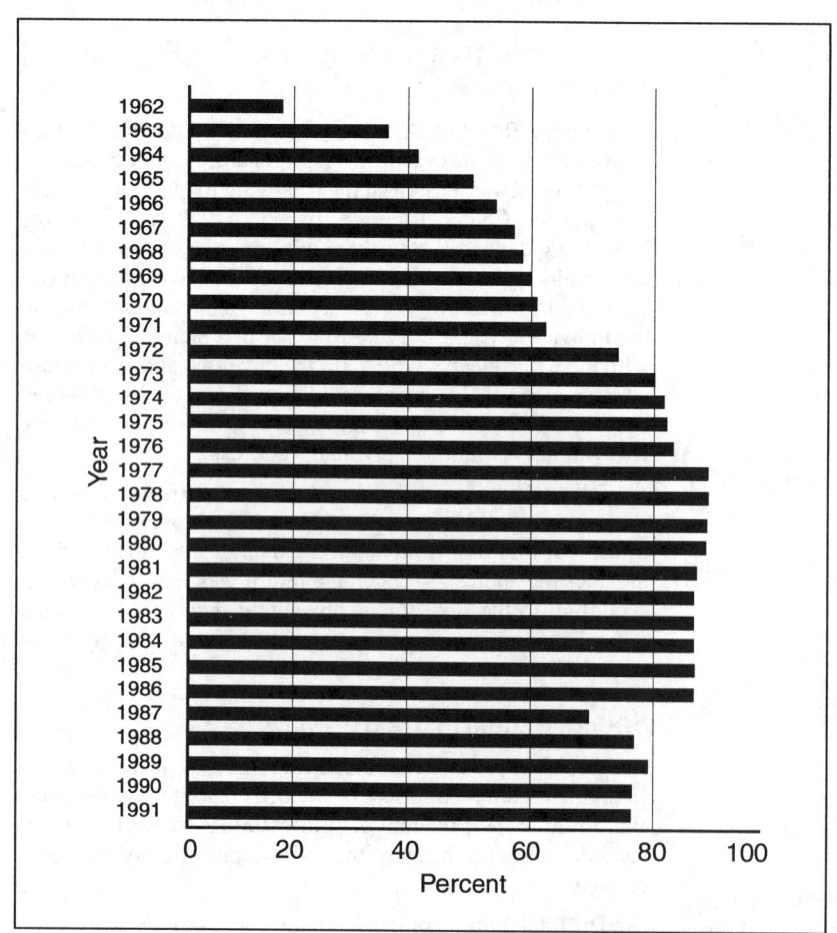

Figure 18-1. Deceased individuals included in the Death Master File versus all U.S. deaths (1962–91) (based on data as of September 1991; reproduced with permission of Cambridge Statistical Research Associates, Inc.).

- Does not give birth places. It gives the state of issuance of the Social Security number, which is often different from the residence at birth.

- Is a research tool—not a source for genealogical data. It is important to follow up on the information given in the index and prove the identity of the individual. Persons who share identical birth dates, names, and residences do exist.

OBTAINING A COPY OF THE ORIGINAL SOCIAL SECURITY APPLICATION

A copy of the original Social Security application (form SS-5) for a deceased individual can be requested by writing to the Social Security Administration, Attention: Freedom of Information Officer, 6401 Security Blvd., Baltimore, MD 21234. The request should include a copy of the death certificate and a statement of relationship to the deceased. The fee is $7.00 if the Social Security number is known; if not, the fee is $16.50.

Beginning in the 1970s, the SSA's paper files were converted into a computer database. The original application forms were microfilmed and then destroyed.[8] The database includes only five of the sixteen questions asked on the original form. Therefore, request a *microprint* from the microfilmed original rather than a computer printout from the database. (The printout for a remarried widow, however, gives both surnames, and this is not on the original application; therefore, it is best to request both the microprint and the printout in such cases.) When there is a claim file, request all documents, such as birth certificate, alien registration card, or naturalization record. Documents exist if a lump sum file was sent. Unfortunately, documents are usually destroyed five years after death.

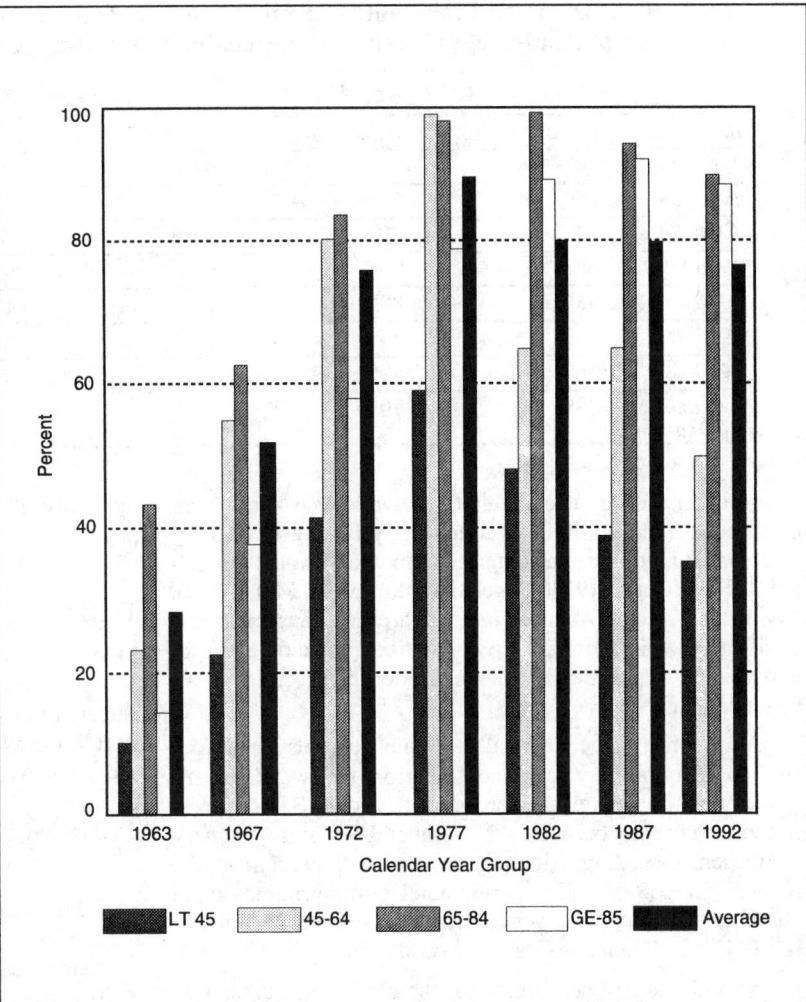

Figure 18-2. Percentage of individuals found on the Death Master File by age group (1963–92) (based on data as of September 1991; reproduced with permission of Cambridge Statistical Research Associates, Inc.).

MILITARY RECORDS

Military records are often used for pre-1900 research, and they can be just as helpful in twentieth-century investigations. America's major twentieth-century wars are described below.

1899–1902: PHILIPPINE INSURRECTION

More than 125,000 American soldiers were sent to the Philippines, and more than 4,000 of them died during this conflict.

1917–1918: WORLD WAR I

More than 4.6 million men and women served in the regular U.S. Army, Navy, and Marine Corps. Of them, 53,403 were killed in action, 77,815 died from disease and other causes, and approximately 202,000 were wounded. New York, Pennsylvania, Illinois, and Ohio furnished the most soldiers.

1941–1945: WORLD WAR II

More than 15.5 million men and women served in the armed forces. Of them, 293,105 died in battle, 96,664 died from other causes, and 659,972 were wounded.

1950–1953: KOREAN WAR

More than 5 million men and women served in the Korean War. Approximately 54,000 of them were killed.

1965–1973: VIETNAM WAR

Over 7 million men and women served during the Vietnam War. Approximately 58,000 of them died.

16 JANUARY–28 FEBRUARY 1991: PERSIAN GULF WAR

More than 500,000 soldiers, including 228,000 from the National Guard and Air National Guard, took part in this conflict. Of them, 148 were killed in action, 407 were wounded, and 121 were killed in non-hostile actions.

Veterans may obtain complete personnel and health records from their own files, or their next of kin may do so if the veteran is deceased or if they have written release-authorization from the veteran. Records are closed to all other persons for a period of seventy-five years after they were created.

Table 18-5. Estimated Probabilities of Finding a Decedent on the Death Master File According to Age and Year of Death (reproduced with permission of Cambridge Statistical Research Associates, Inc.)

	Under Age 45	*Age 45 to 64*	*Age 65 to 84*	*Over Age 84*	*Average All Ages*
Before 1962	Almost nil	Almost nil	Almost nil	Almost nil	Almost nil
1962–64	10%	24%	44%	14%	30%
1965–69	25%	53%	67%	36%	53%
1970–74	44%	80%	84%	56%	73%
1975–79	58%	99%	98%	79%	90%
1980–84	48%	89%	99%	89%	90%
1985–89	38%	63%	93%	89%	81%
1990–	36%	49%	92%	91%	78%
Average All Years	39%	70%	85%	67%	73%

To order military documents from World War I and later, complete Standard Form 180, Request Pertaining to Military Records. This form can be obtained from the National Personnel Records Center (9700 Page Blvd., St. Louis, MO 63132), any of the National Archives regional archives, and most veterans organizations or military installations. State on the form that you are requesting information under the Freedom of Information Act.

A 1973 fire at the National Personnel Records Center destroyed many military personnel files from the twentieth century. Approximately eighty percent of files of U.S. Army personnel discharged between 1 November 1912 and 1 January 1960 were lost. Approximately seventy-five percent of the records for U.S. Air Force personnel with surnames from Hubbard through Z who were discharged between 24 September 1947 and 1 January 1964 were destroyed.

No indexes had been made for the blocks of records that were destroyed; therefore, if a record is not among extant collections, it is difficult to determine whether a person's file was destroyed or whether any such record ever existed. Of approximately 25 million records affected by the fire, about 5 million were recovered.

VETERANS ADMINISTRATION PENSION PAYMENT CARDS

Approximately 2 million pension payment cards (2,539 rolls of microfilm—M850) are at the National Archives and the Family History Library. The cards were created from 1907 to 1930 by the Bureau of Pensions and from 1930 to 1933 by the Veterans Administration (now the Department of Veterans Affairs). They record payments to pensioners on the rolls, 1907 to 1933, except World War I pensioners. The cards are filed alphabetically by the surname of the army or navy invalid or widow.

Information on these cards may include: the name of the veteran, certificate number, unit of service, disability, law under which pensioned, rate of pension, and date of pension. Some cards show the place of residence and date of death of a pensioner and the name of the widow or other recipient of death benefits.[9]

The majority of these cards represent Civil War pensions—veterans who were still living in the twentieth century. John's "Army Invalid" pension payment card gives his death date of 23 November 1924 (figure 18-3). The government reports the name and address of his widow. The "Army Widow" pension payment card gives Angelette's death date of 27 February 1929 (figure 18-4).

WORLD WAR I DRAFT REGISTRATION CARDS

More than 24 million men (male citizens and alien declarants) between the ages of eighteen and forty-five—approximately 23 percent of the population in 1918—were registered in three distinct World War I drafts. Not all men who registered for the draft actually served in the military, and not all men who served in the military registered for the draft. Those who did register for the draft included males born between 1873 and 1900 as follows:

- 5 June 1917: all men aged twenty-one to thirty-one.
- 5 June 1918: all men who had become twenty-one years of age since the previous registration. (A supplemental registration, dated 24 August 1918, covered all men who had become twenty-one years of age after 5 June.)
- 12 September 1918: all men aged eighteen to twenty-one and thirty-one to forty-five.

Information on the World War I cards may include name; age; home address; date and place of birth; occupation; by whom employed; where employed; marital status; race; height, build, color of eyes and hair; prior military service; whether a natural-born citizen, naturalized citizen, alien, or foreign citizen who had declared intention to seek U.S. citizenship (aliens were required to list the country to which they were subject); whether disabled; whether bald; whether the male was solely responsible for the support of a father, mother, wife, child under twelve, or sister or brother under twelve; and whether an exemption from the draft was being claimed (and, if so, on what grounds). They contain no information about an individual's military service. Table 18-6 indicates what information was solicited at each of the registrations.

The records are first arranged alphabetically by state, including Alaska, Hawaii, Puerto Rico, and the District of Columbia. Within the states, the cards are alphabetical by county or city (except for Connecticut, Massachusetts, and Rhode Island, which are alphabetical by names of registrants).

Local boards were established for approximately 30,000 persons in each city or county with a population of more than 30,000. Therefore, registrants who resided in rural areas are relatively easy to locate, because each county had only one draft board. Searches in large cities and some larger counties

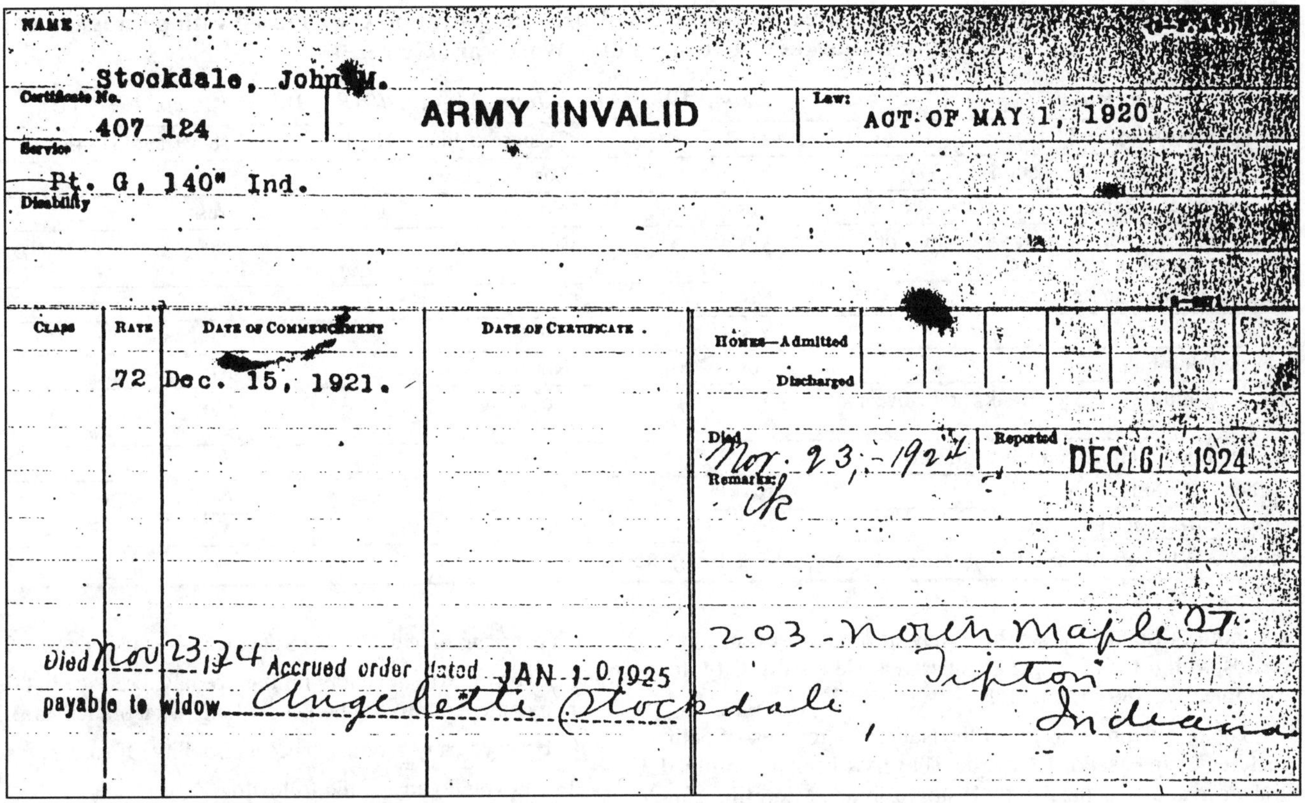

NAME		Stockdale, John M.				(U-10.1.0)
Certificate No. 407 124		ARMY INVALID	Law:	ACT OF MAY 1, 1920		
Service		Pt. G, 140ᵗʰ Ind.				
Disability						

CLASS	RATE	DATE OF COMMENCEMENT	DATE OF CERTIFICATE	HOMES—Admitted					
	72	Dec. 15, 1921.		Discharged					

Died *Nov. 23, 1924* Reported DEC 6 1924

Remarks: *UK*

Died *Nov 23 74* Accrued order dated JAN 10 1925

payable to widow *Angelette Stockdale*

203 North Maple St
Tipton
Indiana

Figure 18-3. Pension payment card for John M. Stockdale.

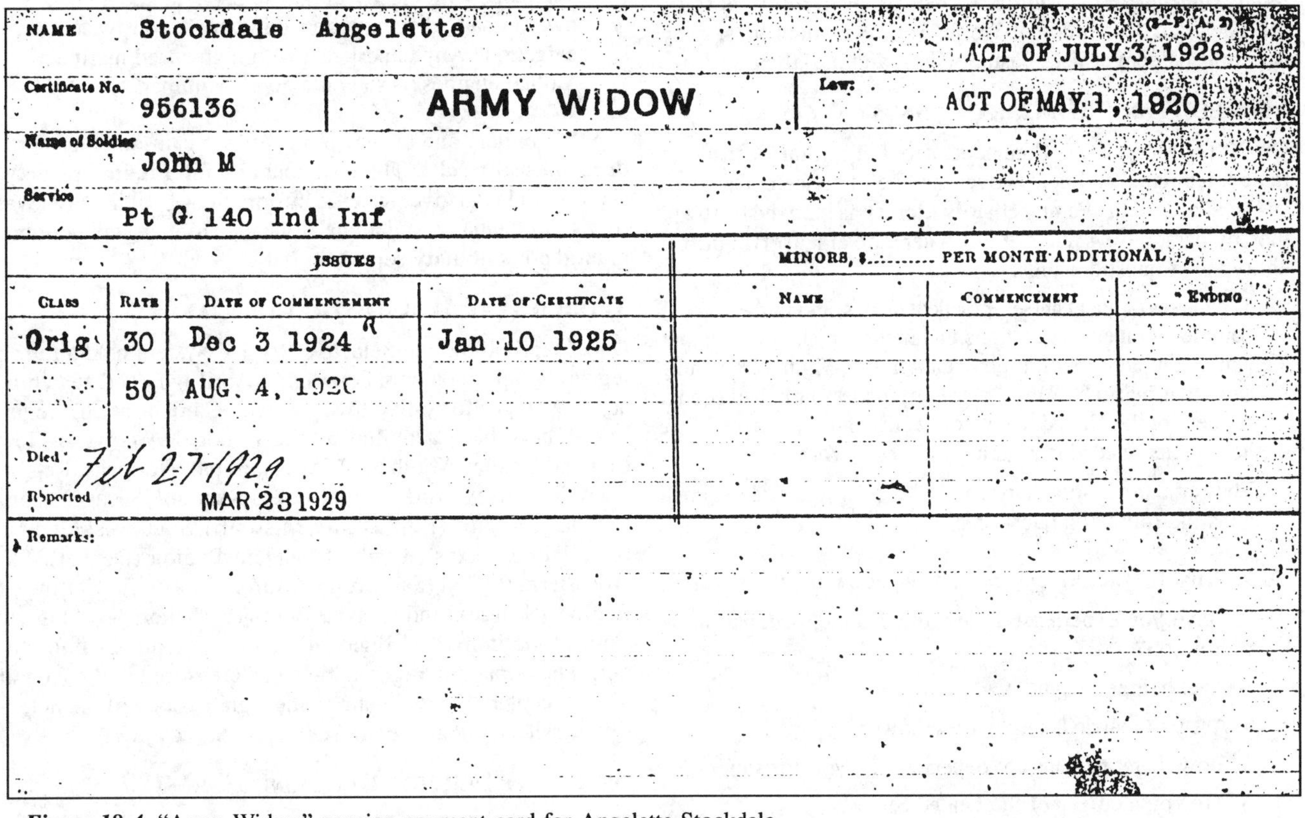

NAME	Stockdale Angelette			(U-P.1.0)
			ACT OF JULY 3, 1926	
Certificate No. 956136	ARMY WIDOW	Law:	ACT OF MAY 1, 1920	
Name of Soldier John M				
Service Pt G 140 Ind Inf				

	ISSUES			MINORS, $...... PER MONTH ADDITIONAL		
CLASS	RATE	DATE OF COMMENCEMENT	DATE OF CERTIFICATE	NAME	COMMENCEMENT	ENDING
Orig	30	Dec 3 1924 ᴿ	Jan 10 1925			
	50	AUG. 4, 1926				

Died *Feb 27-1929*
Reported MAR 23 1929

Remarks:

Figure 18-4. "Army Widow" pension payment card for Angelette Stockdale.

Table 18-6. Information Solicited on World War I Draft Registration Cards (used with permission of Susan Hawkes Cooke and Linda Woodward Geiger*)

Information Solicited	5 June 1917 (A)	5 June, 24 Aug. 1918 (B)	12 Sep. 1918 (C)
Age of men registered	21–31	21 since 5 June 1917	18–21 and 31–45
Birthplace (town, state, nation)	Yes	Yes	No
Present trade, occupation or office	Yes	No	Yes
Dependents (father, mother, wife, child or sibling under 12); state which	Yes	No	No
Nearest relative and address	No		
If bald	Yes	No	No
Married or single	Yes	No	No
Previous military service (rank, branch, years, nation or state)	Yes	No	No
If exemption claimed, on what grounds	Yes	No	No
Father's Birthplace	No	Yes	No
Indian citizen or non-citizen	No	No	Yes

*See "WWI Draft Records," FGS *Forum* 8 (2) (Summer 1996): 8.

are more difficult because there may have been several draft boards within the same geographic area. New York City, for example, had 189 local boards.

The original records are at the National Archives—Southeast Region in East Point, Georgia. They have been microfilmed and are available at the Family History Library. Microfilm copies are at the National Archives regions that serve the respective states.

See Michael Knapp, "World War I Service Records," *Prologue: Journal of the National Archives* (Fall 1990): 300-03, for a detailed description of World War I personnel files, army transport passenger lists, casualty lists, and burial case files.

WORLD WAR I MILITARY CENSUS

On 20 February 1917, Connecticut took a military census of male inhabitants and nurses over the age of sixteen. This census, available at the Family History Library, is indexed by town, then by person (454 microfilms). There are at least two different types of questionnaires.

- The nurses (student nurses, practical nurses, and nurse's aides) completed nineteen questions that include place of birth and permanent address of a relative or friend. Figure 18-5 indicates that Ingrid H. Wester was born in Denmark, had been a resident of the United States for twenty-three years, and that her mother resided in Mamaroneck, New York.

- The regular questionnaire for males over age sixteen contains the following questions:

  1. What is your present trade, occupation or profession?

  2. Have you experience in any other trade, occupation or profession?

  3. Age, height, weight

  4. Are you married, single, or widower?

  5. How many persons are dependent on you for support?

  6. Are you a citizen of the United States?

  7. If not a citizen of the United States have you taken out your first papers?

8. If not a citizen of the United States, what is your nationality?

9. Have you ever done any military or naval service in this or any other country? Where, how long, what branch, rank?

10. Have you any serious physical disability? If so, name it.

11. Can you do any of the following:

Ride a horse? Handle a team? Drive an automobile? Ride a motorcycle? Understand telegraphy? Operate a wireless? Any experience with a steam engine? Any experience with electrical machinery? Handle a boat, power or sail? Any experience in simple coastwise navigation? Any experience with high speed marine gasoline engines? Are you a good swimmer?

The military and citizenship questions can sometimes produce unusual results. The questionnaire for a retired seventy-six-year-old man gives specific information about his Civil War service in the navy, and a questionnaire from an Italian immigrant reports military service in Italy.

WORLD WAR II REGISTRATION CARDS

On 27 April 1942, the Selective Service System held a fourth registration for men born between 28 April 1877 and 16 February 1897 (ages forty-five to sixty-five). Cards from this registration have been acquired by the National Archives—New England Region (Waltham, Massachusetts), Northeast Region (New York, New York), Great Lakes Region (Chicago), Central Plains Region (Kansas City, Missouri), Southwest Regions (Fort Worth, Texas), Rocky Mountain Region (Denver), Pacific Sierra Region (San Bruno, California), Pacific Northwest Region (Seattle), and Alaska Region (Anchorage, Alaska). Contact the individual regional archives for further information. The remaining registration cards are stored in the federal records centers. They remain in the legal custody of the Selective Service System and are subject to privacy laws.

SELECTIVE SERVICE RECORDS, 1940–1975

Draft classification records were maintained from 1940 to 1975. Information about individuals who were registered under the Selective Service Act was recorded in ledger books and is avail-

State of Connecticut.

By direction of an act of the Legislature of Connecticut, approved February 20th, 1917, I am required to procure certain information relative to the resources of the state. I therefore call upon you to answer the following questions.

MARCUS H. HOLCOMB,
Governor.

INSTRUCTIONS: Return this form properly made out, duly signed, to the Bureau of Military Census, Connecticut State Library, Hartford, Conn., not later than ten days after it is received. Failure to make this return within the specified time will be construed as a refusal. Please PRINT your name, giving your own first name, if married, with your unmarried name following in parentheses. Give your present or professional address. In answering questions No. 16 and No. 17, simply write "Yes" or "No."

CONNECTICUT TOWN or CITY _Greenwich_   DATE _Nov 20, 1917_

FULL NAME _Ingrid H. Wester_

STREET ADDRESS AND NUMBER _Lake Ave._   Tel. No. _1800_

1 Graduate of _Greenwich Hospt. Ass'n_   Date _April 1, 1917_

2 Are you a member of your Alumnae Association? _Yes._

3 Line of work since graduation _Supervising_

4 In what line of professional work are you at present employed? _Supervisor in the Greenwich Hospital._

5 Have you any experience in any other occupation or profession? _No._

6 In what department of nursing are you best qualified for service? _Supervising._

7 What is your age? _24 years_   Height _5 ft. 5¾ in._   Weight _117 lbs_

8 Are you a registered nurse? _Yes._   In what state? _Connecticut_ Year _1917._

9 Are you married _No._   Single _Yes._   Widowed _No._

10 If married, Husband's name _____

11 Have you anyone dependent on you for support? _No._   If so, how many? _____

12 Are you a native of the U. S. _No._   (in U.S. 23 yrs.) Where were you born? _Denmark_

13 Have you done any Army or Navy Nursing service in this or any other country? _No._

14 Where _____   How long _____   What branch _____

15 Have you any permanent physical disability? _No._   If so name it _____

16 Could you respond promptly to an emergency call for nursing service in this state? _Yes._

17 Would you volunteer for an emergency call for nursing service outside this state? _Yes._

18 Give reasons, if unable to answer these emergency calls _____

19 Name and permanent address of relative or friend? _Mrs. H. Wester, Mamaroneck, N.Y. (mother)._

Signed: _Ingrid H. Wester_

Figure 18-5. Nurse's questionnaire from the 1917 Connecticut military census.

able to the public. The records list name, date of birth, draft classification, date to report for induction, and, in some cases, date of separation. All requests for information must be made through National Headquarters, Selective Service System, Washington, DC 20435.[10]

WORLD WAR II PRISONERS OF WAR

A computerized database of approximately 120,000 prisoners-of-war who survived World War II (90,000 from the European theater and 30,000 from the Pacific) is available through Cam-

bridge Statistical Research Associates. Information in this database includes name, rank, serial number, service branch, date reported missing, home state, race, area of casualty, last reported date, when liberated, source of report, what country detained by, and prison camp (if known). See Jennifer Davis Heaps, "World War II Prisoner-of-War Records," *Prologue: Journal of the National Archives* 23 (Fall 1991): 324–28.

WORLD WAR II MILITARY SEPARATION PAPERS

Military discharge papers of World War II veterans were often filed with the register of deeds within the county in which the veteran resided; they may also be at the state adjutant general's office or state archive. Some of these records have been microfilmed and are available at the Family History Library. They can be located in the *Family History Library Catalog* under "state-county-military records."

In the case of North Carolina, the separation notice of each veteran claiming residence in North Carolina was sent to the State Selective Service Board. They were filed by county and within county by order number. The Selective Service later turned these over to the state archive, where they remained filed by county but have been rearranged alphabetically by name of veteran. Other states may have followed similar procedures.

MILITARY DEATH INDEX

Korean Conflict

The names of approximately 30,000 to 40,000 soldiers who died in Korea from 1950 to 1957 are in the Korean Conflict Death Database. This is available at the Family History Library (known as the Military Index) and Cambridge Statistical Research Associates. Included is name, branch of military service, country of casualty, type of casualty, Social Security or service number, military pay grade, date of death, home city and state, date of birth, cause of death, race, and sex.

Vietnam War

Approximately 58,000 deaths that occurred during the Vietnam Conflict are included in this database, which is also available at the Family History Library and through Cambridge Statistical Research Associates. Data includes name, branch of military service, country of casualty, type of casualty, Social Security number or service number, military pay grade, date of death, home city and state, service occupation, date of birth, cause of death, race, religious affiliation, age, sex, marital status, date when sent to Vietnam, when the body was recovered, and province of Vietnam. Casualties included in this index occurred in Cambodia, Communist China, Laos, North Vietnam, South Vietnam, and Thailand.

The BRAVO (Brotherhood Rally of All Veterans Organizations) Buddy Search has a list of more then 65,000 Vietnam veterans hoping to re-establish contact with wartime acquaintances. Several other Vietnam newsletters and bulletin boards are dedicated to helping Vietnam veterans—see Lt. Col. Richard S. Johnson, *How to Locate Anyone Who Is or Has Been in the Military: Armed Forces Locator Directory*, 6th ed. (Burlington, N.C.: MIE Publishing, 1995), for complete details. Also see Charles A. Shaughnessy, "Vietnam Records in the National Archives," *Prologue: Journal of the National Archives* 23 (Spring 1991): 69–76.

ARMED SERVICE LOCATORS

The armed forces will assist in locating individuals through their locator services. Requests should include name, service, serial number (usually the person's Social Security number), last known address, date of birth, and last known rank. The National Personnel Records Center for each branch will forward correspondence to the last known address under the following conditions: if the veteran's benefits are affected, if the requestor's veteran or Social Security benefits are dependent upon contacting the veteran, if an estate settlement is involved, or if a financial institution is collecting a debt.

Johnson, *How to Locate Anyone Who is or Has been in the Military: Armed Forces Locator Directory* (cited earlier) includes addresses and telephone numbers for military reunion contacts, veterans' organizations, Vietnam veterans' contacts, military electronic bulletin boards, and numerous other tips for locating military personnel.

VOTER REGISTRATION RECORDS

Current voter registration records are open to public inspection. The data can include name, address, telephone number, party affiliation, date of birth (sometimes birthplace), and, sometimes, Social Security number. Some voter registrations also indicate the date of first registration, which can be helpful in tracking an individual.

The county or city has jurisdiction over voter registration; however, some states also maintain a statewide index to registered voters—usually at the secretary of state's office. Some states will release voter registration information over the telephone; other require a written request or a personal visit.

Retention of voter registration cards can vary greatly, even within the same state. Many offices destroy the cards one year after the registration is invalidated by death or change of address. Others hold the information for a specific time period before purging their files.

Some records have been archived and are available to researchers. Early twentieth-century registrations sometimes include information not often found in current registrations, such as marital status, physical description, occupation, whether a homeowner or tenant, and citizenship data (such as date and court of naturalization). Cambridge Statistical Research Associates has 1994 voters on CD-ROM for the states of Colorado, New York, Ohio, and Texas.

SCHOOL AND UNIVERSITY RECORDS

The Family Educational Rights and Privacy Act of 1974 allows schools to release "directory information" to the public without the consent of a student. However, a student may request that all or part of this information be withheld from the public by making a written request to do so. "Directory information" includes, but is not limited to, the student's name, current address, telephone listing, major, date and place of birth, dates of attendance, degrees and awards received, and previous educational agencies or institutions attended.

Records generated at all levels of education can be helpful in twentieth-century research. Sources include school censuses, yearbooks, alumni records, fraternal organizations, reunion records, and classmates. To identify schools within a specific time period and geographical area, consult a city directory or local library.

SCHOOL CENSUSES

Many school districts have conducted school census enumerations to help plan future expenditures for teachers and textbooks. School censuses vary in content from names and ages (or dates of birth) of each child, names and occupations of parents, and addresses. These reports may be deposited in state archives or within school district archival collections. Some have been microfilmed, such as the school census for Bastrop

County, Texas (1918 to 1936), and are available at the Family History Library.

YEARBOOKS

High school and college yearbooks document an individual's involvement within a school and provide names of classmates. The school library usually has complete or nearly complete collections of school yearbooks. Public libraries generally depend upon donations of yearbooks, so their collections are rarely complete.

The largest archive of yearbooks is the 2,500-volume collection by Seth Poppel, who specializes in collecting yearbooks of celebrities. This is available through Yearbook Archives, 38 Range Dr., Merrick, NY 11566; telephone (516) 867-6280. Also refer to *Memories Magazine's Yearbook* (New York: Doubleday, 1990), which reproduces more than four hundred high school graduation photographs from Poppel's collection.

ALUMNI RECORDS

Most universities and colleges maintain alumni files that sometimes follow the career of a graduate, including details about places of employment, address, and names and dates of birth of children. Alumni directories are published periodically and should be available at the school's library. Biographical questionnaires are sometimes mailed to alumni and included in the student's file.

Francis James Dallet, "University Archives as a Genealogical Resource," *National Genealogical Society Quarterly* (March 1977): 57–74, includes specific titles of published alumni biographies for Harvard University, the College of William and Mary, Yale University, the University of Pennsylvania, Princeton University, Columbia University, Brown University, Rutgers University, Dartmouth College, Hampden-Sidney College in Virginia, Washington College, Washington and Lee University, Dickinson College, St. John's College, the College of Charleston, Franklin and Marshall College, the University of North Carolina at Chapel Hill, the University of Vermont, Williams College, Bowdoin College, the University of Tennessee, Tusculum College, Union College, Middlebury College, and nine British universities.

PERSONAL ADVERTISEMENTS AND BULLETIN BOARDS

Placing a personal advertisement in a local newspaper can sometimes produce results in locating an individual. Adoptees may also want to consider placing an ad in *Reunions Magazine*, P.O. Box 11727, Milwaukee, WI 53211-1727; telephone (414) 263-4567.

Inquiries placed on computer bulletin boards can also bring results in locating an individual. PRODIGY, GEnie, America Online, and CompuServe are subscriber services, and all include a genealogy bulletin board.

There are also privately operated bulletin boards. Many of them are connected through the National Genealogical Conference, which is moderated by the National Genealogical Society Computer Interest Group (NGS/CIG). Write to the National Genealogical Society, 4527 Seventeenth St. N., Arlington, VA 22207-2399 for information on locating a bulletin board in your state.

BIOGRAPHICAL INDEXES AND DATABASES

The variety and extent of biographical indexes is large, as the examples discussed below illustrate—and the availability of indexes and databases will increase rapidly in the computer age. A helpful finding aid for determining names and addresses of organizations that may maintain specialized indexes is Denise M. Allard, *Organizations Master Index* (Detroit: Gale Research Co., 1987). It is a consolidated index to approximately fifty directories, handbooks, yearbooks, encyclopedias, and guides providing information on approximately 150,000 national and international associations, government agencies and advisory organizations, foundations, research centers, museums, religious groups, political organizations, labor unions and other organizations, institutions, and programs of all kinds in the United States, Canada, and worldwide.

BIOGRAPHY AND GENEALOGY MASTER INDEX

Miranda C. Herbert and Barbara McNeil, *Biography and Genealogy Master Index*, 2nd ed., 8 vols. (Detroit: Gale Research Co., 1980; supplement 1982; 1981–85; 1986–90; 1991; first edition published as *Biographical Dictionaries Master Index 1975–76*), and its supplements are essential tools for locating biographical sketches on individuals found in "who's who" types of publications. This multi-volume index of more than 5 million people includes entries from hundreds of sources. Sample sources indexed include "Musicians Since 1900," "Who's Who in American Art," "Who's Who of American Women," "Twentieth-Century Children's Writers," "Directory of American Scholars," and "American Black Writers." Every edition and supplement should be examined because there is no duplication of the entries. A CD-ROM edition of this reference book is available at the Family History Library.

DECEASED PHYSICIAN MASTER FILE

The American Medical Association's (AMA) Deceased Physician Master File (1878 to 1969) contains information about more than 350,000 U.S. physicians. Information in this card file includes dates of birth and death, medical school attended, place of practice, hospital affiliation, and obituary. This file is incomplete for the period from 1878 to 1905 but comprehensive for the period from 1906 to 1969. Membership in the AMA was not a prerequisite for inclusion in the index.

The original cards are being microfilmed by the Genealogical Society of Utah; completion is anticipated for mid-1997. The original cards will be sent to the National Genealogical Society, and the microfilmed copies will become available from the Family History Library in Salt Lake City and its family history centers. Cards from 1930 to 1969 will also become available online (for a fee) from Data Services, (312) 464-5272.

Also see Arthur W. Hafner, ed., *Directory of American Deceased Physicians, 1804–1929,* 2 vols. (Chicago: American Library Association, 1996).

CIRCUS WORLD MUSEUM

The Circus World Museum of the State Historical Society of Wisconsin has a card catalog of more than 700,000 names of circus performers from colonial times to the present.

SOCIETY FOR AMERICAN BASEBALL RESEARCH

The Biographical Committee of the Society for American Baseball Research, P.O. Box 93183, Cleveland, OH 44101, is collecting vital data on all of the 13,000 men who have played in the major leagues since 1871.[11]

EMPLOYMENT RECORDS

Success in obtaining information from employment records varies greatly based upon each employer's access policy and retention schedule. Some employers destroy personnel files after a predetermined period, such as ten years after termination; others retain them indefinitely, sometimes depositing them in local archives.

Employment records can yield varied information, including date of birth, birthplace, and names of parents, as well as details on education, job transfers, and reasons for termination (retirement, job loss, or job change). Some employers also include documents on naturalization, citizenship, or residence abroad. Information on an employee's membership in a local union or labor organization may also be on file.

RAILROAD EMPLOYMENT AND RETIREMENT RECORDS

Railroad employment and retirement records are a useful twentieth-century source. The employment records are generally archived by each railway company, and some have been deposited in museums and historical societies. Retention and survival of records varies tremendously, as does response to inquiries. The types of records, as described in Wendy Elliot, "Railroad Records for Genealogical Research," *National Genealogical Society Quarterly (NGSQ)* 75 (December 1987): 271–77 (an addendum to this article was published in *NGSQ* 79 [June 1991]: 140), may include employment applications, surgeon's certificates, general employment files (these can be destroyed after fifty years under federal regulations, if the company chooses), and history cards (abstracts of employment files prior to destruction—usually maintained permanently).

The U.S. Railroad Retirement Board administers the federal retirement-survivor and unemployment-sickness benefit programs that cover the nation's railroad workers and their families. The majority of the board's records pertain to individuals associated with the rail industry after 1936 who qualified for a railroad retirement annuity. A minimum of ten years' service was required for benefits.

Records are organized by the railroad employee's Social Security number or a Railroad Retirement Board-assigned number prefaced by a letter. The board will provide information on deceased persons for the purpose of genealogical research; however, they will not release information about living beneficiaries without the person's consent. When requesting information about a deceased individual, provide a photocopy of the death certificate and state the relationship to the deceased.

There are nine types of records maintained by the Railroad Retirement Board. For complete content descriptions, see Wendy Elliot's article, noted above.

- Employee's death certificate
- Application for employee (age and service) annuity under the railroad retirement act

- Description and certification as to eligibility of evidence submitted
- Certification in support of employer service for which no records are available
- Application for employee annuity under the Railroad Retirement Act
- Employee's statement of compensated service rendered
- Record of employee's prior service
- Employee registration
- Employee's certificate of termination of service and relinquishment of rights

In the late 1960s, the board initiated a policy approving destruction of individual files thirty years after the last payment is made to the claimant or any beneficiaries in accordance with federal record retention schedules. The destruction was put on hold after genealogists protested. A decision regarding future retention or destruction had not been made as of late 1995. The files were not abstracted or microfilmed before disposal. (The Railroad Retirement Board does not maintain personnel or retirement files of former Atchison, Topeka and Santa Fe Railway employees who died prior to 1970.)

The accessibility and retention of railroad personnel records varies from company to company. Museums and historical societies often house records of local or regional railroads, as do the examples below.

- The California State Railroad Museum Library, 111 I Street, Sacramento, CA 95814, maintains employment records for the Southern Pacific Railroad. Southern Pacific employee cards, 1900 to 1930, are available at the Family History Library.
- The Chicago Historical Society, North Ave. and Clark St., Chicago, IL 60614, has records for the Brotherhood of Sleeping Car Porters.
- The Minnesota State Historical Society, 690 Cedar St., St. Paul, MN 55101, houses records of the Burlington Northern, Northern Pacific, and Great Northern railroad companies.
- The Newberry Library, 60 W. Walton St., Chicago, IL 60610, has records for the Chicago, Burlington, and Quincy Railroad; the Illinois Central Railroad; and the Pullman Standard Car Company.[12]
- Northern Illinois University, University Library, De Kalb, IL 60115, maintains a large collection of records for the Chicago and Northwestern Railroad, including those from the Minneapolis and St. Paul and the Chicago Great Western companies.
- The San Diego Historical Society, 1649 El Prado, San Diego, CA 92101, houses records for the San Diego and Arizona Railroad Company.

It is best to go to the repository in question or to employ a researcher to make a personal search when attempting to research personnel or business records of a railroad company.

See "Insurance Records," below, regarding abstract of life insurance claims of Union Pacific Railroad employees. Also refer to chapter 10, Research in Business, Employment, and

Institutional Records, for more about how to locate and use business records.

U.S. POSTAL SERVICE RECORDS

Effective 21 January 1994, all post offices were directed to cease researching and disclosing addresses of individuals and families except for those requested by government, law enforcement agencies, and courts. The U.S. Postal Service made this change as a matter of public safety for its customers.

If the person you are seeking has a post office address, the street address is not available without a court order. The street address may be given, however, for businesses.

CRIMINAL RECORDS

The National Crime Information Center (NCIC) was established in 1967 in Washington, D.C., by the Federal Bureau of Investigation. It contains nearly 20 million records. Access to the NCIC and related databases is limited by the FBI to law enforcement agencies (approximately 17,000 agencies nationwide are authorized to have access to some of the FBI's computer data). Data in the system includes wanted or missing people, including some data from other countries; stolen vehicles, guns, boats, license plates, and financial securities; criminal histories; information from drivers' licenses; and Secret Service files on threats made against some people under federal protection. The name of a missing child can be entered into the NCIC system.

On the local level, criminal case files are open to the public, but only after full prosecution and sentencing are complete. A criminal may be sent to a federal, state, or county prison or city jail, where additional records are maintained. Some federal prison records may be housed by the National Archives or one of its branches. For example, the Seattle Branch has the records of the U.S. Federal Penitentiary at McNeil Island, Washington, 1890 to 1981.[13] In a similar manner, state prison records are often deposited at a state archive. The California State Archives, for example, has the records from San Quentin (1850 to 1949, plus San Quentin execution books, 1893 to 1967) and Folsom State Prison (1880 to 1949).[14] The Colorado State Archives has the Colorado State Penitentiary records (1878 to 1950).

INSURANCE RECORDS

Insurance companies have extensive data that can be helpful to genealogists. For example, applications often include names, birth dates, and causes of death of immediate family members, such as parents, children, and siblings. The records are usually maintained in the home office, and policies regarding search or release of information vary. If the request concerns a close relative or beneficiary, there is a higher probability of success.

Beware of the tip, often circulated through genealogical society newsletters, to write to Policy Search, American Council of Life Insurance, to determine if an ancestor held an insurance policy. This suggestion is misleading because the service that is offered is to help determine if a policy benefit is due—not whether an individual owned a policy. If the American Council of Life Insurance has sufficient reason for believing a policy benefit is due and such a policy is located, the council will contact the beneficiary directly.

Inquiries regarding insurance payments to beneficiaries of veterans may be sent to the VA Insurance Office, Department of Veterans Affairs, P.O. Box 13399, Philadelphia, PA 19101. Include as much identifying information as possible.

The *Directory of Health/Life Insurance Companies* (Modesto, Calif.: HRS Geriatric Publishing, 1989) lists names and headquarter addresses of the major firms. City directories and state business directories are also helpful in determining which firms operated within a specific area and time period.

An unusual example of insurance claims data becoming available to the public is the abstracts made from original Union Pacific Railroad life insurance records. The original claims are located at the LDS Family History Center in Las Vegas, Nevada. They have been microfilmed and are available at the Family History Library. Information may include Social Security number, sex, race, occupation, birth date, birthplace, address, father's name, mother's name, marriage date, death date, cause of death, place of burial, and spouse's name.

MEDICAL RECORDS

Hospitals, nursing homes, physicians, dentists, and other health care practitioners and facilities hold records valuable to the genealogist. Privacy and record retention are major stumbling blocks in gaining access to such records. Information from medical records will usually be released only to a physician or to the person directly involved. Birth mothers are usually entitled to copies of their hospital records and those of their children; however, if the file indicates an adoption, access may be denied.

If the medical records have been destroyed, an admittance record may still exist indicating the name of the patient, residence, age, date of admittance, and financial arrangements.

CORONERS' RECORDS

If a death certificate indicates that an autopsy (or coroner's inquest) was performed on the deceased, there may be additional information on the official report. A coroner's inquest may include a necropsy report giving technical causes of death, pathology reports, and testimony regarding the circumstances surrounding the death. Inquest files may also include the individual's full name and address, date of the inquest, age, sex, race, marital status, birthplace, how long in the United States, how long in the city, name and birthplace of father, maiden name and birthplace of mother, date of death, date of accident, hour of accident, mental condition, physical condition, height, weight, extent of education, religion, housing conditions, occupation, by whom employed, past occupation, wages or salary due, amount of life insurance, value of personal and real property, military service, number and ages of dependents, and cause of death. A list of names, addresses, and occupations of witnesses and jurors may also be included. See Loretto Dennis Szucs and Ted Naanes, "Dead Men Do Tell Tales," *Ancestry* 12 (2): 6–11 (March/April 1994).

RECORDS OF THE EUGENICS RECORD OFFICE

In 1910, Charles Benedict Davenport founded the Eugenics Record Office at Cold Spring Harbor on Long Island. For the following three decades he and his staff collected data of many varieties on human genetics, including information on physical and psychological characteristics. With the outbreak of World War II, the work of the Eugenics Record Office was suspended, and after Davenport's death in 1944 no one was willing or able to carry on the work. In 1949 the working papers of the Eugenics Record Office were transferred to the Dight Institute at the University of Minnesota in Minneapolis.

Many methods were used in collecting the data, and a variety of files were created as a result. Only the two largest and most important will be mentioned here. The Record of Family Traits was a twelve-page questionnaire, of which more than 20,000 were completed and returned to the Eugenics Record Office. A large proportion of these were completed by college biology students, who were asked to provide information on themselves, parents, grandparents, and siblings. There were also two pages for other relatives of the person who completed the questionnaire; on some forms these extended back to persons born before the revolutionary war.

The second important category of records is the Field Workers' Reports, which consisted of extensive studies of a sizable group of individuals, such as a community in which there was a high incidence of some genetic disorder. There are nearly one hundred of these reports, some of them in excess of one thousand pages.

Although these records cover a relatively small proportion of the population of the United States between the wars, they were collected from all parts of the country, and there is no way to tell in advance who might or might not be represented in the records. What makes this collection especially valuable is the vast and exhaustive set of card indexes, which record every name included in most of the records, including the two categories described above. These indexes allow the researcher to start with either a surname or a place-name and to quickly learn whether there is anything of interest in the collection. The bulk of the papers of the Eugenics Record Office have been microfilmed by the Family History Library. Look in the library's catalog under "United States—Medical Records."

The Record of Family Traits submitted by Harriet H. Shoen from Plainfield, New Jersey, in 1928 (FHL microfilm no. 1711558, file no. SHO-19) serves as an excellent example of the variety of information buried in these files. Harriet was the second child of nine born to Bertram Guy Shoen and Agnes Ruth (Russel) Shoen. The record includes information about Harriet's grandparents, parents, siblings, her father's five siblings, her mother's six siblings, and the children of all these aunts and uncles. The Bible record of the Shoen, Russell, Cook, and Hickok families is also included; it contains birth dates from the early nineteenth century. These Bible records were discovered through the excellent cross-reference indexing system of the Eugenics Record Office. Harriet Shoen added the following comment about her family:

> A number of people on the maternal side of our family have eye and vision defects and liver trouble and gallstones. Twins have not occurred in any side branches of the family that I have been able to discover. Keeping track of the present generation ought to be interesting in this respect, as my paternal grandfather and my maternal grandmother were both identical twins. The one case of twins in my generation were

abnormal having but one naval [sic] cord. There is a strain of inventiveness, artistic talent and constructive ability on both sides of my family. Some have had better chances to develop this than others. There was a strong similarity of temperament between my father and my maternal grandfather—both being moody and hard to live with, so that their wives left them. The Shoen family were very sturdy, healthy people— strongly sexed.

The biographical information on Harriet's grandfather, Ebenezer S. Shoen, includes her comment, "I remember him as a leisurely good-natured old gentleman who amused us children very much telling Civil War stories. An identical twin— member of family of eighteen children of which ten were twins." Harriett also reported the New York unit in which her grandfather served during the Civil War.

MOTOR VEHICLE AND DRIVER'S LICENSE RECORDS

Each state has a Department of Motor Vehicles (DMV) that maintains records of all drivers and their vehicles. Access to these records varies from one state to another; some require only the person's name and date of birth, while some require the driver's license number and/or written permission.

Early and mid-1990s driver's license indexes for Maine, Mississippi, Oregon, Texas, South Carolina, and Wisconsin are available on CD-ROM from Cambridge Statistical Research Associates. Indexes based on motor vehicle records are available for Colorado, Connecticut, Florida, Ohio, New Hampshire, New York, and Texas.

The National Driver's Registration Service was established to help law-enforcement agencies and insurance companies trace individuals with a driver's license suspended or revoked in one state who apply for a driver's license in another state.[15]

Drivers' histories are helpful when they report violations; a follow-up with court records may provide additional clues to help locate the person.

If searching for active-duty military personnel, keep in mind that they usually keep their driver's licenses and car registrations in their home states rather than the states in which they are stationed. Some may even have vehicles registered in more than one state.

A search of motor vehicle registrations (by license plate number or name of vehicle owner) may reveal the name and address of the owner, birth date, the owner's insurance company, date of registration and expiration, lien holder, and description of the vehicle.

The MVR Book: A Motor Services Guidebook (Tempe, Ariz.: BRB Publications, 1993) lists (by state) details regarding access and regulations for all state driver and vehicle records.

IMMIGRATION AND NATURALIZATION RECORDS

Naturalizations and passenger lists are covered fully in chapter 13, Immigration: Finding Immigrant Origins. Refer to that chapter for details on accessing twentieth-century records.

PASSPORTS

Passports were not required by law for U.S. citizens traveling overseas prior to World War I, except during the Civil War. Therefore, passports were only obtained by people who expected to travel in areas that might require one, who wanted more formal identification, and naturalized citizens who needed proof of citizenship to avoid being drafted into military service.[16]

Passport applications from 1906 to 1925 are in the custody of the Civil Reference Branch, Textual Reference Division, National Archives and Records Administration, Suitland, MD 20409.

Passport records created after 1925 are in the custody of the Passport Office, Department of State, Washington, DC 20520. If seeking a passport application filed after 1925, you must provide the name and date of birth and a letter from the applicant granting permission for the search. If seeking the application of a deceased person, submit a copy of the death certificate and a statement of relationship to the deceased.

Passport applications vary in content. They usually contain the name, signature, place of residence, age, and personal description of the applicant; names or number of persons in the family intending to travel; the date; and, where appropriate, the date and court of naturalization. They sometimes contain the exact date and place of birth of the applicant and of the spouse and minor children, if any, accompanying the applicant. If the applicant was a naturalized citizen, the date and port of his or her arrival in the United States, the name of the vessel on which the applicant arrived, and the date and court of naturalization were included.[17]

The Family History Library has microfilmed passport applications, 1795 to 1920 and indexes for the years 1830 to 1831, 1850 to 1852, and 1860 to 1925.

ALIEN REGISTRATION

Since the 1929 Alien Registration Act, aliens have been required to register their current residence and place of employment annually with the federal government. Alien registration cards are filed by aliens at their local post offices. These records are restricted by the terms of the Immigration and Nationality Act of 1952, which reads: "All registration and fingerprint records made under the provisions of this title shall be confidential, and shall be made available only to such persons or agencies as may be designated by the Attorney General."[18]

National Archives Record Group 118 (Attorneys and Marshals) includes a collection of World War I alien files at the National Archives—Central Plains Region in Kansas City, Missouri. This collection consists of alien applications for permits to continue residing within certain restricted zones.

Information on the applications includes the alien's residence, birth, and employment, and a certificate or affidavit in support of the application made by a friend or employer. A second file provides similar information on male and female aliens required to register, but it also includes their fingerprints, military service, and the names and birth dates of their children between ten and fourteen years of age. Both files include physical descriptions and photographs of the aliens.[19]

The Minnesota Historical Society has registration forms completed by non-citizen adults in Minnesota in February 1918 as a result of the 1918 Alien Registration and Declaration of Holdings, under the auspices of the Minnesota Commission of Public Safety. Questions on the form include name, place of birth, years in the country, port of entry, date of arrival, occupation, name of spouse, and names of children.[20]

TEXAS SEAPORT MUSEUM IMMIGRATION DATABASE

The port of Galveston, Texas, is often overlooked by researchers who use the records of the five "major " ports—Baltimore, Boston, New Orleans, New York, and Philadelphia. Yet this important entry point processed large numbers of immigrants, primarily Germans and Eastern Europeans, from the 1840s through 1920. In the early twentieth century, scores of Eastern European and Russian Jews passed through Galveston seeking resettlement in the Midwest and West.

An immigration database has been created at the Texas Seaport Museum, 2016 Strand, Galveston Island, TX 77550. Volunteers using the passenger lists that survived the hurricane of 1900 have extracted each immigrant's name, country of origin, age, sex, and occupation, as well as the ship's name, date of arrival, and port of departure. Included are the occasional miscellaneous notes that appear on the lists, such as deaths at sea. The entries are for the years 1846 to 1871 and 1896 to 1921.

The resulting database, a project of the Galveston Historical Foundation, includes approximately 150,000 names. Visitors to the museum can easily access the database. A printout may be obtained by mail for a small fee.[21]

CANADIAN BORDER CROSSING RECORDS

Approximately 3 million cards dating from 1895 to 1952 provide valuable information about persons who crossed the border between Canada and the United States. Known as the "St. Albans Passenger Arrival Records," they include passengers arriving by train through substations or ports along the borders from Washington to Maine.[22] Each card typically provides name, age, exact place of birth, last residence, occupation, name and address of relative in former country, name and address of relative in the destination city, whether the person's first visit to the U.S., date and vessel of seaport arrival, date and place of border crossing, and physical description.

There are four indexes to these records:

- Soundex Index to Canadian Border Entries Through the St. Albans, Vermont, District, 1895–1924 (M1461, 400 rolls)

- Alphabetical Index to Canadian Border Entries through Small Ports in Vermont, 1895–1924 (M1462, six rolls)

- Soundex Index to Entries Into the St. Albans, Vermont, District Through Canadian Pacific and Atlantic Ports, 1924–1952 (M1463, ninety-eight rolls)

- Card Manifests (alphabetical) of Individuals Entering Through the Port of Detroit, Michigan, 1906–1954 (M1478, 117 rolls)

The St. Albans indexes include the entire United States-Canada border (from the East Coast to the West Coast) from

1895 to 1915. The 1915-to-1924 indexes cover the border east of Buffalo, New York, only.

The passenger lists are reproduced in two series:

- Manifests of Passengers Arriving in the St. Albans, Vermont, District Through Canadian Pacific and Atlantic Ports, 1895–1954 (M1464, 608 rolls)

- Manifests of Passengers Arriving in the St. Albans, Vermont, District Through Canadian Pacific Ports, 1929–1949 (M1465, twenty-five rolls)

This complete series of microfilm (1,168 rolls) is available at the Family History Library, the National Archives in Washington, D.C., and the National Archives—New England Region in Boston. The National Archives regional archives in New York, Philadelphia, Chicago, Kansas City, Denver, San Francisco, and Seattle have M1462, M1463, and M1465 (a total of 129 rolls). The regional archives in Atlanta, Fort Worth, and Los Angeles do not have any of this record group.

ORPHAN TRAIN RESEARCH

From 1854 to 1929, approximately 150,000 homeless children, many of them orphaned, were sent by train from New York to the West. In 1987 the Orphan Train Heritage Society of America, Inc., P.O. Box 496, Johnson, AR 72741-0496, was created as a clearinghouse for information about orphan train riders. It offers a research service for members and nonmembers and publishes a newsletter.

AMERICAN RED CROSS

The American Red Cross provides tracing services to people who have been separated from their families by war, civil disturbance, or changing world conditions. For further information about their tracing service, call 1-800-848-9277 or the local chapter of the American Red Cross.

Through an arrangement with the International Tracing Service of the International Committee of the Red Cross, the American Red Cross Holocaust and War Victims Tracing and Information Center in Baltimore, Maryland, works closely with local chapters in an effort to serve those who were involved in or affected by the events of World War II.

German concentration camp records containing the names of approximately 400,000 people who were interned or died in the camps before and during World War II were released by the Soviet Union in 1989. These documents were recovered by the Soviet army during its advance through Germany in the closing days of World War II. Applicants must provide the relative's name, approximate age at the time of disappearance, their relationship, and the date and place the relative was last seen. It may be a few months or even several years before a response is given because the records at the International Tracing Services, in Arolsen, Germany, are not computerized.

SALVATION ARMY

The Salvation Army's Missing Persons Bureau has thousands of active case files of people looking for missing family members. In 1990, the Missing Persons Services unit in Chicago handled 5,340 new requests and was able to locate ten to fifteen percent of them within the first year.[23] The Salvation Army will search only for close relatives of the inquirer. It will not search for runaway children or handle requests involving adoption or kidnapping of a child by a parent.

Contact your local Salvation Army office for information about the Missing Persons Service. Search inquiries must originate from the headquarters within the region of your residence, regardless of where the search may be conducted. For example, if the inquirer resides in Indiana and is looking for a brother whose last known address was in Florida, the inquiry should go to the central U.S. office, as indicated below.

- Eastern United States—120 W. 14th St., New York, NY 10011 (Connecticut, Delaware, Maine, Massachusetts, New Hampshire New Jersey, New York, Ohio, Pennsylvania, Rhode Island, Vermont)

- Central United States—860 N. Dearborn St., Chicago, IL 60610 (Illinois, Indiana, Iowa, Kansas, Michigan, Minnesota, Missouri, Nebraska, North Dakota, South Dakota, Wisconsin)

- Southern United States—1424 N.E. Expressway, Atlanta, GA 30329 (Alabama, Arkansas, Florida, Georgia, Kentucky, Louisiana, Maryland, Mississippi, North Carolina, Oklahoma, South Carolina, Tennessee, Texas, Virginia, Washington, D.C., West Virginia)

- Western United States—30840 Hawthorne Blvd., Rancho Palos Verdes, CA 90274 (Alaska, Arizona, California, Colorado, Hawaii, Idaho, Montana, Nevada, New Mexico, Oregon, Utah, Washington, Wyoming)

If you are researching an officer of the Salvation Army, the Salvation Army Archives and Research Center, 145 W. 15th Street, New York, NY 10011, has a biographical card index with more than 10,000 cards that list residence, nationality, parents' names, and birth dates of officers.

INFORMATION BROKERS AND PRIVATE INVESTIGATORS

Information brokers and private investigators offer online public record searches for fees ranging from $10.00 and up. To locate an information broker or private investigator, check a telephone directory under "investigators" or "information services." Motor vehicle and driver's records, Uniform Commercial Code (UCC) filings, tax liens, bankruptcy records, voter registrations, criminal histories, credit report headers (in compliance with the Fair Credit Reporting Act),[24] and many other public records can be searched nationwide.

THE EFFECTS OF COMPUTER TECHNOLOGY

Computer technology has affected twentieth-century research tremendously. In a positive vein, more and more electronic databases and indexes are being created to accelerate access to records (see chapter 2). Many records are being kept in machine readable form, but when they become outdated they are usually purged to save time and expense. Some computer data is now unreadable and in danger of being lost forever.[25]

Sources useful to genealogists improve and grow regardless of the time period, but these changes have been more rapid in the twentieth century. A critical point to remember in the twentieth century is that we must avoid total reliance upon the computer. For thorough research, the need for hands-on searching in the dusty corners of repositories will remain, even into the twenty-first century.

ADDRESSES

For a list of state and local government offices which accept telephone orders for birth and death certificates:

Network, Inc.
4512 Central Pike
Hermitage, TN 37076
1-800-255-2414

Births of U.S. citizens in foreign countries:

Passport Services
Correspondence Branch
U.S. Department of State
1425 K St. N.W., Room 386
Washington, DC 20522-1705

Deaths of U.S. citizens (non-military) filed in 1960 or after:

Passport Services
Correspondence Branch
U.S. Department of State
Washington, DC 20522-1705

Deaths of U.S. citizens (non-military) filed before 1960:

National Archives and Records Service
Diplomatic Records Branch
Washington, DC 20408

Deaths of U.S. citizens (military) or civilian employees of the Department of Defense:

National Personnel Records Center
(Military Personnel Records)
9700 Page Ave.
St. Louis, MO 63132-5100

Birth records of alien children adopted by U.S. citizens:

Immigration and Naturalization Service
U.S. Department of Justice
Washington, DC 20536

Births and deaths occurring on vessels or aircraft:

U.S. Department of State
Washington, DC 20522-1705

Census, 1930 to 1990:

U.S. Department of Commerce
Bureau of the Census
P.O. Box 1545
Jeffersonville, IN 47131

Telephone:

U S WEST Communications
421 S.W. Oak
Portland, OR 97204

NYNEX Corporation
100 Church St., Room 920
New York, NY 10007
1-800-338-0646

Social Security Letter Forwarding Service:

Location Services Department
Social Security Administration
6401 Security Blvd.
Baltimore, MD 21234

Social Security applications:

Social Security Administration
Attention: Freedom of Information Officer
6401 Security Blvd.
Baltimore, MD 21234

Social Security Death Index, World War II prisoners of war, Korean conflict, Vietnam Index:

Cambridge Statistical Research Associates, Inc.
53 Wellesley
Irvine, CA 92612
(714) 509-9900
(714) 509-9119 (fax)
1-800-327-2720

Automated Research Systems, Inc.
327 E. 1200 S., Suite 8
Orem, UT 84058
1-800-244-1776

Military:

National Personnel Records Center
9700 Page Blvd.
St. Louis, MO 63132-5100
(314) 263-3901

"BRAVO" Buddy Search
23917 Craftsman Rd.
Calabasas, CA 91364
(818) 999-4174

Yearbooks—celebrities:

Seth Poppel
Yearbook Archives
38 Range Dr.
Merrick, NY 11566

Deceased Physician Master File:

American Medical Association
515 N. State St.
Chicago, IL 60610
(312) 464-5000
(312) 464-4184 (fax)

Circus World Museum:

State Historical Society of Wisconsin

426 Water St.

Baraboo, WI 53913

Society for American Baseball Research:

Society for American Baseball Research

P.O. Box 93183

Cleveland, OH 44101

Railroad retirement:

U.S. Railroad Retirement Board

Office of Public Affairs

844 N. Rush St.

Chicago, IL 60611-2092

Insurance payments—veterans:

VA Insurance Office

Department of Veterans Affairs

P.O. Box 13399

Philadelphia, PA 19101

1-800-669-8477

Suspended or revoked drivers' licenses:

National Driver's Registration Service

U.S. Department of Commerce

1717 H St.

Washington, DC 20510

Passports, 1906 to 1925:

Civil Reference Branch

Textual Reference Division

National Archives and Records Administration

Suitland, MD 20409

Passports after 1925:

Passport Office

Department of State

Washington, DC 20520

Immigration database:

Texas Seaport Museum

2016 Strand

Galveston Island, TX 77550

(409) 763-1877

Orphan train:

Orphan Train Heritage Society of America, Inc.

P.O. Box 496

Johnson, AR 72741-0496

NOTES

1. For further information regarding the Freedom of Information Act and the Privacy Act, refer to Allan Adler, ed., *Litigation Under the Open Federal Government Laws* (American Civil Liberties Union, 1991). (The 1988 edition was titled *Litigation Under the Federal Freedom of Information Act and Privacy Act.*) Write to: ACLU, Publications Department, 122 Maryland Ave. N.E., Washington, DC 20002; 202-544-1681.

Also see David C. Boyle, "Proposal to Amend the United States Privacy Act to Extend Its Protections to Foreign Nationals and Non-Resident Aliens," *Cornell International Law Journal* 22 (Spring 1989). This article includes an excellent historical overview (pp. 286–95) of the Privacy Act and its relation to the Freedom of Information Act.

2. Elizabeth L. Nichols, "Statewide Civil Vital Registration in the United States," *The Genealogical Helper* 34 (May–June 1980): 6–14. This article includes a detailed summary of each state's vital records laws, as well as comments noting special indexes.

3. *Model State Vital Statistics Act and Model State Vital Statistics Regulations,* rev. ed. (Hyattsville, Md.: U.S. Department of Health, Education, and Welfare, Public Health Service, National Center for Health Statistics.) Also see "NGS Asks Greater Access to Vital Records," *National Genealogical Society Newsletter* (January–February 1991): 8.

4. Ted L. Gunderson, *How to Locate Anyone Anywhere Without Leaving Home* (New York: E. P. Dutton, 1989), 56.

5. From a leaflet by Cambridge Statistical Research Associates, 53 Wellesley, Irvine, CA 92612.

6. Ibid.

7. Ibid.

8. Periodically, genealogical societies publish notices that the SSA is going to destroy the original applications and ask concerned genealogists to write to the SSA requesting that the records be placed in the National Archives. These notices are incorrect and unnecessarily alarming. The SSA received written approval from the archivist of the United States to destroy the original paper documents after they were microfilmed. Current applications are microfilmed and retained for five years before destruction.

9. *Guide to Genealogical Research in the National Archives*, rev. ed. (Washington, D.C.: National Archives, 1983), 130.

10. Lt. Col. Richard S. Johnson. *How to Locate Anyone Who Is or Has Been in the Military: Armed Forces Locator Directory,* 4th ed. (Fort Sam Houston, Tex.: Military Information Enterprises, 1991), 83.

11. Robert Charles Anderson, "Baseball Genealogy," *Association of Professional Genealogists Quarterly* 6 (Fall 1991): 59–61.

12. Elisabeth Coleman Jackson and Carolyn Curtis, *Guide to the Burlington Archives in the Newberry Library 1851–1901* (Chicago: Newberry Library, 1949).

13. Loretto Dennis Szucs and Sandra Hargreaves Luebking, *The Archives: A Guide to the National Archives Field Branches* (Salt Lake City: Ancestry, 1988), 278.

14. "Using California State Prison Records in Genealogical Research," *Utah Genealogical Association Newsletter* (Second Quarter 1988): 20–21.

15. Gunderson, *How to Locate Anyone Anywhere Without Leaving Home,* 43–44.

16. *The United States Passport: Past, Present, Future* (Washington, D.C.: Passport Office, Department of State, 1976).

17. *Guide to Genealogical Research in the National Archives,* 246.

18. *Guide to the National Archives of the United States* (Wash-

ington, D.C.: National Archives and Records Administration, 1987), 347.

19. Szucs and Luebking, *The Archives: A Guide to the National Archives Field Branches,* 66.

20. Eichholz, Alice, ed., *Ancestry's Red Book: American State, County and Town Sources,* rev. ed. (Salt Lake City: Ancestry, 1992), 387.

21. "Texas Seaport Museum's Immigration Database," FGS [Federation of Genealogical Societies] *Forum* 3 (3): 8–9 (Fall 1991).

22. Constance Potter, "St. Albans Passenger Arrival Records," *Prologue: Journal of the National Archives* (Spring 1990): 90–93.

23. Joseph E. Miller, "Searching for Family and Friends," *Reunions Magazine* (Spring 1991): 36–39.

24. "What Price Privacy?," *Consumer Reports* (May 1991): 356–60, reports that the nation's credit bureaus keep files on nearly ninety percent of American adults. "Is Nothing Private?," *Business Week* (4 September 1989): 74, reported that credit bureau computers contain 400 million records on 160 million individuals and that the data is shockingly easy and inexpensive to buy without the subject's consent.

25. "Historic Catch-22: As Computers Got Better, Early Data Now Unreadable," *Association of Professional Genealogists Quarterly* 6 (Fall 1991): 61.

BIBLIOGRAPHY

Allard, Denise M. *Organizations Master Index.* Detroit: Gale Research Co., 1987.

Askin, Jayne, and Molly Davis. *Search: A Handbook for Adoptees and Birthparents,* 2nd ed. Phoenix, Ariz.: Oryx Press, 1992.

Burek, Deborah M., ed. *Cemeteries of the U.S.: A Guide to Contact Information for U.S. Cemeteries and Their Records.* Detroit: Gale Research Co., 1944.

Culligan, Joseph J. *When In Doubt Check Him Out.* Hallmark Press, 1993.

_____. *You, Too, Can Find Anybody.* Hallmark Press, 1993.

Dallet, Francis James. "University Archives as a Genealogical Resource," *National Genealogical Society Quarterly* (March 1977): 57–74

Daugherty, Rebecca, ed. *How to Use the Federal FOI Act.* 7th ed. Washington, D.C.: Reporters Committee for Freedom of the Press, 1994.

Directory of Health/Life Insurance Companies. Modesto, Calif.: HRS Geriatric Publishing, 1989.

Eichholz, Alice, ed. *Ancestry's Red Book: American State, County and Town Sources.* Rev. ed. Salt Lake City: Ancestry, 1992.

Elliot, Wendy. "Railroad Records for Genealogical Research." *National Genealogical Society Quarterly (NGSQ)* 75 (December 1987): 271–77. An addendum to this article was published in *NGSQ* 79 (June 1991): 140)

Ferraro, Eugene. *You Can Find Anyone!* Santa Ana, Calif.: Marathon Press, 1986.

Gunderson, Ted L. *How to Locate Anyone Anywhere Without Leaving Home.* New York: E.P. Dutton, 1989.

Haverford College. *Quaker Necrology Index of Haverford College.* 2 vols. Boston: G.K. Hall, 1961.

Heaps, Jennifer Davis. "World War II Prisoner-of-War Records." *Prologue: Journal of the National Archives* 23 (Fall 1991): 324–28.

Herbert, Miranda C., and Barbara McNeil. *Biography and Genealogy Master Index.* 2nd ed. 8 vols. Detroit: Gale Research Co., 1980; supplement 1982; 1981–85; 1986–90; 1991. First edition published as *Biographical Dictionaries Master Index 1975–76.*

Holiday, John. "New Adventures in Research: Contemporary Record Search and Locatology," *APG Quarterly* (Summer 1990): 27–31.

Jarboe, Betty. *Obituaries: A Guide to Sources,* 2nd ed. Boston: G.K. Hall, 1989.

Johnson, Lt. Col. Richard S. *How to Locate Anyone Who Is or Has Been in the Military: Armed Forces Locator Directory,* 6th ed. Burlington, N.C.: MIE Publishing, 1995.

Kemp, Thomas J. *International Vital Records Handbook.* 3rd ed. Baltimore: Genealogical Publishing Co., 1994.

King, Dennis. *Get the Facts on Anyone.* 2nd ed. New York: MacMillan, 1995.

Klunder, Virgil L. *Lifeline: The Action Guide to Adoption Search.* Cape Coral, Fla.: Caradium Publishing, 1991.

Knapp, Michael. "World War I Service Records." *Prologue: Journal of the National Archives* (Fall 1990): 300–03.

Masciangelo, Bill, and Tom Ninkovich. *Military Reunion Handbook.* San Francisco: Reunion Research, 1991.

Memories Magazine's Yearbook. New York: Doubleday, 1990.

The MVR Book: A Motor Services Guidebook. Tempe, Ariz.: BRB Publications, 1993.

The New York Times Obituaries Index, 1858–1968. New York: New York Times, 1970.

The New York Times Obituary Index II, 1969–1978. New York: New York Times, 1980.

Niles, Reg. *Adoption Agencies, Orphanages and Maternity Homes: An Historical Directory.* 2 vols. Garden City, N.Y.: Phileas Deigh Corp., 1981.

Shaughnessy, Charles A. "Vietnam Records in the National Archives." *Prologue: Journal of the National Archives* 23 (Spring 1991): 69–76.

Szucs, Loretto Dennis, and Ted Naanes. "Dead Men Do Tell Tales." *Ancestry Magazine* 12 (2): 6–11 (March/April 1994).

Tillman, Norma Mott. *How to Find Almost Anyone, Anywhere.* Nashville, Tenn.: Rutledge Hill Press, 1994.

Where to Write for Vital Records: Births, Deaths, Marriages, and Divorces. Hyattsville, Md.: U.S. Department of Health and Human Services Publication No. (PHS) 93-1142.

TRACKING URBAN ANCESTORS
CHAPTER CONTENTS

19

TRACKING URBAN ANCESTORS

Loretto Dennis Szucs

From a colonial society of small farms and villages, the United States grew rapidly into a nation dominated by massive urban centers. Early settlers, many of whom had been city dwellers in Europe, congregated in seaport towns along the Atlantic coast. The larger colonial towns became government centers where brisk commerce attracted a continuous influx of immigrants. Most ports became hubs for milling, shipbuilding, and other manufacturing activities.

In the years between the American Revolution and the Civil War, the populations of the major cities increased dramatically. New York was a city of approximately 33,000 in 1790; there were 800,000 people on the island of Manhattan by 1860. Philadelphia's count of 28,000 people in the 1790 census had leaped to more than 565,000 by the 1860 enumeration. Brooklyn (not yet part of New York City), with a population of 5,000 in 1790, was home to more than 265,000 by 1860, distinguishing it as America's third-largest city.

Climate, geography, and the focus on agriculture dictated a slower growth pattern for Southern urbanization. Yet New Orleans had a population of nearly 1,000 as early as 1727, and Charleston was the largest Southern metropolis, with a population of 10,000 by the time of the American Revolution.

Urbanization was not limited to the Atlantic coast; it expanded inland with new frontiers. The cities of Pittsburgh, Louisville, Cincinnati, and St. Louis flourished along the Ohio and Mississippi rivers. With the introduction of steam navigation and the opening of a canal system, the Great Lakes cities of Buffalo, Cleveland, Detroit, Chicago, and Milwaukee sprang up. Even in states and territories where the population was sparse, the extent of urbanization was remarkable. Seattle, Portland, San Francisco, Los Angeles, and Salt Lake City played important roles in the development of the Far West. By 1860, Houston, Galveston, Austin, and San Antonio had also become important cultural, social, and economic centers.[1]

Very early in the process of developing a family history, you will probably encounter the problem of locating information about ancestors who lived in a large American city. The United States today is very much an urban nation—73.5 percent of the population lives in cities—but the trend began well over a century ago.[2] More than fifty percent of the population lived in urban areas as early as 1920. Moreover, many specific ethnic groups had higher percentages of urbanization than the general population. By 1910, approximately seventy-two percent of the foreign-born lived in cities.[3, 4] The economics of migration, as well as the personal goals of the migrants, many of whom hoped to make a fortune and return home, necessitated settlement in urban centers, such as New York, Cleveland, and Chicago. There, burgeoning industries welcomed common laborers, ethnic clusters offered a familiar setting for the homesick, and cheap housing and food let them accumulate savings.

RESEARCH STRATEGIES

Research among the maze of metropolitan records reveals the confusing variety, color, and bustle of the urban surroundings new to the immigrants. Much of the genealogist's knowledge in the use of these resources must be self-taught. No two cities were born of a common history, nor were their political natures, commercial interests, ethnic makeup, or geographical locations ever identical. Research sources readily found in one city may be closed to access or have been destroyed in the next. The experiences of the African American, the German Jew, the Irish Catholic, and the white Anglo-Saxon Protestant frequently differed, and those differences dictate the types of records to be used.

Despite their differences, cities have one thing in common: a reputation for being difficult to research because of their multilayered bureaucracies, the sheer volume of records created by enormous populations, and a lack of printed indexes and access to sources. The advantage is that urban areas often include the resources, human and financial, to preserve and to disseminate information about the past. Also, city governments require more information from their residents than do their rural counterparts.

Historical societies, libraries, and universities collect manuscripts, newspapers, rare books, and similar materials from which sociologists, demographers, urbanologists, and social historians can draw. It is no accident that some of the most dynamic contemporary research is occurring in urban-related topics: the resources are vast.

Many of the sources mentioned in this chapter are further detailed elsewhere in this book. This chapter is specifically designed to identify problems unique to city research and to offer strategies and sources that clarify bureaucratic jurisdictions and make searching massive volumes of urban-created records more manageable.

Perhaps more than in any other phase of genealogical research, it is important to gather as much identifying information as possible about the subject of a search from relatives near and far. Knowing the approximate part of the city, a street name, an occupation, or the name of a church or school can make all the difference when it comes to finding people in city directories or census or any other records, particularly when common names are involved.

As cities grew in population and geographical dimensions, their borders and jurisdictions changed. Larger towns annexed other towns over the years, and if you are not aware of such historical facts, there is a good chance that you will overlook desired information. For example, Boston was divided into various wards, and boundaries were redrawn as new areas were added. To add to the confusion, Beacon Hill, East Boston, Fort Hill, the North End, South Boston, the South Cove, the South End, and the West End are the informal names of sections. Brighton, Charlestown, Dorchester, Roxbury, and West Roxbury were annexed by the city of Boston in the 1860s and 1870s, while Hyde Park did not become Boston until 1912. Sections of present-day Boston are still called by the names of the former towns. Prior to annexation, each town kept its own records. Other towns in the Boston vicinity remain separate municipalities to the present day, including Cambridge and Somerville (both in Middlesex County) and Brookline (in Norfolk County).[5]

Different cities and counties have different record-keeping practices, and it is critical to know of these distinctions. Deeds for Rochester, New York, for example, are kept at the county level, but Baltimore and St. Louis deeds are kept at the city level. There may be different access policies and charges among the city, county, and state levels. Most vital records for Illinois have been microfilmed up to around 1915 (depending on the county). In some cases, microfilmed copies of vital records are easier to obtain through the Family History Library of The Church of Jesus Christ of Latter-day Saints (LDS church) in Salt Lake City or through the Illinois State Archives or one of the local archives.

Because the offices of heavily populated cities and counties are frequently hard to access, and because city and county bureaucracies are typically difficult to work with, it may be far easier in some instances to consult indexes for cities at the nearest family history center of the LDS Family History Library. Many genealogically important city records have been microfilmed by the Genealogical Society of Utah. The society is microfilming on an ongoing basis, so if records or indexes are not yet available, they might be in six months or a year. It is wise to stay informed.

LIBRARY SOURCES

The basic approach to urban genealogy is similar to that followed for any other research problem. Every genealogist begins with certain facts and progresses to the unknown. If tradition says that an individual emigrated from Germany and settled first in Baltimore, educate yourself on the background and existing materials for research in that city. Guides have been published for many major cities which outline in broad terms the location and accessibility of sources, eliminating some blind alleys.

In response to the overwhelming interest in family history and the resulting number of requests in recent years, city libraries have published pamphlets describing their genealogy and local history holdings, hours of operation, and research policies. The Public Library of Cincinnati and Hamilton County, 800 Vine St., Library Square, Cincinnati, OH 45202-2071, publishes a brochure titled *Finding Your Family Roots in Cincinnati,* for example. If you live some distance from the public library in the area of an ancestor's residence, you can write or call to request a descriptive brochure. If no such brochure is available, the library should be able to provide adequate details over the telephone so that you can determine whether a trip to it is in order. Any large library should have a current issue of the *American Library Directory,* a reference volume with essential addresses and telephone numbers for other libraries across the country. Some libraries will even supply lists of researchers, though none of the institutions will specifically recommend or guarantee the quality of the work of individuals listed. If a library is unable to provide a list of researchers, you may wish to contact the Association of Professional Genealogists, 3421 M St. N.W., Suite 236, Washington, DC 20007-3552, for assistance in locating a professional researcher in a particular city.

CITY RESEARCH GUIDES

A number of genealogical and historical guides for specific cities have been published over the past few years, and more are in the development stages. One of the best currently available is Estelle Guzik, ed., *Genealogical Resources in the New York Metropolitan Area* (New York: Jewish Genealogical Society, 1989). Though published by the Jewish Genealogical society, the volume is by no means limited to Jewish sources. The majority of the facilities covered are in New York City, but six suburban counties in New York state and New Jersey are also included. Archives serving the metropolitan area, bureaus of vital records, city clerks, offices, civil, county, and federal courts, genealogical and historical societies, and libraries with genealogical holdings and special collections are but a few of the topics discussed in the volume. Adding greatly to the usefulness of the guide are geographical and mailing addresses, telephone numbers, hours of operation, and directions for driving or reaching the various facilities by public transportation. A knowledge of the basic records maintained by public agencies in these counties of New York and New Jersey will help in locating records in other counties as well. The material is organized geographically so that researchers can coordinate their visits to facilities within a particular area. An earlier but still informative volume is Rosalie F. Bailey, *Guide to Genealogical and Biographical Sources for New York City, 1783–1898* (New York: the author, 1954). Even if New York City is not your area of interest, this work's forty separate categories of records with select bibliographies will give you an analogue for the city in which you are interested. Not all of these will apply to every research problem, but knowing of them can stimulate innovative approaches when other paths seem closed.

Those with Chicago research problems will find help in Loretto Dennis Szucs, *Chicago and Cook County: A Guide to Research* (Salt Lake City: Ancestry, 1996). It covers many genealogical sources and research strategies from vital records to Chicago communities and neighborhoods, occupational and business resources, and miscellaneous sources and addresses.

The volume includes a chronological list of 107 major historical events that affect research in the area. A glance at the chronology pinpoints important changes, such as the incorporation of the city in 1837, the opening of the Illinois and Michigan Canal in 1848, the cholera epidemic and bank panic of 1849, and the Great Chicago Fire of 1871, which destroyed almost all government-created records. "Archives and Manuscript Collections," "Historical Societies," "Gazetteer of Cook County," "Genealogical Societies," "Cemeteries in the Metropolitan Chicago Area," and collections of the Family History Library and its local family history centers, the Newberry Library, and the National Archives—Great Lakes Region in Chicago are among topics described in the eleven appendices of the book. Specific information is provided where the researcher is likely to confront a forbidding bureaucracy.

Robert W. Barnes, *Guide to Research in Baltimore City and County* (Westminster, Md.: Family Line Publications, 1989), provides important details about genealogical information in archives, libraries, repositories, maps, biographical sources, cemeteries, ethnic histories, newspapers, occupational and political sources, and some hard-to-find city records. As the author points out, "Knowing where to look is an important part of the researcher's job. It is extremely frustrating to drive to the Court House at Towson only to find that the records being sought are some ten miles away in Baltimore City, or thirty miles away in the Maryland State Archives."

STATE GUIDES

Unfortunately, there are far too few guides yet available for specific cities, but some statewide compilations may be very helpful where city guides are lacking. Carol W. Bell, *Ohio Guide to Genealogical Sources* (Baltimore: Genealogical Publishing Co., 1988), is a notable example. For instance, if Cleveland is an area of interest, addresses of courts, historical and genealogical societies, and other useful information concerning the city can be found under the heading of Cuyahoga County. Additionally, consulting the county lists can reveal which vital and probate records had already been microfilmed by the Genealogical Society of Utah at the time of the guide's publication. Under the heading "Miscellaneous" there are also land, marriage, Bible, cemetery, church, and other records for the city, available on microfilm at the Ohio Historical Society and the Western Reserve Historical Society. The guide, of course, details valuable collections that will facilitate research in other Ohio counties and cities as well.

Roseann Hogan, *Kentucky Ancestry: A Guide to Genealogical and Historical Research* (Salt Lake City: Ancestry, 1993), is an in-depth study that will facilitate research in any city or rural area in Kentucky. Seven chapters of this work provide historical background and methodology for using both standard and unique sources in the state. Chapter 8 inventories records by county. There are also a number of constructive tips on city records, including the fact that, despite irregular reporting of vital events in the state before 1910, more uniform registration began in the cities of Lexington, Louisville, Newport, and Covington almost twenty-five years earlier. Hogan alerts readers to the fact that Kentuckians have filed more than 500,000 delayed birth certificates, which typically are completed in order to obtain Social Security benefits, and that there is a possibility that even if no official certificate can be found in Frank-

fort, a certificate may have been filed with the Social Security Administration or other government agencies.

If you have research to conduct in Atlanta, Savannah, or any other Georgia city, Robert Scott Davis, Jr., *Research in Georgia* (Easley, S.C.: Southern Historical Press, 1981), is particularly helpful. The volume emphasizes the Georgia Department of Archives and History. Yet another essential guide for a Southern state is Helen Leary, ed., *North Carolina Research: Genealogy and Local History* (Raleigh, N.C.: North Carolina Genealogical Society, 1996).

LIBRARY GUIDES

Guides to library collections can also be direct routes to information on cities. Joseph Oldenburg, *A Genealogical Guide to the Burton Historical Collection: Detroit Public Library* (Salt Lake City: Ancestry, 1988), provides information on city directories, local history sources, newspapers, atlases and maps, and picture collections for the Detroit area as well as some other Michigan counties and other states. Sources that would be difficult for the average researcher to discover are brought to light in this guide. For Detroit and Wayne County, for example, are descriptions of vital records transcribed by the Louisa St. Clair Chapter of the National Society of the Daughters of the American Revolution (DAR) in conjunction with the Work Projects Administration (WPA). The same DAR chapter has transcribed Detroit cemetery and church records and a fifty-three-volume set of *Early Land Transfers, Detroit and Wayne County Michigan, 1703–1869*. Yet another set compiled by the St. Clair DAR chapter is the *Probate Records of Wayne County, Michigan*. Arranged chronologically, the five volumes cover the years 1797 to 1870. Of special interest to anyone with Catholic ancestors in the Detroit area is a collection of church records. "The Archdiocese of Detroit has deposited microfilm copies of the registers of seventy-three Roman Catholic parishes in and around Detroit," according to Oldenburg's guide. Figure 19-1 is a page from the record of the German-American Savings Bank of Detroit. It is from the Charles Kanter papers described in chapter 4, Manuscripts, in the *Guide to the Burton Historical Collection*.

Peggy Tuck Sinko, *Guide to Local and Family History at The Newberry Library* (Salt Lake City: Ancestry, 1987), will prepare the researcher for the fact that, like most other libraries, the Newberry does not have official Chicago or Cook County birth, death, marriage, probate, or land records, but it does have some important yet obscure sources for the city. In addition to all of the available Chicago city directories (1838 to 1928–29), the guide calls attention to "Sam Fink's Marriages and Deaths From Chicago Newspapers, 1834–1889," and the Newberry's unique Chicago and Cook County Biographical File, an ever-growing source.

MULTI-CITY REFERENCE TOOLS

Another extremely useful urban tool with a somewhat unlikely title is Arthur Kurzweil and Miriam Weiner, *The Encyclopedia of Jewish Genealogy* (Northvale, N.J., and London: Jason Aronson, 1991). Whether you have Jewish ancestors or not, this work has substantive chapters on city resources in Arizona, California, Colorado, Connecticut, District of Columbia, Georgia, Illinois, Iowa, Kansas, Kentucky, Maryland, Massachusetts, Michigan, Minnesota, Missouri, Nebraska, New Jer-

Figure 19-1. Depositors' signatures from the records of the German-American Savings Bank of Detroit.

sey, New York, North Carolina, Ohio, Oklahoma, Oregon, Pennsylvania, Texas, Utah, Virginia, Washington, and Wisconsin.

One of the most important reference works is Alice Eichholz, ed., *Ancestry's Red Book: American State, County and Town Sources,* rev. ed. (Salt Lake City: Ancestry, 1992), which covers all U.S. states and cities. The state chapters open with historical segments and proceed to summarize vital, census, land, probate, court, tax, cemetery, church, and military records; local history; maps; periodicals, newspapers, and manuscripts; and archives, libraries, and societies. Each chapter concludes with a table that lists county and town courthouse addresses, dates of formation, parent political units, and the beginning dates of vital and court records. Outline maps showing the counties and county seats complement the chapters on each state.

INDEXES

There are a number of valuable finding tools that have not yet been published. The Baltimore City Archives has, for example, a WPA-compiled name index to the municipal records for 1756 to 1938. The Douglas County Historical Society (Omaha, Nebraska) has the *Omaha World-Herald* Clipping File, a subject and biographic file with 400,000 subject files (including more than 5 million clippings from between 1907 and 1983). The Oregon Historical Society has several biographical sources important for searching cities in that state. A vertical file consisting of newspaper clippings includes 4,000 subjects on state and local history and 1,500 biographies of prominent Oregonians. Also covered are historic structures, ethnic groups, cities, counties, and Portland neighborhoods. A separate "Biography Card File" was put together from books, scrapbooks, newspaper clippings, among other things.

CITY DIRECTORIES

A decided advantage to conducting research in a metropolitan area is the availability of printed directories for most cities,

large and small. There is scarcely a more satisfying or more productive adventure in family history research than finding an ancestor in an old directory, discovering his or her occupation (or multiple occupations), and knowing exactly where in the city he or she lived. The enjoyment grows if you are able to track families for significant time periods. Figure 19-2 is from an 1872 directory for Brooklyn, New York. Chapter 11, Research in Directories, provides an excellent, in-depth description of this important source. However, there are certain concepts and strategies that bear highlighting here.

While directories of residents may date back to a city's earliest days, no directory is all-inclusive. Because the motive behind the printing of most of these books was to sell advertising, the listing of residents was selective. Stephen Thernstrom cites a study of Newburyport, Massachusetts, city directories. "Volumes purporting to list every family in the community were published in January 1849 and January 1851. These have been compared with a list of all laborers resident in Newburyport taken from the Seventh United States Census. Fully forty-five percent of the laboring families found by the diligent census-taker in September and October of 1850 cannot be located in either directory."[6] Thernstrom concludes that, in addition to inadvertently missing many of the city's transient population, "the compiler of the directories either did not know about or did not choose to include many working class families in his volumes." Similar conclusions have been made in studies conducted in other cities. Yet, genuine efforts seem to have been made by some of the publishers. The compilers of the *Chicago 1844 Directory* stated on the first page of the volume:

It has been the design to include in this Directory the names of all persons and all firms in the City, to arrange them alphabetically, and in every instance to give the correct spelling. There may be cases however, where names may have been accidentally inserted in the

Figure 19-2. A page from an 1872 Brooklyn, New York, city directory. It is typical of compilations that exist for most American cities.

HUF—HUG   356   HUG

Huff Wilhelm, mason, h 83 Gerry
Huff William T. h 449 Lafayette av
Huff William T. painter, h 113 Hamilton
Huffington John W. agt. h 99 Pineapple
Huffington John, lab. h 1715 Pacific
Huffington Julia, wid. h 127 Fort Greene pl
Hufnagel Henry F. hairdresser, 644 3d av
Hufnagel John C. furniture, r 18 Hicks, h 18 Hicks
ᴱHufnagel Robert, jeweler, Franklin c Kent
Huffnagle John, engineer, h 379 Van Brunt
ᴱHuffner Josephine, wid. h 49 Orchard
ᴱHug Jacob, carpenter, h 33 McKibbin
ᴱHugal Frederick, driver, h 248 2d
Hugaw Thomas, safemkr. h 321 Warren
Huge Fred, clk. h 97 Myrtle av
Hugerland John, butcher, Clinton c Hamilton av. h Huntington
Huges William, mason, h 953 Pacific
Hugg August, hatter, h 514 Flushing av
Huggar Charles, liquors, 45 Grand
Huggin Mary, wid. h 116 Smith
ᴱHuggins Caroline, h r 179 S. 3d
ᴱHuggins Catherine, wid. h 50 Jefferson
ᴱHuggins James, painter, h 105 S. 1st
Huggins James (Rev.) printer, 37 2Pearl, N. Y. h 91 Tompkins av
Huggins William, shoes, 125 Bridge
ᴱHugh James, peddler, h 1303 Myrtle av
Hughan Samuel, drugs, 130 Pearl, N. Y. h 362 Van Buren
ᴱHughes Albert T. provisions, 1224 Myrtle av
Hughes Alexander, clk. h 230 Warren
Hughes Atha, shades, 68 Water
Hughes Andrew, lab. h 120 Concord
Hughes Andrew, watchman, h Richards c Tremont
ᴱHughes Ann, teacher, h 341 4th
ᴱHughes Ann, wid. h 171 N. 7th
ᴱHughes Ann, wid. liquors, 268 Union av
Hughes Anne, drugs, 513 Atlantic av
ᴱHughes Annie, dressmkr. 250 Grand
Hughes Archy, h 244 Pacific
Hughes Arthur, painter, h 194 Hudson av
Hughes Bernard, carman, h 201 St. Mark's av
Hughes Charles, h 810 B'way
Hughes Daniel, h 128 2d pl
Hughes Daniel, billiards, h 1155 Fulton
ᴱHughes Daniel, liquors, 85 Clymer, h 61 Wythe av
Hughes Daniel, shipmaster, h 493 Hicks
Hughes Edward, h 159 9th
Hughes Edward, blacksmith, h 353 Van Buren
Hughes Edward, carpenter, h 86 Spencer
Hughes Edward, drugs, 86 Spencer
ᴱHughes Edward, engineer, h 263 Mauger
Hughes Edward, lab. h 94 Union
Hughes Edward, liquors, 153 Imlay
Hughes Edward, liquors, 304 Van Brunt
Hughes Edward J. plumber, h 550 Myrtle av
ᴱHughes Edward, sawfiler, h 42 N. 2d
Hughes Edward M. dentist, 1109 De Kalb av
ᴱHughes Edwin, mason, h 214 8th
Hughes Eleanor B. h 65 Hamilton
Hughes Ellen, wid. h 580 Carlton av
ᴱHughes Felix, lab. h 433 1st
Hughes Francis, bartender, h 300 Columbia
Hughes George, hatter, h 187 Throop av

Hughes George, printer, h 21 Canton
Hughes George F. bookkpr. h 254 Flushing
Hughes Harvey, grocer, Park av. c Adelphi, 174 Park av
Hughes Henry, butcher, h 59 Woodhull
Hughes Henry, clk. h 59 Woodhull
Hughes Henry, clk. h 496 State
ᴱHughes Henry, printer, h 10 Gates av
Hughes Henry, shoes, 216 Atlantic av
Hughes Henry, teacher, h 738 Bergen
Hughes Henry A. machinist, h 60 High
ᴱHughes Henry F. pianomkr. 369 B'way
ᴱHughes Henry W. segarmkr. h 291 4th
Hughes H. C. provisions, 113 Park av
Hughes James, h 456 State
Hughes James, barber, h 27 Main
Hughes James, billiards, h 1155 Fulton
Hughes James, bricklayer, h 255 St. Mark's
Hughes James, flour, 694 Myrtle av
Hughes James, hatter, h Degraw n Bond
Hughes James, lab. h 218 Pacific
ᴱHughes James, lab. h ft Greenpoint av
Hughes James, lab. h 58 Little
Hughes James, lab. h 372 Baltic
Hughes James, machinist, h 264 Plymouth
ᴱHughes James, milliner, h 433 First
Hughes James, molder, h 46 Lexington av
ᴱHughes James, patternmkr. h 28 Filmore
ᴱHughes James, paver, h 99 Walton
Hughes James, plasterer, h 73 Kosciusko
ᴱHughes James, teacher, h 356 2d
Hughes James C. bookkpr. h 67 Nevins
ᴱHughes James E. brassfinisher, h 341 4th
Hughes James H. clk. h 247 Front
Hughes Jane, nurse, h 183 Hudson av
ᴱHughes Jane, wid. h 205 Kent
ᴱHughes Jane, wid. h 169 9th
ᴱHughes John, h 45 Withers
Hughes John, blacksmith, h 353 Van Buren
Hughes John, butcher, 329 Court
Hughes John, carman, h r 546 Grand av
ᴱHughes John, carman, h 263 Mauger
Hughes John, carpenter, h 233 Flatbush av
ᴱHughes John, clk. h 29 Grand
ᴱHughes John, cotton, N. Y. h 323 Leonard
Hughes John, drugs, 185 De Kalb av
Hughes John, grainer, h r 463 Dean
ᴱHughes John, jeweler, h 121 Skillman av
Hughes John, lab. h Brooklyn av. n Dean
ᴱHughes John, lab. h 152 India
Hughes John, lab. h 225 16th
ᴱHughes John, lab. h 89 N. 4th
Hughes John, lab. h 227 15th
Hughes John, lab. h 302 Plymouth
ᴱHughes John, liquors, 1st c N. 9th
Hughes John, mason, h 214 Flatbush av
Hughes John, painter, h 14 Prospect
Hughes John, porter, h 664 Atlantic av
Hughes John, salesman, h 60 High
Hughes John, seaman, h 173 Navy
Hughes John, tailor, h 44 Lafayette
Hughes John, wheelwright, h 174 Front
Hughes John H. jr. h 363 Pacific
Hughes John A. bldr. h 363 Pacific
ᴱHughes Joseph, liquors, 365 S. 4th, h 329
Hughes Julia, h 391 Warren
Hughes Lambert R. provisions, Myrtle av c B'way, h 55 Sands

wrong connection, and cases also of incorrect orthography—particularly where persons have been unable to spell, and the names have been written from the sound. Immediate measures will be taken to procure the names of all persons who have accidentally been omitted in this volume; a complete list, corrected from time to time, will be kept at the General Intelligence office, where the public can at times get information in regard to the names, business, and residence of every inhabitant of the City. Persons finding themselves excluded and persons coming to the City hereafter, are requested to call at the above place and have their names enrolled. Very few of our buildings are numbered, the necessity, however, of this can be avoided, if persons occupying buildings permanently, will put themselves to the trifling trouble and expense of putting their names on their doors.[7]

As cautious as publishers claimed to be, however, it is clear that immigrants were consistently omitted from the commercial publications—particularly those immigrants who did not speak English. Frequently, entire ethnic neighborhoods were left out of city compilations. Some groups, such as the Poles in Chicago, independently published city or community directories in their native language to offset such gaps.

Cities often had several directory publishers—Chicago had three in 1871. Consult all of them, for each may contain unique details. Richard Edwards, *Edwards' 1871 Chicago Census Directory* (Chicago: Richard Edwards, 1871), lists not only names, occupations, and addresses of individuals, but also provides a ward number, the number of males, females, and total in residence, as well as the birthplace of the head of household. John Gager, *Gager's 1857 Chicago Directory* (Chicago: John Gager and Co., 1857), includes the birthplace and years of residence in Chicago with the usual information. One publication lists "Miller, Emma, widow," and one by another publisher in the same year adds "Emma, widow of James." Limiting a search to one directory increases the chance of missing precious clues.

TELEPHONE DIRECTORIES

A year or so after Alexander Graham Bell invented the articulating telephone, telephone directories began to appear in cities across the country. In 1878, Chicago had its first published telephone book. It listed mostly business establishments; the remainder were the handful of private citizens who could afford the luxury. Most of the population has been vastly underrepresented in telephone directories—even in later years. As late as 1900, only seventeen people per one thousand had a telephone; by 1920 that number had risen to twenty-three per one thousand. Having a telephone then, as now, did not guarantee inclusion in a telephone book; many elected not to be listed.

In addition to the collections of current directories for cities in the United States that are available in large public and university libraries, there are telephone search services, such as the one provided by Ancestry (P.O. Box 476, Salt Lake City, UT 84110), which provide access to a 90-million-household database of names, addresses, and telephone numbers.

STREET DIRECTORIES

One of the frustrations in research is finding incomplete information in a source—for example, a beautiful old portrait which

bears the name and street address of the photographer but gives no city, or a candid shot of a group of people on the porch of a charming old house at 4124 Trowbridge Street, or a letter which states, "Your brother remains close to the shop in the city but has taken up new quarters on Madison Street." Such information is useless if the town name is unknown. *The Street Directory of the Principal Cities of the United States* (Detroit: Gale Research Co., 1973), originally published by order of the postmaster general in 1908, is an alphabetical listing of streets, avenues, courts, places, lanes, roads, and wharves to which mail was delivered, with references to all the cities and towns where these street names appear. City directories frequently included street guides. See figure 19-3, a street and avenue guide from a 1900 Chicago directory.

GENEALOGICAL SOCIETIES

Genealogical societies at the national, state, and local levels offer educational programs and publications with a strong focus on the locality served. The Dubuque County Genealogical Society (P.O. Box 13, Dubuque, IA 52004-0013), for example, publishes such titles as *A Guide to Microfilmed Records at Carnegie-Stout Public Library, Dubuque, Iowa;* lists of Dubuque city directories, 1856 to 1983; newspapers for the area; an obituary file; and probate and marriage index information. Other society publications are an *Index of Churches and Cemeteries of Dubuque County, Iowa; Burial Records of Dubuque City Cemetery, 1854–1875; Declarations of Intent to Become a Citizen, Dubuque County, Iowa;* and *Roots in Dubuque County, Iowa: A Genealogical Resource Book.*

To find the name and address of the genealogical society in your area of interest, consult Mary Meyers, ed., *Meyer's Directory of Genealogical Societies in the U.S.A. and Canada* (Mt. Airy, Md.: the editor; updated and reissued in even-numbered years).

HISTORY

The importance of understanding the history of any geographical area in genealogical research cannot be overstated. Basic historical overviews of most cities can be found in encyclopedias, but for a better understanding of what types of records may exist or what it was like to live in the times and places of our ancestors, the ever-increasing number of urban studies that are becoming available are among the most encouraging aspects of city research. If a descriptive volume on the city in which you are interested is not on the shelf of your local public library, a large city or university library may have it or be able to borrow it for you through interlibrary loan.

Rita Miller, ed., *Brooklyn, U.S.A.: The Fourth Largest City in America* (New York: Brooklyn College Press, 1979), is an example of a work that provides a sociological view of the city from its original inhabitants to mobility patterns of residents in the 1970s. Discussions of topics and author's notes on subjects as diverse as Kings County in the American Revolution, Bedford-Stuyvesant, Flatbush, the Brooklyn Academy of Music, the Brooklyn Navy Yard, the Brooklyn Dodgers, Neighborhoods of Brooklyn, and even a chapter titled "Kings English: Fact and Folklore of Brooklyn Speech" provide rare insights into Brooklyn as it was in an ancestor's day, as well as providing precious clues for finding record sources.

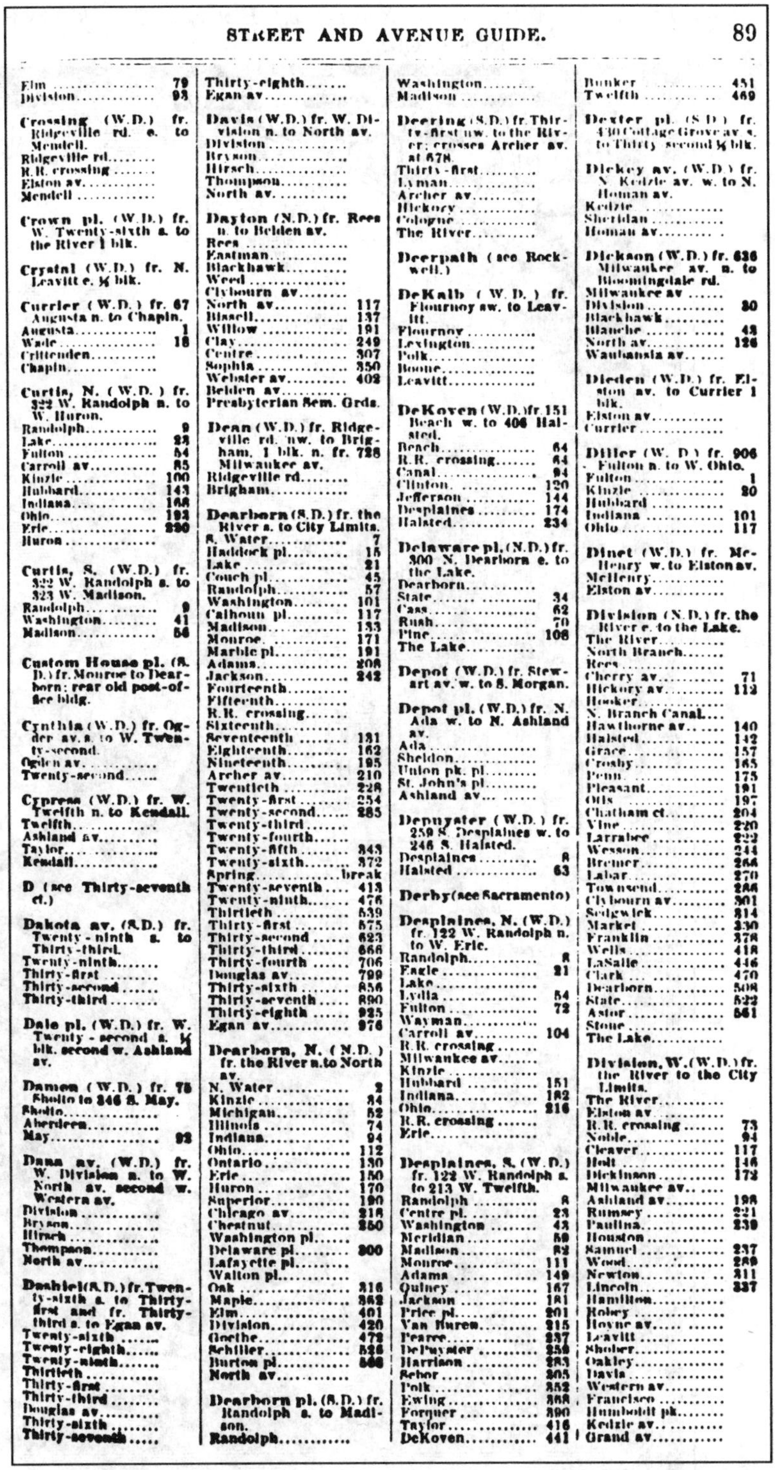

STREET AND AVENUE GUIDE. 89

Elm 79
Division 93

Crossing (W.D.) fr. Ridgeville rd. e. to Mendell.
Ridgeville rd ....
R.R. crossing ....
Elston av ....
Mendell ....

Crown pl. (W.D.) fr. W. Twenty-sixth s. to the River 1 blk.

Crystal (W.D.) fr. N. Leavitt e. ½ blk.

Currier (W.D.) fr. 67 Augusta n. to Chapin.
Augusta 1
Wade 18
Crittenden ....
Chapin ....

Curtis, N. (W.D.) fr. 322 W. Randolph n. to W. Huron.
Randolph 9
Lake 23
Fulton 54
Carroll av 85
Kinzie 100
Hubbard 143
Indiana 168
Ohio 193
Erie 230
Huron ....

Curtis, S. (W.D.) fr. 322 W. Randolph s. to 323 W. Madison.
Randolph 9
Washington 41
Madison 56

Custom House pl. (S.D.) fr. Monroe to Dearborn; rear old post-office bldg.

Cynthia (W.D.) fr. Ogden av. s. to W. Twenty-second.
Ogden av ....
Twenty-second ....

Cypress (W.D.) fr. W. Twelfth n. to Kendall.
Twelfth ....
Ashland av ....
Taylor ....
Kendall ....

D (see Thirty-seventh ct.)

Dakota av. (S.D.) fr. Twenty-ninth s. to Thirty-third.
Twenty-ninth ....
Thirty-first ....
Thirty-second ....
Thirty-third ....

Dale pl. (W.D.) fr. W. Twenty-second s. ½ blk. second w. Ashland av.

Damen (W.D.) fr. 78 Sholto to 346 S. May.
Sholto ....
Aberdeen ....
May 93

Dana av. (W.D.) fr. W. Division n. to W. North av. second w. Western av.
Division ....
Bryson ....
Hirsch ....
Thompson ....
North av ....

Dashiel (S.D.) fr. Twenty-sixth s. to Thirty-first and fr. Thirty-third s. to Egan av.
Twenty-sixth ....
Twenty-eighth ....
Twenty-ninth ....
Thirtieth ....
Thirty-first ....
Thirty-third ....
Douglas av ....
Thirty-sixth ....
Thirty-seventh ....
Thirty-eighth ....
Egan av ....

Davis (W.D.) fr. W. Division n. to North av.
Division ....
Bryson ....
Hirsch ....
Thompson ....
North av ....

Dayton (N.D.) fr. Rees n. to Belden av.
Rees ....
Eastman ....
Blackhawk ....
Weed ....
Clybourn av ....
North av 117
Bissell 137
Willow 191
Clay 249
Centre 307
Sophia 350
Webster av 402
Belden av ....
Presbyterian Sem. Grds.

Dean (W.D.) fr. Ridgeville rd. nw. to Brigham, 1 blk. n. fr. 728 Milwaukee av.
Ridgeville rd ....
Brigham ....

Dearborn (S.D.) fr. the River s. to City Limits.
S. Water 7
Haddock pl 15
Lake 21
Couch pl 45
Randolph 57
Washington 101
Calhoun pl 117
Madison 133
Monroe 171
Marble pl 191
Adams 208
Jackson 242
Fourteenth ....
Fifteenth ....
R.R. crossing ....
Sixteenth ....
Seventeenth 131
Eighteenth 162
Nineteenth 195
Archer av 210
Twentieth 228
Twenty-first 254
Twenty-second 285
Twenty-third ....
Twenty-fourth ....
Twenty-fifth 343
Twenty-sixth 372
Spring .... break
Twenty-seventh 413
Twenty-ninth 476
Thirtieth 539
Thirty-first 575
Thirty-second 623
Thirty-third 666
Thirty-fourth 706
Douglas av 799
Thirty-sixth 856
Thirty-seventh 890
Thirty-eighth 925
Egan av 976

Dearborn, N. (N.D.) fr. the River n. to North av.
N. Water 2
Kinzie 34
Michigan 52
Illinois 74
Indiana 94
Ohio 112
Ontario 130
Erie 150
Huron 170
Superior 190
Chicago av 218
Chestnut 250
Washington pl ....
Delaware pl 300
Lafayette pl ....
Walton pl ....
Oak 316
Maple 362
Elm 401
Division 420
Goethe 472
Schiller 526
Burton pl 566
North av ....

Dearborn pl. (S.D.) fr. Randolph s. to Madison.
Randolph ....

Washington ....
Madison ....

Deering (S.D.) fr. Thirty-first nw. to the River; crosses Archer av. at 678.
Thirty-first ....
Lyman ....
Archer av ....
Hickory ....
Cologne ....
The River ....

Deerpath (see Rockwell.)

DeKalb (W.D.) fr. Flournoy av. to Leavitt.
Flournoy ....
Lexington ....
Polk ....
Boone ....
Leavitt ....

DeKoven (W.D.) fr. 151 Beach w. to 406 Halsted.
Beach 64
R.R. crossing 64
Canal 94
Clinton 120
Jefferson 144
Desplaines 174
Halsted 234

Delaware pl. (N.D.) fr. 300 N. Dearborn e. to the Lake.
Dearborn ....
State 34
Cass 62
Rush 70
Pine 108
The Lake ....

Depot (W.D.) fr. Stewart av. w. to S. Morgan.

Depot pl. (W.D.) fr. N. Ada w. to N. Ashland av.
Ada ....
Sheldon ....
Union pk. pl ....
St. John's pl ....
Ashland av ....

Depuyster (W.D.) fr. 259 S. Desplaines w. to 246 S. Halsted.
Desplaines 8
Halsted 63

Derby (see Sacramento)

Desplaines, N. (W.D.) fr. 122 W. Randolph n. to W. Erie.
Randolph 8
Eagle 21
Lake ....
Lydia 54
Fulton 72
Wayman ....
Carroll av 104
R.R. crossing ....
Milwaukee av ....
Kinzie ....
Hubbard 151
Indiana 182
Ohio 216
R.R. crossing ....
Erie ....

Desplaines, S. (W.D.) fr. 122 W. Randolph s. to 213 W. Twelfth.
Randolph 8
Centre pl 23
Washington 43
Meridian 59
Madison 82
Monroe 111
Adams 149
Quincy 167
Jackson 181
Price pl 201
Van Buren 215
Pearce 237
DePuyster 259
Harrison 283
Bebor 305
Polk 352
Ewing 368
Forquer 390
Taylor 416
DeKoven 441

Bunker 451
Twelfth 469

Dexter pl. (S.D.) fr. 430 Cottage Grove av. s. to Thirty second ½ blk.

Dickey av. (W.D.) fr. N. Kedzie av. w. to N. Homan av.
Kedzie ....
Sheridan ....
Homan av ....

Dickson (W.D.) fr. 636 Milwaukee av. n. to Bloomingdale rd.
Milwaukee av ....
Division 80
Blackhawk ....
Blanche 43
North av 126
Waubansia av ....

Dieden (W.D.) fr. Elston av. to Currier 1 blk.
Elston av ....
Currier ....

Diller (W. D.) fr. 906 Fulton n. to W. Ohio.
Fulton 1
Kinzie 20
Hubbard ....
Indiana 101
Ohio 117

Dinet (W.D.) fr. McHenry w. to Elston av.
McHenry ....
Elston av ....

Division (N.D.) fr. the River e. to the Lake.
The River ....
North Branch ....
Rees ....
Cherry av 71
Hickory av 113
Hooker ....
N. Branch Canal ....
Hawthorne av 140
Halsted 142
Grace 157
Crosby 165
Penn 175
Pleasant 191
Otis 197
Chatham ct 204
Vine 220
Larrabee 222
Wesson 244
Bremer 266
Labar 270
Townsend 286
Clybourn av 301
Sedgwick 314
Market 330
Franklin 378
Wells 418
LaSalle 446
Clark 470
Dearborn 508
State 522
Astor 561
Stone ....
The Lake ....

Division, W. (W.D.) fr. the River to the City Limits.
The River ....
Elston av ....
R.R. crossing 73
Noble 94
Cleaver 117
Holt 146
Dickinson 172
Milwaukee av ....
Ashland av 198
Rumsey 221
Paulina 239
Houston ....
Samuel 237
Wood 289
Newton 311
Lincoln 337
Hamilton ....
Robey ....
Hoyne av ....
Leavitt ....
Sholer ....
Oakley ....
Davis ....
Western av ....
Francisco ....
Humboldt pk ....
Kedzie av ....
Grand av ....

Figure 19-3. A page from a "Street and Avenue" guide from a 1900 Chicago city directory.

Pictorial histories of American cities are enjoying a revival of popularity. Major booksellers in most urban areas usually have significant local history sections where any number of contemporary works can be found. Anyone with Chicago roots can gain a wealth of knowledge about the city from Harold Mayer and Richard Wade, *Chicago: Growth of a Metropolis* (Chicago: University of Chicago Press, 1969). Photographic documentation is especially useful in describing the physical growth and settlement patterns in cities. One thousand photographs and illustrations and an extensive local history bibliography make this well-documented Chicago history volume especially useful.

A valuable aid for laying the groundwork in any city research is John Buenker, Gerald Michael Greenfield, and William J. Murin, *Urban History: A Guide to Information Sources* (Detroit: Gale Research Co., 1981), an annotation of 1,921 scholarly works covering eleven broad topical areas. Pertinent information on every major city is listed in it. Many of the sources cited are standard metropolitan histories; others are contemporary works with bibliographies which are potential gold mines in themselves, pointing to the original sources on which the author based his or her study. Such references can lead directly to manuscripts, special collections, and other hidden tools.

County and municipal histories, long used by family historians, can also provide critical information for furthering city research. While the greatest number of these histories were published in the 1880s and 1890s, dates vary from one locality to another. The two-volume *Kings County History 1683 to 1884: The Civil, Political, Professional and Ecclesiastical History and Commercial and Industrial Record of the County of Kings and the City of Brooklyn, N.Y. From 1683 to 1884* by Henry R. Stiles (New York: W.W. Munsell and Co., 1884) (figure 19-4) is one of several Kings County histories. It focuses on Brooklyn, which was then the third largest city in the United States. A helpful, though by no means all-inclusive, source is P. William Filby, comp., *A Bibliography of American County Histories* (Baltimore: Genealogical Publishing Co., 1985). To learn if there is a published history for Raleigh, North Carolina, for example, you can consult this bibliography (arranged alphabetically by state and then by county) to see that there are several entries for Wake County, one of which is a 1902 publication titled *Historical Raleigh With Sketches of Wake County and Its Important Towns* by Moses N. Amis. As with any other source, it is important to read Filby's preface, in which he explains the criteria used to determine a book's inclusion in his work. "Books beginning with titles such as 'Historical and Biographical' . . . can contain a history of the county and consist in the main of biographies, yet they are often the only histories available." For this reason, Filby included them in his bibliography. On the other hand, he chose not to include books with such titles as "Biographies of Prominent Men . . ." or "Portrait and Biographical Histories. . . ." As Filby points out, these histories must be used with a degree of skepticism, because publishers made up their costs by including only the most flattering biographical sketches of prominent citizens who were their patrons for such projects.

Another bonus for city research is that many histories were generated to appeal to various segments of the population. Not

Figure 19-4. Title page from *Kings County History 1683 to 1884* by Henry Stiles, a typical example of county histories that focus on major American cities.

only will you find volumes that focus on counties or cities, but also those defining local political parties, wards, industries, ethnic groups, neighborhoods, religious groups, and fraternal and social organizations. These groups and others provided additional opportunities for less-prominent citizens to be included in a printed source. Consequently, if your ancestor was not mentioned in a standard city or county work, there is still the possibility of his or her inclusion in one of the smaller histories that frequently included biographical sketches. Most local histories are in non-circulating reference sections of libraries, so it is usually necessary to travel to those special collections.

CENSUS RECORDS

Federal, state, and special censuses are productive genealogical tools, for probably no other records in existence contain more data about families (see chapter 5, Research in Census Records). Searching through the census schedules for a metropolitan area, however, presents special problems.

The Soundex and other census indexes are helpful but somewhat limited, especially in city situations. Often, names were misspelled or completely omitted in transcription from the original schedules. For the 1880 census, only households with children ten years of age or under were listed in the Soundex index. When indexes fail or when they have yet to be created for a densely populated urban area, an educated approach is important. If you know the family's makeup, you can go over a census line by line in hopes that names, ages, birthplaces, and other known facts will catch your eye, even though the name is misspelled or the page barely legible. However, in most cases, this can be extremely time consuming. For the 1850 through 1870 censuses, the ward is the smallest division of the city. Space for the enumerators to identify street names and numbers did not appear on census forms until the 1880 enumeration.

The geographical arrangement of the census schedules makes finding aids vital when searching for urban residents, for in every census year some names were inadvertently left out of census indexes or were misspelled to the extent that they cannot be found in the index. Historian Keith Schlesinger devised a system to locate individuals overlooked by the Soundex. Schlesinger gleaned addresses from city directories, which he found both accurate and accessible, then plotted them on maps of census enumeration districts, which normally followed the boundaries of voting precincts in most cities. Figure 19-5 is a section of an 1880 Chicago map on which enumerator visitation dates are noted. By matching ward and visitation dates to census pages, it is possible to search for the non-indexed individual to one or two enumeration districts. By narrowing the search for the non-indexed individual to one or two enumeration districts, this scheme permits the historian to escape the confinement of the Soundex. Research institutions are beginning to acquire enumerator district maps and finding aids which trace the route taken during the count, and enumeration district boundary descriptions are available on microfilm through the National Archives and Records Administration and in some genealogical library collections. The Newberry Library and Schlesinger have refined several methods for searching the 1850 through 1910 censuses for Chicago. See Keith Schlesinger and Peggy Tuck Sinko, "Urban Finding Aid for Manuscript Census Searches," *National Genealogical Society Quarterly* 69 (September 1981): 171–80. The techniques, of course, are applicable to other cities as well.

Technological advances in recent years have enabled many of the voluminous post-1850 to 1880 census schedules to be indexed, and others are in the process of being indexed. Many statewide and some city indexes are available in book, microfiche, or computer disk formats for that period. Historic Resources, Inc. (P.O. Box 254, Bountiful, UT 84011-0254), offers a growing list of databases, including the 1870 census indices for the cities of Chicago, St. Louis, and Philadelphia. The accuracy of recently produced indexes has improved with increased cross checking of entries before publication. Yet, as in any indexing, some names will inevitably be incorrect or will have been missed entirely, so do not conclude that an ancestor is not in the actual census schedule if his or her name is not found in an index.

As in any other record category, titles can be misleading. The cover of the 1870 census index for Chicago implies that it includes only individuals who lived within the city limits. However, a second title page shows, correctly, that the volume covers not only the city but the thousands of others who lived in townships outside the city but within Cook County—an important distinction.

Several projects are currently under way to index the 1880 federal census schedules. Padraigreen Publishing, P.O. Box 24410, New Orleans, LA 70184-4410, for example, has in progress a project to index the 200,000 individuals in the 1880 census for New Orleans. It is spread over seventeen wards and ninety-two enumeration districts and occupies 4,300 pages. Many metropolitan areas are not treated separately but rather within statewide, every-name index publications, such as the 1880 Ohio census. A few statewide special census schedules have been published.

Considering the rapid rate at which census indexes are being generated, both by commercial entities and by independent volunteer individuals or organizations, it is impractical to list those that are currently available. It is wise, however, to check with libraries, archives, and genealogical societies in the locality of your search to see what kinds of census finding tools are available before embarking on a page-by-page search through a large city census.

To even the casual researcher, the population explosion in the United States can be seen clearly by the increase in the number of census rolls filed for each succeeding census year. In U.S. Bureau of the Census, *A Century of Population Growth 1790–1900* (Washington, D.C.: Government Printing Office, 1909), the Census Bureau reported that in 1790 there were but five cities having populations of 8,000 or more: Boston, New York, Philadelphia, Baltimore, and Charleston. In 1900 the number of cities within the area enumerated in 1790 that had a population of 8,000 or more was 286, an increase of more than fifty-fold.

Despite the population density in 1900 and the large volume of microfilm rolls required to reproduce the census for that year, the 1900 Soundex index is one of the best finding tools available. The 1900 census is indexed for each state and has proved to be the most complete and accurate means for locating individuals in any census year.

Figure 19-5. A section of an 1880 Chicago map on which the census enumerator's visitations have been plotted. Reproduced courtesy of the Newberry Library.

The 1910 federal census presents a major problem, especially for city research. Only twenty-one states are included in the Soundex/Miracode indexing of the census schedules for 1910, and both systems of indexing are noted for their omission rates. Additionally, the quality of microfilming is especially poor, and some Soundex/Miracode cards are so light that they are illegible. When using the Soundex/Miracode for 1910, note that some large cities are indexed separately from their

states. For example, the Alabama cities of Birmingham, Mobile, and Montgomery are independently indexed and not included with the rest of the state. Microfilm numbers are listed at the end of the Soundex/Miracode listing for the state. The same is true for some cities in Georgia, Louisiana, Pennsylvania, and Tennessee.

An excellent finding tool for thirty-nine cities in the 1910 federal population census, however, is *1910 Index to City Streets and Enumeration Districts* (National Archives microfiche publication M1283); it has been reproduced on fifty sheets of microfiche. By determining the street address for an individual in a 1910 city directory, it is possible to search for the street name or number on microfiche, which is arranged alphabetically by name of city and thereafter in alphabetical order or numerical order of the street. Once the enumeration district number is determined from the microfiche, it is usually quick work to locate the actual address for the person or family on the actual census schedule. The city schedules were selected for indexing by the Census Bureau based on the frequency of requests for information. The records were originally in bound volumes, but were unbound for microfilming. With the exception of several of the larger cities, the index for each city occupies a single volume. The original arrangement of the records has been preserved with the exception that the boroughs of Manhattan, the Bronx, Richmond (Staten Island), and Brooklyn are under the heading "New York City." There is no index for the borough of Queens.

Cities indexed by street and enumeration district for the 1910 census are Akron, Ohio; Atlanta; Baltimore; Canton, Ohio; Charlotte, North Carolina; Chicago; Cleveland; Dayton, Ohio; Denver; Detroit; District of Columbia; Elizabeth, New Jersey; Erie, Pennsylvania; Fort Wayne, Indiana; Gary, Indiana; Grand Rapids, Michigan; Indianapolis; Kansas City, Kansas; Long Beach, California; Los Angeles and Los Angeles County; Newark, New Jersey; New York City (including Brooklyn, Manhattan, the Bronx, and Richmond); Oklahoma City, Oklahoma; Omaha, Nebraska; Patterson, New Jersey; Peoria, Illinois; Philadelphia; Phoenix; Reading, Pennsylvania; Richmond, Virginia; San Antonio; San Diego; San Francisco; Seattle; South Bend, Indiana; Tampa, Florida; Tulsa, Oklahoma; Wichita, Kansas; and Youngstown, Ohio.

The 1920 census, though lacking some information categories that some previous census schedules included, has Soundex indexes for every state and territory. Figure 19-6 is an example of the 1920 census schedule for a portion of the twenty-fifth ward of Philadelphia. The 1920 census consists of 2,076 rolls of population schedules and 8,585 rolls of Soundex. Between 1938 and 1940, the WPA prepared approximately 51 million Soundex index cards, based on surname, for all states and territories enumerated in the 1920 census. The indexes were generated to assist the Census Bureau in searches for individuals who needed official proof of age from a period before all states had a uniform system of registering births.

The 1920 Soundex index contains approximately 107 million names and resembles the 1910 Soundex/Miracode in format. For the 1920 Soundex, however, related members in a dwelling were enumerated on a "family card," while boarders, servants, and the like were listed on a separate card.

In the official *Instructions to Enumerators,* issued by the Bureau of the Census on 1 January 1920, item 68 provided the method for canvassing a city block:

> If your district is in a city or town having a system of house numbers, canvass one block or square at a time. Do not go back and forth across the street. Begin each block at one corner, keep to the right, turn the corner, and go in and out of any court, alley, or passageway that may be included in it until the point of starting is

reached. Be sure you have gone around and through the entire block before you leave it.

There is no way of knowing how precisely enumerators followed the fifty pages of small-print instructions, but a diagram was provided with item 68 to show exactly how to proceed on a block divided with alleys and courts.

"Census Enumeration District Description" microfilms are another route for cutting search time in cities. The descriptions, arranged alphabetically by state, county, and city and thereunder by supervisor's district, are available for the 1880, 1900, 1910, and 1920 census schedules. Figure 19-7 is part of a page from the Census Enumeration District Descriptions (1910). It shows Boston's twentieth ward. These finding tools are especially useful for large cities and when institutions, even if enumerated at their street address, were recorded at the end of the schedules for an enumeration district, as they frequently were.

Establishing the whereabouts of your own urban ancestor does not exhaust the possibilities of census schedules. The microfilm contains the raw data necessary to understand the life of a neighborhood. What, for example, was the ethnic and occupational makeup of the street? Did the family settle with or near relatives? When combined with historical or sociological studies, a census can provide a better insight on what it meant to live in a nineteenth-century city.

State censuses, mortality schedules, and other special enumerations should not be overlooked as potential city sources, though few of them are indexed. The New York state census for 1855, for example, is far more important than the federal census because it includes information on the value and construction of the dwelling; the number of families occupying it; household members by name, age, sex, and relation to the head of the family; state or country of birth for each; marital status; profession, trade, or occupation; number of years resident in the city; voting status; and literacy of adults. The 1855 census-takers took the local election districts in each city ward for their districts, enabling the searcher to focus on a desired household faster than in a corresponding federal census, which was organized by ward. While this census does not specify bounds of election districts for New York City, on 7 November 1854 the *New York Times* published the polling places of each of the 128 election districts in the twenty-two wards for the previous election. A number of state and other special censuses have been microfilmed by the Genealogical society of Utah. The listings for the New York state census for the city of Rochester are shown in figure 19-8. Other states took statistics that are particularly valuable to genealogists. The 1925 Iowa state census lists name, place of abode, relationship to head of household, citizenship, education, names of parents (including mother's maiden name), nativity of parents, place of marriage of parents, military service, occupation, and religion. There is a separate index for the 1925 Iowa census, but many state and other special census schedules are not indexed.

VITAL RECORDS

The information contained in vital records (births, marriages, and deaths) varies by the locality and the year (see chapter 3, Research in Birth, Death, and Cemetery Records, and chapter 4, Research in Marriage and Divorce Records). Many cities began collecting vital records information before the states did.

Figure 19-6. A 1920 census schedule showing sheet 7A, 1st supervisor's district, enumeration district 790, twenty-fifth ward of Philadelphia.

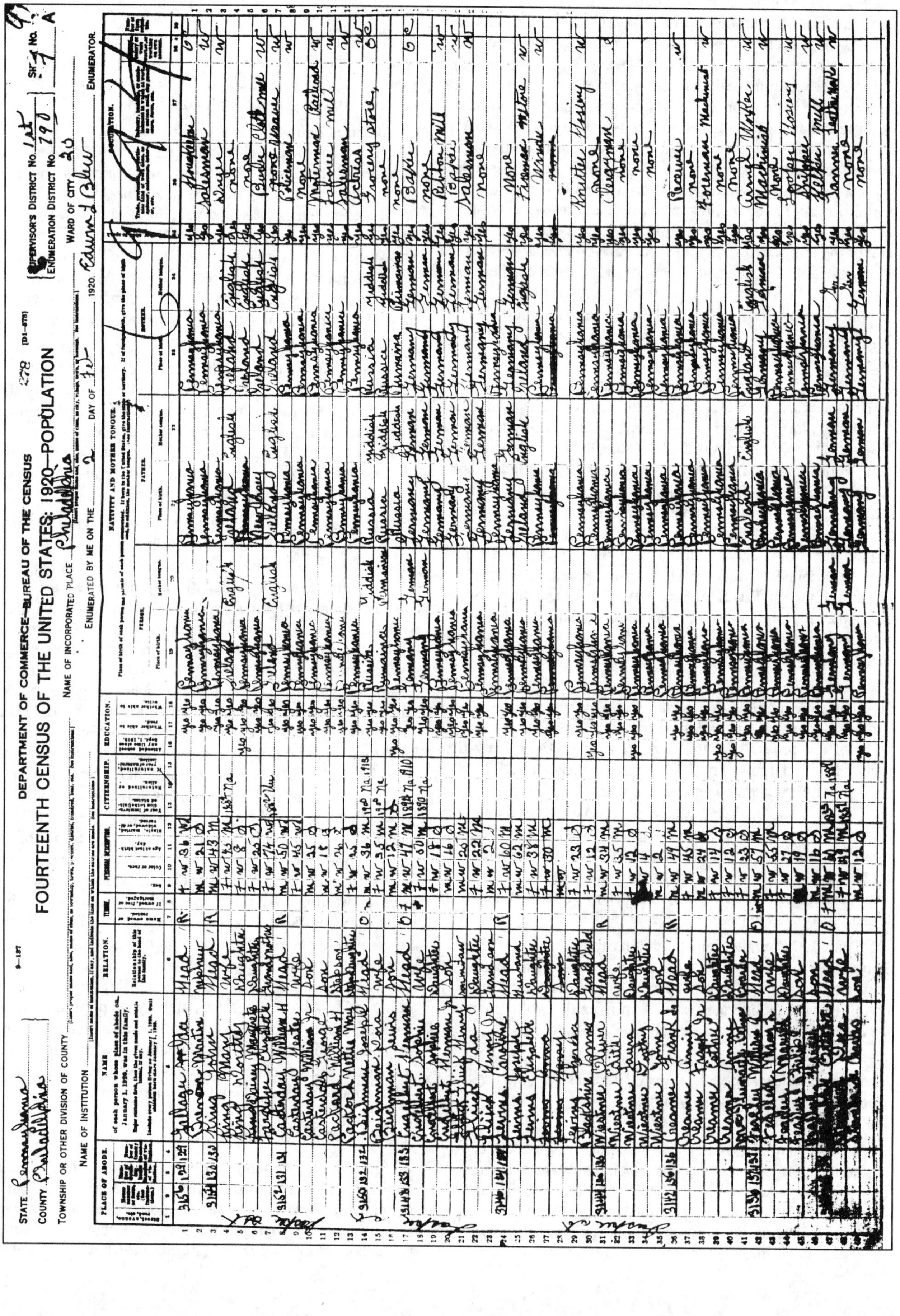

Their interest was partly a response to the overcrowding and greater health problems in cities, and some states with large urban populations were the first to require registration for precisely the same reasons, particularly when the so-called Progressive Movement was strong. Neither Illinois nor New York had statewide registration.

Birth Records

Birth certificates usually indicate the date, time, and place of birth; sex of the baby; the names of the infant and parents; and the attending midwife or physician. The report of birth for Irene Adamski (figure 19-9), January 26, 1910, while not specifying the parents' exact birthplaces in Poland, does provide the family address, the maiden name of the mother, and the father's occupation. One collection (more than 100,000 entries) of midwives' records for Chicago is at Northwestern Memorial Hospital Archives. It was recently made accessible by a microfilming project of the Genealogical Society of Utah and is available from the LDS Family History Library and its family history centers. Similar manuscripts exist for other places, although you must search to locate them. Delayed birth records can be as useful as a record filed at the time of birth, but they are usually filed separately and are often overlooked.

Marriage Records

Marriage certificates often list the man's name and age, the woman's maiden name and age, and the name of the presiding minister or official. If necessary, you can connect the minister to the religious institution through contemporary city directories. The marriage license application is more desirable because it usually has more information, but in some places the application is either no longer extant or not publicly available. Marriage indexes, often compiled from newspapers, are also very useful for pinpointing dates.

In Cincinnati, the marriage records were destroyed when the Hamilton County courthouse burned—not once but three different times (1814, 1849, and 1884). The WPA reconstructed the marriages from surviving pages and compiled a new set of

...mmerce and Labor
THE CENSUS
...TH CENSUS
...APHER

Descriptions of the Enumeration Districts of the .... *Supervisor's District of* ...... Massa chusett

NO. OF E. D.	DESCRIPTION OF ENUMERATION DISTRICT	COUNTY Pop. 1910	RATE OF PAY	INSTRUCTI...
	Boston city (continued)	Suffolk		
1561 Tract 180	~~Ward 20 (part~~ of) Precinct 3 (part of) Bounded by East Cottage and Cresent Ave. Newport, Harbor View, and Dorchester Ave. Savin Hill Ave. Pleasant.	2,186	B	
1562. Tract 181	Ward 20 (part of) Precinct 3 (part of) Bounded by East Cottage Pleasant Sawyer Ave., Cushing Ave., Salcombe, and Stoughton Columbia Road and Edward Everett square.	" 1,549	B	
1563. Tract 182	Ward 20 (part of) Precinct 4 (part of) Bounded by Columbia Road and Columbia square Stoughton, Salcombe, Cushing Ave. and Sawyer Ave. Pleasant Hancock.	" 1,794	B	
1564 Tract 183	Ward 20 (part of) Precinct 4 (part of) Bounded by Columbia Road Hancock High, Church and Eaton square, Quincy.	" 2,565	B	

Figure 19-7. "Descriptions of the Enumeration Districts" of Boston, Massachusetts, showing a portion of the twentieth ward. National Archives micrifilm publication T1224, roll 32.

NEW YORK, MONROE - CENSUS

US/CAN FILM AREA

New York. Secretary of State.
Monroe Co., New York, state census, 1855-1905. -- Salt Lake City : Filmed by the Genealogical Society of Utah, 1970. -- 21 microfilm reels ; 35 mm.

Microreproduction of original records.

Vol. 1	1855	0833737
Vol. 2	1855	0833773
Rochester (pts. 1-2, wards 1-10)	1855	1429808
Vol. 1 Rochester (wards 1-7)	1865	0833774
Vol. 2 Rochester (wards 8-14)	1865	0833775
Vol. 3	1865	0833776
Vol. 4	1865	0833777
Vol. 5	1865	0833778
Vol. 1-2 Rochester (wards 1-8)	1875	0833779
Vol. 3-4 Rochester (wards 9-16)	1875	0833780
Vol. 5-6	1875	0833781
Vol. 7-8	1875	0833782
Vol. 1-8	1892	0833783
Vol. 9-16	1892	0833784
Towns	1892	0833785
Vol. 1-8	1905	0833786
Vol. 9-13	1905	0833787
Vol. 14-18	1905	0833788
Vol. 19-21	1905	0833789
Towns v. 1	1905	0833790
Towns v. 2	1905	0833791

Figure 19-8. State census microfilms, such as these listed for Rochester, New York, can provide invaluable information about city dwellers.

The physician or midwife (when in attendance), or the parent or householder should immediately send this certificate accurately filled out to the County Clerk of the County in which the birth takes place. Penalty for not making report within 30 days, fine of $10 to $100, or imprisonment in jail for 30 days, or both.

WRITE PLAINLY, WITH UNFADING INK—THIS IS A PERMANENT RECORD.

STATE OF ILLINOIS,
Cook County.

101

REPORT OF BIRTH*

VITAL STATISTICS DEPARTMENT—COUNTY CLERK'S OFFICE.

1. † Full Name of Child Irene Adamski
2. Sex female Race or Color (if not of the white race) white
3. Number of Child of this Mother first
4. Date of this Birth Jan. 26 1910
5. Place of Birth, No. 2227 Sacremento ~~St.~~ ave Chicago City ~~Village~~ ~~Town~~
6. Residence of Mother, No. same Street same
7. Place of Birth TOWN STATE OR COUNTRY AGE OF
   a. Father Poland 23
   b. Mother Poland 21
8. Full Name of Mother Kate Adamski
9. Maiden Name of Mother Kate Ratajczck
10. Full Name of Father Frank Adamski
11. Occupation of Father Core Maker
12. Name and Address of Nurse or Attendant (if any)

Reported by A J Strzam M. D. or ~~Midwife~~

Date Jan 29 19.. Residence 2025 Western ave Telephone 1146 Canal

* Each birth should be reported on a separate blank form.
† The baptismal or christian name of child should be certified, if possible, when this certificate is made, and should, in any case, be reported to the County Clerk within a year.
‡ In case of more than one child at a birth, a SEPARATE RETURN must be made for each, and the number of each, in order of birth, stated.

Figure 19-9. Report of birth for Irene Adamski, who was born on 26 January 1910 in Chicago, Cook County, Illinois.

indexes. The Daughters of the American Revolution also reconstructed the marriage records using ministers, diaries, church registers, justice dockets, original certificates, and newspapers. The combination of both sets is more complete for some surnames than the records were before the fires.

DEATH RECORDS

A death certificate usually contains at least the name and age of the decedent; the date, place, and cause of death; the name of the attending physician; and the place of burial. Later records contain more information. In metropolitan areas, you will need at least an approximate death date to request a death records search. With the Social Security number, recorded on the death certificate since 1937, you can often access other sources. Sometimes records are requested on the assumption that a death, birth, or marriage took place within a city's borders when, in fact, the event took place in an adjacent community. An example is figure 19-10. A death record requested for Delia Farr in Chicago, Cook county, Illinois, was returned with the notation "not found." A second request, requiring a second fee but asking for an extended search of suburban Cook County, produced the desired results.

The Genealogical Society of Utah has microfilmed vital records for many municipalities, and the society's family history centers may provide the only opportunity to do a competent search. The sheer volume of documents in the care of the metropolitan agency makes the search difficult; vital statistics agencies are usually overworked, understaffed, and ill-prepared to do lengthy or thorough searches. When the exact date of an event is unknown, the name common or misspelled, or the handwriting questionable or illegible, the complications can become insurmountable. Additionally, vital records are subject to change with little or no notice. State legislation has opened, restricted, and sometimes completely eliminated genealogists' access to the records. If you are making a special trip to a vital records office, you might spare yourself a good deal of frustration by calling ahead to verify access policies and fees.

A few American cities have bound volumes of records. New York City printed vital records by order of the borough governments. Each annual volume was individually indexed. Today these sources are available on microfilm only at the Municipal Archives, Department of Records and Information Services, 52 Chambers St., New York, NY 10007, and the Genealogical Society of Utah and its branches. Below is a borough-by-borough list of the existing birth, death, and marriage records.

Manhattan
Births: July 1847–48; July 1853–97

Deaths: 1795–1804; 1812–1919

Marriages: June 1847–1948; July 1853–65

Brooklyn
Births: 1866–97

Deaths: 1847–53; 1857–1919

Marriages: 1847–52 (Flatbush only)

Bronx
Deaths: 1898–1919

Queens
Deaths: 1898–1919

Various birth, death, and marriage records: 1880s–1890s

Richmond
Deaths: 1898–1919

Staten Island
Various birth, death, and marriage records: 1880s–1890

Special indexes can be of great assistance where they exist. The WPA compiled an index to Chicago deaths, 1871 to 1933, in 1933. Inaccessible except to agency officials until recently, it is now available on microfilm through the Family History Library and its family history centers. See figure 19-11.

FINDING DEATH DATES

Obituaries provide valuable biographical data and, for many people, are the only printed sources with such information. Betty M. Jarboe, *Obituaries: A Guide to Sources,* rev. ed. (Boston: G.K. Hall and Co., 1988), is an invaluable finding aid for obituaries in newspapers and periodicals, particularly when the population of a city makes searching for a death date unusually difficult. A typical citation from this source shows that the Colorado Historical Society Library has files of newspaper birth, marriage, and death notices from the 1860s to the 1940s. Another entry indicates that the New Orleans Public Library has a card file of approximately 523,000 obituary cards which it is expanding by 25,000 new cards per year. *Monroe County, N.Y. Cemetery Record Index,* a 1984 publication of the Rochester Genealogical Society, is another of many entries for metropolitan areas in Jarboe's work.

An unusual example of combining records to find a death date is the case of Solomon Schwartz. His descendants moved away from Chicago, and his death date and burial place were no longer known, although the descendants remembered that he had been buried in a Jewish cemetery. His great-grandchildren could not find his name in the city death index, and they could not use cemetery records because they are arranged chronologically and by lot numbers. However, in the county recorder's records, a deed book marked "Cemeteries" contained original title records arranged by cemetery. Solomon Schwartz's record was in the second Jewish cemetery consulted. Only the number of the conveyance, the date, names of the grantor (cemetery) and the grantee (Solomon), and the legal description of the cemetery lot were given; but further investigation in the cemetery's records proved that it was the correct man.

CORONERS' INQUESTS

Coroners' inquests are infrequently used records. If there is reason to believe that an ancestor died from any violent, unnatural, or unknown cause, the resulting inquest may contain a wealth of information rarely found in other sources. Maryland and Virginia have inquests dating back to the mid-seventeenth century. Many of the deaths reported annually in a city end up in the coroner's files, which are now commonly under the jurisdiction of the city or county medical examiner. Earlier records may contain more details than later files do. Coroners' files may also provide personal histories of the victim through exact birthplaces, dates, names of parents and other relatives, educational and occupational background, military service, Social Security number, and much more. A doctor's statement may incorporate a medical history and physical traits. Eyewitness accounts often contain insights into the character of a victim and record the drama of the death itself. A coroner's verdict concluded early case histories, but more recent reports do not determine guilt. They also provide leads to subsequent court cases. Usually an exact death date is needed, because this record type is usually arranged chronologically, and most are not indexed. Inquests stemming from catastrophes are sometimes grouped under the name of the disaster, such as the Iroquois Theatre Fire. Coroners' inquests combine effectively with news accounts of disasters, which provide casualty lists and background details on each event.

UNDERTAKERS' RECORDS

Undertakers' records often include more detailed information about a decedent than does the official county death certificate. However, mortuaries may be difficult to locate in the city because of shifting neighborhoods. Use city directories to trace a family-owned establishment to a new location in the city (see the section on morticians in chapter 10, Research in Business, Employment, and Institutional Records). A successor might know the whereabouts of records from defunct establishments, and cemeteries that have been in existence for some time are

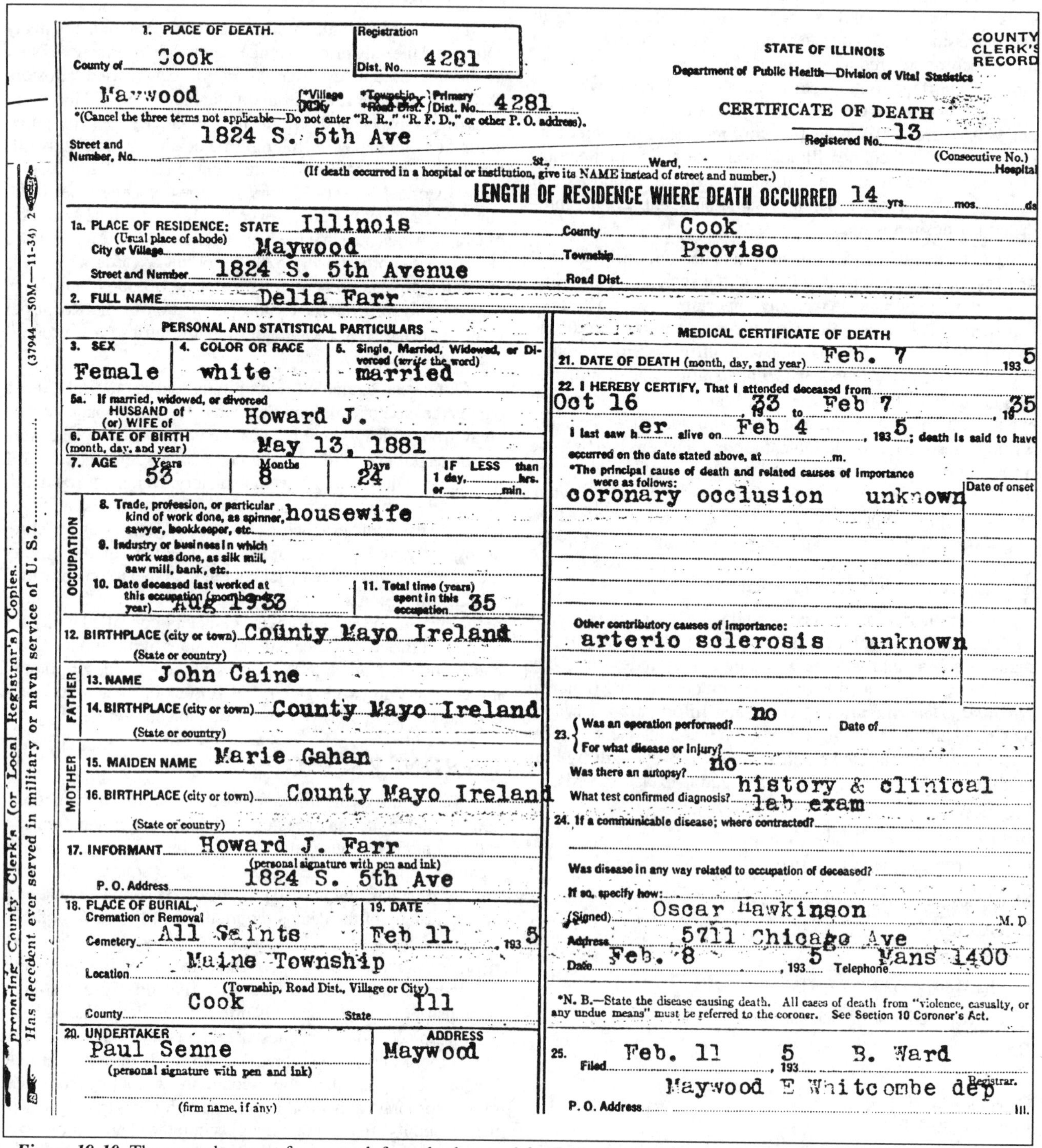

1. PLACE OF DEATH. County of Cook Registration Dist. No. 4281

Maywood (*Village/City) (*Township/Road Dist.) Primary Dist. No. 4281

*(Cancel the three terms not applicable—Do not enter "R. R.," "R. F. D.," or other P. O. address).

Street and Number, No. 1824 S. 5th Ave St., Ward, (If death occurred in a hospital or institution, give its NAME instead of street and number.) Hospital

STATE OF ILLINOIS
Department of Public Health—Division of Vital Statistics
COUNTY CLERK'S RECORD
CERTIFICATE OF DEATH
Registered No. 13 (Consecutive No.)

LENGTH OF RESIDENCE WHERE DEATH OCCURRED 14 yrs. mos. ds

1a. PLACE OF RESIDENCE: (Usual place of abode) STATE Illinois County Cook
City or Village Maywood Township Proviso
Street and Number 1824 S. 5th Avenue Road Dist.

2. FULL NAME Delia Farr

PERSONAL AND STATISTICAL PARTICULARS

3. SEX Female
4. COLOR OR RACE white
5. Single, Married, Widowed, or Divorced (write the word) married
5a. If married, widowed, or divorced HUSBAND of (or) WIFE of Howard J.
6. DATE OF BIRTH (month, day, and year) May 13, 1881
7. AGE Years 53 Months 8 Days 24 IF LESS than 1 day, hrs. or min.

OCCUPATION
8. Trade, profession, or particular kind of work done, as spinner, sawyer, bookkeeper, etc. housewife
9. Industry or business in which work was done, as silk mill, saw mill, bank, etc.
10. Date deceased last worked at this occupation (month and year) Aug 1933
11. Total time (years) spent in this occupation 35

12. BIRTHPLACE (city or town) County Mayo Ireland (State or country)

FATHER
13. NAME John Caine
14. BIRTHPLACE (city or town) County Mayo Ireland (State or country)

MOTHER
15. MAIDEN NAME Marie Gahan
16. BIRTHPLACE (city or town) County Mayo Ireland (State or country)

17. INFORMANT Howard J. Farr (personal signature with pen and ink)
P. O. Address 1824 S. 5th Ave

18. PLACE OF BURIAL, Cremation or Removal
Cemetery All Saints
Location Maine Township (Township, Road Dist., Village or City)
County Cook State Ill
19. DATE Feb 11, 1935

20. UNDERTAKER Paul Senne (personal signature with pen and ink) (firm name, if any)
ADDRESS Maywood

MEDICAL CERTIFICATE OF DEATH

21. DATE OF DEATH (month, day, and year) Feb. 7 1935

22. I HEREBY CERTIFY, That I attended deceased from Oct 16 1933 to Feb 7 1935
I last saw her alive on Feb 4, 1935; death is said to have occurred on the date stated above, at m.
*The principal cause of death and related causes of importance were as follows: coronary occlusion — Date of onset: unknown

Other contributory causes of importance: arterio solerosis — unknown

23. Was an operation performed? no Date of
For what disease or injury?
Was there an autopsy? no
What test confirmed diagnosis? history & clinical lab exam

24. If a communicable disease; where contracted?
Was disease in any way related to occupation of deceased?
If so, specify how:

(Signed) Oscar Hawkinson M. D
Address 5711 Chicago Ave
Date Feb. 8, 1935 Telephone Mans 1400

*N. B.—State the disease causing death. All cases of death from "violence, casualty, or any undue means" must be referred to the coroner. See Section 10 Coroner's Act.

25. Filed Feb. 11, 1935 B. Ward Registrar.
P. O. Address Maywood Ill. E Whitcombe dep

(37944—50M—11-34) 23

Has decedent ever served in military or naval service of U. S.?

preparing County Clerk's (or Local Registrar's) Copies.

Figure 19-10. The second request for a search for a death record for Delia Farr of Chicago. In this case, the record was found.

```
**************************************************************************
ILLINOIS, COOK, CHICAGO - VITAL RECORDS
                                                           +---------------
Chicago (Illinois). Board of Health.                       :U.S. & CAN
    Chicago deaths, 1871-1933.                             :FILM AREA
                                                           +---------------
    Microfilm of original records at the Cook County courthouse, Chicago,
        Illinois.
    Alphabetical listing of Chicago city and county deaths returned to the
        City Board of Health and later forwarded for filing with the county
        clerk.  Includes name, address, date of death, and register number.

    Deaths, A-Bou        1871-1933 --------------------------------- 1295943
    Deaths, Bou-Cul      1871-1933 --------------------------------- 1295944
    Deaths, Cul-Fol      1871-1933 --------------------------------- 1295945
    Deaths, Fol-Haw      1871-1933 --------------------------------- 1295946
    Deaths, Haw-J        1871-1933 --------------------------------- 1295947
    Deaths, K-Lap        1871-1933 --------------------------------- 1295948
    Deaths, Lap-McB      1871-1933 --------------------------------- 1295949
    Deaths, McC-Obr      1871-1933 --------------------------------- 1295971
    Deaths, Obr-Res      1871-1933 --------------------------------- 1295972
    Deaths, Rep-Sik      1871-1933 --------------------------------- 1295973
    Deaths, Sik-Ste      1871-1933 --------------------------------- 1295974
    Deaths, Ste-Wal      1871-1933 --------------------------------- 1295975
    Deaths, Wal-Z        1871-1933 --------------------------------- 1295976
**************************************************************************
```

Figure 19-11. Microfilm index of Chicago deaths from 1871 to 1933 compiled by the Work Projects Administration.

often able to locate files of defunct undertaking establishments. Some genealogical societies have traced the histories of funeral homes in the areas they serve. Records from 398 funeral homes in the Chicago area have been surveyed by Kirk Vandenburg for the South Suburban Genealogical and Historical Society, P.O. Box 96, South Holland, IL 60473. During the process of the survey, every attempt was made to locate records of funeral homes that had changed names or gone out of business. Similar projects have been undertaken by other genealogical societies across the United States.

CEMETERY RECORDS

There is no direct route to cemetery records in metropolitan areas (see chapter 3). Nonsectarian cemeteries generally maintain their own files. Policies vary somewhat, but many cemetery officials will give minimal information over the telephone: names of individuals interred in a single plot, exact grave locations, and current owners of the plot. Additional information usually requires a fee. Since records are, in most instances, cross-indexed by location and chronology, seldom does a comprehensive index exist. The key to cemetery record use is an exact death date for at least one of the individuals buried in a given plot. This, in turn, can lead to names of others in the same place. Many a city has removed the deceased and paved over an old cemetery that was in the way of urban progress. Records for these cemeteries can be especially challenging to track down. Consulting old histories, historical societies, and, of course, genealogical societies in the area of interest is the recommended approach.

Genealogical societies and DAR chapters have been engaged in transcribing and publishing cemetery records for years. Even if these organizations have not been involved in the cemetery work directly, they are usually the first to know about and to advertise such projects in their publications. For example, *The Generator,* the newsletter of the St. Mary's County Genealogical Society (Maryland), announced the publication of *Records of St. Paul's Cemetery 1855–1946* (Elaine O. Zimmerman and Kenneth E. Zimmerman, P.O. Box 276, Woodstock, MD 21163) soon after it was completed. The 2,000 names of German immigrants who were listed in the Baltimore city cemetery in-

clude transfers from the old cemetery owned by the German Evangelical Lutheran Church. As the newsletter suggests, cemetery publications take on additional value because the stones in many have weathered or been vandalized to the extent that they are no longer readable.

For decades it was presumed that Chicago's city cemetery records preceding 1871 had been destroyed in the Great Fire. More than one hundred years after the fire, however, researcher Helen Sclair discovered burial permits and an assortment of cemetery records dating from before the fire and back to Chicago's earliest days. They had been buried in city council files that had been long forgotten in a storage basement. They were later transferred to the Illinois State Archives in Springfield, catalogued as a whole under the city council title, and then transferred to the Illinois Regional Archives at Chicago, where someone with an interest in local history ultimately recognized their genealogical value. The Chicago Genealogical Society is in the process of publishing a book about the rich documentation that is a result of the discovery. There are probably many genealogically significant records hidden in storage or in obscure archive listings in every state.

NEWSPAPERS

An entire chapter of this book is devoted to newspaper research (chapter 12, Research in Newspapers), but a word of caution is in order for the city researcher. In larger cities there were multiple editions of the major daily newspapers, as well as regular runs of community, neighborhood, ethnic, and religious newspapers. To do a thorough search for an event in the life of a city ancestor, all of these publications should be considered. Under the auspices of the United States Newspaper Project, almost every state has its own newspaper preservation projects, which are designed to collect and microfilm all of the extant newspapers in the state for historical purposes. Among the outstanding newspaper collections in the United States is that of the State Historical Society of Wisconsin (second only to the Library of Congress). James L. Hansen, *Wisconsin Newspapers, 1833–1850: An Analytical Bibliography* (Madison, Wis.: State Historical Society of Wisconsin, 1979), describes this collection.

RELIGIOUS SOURCES

Locating urban religious records presents a unique challenge (see chapter 6, Research in Church Records). Population, geography, and ethnicity are confusing enough; but to complicate matters further, different denominations have kept different types of records. For example, presbyteries transferred membership records with the departure of the member. Immigrants commonly chose to worship in their own tongues and often went far out of their neighborhoods to find the congenial atmosphere of the national parish. Churches as well as people responded to the dynamics of cities—some closing, consolidating, or moving as neighborhoods changed, others shifting from their ethnic orientations to accommodate new circumstances. Thus, any researcher having difficulty tracing the church or synagogue of his or her ancestor might save time by backtracking to study the history of that particular religion in the locale of interest. Though finding religious records may be difficult, it usually repays the time and effort spent. Church records usually predate civil records and supply information not found elsewhere—sometimes indicating even the European church or parish where people being married were christened or confirmed.

An invaluable guide for research in this area is the Historical Records Survey of the WPA. WPA workers inventoried church and public records extant in the 1930s for many areas in the United States. Their lists for urban churches are especially valuable. A typical entry for church vital records would contain the name and address of the institution at the time of publication, ethnic orientation (if any), and comprehensive dates for each type of vital record. If the organization housed documents from other congregations, the survey noted that fact and included a range of dates. For example, in *A Guide to Church Vital Statistics Records in California—San Francisco and Alameda Counties* (San Francisco: Northern California Historical Records Survey, 1940), the individual churches are arranged by geographical area and denomination. A summary of baptisms, marriages, and death records follows for each. Additionally, it notes that Holy Family was a Chinese mission while Saint Anthony of Padua was German. In most cases the founding dates are noted.

The obvious limitation to the survey is that many of the records may have since been moved. But it still provides an overview of the span of years during which records were kept and is proof that the records were still in existence at the time of the WPA compilation. It is a very good place to start.

For those inventories which were printed, consult Sargent B. Child and Dorothy P. Holmes, *Bibliography of Research Project Reports*, WPA Technical Series No. 7 (1943. Reprint. Bountiful, Utah: Printing by Faisal, 1979 [as W.P.A. Bibliography 9]). Many inventories were never printed; they can be located by consulting Loretta L. Hefner, *The WPA Historical Records Survey: A Guide to the Unpublished Inventories, Indexes, and Transcripts* (Chicago: Society of American Archivists, 1980).

Some contemporary guides facilitate finding records for certain cities. A local reference librarian should, for example, be able to point to guides such as *Genealogical Resources in the New York Metropolitan Area* and *The Encyclopedia of Jewish Genealogy*. Both of these guides, mentioned earlier in the chapter, contain specific addresses for Jewish material. Jack Bochar, *Locations of Chicago Roman Catholic Churches, 1850–1990* (Geneva, Ill.: the author, 1990), is a time-saving book filled with maps, addresses, microfilm numbers, and historical data relating to hundreds of parishes in that city.

Early city or county histories, biographical sketches, and jubilee books provide other background on religious institutions in a particular area. Illustrations included in county histories often preserve the only surviving images of buildings where city ancestors worshipped (see figure 19-12). Through these descriptions you can trace the development and ethnic makeup of a church. Modern studies also are a tremendous help, and their bibliographies enhance their utility. George Lane and Alginantes Kezys, comps., *Chicago Churches and Synagogues* (Chicago: Loyola University Press, 1981), highlights 125 houses of worship with architectural, historical, or social significance. Further, they provide a detailed description and history of each building and its congregation, ethnic makeup, architectural attributes, and location by exact address and area of city. The acknowledgments and notes provide numerous sources for locating denominational repositories.

A few church records are available in book form or microform. The Newberry Library in Chicago has a large collection of sources from the eastern United States as well as from local institutions. The Detroit Society of Genealogical Research is one of many metropolitan groups engaged in the publication of local church records. The Genealogical Society of Utah has microfilmed church registers from numerous localities, and its family history centers in every state allow access to these records. Also available through the Family History Library is the International Genealogical Index, which is rich in church registers for New York City, Boston, Chicago, Hartford, Indianapolis, Philadelphia, and many other cities (see chapter 2, Databases, Indexes, and Other Finding Aids).

Used in combination with other sources, church vital records can help solve even the most perplexing problems. For example, Karl Johnson was known to have lived at a certain address in Minneapolis for several years near the beginning of the twentieth century, but his death date was unknown. A death index indicated that he had died at that address in 1911. This death year led to a certificate which, in turn, pointed to the cemetery records. The cemetery gave the officiating minister's name, and a directory search identified him as belonging to the Swedish Covenant Church. It had since moved, but inquiries at another congregation of the same denomination pinpointed the new location of the records. Not only did the church have many records of the family, it had a jubilee book with biographical sketches that included Karl Johnson as a founding member. The biography gave his exact birthplace, his date of arrival in the United States, and his residence before settling in Minneapolis.

LAND-REAL ESTATE PROPERTY

Even though the city dweller is not always dependent upon his or her land for a livelihood, that quarter acre is usually as valuable as the agriculturalist's quarter section. Not only the deed books but many court cases bear record of this.

Most American cities are under the jurisdiction of county governments, and city land records are almost always held by the county recorder. City lots, however, may be recorded in volumes separate from county land with their own indexes or finding aids; they are easy to miss.

Figure 19-12. Illustration of the First Place Methodist Episcopal Church. Published in *Kings County History 1683 to 1884* by Henry Stiles (New York: W.W. Munsell and Co., 1884).

The municipal library, designed to collect data useful to the governance of the city, is a good place to learn the procedures of land searching. Plat maps or tract books may be centralized there. Otherwise, detailed plat maps of a city are usually available from municipal agencies or from the recorder of deeds.

If the ancestor you are interested in is consistently listed at a certain address for a number of years in city directories, he or she may have owned that piece of property. Frequent address changes may indicate that he or she was renting. Both of these hypotheses need further proof for verification. The ancestor who rented property in one location may also have owned land in another, especially a vacant lot. To find his or her land records check land indexes of abstracts, tax rolls, and less commonly consulted sources, such as building permits or building improvement files; street, sidewalk, and sewer assessment records; and utility cards for water, lighting, and refuse collection, which also identify an owner with a specific lot or address. These records are normally not subject to privacy laws. Land abstracts compiled from deeds and other property documents by title and abstract companies provide an alternate source when the original land records have been destroyed. They were especially valuable in Chicago after the Great Fire of 1871, when they were used to reestablish property titles in burned areas. Figure 19-13 is a page from "An Examination of Title."

Examination of Title
to

Lot 24 in Block 4 in C. T. Yerkes' Subdivision of Blocks 33. 34. 35. 36. 41. 42
43 and 44 in the Subdivision of Section
19 T. 40 N. R. 14 E. of the 3rd P. M. (except
the South West quarter of the North
East quarter, the South East quarter
of the North West quarter and the
East half of the South East quarter
thereof) in Cook County, Ills.

Last examination made by Handy & Company
dated April 4. 1887.

Affidavit
by
Franklin Hatheway
Doc. 1.505.202

Subscribed and sworn
to July 15. 1891 and re-
corded July 16. 1891 in
Book 3635 page 127.
That he is a resident
of Chicago, Illinois, and is the Secretary of
the Jennings Trust Company, that he was
well and intimately acquainted with
William E. Jones in his life time and was
also well and intimately acquainted
with the family of said William E.
Jones, that he was in the employ of said
William E. Jones at the time of his

MAPS

A solid knowledge of the city's layout as it existed in an ancestor's time is also important. While current maps may provide an introduction and a point of reference, ward boundaries, street names, and street numbers change over the years. A good source of nineteenth-century maps is E.K. Kirkham, *A Handy Guide to Searching in the Larger Cities of the United States* (Logan, Utah: The Everton Publishers, 1974), which includes thirty-nine maps for twenty-three major cities along with their respective street indexes.

Jonathan Sheppard Books (P.O. Box 2020, Plaza Station, Albany, NY 12220) offers a packet of maps reproduced from Fannin's Atlas of 1853, which includes maps for the cities of Baltimore, Boston, Buffalo, Charleston, Chicago, Cincinnati, Milwaukee, New Orleans, New York, Philadelphia, Pittsburgh, St. Louis, San Francisco, and Washington, D.C. Write to the company for prices.

Many American city maps are available for purchase from the photoduplication section of the Library of Congress. Several categories of the library's maps that are especially useful in city research are described in James C. Neagles, *The Library of Congress: A Guide to Genealogical and Historical Research* (Salt Lake City: Ancestry, 1990).

WARD MAPS

Among the maps most used for urban research are ward maps, fire insurance maps, and panoramic or "birds-eye-view" maps. Figure 19-14 is part of a map that shows wards for New York City in 1850. Ward maps are especially important when used in conjunction with city directories in cases when a census index does not exist or when a suspected resident does not appear in an index. By defining the ward boundaries, it is often possible to eliminate hours of wasted search time. Ward boundaries changed frequently from one census enumeration to the next, so it is necessary to coordinate the ward map with the census year. For a good description of early maps, see Michael H. Shelley, *Ward Maps of United States Cities: A Selective Checklist of Pre-1900 Maps in the Library of Congress* (Washington, D.C.: Library of Congress, 1975). Some libraries have maps that are designed to facilitate searching cities in federal census years 1790 to 1920.

FIRE INSURANCE MAPS

The Sanborn Map Company produced some 700,000 sheets of detailed maps for 12,000 cities and towns in North America from 1867 to the present. (Other companies began producing maps as early as 1846.) These maps were used by insurance agents to determine hazards and risk in underwriting specific buildings. They were produced on oversize sheets in pastel colors: olive drab for adobe, pink for stone, blue for brick, yellow for wood, gray for iron. Size, shape, and construction of homes, businesses, and farm buildings; locations of windows, doors, and firewalls; roof types; widths and names of streets; property boundaries; ditches, water mains, and sprinkling systems; and other details are clearly indicated. Individual residents do not appear on the maps by name, although specific addresses are shown. Businesses appear by name. Once you have found your ancestor in census, directory, or utility files, you can determine precisely what house or business the family lived and worked in. It is possible to combine city directories and census entries with fire insurance maps and to locate each resident on the map. "Fire Insurance Maps in the Library of Congress," prepared by the Geography and Map Section of the Library of Congress (Washington, D.C.: 1981), lists the maps available for each town and city. Copies will be supplied upon request from the Library of Congress, Photoduplication Services, Washington, DC 20540. Because their sizes vary, it is wise to write ahead and ask for a cost estimate for each copy. (The pastel colors do not reproduce distinctly in black and white.)

Duplicate copies of the maps are also available at selected libraries across the country and in state historical societies and local public libraries. For example, the maps for Tacoma, Washington, are in the Tacoma Public Library in their original, multicolored form. Those for Utah cities are found at the Utah State Historical Society.

PANORAMIC/BIRDSEYE MAPS

When they exist for an ancestor's hometown, panoramic or "birds-eye-view" maps can add an attractive dimension to a family history. Drawn in perspective, streets and buildings are depicted in them as if from the air. Still prized for their artistic beauty, the commercially motivated drawings were commissioned by chambers of commerce, real estate companies, and businessmen whose establishments were frequently advertised on the borders. The panoramics were especially popular during the Civil War era and will be found in a number of county and municipal histories. A useful guide to these romantic maps is Library of Congress, *Panoramic Maps of Cities in the United States and Canada: A Checklist of Maps in the Collections of the Library of Congress, Geography and Map Division,* 2nd ed. (Washington, D.C.: Library of Congress, 1984).

Metropolitan historical societies may also maintain separate guides to their map collections. Maps may be cataloged by date, enabling the searcher to pinpoint a particular time period to coordinate the city directory-census study. Maps may also be listed by subject. School district and cemetery maps may help to locate records from those agencies. The New York Public Library has one of the largest city map collections in the United States.

Most libraries do not have special equipment for the reproduction of large maps, nor do they allow photocopying because of potential damage to the maps. You may improvise a makeshift map by superimposing wards or old street locations on a current map.

CHANGING BOUNDARIES AND JURISDICTIONS

Over the years, as cities grew, most of them expanded by annexing the small towns at their fringes. Wards assumed different configurations, streets were frequently renamed or they disappeared entirely when a building project came along, some cities changed their numbering systems entirely, and annexations extended city limits on a regular basis. For anyone attempting Philadelphia research, this type of environment is clarified in John Daly and Allen Weinberg, *Genealogy of Philadelphia County Subdivisions,* 2nd ed. (Philadelphia: Department of Records, 1966). Though not always found in published form, it is to the researcher's great advantage to inquire at the state or local level for guides to get through the complexities of metro-

Figure 19-4. 1850 map of New York City showing wards.

politan changes—and there were many! For example, the following towns became part of Boston in the years indicated: East Boston, 1637; South Boston, 1804; Roxbury, 1868; Dorchester, 1870; Brighton, 1874; Charlestown, 1874; West Roxbury, 1874; and Hyde Park, 1912.[8]

In an article titled "American Cities Are (Mostly) Better Than Ever," Richard C. Wade explains:

> Municipal boundaries were wide and continually enlarging. In 1876 St. Louis reached out into neighboring farm land and incorporated all the area now within its city limits. In one swift move, in 1889 Chicago added over 125 square miles to its territory. And in 1898 New York absorbed the four surrounding counties—including Brooklyn, the nation's fourth largest city—making it the Empire City.
>
> As populations grew, there were always fresh areas to build up. This meant that all the wealth, all the commerce, all the industry, and all the talent lay within the city.
>
> More prosperous than either the state or federal governments, the cities needed no outside help; indeed they met any interference with the demand for home rule.[9]

Wade touches on two important points that consistently give researchers problems in urban situations if they have not familiarized themselves with the history of the area. Imagine an individual who believes his ancestors were from Chicago but cannot find them in directories before 1890, though he is sure they were city residents as early as 1880. Had he checked the history against maps of the area where they lived, he would have discovered that they indeed lived in what is now Chicago but was then Austin, Illinois. The town of Austin had its own city directories until the larger city brought it under its wing in 1889. Likewise, a woman searching for a Brooklyn address in the 1920 census was frustrated for some time trying to determine why the numbers she took from the census catalog would not lead her to the right place in the microfilm. Had she known a little bit about Brooklyn, she would have known that while Brooklyn has been part of New York City since 1898, it is in Kings County and not in New York County, where she had been searching.

Home rule can complicate the process of finding urban records. Just when you think you know what kind of records a state keeps and where they are kept, you may find that the city of your interest had an entirely different procedure. For example, Illinois counties have required brides and grooms to answer a number of questions on marriage applications that make them especially valuable for family historians. Cook County, however, under its home rule, did not require that applications be retained by the clerk for many years. Additionally, in other Illinois counties, vital record indices are open for inspection to any member of a state genealogical society, but because the Chicago office processes an average of 1,000 requests per day, a different set of rules prevents researchers from personally searching Cook County indexes. Policies are also subject to sudden changes, so it is wise to call in advance.

There are yet other distinctions that the urban researcher will need to make. For example, areas legally designated as

city-county include San Francisco, Denver, and Honolulu. An area designated as metropolitan is Nashville and Davidson County, Tennessee. Areas subject to some county jurisdiction but operating as cities are Jacksonville, Duval County, Florida; Indianapolis, Marion County, Indiana; New Orleans, Orleans Parish, Louisiana; Baton Rouge, East Baton Rouge Parish, Louisiana; Nantucket, Nantucket County, Massachusetts; Boston, Suffolk County, Massachusetts; New York City Borough/ County, New York: Bronx, Kings (Brooklyn), New York (Manhattan), Queens, and Richmond; and Philadelphia County, Philadelphia. Areas designated as independent cities, not subject to the county: Washington, D.C.; Baltimore City, Maryland; St. Louis, Missouri; Carson City, Nevada.

Independent Virginia city records are detailed in Eichholz, *Ancestry's Red Book: American State, County and Town Sources,* for the following burgs of Virginia: Alexandria, Bedford, Bristol, Buena Vista, Charlottesville, Chesapeake, Clifton Forge, Colonial Heights, Covington, Danville, Emporia, Fairfax, Falls Church, Franklin, Fredericksburg, Galax, Hampton, Harrisonburg, Hopewell, Lexington, Lynchburg, Manassas, Manassas Park, Manchester, Martinsville, Nansemond, Newport News, Norfolk, Norton, Petersburg, Poquoson, Portsmouth, Radford, Richmond, Roanoke, Salem, South Boston, South Norfolk, Staunton, Suffolk, Virginia Beach, Warwick, Waynesboro, Williamsburg, and Winchester.

NATURALIZATION RECORDS

Because so many urbanites were immigrants, naturalization records are yet another type of record which urban researchers commonly mine for information. Until 1906, naturalization was strictly a function of the courts. Prior to that year, an individual could be naturalized in any court of record. Some cities supported county, criminal, municipal, police, marine, and mayor's courts. It was often a matter of choosing which court was close or convenient for the immigrant to approach for citizenship. In October 1906, Congress created the Bureau of Immigration and Naturalization to standardize the system. One by-product was a greatly expanded set of questions for the immigrant to answer; another was retention of duplicate copies of all final petitions in the Washington office of the bureau. After many of the minor courts stopped naturalizing, their records were frequently filed in county or city offices, and many old court records have been dispersed to archives, historical societies, libraries, and a number of unlikely storage places.

Naturalization records require a petition number for reference purposes. This number is usually available through indexes maintained by the court of record where the petition was filed. The New England states, New York City, and Chicago are blessed with comprehensive Soundex indexes which cover local and federal naturalizations. The New York records are further indexed by national group (Germans, Italians, etc.) for several years. When the Soundex fails to supply a reference, as it occasionally does, ancillary records, such as order books (which show all naturalizations approved on a given day) and registers (which list petitioners by first initial of surname), may also exist.

Because naturalization conferred voting rights on aliens, voting records are another possible source of information for the urban genealogist. Voter registration lists included the native-born as well as the naturalized, of course, but have the built-in limitation that they cover only those who made the effort to register. Still, voting records are sometimes indexed or registered by ward, and they can provide an avenue for identification when censuses or directories are not available. Precinct block books might substitute for assessment books in areas where few people owned property. Voting lists can provide a test for community involvement. They reflect local mores in other ways, for the linkage between citizenship and voting was not always visible. Voting did not always guarantee full-fledged citizenship, just as citizenship did not always result in the exercise of the ballot. For anyone writing a detailed family history, a study of official election returns, especially those predating the secret ballot, might prove intriguing as a means of identifying political participation. Many genealogical societies are making it a point to see that voter lists are saved and published whenever possible. The Berkshire Family History Association (P.O. Box 1437, Pittsfield, MA 01202-1437), for example, has published in its quarterlies "Registers of Voters in Pittsfield, Massachusetts—1890."

COURT RECORDS

Court records are potentially the most valuable yet the most underutilized of urban sources (see chapter 7, Research in Court Records). Again, the case volume created by the vast population and the bureaucracy involved may intimidate even an enthusiastic searcher. Court jurisdictions and procedures have puzzled many a researcher, but books on local government can guide you through the maze. By far the most commonly used court records are the probates because of their helpfulness in identifying heirs. Some counties have master indexes for court proceedings, but, more often than not, you must examine registers by year. When names are distinguished only by case number, a search of the docket books may be in order. The shortcut approach is especially good in cities where old cases are warehoused and must be requested a few at a time. Dockets provide a synopsis of the case, the decedent's name and date of death, name of the administrator, and names of widowed spouse and heirs. This information enables the searcher to order the correct case from the warehouse or to retrieve it from its court location without going through all the other cases of the same name. Before visiting any court, it is advisable to call in advance to check on research policies and days and hours of operation. This is a good time to ask if indexes and records are immediately accessible or if storage of actual records in an off-site location will make it necessary to make two or more trips to the court.

City courts can also yield information of value. If the city is subject to county jurisdiction, police courts and local justice courts take care of trivial matters that involve limited fines and fees. More important cases go automatically to county and state tribunals. If the city is independent, however, mayors' courts—hustings (so-called in Virginia, Maryland, and the Carolinas)—had substantial jurisdiction.

Some city courts issued business licenses for taverns, mercantile establishments, hotels, and other shops and received petitions from local citizens regarding many of the functions which are today handled by commissioners or separate agencies of government, such as road repair, runoff water drainage, watch and ward (police patrol and security of business and personal property), volunteer fire department personnel, and numerous other activities necessary to provide services and protection for city dwellers. Another important function was providing for the poor. Among the references to the poor in city court minutes are notices of removals of people and families who were not residents of the city and who might become public charges on the poor rolls. Minutes record that these people were transported to the city line at public expense.

Records for these courts were often printed annually by public order, and these volumes can be found in local public libraries. For example, the printed minutes and reports of city officials for St. Paul, Minnesota, are in the St. Paul Public Library; a second copy is available at the Minnesota Historical Society. The city minutes for Nashua, New Hampshire, are found only in the Nashua Public Library, where there is a complete run of volumes that continue well into the twentieth century. The Genealogical Society of Utah has microfilmed the city court volumes for Savannah, Georgia, and several other southern cities and towns. The minutes of the Mayor's Court of New York City are published in the collections of the New York Historical Society. There is a great interest in city court minutes, and many of them are easy to locate.

Somewhat less well known than probate or other local court records are federal court files. The federal courts have traditionally heard cases involving interstate disputes and often served as courts of appeal for litigation which originated at the local level. In addition, the federal courts were usually indexed by plaintiff and/or by defendant, making the search a time-consuming project.

The material in the files varies with the significance of the case and the state that it reached during the trial process. But depositions describing the acquisition and retention of property were not unusual in land disputes, which often appeared as equity suits. These were often accompanied by maps of the place in question or copies of deeds submitted as exhibits. Such cases can produce thousands of pages of testimony and may detail facts about the family and its environment which are not available elsewhere.

Bankruptcy filings included schedules of assets and liabilities, outlining the business and financial dealings of the bankruptcy claimant. Small partnerships and proprietorships, along with personal bankruptcies, comprised the preponderance of cases heard in bankruptcy court. When federal bankruptcy laws were not in effect, "involuntary" bankruptcies were entered as equity proceedings. Loretto Dennis Szucs, "To Whom I Am Indebted: Bankruptcy Records," *Ancestry* 12 (5) (September–October 1994): 26–27, explores historical events that caused bankruptcies and provides information on how and where to find such files. Federal criminal prosecutions were a minor portion of the case load until the 1920s, when prohibition violations swelled the numbers. Other types of federal cases of genealogical interest include confiscation cases from the Civil War, when the federal government seized the available property of Confederate sympathizers, and personal injury suits against interstate carriers (usually railroads).

The federal government has touched urban residents in ways other than through its courts. The Internal Revenue Service was less visible before World War I than it is now, but an assortment of IRS assessment lists sheds light on the wealth of many individuals during the Civil War and again after 1913. The Civil War-vintage assessments (arranged by collection district and thereunder alphabetically) have been microfilmed; those for the early twentieth century have not. Original monthly assessment lists survive for San Francisco, Denver, Chicago, and Detroit and are deposited in the federal archives and records centers serving those cities. Taxable income was defined at a level which limited the assessment to the middle and upper classes; nevertheless, thousands of entries appear in the volumes pertaining to urban districts.

A source with particular interest to those whose roots lie in the South comes from the records of the Southern Claims Commission, which was organized to settle with Union sympathizers who had supplied Northern forces without compensation. Case files included depositions, affidavits, reports, and receipts. A geographical index, arranged by state and county, allows the researcher to pinpoint people in a specific territory, while the consolidated index serves as a name entry. See *Records of the Commissioners of Claims (Southern Claims Commission), 1871–1880,* micropublication M87 (Washington, D.C.: National Archives and Records Service), and Gary B. Mills, *Civil War Claims in the South: An Index to Claimants Before the Southern Claims Commission, 1871–1880* (Laguna Hills, Calif.: Aegean Park Press, 1980), an accompanying consolidated index. These records are not limited to cities, but the major locales of Atlanta and New Orleans are included.

BUSINESS AND OCCUPATIONAL RECORDS

Bankruptcy and tax records lead naturally to another source: professional, business, and employment records (see chapter 10). Occupational specialization and the related drive to license specific trades or skills both resulted from urbanization and mass society. Many of these collections belong to institutions which lack the resources to undertake extensive searches; indexes and finding aids may prove spotty; and privacy restrictions sometimes limit access. Still, these records are definitely worth searching.

National professional associations, with membership lists often dating back to the 1800s, produce such records. The American Medical Association, for example, keeps files on its members, and a doctor residing in New York after around 1880 had to register his license with the county clerk and submit an affidavit of his admission to practice. Private associations printed directories, almanacs, and collective biographies with information on their members. This filled a dual need, providing exposure for the budding professional and assuring clients of a given skill in a mobile society. Whatever the purpose, the result for the genealogist is additional information about the newly emergent managerial and professional classes.

Increased interest in business regulation during the same time period stemmed from the same concerns and generated another body of records. The demand for honest retailing inspired Boston to inspect the weights and measures of merchants in that city as early as 1881. Inspection reports, an early type of consumer protection, gave the owner's name and address and described any action taken as a result of the visit. Similar departments eventually appeared throughout the country. A parallel to this idea in the private sector was the credit report, developed in 1842 by Dunn and Bradstreet. National in scope and detailed in coverage, the reports in the company archives, now at Harvard University Library, can increase understanding of nineteenth-century business practices as well as knowledge of some particular firms. For example, credit investigators recorded many personal aspects in their reports. One noted that his subject had married well; her name and a comment on her father buttressed the opinion that she was a good risk. While researchers should know of the existence of the Dunn and Bradstreet collection, library restrictions make it extremely difficult to gain access to the records.

If you can identify an ancestor with a specific company or business, you may be able to search the records of that business, assuming that it is still extant or that the records have been deposited in a historical society or corporate archive. Business libraries and archives must usually be examined in person because they simply do not have the personnel to respond to mail requests.

Most major metropolitan areas began as transportation centers, and many records of transportation companies have survived. Maritime records in the National Maritime Museum of San Francisco, the Great Lakes Maritime Institute in Detroit, and the Great Lakes Historical Society in Vermillion, Ohio, near Cleveland, may contain documentation in the form of crew lists or logbooks. The National Archives in Washington, D.C., contains applications for seamen's protection certificates and files on merchant seamen; the National Archives' regional archives are currently acquiring inspection and licensing documents from maritime and riparian ports. Boston, Cleveland, Detroit, and Chicago records have already been transferred; others will follow as they are found.

Rail transportation workers may be traced through corporate archives, union records, or government agencies. The Newberry Library in Chicago has manuscripts from the Chicago, Burlington, and Quincy Railroad and some from the Pullman Standard Car Company. The South Suburban Genealogical Society (P.O. Box 96, South Holland, IL 60473) has indexed more than 1 million Pullman Company records that are on file at the society. The Chicago Historical Society has acquired some files of the Brotherhood of Sleeping Car Porters. The Railroad Retirement Board, also located in Chicago, is the national pensioning agency for rail workers; its records should be interesting to anyone with an ancestor eligible for a railroad pension. The Railroad Retirement Board, however, did not begin operations until the mid-1930s. Records are limited to individuals associated with the rail industry at or since that time or who were receiving private rail pensions, which were assumed by the board in 1937.

Many municipalities have records of city employees dating back to founding days. Police and firefighter pension records often comprise the greater part of municipal collections. Municipal archives and reference libraries are good sources for these records. Sometimes the municipal departments still hold the documents.

The union movement had many of its roots in the major industrial centers of the country, and some records have survived. Wayne State University in Detroit is the site of the Archives of Labor History, which has collected manuscripts from unions all over the country. Its major holdings have come from the United Auto Workers, as might be expected, but some records have come from the American Federation of Teachers, the Newspaper Guild, and the Industrial Workers of the World. The Ohio Historical Society has gathered labor union documents as well, placing many of them in regional repositories, such as the Western Reserve Historical Society in Cleveland.

NEIGHBORHOOD SOURCES

Anyone who reads a city history will immediately realize that only a small fraction of the population gains municipal recognition. A citizen prominent enough to be found in a major printed historical source will easily be found in other likely sources—land, census, church, probate records. For most urban ancestors, however, an often productive search area is the neighborhood. Usually, the neighborhood will have its own library, where a researcher can expect to find more information on that immediate area, including local histories (sometimes still in manuscript form), and even neighborhood newspapers. Community newspapers allowed a great deal of space for local events and personalities ignored by big city newspapers. A local library may also be the place to begin a search for school records, which are sometimes dispersed rather than in compact collections. The school records themselves are usually kept at the municipal level, but the library can provide area school addresses and district jurisdictions.

City neighborhoods and districts may have their own historical societies and museums, which are often affiliated with the public library. Even if they are not, the local librarian may know about them. Neighborhood historical societies, usually run by volunteers, are open at irregular hours and are rarely listed in telephone directories; but when they exist they can be gold mines of information about local residents and may have community photographs, scrapbooks, and personal mementos.

In 1976, the U.S. bicentennial prompted many communities and neighborhoods to investigate their heritage. Old-timers were interviewed, relics came out of attics, and basements gave up documents. Indexes of newspaper obituaries and cemeteries were compiled. Published local studies went to neighborhood libraries and often to university and community college libraries.

Check the main branch of the city public library, the municipal library, and the city or county historical library for neighborhood sources as well. If the ethnic makeup of a neighborhood has changed or if the old neighborhood no longer exists, then the central repository for the city is the logical place to search for needed information. When searching major libraries for neighborhood information, you should check not only listings of the neighborhood itself, but also its surrounding neighbors, especially if they shared a district or area name. The dominant nationality of a neighborhood may also be the key to locating information. Some examples include Germans in Old Town Area, South Side Irish, and Poles of the Milwaukee Avenue District. Still other neighborhoods were settled by mixed ethnic groups that shared a common occupation in a particular part of the city. The garment district, the stockyard area, the steel mill area—all might be classifications in a library card catalog. Modern urban studies frequently focus on specific bibliographies of master's theses, dissertations, or books that can help further searches.

Photograph archives and graphics departments maintained by some libraries may provide photographs of cities, neighborhoods, streets, business establishments, and ancestral homes. The Graphics Department of the Chicago Historical Society catalogs its photographs by street address as well as subject (landmark, neighborhood, event). To draw from this collection you need to know the changes in the names of streets and in the city's numbering system, but such efforts usually add a valuable graphics dimension to the family history. Ask reference personnel for street directories and other such finding aids.

ETHNIC SOURCES

Nowhere is the recent dramatic increase in interest in genealogy more evident than in ethnic research, along with a parallel increase in research guides and tools. Genealogical societies nationwide are bringing sophistication to the collection, preservation, and use of ethnic materials. The microfilming projects of the Genealogical Society of Utah and the Family History Library have brought the records of the world to our doorsteps. Lubomyr Wynar, *Encyclopedic Directory of Ethnic Organizations in the United States* (Littleton, Colo.: Libraries Unlimited, 1976), the first comprehensive guide to major organizations created by various communities, demonstrates the pluralism of the American city. Ethnic presses and organizations are primary indicators of a particular ethnic group's social structure, but interdisciplinary efforts by colleges and universities are also important.

SETTLEMENTS

The settlement house was an institution which served a grassroots clientele in urban areas. Numerous settlements sprang up in working-class neighborhoods, where they sought to reach a maximum number of residents with programs ranging from citizenship classes to ethnic musical societies. Like the unions, papers of settlement houses contain membership lists and minutes of meetings. They also have a wealth of information about happenings in the neighborhood in which they were situated: the daily pulse of life on the surrounding streets, ethnic conflicts, the drive to attain success. Settlements reached only a small proportion of those who resided in the overcrowded tenements beyond their doors, but the larger ones often had 2,000 members on their rolls at any given time.

MUNICIPAL RECORDS

By definition, a municipality is a town or city of any size having the powers of local self-government. Cities have, in most cases, been responsible for preserving and storing their respective histories. The great volumes of material amassed by most municipal governments demand that records be stored off site. Often, state archives step in to save these amazingly detailed records. The Minnesota State Archives, for example, has records for more than one hundred of the state's municipalities.

The records include such administrative information as city council minutes, annual reports, correspondence and subject files; financial records, including payroll registers and registers of receipts and disbursements; municipal court and justice of the peace dockets; cemetery records, including burial registers and lot owner records; police jail registers and registers of tramps lodged in jail; death records; scrapbooks and newsletters; and poll lists and election registers containing the names of persons who voted in elections. Notable among the latter are Minneapolis registers of electors for 1902–23, which contain significant genealogical information. Some municipal records include information about the registration or licensing of saloon keepers, peddlers, and others. Names of city council members appear in the minutes and names of city officials and staff can be found in payroll registers and annual reports.[10]

ARCHIVES

THE NATIONAL ARCHIVES

Unique city sources are often found in the regional system of the National Archives. Loretto Dennis Szucs and Sandra Hargreaves Luebking, in *The Archives: A Guide to the National Archives Field Branches* (Salt Lake City: Ancestry, 1988), point out several of these obscure urban collections. Millions of files from cases heard in the U.S. courts in cities all across the nation have been preserved. Landmarks in history and events that shaped the lives of otherwise unknown citizens have been preserved. The National Archives—New England Region in suburban Boston, for example, has court records for the area that relate to such diverse matters as admiralty disputes, infringement of patent and copyrights, mutiny and murder, illegal manufacturing or sale of alcoholic beverages, and many others. The region also has the original copies of naturalization records of the federal courts for the six New England states dating back to 1790. Federal court records at the National Archives—Central Plains Region in Kansas City provide firsthand accounts of life in urban centers in the "Wild West." Few people would think to look for a Philadelphia source titled "Registers of Aliens, 1798–1812." Available only at the National Archives—Mid-Atlantic Region in Philadelphia, it is a list of individuals who came before the U.S. District Court for the Eastern District of Pennsylvania during the Quasi-War With France. Significant information regarding individuals involved in the San Francisco Earthquake of 1906 can be extracted from materials in a number of record groups at the National Archives—Pacific Sierra Region in San Bruno, California. Some of the least known yet genealogically rich city records are described in *The Archives*.

STATE ARCHIVES

State archives, by their nature, collect, preserve, and make available some of the very best city sources. Almost every state has as its mission to protect those public records of historical value which are created by state agencies and local units of government. These sources are principally in manuscript (unpublished) form. Also available in most state archives are microfilm copies of some federal records as they relate to the state served, such as federal population schedules.

Most state archives will provide a descriptive brochure upon request. The State Archives of Michigan, for example, in its brochure lists a wealth of genealogical materials that are essential to city research in that state. In addition to the federal population census schedules, the Archives of Michigan is typical of other states in having a collection of federal agricultural, manufacturing, mortality, and social statistical censuses. As is the case with most other state archives, Michigan's holds the state-created censuses as well. Tax assessment rolls, Michigan military rosters, Civil War grave registrations, and photograph files are among other rich sources listed. As a courtesy to its patrons, the Michigan Archives brochure also suggests genealogical sources in Michigan state facilities.

Frequently, the quickest and easiest access to records is through state archives. The New Jersey State Archives has a continuing run of statewide registrations of births, marriages, and deaths beginning in 1848, and with indexes through 1923 for births and through 1940 for marriages and deaths. The New Jersey State Archives and 262 other repositories in the state are described in New Jersey Historical Commission, *New Jersey Historical Manuscripts: A Guide to Collections in the State.* (Trenton: New Jersey Historical Commission, 1987).

COUNTY ARCHIVES

A large number of county archives scattered around the United States focus on original records generated by county and city agencies. In the Cuyahoga County (Ohio) Archives, for example, are Cleveland records of birth, marriage, death, naturalization, and divorce; and coroners' case files, voter lists, township and ward maps, atlases for the city of Cleveland, probate estate files, registrations and charters of religious and other societies, journals of Cuyahoga County justices of the peace, county surveyor's records, Cleveland city directories, and more.

MUNICIPAL ARCHIVES

Municipal archives do not exist in every American city, but those that do often preserve unique information that can add interesting details to any family history.

Philadelphia has the oldest city archive in the United States, its archive being established in 1952. For the researcher with research interests in the city, an essential guide is John Daly, *Descriptive Inventory of the Archives of the City of Philadelphia* (Philadelphia: Department of Records, 1970).

The Municipal Archives for the City of New York (New York City Department of Records and Information Services) was established to maintain, catalog, and make available historic New York City government records. Of particular genealogical usefulness is the large collection of vital records for the city (boroughs). While the New York state census records are as yet not available for all years on microfilm or in all offices, the Municipal Archives does have them for Brooklyn (Kings County) for 1855, 1865, 1875, 1905, and 1915. A special New York City Police Census taken in Manhattan and the western Bronx in 1890; almshouse records covering the years 1758 to 1953; some court records from 1808 to 1935; coroner's records for several of the boroughs spanning the years 1823 to 1918; photographs, some 50,000 volumes of voter registrations; real estate valuation records; and more make the New York City Municipal Archives a very important research stop for anyone with roots in the northeastern metropolis.

SPECIAL ARCHIVES

There are also significant institutional archives that preserve and make available original records that have survived in no other form. For example, historical documents acquired by the University of Massachusetts, Boston, reveal stories of poverty from an era before the existence of public welfare programs and detail much about the life of the poor in nineteenth-century America. The archive's collection consists of photographs, yearbooks, and personal dossiers on students and administrators of an institution known as the Boston Asylum and Farm School for Boys that was located on Thompson's Island in Boston Harbor. The Archives Department at the University of Massachusetts, Boston, is the only repository in the area that concentrates on preserving the records of private social welfare agencies. Many of these agencies were started in the nineteenth century in response to social upheavals that proved damaging to American family life. The department also has collections relating to twentieth-century community organizing, social movements, and the history of Dorchester, Massachusetts. Like many other institutional archives, the Archives Department is open to the public (by appointment only).

STATE HISTORICAL SOCIETIES AND LIBRARIES

State historical societies and libraries should not be overlooked because of the rich collections they catalog for cities and for statewide compilations that include cities within the state. The California State Library, for example, holds approximately 640,000 index cards covering 1.2 million items from such sources as newspapers, manuscripts, periodicals, and county histories in the California Information File. Among the treasures at the Connecticut State Library are most of the state's probate estate papers from before 1850 (fewer from 1850 to 1900) and state census records, including a 1917 Connecticut military census that included males ages ten to thirty along with automobile owners, aliens, and nurses. Also at the Connecticut State Library is a master index of individual names compiled from tombstones in more than 2,000 cemeteries in Connecticut that was compiled by the WPA. Obviously, there is urban material to be gleaned from all of these collections and others across the country.

STATEWIDE PROJECTS

Statewide projects are ongoing in almost every state. They comprise yet another important source to be considered in tracking urban dwellers' records. Unfortunately, some of the projects have elected to leave large metropolitan areas out of their compilations, or have left them until last, due to the enormous amount of time and effort required to enter the millions of names into the computer databases.

Hundreds of thousands of marriages have been entered to date in a pre-1900 Illinois Statewide Marriage Index, a continuing joint project of the Illinois State Archives and the Illinois State Genealogical Society. In an effort to replace the missing 1890 federal census, genealogists in California have launched a statewide project to transcribe and computerize names from the voting lists for California for 1890.

Urban research is often intimidating, but, given the vast array of records described in this and other sections of this volume, it is often the most exciting and fruitful dimension of family history research. It pays to stay informed through membership in genealogical organizations. The potential for successful research and great satisfaction in the results is growing daily.

NOTES

1. Raymond A. Mohl, ed., *The Making of Urban America* (Wilmington, Del.: Scholarly Resources, 1988), 3–20.

2. U.S. Department of Commerce press release, 1993.

3. U.S. Bureau of the Census, *Statistical Abstract of the United States: Colonial Times to 1970* (Washington, D.C.: U.S. Government Printing Office, 1975), 11–12.

4. Charles N. Glaab and A. Theodore Brown, *A History of Urban America* (New York: The Macmillan Co., 1967).

5. Eibhlin MacIntosh and Richard C. Wade, "The Irish in Boston," *The Irish at Home and Abroad* 1 (3) (Winter 1993–94).

6. Steven Thernstrom, *Poverty and Progress* (Boston: Harvard University Press, 1964).

7. *Chicago 1844 Directory* (Chicago: Norris Publishers).

8. Alice Eichholz, ed., *Ancestry's Red Book: American State, County and Town Sources,* rev. ed. (Salt Lake City: Ancestry, 1992), 349–68.

9. Richard C. Wade, "American Cities Are (Mostly) Better Than Ever," *American Heritage* 30 (2) (February–March 1979).

10. Minnesota Historical Society Library and Archives Division, *Genealogical Resources of the Minnesota Historical Society: A Guide* (St. Paul: Minnesota Historical Society Press, 1989).

BIBLIOGRAPHY

American Library Directory: A Classified List of Libraries in the United States and Canada, With Personnel and Statistical Data. New York: R.R. Bowker, annual.

Bailey, Rosalie Fellows. *Guide to Genealogical and Biographical Sources for New York City, 1783–1898.* New York: the author, 1954.

Barnes, Robert W. *Guide to Research in Baltimore City and County.* Westminster, Md.: Family Line Publications, 1989.

Bell, Carol Willsey. *Ohio Guide to Genealogical Sources.* Baltimore: Genealogical Publishing Co., 1988.

Bochar, Jack. *Locations of Chicago Roman Catholic Churches 1850–1990.* Geneva, Ill.: the author, 1990.

Buenker, John D., Gerald Michael Greenfield, and William J. Murin. *Urban History: A Guide to Information Sources.* Detroit: Gale Research Co., 1981.

Child, Sargent B., and Dorothy P. Holmes. *Bibliography of Research Project Reports.* WPA Technical Series No. 7. 1943. Reprint. Bountiful, Utah: Printing by Faisal, 1979 (as W.P.A. Bibliography 9).

Daly, John. *Descriptive Inventory of the Archives of the City of Philadelphia.* Philadelphia: Department of Records, 1970.

_____, and Allen Weinberg. *Genealogy of Philadelphia County Subdivisions.* 2nd ed. Philadelphia: Department of Records, 1966.

Davis, Robert Scott, Jr. *Research in Georgia.* Easley, S.C.: Southern Historical Press, 1981.

Edwards, Richard. *Edwards' Chicago Census Directory.* Chicago: Richard Edwards, 1871.

Eichholz, Alice, ed. *Ancestry's Red Book: American State, County and Town Sources.* Rev. ed. Salt Lake City: Ancestry, 1992.

Filby, P. William, comp. *A Bibliography of American County Histories.* Baltimore: Genealogical Publishing Co., 1985.

Gager, John. *Gager's 1857 Chicago Directory.* Chicago: John Gager and Co., 1857.

Geography and Map Section of the Library of Congress. "Fire

Insurance Maps in the Library of Congress." Washington, D.C.: 1981.

Glaab, Charles N., and A. Theodore Brown. *A History of Urban America.* New York: Macmillan, 1967.

Guzik, Estelle, ed. *Genealogical Sources in the New York Metropolitan Area.* New York: Jewish Genealogical Society, 1989.

Hansen, James L. *Wisconsin Newspapers 1833–1850: An Analytical Bibliography.* Madison, Wis.: State Historical Society of Wisconsin, 1979.

Hefner, Loretta L. *The W.P.A. Historical Records Survey: A Guide to Unpublished Inventories, Indexes and Transcripts.* Chicago: Society of American Archivists, 1980.

Hogan, Roseann Reinmuth. *Kentucky Ancestry: A Guide to Genealogical and Historical Research.* Salt Lake City: Ancestry, 1993.

Jarboe, Betty M. *Obituaries: A Guide to Sources.* Rev. ed. Boston: G.K. Hall and Co., 1988.

Kirkham, E.K. *A Handy Guide to Searching in the Larger Cities of the United States.* Logan, Utah: The Everton Publishers, 1974.

Kurzweil, Arthur, and Miriam Weiner, eds. *The Encyclopedia of Jewish Genealogy.* Northvale, N.J., and London: Jason Aronson, 1991.

Lane, George, and Alginantes Kezys, comps. *Chicago Churches and Synagogues.* Chicago: Loyola University Press, 1981.

Leary, Helen F.M., ed. *North Carolina Research: Genealogy and Local History.* Raleigh, N.C.: North Carolina Genealogical Society, 1996.

Library of Congress. *Panoramic Maps of Cities in the United States and Canada: A Checklist of Maps in the Collections of the Library of Congress, Geography and Map Division.* 2nd ed. Washington, D.C.: Library of Congress, 1984.

MacIntosh, Eibhlin, and Kyle J. Betit. "The Irish in Boston." *The Irish at Home and Abroad* 1 (3) (Winter 1993–94).

Mayer, Harold M., and Richard C. Wade. *Chicago: Growth of a Metropolis.* Chicago: University of Chicago Press, 1969.

Meyers, Mary K., ed. *Meyer's Directory of Genealogical Societies in the U.S.A. and Canada.* Mt. Airy, Md.: the editor (updated and reissued in even-numbered years).

Miller, Rita Seiden, ed. *Brooklyn, U.S.A.: The Fourth Largest City in America.* New York: Brooklyn College Press, 1979.

Mills, Gary B. *Civil War Claims in the South: An Index to Claimants Before the Southern Claims Commission, 1871–1880.* Baltimore: Genealogical Publishing Co., 1994.

Minnesota Historical Society Library and Archives Division, *Genealogical Resources of the Minnesota Historical Society: A Guide* (St. Paul: Minnesota Historical Society Press, 1989).

Mohl, Raymond A., ed. *The Making of Urban America.* Wilmington, Del.: Scholarly Resources, 1988.

Neagles, James C. *The Library of Congress: A Guide to Genealogical and Historical Research.* Salt Lake City: Ancestry, 1990.

New Jersey Historical Commission. *New Jersey Historical Manuscripts: A Guide to Collections in the State.* Trenton: New Jersey Historical Commission, 1987.

The Official Catholic Directory. Wilmette, Ill.: P.J. Kenedy and Sons. Annual.

Oldenburg, Joseph F. *A Genealogical Guide to the Burton Historical Collection: Detroit Public Library.* Salt Lake City: Ancestry, 1988.

Schlesinger, Keith, and Peggy Tuck Sinko. "Urban Finding Aid for Manuscript Census Searches," *National Genealogical Society Quarterly* 69 (September 1981): 171–80.

Shelley, Michael H. *Ward Maps of United States Cities: A Selective Checklist of Pre-1900 Maps in the Library of Congress.* Washington, D.C.: Library of Congress, 1975.

Sinko, Peggy Tuck. *Guide to Local and Family History at The Newberry Library.* Salt Lake City: Ancestry, 1987.

The Street Directory of the Principal Cities of the United States. Detroit: Gale Research Co., 1973.

Suelflow, August R. *A Preliminary Guide to Church Records and Repositories.* Chicago: Society of American Archivists, 1969.

Szucs, Loretto Dennis, and Sandra Hargreaves Luebking. *The Archives: A Guide to the National Archives Field Branches.* Salt Lake City: Ancestry, 1988.

_____. *Chicago and Cook County: A Guide to Research.* Salt Lake City: Ancestry, 1996.

_____, "To Whom I Am Indebted: Bankruptcy Records." *Ancestry* 12 (5) (September–October 1994): 26–27.

Thernstrom, Stephen. *Poverty and Progress.* Boston: Harvard University Press, 1964.

United States Bureau of the Census. *A Century of Population Growth.* Washington, D.C.: Government Printing Office, 1909.

_____. *Historical Statistics of the United States: Colonial Times to 1970.* Washington, D.C.: Government Printing Office, 1975.

_____. *Statistical Abstract of the United States: 1993.* 13th ed. Washington, D.C.: 1993.

Wade, Richard. "American Cities Are (Mostly) Better Than Ever." *American Heritage* 30 (2) (February–March 1979).

Works Progress Administration. *A Guide to Church Vital Statistics Records in California.* San Francisco: Northern California Historical Records Survey, 1940.

Wynar, Lubomyr R. *Encyclopedic Directory of Ethnic Organizations in the United States.* Littleton, Colo.: Libraries Unlimited, 1976.

TRACKING THROUGH HEREDITARY AND LINEAGE ORGANIZATIONS

Chapter Contents

20

TRACKING THROUGH HEREDITARY AND LINEAGE ORGANIZATIONS

Grahame Thomas Smallwood, Jr.

Source material for more than 100 hereditary societies and more than 1,000 family organizations throughout the United States is scattered through a wide range of registers, journals, newsletters, and membership rosters. The hereditary societies listed in this chapter are those which are the best known and most active in the United States. *The Hereditary Society Blue Book* contains more detailed information about many additional hereditary societies. Check the genealogical section of your local library for a copy or write to the publisher at P.O. Box 1989, Beverly Hills, CA 90213-1989. Many of the sources needed to establish membership in a hereditary society—vital, military, church, pension, and other records—are discussed in other chapters of this book and are not repeated in this chapter.

Hereditary societies can be classified under seven headings:

- War societies
- Early settler and ship societies
- Colonial societies
- Nationality (ethnic) societies
- Religious societies
- Royal and baronial societies
- Family organizations

Hereditary (or lineage) societies require prospective members to complete an application form showing descent from the qualifying ancestor for that society (figures 20-1, 20-2, and 20-3). The application must be sufficiently documented to prove beyond any doubt the accuracy of the lineage set forth.

Some hereditary societies do not wish to have their mailing addresses published. The majority of these are "by invitation only" societies which require that new members be invited to join by a current member and provide letters of recommendation.

For many of the societies described below, various printed sources are listed. Printed sources can help you prove your lineage to an ancestor who qualifies you to be a member of a hereditary society.

WAR SOCIETIES

The oldest, largest, and best-known of the hereditary societies are those with membership based on the military service of members' ancestors. These societies are listed below in chronological order of military service.

THE ANCIENT AND HONORABLE ARTILLERY COMPANY OF MASSACHUSETTS

> The Armory
> Faneuil Hall
> Boston, MA 02109

Founded in 1637 and chartered by Governor Winthrop in 1638, The Ancient and Honorable Artillery Company of Massachusetts is the oldest military body and chartered organization in America. Membership is limited to 550 regular members, who are not required to have descended from a former member. "Right of descent" membership is open to any male descendant of a former member of the company who served before 1738. Unlike the regular members, "right of descent" applicants may reside outside the New England area.

Printed Works
The Ancient and Honorable Artillery Company of Massachusetts. *Roll of Members of the Military Company of Massachusetts, Now Called the Ancient and Honorable Artillery Company of Massachusetts With a Roster of the Commissioned Officers and Preachers, 1638–1894.* Boston: Alfred Mudge & Son, 1895.

NATIONAL SOCIETY WOMEN DESCENDANTS OF THE ANCIENT AND HONORABLE ARTILLERY COMPANY

> 1234 S. Cumberland Ave.
> Park Ridge, IL 60068-5238

This society was founded in 1927 for female descendants of former members of the Ancient and Honorable Artillery Company of Massachusetts, 1637 to 1774.

Printed Works
History and Lineage Book. 7 vols. The society, 1940, 1950, 1959, 1974, 1980.

THE GENERAL SOCIETY OF COLONIAL WARS

> 1316 Seventh St.
> New Orleans, LA 70115-3319

Figure 20-1. Membership support affidavit of Grahame Thomas Smallwood, Jr., for The Society of Colonial Wars in the Commonwealth of Pennsylvania.

THE SOCIETY OF COLONIAL WARS IN THE COMMONWEALTH OF PENNSYLVANIA

AFFIDAVIT

In support of application for membership ot (give full name)

Grahame Thomas Smallwood, Jr.

Pennsylvania
(State)

Philadelphia
(City or County)

ss.:

Grahame Thomas Smallwood, Jr.   being duly sworn, says:—
(Full name of deponent)

1.   That the applicant was born on ....26 February .... 1919 in Toledo, Ohio
and is a resident of .. Philadelphia, Pennsylvania   (Town, City or County)

2.   That he is the son of ... Graeme Thomas Smallwood .... born in Revere, Mass.
on 2 Aug. 1897, died in ..... Washington, D.C. .... on 25 April 1947
and Dorothy Hubbell ... his wife, born in Toledo, Ohio .... on 17 December 1895
died in .... on .... married in Washington, D.C.
on 12 March 1918

3.   That the said Dorothy Hubbell was the daughter of Edward Parmelee Hubbell
born in Buffalo, N.Y. on 7 February 1869, died in Washington, D.C.
on 8 Aug. 1951, and Ermina Cadwell Pheatt .... his wife, born in Toledo, Ohio
on 28 Dec. 1869 died in Washington, D.C. .... on 9 February 1956
married in Toledo, Ohio ... on 12 February 1895

4.   That the said Ermina C. Pheatt was the daughter of Zebulon Converse Pheatt
born in Cape Vincent, N.Y. on 21 December 1832, died in Toledo, Ohio
on 7 July 1901, and Sarah Amanda Cadwell .... his wife, born in Turin, N.Y.
on 17 Feb. 1832 died in Toledo, Ohio .... on 27 August 1903
married in Cape Vincent, N.Y. on 21 May 1867

5.   That the said Sarah A. Cadwell was the daughter of Joseph Cadwell
born in Lisle, N.Y. on 24 January 1796, died in Cape Vincent, New York
on 2 Aug. 1865, and Julia Bush .... his wife, born in Turin, N.Y.
on 29 July 1802 died in Turin, New York .... on 14 April 1843
married in Turin, N.Y. on 7 January 1827

6.   That the said Julia Bush was the daughter of Oliver Bush
born in Westfield, Mass. on 13 August 1770, died in Turin, New York
on 9 Apr. 1844, and Electa Dewey .... his wife, born in Westfield, Mass
on 16 Nov. 1772, died in Turin, New York .... on 8 February 1849
married in Westfield, Mass on 8 January 1795

7.   That the said Electa Dewey was the daughter of Noble Dewey
born in Westfield, Mass. on 15 June 1752, died in Westfield, Mass.
on 23 Dec. 1830, and Eleanor Pomeroy .... his wife, born in Northampton, Mass
on 20 Oct 1752, died in Turin, New York .... on 6 November 1823
married in Westfield, Mass on 20 August 1772

8. That the said Eleanor Pomeroy was the daughter of Daniel Pomeroy

born in Northampton, Mass. on 27 March 1709, died in Battle of Lake George

on 8 Sept. 1755, and Rachel Moseley his wife, born in

on 1715, died in Northampton, Mass. on 1 February 1797

married in on 4 November 1736

9. That the said was the of

born in on died in

on , and his wife, born in

on , died in on

THAT TO THE BEST OF DEPONENT'S KNOWLEDGE AND BELIEF THE LINE OF DESCENT SET FORTH ABOVE IS LINEAL AND NOT IN ANY CASE BY ADOPTION.

THAT THE SERVICES OF DANIEL POMEROY

in the American Colonial Wars upon which this claim of eligibility to membership is based, were as follows:

Killed at the Battle of Lake George while serving as a Lieutenant in Colonel William's Regiment with his brother Lieut-Colonel Seth Pomeroy.

AUTHORITIES AS TO SERVICE

"The Journals & Papers of Seth Pomeroy" pgs.115,142 Published by the Soc. of Colonial Wars in the State of New York, 1926.; Soc.Col.Wars First Supplement to Index of Ancestor 1941,p.202. Mass. Soc. Col. Wars, 1906, p. 161.

AUTHORITIES AS TO DESCENT

Formal Proof Is Required For Each Statement In Every Generation

Both as to services of ancestor and descent give references to documentary or other authorities and submit same or certified copies.
Allegations of fact based upon tradition cannot be considered. Mere titles of rank in town, church, probate, or registry records, and on gravestones cannot be accepted. Encyclopaedias, genealogies, and histories must have references in them to original authorities. Give volume and page for book references.

ot encroach upon rgin, which is re- or binding.

Generation	References	Generation	References
1 Birth certificate		8 Pomeroy.Gen.A.A.Pomery,1912,p.172 Journals & Papers of Gen.Seth Pomeroy 1926, pgs.115, 142. N.E.Hist.Gen.Reg. vol 43, pgs. 41-43. Mass.Soc. Col.Wars	
2 Birth certificates,Marriage certif. Death certificate.		9 1906, p.161	
3 Death certificates; Marriage certif. Family Bible records.		10	
4 Death certificates; D.A.R.Lineage Book,Vol.135,p.178; Hist. Toledo & Lucas Co.Ohio,pgs.30,422,758		11	
5 Kelloggs in the New World,p.230 ed of 1903; D.A.R.Lineage Book,vol.135, p.178;vol 27,p.40; vol.28,p.113. Cem.Church Recs.DAR 1932,vol 31,p181		12	
6 Dewey Gen.1898,A.M.Dewey,p.273. Westfield Marriages,1781-1835,p.415; Westfield Births (1937), p.56; NYState D.A.R.Records,vol.31,p.180.		13	
7 Pomeroy Gen.A.A.Pomeroy,1912,p.227; Noble Gen.,Boltwood,1878, p. 383; Dewey Gen.,A.M.Dewey,1898,p. 275. Cem.Church Recs.DAR vol.31,p 183. N.E.H.G.R.,vol. 43, p.43.		14	

Figure 20-2. Applicant's genealogical chart of Grahame Thomas Smallwood, Jr., for the Dutch Colonial Society of Delaware.

APPLICANT'S GENEALOGICAL CHART

Dutch Colonial Society of Delaware

THIS WORKING SHEET SHOULD BE RETURNED WITH APPLICATION

Name ..Grahame Thomas Smallwood, Jr... Spouse ....

Descendant of ..Cornelis Maessen van Buren......

1   I am the decendant of

Graeme Thomas Smallwood born on 2 August 1897   at Revere, Massachusetts
died at Washington, D.C. on 25 April 1947   and his (first or   ) spouse
Dorothy Hubbell born on 17 December 1895   at Toledo, Ohio
died at .... on ....   married on 12 March 1918
                                                               Washington, D.C.

2   The said ....Dorothy Hubbell.. was the child of
Edward Parmelee Hubbell born on 7 February 1869   at Buffalo, New York
died at Washington, D.C. on 8 August 1951   and his (first or   ) spouse
Ermina Cadwell Pheatt born on 28 December 1869   at Toledo, Ohio
died at Washington, D.C. on 9 February 1956   married on 12 February 1895
                                                               Toledo, Ohio

3   The said ....Ermina Cadwell Pheatt........................... was the child of
Zebulon Converse Pheatt born on 21 December 1832   at Cape Vincent, New York
died at Toledo, Ohio on 7 July 1901   and his (first or second) spouse
Sarah Amanda Cadwell born on 17 February 1832   at Turin, New York
died at Toledo, Ohio on 27 August 1903   married on 21 May 1867
                                                               Cape Vincant, N.Y.

4   The said ....Zebulon Converse Pheatt..................... was the child of
Isaac Tichenor Pheatt born on 15 April 1808   at Liverpool, New York
died at Toledo, Ohio on 11 May 1859   and his (first or   ) spouse
Ermina Frink born on 15 September 1809   at Herkimer, New York
died at Toledo, Ohio on 11 October 1881   married on 3 December 1829
                                                               Rochester, N.Y.

5   The said ....Isaac Tichenor Pheatt........................... was the child of
David Pheatt born on 1778   at
died at Oswego, New York on 4 September 1834   and his (first or   ) spouse
Harriett Muller bapt born on 18 June 1785   at Kinderhook, New York
died at Oswego, New York on 24 August 1863   married on 1807
                                                               Fulton, New York

6   The said ....Harriett Muller............................... was the child of
Cornelius H. Muller bapt born on 14 April 1759   at Claverack, New York
died at Fulton, New York on ....   and his (first or   ) spouse
Maria Muller born on ....   at ....
died at Hannibal, New York on ....   married on 16 November 1781
                                                               Claverack, N.Y.

7   The said ....Cornelius H. Muller......................... was the child of
Hendrick Muller bapt born on 5 May 1728   at Claverack, New York
died at .... on ....   and his (first or   ) spouse
Harriet van Dusen bapt born on 9 February 1734   at Livingston, New York
died at .... on ....   married on 3 January 1756

8   The said _____ **Harriet (Ariaantje) van Dusen** _____ was the child of

Tobias van Dusen   bapt born on   **16 August 1696**   at   **Claverack, New York**

died at _____ on   **17 October 1781** _____ and his (first or   ) spouse

Ariaantje Muller   bapt born on   **19 July   1696**   at   **Claverack, New York**

died at _____ on   **Before 1772**   married on **21 March 1723**

9   The said _____ **Tobias van Dusen** _____ was the child of

Robert Teuwis van Deusen   born on _____ at _____

died at _____ on _____ and his (first or   ) spouse

Cornelia M.van Buren,   born on bapt.   **1665**   at _____

died at _____ on   **before 1717**   married on **22 September 1689**

10   The said _____ **Cornelia Martense van Buren** _____ was the child of

Marten Cornelius van Buren born on   **1638/9**   at _____

died at _____ on   **13 November 1703**   and his (first or   ) spouse

Maritje Quackenbos   born on _____ at _____

died at   **Albany, New York**   on   **7 May   1683**   married on   **1662**

11   The said _____ **Marten Cornelius van Buren** _____ was the child of

Cornelis Maessen van Buren born on _____ at   **Burmalsen,Gelderland**

died at   **Papsknee, New York**   on   **1648**   and his (first or   ) spouse

Catalyntje Martens   born on _____ at _____

died at   **Papsknee, New York**   on   **1648**   married on   **1635/6**

12   The said _____ was the child of

born on _____ at _____

died at _____ on _____ and his (first or   ) spouse

born on _____ at _____

died at _____ on _____ married on _____

RESIDENCE IN COUNTY AND STATE OF FAMILY IN EACH GENERATION DESIRED

DETAILS SHOWING THE FAMILY DESCENT: Give reference to verify the above statement of birth, marriage and death, by volume and page if reference is made to published work, and a duplicate certified or attested copy of facts where reference is made to Family Bible, tombstone, or other unpublished authority. Statements based upon TRADITION cannot be considered.

1st Gen.   **Birth certificates(Attached)Marriage and Death certificate (attached).**

2nd Gen.   **Marriage certificate (attached); Death notices (attached)**   Hist.Toledo,Lucas Co.

3rd Gen.   **Death certificates (att.); Hough's Hist.Jefferson Co.N.Y.p.115;pgs.30;422;758.**

4th Gen.   **Hist.Toledo,Lucas Co.Ohio.p.438,455,457,693,836;DAR Lineages vol.135,page 178.**

5th Gen.   **Kinderhook,N.Y.,Vosburgh,vol 2,p.144; 1840 Census Oswego;1810 Census Oneida,N.Y.**

6th Gen.   **DAR Patriot Index,1966 p.468;Columbia Co.N.Y.Wills.1935.vol.I,p.31;Claverack Records.**   Dutch Ref.Church

7th Gen.   **NY Gen & Biog.Rec. vol.74,p.16,56,127,147; VanDeusen Gen,Benson,1901,p.48, 133-4.**

8th Gen.   **Van Deusen Gen,Benson,p.47; Van Deusen Gen,A.H.VanD.,1912,p.7,22,35.**

9th Gen.   **Van Buren Fam.,H.van B.Peckham,1913,p.325-337;Van D.Gen.Benson,1901, p. 41.**

10th Gen.   **St.Nicholas Soc.volVIII,1968 p.115;VanBuren Fam,Peckham,1913,p.17-28.**

11th Gen.   **Van Buren Fam.Peckham,1913,pgs.17-28, 51,299; Holland Dames Register,p.102.**

12th Gen. _____

Figure 20-3. Excerpts from the life membership application of Grahame Thomas Smallwood, Jr., for The Order of the Crown of Charlemagne in the United States of America.

National Number

The Order of the Crown of Charlemagne in the United States of America

SUPPLEMENTAL **Lineage Claim**

for

Life Membership

Name of Applicant _____ Grahame Thomas Smallwood, Jr.

Maiden Name _____

Address _____ The Union League

_____ Philadelphia, Pa., 19102

The American Ancestor _____ Alice Freeman wife of John Thompson

_____

is the ancestor through whom my claim of eligibility is based.

S He settled in ___ Roxbury _____ in the colony of ___ Massachusetts Bay ___

on or about ___ 1627☰1640 _____ S He was born ___ ca. 1595 ___ SHe died ___ 11 Feb 1664/5

Endorsed by the undersigned members to whom the applicant is known.

1. Name _____

   Address _____

2. Name _____

   Address _____

The undersigned have investigated and ascertained that the Applicant meets the required qualifications for membership and thus approve this application.

The ~~Life~~ Supplemental Membership fee of $ 40.00 _____ was paid by _____

Date fee received by Treasurer _____   Treasurer General

Date this lineage was approved _____   Genealogist General

Date of election to membership _____   Registrar General

DO NOT WRITE ON THIS MARGIN

10. The said   Elizabeth Wheeler ....was the child of

......Isaac Wheeler...................... born at...................on...1646...............................

died at ....on..5 June 1712........; married on..1668.....................

to ...Martha Park....................... born at ...Wethersfield,Conn..on..1646..............

died at ....on..4 Feb. 1717.......; married at...........................

Proof: ..Wheeler Fam. in Amer. pgs. 354,637,639; Pope's Pioneers Mass.1900, p.490;.....

........Gallup Fam. J.D.Gallup, p.30;..

11. The said   Martha Park ....was the child of

......Thomas Parke................. born an bp.13 Feb. 1615....... at Preston, Eng.............

died at ..Preston, Conn....................on..30 July 1709.....; married on..28 Oct. 1645.......

to ..Dorothy Thompson.............. bp. born at ..Preston Capes,Eng... on..5 July 1624.......

died at ....on after 1709.........; married at...........................

Proof: ..N.E.H.G.R., vol.75, p.135-6; Magna Charta Sureties, Weis, p.125;...................

........Parke Fam. of Conn., F.S.Parke,1906;..

12. The said   Dorothy Thompson...was the child of

......John Thompson.................. born at ...Preston, England....on..ca. 1580-90..........

died at ..Little Preston, England.....on..1626-27...........; married on ca. 1615...........

to ..Alice Freeman.................... born at ....on..ca. 1595...................

died at ..New London, Conn.......on..11 Feb. 1664/5.....; married at...........................

Proof: ..Ancestral Roots, Adams & Weis, 4th Ed. revised p. 28; Blood Royal,.................

........d'Angerville, vol. III, p.428-430; 680-682.T.A.G. VOL 13,p1-8;VOL.29, p.215.

13. The said   Alice Freeman..was the child of

......Henry Freeman of Cranford...... born at.................on..1560.........................

died at ....on.............; married bp. 25 Dec. 1591........

to ..Margaret Edwards.............. born at ....on...........................

died at ....on.............; married at...........................

Proof: ..T.A.G. vol. 13, p.1-8; Ancestral Roots,4th ed. p.28.

14. The said Margaret Edwards...was the child of

......Edward Edwards,gent.of Alwalton born at.................on ca. 1537....................

died at ....on..ca. 1591/2.........; married on...............

to ..Ursula Coles................... of Preston over Hill born at ....on...........

died at ..bur. Alwalton...................on..2 Feb. 1606.......; married at...................

Proof: ..T.A.G. vol 13, p.1-8; Ancestral Roots 4th rev.ed. p.28.

This society was founded in 1893 for male descendants of ancestors who served in the military from the time of the settlement of Jamestown, Virginia, in 1607 to the Battle of Lexington in 1775; or who held office as governor, lord proprietor, etc., or a member of the legislative body of a colony in that time period.

Printed Works

Nearly all of the twenty-nine state societies have published, from time to time, their own registers. Two excellent examples are The Society of Colonial Wars in the State of Connecticut, *Register of Pedigrees and Services of Ancestors* (Hartford: the society, 1941), and The Society of Colonial Wars in the State of Maryland, *Genealogies of the Members and Record of Services of Ancestors* (Baltimore: The Friedenwald Co., 1905), which includes a pedigree chart for each member.

Andrews, Frank DeWitte. *Connecticut Soldiers in the French and Indian War.* Vineland, N.J.: the compiler, 1923.

Benedict, Robert D. "The Pequot War." In *New York Society of Colonial Wars Year Book 1906–1907.* The society, 1907.

Bodge, George Madison. *Soldiers in King Philip's War.* Baltimore: Genealogical Publishing Co., 1967.

Church, Thomas. *The History of Philip's War, Also of the French and Indian Wars at the Eastward, 1716* (see H.N. Dexter's revised edition of 1865).

Drake, Samuel A. *The Border Wars of New England Covering King William's War 1689–1697 and Queen Anne's War 1701–1714* (1897 edition).

Fornance, Joseph K. *The Pennymite Wars.* Philadelphia: The Society of Colonial Wars in the Commonwealth of Pennsylvania, 1941.

General Society of Colonial Wars. *An Index of Ancestors and Roll of Members.* 3 vols. New York, 1922. Hartford, 1941. Baltimore, 1977.

New York Historical Society. *Muster Rolls of the New York Provincial Troops, 1755–1764.* New York: the society, 1892.

Parkman, Francis. *A Half Century of Conflict: Queen Anne's War 1701–1714 and King George's War 1744–1748* (1892 edition).

Wade, Herbert Treadwell. *A Brief History of the Colonial Wars in America, From 1607 to 1775.* Society of Colonial Wars in the State of New York, 1948.

NATIONAL SOCIETY, DAUGHTERS OF COLONIAL WARS

2220 Crescent Dr.
Hampton, VA 23661

This society was organized in 1932 for women descendants of participants in the colonial wars. The membership requirements are very similar to those cited above for The General Society of Colonial Wars.

Printed Works

National Society Daughters of Colonial Wars. *Membership List and Index of Ancestors.* 2 vols. Somerville, Mass.: 1941, 1950.

CONTINENTAL SOCIETY, SONS OF INDIAN WARS

3917 Heritage Hills Dr., No. 104
Bloomington, MN 55437-2633

This society was founded in 1987 for male descendants of Native Americans and non-Native Americans who participated, in any capacity, in actual hostilities, or in any other activity with each other, during the period 1607 to 1900. Eligibility is based upon lineal descent.

Printed Works

The Peace Pipe, published quarterly.

CONTINENTAL SOCIETY, DAUGHTERS OF INDIAN WARS

5071 Willow Point Parkway N.E.
Marietta, GA 30068

Founded in 1988 for female descendants with same qualifications as the Sons of Indian Wars.

Printed Works

The Calumet, published semiannually.

THE SOCIETY OF THE CINCINNATI

Anderson House Library
2118 Massachusetts Ave. N.W.
Washington, DC 20008

This society was founded in 1783 at the close of the revolutionary war by a group of officers of the Continental Line. This mutual friendship society of officers was conceived to "endure as long as they shall endure, or any of their eldest male posterity; and in failure thereof, the collateral branches who may be judged worthy of becoming its members and supporters." Of the 2,269 original members, plus 1,257 who were eligible but did not join or had been killed in battle, approximately 2,000 are presently represented by descendants.

Printed Works

A number of state societies have published their own volumes on members and their ancestors. An excellent example is Francis S. Drake, *Memorials of the Society of the Cincinnati of Massachusetts* (Cambridge: John Wilson & Son, 1873).

Heitman, Francis B. *Historical Register of Officers of the Continental Army During the War of the Revolution, 1914, With Addenda by Robert H. Kelby, 1932.* Baltimore: Genealogical Publishing Co., 1973.

Hume, Edgar Erskine, comp. *Society of the Cincinnati, Rules of the State Societies for Admission to Membership.* Washington, D.C.: the society, 1934.

Metcalf, Bryce. *Original Members and Other Officers Eligible to the Society of the Cincinnati 1783–1838, With the Institutions, Rules of Admission, and Lists of the Officers of the*

General and State Societies. Strasburg, Va.: Shenandoah Publishing House, 1938.

DAUGHTERS OF THE CINCINNATI

122 E. 58th St.
New York, NY 10022

Founded in 1894, the Daughters of the Cincinnati have requirements for membership similar to those of the men's society, with one major exception: more than one member may represent an ancestor at a given time.

Printed Works
A Salute to Courage. New York: Columbia University Press, 1979.

NATIONAL SOCIETY DAUGHTERS OF THE AMERICAN REVOLUTION

1776 D St. N.W.
Washington, DC 20006

Organized in 1890, this society is the largest and best known of the hereditary societies, with a membership exceeding 190,000. Since 1890, some 760,000 women have joined the DAR. Membership is based on descent from an ancestor who served the cause of American independence in the military, as a recognized patriot, or by rendering material aid.

Printed Works
More than two hundred volumes have been printed by various state societies, including membership rosters, lists of ancestors buried in a particular state, and biographies of the founders in various states.

DAR Index of the Rolls of Honor. 4 vols. Washington, D.C.: the society, 1916–40. Reprint. 1980, 4 vols. in 2. These volumes index the ancestors of members as published in 160 volumes of lineage books.

DAR Patriot Index. 2 vols. Washington, D.C.: the society, vol. 1, 1966; vol. 2, 1979. These volumes list the revolutionary soldier with known dates of birth and death, name of wife or wives, rank, and state from which served.

Reamy, Martha, and William Reamy. *Index to the Rolls of Honor.* Baltimore: Genealogical Publishing Co., 1995. This volume contains the names of the 228,639 Union soldiers listed in the twenty-seven volumes of the U.S. Quartermaster's *Roll of Honor.* The original twenty-seven volumes were consolidated into ten volumes and published by the Genealogical Publishing Co. in 1994.

GENERAL SOCIETY SONS OF THE REVOLUTION

Fraunces Tavern
54 Pearl St.
New York, NY 10004

This society was founded in 1876 as a result of the stringent requirements of the Society of the Cincinnati, which made no provision for membership of younger sons of the original members. Membership is based on military service or descent from key civil officials.

Printed Works
Numerous state societies of the Sons of the Revolution have published biennial volumes on membership and ancestry. Two excellent examples are the 1901–03 and 1907–09 *Register of the Sons of the Revolution in the State of Missouri* (St. Louis: Woodward & Tieernan Printing Co.) They contain ancestral lines from nearly all of the thirteen colonies.

Hall, Henry. *Year Book of the Societies Composed of Descendants of the Men of the Revolution.* New York: The Republic Press, 1890. This rare and unusual volume unites the Sons of the Revolution, Sons of the American Revolution, Daughters of the American Revolution, and the Society of the Cincinnati.

NATIONAL SOCIETY SONS OF THE AMERICAN REVOLUTION

National Headquarters
1000 S. 4th St.
Louisville, KY 40203

Organized in 1889, the Sons of the American Revolution (SAR) is the largest hereditary society for men, with chapters in all fifty states, the District of Columbia, France, and England. Membership is based on descent from an ancestor who served in the military, held high official office, or was a patriot in the American cause.

Printed Works
Numerous state societies of the SAR have printed yearbooks containing lineages, etc. The 1893–94 volume of the New York State Society presents a number of engravings of ancestors. The register of the District of Columbia Society for 1896 is another splendid volume.

Cornish, Louis A., and A. Howard Clark. *A National Register of the Society Sons of the American Revolution.* New York: Andrew H. Kellogg Press, 1902. This unusual volume contains the entire list of membership for the National Society to 31 December 1901, including all deceased members, with lines of descent from revolutionary war ancestors.

St. Paul, John, Jr. *The History of the National Society of the Sons of the American Revolution.* New Orleans: Pelican Publishing Co., 1962.

Microfilm
The Genealogical Society of Utah has microfilmed more than 82,500 lineage papers of the National Society SAR and cross-indexed them by the name of the member and the name of the ancestor.

NATIONAL SOCIETY CHILDREN OF THE AMERICAN REVOLUTION

1776 D St. N.W.
Washington, DC 20006

This society was organized under the auspices of the DAR. Membership is limited to boys and girls under the age of twenty-two. Membership requirements are the same as for the DAR and SAR.

HEREDITARY ORDER OF DESCENDANTS OF THE LOYALISTS AND PATRIOTS OF THE AMERICAN REVOLUTION

3917 Heritage Hills Dr., No. 104
Bloomington, MN 55437-2633

This society was organized in 1973 for those who descended from both a loyalist and a patriot of the American Revolution. The loyalist may be a collateral ancestor, but not more distant than the third degree. Application forms show the two lines of descent from the two ancestors.

Printed Works

Brown, Wallace. *The Good Americans: The Loyalists in the American Revolution.* New York: William Morrow & Co., 1969.

_____, *The King's Friends: The Composition and Motives of the American Loyalist Claimants.* Providence: Brown University Press, 1966.

Clark, Murtie June. *The Loyalists in the Southern Campaign of the Revolutionary War.* 3 vols. Baltimore: Genealogical Book Co., 1981.

DeMond, Robert O. *Loyalists in North Carolina during the Revolution.* 1940. Reprint. Hampden, Conn.: Archer Books, 1964.

Hancock, Harold Bell. *Delaware Loyalists.* Wilmington: Historical Society of Delaware, 1940.

Harrell, Isaac Samuel. *Loyalism in Virginia.* Durham, N.C.: Duke University Press, 1926.

Jones, Edward Alfred. *Loyalists in Massachusetts: Their Memorials, Petitions and Claims.* 1930. Reprint. Baltimore: Genealogical Publishing Co., 1969.

Sabine, Lorenzo. *Biographical Sketches of Loyalists of the American Revolution.* 2 vols. 1864. Reprint. Port Washington, N.Y.: Kennikat Press, 1966.

Smith, Paul H. *Loyalists and Redcoats.* Chapel Hill, N.C.: University of North Carolina Press, 1964.

Starke, James H. *The Loyalists of Massachusetts, and the Other Side of the American Revolution.* Boston: the author, 1910.

The United Empire Loyalists: *The Old Empire Loyalist List.* 1885. Reprint. Baltimore: Genealogical Publishing Co., 1976.

Wright, Esther Clark. *Loyalists of New Brunswick.* Fredericton, Nebr.: the author, 1955.

SOCIETY OF THE DESCENDANTS OF WASHINGTON'S ARMY AT VALLEY FORGE

P.O. Box 915
Valley Forge, PA 19481

This society was organized in 1976 at Valley Forge, Pennsylvania, for descendants of soldiers who served in the Continental Army at the Valley Forge encampment in 1777–78.

Printed Works

Chunn, Calvin E. *Not by Bread Alone.* The society, 1981.

Worley, Ramona. *In Search for the Winter Patriot.* The society, 1979.

SOCIETY OF THE WHISKEY REBELLION OF 1794

3311 Columbia Pike
Lancaster, PA 17603

This society was organized in 1959 for male lineal descendants of ancestors who served in the militia to put down the 1794 western Pennsylvania rebellion against Alexander Hamilton's excise tax on whiskey.

MILITARY ORDER OF FOREIGN WARS OF THE UNITED STATES

122 E. 58th St.
New York, NY 10022

This society was organized in 1894. Membership is conferred on officers with active military service in any foreign war from the American Revolution to the Vietnam War. Descendants in the direct male line of such an officer may qualify for hereditary companionship.

Printed Works

Register of Commanderies and Members, Military Order of Foreign Wars of the United States 1894–1900. The order, 1901.

GENERAL SOCIETY OF THE WAR OF 1812

P.O. Box 106
Longwood Estates
Mendenhall, PA 19357

This society was organized 24 September 1814 at Fort McHenry, Baltimore, Maryland, at the close of the War of 1812. It was primarily a Maryland society known as "The Defenders of Baltimore." From 1814 to 1888, all of the presidents were War of 1812 veterans. Membership is limited to male lineal descendants of participants in the military or privateer service of the United States. If the participant had no descendants, one collateral descendant may be admitted to the society.

Printed Works

Biennial and triennial meetings of the general society have published their proceedings for the past ninety years.

General Society of the War of 1812. *The Constitution and Register of Membership of the General Society of the War of 1812.* Washington, D.C.: The Law Reporter Printing Co., 1908.

Ordway, Col. Frederick Ira, Jr., ed. *Register of the General Society of the War of 1812.* The society, 1972.

_____, *Bicentennial Supplement to the 1972 Register.* Ann Arbor, Mich.: Edwards Brothers, 1976.

NATIONAL SOCIETY, UNITED STATES DAUGHTERS OF 1812

1461 Rhode Island Ave. N.W.
Washington, DC 20005

Organized 8 January 1892 on the anniversary of the Battle of New Orleans, the society requires lineal descent from an ancestor who rendered military, naval, or civil service between the close of the American Revolutionary War in 1784 and the close of the War of 1812 in 1815. Military service may be in any one of sixteen recognized engagements between those dates.

Printed Works
1812 Ancestor Index. Norcross, Ga.: Harper Printing Co., 1970. This volume lists some 20,000 established ancestors, names of spouses, the name of the child (and spouse) through whom the member joined, and the state from which the ancestor served.

THE MILITARY SOCIETY OF THE WAR OF 1812

Seventh Regiment Armory
643 Park Ave.
New York, NY 10021

This society was founded in 1826 for descendants of commissioned officers, aides-de-camp, and commanding officers of private armed vessels of the United States who served in the armies and navies in the War of 1812.

AZTEC CLUB OF 1847—THE MILITARY SOCIETY OF THE MEXICAN WAR 1846–1848

6200 Oregon Ave. N.W., No. 114
Washington, DC 20015

This society was organized in 1847 for lineal descendants of commissioned officers of the army, navy, and marines who served in Mexico or Mexican waters during the War with Mexico, 1846 to 1848.

Printed Works
The Aztec Club of 1847: Roster of Members. The society, 1972.

Bauer, K. Jack. *The Mexican War.* New York: the author, 1974.

SAN JACINTO DESCENDANTS

7011 Spring Briar
San Antonio, TX 78209

Anyone who is a direct descendent of a person who participated in the Battle of San Jacinto, 1836, or was assigned to the rear guard at Harrisburg is eligible for membership in this society.

MILITARY ORDER OF THE LOYAL LEGION OF THE UNITED STATES (MOLLUS)

1805 Pine St.
Philadelphia, PA 19103

This society was founded in 1865, the year Lincoln died. Membership is limited to male lineal descendants of commissioned officers in the Union forces, 1861 to 1865, with hereditary membership open to male descendants of a brother or sister of such an officer. Its library contains some 11,000 volumes on the Civil War and numerous regimental histories.

Printed Works
Numerous commanderies throughout the United States have printed rosters for nearly a century. An excellent example is the *Register of the Commandery of the State of Pennsylvania, 1865–1882.*

Roster of the Military Order of the Loyal Legion of the United States. Philadelphia: the order, 1975. Contains membership rosters of sixteen state commanderies.

Loyal Legion Historical Journal. Published periodically by the order for more than forty years.

DAMES OF THE LOYAL LEGION OF THE UNITED STATES

1805 Pine St.
Philadelphia, PA 19103

This society was founded in 1899 as a companion society to MOLLUS. Membership is limited to women descendants of Union army commissioned officers and the wives of members of MOLLUS.

Printed Works
Roster of the Loyal Legion of the United States, as cited above, contains a section devoted to the membership of the Dames of the Loyal Legion.

SONS OF THE UNION VETERANS OF THE CIVIL WAR

Keith G. Harrison
4209 Santa Clara Dr.
Holt, MI 48842-1868

This society was founded in 1881 to perpetuate the memory of the Grand Army of the Republic. Membership is open to all male descendants of soldiers, sailors, and marines who served in the Union cause, 1861 to 1865.

Printed Works
The Banner (1917 Teel Ave., Lansing, MI 48910), a quarterly published by the society, has information on all posts.

AUXILIARY TO THE SONS OF THE UNION VETERANS OF THE CIVIL WAR

This group was organized in 1883 as the Ladies Aid Society. Membership today is in several categories: wives of sons of the Union veterans, widows of sons who were in good standing at death, mothers of sons, and all female lineal relatives.

Printed Works
The Banner, although published by the Sons of the Union Veterans, also includes information on the auxiliary.

DAUGHTERS OF UNION VETERANS OF THE CIVIL WAR, 1861–65

503 S. Walnut St.
Springfield, IL 62704

Organized in 1885, this society is the oldest women's hereditary society in the United States. Membership is limited to lineal descendants of military participants in the Civil War on the Union side.

LADIES OF THE GRAND ARMY OF THE REPUBLIC

This society was organized in 1885, combining the Loyal Ladies League and the Ladies of the Grand Army of the Republic. Membership is open to all mothers, wives, sisters, daughters, granddaughters, blood-kin nieces, and cousins of honorably discharged Union veterans.

UNITED DAUGHTERS OF THE CONFEDERACY

Memorial Building
328 N. Blvd.
Richmond, VA 23220

This group was organized in 1894 for women who are lineal or collateral descendants of men or women who served in the military or civil service of the Confederate States of America, or who gave material aid to the cause.

Printed Works
Davis, Jefferson. *Woman in the South in War Times* and *The Rise and Fall of the Confederate Government* (both available through the society).

CHILDREN OF THE CONFEDERACY

Memorial Building
328 N. Blvd.
Richmond, VA 23220

Organized in 1896 by the United Daughters of the Confederacy, membership in this society is limited to boys and girls under twenty-one years of age who are lineal descendants or nieces or nephews of men or women who served honorably in the Confederate service or of members of the United Daughters of the Confederacy or the Sons of Confederate Veterans.

SONS OF CONFEDERATE VETERANS

P.O. Box 59
Columbia, TN 38402-0059

This group was organized in 1896 under the auspices of the United Confederate Veterans. Membership is limited to male descendants, lineal or collateral, of members of the Confederate military or participants who died in prison, were killed in battle, or were honorably discharged.

MILITARY ORDER OF THE STARS AND BARS

P.O. Box 59
Columbia, TN 38402-0059

This society was organized in 1938 for male descendants, lineal or collateral, of commissioned officers of the Confederate States of America.

NATIONAL ORDER OF THE BLUE AND GRAY

P.O. Box 1301
Vienna, VA 22183

The National Order of the Blue and Gray was founded in 1990 for descendants of ancestors who rendered civil or military service to both the Confederate and Federal governments during their lifetimes, including service in battle under Confederate and Federal authority; in a political role (state level or higher); or as a physician, surgeon, chaplain, or nurse in wartime service.

MILITARY ORDER OF THE WORLD WARS

435 N. Lee St.
Alexandria, VA 22314

Organized in 1919 as The American Officers of the Great War, this society's title was changed in 1920 (in 1942, "War" became "Wars"). Membership is open to male U.S. citizens who served honorably on active duty as commissioned officers between 6 April 1917 and 2 July 1921, or since 16 September 1940. Male descendants of members or of deceased officers are eligible for hereditary membership.

EARLY SETTLER AND SHIP SOCIETIES

These societies (listed below by date of founding) are based on the earliest settlers of a town, state, or geographical area. Societies of early arrivals on specific ships are included as well; they are identified by the name of the ship—that is, *Mayflower, Welcome, Ark, Dove,* etc.

SAINT NICHOLAS SOCIETY OF THE CITY OF NEW YORK

122 E. 58th St.
New York, NY 10022

At the suggestion of Washington Irving, this organization was founded in New York City in 1835 as a society for male descendants of residents of the city of New York or of New York state prior to 1785. Members must be proposed and seconded in writing. Membership is limited.

Printed Works
The Saint Nicholas Society of the City of New York Genealogical Record. 9 vols. New York: the society, 1905–80. These volumes contain the complete lineages of all members, plus biographical sketches of the ancestors.

Talcott, Sebastian Visscher. *Genealogical Notes of New York and New England Families.* 1883. Reprint. Baltimore: Genealogical Publishing Co., 1973.

SOCIETY OF CALIFORNIA PIONEERS

456 McAllister St.
San Francisco, CA 94102

This group was founded in 1850 for male lineal descendants of Californians who were resident before 1 January 1850, the date of statehood.

Printed Works
Bancroft, Hubert H. *California Pioneer Register and Index 1542– 1858: Including Inhabitants of California 1769–1800 and List of Pioneers.* 1884–90. Reprint. Baltimore: Genealogical Publishing Co., 1964.

California State Society Daughters of American Revolution. *Records of the Families of California Pioneers.* Vol. 2. The society, n.d.

Northrup, Marie E. *Spanish-Mexican Families of Early California, 1769–1850.* New Orleans: Polyanthos, 1976.

DAUGHTERS OF THE REPUBLIC OF TEXAS

510 E. Anderson Ln.
Austin, TX 78752

This society was founded in 1891 for female lineal descendants of loyal citizens who established residence in Texas before the state's annexation on 19 February 1846.

Printed Works

See the sources listed for the Sons of the Republic of Texas and:

Morris, Mrs. Harry Joseph, comp. *Daughters of the Republic of Texas: Founders and Patriots of the Republic of Texas—Lineages of Members.* Austin: the author, 1963.

Texas Society of the Daughters of the American Revolution. The *Roster of Texas Daughter's Revolutionary Ancestors* (Houston: the society, 1976).

SONS OF THE REPUBLIC OF TEXAS

5942 Abrams Rd., Suite 222
Dallas, TX 75231

This group was organized in 1893 for male lineal descendants of Texans who were resident prior to annexation on 19 February 1846.

Printed Works

Geue, Chester W., and E.H. Geue. *A New Land Beckoned: German Immigrants to Texas 1844–1847.* Fort Worth: the authors, 1966.

Gracy, Alice Duggan, Jane Sumner, and Emma G.S. Gentry. *Early Texas Birth Records 1838–1870.* 2 vols. Austin: Mrs. H.R. Gentry, 1970–71.

Grammer, Norma Rutledge. *Marriage Records of Early Texas 1824–1846.* Fort Worth: Fort Worth Genealogical Society, 1972.

Miller, Thomas Lloyd. *Bounty and Donation Land Grants of Texas 1835–1888.* Austin: the author, 1967.

Scott, Florence Johnson. *Royal Land Grants of the Rio Grande 1777–1821.* Rio Grande City: Rio Grande City Publishers, 1969.

NATIONAL SOCIETY OF NEW ENGLAND WOMEN

5148 29th Ave. S.
Minneapolis, MN 55417-1331

This group was organized in 1895 for women descendants of any ancestor born in New England before the signing of the U.S. Constitution on 4 March 1789.

ORDER OF THE FOUNDERS AND PATRIOTS OF AMERICA

758 E. Day Ave.
Milwaukee, WI 53217

This society was organized in 1896 for men descended in the male line of either parent from an ancestor who settled in one of the colonies before 13 May 1657 and whose intermediate ancestor, in the same line, served in the American Revolution. Because both founder and patriot must bear the surname of the applicant's father or mother, this has long been regarded as the most difficult lineage society to join.

Printed Works

Colket, Meredith B., Jr. *Founders of Early American Families—Emigrants From Europe 1607–1657.* Oberlin, Ohio: Oberlin Printing Co., 1975. This most unusual volume documents some 3,500 male heads of families who appear to have descendants in the male line to the present day.

The Order of the Founders & Patriots of America Registers. Vol. 1. New York: J.J. Little & Ives Co., 1926. Vol. 2, Arthur Adams, comp. The order, 1940. Vol. 3. New York: the order, 1960. Vol. 4. New Hartford, Conn: the order, 1981.

GENERAL SOCIETY OF MAYFLOWER DESCENDANTS

4 Winslow St.
P.O. Box 3297
Plymouth, MA 02361

This group was founded in 1897 as a society for the lineal descendants of passengers on the *Mayflower,* which arrived in Plymouth harbor in December 1620.

Printed Works

A number of state societies have published excellent volumes with complete lineages of members. An example is Frederick Ira Ordway, Jr., ed., *Register of the Society of Mayflower Descendants in the District of Columbia,* 2 vols. in 1 (Federalsburg, Md.: J.W. Stowell Printing Co., 1970, 1973).

Harding, Anne Borden, ed. *Mayflower Families Through Five Generations: Family of George Soule.* Vol. 1. Plymouth, Mass: the society, 1980.

Kellog, Lucy Mary, ed. *Mayflower Families Through Five Generations: Families of Francis Eaton, Samuel Fuller, and William White.* Vol. 1. Plymouth, Mass: the society, 1975.

The Mayflower Descendant. 34 vols. and a 2-vol. index. Plymouth, Mass: Massachusetts Society, 1899–1937.

Sherman, Robert M., ed. *Mayflower Families Through Five Generations: Families of James Chilton, Richard More, and Thomas Rogers.* Vol. 2. Plymouth, Mass: the society, 1978.

Terry, Milton E., and Anne Borden Harding, comps. *Mayflower Ancestral Index.* Plymouth, Mass.: the society, 1981.

NATIONAL SOCIETY, DAUGHTERS OF FOUNDERS AND PATRIOTS OF AMERICA

Park Lane Building
2025 Eye St. N.W., No. 615
Washington, DC 20006

This group was founded in 1898 for women descended in the direct male line of either parent from an ancestor who settled in any of the colonies between 13 May 1607 and 13 May 1687. (The last date is thirty years later than the men's organization.)

Printed Works

Lineage Book of the National Society of Daughters of Founders and Patriots of America. 45 vols. since 1909. Contains complete proven lineages.

NATIONAL SOCIETY, DAUGHTERS OF UTAH PIONEERS

300 North Main St.
Salt Lake City, UT 84103

This group was founded in 1901 for female lineal descendants of those who came to Utah before the completion of the railroad on 10 May 1869.

Printed Works

Daughters of Utah Pioneers. 30 vols. Salt Lake City: the society, 1939–68.

Jakeman, James T., ed. *Daughters of Utah Pioneers and Their Mothers.* Salt Lake City: the society, 1930. Contains an excellent collection of more than five hundred photographs.

Utah Pioneer Biographies. 44 vols. Salt Lake City: Utah Historical Society, 1935–64.

SOCIETY OF THE FOUNDERS OF NORWICH, CONNECTICUT

348 Washington St.
Norwich, CT 06360

Organized in 1901, this society is open to all interested in the history and preservation of Norwich. Applicants who prove lineal descent from an original proprietor or one of the earliest settlers receive a certificate of descent.

Printed Works

Caulkins, Frances M. *History of Norwich From Its Possession by the Indians to the Year 1866.* 1866. Reprint. Baltimore: Genealogical Publishing Co., 1976.

SONS AND DAUGHTERS OF OREGON PIONEERS

1500 S.W. Spring St.
Portland, OR 97201

This group was organized in 1901 for lineal descendants of settlers in the Oregon Country before statehood, 14 February 1859.

Printed Works

Genealogical Material in Oregon Donation Land Claims Abstracted From Applications. 4 vols. Portland: Genealogical Forum, 1957–62.

"Genealogical Research in Oregon." *National Genealogical Society Quarterly* 47 (1959): 115–48.

Oregon State Archives. *Pioneer Families of the Oregon Terri-tory, 1850.* Bull. 3, Pub. 17. Salem: Oregon State Archives, 1961.

PISCATAQUA PIONEERS

211 Lowell St.
Wilmington, MA 01887

This group was organized in 1905 for lineal descendants of early (before July 1776) settlers on both the New Hampshire and Maine sides of the Piscataqua River and its tributaries.

Printed Works

Noyes, Sybil, Charles Thornton Libby, and Walter Goodwin Davis. *Genealogical Dictionary of Maine and New Hampshire.* 1928–39. Reprint. Baltimore: Genealogical Publishing Co., 1972.

Pope, Charles Henry. *The Pioneers of Maine and New Hampshire, 1623–1660.* Baltimore: Genealogical Publishing Co., 1965.

Society of Piscataqua Pioneers, Register of Members and Ancestors, 1905–1981. The society, 1981.

Spencer, Wilbur D. *Pioneers on Maine Rivers With Lists to 1651.* 1930. Reprint. Baltimore: Genealogical Publishing Co., 1973.

THE WELCOME SOCIETY OF PENNSYLVANIA

415 S. Croskey St.
Philadelphia, PA 19146

This group was founded in 1906 to honor the ship *Welcome,* on which William Penn travelled to his colony. Applicants must prove lineal descent from a passenger arriving on the *Welcome* in October 1682 or on some other vessel arriving in Pennsylvania between 24 December 1681 and 31 December 1682.

Printed Works

McCracken, George E., ed. *Penn's Colony, The Welcome Claimants—Proved, Disproved and Doubtful, With an Account of Some of Their Descendants.* Vol. 2. Baltimore: Genealogical Publishing Co., 1970.

Sheppard, Walter Lee, Jr., ed. *Penn's Colony, Passengers and Ships Prior to 1684.* Vol. 1. Baltimore: Genealogical Publishing Co., 1970.

NATIONAL SOCIETY, SONS OF UTAH PIONEERS

3301 E. 2920 S.
Salt Lake City, UT 84109

This group was organized in 1907 for male lineage descendants of those who came to Utah prior to completion of the railroad, 10 May 1869.

Printed Works

Biographies of the Members of the Salt Lake Chapter, Sons of Utah Pioneers. Salt Lake City: Genealogical Society of Utah, 1980. A collection of sketches contributed by members.

Jackson, Ronald Vern, and David L. Grundvig. *Directory of Individuals Residing in Salt Lake City Wards 1854–1861.* Early Mormon Series, vol. 1. Salt Lake City: the authors, 1982.

List of Pioneers of 1847 With Biographical Notes From the Journal of the History of the Church 1847 and The Historical Record. Vol. 9. Salt Lake City: Genealogical Society of Utah, n.d.

The Pioneer, a monthly publication. 32 vols. to 1983.

NATIONAL SOCIETY, SONS AND DAUGHTERS OF THE PILGRIMS

3917 Heritage Hills Dr., No. 104
Minneapolis, MN 55437

This group was organized in 1908 for lineal descendants of settlers (Pilgrims) in any of the colonies prior to 1700.

Printed Works

Lineages of Members of the National Society of the Sons & Daughters of the Pilgrims 1920–1952. Vol. 2. The society, 1953.

Lineages of Members of the National Society of the Sons & Daughters of the Pilgrims to 1 January 1929. Philadelphia: the society, 1929.

Mayo, Mary E., ed. *Sixteen Hundred Lines to Pilgrims, Lineage Book III.* Ann Arbor, Mich: Edwards Brothers, 1982.

The Pilgrim News-Letter, a semiannual publication with news of various state branches and the annual General Court.

NATIONAL SOCIETY OF OLD PLYMOUTH COLONY DESCENDANTS

24 Pilgrim Dr.
Winchester, MA 01890-3371

This group was organized in 1910. Applicants must prove descent from a man or woman who came to Old Plymouth Colony before 1641.

Printed Works

Davis, William T. *General Register of Plymouth Families, From Ancient Landmarks of Plymouth.* 1899. Reprint. Baltimore: Genealogical Publishing Co., 1977.

Greenlaw, Lucy Hall. *The Genealogical Advertiser.* 4 vols. 1898–1901. Reprint. 4 vols. in 1. Baltimore: Genealogical Publishing Co., 1974. Contains Plymouth Colony marriages, 1693 to 1733, and probate records, 1686 to 1688.

Kingman, Bradford. *Epitaphs From Burial Hill, Plymouth, Massachusetts—1657–1892.* 1892. Reprint. Baltimore: Genealogical Publishing Co., 1977.

Records of Plymouth Colony—Births, Marriages, Deaths, Burials, etc., 1633–1689. 1857. Reprint. *The Records of the Colony of New Plymouth in New England,* vol. 8. Baltimore: Genealogical Publishing Co., 1977.

Wakefield, Robert S. *Plymouth Colony Marriages to 1650.* The author, 1978.

Young, Alexander. *Chronicles of the Pilgrim Fathers of the Colony of Plymouth From 1602–1625.* 1844. Reprint. Baltimore: Genealogical Publishing Co., 1974.

THE SOCIETY OF THE ARK AND THE DOVE

c/o Maryland Historical Society
201 W. Monument St.
Baltimore, MD 21201

This group was founded in 1910 for lineal descendants of Sir George Calvert, the first Lord Baltimore, and settlers who came in *The Ark* or *The Dove* in March 1634.

Printed Works

Maryland Genealogies—A Consolidation of Articles From the Maryland Historical Magazine. 2 vols. Baltimore: Genealogical Publishing Co., 1980. Vol. 1 contains numerous descendants of the Calvert family.

Richardson, Albert L. *The Maryland Original Research Society of Baltimore Bulletin.* 3 issues in 1 vol. Reprint. Baltimore: Genealogical Publishing Co., 1979.

Skordas, Gust. *Early Settlers of Maryland.* 1968. Reprint. Baltimore: Genealogical Publishing Co., 1979. An index of names of immigrants compiled from records of land patents, 1633 to 1680, in the Hall of Records at Annapolis, Maryland.

ORDER OF THE FIRST FAMILIES OF VIRGINIA

5055 Seminary Rd., No. 439
Alexandria, VA 22311

This society was founded in 1912 to honor Virginia, the first permanent English colony on this continent. Membership is by invitation only and is limited to lineal descendants of those who aided in the establishment of the Virginia Colony, 1607 to 1624.

Printed Works

Jester, Annie Lash, and Martha Woodroof Hiden. *Adventurers of Purse and Person: Virginia 1607–1616.* 2nd ed. The society, 1964.

SOCIETY OF INDIANA PIONEERS

Indiana Historical Society
Indiana State Library and Historical Building
315 W. Ohio St.
P.O. Box 88255
Indianapolis, IN 46202

This group was founded in 1916 for lineal descendants of residents of the state during the pioneer period, 1825 to 1850, when the last two counties were added.

Printed Works

There are numerous early county histories for Indiana, plus a large collection in Colleen Ridlen, *Early Marriage Records.*

Cockrum, William M. *A Pioneer History of Indiana.* N.p., 1907.

Heiss, Willard. *Who's Your Hoosier Ancestor?* 3 vols. Indianapolis: the author, 1963–65. Reprinted columns from the *Indianapolis Times.*

McCay, Leonard G. *Indiana Ancestors Index.* Indianapolis: the author, 1975.

LOUISIANA COLONIALS

5 S. Lark St.
New Orleans, LA 70124

This society was founded in 1917 for all lineal descendants of colonists of the Louisiana Territory before it became a state on 30 April 1803.

Printed Works

Arthur, Stanley C., and George C.H. de Kernion. *Old Families of Louisiana.* 1932. Reprint. Baltimore: Genealogical Publishing Co., 1971.

DeVille, Winston. *Gulf Coast Colonials: A Compendium of French Families in Early 18th Century Louisiana.* Baltimore: Genealogical Publishing Co., 1968.

_____. *Louisiana Recruits.* Cottonport, La.: Polyanthos, 1973.

_____. *The New Orleans French 1720–1733.* Baltimore: Genealogical Publishing Co., 1973.

Seebold, Herman deBachelle. *Old Louisiana Plantation Homes and Family Trees.* 2 vols. 1941. Reprint. The author, 1971.

SONS AND DAUGHTERS OF THE FIRST SETTLERS OF NEWBURY, MASSACHUSETTS

P.O. Box 444
Newburyport, MA 01950

This group was founded in 1927 for all lineal descendants of those who settled at Newbury before 1700.

Printed Works

Directory of Ancestors, 1635–1992.

Hoyt, David W. *The Old Families of Salisbury and Amesbury With Some Related Families of Newbury, Haverhill, Ipswich, and Hampton, and of York County, Maine.* 1879–1919. Reprint. Baltimore: Genealogical Publishing Co., 1982.

John J. Currier, of Newbury Port, 1764–1905. 2 vols. 1906–09. Reprint. Baltimore: Genealogical Publishing Co., 1977–78.

SOCIETY OF THE DESCENDANTS OF THE FOUNDERS OF HARTFORD

77 Welles Dr. N.
Newington, CT 06111

This group was organized in 1931 to honor the founder, the Reverend Thomas Hooker, and the early settlers of Hartford, Connecticut. Membership requires lineal descent from an ancestor who settled in Hartford before February 1640.

Printed Works

Barbour, Lucius Barnes. *Families of Early Hartford Connecticut.* 2nd rev. ed. Baltimore: Genealogical Publishing Co., 1982.

JAMESTOWNE SOCIETY

P.O. Box 17426
Richmond, VA 23226

This group was founded in 1936. Membership is open to descendants of stockholders in the Virginia Company of London or of settlers at Jamestown or on Jamestown Island before 1700.

Printed Works

Inman, Joseph Francis. *Historical Highlights of the Jamestowne Society's First Quarter of a Century—Roster of Members 1936–1971.* Richmond: the society, 1971.

The Jamestowne Society—Roster of Members, January 31, 1983. Richmond: the society, 1983. Includes articles of incorporation, bylaws of the society, and the qualifying ancestor of each member.

THE FIRST FAMILIES OF OHIO

P.O. Box 2625
Mansfield, OH 44906

This society was founded in 1964, with membership restricted to members of the Ohio Genealogical Society with proven descent from an ancestor who settled in the territory, now the state of Ohio, before 1820.

Printed Works

The 1890 Howe Historical Collection of eighty-eight Ohio counties has been reprinted in eighty-eight individual pamphlets containing biographies and history.

Dyer, Albion M. *First Ownership of Ohio Lands.* 1911. Reprint. Baltimore: Genealogical Publishing Co., 1982.

Smith, Marjorie, ed. *Ohio Marriages 1790–1897 Extracted from the Old Northwest Genealogical Quarterly.* 1977. Reprint. Baltimore: Genealogical Publishing Co., 1980.

THE ORDER OF THE FIRST FAMILIES OF MISSISSIPPI 1699–1817

W. Cyprus Dr.
Cary, MS 39054

This society was founded in 1967 for lineal descendants of natives or residents of the old territory now included in the state of Mississippi, between the French establishment of Old Biloxi in 1699 and statehood on 10 December 1817.

Printed Works

Gillis, Norman E. *Early Inhabitants of the Natchez District.* The author, 1963.

King, Junie E.S. *Mississippi Court Records 1799–1835.* Beverly Hills: the author, 1936.

McBee, May Wilson. *The Natchez Court Records 1767–1805.* 1953. Reprint. Baltimore: Genealogical Publishing Co., 1979.

Mississippi State Daughters of the American Revolution. *Mississippi Daughters and Their Ancestry.* 2 vols. Starkville, Miss.: Starkville Publishing Co., 1965.

MISSOURI TERRITORIAL PIONEERS

3929 Milton Dr.
Independence, MO 64055

Founded in 1980 for descendants of settlers who lived in Missouri before 1850, or of ancestors who settled one hundred years or more before submission of the applicant's paper.

DESCENDANTS OF THE FOUNDERS OF NEW JERSEY

109 Christopher St.
Montclair, NJ 07042

This organization was founded in 1982 for descendants of founders who were in any area which is now in the state of New Jersey before 13 December 1685.

DESCENDANTS OF THE FOUNDERS OF ANCIENT WINDSOR

P.O. Box 39
Windsor, CT 06095

This organization was founded in 1983 for descendants of people who resided in Windsor, Connecticut, before 1640.

THE HEREDITARY ORDER OF THE FIRST FAMILIES OF MASSACHUSETTS

253 Tremont St.
Melrose, MA 02176

Founded in 1985 for descendants of ancestors who were residents of the Massachusetts Bay Colony before 1650.

FIRST FAMILIES OF GEORGIA

15 Watson Dr.
Newnan, GA 30263

First Families of Georgia was founded in 1986 for descendants of settlers who resided in the territory now known as Georgia from 1733 to 1797.

NATIONAL SOCIETY, FIRST FAMILIES OF MINNESOTA

Arthur L. Finnell
3917 Heritage Hills Dr., No. 104
Bloomington, MN 55437

This group was founded in 1990 for descendants of ancestors who settled in Minnesota before statehood (11 May 1858) in territory that is now the state of Minnesota.

ORDER OF THE FIRST FAMILIES OF RHODE ISLAND AND THE PROVIDENCE PLANTATIONS 1636–1742

Robert Carter Arnold
2500 Q St. N.W., No. 139
Washington, DC 20007

The order was founded in 1991 for descendants of ancestors who resided in the colony of Rhode Island or the Providence plantations, 1636 to 1647.

COLONIAL SOCIETIES

These groups involve descent from ancestors who were active during the colonial period. The cutoff date is generally 4 July 1776, but there are exceptions which are noted below. The following societies are listed in the order of founding.

COLONIAL DAMES OF AMERICA

421 E. 61st St.
New York, NY 10021

The society was founded in 1890 for women of lineal descent from worthy ancestors who held public office or a commission in the armed forces, from the settlement of Jamestown on 13 May 1607 to 19 April 1775. There are chapters in fourteen major cities, the District of Columbia, London, Paris, and Rome.

Printed Works

Ancestral Records and Portraits—A Compilation From the Archives of Chapter 1, Baltimore, Maryland, of The Colonial Dames of America. 2 vols. New York: Grafton Press, 1910.

THE NATIONAL SOCIETY OF THE COLONIAL DAMES OF AMERICA

Dumbarton House
2715 Q St. N.W.
Washington, DC 20007

This society was founded in 1891 for women of lineal descent from residents of the American colonies before 1750 who rendered service to their country before 5 July 1776, including the signers of the Declaration of Independence. There are societies in some forty states and the District of Columbia.

Printed Works

Index of Pennsylvania Ancestors of the National Society of the Colonial Dames in the Commonwealth of *Pennsylvania.* Philadelphia: the society, 1970.

Register of Ancestors, The National Society of the Colonial Dames of America in the Commonwealth of Virginia. Richmond: the society, 1979.

COLONIAL ORDER OF THE ACORN

200 E. 66th St.
Apt. E-507
New York, NY 10021-6728

This order was founded in 1894 for male lineal descendants of people who were residents of American colonies before 4 July 1776. Membership is limited to two hundred, and applicants must be proposed in writing by a proposer and seconder. The society does not emphasize military or civil service and can commemorate events not associated with wars. The New York chapter was the first organized; Maryland and Connecticut chapters were authorized, but it is believed that only the New York chapter is presently active.

Printed Works

Views of Early New York With Illustrative Sketches. New York: the society, 1904.

THE COLONIAL SOCIETY OF PENNSYLVANIA

215 S. 16th St.
Philadelphia, PA 19102

This group was founded in 1895 for male lineal descendants of ancestors who settled before 1700 in any of the American colonies.

Printed Works
The Colonial Society of Pennsylvania: Charter, Constitution, Bylaws, Officers, Members, etc. 4 vols. Philadelphia: the society, 1908, 1914, 1931, 1950. Contains a line of descent for each member.

THE NATIONAL SOCIETY OF THE COLONIAL DAUGHTERS OF THE SEVENTEENTH CENTURY

P.O. Box 200
Harvel, IL 62538

This organization was founded in 1896 for women lineally descended from ancestors who rendered service from 1607 through 1699, according to the society's eligibility list. Membership is by invitation only.

Printed Works
National Society of the Colonial Daughters of the Seventeenth Century, Lineage Book. 8 vols. The society, 1898, 1907, 1916, 1923, 1932, 1942, 1968. The 1968 volume contains the names of more than 1,800 colonists and their qualifying service.

THE HEREDITARY ORDER OF THE DESCENDANTS OF COLONIAL GOVERNORS

3800 Treyburn Dr., No. 309-C
Williamsburg, VA 23185-2875

The order was founded in 1896 for lineal descendants of those men who exercised supreme executive power in the American colonies before 1775. Membership is by invitation only.

Printed Works
Raimo, John W., ed. *The Biographical Directory of American Colonial Governors 1607–1789.* Westport, Conn.: Meckler Books, 1979.

The Pennsylvania Society of Colonial Governors. Vol. 1. Philadelphia: Allen, Lane & Scott, 1916.

THE VERMONT SOCIETY OF COLONIAL DAMES

102 Court St.
Middlebury, VT 05753

This society was organized in 1897 as an independent society for women of lineal descent from ancestors whose service in the colonial period is of public record, such as the founder of a colony, town, or church or those who served in any civil or military capacity.

ORDER OF AMERICANS OF ARMORIAL ANCESTRY

308 Clinton Rd.
Lexington, KY 40502-2354

This order was founded in 1903 for lineal descendants of immigrants in the original colonies who had a proven right to "bear coat armor" in the country of their origin.

Printed Works
Ravenscroft, Ruth Thayer, comp. *Complete Register of Members With Coats of Arms, From 15 September 1903 to 15 December 1964.* Colorado Springs: Lithographic Press, 1965.

"The Roll of Arms." *New England Historical and Genealogical Register.* 1928, 1932, 1936, 1940, 1946, 1954, 1958, 1971, 1979.

Warner, Louis, comp. *Order of Americans of Armorial Ancestry, Officers and Members.* The society, 1979.

DESCENDANTS OF THE SIGNERS OF THE DECLARATION OF INDEPENDENCE

P.O. Box 808
Devon, PA 19333

This society was founded in 1907 for all lineal descendants of those who signed the Declaration of Independence.

Printed Works
Numerous biographies have been published for all of the signers.

Leach, Frank Willing. "Manuscript Collection Containing All the Known Lines of Descent of the Signers." Philadelphia: Historical Society of Pennsylvania.

THE ORDER OF COLONIAL LORDS OF MANORS IN AMERICA

108 N. St.
Roxbury, CT 06783

This society was founded in 1911 for lineal descendants of the order's twenty-seven recognized patroons, lords of the manor, or seigniors. Membership is by invitation only.

Printed Works
Check family genealogies on the following names: Archer, Billop, Brooke, Claggett, de Lotbiniere, Heathcote, Herman, Gardiner (2), Livingston, Lloyd, Mayhew, Melyn, Morris, Paine, Palmer, Pell, Philips, Sewell, Tangier Smith, Sylvester, Van Courtlandt (2), van der Donck, Van Rensselaer, Winthrop, and Wyllys.

THE NATIONAL SOCIETY OF COLONIAL DAMES OF THE XVII CENTURY

1300 New Hampshire Ave. N.W.
Washington, DC 20036

This group was founded in 1915 for women of lineal descent from ancestors who lived in the eleven British colonies of America before 1701 as an immigrant colonist or as a descendant of one.

Printed Works
The Seventeenth Century Review. 25 vols. to 1983.

NATIONAL SOCIETY, DAUGHTERS OF AMERICAN COLONISTS

2205 Massachusetts Ave. N.W.
Washington, D.C. 20008

The society was founded in 1921 for female lineal descendants of those who rendered civil or military service in any of the colonies before 4 July 1776.

Printed Works
The Colonial Courier. 25 vols. to 1983.

NATIONAL SOCIETY OF THE DAMES OF THE COURT OF HONOR

2165 Leafmore Dr.
Decatur, GA 30033

This group was founded in 1921 for female lineal descendants of colonial governors or commissioned officers who served during the American wars, 1607 to 1865; colonial wars and colonial governors, 1607 to 1775; the American Revolution, 1775 to 1783; the War of 1812, 1784 to 1815; the Mexican War, 1836 to 1838; and the Civil War, 1861 to 1865. Membership is by invitation only.

Printed Works
Research sources for all of the war societies also apply to this society.

THE SOCIETY OF DESCENDANTS OF THE COLONIAL CLERGY

12 Westchester Dr.
Auburn, MA 01501

This group was founded in 1933 for lineal descendants of any clergyman regularly ordained, installed, or settled over any Christian church in the original colonies before 4 July 1776.

Printed Works
Weis, Frederick Lewis. *The Colonial Clergy and the Colonial Churches of New England.* Lancaster, Mass.: the society, 1936.

_____. *The Colonial Clergy of Maryland, Delaware, and Georgia.* Lancaster, Mass.: the society, 1950.

_____. *The Colonial Clergy of Virginia, North Carolina and South Carolina.* Boston: the society, 1955.

_____. *The Colonial Clergy of the Middle Colonies, New York, New Jersey and Pennsylvania 1628–1776.* Worcester, Mass.: the society, 1957.

THE NATIONAL SOCIETY OF LORDS OF THE MARYLAND MANORS

3721 Alton Place N.W.
Washington, DC 20016

This society was founded in 1938 for lineal descendants of the first Baron Baltimore, or of one or more of the colonists who were "granted by the Lord Proprietor of Maryland, a manor in fee simple with manorial rights and privileges" before 1722. The society has placed markers at twenty-three manors. Membership is by invitation only.

Printed Works
See sources cited for The Society of The Ark and The Dove.

NATIONAL SOCIETY OF THE CHILDREN OF THE AMERICAN COLONISTS

2205 Massachusetts Ave. N.W.
Washington, DC 20008

This group was founded in 1939 as a kindred society to the National Society of the Daughters of the American Colonists. Any child from birth through twenty-one years of age is eligible through lineal descent from an ancestor who rendered civil or military service to any of the colonists before 4 July 1776.

Printed Works
Sources are the same as for the Daughters of the American Colonists.

NATIONAL SOCIETY, SOUTHERN DAMES OF AMERICA

307 Cindy Lou Ave.
Mandeville, LA 70448

This society was founded in 1962 for women of verified Southern ancestry. Membership is by invitation only.

Printed Works
All lineage volumes on the South apply to this society.

FLAGON AND TRENCHER—DESCENDANTS OF COLONIAL TAVERNKEEPERS

850-A Thornhill Court
Lakewood, NJ 08701

This society was founded in 1962 for men and women who are lineal descendants of anyone who conducted a tavern, inn, ordinary, or other type of hostelry on or before 4 July 1776.

Printed Works
Stryker-Rodda, Harriet, ed. *Colonial Tavernkeepers: Qualifying Ancestors of Flagon and Trencher Members.* 8 vols. The society, 1976, 1977, 1978, 1980, 1982, 1985, 1986, 1991.

ORDER OF DESCENDANTS OF COLONIAL PHYSICIANS AND CHIRURGIEONS

9317 Bent Tree Circle
Wichita, KS 67226

This order was organized in 1974 for men and women who are lineal descendants of physicians, surgeons, or licensed midwives who practiced on the North American continent during the colonial period through 1783. Membership is by invitation only.

Printed Works
Order of Descendants of Colonial Physicians and Chirurgieons Membership Roster. 2 vols. The society, 1978, 1979. Supplements issued 1980, 1981, 1982.

NATIONAL SOCIETY SONS OF AMERICAN COLONISTS

9033 Lyndale Ave. S.
Suite 108
Bloomington, MN 55420

This society was founded in 1958 and reorganized in 1986 for male descendants of ancestors who rendered civil or military service in any of the American colonies before 4 July 1776.

NATIONAL SOCIETY, SONS OF COLONIAL NEW ENGLAND

111 Duke St.
Alexandria, VA 22314

Founded in 1985 for male descendants of people born in any of the six New England colonies before 4 July 1776.

NATIONALITY (ETHNIC) SOCIETIES

Among the oldest lineage societies established in the United States, these include many charitable societies founded for English, Irish, Scottish, and Welsh immigrants in the major port cities of the Atlantic coast. These societies are listed by the date of founding.

THE WELSH SOCIETY OF PHILADELPHIA

450 Broadway
Camden, NJ 08103

This group was organized in 1729 for men of Welsh birth or descent. It is the oldest hereditary society in Philadelphia and was founded as a charitable society to aid distressed Welshmen.

Printed Works

Hartmann, Edward George. *The Welsh Society of Philadelphia—History, Charter and By-Laws, and Membership List.* Philadelphia: the society, 1980. Printed for the 250th anniversary of the society's founding.

THE SAINT ANDREW'S SOCIETY

1218 Chestnut St.
Philadelphia, PA 19107

820 E. 67th St.
Savannah, GA 31405

281 Park Ave. S.
New York City, NY 10010
150 Washington Ave.
Albany, NY 12200

Saint Andrew's Society was established in Charleston, South Carolina, in 1729; Philadelphia, Pennsylvania, in 1747; Savannah, Georgia, in 1750; New York City in 1756; Alexandria, Virginia, in 1780; Albany, New York, in 1803; and Washington, D.C., in 1855. The society is for men of Scottish birth or descent except in Charleston, where there are no restrictions on lineage, although membership is limited to thirty. Later societies have been organized throughout the United States.

Printed Works

An Historical Sketch of the Catalogue of the Saint Andrew's Society of Philadelphia With Biographical Sketches of De-

ceased Members 1749–1913. 2 vols. Philadelphia: the society, 1907–13.

History of the Saint Andrew's Society of the City of Charleston, South Carolina 1729–1929. Charleston: the society, 1929.

Morrison, David Baillie, ed. *Two Hundredth Anniversary, 1756–1956, of the Saint Andrew's Society of the State of New York.* Philadelphia and New York: Clark Printing House, 1956.

Kimmear, Peter. *Historical Sketch of the Saint Andrews Society of the City of Albany 1803–1903.* Albany: Weed-Parsons, 1903.

THE SAINT GEORGE'S SOCIETY

110 Church St.
Charleston, SC 29401

P.O. Box 383
Baltimore, MD 21203

15 E. 26th St.
New York, NY 10010

The society was established in Charleston, South Carolina, in 1733; New York in 1770; Philadelphia in 1722; and Baltimore in 1867. Membership is restricted to men of English birth or ancestry, except for the Charleston Society, which has no ancestry restrictions but limits membership to thirty.

Printed Works

Knauf, Theodore C. *A History of the Society of the Sons of St. George Established at Philadelphia, Etc.* Philadelphia: the society, 1923.

THE SOCIETY OF THE FRIENDLY SONS OF SAINT PATRICK

1218 Chestnut St.
Philadelphia, PA 19107

This group was organized in 1771 in Philadelphia for the relief of immigrants from Ireland, with membership restricted to men of Irish birth or descent.

Printed Works

Campbell, John M. *The History of the Friendly Sons of St. Patrick and the Hibernian Society.* Philadelphia: the society, 1982.

Clark, Dennis J. *A History of the Society of the Friendly Sons of St. Patrick for Relief of Emigrants From Ireland in Philadelphia 1951–1981.* Philadelphia: the society, 1982.

Dougherty, Daniel. *History of the Friendly Sons of St. Patrick for the Relief of Emigrants from Ireland in Philadelphia.* Philadelphia: the society, 1892.

Hood, Samuel. *A Brief Account of the Friendly Sons of St. Patrick.* Philadelphia: the society, 1844.

SAINT DAVID'S SOCIETY OF NEW YORK

71 W. 23rd St.
New York, NY 10010

Saint David's Society was founded in 1835 for men of Welsh birth or who are descended from those connected by ties of consanguinity or marriage. Before this, Welshmen had participated in the Saint David's Benevolent Society, founded in 1801, and the Ancient Britons Benefit Society, founded in 1805.

Printed Works

Saint David's Society of the State of New York—Origin and Purpose of the Society. New York City: the society, n.d.

HOLLAND SOCIETY OF NEW YORK

122 E. 58th St.
New York, NY 10022

The Holland Society was founded in 1885 for male descendants (in the direct male line only) of Dutchmen who were natives or residents of New York or the American colonies before 1675.

Printed Works

Holland Society of New York Yearbook. 38 vols. New York: the society, 1886–1937.

Index to Publications of the Holland Society of New York. New York: the society, 1959.

De Halve Maen. Holland Society of New York quarterly magazine, 1922 to date.

THE NETHERLANDS SOCIETY OF PHILADELPHIA

2522 Lombard St.
Philadelphia, PA 19146

This group was founded in 1892 for male lineal descendants of a Dutch ancestor who settled in the American colonies before 4 July 1776, or who, born in the Netherlands, emigrated to the United States after 1776.

Printed Works

The Netherlands Society of Philadelphia—An Account of the Organization, Purposes and Traditions. Philadelphia: the society, 1966.

SWEDISH COLONIAL SOCIETY

Gloria Dei Church
915 Swanson St.
Philadelphia, PA 19147

This group was founded in 1909 for men and women of lineal descent from Swedish colonists who were in the United States before 1783 (known as Forefather Members) as well as any person interested in the history of the early Swedes in America.

Printed Works

Johnson, Amandus. *The Swedish Settlements on the Delaware, 1638–1664.* 2 vols. 1911. Reprint. Philadelphia: 1969.

The Swedish Colonial Society, Governor Johan Printz Memorial Edition, History, Charter, By-Laws, Officers, Members, Publications, Etc. Philadelphia: the society, 1954.

THE DUTCH SETTLERS SOCIETY OF ALBANY

23 Dresden Court
Albany, NY 12203

This group was founded in 1924 for male and female descendants of pre-1665 residents of Fort Orange, the colony of Rensselaerswick, or the village of Beverwyck.

Printed Works

The Dutch Settlers Society of Albany Yearbook. 48 vols. Albany: the society, 1925–83.

Wilcoxen, Charlotte. *Seventeenth Century Albany: A Dutch Profile.* Albany: Albany Institute, 1981.

Records of the Dutch Reformed Church of Albany, New York 1683–1809 as Excerpted from Year Books of the Holland Society of New York. 1904–27. Reprint. Baltimore: Genealogical Publishing Co., 1978.

RELIGIOUS SOCIETIES

THE HUGUENOT SOCIETY OF AMERICA

122 E. 58th St.
New York, NY 10022

This group was founded in 1883 in New York City for male and female lineal descendants of Huguenot families that immigrated to America before the Edict of Toleration of 28 November 1787.

Printed Works

Collections of the Huguenot Society of America—Registers of the Births, Marriages and Deaths of the Eglise Francois a la Nouvelle York, From 1688 to 1804. Vol. 1 only. New York: the society, 1886.

THE HUGUENOT SOCIETY OF SOUTH CAROLINA

138 Logan St.
Charleston, SC 29401

This organization was founded in 1885 in Charleston, South Carolina, for male and female lineal descendants of Huguenot families that immigrated to America before the Edict of Toleration of 28 November 1787.

Printed Works

DuBose, S., and F. Porcher. *History of the Huguenots of South Carolina.* N.p., 1887.

Transactions of the Huguenot Society of South Carolina. 87 vols. Columbia: the society, 1889–1982.

THE HUGUENOT SOCIETY OF THE FOUNDERS OF MANAKIN IN THE COLONY OF VIRGINIA

4414 Alta Vista Ln.
Dallas, TX 75229-2915

This group was founded in 1922 for male and female lineal descendants of any pre-1786 Huguenot resident of Virginia. Associate membership is provided for descendants from Huguenots who resided outside of Virginia.

Printed Works

R.A. Brock. *Documents, History and Family Genealogy Relating to the Huguenot Emigration to Virginia and to the Settlement of Manakin Town, With an Appendix of Genealogy.* 1886. Reprint. Baltimore: Genealogical Publishing Co., 1979.

The Huguenot. 21 vols. The society, 1924–66.

NATIONAL HUGUENOT SOCIETY

Arthur L. Finnell, Registrar General
9033 Lyndale Ave. S., Suite 108
Bloomington, MN 55420

This group was organized in 1951 as a federation of state societies. In 1983 there were forty-two state society organizations, including the District of Columbia. Individual applicants join a local state society and automatically become a member of the national society.

Printed Works

Stapleton, Rev. Ammon. *Memorials of the Huguenots in America.* Carlisle, Penn: Huguenot Publishing Co., 1901.

Baird, Charles W. *History of the Huguenot Emigration to America.* 2 vols. 1885. Reprint. Baltimore: Regional Publishing Co., 1966.

Forbes, Allan, and Paul F. Cadman. *Boston and Some Noted Emigrés.* Boston: State Street Trust Company, 1938.

NATIONAL SOCIETY DESCENDANTS OF EARLY QUAKERS

Heather Hills Farm
Route 3, P.O. Box 51
Harmony, WV 25243

ROYAL AND BARONIAL SOCIETIES

All of the societies in this grouping, listed by date of founding, require the applicant to trace the ancestry of an immigrant ancestor to his or her native country until noble or royal ancestry is reached. Establishing the proper "gateway" ancestor is the major problem for most applicants. The first two volumes listed below are of great assistance in locating such ancestors. They are the only editions with acceptable proof for the various royal and baronial lineage societies. While the majority of the *Ancestral Roots* ancestry is of the New England area, nearly half of *The Magna Charta* lines are Virginian. *The Complete Peerage* is the most acceptable proof for all peerage lines.

Cokayne, George E., ed. *The Complete Peerage.* 13 vols. London, 1910–59.

Weis, Frederick Lewis. *Ancestral Roots of Sixty Colonists Who Came to New England Between 1623 and 1650. The Lineage of Alfred the Great, Charlemagne, Malcolm of Scotland, Robert the Strong and Some of Their Descendants.* 5th ed., with additions and corrections by Walter Lee Sheppard, Jr. Baltimore: Genealogical Publishing Co., 1976.

———, and Arthur Adams. *The Magna Charta Sureties, 1215: The Barons Named in the Magna Charta 1215 and Some of Their Descendants Who Settled in America 1607–1650.* 3rd

ed., with additions and corrections by Walter Lee Sheppard, Jr. Baltimore: Genealogical Publishing Co., 1979.

ORDER OF THE CROWN IN AMERICA

This society was founded in 1898 as an order for men and women of proven royal descent, with the stipulation that ladies be members in good standing of either the Colonial Dames of America or the National Society of Colonial Dames of America. Membership is limited and by invitation only.

Printed Works

The History, Constitution and Officers of the Order of the Crown in America. The order, 1902, 1917, 1927.

Order of the Crown in America Membership Roster. The order, 1962, 1968, 1971, 1975, 1981, 1986, 1991.

THE BARONIAL ORDER OF MAGNA CHARTA

625 S. Bethlehem Pike
Ambler, PA 19002

This society was founded in 1898 for male lineal descendants of the earls and barons who were elected to be the sureties of the Magna Charta shortly after 19 June 1215. Membership is by invitation only.

Printed Works

Bye, Arthur Edwin. *Magna Charta, King John and The Barons.* Bridgeport, Penn: Chancellor Press, 1967.

Weis, Frederick Lewis, and Arthur Adams. *The Magna Charta Sureties 1215.* 3rd ed., with additions and corrections by Walter Lee Sheppard, Jr. Baltimore: Genealogical Publishing Co., 1979.

THE NATIONAL SOCIETY OF AMERICANS OF ROYAL DESCENT

108 N. St.
Roxbury, CT 06783

This group was founded in 1908 for men and women of proven royal descent. An applicant must be a member of a recognized lineage society of the colonial period, and a female applicant must be a member of either the National Society of the Colonial Dames of America or of the Colonial Dames of America. Applicants also need to be known by at least one member of the group's executive council and be proposed and seconded in writing. Membership is by invitation only.

Printed Works

National Society of Americans of Royal Descent—History, Membership Roster, Constitution and By-Laws. The society, 1960, 1965, 1968, 1971, 1974, 1977, 1980, 1983, 1989.

NATIONAL SOCIETY OF MAGNA CHARTA DAMES

P.O. Box 4222
Philadelphia, PA 19144

The society was founded in 1909 for female descendants of the Magna Charta Sureties of 1215. Membership is by invitation of the council, following proposal by a present member.

Printed Works

Wurts, John S. *Magna Charta*. 8 vols. Philadelphia: the author, 1942.

THE NATIONAL SOCIETY OF DAUGHTERS OF THE BARONS OF RUNNEMEDE

This group was organized in 1921 for women of lineal descent from one or more of the barons who served as sureties of the Magna Charta in 1215. Membership is by invitation only, following proposal by a present member.

Printed Works

National Society Daughters of the Barons of Runnemede— Organization, History and Membership—With Full-Color Arms of the Barons. Athens, Ga.: McGregor Co., 1937. Contains biographical sketches of the "gateway" ancestors of the members and sketches of the founders of the society.

THE MILITARY ORDER OF THE CRUSADES

104 Bladdyn Rd.
Ardmore, PA 19003

The Military Order of the Crusades was founded in 1934 for men of lineal descent from one or more crusaders of the rank of knight or higher who participated in the Crusades, 1096 to 1291. Membership is by invitation only.

Manuscript Documents in Possession of the Order

Perot, William Hannis. List of Crusaders Used as Qualifying Ancestors by the Order to 7 June 1977.

History, Constitution and By-Laws. The order, 1960.

ORDER OF THREE CRUSADES 1096–1192

P.O. Box 6127
Charlottesville, VA 22906

This order was founded in 1936 for men and women of lineal descent from a participant in one of the first three crusades, 1096 to 1192. A pilgrimage to Jerusalem as a religious gesture was not a crusade and is not acceptable. Membership is by invitation only, and applicants must be sponsored by two members and be known to at least one officer of the order.

Printed Works

Order of Three Crusades 1096–1192—History, Constitution and By-Laws, Membership Roster. 4 vols. The order, 1965, 1970, 1976, 1983.

ORDER OF THE CROWN OF CHARLEMAGNE IN THE UNITED STATES OF AMERICA

108 North St.
Roxbury, CT 06783

This society was founded in 1939 for men and women of lineal descent from the Emperor Charlemagne. Membership is by invitation only.

Printed Works

Von Redlich, Marcellus Donald R. *Pedigrees of Some of the Emperor Charlemagne's Descendants.* Vol. 1. West Somerville, Mass: Somerville Printing Co., 1942.

Langston, Aileen Lewers, and J. Orton Buck, Jr., comps. *Pedigrees of Some of the Emperor Charlemagne's Descendants.* Vol. 2. Cottonport, La: Polyanthos, 1974.

Buch, J. Orton, and Timothy Field Beard. *Pedigrees of Some of the Emperor Charlemagne's Descendants.* Vol. 3. Nashville: Ambrose Printing Co., 1978.

DESCENDANTS OF THE ILLEGITIMATE SONS AND DAUGHTERS OF THE KINGS OF BRITAIN

3858 N. Leavitt Ave.
Chicago, IL 60618

This group was founded in 1950 by four fellows of the American Society of Genealogists to improve scholarship and research on all "royal lineages." Membership is open to men and women who can prove their descent, in any line, from the illegitimate son, daughter, grandson, or granddaughter of a king or queen of England, Scotland, or Wales.

A manuscript titled "Royal Bastards From the Time of the Norman Conquest—the Constitution, Annual Reports, Lineages of Descents of Members, Etc." is provided to members in looseleaf form, to be added to three-ring binders as new members join. Approximately two hundred lineages have been approved.

Printed Works

Sheppard, Walter Lee, Jr. "Descendants of the Illegitimate Sons and Daughters of the Kings of Britain." *National Genealogical Society Quarterly* 62 (September 1974): 182–91.

GUILD OF ST. MARGARET OF SCOTLAND

1047 Baseline Rd.
Claremont, CA 91711

The guild was founded in 1975 for descendants of St. Margaret of Scotland; or of an early king or queen of England, Ireland, Scotland, or Wales; or of an ancestor who lived in the British Isles before 1600.

FAMILY SOCIETIES AND ORGANIZATIONS

The proliferation of family societies in the past five years makes it impossible to list all of them in this relatively brief chapter. Many family groups publish extensive family genealogies, newsletters, and bulletins. They also hold family reunions throughout the United States. Sources for information on these family associations include:

Bentley, Elizabeth Petty. *Directory of Family Associations.* Published biannually by Genealogical Publishing Co., 1001 N. Calvert St., Baltimore, MD 21202-3897. Lists addresses, telephone numbers, contact persons and publications of family associations, reunion committees, one-name societies, surname exchanges, and family newsletters.

The Connecticut Nutmegger. Published quarterly by the Connecticut Society of Genealogists, P.O. Box 435, 2906 Main St., Glastonbury, CT 06033. Contains lists of family reunions, clan societies, and family histories, as well as Connecticut vital records. Annual dues and subscriptions are $20.

Newsletter of the International Society for British Genealogy and Family History. Contains listings of family reunions in the United States and in England. The annual fee is $10. The address is P.O. Box 20425, Cleveland, OH 44120.

The National Genealogical Society Newsletter. Published six times a year, the newsletter has a column, "About Families," which covers reunions and publications. The annual membership of $30 includes the excellent *National Genealogical Society Quarterly Magazine.* The mailing address is 4527 17th St. N., Arlington, VA 22207-2363.

LOCATION OF LINEAGE SOCIETY SOURCE MATERIAL

Hereditary Society Blue Book. Edited by Robert R. Davenport. Eastwood Publishing Co., 1995. This annual register of hereditary and lineage societies includes data about founding, insignia, membership requirements, and national address. An extensive "who's who" section is devoted to lineage society leaders.

SUGGESTIONS FOR THE SERIOUS LINEAGE SOCIETY RESEARCHER

Many professional genealogists specialize in preparing lineage papers for their clients. Those certified by the Board for Certification of Genealogists may place the initials C.A.L.S. (Certified American Lineage Specialist) after their names.

A list of certified genealogists throughout the United States is available from the Board for Certification of Genealogists. For a copy, send $3 and a no. 10 self-addressed, stamped envelope with postage for three ounces of first-class mail to P.O. Box 14291, Washington, DC 20044.

A certified American lineage specialist should be familiar with the requirements for membership in all of the major hereditary societies and the format for documenting applications for each society. Individuals make application for membership in the society and receive the worksheets and application forms. The genealogist should never ask for application blanks for a client.

Documentation is frequently misunderstood. The listing of a volume with pertinent page numbers is not sufficient for most societies. Photocopies of all proofs should accompany the application. This will speed up approval by the society's verifying genealogist, who often resides far from a major library and depends entirely on the material submitted. All original copies of vital records, family Bible records, and personal documents should be retained by the applicant. Photocopies from published volumes should include the title page—especially when submitting family Bible records. The page showing the year the Bible was published is vital to establish the fact that the entries were made at that time period.

Never hand-letter applications, no matter how legibly. All applications should be typed or printed. When two copies are required, both should be original copies.

CONTRIBUTORS

Robert Charles Anderson, a native of Bellows Falls, Vermont, now resides in Derry, New Hampshire. He received a B.A. in biochemical sciences from Harvard College in 1971, an M.S. in biology from the California Institute of Technology in 1973, and an M.A. in history from the University of Massachusetts/ Amherst in 1983. He is a certified genealogist and a fellow of the American Society of Genealogists, and he was president of the latter organization from 1989 to 1992. He is also a trustee of the Board for Certification of Genealogists. Bob is currently coeditor of The American Genealogist and director of the New England Historic Genealogical Society's Great Migration Study Project.

Lloyd DeWitt Bockstruck, supervisor of the Genealogy Section of the Dallas [Texas] Public Library, has been on the faculty of the Institute of Genealogy and Historical Research at Samford University in Birmingham, Alabama, since 1974. He is the author of the weekly column "Family Tree" in *The Dallas Morning News.* Author of *Virginia's Colonial Soldiers* and *Revolutionary War Bounty Land Grants Awarded by State Governments,* he has a keen interest in colonial American genealogy, Southside Virginia, and German Ancestry. He was the recipient of the Award of Merit from the National Genealogical Society in 1983 and was named a fellow of the society in 1992. He holds an A.B. *cum laude* in biology from Greenville College, an M.A. in European History from Southern Illinois University, an M.S. in library science from the University of Illinois, and a certificate from the Institute of Genealogy and Historical Research.

Johni Cerny, BS, FUGA, is the founder and president of Lineages, Inc. She received a bachelor of science degree in 1969 from Brigham Young University with majors in social work and genealogical research. She was awarded an associate of arts degree in genealogical research technology from BYU in 1968. Honored by the Utah Genealogical Society, she was made a fellow in 1968. With Arlene Eakle, she edited and authored the first edition of *The Source: A Guidebook of American Genealogy* (1984), and with Wendy Elliott she edited and authored *The Library: A Guide to the LDS Family History Library* (1986). She specializes in tracing the origins and ancestry of German immigrants to the United States and in Pennsylvania-German research, and she compiles the German Emigration Index, a database of German immigrants to the United States whose origins have been documented. She has been engaged in ge-

nealogical research for more than thirty years; in a professional capacity, since 1979.

Richard W. Dougherty holds a Ph.D. in history from the University of Wisconsin-Madison. A Fulbright Scholar at the University of Bonn, Germany, his area of research specialization is tracing immigrant ancestors from Germany and Central Europe. Accredited in German research by the LDS Family History Department, he is also a member of the Concordia Historical Institute, the National Genealogical Society, the Utah Genealogical Association, and the Association of Professional Genealogists. He is the author of chapters on American, German, and central European collections in *The Library: A Guide to the Family History Library,* as well as journal articles and book reviews. Forthcoming projects include a chapter on church records for *The Printed Source: A Guide to Secondary Sources in American Genealogy.*

Arlene H. Eakle, Ph.D., is a professional genealogist with more than twenty-five years of experience and is the owner of The Genealogical Institute. She is an expert in Scots-Irish, Native American, and Southern research, with a ninety-six-percent success rate. She gives one-on-one personalized consultations and has lectured at more than three hundred seminars throughout the United States, Canada, and Europe. Eakle has authored or contributed to more than seventy-five publications, including the first edition of *The Source: A Guidebook of American Genealogy,* and is the author of a four-star video series. She is the first American ever to receive the prestigious Julian Bickersteth Memorial Medal from Canterbury, England.

James L. Hansen, FASG, has been the reference librarian and genealogical specialist at the Library of the State Historical Society of Wisconsin since 1974. He has authored articles on a variety of genealogical topics, a bibliography of territorial Wisconsin newspapers, and a guide to the library in which he works. He has taught beginning and advanced genealogical research courses over Wisconsin's Educational Telephone Network, and is a nationally-known speaker, having lectured on genealogical topics in Wisconsin and around the United States, at the National Institute on Genealogical Research at the National Archives, and at numerous national conferences in the United States and Canada. He was the 1994-95 president of the Association of Professional Genealogists and is a fellow of the American Society of Genealogists.

Kathleen W. Hinckley, CGRS, is owner and operator of Discover Your Roots, a genealogical research firm for family history research throughout the United States. She specializes in twentieth-century research, including adoption and probate. She has served on the boards of trustees for the Board for Certification of Genealogists (1989-95), the Association of Professional Genealogists (1988-93), the Genealogical Speakers Guild (1992-93), and the Federation of Genealogical Societies (1986-88). She is currently executive secretary for the Association of Professional Genealogists and is a senior member of the Professional Private Investigators Association of Colorado.

Sandra Hargreaves Luebking is a professional genealogical and historical researcher. She has a BA degree in anthropology from the University of Illinois at Chicago and has completed graduate course work in history and communications at the University of Illinois at Springfield. She has been a lecturer at the Institute of Genealogy and Historical Research at Samford University since 1979. In 1990 she became the Course 1 coordinator. She is also the intermediate studies coordinator for the Genealogical Institute of Mid-America at the University of Illinois at Springfield; she has held that position since the establishment of the institute in 1994. She is the editor of *Forum,* the national quarterly magazine of the Federation of Genealogical Societies (FGS); *Carolyn Kuhn Royer: A Memoir;* and coeditor of *The Archives: A Guide to the National Archives Field Branches.* The last received a National Genealogical Society "Award for Excellence in Genealogical Methods and Sources." Recent honors are the David S. Vogels Jr. Award (1992) for career contributions to FGS; she was made a fellow of the Utah Genealogical Association (1993); and received the Outstanding IGHR Alumni Award from Samford University (1995).

Kory L. Meyerink, AG, MLS, has been a professional genealogist since 1978. Currently he develops family history products for Infobases, an electronic text publisher. Formerly the Publications Coordinator for the Family History Library, he was responsible for the creation and publication of the library's instructional material. Accredited since 1980 (Germany and Midwest, eastern, and New England United States), he ran a successful free-lance research business, specializing in immigrant origins research, until joining the library staff as a reference consultant in 1986. Kory has served as trustee and executive secretary of the Association of Professional Genealogists and has held many offices in the Utah Society, Sons of the American Revolution. He also belongs to the National Genealogical Society and the Council of Genealogy Columnists, and is currently the president of the Utah Genealogical Association. He completed his masters degree in Library and Information Science at Brigham Young University in 1990 and now teaches genealogy for that university through its Salt Lake Center, as well as on campus at an annual Genealogy and Family History Seminar.

Gary Mokotoff is a leader in the field of Jewish-American genealogy. He is publisher of *Avotaynu,* a magazine of Jewish genealogy; past president of the Association of Jewish Genealogical Societies; and is on the board of directors of JewishGen. He is author of a number of books, including the award-winning *Where Once We Walked,* a gazetteer of Central and Eastern European communities, and *How to Document Victims and Locate Survivors of the Holocaust.* Mokotoff is also known for his application of computer technology to Jewish genealogy—

endeavors which include his coauthorship of the Daitch-Mokotoff Soundex code, the Consolidated Jewish Surname Index, the Jewish Genealogical Family Finder, and the Jewish Genealogical People Finder. He is currently on the board of directors of the Federation of Genealogical Societies and is a member of the Association of Professional Genealogists and Genealogical Speakers Guild.

George J. Nixon is a native of Grants Pass, Oregon. He has been a professional genealogist and native of Salt Lake City since 1976. He has a degree in history from the University of California, Los Angeles. He specializes in Native American research, probate research, and heir tracing. He is a contributing author to *Native American Genealogical Source Book* (Gale Research Co., 1995) and is currently at work on an in-depth Native American methodology book.

Gordon L. Remington, FUGA, a native of Rochester, New York, is a professional genealogist who resides in Salt Lake City. A member of the Association of Professional Genealogists since 1979, he has served three terms on its board and in numerous other capacities. He has also served twice as president of the Professional Chapter of the Utah Genealogical Association, has served on the association's board, and has served as editor of the association's *Genealogical Journal* (1988-93). He is a contributing editor of *The National Genealogical Society Quarterly* and has published articles in *The American Genealogist, The New England Historical and Genealogical Register,* and *The New York Genealogical and Biographical Record,* as well as other national and regional periodicals. In 1992 he was named a fellow of the Utah Genealogical Association.

George R. Ryskamp, JD, AG, is an attorney, author, and accredited genealogist. In 1993, after fifteen years of legal practice in southern California, he joined the History Department of Brigham Young University in Provo, Utah, where he teaches Latin American and southern European family history and the use of American legal documents and concepts in family history. He has researched, lectured, and taught university-level classes in family history throughout the United States and in Spain, Portugal, France, and Mexico. In addition to three books on Hispanic family history research, he has published articles in *National Genealogical Society Quarterly, Brigham Young University Law Review, Spanish American Genealogist,* and *Genealogical Journal of the Society for Hispanic Historical and Ancestral Research.*

Grahame Thomas Smallwood, Jr., is a retired Certified American Lineage Specialist. He was educated in Europe and now lives in Potomac, Maryland. A specialist in preparing lineage papers for hereditary societies, he is himself a member of sixty societies, including the Order of the Founders and Patriots of America (governor-general, 1968-72), Order of Descendants of Colonial Governors (governor-general, 1963-67), National Society Americans of Royal Descent (president-general, 1971-73), Order of Americans of Armorial Ancestry (national president, 1973-76), Baronial Order of Magna Carta (marshal, 1974-76), Military Order of the Crusades (commander-general, 1977-78), Order of the Crown of Charlemagne (president-general, 1987-89), National Society Sons and Daughters of the Pilgrims (governor-general, 1989-91), and Order of the First Families of Rhode Island and Providence Plantations (governor-general, 1995-97). He was the first recipient of the Grahame Thomas Smallwood, Jr. Award of the Association of Professional Genealogists.

Loretto Kathryn Dennis Szucs—"Lou"—holds a B.A. degree in history from Saint Joseph's College in Indiana and has been involved in genealogical research, teaching, lecturing, and publishing for more than twenty-five years. Previously employed as an archives specialist for the National Archives, she is currently managing editor for Ancestry Incorporated. She has served on the Illinois State Archives Advisory Board and on the governing boards of the Chicago Genealogical Society, the South Suburban Genealogical and Historical Society (Illinois), and the Illinois State Genealogical Society. Lou was the founding secretary for the Federation of Genealogical Societies and has held various positions in that organization, including editor of the FGS *Forum.* She is the author of several publications, including *Chicago and Cook County Sources: A Genealogical and Historical Guide;* with Sandra Luebking, she co-authored *The Archives: A Guide to the National Archives Field Branches.* Honors Lou has received include a 1984 citation for the Archivist of the United States for her work to establish the volunteer program at the National Archives' Chicago Regional Archives Branch; a 1987 National Genealogical Society Award of Merit for *Chicago and Cook County Sources;* the 1990 David S. Vogels, Jr., Award for outstanding contributions to the Federation of Genealogical Societies; the 1991 Award for Excellence in Genealogical Methods and Sources from the National Genealogical Society; a 1992 Special Award from the Illinois Genealogical Society; and in 1995 she became a fellow of the Utah Genealogical Association.

David T. Thackery has been curator of Local and Family History at the Newberry Library in Chicago since 1983, where he is responsible for collection development and reference services in genealogy. His writing has been published in a variety of genealogical publications, including *Ancestry Magazine.* He has published a bibliography of African-American family history for the Newberry Library and was co-compiler of an authoritative union list and bibliography of Illinois county land ownership maps and atlases. Thackery has written about various Civil War topics and is currently writing the history of a local regiment from his hometown in Ohio. He holds a bachelor's degree from Ohio's Wittenberg University and two master's degrees from the University of Chicago.

Curt B. Witcher is the manager of the Historical Genealogy Department of the Allen County Library in Fort Wayne, Indiana. He is an active member of the American Library Association, a member of the National Genealogical Society's governing council, and is the president of the Federation of Genealogical Societies. He also serves as the national data input coordinator for the Civil War Soldiers System Names Index Project. He was the founding president of the Indiana Genealogical Society, is an adjunct professor in Indiana University's Continuing Education Program, and is a genealogical instructor and lecturer. Witcher is coeditor of the *Periodical Source Index,* serves on the advisory board of the Passenger and Immigration Index Project for Gale Research, Inc., and is a research consultant for the PBS television series "Ancestors." He was distinguished in 1995 as a fellow of the Utah Genealogical Association (FUGA).

APPENDIX A

National Archives and Records Administration Regional Archives System

The regional archives listed below, except for the Pittsfield Region, receive the permanently valuable, noncurrent records of federal courts and agencies in the areas they serve. All regional archives have extensive holdings of National Archives microfilm publications.

National Archives—New England Region

380 Trapelo Rd.
Waltham, MA 02154
617-647-8100

Covers Connecticut, Maine, Massachusetts, New Hampshire, Rhode Island, and Vermont

National Archives—Pittsfield Region

100 Dan Fox Dr.
Pittsfield, MA 01201
413-443-8458

Has no original records, only microfilmed records relating to genealogy

National Archives—Northeast Region

201 Varick St.
New York, NY 10014
212-337-1300

Covers New York, New Jersey, Puerto Rico, and the Virgin Islands

National Archives—Mid-Atlantic Region

9th & Market Streets, Room 1350
Philadelphia, PA 19107
215-597-3000

Covers Delaware, Maryland, Pennsylvania, Virginia, and West Virginia

National Archives—Southeast Region

1557 St. Joseph Ave.
East Point, GA 30344
404-763-7477

Covers Alabama, Florida, Georgia, Kentucky, Mississippi, North Carolina, South Carolina, and Tennessee

National Archives—Great Lakes Region

7358 S. Pulaski Rd.
Chicago, IL 60629
312-581-7816

Covers Illinois, Indiana, Michigan, Minnesota, Ohio, and Wisconsin

National Archives—Central Plains Region

2312 E. Bannister Rd.
Kansas City, MO 64131
816-926-6272

Covers Iowa, Kansas, Missouri, and Nebraska

National Archives—Southwest Region

501 W. Felix St., P.O. Box 6216
Fort Worth, TX 76115
817-334-5525

Covers Arkansas, Louisiana, New Mexico, Oklahoma, and Texas

National Archives—Rocky Mountain Region

Building 48, Denver Federal Center
P.O. Box 25307
Denver, CO 80225
303-236-0817

Covers Colorado, Montana, North Dakota, South Dakota, Utah, and Wyoming

National Archives—Pacific Southwest Region

24000 Avila Rd.
P.O. Box 6719
Laguna Niguel, CA 92677-6719
714-643-4241

Covers Arizona, southern California, and Clark County, Nevada

National Archives—Pacific Sierra Region

1000 Commodore Dr.
San Bruno, CA 94066
415-876-9009

Covers California except southern California, Hawaii, Nevada except Clark County, American Samoa, and Guam

National Archives—Pacific Northwest Region

6125 Sand Point Way N.E.
Seattle, WA 98115
206-526-6507

Covers Idaho, Oregon, and Washington

National Archives—Alaska Region

654 W. 3rd Ave.
Anchorage, AL 99501
907-271-2441

Covers Alaska

APPENDIX B

State Archives

compiled by Linda S. McCleary, MLS
Public Library Development Consultant
Library Extension Division
Department of Library, Archives and Public Records
Phoenix, Arizona

For additional information regarding the full holdings and unique collections within each archive division, contact the state you are researching.

Alabama Department of Archives and History

624 Washington Ave.
Montgomery, AL 36130
(205) 242-4441
Fax: (205) 240-3433

Alaska State Archives and Records Management Services

141 Willoughby Ave.
Juneau, AK 99802-1720
(907) 465-2275
Fax: (907) 465-2465

Arizona State Archives

Department of Library, Archives and Public Records
1700 W. Washington St.
Phoenix, AZ 85007
(602) 542-4159
Fax: (602) 542-4402

Arkansas History Commission

One Capitol Mall
Little Rock, AR 72201
(501) 682-6900

California State Archives

201 N. Sunrise Ave.
Sacramento, CA 95561
(916) 773-3000
Fax: (916) 773-8249

Colorado Department of Administration

Division of State Archives and Public Records
1313 Sherman St., I-B20
Denver, CO 80203
(303) 866-2055
Fax: (303) 866-2257

Connecticut State Archives

Connecticut State Library
231 Capitol Ave.
Hartford, CT 06106
(203) 566-5650
Fax: (203) 566-2133

Delaware Bureau of Archives and Records Management

Hall of Records
Dover, DE 19901
(302) 739-5318
Fax: (302) 739-6711

Florida State Archives

R. A. Gray Building (M.S. 9A)
Tallahassee, FL 32399-0250
(904) 487-2073
Fax: (904) 488-4894

Georgia Department of Archives and History

Box RPM
330 Capitol Ave., S.E.
Atlanta, GA 30334
(404) 656-5486
Fax: (404) 656-2940

Hawaii State Archives

Iolani Palace Grounds
Honolulu, Hawaii 96813
(808) 586-0310
Fax: (808) 586-0330

Idaho Library and Archives

210 Main St.
Boise, ID 83702

(208) 334-3890
Fax: (208) 334-3198

Illinois State Archives

Archives Building
Springfield, IL 62756
(217) 782-4682
Fax (217) 524-3930

Indiana State Archives

Commission on Public Records
State Office Bldg., Rm. W472
Indianapolis, IN 46204-2215
(317) 232-3373
Fax: (317) 232-3154

State Archives of Iowa

State Historical Society of Iowa
Capitol Complex
600 E. Locust
Des Moines, IA 50319
(515) 281-8837
Fax: (515) 282-0502

Kansas State Historical Society

120 W. Tenth St.
Topeka, KS 66612-1291
(913) 296-3251
Fax: (913) 296-1005

Kentucky Dept. for Lib/Arch.

Public Records Division
Archives Research Room
P.O. Box 537
Frankfort, KY 40602-0537
(502) 875-7000 Ext. 173
Fax: (502) 564-5773

State of Louisiana

Secretary of State
Division of Archives, Records Management, and
History
P.O. Box 94125
Baton Rouge, LA 70804-9125
(504) 922-1206
Fax: (504) 925-4726

Maine State Archives

Capitol—Station House 84
Augusta, ME 04333-0084
(207) 289-5790
Fax: (207) 289-8598

Maryland State Archives

350 Rowe Blvd.
Annapolis, MD 21401
(301) 974-3915

Massachusetts Archives

Office of Secretary of State
Boston, MA 02125
(617) 727-2816
Fax: (617) 727-2826

Michigan State History Bureau

State Archives
Lansing, MI 48906
(517) 373-1401
Fax: (517) 373-0851

Minnesota Historical Society

345 Kellogg Blvd. W.
St. Paul, MN 55102-1906
(612) 297-4502
Fax: (612) 296-9961

Mississippi Department of Archives and History

100 S. State St.
Jackson, MS 39205-0571
(601) 359-6850
Fax: (601) 359-6905

Missouri State Archives

600 W. Main St.
Jefferson City, MO 65102
(314) 751-4717

Montana Historical Society

Division of Library and Archives
225 N. Roberts St.
Helena, MT 59620
(406) 444-4775
Fax: (406) 444-2696

Nebraska State Historical Soc.

1500 R St.
Box 82554
Lincoln, NE 68501
(402) 471-4785
Fax: (402) 471-3100

Nevada State Library and Archives

100 Stewart Street
Carson City, NV 89710
(702) 687-5210

New Hampshire State Archives

71 S. Fruit St.
Concord, NH 03301-2410
(603) 271-2236
Fax: (603) 271-2272

New Jersey State Archives

CN 307, 2300 Stuyvesant Ave.
Trenton, NJ 08625
(609) 530-3203
Fax: (609) 530-6121

New Mexico Commission of Public Records

New Mexico Records and Archives
404 Montezuma Ave.
Santa Fe, NM 87503
(505) 827-7332
Fax: (505) 827-7331

New York State Archives

State Education Department
Albany, NY 12230
(518) 474-1195

North Carolina State Archives

Department of Cultural Resource
109 E. Jones St.
Raleigh, NC 27601-2807
(919) 733-7305
Fax: (919) 733-5679

North Dakota State Archives and Historical Research Library

612 E. Blvd. Ave.
Bismarck, ND 58505-0830
(701) 224-2668
Fax: (701) 224-3000

Ohio Historical Society

Archives/Library Division
1982 Velma Ave.
Columbus, OH 43211-2497
(614) 297-2510
Fax: (614) 297-2411

Oklahoma Department of Libraries

200 North East Eighteenth St.
Oklahoma City, OK 73105-3298
(405) 521-2502
WATS 1-800-522-8116
Fax: (405) 525-7804

Oregon Secretary of State

Archives Division
800 Summer N.E.
Salem, OR 97310
(503) 373-0701
Fax: (503) 373-0659

Pennsylvania State Archives

P.O. Box 1026
Harrisburg, PA 17108-1026
(717) 787-2891

Rhode Island State Archives

337 Westminister St.
Providence, RI 02903-3302
(401) 277-2353
Fax: (401) 277-3199

South Carolina Department of Archives and History

1430 Senate St.
Columbia, SC 29211
(803) 734-8577
Fax: (803) 734-8820

South Dakota Historical Society/State Archives

900 Governors Dr.
Pierre, SD 57501-2217
(605) 773-3458
Fax: (605) 773-6041

Tennessee State Library and Archives

403 Seventh Ave. N.
Nashville, TN 37219-1411
(615) 741-7996
Fax: (615) 741-6471

Texas State Archives Division

Lorenzo de Zavala State Archives and Library Building
P.O. Box 12927
Austin, TX 78711-2927
(512) 463-5480
Fax: (512) 463-5436

Utah State Archives and Records Service

Archives Building, State Capitol
Salt Lake City, UT 84114
(801) 538-3012
Fax: (801) 538-3354

State of Vermont Archives

Secretary of State's Office
26 Terrace Street
Montpelier, VT 05633-1103
(802) 828-2369
Fax: (802) 828-2496

Commonwealth of Virginia

Virginia State Library and Archives
11th St. at Capitol Square
Richmond, VA 23219-3491
(804) 786-2332
Fax: (804) 786-5855

Washington Secretary of State Office

Division of Archives and Records Management
1120 Wash St., S.E.
P.O. Box 40238
Olympia, WA 98504-0238
(206) 753-5485
Fax: (206) 586-5629

West Virginia Archives

Division on Culture and History
1900 Kanawha Blvd. E.
Charleston, WV 25305-0300
(304) 558-0230
Fax: (304) 558-2779

The State Historical Society of Wisconsin

816 State St.
Madison, WI 53706-1488
(608) 264-6480
Fax: (608) 264-6472
Wyoming Archives

Parks and Cultural Resources Division

Barrett Building
Cheyenne, WY 82002
(307) 777-7013
Fax: (307) 777-6289

APPENDIX C

Historical Societies

Alabama Historical Association

P.O. Box 2877
Tuscaloosa, AL 35486

Alaska Historical Library and Museum

P.O. Box G
Eighth Floor, State Office Building
Juneau, AK 99811
Phone: (907) 465-2925

Alaska Historical Society

524 W. Fourth Ave., Suite 208
Anchorage, AK 99501

Arizona Historical Society

Century House Museum
240 Madison Ave.
Yuma, AZ 85364
Phone: (602) 782-1841

Arkansas Historical Association

History Department
Ozark Hall, 12, University of Arkansas
Fayetteville, AR 72701
Phone: (501) 575-5884

Arkansas Historical Society

422 S. Sixth St.
Van Buren, AR 72956

Arkansas History Commission

1 Capitol Mall
Little Rock, AR 72201
Phone: (501) 682-6900

California Historical Society

2090 Jackson St.
San Francisco, CA 94109

Colorado Historical Society

Stephen H. Hart Library
1300 Broadway
Denver, CO 80203
Phone: (303) 866-2305

Connecticut Historical Commission

59 S. Prospect St.
Hartford, CT 06106

Connecticut Historical Society

1 Elizabeth St. at Asylum Ave.
Hartford, CT 06105
Phone: (203) 236-5621

Connecticut League of Historical Societies

P.O. Box 906
Darien, CT 06820

Historical Society of Delaware

Town Hall
505 Market St.
Wilmington, DE 19801
Phone: (302) 655-7161

Florida Historical Society

P.O. Box 3645, University Station
Gainesville, FL 32601

Georgia Historical Society

501 Whittaker St.
Savannah, GA 31499
Phone: (912) 651-2128

Hawaiian Historical Society

560 Kawaiahao St.
Honolulu, HI 96813
Phone: (808) 537-6271

Idaho Historical Society

610 N. Julia Davis Dr.
Boise, ID 83706
Phone: (208) 384-2120
        (208) 334-3356

Illinois State Historical Library

Old State Capitol
Springfield, IL 62701
Phone: (217) 782-4836

Indiana Historical Society

State Library and Historical Building
Family History Section
315 W. Ohio St.
P.O. Box 88255
Indianapolis, IN 46202
Phone: (317) 232-1879

State Historical Society of Iowa

Library/Archives Bureau
State of Iowa Historical Building
600 E. Locust
Des Moines, IA 50319
Phone: (515) 281-5111

State Historical Society of Iowa

Library/Archives Bureau
Centennial Building
402 Iowa Avenue
Iowa City, IA 52240
Phone: (319) 335-3916

Kansas State Historical Society

Archives Division
Memorial Building
120 W. Tenth St.
Topeka, KS 66612
Phone: (913) 296-4776
        (913) 296-3251

Kentucky Historical Society

300 Broadway
Old Capitol Annex
P.O. Box H
Frankfort, KY 40602
Phone: (502) 564-3016

Louisiana Genealogical and Historical Society

P.O. Box 3454
Baton Rouge, LA 70821
Phone: (504) 343-2608

Maine Historical Society

485 Congress St.
Portland, ME 04111
Phone: (207) 774-1822

Maryland Historical Society

201 W. Monument St.
Baltimore, MD 21201
Phone: (301) 685-3750, ext. 359

Massachusetts Historical Society

1154 Boylston St.
Boston, MA 02215
Phone: (617) 536-1608

Historical Society of Michigan

2117 Washtenaw Ave.
Ann Arbor, MI 48104

Michigan Historical Commission

505 State Office Building
Lansing, MI 48913

Minnesota Historical Society

690 Cedar St.
Saint Paul, MN 55101
Phone: (612) 296-2143

Historical and Genealogical Association of Mississippi

618 Avalon Rd.
Jackson, MS 39206

Missouri Historical Society

Research Library and Archives
Jefferson Memorial Building
Forest Park
Saint Louis, MO 63112-1099
Phone: (314) 361-1424

State Historical Society of Missouri

1020 Lowry St.
Columbia, MO 65201
Phone: (314) 882-7083

Nebraska State Historical Society

State Archives Division
1500 R St.
P.O. Box 82554
Lincoln, NE 68501
Phone: (402) 471-4771
        (402) 471-4751

Nebraska State Historical Society Room

Chadron State College
Chadron State Library
Chadron, NE 69337

Nevada State Historical Society

1650 N. Virginia St.
Reno, NV 89503
Phone: (702) 789-0190

Nevada State Museum and Historical Society

700 Twin Lakes Dr.
Las Vegas, NV 89107
Phone: (702) 486-5205

Association of Historical Societies of New Hampshire

Maple St.
Plaistow, NH 03865

New Hampshire Historical Society

30 Park St.
Concord, NH 03301
Phone: (603) 225-3381

New Jersey Historical Society

230 Broadway
Newark, NJ 07104
Phone: (201) 483-3939

Historical Society of New Mexico

P.O. Box 4638
Santa Fe, NM 87501

History Library Museum of New Mexico

Palace of the Governors
Santa Fe, NM 87501

The New York Historical Society

170 Central Park W.
New York, NY 10024-5194
Phone: (212) 873-3400

North Carolina Society of County and Local Historians

1209 Hill St.
Greensboro, NC 27408

State Historical Society of North Dakota

State Archives and Historical Research Library
Heritage Center
612 E. Blvd. Ave.
Bismarck, ND 58505
Phone: (701) 224-2668—Division Office
(701) 224-2091—Reference Desk

Ohio Historical Society

Archives-Library Division
Interstate Route 71 and 17th Ave.
1985 Velma Ave.
Columbus, OH 43211
Phone: (614) 466-1500
(614) 297-2510
(614) 297-2300

Oklahoma Historical Society

Library Resources Division
Wiley Post Historical Building
2100 N. Lincoln Blvd.
Oklahoma City, OK 73105
Phone: (405) 521-2491

Oregon Historical Society

1230 S.W. Park Ave.
Portland, OR 97268
Phone: (503) 222-1741

Heritage Society of Pennsylvania

P.O. Box 146
Laughlintown, PA 15655

Historical Society of Pennsylvania

1300 Locust St.
Philadelphia, PA 19107
Phone: (215) 545-0391

Rhode Island State Historical Society

121 Hope St.
Providence, RI 02909
Phone: (401) 331-8575

South Carolina Historical Society

100 Meeting St.
Charleston, SC 29401
Phone: (803) 723-3225

South Dakota State Historical Society

South Dakota Archives
Cultural Heritage Center
900 Governors Dr.
Pierre, SD 57501
Phone: (605) 773-3804

Tennessee Historical Society

Ground Floor
War Memorial Building
300 Capital Blvd.
Nashville, TN 37243-0084
Phone: (615) 242-1796

Tennessee Historical Commission

Conservation Department
701 Broadway
Nashville, TN 37203
Phone: (615) 742-6717

Texas State Historical Association

2.306 SRH, University Station
Austin, TX 78712

Utah State Historical Society

300 Rio Grande
Salt Lake City, UT 84101
Phone: (801) 533-5808

Virginia Historical Society

428 N. Blvd.
P.O. Box 7311
Richmond, VA 23211
Phone: (804) 342-9677

Washington State Historical Society

Hewitt Library
State Historical Building
315 N. Stadium Way
Tacoma, WA 98403
Phone: (206) 593-2830

West Virginia Historical Society

Division of Archives and History
Department of Culture and History
Science and Cultural Center
Capitol Complex
Charleston, WV 25305
Phone: (304) 348-2277
        (304) 348-0230

The State Historical Society of Wisconsin

816 State St.
Madison, WI 53706
Phone: (608) 262-9590—Reference Librarian
        (608) 262-3338—Reference Archivist
        (608) 262-9580
        (608) 262-2781

Wyoming State Archives

Barrett Building
2301 Central Ave.
Cheyenne, WY 82002
Phone: (307) 777-7826

The Family History Library and Its Centers

compiled by Kory L. Meyerink

The Family History Library is the largest library in the world specializing in collecting genealogical or family history material. Sometimes called the "mecca" of genealogy, the Family History Library attracts many family historians who plan trips and vacation time to come to Salt Lake City, Utah, to use the worldwide collections housed in the library's five-story building.

Because of the scope of the library's collections, as well as the easy access provided by its thousands of branch libraries, it is useful for every family historian to know about the library. Its history dates back to 1894, when the Genealogical Society of Utah was founded to gather and preserve the various records that help people trace their ancestry. Shortly after its founding, the society opened a library which later became the Family History Library. In 1938, the society began preserving records on microfilm. Today, about 250 microfilm camera operators microfilm birth, marriage, death, probate, immigration, military, and many other records in more than fifty countries. Through this microfilming activity, as well as a carefully planned purchasing program, the library has acquired the world's largest collection of genealogical information.

Since 1944, the library (as well as the Genealogical Society of Utah) has been wholly owned and operated by The Church of Jesus Christ of Latter-day Saints. Also known as the LDS church or "Mormon" church, it teaches its members to "seek out their kindred dead" in preparation for the afterlife. However, while the library is maintained as a resource to LDS church members, all persons, regardless of race, creed, or religion, are welcome to visit the library and use its collections and services at no charge. In 1964, a system of branch libraries, now called family history centers, was established to give more people access to the library's resources. These are described further below.

The Family History Library is located at 35 North West Temple St., Salt Lake City, UT 84150 (telephone 801-240-2331). The library is open Monday through Friday from 7:30 a.m. until 10:00 p.m. and on Saturdays from 7:30 a.m. until 5:00 p.m. The library is closed on the following holidays each year: New Years Day, Independence Day, Pioneer Day (a state holiday on or near 24 July), Thanksgiving, Christmas Eve, and Christmas.

MICROFORM COLLECTIONS

The heart of the library's collection is approximately 2 million rolls of microfilmed records (equal to more than 6 million written volumes) and more than 500,000 microfiche. The collection includes records kept by governments, churches of many denominations, other organizations, and individuals. These records include copies of church registers, census records, passenger lists, military records, land, and probate records. Most of the records date from about 1550 to about 1920. Various "rights of privacy" regulations mean that the library has few records of living persons. Also, the library does not have a record of everyone who has ever lived. However, the library does have a substantial collection of records for many areas of the world, particularly countries from which North Americans have ancestors.

North America

The library's largest collection covers the United States. More than half a million microfilm rolls represent every state. At least 100,000 of those rolls are federal records (including census, military, and immigration records). These records come from more than 2,300 archives, county courthouses, and other repositories, particularly from the states east of the Mississippi River. With at least 35,000 rolls for Canada, almost all Quebec church records and many civil records from Ontario and other provinces are included.

British Areas

The more than 155,000 rolls for Great Britain include a comprehensive collection of Scottish records, as well as a very large collection of records from England. The library also has significant collections for Ireland and Wales, with many records also available for Australia and New Zealand.

Europe

With more than half a million rolls of microfilm, the European microfilms form the second-largest collection at the library. They include church and civil records for many areas of Germany and France (more than 100,000 rolls each). Virtually all major genealogical records are available for the Netherlands (90,000 rolls), Belgium (66,000 rolls), Hungary (12,000 rolls), and Luxembourg. The fastest growth in the European collection is for the countries of Italy, Poland, Portugal, Spain, and Switzerland.

Scandinavia

The library's collection of more than 200,000 microfilms for Denmark (95,000 rolls), Sweden (79,000 rolls), Norway (12,000 rolls), and Finland (15,000 rolls) provides virtually comprehensive coverage for these countries.

Latin America

Most church parish records are included in the collections for Mexico (140,000 rolls), Chile (8,000 rolls), and Uruguay. Another 50,000 rolls provide growing, but still incomplete, coverage for the other Latin countries, most notably Argentina, Brazil, and Guatemala (each with at least 8,000 rolls).

Other Areas

Other countries for which the library has comprehensive collections include the Philippines (51,000 rolls), Sri Lanka, many Pacific islands, and many smaller countries. There are partial collections for South Africa and many other countries. The library has a growing collection of family histories for China, Japan, and Korea.

BOOK AND OTHER COLLECTIONS

The library also has more than a quarter of a million volumes of books, including published family histories, local histories, indexes, periodicals, and other research aids. More than half of this collection is also available on microfilm or microfiche. Many thousands of the library's microfilms are reproductions of books that are not available (as books) at the library. Often these are obscure books not easily found in other libraries and which may have been out of print for decades.

The library also has a very useful collection of maps to help place ancestors in geographic perspective and to aid the research process. Several hundred manuscript pedigrees represent the research of previous family historians. Microfilm copies of most of these are also available.

The library's Automated Resource Center houses electronic materials the library has collected and also provides access to the major online services, such as CompuServe and America Online. The collection of compact discs represents virtually every title available that pertains to local or family history.

FamilySearch®

FamilySearch is a computerized collection of genealogical information created by The Church of Jesus Christ of Latter-day Saints. It is available throughout the library. The collection uses compact disc technology to store and retrieve massive amounts of genealogical data. However, it is not available through modem or Internet use (as of 1996). FamilySearch is described in chapter 2, Databases, Indexes, and Other Finding Aids. The following files and programs are part of FamilySearch:

- Ancestral File™
- Family History Library Catalog™
- International Genealogical Index™
- U.S. Social Security Death Index
- U.S. Military Index
- Scottish Church Records

- TempleReady™
- Personal Ancestral File®

FAMILY HISTORY LIBRARY CATALOG

The *Family History Library Catalog* lists and describes each of the microfilms, microfiche, books, compact discs, manuscripts, and all other records in the library. It is the key to understanding the growing collection of the library and having success in your research. Each year almost 100 million new pages of historical documents are preserved and cataloged (about 50,000 rolls). The catalog is available on compact disc and on microfiche, both of which are updated, usually annually. Individuals or institutions may purchase the microfiche version of the catalog, or portions of it. With the catalog, researchers can find records by author, title, subject, locality, or surname. The compact disc version of the catalog allows searches by microfilm or microfiche number or by computer number, but not by author, title, or subject (as of 1996).

LIBRARY SERVICES

Guided tours of the Family History Library are not provided. However, library volunteers provide a short orientation for persons new to the library. Orientation classes can be provided for groups of fifteen to sixty people. Contact the library in advance so that they will be prepared to meet the group's needs.

The library staff does not do research for patrons. However, they will help all library users to understand how to use the facilities. The staff is very friendly and will answer brief reference questions, help locate a town, or determine what records are available for a specific locality. The staff will answer questions received by mail, telephone, fax, E-mail (fhl@byu.edu), and online services (CompuServe, America Online, etc.)

The library has "open stacks" so that patrons can retrieve and use virtually any of the materials personally. Copies of most of the microfilms are immediately available in the library and can be used at any of the more than seven hundred microfilm readers and dozens of microfiche readers. Patrons can photocopy selected portions of books, microfilms, and microfiche inexpensively. Copy machines are available on each floor.

The library also holds classes on the use of the library, its collections, and its computer systems as well as basic research procedures. Classes are often repeated every week or month. Contact the library for a copy of the current month's schedule.

Most of the library's microfilms and microfiche can be lent for use at one of the family history centers. There is a small postage and duplication fee, and this service can only be requested in person at a local family history center. (See below.)

PREPARING TO VISIT THE LIBRARY

Family historians are more successful when they visit the library if they are prepared to effectively use its resources. To do this, gather all the background information you can beforehand, and familiarize yourself with the records you will need to access in your research. Where possible, visit a local family history center before you visit the library. Also note that, while most of the microfilms you will want to use are kept at the library, some are housed in a different location. If you are planning to use recent (new) films, films of obscure sources, or films for countries outside western Europe and Great Britain, contact the library to check on film availability or write the library at least two weeks in advance and request the films you need.

The library has records from many governments, churches, and organizations. Most documents are written in the language of the country where they were made. While you may not need to know the foreign language to use the records, it would be useful to learn a few key words. Most original records are handwritten and in chronological order. Also, they are not indexed, so allow plenty of time at the library to search these records carefully.

You may want to read more about the library when preparing for a visit. A thorough treatment of the library's collection, including a description of many major reference sources for each country or state, is Johni Cerny and Wendy Elliott, *The Library: A Guide to the LDS Family History Library* (Salt Lake City: Ancestry, 1988). For a more recent and briefer guide see Carlyle Parker, *Going to Salt Lake City to Do Family History Research*, 2nd ed. (Turlock, Calif.: Marietta Publishing Co., 1993).

If you wish to share your family information with the library and its patrons while preserving it for future generations, contact the Acquisitions Unit on the third floor of the library for more information (telephone: 801-240-2337).

FAMILY HISTORY CENTERS

The Family History Library currently supports more than 2,500 "branch libraries," called family history centers, throughout the world. As branches of the Family History Library, they can provide access to almost all of the microfilm and microfiche maintained at the main library. Because of the LDS church's interest in genealogical research, these centers have been provided as a way for their members and the entire public to use the resources of the Family History Library (at no charge) without having to travel to Salt Lake City.

Family history centers have been established in most LDS stakes. (A stake is a group of six to twelve "wards" or congregations.) Through them, microfilm and microfiche copies of the records at the Family History Library can be borrowed for a small handling fee. The books at the main library do not circulate, but more than half of them are available on microfilm. Many published sources are under copyright, and in most such cases the Family History Library cannot microfilm them.

Family history centers are found in LDS church buildings throughout the United States and in dozens of foreign countries, generally in or near large population centers. Areas of greater LDS population, such as the western United States, have more family history centers. Usually these centers are about the size of a classroom, and they are equipped with microfilm and microfiche reading machines, computers with the FamilySearch program, a copy of the *Family History Library Catalog,* and other major sources, such as Ancestral File, the International Genealogy Index, and the Accelerated Indexing System's census indexes. The staff are all volunteers with varying experience in genealogical research. Nonetheless, you will generally find them to be quite helpful. In these centers, pa-

trons can use the library resources and request copies of sources not immediately available.

While most centers have a small collection of general reference books, centers do not collect records of the area where they are located. However, because of the size of the Family History Library's collection and the fact that many of the sources are public domain documents and books, most sources that the researcher is seeking are available on microfilm or microfiche and can be sent to any center. Most films are only kept at the centers for a short period of time while patrons use them for their immediate research.

Do not be concerned that these centers are sponsored by a church. Proselyting is not allowed in family history centers. Furthermore, studies have shown that, on average, more than half of their patrons are not members of the LDS church. For more information on family history centers, see pages 2-3 of *The Library* (cited earlier).

Some of the older, larger family history centers have collected several thousand books and hundreds of rolls of microfilm. Some of these "regional" libraries are in or near the cities of San Diego, Los Angeles, Oakland, Sacramento, Phoenix, Provo and Logan, Utah, Las Vegas, Calgary (Alberta), and Pocatello and Rexburg, Idaho.

The following list identifies the cities in each state and Canadian province where major family history centers can be found. This list does not include smaller centers, most of which are open for very few hours, do not have the staff to serve public patrons, and usually do not have microfilm circulation available. When using this list to locate centers near large cities, such as Chicago or Boston, look for surrounding suburban towns. To locate the center in one of the towns listed below, contact a local congregation of The Church of Jesus Christ of Latter-day Saints (see the white pages of a telephone directory) or a local genealogical society. In addition, a list of family history centers in your state can be obtained from the Family History Library.

United States

Alabama
Anniston, Birmingham, Cullman, Decatur, Dothan, Eufaula, Florence, Huntsville, Mobile, Montgomery, Tuscaloosa

Alaska
Anchorage, Bethell, Fairbanks, Juneau, Ketchikan, Sitka, Soldotna, Wasilla

Arizona
Benson, Buckeye, Casa Grande, Cottonwood, Duncan, Eagar, Flagstaff, Globe, Holbrook, Kingman, Mesa, Nogales, Page, Payson, Peoria, Phoenix (7), Prescott, Safford, Scottsdale, Show Low, Sierra Vista, Snowflake, St. Johns, Sun City, Tucson (2), Willcox, Winslow, Yuma

Arkansas
Fort Smith, Hot Springs, Jacksonville, Little Rock, Rogers, Russelville, Springdale

California
Northern California: Anderson, Chico, Eureka, Gridley, Miranda, Mt. Shasta, Quincy, Redding, Susanville, Ukiah, Vacaville, Weaverville, Yuba City, Bay Area, Antioch, Concord, Fairfield, Fremont (2), Los Altos, Menlo Park, Napa, Oakland, Pacifica, San Bruno, San Jose (2), Santa Clara, Santa

Cruz, Santa Rosa, Central California, Auburn, Clovis (2), Fresno (2), Hanford, Manteca, Merced, Modesto (2), Placerville, Sacramento (2), Seaside, Sonora, Stockton, Sutter Creek, Turlock, Visalia, Woodland

Los Angeles County: Burbank, Canoga Park, Carson, Cerritos, Chatsworth, Covina (Spanish), Glendale, Hacienda Heights, Huntington Park, La Crescenta, Lancaster (2), Los Alamitos, Los Angeles, Monterey Park (Spanish), Northridge, Norwalk, Palmdale, Pasadena, Rancho Palos Verdes, Torrance, Valencia, Whittier

Southern California (outside Los Angeles County): Anaheim, Bakersfield (3), Barstow, Blythe, Buena Park, Camarillo, Carlsbad, Chino, Corona, El Cajon, El Centro, Escondido (2), Fontana, Hemet, Huntington Beach, Lake Elsinore, Lompoc, Mission Viejo, Moreno Valley, Needles, Newbury Park, North Edwards, Orange, Palm Desert, Redlands, Ridgecrest, Riverside (3), San Bernardino, San Diego (3), San Luis Obispo, Santa Barbara, Santa Maria, Simi Valley, Thousand Oaks, Upland, Ventura, Victorville, Vista, Westminster

Colorado
Alamosa, Arvada, Aurora, Colorado Springs, Cortez, Craig, Denver, Durango, Fort Collins, Frisco, Grand Junction, Greeley, La Jara, Lakewood, Littleton (2), Longmont, Louisville, Montrose, Northglenn, Paonia, Pueblo, Sterling

Connecticut
Bloomfield, Madison, Mystic, New Canaan, Woodbridge

Delaware
Dover, Wilmington

District of Columbia
(See Maryland)

Florida
Arcadia, Belle Glade, Boca Raton, Bradenton, Ft. Myers, Gainsville, Homestead, Jacksonville, Key West, Lake City, Lake Mary, Largo, Lecanto, Miami, New Port Richey, Orange Park, Orlando, Palm Beach Gardens, Palm City, Panama City, Pensacola, Plantation, Port Charlotte, Rockledge, Tallahassee, Tampa, Winter Haven

Georgia
Albany, Brunswick, Columbus, Douglas, Evans, Jonesboro, Macon, Marietta, Powder Springs, Rome, Roswell, Savannah, Suwanee, Tucker

Hawaii
Hilo, Hawaii; Kailua-Kona, Hawaii; Lihue, Kauai; Kahului, Maui; Honolulu, Oahu (2); Kaneohe, Oahu; Laie, Oahu; Mililani, Oahu; Waipahu, Oahu

Idaho
Arimo, Basalt, Blackfoot (2), Boise (3), Burley, Caldwell, Coeur D'Alene, Driggs, Eagle, Emmett, Grangeville, Hailey, Idaho Falls (3), Lewiston, McCammon, Malad, Montpelier, Moore, Moscow, Mountain Home, Nampa, Pocatello, Preston, Rexburg, Rigby (2), Salmon, Sandpoint, Shelley, Soda Springs, Terreton, Twin Falls, Weiser

Illinois
Buffalo Grove, Champaign, Chicago Heights, Naperville, Nauvoo, O'Fallon, Peoria, Rockford, Schaumburg, Wilmette

Indiana
Bloomington, Columbus, Evansville, Fort Wayne, Indianapolis, Kokomo, Muncie, New Albany, Noblesville, South Bend, Terre Haute, West Lafayette

Iowa
Ames, Cedar Falls, Cedar Rapids, Davenport, Mason City, Sioux City, West Des Moines

Kansas
Dodge City, Emporia, Hutchinson, Olathe, Salina, Topeka, Wichita

Kentucky
Corbin, Hopkinsville, Lexington, Louisville, Martin, Morgantown, Owingsville, Paducah

Louisiana
Alexandria, Baton Rouge, Denham Springs, Monroe, Metairie, Shreveport, Slidell

Maine
Bangor, Cape Elizabeth, Caribou, Farmingdale

Maryland
Annapolis, Ellicott City, Frederick, Germantown, Kensington, Lutherville, Suitland

Massachusetts
Foxboro, Weston, Worcester

Michigan
Ann Arbor, Bloomfield Hills, East Lansing, Escanaba, Grand Blanc, Grand Rapids, Harvey, Hastings, Kalamazoo, Ludington, Midland, Muskegon, Traverse City, Westland

Minnesota
Bemidji, Brooklyn Park, Duluth, Minneapolis, Rochester, St. Paul

Mississippi
Booneville, Clinton, Columbus, Gulfport, Hattiesburg

Missouri
Cape Girardeau, Columbia, Farmington, Frontenac, Hazelwood, Independence, Joplin, Kansas City, Liberty Springfield, St. Joseph

Montana
Billings (2), Bozeman, Butte, Glasgow, Glendive, Great Falls (2), Havre, Helena, Kalispell, Lewiston, Missoula, Stevensville

Nebraska
Gordon, Grand Island, Lincoln, Omaha, Papillion

Nevada
Ely, Elko, Fallon, Henderson, Las Vegas, Logandale, Mesquite, Reno, Tonapah, Winnemucca

New Hampshire
Concord, Nashua, Portsmouth

New Jersey
Cherry Hill, East Brunswick, Morristown, North Caldwell, Short Hills

New Mexico
Alamogordo, Albuquerque (3), Carlsbad, Clovis, Farmington, Gallup, Grants, Las Cruces, Los Alamos, Roswell, Santa Fe, Silver City

New York
Brooklyn, Elmhurst (Spanish), Ithaca, Jamestown, Lake Placid, Liverpool, Loudonville, New York City, Pittsford, Plainview, Rochester, Scarsdale, Vestal, Williamsville, Yorktown

North Carolina
Chapel Hill, Charlotte (2), Durham, Fayetteville, Goldsboro, Greensboro, Hickory, Kinston, Raleigh, Skyland, Wilmington, Winston-Salem

North Dakota
Bismarck, Fargo, Grand Forks, Minot

Ohio
Cincinnati (2), Dayton, Dublin, Fairborn, Kirtland, Perrysburg, Reynoldsburg, Tallmadge, Westlake, Wintersville

Oklahoma
Ardmore, Enid, Lawton, Muskogee, Norman, Oklahoma City (2), Stillwater, Tulsa (2), Woodward

Oregon
Baker City, Beaverton, Bend, Brookings, Central Point, Corvallis, Eugene, Grants Pass, Gresham, Hermiston, Hillsboro, John Day, Klamath Falls, La Grande, Lake Oswego, Lebanon, McMinnville, Medford, Milwaukie, Newport, Northbend, Nyssa, Ontario, Oregon City, Portland (2), Prineville, Roseburg, Scio, St. Helens, Salem (2), Sandy, The Dalles, Tualatin

Pennsylvania
Broomall, Clarks Summit, Erie, Johnstown, Kane, Lancaster, Meridian, Philadelphia, Pittsburgh, Reading, State College, York

Rhode Island
Warwick

South Carolina
Charleston, Columbia, Florence, Greer

South Dakota
Gettysburg, Pierre, Rapid City, Rosebud, Sioux Falls

Tennessee
Bartlett, Chattanooga, Cordova, Franklin, Kingsport, Knoxville, Madison, McMinnville

Texas
Abilene, Amarillo, Austin (2), Bay City, Bryan, Conroe, Coppell, Corpus Christi, Dallas, Denton, Duncanville, El Paso (2), Fort Worth (2), Friendswood, Gilmer, Harlingen, Houston (2), Katy, Kileen, Kingwood, Longview, Lubbock, McAllen, Midland, Odessa, Orange, Pasadena, Plano, Port Arthur, San Antonio (2), Spring, Sugarland, The Colony, Tyler, Victoria, Wichita Falls

Utah (except Davis, Salt Lake, and Utah counties)
Altamont, Beaver, Blanding, Brigham City, Castle Dale, Cedar City, Delta, Duchesne, Enterprise, Escalanate, Eureka, Ferron, Fillmore, Goshen, Helper, Huntington, Hurricane, Hyrum, Kanab, Laketown, Loa, Logan (2), Manti, Marion, Midway, Moab, Monticello, Morgan, Moroni, Mt. Pleasant, Nephi, Ogden, Panguitch, Park City, Parowan, Price, Richfield, Roosevelt, St. George, Tooele, Tremonton, Tropic, Vernal, Wellington, Wendover

Davis County: Bountiful, Farmington (3), Kaysville (2), Layton, Syracuse

Salt Lake County: Bluffdale, Draper, Kearns (3), Magna (2), Midvale, Murray (4), Salt Lake City (13), Sandy (9), South Jordan, West Jordan (3), West Valley City (6)

Utah County: American Fork (2), Lehi, Lindon, Mapleton, Orem (5), Payson, Pleasant Grove (2), Provo (8), Santaquin, Spanish Fork, Springville

Vermont
Berlin

Virginia
Alexandria, Annandale, Bassett, Centreville, Charlottesville, Chesapeake, Dale City, Falls Church, Fredericksburg, Hamilton, Harrisonburg, Midlothian, Newport News, Oakton, Pembroke, Richmond, Salem, Virginia Beach, Waynesboro, Winchester

Washington
Auburn, Bellevue, Bellingham, Bremerton (2), Centralia, Chehalis, Colville, Ellensburg, Elma, Ephrata, Everett, Federal Way, Kirkland, Lake Stevens, Longview, Moses Lake, Mountlake Terrace, Mount Vernon, North Bend, Olympia, Omak, Othello, Port Angeles, Puyallup, Quincy, Richland, Seattle (2), Spokane (4), Sumner, Tacoma, Vancouver (3), Walla Walla, Wenatchee, Yakima

West Virginia
Charleston, Fairmont, Huntington

Wisconsin
Appleton, Eau Claire, Hales Corner, Kenosha, Madison, Shawano, Wausau

Wyoming
Afton, Casper, Cheyenne, Cody, Diamondville, Evanston, Gillette, Green River, Jackson Hole, Laramie, Lovell, Lyman, Rawlins, Riverton, Rock Springs, Sheridan, Worland

Canada

Alberta
Calgary, Cardston, Edmonton, Fort Macleod, Grande Prairie, Lethbridge, Magrath, Medicine Hat, Raymond, Red Deer, Taber

British Columbia
Burnaby, Courtenay, Cranbrook, Fort St. John, Kamloops, Kelowna, Prince George, Surrey, Terrace, Vernon, Victoria

Manitoba
Brandon, Winnipeg

New Brunswick
St. John

Newfoundland
St. John's

Nova Scotia
Dartmouth

Ontario
Brampton, Chatham, Etobicoke, Fort Frances, Glenburnie, Hamilton, Kitchener, London, Oshawa, Ottawa, Sarnia, Sault St. Marie, St. Thomas, Thunder Bay, Timmins, Windsor

Quebec
La Salle, Montreal (French)

Saskatchewan
Regina, Saskatoon

APPENDIX E

Genealogical Societies

compiled by Carol Yocom

The following is a sampling of the hundreds of national, state, regional, and ethnic genealogical societies and umbrella organizations in the United States. For a more comprehensive and current listing, see Mary K. Meyer, *Directory of Genealogical Societies in the USA and Canada,* 10th ed. (Maryland: the compiler, 1994), and *Federation of Genealogical Societies 1996 Membership Directory* (Richardson, Tex.: Federation of Genealogical Societies, 1996).

NATIONAL SOCIETIES

Afro-American Historical and Genealogical Society

P.O. Box 73086
Washington, DC 20056-3086

American-Canadian Genealogical Society

P.O. Box 668
Manchester, NH 03105

American Family Records Association (AFRA)

P.O. Box 15505
Kansas City, MO 64106

American-French Genealogical Society

P.O. Box 2113
Pawtucket, RI 02861

Association of Jewish Genealogical Societies

1485 Teaneck Rd.
Teaneck, NJ 07666

The Belgian Researchers, Inc.

62073 Fruitdale Lane
La Grande, OR 97850

Czechoslovak Genealogical Society

P.O. Box 16225
St. Paul, MN 55116-0225

Federation of Genealogical Societies

P.O. Box 830220
Richardson, TX 75083-0220

German Genealogical Society of America

P.O. Box 291818
Los Angeles, CA 90029

Hispanic Genealogical Society

P.O. Box 810561
Houston, TX 77281-0561

International Genealogy Fellowship of Rotarians

c/o Charles D. Townsend
5721 Antietam Dr.
Sarasota, FL 34231

Irish Genealogical Society

P.O. Box 16585
St. Paul, MN 55116-0585

Irish Family History Forum

P.O. Box 351
Rockville Centre, NY 11571

Italian Genealogy Group

7 Grayson Dr.
Dix Hills, NY 11746

Jewish Genealogical Society, Inc.

P.O. Box 6398
New York, NY 10128

National Genealogical Society

4527 Seventeenth St. N.
Arlington, VA 22207-2399

National Society, Daughters of the American Revolution

Library
1776 D St. N.W.
Washington, DC 20006

New England Historic Genealogical Society

101 Newbury St.
Boston, MA 02116

Northwest Territory Canadian and French Heritage Center

P.O. Box 29397
Brooklyn Center, MN 55429

Orphan Train Heritage Society of America

4912 Trout Farm Rd.
Springdale, AR 72764

Palatines To America

Capital University, Box 101G4
Columbus, OH 43209-1294

POINT [Pursuing Our Italian Names Together]

P.O. Box 2977
Palos Verdes, CA 90274

Polish Genealogical Society of Michigan

Burton Collection
Detroit Public Library
5201 Woodward Ave.
Detroit, MI 48202

Polish Genealogical Society

984 N. Milwaukee Ave.
Chicago, IL 60622

Puerto Rican Hispanic Genealogical Society

25 Ralph Ave.
Brentwood, NY 11717-2424

Scandinavian-American Genealogical Society

P.O. Box 16069
St. Paul, MN 55116-0069

TIARA [The Irish Ancestral Research Association]

P.O. Box 619
Sudbury, MA 01776

ALABAMA

Alabama Genealogical Society

Samford University Library
Box 2296
800 Lakeshore Dr.
Birmingham, AL 35229

Natchez Trace Genealogical Society

P.O. Box 420
Florence, AL 35631-0420

Tuscaloosa Genealogical Society

1439 Forty-Ninth Ave.
East Tuscaloosa, AL 35404

ALASKA

Alaska Genealogical Society

7030 Dickerson Dr.
Anchorage, AK 99504

ARIZONA

Arizona Genealogical Advisory Board

P.O. Box 5641
Mesa, AZ 85211

Arizona State Genealogical Society

P.O. Box 42075
Tucson, AZ 85733

ARKANSAS

Arkansas Genealogical Society

P.O. Box 908
Hot Springs, AR 71902-0908

CALIFORNIA

California Genealogical Society

P.O. Box 77105
San Francisco, CA 94107-0105

California State Genealogical Alliance

c/o Wendy Elliott
4808 E. Garland St.
Anaheim, CA 92807

Conejo Valley Genealogical Society

P.O. Box 1228
Thousand Oaks, CA 91358

Contra Costa Genealogical Society

P.O. Box 910
Concord, CA 94522

Los Angeles Westside Genealogical Society

P.O. Box 10447

Marina del Rey, CA 90295

San Diego Genealogical Society

1050 Pioneer Way

Suite E

El Cajon, CA 92020-1943

Questing Heirs GenSoc, Inc.

P.O. Box 15102

Long Beach, CA 90815-0102

COLORADO

Colorado Genealogical Society

P.O. Box 9218

Denver, CO 80209

Colorado Council of Genealogical Societies

P.O. Box 24379

Denver, CO 80224-0379

The council can provide a list of all genealogical societies in the state if a self-addressed stamped envelope is included with the request.

Columbine Genealogical Society

P.O. Box 2074

Littleton, CO 80161

CONNECTICUT

Connecticut Society of Genealogists

P.O. Box 435

Glastonbury, CT 06033

The Connecticut Ancestry Society

P.O. Box 249

Stamford, CT 06940-0249

DELAWARE

Delaware Genealogical Society

505 Market St. Mall

Wilmingt]on, DE 19801-3091

FLORIDA

Central Florida Genealogical Society

P.O. Box 177

Orlando, FL 32802-0177

Florida Genealogical Society, Inc.

P.O. Box 18624

Tampa, FL 33679-8624

Florida State Genealogical Society

P.O. Box 10249

Tallahassee, FL 32302-2249

Genealogical Society of North Brevard

P.O. Box 897

Titusville, FL 32781

GEORGIA

Georgia Genealogical Society

P.O. Box 54575

Atlanta, GA 30308-0575

HAWAII

Hawaii County Genealogical Society

P.O. Box 831

Keaau, HI 96749

The Sandwich Islands Genealogical Society

Hawaii State Library

478 S. King St.

Honolulu, HI 96813

IDAHO

Idaho Genealogical Society

4620 Overland Rd. No. 204

Boise, ID 83705-2867

ILLINOIS

Chicago Genealogical Society

P.O. Box 1160

Chicago, IL 60690

Fulton County Historical and Genealogical Society

45 N. Park Dr.

Canton, Il 61520-1126

Illinois State Genealogical Society

P.O. Box 10195

Springfield, IL 62791

Jacksonville Area Genealogical and Historical Society

P.O. Box 21

Jacksonville, IL 62651-0021

McLean County Genealogical Society

P.O. Box 488
Normal, IL 61761-0488

Madison County Genealogical Society

P.O. Box 631
Edwardsville, IL 62025

South Suburban Genealogical and Historical Society

P.O. Box 96
South Holland, IL 60473

Genealogical Society of Southern Illinois

John A. Logan College
Route 2 Box 145
Carterville, IL 62918

INDIANA

Allen County Genealogical Society

P.O. Box 12003
Fort Wayne, IN 46862

Indiana Genealogical Society, Inc.

P.O. Box 10507
Fort Wayne, IN 46852-0507

Southern Indiana Genealogical Society

P.O. Box 665
New Albany, IN 47151-0665

Tippecanoe County Area Genealogical Society

909 S. St.
Lafayette, IN 47901

IOWA

Iowa Genealogical Society

P.O. Box 7735
Des Moines, IA 50322-7735

Northeast Iowa Genealogical Society

503 S. St.
Waterloo, IA 50701

Northwest Iowa Genealogical Society

46 First St. S.W.
Le Mars, IA 51031

KANSAS

Kansas Genealogical Society

P.O. Box 103
Dodge City, KS 67801

Kansas Council of Genealogical Societies

P.O. Box 3858
Topeka, KS 66604-6858

Reno County Genealogical Society

P.O. Box 5
Hutchinson, KS 67504-0005

Topeka Genealogical Society

P.O. Box 4048
Topeka, KS 66604-0048

KENTUCKY

Eastern Kentucky Genealogical Society

P.O. Box 1544
Ashland, KY 41105-1544

Kentucky Genealogical Society

P.O. Box 153
Frankfort, KY 40602

Louisville Genealogical Society

P.O. Box 5164 DGS
Louisville, KY 40255-0164

West-Central Kentucky Family Research Association

P.O. Box 1932
Owensboro, KY 42302

LOUISIANA

Baton Rouge Genealogical Society

P.O. Box 80565
SE Station
Baton Rouge, LA 70898

Louisiana Genealogical and Historical Society

P.O. Box 3454
Baton Rouge, LA 70821

MAINE

Maine Genealogical Society

P.O. Box 221
Farmington, ME 04938

MARYLAND

Baltimore County Genealogical Society

P.O. Box 10085
Towson, MD 21204

Historical Society of Charles County

P.O. Box 261
Port Tobacco, MD 20677

Maryland Genealogical Society

201 W. Monument St.
Baltimore, MD 21201

Prince George's County Genealogical Society

P.O. Box 819
Bowie, MD 20718-0819

MASSACHUSETTS

Berkshire Family History Association, Inc.

P.O. Box 1437
Pittsfield, MA 01201

Essex Society of Genealogists

P.O. Box 313
Lynnfield, MA 01940

Massachusetts Genealogical Council

P.O. Box 5393
Cochituate, MA 01778

The Massachusetts Society of Genealogists, Inc.

P.O. Box 215
Ashland, MA 01721-0215

MICHIGAN

The Detroit Society for Genealogical Research

Detroit Public Library
5201 Woodward Ave.
Detroit, MI 48202

Genealogical Society of Washtenaw County, Michigan

P.O. Box 7155
Ann Arbor, MI 48107

Kalamazoo Valley Genealogical Society

P.O. Box 405
Comstock, MI 49041

Michigan Genealogical Council

P.O. Box 80953
Lansing, MI 48908-0593

MINNESOTA

Minnesota Genealogy Society

P.O. Box 16069
St. Paul, MN 55116-0069

MISSISSIPPI

Mississippi Genealogical Society

P.O. Box 5301
Jackson, MS 39216-5301

MISSOURI

Missouri State Genealogical Association

P.O. Box 833
Columbia, MO 65205-0833

Northwest Missouri Genealogical Society

P.O. Box 382
St. Joseph, MO 64502-0382

Ozarks Genealogical Society

P.O. box 3945
Springfield, MO 65808-3945

St. Louis Genealogical Society

9011 Manchester Rd.
Suite No. 3
Brentwood, MO 63144

MONTANA

Montana State Genealogical Society

P.O. Box 555
Chester, MT 59522

Great Falls Genealogy Society

Paris Gibson Square
1400 First Ave.N., Room 30
Great Falls, MT 59401-3299

NEBRASKA

Greater Omaha Genealogical Society

P.O. Box 4011
Omaha, NE 68104

Lincoln-Lancaster Genealogical Society

P.O. Box 30055
Lincoln, NE 68503-0055

Nebraska State Genealogical Society

P.O. Box 5608
Lincoln, NE 68505-0608

NEVADA

Nevada State Genealogical Society

P.O. Box 20666
Reno, NV 89515-0066

Clark County Genealogical Society

P.O. Box 1929
Las Vegas, NV 89125-1929

NEW HAMPSHIRE

New Hampshire Society of Genealogists

P.O. Box 2316
Concord, NH 03302-2316

NEW JERSEY

Gloucester County Historical Society

17 Hunter St.
P.O. Box 409
Woodbury, NJ 08096-0409

Genealogical Society of New Jersey

P.O. Box 1291
New Brunswick, NJ 08903-1291

Monmouth County Genealogy Club

Monmouth County Historical Association
70 Court St.
Freehold, NJ 07728

Morris Area Genealogy Society

P.O. Box 105
Convent Station, NJ 07961

Genealogical Society of the West Fields

550 E. Broad St.
Westfield, NJ 07090

NEW MEXICO

Genealogy Club of the Albuquerque Public Library

423 Central Ave. N.E.
Albuquerque, NM 87102

New Mexico Genealogical Society

P.O. Box 8283
Albuquerque, NM 87198-8283

Southern New Mexico Genealogical Society

1840 Amis Ave.
Las Cruces, NM 88005-1652

NEW YORK

Capital District Genealogical Society

P.O. Box 2175
Empire State Plaza
Albany, NY 12220-0175

Central New York Genealogical Society

P.O. Box 104, Colvin Station
Syracuse, NY 13205

Dutchess County Genealogical Society

P.O. Box 708
Poughkeepsie, NY 12603

New York State Council of Genealogical Organizations

P.O. Box 2593
Syracuse, NY 13220-2593

New York Genealogical and Biographical Society

122 E. 58th St.
New York, NY 10022-1939

Western New York Genealogical Society

P.O. Box 338
Hamburg, NY 14075-0338

NORTH CAROLINA

Carolinas Genealogical Society

P.O. Box 397
Monroe, NC 28111

Forsyth County Genealogical Society

P.O. Box 5715
Winston-Salem, NC 27113-5715

Johnson County Genealogical Society

c/o Public Library of Johnson County
Smithfield, NC 27577

North Carolina Genealogical Society

P.O. Box 1492
Raleigh, NC 27602

Wilkes Genealogical Society

P.O. Box 1629
North Wilkesboro, NC 28659

NORTH DAKOTA

Bismark-Mandan Historical and Genealogical Society

P.O. Box 485
North Wilkesboro, NC 28659

Red River Valley Genealogical Society

P.O. Box 9284
Fargo, ND 58106

OHIO

The Greater Cleveland Genealogical Society

P.O. Box 40254
Cleveland, OH 44140

Ohio Genealogical Society

34 Sturges Ave.
P.O. Box 2625
Mansfield, OH 44906

OKLAHOMA

Federation of Oklahoma Genealogical Societies

P.O. Box 26151
Oklahoma City, OK 73126

Oklahoma Genealogical Society

P.O. Box 12986
Oklahoma City, OK 73157-2986

OREGON

Genealogical Council of Oregon, Inc.

P.O. Box 15169
Portland, OR 97215

Genealogical Forum of Oregon

2130 S.W. 5th Ave.
Suite 220
Portland, OR 97201-4934

Oregon Genealogical Society, Inc.

P.O. Box 10306
Eugene, OR 97440-2306

PENNSYLVANIA

Blair County Genealogical Society

P.O. Box 855
Altoona, PA 16603

Cornerstone Genealogical Society

P.O. Box 547
Waynesburg, PA 15370

Genealogy Society of Pennsylvania

1305 Locust St.
Philadelphia, PA 19107

Historical Society of Western Pennsylvania and Western Pennsylvania Genealogical Society

4338 Bigelow Blvd.
P.O. Box 8530
Pittsburgh, PA 15220-0530

South Central Pennsylvania Genealogical Society

P.O. Box 1824
York, PA 17405-1824

RHODE ISLAND

Rhode Island Genealogical Society

507 Clark's Row
Bristol, RI 02809-1481

SOUTH CAROLINA

Chester District Genealogical Society

P.O. Box 336
Richburg, SC 29729

South Carolina Genealogical Society

P.O. Box 16355
Greenville, SC 29606

SOUTH DAKOTA

Sioux Valley Genealogical Society

200 W. Sixth St.
Sioux Falls, SD 57104-6881

South Dakota Genealogical Society

P.O. Box 490
Winner, SD 57580

TENNESSEE

Jefferson County Genealogical Society

P.O. Box 267
Jefferson City, TN 37760

Middle Tennessee Genealogical Society

P.O. Box 190625
Nashville, TN 37219-0625

Tennessee Genealogical Society

P.O. Box 111249
Memphis, TN 38111-1249

TEXAS

Austin Genealogical Society

P.O. Box 1507
Austin, TX 78767-1507

Dallas Genealogical Society

P.O. Box 12648
Dallas, TX 75225-0648

Houston Area Genealogical Association

2507 Tannehill
Houston, TX 77008-3052

Texas State Genealogical Society

Route 4, Box 56
Sulphur Springs, TX 75482

Tip O' Texas Genealogical Society

410 76 Dr.
Harlingen, TX 78550

UTAH

Utah Genealogical Association

P.O. Box 1144
Salt Lake City, UT 84110

VERMONT

Vermont Genealogical Society

P.O. Box 422
Pittsford, VT 05763

VIRGINIA

Genealogical Research Institute of Virginia

P.O. Box 29178
Richmond, VA 23242-0178

Tidewater Virginia Genealogical Society

P.O. Box 7650
Hampton, VA 23666

Virginia Genealogical Society

5001 W. Broad St. No. 115
Richmond, VA 23230-3023

WASHINGTON

Clark County Genealogical Society

P.O. Box 2728
Vancouver, WA
98668-2728

Eastside Genealogical Society

P.O. Box 374
Bellevue, WA 98009

Washington State Genealogical Society

P.O. Box 1422
Olympia, WA 98507

WEST VIRGINIA

Kanawha Valley Genealogical Society

P.O. Box 8555
South Charleston, WV 25303

West Virginia Genealogical Society

P.O. Box 249
Elkview, WV 25071

WISCONSIN

Milwaukee County Genealogical Society

P.O. Box 27326
Milwaukee, WI 53227-0326

Wisconsin Genealogical Council

6083 Co. Trk. S.
Wisconsin Rapids, WI 54495

Wisconsin State Genealogical Society

2109 Twentieth Ave.
Monroe, WI 53566-3426

WYOMING

Fremont County Genealogical Society

Riverton Branch Library
1330 W. Park Ave.
Riverton, WY 82501

APPENDIX F

Where to Write for Vital Records

This appendix is reproduced from a 1993 publication of the U.S. Department of Health and Human Services titled *Where to Write for Vital Records: Births, Deaths, Marriages, and Divorces.* Some of the prices and other information contained herein may have changed since 1993.

State, Type of Record	Address	Cost of Copy/Remarks
Alabama		
Birth or Death	Center for Health Statistics State Department of Public Health P.O. Box 5625 Montgomery, AL 36103-5625	$12.00/State office has had records since January 1908. Additional copies at same time are $4.00 each. The fee for special searches is $10.00 per hour. Money order or check should be made payable to Center for Health Statistics. Personal checks are accepted. To verify current fees, the telephone number is (205)242-5033.
Marriage	Same as Birth or Death	$12.00/State office has had records since August 1936.
	See remarks	Varies/Probate judge in county where license was issued.
Divorce	Same as Birth or Death	$12.00/State office has had records since January 1950.
	See remarks	Varies/Clerk or Register of Court of Equity in county where divorce was granted.
Alaska		
Birth or Death	Department of Health and Social Services Bureau of Vital Statistics P.O. Box H-O2G Juneau, AK 99811-0675	$7.00/State office has had records since January 1913. Money orders should be made payable to Bureau of Vital Statistics. Personal checks are not accepted. To verify current fees, the telephone number is (907) 465-3391. This will be a recorded message.
Marriage	Same as Birth or Death	$7.00/State office has had records since 1913.
Divorce	Same as Birth or Death	$7.00/State office has had records since 1950.
	See remarks	Varies/Clerk of Superior Court in judicial district where divorce was granted. Juneau and Ketchikan (First District), Nome (Second District), Anchorage (Third District), Fairbanks (Fourth District).
American Samoa		
Birth or Death	Registrar of Vital Statistics Vital Statistics Section Government of American Samoa Pago Pago, AS 96799	$2.00/Registrar has had records since 1900. Money order should be made payable to ASG Treasurer. Personal checks are not accepted. To verify current fees, the telephone number is (684) 633-1222, ext. 214. Personal identification is required before a record will be sent.

State, Type of Record	Address	Cost of Copy/Remarks
Marriage	Same as Birth or Death	$2.00
Divorce	High Court of American Samoa Tutuila, AS 96799	$1.00

Arizona

Birth (long form)	Vital Records Section Arizona Department of Health Services P.O. Box 3887 Phoenix, AZ 85030	$8.00/State office has had records sine July 1909 and abstracts of records filed in counties before then. Check or money order should be made payable to Office of Vital Records. Personal checks are accepted. To verify current fees, the telephone number is (602) 255-3260. This will be a recorded message. Applicants must submit a copy of picture identification or have their request notarized.
Birth (short form)	Same as Birth (long form)	$5.00/Same as Birth (long form)
Marriage	See remarks	Varies/Clerk of Superior Court in county where license was issued.
Divorce	See remarks	Varies/Clerk of Superior Court in county where divorce was granted.

Arkansas

Birth	Division of Vital Records Arkansas Department of Health 4815 West Markham St. Little Rock, AR 72201	$5.00/State office has had records since February 1914 and some original Little Rock and Fort Smith records from 1881. Additional copies of death record, when requested at the same time, are $1.00 each. Check or money order should be made payable to Arkansas Department of Health. Personal checks are accepted. To verify current fees, the telephone number is (501) 661-2336. This will be a recorded message.
Death	Same as Birth	$4.00/Same as Birth
Marriage	Same as Birth or Death	
	See remarks	$5.00/Coupons since 1917.
		Varies/Full certified copy may be obtained from County Clerk in county where license was issued.
Divorce	Same as Birth or Death	$5.00/Coupons since 1923.
	See remarks	Varies/Full certified copy may be obtained from Circuit or Chancery Clerk in the county where the divorce was granted.

California

Birth	Vital Statistics Section Department of Health Services P.O. Box 730241 Sacramento, CA 94244-0241	$12.00/State office has had records since July 1905. For earlier records, write to County Recorder in county where event occurred. Check or money order should be made payable to State Registrar, Department of Health Services or Vital Statistics. Personal checks are accepted. To verify current fees, the telephone number is (916) 445-2684.
Death	Same as Birth	$8.00/Same as Birth
Heirloom Birth	Not available until further notice	$31.00/Decorative birth certificate (11 by 14 inches) suitable for framing.
Marriage	Same as Birth or Death	$12.00/State office has had records since July 1905. For earlier records, write to County Recorder in county where event occurred.

State, Type of Record	Address	Cost of Copy/Remarks
Divorce	Same as Birth or Death	$12.00/Fee is for search and identification of county where certified copy can be obtained. Certified copies are not available from State Health Department.
	See remarks	Varies/Clerk of Superior Court in county where divorce was granted.

Canal Zone

Birth or Death	Panama Canal Commission Vital Statistics Clerk APOAA 34011	$2.00/Records available from May 1904 to September 1979.
Marriage	Same as Birth or Death	$1.00/Records available from May 1904 to September 1979.
Divorce	Same as Birth or Death	$.50/Records available from May 1904 to September 1979.

Colorado

Birth or Death	Vital Records Section Colorado Department of Health 4300 Cherry Creek Dr. South Denver, CO 80222-1530	$12.00/State office has had death records since 1910. State office also has birth records for some counties for years before 1910. Additional copies of the same record ordered at the same time are $6.00.
		Check or money order should be made payable to Colorado Department of Health. Personal checks are accepted. To verify current fees, the telephone number is (303) 756-4464. This will be a recorded message.
Marriage	Same as Birth or Death	Varies/Certified copies are not available from State Health Department. Statewide index of records for 1900-39 and 1975 to present. Fee verification is $12.00.
Divorce	Same as Birth or Death	Varies/Certified copies are not available from State Health Department. Statewide index of records for 1900-39 and 1968 is present. Fee verification is $12.00.
		Copies available from Clerk of District Court in county where divorce was granted.

Connecticut

Birth or Death	Vital Records Department of Health Services 150 Washington St. Hartford, CT 06106	$5.00/State office has had records since July 1897. For earlier records, write to Registrar of Vital Statistics in town or city where event occurred. Check or money order should be made payable to Department of Health Services. Personal checks are accepted. Fax requests are not accepted. Must have original signature on request. To verify current fees, the telephone number is (203) 566-2334. This will be a recorded message.
Marriage	Same as Birth or Death	$5.00/Records since July 1897 at State Registry.
	See remarks	For older records, contact Clerk of Superior Court where marriage occurred.
Divorce	See remarks	Applicant must contact Clerk of Superior Court where divorce was granted. State office does not have divorce decrees and cannot issue certified copies.

Delaware

Birth or Death	Office of Vital Statistics Division of Public Health	$5.00/State office has death records since 1930 and birth records since 1920. Additional copies of

State, Type of Record	*Address*	*Cost of Copy/Remarks*
	P.O. Box 637	the same record requested at the same time are $3.00 each.
	Dover, DE 19903	Check or money order should be made payable to Office of Vital Statistics. Personal checks are accepted. To verify current fees, the telephone number is (302) 739-4721.
Marriage	Same as Birth or Death	$5.00/Records since 1930. Additional copies of the same record requested at the same time are $3.00 each.
Divorce	Same as Birth or Death	Records since 1935. Inquiries will be forwarded to appropriate office. Fee for search and verification of essential facts of divorce is $5.00 for each 5-year period searched. Certified copies are not available from State office.
		$2.00/Prothonotary in county where divorce was granted up to 1975. For divorces granted after 1975 the parties concerned should contact Family Court in county where divorce was granted.

District of Columbia

Birth or Death	Vital Records Branch Room 3009 425 I St. N.W. Washington, DC 20001	$12.00/Office has had death records since 1855 and birth records since 1874 but no death records were filed during the Civil War. Cashier's check or money order should be made payable to D.C. Treasurer. To verify current fees, the telephone number is (202) 727-9281.
Marriage	Marriage Bureau 515 5th St. N.W. Washington, DC 20001	$5.00
Divorce	Clerk, Superior Court for the District of Columbia, Family Division 500 Indiana Avenue, NW Washington, DC 20001	$2.00/Records since 16 September 1956.
	Clerk, U.S. District Court for the District of Columbia Washington, DC 20001	Varies/Records before 16 September 1956.

Florida

Birth Death	Department of Health and Rehabilitative Services Office of Vital Statistics P.O. Box 210 1217 Pearl St. Jacksonville, FL 32231	Birth: $9.00; death: $5.00/State office has some birth records dating back to April 1865 and some death records dating back to August 1877. The majority of records date from January 1917. (If the exact date is unknown, the fee is $9.00 [births] or $5.00 [deaths] for the first year searched and $2.00 for each additional year up to a maximum of $50.00. Fee includes one certification of record if found or certified statement stating record not on file.) Additional copies are $4.00 each when requested at the same time.
		Check or money order should be made payable to Office of Vital Statistics. Personal checks are accepted. To verify current fees, the telephone number is (904) 359-6900. This will be a recorded message.
Marriage	Same as Birth or Death	$5.00/Records since 6 June 1927. (If the exact date is unknown, the fee is $5.00 for the first year searched and $2.00 for each additional year up to a maximum of $50.00. Fee includes one copy of record if found or certified statement stating record not on file.) Additional copies are

State, Type of Record	Address	Cost of Copy/Remarks
		$4.00 each when requested at the same time.
Divorce	Same as Birth or Death	$5.00/Records since 6 June 1927. (If the exact date is unknown, the fee is $5.00 for the first year searched and $2.00 for each additional year up to a maximum of $50.00. Fee includes one copy of record if found or certified statement stating record not on file.) Additional copies are $4.00 each when requested at the same time.

Georgia

State, Type of Record	Address	Cost of Copy/Remarks
Birth or Death	Georgia Department of Human Resources Vital Records Unit Room 217-H 47 Trinity Ave. S.W. Atlanta, GA 30334	$10.00/State office has had records since January 1919. For earlier records in Atlanta or Savannah, write to County Health Department in county where event occurred. Additional copies of same record ordered at same time are $5.00 each except birth cards, which are $10.00 each.
		Money order should be made payable to Vital Records, GA DHR. Personal checks are not accepted. To verify current fees, the telephone number is (404) 656-4900. This is a recorded message.
Marriage	Same as Birth or Death	$10.00/Centralized State records since 9 June 1952. Certified copies are not issued at state office. Inquiries about marriages occurring before 9 June 1952, will be forwarded to appropriate Probate Judge in county where license was issued.
	See remarks	Varies/Probate Judge in county where license issued.
Divorce	See remarks	$2.00 for certification plus $0.50 per page/ Centralized state records since 9 June 1952. Certified copies are not issued at state office. Inquiries will be forwarded to appropriate Clerk of Superior Court in county where divorce was granted.
	See remarks	Clerk of Superior Court in county where divorce was granted.

Guam

State, Type of Record	Address	Cost of Copy/Remarks
Birth or Death	Office of Vital Statistics Department of Public Health and Social Services Government of Guam P.O. Box 2816 Agana, GU, M.I. 96910	$5.00/Office has had records since 16 October 1901. Money order should be made payable to Treasurer of Guam. Personal checks are not accepted. To verify current fees, the telephone number is (671) 734-4589.
Marriage	Same as Birth or Death	$5.00
Divorce	Clerk, Superior Court of Guam Agana, GU, M.I. 96910	Varies

Hawaii

State, Type of Record	Address	Cost of Copy/Remarks
Birth or Death	Office of Health Status Monitoring State Department of Health P.O. Box 2816 Agana, GU, M.I., 96910	$2.00/State office has had records since 1853. Check or money order should be made payable to State Department of Health. Personal checks are accepted for correct amount only. To verify current fees, the telephone number is (808) 586-4533. This is a recorded message.
Marriage	Same as Birth or Death	$2.00
Divorce	Same as Birth or Death	$2.00/Records since July 1951.
	See remarks	Varies/Circuit Court in county where divorce was granted.

State, Type of Record	*Address*	*Cost of Copy/Remarks*

Idaho

Birth	Vital Statistics Unit Idaho Department of Health and Welfare 450 W. State St. Statehouse Mail Boise, ID 83720-9990	$8.00/State office has had records since July 1911. For records from 1907 to 1911, write to County Recorder in county where event occurred.
Wallet card	Same as Birth	$8.00
Death	Same as Birth	$8.00
Heirloom Birth	Same as Birth or Death	$30.00/Decorative birth certificates (8 1/2 by 11 inches and 5 by 7 inches) are suitable for framing. Check or money order should be made payable to Idaho Vital Statistics. Personal checks are accepted. To verify current fees, the telephone number is (208) 334-5988. This is a recorded message.
Marriage	Same as Birth or Death; see remarks	$8.00/Records since May 1947. Earlier records are with County Recorder in county where license was issued. County Recorder in county where license was issued.
Divorce	Same as Birth or Death	$8.00/Records since May 1947. Earlier records are with County Recorder in county where divorce was granted.
	See remarks	Varies/County records in county where divorce was granted.

Illinois

Birth or Death	Division of Vital Records Illinois Department of Public Health 605 W. Jefferson St. Springfield, IL 62702-5097	$15.00/certified copy/$10.00 certification/State office has had records since January 1916. For earlier records and for copies of State records since January 1916, write to County Clerk in county where event occurred (county fees vary). The fee for a search of the state files is $10.00. If the record is found, one certification is issued at no additional charge. Additional certifications of the same record ordered at the same time are $2.00 each. The fee for a full certified copy is $15.00. Additional certified copies of the same record ordered at the same time are $2.00 each. Money orders, certified checks, or personal checks should be made payable to Illinois Department of Public Health. To verify current fees, the telephone number is (217) 782-6553. This will be a recorded message.
Marriage	Same as Birth or Death	$5.00/Marriage Index since January 1962. Selected items may be verified (fee $5.00). Certified copies are not available from state office. For certified copies, write to the County Clerk in county where license was issued.
Divorce	Same as Birth or Death	$5.00/Divorce Index since January 1962. Selected items may be verified (fee $5.00). Certified copies are not available from the state office. For certified copies, write to the Clerk of Circuit Court in county where divorce was granted.

State, Type of Record	*Address*	*Cost of Copy/Remarks*

Indiana

Birth	Vital Records Section State Department of Health 1330 W. Michigan St. P.O. Box 1964 Indianapolis, IN 46206-1964	$6.00/State office has had birth records since October 1907 and death records since 1900. Additional copies of the same records ordered at the same time are $1.00 each. For earlier records, write to Health Officer in city or county where event occurred. Check or money order should be made payable to Indiana State Department of Health. Personal checks are accepted. To verify current fees, the telephone number is (317) 633-0274.
Death	Same as Birth	$4.00
Marriage	Same as Birth or Death	Marriage index since 1958. Certified copies are not available from State Health Department.
	See remarks	Varies/Clerk of Circuit Court or Clerk of Superior Court in county where license was issued.
Divorce	See remarks	Varies/County Clerk in county where divorce was granted.

Iowa

Birth or Death	Iowa Department of Public Health Vital Records Section Lucas Office Building 321 E. 12th St. Des Moines, IA 50319-0075	$6.00/State office has had records since July 1880. Check or money order should be made payable to Iowa Department of Public Health. To verify current fees, the telephone number is (515) 281-4944. This will be a recorded message.
Marriage	Same as Birth or Death	$6.00/State office has had records since July 1880.
Divorce	Same as Birth or Death	Brief statistical record only since 1906. Inquiries will be forwarded to appropriate office. Certified copies are not available from State Health Department.
	See remarks	$6.00/Clerk of District Court in county where divorce was granted.

Kansas

Birth	Office of Vital Statistics Kansas State Department of Health and Environment 900 Jackson St. Topeka, KS 66612-1290	$10.00/State office has had records since July 1911. For earlier records, write to County Clerk in county where event occurred. Additional copies of same record ordered at same time are $5.00 each. Check or money order should be made payable to State Registrar of Vital Statistics. Personal checks are accepted. To verify current fees, the telephone number is (913) 296-1400. This will be a recorded message.
Death	Same as Birth	$7.00
Marriage	Same as Birth or Death	$7.00/State office has had records since May 1913.
	See remarks	Varies/District Judge in county where license was issued.
Divorce	Same as Birth or Death	$7.00/State office has had records since July 1951.
	See remarks	Varies/Clerk of District Court in county where divorce was granted.

State, Type of Record	*Address*	*Cost of Copy/Remarks*

Kentucky

Birth	Office of Vital Statistics Department for Health Services 275 E. Main St. Frankfort, KY 40621	$7.00/State office has had records since January 1911 and some records for the cities of Louisville, Lexington, Covington, and Newport before then. Check or money order should be made payable to Kentucky State Treasurer. Personal checks are accepted. To verify current fees, the telephone number is (502) 564-4212.
Death	Same as Birth	$6.00
Marriage	Same as Birth or Death	$6.00/Records since June 1958.
	See remarks	Varies/Clerk of County Court in county where license was issued.
Divorce	Same as Birth or Death	$6.00/Records since June 1958.
See remarks	$6.00/Records since June 1958.	Varies/Clerk of Circuit Court in count where decree was issued.

Louisiana

Birth (long form)	Vital Records Registry Office of Public Health 325 Loyola Ave. New Orleans, LA 70112	$10.00/State office has had records since July 1914. Birth records for City of New Orleans are available from 1892. Death records are available since 1942. Older birth, death, and marriage records are available through the Louisiana State Archives, P.O. Box 94125, Baton Rouge, LA 70804. Check or money order should be made payable to Vital Records. Personal Checks are accepted. To verify current fees, the telephone number is (504) 568-5152.
Birth (short form)	Same as Birth (long form)	$7.00/Same as Birth (long form)
Death	Same as Birth	$5.00/Same as Birth
Marriage		
Orleans Parish	Same as Birth or Death	$5.00
Other Parishes	See remarks	Varies/Certified copies are issued by Clerk of Court in parish where license was issued.
Divorce	See remarks	Varies/Clerk of Court in parish where divorce was granted.

Maine

Birth or Death	Office of Vital Statistics Maine Department of Human Services State House Station 11 Augusta, ME 04333-0011	$10.00/State office has had records since 1892. Records for 1892-1922 are available at the Maine State Archives. For earlier records, write to the municipality where the event occurred. Additional copies of same record ordered at same time are $4.00 each. Check or money order should be made payable to Treasurer, State of Maine. Personal checks are accepted. To verify current fees, the telephone number is (207) 289-3184.
Marriage	Same as Birth or Death	$10.00/Same as Birth or Death
Divorce	Same as Birth or Death	Same as Birth or Death
	See remarks	Clerk of District Court in judicial division where divorce was granted.

Maryland

Birth or Death	Division of Vital Records Department of Health and Mental Hygiene	$4.00/State office has had records since August 1898. Records for City of Baltimore are available from January 1875.

State, Type of Record	Address	Cost of Copy/Remarks
	Metro Executive Building 4201 Paterson Ave. P.O. Box 68760 Baltimore, MD 21215-0020	Will not do research for genealogical studies. Must apply to State of Maryland Archives, 350 Robe Blvd., Annapolis, MD 21401, (301) 974-3914.
		Check or money order should be made payable to Division of Vital Records. Personal checks are accepted. To verify current fees, the telephone number is (301) 225-5988. This will be a recorded message.
Marriage	Same as Birth or Death	$4.00/Records since June 1951.
	See remarks	Varies/Clerk of Circuit Court in county where license was issued or Clerk of Court of Common Pleas of Baltimore City (for licenses issued in city of Baltimore).
Divorce (verification only)	Same as Birth or Death	No fee/Records since January 1961. Certified copies are not available from state office. Some items may be verified.
	See remarks	Varies/Clerk of Circuit Court in county where divorce was granted.

Massachusetts

State, Type of Record	Address	Cost of Copy/Remarks
Birth or Death	Registry of Vital Records and Statistics 150 Tremont St., Room B-3 Boston, MA 02111	$6.00 (in person); $11.00 (mail request); $3.00 (State Archives)/State office has records since 1901. For earlier records, write to The Massachusetts Archives at Columbia Point, 220 Morrissey Blvd., Boston, MA 02125, (617) 727-2816.
		Check or money order should be made payable to Commonwealth of Massachusetts. Personal checks are accepted. To verify current fees, the telephone number is (617) 727-7388. This will be a recorded message.
Marriage	Same as Birth or Death	Fees are same as Birth or Death/Records since 1901.
Divorce	Same as Birth or Death	Index only since 1952. Inquirer will be directed where to send request. Certified copies are not available from state office.
	See remarks	$3.00/Registrar of Probate Court in county where divorce was granted.

Michigan

State, Type of Record	Address	Cost of Copy/Remarks
Birth or Death	Office of the State Registrar and Center for Health Statistics Michigan Department of Public Health 3423 N. Laguna St. Lansing, MI 48909	$13.00/State office has had records since 1867. Copies of most records since 1867 may also be obtained from County Clerk in county where event occurred. Fees vary from county to county. Detroit records may be obtained from the City of Detroit Health Department for births occurring since 1893 and for deaths since 1897.
		Check or money order should be made payable to State of Michigan. Personal checks are accepted. To verify current fees, the telephone number is (517) 335-8655. This will be a recorded message.
Marriage	Same as Birth or Death	$13.00/Records since April 1867.
	See remarks	Varies/County Clerk in county where license was issued.
Divorce	Same as Birth or Death	$13.00/Records since 1897.
	See remarks	Varies/County Clerk in county where divorce was granted.

State, Type of Record	*Address*	*Cost of Copy/Remarks*

Minnesota

Birth	Minnesota Department of Health Section of Vital Statistics 717 Delaware St. S.E. P.O. Box 9441 Minneapolis, MN 55440	$11.00/State office has had records since January 1908. Copies of earlier records may be obtained from Local Registrar in county where event occurred or for the St. Paul City Health Department if the event occurred in St. Paul. Additional copies of the death record when ordered at the same time are $2.00 each
		Check or money order should be made payable to Treasurer, State of Minnesota. Personal checks are accepted. To verify current fees, the telephone number is (612) 623-5121.
Death	Same as Birth	$8.00/Same as Birth
Marriage	Same as Birth or Death	Statewide index since January 1958. Inquiries will be forwarded to appropriate office. Certified copies are not available from State Department of Health.
	See remarks	$8.00/Local Registrar in county where license was issued. Additional copies of the marriage record when ordered at the same time are $2.00 each.
Divorce	Same as Birth or Death	Index since January 1970. Certified copies are not available from state office.
	See remarks	Varies/Local Registrar in county where divorce was granted.

Mississippi

Birth	Vital Records State Department of Health 2423 N. State St. Jackson, MI 39216	$12.00/State office has had records since 1912. Full copies of birth certificates obtained within 1 year after the event are $7.00. Additional copies of same record ordered at same time are $3.00 each for birth; $2.00 each for death and marriage.
		For out-of-state requests only bank or postal money orders are accepted and should be made payable to Mississippi State Department of Health. Personal checks are accepted only for in-state requests. To verify current fees, the telephone number is (601) 960-7981. A recorded message may be reached at (601) 960-7450.
Birth (short form)	Same as Birth	$7.00
Death	Same as Birth	$10.00
Marriage	Same as Birth or Death	$10.00/Statistical records only from January 1926 to 1 July 1938, and since January 1942.
	See remarks	$3.00/Circuit Clerk in county where license was issued.
Divorce	Same as Birth or Death	Records since January 1926. Certified copies are not available from state office. Index search only available at $6.00 for each 5-year increment. Book and page number for county record provided.
	See remarks	Varies/Chancery Clerk in county where divorce was granted.

Missouri

Birth or Death	Missouri Department of Health Bureau of Vital Records 1730 E. Elm P.O. Box 570	$10.00/State office has had records since January 1910. If event occurred in St. Louis (City), St. Louis County, or Kansas City before 1910, write to the City or County Health Department.

State, Type of Record	*Address*	*Cost of Copy/Remarks*
	Jefferson City, MO 65102-0570	Copies of these records are $3.00 each in St. Louis City and $5.00 each in St. Louis County. In Kansas City, $6.00 for first copy and $3.00 for each additional copy ordered at same time.
		Check or money order should be made payable to Missouri Department of Health. Personal checks are accepted. To verify current fees on birth and death records, the telephone number is (314) 751-6400.
Marriage	Same as Birth or Death	No fee/Indexes since July 1948. Correspondents will be referred to appropriate Recorder of Deeds in county where license was issued.
	See remarks	Varies/Recorder of Deeds in county where license was issued.
Divorce	Same as Birth or Death	No fee/Indexes since July 1948. Certified copies are not available from State Health Department. Inquiries will be forwarded to appropriate office.
	See remarks	Varies/Clerk of Circuit Court in county where divorce was granted.
Montana		
Birth or Death	Bureau of Records and Statistics State Department of Health and Environmental Helena, MT 59620	$10.00/State office has had records since late 1907. Check or money order should be made payable to Montana Department of Health and Environmental Sciences. Personal checks are accepted. To verify current fees, the telephone number is (406) 444-2614.
Marriage	Same as Birth or Death	Records since July 1943. Some items may be verified. Inquiries will be forwarded to appropriate office. Apply to county where license was issued if known. Certified copies are not available from state office.
	See remarks	Varies/Clerk of District Court in county where license was issued.
Divorce	Same as Birth or Death	Records since July 1943. Some items may be verified. Inquiries will be forwarded to appropriate office. Apply to court where divorce was granted if known. Certified copies are not available from state office.
	See remarks	Varies/Clerk of District Court in county where divorce was granted.
Nebraska		
Birth	Bureau of Vital Statistics State Department of Health 301 Centennial Mall S. P.O. Box 95007 Lincoln, NE 68509-5007	$8.00/State office has had records since late 1904. If birth occurred before then, write the state office for information. Check or money order should be made payable to Bureau of Vital Statistics. Personal checks are accepted. To verify current fees, the telephone number is (402) 471-2871. This is a recorded message.
Death	Same as Birth	$7.00/Same as Birth
Marriage	Same as Birth or Death	$7.00/Records since January 1909.
	See remarks	Varies/County Court in county where license was issued.

State, Type of Record	Address	Cost of Copy/Remarks
Divorce	Same as Birth or Death	$7.00/Records since January 1909.
	See remarks	Varies/Clerk of District Court in county where divorce was granted.

Nevada

Birth	Division of Health- Vital Statistics Capitol Complex 505 E. King St. No. 102 Carson City, NV 89710	$11.00/State office has records since July 1911. For earlier records, write to County Recorder in county where event occurred. Check or money order should be made payable to Section of Vital Statistics. Personal checks are accepted. To verify current fees, the telephone number is (702) 687-4480.
Death	Same as Birth	$8.00/Same as Birth
Marriage	Same as Birth or Death	Indexes since January 1968. Certified copies are not available from State Health Department. Inquiries will be forwarded to appropriate office.
	See remarks	Varies/County Recorder in county where license was issued.
Divorce	Same as Birth or Death	Indexes since January 1968. Certified copies are not available from State Health Department. Inquiries will be forwarded to appropriate office.
	See remarks	Varies/County Clerk in county where divorce was granted.

New Hampshire

Birth or Death	Bureau of Vital Records Health and Welfare Building 6 Hazen Dr. Concord, NH 03301	$10.00/State office has had records since 1640. Copies of records may be obtained from state office or from City or Town Clerk in place where event occurred. Additional copies ordered at the same time $6.00 each. Check or money order should be made payable to Treasurer, State of New Hampshire. Personal checks are accepted. To verify current fees, the telephone number is (603) 271-4654. This will be a recorded message.
Marriage	Same as Birth or Death	$10.00/Records since 1640.
	See remarks	$10.00/Town Clerk in town where license was issued.
Divorce	Same as Birth or Death	$10.00/Records since 1808.
	See remarks	Varies/Clerk of Superior Court where divorce was granted.

New Jersey

Birth or Death	State Department of Health Bureau of Vital Statistics South Warren and Market Streets CN 370 Trenton, NJ 08625	$4.00/State office has had records since June 1878. Additional copies of same record ordered at same time are $2.00 each. If the exact date is unknown, the fee is an additional $1.00 per year searched.
	Archives and History Bureau State Library Division State Department of Education Trenton, NJ 08625	For records from May 1848 to May 1878. Check or money order should be made payable to New Jersey State Department of Health. Personal checks are accepted. To verify current fees, the telephone number is (609) 292-4087. This will be a recorded message.

State, Type of Record	*Address*	*Cost of Copy/Remarks*
Marriage	Same as Birth or Death	$4.00/If the exact date is unknown, the fee is an additional $1.00 per year searched.
	Archives and History Bureau State Library Division State Department of Education Trenton, NJ 08625	$2.00/For records from May 1848 to May 1878.
Divorce	Public Information Center CN 967 Trenton, NJ 08625	$10.00/The fee is for a certified Blue Seal copy. Make check payable to Clerk of the Superior Court.

New Mexico

Birth	Vital Statistics New Mexico Health Services Division P.O. Box 26110 Santa Fe, NM 87502	$10.00/State office has had records since 1880. Check or money order should be made payable to Vital Statistics. Personal checks are not accepted. To verify current fees, the telephone number is (505) 827-2338. This will be a recorded message.
Death	Same as Birth	$5.00/Same as Birth
Marriage	See remarks	Varies/County Clerk in county where license was issued.
Divorce	See remarks	Varies/Clerk of Superior Court where divorce was granted.

New York

(except New York City)

Birth or Death	Vital Records Section State Department of Health Empire State Building Tower Building Albany, NY 12237-0023	$15.00/State office has had records since 1880. For records before 1914 in Albany, Buffalo, and Yonkers, or before 1880 in any other city, write to Registrar of Vital Statistics in city where event occurred. For the rest of the state, except New York City, write to state office.
		Check or money order should be made payable to New York State Department of Health. Personal checks are accepted. To verify current fees, the telephone number is (518) 474-3075. This well be a recorded message.
Marriage	Same as Birth or Death	
	See remarks	$5.00/Records from 1880 to present. $5.00/For records from 1880-1907 and licenses issued in the cities of Albany: City Clerk, City Hall, Albany, NY 12207; Buffalo: City Clerk, City Hall, Buffalo, NY 14202; Yonkers: Registrar of Vital Statistics, Health Center Building, Yonkers, NY 10701.
Divorce	Same as Birth or Death	$15.00/Records since January 1963.
	See remarks	Varies/County Clerk in county where divorce was granted.

New York City

Birth or Death	Division of Vital Records New York City Department of Health P.O. Box 3776 New York, NY 10007	$15.00/Office has birth records since 1910 and death records since 1949 for those occurring in the Boroughs of Manhattan, Brooklyn, Bronx, Queens, and Staten Island. For birth records prior to 1910 and death records prior to 1949, write to Archives Division, Department of Records and Information Services, 31 Chambers St., New York, NY 10007.
		Certified check or money order should be made payable to New York City Department of Health. to verify current fees, the telephone numbers are

State, Type of Record	*Address*	*Cost of Copy/Remarks*
		(212) 619-4530 or (212) 693-4637. These are recorded messages.

Marriage

Bronx Borough	City Clerk's Office 1780 Grand Concourse Bronx, NY 10457	$10.00/Records from 1847 to 1865. Archives Division, Department of Records and Information Services, 31 Chambers St., New York, NY
Brooklyn Borough	City Clerk's Office Municipal Building Brooklyn, NY 11201	1007, except Brooklyn records for this period which are filed with County Clerk's Office, Kings County, Supreme Court Building, Brooklyn, NY 11201. Additional copies of same record ordered
Manhattan Borough	City Clerk's Office Municipal Building New York, NY 10007	at same time are $5.00 each. Records from 1866 to 1907. City Clerk's Office in borough where marriage was performed. Records from 1908 to 12 May 1943. New York City residents write to
Queens Borough	City Clerk's Office 120-55 Queen's Boulevard Kew Gardens, NY 11424	City Clerk's Office in the borough of the bride's residence; nonresidents write to City Clerk's Office in borough where license was obtained.
Staten Island Borough (no longer called Richmond)	City Clerk's Office Staten Island Borough Hall Staten Island, NY 10301	Records since 13 May 1943. City Clerk's Office in borough where license was issued.
Divorce		See New York State

North Carolina

Birth or Death	Department of Environment, Health and Natural Resources Division of Epidemiology Vital Records Section 225 N. McDowell St. P.O. Box 29537 Raleigh, NC 27626-0537	$10.00/State office has had records since October 1913 and death records since 1 January 1946. Death records from 1913 through 1945 are available from Archives and Records Section, 109 East Jones St., Raleigh, NC 27611. Additional copies of the same record ordered at the same time are $5.00 each. Check or money order should be made payable to Vital Records Section. Personal checks are accepted. To verify current fees, the telephone number is (919) 733-3526.
Marriage	Same as Birth or Death	$10.00/Records since January 1962.
	See remarks	$3.00/Registrar of Deeds in county where marriage was performed.
Divorce	Same as Birth or Death	$10.00/Records since January 1958.
	See remarks	Varies/Clerk of Superior Court where divorce was granted.

North Dakota

Birth	Division of Vital Records State Capitol 600 E. Blvd. Ave. Bismarck, ND 58505	$7.00/State office has had some records since July 1893. Years from 1894 to 1920 are incomplete. Additional copies of birth records are $4.00 each; death records are $2.00 each. Money order should be made payable to Division of Vital Records. To verify current fees, the telephone number is (701) 224-2360.
Death	Same as Birth	$5.00/Same as Birth
Marriage	Same as Birth	$5.00/Records since July 1925. Requests for earlier records will be forwarded to appropriate office. Additional copies are $2.00 each.
	See remarks	Varies/County Judge in county where license was issued.
Divorce	Same as Birth or Death	Index of records since July 1949. Some items may be verified. Certified copies are not available from State Health Department. Inquiries will be forwarded to appropriate office.

State, Type of Record	Address	Cost of Copy/Remarks
	See remarks	Varies/Clerk of District Court in county where divorce was granted.
Northern Mariana Islands		
Birth and Death	Superior Court Vital Records Section P.O. Box 307 Saipan, MP 96950	$3.00/Office has had records for birth and death since 1945 and records for marriage since 1954. Years from 1945 to 1950 are incomplete.
Marriage	Same as Birth and Death	$3.00/Money order or Bank Cashiers Check should be made payable to Superior Court. Personal checks are not accepted. To verify current fees, the telephone number is (670) 234-6401, ext. 15.
Divorce	Same as Birth or Death	$0.50 per page for Divorce Decree plus $2.50 for certification/Office has had records for divorce since 1960.
Ohio		
Birth or Death	Bureau of Vital Statistics Ohio Department of Health P.O. Box 15098 Columbus, OH 43215-0098	$7.00/State office has had birth records since December 20, 1908. For earlier birth and death records, write to the Probate Court in the county where the event occurred. The State Office has death records which occurred after 31 December 1936. Death records which occurred 20 December 1908- 31 December 1936, can be obtained from the Ohio Historical Society, Archives Library Division, 1985 Velma Avenue, Columbus, OH 43211-2497.
		Check or money order should be made payable to State Treasury. Personal checks are accepted. To verify current fees, the telephone number is (614) 466-2531. This will be a recorded message.
Marriage	Same as Birth or Death	Records since September 1949. All items may be verified. Certified copies are not available from State Health Department. Inquiries will be referred to appropriate office.
	See remarks	Varies/Probate Judge in county where license was issued.
Divorce	Same as Birth or Death	Records since September 1949. All items may be verified. Certified copies are not available for State Health Department. Inquiries will be forwarded to appropriate office.
	See remarks	Varies/Clerk of Court of Common Pleas in county where divorce was granted.
Oregon		
Birth or Death	Oregon Health Division Vital Statistics Section P.O. Box 14050 Portland, OR 97214-0050	$13.00/State office has had records since January 1903. Some earlier records for the City of Portland since approximately 1880 are available from the Oregon State Archives, 1005 Broadway, NE, Salem, OR 97310.
Heirloom Birth	Same as Birth or Death	$28.00/Presentation style calligraphy certificate suitable for framing.
		Money order should be made payable to Oregon Health Division. To verify current fees, the telephone number is (503) 731-4095. This will be a recorded message.
Marriage	Same as Birth or Death	$13.00/Records since January 1906.

State, Type of Record	*Address*	*Cost of Copy/Remarks*
	See remarks	Varies/County Clerk in county where license was issued. County Clerks also have some records before 1906.
Divorce	Same as Birth or Death	$13.00/Records since 1925.
	See remarks	Varies/County Circuit Court Clerk where divorce was granted. County Clerks also have some records before 1925.

Pennsylvania

Birth	Division of Vital Records State Department of Health Central Building 101 S. Mercer St. P.O. Box 1528 New Castle, PA 16103	$4.00; $5.00 for a Wallet Card/State office has had records since January 1906. For earlier records, write to Register of Wills, Orphans Court, in county seat of county where event occurred. Persons born in Pittsburgh from 1870 to 1905 or in Allegheny City, now part of Pittsburgh, for 1882 to 1905 should write to Office of Biostatistics, Pittsburgh, PA 15219. For events occurring in City of Philadelphia from 1860 to 1915, write Vital Statistics, Philadelphia Department of Public Health, 401 North Broad Street, Room 942, Philadelphia, PA 19108. Check or money order should be made payable to Division of Vital Records. Personal checks are accepted. To verify current fees, the telephone number is (412) 656-3100.
Death	Same as Birth	$3.00/Same as Birth
Marriage	See remarks	Varies/Make application to the Marriage License Clerks, County Court House, in county where license was issued.
Divorce	See remarks	Varies/Make application to the Prothonotary Court House, in county seat of county where divorce was granted.

Puerto Rico

Birth or Death	Department of Health Demographic Registry P.O. Box 11854 Fernandez Juncos Station San Juan, PR 00910	$2.00/Central office has had records since 22 July 1931. Copies of earlier records may be obtained by writing to local Registrar (Registrador Demografico) in municipality where event occurred or by writing to central office for information. Money order should be made payable to Secretary of the Treasury. Personal checks are not accepted. To verify current fees, the telephone number is (809) 728-7980.
Marriage	Same as Birth of Death	$2.00
Divorce	Same as Birth or Death	
	See remarks	$2.00 Superior Court where divorce was granted.

Rhode Island

Birth or Death	Division of Vital Records Rhode Island Department of Health Room 201, Cannon Building 3 Capitol Hill Providence, RI 02908-5097	$10.00/State office has had records since 1853. For earlier records, write to Town Clerk in town where event occurred. Additional copies of the same records ordered at the same time are $5.00 each. Money order should be made payable to General Treasurer, State of Rhode Island. To verify current fees, the telephone number is (401) 277-2811. This will be a recorded message.

State, Type of Record	Address	Cost of Copy/Remarks
Marriage	Same as Birth or Death	$10.00/Records since January 1853. Additional copies of the same record ordered at the same time are $5.00 each.
Divorce	Clerk of Family Court 1 Dorrance Plaza Providence, RI 02903	$1.00

South Carolina

Birth or Death	Office of Vital Records and Public Health Statistics South Carolina Department of Health and Environmental Control 2600 Bull St. Columbia, SC 29201	$8.00/State office has had records since January 1915. City of Charleston births from 1877 and deaths from 1821 are on file at Charleston County Health Department. Ledger entries of Florence City births and deaths from 1895 to 1914 are on file at Florence County Health Department. Ledger entries of Newberry City births and deaths from the late 1800s are on file at Newberry County Health Department. These are the only early records obtainable. Additional copies of the same birth records ordered at the same time of certification are $3.00. Check or money order should be made payable to Department of Health and Environmental Control. Personal checks are accepted. To verify current fees, the telephone number is (803) 734-4830.
Marriage	Same as Birth or Death	$8.00/Records since July 1950.
	See remarks	Varies/Records since July 1911. Probate Judge in county where license was issued.
Divorce	Same as Birth or Death	$8.00/Records since July 1962.
	See remarks	Varies/Records since April 1949. Clerk of county where petition was filed.

South Dakota

Birth or Death	State Department of Health Center for Health Policy and Statistics Vital Records 523 E. Capitol Pierre, SD 57501	$5.00/State office has had records since July 1905 and access to other records for some events that occurred before then. Money order should be made payable to South Dakota Department of Health. Personal checks are accepted. To verify current fees, the telephone number is (605) 773-3355. This will be a recorded message.
Marriage	Same as Birth or Death	
	See remarks	$5.00/Records since July 1905. County Treasury in county where license was issued.
Divorce	Same as Birth or Death	
	See remarks	$5.00/Records since July 1905 Varies/Clerk of Court in county where divorce was granted.

Tennessee

Birth (long form)	Tennessee Vital Records Department of Health Cordell Hull Building Nashville, TN 37247-0350	$10.00/State office has had birth records for entire state since January 1914, for Nashville since June 1881, for Knoxville since July 1881, and for Chattanooga since January 1882. State office has had death records for entire state since January 1914, for Nashville since July 1874, for Knoxville since July 1887, and for Chattanooga since 6 March 1872. Birth and death enumeration records by school district are available for July

State, Type of Record	Address	Cost of Copy/Remarks
		1908 through June 1912. Vital Records Office keeps death records for 50 years; older records are maintained by Tennessee Library and Archives, Archives Division, Nashville, TN 37243-0312. For Memphis birth records from April 1874 through December 1887 and November 1898 to 1 January 1914, and for Memphis death records from May 1848 to 1 January 1914, write to Memphis-Shelby County Health Department, Division of Vital Records, Memphis, TN 38105. Additional copies of the same birth, marriage, or divorce records, requested at the same time, are $2.00 each.
		Check or money order should be made to Tennessee Vital Records. Personal checks are accepted. To verify current fees, the telephone number is (615) 741-1763.
Birth (short form)	Same as Birth (long form)	$5.00/Same as Birth (long form)
Death	Same as Birth	$5.00/Same as Birth
Marriage	Same as Birth	$10.00/Records since July 1945.
	See remarks	Varies/County Clerk in county where license was issued.
Divorce	Same as Birth or Death	$10.00/Records since July 1945.
	See remarks	Varies/Clerk of Court in county where divorce was granted.

Texas

State, Type of Record	Address	Cost of Copy/Remarks
Birth	Bureau of Vital Statistics Texas Department of Health 1100 W. 49th St. Austin, TX 78756-3191	$11.00/State office has had records since 1903. Additional copies of same death record ordered at same time are $3.00 each. Check or money order should be made payable to Texas Department of Health. Personal checks are accepted. To verify current fees, the telephone number is (512) 458-7111. This is a recorded message.
Death	Same as Birth	$9.00/Same as Birth
Marriage	See remarks	Records since January 1966. Certified copies are not available from state office. Fee for search and verification of essential facts of marriage is $9.00 each.
		Varies/County Clerk in county where license was issued.
Divorce	See remarks	Records since January 1968. Certified copies are not available from state office. Fee for search and verification of essential facts of divorce is $9.00 each.
		Varies/Clerk of District Court in county where divorce was granted.

Utah

State, Type of Record	Address	Cost of Copy/Remarks
Birth	Bureau of Vital Records Utah Department of Health 288 N. 1460 W. P.O. Box 16700 Salt Lake City, UT 84116-0700	$12.00/State office has had records since 1905. If event occurred from 1890 to 1904 in Salt Lake City or Ogden, write to City Board of Health. For records elsewhere in the state from 1898 to 1904, write to County Clerk in county where event occurred. Additional copies, when requested at the same time, are $5.00 each.
		Check or money order should be made payable to

State, Type of Record	*Address*	*Cost of Copy/Remarks*
		Utah Department of Health. Personal checks are accepted. To verify current fees, the telephone number is (801) 538-6105. This is a recorded message.
Death	Same as Birth	$9.00/Same as Birth
Marriage	Same as Birth or Death	$9.00/State office has had records since 1978. Only short form certified copies are available.
	See remarks	Varies/County Clerk in county where license was issued.
Divorce	Same as Birth or Death	$10.00/State office has had records since 1978. Only short form certified copies are available.
	See remarks	Varies/County Clerk where divorce was granted.

Vermont

State, Type of Record	*Address*	*Cost of Copy/Remarks*
Birth or Death	Vermont Department of Health Vital Records Section Box 70 60 Main St. Burlington, VT 05402	$5.00/State office has had records since 1981. Check or money order should be made payable to Vermont Department of Health. Personal checks are accepted. To verify current fees, the telephone number is (802) 863-7275.
Birth, Death or Marriage	Division of Public Records US Route 2-Middlesex 133 State St. Montpelier, VT 05633	$5.00/Records prior to 1981. To verify current fees, the telephone number is (802) 828-3286. $5.00/Town or City Clerk of town where birth or death occurred.
Marriage	Same as Birth or Death	$5.00/State office has had records since 1981.
	See remarks	$5.00/Town Clerk in town where license was issued.
Divorce	Same as Birth or Death	$5.00/State office has had records since 1981.
	See remarks	$5.00/Town Clerk in town where divorce was granted.

Virginia

State, Type of Record	*Address*	*Cost of Copy/Remarks*
Birth or Death	Division of Vital Records State Health Department P.O. Box 100 Richmond, VA 23208-1000	$5.00/State office has had records from January 1853 to December 1896 and since 14 June 1912. Only the cities of Hampton, Newport News, Norfolk, and Richmond have records between 1896 and 14 June 1912. Check or money order should be made payable to State Health Department. Personal checks are accepted. To verify current fees, the telephone number is (804) 786-6228. This is a recorded message.
Marriage	Same as Birth or Death	$5.00/Records since January 1853.
	See remarks	Varies/Clerk of Court in county or city where license was issued.
Divorce	Same as Birth or Death	$5.00/Records since January 1918.
	See remarks	Varies/Clerk of Court in county or city where divorce was granted.

Virgin Islands

State, Type of Record	*Address*	*Cost of Copy/Remarks*
Birth or Death		
St. Croix	Registrar of Vital Statistics Charles Harwood Memorial Hospital Christiansted St. Croix, VI 00820	$10.00/Registrar has had birth and death records on file since 1840.
St. Thomas and St. John	Registrar of Vital Statistics Knud Hansen Complex Hospital Ground	$10.00/Registrar has had birth records on file since July 1906 and death records since January 1906

State, Type of Record	Address	Cost of Copy/Remarks
	Charlotte Amalie St. Thomas, VI 00802	Money order for birth and death records should be made payable to Bureau of Vital Statistics. Personal checks are not accepted. To verify current fees, the telephone number is (809) 774-9000 ext. 4621 or 4623.
Marriage	Bureau of Vital Records and Statistical Services Virgin Islands Department of Health Charlotte Amalie St. Thomas, VI 00801	Certified copies are not available. Inquiries will be forwarded to the appropriate office.
St. Croix	Chief Deputy Clerk Family Division Territorial Court of the Virgin Islands P.O. Box 929 Christiansted St. Croix, VI 00820	$2.00
St. Thomas and St. John	Clerk of the Territorial Court of the Virgin Islands Family Division P.O. Box 70 Charlotte Amalie St. Croix, VI 00801	$2.00
Divorce	Same as Marriage	Certified copies are not available. Inquiries will be forwarded to appropriate office.
St. Croix	Same as Marriage	$5.00/Money order for marriage and divorce records should be made payable to Territorial court of the Virgin Islands. Personal checks are not accepted.
St. Thomas and St. John	Same as Marriage	$5.00
Washington		
Birth or Death	Department of Health Center for Health Statistics P.O. Box 9709 Olympia, WA 98507-9709	$11.00/State office has had records since July 1907. For King, Pierce, and Spokane counties copies may also be obtained from county health departments. County Auditor of county of birth has registered births prior to July 1907. Check or money order should be made payable to Department of Health. To verify current fees, the telephone number is (206) 753-5936.
Marriage	Same as Birth or Death	$11.00/State office has had records since January 1968.
	See remarks	$2.00/County Auditor in county where license was issued.
Divorce	Same as Birth or Death	$11.00/State office has had records since January 1968.
	See remarks	Varies/County Clerk in county where divorce was granted.
West Virginia		
Birth or Death	Vital Registration Office Division of Health State Capitol Complex Bldg. 3 Charleston, WV 25305	$5.00/State office has had records since January 1917. For earlier records, write to Clerk of County Court in county where event occurred. Check or money order should be made payable to Vital Registration. Personal checks are accepted. To verify current fees, the telephone number is (304) 558-2931.

State, Type of Record	*Address*	*Cost of Copy/Remarks*
Marriage	Same as Birth or Death	$5.00/Records since 1921. Certified copies available from 1964.
	See remarks	Varies/County Clerk in county where license was issued.
Divorce	Same as Birth or Death	Index since 1968. Some items may be verified (fee $5.00). Certified copies are not available from state office.
	See remarks	Varies/Clerk of Circuit Court, Chancery Side, in county where divorce was granted.

Wisconsin

Birth	Vital Records 1 West Wilson St. P.O. Box 309 Madison, WI 53701	$10.00/State Office has scattered records earlier than 1857. Records before 1 October 1907, are very incomplete. Additional copies of the same records ordered at the same time are $2.00 each. Check or money order should be made payable to Center for Health Statistics. Personal checks are accepted. To verify current fees, the telephone number is (608) 266-1371.
Death	Same as Birth	$7.00/Same as Birth
Marriage	Same as Birth	$7.00/Records since April 1836. Records before 1 October 1907, are incomplete. Additional copies of the same record ordered at the same time are $2.00 each.
Divorce	Same as Birth	$7.00/Records since October 1907. Additional copies of the same record ordered at the same time are $2.00 each.

Wyoming

Birth	Vital Records Services Hathaway Building Cheyenne, WY 82002	$8.00/State office has had records since July 1909. Money orders should be made payable to Vital Records Services. To verify current fees, the telephone number is (307) 777-7591.
Death	Same as Birth	$6.00/Same as Birth
Marriage	Same as Birth	$8.00/Records since May 1941.
	See remarks	Varies/County Clerk in county where license was issued.
Divorce	Same as Birth	$8.00/Records since May 1941.
	See remarks	Varies/Clerk of District Court where divorce took place.

Selected Acronyms
and Abbreviations

AASLH	American Association of State and Local History
ABI	*American Biographical Index*
ACPL	Allen County Public Library of Fort Wayne, Indiana
AG	Accredited Genealogist (LDS)
ALA	American Library Association
APG	Association of Professional Genealogists
APGQ	*Association of Professional Genealogists Quarterly*
ASG	American Society of Genealogists
BCG	Board for Certification of Genealogists
BGMI	*Biography Genealogy Master Index*
BYU	Brigham Young University
CAILS	Certified American Indian Lineage Specialist
CALS	Certified American Lineage Specialist
CDA	Colonial Dames of America
CG	Certified Genealogist
CGC	Council of Genealogy Columnists
CGI	Certified Genealogical Instructor
CG-Intern	Certified Genealogist-Intern
CGL	Certified Genealogical Lecturer
CGRS	Certified Genealogical Record Searcher
CIG	Computer Interest Group
DAC	National Society Daughters of the American Colonists
DAR	See NSDAR
DCW	National Society Daughters of Colonial Wars
DFPA	National Society, Daughters of Founders and Patriots of America
DLP	Descendants of Loyalists and Patriots
DUV	Daughters of Union Veterans of the Civil War
FASG	Fellow, American Society of Genealogists
FGS	Federation of Genealogical Societies, publishes *FORUM*
FHC	Family history center (branch of the Family History Library)
FHL	Family History Library
FHLC	*Family History Library Catalog™*
FNGS	Fellow, National Genealogical Society
FUGA	Fellow, Utah Genealogical Association
GEDCOM	Genealogical Data Communications
GENTECH	The Technology in Genealogy Conference
GIM	Genealogical Institute of Mid-America (University of Illinois at Springfield)
GJ	*Genealogical Journal* (of the Utah Genealogical Association)
GPAI	*Genealogical Periodical Annual Index*
GSG	Genealogical Speakers Guild
GSMD	General Society of Mayflower Descendants
GSU	Genealogical Society of Utah
HISGEN	See NEHGS
IGHR	Institute of Genealogical and Historical Research (Samford University, Birmingham, Alabama)
IGI	International Genealogical Index™
IGS	Institute of Genealogical Studies (Dallas Genealogical Society, Dallas, Texas)
ISBGFH	International Society for British Genealogy and Family History
JGS	Jewish Genealogical Society

LDS	Latter-day Saints (The Church of Jesus Christ of Latter-day Saints)
NARA	National Archives and Records Administration
NEHGR	*New England Historical and Genealogical Register* (publication of NEHGS)
NEHGS	New England Historic Genealogical Society (Boston, Massachusetts)
NGS	National Genealogical Society
NGS/CIGNGS	Computer Interest Group; publishes the *NGS/CIG Digest*
NGSQ	*National Genealogical Society Quarterly*
NHS	National Huguenot Society
NIDS	National Inventory of Documentary Sources
NIGR	National Institute on Genealogical Research (Washington, D.C.)
NSCD-17	National Society, Colonial Dames of the 17th Century
NSCD	National Society, Colonial Dames of America
NSDAR	National Society Daughters of the American Revolution
NUCMC	*National Union Catalog of Manuscript Collections*
NYGB	New York Genealogical and Biographical Society
NYGBR	*New York Genealogical and Biographical Society Record*

OCLC	Online Computer Library Center
OFPA	Order of the Founders and Patriots of America
PAF	*Personal Ancestral File®*
PERSI	*Periodical Source Index*
RLIN	Research Libraries Network
SAR	National Society, Sons of the American Revolution
SASE	Self-addressed, stamped envelope
SC	The Society of the Cincinnati
SCV	Sons of Confederate Veterans
SCW	Society of Colonial Wars
SLIG	Salt Lake Institute of Genealogy
TAG	*The American Genealogist*
TG	*The Genealogist*
UDC	United Daughters of the Confederacy
UGA	Utah Genealogical Association
USD 1812	National Society, Daughters of the War of 1812

SOURCES

"Alphabet Soup: Selected Acronyms Used in Genealogy," Phyllis Brown Miller. FGS *Forum* 7 (3) (Fall 1995):11

National Genealogical Society 1996 Conference in the States, Nashville, Tennessee, Syllabus (NGS, 1996).

1995-1996 APG Directory of Professional Genealogists. Edited by Elizabeth Kelley Kerstens. Washington, D.C.: Association of Professional Genealogists, 1995.

Index

This index includes subject entries as well as bibliographic entries for authors and titles. Titles of articles (in periodicals and symposia, for example) are given in quotation marks, whereas titles of complete works (such as books, databases, and computer programs) appear in italics. Works that appear only in the individual chapter bibliographies are not included in this index. Two page references for chapter endnotes are given: one for the page at the end of the chapter on which the endnote appears, and one for the page in the chapter on which reference to the endnote is made (for example, 543n7, 570 denotes a reference on page 543 to note 7, the endnote appearing on page 570).

in newspapers, 462
of orphans, 378–80
Apprentices of Connecticut 1637–1900,
339
Apprentices of Virginia 1623–1800, 339
Apprenticeship Past and Present, 338n3,
355
Approval roll, for Native American tribal
enrollment, 534
Aquayo Hayle, Lolita Rosa, 598, 613
Arapaho tribe, history and records of,
554
Archer, George, 40
*Archer's Directory of Genealogical
Software,* 40
Architects, directories of, 405
Archives
of Assemblies of God, Pentecostal
church records in, 167
of business records, 352, 354
Catholic church records in, 160
of census mortality schedules, 129,
table 128
church, 154, 157, 160–70
burial registers in, 74
clergy records in, 343
directories in, 393
city, 681
city directories in, 386
of colonial records in Spain, 600
of corporations, employment records
in, 347
of The Evangelical Lutheran Church in
America, 164
genealogies in, 457
of Greek Orthodox Archdiocese of
North America, 163
historical, of colleges and universities,
347
immigration records in, 448, 460
Jewish records in, in central and
eastern Europe, 621
manuscript collections in, 15, 353
of Mennonite Church, 166
of Moravian Church, 167
National. *See* National Archives
Native American records in, 523
of New England Yearly Meeting of
Friends, Quaker records at, 168
newspapers in, 419–21
records of untitled nobility in, of Spain
and Latin America, 605, 607
of Reformed Church in America, 168
state, Appendix B
city records in, 680, 681
Confederate military records in, 296
county tax lists in, 263
court records in, 201
defunct business information from,
355
family record collections in, 95
land records in
in Georgia, 270

of New Jersey colony, 276
in New York, 277
in Pennsylvania, 279, 280
in Rhode Island, 280
in South Carolina, 280
naturalization records in, 482
prison records in, 647
of Unitarian-Universalist Association,
169
in urban research, 681, 682
of vital records, Appendix F
Archives and Historical Society,
Evangelical Covenant Church of
America, 163
Archives and Research Center, Salvation
Army, 169
Archives de la Chambre de Commerce et
d'Industrie (Le Havre, France),
emigrant lists at, 492
Archives Nationales de la France,
emigrant lists at, 492
Archives of Labor History (Detroit,
Mich.), 679
Archives of Labor (Wayne State
University, Detroit, Mich.), 346
*Archives of Maryland: Proceedings of
the Court of Chancery of Maryland,
1669–1679,* 201n21, 231
Archives of the Indies (Seville, Spain),
Spanish colonial records in, 625
"Archives of Violence, The," 225
*Archives, The: A Guide to the National
Archives Field Branches,* 104n3, 143,
218n36, 231, 264, 268, 486, 527, 626,
647n13, 649n19, 652, 653, 681
Archivo de Simancas (Valladolid, Spain),
600
guide to, 610
Archivo General de las Indias (Seville,
Spain), 600, 602
emigrant lists at, 494
military records in, 609
Arizona. *See also* State-by-state listing
in 1885 New Mexico census, 126
land records of, 255, 268
*Arizona Index, The: A Subject Index to
Periodicals About the State,* 45
Ark and the Dove, Society of the
(hereditary), 699
Arkansas. *See also* State-by-state listing
federal bounty land grants in, 257
Freedmen's Bureau records in, 580
land records of, 268
War of 1812 bounty land warrants for,
259, 260
Arkansas Land Patents Through 1908,
268
*Arkansas Military Bounty Grants (War of
1812),* 268
Arkansas-Oklahoma Synod, Lutheran
church records at, 164
Arlington National Cemetery, sexton's
records for, 305
Arlington National Cemetery (Virginia),

soldiers and veterans buried at, 301
Armenia, emigration from, history of,
451
Armenian-American records, bibliogra-
phy of, 506
"Army Courts-Martial," 224n37, 231
Arnold, Jonnie B., 577n9, 585
Arraignment, in criminal cases, defined,
178
Arrival lists. *See* Passenger lists
Arthur
Stanely Clisby, 272
Stanley C., 700
Artisans
biographies of, 344
immigration of, laws affecting, 450
Ash, Lee, 353
Ashby, Charlotte M., 132
Ashkenazic Jews, history of, 615
Asia, emigration from, history of, 450–
52
Asian-American records
bibliography of, 506–9, 514
Chinese, census mortality schedules in,
127
Social Security number area codes, 637
Soundex census indexes, names in, 125
of War Relocation Authority for
Japanese-Americans, 221
Assemblies of God, Pentecostal church
records in archives of, 167
Assembly (state legislature), divorces
granted by, 96–98
Assessment lists, for federal taxes, 264
Assocation of Jewish Genealogical
Societies, 626
Association for Gravestone Studies, 77,
82
Association of Jewish Genealogical
Societies (AJGS), 623
Association of Professional Genealogists,
16, 53, 656
"Associations and Associators in the
American Revolution," 227n44, 232
Associations and organizations. *See also*
Genealogical societies; Historical
societies; specific organizations
in city directories, 386
directories of, 385, 405–7
emigrant aid societies, passenger lists
in records of, 463, *illus.* 465
ethnic, 40, 424, 442, 458, 459
hereditary, 704, 705
membership in, monument decorations in relation to, 76
family, 40, 707
directory of, 51
fraternal
in census social statistics schedules,
132
immigration data in records of, 448,
459, 460
of Catholic church, 599